Multimedia Edition

TEACHER'S WRAPAROUND EDITION
ECONOMICS
Principles and Practices

GARY E. CLAYTON, Ph.D.

GLENCOE
Macmillan/McGraw-Hill

New York, New York   Columbus, Ohio   Woodland Hills, California   Peoria, Illinois

About the Author

Gary E. Clayton teaches economics and finance at Northern Kentucky University in Highland Heights, Kentucky. Dr. Clayton received his Ph.D. in Economics from the University of Utah, has taught economics and finance at several universities, and has authored textbooks—including several at the college level—as well as a number of articles in various educational, professional, and technical journals. Dr. Clayton has also appeared on a number of radio and television programs, and was a guest commentator specializing in economic statistics for "Marketplace," which is broadcast on American Public Radio and originates at the University of Southern California.

Dr. Clayton has a long-standing interest in economic education. He has participated in and directed numerous economic education workshops. He received the Outstanding Citizen Certificate of Recognition from the state of Arkansas for his work in economic education. He also received a third-place award in the college division of the International Paper Company competition, an award sponsored by the National Council on Economic Education. He has served as Vice President for the Kentucky Council on Economic Education and received the state's highest honor when he received a commission as an honorary Kentucky Colonel. During the summer months, he participates in various study-abroad programs that take college students to Europe.

Contributing Author

Jack C. Morgan, a former high school economics teacher, is Executive Director of the Kentucky Council on Economic Education and Director of the University of Louisville Center for Economic Education. He is a past president of the National Association of Economic Educators. A Phi Beta Kappa graduate of DePauw University, he received his M.A. from Vanderbilt University and Ph.D. from Purdue University. Dr. Morgan is the coauthor of 3 books about teaching economics and author of more than 40 journal articles. In 1996 Dr. Morgan taught economics to teachers in Perm, Russia.

Glencoe/McGraw-Hill

A Division of The McGraw-Hill Companies

Send all inquiries to:
Glencoe/McGraw-Hill
936 Eastwind Drive
Westerville, Ohio 43081

ISBN 0-02-823556-8 (Student Edition)
ISBN 0-02-823560-6 (Teacher's Wraparound Edition)

Printed in the United States of America.

1 2 3 4 5 6 7 8 9 10   027/046   03 02 01 00 99 98

CONTENTS
Teacher's Wraparound Edition

NOW AVAILABLE
Online Resources from Glencoe Social Studies

Visit the Glencoe Social Studies Web site at *glencoe.com/sec/socialstudies/* for unit-based activities you and your students can explore for this and other Glencoe Social Studies books. There you will also find online versions of our Current Events Update, Economics Update and many more exciting resources.

CONTENTS
Student Edition

Alternate Course Outlines

Economics: Principles and Practices provides ample material for a one-year course in economics. The first semester should focus on Chapters 1-10 of the text, while the second semester should emphasize Chapters 11-21. The program, however, may be adapted to a one-semester course. The following models for one-semester survey economics courses have been designed with respect to the *Master Curriculum Guide in Economics: A Framework for Teaching the Basic Concepts,* a course of study written by the National Council on Economic Education (NCEE).

One-Semester Course
Emphasizing Fundamental, Macroeconomic, and International Economic Concepts

Chapter or Section	Title	Length of Study in Days
1	What Is Economics?	6
2	Economic Systems and Decision Making	6
3	Business Organizations and Economic Institutions	6
Chapter 4, Section 2	The Law of Demand	2
Chapter 5, Section 1	What Is Supply?	2
Chapter 6, Section 1	Prices as Signals	3
7	Competition, Market Structures, and the Role of Government	7
12	The Federal Reserve System and Monetary Policy	7
14	Gross Domestic Product	7
15	Population, Economic Growth, and Business Cycles	6
16	Unemployment, Inflation, and Poverty	6
17	Achieving Economic Stability	6
18	International Trade	6
19	Comparative Economic Systems	7
20	Developing Countries	5
		Total days = 82

One-Semester Course
Emphasizing Fundamental and
Microeconomic Concepts

Chapter or Section	Title	Length of Study in Days
1	What Is Economics?	7
2	Economic Systems and Decision Making	6
3	Business Organizations and Economic Institutions	6
4	Demand	6
5	Supply	7
6	Prices and Decision Making	6
7	Competition, Market Structures, and the Role of Government	7
11	Money and Banking	7
16	Unemployment, Inflation, and Poverty	6
18	International Trade	7
19	Comparative Economic Systems	6
21	Global Economic Challenges	5
Life Skills	Budgeting	6
	Maintaining a Checking Account	
	Filing an Income Tax Return	
	Renting an Apartment	
	Borrowing Money	
	Buying Insurance	
	Paying for College	
	Preparing a Resume	

Total days = 82

National Council
on Economic Education
THE **Economics** America AND **Economics** International PROGRAMS

National Council
on Economic Education
THE **Economics** America AND **Economics** International PROGRAMS

January, 1998

Dear Educator,

The purpose of the Voluntary National Content Standards in Economics is to help raise the quality of economic education in America's schools.

Standards in Economics are for students entering a complex global economy, so that they may fully and effectively participate in it. These Standards are signposts to point the way to economic literacy, not to circumscribe it. They are written for teachers to use to help students learn crucial reasoning and decision-making skills that will serve them well all of their lives.

The fact that economics was one of the nine subject areas in the *Goals 2000: Educate America Act* of 1994 demonstrates its importance as a core subject in America's schools. The National Council on Economic Education was designated by the Department of Education to develop the Standards in Economics.

The Standards were written by a coalition of organizations and individuals representing economists, economic educators, and other national groups committed to the advancement of economic literacy.

The Voluntary National Content Standards in Economics are commended to all who see measures of attainable knowledge as important to the growth of individuals and the health of society and who believe with Jefferson that educated and literate – and, we would now add, economically literate – citizens are essential for democracy to survive and to thrive.

Robert Duvall

Robert F. Duvall, President
National Council on Economic Education

1140 Avenue of the Americas, New York, NY 10036   212.730.7007   fax 212.730.1793   ncee@eaglobal.org

Text Correlation to NCEE Standards

For each standard, students will understand that:	*Economics: Principles and Practices* Chapter and Section coverage:
1 Productive resources are limited. Therefore, people cannot have all the goods and services they want; as a result, they must choose some things and give up others.	**CHAPTER 1** Section 1: Scarcity and the Science of Economics Section 2: Trade-Offs and Opportunity Costs **CHAPTER 21** Section 1: Applying the Economic Way of Thinking
2 Effective decision making requires comparing the additional costs of alternatives with the additional benefits. Most choices involve doing a little more or a little less of something; few choices are all or nothing decisions.	**CHAPTER 1** Section 2: Trade-Offs and Opportunity Costs **CHAPTER 5** Section 3: Supply and the Role of Cost **CHAPTER 10** Section 1: The Economics of Government Spending
3 Different methods can be used to allocate goods and services. People, acting individually or collectively through government, must choose which methods to use to allocate different kinds of goods and services.	**CHAPTER 2** Section 1: Economic Systems **CHAPTER 6** Section 1: Prices as Signals **CHAPTER 19** Section 1: The Spectrum of Economic Systems
4 People respond predictably to positive and negative incentives.	**CHAPTER 2** Section 1: Economic Systems Section 3: Capitalism and Free Enterprise **CHAPTER 6** Section 1: Prices as Signals **CHAPTER 9** Section 1: The Economics of Taxation **CHAPTER 21** Section 2: Economic Incentives and Resources

For each standard, students will understand that:	*Economics: Principles and Practices* Chapter and Section coverage:
5 Voluntary exchange occurs only when all participating parties expect to gain. This is true for trade among individuals or organizations within a nation, and among individuals or organizations in different nations.	**CHAPTER 2** Section 3: Capitalism and Free Enterprise **CHAPTER 18** Section 1: Absolute and Comparative Advantage Section 2: Barriers to International Trade Section 3: Financing and Trade Deficits
6 When individuals, regions, and nations specialize in what they can produce at the lowest cost and then trade with others, both production and consumption increase.	**CHAPTER 1** Section 3: Basic Economic Concepts **CHAPTER 15** Section 2: Economic Growth **CHAPTER 18** Section 1: Absolute and Comparative Advantage
7 Markets exist when buyers and sellers interact. This interaction determines market prices and thereby allocates scarce goods and services.	**CHAPTER 2** Section 1: Economic Systems **CHAPTER 6** Section 2: How Prices are Determined Section 3: The Price System at Work **CHAPTER 7** Section 1: Competition and Market Structures **CHAPTER 18** Section 3: Financing and Trade Deficits
8 Prices send signals and provide incentives to buyers and sellers. When supply or demand changes, market prices adjust, affecting incentives.	**CHAPTER 4** Section 1: What is Demand? **CHAPTER 5** Section 1: What is Supply? **CHAPTER 6** Section 1: Prices as Signals Section 2: How Prices are Determined Section 3: The Price System at Work **CHAPTER 12** Section 3: Monetary Policy, Banking, and the Economy **CHAPTER 21** Section 2: Economic Incentives and Resources
9 Competition among sellers lowers costs and prices, and encourages producers to produce more of what consumers are willing and able to buy. Competition among buyers increases prices and allocates goods and services to those people who are willing and able to pay the most for them.	**CHAPTER 6** Section 2: How Prices are Determined Section 3: The Price System at Work **CHAPTER 7** Section 1: Competition and Market Structures Section 2: Market Failures

For each standard, students will understand that:	*Economics: Principles and Practices* Chapter and Section coverage:
10 Institutions evolve in market economies to help individuals and groups accomplish their goals. Banks, labor unions, corporations, legal systems, and not-for-profit organizations are examples of important institutions. A different kind of institution, clearly defined and well enforced property rights, is essential to a market economy.	**CHAPTER 2** Section 2: Evaluating Economic Performance Section 3: Capitalism and Free Enterprise **CHAPTER 3** Section 1: Business Institutions Section 3: Other Organizations and Institutions **CHAPTER 8** Section 1: The Labor Movement **CHAPTER 13:** Section 1: Savings and the Financial System
11 Money makes it easier to trade, borrow, save, invest, and compare the value of goods and services.	**CHAPTER 11** Section 1: The Evolution of Money Section 2: Early Banking and Monetary Standards **CHAPTER 12** Section 1: The Federal Reserve System Section 2: Monetary Policy
12 Interest rates, adjusted for inflation, rise and fall to balance the amount saved with the amount borrowed, thus affecting the allocation of scarce resources between present and future uses.	**CHAPTER 12** Section 3: Monetary Policy, Banking, and the Economy **CHAPTER 17** Section 3: Stabilization Policies
13 Income for most people is determined by the market value of the productive resources they sell. What workers earn depends, primarily, on the market value of what they produce and how productive they are.	**CHAPTER 1** Section 1: Scarcity and the Science of Economics **CHAPTER 8** Section 3: Labor and Wages Section 4: Employment Trends and Issues **CHAPTER 16** Section 3: Poverty and the Distribution of Income
14 Entrepreneurs are people who take the risks of organizing productive resources to make goods and services. Profit is an important incentive that leads entrepreneurs to accept the risks of business failure.	**CHAPTER 1** Section 1: Scarcity and the Science of Economics **CHAPTER 2** Section 3: Capitalism and Free Enterprise **CHAPTER 15** Section 2: Economic Growth

For each standard, students will understand that:	*Economics: Principles and Practices* Chapter and Section coverage:

15 Investment in factories, machinery, new technology, and the health, education, and training of people can raise future standards of living.

CHAPTER 1
Section 3: Basic Economic Concepts

CHAPTER 3
Section 2: Business Growth and Expansion

CHAPTER 15
Section 2: Economic Growth

CHAPTER 20
Section 1: Economic Development
Section 3: Financing Economic Development

16 There is an economic role for government to play in a market economy whenever the benefits of a government policy outweigh its costs. Governments often provide for national defense, address environmental concerns, define and protect property rights, and attempt to make markets more competitive. Most government policies also redistribute income.

CHAPTER 2
Section 3: Capitalism and Free Enterprise

CHAPTER 3
Section 3: Other Organizations and Institutions

CHAPTER 7
Section 2: Market Failures
Section 3: The Role of Government

CHAPTER 9
Section 1: The Economics of Taxation
Section 2: The Federal Tax System
Section 3: State and Local Tax Systems
Section 4: Current Tax Issues

CHAPTER 10
Section 1: The Economics of Government Spending

CHAPTER 16
Section 3: Poverty and the Distribution of Income

CHAPTER 19
Section 1: The Spectrum of Economic Systems
Section 3: The Transition to Capitalism
Section 4: The Various Faces of Capitalism

17 Costs of government policies sometimes exceed benefits. This may occur because of incentives facing voters, government officials, and government employees, because of actions by special interest groups that can impose costs on the general public, or because social goals other than economic efficiency are being pursued.

CHAPTER 6
Section 3: The Price System at Work

CHAPTER 7
Section 3: The Role of Government

CHAPTER 17
Section 4: Economics and Politics

CHAPTER 18
Section 2: Barriers to International Trade

For each standard, students will understand that:	*Economics: Principles and Practices* Chapter and Section coverage:
18 A nation's overall levels of income, employment, and prices are determined by the interaction of spending and production decisions made by all households, firms, government agencies, and others in the economy.	**CHAPTER 1** Section 3: Basic Economic Concepts **CHAPTER 14** Section 1: Measuring the Nation's Output Section 2: Measuring the Nation's Income Section 3: GDP and Changes in the Price Level **CHAPTER 15** Section 2: Economic Growth Section 3: Business Cycles and Fluctuations **CHAPTER 16** Section 1: Unemployment Section 2: Inflation **CHAPTER 17** Section 2: Macroeconomic Equilibrium
19 Unemployment imposes costs on individuals and nations. Unexpected inflation imposes costs on many people and benefits some others because it arbitrarily redistributes purchasing power. Inflation can reduce the rate of growth of national living standards, because individuals and organizations use resources to protect themselves against the uncertainty of future prices.	**CHAPTER 8** Section 1: The Labor Movement Section 3: Labor and Wages Section 4: Employment Trends and Issues **CHAPTER 16** Section 1: Unemployment Section 2: Inflation **CHAPTER 17** Section 1: The Costs of Economic Instability
20 Federal government budgetary policy and the Federal Reserve System's monetary policy influence the overall levels of employment, output, and prices.	**CHAPTER 10** Section 1: The Economics of Government Spending Section 2: Federal Deficits and the National Debt **CHAPTER 12** Section 1: The Federal Reserve System Section 2: Monetary Policy Section 3: Monetary Policy, Banking, and the Economy **CHAPTER 17** Section 2: Macroeconomic Equilibrium Section 3: Stabilization Policies

The Complete Program

Name   Class   Date

Economic Simulation **1**

SELECTING AND APPLYING FOR A PART-TIME JOB

To the Teacher

Deciding to get a part-time job, then looking for and applying for one, is an important economic experience. Students should think carefully not only about the economic opportunities but the trade-offs and opportunity costs as well. Students should also consider their skills, talents, and personal likes and dislikes when choosing a part-time job. They should be aware of the additional expenses that employment might bring, such as the cost of transportation or the necessity of buying a certain kind of clothing.

This simulation helps students develop an awareness of the kinds of work and wage scales available to them, what information is in "Help Wanted" ads, how a job may impact their education, and whether the actual advantages of getting a job equal the perceived advantages.

A. Prepare for the simulation by making copies for each student of the Employment Section (p. 2), the decision-making worksheet (p. 3), and the job application form (pp. 4–5).

B. Organize students into small groups of three or four. They can work together to discuss the various aspects of the jobs listed, although each student will be responsible for his/her final job choice. They can also provide support for each other in completing the job application.

C. Give each student copies of the employment section and the worksheet, directing their attention first to the Advantages and Opportunity Costs columns. Ask that they first fill out the Advantages section, listing what they expect to get from a part-time job. Explain that they will fill out the Opportunity Costs side after they have chosen a job.

D. Direct their attention to the employment page. Explain that they will have 15 minutes to scan the section and decide on three job possibilities. Tell them to circle those possibilities, list them on the worksheet, and jot down the reasons for their interest. Have

them notice that the wor... to formulate questic... information not given. P... space at the bottom where... a rough estimate of the ... expect to receive for wh... decide to work.

E. Call time at the end of 15 ... students to fill out the Op... column on the worksheet.

F. Distribute copies of the job ... and allow 10 or 15 minutes ... complete it.

G. Wrap Up Discuss with students ... and their feelings about those d... types of jobs seem to be avail... timers? What kinds of requirements ... jobs have? Where else might you find advertisements of employment? How many work hours do you think are reasonable while attending classes? What are the advantages and opportunity costs of having a part-time job? What comments and/or feelings did you have while completing the job application?

Pages shown are reduced. Actual size is 8 1/2" x 11".

T15

Name _____   Class _____   Date _____

PRODUCT
MARKETS
GOODS
SERVICES

Receive Revenue

Provide Goods & Services

Spend Income

Buy Goods & Services

BUSINESS ORGANIZATIONS

INDIVIDU

Resources

Economic Laboratories
provide hands-on applications of economic concepts. Closely tied to chapter content, the labs help students analyze information presented in the text.

Name _____   Class _____   Date _____

Economic Laboratory **1**

THE CIRCULAR FLOW OF ECONOMIC ACTIVITY

Every person living in the United States has several, if not many, roles in the circular flow of the nation's economic activity. Read the following description of a day in the life of Andy and Abby Average. Follow the instructions at the end of each paragraph to fill in the economic activity flow chart provided.

Andy and Abby, the Average twins, live in Anycity, USA. Both are working high school students, trying to make extra dollars for personal needs and wants. **Write their names in the appropriate box on the flow chart.**

Today is Friday, their favorite weekday. It is payday. They sleep later than usual this Friday, too late to fix breakfast, and have to run for the bus. They get off the bus two stops before the high school and pick up a quick breakfast at Bob's Breakfast. Andy and Abby have already purchased one good and used one service. **Write the name of the good and the service in the appropriate box on the flow chart.**

Andy and Abby jog the six blocks from Bob's to Anycity High School. At the entrance to the school, they separate for the day and agree on a meeting spot after school to go to work. At lunchtime, Andy buys lunch at the school's cafeteria, while Abby and some friends go to the mall for lunch. **Add Andy's and Abby's lunch purchases in the appropriate box on the flow chart.**

After school, the twins use one of the high school's rental cars provided for working students. Students pay a flat monthly fee for this service, which covers maintenance, gas, and insurance. **List the service in the appropriate box on the flow chart.**

Abby and Andy punch into work at Pat's Pizza Palace at 3 PM. They work for three hours, and then collect their paychecks from Pat. Before leaving, they buy a pizza for supper and then return the rental car to the school. Finally they catch the 7:30 PM bus home. **Add the good that Andy and Abby purchased in the appropriate box on the flow chart. Then, list on the chart all of the business organizations that Abby and Andy made contact with during the day. Finally, write in the name of Abby's and Andy's factor market.**

Discuss your completed diagram with classmates.

ECONOMIC LABORATORIES

T16   *Pages shown are reduced. Actual size is 8 1/2" x 11".*

RUBRIC
A Slideshow or Photo Essay

S: The slide show or photo essay is an outstanding presentation of the theme. The technical quality of the pictures is excellent. The audience is powerfully affected by the set of pictures.

T: The student has taken pictures that are well focused and lighted. Each picture is composed to clearly show what is intended. The entire set of photographs is _____ enced smoothly, and contains a clear theme. The set has its intended effect on the aud _____ understands the core concepts of the theme and has chosen pictures _____ information to the display. For the photo essay, the pic _____ attractive and very presentable manner.

U: The set of pictures is similar to that receiving a rating _____ are not all excellent.

V: The set of pictures is similar to that receiving a rati _____ good quality.

W: The student has taken pictures that are not well f _____ composed. They do not clearly show what is inte _____ and it is unev _____ resentation of the theme _____ well chosen to pr _____ concepts. The _____ t _____ dience. T _____ not have its _____ inaccurate.

X: The slide _____

Note: If a _____ an _____ a _____

CLASSROOM ASSESSMENT LIST
A Slideshow or Photo Essay

Element	Assessment Points Possible	Earned
1. Each picture in the set is well composed to clearly show what is intended.	_____	_____
_____ Each picture is well focused and lighted appropriately.	_____	_____
_____ lear theme.	_____	_____
	_____	_____
	_____	_____
	_____	_____
	_____	_____
	_____	_____
	_____	_____
	_____	_____

_____ sessed by using the rubric
_____ es the show, it can be

ACTIVITY 12 Performance Assessment

THE PRODUCTION PROCESS

BACKGROUND

Moving goods from where they are produced to the consumer who buys them involves channels of distribution. These channels involve several intricate steps.

MATERIALS

List of consumer goods; scissors, poster board, glue, magazines, newspapers, and catalogs

OBJECTIVES

After completing this activity, students will be able to
- Trace the production process from raw materials to the consumer.
- Identify the stages of the production process and explain the difference between wholesale and retail distribution.
- Illustrate channels of distribution with respect to producers, wholesalers, and retailers including the following:
  a. storage and transportation processing (warehousing)
  b. club warehousing
  c. direct marketing (catalogs)
- Decide "place to sell" and "alternative" selling place.

PROCEDURE

1. Brainstorm with the class various products students might purchase in the marketplace. *(fo _____ clothing, jewelry, etc.)*
2. Choose one of the products the students have mentioned and model it on the chalkboard. For _____ draw a Big Mac using colored chalk. Then explain each ingredient used and how the ingredien _____ through the production process from raw goods producer (e.g., lettuce), through warehousing, _____ consumer.
3. Organize the class into teams or groups of five or less, and from the list generated during the brainstorming process, have each group choose a product to trace through the production and distribution process. Each group member will select a role in producing the product. Possible roles include: raw goods producer, a manufacturer, storage and transportation middle persons, a retailer, _____
4. Instruct the teams to illustrate the stages of the production process for their product on posterboard. Teams will need to make a group decision on the "best" place to sell their product.
5. As an enrichment activity, you may wish to have students present the production for a particular product, using a slide show or a photo essay.

ASSESSMENT

1. Have each team select a spokesperson. This individual will come to the front of the room and present the group's product, using the production process poster that the team created. After each spokesperson has made the presentation, the rest of the team will join him or her for a question and answer session from the teacher and classmates.
2. Have students write a paragraph tracing a new product from raw material to market.

RUBRICS

Poster, oral presentation, a writing, slide show, or photo essay

12

Performance Assessment Activities provide opportunities to implement alternative assessment strategies in your classroom. The booklet also contains rubrics and classroom assessment lists that give teachers the flexibility of monitoring student progress or allowing students to check themselves.

Pages shown are reduced. Actual size is 8 1/2" x 11".

T17

ACTIVITY 7 *Math Practice for Economics*

MAKING MONEY WITH YOUR MONEY

Where do you save your money? Do you put it in a jar or in a dresser drawer? Maybe you put it under your mattress for safekeeping. Have you ever considered depositing the money you want to save in a bank or other depository institution? Different kinds of accounts offer different interest rates. When you earn interest, you make money on your money.

There are two basic types of interest: simple and compound. Simple interest is calculated by multiplying the interest rate by the initial deposit, no matter how long the deposit stays in the bank. Compound interest is calculated by multiplying the rate by the most recent balance in your account (the original deposit plus any interest that's been earned so far).

Imagine that you have $200 to deposit and the interest rate is 3 percent. Use the following equations to complete the chart below:

Simple Interest = Interest Rate x Initial Deposit

Compound Interest = Interest Rate x Most Recent Balance

	Account with Simple Interest (1)	Account with Compound Interest (2)
Initial Deposit		
Interest		
Balance		
Interest		
Balance after second year		
Interest		
Balance after third year		

In addition to figuring different kinds of interest, banks and other institutions offer different types of savings accounts and saving plans.

Say your bank offers a Savers Club account, which requires a minimum deposit of $100 and also requires you to leave the money in the bank for 12 months. If the regular savings account has an interest rate of 2.1 percent and the Savers Club has 3.25 percent interest, how ~~~~~~ ~~~~ vould you make on $150 by putting it in the Savers Club instead of the regular ~~~~~~~~~~~~ _____

_____

Now imagine that you have $500, enc~~~~~~~~~~~~~~~~~~~~~~~~~~~~~~~~~~~~~~requires you to leave your money in the bank for 2 years~~~~~~~~~~~~~~~~~~~~~~~~~r savings account, it offers interest compounded annually, a~~~~~~~~~~~~~~~~~~~~~~more would you make after two years if you put your $500~~~~~~~~~~~~~~~~~~~the regular savings account for the same amount of ti~~~~~~~~~~~~~~~~~~~~

Math Practice for Economics provides activities that help students learn the math most commonly used in building and studying economic models. The activities provide students with real-life examples that help bring economics to life and prepare students to make viable decisions in their own financial lives.

Pages shown are reduced. Actual size is 8 1/2" x 11".

T18

ACTIVITY 8 Free Enterprise

SUPPLY AND DEMAND

There are various nonprice factors that cause shifts in the supply and demand curves, not just movement along the same curves. The chart below indicates several situations that will have an effect on the supply and demand curves for cable television. Read each situation and answer the following questions for each one in the chart. The first situation has been completed as an example.

1. *Which nonprice factor causes the shift in the curve?*
2. *Would the shift be in the supply or demand curve?*
3. *Would there be an increase or decrease in quantity at each price?*
4. *In which direction on a graph would the shift go?*

	Nonprice Factor	Supply or Demand	Increase or Decrease	Direction of Shift
1. A very convincing ad warns parents about the dangers of children's watching too much television.	tastes and preferences	demand curve	decrease	left
2. After a two-month strike, cable installers receive a $1/hour raise.				
3. A new cable company opens.				
4. The cost of renting VCR movies goes down.				
5. New technology makes installing cable less expensive.				
6. A large factory nearby lays off 2,000 workers.				
7. Cable TV begins a very popular children's program.				
8. A cable TV transmitter is severely damaged by a storm and has to be replaced.				

FREE ENTERPRISE

Pages shown are reduced. Actual size is 8 1/2" x 11".

Chapter 2

SECTION 1 GUIDED READING

Answer the following questions as you read Section 1, "Economic Systems,"
in Chapter 2 of your textbook.

1. From what does economic activity stem in a traditional economy?

   _____

   _____

2. What is the main strength of a traditional economy?

   _____

3. What is the main weakness of a traditional economy?

   _____

4. Who makes most of the economic decisions in a command economy?

   _____

5. What is the main strength of a command economy?

   _____

6. What are five weaknesses of a command economy?

   a. _____
   b. _____
   c. _____
   d. _____
   e. _____

7. How are economic decisions made in a market economy?

   _____

8. ~~What~~ t are six strengths of a market economy?

   _____

   _____

   _____

   _____

   _____

   e two main weaknesses of a market economy?

   _____

   _____

Guided Reading Activities help students master chapter information as they read the text. These activities are particularly useful for students who have difficulty with reading comprehension.

Pages shown are reduced. Actual size is 8 1/2" x 11".

CHAPTER 21 Enrichment

A SIMPLE SYMBOL OF A COMPLEX ECONOMY

The wooden pencil is among the most common of objects and the most widely used writing ins_____ world. More than 10 billion new pencils are manufactured each year. You may well have a pencil _____ moment. This common object, however, is a perfect symbol of the global nature of the modern econ_____ typical pencil is the result of factors of production from around the world.

The map below shows how the wooden pencil is truly a global product. Study the map and answe_____ that follow.

Enrichment Activities extend and expand each lesson through motivating activities that engage students in meaningful analyses and interpretations of economics.

Location of Resources Used to Make Wooden Pencils

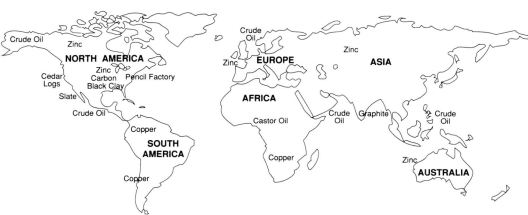

Source: Lawrence C. Wolken, Texas A&M University

1. What African resources are used to make wooden pencils?

_____

2. What Asian resources are used to make wooden pencils?

_____

3. What resources used to make pencils are found in North America?

_____

_____

4. Which continents have deposits of zinc?

_____

5. On which continent are the pencils actually made?

_____

Pages shown are reduced. Actual size is 8 1/2" x 11".

Name _____   Class _____   Date _____

CHAPTER 18 Reteaching

INTERNATIONAL TRADE

Although international trade can bring many benefits, some people object to it because it can take away business from selected industries and jobs from groups of [worke]rs in the United States. Protectionists want tariffs, quotas, and other trade [barrie]rs, while free traders favor fewer trade restrictions. Five arguments for [protect]ion are listed below. For each argument, indicate how protectionists and [free tra]ders stand on the issue.

Protectionists		Free Traders
	National Defense	
	Infant Industries	
	Domestic Jobs	
	Money at Home	
	Balance of Payments	

Pages shown are reduced. Actual size is 8 1/2" x 11".

CHAPTER 15 | Economic Vocabulary Activity

ECONOMIC CROSSWORD PUZZLE

Fill in the terms across and down on the puzzle that match each numbered definition.
Many of the answers are more than one word.

Across

1. even growth path of economy
4. person who studies population characteristics
6. the point of balance if the country could be laid flat and all the people weighed the same
8. average span of years left to people who reach a given age
9. period of economic decline measured by changes in real GDP
10. high birthrate from 1946–1964
11. replenishable natural raw materials
14. relative number of children and elderly per 100 working-age people
15. groups of people of 2,500 or more, or people living in incorporated towns
17. diagram showing the breakdown of groups by age and sex

Down

2. 1930s currency printed by towns
3. growth rate of output per unit of labor input
5. economic state with shortages, unemployment, and excess capacity
7. taxed incomes and properties
12. period of economic recovery
13. official count of all people
16. point where real GDP stops growing

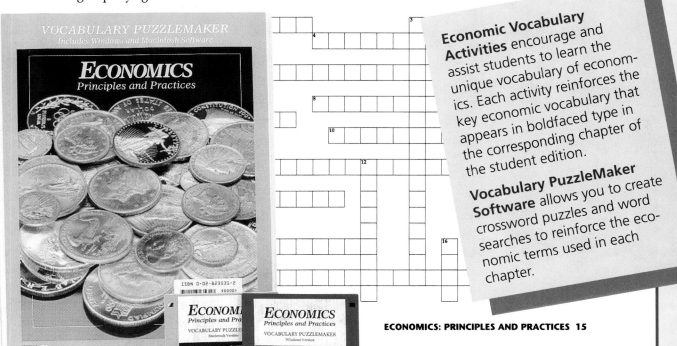

VOCABULARY PUZZLEMAKER
Includes Windows and Macintosh Software

ECONOMICS
Principles and Practices

ISBN 0-02-823531-2

ECONOMICS
Principles and Practices
VOCABULARY PUZZLEMAKER
Macintosh Version

ECONOMICS
Principles and Practices
VOCABULARY PUZZLEMAKER
Windows Version

McGraw Hill / Glencoe McGraw-Hill

Economic Vocabulary Activities encourage and assist students to learn the unique vocabulary of economics. Each activity reinforces the key economic vocabulary that appears in boldfaced type in the corresponding chapter of the student edition.

Vocabulary PuzzleMaker Software allows you to create crossword puzzles and word searches to reinforce the economic terms used in each chapter.

ECONOMICS: PRINCIPLES AND PRACTICES 15

Pages shown are reduced. Actual size is 8 1/2" x 11".

ACTIVITY **5** *Consumer Application*

GOVERNMENT REGULATION

In the American economy, the questions of what to produce and how to produce it are not answered completely by market forces. Government also plays a role by establishing regulations to guarantee the quality of goods and services. Considering the government regulations involved in making a simple consumer item, such as pizza, will give you some idea of the role government plays. Study the pictogram below, and then answer the questions that follow.

Mozzarella cheese—Must be at least 30%, but no more than 45%, fat and come from pasteurized cow's milk.

Beef—Ground beef must be no more than 30% fat.

Crust—Each pound of flour must contain 2.9 mg thiamine, 24 mg niacin and at least 13—but not more than 16—mg of iron.

Pepperoni—18 to 21% protein content required. Meat used in school lunches must pass daily USDA inspections at the plant.

Italian sausage—Uncured, unsmoked sausage must be at least 85% meat. If it consists of more than 13% extenders, it must carry the notice "texturized soy flour added."

Tomato sauce— Must be the "reddish" variety, with at least 24% "natural tomato soluble solids."

Anchovies—Must be packed in oil and in a solution of at least 12% salt.

Mushrooms—Only vitamin C—up to 37.5 mg per ounce—and water allowed in canned mushrooms.

List three or more ingredients that go into making your favorite pizza. Beside each ingredient, guess the [pur]pose of the government regulation controlling its use.

_____

_____

_____

_____

[Foo]d and Drug Administration and the Department of Agriculture have about 310 regulations con-[trolling] pizza ingredients. What other reasons can you think of for these regulations?

_____

_____

[What nega]tive effects might such regulations have on consumers?

_____

_____

_____

_____

Consumer Application Activities show students how the basic economic concepts they have learned can be applied to real-life financial situations.

Pages shown are reduced. Actual size is 8 1/2" x 11".

CHAPTER 6 | *Reinforcing Economic Skills*

INTERPRETING POLITICAL CARTOONS

Political cartoons are entertaining and powerful ways to express opinions about political and economic issues. Study the cartoon below, then answer the questions that follow.

Source: *Cincinnati Post*, November 26,

> **Reinforcing Economic Skills** activities help students develop and reinforce a wide range of skills. Each activity correlates to the skill taught in that chapter of the student edition.

1. Who do the two seated men represent?

_____

2. What do the background and the servant represent?

_____

3. a. What is the man complaining about?

_____

b. Who are the "they" referred to in the cartoon?

_____

4. What is the main point of this cartoon?

_____

_____

5. Do you think the cartoon makes its point effectively, or would a written editorial be more effective? Explain your answer.

_____

Pages shown are reduced. Actual size is 8 1/2" x 11".

ACTIVITY **12** *Cooperative Learning*

MARKETING

GROUP PROJECT

Although price is certainly one major factor affecting a consumer's decision to buy, many other factors also influence this decision. Each company spends a great deal of time and effort determining what these factors are and how to market its product to address them. This research can help the company develop an effective strategy that combines the "four Ps" of marketing: product, price, place, and promotion. As part of a marketing team, develop a marketing strategy and a short advertisement for a product of your choice.

Marketing Strategy

Product	Price	Place	Promotion
What type of packaging will you use? Will you include a warranty or rebate offer? What type of logo or trademark will be used to identify the product?	Estimate your costs of production, advertising, selling, and distribution. How much will you charge the consumer? How much profit do you hope to make?	How are you going to sell the product: by mail, phone, door-to door? What type of store will sell the product?	How will you advertise the product: in newspapers, radio announcements, TV commercials, or direct-mail pieces? Will you rely on just one form of advertisement? Consider offering coupons, free samples, gifts, etc.

COOPERATIVE GROUP PROCESS

1. **Decision-Making** Organize into groups of at least 8 students. As a group, choose a product that your company will package, distribute, and market. Use your imaginations. The product you decide on may be a different version of an already existing item or a completely new creation. Try to limit your choice to a simple product or service, such as a new fast food or pet-walking service. Then assign two or more group members to work on each of the "four Ps" of marketing.
2. **Subgroup Work** Each marketing team conducts research about similar products already on the market using as a guide the planning questions included in the chart for its assigned topic. One person on each team records suggestions made by subgroup members for the group's product. Suggestions are discussed and accepted or rejected. Depending on the assigned topic, artwork or a written summary is prepared to exhibit or explain how the product will be packaged, how much it will cost, where it will be sold, or what advertising will be used.
3. **Group Sharing** The main group reconvenes. Each marketing team describes how it answered the questions for its topic by presenting its artwork or reading its summary. Offer constructive feedback and attempt to solve problems and address concerns.
4. **Group Work** Using the recommendations of each marketing team, work together to create a short TV commercial to advertise your product to the class.
5. **Analysis** Other groups identify the "marketing ploys" used in ea~~~ discusses what influence these have on their decision to buy.

GROUP PROCESS QUESTIONS

Were the goals of this assignment clear?

Did each member share information?

Did members respect each other's point of view and give helpful ~

What would you change to make the group work more enjoyable?

Cooperative Learning Activities reinforce learning and build management and interpersonal skills by requiring students to work together to acquire, organize, and present information.

Most people would probably opt for a little more respectability and reliability. They should go for Strategy 2 or 3. (My wife, after driving a thirteen-year-old Volvo . . . went for Strategy 2. A bit reckless, but she deserves it.)

Whatever you decide, remember that you're trading off comfort, luxury, convenience, reliability, and self-respect for money! Just to help you get through the hard times, here are a few ways to visualize the reward.

$50,000 = A two-week trip every year for twenty years to Hawaii (or Europe, or Hoboken, New Jersey). . . .

$50,000 = A wonderful intimate dinner for two twice a month in the fanciest restaurant you can think of. . . .

$50,000 = A year off from work!

$50,000 = 5,000 anchovy pizzas. Think about this. 5,000 pizzas is ten pizzas a week for ten years; that's almost two a day EVERY DAY. You could eat pizza for ten years on the money you save on this strategy. A truly awesome thought.

From *Car Talk* by Tom and Ray Magliozzi. Copyright © 1991 by Tom and Ray Magliozzi. Used by permission of Dell Books, a division of Bantam Doubleday Dell Publishing Group, Inc.

ANALYZING THE READING

1. What does a person gain by buying an older car?

2. What does a person gain by buying a newer car?

3. How much money co[...]

4. What personal probler[...]

5. Which car-buying strate[...]

12

Name   Class   Date

READING 6   *Primary & Secondary Sources*

CAR TALK

Buying a car is a serious business—but that doesn't mean it can't be fun. Tom and Ray Magliozzi, known as "Click and Clack," dispense humorous but sound car advice to millions on their radio show "Car Talk" and through their book of the same name, from which the following is excerpted. As you read their advice, think about how the savings you make through careful buying add up over time. Then answer the questions that follow.

Our car-buying lives stretch over fifty years (from age twenty to age seventy, at least). And doing the wrong thing for fifty years adds up to a huge pile of money, like maybe $100,000 or $150,000! That is, the difference between a smart car-buying strategy and a not-so-smart strategy can mean a *difference* of more than $100,000 in your pocket (or under your mattress). . . .

There are all kinds of car-buying strategies. They range from buying a new car every year to buying the "best" heap you can find for under five hundred bucks. The latter is *always* cheaper. Don't let anybody tell you any different! If you buy a new car every year, you will always be paying the bank at least $4,000 every year. Always! And even a heap will last a year. (And if it doesn't, you could buy *eight* $500 heaps for $4,000). So, this strategy is always cheaper—in dollars. Of course, if you add in the psychological costs of headaches, worry, the inconvenience of breaking down, the embarrassment of driving a heap, then it's a different story. The guy with the new car has much more comfort, luxury, convenience, and reliability than you do.

You have *traded* these things for *money*.

So who needs headaches, worry, embarrassment? The problem is that we all at some point in our lives have owned the proverbial sled. And we remember in great detail all those headaches. And now . . . we are willing to pay to avoid them.

But here's the great discovery that has been made in the Click and Clack Institute of Paranormal Psychology and Charm School: You can have your cake and eat it too!

There are strategies that lie between the two extremes mentioned above, and they work. If you adopt one of these in-between strategies, you can not only pocket a pile of money but you

can also avoid most if not all of the inconveniences. . . .

[H]ere are the strategies to be considered:
1. Buy a new car every two [...]
2. Buy a three-year-[...] seven years.
3. Buy a seven-year c[...] three years.
4. Buy a nine-year-old [...]

[T]he difference betwee[...] heap) and Strategy 1 (new [...] is fifty thousand dollars. Tha[...] fifty grand under your mat[...]

> **There are all kin[...] buying strategies. T[...] from buying a new [...] year to buying the "l[...] you can find . . .**

twenty years, if you buy a heap instead of buying a new car every two years.

That's the biggest [difference in the strategies] but we don't necessarily recommend that everyone select Strategy 4. After all, we are talking about a *trade-off*, and in order to realize this much of a gain, you have to trade off an awful lot—mostly in the form of reliability, but also in the form of prestige. Most people's egos can't deal with what other people think about a person who's driving around in a nine-year-old rust bucket. (My car is *twenty-seven* years old; that tells you something about how much self-respect I have left. This is obviously the strategy for the real cheapskate.)

PRIMARY & SECONDARY SOURCE READINGS   11

Primary and Secondary Source Readings provide interesting supplemental readings that help students learn practical applications of economics in their nation and the world. Each activity includes a reading and questions that allow students to use the critical thinking skills taught throughout the course.

Pages shown are reduced. Actual size is 8 1/2" x 11".

Focus Activities

The Bank Panic of 1907

A bank panic that occurred in 1907 led to actions and legislation that created a central bank for the United States.

Focus Activity Transparencies provide 100 high-interest, visually motivating transparencies that allow you to introduce each text section with an arresting visual in order to pique student interest in the major concepts of the section. An accompanying **Focus Activity Sheet** as well as a **Teaching Strategy** page is provided for each transparency.

...cribe wha...
about this ban...

2. When a bank...
followed. How...

Focus Activities

Focus Activities

...e Changing Role of Marketing

...se print media advertisements—one from 1899, the other from 1994—present different marketing styles and strategies.

Reproduced from a Sears Roebuck catalog, 1899.
Advertisement from 1899

Photo courtesy of Chrysler Corporation.
Advertisement from 1994

1. What are some of the differences between the two advertisements?

2. How have marketing strategies developed between 1899 and 1994?

Focus Activities

Pages shown are reduced. Actual size is 8 1/2" x 11".

T28

Economic Concepts

The bar graph shows the differences in median wages for males and females in the United States. It compares the percentage of median female income to median male income. For example, in 1990 the median income for women was 71.1 percent of the median income for men.

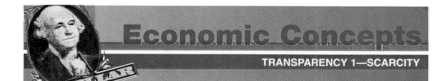

Median Female Income as a Percentage of Male Income

1. According
   income. If f
   make for ev

2. What would

Economic Concepts

Economic Concepts

The cartoon depicts a very common situation: a long list of wants and the dilemma of how to pay for them. It illustrates the economic concept of scarcity: unlimited wants and limited resources.

1. Based on the transparency, what things are requested? Are these wants or needs?

2. What is the scarce resource?

Economic Concepts

Economic Concepts Transparencies provide 22 transparencies, each keyed to one of the economic concepts identified by the National Council on Economic Education. Self-contained student activities that accompany each transparency can be assigned for homework or for independent practice. Teaching pages include clear objectives, activities, and discussion questions.

Pages shown are reduced. Actual size is 8 1/2" x 11".

Economic Forms

X-Y Axis Line Graph

Economic Forms Transparencies provide you with 8 blank forms commonly used in the study of economics. Student activity sheets reproduce these forms, and teaching strategies that accompany each transparency provide you with a wealth of opportunities for classroom instruction.

Economic Forms

CHAPTER 14

Audiocassette Test

GROSS DOMESTIC PRODUCT

Directions: After listening to the cassette tape for Chapter 14, complete the following items.

▨ **Write** the type of income next to each definition using the following abbreviations: **GNP** (Gross National Product), **NNP** (Net National Product), **GDP** (Gross Domestic Product), **PI** (Personal Income), **DPI** (Disposable Personal Income), **NI** (National Income). (10 points each)

___ 1. total income of consumers before income taxes are subtracted

___ 2. GNP minus capital consumption allowances

___ 3. the dollar value of final goods, services, and structures produced in one year with labor and property supplied by U.S. residents

___ 4. NNP minus all taxes—except corporate profits tax—that businesses pay as a cost of doing business

___ 5. (C+I+G+F)

___ 6. consumer income after incom___

___ 7. the dollar amount of all final___ one year

▨ **Circle** the term in parentheses ___

8. Businesses include (retained earni___ taxes.

9. Government sector expenditure___ this money is used by others to___

10. When the GDP hasn't been ad___

11. Secondhand sales are not cou___ (they are used to make other pr___

12. The cost of the new market___ ___tion rate).

CHAPTER DIGESTS AUDIOCASSETTES

ECONOMICS
Principles and Practices

CHAPTER 14

Audiocassette Activity

GROSS DOMESTIC PRODUCT

Directions: As you listen to the cassette tape for Chapter 14, complete the following items.

▨ **Match** the following terms to the correct definitions.

___ 1. nonmarket transactions

___ 2. gross private domestic investment

___ 3. output-expenditure model

___ 4. national income accounting

___ 5. capital consumption allowances

___ 6. implicit GDP price deflator

a. A system used to study production, consumption, savings, and investment

b. Products used in making other products that are already counted in GDP

c. Services provided by homemakers

d. The depreciation of capital stock that occurs because of production

e. Expenditures that the investment sector makes

f. Measures price changes in GDP and removes the effects of inflation

___ Shows aggregate demand by all sectors

___ ow.

___ hanges in the

___ ports.

___ hold.
___ er.

___ reflected by the
___ nal income.
___ ed earnings.

___ s a value of

d. none of these

___ aid payments.
___ s and tips.

**CHAPTER DIGESTS AUDIOCASSETTE
ACTIVITIES AND TESTS**

ECONOMICS
Principles and Practices

Includes
• Chapter Summaries on Audiocassette
• Chapter Activities
• Tests

G30892.08

Pages shown are reduced.

Spanish Resources include vocabulary activities, reteaching activities, and 22 section quizzes, and 22 Economic Concepts transparencies packaged in an easy-to-use binder. **Spanish Chapter Digest Audiocassettes** are also available.

Name _____   Class ___ Date ___ Score ___

Chapter 1

SECTION 3 QUIZ

MATCHING

Match each item in Column A with the items in Column B.
Write the correct letters in the blanks. (10 points each)

A

_____ 1. needs
_____ 2. wants
_____ 3. goods
_____ 4. services
_____ 5. market

A. tangible commodities
B. means of expressing need
C. location or other mechan___
   to exchange economic p___
D. basic requirements for s___
E. works that are perform___

MULTIPLE CHOICE

In the blank at the left, write the letter of the choice that best comple___
the statement or answers the question. (10 points each)

___mething to have value, it must
___of money.

c. be
d. ne___

___le of a servi___
c. ___

Name _____   Class ___ Date ___ Score ___

Chapter 1

SECTION 2 QUIZ

MATCHING

Match each item in Column A with the items in Column B.
Write the correct letters in the blanks. (10 points each)

A

_____ 1. opportunity cost
_____ 2. production possibilities
   frontier
_____ 3. trade-off
_____ 4. decision-making grid

B

A. an alternative choice
B. a tool that can be used to help make an economic decision by
   identifying alternatives and criteria to evaluate the alternatives
C. the classic example used to illustrate opportunity costs along the
   production possibilities frontier
D. the cost of the next best alternative when a choice is made
   ___enting various combinations of goods and services
   ___uce when all resources are fully employed

___pletes

___p between trade-offs and opportunity costs?
___offs are made.
___offs.
___n economic decision.
___unity costs.

___l for $35.00. Which of the following is an

___oney on a soccer ball
___ave been bought for $35.00

___d the tax paid on the ball

___eristic of a production possibilities frontier?
___ty costs.
___productive resources.
___description and analysis.
___ls for goods and services.

___o goods is producing on its production possibilities
___of good A means that
___ced.   c. ___ood B must be produced.
___e pro___   ___ne opportunity costs involved.

Name _____   Class ___ Date ___ Score ___

Chapter 1

SECTION 1 QUIZ

MATCHING

Match each item in Column A with the items in Column B.
Write the correct letters in the blanks. (10 points each)

A

_____ 1. scarcity
_____ 2. entrepreneurs
_____ 3. capital
_____ 4. labor
_____ 5. land

B

A. factor of production that includes all natural resources
B. factor of production that includes the tools, equipment, and
   factories used in the production of goods and services
C. factor of production that includes people and their efforts, abilities,
   and skills
D. condition that arises because society does not have enough
   resources to produce all the things people would like to have
E. factor of production that involves risk-takers in search of profits

MULTIPLE CHOICE

In the blank at the left, write the letter of the choice that best completes
the statement or answers the question. (10 points each)

_____ 6. Which of the following is NOT a basic economic question?
   a. WHAT to produce
   b. WHEN to produce
   c. FOR WHOM to produce
   d. HOW to produce

_____ 7. The study of economics includes all of the following EXCEPT
   a. description.
   b. analysis.
   c. explanation.
   d. financing.

_____ 8. What is the fundamental problem of economics?
   a. scarcity
   b. capital
   c. the factors of production
   d. labor

_____ 9. Which of the following is NOT a capital good?
   a. a bulldozer at a construction site
   b. a cash register at a clothing store
   c. an oven at a bakery
   d. a television set for sale at an appliance store

_____ 10. What is the best explanation of "There Is No Such Thing As A Free Lunch" (TINSTAAFL)?
   a. Businesses try to attract consumers with "free" offers that are really not free.
   b. There is always a cost when something is produced.
   c. The factors of production are the means for a society to produce and distribute goods
      and services.
   d. Every society must answer the three basic economic questions.

Section Quizzes provide a
quick, effective way to monitor the daily progress of your
students.

Pages shown are reduced.
Actual size is 8 1/2" x 11".

CHAPTER 5 TEST   Form B

MATCHING

Match each item in Column A with the items in Column B. Write the correct letters in the blanks. (3 points each)

A

_____ 1. evaluation of extra costs and extra benefits of an action
_____ 2. number of units sold multiplied by the average price per unit
_____ 3. the raw materials needed for production
_____ 4. extra output gained by adding one more unit of input
_____ 5. a period of production that allows change only to the amount of variable inputs
_____ 6. relates changes in output to different amounts of a variable input while other inputs are fixed
_____ 7. the total fixed cost
_____ 8. third stage of production
_____ 9. amount of a product sellers offer at every possible market price
_____ 10. graphic presentation of supply schedule

B

A. production function
B. inputs
C. supply
D. overhead
E. marginal analysis
F. supply curve
G. negative returns
H. marginal product
I. short run
J. total revenue

MULTIPLE CHOICE

In the blank at the left, write the letter of th_ ... _tement or answers the question. (4 points each)

_____ 11. If a firm can react quickly t_ products, then supply is li_
    a. elastic.
    b. unit elastic.

_____ 12. Depreciation is the
    a. purchasing of new e_
    b. cost of shipping goo_

_____ 13. The profit-maximizing_
    a. total cost equals tot_
    b. marginal cost equal_
    _ total production is_
    _ l costs are min_

CHAPTER 5 TEST   Form A

MATCHING

Match each item in Column A with the items in Column B. Write the correct letters in the blanks. (3 points each)

A

_____ 1. business expenses that change as production changes
_____ 2. describes the relationship between input and output
_____ 3. one of the stages of production
_____ 4. expenses that a business incurs even if the plant is idle and output is zero
_____ 5. the reaction of quantity supplied to a price change
_____ 6. the amount producers bring to market
_____ 7. the sum of fixed and variable costs
_____ 8. total revenue equals total cost
_____ 9. quantity supplied varies directly with price
_____ 10. a government payment to protect a certain type of economic activity

B

A. Law of Supply
B. supply elasticity
C. total cost
D. subsidy
E. Law of Variable Proportions
F. break-even point
G. variable costs
H. diminishing returns
I. quantity supplied
J. fixed costs

MULTIPLE CHOICE

In the blank at the left, write the letter of the choice that best completes the statement or answers the question. (4 points each)

_____ 11. The basic decision for a supplier is
    a. how much to produce without regard to demand.
    b. the amount to offer for sale at various prices.
    c. the willingness of consumers to purchase.
    d. the ability of consumers to purchase.

_____ 12. The factor that would cause the supply curve to shift to the right is
    a. higher taxes.
    b. a decrease in government subsidies.
    c. an increase in the cost of inputs.
    d. an increase in the number of sellers.

_____ 13. The extra cost incurred by producing one additional unit of a product is called
    a. total cost.
    b. variable cost.
    c. marginal cost.
    d. fixed cost.

_____ 14. The schedule of quantities that would be offered for sale at all possible prices that could prevail in the market is called
    a. trade-offs.
    b. elastic demand.
    c. opportunity costs.
    d. supply.

_____ 15. Demand is based on consumer purchase, whereas supply is based on
    a. the ability to purchase.
    b. the willingness to purchase.
    c. producers offering products for sale.
    d. offering a wide range of prices.

Chapter Tests (Forms A and B) evaluate student understanding of the main chapter facts and ideas. **Unit Tests** measure student comprehension of major concepts in economics.

Economics: Principles and Practices Testmaker software allows you to customize section, chapter, and unit tests. Use the existing database to create tests covering one or more sections, chapters, or units. In addition, you can edit the more than 3,000 database questions or add your own. The software is available in Macintosh or Windows formats.

BUSINESS ORGANIZATIONS

Local Objectives	TWE – Teacher's Wraparound Edition TCR – Teacher's Classroom Resources
	Objectives 1. Describe the characteristics of the sole proprietorship. 2. Understand the strengths and weaknesses of the partnership. 3. Describe the structure and features of the corporation.
	Focus __ Bellringer and Motivational Activities, TWE, p. 54 __ *Focus Activity Transparency 23*, TCR __ Preteaching Vocabulary, TWE, p. 54 __ Chapter Digests Audiocassette (English and Spanish)
	Teach **Guided Practice** __ Activities, TWE, pp. 55–57 __ Meeting Special Needs, TWE, p. 55 __ NBR's Economics In Action Video Program __ *Economic Concepts Transparency 5*, TCR (English and Spanish) __ *Cooperative Learning Activities*, TCR, p. 9 __ *Economic Simulations 1*, TCR __ *Economic Laboratories 1*, TCR **Independent Practice** __ Activities, TWE, pp. 58–60 __ *Guided Reading Activities*, TCR, p. 7 __ *Math Practice for Economics*, TCR, p. 8 __ *Primary and Secondary Source Readings*, TCR, pp. 17–18 __ *Reinforcing Economic Skills*, TCR, p. 3 __ *Free Enterprise Activities*, TCR, pp. 9, 11 __ *Performance Assessment Activities*, TCR, p. 8
	Assess __ Check for Understanding, TWE, p. 60 __ Meeting Lesson Objectives, TWE, p. 61 __ *Section Quizzes*, TCR, p. 7 (English and Spanish) __ Evaluate, TWE, p. 62
	Reteaching __ Reteach, TWE, p. 62
	Enrichment __ Enrich, TWE, p. 62
	Close __ Close, TWE, p. 62

Reproducible Lesson Plans let you spend less time planning and more time teaching.

Pages shown are reduced. Actual size is 8 1/2" x 11".

Multimedia Resources

Stocktracker Software is a simulation of stock trading that teaches students the effects of news events on stock prices.

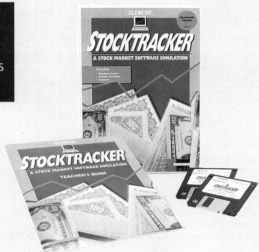

Chapter Challenger Interactive Review Software reinforces the economic terms used in each chapter. A complete bank of multiple choice questions allows students to test their understanding of basic economic concepts at the unit, chapter, or section levels. A tutorial explains why incorrect answers to the questions are wrong.

Nightly Business Report: Economics In Action Videos teach students economic concepts through stimulating television features. Available on laser discs or videotape, these 30 high-interest video segments were produced in conjunction with the award-winning staff and crew of *Nightly Business Report*. A student activity sheet and teaching strategies accompany each video segment.

Interactive Economics! CD-ROM and software make learning economics fun and easy. The 10 lessons help your students master important economic concepts.

MindJogger Videoquiz offers preview, review, and reinforcement of chapter content in a game-show environment. Available in videodisc and VHS formats.

ECONOMICS
Principles and Practices

GARY E. CLAYTON, Ph.D.

GLENCOE
McGraw-Hill

New York, New York   Columbus, Ohio   Woodland Hills, California   Peoria, Illinois

ABOUT THE AUTHOR

Gary E. Clayton teaches economics and finance at Northern Kentucky University in Highland Heights, Kentucky. Dr. Clayton received his Ph.D. in Economics from the University of Utah, has taught economics and finance at several universities, and has authored textbooks—including several at the college level—as well as a number of articles in various educational, professional, and technical journals. Dr. Clayton has also appeared on a number of radio and television programs, and was a guest commentator specializing in economic statistics for "Marketplace," which is broadcast on American Public Radio and originates at the University of Southern California.

Dr. Clayton has a long-standing interest in economic education. He has participated in and directed numerous economic education workshops. He received the Outstanding Citizen Certificate of Recognition from the state of Arkansas for his work in economic education. He also received a third-place award in the college division of the International Paper Company competition, an award sponsored by the National Council on Economic Education. He has served as Vice President for the Kentucky Council on Economic Education and received the state's highest honor when he received a commission as an honorary Kentucky Colonel. During the summer months, he participates in various study-abroad programs that take college students to Europe.

Glencoe/McGraw-Hill

A Division of The **McGraw·Hill** *Companies*

Send all inquiries to:
Glencoe/McGraw-Hill
936 Eastwind Drive
Westerville, Ohio 43081

ISBN 0-02-823556-8   (Student Edition)
ISBN 0-02-823560-6   (Teacher's Wraparound Edition)

Printed in the United States of America.
1 2 3 4 5 6 7 8 9 10 027/046 03 02 01 00 99 98

CONTENTS

CONTENTS

PROFILES IN ECONOMICS

JANET YELLEN
ECONOMIST
page 242

OPRAH WINFREY
ENTREPRENEUR
page 278

ALAN GREENSPAN
ECONOMIST
page 301

EDWARD T. LEWIS
ENTREPRENEUR
page 324

JOHN MAYNARD KEYNES
ECONOMIST
page 353

WALTER E. WILLIAMS
ECONOMIST
page 382

WILMA MANKILLER
ENTREPRENEUR
page 398

MILTON FRIEDMAN
ECONOMIST
page 435

BILL GATES
ENTREPRENEUR
page 452

KARL MARX
ECONOMIC HISTORIAN
page 476

W. ARTHUR LEWIS
ECONOMIST
page 503

THOMAS MALTHUS
ECONOMIST
page 526

ECONOMICS IN ACTION
Video Activities

INTERACTIVE ECONOMICS!
Computer Activities

SURFING THE "NET"
Web Activities

Technology Activities

CASE STUDIES: ISSUES IN FREE ENTERPRISE

Skills

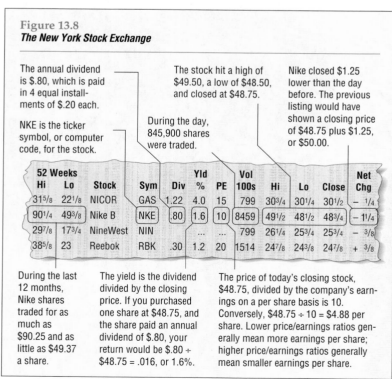

Figure 13.8
The New York Stock Exchange

The annual dividend is $.80, which is paid in 4 equal installments of $.20 each.

NKE is the ticker symbol, or computer code, for the stock.

The stock hit a high of $49.50, a low of $48.50, and closed at $48.75.

During the day, 845,900 shares were traded.

Nike closed $1.25 lower than the day before. The previous listing would have shown a closing price of $48.75 plus $1.25, or $50.00.

52 Weeks Hi	Lo	Stock	Sym	Div	Yld %	PE	Vol 100s	Hi	Lo	Close	Net Chg
31⁵/₈	22¹/₈	NICOR	GAS	1.22	4.0	15	799	30³/₄	30¹/₄	30¹/₂	– ¹/₄
90¹/₄	49³/₈	Nike B	NKE	.80	1.6	10	8459	49¹/₂	48¹/₂	48³/₄	– 1¹/₄
29⁷/₈	17³/₄	NineWest	NIN	...	...		799	26¹/₄	25³/₄	25³/₄	– ³/₈
38⁵/₈	23	Reebok	RBK	.30	1.2	20	1514	24⁷/₈	24³/₈	24⁷/₈	+ ³/₈

During the last 12 months, Nike shares traded for as much as $90.25 and as little as $49.37 a share.

The yield is the dividend divided by the closing price. If you purchased one share at $48.75, and the share paid an annual dividend of $.80, your return would be $.80 ÷ $48.75 = .016, or 1.6%.

The price of today's closing stock, $48.75, divided by the company's earnings on a per share basis is 10. Conversely, $48.75 ÷ 10 = $4.88 per share. Lower price/earnings ratios generally mean more earnings per share; higher price/earnings ratios generally mean smaller earnings per share.

HELP WANTED

DID YOU KNOW?

CONTENTS
Charts, Graphs, and Maps

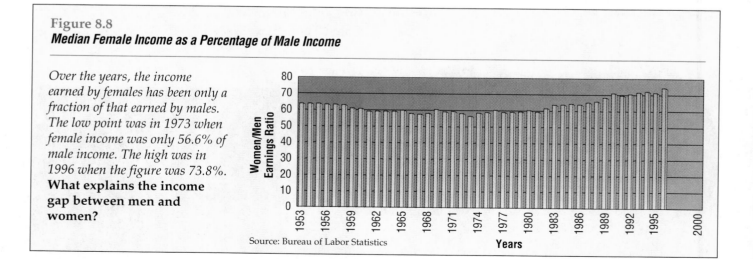

Figure 8.8
Median Female Income as a Percentage of Male Income

Over the years, the income earned by females has been only a fraction of that earned by males. The low point was in 1973 when female income was only 56.6% of male income. The high was in 1996 when the figure was 73.8%. **What explains the income gap between men and women?**

Source: Bureau of Labor Statistics

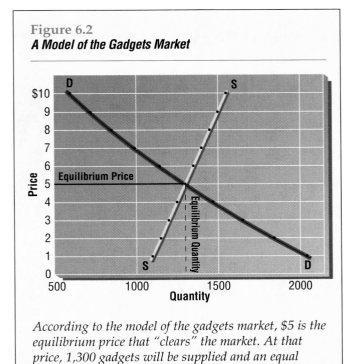

Figure 6.2
A Model of the Gadgets Market

According to the model of the gadgets market, $5 is the equilibrium price that "clears" the market. At that price, 1,300 gadgets will be supplied and an equal number purchased. **What happens to the supply of gadgets if the price is lowered to $3?**

CONTENTS

Figure 16.4

The Declining Value of the Dollar

When the price level goes up, the purchasing power of the dollar goes down. When the price level goes down, as it did during the Great Depression, the purchasing power of the dollar goes up. Today, the dollar buys about 5 percent of the goods and services it purchased in 1900. **If inflation continues, what will happen to the purchasing power of the dollar?**

Source: U.S. Department of Commerce

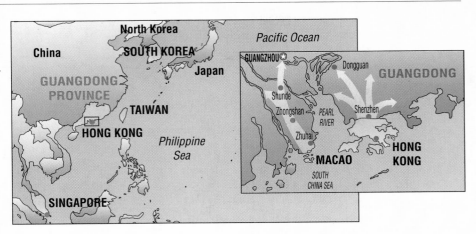

Figure 19.3
Capitalism in Asia—The Asian Tigers

Because of the dynamic growth and economic progress made by South Korea, Hong Kong, Singapore, and Taiwan since the end of World War II, they are sometimes called the "Asian Tigers." Some observers have even suggested that the Guangdong Province of mainland China could be added to this list. **How have the Asian Tigers relied on capitalism to spur their economic growth?**

Basic Concepts in Economics

These 21 basic economic concepts are adapted from *A Framework for Teaching Basic Economic Concepts* published by the **National Council on Economic Education**.

FUNDAMENTAL ECONOMIC CONCEPTS

1. Scarcity and Choice

Scarcity is the universal problem that faces all societies because there are not enough resources to produce everything people want. Scarcity requires people to make **choices** about the goods and services they use.

2. Opportunity Cost and Trade-Offs

Opportunity cost is the forgone benefit of the next best alternative when scarce resources are used for one purpose rather than another. **Trade-offs** involve choosing less of one thing to get more of something else.

3. Productivity

Productivity is a measure of the amount of output (goods and services) produced per unit of input (productive resources) used.

4. Economic Systems

Economic systems are the ways in which people organize economic life to deal with the basic economic problem of scarcity.

5. Economic Institutions and Incentives

Economic institutions include households and families and formal organizations such as corporations, government agencies, banks, labor unions, and cooperatives. **Incentives** are factors that motivate and influence human behavior.

6. Exchange, Money, and Inter-dependence

Exchange is a voluntary transaction between buyers and sellers. It is the trading of a good or service for another good or service, or for money. **Money** serves as a medium of exchange. **Interdependence** means that decisions or events in one part of the world or in one sector of the economy affect decisions and events in other parts of the world or sectors of the economy.

MICROECONOMIC CONCEPTS

7. Markets and Prices

Markets are arrangements that enable buyers and sellers to exchange goods and services. **Prices** are the amounts of money that people pay in exchange for a unit of a particular good or service.

8. Supply and Demand

Supply is defined as the different quantities of a resource, good, or service that will be offered for sale at various possible prices during a specific time period. **Demand** is defined as the different quantities of a resource, good, or service that will be purchased at various possible prices during a specific time period.

9. Competition and Market Structure

Competition is the struggle between businesses that strive for the same customer or market. Competition depends on **market structure**—the number of buyers and sellers, the extent to which firms can control price, the nature of the product, the accuracy and timeliness of information, and the ease with which firms can enter and exit the market.

10. Income Distribution

Income distribution refers to the way the nation's income is distributed by function—to those who provide productive resources—and by recipient, primarily individuals and families.

11. Market Failures

Market failures occur when there are inadequate competition, lack of access to reliable information, resource immobility, externalities, and the need for public goods.

12. The Role of Government

The **role of government** includes establishing a framework of law and order in which a market economy functions. The government plays a direct and an indirect role in the economy as both a producer and a consumer of goods and services.

MACROECONOMIC CONCEPTS

13. Gross Domestic Product

Gross Domestic Product (GDP) is defined as the market value of the total output of all final goods and services produced within a country's boundaries during one year.

14. Aggregate Supply and Aggregate Demand

Aggregate supply is the total amount of goods and services produced by the economy during a period of time. **Aggregate demand** is the total amount of spending on goods and services in the economy during a period of time.

15. Unemployment

Unemployment is defined as the number of people without jobs who are actively seeking work. This is also expressed as a rate when the number of unemployed is divided by the number of people in the labor force.

16. Inflation and Deflation

Inflation is a sustained increase in the average price level of the entire economy. **Deflation** is a sustained decrease in the average price level of an entire economy.

17. Monetary Policy

Monetary policy consists of actions initiated by a nation's central bank that affect the amount of money available in the economy and its cost (interest rates).

18. Fiscal Policy

Fiscal policy consists of changes in taxes, in government expenditures on goods and services, and in transfer payments that are designed to affect the level of aggregate demand in the economy.

INTERNATIONAL ECONOMIC CONCEPTS

19. Absolute and Comparative Advantage and Barriers to Trade

Absolute advantage and comparative advantage are concepts that are used to explain why trade takes place. Comparative advantage is based on opportunity cost and refers to a country's ability to produce goods and services relatively more efficiently. **Barriers to trade** deny citizens the benefits of relatively more efficient production in other countries.

20. Exchange Rates and the Balance of Payments

An **exchange rate** is the price of one nation's currency in terms of another nation's currency. The **balance of payments** of a country is a statistical accounting which records, for a given period, all payments that the residents, businesses, and governments of one country make to the rest of the world as well as the receipts that they receive from the rest of the world.

21. International Aspects of Growth and Stability

International aspects of growth and stability are more important today than in the past because all nations are much more interdependent.

Unit Goals

After studying this unit, students will be able to:

1. **Define** *economics* and its fundamental principles.

2. **Differentiate** between traditional, command, and market economies and discuss the major characteristics of the American free enterprise economy.

3. **Identify** the major types of economic organizations in the United States.

Unit Overview

Unit 1 provides a basic introduction to and an overview of economics. **Chapter 1** focuses on the fundamental economic problem of scarcity and introduces terms necessary to the study and understanding of economics. Additional concepts that deal with decision making are developed in **Chapter 2,** which focuses on the different economic systems. **Chapter 3** explains the different kinds of economic institutions that operate in our economy to bring resources and consumers together.

⌒ If time does not permit teaching the entire unit, use the **Chapter Digests Audiocassettes** to highlight chapter content.

Connecting with Past Learning

Ask students what they think of when they hear the word *economics*. Write their responses on the chalkboard and have them use this information to develop a working definition of *economics*. As students study the unit, have them adjust the definition.

UNIT 1

FUNDAMENTAL ECONOMIC CONCEPTS

CHAPTER 1
What Is Economics?

CHAPTER 2
Economic Systems and Decision Making

CHAPTER 3
Business Organizations and Economic Institutions

Our nation cannot afford to have high school students who lack the basic skills to understand vital economic issues. . . . Without a solid education in economics at the pre-college level, many adults will never have the slightest chance of learning how the economy functions and their roles in the wealth-creating process.

—William B. Walstad, Professor of Economics,
December 28, 1988

§ Economics and You

In this unit, discover what part economics plays in the following situations:

- You must choose between buying gas for your car or taking your friend out for pizza.
- Your friend from Russia is stunned by all the shoes available at your local shoe store.
- The same product is less expensive at a department store than at a specialty shop.

4 UNIT 1: *Fundamental Economic Concepts*

$$ *Economics and You*

The first situation above—choosing between buying gas or pizza—is an example of what economists call *opportunity cost*—the cost of the next best alternative of money, time, or resources when one choice is made rather than another. The second situation is an illustration of how different economic systems answer such basic economic questions as *WHAT to produce.* The third situation is an illustration of how a business organization's "bigness" can lead to more efficiency and lower consumer prices.

A farmer harvests his crop by implementing the factors of production—land, labor, entrepreneurship, and capital.

Introducing the Unit

Organize students in pairs and ask pair members to interview their partners to obtain the following information:

1. Give an example of a want.

2. What inputs are necessary to produce the want? *(i.e., factors of production—land, labor, capital, and entrepreneurship)*

3. Do you have any part in the process necessary to get your want? *(i.e., Do you work?)*

4. What can you do to get your want?

After each person has been interviewed, ask the class what is necessary in our society to obtain their wants. Point out that wants are purchased in the marketplace and cost money that most people must earn by selling their labor, or working. In other words, we trade our productive efforts to satisfy our wants.

Unit Project

Have each student choose a product or service. As new concepts and vocabulary are introduced in Unit 1, have students apply what they have learned to their product or service. When factors of production are discussed, for example, students should list those for their choice. In the same way, students should identify their product or service as a want or need, whether it has utility and value, how it would be manufactured and sold in the three types of economic systems, and so on.

Examining the Photograph

Ask students to identify what in the photograph represents each of the four factors of production. Record their responses on a flip chart. After students have studied the discussion of factors of production in Chapter 1, display the flip chart and have them review and adjust their original suggestions. *(land—fertile field; labor—tractor driver; capital—tractor, harvester; entrepreneurship—management skills of farmer, which brought the other factors together)*

5

CHAPTER ORGANIZER

Daily Objectives	Reproducible Resources	Multimedia Resources
Section 1 **Scarcity and the Science of Economics** 1. **Explain** the nature of scarcity and show its relationship to economics. 2. **Describe** the factors of production. 3. **Examine** the three basic economic questions each society must decide. 4. **Define** economics and identify the four key elements within its scope.	▭ Reproducible Lesson Plan 1-1 ▭ Guided Reading Activity 1-1 ▭ Cooperative Learning Activity 1 ▭ Consumer Application Activity 1 ▭ Math Practice for Economics 1 ▭ Free Enterprise Activity 3 ▭ Primary and Secondary Source Reading 1 ▭ Performance Assessment Activity 1 ▭ Reinforcing Economic Skills 1 ▭ Section Quiz 1-1*	Focus Activity Transparency 1 Vocabulary PuzzleMaker Chapter Challenger Interactive Review Software Testmaker MindJogger Videoquiz NBR's Economics in Action Video Program
Section 2 **Trade-Offs and Opportunity Costs** 1. **Understand** that trade-offs are present whenever choices are made. 2. **Discover** that trade-offs are costs in the form of opportunities given up when one course of action is chosen instead of another. 3. **Evaluate** the opportunity cost that an economy faces when resources are allocated to the production of one good instead of another.	▭ Reproducible Lesson Plan 1-2 ▭ Guided Reading Activity 1-2 ▭ Section Quiz 1-2*	Focus Activity Transparency 2 Vocabulary PuzzleMaker Chapter Challenger Interactive Review Software Testmaker Interactive Economics!
Section 3 **Basic Economic Concepts** 1. **Understand** the difference between needs and wants, and goods and services. 2. **Explain** the relationship among value, utility, and wealth. 3. **Describe** the importance of productivity. 4. **Understand** the importance of economics to the American free enterprise system.	▭ Reproducible Lesson Plan 1-3 ▭ Guided Reading Activity 1-3 ▭ Section Quiz 1-3*	Focus Activity Transparency 4 Vocabulary PuzzleMaker Chapter Challenger Interactive Review Software Testmaker NBR's Economics in Action Video Program Interactive Economics!
Chapter Review and Evaluation	▭ Enrichment Activity 1 ▭ Reteaching Activity 1* ▭ Economic Vocabulary Activity 1* ▭ Chapter 1 Test, Forms A and B	Chapter Digests Audiocassette Activities and Tests* Testmaker Mindjogger Videoquiz

Also available in Spanish

 Blackline Master   Transparency   CD-ROM   Software   Videodisc   Audiocassette

⏱ OUT OF TIME? Assign the Chapter 1 Digest Audiocassette and the corresponding Chapter Digest activities and tests.

VOLUNTARY NATIONAL CONTENT STANDARDS IN ECONOMICS

Emphasized in Chapter 1

Content Standard 1 *Students will understand that:*
Productive resources are limited. Therefore, people cannot have all the goods and services they want; as a result, they must choose some things and give up others.

Content Standard 2 *Students will understand that:*
Effective decision making requires comparing the additional costs of alternatives with the additional benefits. Most choices involve doing a little more or a little less of something; few choices are all-or-nothing decisions.

Economics America *Resources Available From NCEE*

- *Voluntary National Content Standards in Economics*
- *Capstone: The Nation's High School Economics Course*
- *Civics and Government*
- *Geography: Focus on Economics*
- *Personal Decision Making: Focus on Economics*

To order these materials, or to contact your state Council on Economic Education about workshops and programs, call 1-800-338-1192 or visit http://www.nationalcouncil.org**.**

PERFORMANCE ASSESSMENT

The following chapter projects may be assigned at the beginning of the chapter and used for performance assessment.

Multicultural Heritage Point out that many of the choices people make among their unlimited wants are influenced by culture. Young people, for example, usually buy clothes or music that is different from older generations' styles. Similarly, people of diverse ethnic backgrounds usually buy different types of food. Have students interview 10 people—students and teachers, family members, or neighbors—and ask them to identify three goods and three services they have purchased recently. In a follow-up class analysis of the interview findings, ask students to determine which of the most frequently mentioned choices were culturally determined. (*Answers may vary but might include haircuts, designer jeans, pizza, or popular videotapes or compact discs.*)

Cooperative Learning Have students apply economic decision making by constructing a grid similar to Jesse's Decision-Making Grid on page 15. Organize students into groups of four or five. Instruct groups to select a gift appropriate for a high school graduate. First, ask groups to brainstorm about possible high school graduation gifts and about the criteria that might be used to evaluate gift suggestions. Next, have each group organize the information developed during its brainstorming session into a grid. Then have group members discuss the criteria and record the evaluation of each gift suggestion with a yes or no on the grid. Finally, have groups select the most appropriate gift, based on the suggestion that has the largest number of positive responses to criteria. Invite groups to present and justify their decisions to the class. In a class discussion, compare the choices by the different groups and the reasons for those choices.

ADDITIONAL RESOURCES

Readings for the Student

Heilbroner, Robert L., and Lester Thurow. *Economics Explained*, revised ed. New York: Simon & Schuster, 1994. Explains the fundamentals of economics in straightforward language.

Pass, Christopher, et al. *The HarperCollins Dictionary of Economics.* New York: HarperCollins, 1991. Invaluable resource that uses illustrations and examples to define key economic concepts.

Readings for the Teacher

Brenneke, Judith Staley, ed. *An Economy at Risk: Does Anyone Care?* Atlanta: Georgia State University Business Press, 1992. Presents a rationale for including economics in elementary and secondary education.

Multimedia

Economics U$A: Resources & Scarcity/Markets & Prices. The Annenberg/CPB Collection, 19 Gregory Drive, South Burlington, VT 05403. Color video, 60 mins. First 30–minute program on video discusses the basic economic problem of scarcity.

An Introduction to Economics. Knowledge Unlimited, 1994. Available from Social Studies School Service, 10200 Jefferson Boulevard, P.O. Box 802, Culver City, CA 90232–0802. VHS videocassette, teacher's guide. Explains fundamentals of economics by examining U.S. economy in action.

Chapter Overview

Economics is the study of the ways in which societies use the limited resources available to them to satisfy the unlimited wants of their citizens. Thus, **Chapter 1** introduces students to the concept of scarcity and the necessity of making choices.

GLENCOE
TECHNOLOGY

VIDEODISC
MindJogger Videoquiz

Use MindJogger to preview the Chapter 1 content

 Chapter 1
Disc 1, Side A

 Also available in VHS.

inter**NET**
CONNECTION

Resources for Chapter 1 on the World Wide Web*

National Council on Economic Education

http://www.nationalcouncil.org/

Economic resources for K-12 teachers

http://ecedweb.unomaha.edu/teach2.htm

Sites subject to change.

As a consumer, you must make choices from many alternatives.

VISUAL INSTRUCTION

Encourage students to suggest how the photograph illustrates choices. *(different styles, colors, and sizes of sneakers)* Point out that economics includes the study of WHAT is produced, HOW the production takes place, and FOR WHOM the production is intended.

 Extra Credit Project

Have students create a television-viewing log for news items presented on the nightly news. Suggest that some students watch national newscasts on the networks, that others watch CNN national newscasts, and that still others watch local newscasts.

They should record the date, the subject of the item, and the length of time given to the item. When study of the chapter is completed, have students compare and discuss their logs, noting how much news is devoted to economic issues.

CHAPTER 1

What Is Economics?

SECTION 1
Scarcity and the Science of Economics

SECTION 2
Trade-Offs and Opportunity Costs

SECTION 3
Basic Economic Concepts

CHAPTER PREVIEW

People to Know

• Adam Smith
• Credit Manager

Applying Economic Concepts to Your Life

Trade-Offs Resources are scarce. Time is scarce. Sometimes it seems as if you have a million things to do, and you just don't know what to do first. You may have many alternatives to select from, and you have to make choices—but which choice is the right one? One choice may prevent another. Believe it or not, the study of economics will help you become a *better* decision maker because it helps you develop a "way of thinking" about *trade-offs* and decision making.

Journal Writing

For one week, keep track of all your economic decisions—the money you spend, the items you buy, the choices you make. Be aware of each decision and your reasons for making it.

CHAPTER 1: *What Is Economics?* **7**

FOCUS

Section Objectives

1. Explain the nature of scarcity and show its relationship to economics.
2. Describe the factors of production.
3. Examine the three basic economic questions each society must decide.
4. Define economics and identify the four key elements within its scope.

Bellringer

Prior to taking roll at the beginning of the class period, display Focus Activity Transparency 1 on the overhead projector and assign the accompanying Student Activity.

Motivational Activity

Discuss students' responses to the activity sheet that accompanies Focus Activity Transparency 1.

Preteaching Vocabulary

Have students provide examples of scarce resources in their daily lives.

Use the **Vocabulary PuzzleMaker** to create crossword and word search puzzles.

TEACH

Guided Practice

L1 *Bulletin Board* Have students bring to class photographs or magazine clippings that illustrate scarce economic resources. Then have volunteers create an annotated bulletin-board display titled *Scarcity.* **LEP**

SECTION 1
Scarcity and the Science of Economics

Section Preview

Objectives

After studying this section, you will be able to:

1. **Explain** the nature of scarcity and show its relationship to economics.
2. **Describe** the factors of production.
3. **Examine** the three basic economic questions each society must decide.
4. **Define** economics and identify the four key elements within its scope.

Key Terms

scarcity, factors of production, land, capital, financial capital, labor, entrepreneur, economics

Applying Economic Concepts

Scarcity We never seem to have enough! If you were asked to make a list of items you would like to have—and if the list could be as long as you wanted—it might take several days to finish the task. If we asked others to do the same, we would probably end up with more items than we could ever hope to produce. This is the essence of *scarcity*—a condition caused by unlimited wants in a world of limited resources.

Many things in life seem to be "free" when, actually, they are not. For example, you may think you are being treated to a "free" lunch when your friend uses a "buy one, get one free" coupon at a restaurant. While you may not pay for it then and there, someone had to pay the farmer for raising the food, the truck driver for delivering the food, the chef for preparing the food, and the server for serving the food. Who is that "someone"? Although it may come as a surprise, that someone may be you!

TINSTAAFL

When a business offers someone a "free" lunch, the price of that lunch is usually buried somewhere in the price the firm charges for its products. The "free" lunch may be offered to make a sale. If the person later orders services or products from the business, the firm will recover some, if not all, of the cost of the lunch.

If the individual does not buy, then someone else will pay for the lunch by paying higher prices. The more a business gives away "free," the more it has to charge for the items it produces and sells. In the end, someone always pays for the supposedly "free" lunch. **1**

Unfortunately, most things in life are not free because someone has to pay for the production in the first place. Economic educators have a term, *TINSTAAFL*, which describes this concept. In short, this term means that *There Is No Such Thing As A Free Lunch.* This concept is one of the keys to understanding the fundamental economic problem.

The Fundamental Economic Problem

The fundamental economic problem facing all societies is that of **scarcity**—the condition that arises because society does not have enough resources to produce all the things people would like to have. The problem of scarcity is not, as some people might think, caused by a shortage of money. ☑

Suppose that everyone in a society suddenly became wealthier than they ever thought possible. Even if everyone became millionaires, they would still go without many of the things they want and need. Who would want to work? Most people would probably try to spend their money on houses, boats, cars, vacations, and other things. At first, store owners would be delighted to sell their merchandise. The supply of items

---

Classroom Resources for SECTION 1

- Reproducible Lesson Plan 1-1
- Guided Reading Activity 1-1
- Cooperative Learning Activity 1
- Consumer Application Activity 1
- Math Practice for Economics 1
- Free Enterprise Activity 3
- Primary and Secondary Source Reading 1
- Performance Assessment Activity 1

- Reinforcing Economic Skills 1
- Section Quiz 1-1
- Spanish Section Quiz 1-1
- Focus Activity Transparency 1
- NBR's Economics in Action Video Program
- Testmaker
- Vocabulary PuzzleMaker
- Chapter Challenger Interactive Review Software
- MindJogger Videoquiz

Figure 1.1
Scarcity

Seemingly Unlimited Wants | Limited Resources

SCARCITY

CHOICES

WHAT To Produce | HOW To Produce | FOR WHOM To Produce

Scarcity is the fundamental economic problem that forces consumers and producers to use resources wisely. **Why is scarcity not caused by a shortage of money?**

Factors Of Production

The reason people cannot satisfy all their wants and needs is the scarcity of productive resources. These resources, or **factors of production**, are land, capital, labor, and entrepreneurship. They provide the means for a society to produce and distribute its goods and services. 2

Land

In economics, **land** refers to the "gifts of nature," or natural resources not created by human effort. "Land" includes deserts, fertile fields, forests, mineral deposits, cattle, whales, sunshine, and the climate necessary to grow crops.

Because only so many natural resources are available at any given time, economists tend to think of land as being fixed, or in limited supply. Not enough good farmland exists to feed all of the earth's population, nor enough sandy beaches for everyone to enjoy, nor enough minerals to meet our expanding energy needs indefinitely.

Capital

Another factor of production is **capital**—the tools, equipment, and factories used in the production of goods and services. Such items also are called capital goods to distinguish them from **financial capital**, the money used to buy the tools and equipment used in production.

Capital is unique in that it is the result of production. A bulldozer, for example, is a capital good used in construction. It was built in a factory, however, which makes it the result of earlier production. Like the bulldozer, the cash register in a neighborhood store is a capital good. It, too, is the result of earlier

in the stores would not last long, however. With few people working, it would be almost impossible to order more inventory from factories. Shelves would soon be empty, and there would be nothing left to buy.

The huge increase in everyone's income would not solve the economic problem of scarcity. Most likely, it would have the opposite effect—the entire economy would come to a halt until people found that their money was practically, if not totally, worthless. Thus, the problem of scarcity is not caused by a shortage of money, but by a lack of resources needed to make all the things people want.

Cooperative Learning
Assign Cooperative Learning Activity 1.

L2 *Analyzing Information*
List on the chalkboard a number of economic activities; for example, producing toys, providing financial advice, teaching economics. Call on volunteers to identify the factors of production used in these.

Economics in Action

Chapter 2
Disc 1, Side 1
Title: *What Is Economics?*
Subject: Concept of scarcity and trade-offs
Ask: If an item that everyone needs is scarce, how can it be allocated? *(Answers may include through rationing programs.)*

 Also available in VHS.

VISUAL INSTRUCTION

Answer to Caption:
Money has no impact on meeting unlimited wants with limited resources.

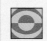

QUICK CHECK

Checking Understanding
1. Why is there no such thing as a "free" lunch?
2. What are the four factors of production?

Applying Economic Concepts
Scarcity During World War II, silk and nylon were used for making parachutes. As a result, women's stockings became scarce. Women dealt with this scarcity by painting their legs with makeup, simulating nylons, or by drawing seams up the backs of their legs.

CHAPTER 1: *What Is Economics?* **9**

Meeting Special Needs

Study Strategy The objectives given in the Section Preview feature provide a valuable tool for focusing students on the main ideas. Point out that the tasks required by the objectives are signaled in the first word. Some emphasize information collection ("List," "Identify"), while others call for description ("Describe," "Explain"). Still others ask students to compare, analyze, and so on. Ask students to look through all the objectives and note the first word of each. Discuss the kinds of responses required.

QUICK CHECK

ANSWERS

1. "Free" items force a business to charge more for items it sells.
2. land, labor, capital, entrepreneurship

Independent Practice

 Guided Reading Assign Guided Reading Activity for Section 1. **LEP**

Consumer Application Assign Consumer Application Activity 1.

Math Practice Assign Math Practice for Economics 1.

Free Enterprise Assign Free Enterprise Activity 3.

Readings Assign Primary and Secondary Source Reading 1.

Performance Assessment Assign Performance Assessment Activity 1.

L2 Designing a Poster Have students work individually or in small groups to design a poster that illustrates the three basic economic questions. **LEP**

L3 Writing Commercials Have students write storyboards for a television commercial "selling" economics as a subject that should be studied by the class. The commercial should describe the nature of economics, discuss the relevance of the subject to class members, and point out how they may benefit from an understanding of the subject.

VISUAL INSTRUCTION

Have students consider which, if any, of the four factors of production is the most important.

Answer to Caption:

minerals (diamonds), diamond-cutting machines, diamond cutters, jewelers

---

production and is used for the record keeping associated with the sale of goods and services.

Labor

A third factor of production is **labor**—people with all their efforts, abilities, and skills. This category includes all people except for a unique group of individuals called entrepreneurs, which we single out because of their special role in the economy.

Unlike land, labor is a resource that may vary in size over time. Historically, factors such as population growth, immigration, famine, war, and disease have had a dramatic impact on both the quantity and quality of labor.

Entrepreneurs

Some workers have a special status because they are the innovators responsible for much of the change in our economy. These people are called entrepreneurs. An **entrepreneur** is a risk-taker in search of profits.

Entrepreneurs often are thought of as the driving force in the American economy because they exhibit a knack for starting a new business or bringing new products to market. Their initiative combines the resources of land, labor, and capital into new products. **1**

Three Basic Questions

To provide for the needs of its people, a society must answer three basic economic questions. In so doing, it makes decisions about the ways its limited resources are going to be used.

Figure 1.2
The Factors of Production

THE FACTORS OF PRODUCTION

LAND   CAPITAL   LABOR   ENTREPRENEURS

LAND *includes the "gifts of nature," or natural resources not created by human effort.*

CAPITAL *includes the tools, equipment, and factories used in production. Capital is unique in that it is the result of production.*

LABOR *includes people with all their efforts and abilities, excluding those individuals with unique entrepreneurial abilities.*

ENTREPRENEURS *include those unique risk-taking individuals who have the ability to start a new business or bring a product to market.*

The productive resources in a modern economy include LAND, CAPITAL, LABOR, and ENTREPRENEURIAL ABILITY. All four factors of production are necessary for production to take place. **What four factors of production are necessary to bring jewelry to consumers?**

$ Free Enterprise Activity $

Just as consumers are faced with scarcity of goods and services, entrepreneurs must deal with scarcity of the other three factors of production—land, capital, and labor. Have students imagine they are entrepreneurs in the business of producing and selling widgets. Inform them that the price of the raw material used for making widgets has doubled. Encourage students to make economic predictions about what will happen in the widget business. *(Fewer widgets will be produced; the price of widgets will go up; consumers will purchase fewer widgets.)*

What To Produce

The first question is that of WHAT to produce. Should a society devote most of its resources to producing military equipment or to other items such as food, clothing, or housing? Suppose the decision is to produce housing. Should its limited resources then be used for low-income, middle-income, or upper-income housing? How many of each will be needed? A society cannot have everything its people want, so it must decide WHAT to produce.

How To Produce

A second question is that of HOW to produce. Should factory owners use assembly-line methods that require little labor, or should they use less equipment and more workers? If an area has many unemployed people, the second method might be better. On the other hand, assembly-line methods in countries where capital is widely available usually have lower production costs. Lower costs make many manufactured items less expensive and, therefore, available to more people.

For Whom To Produce

The third question deals with FOR WHOM to produce. After a society decides WHAT and HOW to produce, the items produced must be allocated to someone. If the society decides to produce housing, should it be distributed to workers, professional people, or government employees? Perhaps another group is more deserving. Who decides? In the end, the result is the same. If not enough houses exist for everyone, a choice must be made as to who will receive the existing supply.

These three choices about WHAT, HOW, and FOR WHOM to produce are not easy for any society to make. Nevertheless, a society has few options. It must answer the three basic questions as long as there are not enough resources to satisfy the fundamental economic problem of scarcity. Different societies answer these questions in different ways. 2

The Meaning and Scope of Economics

Economics is the study of human efforts to satisfy what appear to be unlimited and competing wants through the careful use of relatively scarce resources. It is also a social science because it deals with the behavior of people as they cope with the fundamental problem of scarcity.

Description

Economics deals with the *description* of economic activity. It is concerned with what is produced and who gets how much, as well as with topics such as unemployment, inflation, international trade, the interaction of business and labor, and the effects of government spending and taxes. Description, however, is not enough because description alone leaves many important "why" and "how" questions unanswered.

Analysis

In order to answer such questions, economics must focus on the *analysis* of economic activity as well. Why, for example, are prices of some items high while others are low? Why are incomes higher in some states than in others? How do taxes affect people's desire to work and save?

Checking Understanding	Applying Economic Concepts
1. Why are entrepreneurs considered the "driving force" in the American economy? 2. Why must a society face the choices about WHAT, HOW, and FOR WHOM to produce?	**Entrepreneurs** Think of a local entrepreneur—maybe even yourself! What factors of production did the entrepreneur combine into a new product?

CHAPTER 1: *What Is Economics?* **11**

ASSESS

Check for Understanding

Assign Section 1 Review as homework or an in-class activity.

Use **Chapter Challenger Interactive Review Software** to review Section 1.

> ### MEETING LESSON OBJECTIVES
>
> Each objective below is tested by the questions that follow it in parentheses.
> 1. **Explain** the nature of scarcity and show its relationship to economics. **(1, 2, 6, 7)**
> 2. **Describe** the factors of production. **(1, 3)**
> 3. **Examine** the three basic economic questions each society must decide. **(4)**
> 4. **Define** economics and identify the four key elements within its scope. **(1, 5)**

ANSWERS

1. because they exhibit a knack for starting a new business or bringing new products to market
2. because there are not enough resources to satisfy the problem of scarcity

Evaluate

Assign the Section 1 Quiz in the TCR or use the *Economics: Principles and Practices* Testmaker to create a customized quiz. Spanish Section Quizzes are available in the Spanish Resources Binder.

Reteach

Call on students to define the key terms listed in the Section Preview. Call on others to give an example or illustration of each term.

Enrich

Provide students with copies of business and financial newspapers and magazines, such as *The Wall Street Journal, Forbes,* and *Business Week.* Have students search through their publications to locate and discuss articles that address the concepts they have examined in the chapter.

CLOSE

Ask students to look up the definition of *social science* in the dictionary. Write the definition on the chalkboard. Direct students to the definition of *economics* on page 11 and the key elements within the scope of economics on pages 11–12. Have students discuss how the definition of social science matches the meaning and scope of economics as defined in the text.

HELP WANTED

Credit Manager

▼

A growing business requires a credit manager to decide whether to extend credit to clients—either companies or individuals. Duties include analyzing financial reports submitted by client companies, checking on their management, and reviewing credit agency reports on their promptness in paying bills. Credit policies to be met by individuals applying for credit also must be drawn up. You must also be able to set up office procedures and oversee other employees in the credit department. Required skills are analyzing detailed information, drawing conclusions, and speaking and writing effectively. Computer skills are helpful.

▼

Education: Degree in business administration
Median Salary: $39,700

Explanation

Economics is also concerned with the *explanation* of economic activity. After economists understand how things work, it is useful and even necessary to communicate this knowledge to others. In this manner, the study of economics helps us better understand our world.

Prediction

Finally, economics is concerned with *prediction*, anticipating the likely consequences of different courses of action. Suppose a community wants to raise revenue to build a health-care facility. Should the funds be raised through voluntary contributions, payroll taxes, property taxes, or by some other means? Economists can help predict the consequences of different courses of action, but the final choice is still up to the people in the community.

In the end, the scope of economics is limited to four key elements—description, analysis, explanation, and prediction. Economists study what is, or tends to be, and how it came to be. Economists can be compared to nuclear physicists who can explain how to make a nuclear bomb and what damage the bomb can do. As scientists, however, they are not expected to judge whether or not the bomb should be used in war. People must make up their own minds about that.

Economists do not hand down economic rules for people to obey. Deciding what is to be done is the responsibility of all citizens in a democratic society. The study of economics will not lead to ethical judgments for economic problems, but it will help us to become more informed citizens and better decision makers.

SECTION 1 REVIEW

Reviewing Terms and Facts

1. **Define** scarcity, factors of production, land, capital, financial capital, labor, entrepreneur, economics.
2. **Describe** the fundamental economic problem.
3. **Describe** the factors of production.
4. **List** the three basic economic questions any society must answer.

5. **Identify** the four key elements that define the scope of economics.

Critical Thinking

6. **Analyzing Information** Give an example of a supposedly "free" item that you see every day. Explain why the item is not really free by stating who or what actually pays for it.

Applying Economic Concepts

7. **Scarcity** How does scarcity affect your life? Provide several examples of items you have had to do without because limited resources could not keep up with your wants.

Answers to SECTION 1 REVIEW

1. All vocabulary words are defined in the Glossary.

2. scarcity—where seemingly unlimited wants have to be met with limited resources

3. land—natural resources not created by human effort; capital—tools, equipment, and factories used in production of goods and services; labor—people with all their efforts, abilities, and skills; and entrepreneurs—risk-takers in search of profits

4. WHAT to produce? HOW to produce? FOR WHOM to produce?

5. Description, analysis, explanation, prediction

6. Students may propose a "buy one meal, get another free" deal at a restaurant. They may suggest that the purchaser might pay for the meal later in repeat business at the restaurant, or that others may pay through higher prices for meals not on special offer.

7. Examples may include concert tickets, "limited edition" CDs, or clothes.

ECONOMIC SKILL

Interpreting Line Graphs

"A picture is worth a thousand words." How many times have you heard that expression? Often it is true. A graph, like a picture, can present much information in a more concise way than words. Graphs are drawings that compare numerical values. Graphs often are used to compare changes over time or differences between places, groups of items, or other related events.

Explanation

The line graph is a common type of graph. The information being compared usually appears on the left side of the graph—the vertical axis—with time appearing along the bottom of the graph—the horizontal axis. Dots or other symbols are sometimes used to show numerical values, and they are frequently connected with a line to keep the information from getting mixed up with other values in the graph.

The steps involved in interpreting line graphs are:

a. Read the title of the graph. This should tell you what to expect or look for.
b. Familiarize yourself with the information on the horizontal axis.
c. Familiarize yourself with the information on the vertical axis.
d. Examine where the dots are placed on the graph.
e. Determine what the line(s) or curve(s) symbolizes. Sometimes the lines are even labeled to make the graph easier to read.
f. Compare the line(s) in the graph to the horizontal and vertical axes to determine the point being made.

Practice

Examine the line graph, then answer the questions that follow.

1. What does the line graph show?
2. What information is presented along the horizontal axis?
3. What information is presented along the vertical axis?
4. How did consumers spend most of their money in 1961?
5. In which category in 1961 did consumers spend the least?
6. What do all the expenditures add up to in 1961?
7. What kinds of changes took place over time?
8. Which category of consumer expenditures was the largest in 1997?

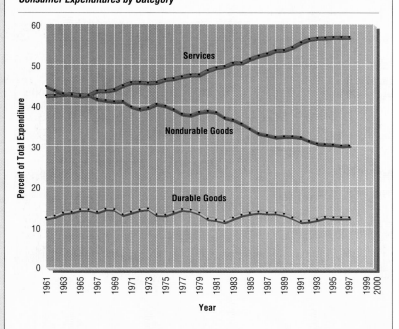

Figure 1.3
Consumer Expenditures by Category

Services

Nondurable Goods

Durable Goods

Percent of Total Expenditure (vertical axis: 0, 10, 20, 30, 40, 50, 60)

Year (horizontal axis: 1961, 1963, 1965, 1967, 1969, 1971, 1973, 1975, 1977, 1979, 1981, 1983, 1985, 1987, 1989, 1991, 1993, 1995, 1997, 1999, 2000)

Source: *Economic Report of the President, 1997*

Additional Practice

For further practice interpreting line graphs, complete the Reinforcing Skills exercise in the Chapter 1 Review on page 29.

TEACHING

SKILLS

TEACH

Direct students' attention to the graph on page 16. Ask students how that graph is similar to the line graph on this page. (*They both compare numerical information.*) How is it different from the line graph on this page? (*The graph on page 16 compares quantities at one moment in time; the line graph here shows how quantities changed over time.*)

Have students collect data for five days on one of these topics: high and low stock prices, school attendance of boys and girls, or any other readily available figures that can be collected daily. Then have students organize their data on a line graph.

Skills Practice

For additional practice, have students complete Reinforcing Economic Skills 1.

? DID YOU KNOW

Americans love to shop! Experts estimate that approximately 20 square feet of retail store space exists for every man, woman, and child in the United States. This compares to approximately 2 square feet per person in Great Britain.

Answers to SKILL

1. the level or percentage of consumer expenditures in particular categories over a period of time
2. the years from 1959 to 1997
3. the percentage of total expenditures each particular category represents
4. on nondurable goods
5. durable goods
6. 100 percent; 13 percent on durable goods, 47 percent on nondurable goods, and 40 percent on services
7. Consumers shifted expenditures from nondurable goods to services.
8. services

FOCUS

Section Objectives

1. Understand that trade-offs are present whenever choices are made.

2. Discover that trade-offs are costs in the form of opportunities given up when one course of action is chosen instead of another.

3. Evaluate the opportunity cost that an economy faces when resources are allocated to the production of one good instead of another.

Bellringer

 Prior to taking roll at the beginning of the class period, display Focus Activity Transparency 2 on the overhead projector and assign the accompanying Student Activity 2.

Motivational Activity

Discuss students' responses to the activity sheet that accompanies Focus Activity Transparency 2.

Preteaching Vocabulary

Have students recall some recent choices they have made and identify the opportunity cost for each decision.

Use the **Vocabulary PuzzleMaker** to create crossword and word search puzzles.

VISUAL INSTRUCTION

Ask students to discuss how the concept of opportunity cost might help them to better organize their time.

Answer to Caption:

Answers will vary.

SECTION 2
Trade-Offs and Opportunity Costs

Section Preview

Objectives

After studying this section, you will be able to:

1. **Understand** that trade-offs are present whenever choices are made.

2. **Discover** that trade-offs are costs in the form of opportunities given up when one course of action is chosen instead of another.

3. **Evaluate** the opportunity cost that an economy faces when resources are allocated to the production of one good instead of another.

Key Terms

trade-offs, opportunity cost, production possibilities frontier

Applying Economic Concepts

Trade-Offs What did you do last night—homework, watch TV, listen to CDs, visit a friend? Because you could not do all those things at once, you had to make a choice. Your decision to do one thing instead of another involved a *trade-off*. Trade-offs are alternatives, and they have costs that can be expressed as the next best option that you gave up in order to do something else. If you think about it, life is full of trade-offs.

The process of making a choice is not always easy. Still, individuals, businesses, government agencies, and any other groups that try to satisfy people's wants and needs must make decisions. To become a good decision maker, you need to know how to identify the problem, and then analyze all your alternatives in a way that carefully considers the costs and benefits of each possibility. **1**

Trade-Offs Among Alternatives

Because people cannot have everything they want, they face **trade-offs,** or alternative choices, when spending their income or time. While choices are not always easy to make, a decision-making grid such as that in **Figure 1.4** shows one way to approach such problems. This grid summarizes a decision made by Jesse, a newspaper carrier whose dilemma was to spend a gift of $50 in the best way possible.

Jesse discovered that several alternatives seemed appealing—a soccer ball, jeans, a portable cassette player, several CDs, and concert tickets. At the same time, he realized that each item had advantages and

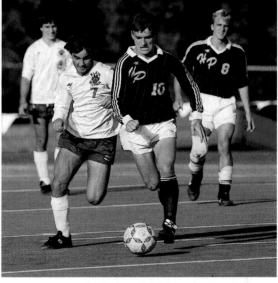

Opportunity Cost *These students have considered the opportunity costs of playing soccer instead of another activity.* **What may be an opportunity cost of playing organized sports?**

14 UNIT 1: *Fundamental Economic Concepts*

Classroom Resources for SECTION 2

- Reproducible Lesson Plan 1-2
- Guided Reading Activity 1-2
- Section Quiz 1-2
- Spanish Section Quiz 1-2

- Focus Activity Transparency 2
- Interactive Economics!
- Testmaker
- Vocabulary PuzzleMaker
- Chapter Challenger Interactive Review Software

Figure 1.4
Jesse's Decision-Making Grid

ALTERNATIVES	CRITERIA				
	Costs $50 or Less?	Durable?	Will Parents Approve?	Future Expenses Unnecessary?	Can Use Anytime?
Several CDs	yes	yes	yes	yes	no
Concert Tickets	yes	no	no	no	no
Cassette Player	yes	yes	yes	no	yes
Soccer Ball	yes	yes	yes	yes	no
Jeans	yes	yes	yes	yes	yes

Adapted from Trade-Offs, © 1978 Agency For Instructional Technology (AIT)

A decision-making grid is a good way to list and then evaluate alternatives when a decision must be made.
What do economists mean when they talk about *costs*?

disadvantages. Some items were more durable than others, and some might require his parents' consent. Some even had additional costs while others did not—the cassette player required batteries and the concert tickets required the use of his parents' car.

To help with his decision, Jesse drew a grid that listed his alternatives and several criteria to judge them. Then he evaluated each alternative with a "yes" or "no." In the end, Jesse chose the jeans because they satisfied more of his criteria than any other alternative.

Using a decision-making grid is an effective way to analyze an economic problem. Among other things, it forces you to consider a number of relevant alternatives. For another, it requires you to identify the decision criteria used to evaluate the alternatives. Finally, it forces you to evaluate each alternative based on the criteria.

Opportunity Cost

People often think of cost in terms of dollars. To an economist, however, cost often means more than the price tag placed on a good or service. Instead, economists think in terms of **opportunity cost**—the cost of the next best alternative use of money, time, or resources when one choice is made rather than another.

When Jesse decided on the jeans, his opportunity cost was the next best choice—the soccer ball or the cassette player—that he gave up. Suppose a person spends $5,000 on a used car. The opportunity cost of the purchase is the value of the stereo, apartment, vacation, or other items and activities that could have been bought with money spent on the car.

Even time has an opportunity cost. Suppose your friend had a chance to earn $50 for a morning's work but ended up oversleeping because the alarm never

Checking Understanding

1. What do you need to know to become a good decision maker?

Applying Economic Concepts

 Trade-Offs In Figure 1.4, Jesse's criteria included expense, durability, parental consent, and so on. What criteria would you use to evaluate alternatives? Why?

CHAPTER 1: *What Is Economics?* **15**

TEACH

Guided Practice

L2 Analyzing Information
Encourage students to imagine they are officers of a school social club who must decide how to spend a $500 grant. Call on volunteers to explain the procedure they would follow in making their decision. (Refer students to Figure 1.4 on page 15.)

INTERACTIVE ECONOMICS!

CD-ROM Opportunity Costs

Have students complete the "Economics Lab" and "Math Practice" sections of the lesson on opportunity costs. Students will determine whether firms have an absolute advantage or a comparative advantage of certain goods. Based on this information, students will decide which goods the firms should produce.

Supplied in both CD-ROM and diskette versions.

VISUAL INSTRUCTION

Ask students how and why their choices for purchases and evaluation criteria might differ from Jesse's.

Answer to Caption:
the cost of the next best alternative use of time, money, or resources when one choice is made rather than another

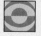

Meeting Special Needs

Study Strategy As you present the information in this section, model the following process for students with weak reading skills. Explain the value of using a study strategy such as SQ3R (Survey, Question, Read, Recite, Review). Tell stu-

dents that the skills in this strategy will be taught and practiced throughout the text. Ask students if the text looks "hard" or "easy" to them. Note which students might have difficulty comprehending the material.

ANSWERS

1. how to identify the problem and to analyze all alternatives that consider the costs and benefits of each possibility

Independent Practice

📂 **Guided Reading** Assign Guided Reading Activity for Section 2. **LEP**

L2 Creating Cartoons Have students draw cartoons illustrating the concept of opportunity cost. **LEP**

ASSESS

Check for Understanding

Assign Section 2 Review as homework or an in-class activity.

💿 Use **Chapter Challenger Interactive Review Software** to review Section 2.

MEETING LESSON OBJECTIVES

Each objective below is tested by the questions that follow it in parentheses.

1. **Understand** that trade-offs are present whenever choices are made. **(1, 2, 4, 5)**

2. **Discover** that trade-offs are costs in the form of opportunities given up when one course of action is chosen instead of another. **(1, 2, 3, 4, 5)**

3. **Evaluate** opportunity cost of allocating resources to production of one good instead of another. **(1, 3)**

VISUAL INSTRUCTION

Ask students to define *opportunity cost* in their own words.

Answer to Caption:

consumers and privately owned businesses

Lesson 1 of Interactive Economics! to learn more about "Opportunity Costs."

Figure 1.5
The Production Possibilities Frontier

A. When resources are fully used, a country can produce anywhere along its production frontier.

The opportunity cost of producing more guns is the amount of butter given up.

B. When all resources are not fully used, a country cannot reach its potential.

The opportunity cost of unemployment is 200 units of butter.

The production possibilities frontier is used by economists to illustrate the maximum amount of goods and services possible if all factors of production are fully employed. **In a free enterprise economy, who decides the WHAT to produce question?**

went off. In this case, the opportunity cost of the morning's rest was $50.

When economists talk about costs, they are talking in terms of alternatives that are given up. Thus, part of making economic decisions involves recognizing and evaluating alternatives as well as making choices from among the alternatives.

The Production Possibilities Frontier

A popular model economists use to illustrate the concept of opportunity cost is the **production possibilities frontier**. The frontier is a diagram representing various combinations of goods and/or services an economy can produce when all productive resources are fully employed. In the classic example, a mythical country called Alpha has a limited supply of resources and produces two kinds of goods—guns and butter. At current production levels, Alpha produces 50 units of guns and 800 units of butter annually. Point **a** in Graph **A** on **Figure 1.5** represents this level.

Now, suppose that Alpha decided it did not have enough guns to protect itself. It could then shift resources from the production of butter into the production of guns. This might make butter production drop to 400 units, and allow gun production to rise to 100 units. Point **b** in Graph **A** represents this new combination of output. The opportunity cost of producing the additional 50 units of guns is the 400 units of butter given up.

Points **a** and **b** represent only two possible mixes of output. If Alpha needed more butter, it could shift enough resources to produce at point **c** in Graph **A**. The production possibilities frontier, which appears as a smooth curve in **Figure 1.5**, is made up of a large number of combinations of output such as those represented by points **a**, **b**, and **c**.

It is also possible for Alpha to produce the mix of output shown at point **a'** in Graph **B**. In this case, all resources are not fully employed. Workers in the

16 Unit 1: *Fundamental Economic Concepts*

$ Free Enterprise Activity $

An important benefit of the American free enterprise system is the freedom to choose, or to make economic decisions. Ask students to search current newspaper articles looking for examples of economic decisions. They should list each decision, indicate whether it is an individual or group decision, name the opportunity costs in each decision, and describe the economic benefits expected from the decision.

butter industry, for example, may be on strike, causing the output of butter to fall to 600 units. In this case, the opportunity cost of the strike would be the 200 units of butter not produced because of idle resources.

Production at **a'** could also be the result of other idle resources such as factories that have been built but are not being used. Workers may have chosen to enjoy four weeks of vacation a year rather than two. As long as some resources are not used, the country cannot produce on its frontier—which is another way of saying that it cannot reach its full production potential.

The production possibilities frontier is just one of the many tools used by economists to describe the economy. Realistically, economies are able to produce more than two goods or services, but the concept is easier to illustrate if only two products are examined. Even so, a simple model such as Figure 1.5 is sometimes all that economists need to analyze an actual problem.

...I REALIZE YOU'RE ALL STARVING, BUT LET'S FACE THE FACTS

THE HUNS HAVE FIVE CATAPULTS... WE ONLY HAVE THREE

THEREFORE, IN THE INTEREST OF NATIONAL DEFENSE, I MUST CONFISCATE YOUR CROPS...

...AND SELL THEM TO THE HUNS FOR ENOUGH MONEY TO BUILD TWO MORE CATAPULTS

WELL.... WHAT DID THEY THINK OF MY SPEECH?

THEY HAVE THEIR OWN WORD FOR IT

WHAT'S THAT?

FINKONOMICS

Trade-Offs *In the cartoon, the king faces a trade-off between crops and catapults.* **What is the opportunity cost of obtaining two more catapults?**

SECTION 2 REVIEW

Reviewing Terms and Facts

1. **Define** trade-offs, opportunity cost, production possibilities frontier.
2. **Describe** how the rows and columns in a decision-making grid are related to trade-offs and opportunity costs.
3. **Explain** how opportunity cost is involved when resources are shifted from the production of one good to another.

Critical Thinking

4. **Making Generalizations** Explain the advantages of using a decision-making grid to evaluate alternatives.

Applying Economic Concepts

5. **Trade-Offs** Identify several possible uses of your time that will be available to you after school today. What will you actually do, and what will be the opportunity cost of your decision?

CHAPTER 1: *What Is Economics?* **17**

Background

In his research for *An Inquiry into the Nature and Causes of the Wealth of Nations,* Smith analyzed the manufacture of pins and showed that productivity increased when workers specialized in one step in the manufacturing process. In addition, Smith's "invisible hand" theory led him to strongly criticize the British policy of mercantilism, which curtailed free trade and production.

TEACH

An Inquiry into the Nature and Causes of the Wealth of Nations was published in 1776, the same year that the Declaration of Independence was issued. Ask students to identify any common themes in the book and the document. *(individual rights)*

PROFILES IN ECONOMICS

ADAM SMITH
(1723–1790)

Adam Smith was a Scottish economist and philosopher. His best-known work, *An Inquiry into the Nature and Causes of the Wealth of Nations,* was published in 1776. More commonly called *The Wealth of Nations,* the book offered a detailed description of life and trade in English society. It also scientifically described the basic principles of economics for the first time.

After graduating from Glasgow University in Scotland, Smith traveled to England and enrolled at Oxford University. His stay lasted six years.

Smith returned to Scotland to lecture at Edinburgh

Buyers and sellers meet at the Covent Garden Market.

University and Glasgow University, where he was immensely popular with his students. He also traveled extensively. While in Europe, Smith met and exchanged ideas with French writer Voltaire, Benjamin Franklin, and the French economist Quesnay. His travels helped him formulate the ideas put forth in *The Wealth of Nations.*

PRODUCTIVITY AND WEALTH Smith observed that labor becomes more productive as each worker becomes more skilled at a single job. He said that new machinery and the division and specialization of labor would lead to an increase in production and greater wealth for the nation. Smith also argued that wealth was the sum of the nation's goods produced by labor, regardless of who owned those goods.

INVISIBLE HAND One of Smith's most important contributions dealt with competition in the marketplace. He argued that competition, together with the free market system, would act as an *invisible hand* that guided resources to their most productive use. He believed that under competitive conditions, individuals acting naturally in their own self-interest, and with a minimum of government intervention, would bring about the greatest good for society as a whole.

LAISSEZ-FAIRE *The Wealth of Nations* was ridiculed by the aristocracy in Parliament. Businesspeople, however, were delighted to have a moral justification for their growing wealth and power. Eventually, the doctrine of *laissez-faire,* meaning no government intervention in economic affairs, became the watchword of the day in Great Britain.

Examining the Profile

1. **Making Generalizations** Summarize Smith's philosophies on productivity, wealth, the invisible hand, and the role of government in the economy.

2. **For Further Research** Research Smith's views and the effects of his economic philosophies on the American free enterprise system.

Answers to Examining the Profile

1. **productivity:** more highly skilled workers, new technology, and specialization lead to greater productivity; **wealth:** sum of all the nation's goods produced by labor, regardless of who owns those goods; **the invisible hand:** competition and the market system working together guide resources to their most productive use; **the role of government in the economy:** government intervention in the economy should be kept to a minimum

2. Students should be encouraged to write one page on the impact of Smith's philosophies on the American free enterprise system.

Section Preview

Objectives

After studying this section, you will be able to:

1. **Understand** the difference between needs and wants, and goods and services.
2. **Explain** the relationship among value, utility, and wealth.
3. **Describe** the importance of productivity.
4. **Understand** the importance of economics to the American free enterprise system.

Key Terms

need, want, free product, economic product, good, consumer good, capital good, durable good, nondurable good, service, consumer, consumption, conspicuous consumption, value, paradox of value, utility, wealth, production, productivity, specialization, division of labor, human capital, economic interdependence, market, factor market, product market, standard of living, free enterprise economy

Applying Economic Concepts

Conspicuous Consumption Do you have an expensive item that you enjoy showing off? *Conspicuous consumption*, the use of an expensive good, service, or other extravagant purchase to impress others, is fairly common. More than likely, this economic term applies to someone you know.

FOCUS

Section Objectives

1. Understand the difference between needs and wants, and goods and services.
2. Explain the relationship among value, utility, and wealth.
3. Describe the importance of productivity.
4. Understand the importance of economics to the American free enterprise system.

Bellringer

Prior to taking roll at the beginning of the class period, display Focus Activity Transparency 4 on the overhead projector and assign the accompanying Student Activity 4.

Motivational Activity

Discuss students' responses to the activity sheet that accompanies Focus Activity Transparency 4.

Preteaching Vocabulary

Have students illustrate how the terms are related by using them in sentences.

Use the **Vocabulary PuzzleMaker** to create crossword and word search puzzles.

E conomics, like any other social science, has its own vocabulary. To understand economics, a review of some key terms is necessary. Fortunately, most economic terms are widely used, and many will already be familiar.

Needs and Wants

Sometimes we hear a term so often we do not even know that it is a basic economic concept. Two terms, *needs* and *wants*, are cases in point.

Needs and Wants *Food represents a basic need related to survival, while a sports car and CD player are usually considered wants.* **Which of your needs might be considered wants by other societies?**

VISUAL INSTRUCTION

Call on volunteers to give other examples of needs and wants.

Answer to Caption:
Answers will vary.

Classroom Resources for SECTION 3

- Reproducible Lesson Plan 1-3
- Guided Reading Activity 1-3
- Section Quiz 1-3
- Spanish Section Quiz 1-3
- Focus Activity Transparency 4
- NBR's Economics in Action Video Program
- Interactive Economics!
- Enrichment Activity 1
- Reteaching Activity 1

- Spanish Reteaching Activity 1
- Economic Vocabulary Activity 1
- Spanish Economic Vocabulary Activity 1
- Chapter 1 Test, Form A and Form B
- English and Spanish Audiocassettes
- Testmaker
- Vocabulary PuzzleMaker
- Chapter Challenger Interactive Review Software
- MindJogger Videoquiz

Need

A **need** is a basic requirement for survival. People have basic needs such as food, clothing, and shelter. People also have higher level needs, such as communication, love, acceptance, knowledge, hope, and accomplishment. These needs are part of the makeup of each person.

Want

A **want** is a means of expressing a need. Food, for example, is a basic need related to survival. To satisfy this need, a person may "want" a pizza, hamburger, taco, or other favorite food. Any number of foods will satisfy the basic need for nourishment. Given a person's budget, some choices might seem reasonable while others might not. The point is that the range of things represented by the term *want* is much broader than that represented by the term *need*. ☑

Goods, Services, and Consumers

Some things, such as sunshine or air, are known as **free products** because they are so plentiful. No one could possibly own them, and no price can be attached to them. Some are so important that life would be impossible without them. Even so, free products are not scarce enough to be a major concern in the study of economics.

Instead, economics is concerned with **economic product**s—goods and services that are useful, relatively scarce, and transferable to others. Economic products are scarce in an economic sense. That is, one cannot get enough to satisfy individual wants and needs. Because of these characteristics, economic products command a price.

Goods

The terms *goods* and *services* are used to describe the many things people desire. A **good** is a tangible commodity like a book, car, or compact disc player. A **consumer good** is intended for final use by individuals. A manufactured good used to produce other goods and services is called a **capital good**. An example of a capital good would be a robot welder in a factory, an oven in a bakery, or a computer in a high school.

Any good that lasts three years or more when it is used on a regular basis is called a **durable good**. Durable goods would include both capital goods such as robot welders and consumer goods such as automobiles. A **nondurable good** is an item that lasts for less than three years when it is used on a regular basis. Examples of nondurable goods include food, writing paper, and most clothing items. **1**

Services

The other type of economic product is a **service**, or work that is performed for someone. Services include haircuts, home repairs, and forms of entertainment such as concerts. They also include the work that doctors, lawyers, and teachers perform.

Figure 1.6
Goods and Services

Economics is a social science concerned with the problem of scarcity. Therefore, economists primarily study economic, or scarce, products. **What is the difference between free products and economic products?**

PRODUCTS
- Free (Plentiful)
- Economic (Scarce)
  - GOODS (Tangibles)
    - Consumer Goods
    - Capital Goods
  - SERVICES (Intangibles)

Wealth *Forests and farmland are natural resources and items of wealth.* **Why are natural resources considered part of the nation's wealth?**

The difference between a good and a service is that a service is something that cannot be touched or felt.

Consumers

People who use goods and services to satisfy wants and needs are **consumers**, and they play an important role in many economies. As consumers, people indulge in **consumption**—the process of using up goods and services in order to satisfy wants and needs.

Some consumers carry the process of consumption to extreme limits. **Conspicuous consumption**—the use of a good or service to impress others—is fairly common. A person may wear expensive jewelry or drive a flashy car. While that person obviously enjoys the use of these items, at least part of the enjoyment comes from showing off his or her expensive tastes to others.

Value, Utility, and Wealth

In economics, **value** refers to something that has a worth that can be expressed in dollars and cents. Someone may say, for example, that he or she has a valuable coin, antique doll, baseball card, or model train collection. In each case, value is determined by the price someone would pay for the item. Why, however, does something have value, and why are some things worth more than others? To answer these questions, it helps to review an early problem faced by economists.

Paradox of Value

Early economists observed that some things, such as water, were essential to life yet had little monetary value. Other things, such as diamonds, were not essential but had much higher value. The problem

L2 *Analyzing Information*
Encourage students to imagine they are managers of the Straight and True Paper Airplane Company. Call on volunteers to describe airplane-construction procedures that might be followed if the company were a one-person operation. Ask others how airplanes might be made if the company's staff consisted of 12 people who specialized in various tasks. Which company would be more efficient? Why?

 CURRICULUM CONNECTIONS

Sociology The term *conspicuous consumption* was coined by economist and social critic Thorstein Veblen in his study *The Theory of the Leisure Class* (1899).

 VISUAL INSTRUCTION

Ask students to identify other natural resources that are items of wealth.

Answer to Caption:

They are useful, scarce, transferable, and tangible.

 ANSWERS

1. **Durable good:** item that lasts three years or more when used on a regular basis; **nondurable good:** item that lasts less than three years when used on a regular basis

 QUICK CHECK

Checking Understanding

1. What is the difference between a durable good and a nondurable good?

Applying Economic Concepts

☑ **Needs vs. Wants** Advertisers often present wants as needs to promote their products. Provide an example of an advertisement that influenced you to view a want as a need.

$ Free Enterprise Activity $

Have students apply their understanding of several of the economic terms found in Section 3. They can do this by giving an illustration—not used in the text—for each of the following fundamental economic concepts: consumer durable goods (*e.g., refrigerators, dishwashers, CD players*); consumer nondurable goods (*e.g., soap, gasoline*); conspicuous consumption (*e.g., fur coat, "superstar" athletic shoes*); wealth (*e.g., automobile, computer, pen*); human capital (*e.g., education, ideas*).

L1 *Brainstorming* Organize students into groups of four or five. Instruct groups to brainstorm ways in which people might invest in human capital. Call on groups to report their lists to the class. Note the most often-mentioned methods on the chalkboard. Then ask the class to prioritize these methods in terms of their importance to the economy. **LEP**

Independent Practice

📂 **Guided Reading** Have students complete Guided Reading Activity for Section 3. **LEP**

L1 *Categorizing* Have students record all the purchases they have made over the last month. Direct them to categorize each purchase into one of three groups—durable goods, nondurable goods, and services. Have students compare their lists. **LEP**

L2 *Economic Interdependence* Have students list the various ways they are dependent on others and how others are dependent on them. Ask students to compare their lists, noting those ways that illustrate economic interdependence.

L3 *Conducting Interviews* Instruct pairs of students to interview local jewelers. Interviewers should ask the jewelers to explain why diamonds and other precious stones are so expensive. Have pairs make an oral presentation that relates their findings to the paradox of value.

became known as the diamond-water paradox, or the **paradox of value**, and the solution to the problem helps us determine the nature of value.

At first, it seemed paradoxical that so many essentials had little value while other items had much higher value. Later, economists decided that part of the reason was due to scarcity. For example, water is so plentiful in many areas that it has little or no value. On the other hand, diamonds are so scarce that they have great value. In order for something to have value, then, it has to be somewhat scarce. Scarcity by itself, however, is not enough to create value.

Utility

For something to have value, it must also have **utility**, or the capacity to be useful to someone. Utility is not something that is fixed or measured, like weight or height. Instead, the utility of a good or service may vary from one person to the next. One person may get a great deal of enjoyment from a home computer; another may get very little. One person may enjoy a rock concert; another may not. A good or service does not have to have utility for everyone, only utility for some.

For something to have value, it must be scarce and have utility. This is the solution to the paradox of value. Diamonds are scarce and have utility—and therefore a value that can be stated in monetary terms. Water has utility, but is not scarce enough in most places to give it much value.

Wealth

Another concept is **wealth**—the sum of those economic products that are tangible, scarce, useful, and transferable from one person to another. Most economic goods are counted as wealth, but services are not. The reason for this is that it is difficult to measure the value of services accurately.

For example, it is difficult to measure the contribution people's abilities and talents make to a nation's wealth. If a country's material possessions were taken away, its people, through their skilled efforts, would probably restore these possessions. On the other hand, if a country's people were taken away, its wealth would deteriorate.

A country's total wealth is the stockpile of useful, scarce, transferable, and tangible things in existence at a given time. The nation's wealth includes all such items as natural resources, factories, stores, houses, motels, theaters, furniture, clothing, books, video games, and even footballs.

Productivity

When the factors of production—land, labor, entrepreneurship, and capital—are present, **production**, or the process of creating goods and services, can take place. Even the production of the service called education requires the factors of production. The chalkboards, desks, and audiovisual equipment used in schools are capital goods. Another requirement is labor, represented by the services of teachers, administrators, and other employees. Land, such as the iron ore, granite, and timber used to make the building and desks, as well as the lot where the school is located, also is needed. It is nearly impossible to provide the service of education without all the factors of production.

The efficient use of productive resources is called **productivity**. Productivity goes up whenever more output can be produced with the same amount of inputs. Productivity also goes up if the same output can be produced with fewer inputs.

Productivity is usually discussed in terms of labor, but it applies to all factors of production. For this reason, business owners try to buy the most efficient capital goods, and farmers try to use the most fertile land for their crops. In a world of relatively scarce resources, productivity is a key issue.

Specialization of Labor

Increases in productivity often occur when people specialize. In economics, **specialization** means that productive inputs do whatever task they are able to do best. For example, an excellent carpenter with average skills in other areas might want to build a house. Even if the carpenter could build the entire house without any help, it might be better to hire other workers who specialize in foundations, plumbing, and electrical wiring. The carpenter might even

---

Extending the Content

Capital Goods To produce most goods and services, it takes all four factors of production—land, labor, capital, and entrepreneurs. Although a nation may have abundant natural resources, human labor, and entrepreneurship, it may not have enough capital goods to produce needed consumer goods and services. Thus, its people may still be denied a high standard of living. For example, although some developing nations have large supplies of labor and natural resources, they are barely able to provide enough food for their people because they lack machinery, equipment, and factories.

save money by first working for someone else, and then using the money to hire the specialized workers.

Specialization, also known as the **division of labor**, takes place when workers perform fewer tasks more frequently. A worker who performs several tasks many times every day is likely to become more proficient than a worker who performs hundreds of different tasks once a week.

Labor is not the only factor of production that can specialize. Complex industrial robots are often built to perform one or two simple assembly-line tasks. Regions, countries, and states even specialize. Idaho specializes in potatoes, Iowa specializes in corn, and Texas specializes in oil, cotton, and cattle. **1**

Human Capital

Finally, productivity tends to increase when firms invest in **human capital**, the sum of skills, abilities, health, and motivation of people. Investments by government and businesses in training, health care, and employee motivation tend to increase the amount of production that takes place with a given amount of labor. Employers are usually rewarded with higher quality products and increased profits. Workers often benefit from higher pay, better jobs, and more satisfaction with their work and leisure.

Economic Interdependence

The American economy has a remarkable degree of **economic interdependence**. This interdependence means that actions in one part of the country or the world have an economic impact on what happens elsewhere. Bad weather in one part of the world can affect sugar prices in the United States, and a change in sugar prices can affect the price of snack foods and

the demand for sugar substitutes. Because of this interdependence, we need to understand how all the parts fit together.

The Circular Flow of Economic Activity

To the economist, a **market** is a location or other mechanism that allows buyers and sellers to deal readily in a certain economic product. Markets may

Figure 1.7
Relationship Between Income & Education

Education	Median Income for Males	Females
Less than 9th Grade	$20,153	$15,150
9th to 12th Grade (no diploma)	$25,283	$17,313
High School Graduate & Equivalency	$32,521	$21,893
Some College, no degree	$38,491	$25,889
Associate Degree	$39,873	$28,403
Bachelor Degree	$52,354	$36,555
Master's Degree	$70,859	$44,471
Professional Degree	$112,873	$90,711
Doctorate Degree	$86,436	$62,169

Source: U.S. Department of Commerce, Bureau of the Census

A formal education is one way to invest in human capital. **How does this type of investment pay off for both employers and employees?**

CHAPTER 1: *What Is Economics?* **23**

Checking Understanding

1. In what does your state or community specialize? Why?

Applying Economic Concepts

 Economic Interdependence How do you get to school or work each day? Chances are that you depend on someone else, perhaps someone you don't even know such as a bus driver or subway operator. Most activity involves similar economic interdependence.

 VISUAL INSTRUCTION

One generalization that can be drawn from the chart is that income increases as level of education rises. Ask students to draw another generalization. *(Men receive higher incomes than women at all levels of education.)*

Answer to Caption:

Employers are usually rewarded with higher-quality products and increased profits. Employees usually enjoy higher pay, better jobs, and more satisfaction.

INTERACTIVE ECONOMICS!

CD-ROM Circular Flows

Have students study the Lesson 2 "Tutorial," which focuses on circular flows. Students will see how the basic two-sector model works. After students read the "Tutorial," have them attempt to complete the "Economics Lab" dealing with circular flows. The lab includes the third sector—government—in the circular flow, so have students click and drag the correct terms to only the outer circular flow dealing with the business and household sectors.

Supplied in both CD-ROM and diskette versions.

Cultural Diversity and Economics

A Valuable Animal In the past, the camel was a highly prized possession in many Arab countries. This hardy animal, which could travel for days without water and was seemingly unaffected by the heat, was indispensable for long journeys across the desert. Wealth and social standing were measured, in part, by the number of camels a person owned. Today, however, cars and trucks are the favored means of travel throughout Southwest Asia. Even so, in some Arab countries ownership of camels remains a mark of wealth.

 ANSWERS

1. Answers will vary. Encourage students to consider such factors as natural resources, location, and so on when answering the *Why?* of the Quick Check.

be local, regional, national, or global. All markets are similar, however, in that their economic activity has a distinct circular flow.

How does this circular flow operate? Individuals earn their incomes in **factor markets**—the markets where productive resources are bought and sold. Here, entrepreneurs hire labor for wages and salaries, land is provided in return for rent, and money is loaned for interest or invested for a profit. When individuals receive their incomes, they spend it in **product markets**—markets where producers offer goods and services for sale. **1**

In a similar way, business firms receive payments in the product markets when they sell goods and services to individuals. This pays for the land, labor, and capital bought in the factor markets. These resources are then used to manufacture additional products that are sold in the product markets.

Figure 1.8 illustrates the circular flow of economic activity that links economic markets, money, resources, businesses, and consumers. In the diagram, money circulates on the outside to illustrate payments for goods, services, and factors of production, which flow in the opposite direction on the inside.

Investing in the Future

Most Americans are concerned about their **standard of living**—the quality of life based on the possession of necessities and luxuries that make life easier. How can you be assured of achieving a higher standard of living in the future than you now have?

As individuals, we know that we can have more in the future if we save by putting our money in the bank, or if we invest in human capital by obtaining additional skills. Investments in education, illustrated in **Figure 1.7**, can have substantial payoffs. These types of investments, however, require that we make a sacrifice today so we can have a better life in the future.

Businesses, governments, and other organizations face the same choices as do individuals. Investments in physical capital or in projects that increase health or productivity today will increase future production and promote economic growth. Faster economic growth, in turn, increases the amount of goods and services available to us in the future, thereby increasing our standard of living. In the end, the trade-off between present and future consumption faces all of us.

 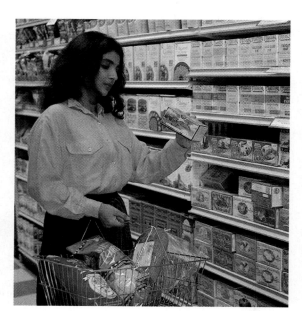

Economic Interdependence *If poor weather or disease causes coffee production to decrease, coffee drinkers in the United States may switch to drinking tea.* **How might you be affected by war in an oil-producing country?**

24 Unit 1: *Fundamental Economic Concepts*

 $ Free Enterprise Activity $

Point out that in a free enterprise system, the emphasis is on the individual. Identify some roles the individual may play in a free enterprise system, including consumer, producer, owner of factors of production, voting citizen, investor, and saver. Next, have students assume each role, explaining why their assigned role is important in a free enter-

prise economy and illustrating how their role is interdependent with others. Direct the rest of the class to discuss and add to the students' descriptions.

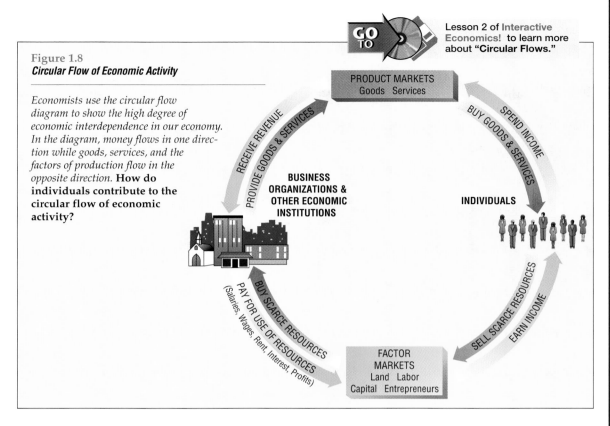

Figure 1.8
Circular Flow of Economic Activity

Economists use the circular flow diagram to show the high degree of economic interdependence in our economy. In the diagram, money flows in one direction while goods, services, and the factors of production flow in the opposite direction. **How do individuals contribute to the circular flow of economic activity?**

GO TO Lesson 2 of *Interactive Economics!* to learn more about "Circular Flows."

PRODUCT MARKETS
Goods   Services

RECEIVE REVENUE

PROVIDE GOODS & SERVICES

SPEND INCOME

BUY GOODS & SERVICES

BUSINESS ORGANIZATIONS & OTHER ECONOMIC INSTITUTIONS

INDIVIDUALS

PAY FOR USE OF RESOURCES
(Salaries, Wages, Rent, Interest, Profits)

BUY SCARCE RESOURCES

SELL SCARCE RESOURCES

EARN INCOME

FACTOR MARKETS
Land   Labor
Capital   Entrepreneurs

The Road Ahead

The study of economics does more than explain how people deal with scarcity. It provides insight as to how incomes are earned and spent, how jobs are created, and how the economy works on a daily basis. It also provides a more detailed understanding of a **free enterprise economy**—one in which consumers and privately owned businesses, rather than the government, jointly make the majority of the WHAT, HOW, and FOR WHOM decisions.

In addition, the study of economics will provide a working knowledge of property rights, competition, supply and demand, the price system, and the economic incentives that make the American economy function. Along the way, topics such as unemployment, the business cycle, inflation, and economic growth will be covered. The role of business, labor, and government in the American economy also will be examined. Finally, the relationship of the United States economy to the international economy will be explored. ✔

QUICK CHECK

Checking Understanding

1. What is the difference between a factor market and a product market?

Applying Economic Concepts

✔ **Economic Interdependence**   In today's global economy, United States consumers and businesses are directly affected by events around the world. Now, more than ever, understanding economics is vital to understanding how you will be affected by social and political forces.

CHAPTER 1
SECTION 3

Evaluate

📁 📁 💻 Assign the Section 3 Quiz in the TCR or use the *Economics: Principles and Practices* Testmaker to create a customized quiz. Spanish Section Quizzes also are available in the Spanish Resources Binder.

Reteach

Ask students to find examples in their own lives in which they are specializing.

📁 📁 Have students complete Reteaching Activity 1. Spanish Reteaching Activities also are available in the Spanish Resources Binder.

VISUAL INSTRUCTION

Other types of circular flow diagrams can be found on pages 321 and 358.

Answer to Caption:
They sell their scarce resources for income, and then spend their income to buy goods and services.

QUICK CHECK

ANSWERS

1. **factor market:** where productive resources are bought and sold; **product market:** where producers sell goods and services

---

Extending the Content

A Fifth Factor of Production?   Some economists believe that technology should be considered one of the factors of production. These economists stress that technological inventions have been important in stimulating the economy. They point to the invention of the automobile and the subsequent development of mass production as an example. They also refer to the more recent improvements in computers and the influence this technology has had on information processing and jobs in the service sector. Those economists who disagree usually suggest that technology is simply an aspect of entrepreneurship or advances in the production of capital goods.

Enrich

Refer students to the circular flow diagram on page 25. Have students construct a similar circular flow diagram that represents their own economic activity if they have a job, or the economic activity of a family member if they do not.

 Have students complete Enrichment Activity 1.

CLOSE

Ask students to discuss what everyday benefits they might derive from the study of economics.

VISUAL INSTRUCTION

Have students identify the economic issues that played a role in a recent local, state, or national election.

Answer to Caption:

It provides voters with a better understanding of election issues and, therefore, enables them to make more informed decisions about the candidates.

Economics and Politics *Economic issues play a major role in presidential campaigns.* **How does the study of economics help people make more informed choices in the voting booth?**

The study of economics helps people become better decision makers. Economic issues often are debated during political campaigns, and voters need to understand the issues before deciding which candi-

date to support. A voter may have to decide between the candidate who favors higher taxes and more government spending and the candidate who favors lower taxes and less government spending. Other candidates may favor limiting imports, and even others may favor free trade.

The study of economics does not provide voters with clear-cut answers to all questions. It does help them have a better understanding of the issues involved, however. In doing so, the study of economics helps people make more informed choices in the voting booth.

Textbook economics can be divided into neat sections for study, but the real world is not so orderly. Most people live in dynamic societies in which things are constantly changing. Events take place daily, and economies almost always are in a state of flux. In addition, the people of the world differ. Not everyone has the same kind or degree of ambition, strength, greed, or luck. Opinions also differ, and some issues never seem to be settled.

No matter what road people decide to take, they will not have a smooth, easy ride. In practice, the world of economics is complex and the road ahead is bumpy. Studying and understanding economics, however, is vital to understanding many of the political and social forces operating around us.

SECTION 3 REVIEW

Reviewing Terms and Facts

1. **Define** need, want, free product, economic product, good, consumer good, capital good, durable good, nondurable good, service, consumer, consumption, conspicuous consumption, value, paradox of value, utility, wealth, production, productivity, specialization, division of labor, human capital, economic interdependence, market, factor market, product market, standard of living, free enterprise economy.

2. **Explain** the conditions that must be present for something to have value.

3. **Provide** three examples of items that could be considered as wealth.

4. **Explain** the importance of productivity.

Critical Thinking

5. **Determining Cause and Effect** How does education relate to the productivity of human capital?

Applying Economic Concepts

6. **Production** Using a product that is familiar to you, explain how each of the factors of production was used in its production.

Answers to SECTION 3 REVIEW

1. All vocabulary words are defined in the Glossary.

2. To have value, an item must be relatively scarce and have utility.

3. Answers will vary but might include natural resources, factories, stores, houses, motels, theaters, furniture, clothing, books, video games, or footballs.

4. When there are limited resources to meet unlim-

ited wants, productivity—the efficient use of productive resources—is absolutely essential.

5. Investment in training and other forms of education tends to increase the amount of production that takes place with a given amount of labor. ,

6. Answers will vary. Refer students to the "biographies" they wrote for the Guided Practice activity on page 20.

ECONOMICS IN ACTION

What Is Economics?

Setting Up the Video

With your classmates, view "What Is Economics?" on the videodisc *Economics in Action*. The video focuses on the economic concept of scarcity. A news report on pork bellies, for example, points out that the price of bacon rose because McDonald's®, Wendy's®, Taco Bell®, and other fast-food chains started using bacon on their sandwiches. The video concludes that because all resources are inherently limited, society as a whole must decide how it wants to allocate them.

Chapter 2
Disc 1, Side 1

View the video by scanning the bar code or by entering the chapter number on your keypad and pressing Search. *(Also available in VHS format.)*

Hands-On Activity

Recognize the economic trade-offs in your own life. Make two columns on a piece of paper. In one column, list the things you feel you need to buy each week. In the other column, list the things you want to buy. Which column has more items? What is the difference between a need and a want? About how much money is required to satisfy your weekly needs and wants?

NIGHTLY BUSINESS REPORT
Economics in Action

Chapter 2
Disc 1, Side 1
Title: *What Is Economics?*

If you do not have access to a videodisc player, the **Economics in Action** programs are available in VHS.

INTERACTIVE ECONOMICS!

Circular Flows

Introduction

Lesson 2 of *Interactive Economics!* describes how the basic parts of the economy work together. In the market economy of the United States, people in one part of the country are both affected by and dependent on the actions of other people in different parts of the country.

The circular flow model is a popular tool that economists use to show the dynamic workings of a market economy. More than any other tool, it helps to show the economic interdependency of different segments of the economy and the way in which markets link these components together.

Using the Software

1. Select "Circular Flows" from the Main Menu.
2. Read the introduction, then click on and review "Households and Businesses."
3. Repeat the process for "Adding Government to the Circular Flow."
4. Click on "Economics Lab." Complete the lab by clicking and dragging the correct terms to their proper place in the circular flow of economic activity.
5. Print your completed lab.

INTERACTIVE ECONOMICS!

Before students complete the "Economics Lab" in Lesson 2, ask them the following questions:

1. What are the four components of a two-sector circular flow model? *(business sector, household or consumer sector, product market, factor market)*
2. What additional component is added to a three-sector circular flow model? *(government)*
3. What does the word *household* mean, according to the U.S. Bureau of the Census? *(everyone living together in a separate living quarters even if they are not all related by blood, marriage, or adoption)*
4. What is included in the business sector of the economy? *(partnerships, proprietorships, corporations, nonprofit organizations, entrepreneurs)*
5. What is bought and sold in the factor market? *(land, labor, and capital)*
6. What is bought and sold in the product market? *(goods and services)*

27

TEACHER NOTES

Answers

Reviewing Key Terms

1. h	6. b
2. g	7. c
3. j	8. f
4. a	9. e
5. d	10. i

Reviewing the Facts

1. because someone ends up paying—usually through higher prices—for the products that businesses give away for "free"

2. having only limited resources to meet seemingly unlimited wants

3. WHAT to produce? HOW to produce? FOR WHOM to produce?

4. It deals with people's behavior as they cope with scarcity.

5. the alternative choices people face when spending their income or time

6. the cost of the next best alternative use of money, time, or resources when one choice is made rather than another

7. opportunity cost

8. Needs are necessary for survival; wants are ways of expressing needs.

9. Free products are plentiful, not owned by anybody, and cannot have a price attached to them. Economic products are

---

CHAPTER 1 REVIEW

Reviewing Key Terms

Write the key term that best completes the following sentences.

a. scarcity	f. capital goods
b. human capital	g. value
c. utility	h. consumer goods
d. opportunity cost	i. consumers
e. factors of production	j. services

1. Economic products designed to satisfy people's wants and needs are called _____.
2. The _____ of a CD player can be expressed in dollars and cents.
3. Haircuts, repairs to home appliances, and entertainment are examples of _____.
4. _____ arises because society does not have enough resources to produce all the things people would like to have.
5. The _____ of going to a football game instead of working would include the money not earned at your job.
6. _____ is the sum of the skills, abilities, health, and motivation of people.
7. _____ is another name for the capacity of a product to be useful.
8. The only factors of production that are themselves the result of earlier production are _____.
9. Land, labor, entrepreneurship, and capital are _____.
10. People who use goods and services to satisfy their wants and needs are called _____.

Reviewing the Facts

SECTION 1 *(pages 8–12)*
1. **Explain** why economists say there is no such thing as a "free" lunch.
2. **Identify** the cause of scarcity.
3. **List** the three basic economic questions each society must face.
4. **Explain** why economics is considered a social science.

SECTION 2 *(pages 14–17)*
5. **Explain** the meaning of a trade-off.
6. **Describe** the nature of an opportunity cost.
7. **Identify** the economic concept illustrated by the production possibilities frontier.

SECTION 3 *(pages 19–26)*
8. **Explain** the difference between a need and a want.
9. **Distinguish** between free products and economic products.
10. **Discuss** why services are excluded when the wealth of a nation is measured.
11. **Name** the factors of production used in production.
12. **Explain** why economists argue that productivity is important.
13. **Distinguish** between product markets and factor markets.
14. **Explain** why economic education is important.

Critical Thinking

1. **Drawing Conclusions** Think of circumstances that could change a free product to an economic one. What are they, and what characteristics must the new economic products have?
2. **Determining Cause and Effect** Suppose that Alpha, in **Figure 1.5** on page 16, decided to produce more butter and fewer guns. What would Alpha have to do to make the change? What would be the opportunity cost of producing more butter? What conditions would have to be met for the new mix of guns and butter to be on the production possibilities frontier?
3. **Analyzing Information** How will the study of economics help you become a better decision maker?
4. **Synthesizing Information** Examine the circular flow diagram in **Figure 1.8** on page 25 and explain how you fit into one or more parts of the overall process.

---

scarce, their ownership is transferable, and they command a price.

10. because they are intangible and it is difficult to measure accurately their value

11. land, labor, capital, and entrepreneurs

12. Productivity is the efficient use of productive resources. The more efficiently productive resources are used, the greater the number of goods and services produced.

13. Product markets are where producers offer goods and services for sale. Factor markets are where productive resources are bought and sold.

14. It helps people become better decision makers.

Critical Thinking

1. For example, if water quality deteriorates, clean water becomes scarce and, thus, becomes an economic good. New economic goods must be scarce, have transferable ownership, and have monetary value.

Applying Economic Concepts

1. **Scarcity** What effect would a large increase in every citizen's income have on the economy of a nation?

2. **Trade-Offs and Opportunity Cost** If you decide to go to college after graduation from high school, what will be the opportunity cost of that decision? Use a specific example.

Reinforcing Skills

INTERPRETING LINE GRAPHS

Examine the line graph below, then answer the following questions.

1. What is the subject of this line graph?
2. What information is shown along the horizontal axis?
3. What information is shown along the vertical axis?
4. Do the series shown in the graph reflect spending by all consumers? Explain.
5. Which category of consumer spending has increased the most over the years? By how much?
6. How have housing expenditures changed between 1959 and 1997?

Figure 1.9
Consumer Expenditures on Selected Services

Percent of Total Consumer Spending on Services

Housing
Medical Care
Transportation
Electricity & Gas

Year: 1959 1961 1963 1965 1967 1969 1971 1973 1975 1977 1979 1981 1983 1985 1987 1989 1991 1993 1995 1997 1999 2000

Source: *Economic Report of the President*, 1997

Individual Activity

Imagine that you must spend $50. Make a list of three to five alternatives from which you could choose. State the criteria you feel are most important in helping you judge the alternatives you have listed. Use the decision-making grid to evaluate each alternative. Make your decision.

Cooperative Learning Activity

In groups, create an ideal economic society, listing the kinds of natural, human, and manufactured resources you would include in it. Then, compare the lists of all the groups. What prevents us from having all these resources?

Technology Activity

Using a Spreadsheet

In the **Journal Writing** activity on page 7, you were asked to keep track of all your "economic decisions" for one week. Use your data to create a spreadsheet, highlighting your weekly spending habits.

1. In cells B1 through E1, type *Food, Clothing, Entertainment*, and *Other*. In cell F1, type *TOTAL*.
2. In cells A2 through A8, type the days of the week, starting with *Monday* in cell A2. In cell A9, type *TOTAL*.
3. In cells B2 through E2, enter the amount spent in each category on Monday. Repeat this process for the other six days.
4. In cell F2, use a formula such as =SUM (B2:E2) to calculate total expenditures on Monday. Click and drag this formula to cells F3 through F8 to find the other weekday sums.
5. Compute total expenditures for cells B9-F9.

Applying Economic Concepts

1. Students may suggest that many people would stop working and the economy would temporarily come to a halt.

2. Specific answers will vary, but the opportunity cost is whatever students would not be able to do or buy because of the time and money they spend going to college.

Reinforcing Skills

1. consumer spending on selected categories of services

2. time as measured in years

3. the percent of total consumer spending on various categories of services

4. no, only selected categories of services; consumer spending on goods is not shown

5. medical care; it has increased from about 9.5 percent of total consumer expenditures on services to 15 percent

6. Housing started at 14 percent in 1959, reached 16.3 percent in 1981, and fell to 14.8 percent in 1997.

? BONUS TEST QUESTION

Imagine that everyone won the state lottery, which paid $1 million each year for the next 20 years. Would scarcity end? Explain. *(No. No one would want to work to produce the items people would want to buy.)*

2. Resources have to be shifted from guns to butter. The opportunity cost of producing more butter is the production of fewer guns. All of Alpha's productive resources would have to be employed.

3. Studying economics helps people to identify and evaluate all possible alternatives in a decision.

4. Students may mention that they are individuals who purchase goods and services in product markets. Other students might mention that they sell their scarce productive resources in factor markets.

CHAPTER 2 PLANNING GUIDE

CHAPTER ORGANIZER

Daily Objectives	Reproducible Resources	Multimedia Resources
Section 1 **Economic Systems** 1. **Describe** the characteristics of the traditional economy. 2. **Explain** the strengths and weaknesses of the command economy. 3. **Examine** the strengths and weaknesses of a market economy.	Reproducible Lesson Plan 2-1 Guided Reading Activity 2-1 Cooperative Learning Activity 2 Consumer Application Activity 2 Math Practice for Economics 2 Free Enterprise Activities 1, 2, 6 Primary and Secondary Source Reading 2 Performance Assessment Activity 2 Reinforcing Economic Skills 2 Section Quiz 2-1*	Focus Activity Transparency 5 Economic Concepts Transparency 4 Vocabulary PuzzleMaker Chapter Challenger Interactive Review Software Testmaker MindJogger Videoquiz NBR's Economics in Action Video Program
Section 2 **Evaluating Economic Performance** 1. **Describe** the basic economic and social goals used to evaluate economic performance. 2. **Examine** the trade-offs among economic and social goals.	Reproducible Lesson Plan 2-2 Guided Reading Activity 2-2 Section Quiz 2-2*	Focus Activity Transparency 7 Vocabulary PuzzleMaker Chapter Challenger Interactive Review Software Testmaker
Section 3 **Capitalism and Free Enterprise** 1. **Explore** the characteristics of a free enterprise system. 2. **Describe** the role and importance of the entrepreneur. 3. **Examine** the role of the consumer as "sovereign" of the economy. 4. **Describe** the role that government plays in a free enterprise economy.	Reproducible Lesson Plan 2-3 Guided Reading Activity 2-3 Section Quiz 2-3*	Focus Activity Transparency 6 Vocabulary PuzzleMaker Chapter Challenger Interactive Review Software Testmaker NBR's Economics in Action Video Program
Chapter Review and Evaluation	Enrichment Activity 2 Reteaching Activity 2* Economic Vocabulary Activity 2* Chapter 2 Test, Forms A and B	Chapter Digests Audiocassette Activities and Tests* Testmaker MindJogger Videoquiz

Also available in Spanish

 Blackline Master   Transparency   CD-ROM   Software   Videodisc   Audiocassette

OUT OF TIME? Assign the Chapter 2 Digest Audiocassette and the corresponding Chapter Digest activities and tests.

National Council on Economic Education

THE **Economics** America AND **Economics** International PROGRAMS

VOLUNTARY NATIONAL CONTENT STANDARDS IN ECONOMICS
Emphasized in Chapter 2

Content Standard 3 *Students will understand that:* Different methods can be used to allocate goods and services. People, acting individually or collectively through government, must choose which methods to use to allocate different kinds of goods and services.

Content Standard 16 *Students will understand that:* There is an economic role for government to play in a market economy whenever the benefits of a government policy outweigh its costs. Governments often provide for national defense, address environmental concerns, define and protect property rights, and attempt to make markets more competitive. Most government policies also redistribute income.

EconomicsAmerica *Resources Available From NCEE*

- *Capstone: The Nation's High School Economics Course*
- *Civics and Government: Focus on Economics*
- *Economics and Entrepreneurship*
- *Economics in Transition: Command to Market*
- *United States History: Eyes on the Economy, Vol. II*
- *World History: Focus on Economics*

To order these materials, or to contact your state Council on Economic Education about workshops and programs, call 1-800-338-1192 or visit http://www.nationalcouncil.org.

PERFORMANCE ASSESSMENT

The following chapter projects may be assigned at the beginning of the chapter and used for performance assessment.

Multicultural Heritage List on the chalkboard the names of several nations—Great Britain, Mexico, Japan, South Korea, North Korea, China, Hungary, Poland, Indonesia, and Saudi Arabia, for example—and have each student choose a nation to research. Next, direct students to the Critical Thinking Skill on page 37. Instruct them to follow the listed steps to gather either current or historical information about the economic system of their selected nation. Suggest that they focus on the extent to which the system has characteristics of traditional, command, or market economies. Then have students follow the steps for formulating questions to learn about their selected country's culture. Finally, ask students to gather the information in a report, showing direct relationships between the country's culture and characteristics of its economic system. Call on students to present their reports to the class.

Cooperative Learning Organize students into five groups. Assign each group one of the economic roles of government—protector, provider, consumer, regulator, and promoter of national goals. Direct groups to construct a four-page annotated pictorial essay on their assigned roles, using current and historical materials. Ensure that group members share the various tasks involved—research, writing, artwork, layout and design, and so on—among themselves. Call on group representatives to present and discuss their essays to the class.

ADDITIONAL RESOURCES

Readings for the Student

Dunnan, Nancy. *Entrepreneurship.* Englewood Cliffs, NJ: Silver Burdett, 1990. Provides a thorough introduction to the process of entrepreneurship.

Stein, Herbert, and Murray Foss. *The New Illustrated Guide to the American Economy.* Washington, DC: American Enterprise Institute, 1995. Uses full-color illustrations to help students visualize key economic concepts.

Readings for the Teacher

Casler, Stephen D. *Introduction to Economics.* New York: HarperCollins, 1992. Well-organized and thorough survey of the subject.

Multimedia

Chickenomics: A Fowl Approach to Economics. World Research Incorporated Education, 968 Emerald Street, Suite 6700, P.O. Box 9059, San Diego, CA 92169–0059. Color video, 30 mins. Teaches basic aspects of a market economy with the help of the San Diego Chicken.

Economics in a Changing World: Where Do I Fit in? Churchill Media, 1995. Available from Social Studies School Service, 10200 Jefferson Boulevard, P.O. Box 802, Culver City, CA 90232-0802. VHS Videocassette. First video, *Basic Economic Principles,* 27 min., covers topics of scarcity and the basic tools of economics.

Chapter Overview

Chapter 2 examines the three types of economic systems—traditional, command, and market. The chapter also lists and explains the seven economic and social goals shared by most Americans. The chapter concludes with a discussion of capitalism.

GLENCOE
TECHNOLOGY

VIDEODISC
MindJogger Videoquiz

Use MindJogger to preview the Chapter 2 content.

Chapter 2
Disc 1, Side A

 Also available in VHS.

interNET
CONNECTION

Resources for Chapter 2 on the World Wide Web*

National Council on Economic Education

http://www.nationalcouncil.org/

Soviet Union's command economy

http://www.interknowledge.com/russia/rushis07.htm

Native Americans' traditional economic systems

http://hanksville.phast.umass.edu/misc/NAculture.html

Sites subject to change.

In a market economy, consumers have the opportunity to choose from a variety of goods and services.

VISUAL INSTRUCTION

Ask how the photograph illustrates choice. *(many different stores that offer variety of goods and services to consumers)*

✚ Extra Credit Project

Organize students into groups of three or four. Direct groups to develop a lesson plan and teaching materials for a 30-minute class, suitable for junior-high students, titled "Free Enterprise—The American Economic System." (See Section 3 CLOSE activity.)

CHAPTER 2

Economic Systems and Decision Making

SECTION 1
Economic Systems

SECTION 2
Evaluating Economic Performance

SECTION 3
Capitalism and Free Enterprise

CHAPTER PREVIEW

People to Know

• Anita Roddick
• Real Estate Agent

Applying Economic Concepts To Your Life

Consumer Sovereignty Have you ever asked, "Why doesn't someone invent a product that does this?" Or, "Whose idea was it to make that?" In effect, you're asking who decides the "WHAT to produce" question in our society. Government? Businesses? Another group? You're right if you said government and businesses, but another group bigger than both of those combined is the most influential. Consumers—including you—ultimately decide WHAT will be produced.

Journal Writing

For one week, be an inventor and write down ideas for products or services that you think should be produced. Keep in mind that your products should appeal to many consumers.

Connecting to Past Learning

Ask students to recall the meaning of the term *consumer* (*someone who uses goods and services to satisfy needs and wants*). Then call on volunteers to discuss the role that the consumer plays in the American economy. End the discussion by mentioning that in this chapter, students will learn how the consumer plays a primary role in the American free enterprise economy.

Applying Economics

Write the following words on the chalkboard: *traditional, command, market.* Have students give examples of how these words are used in everyday life. For example, the term *traditional* might be used to refer to the practice of family and friends gathering to celebrate Thanksgiving. Next, point out that these three terms have a special meaning in economics because they are applied to different forms of economic systems. Have students consider the everyday meanings of the terms as they try to identify the nature of economic systems the terms might be used to characterize.

 PERFORMANCE ASSESSMENT

Refer to page **30B** for a Performance Assessment activity for this chapter. Also see the **Performance Assessment Activities** booklet for additional suggestions.

Economic Portfolio

In the **Journal Writing** activity above, students are asked to come up with ideas for new products or services. Encourage students to group their ideas into categories—Household Items, Study Aids, Games and Entertainment, for example. In addition, suggest that they include one or two reasons why consumers would want to buy each item. Then inform students that after they have completed study of Chapter 2, they will be asked to develop an advertising brochure persuading a consumer to purchase one of their new products. Refer students to the **Technology Activity** in the Chapter 2 Review.

Key to Ability Levels — **Teaching strategies have been coded for varying learning styles and abilities:**
L1 - Basic (activities for all students)   **L2 - Average** (activities for average to above-average students)
L3 - Challenging (activities for above-average students)   **LEP - Limited English Proficiency**

FOCUS

Section Objectives

1. Describe the characteristics of the traditional economy.
2. Explain the strengths and weaknesses of the command economy.
3. Examine the strengths and weaknesses of a market economy.

Bellringer

Prior to taking roll at the beginning of the class period, display Focus Activity Transparency 5.

Motivational Activity

Discuss students' responses to the activity sheet that accompanies Transparency 5.

Preteaching Vocabulary

Ask students to define *market economy*, basing their definition on information they learned in Chapter 1. **LEP**

Use the **Vocabulary PuzzleMaker** to create crossword and word search puzzles.

TEACH

Guided Practice

L1 *Constructing a Chart* Call on volunteers to identify how each of the three types of economies answer each economic question. Then have students construct a chart titled "Comparing Economic Systems: Answering the Three Basic Questions." **LEP**

Section Preview

Objectives

After studying this section, you will be able to:

1. **Describe** the characteristics of the traditional economy.
2. **Explain** the strengths and weaknesses of the command economy.
3. **Examine** the strengths and weaknesses of a market economy.

Key Terms

economy, economic system, traditional economy, command economy, market economy

Applying Economic Concepts

Tradition Do your parents want you to follow in their footsteps? Enter the same profession? Take over the family business? Attend the same college they went to? *Tradition* plays a stabilizing role in our lives. Even the American free enterprise economy, characterized by freedom and competition, has some elements of tradition.

The survival of any society depends on its ability to provide food, clothing, and shelter for its people. Because these societies face scarcity, decisions concerning WHAT, HOW, and FOR WHOM to produce must be made.

All societies have something else in common. They have an **economy,** or **economic system**—an organized way of providing for the wants and needs of their people. The way in which these provisions are made determines the type of economic system they have. Three major kinds of economic systems exist—traditional, command, and market.

Traditional Economy

Many of our actions spring from habit and custom. Why, for example, do so many people eat turkey on Thanksgiving? Why does the bride toss the bouquet at a wedding? Why do most people shake hands with strangers, or leave tips in restaurants? For the most part, these practices have been handed down from one generation to the next and have become tradition.

In a society with a **traditional economy,** the allocation of scarce resources and nearly all other economic activity stems from ritual, habit, or custom. Habit and custom also dictate most social behavior. Individuals are not free to make decisions based on what they

want or would like to have. Instead, their roles are defined by the customs of their elders and ancestors. They know what goods and services will be produced, how to produce them, and how such goods and services will be distributed. **1**

The Inuit society of northern Canada in the last century is an example of a traditional economy. For generations, parents taught their children how to survive in a harsh climate, make tools, fish, and hunt. Their children, in turn, taught these skills to the next generation.

The Inuit hunted, and it was traditional to share the spoils of the hunt with other families. If a walrus or bear was taken, hunters divided the kill evenly into as many portions as there were heads of families in the hunting party. The hunter most responsible for the kill had first choice, the second hunter to help with the kill chose next, and so on. Later, members of the hunting party shared their portions with other families, because the Inuit shared freely and generously with one another.

The hunter had the "honor" of the kill and the respect of the village—rather than a physical claim to the entire kill itself. Because of this tradition of sharing, and as long as skilled hunters lived in the community, a village could survive the long harsh winters. This custom was partially responsible for the Inuit's survival in northern Canada for thousands of years.

32 UNIT 1: *Fundamental Economic Concepts*

Classroom Resources for SECTION 1

- Reproducible Lesson Plan 2-1
- Guided Reading Activity 2-1
- Cooperative Learning Activity 2
- Consumer Application Activity 2
- Math Practice for Economics 2
- Free Enterprise Activities 1, 2, 6
- Primary and Secondary Source Reading 2
- Performance Assessment Activity 2
- Reinforcing Economic Skills 2
- Section Quiz 2-1

- Spanish Section Quiz 2-1
- NBR's Economics in Action Video Program
- Focus Activity Transparency 5
- Economic Concepts Transparency 4
- Testmaker
- Vocabulary PuzzleMaker
- Chapter Challenger Interactive Review Software
- MindJogger Videoquiz

Traditional Economy *This Pueblo artist in New Mexico uses her ancestors' techniques for weaving.* **What drives economic activity in a traditional economy?**

Strengths

The main strength of a traditional economy is that everyone knows which role to play. Little uncertainty exists over WHAT to produce. If you are born into a family of hunters, you hunt. If you are born into a family of farmers, you farm. Likewise, little uncertainty exists over HOW to produce, because you do everything the same way your parents did. Finally, the FOR WHOM question is determined by the customs and traditions of the society. Life is generally stable, predictable, and continuous.

Weaknesses

The main drawback of the traditional economy is that it tends to discourage new ideas and new ways of doing things. The traditional society even punishes people for breaking rules or acting differently. The lack of progress leads to a lower standard of living than other types of economic societies have. **2**

Command Economy

Other societies have a **command economy**—one in which a central authority makes most of the WHAT, HOW, and FOR WHOM decisions. Economic decisions are made at the top, and people are expected to go along with choices their leaders make. Command economies can be found in North Korea, Cuba, and the People's Republic of China. Until recently, the communist bloc countries of Eastern Europe and the former Soviet Union also had command economies.

In the former Soviet Union, for example, the government made major economic choices. The State Planning Commission directed nearly all aspects of the Soviet economy. It determined needs, decided goals, and set production quotas for major industries.

If the State Planning Commission wanted to stress growth of heavy manufacturing, it shifted resources from consumer goods to that sector. If it wanted to strengthen national defense, it directed resources to the production of military equipment and supplies.

QUICK CHECK

Checking Understanding

1. How are roles defined in a traditional economy?
2. What is the main weakness of a traditional economy?

Applying Economic Concepts

☑ **Traditional Economy** Elements of tradition carry over from one generation to the next in many American "household economies." Ask your parents what traditions they learned in regard to chores and money management.

Cooperative Learning
Assign Cooperative Learning Activity 2.

GLENCOE
TECHNOLOGY

NIGHTLY BUSINESS REPORT

Economics in Action

Chapter 3
Disc 1, Side 1

Title: *Economic Systems & the American Economy*

Subject: How America's free enterprise system works

Ask: What are some examples of government's role in the American economy *(Answers may include requiring businesses to pay workers a minimum wage and requiring them to meet environmental standards.)*

  Also available in VHS.

VISUAL INSTRUCTION

Prompt students to note the traditional elements shown in the photograph. *(Traditional-style loom, artist works by hand, and so on.)*

Answer to Caption:
ritual, habit, or custom

QUICK CHECK

ANSWERS

1. by the customs of the people's elders or ancestors
2. It tends to discourage new ideas and new ways of doing things.

L2 Journalism Write the following statement on the chalkboard: Dollar votes tell producers what consumers want. Tell students that this is the headline of a brief newspaper article on the role of the consumer in a market economy and ask them to write the article.

Independent Practice

Guided Reading Assign Guided Reading Activity for Section 1. **LEP**

L1 Illustrating Ideas Have students use library resources to find visual images that illustrate each of the three economic systems. Call on volunteers to present and justify their selections in an oral report. **LEP**

L2 Applying Ideas Have students write a paragraph explaining how each of the three types of economic systems might respond to the introduction of new technology. For guidance, suggest that students consider how each system views new ideas. Select students to present and discuss their paragraphs.

DID YOU KNOW

The word *market* derives from the Latin word *mercari*, which means "to trade." Its first use in its present meaning—the place where trading goes on—probably appeared in the twelfth century.

DID YOU KNOW?

Modern Times Meet Tradition In 1993 the Northwest Territories government in northern Canada proposed an alternate way for Inuit peoples to pay alimony to former spouses. Instead of making alimony payments in Canadian dollars, the Inuit would be able to use the Arctic's more traditional currencies: caribou, seal, and whale blubber. Payment could also be made in the form of firewood, animal skins, fish, or even chunks of icebergs.

Strengths

The main strength of a command system is that it can change direction drastically in a relatively short time. The former Soviet Union went from an agricultural society to a leading industrial nation in just a few decades. It did so by emphasizing heavy industry and industrial growth rather than the production of consumer goods.

During this period, the central planning agency shifted resources around on a massive scale. Consumer goods were virtually ignored, and when the country faced a shortage of male workers on construction projects, the government put women to work with picks, shovels, and wheelbarrows.

Weaknesses

Several important drawbacks limit the command economy. One is that the command system is not designed to meet the wants and needs of individuals. In the case of Soviet industrial development, an entire generation was forced to do without such consumer goods as cars, home appliances, and adequate housing. People often were told to sacrifice for the good of the state and the benefit of future generations.

A second weakness of the command economy is the lack of incentives for people to work hard. In most command economies, workers with different skills and responsibilities receive similar wages. In addition, people seldom lose their jobs, regardless of the quality of

their work. As a result, some people work just hard enough to fill production quotas set by planners.

This pattern can have unexpected results. At one time in the former Soviet Union, central planners set production quotas for electrical motors to be measured in tons of output per year. Workers soon discovered that the easiest way to fill the quota was to add weight to the motors. As a result, Soviet workers made some of the heaviest electrical motors in the world. They also produced some of the heaviest chandeliers in the world for the same reason. Some were so heavy that they fell from ceilings.

A third weakness is that the command economy requires a large decision-making bureaucracy. Many clerks, planners, and others are needed to operate the system. Most decisions cannot be made until after consulting a number of people and processing a large amount of paperwork. These procedures slow decision making and raise the costs of production.

Yet a fourth weakness of a command economy is that it does not have the flexibility to deal with minor, day-to-day problems. Even when some change is needed, the sheer size of the bureaucracy discourages even the smallest adjustments. As a result, command economies tend to lurch from one crisis to the next—or collapse completely as in the case of the former Soviet Union.

Finally, people with new or unique ideas find it difficult to get ahead in a command economy. Opportunities for individual initiative are rare. Each person is expected to perform a job in a factory, in the bureaucracy, or on a farm, according to the economic decisions made by central planners.

Market Economy

In a **market economy,** people and firms act in their own best interests to answer the WHAT, HOW, and FOR WHOM questions. In economic terms, a market is an arrangement that allows buyers and sellers to come together in order to exchange goods and services. A market could be in a specific location, such as a farmers' market or a flea market. A list of phone numbers for lawn-mowing services posted on a local bulletin board also acts as a market. As long as a mechanism exists for buyers and sellers to get together, a market can exist.

$ Free Enterprise Activity $

Prepare a one-page handout listing the six strengths of a market economy, leaving space under each strength. Distribute copies of the handout to the class and instruct students to find at least two current examples of each strength from newspapers, magazines, radio, or television. Have them enter brief descriptions of examples under the appropriate strength. Allow students one week to complete the assignment. Upon completion, have students compare and discuss their examples.

In a market economy, people's decisions act as votes. When consumers buy a particular product, they are casting their dollar "votes" for that product. After the "votes" are counted, producers know what people want. Because producers are always looking for goods and services that consumers will buy, the consumer plays a key role in determining WHAT to produce.

Strengths

An ideal market economy has several advantages over traditional and command economies. First, a market economy can adjust to change over time. During the gasoline shortage of the 1970s, for example, consumers reduced their demand for large, gas-guzzling automobiles and increased their demand for smaller, fuel-efficient ones. Because automakers still wanted to sell cars, they moved resources from the production of large cars to small ones.

When gas prices leveled off in 1985 and then declined in 1986, the trend slowly began to reverse. Consumers wanted to buy large cars again, so automakers adjusted by making larger yet more fuel-efficient automobiles. Changes in a market economy, then, tend to be gradual. Unlike the traditional economy, change is neither prohibited nor discouraged. Unlike the command economy, change is neither delayed because of bureaucracy, nor suddenly forced on people by others.

A second major strength of the market economy is the freedom that exists for everyone involved. Producers may make whatever they think will sell. They also decide the HOW question by making their products in the most efficient manner. Consumers, on the

🖿 **Consumer Application** Assign Consumer Application Activity 2.

🖿 **Math Practice** Assign Math Practice for Economics 2.

🖿 **Free Enterprise** Assign Free Enterprise Activities 1, 2, and 6.

🖿 **Readings** Assign Primary and Secondary Source Reading 2.

🖿 **Performance Assessment** Assign Performance Assessment Activity 2.

ASSESS

Check for Understanding

Assign Section 1 Review as homework or an in-class activity.

💿 Use **Chapter Challenger Interactive Review Software** to review Section 1.

VISUAL INSTRUCTION

Call on volunteers to suggest words that summarize some aspect of each of the three economic systems. *(Sample: Traditional—static; command—rigid; market—flexible.)*

Answer to Caption:

must be reasonably competitive, resources must be reasonably free to move from one activity to another, adequate information available to everyone

---

Figure 2.1
Comparing Economic Systems

	Traditional	Command	Market
STRENGTHS	*Sets forth certain economic roles for all members of the community *Stable, predictable, and continuous life	*Capable of dramatic change in a short time *Does not meet wants and needs of consumers *Lacks effective incentives to get people to work	*Is able to adjust to change gradually *Individual freedom for everyone *Notable lack of government interference *Decentralized decision making *Incredible variety of goods and services *High degree of consumer satisfaction
WEAKNESSES	*Discourages new ideas and new ways of doing things *Stagnation and lack of progress	*Requires large bureaucracy, which consumes resources *Has little flexibility to deal with small, day-to-day changes *New and different ideas discouraged, no room for individuality	*Rewards only productive resources. Many people are too young, too old, or too sick to work. *Must guard against market failures

Every society has an economic system, or an organized way of answering the WHAT, HOW and FOR WHOM questions. The type of system that is best for a society depends on the ability of that system to satisfy people's wants and needs, and to fulfill its economic goals. **What conditions must be met for a market economy to be effective?**

CHAPTER 2: *Economic Systems and Decision Making* **35**

Extending the Content

Ideal Types Social scientists refer to the three kinds of economic systems as *ideal types*. An ideal type is a simplified description of a particular phenomenon, focusing on the phenomenon's usual, common, and typical features. In other words, an ideal type provides a picture of the essential nature of the phenomenon and, thus, makes the task of analysis much easier. Ideal types rarely, if ever, exist in reality, and most economic systems have ele-

ments of one or more types. A socialist economic system, for example, may have elements of the command and market ideal types. The government owns and controls important means of production. At the same time, however, consumer decisions on what to purchase may help to influence what is produced with the means of production.

MEETING LESSON OBJECTIVES

Each objective below is tested by the questions that follow it in parentheses.

1. **Describe** the characteristics of the traditional economy. **(1, 2)**
2. **Explain** the strengths and weaknesses of the command economy. **(1, 3, 5)**
3. **Examine** the strengths and weaknesses of a market economy. **(1, 4, 5, 6)**

Evaluate

📁 📁 💻 Assign the Section 1 Quiz in the TCR or use the *Economics: Principles and Practices* Testmaker. Spanish Section Quizzes also are available in the Spanish Resources Binder.

Reteach

Copy the strengths and weaknesses of the three economic systems onto flash cards. Display cards one at a time and call on volunteers to name the economic system described by each card.

Enrich

Have students consider their part in the market economy. Ask them to think about the goods and services they consume or the jobs they hold.

CLOSE

Have students discuss which of the three economic systems they would prefer to live under and why.

36

---

other hand, may spend their money on whatever goods and services they wish.

A third strength is the relatively small degree of government interference. Except for certain important concerns, such as national defense and environmental protection, the government tries to stay out of the way so that buyers and sellers can go about their business. As long as competition exists, the market economy tends to take care of itself.

A fourth advantage is that decision making in a market economy is decentralized. Literally billions—if not trillions—of individual economic decisions are made daily. Collectively, these decisions direct scarce resources into uses that consumers favor. Because individuals make these decisions, everyone has a voice in the way the economy runs.

A fifth strength of the market economy is the incredible variety of goods and services provided to consumers. Almost any product can and will be produced if a buyer for it exists. Recent products include everything from pocket computers to 24-hour cable television cartoon networks to pump basketball shoes. In short, if a product can be imagined, if it can be produced, and if consumers are willing to buy it, that product will be produced in a market economy.

A sixth strength is the high degree of consumer satisfaction. The wide range of products available in a market economy makes it possible for almost everyone to satisfy their tastes. In addition, a choice one group makes does not mean that another group cannot have what it wants. If 51 percent of the people want blue shirts, and 49 percent want white ones, people in both groups can still get what they want. Unlike an election, the minority does not have to live with choices the majority makes.

Weaknesses

The primary weakness of the market economy deals with the FOR WHOM question. In general, rewards in a market economy go to the most productive resources. This distribution system may be fine in the case of land or capital, but it can be a problem for the productive resource called labor. Some people may be too young, too old, or too sick to support themselves. These people would have difficulty surviving in a pure market economy without the government or private groups providing for their basic needs.

In addition, markets sometimes do not work as they should. Markets work best when three conditions are met. First, markets must be reasonably competitive, allowing producers to compete with one another to offer the best value for the price. Second, resources must be reasonably free to move from one activity to another. Workers, for example, need the freedom to change jobs if they do not like the ones they have. Likewise, producers need the freedom to produce the goods and services the best way they know how. Third, everyone should have access to adequate information so that alternatives can be known and wise choices made. If any of these conditions are not met, the market itself may fail.

SECTION 1 REVIEW

Reviewing Terms and Facts

1. **Define** economy, economic system, traditional economy, command economy, market economy.
2. **Identify** the strengths and weaknesses of a traditional economy.
3. **List** the strengths and weaknesses of a command economy.
4. **Name** six strengths of a market economy.

Critical Thinking

5. **Making Comparisons** How are the WHAT, HOW, and FOR WHOM questions answered in the command and market economies?

Applying Economic Concepts

6. **Consumer Sovereignty** Give an example of a recent product that has succeeded and a product that has failed in our market economy because of consumers' influence.

Answers to SECTION 1 REVIEW

1. All vocabulary words are defined in the Glossary.

2. Strengths: sets economic roles for all members of society, life is stable, predictable, continuous; **Weaknesses:** discourages new ideas, new ways of doing things, lower standard of living

3. Strengths: capable of great change in short time period; **Weaknesses:** does not meet needs and wants of consumers, lacks effective incentives for people to work hard, requires large bureaucracy, has little flexibility, new ideas discouraged

4. able to adjust to change gradually; individual freedom for everyone; lack of government interference; decision making decentralized; produces great variety of goods and services; high degree of consumer satisfaction

5. command: central authority answers questions; market: people and firms acting in own interests provide answers

6. Answers will vary.

TECHNOLOGY SKILL

Using a Computerized Card Catalog

Imagine that your teacher asks you to write a report about the traditional economy of the Inuit. How should you begin the task? The teacher suggests that you start by asking effective questions and then using a computerized card catalog to help you find the answers you need.

Explanation

Effective questions are those that help you "get to the point" and allow you to better understand any given topic. Begin by asking general questions, then narrow your focus through specific questions. For example, you may begin by asking "Who are the Inuit?" Then ask, "What specific tasks and roles do members of their society perform? How do the Inuit learn their economic roles?"

Now use the computerized card catalog in your school or local library to find books and other resources that will provide answers to your questions. Type in a subject heading—for example, the *Inuit.* You will access the online, or computerized, card catalog that lists all the library's resources for that topic. The computer will list on screen the titles of books, magazines, videotapes, audiocassettes, or CDs that pertain to the Inuit.

The "card" that appears on screen will provide other information as well, including the year the work was published or released, who published or produced it, what media type it is, and the language it is written or recorded in. Then check to find the classification (culture, economics, etc.) and call number under which it is shelved.

Practice

This chapter talks about the strengths and weaknesses of the former Soviet Union's State Planning Commission. Use the computerized card catalog to find additional information on this organization:

1. Type in "Soviet Union".
2. From the list of subjects that appears on the screen, determine which might apply to the State Planning Commission during the years 1925-1955.
3. Follow the instructions on the computer screen to display all the titles under each subject you selected.
4. Determine which of the books, videos, audiocassettes, and CDs now on the screen you want to learn more about.

An Inuit woman prepares fish the way her ancestors did.

Additional Practice

For further practice in using a computerized card catalog, complete the Reinforcing Skills exercise in the Chapter 2 Review on page 51.

TEACHING SKILLS

TEACH

This skill introduces the use of the computer in finding library materials. After students have read the **Explanation**, ask them what they would do to find out about the economy of their state. Encourage them to develop a list of the kinds of questions that would help them gather appropriate information. As a guide, suggest that most questions they need to ask begin with the words *What, Where, When, Who, Why,* or *How.*

Then direct students to use the library computer to find resources that will provide answers to their questions. Point out to students the advantage of a computerized card catalog—the ability of the computer to narrow the students' search for information. If the student does not know or remember the name of a specific book or author, the subject heading can guide the student in the right direction.

Skills Practice For additional practice, have students complete Reinforcing Economic Skills 2.

? DID YOU KNOW

The word *economy* is derived from the Greek *oikonomia,* which refers to "house" or "household" (oikos) and "to manage" or "management" (nemein).

Answers to SKILL

Students' answers will vary depending on the computer program in use and the resources available in the library system. Students' resources should focus on the role, successes, failures, and ramifications of the Soviet Union's State Planning Commission.

FOCUS

Section Objectives

1. Describe the basic economic and social goals used to evaluate economic performance.

2. Examine the trade-offs among economic and social goals.

Bellringer

 Prior to taking roll at the beginning of the class period, display Focus Activity Transparency 7 on the overhead projector and assign the accompanying Student Activity 7.

Motivational Activity

Discuss students' responses to the activity sheet that accompanies Focus Activity Transparency 7.

Preteaching Vocabulary

Ask students to define *inflation* in their own words. Then have students explain why inflation is a special problem for people living on fixed incomes.

Use the **Vocabulary PuzzleMaker** to create crossword and word search puzzles.

VISUAL INSTRUCTION

Ask students to identify the economic goal that the photograph illustrates. *(economic equity)*

Answer to Caption:

They serve as benchmarks that help people to determine if the system is meeting their economic needs.

SECTION 2
Evaluating Economic Performance

Section Preview

Objectives

After studying this section, you will be able to:

1. **Describe** the basic economic and social goals used to evaluate economic performance.

2. **Examine** the trade-offs among economic and social goals.

Key Terms

Social Security, inflation, fixed income

Applying Economic Concepts

Freedom and Equity Do you have enough *freedom* to do the things you want? Do your parents and friends treat you in an *equitable,* or fair, manner? More than likely, your answers to questions such as these have an effect on your happiness and satisfaction with life. People tend to ask the same types of questions about their economy. Does it allow them economic freedom? Is it equitable? The answers to these and other questions help us determine whether or not we are satisfied with our economic system.

Whether a particular economic system is best for a society depends on its ability to satisfy the needs of its people. These needs are, in part, defined by the economic and social goals the society sets for itself. Goals are important because they serve as benchmarks that help people determine if the system meets their needs. If a system meets most—but not all—of the needs, people may demand laws to change the system until their needs are met.

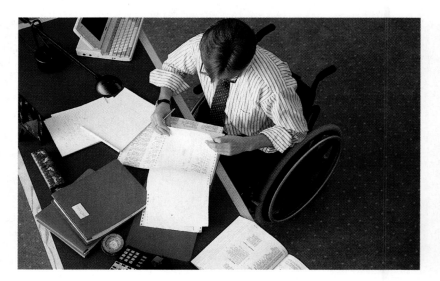

Economic and Social Goals
Federal legislation makes it illegal to discriminate against handicapped persons. **Why are economic goals important?**

Classroom Resources for SECTION 2

📁 Reproducible Lesson Plan 2-2
📁 Guided Reading Activity 2-2
📁 Section Quiz 2-2
📁 Spanish Section Quiz 2-2

🔦 Focus Activity Transparency 7
💿 Testmaker
💿 Vocabulary PuzzleMaker
💿 Chapter Challenger Interactive Review Software

Economic and Social Goals *The floods of 1997 displaced thousands of people. Here, the Ohio River has almost turned Riverfront Stadium in Cincinnati into an island.* **What goal of the American economy was set to provide for those in need?**

Economic and Social Goals

In the United States, people share many broad social and economic goals. While it might be difficult to find them listed in any one place, they are repeated many times in the statements that friends, relatives, community leaders, and elected officials make. We can categorize those statements into seven major economic and social goals.

Economic Freedom

In the United States, people place a high value on the freedom to make their own economic decisions.

People like to choose their own occupation, employer, and uses for their money. Business owners like the freedom to choose where and how they produce. The belief in economic freedom, like political freedom, is one of the cornerstones of American society. **1**

Economic Efficiency

Americans recognize that resources are scarce and that factors of production must be used wisely. If resources are wasted, fewer goods and services can be produced and fewer wants and needs can be satisfied. Economic decision making must be efficient so that benefits gained are greater than costs incurred.

QUICK CHECK

Checking Understanding

1. What are some of the economic choices people and producers in the United States are free to make?

Applying Economic Concepts

 Economic Efficiency In 1813 Francis Lowell combined all the stages of textile production—spinning, weaving, bleaching, dyeing, and printing—under one roof. His efficient mill launched the nation's industrial revolution, changing manufacturing from the home to the factory.

CHAPTER 2: *Economic Systems and Decision Making* **39**

TEACH

Guided Practice

L2 *Analyzing Information* List on the chalkboard the seven economic and social goals discussed in the section. Ask students to suggest which goals might conflict and why. Then have students write sentences suggesting what trade-offs might solve conflicts.

L3 *Debate* Lead the class in a debate on the following: The most important economic and social goal is economic freedom. As the debate progresses, have students note the major pro and con arguments. Then have students use their notes to write a persuasive essay supporting or challenging the statement.

Independent Practice

Guided Reading Assign Guided Reading Activity for Section 2. **LEP**

VISUAL INSTRUCTION

Call on volunteers to identify a recent event that threatened economic security in their community.

Answer to Caption
economic security

QUICK CHECK
ANSWERS

1. People: occupation, employer, uses for money; Producers: where and how to produce

Economic Equity

Americans have a strong sense of justice, impartiality, and fairness. Many people, for example, believe in equal pay for equal work. As a result, it is illegal to discriminate on the basis of age, sex, race, religion, or disability in employment. In addition, laws protect consumers against false advertising, unfair pricing, and dangerous products. Many private businesses even have retirement programs for their employees.

Economic Security

Americans desire protection from such adverse economic events as layoffs and illnesses. States have set up funds to help workers who lose their jobs. Many employers have insurance plans to cover the injuries and illnesses of their workers. On the national level, Congress has set up **Social Security**—a federal program of disability and retirement benefits that covers most working people.

Full Employment

When people work, they earn income for themselves while they produce goods and services for others. If people do not have jobs, however, they cannot support themselves or their families, nor can they produce output for others. As a result, people want their economic system to provide as many jobs as possible.

Price Stability

Another goal is to have stable prices. If **inflation**—a rise in the general level of prices—occurs, workers need more money to pay for food, clothing, and shelter. People on a **fixed income**—an income that does not increase even though prices go up—find that bills are harder to pay and that planning for the future is more difficult. Price stability makes budgeting easier and adds a degree of certainty to the future.

Economic Growth

The last major goal of most Americans is economic growth. Most people hope to have a better job, a newer car, better clothes, their own home, and a number of other things in the future. Growth is needed so that people can have more goods and services in the future. Because the population is likely to grow, economic growth is necessary to meet everyone's future needs.

Future Goals?

The seven goals listed above are ones on which most people seem to agree. As our society evolves, however, it is entirely possible that new goals may be added. Do people feel that a cleaner environment is important enough to be added to the list of goals? Should we add the preservation of an endangered species such as the spotted owl, humpback whale, or timber wolf to the list? In the end, Americans themselves must decide on the goals important to them.

Economic and Social Goals *Price stability is especially important to those people who have fixed incomes.* **What is a fixed income?**

$ *Free Enterprise Activity* $

Write the following incomplete sentence on the chalkboard: The economic and social goal of _____ is illustrated in the economy by _____. Organize students into pairs and have each pair complete seven sentences—one for each of the social and economic goals. (Suggest the following as an example: *The economic and social goal of economic freedom is illustrated in the economy by the choices people can make on how to spend their money.* After the activity is completed, ask pairs to share their sentences with the class.

Economic and Social Goals
A new pipeline in Alaska provides more oil for American consumers. At the same time, however, it disrupts the ecosystem of the Alaskan wilderness. **What other trade-offs can you cite?**

Trade-Offs Among Goals

People sometimes have different ideas about how to reach a goal. At other times, the goals themselves might conflict. Even economic policies have opportunity costs. A policy that keeps foreign-made shoes out of the United States could help the goal of full employment in the local shoe industry. This policy might work against individual freedom, however, if people ended up with fewer choices. A new shopping center built near the highway may stimulate economic growth. At the same time, it may threaten the stability and security of downtown merchants.

Even an increase in the minimum wage might involve a conflict of goals. On one hand, people might argue that an increase is the equitable, or "right," thing to do. Others might argue that increasing the minimum wage raises unemployment and restricts the freedom of employers to pay wages that they think are fair.

For the most part, people, businesses, and government usually are able to resolve conflicts of goals. Fortunately, the economic system of the United States is flexible enough to allow choices, accommodate compromises, and still satisfy the majority of Americans most of the time.

SECTION 2 REVIEW

Reviewing Terms and Facts

1. **Define** Social Security, inflation, fixed income.
2. **List** seven major goals of the United States economy.
3. **Explain** how an increase in the minimum wage might involve a conflict of goals.

Critical Thinking

4. **Analyzing Information** What characteristics does the United States economy have that allow it to resolve conflicts among goals?

Applying Economic Concepts

5. **Freedom and Equity** How do laws against false advertising promote economic equity?

Evaluate

Assign the Section 2 Quiz in the TCR or use the *Economics: Principles and Practices* Testmaker to create a customized quiz. Spanish Section Quizzes also are available in the Spanish Resources Binder.

Reteach

Have students summarize the main ideas of the section in an outline.

Enrich

Write on the chalkboard the terms *scarcity* and *economic growth*. Ask students to write a short paragraph explaining the relationship between the two terms. Call on volunteers to read and discuss their paragraphs.

CLOSE

Have students rank the economic and social goals in order of importance as they see them. Select students to present and justify their rankings.

 VISUAL INSTRUCTION

Have students discuss the following: How big a role should environmental concerns play in the making of economic decisions?

Answer to Caption:
Answers will vary. Refer students to the discussion of trade-offs on this page.

Answers to SECTION 2 REVIEW

1. All vocabulary words are defined in the Glossary.

2. economic freedom, economic efficiency, economic equity, economic security, full employment, price stability, economic growth

3. Many people would say that an increase in the minimum wage would further the goal of economic equity because it is a fair thing to do. Others might argue that it conflicts with the goal of full employment by raising unemployment, and with the goal of economic freedom by preventing employers from paying what they feel are reasonable wages.

4. It is flexible enough to allow choices and accommodate compromises and still satisfy the majority of the people most of the time.

5. They prevent unscrupulous business owners from telling falsehoods. They promote economic equity by ensuring that justice and fairness prevail in the market.

Background

Anita Roddick has a knack for publicity. She located her first Body Shop next to a funeral parlor. The director of the funeral parlor, concerned that people might confuse the two businesses, complained. Roddick leaked the story to the press, and people soon visited her store to see what the fuss was about.

Roddick has a strong environmental awareness. "Businesses," Roddick argues, "should minimize the environmental impact of their operations at all times." To this end, The Body Shop undertakes an "ecological audit" each year. The audit measures the ecological impact of the use of raw materials and products and discovers whether production methods are energy efficient and pollution free. In this way, Roddick says, The Body Shop's "final products are ecologically sound from cradle to grave."

TEACH

After students have read the Profile, point out that Roddick's methods have been referred to as "socially responsible business." Then divide the class into two groups. Have one group develop arguments supporting the idea that businesses have an obligation to be socially responsible. Have the other group draw up arguments in support of the idea that businesses help enough by being profitable and hiring workers. Call on students from both sides of the class to present and discuss their arguments.

PROFILES IN ECONOMICS

ANITA RODDICK
(1942–)

Anita Roddick is a self-described former hippie, social activist, and wildly successful entrepreneur. In 1976 Anita and Gordon Roddick opened their first store—The Body Shop—in Brighton, England, with a $6,500 loan.

Born in the small English town of Littlehampton, Roddick worked in the family cafe. She graduated from the Maude Allen Secondary Modern School for Girls and nearly pursued a career as an actress. Instead, she studied English, history, and art at the University of Bath.

Roddick traveled extensively. Her sense of humor and adventurous spirit marked her as a maverick. Her company, The Body Shop, has proven to be a maverick, too.

The Body Shop employs people in Nepal to create handmade paper from recycled materials.

COSMETICS Anita Roddick produces cosmetics. The Body Shop, however, is quite different from other cosmetics industries.

Roddick's cosmetics are made from natural ingredients and renewable resources, which she discovered during her many travels. They are sold in inexpensive biodegradable or refillable containers. In addition, her products are never tested on animals.

ENVIRONMENTALLY AWARE Roddick is sensitive to women's issues and global concerns. "I hate the beauty business," she declared in her autobiography. "It is a monster industry selling unattainable dreams. It lies. It cheats. It exploits

women." The Body Shop, therefore, does not promote idealized notions of beauty. Anthropologists are hired to study how people in different cultures care for their skin and hair. Roddick then encourages local communities in developing countries to grow the natural ingredients used in her cosmetics.

Roddick is deeply involved with education and the campaign to preserve the rain forests. Her company trucks are painted with slogans such as IF YOU THINK EDUCATION IS EXPENSIVE, TRY IGNORANCE and THE INDIANS ARE THE CUSTODIANS OF THE RAIN FORESTS, THE RAIN FORESTS ARE THE LUNGS OF THE WORLD. IF THEY DIE, WE DIE.

FRANCHISING POLICY Roddick is a shrewd entrepreneur. When others clamored to open their own Body Shop stores, Roddick and her husband franchised the company. Store managers finance their own stores in return for the use of The Body Shop name and its products. By 1997, almost 1,500 stores had opened in 46 countries.

Examining the Profile

1. **Making Comparisons** What makes The Body Shop different from other cosmetics companies?

2. **For Further Research** Research and write about the effects of Roddick's TRADE NOT AID policies with developing nations.

42   UNIT 1: *Fundamental Economic Concepts*

Answers to Examining the Profile

1. The Body Shop does not promote idealized notions of beauty. Its products are made from natural ingredients and renewable resources, never tested on animals, and sold in cheap biodegradable or reusable containers. In the search for new products, it studies skin- and hair-care methods in other cultures. It also encourages communities in developing countries to grow the natural ingredients used in its products.

2. Suggest that students focus on the economic impact of Roddick's policies.

Section Preview

Objectives

After studying this section, you will be able to:
1. **Explore** the characteristics of a free enterprise system.
2. **Describe** the role and importance of the entrepreneur.
3. **Examine** the role of the consumer as "sovereign" of the economy.
4. **Describe** the role that government plays in a free enterprise economy.

Key Terms

capitalism, competition, voluntary exchange, private property, profit, profit motive, consumer sovereignty, mixed economy, modified private enterprise economy

Applying Economic Concepts

Voluntary Exchange Who benefits when you buy something—you or the seller? As long as the transaction involves a *voluntary exchange*, you may both benefit—or the exchange would not have happened in the first place. The market economy is very popular because of voluntary exchange—everybody benefits when a transaction takes place.

A market economy is normally based on **capitalism**, a system in which private citizens own the factors of production. Capitalism thrives on **competition**—the struggle among sellers to attract consumers while lowering costs. Buyers, like sellers, also compete to find the best products at the lowest prices. In this way, goods and services are allocated to those who are willing and able to pay for them.

Free enterprise is another term used to describe the American economy. In a free enterprise economy, competition is allowed to flourish with a minimum of government interference.

Competition and Free Enterprise

A free enterprise economy has four important characteristics—economic freedom, voluntary exchange, private property rights, and the profit motive. These characteristics satisfy many of the economic goals that most Americans seem to share, and they make competition possible.

Economic Freedom

Economic freedom is a characteristic of capitalism often taken for granted. Individuals as well as busi-

nesses enjoy this freedom. People, for example, have the freedom to choose their occupation and their employer. To a lesser extent, they can choose to work where and when they want. They may work on the West Coast, East Coast, or in Alaska. They may work days, nights, indoors, outdoors, in offices, or in their homes.

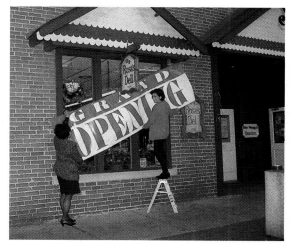

Economic Freedom *The freedom to own a business is a hallmark of free enterprise.* **What other characteristics does a free enterprise economy have?**

CHAPTER 2: *Economic Systems and Decision Making* **43**

TEACH

Guided Practice

L2 Analyzing Ideas On the chalkboard draw a concept web with "Economic Freedom" at the center and "Voluntary Exchange," "Private Property," and "Profit Motive" around it. Call on volunteers to explain the relationship of each satellite idea to the central idea of economic freedom.

GLENCOE
TECHNOLOGY

NIGHTLY BUSINESS REPORT

Economics in Action

Chapter 4

Disc 1, Side 1

Title: *Your Role as a Consumer*

Subject: Consumers' choices, income, and consumer protection

Ask: What are some ways in which the federal government helps the consumer? *(sets safety standards for automobiles; inspects and grades meat, poultry, and dairy products; tests new drugs)*

 Also available in VHS.

VISUAL INSTRUCTION

Call on volunteers to explain why the profit motive is so important to free enterprise.

Answer to Caption:

both tangible items, such as houses and cars, and intangible items, such as skills and talents

44

DID YOU KNOW?

Private Property Early Americans believed so strongly in the right to private property that they incorporated this right into law. The 1st Congress proposed the Fifth Amendment, which was ratified in 1791. The amendment states that private property shall not be taken for public use without just compensation. The Fourteenth Amendment prevents any state from depriving people of their property without due process of law.

With economic freedom, people can choose to have their own business or to work for someone else. They can apply for jobs, and they have the right to accept or reject employment if offered. Economic freedom also means that people can leave jobs and move on to others that offer greater opportunity.

Businesses also enjoy economic freedom. They are free to hire the best workers, and they have the freedom to produce the goods and services they feel will be the most profitable. Businesses can make as many or as few goods and services as they want, and they can sell them wherever they please. They have the right to charge whatever price they feel is profitable, and they are free to risk success or failure.

Voluntary Exchange

A second characteristic of capitalism is **voluntary exchange**—the act of buyers and sellers freely and willingly engaging in market transactions. Moreover, transactions are made in such a way that both the buyer and the seller are better off after the exchange than before it occurred. Buyers, for example, can do many things with their money. They can deposit it in the bank, hide it under a mattress, or exchange it for goods or services. If they spend their money on a product, they must believe that the item being purchased is of greater value to them than the money they gave up. **1**

Figure 2.2
Characteristics of Free Enterprise and Capitalism

Economic Freedom
People may choose their jobs, employers, and how to spend their money.
Businesses may choose what products to sell and what to charge for them.

Voluntary Exchange
Buyers and sellers may engage freely and willingly in market transactions.

Private Property
People may control their possessions as they wish.

Profit Motive
People and organizations may improve their material well-being by making money.

The terms free enterprise *and* capitalism *are often used to describe a market system in which the factors of production are owned by private citizens, and businesses are allowed to compete for profits with a minimum amount of government interference.* **What items are included under the category of private property?**

Meeting Special Needs

Inefficient Readers Students often benefit by using a form of rapid "reading" called *scanning* to locate specific information. Model the scanning procedure by sliding your finger rapidly down the middle of both columns on page 45. Tell students to demonstrate scanning to find the word *profit* on page 46. Time students as they search the rest of the section for the word *profit*.

With voluntary exchange, sellers also have many opportunities to sell their products. If they exchange their goods and services for cash, they must feel that the money received is more valuable than the product being sold, or they would not sell in the first place. In the end, the transaction benefits both buyer and seller or it would not have taken place. Both the buyer and the seller got something they believed had more value than the money or products given up.

Private Property

Another major feature of capitalism and free enterprise is **private property,** the concept that people have the right and privilege to control their possessions as they wish. Private property includes both tangible items such as houses and cars and intangible items such as skills and talents. People are free to make decisions about their property and their own abilities. They have the right to use or abuse their property as long as they do not interfere with the rights of others. People can also sell or not sell their abilities or services as they see fit. ☑

Private property gives people the incentive to work, save, and invest. When people are free to do as they wish with their property, they are not afraid to use, accumulate, or lend it. Private property also helps give people the incentive to get ahead. People know that if they succeed, they will be able to keep any rewards they might earn. 2

Profit Motive

Under free enterprise and capitalism, people are free to risk their savings or any part of their wealth in a business venture. If the venture goes well for them, the people will earn rewards for their efforts. If things go poorly, they could lose part or even all of the

investment. The very possibility of financial gain, however, leads many people to become entrepreneurs, or those who risk entering business in hopes of earning a profit.

What, however, is profit? Consider the earlier case of voluntary exchange. Remember that the buyer gives up money to obtain a product, and the seller gives up the product to obtain money. Unless both parties believe they will be better off afterward than

---

L1 *Classifying* Point out that some economists classify consumer decisions in three major categories—habitual, impulsive, or rational. Habitual decisions are those made routinely, such as purchasing gasoline for a car. Impulsive decisions are those made on the spur of the moment—when a consumer goes to the store intending to buy bread but returns with a chocolate bar, for example. Rational decisions are given great thought and usually involve the purchase of an expensive item, such as a car. Have students provide three examples for each classification and explain why they classified the choices as they did. **LEP**

L3 *Debate* Write the following statement by Abraham Lincoln on the chalkboard: Government should "do for the people what they wish to have done but cannot do as well or at all in their individual capacities." Call on volunteers to debate this characterization of government's economic role. At the close of the debate, have students write a persuasive essay that supports or challenges Lincoln's statement.

QUICK CHECK

Checking Understanding

1. What is *voluntary exchange*?
2. What incentives does private property give people?

Applying Economic Concepts

☑ **Private Property** The right to inherit property is another feature of private ownership in a capitalist system. In the United States, people may arrange to leave their property to whomever they choose after they die.

QUICK CHECK

ANSWERS

1. the act of buyers and sellers freely and willingly engaging in market transactions
2. to work, save, invest, and succeed

$ Free Enterprise Activity $

Organize students into three groups to conduct interviews. The goal of the interviews is to establish how various groups of people view the term *free enterprise.* Work with groups to develop a list of questions dealing with the characteristics of free enterprise. Then have members of one group interview local business owners or managers, members

of the second group interview employees at local businesses, and members of the third group interview shoppers at a mall or shopping area. Ask groups to collate their findings and present them to the class in the form of an oral report. Have students discuss the reasons for any differences in views among the interview subjects.

Independent Practice

📂 **Guided Reading** Assign Guided Reading Activity for Section 3. **LEP**

L1 **Understanding Ideas** Ask students to create a list of all the things they consider to be their private property. Have them note next to each item on the list the ways in which they are free to use the property. Encourage students to compare their lists. **LEP**

L2 **Advertising** Have students work in small groups to develop print advertisements (or radio or television spots if audio or video equipment is available) designed to persuade people to become entrepreneurs. Encourage groups to display or broadcast their advertisements.

ASSESS

Check for Understanding

Assign Section 3 Review as homework or an in-class activity.

🖥 Use the **Chapter Challenger Interactive Review Software** to review Section 3.

VISUAL INSTRUCTION

Ask students to name other well-known entrepreneurs.

Answer to Caption:

because he organizes and manages the factors of production in order to make a profit

Entrepreneurship *John Johnson started* Ebony *magazine in 1945. Today, his business has sales of $275 million annually.* **Why is Johnson considered an entrepreneur?**

before, neither will make the exchange. When exchange takes place, it does so only because both parties feel they will make a profit.

Profit, then, is the extent to which persons or organizations are better off at the end of a period than they were at the beginning. The **profit motive**—the driving force that encourages people and organizations to improve their material well-being—is largely responsible for the growth of a free enterprise system based on capitalism.

The Role of the Entrepreneur

The entrepreneur is one of the most important people in the economy. The entrepreneur organizes and manages land, labor, and capital in order to seek the reward called profit.

Entrepreneurs often start up new businesses. They are the ones who open new restaurants, automobile repair shops, video arcades, and computer stores. They include people who may have worked for others at one time, but have decided to quit and start their own businesses. Entrepreneurs want to be "their own boss" and are willing to risk everything to make their dreams come true. ☑

Many entrepreneurs fail. Of course, others survive and manage to stay in business with varying degrees of success. A few, and only a very few, manage to become fantastically wealthy and famous. Some of the better-known ones include Bill Gates, who founded Microsoft, John Johnson of Johnson Publishing Co., and Mary Kay Ash, who founded Mary Kay Cosmetics.

Despite the rate of failure among entrepreneurs, the dream of success is often too great to resist. The entrepreneur is both the spark plug and the catalyst of the free enterprise economy. When an entrepreneur is successful, everybody benefits. The entrepreneur is rewarded with profits, a growing business, and the satisfaction of a job well done. Workers are rewarded with more and better-paying jobs. Consumers are rewarded with new and better products. The government is rewarded with a higher level of economic activity and higher tax receipts. These receipts can be used to build roads, schools, and libraries for people not even connected with the original entrepreneur. 1

Nor does it stop there. Profits an entrepreneur generates attract an interest in the industry. When this happens, new firms rush in to "grab a share" of the profits. To remain competitive and stay in business, the original entrepreneur may have to improve the quality or cut prices, which means that customers can buy more for less. In the end, the entrepreneur's search for profits can lead to a chain of events that involves new products, greater competition, more production, higher quality, and lower prices for consumers.

The Role of the Consumer

In the United States, consumers often are thought of as having power in the economy because they determine which products are ultimately produced. For example, a company may try to sell a certain item to the public. If consumers like the product, it will sell, and the producer will be rewarded for his or her efforts. If consumers reject the product and refuse to

---

Extending the Content

Private Property as a Natural Right In the eighteenth century, most Americans accepted the idea that private property was a natural right; that is, a right endowed to us by nature that cannot be withdrawn or surrendered. As the revolutionary leader Samuel Adams noted, it is an "unalterable law in nature, that a man should have the free use and sole disposal of the fruit of his honest industry, subject to no control." Have students discuss the following questions: Do you agree that there is such a thing as natural rights? If so, is private property among these rights? Why or why not?

The Role of Government *Among other goods and services, local governments build and maintain city parks.* **How do state and local governments act as regulators?**

purchase it, the firm may go out of business. **Consumer sovereignty** describes the role of the consumer as sovereign, or ruler, of the market. More commonly, this is expressed in a different way by saying that "the customer is always right."

In recent years, producers have had outstanding successes with various products, including home video games, certain dolls, toy robots, and personal computers. Most consumers rejected other products, such as gasohol—gasoline with a 10 percent grain alcohol content—and diesel engines for cars.

Consumers' wants change constantly as modern communications and travel expose people to new ideas and products. Millions of consumers have home computers, even though they were barely known just 20 years ago. Americans use goods and services from every geographic area. Californians

soak their waffles in maple syrup made in Vermont, and New Englanders enjoy vegetables grown in Texas's Rio Grande Valley. Many Americans buy Japanese automobiles, Persian rugs, African purses, and European works of art.

Consumers, then, play an important role in the American free enterprise economy. They have a say in what is—and what is not—produced when they express their wants in the form of purchases in the marketplace. **2**

The Role of Government

Government—whether national, state, or local—has an economic role to play that reflects the desires, goals, and aspirations of its citizens. Government has

QUICK CHECK

Checking Understanding

1. What aspects of the economy benefit when an entrepreneur succeeds?
2. How do American consumers express their wants?

Applying Economic Concepts

Entrepreneurship Starting a business sometimes involves finding a new way to put together existing products and methods. Ray Kroc founded the McDonald's food chain, but he did not invent the hamburger or the drive-in restaurant.

47

Evaluate

📁 📁 💿 Assign the Section 3 Quiz in the TCR or use the *Economics: Principles and Practices* Testmaker to create a customized quiz. Spanish Section Quizzes also are available in the Spanish Resources Binder.

Reteach

Have students write two summary paragraphs, one on the characteristics of free enterprise and the other on the role of entrepreneurs, consumers, and the government in the free enterprise system.

📁 📁 Have students complete Reteaching Activity 2. Spanish Reteaching Activities also are available in the Spanish Resources Binder.

Enrich

Have students research and report on the various ways in which the federal government plays the role of promoter of national goals.

📁 Have students complete Enrichment Activity 2.

CLOSE

Call on groups to make brief presentations on the lesson plans they developed for the Extra Credit Project on page 30. Then have students discuss the following: What makes the free enterprise system unique?

48

---

become involved in the economy because Americans want it to. Consequently, it has become a protector, provider of goods and services, consumer, regulator, and promoter of national goals. The role of government is normally justified whenever its benefits outweigh its costs.

Protector

As protector, the United States government enforces laws such as those against false and misleading advertising, impure food and drugs, environmental hazards, and unsafe automobiles. It also enforces laws against abuses of individual freedoms. Employers, for example, cannot discriminate against workers because of their age, sex, race, or religion. In short, the government protects property rights, enforces contracts, and generally tries to make sure that everyone follows the "rules of the game" to ensure an efficient and fair economy.

Provider and Consumer

All levels of government provide goods and services for citizens. The national government supplies defense services, for example. State governments provide education and public welfare. Local governments often provide parks, libraries, and bus services. In the process, government consumes factors of production just like any other form of business.

Regulator

In its role as a regulator, the national government is charged with preserving competition in the marketplace. It also oversees interstate commerce, communications, and even entire industries such as banking and nuclear power. Many state governments regulate insurance rates and automobile registrations. Even local governments regulate business activity with their control over the granting of building and zoning permits.

Promoter of National Goals

Government reflects the will of a majority of its people. Many functions of government reflect people's desire to modify the economic system to achieve the economic goals of freedom, efficiency, equity, security, full employment, price stability, and economic growth. A government program such as Social Security, as well as laws dealing with the minimum wage and child labor, reveal how Americans have modified their free enterprise economy.

Because of these modifications, the United States is said to have a **mixed economy** or a **modified private enterprise economy**—one in which people carry on their economic affairs freely but are subject to some government intervention and regulation. This system most likely will undergo further change as the goals and objectives of the American people change.

SECTION 3 REVIEW

Reviewing Terms and Facts

1. **Define** capitalism, competition, voluntary exchange, private property, profit, profit motive, consumer sovereignty, mixed economy, modified private enterprise economy.
2. **List** the four major characteristics of capitalism.
3. **Describe** the role of the profit motive in a free enterprise system.

4. **Explain** the importance of the consumer in a free enterprise economy.
5. **Identify** the four roles of the government in the American economy.

Critical Thinking

6. **Determining Cause and Effect** How have Americans' varying economic goals modified their free enterprise economy?

Applying Economic Concepts

7. **Voluntary Exchange** Cite at least three examples of voluntary exchanges you made this week. How are you better off by having made the exchanges? Did the person with whom you exchanged gain, too? How?

48 Unit 1: *Fundamental Economic Concepts*

Answers to SECTION 3 REVIEW

1. All vocabulary words are defined in the Glossary.

2. economic freedom, voluntary exchange, private property, profit motive

3. It is largely responsible for the growth of free enterprise—without the opportunity to improve their material well-being, few people would risk entering business.

4. They determine what is, and what is not, produced when they express their wants in the form of

purchases in the marketplace.

5. protector, provider and consumer, regulator, promoter of national goals

6. They have increased government intervention in the economy in the form of such programs as Social Security and laws dealing with such subjects as the minimum wage and child labor.

7. Answers will vary. As guidance, refer students to the discussion of voluntary exchange on pages 44–45.

ECONOMICS IN ACTION

Economic Systems & the American Economy

Setting Up the Video

With your classmates, view "Economic Systems & the American Economy" on the videodisc *Economics in Action*. The video describes the United States' economic system as a free enterprise economy, one in which the market makes all decisions. A news segment then considers the Cuban economy, which was once completely controlled by the government.

**Chapter 3
Disc 1, Side 1**

View the video by scanning the bar code or by entering the chapter number on your keypad and pressing Search. *(Also available in VHS format.)*

Hands-On Activity

List 10 items you or your family buy in a typical week. Place a checkmark next to the purchases you think include some level of government involvement. Then reconsider your list by asking the following questions: Was there a tax? Did the product require any kind of government inspection? Did any of the products' ingredients require government inspection? As a class, pick one item—pizza, for example—and trace the involvement of government in all stages of the product's development.

GLENCOE TECHNOLOGY

Economics in Action

Chapter 3

Disc 1, Side 1

Title: *Economic Systems & the American Economy*

 If you do not have access to a videodisc player, the **Economics in Action** programs are also available in VHS.

SURFING THE "NET"

China's Economy

Economic systems help societies provide for the wants and needs of their people. The three systems that have evolved over time are the traditional, market, and command economies. In a command economy, a central authority decides the three basic questions of economics—WHAT, HOW, and FOR WHOM to produce. The individual has little or no role in economic planning.

The People's Republic of China has a command economy. Information about China's economy can be found on the Internet.

Getting There

1. Use a search engine. Type in the word *China*.
2. After typing in *China*, enter words like the following to focus your search: *central planning, goods and services, government controls*.
3. The search engine will provide you with a number of links to follow. Links are "pointers" to different sites on the Internet and often appear as blue, underlined words.

What to Do When You Are There

Click on the links to navigate through the pages of information. Gather your findings. Using the findings, write several paragraphs describing the command economy of China—WHAT it produces, HOW it produces goods, and FOR WHOM the goods are allocated.

INTERNET SITES

The following are possible sites for completing the "Net" activities:

Made in China
http://china.utopia.com/

China's Ninth Five-Year Plan
http://www.edu.cn/undp/agenda21/5year.htm

Sustainable Agriculture and Food Security
http://www.edu.cn/undp/shd/agricult.htm

Not on the "Net"...

If students have limited or no access to the Internet, have them complete the activity "China's Economy" by using the computerized card catalog at the school or local library. At the *s:* prompt, students should type in *China*. They should then use the call numbers to find the books and other resources they need to complete their research.

49

Internet addresses that you find useful can be noted in the space below for quick reference.

_____   _____
_____   _____
_____   _____
_____   _____
_____   _____
_____   _____

GLENCOE
TECHNOLOGY

 VIDEODISC
MindJogger Videoquiz

Use MindJogger to review
the Chapter 2 content.

 Chapter 2
Disc 1, Side A

Also available in VHS.

Answers

Reviewing Key Terms

1. b		**6.** d	
2. a		**7.** i	
3. e		**8.** g	
4. f		**9.** h	
5. j		**10.** c	

Reviewing the Facts

1. major strength: everyone
knows which role to play;
weakness: discourages
new ideas

2. does not meet needs and
wants of consumers; lacks
effective incentives for people to work hard; requires
large bureaucracy that consumes resources; has little
flexibility; new ideas and
individuality discouraged

3. When consumers buy a
particular product, they cast
dollar "votes." By counting
these "votes," producers
learn what people want.

4. A traditional economy often
punishes those who attempt
to change the way things are
done. A command economy
has problems adjusting to
changes because it is so
inflexible. A market economy is flexible and can adjust to change.

5. Economic freedom—people
place high value on the
freedom to make their own
economic decisions; eco-
nomic efficiency—recogni-
tion that resources are scarce
and need to be used wisely;

50

Reviewing Key Terms

*Write the letter of the key term that best matches each
definition below.*

a. economic system		**f.** inflation	
b. consumer sovereignty		**g.** command economy	
c. voluntary exchange		**h.** fixed income	
d. private property		**i.** traditional economy	
e. profit motive		**j.** capitalism	

1. the idea that people rule the market
2. a society's organized way of providing for its
people's wants and needs
3. the driving force that encourages people to
improve their material well-being
4. a rise in the general level of prices
5. a system in which the factors of production are
owned by private citizens
6. the right and privilege to control one's own possessions
7. an economic system in which habit and custom
dictate most economic and social behavior
8. an economic system in which a central authority
makes economic decisions
9. the situation in which the money one receives
does not increase even though prices go up
10. the act of buyers and sellers freely conducting
business in a market

Reviewing the Facts

SECTION 1 *(pages 32–36)*

1. **Describe** the main strength and weakness of a
traditional economy.
2. **List** the five major weaknesses of the command
economy.
3. **Explain** how consumers influence a market
economy.
4. **Describe** how a market economy, a traditional
economy, and a command economy adapt to
change.

SECTION 2 *(pages 38–41)*

5. **Describe** the seven major economic goals upon
which most Americans seem to agree.
6. **Identify** the objective of Social Security.
7. **Explain** how any two of the seven major economic goals might conflict.
8. **Explain** the importance of setting economic
goals.

SECTION 3 *(pages 43–48)*

9. **State** how people and businesses benefit from
economic freedom.
10. **Explain** the importance of the entrepreneur in a
free enterprise economy.
11. **Provide** examples of how the government acts as
protector, provider and consumer of goods and
services, regulator, and promoter of national
goals.

Critical Thinking

1. **Checking Consistency** Some people believe the
profit motive conflicts with the goals of economic security and equity. Do you agree or disagree? Why or why not?
2. **Determining Cause and Effect** How can the
movement of people and the communication of
ideas affect the type of economic system a society has?

Applying Economic Concepts

1. **Tradition** Most people tip for service in restaurants, but not for service at clothing stores or gas
stations. Explain how this illustrates economic
behavior by tradition rather than by market or
command.
2. **Freedom and Equity** Explain the role you as a
consumer must play in obtaining economic
equity for yourself.
3. **Economic Incentives** What incentive does owning private property give people?

economic equity—feeling that the economy should
be ruled by justice, impartiality, and fairness; economic security—desire for protection from adverse
economic events; full employment—desire for the
economic system to provide as many jobs as possible; price stability—desire for stable prices; economic growth—desire for economy to produce
more and better goods and services

6. to provide economic security for disabled and retired workers

7. Conflicts will vary.

8. They serve as benchmarks that help people determine if the system is meeting their economic needs.

9. People are free to choose their employer, where and
when they work, and how they spend their money.
Businesses are free to hire the best workers, to decide what and how to produce and what prices to
charge.

Reinforcing Skills

USING A COMPUTERIZED CARD CATALOG

Use the computerized card catalog at your school or local library to find out more about an American entrepreneur and his or her role in shaping the American economy. Before you do any research, however, ask effective questions to help you narrow your topic:

1. Whom shall I research?
2. What did he or she invent or promote?
3. How did he or she become a successful entrepreneur?
4. What effect did this entrepreneur have on the American economy?

Use the answers to these questions to help you type in subject headings on the computerized card catalog. From the list of subjects that appears on the screen, determine which might provide answers to your questions. Follow the instructions on the computer screen to display all the titles under each subject you selected. Identify and print out at least four resources—books, videotapes, CDs, or audiocassettes—you can use to write your report.

Individual Activity

Interview a local entrepreneur to learn what influenced that person to become an entrepreneur. What risks and challenges did he or she face in getting started? How did the entrepreneur learn about the business? How does one go about setting up a business in the area? What functions and/or regulations are performed by the local government? Do these regulations appear to be related to the seven goals stated in the chapter? After the interview, share your findings with the rest of the class.

Cooperative Learning Activity

Working in groups of three, select three nations that typify the three types of economic systems discussed in this chapter. Describe what has or has not been accomplished in the country because of the type of economic system that exists there. Include any other information that is relevant, such as the amount and pace of change that has occurred recently in the economy. As a group, prepare a chart—similar to **Figure 2.1** on page 35—that briefly states your findings. Then have each member of your group take part in presenting the information in your chart to the rest of the class.

Technology Activity
Using a Word Processor

In the **Journal Writing** activity on page 31, you were asked to write ideas for products and services you would like to produce. Take one of your ideas and develop a brochure on the word processor to advertise your product or service.

Make a three-panel brochure, using a portrait layout, with a detachable flap to be returned to you. On the main part of your brochure, describe your product or service. Use glowing adjectives and strong reasons to convince consumers to buy your product or service. Incorporate clip art and decorative fonts to make the brochure attractive. Arrange the text in columns so that it fits neatly on the brochure.

On one side of the detachable flap, put your name and address. On the reverse side, put a short order form that includes the buyer's name, address, and phone number. Print several brochures and share them with class members.

2. Most students will suggest freedom of movement of people and ideas is the hallmark of a market economy. Lack of movement, however, is a tendency of traditional and command economies.

Applying Economic Concepts

1. Most students will note that tenets of a command economy or market economy would require that all services or no services be tipped. Tipping for restaurant service is a long-established tradition that people are expected to observe.

2. Answers will vary. Suggestions might include reporting unfair pricing or false advertising.

3. Private property gives people the incentives to work harder, to save, to invest, and to succeed.

Reinforcing Skills

Students' titles will vary. Refer students to the Technology Skill on page 37.

BONUS TEST QUESTION

Ask students to identify the type of economy in which the following decisions might be made:

1. After hearing complaints about postal service, Jack starts a delivery service. *(market)*

2. Production has remained the same for generations. *(traditional)*

3. A proposal to introduce new production methods is held up for months while paperwork is prepared. *(command)*

10. When entrepreneurs succeed, they benefit by gaining profits; workers benefit through jobs and higher wages; consumers benefit by having more and better products to buy; and government benefits through greater tax revenues.

11. Possible answers: protector—enforces laws against false advertising; provider and consumer—provides highways, uses productive resources; regulator—oversees interstate commerce; promoter of goals—minimum wage promotes equity.

Critical Thinking

1. Some students might argue that the profit motive does conflict with those goals, pointing out that business owners, in their drive for profits, might use false or misleading advertising, set prices too high, or not pay reasonable and fair wages. Others may argue that there is no conflict, because the drive for profits eventually leads to economic success for entrepreneurs and benefits for all.

CHAPTER 3 PLANNING GUIDE

CHAPTER ORGANIZER

Daily Objectives	Reproducible Resources	Multimedia Resources
Section 1 **Business Organizations** 1. **Describe** the characteristics of the sole proprietorship. 2. **Understand** the strengths and weaknesses of the partnership. 3. **Describe** the structure and features of the corporation.	Reproducible Lesson Plan 3-1 Guided Reading Activity 3-1 Cooperative Learning Activity 9 Math Practice for Economics 8 Free Enterprise Activities 9, 11 Primary and Secondary Source Reading 9 Economic Simulation 1 Economic Laboratory 1 Performance Assessment Activity 8 Reinforcing Economic Skills 3 Section Quiz 3-1*	Focus Activity Transparency 23 Economic Concepts Transparency 5 Vocabulary PuzzleMaker Chapter Challenger Interactive Review Software Testmaker MindJogger Videoquiz NBR's Economics in Action Video Program Interactive Economics!
Section 2 **Business Growth and Expansion** 1. **Describe** two ways that businesses in the United States can expand and grow. 2. **Describe** the characteristics of the conglomerate. 3. **Explain** the nature of the multinational corporation and the way it differs from the conglomerate.	Reproducible Lesson Plan 3-2 Guided Reading Activity 3-2 Section Quiz 3-2*	Focus Activity Transparency 24 Vocabulary PuzzleMaker Chapter Challenger Interactive Review Software Testmaker NBR's Economics in Action Video Program
Section 3 **Other Organizations and Institutions** 1. **Describe** the purpose of various nonprofit organizations 2. **Explain** the direct and indirect role of government in our economy.	Reproducible Lesson Plan 3-3 Guided Reading Activity 3-3 Section Quiz 3-3*	Focus Activity Transparency 25 Vocabulary PuzzleMaker Chapter Challenger Interactive Review Software Testmaker
Chapter Review and Evaluation	Enrichment Activity 3 Reteaching Activity 3* Economic Vocabulary Activity 3* Chapter 3 Test, Forms A and B	Chapter Digests Audiocassette Activities and Tests* Testmaker MindJogger Videoquiz

*Also available in Spanish

 Blackline Master   Transparency   CD-ROM   Software   Videodisc   Audiocassette

OUT OF TIME? Assign the Chapter 3 Digest Audiocassette and the corresponding Chapter Digest activities and tests.

National Council on Economic Education

THE **Economics** America AND **Economics** International PROGRAMS

VOLUNTARY NATIONAL CONTENT STANDARDS IN ECONOMICS
Emphasized in Chapter 3

Content Standard 10 *Students will understand that:*
Institutions evolve in market economies to help individuals and groups accomplish their goals. Banks, labor unions, corporations, legal systems, and not-for-profit organizations are examples of important institutions. A different kind of institution, clearly defined and well enforced property rights, is essential to a market economy.

Content Standard 16 *Students will understand that:*
There is an economic role for government to play in a market economy whenever the benefits of a government policy outweigh its costs. Governments often provide for national defense, address environmental concerns, define and protect property rights, and attempt to make markets more competitive. Most government policies also redistribute income.

Economics America *Resources Available From NCEE*

- *Capstone: The Nation's High School Economics Course*
- *Civics and Government: Focus on Economics*
- *Economics and Entrepreneurship*
- *Focus: High School Economics*
- *Learning from the Market: Integrating the Stock Market Game"™ across the Curriculum*
- *United States History: Focus on Economics*

To order these materials, or to contact your state Council on Economic Education about workshops and programs, call 1-800-338-1192 or visit http://www.nationalcouncil.org.

PERFORMANCE ASSESSMENT

The following chapter projects may be assigned at the beginning of the chapter and used for performance assessment.

Multicultural Heritage Many American companies import and export economic products and services throughout the world, and often encounter cultural traditions different from their own. When business people meet in the United States, for example, they often shake hands. In Japan, however, business people greet each other by bowing. Failure to honor such traditional courtesies may have a negative impact on a company's efforts to do business in foreign countries.

Have students write to a number of American companies that do business with foreign countries to discover any foreign cultural or business practices those companies have integrated into their operations. Call on students to report responses to the class.

Cooperative Learning Organize students into four groups, and assign each group one of the following topics: sole proprietorships, partnerships, corporations, other business organizations and institutions. Tell the groups they have been hired by the local Chamber of Commerce to design a museum exhibit on their assigned topic. The exhibit should include relevant historical information, strengths and weaknesses, and several examples of the assigned business organization. Suggest that group members share among themselves the various tasks: layout and design, artwork, writing of exhibit guidebook, and so on. Have groups display their exhibits prominently in the classroom.

ADDITIONAL RESOURCES

Readings for the Student

Drucker, Peter F. *Concept of the Corporation.* New Brunswick, NJ: Transaction Publishers, 1993. New edition of the classic study of the American corporation.

Readings for the Teacher

Drucker, Peter F. *Concept of the Corporation.* New Brunswick, NJ: Transaction Publishers, 1993. New edition of the classic study of the American corporation.

Multimedia

The Business File. Public Broadcasting Service, 1320 Braddock Place, Alexandria, VA 22314–1698. Video series, 30 minutes each. *Forming a Business: Corporations* and *Forming a Business: Proprietorships and Partnerships* provide detailed information on business organizations in the American economy.

Karen's Magic Flute. Instructional Video, P.O. Box 21, Maumee, OH 43537. Video, 30 minutes. Follows an entrepreneur as her business grows from proprietorship to partnership to corporation.

INTRODUCING
CHAPTER 3

Chapter Overview

Chapter 3 introduces economic institutions. **Section 1** describes the three types of business organizations—proprietorships, partnerships, and corporations. **Section 2** details how businesses combine to expand. **Section 3** discusses other institutions that play a role in the American economy.

GLENCOE
TECHNOLOGY

VIDEODISC
MindJogger Videoquiz

Use MindJogger to preview the Chapter 3 content.

Chapter 3
Disc 1, Side A

 Also available in VHS.

inter**NET**
CONNECTION

Resources for Chapter 3 on the World Wide Web*

National Council on Economic Education

http://www.nationalcouncil.org/

Better Business Bureau
http://www.bbb.org/

Small Business: Organization and Operations

http://www.nolo.com/ChunkSB/SB.index.html

*Sites subject to change.

VISUAL INSTRUCTION

Ask students to suggest other types of businesses that might be owned by a sole proprietor. Have them review their suggestions as they read Section 1.

This sole proprietor owns and operates a flower shop to make a profit.

Extra Credit Project

Have students compile an illustrated dictionary of business terms by using all the "Key Terms" introduced in the section previews of Chapter 3.

CHAPTER 3

Business Organizations and Economic Institutions

SECTION 1
Business Organizations

SECTION 2
Business Growth and Expansion

SECTION 3
Other Organizations and Institutions

CHAPTER PREVIEW

People to Know

- Kenneth Chenault
- Sales Clerk

Applying Economic Concepts to Your Life

Economic Institutions Do you work at a business? Belong to a church? Participate in a club? The United States has many different *economic institutions* that use, or represent, the factors of production needed to satisfy the needs and wants of consumers. Chances are these businesses and economic institutions play a significant role in your life.

Journal Writing

As you make purchases during the week, keep a record of all the businesses you visit. Classify each business according to its formal structure—sole proprietorship, partnership, corporation, or cooperative. In some cases, the firm's name may reveal the form of organization. In other cases you may have to ask the manager.

CHAPTER 3: *Business Organizations and Economic Institutions* **53**

INTRODUCING
CHAPTER 3

Connecting to Past Learning

List a number of economic goods and services on the chalkboard and ask students to identify the factors of production used to produce each item. Note student responses under the appropriate good or service and circle each group of factors of production. Then, while pointing to the circles, tell students that this chapter describes the various economic institutions that use productive resources to create goods and services.

Applying Economics

Have students ask older family members and neighbors to list the different economic institutions to which they belong. The list might include consumer or service cooperatives, schools, professional associations, churches, and labor unions. Have students share the results of their polls, and point out that an individual may be a member of several different economic institutions at the same time.

 PERFORMANCE ASSESSMENT

Refer to page **52B** for a Performance Assessment activity for this chapter. Also see the **Performance Assessment Activities** booklet for additional suggestions.

Economic Portfolio

In the **Journal Writing** activity, students are asked to classify the businesses they visit for one week. Suggest that students also note the kinds of goods and services offered at each business. Have students identify any patterns in the types of goods and services provided by particular forms of business organizations.

Key to Ability Levels — Teaching strategies have been coded for varying learning styles and abilities:
L1 - Basic (activities for all students)   **L2 - Average** (activities for average to above-average students)
L3 - Challenging (activities for above-average students)   **LEP - Limited English Proficiency**

FOCUS

Section Objectives

1. Describe the characteristics of the sole proprietorship.
2. Understand the strengths and weaknesses of the partnership.
3. Describe the structure and features of the corporation.

Bellringer

 Prior to taking roll at the beginning of the class period, display Focus Activity Transparency 23 on the overhead projector.

Motivational Activity

Discuss students' responses to the activity sheet that accompanies Transparency 23.

Preteaching Vocabulary

Ask students to skim the section to find the definitions of *proprietorship, partnership*, and *corporation*. Then call on volunteers to give specific examples of each that can be found in their community.

Use the **Vocabulary PuzzleMaker** to create crossword and word search puzzles.

⊙ VISUAL INSTRUCTION

Ask : Would you want to be "your own boss"? Why or why not?

Answer to Caption:

easy to establish or discontinue, do not have to share profits, no separate income taxes, personal satisfaction

---

Section Preview

Objectives

After studying this section, you will be able to:

1. **Describe** the characteristics of the sole proprietorship.
2. **Understand** the strengths and weaknesses of the partnership.
3. **Describe** the structure and features of the corporation.

Key Terms

economic institution, business organization, sole proprietorship, unlimited liability, inventory, fringe benefit, limited life, partnership, general partnership, limited partnership, articles of partnership, limited liability, corporation, incorporate, charter, stock, stockholder, shareholder, dividend, common stock, board of directors, preferred stock, proxy, bond, principal, interest, organizational chart, bankruptcy, unlimited life, revenue

Applying Economic Concepts

Stockholders More than likely, someone you know is a *stockholder*, or part owner, of a major corporation—perhaps IBM, General Motors, Disney, a local bank, or some other company. The United States has more than 3.5 million corporations, and it is not unusual for medium-sized corporations to issue several million shares of stock each. No wonder so many people are stockholders!

I n the United States, many important decisions are made by **economic institutions**—persons and organizations that use or represent the factors of production. One of the major economic institutions is the **business organization**—a profit-seeking enterprise that serves as the main link between scarce resources and consumer satisfactions. Most farms, corner drugstores, hospitals, clothing and shoe stores, computer manufacturers, trucking companies, and law firms fall into this category. These businesses compete with one another for the chance to satisfy consumers' wants and needs.

Sole Proprietorships

The most common form of business organization in the United States today is the **sole proprietorship**—a business owned and run by one person. Although the most numerous of all business organizations, sole proprietorships generally are smallest in size. They collectively have only a fraction of the total sales of all business. Even so, they often are relatively the most profitable. As **Figure 3.3** on page 63 shows, sole proprietorships today earn almost one-fourth of all business profits. ✔

Sole Proprietorship *This baker has established a sole proprietorship so that he can be "his own boss."* **What are other reasons for establishing sole proprietorships?**

Classroom Resources for SECTION 1

- Reproducible Lesson Plan 3-1
- Guided Reading Activity 3-1
- Cooperative Learning Activity 9
- Math Practice for Economics 8
- Free Enterprise Activities 9, 11
- Primary and Secondary Source Reading 9
- Economic Simulation 1
- Economic Laboratory 1
- Performance Assessment Activity 8
- Reinforcing Economic Skills 3

- Section Quiz 3-1
- Focus Activity Transparency 23
- Economic Concepts Transparency 5
- NBR's Economics in Action Video Program
- Interactive Economics!
- MindJogger Videoquiz
- Testmaker
- Vocabulary PuzzleMaker
- Chapter Challenger Interactive Review

Forming a Sole Proprietorship

The sole proprietorship is the easiest form of business to start. No single way exists for setting up a sole proprietorship, and it involves almost no red tape except for occasional licenses and fees required by government agencies. Most sole proprietorships open for business as soon as they set up operations.

Someone could start a sole proprietorship simply by setting up a lemonade stand in his or her front yard. Someone else might decide to mow lawns, do gardening, open a grocery store, run a gas station, or open a restaurant. A sole proprietorship can be run out of a home or from an office space in a professional building. Sole proprietorships represent many different types of businesses.

Economic Strengths

The first strength of a sole proprietorship is the ease with which it may be started. If someone has an idea or an opportunity to make a profit, he or she has only to decide to go into business and then do it.

The second strength is the relative ease in managing a sole proprietorship. Decisions may be made quickly, without having to consult a co-owner, boss, or "higher-up." This gives the owner considerable flexibility, which is very important in some kinds of economic activity. If a problem comes up, the owner can make an immediate decision. **1**

A third strength is that the owner may enjoy the profits of good management without having to share them with other owners. The possibility of suffering a loss exists, but the lure of profits makes people willing to take risks.

Fourth, the sole proprietorship does not have to pay business income taxes because the business is not recognized as a separate legal entity. The owner still

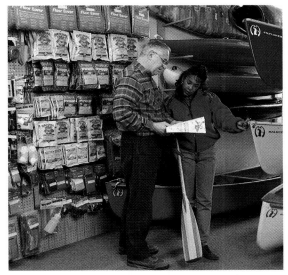

Sole Proprietorships *Most sole proprietorships are small like this outdoor recreation shop.* **How does one set up a sole proprietorship?**

must pay individual income taxes on profits taken from the sole proprietorship, but the business itself is exempt from any tax on income. Aside from one or two minor reports, the owner does not even have to fill out any complicated tax forms beyond those normally required for wage and salary purposes at the end of the year.

Suppose, for example, Mr. Winters owns and operates a small hardware store in a local shopping center, as well as a small auto repair business in a garage next to his home. Because neither business depends on the other, and because the only thing they have in common is ownership, the two businesses appear as separate and distinct economic activities. For tax purposes,

QUICK CHECK

Checking Understanding
1. Who makes the decisions in a sole proprietorship?

Applying Economic Concepts
✓ **Market Structures** Sole proprietorships account for more than 70 percent of American businesses, yet only 6 percent of total sales.

TEACH

Guided Practice

L1 *Generalizing* On the chalkboard draw a table with *Sole Proprietorship, Partnership,* and *Corporation* as vertical headings and *Features, Strengths,* and *Weaknesses* as horizontal headings. Ask students to complete the table. **LEP**

GLENCOE
TECHNOLOGY

NIGHTLY BUSINESS REPORT

Economics in Action

Chapter 12
Disc 1, Side 2
Title: *Business Organizations*
Subject: Factors to consider when starting a business
Ask: What are three important planning activities to undertake before starting a business? *(Answers may include conducting a feasibility study to see if the business will attract customers, developing a business plan, and arranging for financing.)*

 Also available in VHS.

 VISUAL INSTRUCTION

Ask students to explain why sole proprietorships tend to be small.

Answer to Caption:
There is no single way, and most sole proprietors set up simply by starting to do business.

Meeting Special Needs

Inefficient Readers Students with problems decoding unfamiliar words often skip over them. Many times, however, they are successful in comprehending the words based on the context of the sentence. Ask students to scan Section 1 for words with which they are unfamiliar. Ask them to write these words in their notebooks and to guess at the meanings based on the context. Some words that may need definition or review are: *relatively, liability, capital, minimum, entity, dividend, investment, revenue, chartered.*

 QUICK CHECK

ANSWERS

1. the owner

Partnership *Partnerships represent about 7 percent of all business organizations in the United States.* **What may partnership agreements contain?**

however, everything is lumped together at the end of the year. When Mr. Winters files his personal income taxes, the profits from each business, along with wages and salaries earned from other sources, are combined. He does not pay taxes on each of the businesses separately.

A fifth strength of sole proprietorship is psychological. Many proprietors feel a certain amount of personal freedom by being their own boss. They also feel their satisfaction is worth more than a higher salary they might earn working for someone else. Some have a strong desire to see their name in print, have dreams of great wealth or community status, or want to make their mark in history.

A sixth strength is the ease of getting out of business if the owner decides to do so. The owner simply stops offering goods or services for sale. No complicated legal or tax considerations must be met.

Economic Weaknesses

One of the main weaknesses of a sole proprietorship is that the owner has **unlimited liability**. This means that the owner is personally and fully responsible for all losses and debts of the business. If the business fails, the owner's personal possessions may be taken away to satisfy business debts.

Consider, for example, the earlier case of Mr. Winters who owns and operates two businesses. If the

hardware business should fail, Mr. Winters's personal wealth, which includes the automobile repair shop, may be legally taken away to pay off debts arising from the hardware store.

A second weakness of a sole proprietorship is the difficulty in raising financial capital. Generally, a great deal of money is needed to set up a business, and even more is required to support its expansion. A problem may arise because the personal financial resources available to most sole proprietors are limited. Banks and other lenders usually do not want to lend money to new or very small businesses. The sole proprietor often raises financial capital by tapping savings or borrowing from family members.

A third weakness concerns size and efficiency. A business usually needs to be a certain size before it can operate efficiently. A retail store, for example, may need to hire a minimum number of employees just to be open during normal business hours. It may also need to carry a minimum **inventory**—a stock of finished goods and parts in reserve—to satisfy customers or to keep production flowing smoothly. The proprietor must have the financial capital to hire enough labor and inventory to operate efficiently.

A fourth weakness is that the proprietor often has limited managerial experience. The owner-manager of a small company may be an inventor who is highly qualified as an engineer but lacks the "business sense" or time to oversee the orderly growth of the

---

$ Free Enterprise Activity $

Ask students to imagine they are entrepreneurs who have developed a product that is bound to succeed—a frisbee that, when heated, can be eaten like a pizza. Ask students to consider how they would organize to manufacture and sell their new product. Have them write an essay stating which form of business organization they would choose, defending their choice in terms of the strengths and weaknesses of the form of business organization.

company. This owner may have to hire others to do the types of work—sales, marketing, and accounting—that he or she cannot do.

A fifth weakness is the difficulty of attracting qualified employees. Because proprietorships tend to be small, employees often have to be skilled in several areas. In addition, many top high-school and college graduates are more likely to be attracted to positions with larger, well-established firms than small ones. This tendency is especially true when the larger firms offer **fringe benefits**, or employee benefits in addition to wages and salaries. Fringe benefits include paid vacations, sick leave, retirement, and health or medical insurance.

A sixth weakness of the sole proprietorship is **limited life**. This means that when the owner dies, quits, or sells the business, the firm itself legally ceases to exist. 1

Partnerships

A **partnership** is a business jointly owned by two or more persons. It shares many of the same strengths and weaknesses of a sole proprietorship. Collectively, partnerships represent about 7 percent of all business organizations in the United States, but they have only a small fraction of total business sales and profits.

Types of Partnerships

The most common form of partnership is a **general partnership**, one in which all partners are responsible for the management and financial obligations of the business. In a **limited partnership**, at least one partner is not active in the daily running of the business, although he or she may have contributed funds to finance the operation. 2

Partnership *Finding the right partner or partners is essential in a partnership.* **What is the difference between a general partnership and a limited partnership?**

Forming a Partnership

Like a proprietorship, a partnership is relatively easy to start. Because more than one owner is involved, formal legal papers called **articles of partnership** usually are drawn up to specify arrangements between partners. Although not always required, these papers state ahead of time how profits—or losses—are divided.

The partnership articles may specify that the profits be divided equally or by any other arrangement suitable to the partners. They also may state the way future partners can be taken into the business and the way the property of the business will be distributed if the partnership ends.

 QUICK CHECK

Checking Understanding
1. What happens to a sole proprietorship when the owner dies?
2. What is the most common form of partnership?

Applying Economic Concepts
☑ **Market Structures** Partnerships are not limited to retail outlets. Many law firms, doctors, and dentists form partnerships as well.

CHAPTER 3: *Business Organizations and Economic Institutions* **57**

L3 *Writing* To emphasize the importance of corporations in the American economy, provide students with recent issues of *Fortune, Forbes, Business Week, The Wall Street Journal,* or the business sections of various newspapers. Direct students to review their periodicals to locate articles about corporations. Suggest that they make notes on the various items they find. Then ask students to write a few paragraphs on their findings, using the key terms introduced in the discussion on corporations on pages 59–62. Call on volunteers to read their paragraphs to the class.

VISUAL INSTRUCTION

Ask students to discuss the qualities they would look for in a business partner. *(possible responses: business skills, trustworthiness, access to funding)*

Answer to Caption:
In a general partnership, all partners are responsible for management and financial obligations of the business. In a limited partnership, at least one partner is not active in running the business.

 QUICK CHECK ANSWERS
1. It legally ceases to exist.
2. general partnership

Extending the Content

Sole Proprietorships and Partnerships
Although sole proprietorships and partnerships account for only a small part of total business sales, they still play a very important role in the overall economy. These relatively small operations usually have close personal ties with their customers and often are the first to notice—and respond to—changes in consumer demand. In addition, small businesses are able to produce certain specialty items—fine jewelry, for example—more economically than larger companies.

Economic Strengths

Like the sole proprietorship, the first strength of the partnership is its ease of establishment. Even the costs of the partnership articles are minimal if they are spread over several partners.

Ease of management is the second strength. Generally, each partner brings different ideas and areas of expertise to the business. One partner might have a talent for marketing, another for production, another for bookkeeping and finance, and yet another for shipping and distribution. The partners usually agree ahead of time to consult with each other before making any major decisions.

Because the partnership is not a separate legal entity, a third strength is the lack of special taxes on a partnership. As in a proprietorship, the partners withdraw profits from the firm and then pay individual income taxes on them at the end of the year. The only minor difference is that each partner has to submit a special schedule to the Internal Revenue Service detailing the profits from a partnership. This schedule is for informational purposes only and does not give a partnership any special legal status.

Fourth, partnerships can usually attract financial capital more easily than proprietorships. They generally are a little bigger and, if established, have a better chance at getting a bank loan. If money cannot be borrowed, the existing partners can always take in new partners who bring financial capital with them as part of their price for joining the business. **1**

A fifth strength of a partnership is the slightly larger size, which makes efficiency easier to reach. In some areas, such as medicine and law, a relatively small firm with three or four partners may be just the right size for the market. Other partnerships, such as accounting firms, may have literally hundreds of partners offering services throughout the United States.

A sixth strength is that many partnerships find it easier to attract top talent into their organizations. Because most partnerships today offer specialized services, top graduates seek out the more prestigious firms to apply their recently acquired skills in law, accounting, and other fields.

Lesson 10 of Interactive Economics! **to learn more about "Stocks."**

Figure 3.1
Stock Ownership

To own a share of stock is to own part of the company that sells the stock. If a corporation has a total of 200 shares of stock, and if you could somehow divide the firm into 200 equal parts, the owner of a single share of stock would own $1/200^{th}$ of the corporation. A common stockholder, then, owns part of a company's plant and equipment and has a voice in how the business is managed. **How does common stock differ from preferred stock?**

Cultural Diversity and Economics

Corporations The first recorded use of the word *corporation* appeared in the works of Tertullian, one of the founders of the Christian church, in A.D. 190. Tertullian employed the term, which he derived from the Latin word *corporare*, "to make into a body," in his writings on church law. The word first appeared in English in the fifteenth century, and referred to the trade guilds of merchants. By the seventeenth century, the word had begun to be used in its modern-day sense.

Economic Weaknesses

The main weakness of a general partnership is that each partner is fully responsible for the acts of all other partners. If one partner causes the firm to suffer a huge loss, each partner is fully and personally responsible for the loss. This weakness is the same as the unlimited liability feature of a sole proprietorship. It is more complicated, however, because more owners are involved. As a result, most people are extremely careful when they choose a business partner. **2**

In the case of a limited partnership, the limited partner is not fully liable for the losses and debts of the business. This principle is known as **limited liability** and means that the investor's responsibility for the debts of the business is limited by the size of his or her investment in the firm. If the business fails, or if huge debts remain, the limited partner loses only the original investment, and the other partners must make up the rest.

A second weakness of the partnership is that it has limited life. As with sole proprietorships, when a partner dies, quits, or a new partner is added, the original firm legally ceases to exist. A business can, however, still exist in the eyes of the public even though it goes through a legal change. For example, the partnership of A, B, and C may be known as the Widget Company. If a change in ownership occurs, the new partnership may reach an agreement with the old one that allows it to use the same name.

A third weakness is the potential conflict between partners. Sometimes partners discover that they do not get along, and they either have to work together or leave the business. If the partnership is very large, it is fairly easy for these types of problems to develop, even though everyone thought they would get along well in the first place.

Corporations

Although many sole proprietorships and partnerships can be found in the United States, approximately 90 percent of all business is done by corporations. A **corporation** is a form of business organization recognized by law as a separate legal entity having all the rights of an individual. A corporation has the right to buy and sell property, enter into legal contracts, and sue and be sued.

Forming a Corporation

Unlike a sole proprietorship or partnership, a corporation is a very formal and legal arrangement. People who would like to **incorporate**, or form a corporation, must file for permission from the national government or the state where the business will have its headquarters. If approved, a **charter**—a government document that gives permission to create a corporation—is granted. The charter states the name of the company, address, purpose of business, and other features of the business.

The charter also specifies the number of shares of **stock**, or ownership parts of the firm. These shares are certificates of ownership and are sold to investors called **stockholders** or **shareholders**. The money is then used to set up the corporation. If the corporation is profitable, it may eventually issue a **dividend**—a check representing a portion of the corporate earnings or profits—to each stockholder.

Corporate Structure

After an investor purchases stock, he or she becomes an owner and has certain ownership rights. The extent of these rights, however, depends on the

---

Checking Understanding	**Applying Economic Concepts**
1. Why are partnerships able to attract more capital than sole proprietorships? 2. What is the main weakness of a general partnership?	**Market Structures** The United States has more than 3.5 million corporations. This figure represents about 19 percent of American business organizations.

CHAPTER 3
SECTION 1

📖 *Math Practice* Assign Math Practice for Economics 8.

📖 *Free Enterprise* Assign Free Enterprise Activities 9 and 11.

📖 *Readings* Assign Primary and Secondary Source Reading 9.

INTERACTIVE ECONOMICS!

💿 **CD-ROM Personal Finance**

Have students study the Lesson 10 "Tutorial," which focuses on stocks, stock markets, and mutual funds. Students will see how corporations and the stock market work. After students read the "Tutorial," have them attempt to complete the "Economics Lab" dealing with terms related to personal finance.

💾 *Supplied in both CD-ROM and diskette versions.*

QUICK CHECK ANSWERS

1. because they are bigger than sole proprietorships, often have a better chance of getting bank loans, can take in new partners who bring financial capital with them

2. Unlimited liability: partner is responsible for the acts of all other partners.

$ Free Enterprise Activity $

Organize students into small groups and randomly assign groups one of the three forms of business organizations. Then tell them that their organization must develop a marketing and advertising strategy for a new product: the Wonderful Wacky Widget. Have groups describe the details of their strategy and the procedures their organization would follow to develop the strategy. Suggest that they consider such questions as: Who makes the decisions on the strategy? From where will financing come? How complex will the strategy be? and so on. Call on groups to give an oral presentation on their procedures.

Simulation Assign
Economic Simulation 1.

 Simulation Assign
Economic Simulation 1.

 Laboratory Assign
Economic Laboratory 1.

 Performance Assessment Assign Performance
Assessment Activity 8.

L2 Illustrating Ideas Have
students use library resources
to locate an annual report of a
major American corporation.
Have them use information in
the report on the corporation's
organizational structure to
construct an organizational
chart similar to that on page 60.
Call on volunteers to display
and discuss their charts.

ASSESS

Check for Understanding

Assign Section 1 Review
as homework or an in-class
activity.

[icon] Use **Chapter Challenger
Interactive Review Software** to
review Section 1.

[icon] **VISUAL
INSTRUCTION**

Ask students: To whom
are vice presidents answerable? *(the president)* To
whom is the president answerable? *(board of directors)*

Answer to Caption:

about 90 percent

Figure 3.2
Ownership, Control, and Organization of the Typical Corporation

THE OWNERS
Shareholders elect the

BOARD OF DIRECTORS
who selects

THE PRESIDENT
who hires

VICE PRESIDENT
Sales

| Domestic | International |

VICE PRESIDENT
Production

| Quality Control | Research & Development |

VICE PRESIDENT
Finance

| Payroll |

Corporations frequently use an organizational chart to provide a picture of the way the different parts of the organization are related. The chart shows the chain of command starting with the board of directors and ending with the individual employees. The stockholders are not directly involved in the chain of command because they elect the board of directors to represent their interests. **What percent of American business is conducted by corporations?**

type of stock the investor purchases. The two types of stock available to the investor are common and preferred.

Common stock represents basic ownership of a corporation. The owner of common stock usually receives one vote for each share of stock owned. This vote is used to elect a **board of directors** whose duty is to direct the corporation's business by setting broad policies and goals. The board also hires a professional management team to run the business on a daily basis.

Preferred stock represents nonvoting ownership of the corporation. Owners of preferred stock receive dividends before common stockholders. If the corporation goes out of business, and if some property and funds remain after other debts have been paid, preferred stockholders get their investment back before common stockholders. They do not, however, have the right to elect representatives to the board of directors.

In theory, a stockholder who owns a majority of a corporation's common stock can elect board members and control the company. If the corporation is very small, the stockholder might even elect himself or herself—and other family members—to the board of directors.

In practice, this is not done very often, because most corporations are so large and the investment by the typical stockholder is so small. Most small stockholders either do not vote, or they turn their votes over to someone else. This is done with the use of a **proxy**, a ballot that gives a stockholder's representative the right to vote on corporate matters. **1**

Economic Strengths

The main strength of a corporation is the ease of raising financial capital. If the corporation needs more capital, it can sell stock to investors. The revenue can then be used to finance or expand operations.

Extending the Content

Bankruptcy If a firm files for bankruptcy under *Chapter 7*, it simply liquidates and goes out of business. If it files bankruptcy under *Chapter 11*, it is given one year to reorganize and is allowed to stay in business. Individuals with regular incomes may file bankruptcy under *Chapter 13*, which is less complicated and less expensive than filing under *Chapter 11*.

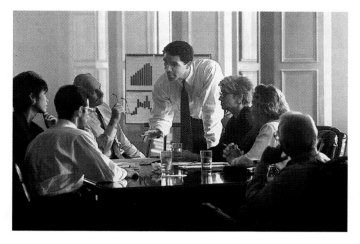

Corporations *Owners of common stock elect a board of directors that, in turn, hires managers to run the business.* **How do common stockholders differ from preferred stockholders?**

In addition to selling stock, a corporation may decide to issue bonds. A **bond** is a written promise to repay the amount borrowed at a later date. **2** The amount borrowed is known as the **principal**. While the money is being borrowed, the corporation pays **interest**, the price paid for the use of another's money.

A second strength of a corporation is that the directors of the corporation can hire the best management available to run the firm. If the corporation is big enough, it can hire specialized talent in nearly all areas. Although some owners may know little or nothing about the business, the people who are running it do. Because the structure of a corporation is usually complex, a diagram called an **organizational chart** like Figure 3.2 is used to show how the different parts of a corporation are related.

A third strength of a corporation is that it provides limited liability for its owners. The corporation, not its owners, is fully responsible for its debts and obligations. Suppose, for example, a court finds that a cor-

poration owes a huge amount of money. The corporation might first try to work out some payment terms with the court. If that fails, it might try to satisfy its debt by selling off some assets of the corporation. If, however, the corporation cannot pay off the debt, it can declare **bankruptcy**, court-granted permission to not pay some or all of its debts, which forces it out of business. Under such circumstances, the investors (stockholders) would lose only their investment in the company, the amount limited to the money invested in stock. They would lose nothing else.

Because limited liability is so attractive, many firms incorporate just to take advantage of it. Suppose Mr. Winters who owns the hardware store and the auto repair business now decides to set up each business as a corporation. If the hardware business should fail, his personal wealth, which includes the automobile repair business, is safe. Mr. Winters may lose all the money invested in the hardware business, but that would be the extent of his loss. ☑

 QUICK CHECK

Checking Understanding

1. How do most small stockholders vote on corporate business?
2. What is a corporate bond?

Applying Economic Concepts

☑ **Business Organizations** Women own about one-third of all businesses in the U.S. The highest growth rates of women-owned companies are in industries traditionally not associated with women—construction, wholesale trade, agricultural services, manufacturing, and transportation.

CHAPTER 3: *Business Organizations and Economic Institutions* **61**

Extending the Content

Regulation State charters issued during the 1800s, for the most part, greatly restricted the powers of corporations. By the end of the century, however, courts and legislatures, yielding to pressure from business interests, began to ease controls on corporate activities. Exposés of business corruption by muckraking journalists at the turn of the century stirred demands for renewed restrictions. As a result, federal and state governments passed laws regulating practically every aspect of corporate operations.

A fourth strength of a corporation is **unlimited life**, meaning that the business continues to exist even when ownership changes. The corporate organization is recognized as a legal entity, or separate unit, so long as it continues to stay in business. Even if ownership changes, the name of the company stated in its charter stays the same, and the corporation continues to do business.

A fifth strength of the corporation is the ease of transferring ownership. If a person owns stock in a corporation but no longer wants to be an owner, he or she simply sells the stock to someone else, who then becomes an owner. It is much easier for the owner of a corporation to leave the business than for sole proprietors or partners to find buyers for their portions of ownership should they decide to leave.

Economic Weaknesses

One weakness of the corporate structure is the difficulty and expense of getting a charter. Depending on the state, attorney's fees and filing expenses can run from a few hundred to several thousand dollars. Because of this expense, many people prefer to set up sole proprietorships or partnerships.

Another weakness of the corporation is that the owners, or shareholders, have little say in how the business is run after they have voted for members of the board of directors. Many investors purchase stock because they hope to receive a dividend. Others buy stock hoping that it will increase in value over time so they can sell it for a profit. In most cases, however, the ability of the shareholder to influence corporate policy is limited to voting for the board of directors.

Because the corporation is recognized as a separate legal entity, it has to pay income taxes just like private individuals. The corporation is required to keep detailed records of **revenues**—receipts from sales, dividends, interest, or other operations—and expenses so that it can pay taxes on its profit.

Finally, corporations are subject to more government regulation than either sole proprietorships or partnerships. Corporations must register with the state in which they are chartered. If a corporation wants to sell its stock to the public, it must register with the federal Securities and Exchange Commission (SEC). It may also have to provide certain financial information about sales and profits. Even an attempt to take over another business may require federal government approval.

SECTION 1 REVIEW

Reviewing Terms and Facts

1. **Define** economic institution, business organization, sole proprietorship, unlimited liability, inventory, fringe benefit, limited life, partnership, general partnership, limited partnership, articles of partnership, limited liability, corporation, incorporate, charter, stock, stockholder, shareholder, dividend, common stock, board of directors, preferred stock, proxy, bond, principal, interest, organizational chart, bankruptcy, unlimited life, revenue.

2. **Describe** the characteristics of the sole proprietorship.

3. **List** the strengths and weaknesses of the partnership.

4. **Explain** the strengths and weaknesses of the corporation.

Critical Thinking

5. **Predicting Consequences** When a corporation wants to introduce a potentially profitable but risky product, it frequently sets up a separate company that has its own corporate structure. Why do you think the corporation does this?

Applying Economic Concepts

6. **Economic Institutions** Find someone you know who owns shares of stock. Ask that person if their shares are common or preferred, and how often that person has a chance to vote for the management of that company. Research to find out the number of ownership shares issued by the corporation.

Answers to SECTION 1 REVIEW

1. All words are defined in the Glossary.

2. owned by one individual; all decisions made by owner; owner receives all profits, but personally responsible for all debts, losses; limited life

3. **strengths:** ease of establishment, ease of management, no special taxes, usually can attract financing, more efficient, can attract top talent; **weaknesses:** all partners equally responsible for business losses (except in limited partnerships), limited life, potential conflict among partners

4. **strengths:** ease of raising financial capital, can hire best managers, limited liability for owners, unlimited life, ease of transferral of ownership; **weaknesses:** sometimes difficult or expensive to get charter, shareholders have little say, has to pay income taxes, subject to more government regulation

5. limited liability—the first corporation limits its exposure by setting up a separate corporation

6. Have students present their findings in a report.

ECONOMIC SKILL

Reading a Circle Graph

Have you ever sat at a dinner table and watched someone dish out pieces of apple pie? When the pie is cut evenly, everybody gets the same size slice. If one slice is cut a little larger, however, someone else gets a smaller piece.

Explanation

A circle graph is like a sliced pie; often, it is even called a pie chart. Circle graphs show relationships among the parts of a whole and are used to show proportion rather than absolute amounts. By looking at a circle graph, you can see how the sections compare with each other in size. The size of these sections is determined by converting percentages to degrees, based on 360° in a circle.

To read a circle graph, follow these steps:
• Examine the graph to deter- mine the subject of discussion.
• Identify the "slices" of the pie to see what each is supposed to represent. Sometimes each section is labeled directly on the graph; at other times you will have to refer to a key on the graph.
• Look for numerical information included to help determine the relative size of the slices.
• Draw conclusions based on this information.

Practice

The "Numbers" circle graph in Figure 3.3 may be analyzed in the following way:

• The whole—the uncut pie— represents the total number of business organizations in the United States.
• There is one section or "slice" for each form of business organization—sole proprietorship, partnership, and corporation.
• Numerical labels are given to indicate the exact percentages of each form of organization.
• Sole proprietorships are the most numerous; partnerships the least.

Examine the other two circle graphs in Figure 3.3, then answer the questions that follow.
1. Can you tell the total number of business organizations by looking at these graphs? Explain.
2. Is any single form of business organization responsible for more than one-half of the nation's sales? Explain.
3. Is it easy to conclude the answer to question 2 without looking at the percentages? Why or why not?
4. What percent of total sales do corporations have? How do you know?
5. Which form of business organization is relatively the most profitable (or has the largest percentage of net income for their sales)?

Figure 3.3
Corporations, Partnerships, and Sole Proprietorships

- Corporations
- Partnerships
- Sole Proprietorships

Sales: 89%, 5%, 6%

Numbers: 74%, 19%, 7%

Net Income (Profit): 69%, 22%, 9%

Source: *1997 Statistical Abstract of the United States*

Additional Practice

For further practice in reading circle graphs, complete the Reinforcing Skills exercise in the Chapter 3 Review on page 74.

CHAPTER 3: *Business Organizations and Economic Institutions* **63**

Answers to SKILL

1. no, only a percentage

2. Yes; the sales circle shows that corporations are responsible for more than 50 percent of sales.

3. Yes; the portion representing corporations obviously occupies more than one-half of the circle.

4. 89 percent; because sole proprietorships and partnerships account for only 11 percent of total sales.

5. sole proprietorships; with only 6 percent of sales, they receive about 22 percent of the profits

FOCUS

Section Objectives

1. Describe two ways that businesses in the United States can expand and grow.

2. Describe the characteristics of the conglomerate.

3. Explain the nature of the multinational corporation and the way it differs from the conglomerate.

Bellringer

Prior to taking roll at the beginning of the class period, display Focus Activity Transparency 24 on the overhead projector and assign the accompanying Student Activity 24.

Motivational Activity

Discuss students' responses to the activity sheet that accompanies Focus Activity Transparency 24.

Preteaching Vocabulary

Ask students to speculate on the meanings of the key terms listed in the Section Preview. Have them check the accuracy of their speculations by finding the correct definitions in the text. **LEP**

Use the **Vocabulary PuzzleMaker** to create crossword and word search puzzles.

SECTION 2
Business Growth and Expansion

Section Preview

Objectives

After studying this section, you will be able to:

1. **Describe** two ways that businesses in the United States can expand and grow.

2. **Describe** the characteristics of the conglomerate.

3. **Explain** the nature of the multi-national corporation and the way it differs from the conglomerate.

Key Terms

merger, horizontal merger, vertical merger, conglomerate, multinational

Applying Economic Concepts

Merger Have you ever noticed that the names of businesses, banks, and other financial institutions seem to keep changing? Sometimes firms change their names because they want to improve their image. More often, the names change because of a *merger*, when two or more businesses combine to form a single enterprise.

A business can grow by investing in factories, machinery, and new technologies. A business can also expand by engaging in a **merger**—a combination of two or more businesses to form a single firm.

Business Combinations

Mergers take place for a variety of reasons. A firm may seek a merger to become more efficient, to acquire a new or better product, to eliminate a rival, or even to change its image. Mergers are classified according to the types of activities that are involved, and corporate identities are sometimes altered during the process.

Reasons for Merging

Efficiency is one of the major reasons for a merger. When two firms merge, they no longer need two presidents, two treasurers, and two personnel directors. The firm can have more retail outlets or manufacturing capabilities without significantly increasing management costs. In addition, the new firm can standardize its products, get better discounts by making volume purchases, and make more effective use of its advertising.

When one corporation merges with another, one of the two usually gives up its separate legal identity.

Sealtest, for example, merged with Southern Dairies when it bought Southern's common stock from investors. Southern then lost its corporate identity when its name was changed to Sealtest.

Sometimes the firm that is bought keeps its name for public relations purposes. When Kraft Foods later merged with Sealtest by buying Sealtest stock, the two became one legal entity. Because Sealtest was a brand name many people trusted, however, Kraft continued to use the Sealtest label on many of its dairy products.

At other times, the name of the new company may reflect the identities of both companies that merged. When Chase National Bank and Bank of Manhattan merged, the new organization was called the Chase Manhattan Bank of New York—a name later changed to Chase Manhattan Corporation to reflect its geographically expanding business.

In some cases, firms merge to catch up with, or even eliminate, their rivals. Royal Caribbean Cruises acquired Celebrity Cruise Lines in 1997 and nearly doubled in size, becoming the second largest cruise line behind Carnival. When the office supply store Staples tried to acquire Office Depot in the same year, however, the government blocked the merger on the grounds that it would reduce competition in the industry.

Finally, a company may use a merger to *lose* its corporate identity. In 1997 ValuJet merged with AirWays to form AirTran Holdings Corporation. The new com-

---

Classroom Resources for SECTION 2

Reproducible Lesson Plan 3-2
Guided Reading Activity 3-2
Section Quiz 3-2
Spanish Section Quiz 3-2

Focus Activity Transparency 24
NBR's Economics in Action Video Program
Testmaker
Vocabulary PuzzleMaker
Chapter Challenger Interactive Review Software

Figure 3.4
Business Combinations

HORIZONTAL MERGER

NICKEL SAVINGS BANK + PEOPLE'S BUILDING & LOAN ASSOCIATION = NICKEL SAVINGS & LOAN ASSOCIATION

BOSTON ENTERPRISES = FAST DELIVERY, INC.

VERTICAL MERGER

HICKORY TREE FARMS + BOSTON ENTERPRISES

Horizontal mergers *involve businesses that make the same product or provide the same service. Sometimes, the name of the new company reflects the identity of the firms that merged.*
Vertical mergers *take place when firms taking part in different steps of manufacturing or marketing come together. Sometimes, one of the companies may lose its identity as a result of the merger.* **Why do companies merge?**

pany flew the same planes and routes as the original company, but AirTran hoped the name change would help the public forget ValuJet's tragic 1996 Everglades crash that claimed 110 lives.

Horizontal Merger

Economists generally recognize two types of mergers. The first is a **horizontal merger**, which takes place when two or more firms that produce the same kind of product join forces. The merger of the two banks, Chase National and the Bank of Manhattan, is one example.

Vertical Merger

The second is a **vertical merger**, which takes place when firms involved in different steps of manufacturing or marketing come together. An example is the U.S. Steel Corporation, now a subsidiary of USX. At one time, through separate companies, USX mined its own ore, shipped it across the Great Lakes, smelted it, and made steel into many different products. Vertical mergers take place when companies believe that it is

important to protect themselves against the loss of suppliers.

Conglomerates

A corporation may become so large through mergers and acquisitions that it becomes a conglomerate. A **conglomerate** is a firm that has at least four businesses, each making unrelated products, none of which is responsible for a majority of its sales.

Diversification is one of the main reasons for conglomerate mergers. Firms believe that if they do not "put all their eggs in one basket," their overall sales and profits will be protected. Isolated economic happenings, such as bad weather or the sudden change of consumer tastes, may affect some product lines at some point, but not all at one time.

During the 1970s and early 1980s, conglomerate mergers were popular in the United States. The cigarette and tobacco firm of R. J. Reynolds became a conglomerate, at one time owning the largest containerized shipping firm in the country (Sea-Land),

CHAPTER 3: *Business Organizations and Economic Institutions* **65**

TEACH

Guided Practice

L1   Vocabulary Write the terms *merger, conglomerate,* and *multinational* on the chalkboard. Then have students write descriptions of the terms. **LEP**

GLENCOE TECHNOLOGY

NIGHTLY BUSINESS REPORT

Economics in Action

Chapter 12
Disc 1, Side 2

Title: *Business Organizations*

Subject: Factors to consider when starting a business

Ask: What are the three basic types of business organizations? *(sole proprietorship, partnership, corporation)*

 Also available in VHS.

VISUAL INSTRUCTION

Ask students why Boston Enterprises merged with Fast Delivery, Inc. *(to protect themselves against the loss of transportation services)*

Answer to Caption:

to grow or to become more efficient

L2 **Debate** Lead the class in a debate of the following: Business mergers are good for the American free enterprise system.

Independent Practice

📁 **Guided Reading** Assign Guided Reading Activity for Section 2. **LEP**

L2 **Journalism** Have students choose two corporations in the community and imagine they have merged. Ask students to write a fictitious newspaper article about the merger and its results.

L3 **Writing** Have students use library resources to write a research paper on an American multinational corporation.

ASSESS

Check for Understanding

Assign Section 2 Review as homework or an in-class activity.

💿 Use the **Chapter Challenger Interactive Review Software** to review Section 2.

VISUAL INSTRUCTION

For homework, ask students to create a similar diagram for a conglomerate of their choice.

Answer to Caption:

A conglomerate's businesses make unrelated products; a multinational has operations in different countries.

Figure 3.5
Conglomerate Structure

A conglomerate is a firm that has at least four businesses, each of which makes unrelated products and none of which is responsible for a majority of its sales. Fortune Brands is a high-profile American conglomerate with a wide range of products. **How does a conglomerate differ from a multinational?**

Office Products
ACCO office supplies
Swingline staplers
Day-Timers personal organizers

Distilled Spirits

Hardware and Home Improvement
Moen faucets
Master Lock
Waterloo toolboxes

Sporting Equipment
Titleist golf balls
Foot-Joy golf shoes
Bulls Eye Putters

DID YOU KNOW?

What's In a Name? On June 1, 1908, a horizontal merger took place that created one of the most interesting names in banking. The Third National Bank and the Fifth National Bank merged to become the Fifth Third National Bank of Cincinnati. In 1975, it became the Fifth Third Bancorp. Because of its unique history and the high visibility of the "Fifth Third" title, this part of the name was never in jeopardy. Today, the Fifth Third Bancorp is one of the largest banks in the Midwest, and one of the most profitable in the country.

the nation's second largest fast-food chain (Kentucky Fried Chicken), the nation's largest fruit and vegetable processor (Del Monte), and the second largest producer of wine and distilled spirits (Heublein).

Since the late 1980s, interest in forming new conglomerates in the United States has declined. In Asia, however, conglomerates such as Samsung, Gold Star, and Daewoo are still dominant in Korea, as are Panasonic, Sony, and Mitsubishi in Japan.

Multinationals

Other large corporations have become multinational in scope. A **multinational** is a corporation that has manufacturing or service operations in a number of different countries. It is, in effect, a citizen of several countries at one time. As such, a multinational is

💲 Free Enterprise Activity 💲

To emphasize the role of large business corporations in the American free enterprise system, select a number of large corporations that produce and sell a variety of consumer goods and services. You might designate Proctor and Gamble, Philip Morris, PepsiCo, Gannett, and H. J. Heinz, for

example. Organize the class into a similar number of groups and assign each group one of the large corporations. Have groups research the goods and services their corporation produces and sells. Then have groups illustrate those products in a bulletin-board display.

subject to the laws of, and is likely to pay taxes in, each country where it has operations.

Multinationals are important because they have the ability to move resources, goods, services, and financial capital across national borders. A multinational with its headquarters in Canada, for example, is likely to sell bonds in France. The proceeds may then be used to expand a plant in Mexico that makes products for sale in the United States.

Multinationals may also be conglomerates if they make a number of unrelated products, but they are more likely to be called a multinational if they conduct their operations in several different countries.

Economic Strengths

Multinationals are usually welcomed for three reasons. First, multinationals help spread new technology worldwide. Second, they generate new jobs in areas where jobs are needed. Third, multinationals produce tax revenues for the host country. Many developing nations find the new technology, jobs, and revenue that multinationals provide helpful in improving their nations' economies.

Economic Weaknesses

Multinationals have several drawbacks. Because they are large and wealthy, they may influence the political life of a host nation. Multinationals also may

exploit the economy of the host nation by paying low wages to workers, by exporting scarce natural resources, or by adversely interfering with the development of local businesses. In addition, workers in major industrialized nations sometimes argue that when multinationals build a plant abroad, they take away jobs at home.

HELP WANTED

Sales Clerk
▼

Local proprietor needs well-groomed, patient, and friendly sales clerk to stock shelves, take inventory, and deal directly with customers. You must be able to demonstrate the product, record the sales transaction and, if necessary, arrange for the product's safe delivery. Ability to work under pressure is helpful. Other required skills include a strong working knowledge of business math for calculating prices and taxes, and the ability to speak clearly and tactfully. Both part-time and full-time hours available.

▼

Education: High-school diploma
Salary: $5.15/hour plus commission

SECTION 2 REVIEW

Reviewing Terms and Facts

1. **Define** merger, horizontal merger, vertical merger, conglomerate, multinational.
2. **Describe** the two ways a business can merge.
3. **Explain** why corporations may become conglomerates.
4. **List** the strengths and weaknesses of multinationals.

Critical Thinking

5. **Evaluating Information** In a newspaper or magazine, find an article about a merger. What companies merged? What reasons, if any, were given for the merger? Was the merger horizontal or vertical? How can you tell?

Applying Economic Concepts

6. **Merger** Locate and report on an example of a merger in your community. Start by looking for a business that recently changed its name. Inquire to find out if it was a vertical or a horizontal merger. Ask about the previous names of the firms involved in the merger, and find out why they selected the current name for the merged enterprise.

MEETING LESSON OBJECTIVES

Each objective below is tested by the questions that follow it in parentheses.

1. **Describe** two ways that businesses in the United States can expand and grow. **(1, 2, 5, 6)**
2. **Describe** the characteristics of the conglomerate. **(1, 3)**
3. **Explain** the nature of the multinational corporation and the way it differs from the conglomerate. **(1, 4)**

Evaluate

📁 📁 💻 Assign the Section 2 Quiz in the TCR or use the *Economics: Principles and Practices* Testmaker to create a customized quiz. Spanish Section Quizzes also are available in the Spanish Resources Binder.

Reteach

Provide students with examples of different kinds of mergers. Ask students to categorize the mergers as horizontal or vertical.

Enrich

Direct students to construct a time line showing how a major American corporation has grown over the years.

CLOSE

Ask students to discuss the following statement in relation to the role that multinationals play in the global economy: "The world is shrinking."

Answers to SECTION 2 REVIEW

1. All vocabulary words are defined in the Glossary.

2. horizontal mergers, when two or more firms that produce the same product join forces, and vertical mergers, when firms in different steps of manufacturing or marketing come together

3. They wish to diversify to protect their sales and profits from isolated economic happenings.

4. **Strengths:** help spread new technology worldwide, generate new jobs in areas where they are

needed, produce tax revenues for host countries; **weaknesses:** may influence political life in host country, may exploit economy of host country, may shift jobs from industrialized countries to host countries

5. Answers will vary. Have students present their findings in a written report.

6. Answers will vary. Have students compare and discuss their findings.

67

Background

American Express Company had revenues of $15.8 billion in 1996. Chenault's steady climb up the corporate ladder was watched by other African Americans who were eager to see the glass ceiling broken. "There have been a number of people before and after me who clearly possess the capabilities to run a large firm," stated Chenault. "That's why it's so important to look at me not as an exception but rather as someone who was given the opportunity to succeed."

TEACH

Ask students to research the highest ranking African Americans in the corporate arena of the United States. Students may want to research past issues of *Black Enterprise* magazine, *Forbes*, and *Business Week*.

School TO WORK

Banking Have students visit a local bank to interview someone in its human resources department. They should learn what qualities and training banks look for in tellers. Have students conclude their interviews by asking how current technological changes are affecting the jobs of tellers.

KENNETH I. CHENAULT
(1952–)

What does it take to become president of one of America's largest and most prestigious corporations? If you've ever asked yourself this question, you might want to meet Kenneth Chenault to find the answer. At age 45, Chenault became president and chief operating officer (COO) of American Express®, the sixty-fifth largest U.S. company in terms of annual sales.

Chenault is the first African American to serve as president of a top-100 company. Some people have compared him to Jackie Robinson, the baseball great who broke the color barrier

American Express®, a global travel and financial services firm, was founded in 1850.

in 1947. Coincidentally, Chenault became COO in 1997, the same year professional baseball honored Robinson's fiftieth anniversary.

STEPPING STONES
Remarkably, Kenneth Chenault did not start his career in business. Instead, he obtained an undergraduate degree in history, and then earned a law degree at Harvard. He had keen instincts for business, however, and worked for a management consulting firm before joining American Express in 1981.

AMERICAN EXPRESS At first Chenault was responsible for strategic planning. Later, his ability to achieve results propelled him up through the corporate ranks, providing new challenges and opportunities. Finally, as president and COO, Chenault was responsible for integrating strategies across all of American Express Company's business units. He has been in the forefront of the company's efforts to increase market share by expanding product offerings, globalizing the business, and helping to open American Express's card network to bank partners around the world. Chenault is also responsible for global advertising and brand management.

How does Chenault view his responsibilities as the highest-ranking African American in corporate America?

"With American Express being a large, publicly held company, I would be scrutinized under any circumstances. If you don't enhance shareholder value, it doesn't matter who you are, you will have a problem. . . . [I]f I do well, I would be very hopeful that it would encourage other companies to give people the opportunity to succeed."

This is exactly the type of realistic and insightful analysis that shareholders at American Express want to hear.

Examining the Profile

1. **Analyzing Information** How has Chenault increased American Express's market share?

2. **For Further Research** Research and write about Chenault's philanthropic achievements in New York City.

Answers to Examining the Profile

1. by expanding product offerings, globalizing the business, and helping to open the company's card network to bank partners around the world

2. Answers will vary. Chenault is a recipient of the Friend of the Children Award from Rheedlan Centers for Children and Families, an American Black Achievement Award, the ROBIE Award for Achievement in Industry from the Jackie Robinson Foundation, the Ceiling Breaker Award from Wharton University, and a Corporate Patron of the Arts from the Studio Museum of Harlem.

Other Organizations and Institutions

Section Preview

Objectives

After studying this section, you will be able to:
1. **Describe** the purpose of various nonprofit organizations.
2. **Explain** the direct and indirect role of government in our economy.

Key Terms

nonprofit organization, cooperative, co-op, consumer cooperative, service cooperative, credit union, producer cooperative, labor union, collective bargaining, professional association, chamber of commerce, Better Business Bureau, public utility

Applying Economic Concepts

Nonprofit Organizations At one time or another, you have probably joined a church, club, or civic organization. Why did you join? To earn money? Probably not. Likewise, many of these organizations do not seek to earn profits, although they do share other characteristics of a business. They are *nonprofit organizations,* and they exist for reasons other than making money for their members.

Section Objectives

1. Describe the purpose of various nonprofit organizations.
2. Explain the direct and indirect role of government in our economy.

Bellringer

Prior to taking roll at the beginning of the class period, display Focus Activity Transparency 25 on the overhead projector.

Motivational Activity

Discuss students' responses to the activity sheet that accompanies Focus Activity Transparency 25.

Preteaching Vocabulary

Refer students to the list of key terms in the Section Preview and have them use the words in sentences. **LEP**

Use the **Vocabulary PuzzleMaker** to create crossword and word search puzzles.

TEACH

Guided Practice

L1 *Designing a Poster*
Organize students into six groups and assign each group one of the following: consumer cooperative, service cooperative, producer cooperative, labor union, professional association, business association. Direct groups to design a poster advertising the kinds of services their assigned organization offers. **LEP**

Business organizations operate in hopes of earning a profit for their owners. Other economic organizations, including schools, churches, hospitals, and cooperative associations, operate on a "not-for-profit" basis. Still others, like labor unions and professional organizations, represent their members in matters of pay, working conditions, and the public perception of their members. Government is an economic institution as well.

Nonprofit Organizations

Many economic institutions, such as schools, medical care facilities, and churches, operate as **nonprofit organizations**. Similar to their profit-seeking counterparts, they work in a businesslike way to make the best use of scarce resources. The main difference is that nonprofit organizations do not seek financial gain for their members. They often provide goods and services to consumers while they pursue other rewards such as improving educational standards, seeing the sick become well, and helping those in need.

Many nonprofit organizations are legally incorporated to take advantage of the unlimited life feature. They are similar to profit-seeking businesses, but do not issue stock, pay dividends, or pay income taxes. Other examples include private welfare groups,

adoption agencies, and youth or civic clubs. Their activities often produce revenues and expenses, but they keep the surplus to further the work of the institution.

Nonprofit organizations make use of the factors of production and serve many needs. Their efforts are difficult to analyze economically, however, because the value of their products is not easy to measure. Even so, the large number of these organizations shows that they are an important part of the productive process.

Cooperative Associations

Another example of a nonprofit economic organization is the **cooperative**, or **co-op**. A cooperative is a voluntary association of people formed to carry on some kind of economic activity that will benefit its members. Cooperatives fall into three major classes—consumer, service, and producer.

Consumer Cooperative

A **consumer cooperative** is a voluntary association that buys bulk amounts of goods, such as food and clothing, on behalf of its members. Its aim is to offer its members products at prices lower than those charged by regular businesses.

CHAPTER 3: *Business Organizations and Economic Institutions* **69**

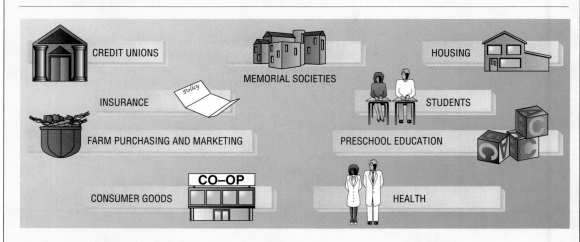

Figure 3.6
Cooperatives in the United States

CREDIT UNIONS
MEMORIAL SOCIETIES
HOUSING
INSURANCE
Policy
STUDENTS
FARM PURCHASING AND MARKETING
PRESCHOOL EDUCATION
CO–OP
CONSUMER GOODS
HEALTH

Source: National Cooperative Business Association.

The cooperative, *or* co-op, *is a voluntary association of people formed to carry on some kind of economic activity that will benefit its members.* **How do the three kinds of cooperatives differ?**

Service Cooperative

A **service cooperative** deals with services rather than goods. Service co-ops offer members insurance, credit, and other similar services. One example of a service co-op is a **credit union** made up of employees from a particular company or government agency.

Credit unions receive their funds from members. In return, members earn interest on their deposits and may borrow money from the credit union. In most cases, they can borrow at better rates and more quickly than they could from for-profit banks or commercial loan companies. **1**

Producer Cooperative

A **producer cooperative** helps members sell their products. In the United States, most cooperatives of this kind are made up of farmers. The co-op helps the farmers sell their crops directly to central markets or to companies that use the members' products. Some co-ops, such as the Ocean Spray cranberry co-op,

market their products directly to consumers. Any savings that the producer co-op makes in marketing costs go to its members.

Labor Unions

Another important economic institution is the **labor union**. A labor union, such as the United Auto Workers, is an organization formed to work for its members' interests in various employment matters. The union speaks for workers when disputes arise over pay, working hours, and other job-related matters. Labor union representatives also negotiate with management for benefits such as health care coverage, life insurance, and vacations. **Collective bargaining** refers to the negotiations between representatives of labor and management.

In the early days of organized labor in the United States, most unions were local. Later, some unions joined with others to become more powerful. In time, the labor movement reached most parts of the country, spread into Canada, and joined the international labor movement. Today most local unions are affiliated with a national or an international organization. Part of the local union dues that union members and workers pay goes to support the activities of the parent organization.

Professional and Business Organizations

Many workers belong to professional societies, trade associations, or academies. While these groups are similar to unions, they do not work in quite the same way.

Professional Associations

One such organization is a **professional association**—a group of people in a specialized occupation that works to improve the working conditions, skill levels, and public perceptions of the profession. Some professional associations require members of the profession to join; others have voluntary membership.

Many college professors belong to the American Association of University Professors. Lawyers belong to the American Bar Association, and some business leaders belong to the Financial Executives Institute or the American Management Association. Many social studies teachers belong to the National Education Association or the National Council for the Social Studies.

Business Associations

Often, businesses organize to promote their collective interest. Most cities and towns have a **chamber of commerce** that promotes the welfare of its members and the community. The typical chamber sponsors activities ranging from educational programs to neighborhood clean-up campaigns to lobbying for favorable business legislation.

Some business associations help protect the consumer. The **Better Business Bureau**, a nonprofit organization sponsored by local businesses to provide general information on companies, is one of these. It maintains records on consumer inquiries and complaints and sometimes offers various consumer education programs. **2**

Government

All levels of government play a dual role as links between consumers and resources. Sometimes government has a direct role, while at other times the role is more indirect.

Direct Role of Government

Many government agencies produce and distribute certain goods and services to consumers, giving government a direct role in linking consumers and resources. The federal government, for example, owns and operates the Tennessee Valley Authority (TVA). The TVA is a government corporation that uses the factors of production to produce electric power for a 7-state area in the South. ☑

The federal government also uses many scarce resources to create a service that benefits all Americans—national defense. State and local governments use the factors of production to provide police and fire protection, rescue services, schools, and court systems. At the same time, all levels of government help develop and maintain roads, libraries, and parks. In

---

Checking Understanding

1. Why do many people prefer to deal with credit unions rather than banks?
2. What is the Better Business Bureau?

Applying Economic Concepts

☑ **Role of Government** The TVA was one of President Franklin Roosevelt's New Deal programs designed to combat the Great Depression. It built dams to generate power and bring electricity to the rural South.

$ Free Enterprise Activity $

Point out that the first successful cooperative in the United States—the Philadelphia Contributionship for the Insurance of Houses from Loss of Fire—was organized by Benjamin Franklin in 1752. It is still operating today, making it the oldest continuously operating cooperative in the country.

Have students research the development of cooperatives in the United States, from their beginnings in the mid-1700s to the present day. Suggest that students present their findings in a written report that discusses how the focus of cooperatives has expanded over the years.

L1 *Using Photographs* Have students search newspapers for photographs that illustrate the dual role of government. Ask volunteers to discuss their selections with the class. **LEP**

ASSESS

Check for Understanding

Assign Section 3 Review as homework or an in-class activity.

💿 Use **Chapter Challenger Interactive Review Software** to review Section 3.

MEETING LESSON OBJECTIVES

Each objective below is tested by the questions that follow it in parentheses.

1. **Describe** the purpose of various nonprofit organizations. **(1, 2, 5)**
2. **Explain** the direct and indirect role of government in our economy. **(3, 4)**

Evaluate

🗁 🗁 💿 Assign the Section 3 Quiz in the TCR or use the *Economics: Principles and Practices* Testmaker to create a customized quiz. Spanish Section Quizzes also are available in the Spanish Resources Binder.

QUICK CHECK

ANSWERS

1. because they can borrow at better rates and more quickly
2. a nonprofit organization sponsored by local business to provide information on companies

Reteach

For each of the five major headings, have students write a newspaper headline that states the main idea of the content under the heading.

  Have students complete Reteaching Activity 3. Spanish Reteaching Activities also are available in the Spanish Resources Binder.

Enrich

Ask students to write an editorial discussing the importance of nonprofit organizations to the American economy.

Have students complete Enrichment Activity 3.

CLOSE

Ask students to discuss which of the institutions examined in Section 3 has the most impact on their lives and why.

VISUAL INSTRUCTION

Ask: What government role does the photograph illustrate—direct or indirect? *(direct)*

Answer to Caption:

regulator of economy, provider of financial benefits that give people purchasing power they otherwise would not have

---

these ways, government plays a direct part in the productive process.

Indirect Role of Government

The government plays an indirect role when it acts as an umpire to make sure the market economy operates as the rules say it should. One such case is the regulation of **public utilities**—investor- or municipal-owned companies that offer an important service to the public, such as water or electric service. Because most public utilities have no competitors, some government controls usually are needed. Government established regulatory control of the cable television industry in 1993 because it felt that some operators were charging too much. Without competition, utilities and other companies having exclusive rights in certain areas may not offer reasonable services at reasonable rates.

The government also plays an indirect role when it grants money to people in the form of Social Security, veterans benefits, financial aid to college students, and unemployment compensation. These payments give people a power they otherwise might not have—the power to "vote" in the market. When people cast votes in the form of dollars, they make their demands felt in the market. This power influences the production of goods and services that, in turn, affects the allocation of scarce resources.

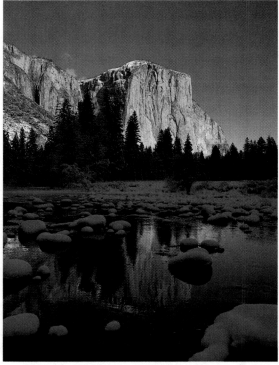

The Role of Government *The federal government helps maintain the beauty of Yosemite National Park.* **What indirect roles does the government play?**

SECTION 3 REVIEW

Reviewing Terms and Facts

1. **Define** nonprofit organization, cooperative, co-op, consumer cooperative, service cooperative, credit union, producer cooperative, labor union, collective bargaining, professional association, chamber of commerce, Better Business Bureau, public utility.
2. **Identify** several nonprofit organizations in your community.
3. **Explain** the dual role of government as an economic institution.

Critical Thinking

4. **Evaluating Information** Make a list of 10 activities performed by your local government: for example, goods and services provided, regulations issued, laws enforced, and so on. Classify each as to its direct or indirect influences on the local economy.

Applying Economic Concepts

5. **Nonprofit Organizations** Name a nonprofit organization that you or one of your friends have joined. State the purpose of the organization, and then compare its activities to profit-making organizations. If your organization collects more than it spends, what does it do with the extra money?

---

72 UNIT 1: *Fundamental Economic Concepts*

Answers to SECTION 3 REVIEW

1. All vocabulary words are defined in the Glossary.

2. Answers will vary. Encourage students to provide at least one example of each organization discussed in the section.

3. Government plays a direct role when it acts as a producer and consumer of goods and services; it plays an indirect role when it acts as regulator of the economy and provides payments to people to maintain their purchasing power.

4. Lists will vary. Encourage students to compare and discuss their lists.

5. Answers will vary.

ECONOMICS IN ACTION

Business Organizations

Setting Up the Video

With your classmates, view "Business Organizations" on the videodisc *Economics in Action*. The video focuses on factors to consider when starting a business. Guidelines that entrepreneurs can use to plan for success are given. The video also explains how to read a daily stock listing for information about the business performance of a corporation.

Hands-On Activity

Create a database with examples of local, state, or national businesses for each type of business organization. Create fields such as Proprietorship, Partnership, and Corporation. Print your results and share your findings with the rest of the class.

Chapter 12
Disc 1, Side 2

View the video by scanning the bar code or by entering the chapter number on your keypad and pressing Search. *(Also available in VHS format.)*

SURFING THE "NET"

Forming a Business

In this chapter you learned that business organizations can be set up in one of three ways—as a sole proprietorship, as a partnership, or as a corporation. Sole proprietorships are small, easy-to-manage enterprises one person owns. Partnerships are owned by two or more persons and are, for the most part, slightly larger in size than sole proprietorships. Stockholders own corporations, which are run by a professional management team selected by a board of directors. You can learn more about business organizations on the Internet.

Getting There

1. Use a search engine. Type in the words *business organization*.

2. After typing in *business organization*, enter words like the following to focus your search: *proprietorship, partnership, corporation*.

3. The search engine will provide you with a number of links to follow. Links are "pointers" to different sites on the Internet and often appear as blue, underlined words.

What to Do When You Are There

Using the findings, plan your own business. Will you be a sole proprietor or a partner or will you incorporate and sell stock? What steps will you first take to start your business? Outline your product and your business decisions on poster board to display in the classroom.

73

MULTIMEDIA ACTIVITIES

GLENCOE
TECHNOLOGY

NIGHTLY BUSINESS REPORT

Economics in Action

Chapter 12

Disc 1, Side 2

Title: *Business Organizations*

If you do not have access to a videodisc player, the **Economics in Action** programs are also available in VHS.

INTERNET SITES

The following are possible sites for completing the "Net" activities:

Business Plan Checklist
http://www.ceimaine.org/business/plan/home.htm

Pick a Memorable Name for Your Business
http://www.nolo.com/ChunkSB/SB6.HTML

Not on the "Net"...

If students have limited or no access to the Internet, have them complete the activity "Forming a Business" by using the computerized card catalog at the school or local library. At the *s:* prompt, students should type in *business organization*. They should then use the call numbers to find the books and other resources they need to help complete their activity.

INTERNET ADDRESS BOOK

Internet addresses that you find useful can be noted in the space below for quick reference.

_____   _____
_____   _____
_____   _____
_____   _____
_____   _____
_____   _____

Answers

Reviewing Key Terms

1. corporations
2. corporations
3. may be all 4
4. corporations; nonprofit organizations
5. nonprofit organizations
6. corporations
7. corporations; nonprofit organizations
8. corporations; nonprofit organizations
9. nonprofit organizations
10. nonprofit organizations
11. partnerships
12. partnerships
13. corporations; nonprofit organizations
14. nonprofit organizations
15. corporations

Reviewing the Facts

1. **strengths:** ease of establishment, ease of management, owner keeps all profits, no separate taxes, psychological benefits, ease of getting out of business; **weaknesses:** unlimited liability, difficulty in raising financial capital, may be too small to be really efficient, owner may have limited business experience, may have difficulty attracting quality employees, limited life

2. **strengths:** ease of establishment, ease of management, no separate taxes, usually can attract financing, more

Reviewing Key Terms

Classify each of the numbered terms below into the following categories (some terms may apply to more than one category):

> Sole Proprietorships
> Partnerships
> Corporations
> Nonprofit Organizations

1. bond
2. stock
3. organizational chart
4. incorporate
5. cooperative
6. dividend
7. unlimited life
8. charter
9. labor union
10. professional association
11. limited partner
12. general partnership
13. board of directors
14. credit union
15. proxy

Reviewing the Facts

SECTION 1 *(pages 54–62)*
1. **Explain** the strengths and weaknesses of a sole proprietorship.
2. **Identify** the strengths and weaknesses of a partnership.
3. **Explain** the structure and strengths of a corporation.

SECTION 2 *(pages 64–67)*
4. **Describe** the difference between a horizontal and a vertical merger.
5. **Explain** why a corporation would choose to become a conglomerate.
6. **Identify** the characteristics of a multinational corporation.

SECTION 3 *(pages 69–72)*
7. **Describe** the difference between a nonprofit institution and other forms of business organizations.
8. **List** three examples of cooperative associations.
9. **Describe** the purpose of a labor union.
10. **Identify** three types of business or professional organizations.
11. **Compare** the direct and the indirect roles of government.

Critical Thinking

1. **Making Comparisons** If you were planning to open your own business, which form of business organization would you prefer—sole proprietorship, partnership, or corporation? Give reasons for your answer.
2. **Evaluating Information** Do you think mergers are beneficial for the United States economy? Defend your response.

Applying Economic Concepts

1. **Economic Institutions** Cite a case in your community where a cooperative would fulfill a definite economic need. Explain why you think so, and then tell what kind of cooperative you would set up.
2. **The Role of Government** Which do you think is more appropriate—the direct or indirect role of government? Defend your position.

Reinforcing Skills

READING A CIRCLE GRAPH
Study the circle graph on page 75, then answer the following questions.
1. What does the whole of the circle graph represent?
2. How many industrial groups are represented in the graph?
3. Which industry has relatively more partnerships?

---

efficient, can attract top talent; **weaknesses:** all partners equally responsible for business losses (except limited partnerships), limited life, potential conflict among partners

3. Structure: a board of directors, elected by owners of common stock, sets broad policies and goals. The board hires a professional management team to run the business on a daily basis. The corporation's strengths include ease of raising financial capital, ability to hire best managers, limited liability for own-

ers, unlimited life, and ease of transferral of ownership.

4. horizontal merger: two or more firms that produce the same product join forces; vertical merger: firms in different steps of manufacturing or marketing come together

5. Its overall sales and profits will be protected from isolated economic happenings.

6. A multinational is a corporation that has manufacturing or service operations in a number of different countries.

4. Can you tell exactly how many partnerships are in the Finance and Insurance industry? Explain.

5. Which industries have the fewest number of partnerships?

Individual Activity

List the strengths and weaknesses of each type of business organization discussed in Chapter 3. Then share the list with the owner of a business in your community. Ask the owner how his or her business is organized. Ask which items on the list were the most influential in deciding how to organize the business and if any additional items should be added to the list. Write a summary report stating whether you think that the form of business organization chosen was the best for the business.

Cooperative Learning Activity

Organize into small groups of three or four for the purpose of designing a new business. First, decide on a hypothetical product your firm would like to produce. Then consider how each of the following lettered items will affect the formal structure (proprietorship, partnership, or corporation) of the business.

(a) the risk of the product

(b) the amount of financial capital needed to open the business

(c) your willingness to share the profits with other owners

(d) the cost and amount of paperwork involved with the start-up of the business

(e) the amount of personal liability you are willing to assume for the actions of others

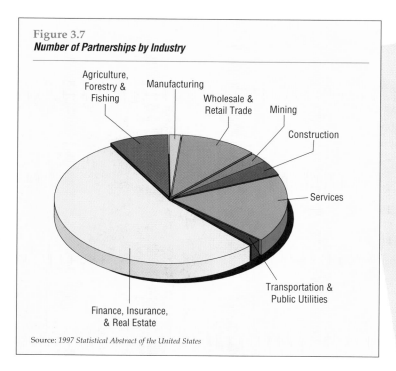

Figure 3.7
Number of Partnerships by Industry

Agriculture, Forestry & Fishing

Manufacturing

Wholesale & Retail Trade

Mining

Construction

Services

Transportation & Public Utilities

Finance, Insurance, & Real Estate

Source: *1997 Statistical Abstract of the United States*

Technology Activity

Developing a Multimedia Presentation

With the increase in multinational corporations, many American citizens are interacting more and more with different cultures in other countries. Imagine that you and a partner have set up a multinational corporation. Select a country and research its culture in relation to business protocol. Develop a video for your employees who are soon to join you in that country. Demonstrate procedures and key words your employees will need to know in order to properly conduct business in the country. Show your completed video to the class.

Applying Economic Concepts

1. Answers will vary. Some students might note that there are few grocery stores in their neighborhood, so a food cooperative would fulfill this economic need.

2. Answers will vary. Some students may suggest that the direct role is most important, because people depend upon the products—highways, for example—that government produces. Others might support the indirect role, arguing that it ensures the fair and efficient operation of the market economy.

Reinforcing Skills

1. The relationships among the parts of a whole. The whole is the total number of partnerships, whereas the parts represent the number of partnerships in various industrial groups.

2. 8

3. Finance, Insurance, and Real Estate

4. No, because no totals are given. In addition, the Finance and Insurance industries are combined with Real Estate.

5. Transportation and Public Utilities and Manufacturing tied at 1.6 percent each.

 BONUS TEST QUESTION

How can stockholders control the operations of a corporation? Why is this power usually limited?

(through exercising their right to vote in elections for the board of directors; Stockholders rarely hold enough stock to influence elections.)

7. A nonprofit organization does not seek financial gain for its members.

8. consumer cooperative, such as a food co-op; service cooperative, such as a credit union; producer cooperative, such as a farmers' co-op

9. to work for its members' interests in various employment matters

10. professional association (American Bar Association); business association organized to promote members' interests (chamber of commerce); business association established to help consumers, (Better Business Bureau)

11. **direct role:** producer and consumer of goods and services; **indirect role:** regulator or makes payments to individuals

Critical Thinking

1. Answers will vary.

2. Options: Mergers are beneficial, leading to more efficient use of resources. They are harmful, leading to the loss of jobs and the concentration of economic power.

BUSINESS ETHICS AND CORPORATE RESPONSIBILITY

FOCUS

Ask students to name several brands of items they feel are important to own. Why do students buy these brands? Is their decision based on the price of the item? Is it based on the quality or name brand of the item? Then ask students if they have ever *not purchased* a product from a particular company because of the company's reputation or its actions. If so, point out that the student has made a purchasing decision based on the company's ethical behavior.

TEACH

L1 *Applying Basic Concepts*
Write "PRO" and "CON" on the chalkboard and ask students to identify the major points of the two arguments about ethics in business. Note responses under the appropriate heading. Then have students write a summary paragraph for each of the arguments, using information on the chalkboard. Ensure that they include such basic economic terms as *profit, profit motive,* and *free enterprise economy* in writing their paragraphs.

conomists believe that the profit motive—the driving force that encourages people and organizations to improve their material well-being—is largely responsible for the growth of the United States' free enterprise system. Corporate leaders believe that the profit motive is essential for the "bottom line," or company profits. Increasingly, however, businesses are being questioned about ethics—their system of moral principles or values—in their quest for profits. Should ethics be a part of business practices?

Pro

I believe that good business ethics is good for the bottom line and good for shareholder value.

As corporations, we live at the sufferance of the public. If we don't behave well, we can be regulated, we can be sued, all sorts of bad things can happen to us. And everyday, it seems, yet another company is the subject of the "wrong kind" of story in the Wall Street Journal. Stories about sexual harassment, environmental contamination, antitrust infractions, illegal foreign payments, fraudulent financial reporting and race issues. Today, companies cannot afford negative publicity. Loss of confidence in an organization is the single greatest cost of unethical behavior. Once the media gets hold of that story, your customers will avoid you like the plague. An essential part of an ethics process is identifying issues that would mortify a chief executive if he were to read about them on the front page of the newspapers.

—STEPHEN BUTLER, "BUSINESS ETHICS AND CORPORATE RESPONSIBILITY," *VITAL SPEECHES OF THE DAY*, 1997

- provide in-service training and customer service that exceeds our customers' expectations;

- provide opportunity for personal and professional growth to our employees, who are essential to our success;

- ensure reasonable and competitive earnings and long-term investment growth for our owners.

▲ *Most corporations publicly stress honesty and a concern for their employees and customers in their corporate mission statements.*

▼ *Problems may occur if employees receive an unspoken message "just get the job done, whatever it takes."*

About the Speakers

 Stephen Butler is CEO of KPMG Peat Marwick.

 Daniel Kadlec is a writer and editor for *Time Magazine.*

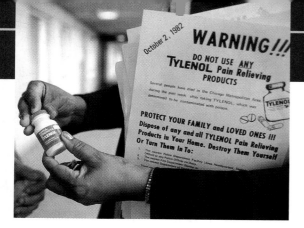

▲ *In the 1980s, ethically responsible Johnson and Johnson pulled every bottle of Tylenol off the shelves after several bottles were tampered with.*

For some companies, increasing profits means using child ▶ *labor or other unethical business practices.*

Con

A deeper concern is that American business, which is now the envy of the world for its profitability and ruthless efficiency, could fall off that pedestal if it takes on too many social issues. "Business exists to make a profit," says John Hood, president of the John Lock Foundation, a North Carolina-based public-policy think tank. "When you lose sight of that, you lose the unique benefits that come from being highly focused in a competitive market."

Cost-cutting CEOs like Al Dunlap would certainly agree. "Chainsaw Al" wiped out a $5 million annual philanthropy budget when he took over at Scott Paper a few years ago. Now, at Sunbeam, he's eliminated that company's $1 million-a-year giving program. "The purest form of charity is to make the most money you can for shareholders and let them give to whatever charities they want," Dunlap says.

—DANIEL KADLEC, "THE NEW WORLD OF GIVING," *TIME MAGAZINE*, MAY 5, 1997

Analyzing the Case Study

1. Why do economists and corporate leaders believe the profit motive is important?

2. What, according to Stephen Butler, is the result of unethical behavior?

3. According to Daniel Kadlec, what may happen to American business if it takes on too many social issues?

4. With which opinion do you agree? Why?

UNIT 1: *Fundamental Economic Concepts* **77**

77

Unit Goals

After studying this unit, students will be able to:

1. **Explain** how supply and demand interact to determine price.
2. **Describe** the major types of economic markets in the United States.

Unit Overview

Unit 2 examines major markets with respect to the degree of competition within each type and how this affects buyers and sellers. **Chapter 4** explains the concept of demand, while **Chapter 5** discusses supply, the theory of production, and profit maximization. **Chapter 6** brings demand and supply together in a relationship focusing on price and explains how the price system operates. **Chapter 7** introduces competition and market structures. It also discusses market failures and the government's role in the economy.

> If time does not permit teaching the entire unit, use the **Chapter Digests Audiocassettes** to highlight chapter content.

Connecting with Past Learning

Remind students that in Unit 1 they studied decision making and choices. Mention that in Unit 2 they will examine competition and the importance of price in buyer and seller decision making. As students study the unit, have them consider how price affects the economic decisions they make.

UNIT 2

MICRO-ECONOMICS

CHAPTER 4
Demand

CHAPTER 5
Supply

CHAPTER 6
Prices and Decision Making

CHAPTER 7
Competition, Market Structures, and the Role of Government

The law of supply and demand is learned in infancy. The infant demands a clean diaper and is willing to supply peace and quiet in exchange. Mother demands peace and quiet and is willing to supply a clean diaper in exchange. The terms of trade are arranged. . . . One scream equals one diaper. The price of one diaper is one scream.

—Jude Wanniski, *The Way the World Works*, 1989

Economics and You

In this unit, discover what part economics plays in the following situations:
- Tickets for some professional sporting events are often sold out.
- The price of local farm products such as corn and tomatoes decreases during the summer.
- The government regulates your local cable television company.

78 UNIT 2: *Microeconomics*

$$ *Economics and You*

The first example above is an illustration of a *shortage*—where the quantity demanded is greater than the quantity supplied at a given price. Through adjustments in supply and demand, an equilibrium price—a price where quantity demanded is equal to the quantity supplied—can be reached.

The second example is an illustration of how various factors, such as supply and demand elasticity, affect prices. An increase in supply, coupled with inelastic demand, would account for this seasonal price change.

The third example is an illustration of one of the roles government plays in the economy—regulating the activities of monopolies to prevent price gouging by greedy operators.

The forces of supply and demand are embodied in the buyers and sellers at the New York Stock Exchange.

Introducing the Unit

Ask students to select a business in their community that they patronize. Have them write a short analysis of the business by responding to the following items:

1. Name and location of the business.

2. Why do you purchase from this business? *(Answers will vary, but may include convenience, price, service, attractiveness of store, and quality of product.)*

3. What is the competition for the business that you selected? *(Answers should note stores nearby, malls, mail order, and so on.)*

4. How does the selected business compete? *(Answers may include price competition, sales, advertising, special service, and so on.)*

In a class discussion, have students share their reports. Then point out that in this unit, students will study how prices are determined, how businesses compete, and the roles that consumers and businesses play in our economy.

Unit Project

Have students work individually or in small groups to develop a collection of magazine and newspaper articles that deal with changes in price for consumer goods or services and for the four factors of production. For each article, students should indicate how the price was affected by a change in supply and demand. Have individuals or groups share and discuss their collections.

Examining the Photograph

Ask: Who represents supply? *(sellers)* Who represents demand? *(buyers)* Point out that, in a market economy, supply and demand work together to determine price. Then ask students to speculate in a brief paragraph on how prices might be set by the actions of buyers and sellers. Provide guidance by mentioning that, in general, buyers will buy more at lower prices and sellers will sell more at higher prices. *(Paragraphs may vary, but should focus on the attempts to balance the desires of buyers with those of sellers.)* As students work through the unit, have them review and adjust their paragraphs.

CHAPTER ORGANIZER

Daily Objectives	Reproducible Resources	Multimedia Resources
Section 1 **What Is Demand?** 1. **Explain** the meaning and concept of demand. 2. **Explain** the purpose of a demand schedule. 3. **Illustrate** the concept of demand in the form of a graph.	▱ Reproducible Lesson Plan 4-1 ▱ Guided Reading Activity 4-1 ▱ Cooperative Learning Activity 8 ▱ Consumer Application Activity 8 ▱ Primary and Secondary Source Reading 8 ▱ Reinforcing Economic Skills 4 ▱ Section Quiz 4-1*	⬚ Focus Activity Transparency 26 ⬚ Vocabulary PuzzleMaker ⬚ Chapter Challenger Interactive Review Software ⬚ Testmaker ⬚ MindJogger Videoquiz ⬚ Interactive Economics!
Section 2 **The Law of Demand** 1. **Explain** the causes of a change in quantity demanded. 2. **Describe** the factors that could cause a change in demand. 3. **Understand** the relationship between the demand curve and diminishing marginal utility.	▱ Reproducible Lesson Plan 4-2 ▱ Guided Reading Activity 4-2 ▱ Section Quiz 4-2*	⬚ Focus Activity Transparency 28 ⬚ Vocabulary PuzzleMaker ⬚ Chapter Challenger Interactive Review Software ⬚ Testmaker ⬚ NBR's Economics in Action Video Program ⬚ Interactive Economics!
Section 3 **Elasticity of Demand** 1. **Analyze** the elasticity of demand for a product. 2. **Explain** the three determinants of demand elasticity.	▱ Reproducible Lesson Plan 4-3 ▱ Guided Reading Activity 4-3 ▱ Math Practice for Economics 9 ▱ Performance Assessment Activity 9 ▱ Section Quiz 4-3*	⬚ Focus Activity Transparency 29 ⬚ Economic Concepts Transparency 8 ⬚ Vocabulary PuzzleMaker ⬚ Chapter Challenger Interactive Review Software ⬚ Testmaker ⬚ NBR's Economics in Action Video Program ⬚ Interactive Economics!
Chapter Review and Evaluation	▱ Enrichment Activity 4 ▱ Reteaching Activity 4* ▱ Economic Vocabulary Activity 4* ▱ Chapter 4 Test, Forms A and B	⬚ Chapter Digests Audiocassette Activities and Tests* ⬚ Testmaker ⬚ MindJogger Videoquiz

Also available in Spanish

 Blackline Master   Transparency   CD-ROM   Software   Videodisc   Audiocassette

⧗ OUT OF TIME? Assign the Chapter 4 Digest Audiocassette and the corresponding Chapter Digest activities and tests.

National Council on Economic Education

THE **Economics** America AND **Economics** International PROGRAMS

VOLUNTARY NATIONAL CONTENT STANDARDS IN ECONOMICS
Emphasized in Chapter 4

Content Standard 8 *Students will understand that:*
Prices send signals and provide incentives to buyers and sellers. When supply or demand changes, market prices adjust, affecting incentives.

EconomicsAmerica *Resources Available From NCEE*

- *Capstone: The Nation's High School Economics Course*
- *MCG: Economics and Entrepreneurship*
- *Economics and the Environment*
- *Focus: High School Economics*
- *Personal Decision Making: Focus on Economics*

To order these materials, or to contact your state Council on Economic Education about workshops and programs, call 1-800-338-1192 or visit http://www.nationalcouncil.org.

PERFORMANCE ASSESSMENT

The following chapter projects may be assigned at the beginning of the chapter and used for performance assessment.

Multicultural Heritage Paralleling the demand by consumers for goods and services, producers have a demand for the four factors of production to produce those goods and services. Ask students to consider producers' demand for one particular factor of production—labor. Point out that in the past, the price some producers were willing to pay for labor was influenced by prejudice and discrimination. In recent years, however, federal legislation has outlawed such practices. Have students monitor newspapers for one week, clipping classified advertisements for jobs. Ask students to determine whether these job openings have any indication of an antidiscrimination policy, such as an equal-employment opportunity statement or statements against hiring based on race, religion, place of birth, sex, age, or physical disadvantage. Encourage students to compare their advertisements. Then have them discuss how discrimination and equal-employment opportunities affect the demand for labor.

Cooperative Learning Organize students into six groups and assign each group a specific good or service, such as a late-model sports car, repair of a malfunctioning VCR, tickets for the premier of a new movie, jeans, allergy medicine, and bread. Instruct groups to analyze the demand for their assigned goods or services by applying the meaning of demand (desire, ability, and willingness to buy), and to determine the elasticity of demand for their goods or services by using the criteria in Figure 4.5 on page 97. Have group representatives present their findings to the class. Then have the class tabulate the findings in a chart similar to Figure 4.5.

ADDITIONAL RESOURCES

Readings for the Teacher

Keenan, Diane, et al. *Economics U$A: High School Activity Packs.* The Annenberg/CPB Collection, 1992. Companion to the video series of the same name (see Multimedia entry below), providing background information and lesson ideas on economic concepts.

Supply and Demand. Gainesville, FL: Center for Economic Education, University of Florida, 1996. Resource guide providing ideas on how to teach this basic principle of the free market system.

Multimedia

Economics U$A: The Firm/Supply & Demand. The Annenberg/CPB Collection, 19 Gregory Drive, South Burlington, VT 05403. Color video, 60 mins. Second 30-minute program on video discusses the dynamics of supply and demand.

You Can't Always Get What You Want. Instructional Video, P.O. Box 21, Maumee, OH 43537. Color video, 30 mins. Teaches the principle of supply and demand by focusing on the activities at a gift shop.

Chapter Overview

Chapter 4 introduces microeconomics and gives an explanation of demand and its characteristics. **Section 1** defines demand and the conditions necessary for it to exist. **Section 2** distinguishes between a change in quantity demanded and a change in demand. **Section 3** analyzes demand elasticity.

GLENCOE
TECHNOLOGY

VIDEODISC
MindJogger Videoquiz

Use MindJogger to preview the Chapter 4 content.

Chapter 4
Disc 1, Side A

 Also available in VHS.

*inter*NET
CONNECTION

Resources for Chapter 4 on the World Wide Web*

National Council on Economic Education
http://www.nationalcouncil.org/

The Wall Street Journal Classroom Resources
http://info.wsj.com/classroom

Consumer World
http://www.consumerworld.org

*Sites subject to change.

VISUAL INSTRUCTION

Ask students to identify actions they have exhibited in the last few days that exemplify demand.

People waiting in line to see a movie exemplify demand—the desire, ability, and willingness to pay.

✚ Extra Credit Project

Have students work in small groups to develop a four-page annotated pictorial essay illustrating the nature of demand, the Law of Demand, and demand elasticity. After studying the chapter, have groups display and discuss their essays.

CHAPTER 4

Demand

SECTION 1
What Is Demand?

SECTION 2
The Law of Demand

SECTION 3
Elasticity of Demand

CHAPTER PREVIEW

People to Know

• Ninfa Laurenzo
• Buyer

Applying Economic Concepts to Your Life

Demand Why is it unlikely that you will find many boat dealerships in a desert? Or many advertising agencies in a rural area? Before a business sets up shop, it researches the potential *demand* for its product. If consumers don't have the desire, ability, or willingness to buy the product, the business will not succeed.

Journal Writing

For one week, keep a journal of your expenditures. Separate the items into goods and services, being specific about the nature of the entries and the amount spent on each. If you buy gas for your car, for example, make a note of whether the gas is regular, premium, or some other type.

CHAPTER 4: *Demand* **81**

Connecting to Past Learning

Write the terms *scarcity, goods and services, opportunity cost,* and *dollar "votes"* on the chalkboard. Direct students to write sentences using each term in association with the term *demand.* The sentences should demonstrate what, if any, understanding students have of the concept of demand. As they study Chapter 4, have them review and adjust their sentences to reflect the precise relationship between the various terms and demand.

Applying Economics

Ask students to name consumer goods and services that they would like to have. Note responses on the chalkboard. Then lead the students in a discussion of each item from the perspective of the conditions necessary for demand— desire, ability, and willingness to buy. Erase those items for which demand does not exist, and stress that merely wanting an item does not mean that you have a demand for that item.

PERFORMANCE ASSESSMENT

Refer to page **80B** for a Performance Assessment activity for this chapter. Also see the **Performance Assessment Activities** booklet for additional suggestions.

Economic Portfolio

In the **Journal Writing** activity above, students are asked to log their expenditures for one week. Suggest that students consider for each entry in their journals the following questions: Could I have delayed this purchase? Do adequate substitutes for this item exist? Did the purchase use a large portion of my income? Tell students that they will need to consider such points to complete a table at the end of the chapter. Refer students to the **Technology Activity** in the Chapter 4 Review on page 101.

Key to Ability Levels — Teaching strategies have been coded for varying learning styles and abilities:
L1 - Basic (activities for all students) **L2 - Average** (activities for average to above-average students)
L3 - Challenging (activities for above-average students) **LEP - Limited English Proficiency**

FOCUS

Section Objectives

1. Explain the meaning and concept of demand.
2. Explain the purpose of a demand schedule.
3. Illustrate the concept of demand in the form of a graph.

Bellringer

 Prior to taking roll at the beginning of the class period, display Focus Activity Transparency 26.

Motivational Activity

Discuss students' responses to the activity sheet that accompanies Transparency 26.

Preteaching Vocabulary

Have students write questions for which each key term is an answer.

Use the **Vocabulary PuzzleMaker** to create crossword and word search puzzles.

◎ VISUAL INSTRUCTION

Ask students to identify unsuitable locations for the music store.

Answer to Caption:
This could be a good location if many potential customers and a stereo store are nearby.

Section Preview

Objectives

After studying this section, you will be able to:

1. **Explain** the meaning and concept of demand.
2. **Explain** the purpose of a demand schedule.
3. **Illustrate** the concept of demand in the form of a graph.

Key Terms

demand, microeconomics, demand schedule, demand curve

Applying Economic Concepts

Demand In a market economy, your opinions count when you cast your dollar "votes" for the goods and services you like best. You express your *demand* for a product when you are willing and able to purchase it.

Most people think of demand as being the desire to have or to own a certain economic product. In this sense, anyone who would like to own a swimming pool could be said to "demand" one. In order for demand to be counted in the marketplace, however, wanting a product must coincide with the ability and willingness to pay for it. Only those people with **demand**—the desire, ability, and willingness to buy a product—can compete with others who have similar demands. **1**

Demand, like many other topics in this unit, is a microeconomic concept. **Microeconomics** is that part of economics that deals with behavior and decision making by small units, such as individuals and firms. Collectively, these micro concepts help explain how prices are determined and how individual economic decisions are made.

An Introduction to Demand

A knowledge of demand is essential to understand how a market economy works. Knowledge of demand is also important for sound business planning.

Suppose you are planning to start a television repair business. Before you begin, you need to know where the demand is. You should set up your shop in a neighborhood with many television sets and few repair shops. Less demand for your services would exist in areas having few television sets and many repair shops.

After you think you know where to locate the shop, how do you measure the demand for your services? You may visit other shops and gauge the reactions of consumers to different prices. You may poll consumers about prices and determine demand from this data. You could study data compiled over past years, which would show consumer reactions to higher and lower prices. ▼

Location *The owner of a music store has set up shop near a stereo business.* **Why is this location a good one?**

Classroom Resources for SECTION 1

- 📁 Reproducible Lesson Plan 4-1
- 📁 Guided Reading Activity 4-1
- 📁 Cooperative Learning Activity 8
- 📁 Consumer Application Activity 8
- 📁 Primary and Secondary Source Reading 8
- 📁 Reinforcing Economic Skill 4
- 📁 Section Quiz 4-1
- 📁 Spanish Section Quiz 4-1

- 🔦 Focus Activity Transparency 26
- ◎ Testmaker
- ◎ Vocabulary PuzzleMaker
- ◎ Chapter Challenger Interactive Review Software
- ◉ MindJogger Videoquiz
- 👤 Interactive Economics!

Lesson 3 of Interactive Economics! to learn more about "Demand Schedules and Curves."

Figure 4.1
The Demand for Compact Discs

A. Demand Schedule

Price per CD	Number of CDs Demanded
$27	10
24	13
21	18
18	25
15	37
12	58
9	94
6	162
3	300

The demand schedule is a listing that shows the amount demanded at each and every price. The demand curve shows the same information in the form of a graph. The graph shows that the demand curve is downward sloping, which means that more will be demanded at lower prices, and less at higher prices. **Why do you suppose that is true?**

All of these methods would give you a general idea as to the desire, willingness, and ability of people to pay. Gathering precise data on how consumers actually behave, however, is not easy. Even so, it is possible to treat the concept of demand in a more formal manner. Economists use schedules and diagrams to represent approximations of consumer behavior. Surveys, a valuable part of economic analysis, often strengthen predictions about people's behavior. **2**

The Demand Schedule

If you asked people in different industries about the demand for their products, you would get many different answers. A person in the oil industry might say that the demand for oil is 46 million barrels per day. Someone in agriculture might say that the daily demand for wheat is 10 million bushels. Someone in the steel industry might say that the demand for steel is 2 million tons per day.

QUICK CHECK

Checking Understanding

1. How do economists define demand?
2. What tools do economists use to measure demand?

Applying Economic Concepts

 Role of Government The Small Business Administration, an agency of the federal government, aids people who want to go into business. Part of this service includes conducting workshops where potential business owners learn how to gauge demand and set prices.

CHAPTER 4: *Demand* **83**

TEACH

Guided Practice

L1 Understanding Ideas Ask students how many soft drinks they would buy at 25¢ a can, at 50¢, at $1, at $1.50, and so on. Note prices and quantities on the board. Then ask students to write a generalization about demand based on these figures. (*As price rises, quantity demanded decreases.*) **LEP**

 Cooperative Learning Assign Cooperative Learning Activity 8.

Independent Practice

Guided Reading Assign Guided Reading Activity for Section 1. **LEP**

Consumer Application Assign Consumer Application Activity 8.

Readings Assign Primary and Secondary Source Reading 8.

VISUAL INSTRUCTION

Point out that the relationship shown by the schedule and curve is true for practically every economic product.

Answer to Caption:

At lower prices, people will have greater desire, willingness, and ability to buy products.

QUICK CHECK

ANSWERS

1. the desire, ability, and willingness to buy
2. observations and surveys

ASSESS

Check for Understanding

Assign Section 1 Review as homework or an in-class activity.

🖭 Use the **Chapter Challenger Interactive Review Software** to review Section 1

MEETING LESSON OBJECTIVES

Each objective below is tested by the questions that follow it in parentheses.

1. **Explain** the meaning and concept of demand. **(1, 2, 4, 5)**

2. **Explain** the purpose of a demand schedule. **(3)**

3. **Illustrate** the concept of demand in the form of a graph. **(3)**

Evaluate

🗀 🗀 🖭 Assign the Section 1 Quiz in the TCR or use the *Economics: Principles and Practices* Testmaker. Spanish Section Quizzes also are available in the Spanish Resources Binder.

Reteach

Have students write a summary of the section using the key terms.

Enrich

Encourage students to interview managers to discover how they measure demand for their products.

CLOSE

Ask students to draw a cartoon that illustrates the relationship between price and demand.

Although each person is in a different industry, they all have one thing in common. Each person has a general idea about current sales, and each sees demand as measured in terms of the sales volume in his or her own industry.

Economists, however, want to know more than the amount purchased at a certain price. They also want to know how much will be bought at higher and lower prices. The average price of crude oil may have been $17 per barrel last year, with 16 million barrels demanded at that price. How much oil would have been demanded if the price had been $21 or $12 per barrel? In economic analysis, demand means that the full range of possibilities has been considered.

Economists want to see the market as a whole. They want to know the amount people will demand at each and every possible price. The result, shown in **Figure 4.1**, is a **demand schedule**—a listing that shows the quantity demanded at all prices that might prevail in the market at a given time.

DID YOU KNOW?

Beams and Bar Codes The scanners used at checkouts do more than record prices and maintain inventory. Scanners also keep track of advertising campaigns, product displays, and coupon activity.

Demand Illustrated

To see how an economist would analyze demand for an economic product, look at the demand schedule in panel A of **Figure 4.1**. The data in the schedule represent an estimate of the demand for compact discs in a certain store on a given day.

The schedule shows that if the price is $27 per disc, people would demand only 10 CDs. At a slightly lower price—$21—people would demand 18 CDs. As the price gets lower and lower, even more CDs would be demanded.

The demand for CDs also can be shown graphically. To do so, the information in the schedule simply is transferred to a graph. On the graph in **Figure 4.1**, point **a** shows that at a price of $15, people will buy 37 CDs. Point **b** shows the quantity demanded at $9, and so on. After all the price-quantity observations listed in the schedule have been transferred to the graph, the points are connected to form the curve that is labeled **DD**.

The curved line **DD** is the **demand curve** for CDs. The curve, like the schedule, tells the quantity that consumers will demand at each and every price. Both the demand schedule and the demand curve illustrate demand. The schedule presents the information in the form of a table. The curve, which is always downward-sloping, presents the information in the form of a graph.

SECTION 1 REVIEW

Reviewing Terms and Facts

1. **Define** demand, microeconomics, demand schedule, demand curve.
2. **Explain** how the common view of demand is different from the economist's view of demand.
3. **Describe** the relationship between the demand schedule and demand curve.

Critical Thinking

4. **Determining Cause and Effect** Explain how your dollars act as "votes" for the products you like best.

Applying Economic Concepts

5. **Demand** Record the names and approximate prices of the last two items you purchased. In general, would you have spent your money differently if the price of each item was twice as high? Would you have spent your money differently if each of the items cost half as much as it did? Explain your responses.

Answers to SECTION 1 REVIEW

1. All vocabulary words are defined in the Glossary.

2. Common view—the desire to have a certain economic product; Economists' view—not only desire to own product, but also ability and willingness to buy product.

3. Both provide information about demand—the schedule in the form of a table and the curve in the form of a graph.

4. By casting your dollar "votes" for a particular product, you express your demand for that product. Producers respond to the demand by producing more of the product.

5. Items will vary, but answers should stress that spending behavior would be different because the quantity demanded would be less when price doubles and more when price is halved.

CRITICAL THINKING SKILL

Determining Cause and Effect

As you read a mystery novel, you may try to figure out which events or actions caused the principal character to act in specific ways. When you read economics, you can make better sense of actions if you determine cause-and-effect relationships.

Explanation

A *cause* is any condition, person, or event that makes something happen. What happens as a result of a cause is known as an *effect*. The connection between what happens and what makes it happen is known as a cause-and-effect relationship.

A cause may have both immediate and long-term effects. An *immediate cause* leads directly to an event. If you are exposed to a virus, for example, you may catch a cold. Other indirect, underlying causes, however, may have contributed to the cold, such as lack of sleep or poor diet.

The following guidelines will aid you in identifying cases of cause-and-effect relationships in written material:

- Look for "clue words" that alert you to cause and effect, such as *because, led to, brought about, produced, as a result of, so that, thus, since, outcome, as a consequence, resulted in, gave rise to,* and *therefore.*
- Look for logical relationships between events, such as "She did this, and that happened."
- Cause and effect is usually expressed in more than one sentence or paragraph. Look for similar events in another time or place, and examine that event for similar causes and effects.

High gasoline prices may cause more mass transit systems to be developed.

Practice

Several examples of cause-and-effect relationships as they relate to the Law of Demand are written below. Decide which action(s) is the cause and which is the effect. Remember that one cause may produce several effects, or one effect may result from several causes. Rewrite the sentences as one sentence, tying them together with a cause-and-effect clue word.

1. a. More cassette tapes are demanded.
   b. The price of cassette players goes down.

2. a. A substitute for gasoline is available.
   b. The price of gasoline goes down.

3. a. The price of bakery goods goes down.
   b. The price of sugar goes down.
   c. Customers buy more bakery goods.

Additional Practice

For further practice in determining cause and effect, complete the Reinforcing Skills exercise in the Chapter 4 Review on page 101.

CHAPTER 4: *Demand* **85**

FOCUS

Section Objectives

1. Explain the causes of a change in quantity demanded.

2. Describe the factors that could cause a change in the level of demand.

3. Understand the relationship between the demand curve and diminishing marginal utility.

Bellringer

 Prior to taking roll at the beginning of the class period, display Focus Activity Transparency 28.

Motivational Activity

Discuss students' responses to the activity sheet that accompanies Transparency 28.

Preteaching Vocabulary

Ask students to suggest how a change in demand and a change in the quantity demanded might differ. **LEP**

Use the **Vocabulary PuzzleMaker** to create crossword and word search puzzles.

◎ VISUAL INSTRUCTION

Ask: What in the picture suggests the store owner has taken steps to stimulate consumer demand? *(the "Sale" sign)*

Answer to Caption:

It reflects the inverse relationship between price and quantity demanded—as price falls, quantity demanded rises.

Section Preview

Objectives

After studying this section, you will be able to:

1. **Explain** the causes of a change in quantity demanded.

2. **Describe** the factors that could cause a change in demand.

3. **Understand** the relationship between the demand curve and diminishing marginal utility.

Key Terms

Law of Demand, change in quantity demanded, income effect, substitution effect, change in demand, substitutes, complements, marginal utility, diminishing marginal utility

Applying Economic Concepts

Change in Demand More than likely, the number of CDs you buy is affected by your income. Would you buy more if you got a new job that paid twice as much? Would you buy fewer CDs if you lost your job or if your allowance stopped? A *change in demand* happens whenever you or others change the amount of a product you buy—even though the price of that product remains unchanged.

The exact prices and quantities illustrated in the demand schedule in Figure 4.1 point out an important feature of demand in general. That is, relatively high prices are associated with relatively low quantities demanded. Similarly, low prices are associated with high quantities demanded. This relationship of demand and price is expressed by the **Law of Demand,** which states that the demand for an economic product varies inversely with its price. **1**

The correlation between demand and price does not happen by chance. Common sense and simple observation show that the Law of Demand works. For consumers, price is an obstacle to buying. When prices fall, consumers generally buy more. We all see the Law of Demand at work when consumers flock to stores on bargain days and during special sales when prices are temporarily reduced. ✔

Change in the Quantity Demanded

The table and graph in Figure 4.2 show that 37 CDs are demanded at a price of $15 each. When the price falls to $9, however, 94 CDs are demanded. This movement *along* the demand curve shows a **change in quantity demanded**—or a change in the quantity

of the product purchased in response to a change in price. An examination of the income and substitution effects helps explain why this happens.

Law of Demand *If the price of bicycle gear drops, this shopper will be better able and more willing to buy a helmet.* **How does this situation reflect the Law of Demand?**

86 UNIT 2: *Microeconomics*

Classroom Resources for SECTION 2

📁 Reproducible Lesson Plan 4-2
📁 Guided Reading Activity 4-2
📁 Section Quiz 4-2
📁 Spanish Section Quiz 4-2

🔖 Focus Activity Transparency 28
◉ NBR's Economics in Action Video Program
▣ Testmaker
▣ Vocabulary PuzzleMaker
▣ Chapter Challenger Interactive Review Software
◉ Interactive Economics!

Lesson 3 of Interactive Economics! to learn more about "A Change in Demand."

Figure 4.2
A Change in Demand for Compact Digital Discs

A. New Demand Schedule

Price per CD	Original Quantity of CDs Demanded	New Quantity of CDs Demanded
$27	10	14
24	13	18
21	18	25
18	25	36
15	37	52
12	58	81
9	94	132
6	162	227
3	300	420

B. New Demand Curve (D,D₁)

A change in demand means that people are willing to buy a different quantity at each and every price. An increase in demand occurs when the demand curve shifts to the right to D_1D_1. A decrease in demand occurs when the demand curve shifts to the left. **What might cause a change in demand for CDs?**

TEACH

Guided Practice

L1 Demonstrating Concepts
Write: (1) minimum wage raised to $6.00 per hour; (2) prices of CD players fall; (3) powerful advertisements make CDs much more appealing. Ask what would happen to the demand for CDs and why. *(Demand would increase in all situations; Reasons: 1. rise in income enables consumers to buy more at all prices; 2. because CD players and CDs are complementary goods; 3. consumer tastes change, stimulated by advertising.)*

 VISUAL INSTRUCTION

Ask: Does D_1D_1 indicate an increase or a decrease in demand? *(increase)*

Answer to Caption:

consumer income, consumer tastes, change in prices of related products

 INTERACTIVE ECONOMICS!

CD-ROM Demand

Have students review "A Change in Demand" and "A Change in the Quantity Demanded." Then have them draw two graphs—one showing a change in quantity demanded, the other showing a change in demand.

Supplied in both CD-ROM and diskette formats.

The Income Effect

When prices drop, consumers pay less for the product and, as a result, have some extra real income to spend. At a price of $15 per CD, consumers spent $555 to buy 37 CDs. If the price drops to $9, they will spend only $333 on the same quantity. The consumers are now $222 richer because of the drop in price, and they may spend more on CDs.

Part, but not all, of the increase from 37 to 94 units purchased is due to consumers feeling richer. This change in the amount purchased is known as the **income effect,** or the change in quantity demanded because of a change in the consumer's real income when the price of a commodity changes. **2**

The Substitution Effect

A lower price also means that CDs will be relatively less expensive than other goods and services such as concerts, movies, and other forms of entertainment. As a result, consumers will have a tendency to purchase more CDs relative to these products. The **substitution effect** is the change in quantity demanded because of the change in the relative price of the product.

The rest of the increase from 37 to 94 CDs purchased that is not due to the income effect is a result of the substitution effect. Together, the income and substitution effects explain why consumers increase consumption of CDs to 94 when the price drops from $15 to $9.

 QUICK CHECK

Checking Understanding

1. What is the relationship between price and quantity demanded?
2. How does the income effect explain the change in quantity demanded that takes place when the price goes down?

Applying Economic Concepts

☑ **Economic Systems** The Law of Demand is a powerful force in our market economy. In a command economy, however, central planners choose WHAT is produced and their prices. Most command economies have failed, in part because they ignore consumer demand.

CHAPTER 4: *Demand* **87**

 Meeting Special Needs

Poor Learners Most students are familiar with the study system known as "SQ3R" (Survey, Question, Read, Recite, Review), but those with reading and learning problems often have difficulty surveying information. One task involved in surveying is predicting what kind of information will be given in a piece of text. Ask students to consider whether the text under each subhead in Section 2 will *describe* events or *discuss concepts and ideas* that shape events.

  ANSWERS

1. quantity demanded varies inversely to price
2. Because of the fall in price, consumers have more real income, some of which may be spent to buy more of the product.

Independent Practice

 Guided Reading Assign Guided Reading Activity for Section 2. **LEP**

L3 *Using Illustrations*
Encourage students to imagine they must teach the meaning of this section's key terms to a sixth-grade class. Have them create annotated illustrations—graphs, diagrams, drawings—for each term. Call on volunteers to present their "lessons" to the class.

 VISUAL INSTRUCTION

Ask: What advertising technique is illustrated here? *(famous athlete promoting a product)* Would you be swayed by this technique? Why or why not?

Answer to Caption:
The curve shifts to the right.

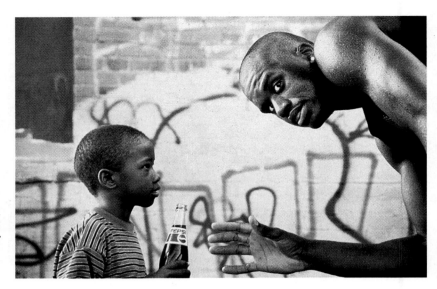

Consumer Tastes *Advertisers may spend millions of dollars annually to increase the popularity of their products.* **What happens to the demand curve for a product if consumers buy more of it at each and every price?**

Change in Demand

Sometimes we observe that people are willing to buy different amounts at the same prices. This is known as a **change in demand** and is different from a change in quantity demanded. When the *quantity demanded* changes, it does so because of a change in the price of the product, and movement occurs along the current demand curve. When there is a *change in demand,* the entire demand curve shifts—to the right to show an increase in demand or to the left to show a decrease in demand for the product. Therefore, a change in demand results in an entirely new curve.

A change in demand is illustrated in the schedule and graph in **Figure 4.2.** The schedule shows that people are willing to buy more at each and every price. At a price of $15, for example, consumers are now willing to buy 52 CDs instead of 37. At $9, they are willing to buy 132 CDs instead of 94. When this information is transferred to the graph, the demand curve appears to have shifted to the right to show an increase in demand.

Demand can change for several reasons. Changes in consumer incomes, consumer tastes, or the prices of related goods all can cause demand to change. When this happens, however, a new schedule must be constructed to reflect the new demand at all of the possible prevailing prices. **1**

Consumer Income

Changes in consumer income can cause a change in demand. As incomes rise, consumers are able to buy more products at each and every price. When this happens, the demand curve generally shifts to the right. If incomes decline, consumers buy less of a good at each and every price. The demand curve then shifts to the left, showing a decrease in demand.

Consumer Tastes

Advertising, news reports, trends, and even seasons can affect consumer tastes. For example, when a product is advertised, its popularity increases and people tend to buy more of it. If consumers want more of an item, they would buy more of it at each and every price. As a result, the demand curve shifts to the right. On the other hand, if people tire of a product, they would buy less at each and every price, causing the demand curve to shift to the left.

Prices of Related Products

A change in the price of related products can cause a change in demand. Some products are known as **substitutes** because they can be used in place of other products. Butter and margarine are classic examples

---

$ *Free Enterprise Activity* **$**

To increase students' understanding of the effects of a change in demand in a free enterprise economy, present the following scenario: A disease destroys much of the coffee crop in South America. How might this affect the price of coffee? The demand for substitute products? The demand for

complementary products? *(price increases; demand for substitute drinks, such as soft drinks and juices, might increase; demand for complementary products, such as sugar, might fall)* Have students present these changes in the form of graphs.

HELP WANTED

Buyer
▼

A large clothing store seeks a buyer to purchase merchandise for resale to the public. You will determine what clothing we offer for sale, finding the best available merchandise at the lowest possible price. Duties include anticipating consumer demand, staying informed about new products, attending trade shows, visiting clothing manufacturers, placing orders, and checking shipments. You also are responsible for assisting in sales promotions and advertising campaigns, as well as checking on clothing displays. Buyers must have the ability to plan, make decisions quickly, work under pressure, and identify products that will sell.

▼

Education: College degree
Salary range: $24,100-$43,000

of substitutes, and a change in the price of one can affect the demand for the other.

An increase in the price of butter could cause the demand for margarine to increase. Likewise, an increase in the price of margarine would cause the demand for butter to increase. In general, the demand for a product tends to increase if the price of its substitute goes up. The demand for a product tends to decrease if the price of its substitute goes down. **2**

Other related goods are known as **complements,** because the use of one increases the use of the other. Film and cameras are two complementary goods. A decrease in the price of cameras means that more cameras will be sold, and that the demand for film will

increase. In the same way, an increase in the price of cameras will cause a decrease in the demand for film. Thus, an increase in the price of one good usually leads to a decrease in the demand for its complement.

The Gillette Corporation makes razor handles and razor blades. To generate a high demand for their products, the price of razor handles is kept low. The profit earned on each razor handle is very small, but the razor blades are sold at very profitable prices. As a result, the company is able to use the profits on the blades to more than offset the profits lost on the handles. Given the complementary nature of the two products, it is unlikely that demand for Gillette blades would have been as high if the handles had been more expensive.

Diminishing Marginal Utility

By selecting from among alternative ways of spending their incomes, consumers try to get the most useful and most satisfactory combination of goods and services. In economics, remember, this usefulness or satisfaction from consumption is called utility.

How do people decide which economic products will provide them with the greatest utility? One answer is found in an analysis of what economists call **marginal utility**—the extra usefulness or satisfaction a person gets from acquiring one more unit of a product. Marginal utility is the amount of satisfaction added "at the margin."

For example, how much satisfaction would you get from a single glass of ice-cold lemonade after playing a hard game of tennis or basketball on a hot summer afternoon? Whatever amount you get is the marginal utility of that particular glass of lemonade. If you still are a little thirsty after drinking one glass of lemonade, you may decide to drink another. How much

QUICK CHECK

Checking Understanding	**Applying Economic Concepts**
1. What is the difference between a change in demand and a change in quantity demanded? 2. Why are butter and margarine considered substitute goods?	☑ **Demand** Economists classify a few goods as inferior goods. Demand for these goods varies inversely with income. People who are laid off may increase their demand for rice, potatoes, and bologna, even though their income goes down.

Extending the Content

Measuring Marginal Utility In some ways, marginal utility frustrated early economists because they wanted a numerical measure of utility, much like prices or quantity demanded. They tried a hypothetical measure called a *util,* but they soon had to abandon any notions of exact measurement because utility is so subjective. To illustrate, if 20

people were asked how much satisfaction they received from a second glass of lemonade, each one would give a different answer. Economists later developed the concept of indifference curves (a topic usually covered in college classes), which can be used to derive all of the propositions in economics without having to actually measure utility.

L2 Analyzing Media Have students monitor newscasts and newspapers to find three stories that discuss demand. Have them explain how the demand in each situation affects price.

ASSESS

Check for Understanding

Assign Section 2 Review as homework or an in-class activity.

◉ Use the **Chapter Challenger Interactive Review Software** to review Section 2.

MEETING LESSON OBJECTIVES

Each objective below is tested by the questions that follow it in parentheses.

1. **Explain** the causes of a change in quantity demanded. **(1, 2, 4, 5)**

2. **Describe** the factors that could cause a change in the level of demand. **(1, 2, 5)**

3. **Understand** the relationship between the demand curve and diminishing marginal utility. **(3)**

QUICK CHECK
ANSWERS

1. change in quantity demanded indicated by consumers' willingness to buy a different quantity at a new price; change in demand indicated by consumers' willingness to buy different amounts at all prices

2. because they can be used in place of each other

extra satisfaction will you get from the second glass? Once again, the extra satisfaction you get is the marginal utility of the second glass.

Consumers generally keep on buying a product until they reach a point where the last unit consumed gives enough, and only enough, satisfaction to justify the price. In the case of the lemonade, the marginal utility of the first glass probably is far greater than the initial amount you paid for the drink. Even the second glass may yield satisfaction greater than the price. In time, however, the marginal utility of still one more glass of lemonade will be less than its price. Sooner or later, the very thought of one more glass of lemonade may make you ill. When you reach the point that the marginal utility is less than the price, you will stop buying.

The lemonade example illustrates the principle of **diminishing marginal utility.** The principle states that the more units of a certain economic product a person acquires, the less eager that person is to buy still more. As people's wants for a particular product become more fully satisfied, they become less willing to spend their limited incomes to buy more of that product.

The principle of diminishing marginal utility can also be used to explain the downward-sloping nature of the demand curve. A shopper may decide to buy two sweaters at one price, for example, but would not

Diminishing Marginal Utility *These people cannot possibly eat another slice of pizza.* **How does this situation reflect the principle of diminishing marginal utility?**

buy three unless the price is even lower. The consumer gets the most utility from the first sweater, a little less from the second, and even less for the third. As a result of the diminishing marginal utility from each successive purchase, lower prices are necessary to encourage the shopper to buy more sweaters. In short, people will buy less at high prices and more when the price goes down.

SECTION 2 REVIEW

Reviewing Terms and Facts

1. **Define** Law of Demand, change in quantity demanded, income effect, substitution effect, change in demand, substitutes, complements, marginal utility, diminishing marginal utility.
2. **Describe** the difference between a change in quantity demanded and a change in demand.
3. **Explain** how the principle of diminishing marginal utility can be used to explain the shape of the demand curve.

Critical Thinking

4. **Drawing Conclusions** What happens to the price and the quantity of goods or services sold when a store runs a sale? How do these factors relate to the downward-sloping demand curve?

Applying Economic Concepts

5. **Change in Demand** Name a product that you recently bought because it went on sale. Identify

at least one substitute for that product, and a complement if possible. What happened to your demand for the substitute good when you purchased the sale item? What happened to your demand for the complementary item when you purchased the sale item? Distinguish between a change in quantity demanded and a change in demand.

PROFILES IN ECONOMICS

NINFA LAURENZO

Ninfa Laurenzo's story is a remarkable one. Widowed with 5 children in 1969, and faced with bankruptcy in 1973, she fought her way back to head a thriving, multimillion dollar corporation that operates many restaurants and employs thousands of people. What happened between 1973 and 1998, and why was Laurenzo so successful?

In many ways, Ninfa Maria Laurenzo was similar to many other small business owners in America. She and her husband, Tommy Laurenzo, started a business making and wholesaling

Laurenzo and her son show off Ninfa's cuisine.

tortillas and pizza dough—a mix of products reflecting Laurenzo's Hispanic and her husband's Italian heritage—in Houston's barrio. Laurenzo was left with the small family business and five children after her husband's death.

NINFA'S, INC. As she struggled with the factory, debts mounted, and Laurenzo was soon hard-pressed to try something else. As a last resort, she mortgaged her house and, with a $5,000 loan from a friend, opened a small restaurant in a corner of the factory. The restaurant had 10 tables, and Laurenzo used the pots, pans, dishes, and silverware from her family kitchen. In July 1973, the restaurant opened to the public with $16 in the cash register and only her children to help.

One week later, a fire destroyed a portion of it, which had to be rebuilt. When it reopened, it offered a small but unique menu that combined the best of Mexican regional cuisine with some of the family's favorite Italian dishes. The food was well received, and the prices were right. Despite a modest expansion of the restaurant, the line of customers waiting for a table still stretched out into the street. A second restaurant was opened in 1976, followed by a third in 1977, and a fourth in 1978. Today, Ninfa's, Inc., includes 21 full-service restaurants known for their gourmet Mexican food.

EXPANSION Laurenzo, however, did not stop. In 1987 she opened the first of many Bambolino's Italian Kitchens. She also has been involved in other ventures, including Cajun restaurants, steak houses, a large catering division, and franchising the Mexican restaurant chain. And today she is as well known for her charity work as she is for her business ventures.

Laurenzo's success was the result of a number of factors. Above all, she had an idea, a quality product, and the willingness to take enormous risks to make it work.

Examining the Profile

1. **Making Generalizations** How does Ninfa Laurenzo epitomize the entrepreneur's role in the American economy?

2. **For Further Research** Research to discover other entrepreneurial restauranteurs and how they made their niche in the American economy.

CHAPTER 4: *Demand* **91**

Answers to Examining the Profile

1. She had an idea and the willingness to take enormous risks to make that idea work. In addition, the whole economy benefitted from her success.

2. Answers will vary. Suggest that students gather information on at least two entrepreneurial restauranteurs.

FOCUS

Section Objectives

1. Analyze the elasticity of demand for a product.
2. Explain the three determinants of demand elasticity.

Bellringer

Prior to taking roll at the beginning of the class period, display Focus Activity Transparency 29 on the overhead projector and assign the accompanying Student Activity 29.

Motivational Activity

Discuss students' responses to the activity sheet that accompanies Focus Activity Transparency 29.

Preteaching Vocabulary

Ask students to give the common definition of *elasticity*. Then ask them to speculate how this term might be applied to demand. Have them check the accuracy of their responses as they read through the section. **LEP**

Use the **Vocabulary PuzzleMaker** to create crossword and word search puzzles.

Section Preview

Objectives

After studying this section, you will be able to:

1. **Analyze** the elasticity of demand for a product.
2. **Explain** the three determinants of demand elasticity.

Key Terms

demand elasticity, elastic, inelastic, unit elastic

Applying Economic Concepts

Elasticity of Demand Why are you charged a premium price when a new movie first comes out? Why do prices tend to go down after the movie has been out for a few months? The answer is that the producer is maximizing the revenue collected from you and your friends. The *elasticity of demand* for a product helps to determine how the product will be priced—and how much you will pay for the product.

The Law of Demand shows that people buy more of an economic product at lower prices than at higher ones. It does not tell how much more, however. Likewise, if prices go up, sales will go down. How much will sales go down, however? If a business owner is thinking about raising prices, how much will be lost in sales?

Demand Elasticity

The answer to these questions is found in the concept of **demand elasticity**—a term used to indicate the extent to which changes in price cause changes in the quantity demanded.

Elastic Demand

The demand for most products is such that consumers do care about changes in price. Demand is **elastic** when a relatively small change in price causes a relatively large change in the quantity demanded. The demand for T-bone steaks, for example, generally is regarded as elastic. At a regular price of $5.59 per pound, only a certain number of people will buy it. If it is put on sale for $3.39 per pound, however, consumers may rush to buy this kind of steak.

Inelastic Demand

For other products, demand may be largely **inelastic,** which means that a given change in price causes a relatively smaller change in the quantity demanded. A higher or lower price for table salt probably will not bring about much change in the quantity bought because people can consume only so much salt. Even if the price was cut in half, the quantity demanded might not rise very much, if at all. Then, too, the portion of a person's annual budget that is spent on salt is so small that even if the price doubled, it would not make much difference to consumers.

Specific vs. General Market

When considering the elasticity of demand for a product, it is necessary to define the market being studied. The demand for gasoline at a particular gas station is likely to be very elastic. If the station raised prices by 10 percent, the amount of gasoline sold would drop significantly because some customers would buy it elsewhere. If the station lowered prices by 10 percent, the amount of gasoline sold would go up a great deal because people would go out of their way to buy "cheap" gasoline.

On the other hand, the demand for gasoline in general is likely to be inelastic. If all gas stations raised

---

Classroom Resources for SECTION 3

- Reproducible Lesson Plan 4-3
- Guided Reading Activity 4-3
- Math Practice for Economics 9
- Performance Assessment Activity 9
- Section Quiz 4-3
- Focus Activity Transparency 29
- Economic Concepts Transparency 8
- NBR's Economics in Action Video Program
- MindJogger Videoquiz

- Enrichment Activity 4
- Reteaching Activity 4
- Economic Vocabulary Activity 4
- Chapter 4 Test, Form A and Form B
- English and Spanish Audiocassettes
- Testmaker
- Vocabulary PuzzleMaker
- Chapter Challenger Interactive Review Software
- Interactive Economics!

Lesson 3 of Interactive Economics! to learn more about "Demand Elasticity."

Figure 4.3
The Total Receipts Test for Demand Elasticity

The key to determining demand elasticity is to examine how revenue changes as prices change. If prices and revenues move in opposite directions, the demand curve is elastic. If prices and revenues move in the same direction, demand is inelastic. Demand is unit elastic if there is no change in revenue when the price changes. **Why is an understanding of elasticity important for businesses?**

Type Of Elasticity	Change In Price	Change In Total Receipts	Movement Of Price And Total Receipts
Elastic	↓	↑	Opposite
Inelastic	↓	↓	Same
Unit Elastic	↓	No Change	

CHAPTER 4: *Demand* **93**

TEACH

Guided Practice

L1 **Vocabulary** To explain the concept of elasticity, it might be helpful to associate the word with its synonym, *flexibility.* Point out that when demand for a product is elastic, the consumer can be flexible and delay the purchase or buy a substitute. When demand is inelastic, the consumer cannot be flexible and must purchase the product no matter what the price. Have students write their own explanations of the concept using other synonyms. *(adaptability, adjustability)* **LEP**

GLENCOE
TECHNOLOGY

NIGHTLY BUSINESS REPORT

Economics in Action

Chapter 6

Disc 1, Side 1

Title: *What Is Demand?*

Subject: Differentiating between elastic and inelastic demand

Ask: What is inelastic demand? *(when a change in price is unlikely to significantly affect quantity demanded)*

 Also available in VHS.

VISUAL INSTRUCTION

Point out that, in general, demand for luxuries tends to be elastic.

Answer to Caption:

It gives an indication of how much sales will change in response to price changes.

prices by 10 percent, consumers would have to pay the higher price or drive less. The law of downward-sloping demand indicates that less gasoline would be bought, but chances are that most people would not reduce their demand for gasoline by very much.

Economists, then, are careful when discussing the elasticity of demand. It makes a great deal of difference, for example, whether the elasticity of demand for gasoline refers to the gasoline a particular gas station sells or to gasoline in general.

Total Receipts Test

To understand the importance of elasticity, it is useful to look at the impact of a price change on total receipts. This analysis of the effects of a price change is sometimes called the total receipts test.

How to Determine Total Receipts

Total receipts, or total revenue, are determined by multiplying the price of a product by the quantity sold. By observing changes in a company's total receipts when the price changes, we can test for elasticity.

If demand for a product is elastic, the amount consumers buy will go up sharply when the price is lowered only a little. The increase in sales at the lower price means a large enough increase in total receipts to surpass the total receipts earned at the original price.

If demand is inelastic, a lower price would mean a small increase in the quantity demanded. Increased sales would not be enough, however, for total receipts to rise.

The total receipts test also works the opposite way. If demand is elastic, higher prices will mean lower total receipts because the quantity demanded goes down sharply. The quantity demanded also goes down when demand is inelastic, but by much less than before. The result is that total revenue actually increases when prices are raised on inelastic goods.[1]

Three Results

The relationship between changing prices and total receipts or revenues is summarized in **Figure 4.3**. In each of the demand curves, the impact on total revenues of a decrease in price from $3 to $2 is shown.

The demand curve in Graph **A** is elastic. When the price drops by $1 per unit, the increase in the quantity demanded is large enough to raise total revenues from $6 to $8.

The demand curve in Graph **B** is inelastic. In this case, when the price drops by $1, the increase in the quantity demanded is not enough to prevent revenues from falling below $6. The demand curve in Graph **C** is called **unit elastic** because total revenues neither increase nor decrease when the price changes.

The three changes noted in the graphs are recorded in the table, which shows that the key to elasticity is the way that revenues and prices change. If revenues and prices move in opposite directions, demand is elastic. If they move in the same direction, demand is inelastic. If there is no change in revenue, demand is unit elastic.

Even though all the price changes illustrated are decreases, the results would be the same if prices had gone up instead of down. If the price rises from $2 to $3 in Graph **A,** for example, receipts fall from $8 to $6. Prices and revenues still move in opposite directions as shown in the table. The results of the summary table are also valid for the demand curves in Graphs **B** and **C**.

Total Receipts Illustrated

Observe the demand for sugar, as shown in the demand schedule and graph in **Figure 4.4**. Between 60 and 70 cents per pound, the demand for sugar is elastic. When the price falls from 70 cents to 60 cents, total receipts rise. When the price increases from 60 cents to 70 cents, total receipts go down. Prices and revenues thus move in opposite directions, so the demand curve is elastic in this region.

Between the prices of 40 to 50 cents per pound, however, the demand is inelastic. If the price is lowered within this span, the total receipts also would be lower. Receipts decrease because consumers are not responsive to changes in price below a certain level. If the price is increased from 40 cents to 50 cents, the total receipts would increase. Therefore, the key to the inelastic demand curve is that changes in price and changes in revenue are in the same direction.

Elasticity, then, is something that reveals how price changes affect revenues. Whether the demand for a product is elastic, inelastic, or unit elastic depends on

Figure 4.4
Elasticity of Demand for Granulated Sugar

A. Demand Schedule

Price per Pound	Number of Pounds Demanded	Total Receipts
$ .80	1,250	$1,000
.70	1,500	1,050
.60	2,000	1,200
.50	2,500	1,250
.40	3,000	1,200
.30	4,000	1,200
.20	5,000	1,000
.10	6,000	600

B. Demand Curve

The elasticity of demand changes as prices change. At any price between $.80/lb and $.50/lb, demand is elastic because total receipts go up as prices go down. The revenue is unchanged between $.40 and $.30, which means that demand is unit elastic. When the price drops below $.30/lb, demand is inelastic because a drop in price causes a drop in revenue. **Which price will maximize total receipts?**

the price range and the product being considered. The total receipts test will determine the proper classification of the product.

Elasticity and Pricing Policies

An understanding of elasticity helps businesses determine pricing policies that can be used to increase revenues. Physicians, for example, normally have an inelastic demand for their services. To raise their revenues, they simply raise their prices. On the other hand, the owner of a neighborhood gas station has an elastic demand for products. To increase revenues,

prices must be lowered. If the owner raised prices, customers would go to other stations, and the gas station's total revenues would fall.2

Analysis of demand elasticity has also helped telephone companies. The demand for local telephone services tends to be inelastic. As a result, the phone rates for local phone services have risen over the years. Demand for long-distance services, however, tends to be elastic. Phone companies tend to lower long-distance rates to increase the total revenue collected from consumers.

It may seem paradoxical, but the telephone industry has discovered that it can increase the amount of

Checking Understanding

1. How do economists use the total receipts test to determine whether the demand for a product is elastic or inelastic?
2. Why is it important for businesses to understand elasticity?

Applying Economic Concepts

 Role of Government The federal government regulates the price of telephone services because telephone companies have monopolies in each market. Without regulation, the companies could charge whatever they pleased.

CHAPTER 4: *Demand* **95**

Independent Practice

Guided Reading Assign Guided Reading Activity for Section 3. **LEP**

L2 **Writing** Have students imagine they are advisers to a legislative panel charged with developing a program to raise revenue on the sales of certain goods and services. Ask students to write reports for the panel, explaining—with examples—why demand elasticity plays a role in its task. Reports should also offer reasoned suggestions of products that might be taxed. Call on volunteers to read their reports to the class.

VISUAL INSTRUCTION

Point out that the total receipts test described on page 94 can be used to estimate elasticity between any two of the prices listed on the schedule.

Answer to Caption:
$.50

ANSWERS

1. If total receipts go up as price goes down, or go down as price goes up, demand is elastic. If total receipts go down as price goes down, or go up as price goes up, demand is inelastic.
2. It helps businesses determine pricing policies that can be used to increase revenues.

📂 **Math Practice** Assign Math Practice for Economics 9.

📂 **Performance Assessment** Assign Performance Assessment Activity 9.

INTERACTIVE ECONOMICS!

💿 **CD-ROM Demand**

Have students study the "Advanced Topics Menu" of Lesson 3, which focuses on determinants of demand elasticity. After clicking on the information provided, students should list the underlying determinants of elasticity on note cards. Have students quiz each other with their cards.

💾 *Supplied in both CD-ROM and diskette formats.*

ASSESS

Check for Understanding

Assign Section 3 Review as homework or an in-class activity.

VISUAL INSTRUCTION

Ask students to discuss which of the three determinants they think has the most impact on demand elasticity and why.

Answer to Caption:

Elastic, because it is a luxury whose purchase can be delayed, other luxuries are available, and it uses a large portion of income.

Demand Elasticity *The elasticity of demand for a product varies according to needs, substitutes, and amount of income for the purchase.* **Do you think the demand for a boat is elastic or inelastic? Why?**

revenue collected from consumers by lowering long-distance rates and raising local rates. Both pricing policies were predicted by examining the elasticity of demand for the services.

An understanding of demand elasticity also explains why the government taxes products with relatively inelastic demands. High taxes often are placed on utility services, tobacco, and alcoholic beverages because the demand for these products is relatively inelastic. People will pay almost any price, within limits, for these goods. A moderate tax on cigarettes, for example, has only a minor impact on the amount sold even though the price goes up. ✅

Determinants of Demand Elasticity

We can estimate the elasticity of demand for a product by considering three factors: the urgency of need, the availability of adequate substitutes, and the amount of income required to buy the item.

Can the Purchase Be Delayed?

A consumer's need for a product is sometimes urgent and cannot be put off. One example is the case

of insulin. If a diabetic needs insulin, an increase in its price is not likely to make him or her put off buying the drug. The demand for tobacco also tends to be inelastic because the product is addictive.[1]

In a less extreme case, such as the need for a tank of gasoline, the consumer might be able to wait a day or two. A limit still exists on the ability to go without, however. In such a case, the demand for the product is likely to be inelastic, so an increase in price causes only a small reduction in the amount bought.

A 50 percent drop in the price of insulin or gasoline probably would not cause a sustained increase in the amount bought. Sales may initially rise because of the lower price, but limits exist as to stockpiling these goods. A drop in the price of insulin probably would not cause the consumer to actually use more. A drop in the price of gasoline probably would have more of an impact on purchases in the long run than in the short run.

If the product were tomatoes or T-bone steaks instead of insulin or gasoline, people might react differently to price changes. If their prices increased, consumers could delay buying either of these items without suffering any great inconvenience. Consumers might buy much more if the price dropped significantly.

The ability to postpone the purchase of a product, then, is one of the determinants of elasticity. If the

---

Extending the Content

Elasticity Elasticity is a measure of responsiveness. Have students think of elasticity in terms of the percentage change in the dependent variable (quantity) caused by a given percentage change in the independent variable (price). Thinking about elasticity in this way will make the concept easier for students to understand when they get to supply elasticity in the next chapter.

Lesson 3 of Interactive Economics! to learn more about "Demand Elasticity."

Figure 4.5
Estimating the Elasticity of Demand

Determinants of Elasticity Yes (elastic) No (inelastic)	ECONOMIC PRODUCTS							
	Tomatoes	T-bone Steak	Table Salt	Gasoline from a Particular Station	Gasoline in General	Services of Medical Doctors	Insulin	Butter
Can Purchase Be Delayed?	yes	yes	no	yes	no	no	no	yes
Are There Adequate Substitutes?	yes	yes	no	yes	no	no	no	yes
Does Purchase Use A Large Portion Of Income?	no	no	no	yes	yes	yes	no	no
Type Of Elasticity	Elastic	Elastic	Inelastic	Elastic	Inelastic	Inelastic	Inelastic	Elastic

The elasticity of demand can usually be estimated by examining the answers to three key questions. All three answers do not have to be the same in order to determine elasticity, and in some cases the answer to a single question is so important that it alone might dominate the answers to the other two. **If you applied the three questions to a college education, what would be the elasticity of demand for higher education?**

Use the **Chapter Challenger Interactive Review Software** to review Section 3.

MEETING LESSON OBJECTIVES

Each objective below is tested by the questions on page 98 that follow it in parentheses.

1. **Analyze** the elasticity of demand for a product. **(1, 2, 5)**

2. **Explain** the three determinants of demand elasticity. **(3, 4, 5)**

Evaluate

 Assign the Section 3 Quiz in the TCR or use the *Economics: Principles and Practices* Testmaker to create a customized quiz. Spanish Section Quizzes also are available in the Spanish Resources Binder.

 VISUAL INSTRUCTION

Have students apply the three determinants of demand elasticity to recent purchases.

Answer to Caption:

Elastic, because it is a purchase that can be delayed; substitutes, such as training for a trade, are available; and it would use a large portion of income.

purchase can be delayed, the demand for the product tends to be elastic. If it cannot be delayed, the demand tends to be inelastic.

Are Adequate Substitutes Available?

If adequate substitutes are available, consumers can switch back and forth between a product and its substitute to take advantage of the best price. If the price of steaks and butter goes up, buyers can switch to chicken and margarine. With enough substitutes, even small changes in the price of a product will cause people to switch. When this happens, the quantity sold at a single store may change a great deal, significantly impacting the store's total receipts.

If a product has many substitutes, the demand for it tends to be elastic. The fewer substitutes available for a product, the more inelastic the demand. **2**

Does the Purchase Use a Large Portion of Income?

The third determinant is the amount of income required to make the purchase. The demand for table

 QUICK CHECK

Checking Understanding

1. Why is the demand for insulin inelastic?
2. Why is the demand for a product with many substitutes elastic?

Applying Economic Concepts

 Taxation A key part of President Clinton's 1993 health-care reform plan was a hefty tax on cigarettes. The administration contended that because smokers had higher health-care costs, they should pay more to fund national insurance.

CHAPTER 4: *Demand* **97**

QUICK CHECK

ANSWERS

1. lack of adequate substitutes for insulin

2. because consumers can switch among the various substitutes

Extending the Content

Cross Elasticity Demand elasticity measures the extent to which changes in price of a product affect the quantity demanded of that product. Economists are also interested in *cross elasticity*—how price changes for one product affect the quantity demanded of another product. In cross elasticity between substitutes, price and demand move the same way. For example, a rise in the price of butter leads to a rise in the quantity demanded of margarine. With cross elasticity between complements, however, price and demand move in opposite directions. A rise in the price of cameras, for instance, will result in a fall in the demand for film.

salt tends to be inelastic because a container usually costs less than a dollar and lasts several months. An increase in price is not likely to be noticed by the buyer or to affect the amount bought.

The purchase of a new car, however, is another matter. Because the average price of a new car is likely to be around $18,000, even a small increase can amount to several hundred extra dollars. People tend to be more sensitive to price increases or decreases on expensive items than on less expensive ones. When the products require a large portion of income, the demand tends to be elastic. When they require a small portion of income, the demand tends to be inelastic.

The three major determinants of demand elasticity are summarized in Figure 4.5. Some products, such as table salt, are easy to classify. Unless a salt-free diet is required for medical reasons, the consumption of salt is something that generally is not postponed. Salt is a product for which there are few adequate substitutes, and it requires only a small portion of income. Therefore, the demand for salt is inelastic.

Other cases are not as clear-cut. The demand for the services of doctors tends to be inelastic even though such services require a large portion of income. The lack of adequate substitutes and the reluctance to put off seeing a doctor when one is sick make the demand for such services inelastic. In the case of other products such as steak, tomatoes, and butter, the amount of

"Scalpel . . ."

Elasticity *If doctors' fees dropped significantly, there would be only a small change in quantity demanded.* **Why is this true?**

income required to purchase them probably is less important than the availability of substitutes and the ability to put off buying these products.

SECTION 3 REVIEW

Reviewing Terms and Facts

1. **Define** demand elasticity, elastic, inelastic, unit elastic.
2. **Explain** how total receipts are determined.
3. **List** the three determinants of demand elasticity.

Critical Thinking

4. **Making Generalizations** Determine your demand elasticity for air travel during holidays by answering these three questions: Can the purchase of a round-trip ticket be delayed? Are adequate substitutes available for air travel? Does the purchase consume a large portion of your income? Write a summary statement explaining your demand elasticity for air travel during holidays.

Applying Economic Concepts

5. **Demand Elasticity** Why are people willing to pay more for a movie when it first comes out, and why are movie theaters willing to lower the prices after the movie has been out for awhile? Analyze the three determinants of demand elasticity for new movies, as well as movies that have been out for several months, to see if theaters are maximizing their revenues in each case.

Answers to SECTION 3 REVIEW

1. All vocabulary words are defined in the Glossary.

2. by multiplying the price of the product by the quantity sold

3. Can the purchase be delayed? Are adequate substitutes available? Does the purchase use a large portion of income?

4. Answers may vary. Students may note that the purchase can be delayed if they are willing to take their trip at another time. Distance to be traveled and time available will determine whether students consider substitutes. The purchase consumes a large portion of income.

5. because it is a new product; to attract people who were unwilling to buy at the higher price; Most students will note that demand for new movies tends to be inelastic, so higher prices will increase revenues. Demand for older movies, however, is more elastic, and lower prices probably will increase revenues.

MULTIMEDIA
ACTIVITIES

ECONOMICS IN ACTION

What Is Demand?

Setting Up the Video

With your classmates, view "What Is Demand?" on the videodisc *Economics in Action*. The video focuses on the effect of prices on the demand for an item. Using the airline industry as an example of elastic demand, the video describes how lowering air fares increased the quantity of air travel demanded. It also portrays medical care as an inelastic demand in which price changes do not significantly affect quantity demanded.

Chapter 6
Disc 1, Side 1

View the video by scanning the bar code or by entering the chapter number on your keypad and pressing Search. *(Also available in VHS format.)*

Hands-On Activity

Recognize the elastic and inelastic goods and services in your own life. Take an imaginary trip to a supermarket with this shopping list: frozen pizza, milk, soda, sugar, salt, candy, bread, laundry detergent, lobster, and breakfast cereal.Which items are subject to elastic demand and which are subject to inelastic demand? Provide explanations for each of your answers.

INTERACTIVE ECONOMICS!

Demand

Introduction

Lesson 3 of *Interactive Economics!* describes the concept of demand, which summarizes people's willingness, ability, and desire to purchase products in the market.

Demand is also a hypothetical concept in the sense that it summarizes the quantities people are willing to purchase over a wide range of prices that could possibly occur in the market.

Demand can be shown as a schedule or as a downward-sloping demand curve. Both presentations tell us that people are willing to purchase more at lower prices and less at higher prices.

Using the Software

1. Select "Demand" from the Main Menu.
2. Read the introduction, then click on "Continue With the Lesson."
3. Click on "A Change in Demand" and review the lesson. Repeat this process for subsequent lessons.
4. Then click on "Economics Lab." Complete the lab by clicking and dragging the appropriate titles and characteristics to their proper locations on each graph.
5. Print your completed lab.

99

TEACHER NOTES

_____

_____

_____

_____

_____

_____

_____

GLENCOE
TECHNOLOGY

VIDEODISC
MindJogger Videoquiz

Use MindJogger to review
the Chapter 4 content.

Chapter 4
Disc 1, Side A

Also available in VHS.

Answers

Reviewing Key Terms

1. E
2. B (also C)
3. D (also C)
4. G
5. A (also D, E, F, G)
6. B (possibly C)
7. F

Reviewing the Facts

1. the desire for an economic product coupled with the ability and willingness to pay for it

2. Schedule: listing showing the quantities demanded at all prices that prevail in the market. Curve: curve on a graph that represents the amount demanded at each and every price. They both illustrate information about demand.

3. Because of diminishing marginal utility, consumers buy less at high prices and more at low prices.

4. Change in quantity demanded means that consumers buy a different quantity of a product if that product's price changes. Change in demand means that consumers have changed their minds about the amount they would buy at each and every price.

100

Reviewing Key Terms

Match each word or phrase below with the correct illustration. Some will have more than one answer.

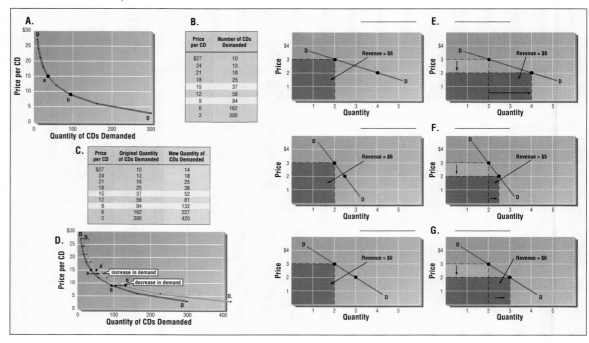

1. elastic demand
2. demand schedule
3. change in demand
4. unit elastic
5. demand curve
6. schedule showing change in quantity demanded
7. inelastic demand

Reviewing the Facts

SECTION 1 (*pages 82–84*)
1. **Explain** what demand means in economics.
2. **Describe** a demand schedule and a demand curve. How are they alike?
3. **Explain** why the demand curve is downward-sloping.

SECTION 2 (*pages 86–90*)
4. **Describe** the difference between a change in quantity demanded and a change in demand.
5. **Identify** the three factors that can cause a change in the level of demand.
6. **Explain** how the principle of diminishing marginal utility is related to the downward-sloping demand curve.

SECTION 3 (*pages 92–98*)
7. **Describe** the difference between elastic demand and inelastic demand.
8. **Explain** how the total receipts test can be used to determine demand elasticity.
9. **List** the three determinants of demand elasticity and describe their effects on the demand curve.

5. change in consumer income, consumer tastes, prices of related products

6. Because marginal utility diminishes with each successive purchase of a product, lower prices are necessary to encourage consumers to make more purchases. Consumers buy less at high prices and more at low prices—the principle illustrated by the downward slope of the demand curve.

7. elastic demand: when a relatively small change in price causes a relatively large change in quantity demanded; inelastic demand: given change in price causes a relatively smaller change in quantity demanded

8. by examining the way total receipts change when price changes

9. Can the purchase be delayed? If purchase can be delayed, demand tends to be elastic; if it cannot be delayed, demand tends to be inelastic. Are ade-

Critical Thinking

1. **Making Generalizations** Do you think the Law of Demand accurately reflects most people's behavior regarding certain purchases? Explain.
2. **Analyzing Information** List several examples of products that are so important that their use cannot be delayed or postponed. What type of demand elasticity do these products have?

Applying Economic Concepts

1. **Demand** How do you think the demand for pizza would be affected by (1) an increase in everyone's pay; (2) an increase in the cost of gasoline; and (3) a decrease in the price of hamburgers? Explain your answers.
2. **Demand Elasticity** How would you, as a business owner, be likely to change the price of your product if you knew the demand elasticity of that product?

Reinforcing Skills

DETERMINING CAUSE AND EFFECT

For each statement below, write a sentence that is either a cause or an effect of the action in the statement.
1. *Cause:* The price of football tickets rises.
   Effect:
2. *Cause:*
   Effect: A record number of customers shopped at Sweater City today.
3. *Cause:* The price of gold drops.
   Effect/Cause:
   Effect:

Individual Activity

List five items you buy regularly. Use the determinants of demand elasticity in **Figure 4.5** on page 97 to classify each item and determine its overall elasticity. If the price of each item increased, what would happen to the total amount of money you would spend on each? What would happen to the amount spent if the price of each item decreased? Use the total receipts test to check your conclusions.

Cooperative Learning Activity

Working in teams of four, have each team interview four students in the school, asking the following questions: (a) What three purchases have you made recently? (b) Do any of these purchases represent a recent change in your buying habits? (c) Was the change caused by a change in income, a change in preference, or a change in the price of substitutes or complements?

After completing the interviews, each team should summarize the information it obtained. Categorize the purchases in which there was a change in demand according to the three reasons listed above. Each team should report its findings.

Technology Activity

Using a Word Processor

In the **Journal Writing** activity on page 81, you were asked to list your expenditures for one week, separating the items into goods and services. Using a word processor, place this information—along with a description of the elasticity of the goods and services you purchased—into a table.
1. Click the "table" icon on your word processor.
2. Click open three columns across, then drag the cursor down as many rows as you have items.
3. When your table appears, type in "Goods and Services" in the top of column 1, "Elastic or Inelastic?" in the top of column 2, and "Reason" in the top of column 3.
4. Type in your list of expenditures in column 1, noting whether each is a good or a service.
5. Complete the rest of the chart by labeling each good and service as either elastic or inelastic. Then describe the reason you chose that label for each item.
6. Print out your completed chart.

Applying Economic Concepts

1. (1) The demand for pizza would increase, because consumers would have more income to spend on all products. (2) The demand for pizza would decrease, because consumers would have less income to spend on all products. (3) The demand for pizza may decrease, because the price of a substitute—hamburgers—has decreased.

2. If demand was elastic, business owners might lower price slightly to generate increase in demand. If demand was inelastic, business owners might leave price at its present level or even raise it slightly.

Reinforcing Skills

1. Answers may vary. Possible response: As a result, demand for tickets falls.

2. Answers may vary. Possible response: The managers of Sweater City cut prices by 50 percent.

3. Answers may vary. Possible response: This leads to a fall in the price of jewelry. As a consequence, demand for jewelry rises.

? BONUS TEST QUESTION

What effect will the following situations have on total receipts?
1. Price falls and demand is elastic. *(receipts rise)*
2. Price rises and demand is inelastic. *(receipts rise)*
3. Price rises and demand is unit elastic. *(no effect)*
4. Price rises and demand is elastic. *(receipts fall)*
5. Price falls and demand is inelastic. *(receipts fall)*

---

quate substitutes available? If substitutes are available, demand tends to be elastic; if few are available, demand tends to be inelastic. Does the purchase use a large portion of income? If a large portion of income is used, demand tends to be elastic; if only a small portion is used, demand tends to be inelastic.

Critical Thinking

1. Answers will vary, but most students will note that whenever prices fall, consumers tend to demand more of a product.

2. Products will vary, but might include drugs such as insulin, dietary requirements such as salt, and medical services. Demand for these will tend to be inelastic because their purchase cannot be delayed and few, if any, adequate substitutes exist.

CHAPTER ORGANIZER

Daily Objectives	Reproducible Resources	Multimedia Resources
Section 1 **What Is Supply?** 1. **Understand** the meaning and concept of supply. 2. **Explain** the difference between the supply schedule and the supply curve. 3. **Explain** what is meant by a change in quantity supplied. 4. **Specify** the reasons for a change in supply.	Reproducible Lesson Plan 5-1 Guided Reading Activity 5-1 Cooperative Learning Activity 11 Math Practice for Economics 10 Primary and Secondary Source Reading 7 Performance Assessment Activity 10 Reinforcing Economic Skills 5 Section Quiz 5-1*	Focus Activity Transparency 30 Vocabulary PuzzleMaker Chapter Challenger Interactive Review Software Testmaker MindJogger Videoquiz NBR's Economics in Action Video Program Interactive Economics!
Section 2 **The Theory of Production** 1. **Explain** the theory of production. 2. **Understand** the importance of marginal product and its application to economics. 3. **Describe** the three stages of production and how they relate to the concept of diminishing returns.	Reproducible Lesson Plan 5-2 Guided Reading Activity 5-2 Section Quiz 5-2*	Focus Activity Transparency 31 Economic Concepts Transparency 3* Vocabulary PuzzleMaker Chapter Challenger Interactive Review Software Testmaker NBR's Economics in Action Video Program Interactive Economics!
Section 3 **Supply and the Role of Cost** 1. **Identify** the relationship between productivity and cost. 2. **Define** four key measures of cost. 3. **Identify** two key measures of revenue.	Reproducible Lesson Plan 5-3 Guided Reading Activity 5-3 Section Quiz 5-3*	Focus Activity Transparency 32 Vocabulary PuzzleMaker Chapter Challenger Interactive Review Software Testmaker NBR's Economics in Action Video Program Interactive Economics!
Chapter Review and Evaluation	Enrichment Activity 5 Reteaching Activity 5* Economic Vocabulary Activity 5* Chapter 5 Test, Forms A and B	Chapter Digests Audiocassette Activities and Tests* Testmaker MindJogger Videoquiz

*Also available in Spanish

 Blackline Master   Transparency   CD-ROM   Software   Videodisc   Audiocassette

00:00 **OUT OF TIME?** Assign the Chapter 5 Digest Audiocassette and the corresponding Chapter Digest activities and tests.

National Council on Economic Education

THE **Economics** America AND **Economics** International PROGRAMS

VOLUNTARY NATIONAL CONTENT STANDARDS IN ECONOMICS
Emphasized in Chapter 5

Content Standard 2 *Students will understand that:*
Effective decision making requires comparing the additional costs of alternatives with the additional benefits. Most choices involve doing a little more or a little less of something; few choices are all-or-nothing decisions.

Content Standard 8 *Students will understand that:*
Prices send signals and provide incentives to buyers and sellers. When supply or demand changes, market prices adjust, affecting incentives.

Economics America *Resources Available From NCEE*

- *Capstone: The Nation's High School Economics Course*
- *Economics and the Environment*
- *Focus: High School Economics*
- *MCG: Economics and Entrepreneurship*
- *Personal Decision Making: Focus on Economics*

To order these materials, or to contact your state Council on Economic Education about workshops and programs, call 1-800-338-1192 or visit http://www.nationalcouncil.org.

PERFORMANCE ASSESSMENT

The following chapter projects may be assigned at the beginning of the chapter and used for performance assessment.

Multicultural Heritage Many immigrants who came to the United States wanted to improve their economic condition. From this perspective, these immigrants became a part of the productive process that supplies goods and services. Have students select an immigrant group and conduct historical research about the group as a part of the labor force. Ask students to write newspaper articles about the role of their selected immigrant group in the productive process. Suggest that, in their articles, students apply terms introduced in Chapter 5, such as *productivity, cost of inputs, variable costs,* and *marginal costs.* Students might combine their articles into a "special edition" of an economics newspaper dealing with the role of immigrants in supplying goods and services in the American economy.

Cooperative Learning Organize students into groups of four and secretly assign each group a concept developed in Chapter 5. Have the groups brainstorm ideas for a skit, scenario, or charade that illustrates their assigned concept. Then have groups use these ideas to develop a script. Call on groups to perform their skits, scenarios, or charades for the class. Have class members attempt to identify the concept being portrayed.

ADDITIONAL RESOURCES

Readings for the Teacher

Keenan, Diane, and Mark H. Maier. *Economics Live! Learning Economics the Collaborative Way.* 1994. Reproducible lessons designed to acompany general economics courses. Incorporates cooperative learning techniques.

Supply and Demand. Gainesville, FL: Center for Economic Education, University of Florida, 1996. Resource guide providing ideas on how to teach this basic principle of the free market system.

Multimedia

Economics U$A: The Firm/Supply & Demand. The Annenberg/CPB Collection, 19 Gregory Drive, South Burlington, VT 05403. Color video, 60 mins. Second 30-minute program on video discusses the dynamics of supply and demand.

Supply and Demand. Greenhouse Films/Social Studies School Service, 10200 Jefferson Boulevard, P.O. Box 802, Culver City, CA 90232-0802. Color video, 15 mins. Real-life scenarios are used to explain basic economic forces of supply and demand.

The Illustrious Yet Elusive World of Microeconomics. Cerebellum, 1995. Video, 113 mins. The Standard Deviants mix comedy and concepts to help students master supply and demand.

Chapter Overview

Chapter 5, which deals with the supply side of the market, is a natural continuation of the preceding chapter on demand. **Section 1** focuses on the nature of supply. **Section 2** introduces the theory of production, which explains how output varies when inputs change. **Section 3** explains the role of costs in determining productivity, and provides an analysis of total and marginal revenues.

GLENCOE
TECHNOLOGY

VIDEODISC
MindJogger Videoquiz

Use MindJogger to preview the Chapter 5 content.

Chapter 5
Disc 1, Side B

Also available in VHS.

inter**NET**
CONNECTION

Resources for Chapter 5 on the World Wide Web*

National Council on Economic Education
http://www.nationalcouncil.org/

USA Today Money
http://www.usatoday.com/money/mfront.htm

CNN Financial Newss
http://www.cnnfn.com

*Sites subject to change.

VISUAL INSTRUCTION

Point out that British economist Alfred Marshall described economics as "an inquiry into the balancing of the forces of demand and supply."

The higher the price of CDs, the more will be offered for sale.

Extra Credit Project

Have students monitor television newscasts and newspapers to find three stories that discuss supply. Have students write a brief explanation of how the situation in each story might affect price and supply.

CHAPTER 5

Supply

SECTION 1
What Is Supply?

SECTION 2
The Theory of Production

SECTION 3
Supply and the Role of Cost

CHAPTER PREVIEW

People to Know

- Dave Thomas
- Market Researcher

Applying Economic Concepts to Your Life

Law of Supply How many hours do you spend studying every night? How many hours would you study if you were paid $1 an hour? $10 an hour? If you would study more for a higher price, you are following the *Law of Supply*, which states that the quantity supplied varies directly with its price.

> ### Journal Writing
>
> For one week, record every service or job you perform for someone else. Include any part-time jobs as well as errands, housekeeping chores, and baby-sitting, if pertinent. Organize the services and the amount of time spent on each into two columns: Paid Work and Unpaid Work.

Connecting to Past Learning

Call on volunteers to describe the nature of demand. *(Demand is concerned with how prices affect consumers' spending behavior. Essentially, consumers will demand more at low prices and less at high prices.)* Then point out that supply is almost the mirror image of demand. It describes, in effect, the other "half" of the market, which provides products to those who demand them.

Applying Economics

Ask students if they play a role as producers in the market. As guidance, remind students that producers provide services as well as goods. Then ask if any students have part-time jobs or do baby-sitting or household chores for an allowance. Point out that by taking part in these activities, they are acting as producers supplying an economic product—their labor—to buyers in the marketplace.

PERFORMANCE ASSESSMENT

Refer to page **102B** for a Performance Assessment activity for this chapter. Also see the **Performance Assessment Activities** booklet for additional suggestions.

Economic Portfolio

As students make their **Journal Writing** entries, suggest that they consider their attitudes toward working for pay and working without pay. Have students describe any difference in attitude they may have toward unpaid work. Then have them write a paragraph explaining why students should get paid for the hours they spend studying and going to school.

Key to Ability Levels — Teaching strategies have been coded for varying learning styles and abilities:

L1 - Basic (activities for all students)   **L2 - Average** (activities for average to above-average students)
L3 - Challenging (activities for above-average students)   **LEP - Limited English Proficiency**

103

FOCUS

Section Objectives

1. Understand the meaning and concept of supply.

2. Explain the difference between the supply schedule and the supply curve.

3. Explain what is meant by a change in quantity supplied.

4. Specify the reasons for a change in supply.

Bellringer

 Prior to taking roll at the beginning of the class period, display Focus Activity Transparency 30.

Motivational Activity

Discuss students' responses to the activity sheet that accompanies Transparency 30.

Preteaching Vocabulary

Call on volunteers to tell what they think each key term means. Have students check their suggestions by finding the terms in the Glossary. **LEP**

Use the **Vocabulary PuzzleMaker** to create crossword and word search puzzles.

⊙ VISUAL INSTRUCTION

Ask: Why might the various models be priced differently? (*Cost of producing each model may be different.*)

Answer to Caption:

Generally, the higher the price, the greater the quantity offered for sale.

Section Preview

Objectives

After studying this section, you will be able to:

1. **Understand** the meaning and concept of supply.

2. **Explain** the difference between the supply schedule and the supply curve.

3. **Explain** what is meant by a change in quantity supplied.

4. **Specify** the reasons for a change in supply.

Key Terms

supply, supply schedule, supply curve, Law of Supply, quantity supplied, change in quantity supplied, change in supply, subsidy, supply elasticity

Applying Economic Concepts

Supply If someone asks you to supply baby-sitting or yard work services after school, what is the first thing that comes to mind? If you are like most people, the answer is pay—and the higher the pay, the more work you are willing to supply. *Supply* is the amount of production—in this case, your efforts—provided over a wide range of prices.

When economists consider demand, they are interested in people's willingness and ability to purchase a product over a wide range of prices. In the case of supply, economists are concerned with people's ability and willingness to offer products for sale over a wide range of prices. **1**

An Introduction to Supply

Economists are concerned with the market as a whole. They want to know how much of a certain product sellers will supply at each and every possible market price. **Supply**, then, may be defined as a schedule of quantities that would be offered for sale at all possible prices that could prevail in the market. The supply of television sets, for example, is the number of sets that manufacturers will likely produce if the prevailing market is $700, $500, $300, or any other price.

Everyone who offers an economic product for sale is a supplier. When you look for a job, you offer your services for sale. Your economic product is your labor, and you would probably be willing to supply more labor for a high wage than you would for a low one. ☑

All suppliers of economic products must make a similar decision. Each supplier must decide how much to offer for sale at various prices—a decision made according to what is best for the individual

Supply *Suppliers offer different models of electronic equipment at various prices.* **How does the price of a product affect the quantity offered for sale?**

seller. What is best depends, in turn, upon the cost of producing the goods or services. Still, it is reasonable to predict that the higher the price, the greater the quantity the seller will offer for sale.

Classroom Resources for SECTION 1

- 🗂 Reproducible Lesson Plan 5-1
- 🗂 Guided Reading Activity 5-1
- 🗂 Cooperative Learning Activity 11
- 🗂 Math Practice for Economics 10
- 🗂 Primary and Secondary Source Reading 7
- 🗂 Performance Assessment Activity 10
- 🗂 Reinforcing Economic Skill 5
- 🗂 Section Quiz 5-1
- 🗂 Spanish Section Quiz 5-1

- 🖋 Focus Activity Transparency 30
- ⊙ NBR's Economics in Action Video Program
- ⊡ Testmaker
- ⊡ Vocabulary PuzzleMaker
- ⊡ Chapter Challenger Interactive Review Software
- ⊙ Interactive Economics!
- ⊙ MindJogger Videoquiz

Lesson 4 of Interactive Economics! to learn more about "Supply Schedules and Curves."

CHAPTER 5
SECTION 1

Figure 5.1
The Supply of T-Shirts

A. Supply Schedule

Price per T-Shirt	Quantity of T-Shirts Supplied
$30	350
27	330
24	300
21	240
18	190
15	140
12	70
9	20
6	0

B. Supply Curve (SS)

The supply schedule is a listing that shows the quantity supplied at each and every price. The supply curve shows the same information in the form of a graph. The figure shows that the supply curve is upward sloping, which means that less will be supplied at lower prices, and more at higher prices. **How does the Law of Supply differ from the Law of Demand?**

Supply and the Supply Schedule

Suppose you are a Student Council officer whose job is to obtain T-shirts for every senior in your class. Because you will need so many shirts, you will want to get the best possible price. To do this, you could make inquiries, meet with manufacturers, and then ask for bids.

You would discover that when you offer a low price, some suppliers would not be interested in your business at all, and others would offer only small quantities. At a price of $9 a shirt, for example, suppliers might offer only 20 shirts. If you offered a higher price, such as $21 a shirt, they might be willing to supply 240 shirts.

After you gather all the data, you can construct a **supply schedule** like the one in panel **A** of **Figure 5.1**. The supply schedule tells the quantities offered at each and every possible market price.

Supply Curve

The data presented in the supply schedule also can be shown graphically. The **supply curve**, labeled **SS** in **Figure 5.1**, slopes upward and to the right to reflect the tendency of suppliers to offer greater quantities for sale at higher prices. **2**

The supply curve is the opposite of the demand curve. If you hold **Figure 5.1** in front of a mirror, you

Checking Understanding	**Applying Economic Concepts**
1. How does supply differ from demand? 2. Why does the supply curve slope upward and to the right?	**Role of Government** In our modified market economy, the federal government guarantees most workers a minimum wage of $5.15 per hour.

Guided Practice

L2 Illustrating Ideas Draw a two-column table on the board with *Pay Per Hour* and *Students Willing to Work* as column headings. In the *Pay* column, list the figures $1 through $10. Next, state that you need help to clean and rearrange the classroom. Ask who would be interested in the job at a wage of $1 an hour. Record the number and repeat the process for all other hourly rates. Tell students they have provided an example of the Law of Supply. Have students use the data in the chart to construct a graph similar to Figure 5.1. **LEP**

Cooperative Learning
Assign Cooperative Learning Activity 11.

 VISUAL INSTRUCTION

Point out that a change in the quantity supplied is represented as a movement along the curve.

Answer to Caption:

For the Law of Supply, quantity varies directly with the price, not inversely as with the Law of Demand.

ANSWERS

1. supply: ability and willingness to offer products for sale over a wide range of prices; demand: ability and willingness to purchase products over a wide range of prices

2. to reflect the tendency of suppliers to offer greater quantities for sale at higher prices

---

Meeting Special Needs

Language Delayed One of the most common problems of students with language difficulties is an inability to ask questions of their teachers. Form small groups to practice developing questions about information in Section 1. Reward groups for the following achievements: producing the most questions and producing the most varied questions.

GLENCOE
TECHNOLOGY

NIGHTLY BUSINESS REPORT

Economics in Action

Chapter 8

Disc 1, Side 1

Title: *What Is Supply?*

Ask: What is the Law of Supply? *(The higher the price, the more producers will offer for sale.)*

  Also available in VHS.

L2 *Cause and Effect* Ask students to identify what happens—and why—to the supply curve for CDs in the following situations:

1. Cost of materials used to make CDs falls. *(Shifts to right—supply increases because price of inputs falls.)*

2. New training methods improve worker efficiency. *(Shifts to right—supply increases due to increased productivity.)*

3. Innovative process for pressing CDs introduced. *(Shifts to right—supply increases because new technology lowers production costs.)*

4. Leading CD producer goes out of business. *(Shifts to left—supply decreased by supplier leaving the market.)*

Independent Practice

☞ **Guided Reading** Assign Guided Reading Activity for Section 1. **LEP**

☞ **Math Practice** Assign Math Practice for Economics 10.

☞ **Readings** Assign Primary and Secondary Source Reading 7.

106

---

will see what looks like a demand curve. Just as the demand curve showed that greater amounts would be bought at lower prices, the supply curve shows that greater amounts will be offered for sale at higher prices.

Law of Supply

The tendency of suppliers to offer more for sale at high prices than at low prices forms the basis for the **Law of Supply**. The law states that the quantity supplied, or offered for sale, varies directly with its price. In other words, if prices are high, suppliers will offer greater quantities for sale. If prices are low, they will offer smaller quantities for sale. **1**

Change in Quantity Supplied

The amount that producers bring to market at any one price is called the **quantity supplied**. A **change in quantity supplied** is the change in amount offered for sale in response to a change in price.

In **Figure 5.1**, for example, 350 T-shirts are supplied when the price is $30. If the price decreases to $24, 300 T-shirts are supplied. If the price then changes to $21, 240 T-shirts are supplied. These changes illustrate a change in the quantity supplied, which is also represented as a movement *along* the supply curve.

In a competitive economy, producers generally react to changing prices in just this way. While the interaction of supply and demand usually determines the final price for the product, the producer has the freedom to adjust production. If the price falls, the producer may offer less for sale, or even leave the market altogether if the price goes too low. If prices rise, the producer may offer more units for sale to take advantage of the better prices.

Change in Supply

Sometimes producers offer different amounts of products for sale at all possible prices in the market. This is known as a **change in supply**.

The schedule and graph in **Figure 5.2** illustrate a change in supply. The schedule in panel **A** shows an increase in supply—with more T-shirts brought to market at each and every price. At the original price of $21

---

per shirt, 240 shirts were available. After the change in supply, 298 shirts were produced for the same price. The schedule shows a similar increase at every price, resulting in the supply curve shifting to S_1S_1.

For a decrease in supply to occur, less would be offered for sale at each and every price, and the supply curve would shift to the left. Changes in supply, whether increases or decreases, occur for the following reasons.

Cost of Inputs

A change in the cost of inputs could cause a change in supply. In the T-shirt illustration, supply may have increased because of a decline in the cost of such inputs as cotton or ink. If the price of the inputs goes down, producers can produce more T-shirts at each and every price.

An increase in the cost of inputs has the opposite effect. If cotton, ink, and labor costs rose, producers would not be willing to produce as many shirts at each and every price. Instead, they would offer fewer products for sale, and the supply curve would shift to the left.

Productivity

If management motivates its workers to do a better job or if workers are trained to work more efficiently, productivity increases. More T-shirts would be produced during every production period. The supply curve shifts to the right because more shirts are produced at every possible price in the market.

If workers are unmotivated, untrained, or unhappy, productivity decreases. The supply curve shifts to the left because fewer goods are brought to the market at every possible price.

Technology

New technology tends to shift the supply curve to the right. The introduction of a new machine, chemical, or industrial process can affect supply by lowering the cost of production. When production costs go down, the producer is usually willing to produce more goods and services at each and every price in the market. **2**

New technologies do not always work as expected, of course. Equipment might break down or parts

---

$ Free Enterprise Activity $

The productivity of the factors of production can have a major impact on the costs of doing business and, therefore, on the supply of goods and services available to consumers. Invite a local business person to talk to the class about the importance of productivity in his or her business. In a follow-up discussion, ask students to speculate about the effects of changes in productivity on supply.

Lesson 4 of Interactive Economics! to learn more about "A Change in Supply."

Figure 5.2
A Change in the Supply of T-Shirts

A. New Supply Schedule

Price per T-Shirt	Original Number of T-Shirts Supplied	New Number of T-Shirts Supplied
$30	350	430
27	330	406
24	300	370
21	240	298
18	190	238
15	140	178
12	70	94
9	20	34
6	0	0

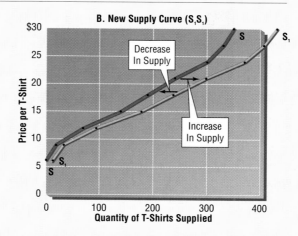

B. New Supply Curve (S,S₁)

A change in supply means that producers are willing to offer a different quantity for sale at each and every price. An increase in supply occurs when the supply curve shifts to the right. A decrease in supply occurs when the supply curve shifts to the left. **How does a change in supply differ from a change in quantity supplied?**

might be difficult to obtain, which would shift the supply curve to the left. These examples are exceptions, however. New technology almost always increases supply.

Number of Sellers

Another factor affecting changes in supply is the number of sellers in the market. Because the supply curve represents the different quantities that *all* producers offer at various prices, supply increases—or shifts to the right—when more suppliers enter the market.

If some suppliers leave the market, fewer products are offered for sale at all possible prices. Supply decreases, and the supply curve shifts to the left.

Taxes and Subsidies

Taxes have the same impact as an increase in the cost of inputs. If the producer's inventory is taxed or fees are paid to receive a license to produce, the cost of production goes up. This causes the supply curve to shift to the left. When production costs go down, supply increases and the supply curve shifts right.

Checking Understanding

1. Why are sellers likely to supply more goods when prices are high?
2. Why does new technology shift the supply curve to the right?

Applying Economic Concepts

 Competition When Dallas-based Southwest Airlines expanded its low-cost, no-frills service nationwide in the 1990s, other airlines scrambled to lower their prices to remain competitive. Consumers benefited from lower prices.

CHAPTER 5: *Supply* **107**

Extending the Content

Changing Supply of Farmland The supply of arable farmland, it would appear, is fairly constant. Over a relatively long period of time, however, the supply of arable land can change because alternative uses for the land are developed. For example, suburban developments, new highways, and shopping centers may encroach upon farmland, thereby decreasing the available amount of arable land.

Subsidies—government payments to individuals, businesses, or other groups to encourage or protect a certain type of economic activity—have the opposite effect of taxes. Subsidies lower the cost of production and encourage producers to stay in the market.

Historically, farmers have received substantial subsidies to support their income. Many farmers would have gone out of business without a supporting subsidy. When the government grants a subsidy, production costs go down. Producers stay in the market, thus increasing supply. When subsidies are repealed, costs go up, producers leave the market, and the supply curve shifts to the left.

Expectations

Expectations, or the anticipation of future events, can affect the supply curve in two ways. If producers think the price of their product is likely to go up, they may withhold some of the supply, causing the market supply to decrease. The supply curve shifts to the left.

On the other hand, producers may expect lower prices for their output in the future. In this situation, they will try to produce and sell as much as possible right away. The supply curve shifts to the right.

Government Regulations

Government regulations also cause a change in supply. When the government mandates new auto safety features such as stronger bumpers, air bags, and emission controls, cars cost more to produce. Producers adjust to the higher cost imposed by the safety standards by producing fewer cars at each and every price in the market.

GO TO ▸ Lesson 4 of Interactive Economics! to learn more about "The Elasticity of Supply."

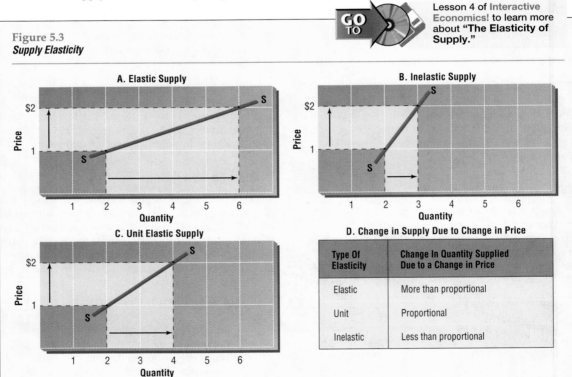

Figure 5.3
Supply Elasticity

A. Elastic Supply

B. Inelastic Supply

C. Unit Elastic Supply

D. Change in Supply Due to Change in Price

Type Of Elasticity	Change In Quantity Supplied Due to a Change in Price
Elastic	More than proportional
Unit	Proportional
Inelastic	Less than proportional

The elasticity of supply, like the elasticity of demand, is a measure of responsiveness. The key to elasticity is the way the dependent variable (quantity supplied) changes in response to a change in the independent variable (price). **What determines whether a business's supply curve is elastic or inelastic?**

Cultural Diversity and Economics

Across the United States, consumers are able to pick up a telephone and order an array of dishes for delivery from a Chinese restaurant. Recent changes in China, which introduced certain aspects of free enterprise into the economy, have enabled the Chinese to do the same thing. Production costs, however, severely limit what meal-delivery companies are able and willing to supply. Service is provided only at lunchtime and for special occasions, such as birthday parties or wedding banquets. Only one or two dishes are offered, orders must be in bulk and, frequently, must be made a day in advance. As the entrepreneurial spirit is allowed to flourish, most economists believe supply will improve.

In general, increased—or tighter—government regulations restrict supply. The regulations increase the cost of inputs or add new features to the product. Relaxed government regulations allow producers to lower the cost of production and to reduce features on products, which results in a shift of the supply curve to the right.

Elasticity of Supply

Just as demand has elasticity, there is elasticity of supply. **Supply elasticity** tells the way in which changes in the quantity supplied are affected by changes in price. If a small increase in price, for example, causes a relatively larger increase in output, the supply curve is said to be elastic. If the quantity supplied changes very little, supply is inelastic.

Supply Elasticities

Three kinds of supply elasticity are illustrated in Figure 5.3. The supply curve in Graph **A** is elastic, because the change in price causes a relatively large change in quantity supplied. Doubling the price from $1 to $2 causes the quantity brought to market to triple.

Graph **B** shows an inelastic supply curve, because the change in price causes a relatively smaller change in quantity supplied. When the price is doubled from $1 to $2, the quantity brought to market goes up only 50 percent, or from 2 to 3.

Graph **C** shows a unit elastic supply curve. In this case, a given change in price causes a proportional change in the quantity supplied. The price doubles from $1 to $2, which causes the quantity brought to market also to double.

Determinants of Supply Elasticity

The extent to which a business's supply curve is elastic or inelastic depends on the nature of its production. The supply curve of shale oil, for example, is likely to be inelastic in the short run. No matter what price is being offered, companies will find it difficult to increase output because of the huge amount of capital and technology needed before production can be increased very much.

The supply curve is likely to be elastic, however, for kites, candy, and other products that can be made quickly without huge amounts of capital and skilled labor. If consumers are willing to pay twice the price for any of these products, most producers will be able to gear up quickly to significantly increase production.

Comparing Demand and Supply Elasticity

Basically, little difference exists between supply elasticity and demand elasticity. If quantities are being purchased, the concept is demand elasticity. If quantities are being brought to market for sale, the concept is supply elasticity. Elasticity for both supply and demand is a measure of responsiveness to a change in price.

SECTION 1 REVIEW

Reviewing Terms and Facts

1. **Define** supply, supply schedule, supply curve, Law of Supply, quantity supplied, change in quantity supplied, change in supply, subsidy, supply elasticity.
2. **Describe** the difference between the supply schedule and the supply curve.
3. **Explain** the difference between a change in quantity supplied and a change in supply.
4. **List** the factors that can cause an increase or decrease in supply.

Critical Thinking

5. **Determining Cause and Effect** According to the Law of Supply, how does price affect the quantity offered for sale?

Applying Economic Concepts

6. **Supply** Provide an example of an economic good whose producer would increase the quantity supplied if price were to go up.

CHAPTER 5: *Supply* **109**

Answers to SECTION 1 REVIEW

1. All vocabulary words are defined in the Glossary.

2. Supply schedule provides information on supply in chart form; supply curve offers same information in graph form.

3. Change in quantity supplied: change in amount offered for sale in response to price change. Change in supply: when different amounts are offered for sale at all possible prices.

4. costs of inputs, productivity, technology, number of sellers, taxes and subsidies, expectations, government regulations

5. Sellers will offer more at higher prices and less at lower prices.

6. Examples will vary.

MEETING LESSON OBJECTIVES

Each objective below is tested by the questions that follow it in parentheses.

1. **Understand** the meaning and concept of supply. **(1, 5, 6)**
2. **Explain** the difference between the supply schedule and the supply curve. **(1, 2)**
3. **Explain** what is meant by a change in quantity supplied. **(1, 3)**
4. **Specify** the reasons for a change in supply. **(4)**

Evaluate

🗂 🗂 💻 Assign the Section 1 Quiz in the TCR or use the *Economics: Principles and Practices* Testmaker. Spanish Section Quizzes also are available in the Spanish Resources Binder.

Reteach

Have students construct a chart showing the similarities and differences between all aspects of demand and supply.

Enrich

Have students write a report on how a technological innovation like the microchip affected production in the computer industry.

CLOSE

Ask students to write a poem, a proverb, or a riddle that illustrates the relationship between price and supply.

TEACH

Call on a volunteer to explain the difference between a news story and an editorial. Next, work through the steps of the explanation, pointing out that the writer's opinion is often signaled by loaded words and other devices that are designed to persuade the reader. Then ask: Does an editorial provide a balanced view? Why or why not? (*No; it provides an opinion. Its purpose is to persuade.*) Conclude by mentioning that American newspapers offer their readers the opportunity to challenge editorial positions through the "Letters to the Editor" column or the op-ed page.

Skills Practice For additional practice, have students complete Reinforcing Economic Skills 5.

ECONOMIC SKILL

Analyzing Editorials

American newspapers have a long tradition of taking stands on economic issues. Editors make a sharp distinction between news stories, which make up most of the contents of the daily paper, and editorials, which are placed in a special section. Unlike a news story, whose purpose is to inform, the purpose of an editorial is to persuade the reader to accept a certain point of view.

Explanation

To analyze an editorial, follow these steps:
- Determine what topic is being discussed.
- Read the editorial carefully to find out what opinion the editors are expressing on that topic.
- Note the arguments and evidence they present to back up their opinion.
- Decide whether you think the editorial is persuasive. Ask: Do I have enough information to form an opinion on this issue?

Practice

Read the editorial below, which appeared in *The Wall Street Journal* on July 26, 1993. Then answer the questions that follow.

1. What is the topic under discussion?
2. What opinion does the writer express about post-industrial society?
3. What evidence and arguments does the writer present to back up his or her opinion?
4. Do you have enough information to make a decision about whether you agree with the writer's point of view? If not, what other information would you need?

> *Most of us in post-industrial society, unlike our not-so-distant ancestors, don't make useful things. . . . we deal in intangible merchandise, such as this little essay, or arguments laid down in a legal brief, or lectures to post-graduate students. . . .*
>
> *The fundamental problem of the post-industrial age has to do with measuring the social value of these activities.*
>
> *In a post-industrial society, where people have no direct sense of how much medical malpractice suits or paper shuffling bureaucracy costs, it also becomes very hard to measure whether the society as a whole is moving toward greater well-being or is retrogressing. In a lecture on BBC4 TV last March, business tycoon Sir James Goldsmith . . . observed that the size of the U.S. economy has quadrupled in the last 50 years and science and technology have achieved incredible innovations. "And yet, American society is deeply ill," he said.*
>
> *"American cities that are wracked with crime, drug taking, alcoholism, suicide and family breakdown are, according to official figures, considered 'richer' than many of the cities that have survived elsewhere in the world and which are still rich in stability and contentment." In short, it is relatively easy to measure the total output of a society, but is not so easy to measure the quality of that output.*
>
> *In the post-industrial age, it thus becomes more necessary to measure human progress subjectively, for example through opinion polls. We know that a very high proportion of the people of the industrial world today are unhappy with government, which may mean they are not especially happy with the quality of their lives.*
>
> —excerpts from "Global View" by George Melloan, *The Wall Street Journal*, July 26, 1993.

Additional Practice

For further practice in analyzing editorials, complete the Reinforcing Skills exercise in the Chapter 5 Review on page 124.

Answers to SKILL

1. the quality of life in the post-industrial age
2. It is difficult to measure whether post-industrial society is moving toward greater well-being or is retrogressing.
3. It is easy to measure society's total output, but not so easy to measure the quality of that output. In support, the writer offers a point made by Sir James Goldsmith: while the U.S. economy has grown by leaps and bounds, and science and technology have achieved incredible innovations, American society is beset with social ills—crime, drugs, alcoholism, suicide, family breakdown, and so on.
4. Students might suggest they need statistical information that backs up some of the writer's statements.

Section Preview

Objectives

After studying this section, you will be able to:

1. **Explain** the theory of production.

2. **Understand** the importance of marginal product and its application to economics.

3. **Describe** the three stages of production and how they relate to the concept of diminishing returns.

Key Terms

theory of production, short run, long run, Law of Variable Proportions, production function, raw materials, total product, marginal product, stages of production, diminishing returns

Applying Economic Concepts

Diminishing Returns Have you ever worked too hard at something—where the outcome of your efforts started to get smaller and smaller even though you "kept at it"? Sometimes you reach a stage of *diminishing returns*, a stage where you still make progress but at a diminished rate.

Suppliers face a complex task. The production of an economic good or service requires a combination of land, labor, capital, and entrepreneurship. Some combinations are more efficient than others, and all combinations affect both output and the cost of production. The **theory of production** deals with the relationship between the factors of production and the output of goods and services. It looks at how output changes when inputs change.

The theory of production generally is based on the **short run**, a period of production that allows producers to change only the amount of variable inputs—usually assumed to be labor. This contrasts with the **long run**, a period of production long enough for all inputs, including capital, to vary.

Law of Variable Proportions

The **Law of Variable Proportions** states that in the short run, output will change as one input is varied while the others are held constant. Although the name of the law is probably new to you, the concept is not.

If you prepare chili, you know that one teaspoon of chili powder will make the chili taste better. Two teaspoons may make it taste better yet. If you keep adding chili powder, however, at some point the chili begins to taste terrible. Basically, preparing chili provides an

example of the Law of Variable Proportions at work. As the amount of the input—the chili powder—varies, so does the output—the quality of the chili.

In an economic sense, the Law of Variable Proportions deals with the relationship between the input of productive resources and the output of final products. The law helps answer the question, How is the output of the final product affected as more units of one variable input or resource are added to a fixed amount of other resources?

Al, do whatever you have to do to increase productivity. Threaten, cajole, fire at will. Have fun.

Productivity *The economist would not consider this advice to Al the best way to increase productivity.* **On what is the theory of production based?**

TEACH

Guided Practice

L2 *Role Play* Draw a two-column chart on the chalkboard, using *Number of Workers* and *Total Product* as column headings. Then provide a student with a stack of papers and a stapler. Ask the student to work at stapling sets of five sheets of paper together for 45 seconds. At the end of the time period, count the number of sets and enter the result in the *Product* column and a 1 in the *Workers* column. Repeat the process using two, three, four, and five students working together. Have students discuss how this activity illustrates the Law of Variable Proportions.

VISUAL INSTRUCTION

Declining output has nothing to do with the abilities of workers, because the Law of Variable Proportions assumes that all units of variable input are of equal quality.

Answer to Caption:

All three stages help businesses decide the number of variable inputs to use in production.

INTERACTIVE ECONOMICS!

CD-ROM Supply

Have students click on "Production, Cost, and Profit Maximization." Then have students imagine that they are managers of a factory. Have them decide what products they will manufacture and how many employees they will need to hire. Have them offer explanations for each new hire.

💾 *Supplied in both CD-ROM and diskette formats.*

A farmer, for example, may have all the land, machines, workers, and other items needed to produce a crop. The farmer, however, may have some questions about the use of fertilizer. How will the crop yield be affected if different amounts of fertilizer are added to fixed amounts of the other inputs? In this case, the variable input is the fertilizer added per acre.

Perhaps a plant manager wants to know, given the existing machines and equipment, how the final output would be affected if one or several workers are hired. The Law of Variable Proportions will also help answer this question.

Of course, it is possible for all inputs to be varied at the same time. The farmer may want to know what will happen to output if not only the fertilizer but also the quantities of the other factors of production are varied. The plant manager may be interested in finding out what will happen if the company not only hires more workers, but also buys several new machines and other equipment. When more than one factor of production is varied, however, it becomes harder to tell what the effect on final output will be.

The Production Function

The Law of Variable Proportions can be illustrated by using a **production function**—a concept that relates changes in output to different amounts of a single input while other inputs are held constant. The production function can be illustrated with a schedule such as the one in panel **A** of **Figure 5.4**, or with a graph like the one in panel **B**. **1**

The first two columns in the production schedule list hypothetical figures on a business's output as the number of workers is varied from 0 to 10. With no workers, for example, there is no output. If the number of workers increases by one, output rises to 14. Add yet another worker and total output rises to 42.

This information is used to construct the production function that appears in the graph. The variable input is shown on the horizontal axis with total production on the vertical axis.

In this example, only the number of workers changes, and all other productive resources remain the same. No changes occur in the amount of machinery used, the level of technology, or quantities of **raw materials**—unprocessed natural products used in

---

GO TO Lesson 4 of Interactive Economics! to learn more about "Production, Cost, and Profit Maximization."

Figure 5.4
The Law of Variable Proportions

A. Production Schedule Using Varying Amounts of Labor

Number of Workers	Total Product (In Units)*	Marginal Product (In Units)*	
0	0	0	Stage I
1	14	14	
2	42	28	
3	75	33	
4	112	37	
5	150	38	
6	180	30	Stage II
7	203	23	
8	216	13	
9	207	–9	Stage III
10	190	–17	

*All figures refer to production/productivity per worker per day.

B. Production Function Using Varying Amounts of Labor

The Law of Variable Proportions shows how total output will change when all inputs except one are fixed. The law can be illustrated as a production schedule as in A, or as the production function shown in B. In this example, labor is the variable input, while all other variables are held constant. **How are the three stages of production related to the Law of Variable Proportions?**

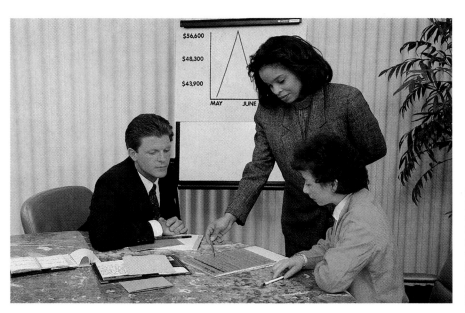

Production Function
In most companies, managers hold regular production meetings at which they evaluate past performance and set future goals. **Why is the use of the production function important in business?**

production. Under these conditions, any change in output must be the result of the variation in the number of workers.

Total Product

The second column in the production schedule in **Figure 5.4** shows **total product**, or total output produced by the firm. The numbers seem to indicate that the plant barely operates when it has only a few workers. Perhaps the workers find it difficult to attend the machines, keep the supply of raw materials flowing smoothly, or remove and package the finished product. These same workers may also have to keep the plant clean and perform other maintenance. Some machines may stand idle much of the time.

As more workers are added, however, total product rises. More machinery can be operated, and plant output rises. Workers can specialize in certain jobs, so that each worker's special talents can be used to the fullest. One group of workers may run the machines while another takes care of maintenance. A third may handle the assembly work. By working in this way—as a coordinated whole—the firm can be very productive. ☑

As even more workers are added, output rises but at a slower rate. Eventually, total product goes as high as it can. Adding the ninth and tenth workers causes total output to go down because these workers just get in the way of the others. Although the ideal number of workers cannot be determined until costs are considered, it is clear that the ninth and tenth workers will not be hired. **2**

 QUICK CHECK

Checking Understanding
1. What does a production function show?
2. What point must eventually be reached if companies continue adding workers?

Applying Economic Concepts
☑ **Division of Labor** Henry Ford developed the assembly line in the early 1900s. He found that productivity increased dramatically if each worker repeated the same task—attaching the gas tank, for example—over and over. By 1922 the company earned $264,000 a day.

CHAPTER 5: *Supply* **113**

 $ Free Enterprise Activity $

Productivity—the output per unit of one of the factors of production—is measured in different ways. The productivity of labor, for example, is gauged by output per hour worked. Because a higher rate of output per hour worked will lead to increased profits, businesses are constantly seeking ways to boost labor productivity. The methods businesses use to achieve this goal include providing attractive working environments, offering pay

incentives and bonuses, subsidizing further education so that workers gain new skills, investing in modern capital equipment, and building larger, more efficient plants.

Have students work in small groups to research the ways local businesses have tried to increase labor productivity. Suggest that groups present their findings in a brief oral report.

CHAPTER 5
SECTION 2

GLENCOE
TECHNOLOGY

NIGHTLY BUSINESS REPORT
Economics in Action

Chapter 8
Disc 1, Side 1
Title: *What Is Supply?*
Subject: Marginal product
Ask: **What is marginal product?** *(the additional output that comes from each worker or other factor added to production)*

 Also available in VHS.

Using Transparencies
Display Economic Concepts Transparency 3. Spanish Transparencies also are available.

Independent Practice

📂 **Guided Reading** Assign Guided Reading Activity for Section 2. **LEP**

VISUAL INSTRUCTION

Ask: What economic law does the production function illustrate? *(Law of Variable Proportions)*

Answer to Caption:
It shows how output might change when inputs are varied.

QUICK CHECK
ANSWERS

1. It relates changes in output to different amounts of a single input while other inputs are held constant.
2. where total output goes down because added workers get in the way of others

113

Stages of Production
As workers are added to this assembly line, output increases—but only to a certain point. **What would happen if company officials doubled the number of workers in this factory?**

Marginal Product

The measure of output shown in the third column of the production schedule in **Figure 5.4** is one of the more important concepts in economics. The measure is known as **marginal product**, the extra output generated by adding one more unit of variable input. Another way to explain marginal product is to say that it is the change in total product caused by the addition of one more unit of variable input.

Note that the marginal productivity of the fifth worker is 38 units, which is more than that of any preceding worker. After the fifth worker is added, however, each worker adds less to the total output. The marginal product of the seventh worker is 23 units of output, and the marginal product of the eighth falls to 13. By the time we get to the ninth worker, marginal product is negative, which is why the ninth worker will not be hired.

Three Stages of Production

When it comes to determining the optimal number of variable units to be used in production, changes in marginal product are of special interest. **Figure 5.4** shows the three **stages of production**—increasing returns, diminishing returns, and negative returns—that are based on the way marginal product changes as variable inputs are added.

STAGE I: Increasing Returns

Hiring the first five workers illustrates the first stage of the Law of Variable Proportions. Each worker contributes more than the previous worker to total output. The first stage is defined as the stage where marginal product is increasing.

In this first stage, the individual workers may not be able to handle the equipment efficiently because of too much machinery and other resources per worker. Not enough workers are present to handle the job well. As the number of workers rises, however, the workers use the available resources better. The result of all this is increasing returns per worker.

As long as each new worker hired contributes more to total output than the worker before, total output rises at a faster rate. Because marginal output increases by larger amounts every time a new worker is added, Stage I is known as the stage of increasing returns.

Companies, however, would not knowingly produce in Stage I for very long. As a firm discovered that each new worker added more output than the last, the firm would be tempted to hire another worker. After all, if the fourth worker produced more than the third, and if the fifth worker added more output than the fourth, a sixth worker would be hired.

STAGE II: Diminishing Returns

In Stage II, the total production keeps growing but by smaller and smaller amounts. Any additional workers hired may stock shelves, package parts, and do other jobs that leave the machine operators free to

spend more time at the machines. The increase in total production, however, is less than it was when the other workers were hired. Each worker, then, makes a diminishing but positive contribution to total output.

Stage II illustrates the principle of **diminishing returns**. As more units of a certain variable input are added to a constant amount of other resources, total output keeps rising, but only at a diminishing rate. In Figure 5.4, the addition of the seventh worker adds 23 new units of output, but the eighth worker adds only 13.

STAGE III: Negative Returns

Adding the ninth and tenth workers makes an even greater difference. Too many workers have been hired, and they are getting in each other's way. Marginal product is negative and total plant output decreases. Labor service, which could be used to advantage in some other job area, is wasted.

Most companies would not hire workers whose addition would cause total production to decrease. Therefore, the number of workers hired would be found only in Stage II. The exact number of workers hired depends on the cost of each worker. If the cost is low, eight workers might be hired. If the cost is high, fewer than eight but no less than six workers would be hired.

MEETING LESSON OBJECTIVES

Each objective below is tested by the questions that follow it in parentheses.

1. **Explain** the theory of production. **(1)**
2. **Understand** the importance of marginal product and its application to economics. **(1, 2, 3, 4)**
3. **Describe** the three stages of production and how they relate to the concept of diminishing returns. **(3, 4, 5)**

Evaluate

Assign the Section 2 Quiz in the TCR or use the *Economics: Principles and Practices* Testmaker. Spanish Section Quizzes also are available in the Spanish Resources Binder.

Reteach

Have students write a paragraph that applies the Law of Variable Proportions to the three stages of production.

Enrich

Ask students to investigate different types of job specialization used by businesses. Have them present their findings in a report that shows the role specialization plays in production.

CLOSE

Have students discuss the following statement: The most important economic concept for business managers to understand is that of marginal product.

SECTION 2 REVIEW

Reviewing Terms and Facts

1. **Define** theory of production, short run, long run, Law of Variable Proportions, production function, raw materials, total product, marginal product, stages of production, diminishing returns.
2. **Explain** how marginal product is related to total product and how it is measured.

3. **Describe** how marginal product changes in each of the three stages of production.

Critical Thinking

4. **Demonstrating Reasoned Judgment** You need to hire workers for a project you are directing. You may add one worker at a time in a manner that will allow you to measure the added contribution of each

worker. At what point will you stop hiring workers? Relate this process to the three stages of the production function.

Applying Economic Concepts

5. **Diminishing Returns** Provide an example of a time when you entered a period of diminishing returns or even negative returns. Explain why this might have occurred.

CHAPTER 5: *Supply* **115**

Answers to SECTION 2 REVIEW

1. All vocabulary words are defined in the Glossary.
2. Marginal product is the change in total product caused by the addition of one more unit of variable input. It is extra output generated by adding one more unit of variable input.
3. Stage I—positive and increasing; Stage II—positive but decreasing; Stage III—negative

4. Somewhere in Stage II; In Stage I, as each worker is added, total product and marginal product increase. In Stage II, as each worker is added, marginal product is positive but decreasing. At end of Stage II, total product is maximized, and in Stage III, as each worker is added, total product decreases because marginal product is negative.
5. Examples will vary.

PROFILES IN ECONOMICS

DAVE THOMAS
(1932–   )

Dave Thomas—founder of Wendy's Old Fashioned Hamburgers restaurants—was a millionaire at age 35, but he didn't make his fortune in hamburgers. He made his first millions by selling Kentucky Fried Chicken (KFC).

GROWING UP Thomas was born in 1932. He never knew his birth parents but was adopted at six weeks old. His mother died when he was five, and his father moved frequently, looking for work. During these moves, Thomas ate in many restaurants, and he liked what he saw—families

Over 5,000 Wendy's restaurants operate in 35 countries.

eating together. He decided that he would someday have his own family restaurant.

The constant moving proved challenging for Thomas, who always found himself the new kid on the block. For a sense of stability, he turned to work at age 12. He was fired from his first two jobs; one over a misunderstanding with his boss, the other when it was discovered that he wasn't 16. His third job at age 12 was a turning point: he was befriended by the owners of a restaurant who were impressed with his work ethic.

At age 15, Thomas made what he calls the biggest mistake of his life—dropping out of high school. After a stint in the army, he returned to the restaurant busi-

ness. In the 1950s, he met Colonel Harland Sanders, founder of KFC restaurants. Thomas worked for several floundering KFC stores in Columbus, Ohio, and became a millionaire when he returned them to profitability in 1968.

HAMBURGERS While working for KFC, Thomas remained interested in hamburgers. He opened his first Wendy's Old Fashioned Hamburgers restaurant in 1969, naming the restaurant after his 8-year-old daughter Melinda Lou, nicknamed "Wendy."

Competitors scoffed at Thomas, but his homey, comfortable restaurants grew and prospered. When Thomas began franchising the restaurant, his concept exploded. More than 1,000 Wendy's opened in the first 100 months. That rapid growth continues. Thomas has received every major award in the restaurant industry.

Thomas has been just as successful in his personal life. He has devoted considerable time to promoting child adoption, and he became the national White House spokesperson for the movement in 1990.

Examining the Profile

1. **Evaluating Information** With which aspect of Thomas's entrepreneurship are you most impressed? Why?

2. **For Further Research** Research Thomas's advertising strategies, summarizing his rise as an American folk hero.

Answers to Examining the Profile

1. Answers will vary. Some students will mention Thomas's perseverance in getting the job done. Others might mention his inventive approaches to marketing his product.

2. Answers will vary. Encourage students to analyze the success of Clara Peller's "Where's the Beef?" advertisement.

Section Preview

Objectives	Key Terms	Applying Economic Concepts
After studying this section, you will be able to: 1. **Identify** the relationship between productivity and cost. 2. **Define** four key measures of cost. 3. **Identify** two key measures of revenue.	fixed cost, overhead, depreciation, variable cost, total cost, marginal cost, total revenue, marginal revenue, marginal analysis, break-even point, profit-maximizing quantity of output	**Marginal Cost** Have you thought about what you will do after graduating from high school? Go to college? Get a job? Have you considered the cost of these options? Economists view options in terms of *marginal cost*—in this case, the additional cost of getting more education versus the cost of going directly into the job market.

An analysis of the Law of Variable Proportions tells us that a business should hire enough labor to produce in Stage II. Before we can specify the exact number of variable inputs, however, we must consider the relationship between productivity and costs.

Productivity and Cost

Different grades of coal, wood, steel, cotton, and glass, as well as most other raw materials, have different productivities. Businesses that use raw materials in manufacturing must decide which grade best suits their needs. Because efficiency is related to both cost and productivity, it is important that care be taken in selecting the proper materials.

Suppose an electric power company that uses coal can choose from among three different grades. Grade A coal sells for $40 per ton, grade B for $33, and grade C for $30. The cost and productivities of each is shown in the chart in **Figure 5.5**. Notice that grade A coal would be more productive than the other two, yielding 2,500 kilowatt-hours of electric power for each ton of coal used.

If we consider the cost effectiveness of the different grades of coal, the figure shows that grade A costs 1.6 cents per kilowatt-hour generated. Grade C also has a cost of 1.6 cents per kilowatt-hour, while grade B has a cost of 1.5 cents.

Both grade C, which is the cheapest and least productive, and grade A, which is the most expensive and most productive, cost more per final unit than grade B. Grade B is the most efficient from a cost point of view.

Figure 5.5
Productivity, Cost, and Efficiency of Various Grades of Coal

Grades of Coal	Price Per Ton	Kilowatt Hours of Electric Power per Ton of Coal Used (Estimated)	Production Cost per Kilowatt Hour of Electric Power
A	$40	2500	1.6¢
B	$33	2200	1.5¢
C	$30	1875	1.6¢

Different grades of coal have different productivities. The most efficient grade is not always the most, or the least, expensive. **Why is it necessary for businesses to consider productivity as well as cost?**

CHAPTER 5: *Supply* **117**

This example shows that both productivity and cost must be considered to make the best production decision. This also holds true for a manufacturer of razor blades that must consider the different grades of steel, as well as for a hotel that must consider the different grades of carpeting. In the end, efficient production is a function of the quality and cost of inputs used.

Measures of Cost

Because the cost of inputs influences efficient production decisions, a business must analyze costs before making its decisions. To make the decision-making process easier, cost is divided into several different categories.

Fixed Cost

The first kind of cost is **fixed cost**—the cost that a business incurs even if the plant is idle and output is zero. It makes no difference whether the business produces nothing, very little, or a large amount. Total fixed cost, or **overhead**, remains the same. ✓

Fixed costs include salaries paid to executives, interest charges on bonds, rent payments on leased properties, and local and state property taxes. Fixed costs also include **depreciation**—the gradual wear and tear on capital goods over time and through use. A machine, for example, will not last forever because its parts will wear out slowly and, after a time, break.

Fixed costs do not change when output changes. Consider the table in **Figure 5.6**, which is an extension of the production schedule in **Figure 5.4**. Regardless of the level of total output, the total fixed cost amounts to $70, as shown in the fourth column of the table. Because executive salaries, interest payments, taxes, and other overhead charges do not change with changes in output, fixed costs never vary.

Variable Cost

Another kind of cost is **variable cost**—a cost that does change when the business rate of operation or output changes. While fixed costs generally are associated with machines and other capital goods, variable costs generally are associated with labor and raw materials. Workers may be laid off or used again as output changes. Other examples of variable costs include the electric power to run the machines or freight charges on shipments of the final product.

In **Figure 5.6** the assumption has been made that the only variable cost is labor. If one worker costs $46 per day, the total variable cost for one worker is $46. Two workers, or two units of variable input, cost $92, and so on.

Fixed Costs *Whether this computer graphics firm is producing to its full capacity (left) or is idle (right), the firm still incurs fixed costs.* **What do fixed costs generally include?**

Figure 5.6
Marginal Product, Cost, and Revenues

STAGES OF PRODUCTION	PRODUCTION SCHEDULE			COSTS				REVENUES		Total Profits
	Number of Workers	Total Product	Marginal Product	Total Fixed Costs +	Total Variable Costs =	Total Costs	Marginal Costs	Total Revenue	Marginal Revenue	
STAGE I	0	0	0	70	0	70		0		−70
	1	14	14	70	46	116	3.29	28	2.00	−88
	2	42	28	70	92	162	1.64	84	2.00	−78
	3	75	33	70	138	208	1.39	150	2.00	−58
	4	112	37	70	184	254	1.24	224	2.00	−30
	5	150	38	70	230	300	1.21	300	2.00	0
STAGE II	6	180	30	70	276	346	1.53	360	2.00	14
	7	203	23	70	322	392	2.00	406	2.00	14
	8	216	13	70	368	438	3.54	432	2.00	−6
STAGE III	9	207	−9	70	414	484	—	414	2.00	−70
	10	190	−17	70	460	530	—	380	2.00	−150

The concepts of marginal product, marginal cost, and marginal revenue are central to economic analysis. Marginal product is used to define the three stages of production. Marginal cost and marginal revenue are used to determine the profit-maximizing quantity of output. **How do total costs differ from marginal costs?**

Total Cost

The **total cost** of production is the sum of the fixed and variable costs. Total cost takes in all the costs a business faces in the course of its operations. The business represented in Figure 5.6, for example, might employ six workers—costing $46 each for a total of $276—to produce 180 units of total output. If no other variable costs existed, and if fixed costs amounted to $70, the total cost of production would be $346. **1**

If the workers go on strike, the total cost of production would fall to $70 even though no output is produced. The total cost of production is equal to the fixed costs plus the variable costs, which, in this case, are zero if the workers are on strike.

Marginal Cost

The other measure of cost is **marginal cost**—the extra cost incurred when a business produces one additional unit of a product. Because fixed costs do not change from one level of production to another, marginal cost is the increase in variable costs that stems from using additional factors of production. **2**

Checking Understanding

1. How do businesses calculate total costs?
2. What are the four measures of cost that businesses must consider?

Applying Economic Concepts

Investment In recent years many companies have relocated to the Sunbelt where wages and rents are lower than in the North. Even foreign firms have moved there. BMWs are assembled in South Carolina; Mercedes Benz in Alabama.

For example, Figure 5.6 shows that the addition of the first worker increased the total product by 14 units. Because total variable costs increased by $46, each of the additional 14 units cost $3.29. If another worker is added, 28 more units of output will be produced for an additional cost of $46. The marginal, or extra, cost of each unit of output is $46 divided by 28, or $1.64.

Practical Applications of Cost Principles

The combination, or mix, of inputs affects supply. If most of the costs of a certain business are fixed and only a few costs vary with output, total output could be increased with very little additional cost.

Gas Stations

Consider, for example, a self-serve gas station with several pumps and a single attendant who works in an enclosed booth on the lot. This operation is likely to have large fixed costs. These include overhead expenses such as the cost of the lot, the pumps and tanks, and the taxes and licensing fees paid to state and local governments.

The variable costs, on the other hand, are likely to be quite small. These include the hourly wage paid to the employee, the cost of electricity for lights and pumps, and the cost of the gas sold. When all costs are included, however, the ratio of variable to fixed costs is small.

As a result, it does not cost much more for the owner to operate the station 24 hours a day, seven days a week. The extra cost of keeping the station open between the hours of midnight and 6:00 A.M. is minimal. The extra wages, the electricity, and other variable costs are minor and may well be covered from the profits of the extra sales. **1**

Another gas station may have a different mix of costs. Suppose a full-service station located nearby offers the services of a mechanic as well as several attendants who wait on customers.

If the station has been around long enough, management may even own the land. Taxes and occupation licenses may have to be paid, but fixed costs are likely to be less than those of the other gas station. The need for the attendants and the mechanic, however, means that the variable costs are higher in comparison to fixed costs. As a result, this station is likely to operate for fewer hours and during the busiest time of the day. Thus, the mix of inputs and the nature of their costs has an impact on the amount of service offered by the owner.

Movie Theaters

A movie theater operator is faced with a similar situation. After the decision is made to show a movie, it makes little difference in cost as to whether 10 or 1,000 people come to the theater per day. The operating expenses are about the same regardless of how many customers show up.

Because marginal costs are low, little extra expense is involved in showing a movie in the early afternoon. The owner is concerned about recovering the large fixed costs and is more likely to schedule a number of movies at different times and prices throughout the day. ☑

Measures of Revenue

Businesses use two key measures of revenue to decide what amount of output will produce the greatest profits. The first is total revenue, and the second is marginal revenue.

> ### DID YOU KNOW?
>
> **Maharaja Mac** The supply of a product is often influenced by religion and culture. When McDonald's® expanded into India, for example, it did not offer its Big Mac because most Indians are Hindu who do not eat beef. Instead, McDonald's® introduced its Maharaja Mac, which consists of two all-mutton (sheep) patties. And because many Indians are vegetarians, McDonald's® rounded out the menu with Vegetable McNuggets and Vegetable McBurgers.

120 UNIT 2: *Microeconomics*

Total Revenue

The **total revenue** is the number of units sold multiplied by the average price per unit. If 42 units are sold at $2 each, the total revenue is $84.

The total revenue column in Figure 5.6 shows this measurement. If each unit brings an average of $2, then 14 units of total product generates $28 of total revenue, 75 units generates $150, and so on.

Marginal Revenue

Marginal revenue is the extra revenue associated with the production and sale of one additional unit of output. It is the most useful measure of revenue both for businesses and economists.

The marginal revenues in Figure 5.6 are determined by dividing the change in total revenue by the marginal product. When a business has no workers, it produces no output, and it receives no revenue. When it adds the first worker, total output jumps to 14 units, and $28 of total revenue is generated. Because the $28 is earned from the sale of 14 units of output, each unit must have added $2. Therefore, the marginal, or extra, revenue each unit of output brings in is $2.

Whenever an additional worker is added, the marginal revenue computation remains the same. If the business employs five workers, it produces 150 units of output and generates $300 of total revenue. If a sixth worker is added, output increases by 30 units, and total revenues increase to $360. To have increased total revenue by $60, each of the 30 additional units of output must have added $2.

If each unit of output sells for $2, the marginal revenue earned by the sale of one more unit is $2. For this reason, the marginal revenue appears to be constant at $2 for every level of output. While marginal revenue is constant in Figure 5.6, however, this will not

always be the case. Businesses often find that marginal revenues start high and then decrease as more and more units are produced and sold. **2**

Marginal Analysis

Economists use **marginal analysis**, a type of decision making that compares the extra benefits to the

HELP WANTED

Market Researcher
▼

We are a consulting company seeking a market researcher. You must gather, record, and analyze facts about products and sales. Information may be gathered from company or government records, published materials, statistical files, and other sources. You may need to print and circulate questionnaires, or survey people over the phone or door-to-door. The information you gather will be used to prepare forecasts of future sales trends, offer recommendations on product design, and define the market toward which advertising should be directed. Strong analytical and writing skills and experience with computerized data are essential. Courses in marketing, statistics, English composition, speech, psychology, and economics are required.

▼

Education: college degree
Salary Range: $19,000-$68,000

Checking Understanding

1. Why are the extra costs of operating a gas station 24 hours a day minimal?
2. How does marginal revenue differ from total revenue?

Applying Economic Concepts

 Demand Theater owners generally lower prices during the day, hoping that lower prices will increase demand during an otherwise lax period. Airlines follow the same principle by drastically cutting fares to Europe in the winter when demand is usually very low.

Cultural Diversity and Economics

India During its early years as an independent nation, India had to import most of its manufactured goods. Over time, however, that has changed. Today, as in the distant past, textile manufacturing is the most important industry. The handicraft industry also is important. India produces a great variety of other products as well, including sewing machines, bicycles, tractors, automobiles, ships, locomotives, and airplanes. In the high-tech area, India has developed and manufactured electronics, radios, televisions, computers, computer software, and satellites.

ASSESS

Check for Understanding

Assign Section 3 Review as homework or an in-class activity.

■ Use **Chapter Challenger Interactive Review Software** to review Section 3.

MEETING LESSON OBJECTIVES

Each objective below is tested by the questions on page 122 that follow it in parentheses.

1. **Identify** the relationship between productivity and cost. **(2, 3)**
2. **Define** four key measures of cost. **(1, 5, 6, 7)**
3. **Identify** two key measures of revenue. **(3, 6)**

MATH PRACTICE

Have students determine the fixed costs and variable costs of owning a car. (*Fixed costs—cost of car or monthly payments, insurance; variable costs—gas, oil, service, maintenance.*)

ANSWERS

1. Variable costs are minor and may be covered by profits from extra sales.
2. Total revenue is the number of units sold multiplied by average price per unit. Marginal revenue is extra revenue associated with the production and sale of one additional unit of output.

Evaluate

📁 📁 🖥 Assign the Section 3 Quiz in the TCR or use the *Economics: Principles and Practices* Testmaker to create a customized quiz. Spanish Section Quizzes also are available in the Spanish Resources Binder.

Reteach

On the chalkboard, copy key statements from Section 3, but change them in some way to make the statements false. Tell students to write the statements correctly.

📁 📁 Have students complete Reteaching Activity 5. Spanish Reteaching Activities also are available in the Spanish Resources Binder.

Enrich

Have students interview local business owners and managers, asking them to define *profit* and explain why profit maximizing is important to them.

📁 Have students complete Enrichment Activity 5.

CLOSE

Ask students to consider which, if any, of society's economic goals are furthered by profit maximization. *(economic freedom, economic efficiency)*

extra costs of an action. Marginal analysis is helpful in a number of situations, including break-even analysis and profit maximization.

Break-even Analysis

When the business represented in Figure 5.6 employs its first worker, it generates total revenue of $28 and total costs of $116, giving it a total profit of $-88. The addition of the next worker increases total revenue to $84 and total costs to $162, which changes total profits to $-78. As more workers are added, total profits eventually become positive.

Eventually the business reaches the **break-even point**—the total output or total product the business needs to sell in order to cover its total costs. In Figure 5.6, the break-even point is 150 units of total product.

Profit Maximization

A business wants to do better than break even, however. It wants to make as much profit as it can. We already know that the business represented in Figure 5.6 will break even when it hires the fifth worker. How many workers and what level of output will be needed to generate the maximum profits?

The business can make this decision by comparing marginal costs and marginal revenues. The business would probably hire the sixth worker, for example, because the extra output would only cost $1.53 to produce and would generate $2 in revenues. In general, as long as the marginal cost is less than the marginal revenue, the business will keep hiring workers.

Having made a profit on the sixth worker, most likely the business would go ahead and hire the seventh. This time, however, the cost of the additional output would equal the additional revenue earned when the product was sold. The addition of the seventh worker neither adds to, nor takes away from, total profits. The company would not hire the eighth worker because the seventh one did not make a positive contribution toward total profits.

When marginal cost is less than marginal revenue, new inputs should be hired and output should expand. The **profit-maximizing quantity of output** is reached when marginal cost and marginal revenue are equal. In Figure 5.6, profits are maximized when the seventh worker is hired. Other combinations may generate the same amount of profits, but no other combination will be more profitable. The difference between total revenue and total cost is maximum here.

SECTION 3 REVIEW

Reviewing Terms and Facts

1. **Define** fixed cost, overhead, depreciation, variable cost, total cost, marginal cost, total revenue, marginal revenue, marginal analysis, break-even point, profit-maximizing quantity of output.
2. **Explain** the relationship between productivity and cost.
3. **Identify** two key measures of revenue.
4. **Explain** the use of marginal analysis for break-even and profit-maximizing decisions.

Critical Thinking

5. **Analyzing Information** Many oil-processing plants operate 24 hours a day, using several shifts of workers to maintain operations. How do you think a plant's fixed and variable costs affect its decision to operate around the clock?
6. **Checking Consistency** In Figure 5.6, total profits are the same after the sixth worker is hired as after the seventh worker is hired. Why should the company hire the seventh worker?

Applying Economic Concepts

7. **Marginal Cost** What is the marginal cost of your decision to buy a new car when you graduate? How much more would a new car cost than a used one?

Answers to SECTION 3 REVIEW

1. All vocabulary words are defined in the Glossary

2. Increases or decreases in productivity generally will have an inverse effect on cost.

3. total revenue, marginal revenue

4. By comparing the marginal revenue and the marginal cost of adding units of variable input, break-even and profit-maximizing points can be established.

5. When variable costs are small relative to fixed costs, the additional cost of operating around the clock is low.

6. because with six workers the profit-maximizing quantity of output had not been reached; This occurs with the hiring of the seventh worker. Other combinations may generate the same amount of profits, but none are more profitable.

7. Answers will vary.

ECONOMICS IN ACTION

What Is Supply?

Setting Up the Video

With your classmates, view "What Is Supply?" on the videodisc *Economics in Action.* The video focuses on factors that affect the quantity supplied of a product and explains that higher prices generally prompt producers to increase the quantity supplied. This concept is explained through the example of coffee producers. The video then considers ways that producers try to increase productivity and marginal product.

 Chapter 8
Disc 1, Side 1

View the video by scanning the bar code or by entering the chapter number on your keypad and pressing Search. *(Also available in VHS format.)*

Hands-On Activity

Imagine that you are a video games manufacturer. List the factors that would cause you to increase or decrease the quantity supplied of the video games you produce. How would you go about making such changes in your manufacturing plant? When focusing on your production, consider the following aspects: labor, equipment, technology, price, and marketing. Share your list with the class.

INTERACTIVE ECONOMICS!

Supply

Introduction

Lesson 4 of *Interactive Economics!* describes the concept of supply, which summarizes the willingness of producers to offer products for sale in the market.

Supply is also a hypothetical concept in the sense that it describes the quantities producers are willing to provide over a wide range of possible prices.

Supply can be shown as a schedule or as an upward-sloping supply curve. Both presentations tell us that producers are willing to offer more at higher prices and less at lower prices.

Using the Software

1. Select "Supply" from the Main Menu.
2. Read the introduction to "Supply," then click on "Supply Schedules and Curves."
3. After reviewing the lesson, click on "A Change in Supply." Repeat this process for "A Change in Quantity Supplied."
4. Finally, click on the "Advanced Topics Menu" and review both topics.
5. Then click on "Economics Lab." Complete the lab by clicking and dragging the appropriate titles and characteristics to their proper locations on each graph.
6. Print your completed lab.

123

Economics in Action

Chapter 8

Disc 1, Side 1

Title: *What Is Supply?*

 If you do not have access to a videodisc player, the **Economics in Action** programs are also available in VHS.

INTERACTIVE ECONOMICS!

Before students complete the "Economics Lab" in Lesson 4, ask them the following questions:
1. What drives suppliers to produce more? (*profit motive*)
2. What is the profit-maximizing quantity of output? (*where the marginal cost of producing the last unit of output is equal to the marginal revenue it receives from the sale of that unit*)
3. What is movement along the supply curve called? (*change in quantity supplied*)
4. What is movement of the supply curve called? (*change in supply*)
5. What are some things that cause a change in supply? (*changes in costs of inputs, productivity, technology, the number of sellers, taxes and subsidies, expectations, and government regulations*)

TEACHER NOTES

_____

GLENCOE TECHNOLOGY

VIDEODISC
MindJogger Videoquiz

Use MindJogger to review the Chapter 5 content.

 Chapter 5
Disc 1, Side B

Also available in VHS.

Answers

Reviewing Key Terms

1. c	6. e
2. d	7. f
3. b	8. a
4. j	9. i
5. g	10. h

Reviewing the Facts

1. the quantities of a product offered for sale at all possible prices that could prevail in the market

2. The supply schedule provides information on supply in chart form; the supply curve offers the same information in graph form.

3. the change in the amount of a product offered for sale in response to price change

4. costs of inputs, productivity, technology, number of sellers, taxes and subsidies, expectations, government regulations

5. In the short run, output will change as one input is varied while others remain constant.

6. Total product is total output produced by a firm; marginal product is extra output generated by adding one more unit of variable input.

7. increasing returns, diminishing returns, and negative returns

Reviewing Key Terms

Write the letter of the key term that best matches each definition below.

a. depreciation
b. diminishing returns
c. fixed cost
d. marginal analysis
e. marginal product
f. marginal revenue
g. production function
h. profit-maximizing quantity of output
i. total cost
j. variable cost

1. a production cost that does not change as total business output changes
2. decision making that compares the additional costs with the additional benefits of an action
3. associated with Stage II of production
4. a production cost that changes when output changes
5. a graphical representation of the theory of production
6. the additional output produced when one additional unit of input is added
7. change in total revenue from sale of one additional unit of output
8. the gradual wearing out of capital goods
9. the sum of variable and fixed costs
10. when marginal revenue equals marginal cost

Reviewing the Facts

SECTION 1 *(pages 104–109)*
1. **Describe** what is meant by supply.
2. **Distinguish** between the supply schedule and the supply curve.
3. **Explain** what is meant by a change in quantity supplied.
4. **Identify** the factors that cause a change in supply.

SECTION 2 *(pages 111–115)*
5. **Describe** the Law of Variable Proportions.
6. **Explain** the difference between total product and marginal product.
7. **Identify** the three stages of production.

SECTION 3 *(pages 117–122)*
8. **Describe** the relationship between marginal cost and total cost.
9. **Identify** four measures of cost.
10. **Describe** one practical application of cost principles.

Critical Thinking

1. **Determining Cause and Effect** Explain why companies with very large fixed costs and small variable costs are most likely to operate or stay open for extended periods.
2. **Making Generalizations** Why might production functions tend to differ from one firm to another?

Applying Economic Concepts

1. **Marginal Analysis** Give an example of a recent decision you made in which you used the tools of marginal analysis.
2. **Diminishing Returns** Label the following actions according to their placement in the stages of production: (a) After many hours of studying, you are forgetting some of the material you learned earlier. (b) You are studying for a test and learning rapidly. (c) After a few hours, you are still learning but not as fast as before.

Reinforcing Skills

ANALYZING EDITORIALS

Read the following editorial, which appeared in *The Wall Street Journal* on June 19, 1997. Then answer the questions that follow.

Anyone wondering what's in store for China in the post-Deng Xiaoping era should look at those most likely to enjoy the positions of power and status in coming years: the children of Chinese officials. But don't look for them in China; hundreds are across the Pacific in American universities. The fact that so many children of the [ruling elite] study in the U.S. is not only a sign of how much

8. Marginal cost is the change in total cost incurred by producing one additional unit of a product.

9. total cost, fixed cost, variable cost, marginal cost

10. Answers may vary, but students will cite one of the applications discussed on page 120.

Critical Thinking

1. Fixed costs will be incurred whether the company is operating or not. Because variable costs are small,

increased costs of operating for extended periods will be minimal and may be covered by extra revenue generated during extended operation.

2. The production function depends upon the way output changes when differing amounts of variable input are added. Because different firms have different technologies and use different amounts of variable inputs, the production function for each firm will vary. Examples will differ, but students might compare an automobile factory, which may

China has changed in recent decades. It may also be the best guarantee possible that China will continue its current [economic] reform track.

An estimated 250,000 Chinese students entered American universities between 1978 and 1996, and some 40,000 are there now, making them the largest group of foreign students in the U.S. . . . After earning a degree . . . they return to China to take important positions in government, universities, or private companies.

1. What topic is being discussed?
2. What opinion does the writer express?
3. What evidence and arguments does the writer present to back up his or her opinion?

Individual Activity

Calculate the marginal cost of going to college. First, list the expenses you would incur if you went to college, including tuition, room and board, books, and transportation. Then list any revenues you might receive in the form of scholarships, part-time jobs, and so forth. Combine the two to find out how much money you might have at the end of the year.

Next, list the expenses you would incur if you elected to go to work, including clothes, car, rent, and so on. Offset these expenses with your income to find out how much money you would have at the end of the year. Finally, compare the two estimates. The difference is the marginal cost of your education.

Cooperative Learning Activity

Working in pairs, use the following steps to learn more about costs. (1) Interview a local business owner to learn more about that business's costs. (2)

Select a time period to analyze, such as one week or one month. (3) Make a list of all inputs used during that period of time. (4) For each type of cost, make an estimate of the dollars spent, given the current rate of output or sales. Construct a matrix similar to the one below, and record this information in the first two columns. Ask how the dollar amount might change for each type of cost if output or sales were to fall by 50 percent, and record this in the third column. Do the same for a doubling of sales or output, and record this information in the fourth column. (5) Based on the estimates for three different levels of output, decide whether each cost is fixed or variable.

Costs	$ Spent at Current Output Level	$ Spent with Output Down 50%	$ Spent with Output Doubled	Cost Classification
1.				
2.				
3.				

Technology Activity

Building a Database

In the **Journal Writing** activity on page 103, you were asked to log all the services and jobs you supply for others for one week. Use this information to help build an "employment" database.

1. Define and name the fields in your database. The following can be used as examples:

Field Name	Field Type
Job/Service	Text
Employer's Name	Text
Employer's Phone	Number
Hourly Wage/Fee	Number
Hours Worked	Number

2. Save the database.
3. Change field size as needed so that all information in each field is visible.
4. Use the speller, proofread, and preview the database. Save the database again.
5. Print your database while in list view.

CHAPTER 5: *Supply* **125**

foreign students in U.S. universities. Many Chinese students are members of the Chinese elite.

4. Answers will vary, but students may suggest they would need more information on the past history or probability of Chinese youth influencing their elders, or information on similar situations in other countries.

? BONUS TEST QUESTION

Which measure of revenue is the most useful for business decisions? Why? *(marginal revenue; By comparing marginal revenues and marginal costs, businesses are able to determine how many workers and what level of output are needed to maximize profits.)*

have hundreds of workers, with a real estate office, which may employ few people.

Applying Economic Concepts

1. Examples will vary. Remind students that they make marginal decisions every time they spend money. Even when they buy a candy bar, their decision to purchase is a result of weighing the extra satisfaction derived from the candy bar against the extra amount of income that must be spent to get it.

2. (a) Stage III—negative returns; (b) Stage I—increasing returns; (c) Stage II—diminishing returns

Reinforcing Skills

1. changing attitudes in China

2. that economic and political reforms will continue because many Chinese children are being educated in the West

3. Chinese students make up the largest group of

CHAPTER ORGANIZER

Daily Objectives	Reproducible Resources	Multimedia Resources
Section 1 **Prices as Signals** 1. **Explain** how prices act as signals to both producers and consumers. 2. **Describe** the advantages of using prices as a way to allocate economic products. 3. **Understand** the difficulty of using rationing and other nonprice criteria to allocate scarce goods and services.	☞ Reproducible Lesson Plan 6-1 ☞ Guided Reading Activity 6-1 ☞ Cooperative Learning Activity 12 ☞ Consumer Application Activity 3 ☞ Math Practice for Economics 11 ☞ Free Enterprise Activities 5, 8 ☞ Primary and Secondary Source Reading 12 ☞ Performance Assessment Activity 11 ☞ Reinforcing Economic Skills 6 ☞ Section Quiz 6-1*	🔦 Focus Activity Transparency 33 💿 Vocabulary PuzzleMaker 💿 Chapter Challenger Interactive Review Software 💾 Testmaker 📀 MindJogger Videoquiz 💿 Interactive Economics!
Section 2 **How Prices Are Determined** 1. **Understand** how prices are determined in competitive markets. 2. **Explain** the importance of an economic model.	☞ Reproducible Lesson Plan 6-2 ☞ Guided Reading Activity 6-2 ☞ Section Quiz 6-2*	🔦 Focus Activity Transparency 34 💿 Vocabulary PuzzleMaker 💿 Chapter Challenger Interactive Review Software 💾 Testmaker 💿 Interactive Economics! 📀 NBR's Economics in Action Video Program
Section 3 **The Price System at Work** 1. **Explain** how prices allocate resources between markets. 2. **Describe** the consequence of having a fixed price in a market. 3. **Apply** your knowledge of demand elasticity to predict the size of a price change. 4. **Understand** what is meant when markets talk.	☞ Reproducible Lesson Plan 6-3 ☞ Guided Reading Activity 6-3 ☞ Section Quiz 6-3*	🔦 Focus Activity Transparency 35 🔦 Economic Concepts Transparency 8* 💿 Vocabulary PuzzleMaker 💿 Chapter Challenger Interactive Review Software 💾 Testmaker 📀 NBR's Economics in Action Video Program 💿 Interactive Economics!
Chapter Review and Evaluation	☞ Enrichment Activity 6 ☞ Reteaching Activity 6* ☞ Economic Vocabulary Activity 6* ☞ Chapter 6 Test, Forms A and B	🎧 Chapter Digests Audiocassette Activities and Tests* 💾 Testmaker 📀 MindJogger Videoquiz

*Also available in Spanish

 Blackline Master   Transparency   CD-ROM   Software   Videodisc   Audiocassette

⏱ OUT OF TIME? Assign the Chapter 6 Digest Audiocassette and the corresponding Chapter Digest activities and tests.

National Council on Economic Education

THE **Economics** America AND **Economics** International PROGRAMS

VOLUNTARY NATIONAL CONTENT STANDARDS IN ECONOMICS
Emphasized in Chapter 6

Content Standard 4 *Students will understand that:*
People respond predictably to positive and negative incentives.

Content Standard 7 *Students will understand that:*
Markets exist when buyers and sellers interact. This interaction determines market prices and thereby allocates scarce goods and services.

Content Standard 8 *Students will understand that:*
Prices send signals and provide incentives to buyers and sellers. When suppy or demand changes, market prices adjust, affecting incentives.

Content Standard 17 *Students will understand that:*
Cost of government policies sometimes exceed benefits. This may occur because of incentives facing voters, government officials, and government employees, because of actions by special interest groups that impose costs on the general public, or because social goals other than economic efficiency are being pursued.

Economics America *Resources Available From NCEE*

PERFORMANCE ASSESSMENT

The following chapter projects may be assigned at the beginning of the chapter and used for performance assessment.

Multicultural Heritage Have students work in pairs to complete the following activity. Direct pairs to use library resources to investigate a number of products—different kinds of food, items of clothing, transportation, and so on—used in everyday life in another country. Pairs should endeavor to find the most recent prices for the products they select. Then have each pair develop an illustrated newspaper article titled, "Products and Prices in [name of selected country]." Display the articles, grouped according to continent, on the bulletin board. Use the display as the starting point for a discussion of the relationship among supply, demand, and prices in the various countries.

Cooperative Learning Organize students into groups of four or five. Encourage groups to imagine they live in an economic system in which price is not used to allocate products. Have groups brainstorm to develop lists of methods to allocate products other than by market price. (Methods suggested might include rationing; "first come, first served"; and various forms of lottery.) Have each group select one method from its list and write a brief explanation of how that method might work in allocating products that students use.

ADDITIONAL RESOURCES

Readings for the Student

Economic Activity and Markets. Federal Reserve Bank of St. Louis, P.O. Box 442, St. Louis, MO 63166. Explains how the economic activity of individuals is coordinated in producing goods and services.

Multimedia

Foundations of Wealth. Films for the Humanities/Social Studies School Service, 10200 Jefferson Boulevard, P.O. Box 802, Culver City, CA 90232–0802. Color video series, 12 mins. each. *Price and the Consumer* and *Price and the Producer* explain the relationship among supply, demand, and prices.

South Dakota: An Economics and Mathematics Simulation. Educational Activities/Social Studies School Service, 10200 Jefferson Boulevard, P.O. Box 802, Culver City, CA 90232–0802. Software, Apple. Simulation illustrating supply and demand in a free market economy.

Chapter Overview

Chapter 6 ties together students' previous learning on economic markets, demand, and supply. **Section 1** discusses prices as signals to producers and consumers. **Section 2** explains how equilibrium prices are determined, and describes shortages and surpluses. **Section 3** describes how prices operate in the economy as a whole.

GLENCOE
TECHNOLOGY

VIDEODISC
MindJogger Videoquiz

Use MindJogger to preview the Chapter 6 content.

 Chapter 6
Disc 1, Side B

 Also available in VHS.

inter**NET**
CONNECTION

Resources for Chapter 6 on the World Wide Web*

National Council on Economic Education
http://www.nationalcouncil.org/

A Business Researcher's Interests
http://www.brint.com/interest.html

U.S. Business Advisor
http://www.business.gov/

*Sites subject to change.

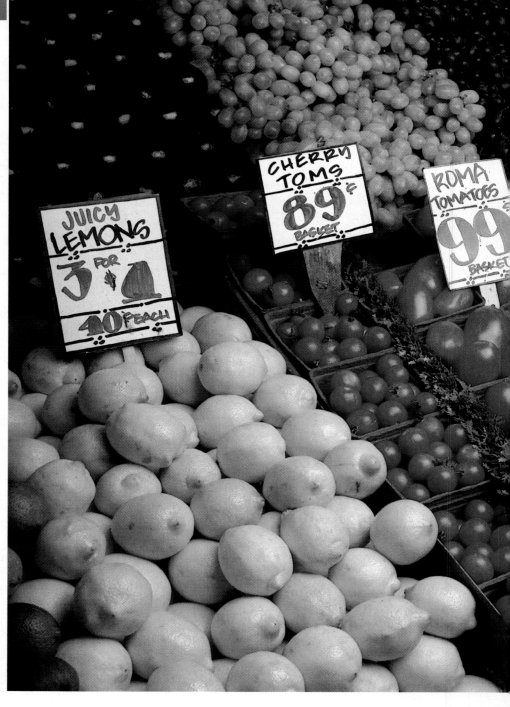

Prices for products in a market economy are determined by the interaction of supply and demand.

VISUAL INSTRUCTION

Point out that in Chapter 6, students will learn how supply and demand interact to determine price.

 Extra Credit Project

Have students write essays on the role that prices play in the market economy. Suggest that they illustrate their essays with examples, charts, and graphs. Call on volunteers to present and discuss their essays.

CHAPTER 6

Prices and Decision Making

SECTION 1
Prices as Signals

SECTION 2
How Prices Are Determined

SECTION 3
The Price System at Work

CHAPTER PREVIEW

People to Know

• Gary Becker
• Budget Analyst

Applying Economic Concepts to Your Life

Price What factors do you consider when you make a decision to buy something? You probably consider color, style, usefulness, and, of course, *price*. Price may be one of the most important factors of all. Economists certainly think so, because they regard the price of an item as a signal to both buyers and sellers.

Journal Writing

Visit an area shopping mall and look for examples of surpluses and shortages, making a list of from 5 to 10 items for each concept. Almost any sale item can be an example of surplus. Rain checks or sellouts of an item signal a shortage.

CHAPTER 6: *Prices and Decision Making* **127**

INTRODUCING CHAPTER 6

Connecting to Past Learning

Call on volunteers to define the Law of Demand and the Law of Supply. Ask other volunteers to draw typical demand and supply curves on the chalkboard. Then combine the two curves and point out that where the two curves intersect establishes the price. Conclude by mentioning that the price mechanism is the focus of this chapter.

Applying Economics

Point to an item in the classroom that students are likely to have purchased, such as a ballpoint pen. Tell students the price you paid for the pen was $0.50, and ask if they have ever paid a higher or lower amount for a similar pen. Next, as a lead-in to a discussion about who determines prices in the American economy, ask who decides how much the pen should cost. Because students' answers are likely to be supply-oriented, have them consider how consumers' wants and needs help determine price. Finally, point out the two main elements that determine price are supply and demand.

 PERFORMANCE ASSESSMENT

Refer to page **126B** for a Performance Assessment activity for this chapter. Also see the **Performance Assessment Activities** booklet for additional suggestions.

Economic Portfolio

As students develop their lists in the **Journal Writing** activity above, have them consider the causes of surpluses and shortages and the ways in which producers react to these two situations.

Key to Ability Levels — Teaching strategies have been coded for varying learning styles and abilities:
L1 - Basic (activities for all students) **L2 - Average** (activities for average to above-average students)
L3 - Challenging (activities for above-average students) **LEP - Limited English Proficiency**

SECTION 1
Prices as Signals

FOCUS

Section Objectives

1. Explain how prices act as signals to both producers and consumers.
2. Describe the advantages of using prices as a way to allocate economic products.
3. Understand the difficulty of using rationing and other nonprice criteria to allocate scarce goods and services.

Bellringer

Prior to taking roll at the beginning of the class period, display Focus Activity Transparency 33.

Motivational Activity

Discuss students' responses to the activity sheet that accompanies Transparency 33.

Preteaching Vocabulary

Ask students to define *rationing* and to provide one or two real examples. **LEP**

Use the **Vocabulary PuzzleMaker** to create crossword and word search puzzles.

TEACH

Guided Practice

L2 Journalism Write the following "headlines" on the chalkboard: PRICES DECIDE WHAT, PRICES DECIDE HOW, PRICES DECIDE FOR WHOM. Then have students write a news story to accompany one of the "headlines."

Cooperative Learning Assign Cooperative Learning Activity 12.

Section Preview

Objectives

After studying this section, you will be able to:

1. **Explain** how prices act as signals to both producers and consumers.
2. **Describe** the advantages of using prices as a way to allocate economic products.
3. **Understand** the difficulty of using rationing and other nonprice criteria to allocate scarce goods and services.

Key Terms

rationing, ration coupon

Applying Economic Concepts

Rationing Have you and your friends ever tried to share something—a candy bar, cake, or pizza—when there really wasn't enough to go around? If so, you already know about the difficulties of sharing something fairly. Sharing is a form of rationing, or allocation, and it is an important concept in economics.

Prices play an important role in our economy. They act as signals that convey information to the buyers and sellers in a market. A high price is a signal for producers to produce more and for buyers to buy less. A low price is a signal for producers to produce less and for buyers to buy more. **1**

Advantages of Prices

Prices serve as a link between producers and consumers. In doing so, they help decide the three basic WHAT, HOW, and FOR WHOM questions all societies face. Without prices, the economy would not run as smoothly, and allocation decisions would have to be made some other way, perhaps by some form of government bureaucracy. Prices perform the allocation function very well for several reasons.

Neutral

First, prices in a free market economy are neutral. They favor neither the producer nor the consumer. Instead, they are a result of competition between buyers and sellers. The more competitive the market, the more efficient the price adjustment process.

If the market is less competitive, prices tend to favor some groups more than others.

Flexible

Second, prices in a market economy are surprisingly flexible. Unforeseen events such as weather, strikes, natural disasters, and even wars affect the prices for many items. Buyers and sellers react to the new level of prices and adjust their consumption and production accordingly. Before long, the system functions smoothly again as it had before. The ability of the price system to absorb unexpected "shocks" is one of the strengths of a market economy.

Price flexibility also allows the market economy to accommodate change. The development of the personal computer provides an example. At first, personal computers were relatively scarce and expensive. Their high prices attracted new producers. The resulting competition, along with advances in technology and production methods, soon drove prices lower. Consumers wanted more computers at lower prices, and more were manufactured to meet the demand. Thus, a major innovation—the computer—entered the economy with the help of the price system and without the involvement of government or one of its bureaucracies.

Price Flexibility *The computer on the left is an older model. The computer on the right is a newer model. If the prices for both computers were adjusted for inflation, the earlier model would cost more.* **Why do you think this is so?**

Freedom of Choice

Third, the price system provides for maximum freedom of choice for everyone. Because a market economy typically provides a variety of products at a wide range of prices, consumers have many choices available to them. If the price is too high, a lower-priced product can usually be found. Even if a suitable alternative cannot be found, no one forces the consumer to pay a certain price for a product in a competitive market economy. **2**

In command economies, such as those found in Cuba and North Korea, consumers face limited choices. Government planners, rather than prices, allocate both resources and products. The government usually decides if a product will be produced, and then limits the product's variety to keep production costs down. Items such as food, transportation, and housing often are offered to citizens at artificially low prices, but seldom are enough produced to satisfy everyone. Many people go without.

No Administrative Cost

Fourth, prices have no cost of administration. Competitive markets tend to find their own prices without outside help or interference. No bureaucrats need to be hired, no committees formed, no laws passed, or other decisions made. Even when prices adjust from one level to another, the change is usually so gradual that people hardly notice.

Checking Understanding

1. What signal does a high price send to buyers and sellers?
2. How does the price system provide for freedom of choice?

Applying Economic Concepts

☑ **Economic Systems** One of the challenges that the former command economies of eastern Europe face is rapidly rising prices. Under communism the government set artificially low prices. When supply and demand were allowed to set prices, costs skyrocketed.

L1 *Organizing Information*
Have students draw a chart using *Price Allocation* and *Nonprice Allocation* as horizontal headings, and *Neutral, Flexible, Freedom of Choice, No Administrative Costs,* and *Efficient* as vertical headings. Ask them to complete the chart by writing brief explanations of how the two allocation systems do or do not exhibit the listed characteristics. **LEP**

VISUAL INSTRUCTION

Ask students how the computer illustrates the flexibility of the price system. *(At first, computers were scarce and relatively expensive. This attracted more producers. Resulting competition, advances in technology, and production methods forced prices down.)*

Answer to Caption:

because earlier models were relatively scarce and more expensive

ANSWERS

1. Buyers should buy less and sellers should offer more for sale.
2. If the price of one product is too high, a lower-priced alternative usually can be found.

INTERACTIVE
ECONOMICS!

CD-ROM Price Determination

Have students click on "Prices as Signals." Then have them quiz a partner on the way prices act as signals to consumers and producers.

 Supplied in both CD-ROM and diskette formats.

Meeting Special Needs

Study Strategy Learning disabled students often have difficulty generalizing the use of a strategy from one situation to another. They need to have periodic review of both the steps of the strategy they are using and the procedures that are used in each of the steps. Tell students that in this section they are going to use the study strategy independently. Have each student make a chart with grids to self-evaluate each one of the following: Did I skim for the title, headings, main ideas? Did I ask questions? Did I answer my questions?

📁 **Guided Reading** Assign Guided Reading Activity for Section 1. **LEP**

L1 Application Present students with the following situation: You want to buy a particular item, but buying it will use up a large amount of your income. Direct students to write a paragraph explaining how prices will help them to decide whether to buy the item. Have students compare their paragraphs.

📁 **Consumer Application** Assign Consumer Application Activity 3.

📁 **Math Practice** Assign Math Practice for Economics 11.

📁 **Free Enterprise** Assign Free Enterprise Activities 5 and 8.

📁 **Readings** Assign Primary and Secondary Source Reading 12.

📁 **Performance Assessment** Assign Performance Assessment Activity 11.

VISUAL INSTRUCTION

Point out that in command economies low prices are usually set for necessities, such as food, and public services, such as mass transit.

Answer to Top Caption:

Prices are neutral and flexible, they offer freedom of choice, they have no administrative costs, and they work efficiently.

Answer to Bottom Caption:

Production was limited.

"They call it a sticker price because it shows how hard they're going to stick us."

Prices *This consumer has a negative view of prices.* **What are the positive aspects of prices in a market economy?**

Efficient

Finally, prices are efficient because they are easily understood by everyone. This allows people to make decisions quickly and efficiently, with a minimum of time and effort. Suppose that you want to buy a prod-

uct that is in short supply. You can still go ahead with the purchase if you can afford its high price. On the other hand, the purchase can be postponed, a substitute can be found, or you can otherwise adjust your behavior.

Prices are even used to influence driving behavior. In some parts of Hong Kong, for example, traffic congestion is a major problem. To encourage drivers to change their driving habits, a system of variable tolls is used with higher tolls during rush hours and lower rates at other times.

Other nonprice allocation systems may require people to fill out application forms, wait in lines, obtain permits, or meet other criteria in order to obtain the scarce good or service. All of these methods allocate resources, but they usually take time and effort. Imagine the frustration you would feel if you stood in line for hours to purchase a product at an artificially low price—only to find that the good sold out just as you reached the head of the line. **1**

Allocations Without Prices

Think what life would be like without a price system. How would a car dealer allocate a limited sup-

Nonprice Allocation *In command economies such as that in the former Soviet Union, government planners set artificially low prices.* **How did this type of nonprice allocation affect the amount of goods produced?**

💲 Free Enterprise Activity 💲

Organize students into five groups and assign each group one of the five advantages of prices—neutral, flexible, freedom of choice, no administrative cost, and efficient. Direct groups to identify a real example of their assigned advantage in opera-

tion. Have groups develop a brief presentation on their example. Presentations could take the form of an illustrated lecture, a skit, a television or radio news story, or a small museum exhibit. Call on groups to make their presentations to the class.

ply of sports cars? Would intelligence, or perhaps good looks, or even political connections, determine who could get a car? Most people probably view these criteria as unfair.

Still, without prices, some other system must be used to allocate scarce goods and services. One such method is **rationing**—a system under which a government agency decides everyone's fair share. Under such a system, people receive a **ration coupon,** similar to a ticket or a receipt, that entitles the holder to purchase a certain amount of the product. Rationing has been used before, especially during wartime, but many problems are associated with it. ☑️

The Problem of Fairness

The first problem with rationing is that almost everyone feels his or her share is too small. During the oil crisis of the early 1970s, for example, the government made plans for, but never implemented, a gas rationing program. One of the major problems with the program was determining how to allocate the gas rationing coupons. Some people argued that the only fair way to allocate gas was to give everyone exactly the same number of coupons. Drivers of newer and more fuel-efficient cars, however, got farther on a gallon of gas than someone who owned an older gas-guzzler. Those who used public transportation needed even fewer coupons.

Consumers debated about who needed gas the most. Driving distances also were debated. Those who lived in western states claimed that, because they drove longer distances than their eastern counterparts, westerners should receive more coupons. Some advocated rationing coupons according to the number of cars registered, so that every owner got "X" number of coupons per car. This plan discriminated against the large family with only one car, and

it seemed to favor young couples who owned two or even three cars.

Some people thought they were more important than others. Should politicians and government bureaucrats get a certain allocation before the remaining coupons are divided among the rest of the citizens? Any number of ways to allocate gas coupons existed, but fairness was still a difficult issue. **2**

QUICK CHECK

Checking Understanding

1. What nonprice systems help allocate resources in a market economy?
2. What are the major problems with rationing?

Applying Economic Concepts

☑️ **Rationing** The United States used rationing during World War II. Families received ration coupons for goods such as meat and butter based on the number of people in the household. Coupons had to be presented at the time the purchase was made.

L2 *Rationing* Give each student a slip of paper that reads "Good for 10 points on test grade." Tell them that for the next 10 minutes, they may trade their points for other items. Then explain that the type of exchange that just took place also happens under a system of rationing. Have students write how a price system differs from a rationing system in determining supply and demand.

ASSESS

Check for Understanding

Assign Section 1 Review as homework or an in-class activity.

💻 Use **Chapter Challenger Interactive Review Software** to review Section 1.

MEETING LESSON OBJECTIVES

Each objective below is tested by the questions that follow it in parentheses.

1. **Explain** how prices act as signals. **(4)**
2. **Describe** the advantages of using prices as a way to allocate economic products. **(2)**
3. **Understand** the difficulty of using rationing and other nonprice criteria to allocate scarce goods and services. **(1, 3, 5)**

Extending the Content

Rationing During World War II, there were critical shortages of many consumer goods because productive resources were being used for the war effort. Because of these shortages, prices rose. In an attempt to control this inflation and provide equitable distribution of scarce goods, the federal government established the Office of Price

Administration (OPA). The OPA set up nearly 6,000 boards nationwide that administered the rationing of such goods as meat, butter, shoes, tires, and gasoline. Ration books containing coupons were issued to each family. In order to purchase any rationed item, a coupon had to be used.

QUICK CHECK

ANSWERS

1. filling out application forms, waiting in lines, obtaining permits, or meeting other criteria

2. establishing a system that is efficient yet fair

High Administrative Cost

A second problem with rationing is the cost. Someone has to pay for printing coupons and the salaries of the people who distribute them. In addition, no matter how much care is taken, some coupons will be stolen, sold, or counterfeited and used to consume the product allocated for someone else.

In the case of the gas shortage of the 1970s, millions of coupons were actually printed and stored in warehouses around the country. The plan called for the coupons to be distributed at local post offices. Committees set up in every community would hear and then rule on hardship cases. The plan would have been expensive to implement. In addition to the cost of printing, shipping, storing, and even guarding the coupons, additional postal and other administrative workers would have had to be hired to distribute the coupons and deal with complaints.

Diminished Incentives

A third problem is that rationing has a negative impact on people's incentive to work and produce. Even if the system was set up so that everyone received an equal share, why should one person work harder than another when each would share equally in the stock of goods and services? What would motivate either person to work at all?

People sometimes lose the incentive to use the rationed good in a careful manner. In the case of the gas rationing coupons, would people have used the

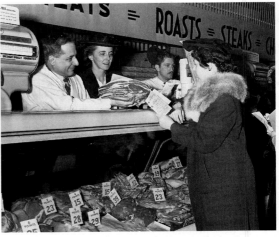

Rationing *During World War II, shoppers had to buy meat with ration coupons.* **How are prices determined in a rationing system?**

gas wisely after they had enough coupons? Some people would still drive rather than carpool or take a bus. Others would be tempted to use all the gas they got even if they did not need it.

Nonprice allocation mechanisms, such as rationing, raise a number of issues that do not need to be addressed under a price allocation system. As long as we have prices, goods can be allocated through a system that is neutral, efficient, flexible, inexpensive, and full of choices.

SECTION 1 REVIEW

Reviewing Terms and Facts

1. **Define** rationing, ration coupon.
2. **List** five advantages of using prices to allocate goods and services.
3. **Explain** the difficulties of allocating goods and services without a price system.

Critical Thinking

4. **Determining Cause and Effect** List five items you would like to buy. How does the price of each item affect your decision to allocate your scarce resources—your money and your time? Describe the way in which prices act as signals to help you make your decisions.

Applying Economic Concepts

5. **Rationing** From your own experience, describe a situation that required some form of rationing. What criteria were used to allocate the good or service, and what were some of the problems with each of the criteria?

Answers to SECTION 1 REVIEW

1. All vocabulary words are defined in the Glossary.

2. Prices are neutral, flexible, offer freedom of choice, have no administrative costs, and work efficiently.

3. establishing a fair system of allocation, the cost of administering the system, the negative impact the system has on people's incentive to work and produce

4. Items will vary. Students will note that price will play a major role in their decision to buy. High prices will signal that they should probably delay their purchase or look for a cheaper alternative. Low prices will signal that they should buy.

5. Answers will vary. As guidance, suggest that students review the material on pages 128, 130–132 before answering the question.

Interpreting Political Cartoons

TEACH

Do you turn to the comics section of the newspaper first? Most people enjoy reading comic strips, but newspapers have another type of cartoon known as the *political cartoon*—a drawing that gives visual commentary on current events.

Explanation

In political cartoons, artists use humor and satire to express opinions about political and economic issues. The purpose of most political cartoons is to inform and influence public opinion in an entertaining way. Because political cartoons reflect the opinions of individual artists, they usually appear on the editorial pages of newspapers.

To interpret the meaning of a political cartoon, study its pictures, words, and symbols to discover its main idea and point of view. Cartoonists often exaggerate drawings to make their points more forcefully. For example, a group of poor people may be represented by one very thin person. Cartoonists also use symbols. The figure of Uncle Sam, for example, is a symbol for the United States government.

Follow these steps to interpret political cartoons.
- Read the title and information in the cartoon to determine its general topic.
- Analyze the symbols in the cartoon.
- Identify the main idea and the cartoonist's point of view.

Practice

Study the cartoon and answer the questions below.
1. Who does the man sitting on the table represent?
2. Who does the second man represent?
3. What is the second man doing?
4. What is the main point of this cartoon?
5. What do you think the cartoonist's attitude is about this issue?
6. How did you form that conclusion?

Call on volunteers to identify the purpose of political cartoons and to list some of the techniques that cartoonists use. *(purpose: to inform and to influence public opinion in an entertaining fashion; techniques: exaggeration, symbols)* Then lead students through the steps to be followed to interpret political cartoons. Have students apply the steps to the cartoon on page 130.

📂 **Skills Practice** For additional practice, have students complete Reinforcing Economic Skills 6.

HEALTH CARE in AMERICA

CHECK BOOK

DANZIGER
The Christian Science Monitor
Los Angeles Times Syndicate

Additional Practice

For further practice in interpreting political cartoons, complete the Reinforcing Skills exercise in the Chapter 6 Review on page 149.

CHAPTER 6: *Prices and Decision Making* **133**

Answers to SKILL

1. American people seeking health care
2. American health care providers or doctors
3. He is examining the patient's checkbook to see if it is breathing; in other words, whether or not the patient has money.
4. That health care providers are interested only in making money, not in providing service to patients.

5. Answers may vary, but most students will suggest that the cartoonist feels that the health-care system has failed the people it was established to serve.

6. Answers may vary, but most students will note that the doctor appears to have no interest in the patient.

SECTION 2

How Prices Are Determined

FOCUS

Section Objectives

1. Understand how prices are determined in competitive markets.
2. Explain the importance of an economic model.

Bellringer

Prior to taking roll at the beginning of the class period, display Focus Activity Transparency 34.

Motivational Activity

Discuss students' responses to the activity sheet that accompanies Transparency 34.

Preteaching Vocabulary

Ask students to define the terms *surplus* or *shortage* in their own words. Then ask them to offer an example of these two economic situations. **LEP**

Use the **Vocabulary PuzzleMaker** to create crossword and word search puzzles.

TEACH

Guided Practice

L1 *Illustrating Ideas* Draw students' attention to Figure 6.2 on page 136. Ask them to think of a pair of scissors whose blades, working in unison, make a clean cut through paper. Then point out that the supply and demand curves are like the scissors. When they work together, they perform a function. Ask students to write a sentence that summarizes how supply and demand determine price. **LEP**

Section Preview

Objectives

After studying this section, you will be able to:
1. **Understand** how prices are determined in competitive markets.
2. **Explain** the importance of an economic model.

Key Terms

economic model, market equilibrium, surplus, shortage, equilibrium price, loss leader

Applying Economic Concepts

Equilibrium Price Have you ever sold something to a friend? Perhaps you wanted to sell at one price and your friend wanted to buy at another. After some compromise, you probably agreed on a price, and the exchange took place. Your price was an *equilibrium price*, or one that clears the market.

In a market economy, everyone who participates in the market jointly determines prices. Prices are considered neutral and impartial.

The Adjustment Process

In economic markets, buyers and sellers have exactly the opposite hopes and intentions. Buyers want to find good buys at low prices. Sellers hope for high prices and profits. Neither side can get exactly what it wants, so some adjustment is necessary to reach a compromise. Even so, both sides benefit as long as the process is voluntary, or the transaction would not have occurred in the first place.

To understand how the adjustment takes place, suppose a new product called a *gadget* is introduced. The gadget, for illustrative purposes, is an innovative home security device. Because the product is new, producers cannot be sure what price to charge for it. They will have to experiment and see if the market forces of supply and demand will help resolve the issue.

An Economic Model

In order to demonstrate how a market works, we can use an **economic model**—a set of assumptions that can be listed in a table, illustrated with a graph, or even stated algebraically—to help analyze behavior and predict outcomes. Information about the market is shown in Figure 6.1, where the price and consumer demand

for gadgets appear in the first two columns and the quantity supplied appears in the third column. **1**

The demand schedule in columns 1 and 2 reflects the Law of Demand—as the price goes down, more gadgets are demanded. Likewise, the supply schedule in columns 1 and 3 reflects the Law of Supply—as the price goes up, the gadget-makers are willing to supply more. These schedules can also be illustrated graphically as in Figure 6.2, where supply and demand curves appear in the same diagram.

The demand curve in Figure 6.2 represents the ability and willingness of consumers to purchase the product. The supply curve in Figure 6.2 represents the ability and willingness of suppliers to offer various quantities of gadgets over a range of different prices. When we put the supply curve and the demand curve together, we have a visual representation of all the buyers and sellers in the market.

Market Equilibrium

In a competitive market, the adjustment process moves toward **market equilibrium**—a situation in which prices are relatively stable, and the quantity of goods or services supplied is equal to the quantity demanded. In terms of the economic model in Figure 6.2, equilibrium is reached when the price is $5, and the quantity supplied is 1,300 units. **2**

How does the market find the equilibrium price of $5 on its own, and why is the quantity supplied exactly equal to the quantity demanded at this price?

Classroom Resources for SECTION 2

- Reproducible Lesson Plan 6-2
- Guided Reading Activity 6-2
- Section Quiz 6-2
- Spanish Section Quiz 6-2
- Focus Activity Transparency 34
- NBR's Economics in Action Video Program

- Testmaker
- Vocabulary PuzzleMaker
- Chapter Challenger Interactive Review Software
- Interactive Economics!

Lesson 5 of Interactive Economics! to learn more about "How Prices Are Determined."

Figure 6.1
The Demand and Supply Schedules for Gadgets

Price (in dollars)	Quantity Demanded	Quantity Supplied	Shortage/ Surplus	
$10	600	1550	950	SURPLUS
9	720	1500	780	
8	850	1450	600	
7	990	1400	410	
6	1140	1350	210	
5	1300	1300	0	EQUILIBRIUM
4	1470	1250	-220	SHORTAGE
3	1650	1200	-450	
2	1840	1150	-690	
1	2040	1100	-940	

The demand schedule for gadgets appears in the first two columns. The supply schedule appears in columns one and three. If you compare the quantities demanded and supplied at every price, you can see there is a surplus at every price at $6 and above, and a shortage at every price at $4 and below. $5 is the equilibrium price that balances the quantity demanded with the quantity supplied. **How is an equilibrium price reached?**

Why did the market not reach equilibrium at $7, or $6, or at some other price? In order to answer these questions, we have to examine the reactions of the buyers and sellers to various market prices.

Surplus

Because the market for gadgets is new, no one knows what the equilibrium price will be. If suppliers guess that the price will be $7 per gadget, they will want to produce 1,400 units for sale. As Graph **A** in **Figure 6.3** shows, consumers will buy only 990 of the 1,400 gadgets at a price of $7, leaving a surplus of 410.

A **surplus** is a situation in which the quantity supplied is greater than the quantity demanded at a given price. Suppliers may have built up inventories in their warehouses, only to find that they did not receive enough orders for the product. If the suppliers want to dispose of the surplus, they need to lower their price to attract more buyers. At a lower price, suppliers will also offer fewer gadgets for sale during the next trading period. The result is that a surplus causes the price to go down, the quantity demanded to rise, and the quantity supplied to be reduced. As long as the price is flexible, the surplus will only be temporary.

 Checking Understanding

1. Why do economists use economic models?
2. What is market equilibrium?

Applying Economic Concepts

Surplus The complex system of federal price supports contributed greatly to persistent surpluses in American agriculture. These price supports were introduced during the Great Depression and were finally phased out beginning in 1997.

CHAPTER 6: *Prices and Decision Making* **135**

GLENCOE
TECHNOLOGY

NIGHTLY BUSINESS REPORT
Economics in Action

Chapter 11
Disc 1, Side 2
Title: *Supply and Demand*
Subject: How supply and demand affect prices
Ask: What factor mentioned in the video contributes to changes in demand? *(The increase in the price of related goods causes an increase in demand.)*

Also available in VHS.

VISUAL INSTRUCTION

Answer to Caption:
Surpluses and shortages put pressure on prices and quantities supplied, forcing the market to seek equilibrium.

 ANSWERS

1. to help analyze behavior and predict outcomes
2. when prices are relatively stable, and quantity supplied is equal to quantity demanded

---

INTERACTIVE ECONOMICS!

 CD-ROM Price Determination

Have students review "How Prices Are Determined." Then have them define "surplus" and "shortage."

 Supplied in both CD-ROM and diskette formats.

L2 *Analyzing Ideas* Direct students to examine Figure 6.3 on page 137. Call on volunteers to explain how these graphs illustrate the price adjustment process. Then lead the class in a discussion of the importance of the process in the American economy. In the discussion, ask students to consider the following questions: Whose needs are being served by the process? In what ways? How would allocations be made if the process did not operate?

Independent Practice

 Guided Reading Assign Guided Reading Activity for Section 2. **LEP**

L2 *Market Model* Have students construct demand and supply schedules and a market model for a brand of blue jeans, using the information below. Then ask at what prices surpluses and shortages appear.

Price	Demand	Supply
$22	60,000	20,000
24	50,000	28,000
26	44,000	32,000
28	36,000	36,000
30	30,000	40,000
32	24,000	46,000

⊙ VISUAL INSTRUCTION

Ask: Will there be a surplus or shortage of gadgets at the following prices: $8? *(surplus)* $5.50? *(surplus)* $4? *(shortage)*

Answer to Top Caption:

quantity supplied decreases

Answer to Bottom Caption:

Demand will be so great that there will be a shortage.

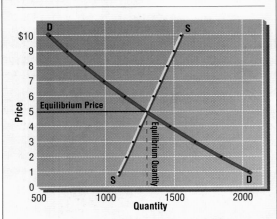

Figure 6.2
A Model of the Gadgets Market

According to the model of the gadgets market, $5 is the equilibrium price that "clears" the market. At that price, 1,300 gadgets will be supplied and an equal number purchased. **What happens to the supply of gadgets if the price is lowered to $3?**

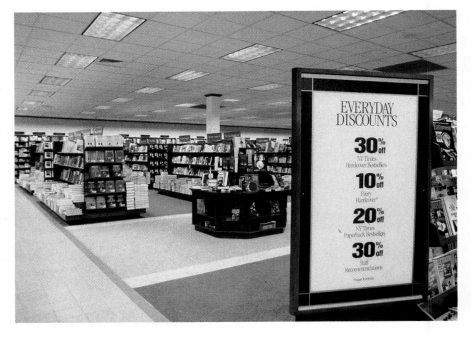

Price Adjustment
Bookstores and other businesses often price certain goods below cost to attract customers. **What may result if the price for a given product is set too low?**

Shortage

If $7 is too high, the producers might consider $4 on the second day. At that price, the quantity supplied changes to 1,250 gadgets. As Graph **B** in **Figure 6.3** shows, however, the $4 price is too low. At $4, the demand curve shows that consumers would buy 1,470 gadgets. Because only 1,250 are available, a shortage of 220 results.

A **shortage** is a situation in which the quantity demanded is greater than the quantity supplied at a given price. When a shortage in the market happens, producers have no more gadgets to sell even though additional buyers are willing to purchase the product at the existing price. Producers wish that they had charged higher prices for their products. The result is that a shortage causes the price and the quantity supplied to increase in the next trading period.

While our model does not show exactly how much the price will go up, we can assume that the next price will be less than $7, which we already know is too high. If the new price is $6, a surplus of 210, as seen in Graph **C** in **Figure 6.3**, will result. This surplus will cause the price to drop, but probably not below $4, which already proved to be too low.

$ Free Enterprise Activity $

To help students understand the role of price in dealing with a surplus, and to give them some math practice, provide them with the following problem. At the end of spring, the manager of a clothing store notices that his stockroom is stacked with designer sweaters priced at $80 each. To clear his stock, the manager decides to mark down the sweater price by 45 percent. What will be the markdown price of the sweaters?

For students who need guidance, explain that the markdown price is determined by: 1. multiplying the regular price by the percentage of markdown, and 2. subtracting the result from the regular price. *(1. $80 × 45% = $36; 2. $80 – $36 = $44. The markdown price is $44.)*

Figure 6.3
Dynamics of the Price Adjustment Process in the Gadgets Market

A. DAY 1: A price of $7 causes a surplus of 410.

B. DAY 2: The previous surplus causes the price to drop. The new price is too low and a shortage develops.

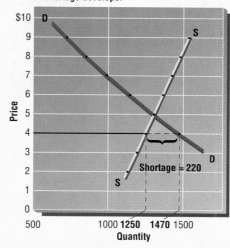

C. DAY 3: The shortage in Day 2 causes the price to rise. The new price is too high.

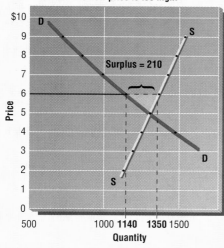

D. DAY 4: The surplus in Day 3 causes the price to drop, and equilibrium is reached.

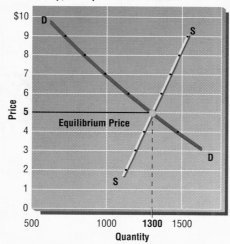

In a competitive market, prices tend to gravitate toward equilibrium as a result of the constant pressures from temporary surpluses and shortages. **What is the difference between a surplus and a shortage?**

CHAPTER 6: *Prices and Decision Making* **137**

Lesson 5 of Interactive Economics! to learn more about "How Prices Are Determined."

CHAPTER 6
SECTION 2

L1 *Advertising* Have students scan grocery advertisements in newspapers for a few days to identify items they think are loss leaders. Call on volunteers to present their advertisements and explain why the items are loss leaders. Have students create a collage with their advertisements and use it as a starting point for a discussion on how loss leaders are used to create demand. **LEP**

ASSESS

Check for Understanding

Assign Section 2 Review as homework or an in-class activity.

 Use **Chapter Challenger Interactive Review Software** to review Section 2.

DID YOU KNOW

Economists sometimes refer to a surplus as *excess supply* and a shortage as *excess demand.*

VISUAL INSTRUCTION

Ask students what price change might be signaled by the existence of a surplus. *(fall in price)*

Answer to Caption:

surplus: when quantity supplied is greater than quantity demanded at given price; shortage: when quantity demanded is greater than quantity supplied at given price

---

Extending the Content

Economic Reasoning Analyzing the steps in a chain of events triggered by a particular change in the economy is called economic reasoning. For example, a large decrease in the price of oil may start the following chain of events. The price of gas goes down. Demand for automobiles increases. To meet this demand, automakers step up production of new cars, hiring more workers to meet new production levels. This increase in employment means that more people have money to spend.

Perhaps more people will travel. This, in turn, leads to increased income for recreation areas, restaurants, hotels, and motels.

Ask students to apply economic reasoning to the following change: a large firm locates in your community. *(Employment rises; newly employed people have money to spend on goods and services; sales increase for businesses in the community; these businesses purchase new inventory, increase advertising, hire more workers, etc.)*

137

DID YOU KNOW?

Brazil's Millionaires In 1993 inflation made almost everyone in Brazil a millionaire. Instead of being happy, however, Brazilians were going crazy. The monthly minimum wage was 3.3 million *cruzeiros*, or about $80 in American currency. A two-bedroom apartment cost 3 billion *cruzeiros*. To keep people from having to lug around suitcases of cash, banknotes in ever-larger denominations appeared every three months.

Equilibrium Price

When the price drops to $5, as shown in Graph **D** in **Figure 6.3**, the market finds its **equilibrium price.** The equilibrium price is the price that "clears the market" in that there is neither a surplus nor a shortage at the end of the trading period. While the model of the market cannot show exactly how long it will take to reach equilibrium, equilibrium will be reached.

Because of the pressure that temporary surpluses and/or shortages put on prices and quantities supplied, the market tends to seek its own equilib-rium. Prices in the gadget market will eventually reach and then stay at $5, with production at 1,300 units, until something disturbs the market.

A Touch of Realism

The theory of competitive pricing represents a set of ideal conditions and outcomes. The theory serves as a model by which to measure the performance of other less competitive market structures.

Many markets do come close to the ideal. The prices of gasoline, foods, and many other items in your community will be relatively close from one store to the next. When the prices of these items do vary, it may be because the buyers are not well informed. A store may also be promoting a certain item as a **loss leader**—an item specially priced below cost to attract customers.

Fortunately, markets only have to be competitive, rather than perfect, to be useful. The great advantage of competitive markets is that they allocate resources efficiently. As sellers compete to meet consumer demands, they are forced to lower costs and prices. At the same time, competition among buyers helps prevent prices from falling too far, and helps allocate goods and services to those who are willing and able to pay.

SECTION 2 REVIEW

Reviewing Terms and Facts

1. **Define** economic model, market equilibrium, surplus, shortage, equilibrium price, loss leader.
2. **Describe** how surpluses and shortages help the market find the equilibrium price.
3. **Explain** the importance of an economic model.

Critical Thinking

4. **Making Inferences** What do merchants usually do to move items that are overstocked? What does this tell you about the equilibrium price for the product?

Applying Economic Concepts

5. **Equilibrium Price** Choose one good or service—for example, unleaded gasoline, a gallon of milk, a local newspaper, a haircut. Visit at least four stores that carry the product, and note its price at each location. What do the individual prices tell you about the equilibrium price for the good or service?

Answers to SECTION 2 REVIEW

1. All vocabulary words are defined in the Glossary.

2. Surpluses indicate that prices should be lowered; shortages indicate that prices should be increased. Through this process, equilibrium eventually will be reached.

3. It shows how markets work by helping analyze behavior and predict outcomes.

4. They lower the price of the items. The equilibrium price for the product is lower than the present price.

5. Answers will vary. Students will note that if there is little difference in prices, the equilibrium price has been reached. If there is a wide variation in prices, price adjustment is still going on.

PROFILES IN ECONOMICS

GARY BECKER
(1930–   )

Gary Stanley Becker is a professor of economics at the University of Chicago and a fellow of the Hoover Institution at Stanford. In 1992 he received the Nobel Prize in economics for his work applying economic analysis to social problems, including crime and punishment, racial and gender discrimination, the formation and breakup of families, drug and substance abuse, and the formation and importance of human capital.

ECONOMIC BASIS OF SOCIAL PROBLEMS Professor Becker views individual behavior as being based on the economic incentives of the marketplace

College graduates reflect an investment in human capital.

and rational self-interest. He believes that costs and benefits interact to help explain human behavior. Shortly after winning the Nobel Prize, he described his theory:

The number of children a couple has depends on the costs and benefits of child rearing. . . . [C]ouples tend to have fewer children when the wife works and has a better-paying job, when subsidies and tax deductions for dependents are smaller, when the cost of educating and training children rises, and so forth.
—Viewpoint, *Business Week*, November 2, 1992

Professor Becker has extended economic analysis into areas normally studied by other social disciplines. He recognizes the contributions made by other social sciences in explaining human behavior, however. Becker argues, for example, that the sociologist helps explain human behavior by identifying the broad social forces, such as peer group pressure, that cause some people to act as they do. When the sociologist's view is combined with the economic theory of costs, benefits, and personal welfare, an explanation for individual behavior becomes more powerful.

In the case of drug and substance abuse, Becker argues that, although addictive behavior has a psychological and a biological basis, the economist can help point out some of the economic circumstances that encouraged people to first become addicted. Economists can also help explain how a change in these economic circumstances—including housing, employment, and better career opportunities—might affect the addiction.

HUMAN CAPITAL Professor Becker helped popularize interest in the topic of human capital. He frequently uses the differences in earnings among high school dropouts, high school graduates, and college graduates to reinforce the point that education and training are rewarded in the marketplace.

Examining the Profile

1. **Identifying Cause and Effect** How can costs help explain why American families have grown smaller?

2. **For Further Research** Research the relationship between periods of economic growth and/or decline and the status of criminal activity during the same periods. Summarize your findings in a statistical table.

Answers to Examining the Profile

1. Many mothers have to work to help pay the family bills. The high cost of child care makes it expensive for working mothers to have large families. Working couples with no children face the temporary loss of income if they decide to have a child. The high cost of a college education may also discourage some families from having many children.

2. Tables will vary. Encourage students to display and discuss their tables.

FOCUS

Section Objectives

1. Explain how prices allocate resources between markets.
2. Describe the consequence of having a fixed price in a market.
3. Apply your knowledge of demand elasticity to predict the size of a price change.
4. Understand what is meant when markets talk.

Bellringer

 Prior to taking roll at the beginning of the class period, display Focus Activity Transparency 35.

Motivational Activity

Discuss students' responses to the activity sheet that accompanies Transparency 35.

Preteaching Vocabulary

Ask students to write sentences using each key term. Have them check the meanings as they work through the section. **LEP**

Use the **Vocabulary PuzzleMaker** to create crossword and word search puzzles.

VISUAL INSTRUCTION

Ask students to suggest why predicting prices may be difficult for farmers. *(Changes in weather may make it difficult for farmers to predict size, quality of harvest.)*

Answer to Caption:

how much to buy and how much to sell

SECTION 3
The Price System at Work

Section Preview

Objectives

After studying this section, you will be able to:
1. **Explain** how prices allocate resources between markets.
2. **Describe** the consequence of having a fixed price in a market.
3. **Apply** your knowledge of demand elasticity to predict the size of a price change.
4. **Understand** what is meant when markets talk.

Key Terms

rebate, price ceiling, minimum wage, price floor, target price, non-recourse loan, deficiency payment

Applying Economic Concepts

Shortage If you are planning to go to college, you should be aware some large universities actually turn students away because of a shortage of classroom space. This *shortage* is partially due to tuition. When tuition is too low, too many people have the ability and willingness to pay. Colleges and universities must then rely on nonprice criteria—state residency, class standing, and SAT or ACT scores—to allocate the existing spaces.

Prices are important because they help producers and consumers make decisions. The overall economy, however, is made up of many markets for many different products. In order to understand how the economy operates as a whole, the role of prices in this larger setting must be examined.

Prices as a System

A price in any given resource market helps sellers decide where to sell their resources and producers where to buy them. The same is basically true of all prices collectively. Prices serve as signals that allocate resources between markets.

Consider the way in which higher oil prices affected producers' and consumers' decisions in the 1970s. During this time, the price of oil went from $5 a barrel to as much as $40. Because the demand for oil is basically inelastic, people had to spend a greater part of their income on energy. Higher energy costs left them with less to spend elsewhere, a fact that affected other markets. ✔

The market for full-size automobiles was one of the first industries to feel the effects. Because most large cars did not get good gas mileage, people bought fewer big cars and more foreign-made, smaller

automobiles. As the demand for big cars fell, producers ended up with unsold inventories of automobiles.

At first, automakers thought the increase in gas prices would be temporary, so they were reluctant to introduce smaller, more fuel-efficient models. As time went on, however, the surplus of unsold cars remained. To move their inventories, manufacturers began to offer a **rebate**—a partial refund of the original price of the product. The rebate was the

Prices *Farmers, like economists, try to predict changes in prices.* **What do prices tell buyers and sellers?**

Classroom Resources for SECTION 3

- Reproducible Lesson Plan 6-3
- Guided Reading Activity 6-3
- Section Quiz 6-3
- Focus Activity Transparency 35
- Economic Concepts Transparency 8
- NBR's Economics in Action Video Program
- Enrichment Activity 6
- Reteaching Activity 6
- Economic Vocabulary Activity 6

- Chapter 6 Test, Form A and Form B
- English and Spanish Audiocassettes
- Testmaker
- Vocabulary PuzzleMaker
- Chapter Challenger Interactive Review Software
- MindJogger Videoquiz
- Interactive Economics!

same as a temporary price reduction, because consumers were offered $500, $600, and even $1,000 back on each new car they bought.

At the same time, automakers began reducing their production of large cars. Plants were closed, workers were laid off, and companies started to change to small car production. Many of the automobile workers who lost their jobs found new ones in other industries.

The result of higher prices in the international oil market was a shift of productive resources out of the large car market into other markets. Although the process was a painful one for those involved, it was a necessary one for a market economy. **1**

What Happens When Prices Are Fixed?

Up to now, we have assumed that the market was reasonably competitive, and that prices, along with quantities offered for sale, were allowed to fluctuate. However, what happens when actions by special interest groups result in government policies that fix the prices people either receive or pay?

This situation often occurs in the case of price supports, which prevent the price system from effectively transmitting information in the market. Many economists argue that fixed prices are examples of government policies whose costs usually outweigh their benefits.

Price Ceilings

Some cities, especially New York City, have experimented with rent controls to make housing more affordable. When rents are capped at artificially low rates, however, persistent "housing shortages" usually result.

Lesson 5 of Interactive Economics! to learn more about "Price Ceilings and Floors."

Figure 6.4
Price Ceilings and Permanent Shortages

In housing markets, a rent control is the same as a price ceiling.

A shortage is created whenever a price ceiling is lower than the equilibrium price. In the figure, a ceiling price of $500 per month results in 2.4 million apartments demanded with only 1.6 million being supplied—leaving a shortage of .8 million, or 800,000 apartments. **Why are price ceilings established?**

The case of a **price ceiling,** the maximum legal price that can be charged, is shown in **Figure 6.4.** Without the ceiling, the market establishes monthly rents at $700. Two million apartments would be supplied and rented at that rate. If authorities thought $700 was too high, they could arbitrarily establish a price ceiling at $500 a month. Consumers, of course, would love the lower price and might demand 2.4 million apartments as a result. Landlords, on the other hand, would just as soon convert some apartments to other uses that offer higher returns. Therefore, only 1.6 million apartments would be offered at $500 per month. **2**

Checking Understanding

1. What was the result of higher prices in the international oil market?
2. How do price ceilings affect quantity supplied?

Applying Economic Concepts

☑ **Market and Prices** The cost of motor fuel—gasoline, ethanol, and diesel—more than tripled during the 1970s before dropping significantly in the mid-1980s.

CHAPTER 6: *Prices and Decision Making* **141**

TEACH

Guided Practice

L3 *Debate* Have students debate the following: "The minimum wage should be increased." Prior to the debate, ask students to use library resources to find information on the history of the minimum wage in the United States, and to interview fellow students who have minimum-wage jobs or local business owners who have employees earning the minimum wage. After the debate, encourage all class members to challenge or question the views presented in the debate.

VISUAL INSTRUCTION

Ask students: What economic laws explain why there is a shortage when price ceilings are set? (*Law of Supply—producers produce less at lower prices. Law of Demand—consumers demand more when prices are low.*)

Answer to Caption:

because the authorities think the market price is too high

ANSWERS

1. a shift of productive resources out of the large car market into other markets
2. Quantity supplied decreases.

Meeting Special Needs

Reading Disability Reading comprehension is often greatly aided by presentation of background information or "schema." The schema is developed from the reader's current knowledge and then extended with new information from text, lecture, pictures, and media. Have students with reading comprehension problems discuss price ceilings from the point of view of a landlord and then a tenant. Have them discuss price floors from the point of view of an employer and then an employee. Then have them read Section 3.

Lesson 5 of Interactive Economics! to learn more about "Price Ceilings and Floors."

Figure 6.5
Price Floors and Permanent Surpluses

A price floor of $5.15 an hour for labor attracts 14 million workers. Employers, however, only want to employ 10 million workers at that price. The result is a surplus of 4 million workers who would like to work at the $5.15 price floor but cannot find jobs. **What might happen to the surplus if the hourly wage fell below the equilibrium price?**

The result would be a shortage of 800,000 apartments, the difference between the 2.4 million demanded and the 1.6 million supplied. Are consumers better off? Perhaps not. More than likely, the better apartments were converted to condos or offices—leaving the poorer ones to be rented.

In addition, 800,000 people are now unhappy because they cannot get an apartment, although they are willing and able to pay for one. Prices no longer allocate apartments. Instead, landlords resort to long waiting lists or other nonprice criteria to assign apartments.

Rent controls freeze a landlord's total revenue and threaten his or her profits. As a result, the landlord tries to lower costs by providing the absolute minimum upkeep, thereby protecting profits. Landlords may have no incentive whatsoever to add additional apartments if they feel rents are too low.

The price ceiling, like any other price, affects the allocation of resources—but not in the way intended. The attempt to limit rents makes some people happy—the ones that get the apartments. Instead of providing affordable rental units to all, however,

apartments (scarce resources) are shifted out of the rental market and into the condo and business office markets. Some apartment buildings may even be torn down to make way for shopping centers, factories, or high-rise office buildings. **1**

Price Floors

Occasionally, prices are considered too low, and some people believe they should be kept higher. The **minimum wage,** the lowest legal wage that can be paid to most workers, is a case in point. The minimum wage is actually a **price floor,** or lowest legal price that can be paid for a good or service.

Figure 6.5 uses a minimum wage of $5.15 per hour. At this wage in the figure, 14 million people would want to offer their services. According to the demand curve for labor, however, only 10 million would be hired—leaving a surplus of 4 million workers.

The figure also shows that without the minimum wage, the actual demand and supply of labor would establish an equilibrium price of $4.00 per hour. At this wage, 12 million workers would offer their services and exactly the same number would be hired—which means that there would be no shortage in the labor market.

Many economists argue that the minimum wage actually increases the number of people who do not have jobs because employers hire fewer workers. In the case of **Figure 6.5,** the number of people who do not get jobs amounts to 2 million—the difference between the number that would work at the equilibrium price (12 million), and the number that would actually work at the higher wage of $5.15 per hour. **2**

Is the current minimum wage higher or lower than the wage that would prevail in its absence? The answer to that question is not always clear, and it may vary from one market to another, as well as from one part of the country to another. Consider wages in your area. Do you think that your employer would pay you less if he or she were allowed to do so? Your response will provide a partial answer to the question.

Predicting Prices

Economists are concerned with both explanation and prediction. They use their models of the market to explain how the world around them works and to

Lesson 5 of Interactive Economics! to learn more about "Price Adjustments and Market Elasticities."

Figure 6.6
Changes in Supply and the Elasticity of Demand

A.

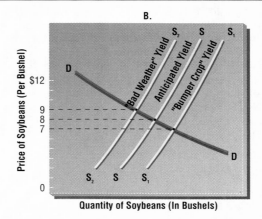
B.

Seasonal price changes in agriculture are often caused by changes in supply. The size of the price change also depends on the elasticity of demand for the product. The less elastic the demand, as in the diagram on the left, the larger the price change. The more elastic the demand, as in the diagram on the right, the smaller the price change. **What other factors may cause a change in prices?**

predict how certain events might affect the economy in the future. Even changes in prices can be explained and sometimes predicted. A change in price normally results from a change in supply, a change in demand, or changes in both. Demand elasticity also turns out to be important in predicting prices.

Changes in Supply

Consider the case of agriculture, in which wide swings in prices from one year to the next are fairly typical. A farmer may keep up with all the latest

developments and have the best advice experts can offer. Even so, the farmer never is sure what price to expect for the crop. A soybean farmer may put in 500 acres of beans, expecting a price of $8 a bushel. The farmer knows, however, that the actual price may end up being anywhere from $5 to $12. The same is true for the cotton farmer who expects 80 cents a pound but may end up getting anywhere from 40 cents to $1.50.

One of the main reasons for the variation in agricultural prices is that weather influences farm output. After planting, all the farmer can do is wait. If it rains too much, the seeds will be washed away and the

Checking Understanding

1. What was the unintended effect of rent controls?
2. How do many economists think the minimum wage affects unemployment?

Applying Economic Concepts

☑ **Role of Government** Many rent controls cap the amount a landlord can raise the rent for a current tenant only. When a new tenant takes the apartment, the forces of supply and demand set the rent. As a result, tenants with similar apartments might pay widely varying rents.

CHAPTER 6: *Prices and Decision Making* **143**

 Using Transparencies
Display Economic Concepts Transparency 8. Spanish Transparencies also are available.

VISUAL INSTRUCTION

Farmers often receive a higher price for crops after a bad harvest than they do after a bumper harvest. Why? *(because demand for food tends to be inelastic and supply is reduced)*

Answer to Caption:
changes in demand

Extending the Content

Price Changes, Supply, and Demand The Civil War almost halted American exports of cotton to England. As a result, the price of cotton in Liverpool rose from 8 pence (English pennies) per pound in 1860 to 31½ pence per pound in 1864. There was a subsequent decrease in the demand for people working in the cotton industry. Another result of the price increase was the great increase in production of substitute fabrics. In Ireland, flax

production quadrupled from 1861 to 1864. During this relatively short period, then, the increase in the price of cotton caused changes in the demand for workers and in the production and demand for substitute fabrics. Ask students to draw diagrams showing the shift in the demand and supply curves for cotton and various substitutes in the first half of the 1860s.

ANSWERS

1. Some apartments shifted out of rental market.
2. It increases the number of people out of work, because employers hire fewer workers at higher wages.

Independent Practice

📂 **Guided Reading** Assign Guided Reading Activity for Section 3. **LEP**

L2 Rebates Have students interview local car dealers to find out if and why they offer rebates on new cars. Select students to present their findings to the class. Then have students discuss how supply and demand influence, or are influenced by, rebates.

L3 Research Have students research the use of price ceilings in the United States. Suggest that students consider the following questions: What were the circumstances that led to the imposition of price ceilings? How long were they used? Were they successful? Why or why not?

VISUAL INSTRUCTION

Ask students to identify a recent situation that resulted in a change in the demand for gold.

Answer to Caption:

bad news, such as war, disasters, or possible recessions

INTERACTIVE ECONOMICS!

CD-ROM Price Determination

Have students click on "Price Ceilings and Floors." Then have them write a paragraph describing the advantages and disadvantages of a price ceiling on rents. *(Advantage: to control prices of rents; disadvantage: shortage of rental units)*

Supplied in both CD-ROM and diskette formats.

---

farmer must replant. If it rains too little, the seeds will not sprout. Even if the weather is perfect during the growing season, rain can still prevent the harvest from being gathered. The weather, then, can cause a change in supply.

The result, shown in Graph **A** in **Figure 6.6**, is that the supply curve is likely to shift, causing the price to go up or down. At the beginning of the season, the farmer may expect supply to look like curve **SS**. If a bumper, or record, crop is harvested, however, supply may look like **S₁S₁**. If bad weather strikes, supply may look like **S₂S₂**. Because the demand for food generally is inelastic, a small change in supply is enough to cause a large change in the price.

Demand Elasticity

What would have happened to prices if the demand for soybeans were highly elastic, as in Graph **B** of **Figure 6.6**? The results would be quite different. Because this demand curve is much more elastic, the

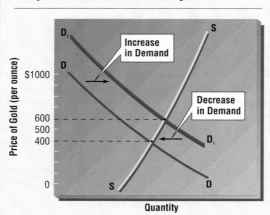

Figure 6.7
Changes in Demand Cause Price Changes

A change in demand is an important cause of fluctuating prices. An increase in demand increases the equilibrium price, and a decrease in demand lowers the price. Changes in consumer incomes, changes in tastes, and changes in the prices of related goods all can cause a change in demand. **What factors might increase the demand for gold?**

prices would only range from $7 to $9 a bushel instead of from $5 to $12 a bushel.

Economists consider demand elasticity whenever a change in supply occurs. When a given change in supply is coupled with an inelastic demand curve, as in Graph **A** in **Figure 6.6**, price changes a great deal. When the same change in supply is coupled with a very elastic demand curve, such as that in Graph **B** of **Figure 6.6**, the change in price is much smaller.

Changes in Demand

Changes in demand also may affect the price of a good or service. **Figure 6.7** shows how changes in demand for gold—coupled with a relatively fixed supply of gold—cause wide fluctuations in its price. Bad news, such as war, possible recessions, or other disasters, might cause people to suddenly increase their demand for gold to **D₁D₁**. This change in demand drives the price of gold to $600 an ounce.

Good news, such as peace agreements, economic growth, or a lower rate of inflation, might cause a decrease in demand to **DD**. The price of gold would then drop sharply to $400 an ounce.

Agricultural Price Supports

In the 1930s, the federal government established the Commodity Credit Corporation (CCC), an agency in the Department of Agriculture. The CCC's job was to help stabilize agricultural prices. The stabilization took two basic forms—the first involving loan supports and the second involving deficiency payments. Both made use of **target prices,** which are essentially floor prices for farm products.

Loan Supports

Under the loan support program, a farmer could borrow money from the CCC at a target price. In return, the farmer pledged his or her crops as security. The loan was then used to plant, maintain, and harvest the crop. The farmer could either sell the crop in the market and use the proceeds to repay the CCC loan, or the farmer could keep the proceeds of the loan and let the CCC take possession of the crop. Because the loan was a **non-recourse loan**, the farmer,

---

Cultural Diversity and Economics

Rice Rice is sacred to the Japanese. In the Shinto religion, for example, each grain of rice is considered a deity. From childhood, the Japanese are taught that rice is a part of their national identity. Rice producers, too, have a sacred aura, and successive Japanese governments have taken steps to protect them from the incursions of imported

foreign rice. The resulting closed market for rice created an artificial shortage in Japan, forcing consumers to pay several times higher than the world price. Years of pressure from foreign governments and from Japanese consumers, however, led the Japanese government to ease restrictions on rice imports in 1993.

Lesson 5 of Interactive Economics! to learn more about "Price Ceilings and Floors."

Figure 6.8
Agricultural Price Supports

Under the CCC loan program in Graph A, the farmer pledges 10,000 bushels of wheat at the $4 target price to receive a $40,000 non-recourse loan. The farmer sells as much wheat as possible at or above the target price in the open market, and then defaults on the remainder of the loan, allowing the CCC to take control of 3,000 bushels of wheat. Under the deficiency payment program in Graph B, the farmer sells all 10,000 bushels on the market at $2.50 a bushel, and then receives a deficiency payment in the amount of $1.50 times 10,000, or $15,000 from the CCC. Either way, the farmer receives at least $40,000 for the wheat. **Which program avoids storage problems for the CCC?**

if unable to repay the money, faced no additional penalties other than forfeiting the crop.

Graph **A** in **Figure 6.8** illustrates the CCC loan program. The target price at the beginning of the year was set at $4 a bushel for wheat. A farmer pledged 10,000 bushels of wheat to the CCC and received a $40,000 loan in return. When the crop was harvested, the farmer sold only 7,000 bushels in the market at $4/bushel, and repaid $28,000 of the CCC loan.

The farmer then forfeited the remaining 3,000 bushels of wheat to the CCC and kept the remainder of the loan, represented by the shaded area in the figure. In the end, the farmer received $4 a bushel for each of the 10,000 bushels produced—with 7,000 bushels sold in the market and the remaining 3,000 picked up by the CCC. Without the loan program, the farmer would have produced 9,000 bushels and sold them at $3 each for a total revenue of $27,000.

Deficiency Payments

The problem with the CCC loan program was that the CCC soon faced enormous stockpiles of food. Surplus wheat was stored in rented warehouses or on open ground. Surplus milk was made into cheese and stored in underground caves. How could the CCC support farm prices, yet avoid the embarrassingly large surpluses?

The answer was to have farmers sell the crops on the open market for the best price they could get, and have the CCC make up the difference with a deficiency payment. A **deficiency payment** is a check sent to farmers that makes up the difference between the actual market price and the target price.

Graph **B** in **Figure 6.8** illustrates the deficiency payment program. The farmer made $25,000 selling 10,000 bushels at $2.50 each, which was $1.50 below the target price of $4.00 a bushel. The farmer, therefore, received deficiency payments of $1.50 times 10,000 bushels, or the $15,000 represented by the shaded area. When the deficiency payment was added to the $25,000 market sale, the farmer made $40,000—the same as under the loan program. In this case, however, the CCC does not have the problem of a surplus.

In exchange for the CCC price supports, farmers often had to promise to limit production. In some cases, aerial photographs were taken to verify that the acreage was within the limits of the quota.

CHAPTER 6: *Prices and Decision Making* **145**

$ Free Enterprise Activity $

Inform students that many people compare prices of grocery items by checking the unit price. This can be calculated by dividing the price by the number of units. The unit price of a 15–ounce box of cereal that costs $2.25 is $0.15, for example. ($2.25 ÷ 15 = $0.15) Remind students that the units of measure must be the same to compare unit price. In other words, pounds cannot be compared with 14 ounces of coffee unless one or the other measure is converted. Assign students four or five products to compare at various grocery stores and supermarkets. They should compare at least two brands of each product, using the unit price of each. For each product, have them choose the brand that is the better buy according to unit price. Have students compare their findings.

Evaluate

Reteach

Direct students to write a paragraph that explains how the price system operates.

Have students complete Reteaching Activity 6. Spanish Reteaching Activities also are available in the Spanish Resources Binder.

Enrich

Have students collect examples of "when markets talk" by reading newspapers and periodicals, watching television news, and listening to the radio. Ask students to share their examples with the class and discuss how the market reacted to certain events.

Have students complete Enrichment Activity 6.

CLOSE

Remind students that prices can be viewed as signals. Ask them to create a logo or symbol that illustrates this idea.

Reforming Price Supports

In an effort to make agricultural output responsive to market forces, Congress passed the Federal Agricultural Improvement and Reform (FAIR) Act of 1996. Under this law, eligible producers of grains, cotton, and rice can enter into a 7-year program that allows them almost complete flexibility to plant any crop on any land. Other products, such as milk, sugar, fruits, and vegetables, are not affected.

Under the new law, cash payments take the place of price supports and deficiency payments. Because these new payments are expected to be as large as the ones they replace, however, the overall cost of farm programs will not go down while the new law is in effect.

When the program expires in the year 2002, farmers will cease to receive all payments. By then, they are expected to have enough experience with the laws of supply and demand to no longer need government help.

When Markets Talk

Markets are highly impersonal mechanisms that bring buyers and sellers together. Although markets do not talk in the usual sense of the word, they do communicate in that they speak collectively for all of the buyers and sellers who trade in the markets. Markets are said to talk when prices in them move up or down significantly.

Suppose the federal government announced that it would raise personal income taxes and corporate taxes to balance the federal budget. If investors thought this policy would not work or that other policies might be better, they might decide to sell some of their stocks and other investments for cash and gold, which could be used in case of an emergency. As the selling takes place, stock prices would fall, and gold prices would rise. It could be said that, in effect, the market voiced its disapproval of the new tax policy.

In a sense, then, the market did talk. Individual investors made decisions on the likely outcome of the new policy and sold stocks for cash or gold. Together, their actions were enough to influence stock prices and to send a signal to the government that investors did not favor the policy.

If investors' feelings were divided about the new policy, some would sell while others bought stocks. As a result, prices might not change, and the message would be that, as yet, the markets have not made up their minds.

SECTION 3 REVIEW

Reviewing Terms and Facts

1. **Define** rebate, price ceiling, minimum wage, price floor, target price, non-recourse loan, deficiency payment.
2. **Describe** two effects of having a fixed price other than the equilibrium price forced on a market.
3. **Explain** why price changes are more moderate when demand is highly elastic.
4. **Describe** how markets speak collectively for buyers and sellers.

Critical Thinking

5. **Determining Cause and Effect** The price of fresh fruit over the course of a year may go up or down by as much as 100 percent. Explain the causes for these changes in terms of changes in demand, changes in supply, and the elasticity of demand for fresh fruit.

Applying Economic Concepts

6. **Shortage** Identify a shortage of employees in your community—for example, not enough skilled doctors, teachers, or piano tuners. Use your knowledge of prices to explain how different wages or salaries could be used to remedy the shortage.

Answers to SECTION 3 REVIEW

1. All vocabulary words are defined in the Glossary.

2. Shortages are created if price ceilings are set below the equilibrium price. Surpluses are created if price floors are set higher than the equilibrium price.

3. because buyers can delay their purchase or find alternates

4. when prices move up or down significantly, signaling the collective decisions of buyers and sellers

5. Supply will be affected by the seasons and weather, and because demand tends to be stable and slightly inelastic, a change in supply is enough to cause a large change in price.

6. Answers will vary, but most students will note that the shortage of different kinds of labor could be adjusted by offering higher wages or salaries.

ECONOMICS IN ACTION

Supply and Demand

Setting Up the Video

With your classmates, view "Supply and Demand" on the videodisc **Economics in Action.** The video focuses on the effect of supply and demand on prices of recycled products. It then explores inelastic demand in the case of medical services, for which price changes may not significantly affect the level of demand.

Chapter 11
Disc 1, Side 2

View the video by scanning the bar code or by entering the chapter number on your keypad and pressing Search. *(Also available in VHS format.)*

Hands-On Activity

Imagine that a major storm (or heat wave) will hit town next week. What goods and services would people need after the storm, and how would you expect the cost of these items to compare to their cost before the storm? List the items as well as the factors that might account for the difference in their cost. Share your list with the class.

INTERACTIVE ECONOMICS!

Price Determination

Introduction

Lesson 5 of **Interactive Economics!** deals with prices. Because of the information they convey, prices are central to the way a market economy works.

Prices serve as signals to both producers and consumers. High prices are signals for producers to supply more and for consumers to purchase less. Low prices do just the opposite. The market itself determines prices, which react quickly to changing market conditions.

Using the Software

1. Select "Price Determination" from the Main Menu.

2. Read the introduction to "Price Determination," then click on "Prices as Signals."

3. After reviewing the information, click on "How Prices Are Determined" and repeat the process.

4. Finally, click on the "Advanced Topics Menu" and read about price adjustments and market elasticities.

5. Then click on "Economics Lab." Complete the lab by clicking and dragging the appropriate graphs to their cause identified in the illustration.

6. Print your completed lab.

147

MULTIMEDIA ACTIVITIES

GLENCOE TECHNOLOGY

NIGHTLY BUSINESS REPORT

Economics in Action

Chapter 11
Disc 1, Side 2

Title: *Supply and Demand*

If you do not have access to a videodisc player, the **Economics in Action** programs are also available in VHS.

INTERACTIVE ECONOMICS!

Before students complete the "Economics Lab" in Lesson 5, ask them the following questions:

1. When the demand curve shifts to the right, what is the result? *(a temporary shortage at the old price)*

2. When the demand curve shifts to the left, what is the result? *(a temporary surplus will arise at the old price)*

3. What happens when there is an increase in supply? *(a temporary surplus at the old price)*

4. What happens when there is a decrease in supply? *(a temporary shortage at the old price)*

5. What degree of change in price occurs when both the demand and supply curves are elastic? *(small changes in price)*

TEACHER NOTES

GLENCOE
TECHNOLOGY

VIDEODISC
MindJogger Videoquiz

Use MindJogger to review
the Chapter 6 content.

 Chapter 6
Disc 1, Side B

Also available in VHS.

Answers

Reviewing Key Terms

1. d
2. a
3. e
4. c
5. c

Reviewing the Facts

1. Prices are neutral, favoring neither producer nor consumer, and flexible, allowing the market economy to accommodate change. Prices provide the maximum freedom of choice for producers and consumers. In addition, prices have no administrative costs. Finally, prices are efficient because they are easily understood by everyone.

2. establishing a fair system of allocation, the cost of administering the system, the negative impact the system has on people's incentive to work and produce

3. Examples will vary, but may include any of the graphic illustrations in the chapter.

4. They provide signals that the equilibrium price has not yet been reached. Shortages signal that equilibrium price is higher than present price, and price needs to increase. Surpluses signal that equilibrium price is lower than present price, and prices need to decrease.

148

Reviewing Key Terms

Write the key term that is an effect of the five causes stated below. Some causes may have more than one effect.

1. **Cause:** The government tries to keep prices down by legislating price ceilings. **Effect:** _____
2. **Cause:** The government wants to allocate scarce goods and services without the help of a price system. **Effect:** _____
3. **Cause:** A reasonably competitive market is experiencing alternating, yet consecutively smaller, surpluses and shortages. **Effect:** _____
4. **Cause:** People decide that farmers should receive a higher price for milk and cheese, so a price floor for these products is established. **Effect:** _____
5. **Cause:** A market is at equilibrium, but the product falls out of style before producers can reduce production. **Effect:** _____

a. rationing
b. economic model
c. surplus
d. shortage
e. equilibrium price
f. loss leader
g. price ceiling
h. price floor

Reviewing the Facts

SECTION 1 *(pages 128–132)*

1. **Describe** five advantages of using price as an allocating mechanism.
2. **List** three problems of allocating goods and services using nonprice-related methods.

SECTION 2 *(pages 134–138)*

3. **Cite** an example of an economic model used in this chapter.
4. **Explain** the role of shortages and surpluses in competitive markets.

SECTION 3 *(pages 140–146)*

5. **Explain** what is meant by a "system" of prices.
6. **Explain** why shortages and surpluses are not temporary when price controls are used.

7. **Describe** two causes of a price change in a market.
8. **Explain** what is meant by the statement that markets talk.

Critical Thinking

1. **Predicting Consequences** Suppose that your state wanted to make health care more affordable for everyone. To do this, state legislators put a series of price controls—price ceilings—in place that cut the cost of medical services in half. What would happen to the demand for medical services at the new, lower price? What would happen to the supply of medical services that doctors would be willing to provide at the new, lower price? Where do you think new doctors would prefer to set up practice? Explain the reasons for your answers.

2. **Making Generalizations** Some people argue that an equilibrium price is not a fair price. Explain why you agree or disagree with this argument.

Applying Economic Concepts

1. **Rationing** Suppose that a guest speaker visited your class and left 20 ballpoint pens as samples—not knowing that there were 30 students in the class. Devise a nonprice rationing system that would fairly allocate the scarce item to everyone in the class.

2. **Equilibrium Price** Many people feel that the minimum wage is too low. If it increased by $1 per hour, what would happen to the number of students who would want to work after school? What would happen to the number of workers that stores in your community would want to hire? Would the combination of these factors cause a shortage or a surplus of workers in your community? Provide an explanation for each of your answers.

---

5. that, collectively, prices serve as signals that allocate resources among the many markets that make up the economy

6. At lower prices there is no incentive for producers to produce more; shortages, therefore, will continue. Conversely, at higher prices consumers have no incentive to buy, so surpluses remain.

7. a change in supply, a change in demand, or a change in both

8. that markets reflect the collective judgments of all buyers and sellers in them

Critical Thinking

1. Answers will vary. Points that students will note include: because demand for medical services tends to be inelastic, the quantity demanded will increase only moderately. Because prices for services would be set below market level, there would be less incentive for doctors to offer services. Quantity sup-

Reinforcing Skills

INTERPRETING POLITICAL CARTOONS

Study the political cartoon below and then answer the following questions.

1. Who does the person represent?
2. What is happening to this person?
3. Describe the appearance of the person.
4. To what is the person connected?
5. What is the main point of this cartoon?
6. What is the cartoonist's attitude about this issue?

Individual Activity

Construct an economic model by following these steps: (1) Select a product and list the kinds of inputs and their costs required in the product's manufacturing. (2) Construct a hypothetical supply curve for the product. (3) Determine the demand elasticity for the product: Does it have many substitutes? Can its purchase be postponed? Does it consume much income? (4) Construct a demand curve and combine it with the supply curve in a single graph. This is your economic model. (5) Finally, make reasonable predictions about the future price of your product.

Cooperative Learning Activity

Many groceries display the unit price—the cost per unit—of food items on their shelves. You can calculate unit price by dividing the price by the quantity. The unit price of a 15-ounce box of cereal that costs $3.75 is $0.25. When comparing unit price, the units of measure must be the same. Three pounds of coffee cannot be compared to 14 ounces of coffee, for example, until one or the other measure is converted.

Working in groups of five, compare the prices of at least two brands of one of these products: orange juice, coffee, chicken soup, frozen pizza, and flour. Calculate the unit price of each brand, and choose the brand that is the better buy for each food product. Share your findings with your group and then with the class as a whole.

Technology Activity

Using a Spreadsheet

Use your personal buying decisions to create a spreadsheet and graph showing how a market equilibrium price is reached.
1. Select a product that costs about $5.00.
2. In cells A1 through C1, enter the words *Price, Demand,* and *Supply.*
3. In cells A2 through A11, enter prices that range from $1.00 to $10.00.
4. In the next two columns, enter quantities that might be demanded and supplied at those prices.
5. Highlight the three columns on the spreadsheet, then click on "Chart Wizard" or a similar icon, or click on "Insert" and then "Chart."
6. Click on "line graph," then highlight a 2-line chart sub-type.
7. Follow the spreadsheet directions to title your graph (see Figure 6.2 on page 136).

CHAPTER 6: *Prices and Decision Making* **149**

---

incentive for workers to sell their labor. Therefore, the number of students wanting to work after school would increase. The higher cost of labor, however, would result in store managers hiring fewer workers. As a result, there would be an excess supply, or surplus, of workers.

Reinforcing Skills

1. United States taxpayer
2. Blood is being siphoned from the American taxpayer.
3. gaunt, weak
4. other countries
5. that foreign aid is draining the American taxpayer
6. The cartoonist feels that American taxpayers' money is helping other countries at the expense of the health of the American economy.

? BONUS TEST QUESTION

Have students identify what will happen to prices in the following situations:

1. Supply decreases and demand is elastic. (*prices rise slightly*)
2. Supply increases and demand is inelastic. (*prices fall markedly*)
3. A surplus exists. (*prices fall*)
4. Supply remains constant but demand increases. (*prices rise*)
5. A shortage exists. (*prices rise*)

---

plied, therefore, probably would decrease. New doctors probably would want to set up practice in states where there were no price ceilings. The price they would receive for their services would be set by the market.

2. Answers will vary, but may include the following: A market price is collectively determined by a large number of buyers and sellers. As a result, it is the best and fairest price for the majority. Or: Because

buyers always want lower prices and sellers always want higher prices, it is hard to establish what is "fair."

Applying Economic Concepts

1. Rationing systems will vary. Students may suggest that the system would have to establish a set amount of time for each student to use a pen.

2. Answers may vary. Most students would note that at a higher minimum wage, there would be more

CHAPTER ORGANIZER

Daily Objectives	Reproducible Resources	Multimedia Resources
Section 1 **Competition and Market Structures** 1. **Explain** the characteristics of pure competition. 2. **Understand** the nature of monopolistic competition. 3. **Describe** the behavior and characteristics of the oligopolist. 4. **Identify** several types of monopolies.	Reproducible Lesson Plan 7-1 Guided Reading Activity 7-1 Cooperative Learning Activity 10 Consumer Application Activities 5, 10 Math Practice for Economics 12 Free Enterprise Activities 10, 12 Primary and Secondary Source Reading 10 Economic Simulation 3 Economic Laboratory 3 Performance Assessment Activity 12 Section Quiz 7-1*	Focus Activity Transparency 39 Economic Concepts Transparencies 7, 9* Vocabulary PuzzleMaker Chapter Challenger Interactive Review Software Testmaker MindJogger Videoquiz NBR's Economics in Action Video Program
Section 2 **Market Failures** 1. **Discuss** the problems caused by inadequate competition. 2. **Understand** the importance of having adequate information. 3. **Describe** the nature of resource immobility. 4. **Explain** the nature of positive and negative externalities.	Reproducible Lesson Plan 7-2 Guided Reading Activity 7-2 Reinforcing Economic Skills 7 Section Quiz 7-2*	Focus Activity Transparency 40 Economic Concepts Transparency 11* Vocabulary PuzzleMaker Chapter Challenger Interactive Review Software Testmaker NBR's Economics in Action Video Program
Section 3 **The Role of Government** 1. **Discuss** the major antitrust legislation in the United States. 2. **Understand** the need for limited government regulation. 3. **Explain** the value of public disclosure. 4. **Discuss** the modifications to our free enterprise economy.	Reproducible Lesson Plan 7-3 Guided Reading Activity 7-3 Section Quiz 7-3*	Focus Activity Transparency 41 Economic Concepts Transparency 12* Vocabulary PuzzleMaker Chapter Challenger Interactive Review Software Testmaker
Chapter Review and Evaluation	Enrichment Activity 7 Reteaching Activity 7* Economic Vocabulary Activity 7* Chapter 7 Test, Forms A and B	Chapter Digests Audiocassette Activities and Tests* Testmaker MindJogger Videoquiz

Also available in Spanish

 Blackline Master   Transparency   CD-ROM   Software   Videodisc   Audiocassette

 OUT OF TIME? Assign the Chapter 7 Digest Audiocassette and the corresponding Chapter Digest activities and tests.

National Council
on Economic Education

THE **Economics** America AND **Economics** International PROGRAMS

VOLUNTARY NATIONAL CONTENT STANDARDS IN ECONOMICS
Emphasized in Chapter 7

Content Standard 9 *Students will understand that:*
Competition among sellers lowers costs and prices, and encourages producers to produce more of what consumers are willing and able to buy. Competition among buyers increases prices and allocates goods and services to those people who are willing and able to pay the most for them.

Content Standard 16 *Students will understand that:*
There is an economic role for government to play in a market economy whenever the benefits of a government policy outweigh its costs. Governments often provide for national defense, address environmental concerns, define and protect property rights, and attempt to make markets more competitive. Most government policies also redistribute income.

EconomicsAmerica *Resources Available From NCEE*

- *Capstone: The Nation's High School Economics Course*
- *Civics and Government: Focus on Economics*
- *Economics and the Environment*
- *Economics in Transition: Command to Market*
- *Focus: High School Economics*
- *United States History: Eyes on the Economy, Vol. II*
- *United States History: Focus on Economics*
- *World History: Focus on Economics*

To order these materials, or to contact your state Council on Economic Education about workshops and programs, call 1-800-338-1192 or visit http://www.nationalcouncil.org.

PERFORMANCE ASSESSMENT

The following chapter projects may be assigned at the beginning of the chapter and used for performance assessment.

Multicultural Heritage Invite someone who has observed market structures in another country to share his or her observations and experiences with students. Before the speaker arrives, ask students to read the textbook pages that discuss market structures, market failures, and the role of government in the market. Have students prepare questions about how these topics are addressed in the speaker's country. After the presentation and questions, you may want to assign library research about businesses and competition in the country presented. Next, have students write a brief essay contrasting competition in the United States and the country discussed in the presentation. Call on volunteers to read their essays to the class.

Cooperative Learning Organize the class into four groups and assign each group one of the four market structures—pure competition, monopolistic competition, oligopoly, and monopoly—discussed in Chapter 7. Instruct groups to identify and visit local businesses that exhibit characteristics of their market structure. Have groups prepare a list of common questions to ask managers regarding the number of firms in the industry, the ability of firms to influence price, product differentiation, and ease of entry into the market.

After the visits and interviews, have groups summarize the information obtained and present their findings to the class. Emphasize that these presentations should compare the businesses visited with the market structures discussed in the chapter.

ADDITIONAL RESOURCES

Readings for the Student

Slavin, Stephen L. *Economics: A Self-Teaching Guide.* New York: John L. Wiley, 1988. A chapter of this book deals with the four theoretical models of competition. Periodic exercises help readers to evaluate their comprehension.

Readings for the Teacher

Keenan, Diane, et al. *Economics USA: High School Activity Packs.* The Annenberg/CPB collection, 1992. Companion text for the video series mentioned below. Provides lesson ideas and related tests on the theoretical models of competition.

Multimedia

Economics U$A: Perfect Competition and Inelastic Demand/Economic Efficiency. The Annenberg/CPB Collection, 19 Gregory Drive, South Burlington, VT 05407–2345. Color video, 60 mins. The first 30-minute segment of the video discusses the characteristics of perfect competition.

Economics U$A: Monopoly/Oligopolies. The Annenberg/CPB Collection, 19 Gregory Drive, South Burlington, VT 05407–2345. Color video, 60 mins. Discusses the nature of these two theoretical models of competition.

INTRODUCING
CHAPTER 7

Chapter Overview

This chapter explains competition and market structures and how inadequate competition causes problems. **Section 1** explains the four market structures: pure competition, monopolistic competition, oligopoly, and monopoly. **Section 2** describes how market failures can occur when there is inadequate competition. **Section 3** discusses antitrust legislation and the need for limited government regulation of markets.

GLENCOE
TECHNOLOGY

VIDEODISC
MindJogger Videoquiz

Use MindJogger to preview the Chapter 7 content.

 Chapter 7
Disc 1, Side B

Also available in VHS.

inter**NET**
CONNECTION

Resources for Chapter 7 on the World Wide Web*

National Council on Economic Education

http://www.nationalcouncil.org/

The Market Research Center

http://www.asiresearch.com/

Antitrust Policy

http://www.antitrust.org/

Advertising Age

http://www.adage.com/

*Sites subject to change.

Advertisers try to convince consumers that their product is better, hoping they will be willing and able to purchase more at a higher price.

 Extra Credit Project

As students study the chapter, have them monitor newspapers and current events magazines to find stories about competition in the economy. Direct them to write summaries of three stories they locate.

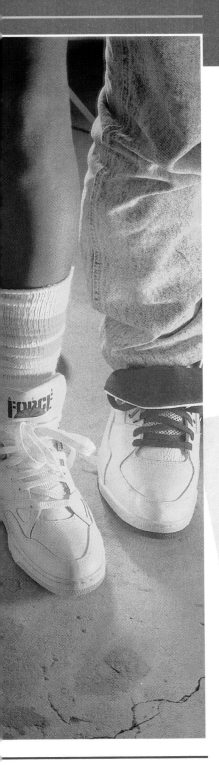

CHAPTER 7

Competition, Market Structures, and the Role of Government

SECTION 1
Competition and Market Structures

SECTION 2
Market Failures

SECTION 3
The Role of Government

CHAPTER PREVIEW

People to Know

- Charles Wang
- Environmental Health Inspector

Applying Economic Concepts in Your Life

Market Structures Why are some products available at competitive prices? Why are other products priced higher? Factors such as demand and supply determine the price of a product. The nature of the business where you bought the product also plays a role in how much it costs. It pays to learn about competition and *market structures*.

Journal Writing

Choose a product offered by several producers that is advertised in newspapers or magazines. For one week, clip and save at least three different advertisements about your product. In your journal, evaluate each advertisement and summarize why you would or would not buy a particular brand.

Connecting to Past Learning

Call on a student to identify the primary aim of businesses. *(to maximize profits)* Next, ask another student to define the term *competition*. *(striving against others to reach an objective)* Then have students speculate how competition might play a role in profit maximization. Suggest that they check and adjust their speculations as they work through the chapter.

Applying Economics

In the classroom, display a number of advertisements for various products. Ask students to identify the purpose of these advertisements. *(attract attention, provide information, persuade consumers to buy)* Then have students discuss why advertising is necessary in a market economy. *(to reinforce product differentiation)*

PERFORMANCE ASSESSMENT

Refer to page **150B** for a Performance Assessment activity for this chapter. Also see the **Performance Assessment Activities** booklet for additional suggestions.

VISUAL INSTRUCTION

Point out that advertising is only one technique that producers may use in a competitive market. Ask students to suggest other techniques that producers might use. *(changing prices, improving product quality, offering special services with product, and so on)*

Economic Portfolio

As students perform the **Journal Writing** activity above, ask them to pay special attention to the advertising techniques that make the products attractive. Mention that this will help them to complete the **Technology Activity** in

the Chapter Review—describing a product in such a way that consumers will want to buy it.

Key to Ability Levels — Teaching strategies have been coded for varying learning styles and abilities:
L1 - Basic (activities for all students) **L2 - Average** (activities for average to above-average students)
L3 - Challenging (activities for above-average students) **LEP - Limited English Proficiency**

FOCUS

Section Objectives

1. Explain the characteristics of pure competition.
2. Understand the nature of monopolistic competition.
3. Describe the behavior and characteristics of the oligopolist.
4. Identify several types of monopolies.

Bellringer

 Prior to taking roll at the beginning of the class period, display Focus Activity Transparency 39.

Motivational Activity

Discuss students' responses to the activity sheet that accompanies Transparency 39.

Preteaching Vocabulary

Have students write sentences that use each key term in its economic context. **LEP**

Use the **Vocabulary PuzzleMaker** to create crossword and word search puzzles.

? DID YOU KNOW

The term *laissez-faire* originated with a group of eighteenth-century French economists who supported free trade. Their slogan, *laissez faire, laissez passer* ("let us alone, let us have free circulation of goods") was adopted by Adam Smith to describe the principle of no government interference in the economy.

SECTION 1
Competition and Market Structures

Section Preview

Objectives

After studying this section, you will be able to:
1. **Explain** the characteristics of pure competition.
2. **Understand** the nature of monopolistic competition.
3. **Describe** the behavior and characteristics of the oligopolist.
4. **Identify** several types of monopolies.

Key Terms

laissez-faire, industry, market structure, pure competition, imperfect competition, monopolistic competition, product differentiation, nonprice competition, oligopoly, collusion, price-fixing, price war, independent pricing, price leadership, monopoly, natural monopoly, franchise, economies of scale, geographic monopoly, technological monopoly, patent, copyright, government monopoly

Applying Economic Concepts

Product Differentiation Name a popular brand of shoes or clothing that you simply must have. Can you name several competing brands that you consider to be poor substitutes? If so, *product differentiation* exists—and you will pay more because of it.

When Adam Smith published *An Inquiry into the Nature and Causes of the Wealth of Nations* in 1776, the average factory was small, and most business was competitive. **Laissez-faire,** the philosophy that government should not interfere with commerce, or trade, dominated Smith's writing. *Laissez-faire* is a French term that means "allow them to do." Under laissez-faire, the role of government is confined to protecting private property, enforcing contracts, settling disputes, and protecting businesses against foreign goods.

By the late 1800s, however, competition was weakening. In some markets, a series of mergers and acquisitions combined many small firms into a few very large businesses. As industries developed— **industry** meaning the supply side of the market, or all producers collectively—the nature of competitive markets changed.

Today, economists classify markets according to conditions that prevail in them. They ask questions such as: How many suppliers are there? How large is each supplier? Do the firms have any influence over price? How much competition exists between firms? What kind of economic product is involved? Are all firms in the market selling exactly the same product, or simply similar ones? Is it easy or difficult for new firms to enter the market?

The answers to these questions help determine **market structure,** or the nature and degree of competition among firms operating in the same industry. Markets are classified according to certain structural characteristics, and economists have names for these different market structures—pure competition, monopolistic competition, oligopoly, and monopoly. **1**

Pure Competition

An important type of market structure is **pure competition.** This market situation includes independent and well-informed buyers and sellers of exactly the same economic product. Five major conditions characterize purely competitive markets. ✔

Conditions for Pure Competition

The first condition is that a large number of buyers and sellers exist. No single buyer or seller is large enough or powerful enough to affect the price of the product.

The second condition is that buyers and sellers deal in identical products. Buyers do not prefer one seller's merchandise over another's. No difference in quality, no brand names, and no need to advertise exist. Think

---

Classroom Resources for SECTION 1

- Reproducible Lesson Plan 7-1
- Guided Reading Activity 7-1
- Cooperative Learning Activity 10
- Consumer Application Activities 5, 10
- Math Practice for Economics 12
- Free Enterprise Activities 10, 12
- Primary and Secondary Source Reading 10
- Economic Simulation 3
- Economic Laboratory 3
- Performance Assessment Activity 12

- Section Quiz 7-1
- Focus Activity Transparency 39
- Economic Concepts Transparencies 7, 9
- NBR's Economics in Action Video Program
- Testmaker
- Vocabulary PuzzleMaker
- Chapter Challenger Interactive Review Software
- MindJogger Videoquiz

Pure Competition *A farm market is a practical example of pure competition.* **What five major conditions characterize purely competitive markets?**

about the market for table salt. Because salt is always the same chemical— sodium chloride—no one brand of salt should be higher in price than any other.

The third condition is that each buyer and seller acts independently. As long as everyone acts independently, sellers compete against one another for the consumer's dollar. Buyers also compete against each other and against the seller to obtain the best price. The competition between buyers and sellers is one of the forces that keeps prices low.

The fourth condition is that buyers and sellers be reasonably well-informed about items for sale. If a store offered an item for sale at a low price, customers would know about it. Because all products are exactly the same, customers would have little reason to remain loyal to one seller. If sellers were reasonably well-informed of other sellers' prices, they would have to keep their own prices low to attract customers.

The fifth condition of a purely competitive market is that buyers and sellers be free to enter into, conduct, or get out of business. This freedom makes it difficult for a single producer in any industry to keep the market just to itself. Producers have to keep prices competitive, or new firms will enter the industry and take away some of their business.

Profit Maximization

Under pure competition, each individual firm is too small to influence price. Therefore, the firm views demand differently than the industry does. In a purely competitive market, supply and demand in the entire industry establishes the equilibrium price. After that price is set, each competitive firm selects a level of output that will maximize its profits at the market price. **2**

QUICK CHECK

Checking Understanding

1. What are the four basic market structures?
2. How is price established in a purely competitive market?

Applying Economic Concepts

☑ **Competition** The concept of perfectly competitive markets can also be applied to labor. A perfectly competitive labor market exists when there are so many workers and employers that no firm or worker can affect wage rates.

TEACH

Guided Practice

L1 *Illustrating Ideas* Call on a volunteer to identify the defining feature of the four market structures. *(extent of competition in each)* Then point out that this can be illustrated by placing the market structures on a continuum with limits of "Most Competitive" and "Least Competitive." *(pure competition, monopolistic competition, oligopoly and monopoly)* Direct students to draw an annotated or illustrated continuum for competition. Call on volunteers to present and explain their diagrams. **LEP**

 VISUAL INSTRUCTION

Point out that there are no purely competitive industries in the United States. Certain forms of agriculture, however, come close to the model of pure competition.

Answer to Caption:

large number of buyers and sellers, buyers and sellers deal in identical products, buyers and sellers act independently, buyers and sellers well informed, ease of entry into market

QUICK CHECK

ANSWERS

1. pure competition, monopolistic competition, oligopoly, monopoly
2. Supply and demand in the industry sets price.

Meeting Special Needs

Specialized Learners Have students who learn best by reading to research the early economic life of your state, including information about early industry, government regulation, and specialization. Have students who prefer visual or hands-on learning experiences draw detailed pictures showing the early economy of your state. Those students who undertook research projects should read them to the class, and ask students who made drawings to display them on the bulletin board. **LEP**

? DID YOU KNOW

In a purely competitive market, individual firms have no control over the price mechanism. Market price is a given that the individual firm cannot influence. For this reason, economists refer to purely competitive firms as *price takers*.

VISUAL INSTRUCTION

Point out that the demand curve for the purely competitive firm is horizontal and perfectly elastic. This means that at the market price, suppliers can sell as much of the product as they want.

Answer to caption:

because all five conditions of pure competition rarely exist at the same time

---

The relationship between firm and industry is shown graphically in **Figure 7.1**. In Graph **A**, the market forces of supply and demand set the equilibrium price at $5. This price of $5, as shown in Graph **B**, now becomes a horizontal demand curve facing each competitive firm. Regardless of how many gadgets the firm makes or wants to make, it receives the market price of $5 each. Because it receives an additional $5 for every additional gadget it produces, the marginal revenue for the perfectly competitive firm is $5, the same as its price.

Just how many gadgets the company produces depends on its costs of production. Suppose the firm expands its production from zero to one gadget. The extra, or marginal, cost of producing the first gadget is $.93, shown in the table below Graph **B** of **Figure 7.1**. Producing the first gadget will be profitable for the firm, because the gadget can be sold for $5. What

happens when the firm produces the second gadget? This is also profitable because the marginal cost of the second unit is $2.90, and it can be sold for $5.

When the firm produces the third unit, however, marginal cost increases to $5. The firm does not lose any money on the sale, but with increasing marginal costs and fixed marginal revenues, it will not expand production beyond three gadgets. In the end, the purely competitive firm will increase production to the point where its marginal cost is equal to its marginal revenue. Then it will sell that output at the equilibrium price already determined by the market forces of supply and demand.

A Theoretical Situation

If all five conditions for pure competition are satisfied, no single buyer or seller would be able to affect

Figure 7.1
Pure Competition: Market Price and Profit Maximization

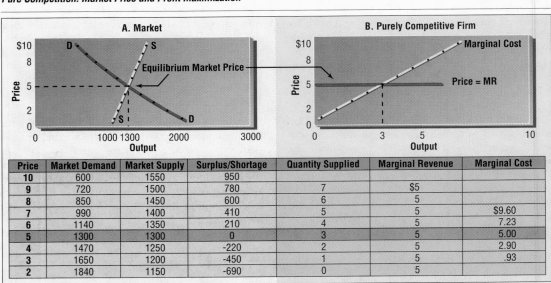

Price	Market Demand	Market Supply	Surplus/Shortage	Quantity Supplied	Marginal Revenue	Marginal Cost
10	600	1550	950			
9	720	1500	780	7	$5	
8	850	1450	600	6	5	
7	990	1400	410	5	5	$9.60
6	1140	1350	210	4	5	7.23
5	1300	1300	0	3	5	5.00
4	1470	1250	-220	2	5	2.90
3	1650	1200	-450	1	5	.93
2	1840	1150	-690	0	5	

*When the market in **A** is purely competitive, the forces of supply and demand set the equilibrium price. The purely competitive firm treats this price as its demand curve, because it is the only price that matters. In other words, the firm in **B** will receive $5 for its output regardless of how much it produces. The $5 market price, therefore, becomes a constant marginal revenue amount. In order to maximize its profits, the firm will produce the quantity of output where its marginal cost is equal to its marginal revenue. This firm will maximize its profits when it produces 3 units for sale at the equilibrium price of $5 each.* **Why is pure competition a theoretical situation?**

$ Free Enterprise Activity $

To demonstrate the concept of product differentiation, have students take part in a blind taste test of a variety of colas. First, ask students to note the name of their favorite brand of cola and to list reasons they like it. Suggest that they limit their reasons to physical attributes—taste, color, aroma,

effervescence, and so on. Then conduct the taste test and determine how many students picked the brand they named as their favorite. Conclude by leading a class discussion on why product differentiation may be as much a matter of perception as of reality.

price. No preferred brands would exist because all products would be identical. No single seller would try to sell a product at a price higher than the prevailing market price because most or all customers would go to other sellers. No restrictions or barriers to keep either buyers or sellers from doing business would exist.

For these reasons, competition in its purest form is a theoretical situation. Few, if any, purely competitive markets exist, although local truck, or vegetable, farming comes close to satisfying all of the conditions. In this market, many sellers offer nearly identical products. The sellers do not band together to try to control prices, and both buyers and sellers have reasonable knowledge of the products and their prices. Finally, anyone who wants to enter the business by growing tomatoes, corn, or other products could do so with little difficulty. **1**

Why do economists study pure competition if it is largely theoretical? Pure competition is used as a benchmark to help evaluate other market structures. All market situations that lack one or more of the conditions of pure competition are given the general name of **imperfect competition.** Most firms and industries in the United States fall under this broad classification. Economists generally divide imperfect competition into three categories—monopolistic competition, oligopoly, and monopoly. **2**

Monopolistic Competition

Monopolistic competition is the market structure that has all the conditions of pure competition except for identical products. By making its product a little different, the monopolistic competitor tries to attract more customers and monopolize a small portion of the market.

Monopolistic Competition *Competitors in the same market generally can produce the same product for about the same cost.* **Why, then, do prices vary greatly for similar products?**

Product Differentiation

The characteristic that separates monopolistic competition from pure competition is called **product differentiation.** Although the product being sold is similar from one firm to another, it is not identical. The differences among the products may be real or perceived. The differentiation may even be extended to store location, store design, manner of payment, delivery, decorations, service, and so on.

Checking Understanding	**Applying Economic Concepts**
1. What business comes closest to the purely competitive model? 2. What are the three categories of imperfect competition?	**Advertising** The advertising industry tries to build product differentiation in consumers' minds. Ads often suggest that wearing certain clothes or fragrances will make the consumer more attractive and happier.

L2 *Demonstrating Ideas*
Organize students into four groups and assign each group one of the four market structures. Direct each group to develop some form of scenario, charade, or skit that might be used to teach the rest of the class the major characteristics of its assigned market structure. Call on groups to make their presentations to the class. After all presentations have been made, lead the class in a discussion of the similarities and differences among the market structures.

Cooperative Learning
Assign Cooperative Learning Activity 10.

Using Transparencies
Display Economic Concepts Transparencies 7 and 9. Spanish Transparencies also are available.

VISUAL INSTRUCTION

Ask students to distinguish between pure competition and monopolistic competition. (*Monopolistic competition is characterized by product differentiation.*)

Answer to Caption:
because of product differentiation

ANSWERS

1. truck farming
2. monopolistic competition, oligopoly, monopoly

Extending the Content

Agriculture and Pure Competition Few markets in modern society meet the conditions of the purely competitive market model. However, the grain market for number two yellow corn—a standard product that does not vary—fits this description very closely. There are many farmers who grow and sell number two yellow corn, as well as a large number of buyers who purchase the corn. The farmers do not advertise, nor do they band together to control price. In addition, there is open communication between buyers and sellers about the market price. The grain market for number two yellow corn, however, falls short of satisfying the fifth condition for pure competition—ease of access to the market. Entry is limited because it takes a sizeable investment to start a farm focusing on the growing of grain.

L3 *Advertising* List the following products on the chalkboard: jeans, shampoo, perfume, gasoline, aspirin. Ask students to name their favorite brands of these items, explaining why they made particular choices. Point out that this is an illustration of product differentiation, because student preferences were based on slight differences among several brands. Continue by stressing that clever advertising may have created a perception of difference, and note that real differences may not exist. Then organize students into groups and have them develop storyboards for an advertisement for one of the items listed on the chalkboard that emphasizes product differentiation. Have groups display their storyboards.

Independent Practice

 Guided Reading Assign Guided Reading Activity for Section 1. **LEP**

VISUAL INSTRUCTION

Have students identify the advertising technique used in the photograph. *(linking a product to superlative athletic performance)*

Answer to Caption:

Answers will vary. Students should note that producers who have successfully differentiated their products in the minds of buyers can charge higher prices.

Many examples of differentiated products can be found. Some brands of athletic footwear have special shock-absorbing soles. Others have certain construction materials to reduce weight. Still others can be inflated to provide additional ankle support. In this case, the differences between the products are real. For different brands of aspirin, however, the difference may be largely imaginary. Federal law states that all aspirin must contain certain chemicals in certain proportions, yet many people believe that some highly advertised brands are better than others.

Nonprice Competition

When a product is differentiated, **nonprice competition** takes the place of price competition. Nonprice competition happens when advertising or other promotional campaigns try to convince buyers that the product is somehow better than another brand. Therefore, monopolistic competitors usually advertise or promote heavily to make their products seem different from everyone else's. The idea is to make the consumer think that the product is so special, or so exclusive, that nothing else really competes with it.

If the seller can differentiate a product in the mind of the buyer, the firm may be able to raise the price a little above its competitors' prices. This concept explains why producers of jeans such as Guess, Bugle Boy, Levi's, Calvin Klein, or Jordache spend so much on advertising and promotion. ☑

Profit Maximization

In monopolistic competition, similar products generally sell within a narrow price range without greatly affecting the seller's or competitor's total sales. The monopolistic aspect of this competition is the seller's ability to raise the price within this narrow range. The competitive aspect is that if sellers raise or lower the price enough, customers will forget minor differences and change brands.

The profit maximization behavior of the monopolistic competitor is no different from that of other firms. The firm produces the quantity of output where its marginal cost is equal to its marginal revenue, and then sells the product for whatever the market will bear. If the firm has successfully convinced consumers that its product is better, it can charge a higher price. If it did not convince consumers, it would not be able to

charge as much. For this reason, we seldom see a single price for athletic shoes, jeans, cosmetics, or other differentiated products.

The monopolistic competitor faces the same ease of market entry as the perfect competitor. With little to stop entry into the industry, the possibility of profits will draw new firms, each of which will produce a product only a little different from the ones already on the market. In time, both the number of firms in a particular industry and the supply of the product will become fairly stable with no great profits or losses. **1**

Oligopoly

A market situation in which a few very large sellers of a product dominate is known as **oligopoly.** The product of an oligopolist may be differentiated—as in the auto industry, or standardized—as in the steel

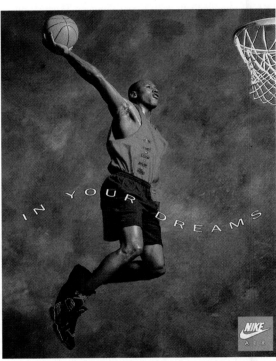

Nonprice Competition *If advertisers can make you believe their product is better than others, you might pay more for it.* **How has nonprice competition affected your buying habits?**

Cultural Diversity and Economics

Home Sweet Home? In an effort to make their products seem different from everyone else's, some sellers appeal to the ethnic background of consumers. To establish the authenticity of their products, for example, food producers might claim that they are made according to recipes "our grandmother brought over from the old country." Or they might suggest that "one taste and you are transported back to the old country." Direct students to locate advertisements that use this approach. Have them compare and discuss their findings.

industry. The exact number of firms in the industry is not as important as the ability of any single firm to cause a change in output, sales, and prices in the industry as a whole. Because of these characteristics, oligopoly is further from pure competition than is monopolistic competition.

In the United States, many markets are already oligopolistic, and many more are becoming so. Pepsi and Coke dominate the soft drink market. McDonald's, Burger King, and Wendy's dominate the fast-food industry. A few large corporations dominate other industries such as the domestic airline industry, the domestic automobile industry, and long-distance telephone service.

Interdependent Behavior

Because so few firms are part of an oligopoly, whenever one firm does something, the other firms usually follow. If one airline announces discount fares, for example, all the other airlines generally match the lower prices in a matter of days, if not hours. Each oligopolist knows that the other firms in the industry have considerable power and influence. Therefore, firms tend to act together rather than let anyone upset the status quo.

Sometimes the interdependent behavior takes the form of **collusion,** a formal agreement to set prices or to otherwise behave in a cooperative manner. One form of collusion is **price-fixing**—agreeing to charge the same or similar prices for a product. In almost every case, these prices are higher than those determined under competition. The firms also might agree to divide the market so that each is guaranteed to sell a certain amount. Because collusion usually restrains trade, it is against the law. Even so, neither the threat of heavy fines nor jail sentences has kept some collusion from taking place.

Pricing Behavior

While an oligopolist can lower the price of its product at any time, the firm knows that other oligopolists are likely to follow suit very quickly. When one firm lowers prices, it could lead to a **price war,** or a series of price cuts by all producers that may lead to unusually low prices in the industry. For a short period, the prices might even be lower than the cost of production for many of the firms.

Raising prices is risky, too, unless the firm knows that rivals will follow. Otherwise, the higher-priced firm will lose sales to its lower-priced competition. Because of this potential to lose profits with price changes, oligopolists generally prefer to compete on a nonprice basis. **2**

Nonprice competition has the advantage of making it more difficult for rivals to react. If an oligopolist finds a new advertising gimmick or a way to change the product itself, the other firms are at a disadvantage for awhile. It takes them longer to catch up and to develop a better advertising campaign or a new physical attribute for their own products.

Some oligopolists follow a policy of **independent pricing.** The oligopolist sets its own price based on demand, the cost of inputs, and other factors. **Price leadership** takes place when one firm, sometimes the biggest and most powerful in the industry, takes the lead and initiates most of the price changes. The other firms follow because they fear a price war or because they believe they will be better off financially by doing so.

Profit Maximization

The oligopolist, like any other firm, maximizes its profits when it finds the quantity of output where its marginal cost is equal to its marginal revenue. Having

L1 **Recognizing Ideas** Ask students to identify three businesses in the community that are in monopolistic competition. Direct students to write a brief description of the competitive strategies employed by these businesses. Call on volunteers to read their descriptions to the class.

 Consumer Application Assign Consumer Application Activities 5 and 10.

Math Practice Assign Math Practice for Economics 12.

Free Enterprise Assign Free Enterprise Activities 10 and 12.

LINKING PAST AND PRESENT

Many firms hire specialist companies, such as advertising agencies, to plan and execute advertising campaigns. The first successful advertising agency was established by George Presbury Rowell in 1864. Rowell's initial campaign involved planning a theatrical program for the holiday season in Boston.

ANSWERS

1. ease of entry and the opportunity to make profits
2. because if rivals do not follow suit, price rise will cause them to lose sales to lower-priced competition

Checking Understanding	Applying Economic Concepts
1. What draws new firms into a monopolistically competitive market? 2. Why are oligopolists usually reluctant to raise prices?	☑ **Advertising and Market Structures** If a firm advertises, you can be sure that it is neither a perfect competitor (because there is no need to advertise a homogeneous product) nor a monopolist (who has no competition).

CHAPTER 7: *Competition, Market Structures, and the Role of Government* **157**

$ Free Enterprise Activity $

Have students select one of the four types of markets described in Section 1—pure competition, monopolistic competition, oligopoly, and monopoly. Ask students to imagine they are entrepreneurs in the selected market and write an essay describing their entrepreneurial activities. They should apply their understanding of the characteristics of the selected market in their essays.

Readings Assign
Primary and Secondary Source
Reading 10.

 Simulation Assign
Economic Simulation 3.

 Laboratory Assign
Economic Laboratory 3.

 Performance Assessment
Assign Performance
Assessment Activity 12.

L3 Research Encourage
students to research one of the
following: fast-food industry,
soft drink industry, domestic
airlines, automobile industry,
long-distance telephone service. Have students write a report showing how the subject
of their research matches the
characteristics and behavior of
an oligopoly. Ask volunteers to
share their reports with the
class.

VISUAL INSTRUCTION

Ask students how the
store in the photograph
might lose its monopoly. *(If
the store made huge profits,
another store might open to
compete. If the store's prices
were too high, another store
might open and take advantage
of the situation by charging
lower prices.)*

Answer to Caption:

*Natural monopoly is a market
situation where costs are minimized by having one producer;
geographic monopoly exists
because of its location.*

---

found this level of production, the oligopolistic company proceeds to charge whatever the market will
bear.

The final price for the product is likely to be higher
than it would be under monopolistic competition,
and much higher than it would be under pure competition. Even when oligopolists do not collude formally, they still tend to act conservatively and seldom
protest price hikes by their rivals.

Monopoly

The final category of economic markets is the exact
opposite of pure competition. A pure **monopoly** is a
market situation with only one seller of a particular
economic product that has no close substitutes. The
American economy has very few cases of pure
monopolies.

Several factors prevent pure monopolies from
occurring. First, the American people traditionally
have disliked monopolies and have tried to outlaw
them. Second, it is usually easy to find a reasonably
close substitute for most products. Margarine can be
used instead of butter, for example, and private automobiles can be substituted for bus, train, and airplane
transportation. Third, new technologies often introduce products that compete with existing monopo-

lies. The development of the fax machine, for example, allows businesses to send electronic letters that
compete with the United States Postal Service.

Although no example of a pure monopoly exists,
some—such as the local telephone company—are
fairly close. Even the telephone company faces competition from other communication companies and
the United States Postal Service, however. For all
practical purposes, a monopoly situation does not
have to be completely pure to qualify as a monopoly.
When economists talk about monopolies, they really
are talking about near monopolies—situations that
are close to being pure.

Natural Monopoly

Sometimes the very nature of an industry dictates
that society would be served best by a monopoly. A
natural monopoly—a market situation where costs
are minimized by having a single firm produce the
product—is one example.

Two or more competing telephone companies serving the same area would be wasteful if they each
needed their own telephone poles and lines. Imagine
the confusion that would result if four or five competing transit company buses raced each other to the corner to pick up waiting passengers. Think what our city
streets would be like if several competing water or gas

Geographic Monopoly
*A lone store in an isolated
area enjoys a geographic
monopoly.* **How does a
geographic monopoly
differ from a natural
monopoly?**

Extending the Content

The Kinked Demand Curve Noted in the student's text on page 157, oligopolists are willing to
lower prices because they feel that their rivals will
follow suit. They are reluctant to raise prices, however, because they cannot be certain that competitors will do the same. Economists sometimes use a

kinked demand curve to explain this situation. On
this curve, demand for products at prices above the
present price is highly elastic. At prices below the
present price, however, demand is less elastic and
may become inelastic.

companies all kept putting in or repairing water and gas lines.

To avoid such problems, government often gives a public utility company permission to act as a natural monopoly. This arrangement is known as a **franchise.** It gives a company the exclusive right to do business in a certain area without competition. By accepting such franchises, the companies also accept a certain amount of government regulation.

Another justification for the natural monopoly is lower cost. Suppose the cost of production goes down as a firm grows larger and larger. It would make sense for the firm to grow as much as possible to reduce its production costs. This growth results from **economies of scale,** a situation in which the larger the firm grows, the more efficiently it uses its personnel, plant, and equipment.

Geographic Monopoly

Sometimes a business has a monopoly simply because of its location. A drugstore operating in a town that is too small to support two or more such businesses becomes a **geographic monopoly** because no other business in the immediate area offers any competition. Likewise, the owner of the only gas station on a lonely interstate highway exit also has a type of geographic monopoly. Drivers on the interstate are usually not aware of other gas stations in the area.

A geographic monopoly may not always be able to maintain its status. If the only drugstore in a small town began to make a great deal of money, another may soon come along and compete. If the gas station along the interstate keeps its prices too high, other stations will open to take advantage of the profits.

Technological Monopoly

The special privileges given to those who invent a new product or process lead to another kind of monopoly called a **technological monopoly.** In this type of monopoly, a firm or individual has discovered a new manufacturing technique or has invented or created something entirely new.

Figure 7.2
Market Structures and Their Characteristics

	Number of Firms in Industry	Influence Over Price	Product Differentiation	Advertising	Entry Into Market	Examples
Pure Competition	Many	None	None	None	Easy	Perfect: None Near: Truck Farming
Monopolistic Competition	Many	Limited	Fair Amount	Fair Amount	Easy	Gas Stations Women's Clothing
Oligopoly	Few	Some	Fair Amount	Fair Amount	Difficult	Automobiles Aluminum
Pure Monopoly	One	Extensive	None	None	Almost Impossible	Perfect: None Near: Electricity

The term market structure *refers to the nature and degree of competition among firms operating in the same industry. Individual market structures—pure competition, monopolistic competition, oligopoly, and monopoly—are determined by the five characteristics listed in the columns above.* **In which market structure does nonprice competition play a major role?**

CHAPTER 7: *Competition, Market Structures, and the Role of Government* **159**

Extending the Content

Market Share The market share is the portion of total sales that an individual firm has. Businesses like to see their market share grow, especially at the expense of another firm's market share. Even when the total sales of a product remain the same, an individual firm can increase its market share and can experience growth and increased profits.

Market share is illustrated in the sale of pre-pared iced tea in supermarkets. In early 1993, Snapple had a 44% market share. Lipton lost market-share leadership and dropped to 19%. Nestea had 16%. Ask students to interview the managers of supermarkets to determine the products that have the largest market share. Examples might include cereals or soft drinks.

ASSESS

Check for Understanding

Assign Section 1 Review as homework or an in-class activity.

 Use **Chapter Challenger Interactive Review Software** to review Section 1.

MEETING LESSON OBJECTIVES

Each objective below is tested by the questions on page 161 that follow it in parentheses.

1. **Explain** the characteristics of pure competition. **(1, 2)**

2. **Understand** the nature of monopolistic competition. **(1, 3, 7)**

3. **Describe** the behavior and characteristics of the oligopolist. **(1, 4, 6)**

4. **Identify** several types of monopolies. **(1, 5)**

VISUAL INSTRUCTION

Ask students why the monopolist is called a "price maker." *(Because a monopoly is the sole supplier of a product, it can control the quantity supplied and, therefore, establish prices.)*

Answer to Caption:

Americans traditionally have disliked monopolies and have tried to outlaw them; usually easy to find close substitute for most products; new technologies often produce products to compete with monopolies

---

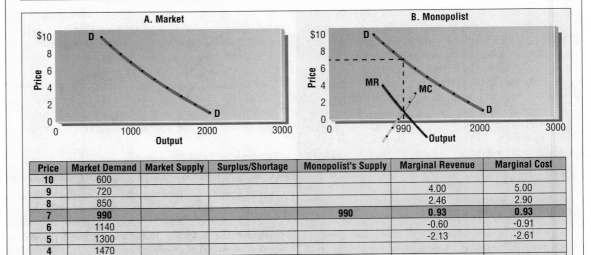

Figure 7.3
Monopoly: Market Price and Profit Maximization

Price	Market Demand	Market Supply	Surplus/Shortage	Monopolist's Supply	Marginal Revenue	Marginal Cost
10	600					
9	720				4.00	5.00
8	850				2.46	2.90
7	990			990	0.93	0.93
6	1140				-0.60	-0.91
5	1300				-2.13	-2.61
4	1470					
3	1650					
2	1840					

Because the monopolist is a "price maker," there is no supply curve for the market in A. Instead, the monopolist examines the market demand curve, and then decides how much to produce. In B, marginal revenue is computed from the market demand and then compared to marginal costs. The profit-maximizing quantity of output occurs at 990 gadgets, or where marginal costs are just equal to marginal revenue. After the monopolist determines that 990 gadgets will be produced, they will be priced for sale at $7 each. **What factors prevent pure monopolies from occurring?**

Article I, Section 8, of the Constitution of the United States gives Congress the power:

to promote the progress of science and useful arts, by securing for limited times to authors and inventors the exclusive right to their respective writings and discoveries.

DID YOU KNOW?

Monopsony A market structure opposite the monopoly is the monopsony. Whereas a monopoly is a single seller, a monopsony is a single buyer. A monopsony exists in the market for astronaut services, with the United States government being the single buyer.

The government fulfills this mandate by granting a **patent**—an exclusive right to manufacture, use, or sell any new and useful art, machine, manufacture, or composition of matter, or any new and useful improvement thereof. Inventions are covered for 17 years and designs can be patented for shorter periods, after which they become public property available for the benefit of all.

Art and literary works are protected in much the same way through a **copyright.** It gives authors or artists the exclusive right to publish, sell, or reproduce their work for their lifetime plus 50 years.

Government Monopoly

Still another kind of monopoly is a **government monopoly**—a business the government owns and

---

Extending the Content

Franchises Franchises other than those issued by the government exist in the marketplace. These are issued by a company giving permission to a person or group to use its name and sell its products. Such franchises have became an important aspect of the American economy, and sales by all franchise operations now exceed $1 trillion annually. The fast-food restaurant is probably the franchise that Americans are most familiar with. For example, 90

percent of people more than 12 years old eat regularly at a fast-food franchise.

Have students name other franchises with which they are familiar. Then ask them to note how often they make purchases from franchises. Have students work in groups to prepare charts and graphs showing the frequency and volume of their franchise purchases.

operates. Government monopolies are found at the national, state, and local levels. In most cases, they involve products people need that private industry may not adequately provide.

At the local level, many towns and cities have monopolies that oversee water use. Some states control alcoholic beverages by requiring that they be sold only through state stores. At the national level, the government tightly controls the processing of weapons-grade uranium for military purposes.

Profit Maximization

Monopolies maximize profits the same way as other firms—they equate marginal cost with marginal revenue to find the profit-maximizing quantity of output. Suppose, for example, that the gadgets industry was dominated by a monopolist, instead of by many small producers as was the case in Figure 7.1. In addition, assume that the main difference between the monopolist and the pure competitor in Figure 7.1 is size, with the monopolist being hundreds of times larger than the pure competitor.

The market for gadgets in Graph A in Figure 7.3 shows only a demand curve and no supply curve. This situation occurs because the monopolist is the only supplier of gadgets. The monopolist is able to set a price and quantity of output most profitable to itself.

At a price of $10, the monopolist could sell 600 units for a total of $6,000. If the price dropped to $9, 720 gadgets could be sold for $6,480. Because an additional 120 units generated an additional $480 in total revenue, the extra, or marginal, revenue from the sale of each gadget must have been $480 divided by 120, or $4. The $4 is shown in the second column in Table B in Figure 7.3. The marginal revenue generated by expanding production to 850 units, 990 units, and so on, is computed the same way.

The marginal cost for the monopolist is shown in the third column in Table B of Figure 7.3. Marginal cost is initially low, but it steadily increases as production increases. By the time output reaches 990 units, the marginal cost is $.93, and goes even higher at higher levels of output.

When the monopolist equates marginal cost with marginal revenue, it finds that the profit-maximizing quantity of output is 990 units. These 990 gadgets will be sold for $7 each. Therefore the monopolist produces fewer gadgets than do the hundreds of pure competitors in Figure 7.1—990 gadgets instead of 1300—yet charges a higher price for each gadget.

SECTION 1 REVIEW

Reviewing Terms and Facts

1. **Define** laissez-faire, industry, market structure, pure competition, imperfect competition, monopolistic competition, product differentiation, nonprice competition, oligopoly, collusion, price-fixing, price war, independent pricing, price leadership, monopoly, natural monopoly, franchise, economies of scale, geographic monopoly, technological monopoly, patent, copyright, government monopoly.

2. **List** the five characteristics of pure competition.
3. **Describe** how the monopolistic competitor differs from the pure competitor.
4. **Explain** why the actions of one oligopolist affects others in the same industry.
5. **List** four types of monopolies.

Critical Thinking

6. **Synthesizing Information** Provide at least two examples of oligopolies in the United States today.

Applying Economic Concepts

7. **Product Differentiation** Make a list of as many clothing stores in your community as possible. Describe how each store tries to differentiate its products from the others.

CHAPTER 7: *Competition, Market Structures, and the Role of Government* **161**

CHAPTER 7
SECTION 1

Evaluate

 Assign the Section 1 Quiz in the TCR or use the *Economics: Principles and Practices* Testmaker to create a customized quiz. Spanish Section Quizzes also are available in the Spanish Resources Binder.

Reteach

To reinforce an understanding of market structures, have students develop an annotated outline of the section.

Enrich

Invite a farmer or member of a farm association to speak to the class about how market conditions affect farming. Have students use information gleaned from the talk to write an essay titled "The Economics of Farming."

CLOSE

Have students write a brief report on the role of competition in the American free enterprise economy.

LINKING PAST AND PRESENT

The U.S. Patent Office issued its first patent in 1790. It was for a new method of making potash. A little more than 200 years later, in 1991, it issued the 5,000,000th patent—for a genetically engineered microbe.

Answers to SECTION 1 REVIEW

1. All vocabulary words are defined in the Glossary.
2. large number of buyers and sellers, buyers and sellers deal in identical products, buyers and sellers act independently, buyers and sellers well informed, ease of entry into market or business
3. Monopolistic competitors differ from pure competitors in that they practice product differentiation.

4. Because there are so few firms, whenever one does something, the others usually follow.
5. natural monopoly, geographic monopoly, technological monopoly, government monopoly
6. Answers will vary but may include fast-food industry, soft drink industry, domestic airlines, automobile industry, or long-distance telephone service.
7. Answers should focus on advertising and other forms of promotion.

CA's economic setbacks in the early 1990s were caused, in part, by the purchase of a software company whose products, by and large, were incompatible with the systems of CA's major customers. Further, a recession and then the Persian Gulf War dampened business investments in the United States and throughout the world.

TEACH

Ask students to discuss why Charles Wang thinks it's important for CEOs to have a working knowledge of PCs. *(Students will note that computers play such a large role in business operations now, and that role almost certainly will grow in the future. CEOs, if they are to understand the operations of their companies, should know how to use a PC.)*

School TO WORK

Computer Programmer
To learn more about computer programming, volunteer to serve as a teacher's aide in your school's computer department, or volunteer as an assistant at a local business that utilizes programmers. Use your experience as a volunteer to find out what particular skills programmers must have.

PROFILES IN ECONOMICS

CHARLES WANG
(1944–   )

"There are CEOs who brag about never having touched a PC," says Charles Wang, head of Computer Associates International (CA). "I say to them, 'Get your head out of the sand, kid.'" Wang's aggressive approach has helped him propel his company of 4 employees to one that earns more than $4 billion in computer software sales a year. Currently, Computer Associates is the largest independent supplier of software for business computing.

HUMBLE BEGINNINGS Born in Shanghai, China, in 1944, Charles Wang (WONG) and his family fled the communist regime in 1952 to settle in

Wang supplies on-site fitness facilities and child development centers for CA employees.

the United States. Wang attended Queens College in New York and opened an American subsidiary

of the Swiss-owned Computer Associates in New York City in 1976. Wang began operations with one product.

A SPECTACULAR SUCCESS Wang believed that the best way to help the fledgling company grow was to purchase existing software firms and market their products. He hoped this approach would spare his company the risk of developing its own products while allowing CA to get products to market sooner. Following this approach, Computer Associates purchased a number of firms throughout the

1980s. The firm was so successful that sales increased from $85 million in 1984 to $1 billion in 1989.

Although sales were robust that year, the company faced numerous challenges in the recession of 1990-1991. Despite these difficulties, Wang remained optimistic about the future of his company and launched a campaign to purchase still other companies. His efforts were amply rewarded, and CA soon found itself back on the fast track.

PROGRESSIVE MANAGING Despite its enormous growth, the company still remains focused on people. Wang supplies on-site fitness facilities and child development centers for CA employees. He brought together 2,000 members of CA's development staff for "Nerd Weekend"—a celebration for the people who fueled CA's growth. He also sponsors "Technology Boot Camps" to help chief executives get over their fear and ignorance of computers. In 1994, he wrote *Techno Vision*, a book urging business people to start thinking like technology people, and vice versa. How has Wang accomplished so much? "I love it when people say it can't be done," he says. "I love the challenge."

Examining the Profile

1. **Analyzing Ideas** What business strategy helped Wang's fledgling company become so successful?

2. **For Further Research** Find out the current status of Computer Associates' sales. Write a summary of your findings.

Answers to Examining the Profile

1. Wang purchased existing software firms and marketed their products.

2. Answers will vary. Encourage students to compare and discuss their summaries.

Section Preview

Objectives

After studying this section, you will be able to:

1. **Discuss** the problems caused by inadequate competition.
2. **Understand** the importance of having adequate information.
3. **Describe** the nature of resource immobility.
4. **Explain** the nature of positive and negative externalities.

Key Terms

market failure, externality, negative externality, positive externality, public good

Applying Economic Concepts

Market Failure Have you ever felt that the perfect job is waiting for you—but you just can't seem to find it? If so, you're experiencing market failure. A *market failure* usually occurs when we don't have adequate information about the market. The result is that productive resources—including you—do not reach their maximum potential.

Those who favor a free enterprise system believe it brings about an efficient and automatic allocation of material and human resources for the benefit of the whole economy. Markets work best when four conditions are met: Adequate competition must exist in all markets. Buyers and sellers must be reasonably well-informed about conditions and opportunities in these markets. Resources must be free to move from one industry to another. Finally, prices must reasonably reflect the costs of production, including the rewards to entrepreneurs.

Sometimes, markets fail to perform as expected, and problems develop. A **market failure** occurs when any of the four conditions described above alter significantly. The most common market failures involve cases of inadequate competition, inadequate information, resource immobility, external economies, and public goods. These failures occur on both the demand and supply sides of the market.

Inadequate Competition

Over time, mergers and acquisitions have resulted in increasingly larger and fewer firms dominating various industries. The result, in extreme cases, is a monopoly.

Dangers of Monopolies

The greatest danger of a monopoly is that it denies consumers the benefit of competition. People cannot depend on the free market system to allocate resources efficiently, or to bring the greatest satisfaction. Instead, they must depend on the monopolist who is "above the market."

When a monopoly has gained control of an industry, it can use its position to prevent competition and restrict production. This situation brings about artificial shortages that cause higher prices.

Another danger of monopolies concerns resource allocation. Competition makes businesses become more efficient in using resources. Because monopolies are not under those pressures, however, they may waste and misallocate scarce resources.

Economic and Political Power

Inadequate competition may enable a business to influence politics by wielding its economic might. In the past, some large firms have used their huge capital resources to further the political careers of their owners, relatives, and friends.

A large corporation does not even have to be a monopoly for its economic power to translate to political power, although it certainly helps. A large

---

Classroom Resources for SECTION 2

- Reproducible Lesson Plan 7-2
- Guided Reading Activity 7-2
- Reinforcing Economic Skills 7
- Section Quiz 7-2
- Spanish Section Quiz 7-2

- Focus Activity Transparency 40
- Economic Concepts Transparency 11
- NBR's Economics in Action Video Program
- Testmaker
- Vocabulary PuzzleMaker
- Chapter Challenger Interactive Review Software

Section Objectives

1. Discuss the problems caused by inadequate competition.
2. Understand the importance of having adequate information.
3. Describe the nature of resource immobility.
4. Explain the nature of positive and negative externalities.

Bellringer

Prior to taking roll at the beginning of the class period, display Focus Activity Transparency 40 and assign the accompanying Student Activity 40.

Motivational Activity

Discuss students' responses to the activity sheet that accompanies Focus Activity Transparency 40.

Preteaching Vocabulary

Refer students to the list of key terms in the Section Preview. Have students write questions for which each term is an answer. **LEP**

Use the **Vocabulary PuzzleMaker** to create a crossword or word search puzzle.

TEACH

Guided Practice

L1 *Understanding Ideas*
Write the following on the chalkboard: *Inadequate Competition, Inadequate Information, Resource Immobility, Externalities, Public Goods.* Call
(continued)

on volunteers to provide examples of each form of market failure. Then have students write a brief explanation of the concept of market failure.

L2 *Environment* Briefly review externalities with students, pointing out that economists use a number of other names for this market failure—spillovers, neighborhood effects, and social costs and benefits, for example. Then have students identify and discuss developments in their state that have created either negative or positive environmental externalities.

GLENCOE
TECHNOLOGY

NIGHTLY BUSINESS REPORT

Economics in Action

Chapter 14

Disc 1, Side 2

Title: *Competition and Monopolies*

Subject: Competition in a free enterprise economy

Ask: What is the greatest danger of monopolies? *(Consumers denied the benefits of competition.)*

Also available in VHS.

VISUAL INSTRUCTION

Ask: How might the government approach the situation of inadequate competition? *(by establishing policies geared to maintain or increase competition)*

Answer to Caption:

Students may suggest that a corporation, in order to get tax breaks from government, might threaten to move.

Maintaining Competition *Unlike consumer industries, there are a limited number of potential customers for military goods, such as these F16s manufactured by Lockheed in Fort Worth, Texas. Maintaining adequate competition is a difficult but worthwhile goal because competitive markets tend to police themselves and require less government intervention.* **How do large corporations sometimes wield political as well as economic power?**

corporation, for example, may want the state or local government to give it tax breaks or some other considerations. If the government refuses, the corporation may threaten to move its plant elsewhere, causing economic loss to the community. Because the community does not want to risk the loss, the corporation may get its way. ✓

Both Sides of the Market

If we consider the supply side of the market, it is clear that purely competitive or monopolistically competitive markets usually have enough firms to ensure competition. When it comes to oligopoly, however, we know that the temptation to collude is strong. No competition exists at all if a monopolist dominates the supply side of the market.

Inadequate competition may happen on the demand side of the market as well. In most cases, such as in the consumer goods and services markets,

numerous buyers can be found. How many consumers, though, will buy incredibly large office buildings, super computers, or M-1 tanks and high technology fighter jets?

Maintaining adequate competition is a difficult but worthwhile goal. If markets can be kept reasonably competitive, they tend to police themselves and require less government intervention. Accordingly, many government policies are geared to maintain or increase competition rather than to actually regulate a less competitive market. **1**

Inadequate Information

If resources are to be allocated efficiently, everyone—consumers, businesspeople, and government officials—must have adequate information about market conditions. A secretary or an accountant may receive a competitive wage in the automobile industry,

---

Meeting Special Needs

Reading Disability Practice a focused reading exercise with students who experience reading comprehension problems. Have students read the subsection "Inadequate Information." When students have finished reading, have them write in their notebooks what they remember of the subsection. Then have them reread the subsection to look

for answers to the following questions: What is needed to allocate resources efficiently? How can information be obtained? Ask students to check whether they wrote this information in their notebooks. If not, discuss why they might have left it out.

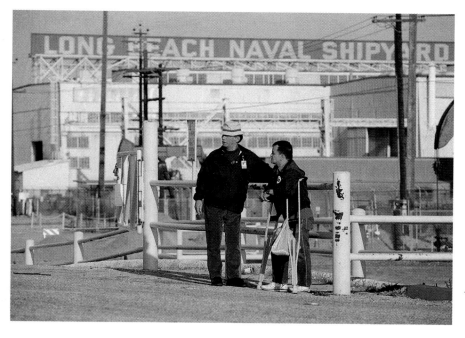

Resource Immobility
Although closing military bases may save taxpayers' dollars, the federal employees who worked at the base may be unable to find other jobs in the community. **When is resource immobility not a problem?**

 Using Transparencies
Display Economic Concepts Transparency 11. Spanish Transparencies are also available.

Independent Practice

Guided Reading Assign Guided Reading Activity for Section 2. **LEP**

L2 *Informative Writing*
Have students find newspaper articles about federal, state, or local public goods. Ask them to write short essays summarizing what the article is about and analyzing why the public good discussed is not provided by markets.

 VISUAL INSTRUCTION

Ask: Why might the resources pictured not be free or willing to move? *(Some of the workers might not be able to sell their homes, others might not be willing to leave the area for jobs elsewhere.)*

Answer to Caption:

One situation students might cite is when resources have alternatives—as when a store owner decides to stop selling shoes and open a video store.

but are wages for the same skills higher in the insurance industry, or in the banking industry? A business may use its plant and equipment efficiently in the shoe industry, but would it be better off manufacturing tents and backpacking equipment? Even the treasurer of a small community needs to know if the town's surplus funds can earn a higher return if invested in Dallas, New York, Indianapolis, or Seattle. Information about conditions in many markets is needed before these questions can be answered.

Some information is easy to obtain, such as want ads or sale prices in the local newspaper. Other information is more difficult to obtain. An investor might write to several companies for information about their earnings and dividends. The investor might visit a local library to research various companies.

A free enterprise economy requires an incredible amount of information if resources are to be allocated efficiently. When adequate information is not available, it is difficult to employ resources to their fullest for the maximum benefit of society.

Resource Immobility

One of the more difficult problems in any economy is that of resource immobility. The efficient allocation of resources requires that land, labor,

 QUICK CHECK

Checking Understanding

1. Why is maintaining adequate competition a worthwhile goal?

Applying Economic Concepts

☑ **Market Failures** Large corporations often employ lobbyists at the state and national levels who try to persuade lawmakers to support legislation favorable to the company.

 QUICK CHECK

ANSWERS

1. If markets can be kept reasonably competitive, they tend to police themselves and require less government intervention.

 Free Enterprise Activity $

List several public goods or services on the chalkboard—flood control, national defense, county roads, fire protection, and police protection, for example. Organize students into several small groups and assign each group one of the listed public goods. Have groups develop a brief oral presentation giving reasons their assigned item should remain a public good or why it should be provided as a private good by competitive markets. Have groups make and discuss their presentations.

L3 *Critical Thinking* Provide students with a number of instances of externalities—water or air pollution, traffic congestion, increased business at a restaurant after construction of a highway ramp, for example. Ask students to develop strategies for correcting external costs and benefits. (As an example, suggest that businesses that pollute might be charged a special "clean-up" tax.) Have students compare and discuss their strategies.

ASSESS

Check for Understanding

Assign Section 2 Review as homework or an in-class activity.

 Use **Chapter Challenger Interactive Review Software** to review Section 2.

 DID YOU KNOW

As interdependence increases, so do negative externalities.

VISUAL INSTRUCTION

Call on a volunteer to explain why externalities are considered market failures. (*Their costs and benefits are not reflected in market prices.*)

Answer to Caption:

Negative externality; because people living near the airport had nothing to do with expansion but may experience considerable inconvenience from construction, airplane noise, or fall in the value of their property

166

Externalities *Most economic activities generate externalities.* **Do you think the nearby airport expansion was a positive or a negative externality for the people living in this neighborhood? Why?**

entrepreneurs, and capital be free to move to markets where returns are the highest.

Sometimes this movement is not a problem. The secretary looking for a job in a large city usually has many choices. Aside from salary, concerns may center around the longer drive to work, finding a parking space, or walking a long distance from the bus stop. A store owner may quit selling shoes and decide to open a video rental or pizza parlor instead.

At other times, resources are simply not free or willing to move. What happens when a large auto assembly plant closes, leaving hundreds of workers without employment? Certainly some workers can find jobs in other industries, but not everyone can. Some workers may not be able to sell their homes. Other workers may not want to move away from friends and relatives to find new, higher-paying jobs in other cities.

Consider the problems caused when the national government closes military bases to save taxpayers' dollars. Thousands of workers are laid off in communities that have no immediate means of employing them. Resource mobility, assumed as an ideal in the

competitive free enterprise economy, is much more difficult to accomplish in the real world. When resources are immobile or refuse to move, markets do not function as efficiently as they could.

Externalities

Many activities generate some kind of **externality,** or economic side effect that either benefits or harms a third party not directly involved in the activity.

Negative Externality

If an economic action harms a third party, the side effect is called an external cost, or **negative externality.** Suppose that a city undertakes a major expansion of the local airport to attract more businesses and jobs. People who live near the airport are likely to experience considerable inconvenience from construction, as well as from additional airport noise after the additional runways are built. These people may have

166 UNIT 2: *Microeconomics*

Extending the Content

A New Approach to Pollution Costs A new strategy for internalizing the costs of pollution is gaining favor throughout the United States. This approach involves a pollution-control agency that establishes the amount of pollution allowed in an area—1,000 tons of pollutants may be discharged into a river, for example. At first, pollution permits, which add up to 1,000 tons, are either given or sold to businesses that discharge materials into the river. Businesses that need to discharge more than they

are permitted may purchase permits from other businesses, or they may develop production methods that limit pollution. As time goes on, fewer permits are issued, forcing firms to reduce pollution or pay more for increasingly scarce permits—making pollution an internal cost of production to be borne by the producers and their customers. Pollution permits are discussed further on page 530.

had nothing to do with the airport expansion, but they suffer negative externalities from its construction.

Positive Externality

If the economic action benefits a third party, the beneficial side effect is called an external benefit, or **positive externality.** People living on the other side of town may benefit from the additional jobs generated by the airport expansion. A restaurant may sell more meals and hire more workers. Both the restaurant and the workers hired will gain from the positive externalities, or benefits, of the airport expansion.

Externalities as Market Failures

Externalities are classified as market failures because their costs and benefits are not reflected in the market prices paid by the buyers and sellers of the original product. Does the airline or the air traveler compensate the home owner for the diminished value of the home located near the new runway extension? Does the restaurant owner share the additional good fortune derived from the new business with the airline or the air traveler? In both cases

the answer is no. As a result, the prices that air travelers pay for air travel may not really reflect the external costs and benefits that the airport expansion generates.

Public Goods

Another form of market failure is the need for public goods. **Public goods** are those products, such as highways, flood control, national defense, and police and fire protection, that are collectively consumed by the population. The market, if left to itself, does not supply these items or only supplies them inadequately.

A market economy produces only those items that can be withheld if people refuse to pay for them. It would be difficult, for example, to get everyone to pay for a public good such as national defense. In addition, it would be difficult to withhold national defense from single individuals. The result is that the market economy does not produce national defense.

Although the market is very successful in satisfying individual wants and needs, it fails to satisfy them on a collective basis. If public goods are to be supplied, the government usually has to provide them.

SECTION 2 REVIEW

Reviewing Terms and Facts

1. **Define** market failure, externality, negative externality, positive externality, public good.
2. **Explain** why markets need adequate competition and information.
3. **Explain** why resources are not always mobile and willing to move.
4. **Identify** two types of externalities.
5. **Explain** why the need for public goods is a form of market failure.

Critical Thinking

6. **Determining Cause and Effect** State one possible positive externality and one possible negative externality from the closing of a military base.

Applying Economic Concepts

7. **Market Failures** Cite at least two examples of situations in your community in which resources did not move from one market or industry to another because they were either unable or unwilling to move.

MEETING LESSON OBJECTIVES

Each objective below is tested by the questions that follow it in parentheses.

1. **Discuss** the problems caused by inadequate competition. **(2, 7)**
2. **Understand** the importance of having adequate information. **(2)**
3. **Describe** the nature of resource immobility. **(3, 7)**
4. **Explain** the nature of positive and negative externalities. **(1, 4, 6)**

Evaluate

Assign the Section 2 Quiz in the TCR or use the *Economics: Principles and Practices* Testmaker. Spanish Section Quizzes also are available.

Reteach

Ask students to write five newspaper headlines that summarize the five market failures discussed in the section.

Enrich

Invite the mayor or a police officer to visit the class and discuss negative and positive externalities in your community.

CLOSE

Ask students to choose the one factor they believe is the most serious obstacle to efficient market competition and to justify their choices in writing.

Answers to SECTION 2 REVIEW

1. All vocabulary words are defined in the Glossary.

2. Without adequate competition and information, productive resources will not be allocated efficiently.

3. Some workers might be tied to a particular area because they are unable to sell their homes. Others might not be willing to leave the area for jobs elsewhere.

4. negative externalities, positive externalities

5. because the market fails to satisfy needs and wants on a collective basis

6. Possible answers: positive externality—military base may have been operating machinery that discharged pollution, and the pollution ends with base closing; negative externality—businesses near base would lose customers and have to lay off workers.

7. Have students review the text on pages 165–166 before answering the question.

Point out to students that the information on page 168 is just the basics. Provide them with further tips for using a word processor.

SEARCHING FOR AND REPLACING TEXT If students find that they have misspelled a word or used an incorrect word, they should not look through the whole document to find that word. Have them use the "search" and "replace" functions on their software to have the computer find every instance where they used the word, and then they can correct it.

MORE FORMATTING TIPS Special tools in many word processing programs allow students to change the fonts or typeface of their reports and add simple graphics to their text. Have students read their software instructions to learn how to divide copy with thick lines, set off a feature by placing it in a box, or illustrate statistics with a graph.

FOOTNOTES, ENDNOTES, BIBILIOGRAPHIES Most word processing software includes steps for including footnotes, endnotes, and bibliographies. Have students place the cursor where they want the footnote, for example, to be referenced. Then have students click on the "Insert" and "Footnote" keys or follow the computer's instructions to add the footnote. Remind students that there is often an "Undo" or a "Help" button to provide assistance.

Skills Practice For additional practice, have students complete Reinforcing Economic Skills 7.

TECHNOLOGY SKILL

Using a Word Processor

Has your teacher ever asked you to turn in a report that had to be typed and formatted correctly? Word processing software can help you create these reports easily.

Explanation

Most word processing programs perform the same basic functions. A few simple commands are all you really need to know to begin creating and moving text around on your computer.

- CREATING A DOCUMENT (FILE) When you start your word processor, the screen will probably show either a blank document or a main menu, which lists several options for using your computer. If you see a blank document, you are ready to enter text. If you see a main menu, select the option that says "Create a document" or "Open a file." A blank document appears on your screen and you'll be ready to write.

- CUTTING AND PASTING TEXT "Cutting and pasting" is another name for moving text from one place to another. First, highlight the text you want to move (follow your computer's instructions for highlighting). Click on the "cut" button, and the text disappears. Then move your cursor to the spot where you want to place the text. Click the "paste" button, and the cut text appears in the new position.

- FORMATTING TEXT Do you want your text to have special margins on the sides, top, and bottom? Should certain words appear in boldfaced type and other words underlined? Do you want your text to be single-spaced or double-spaced? Press the "Format" button and follow the directions to tell the computer how you want your text to look.

- SAVING YOUR DOCUMENT Before you turn off your word processor, save your text either onto the computer's hard drive or onto a floppy disc. Name the document so you can later identify what the file contains.

Practice

1. Open a new word processing file.

2. Type a heading using your own name, your teacher's name, and today's date.

3. Type the title of the excerpt to the left in all caps, centered.

4. Type the body of the excerpt.

5. Insert your own text stating whether you agree or disagree with the excerpt and why.

6. Save your document as INVENTIONS. Print and then close the document.

Not All Inventions are Created Equal

From chewing gum to electricity, all inventions are an effort to raise our living standards. A few make it, most don't, but some inventions are clearly more earthshaking than others. Perhaps the best way to judge an invention's significance is by its extent of spillovers—connections to other goods and services that it either makes possible or makes cheaper to produce. Here are the top 10 inventions and discoveries of modern times—open, of course, to dispute.

Top 10 Inventions and Discoveries
1. *Electricity, 1873*
2. *Microprocessor, 1971*
3. *Computer, 1946*
4. *DNA, 1953*
5. *Telephone, 1876*
6. *Automobile, 1886*
7. *Internet, 1991*
8. *Television, 1926*
9. *Refrigeration, 1913*
10. *Airplane, 1903*

—*The Economy at Light Speed*, Federal Reserve Bank of Dallas

Additional Practice

For further practice in using a word processor, complete the Reinforcing Skills exercise in the Chapter 7 Review on page 174.

Answers to SKILL

Paragraphs will vary, but students should either explain why they agree with the listing or give alternatives for the list and explain why they chose those inventions and discoveries.

The Role of Government

Section Preview

Objectives

After studying this section, you will be able to:

1. **Discuss** the major antitrust legislation in the United States.
2. **Understand** the need for limited government regulation.
3. **Explain** the value of public disclosure.
4. **Discuss** the modifications to our free enterprise economy.

Key Terms

trust, price discrimination, cease and desist order, public disclosure

Applying Economic Concepts

Public Disclosure Do you have a credit card or a car loan? Did you notice that someone took the time to explain the size of monthly payments, the computation of the interest, and other important terms of the agreement? Disclosing this information is not merely an act of kindness on the part of the business. It is required by a federal *public disclosure* law so that you are a better-informed consumer.

Today, government has the power to maintain competition and to regulate certain monopolies that exist for the public welfare. In some cases, government has taken over certain economic activities and runs them as government-owned monopolies.

Antitrust Legislation

In the late 1800s, the United States passed laws to restrict monopolies, combinations, and **trusts**—legally formed combinations of corporations or companies.

Sherman Antitrust Act

In 1890 Congress passed the Sherman Antitrust Act "to protect trade and commerce against unlawful restraint and monopoly." The Sherman Act, described in Figure 7.4, was the country's first significant law against monopolies. It sought to do away with restraints and monopolies that hindered competition or made competition impossible.

By the early 1900s, a number of business organizations had been convicted under the Sherman Act. In 1911 the Supreme Court declared that the Standard Oil Company was practicing "unreasonable" restraint of trade and ordered that it be broken up into several smaller, independent companies.

Clayton Antitrust Act

The Sherman Act laid down broad foundations for maintaining competition. The act was not specific enough, however, to stop practices that restrained trade and competition. In 1914 Congress passed the Clayton Antitrust Act to give the government greater power against monopolies. Among other provisions, this act outlawed **price discrimination**—the practice of charging customers different prices for the same product—in cases where it might lead to monopoly or lessen competition.

Federal Trade Commission Act

The Federal Trade Commission Act was passed in the same year to enforce the Clayton Act. The act set up the Federal Trade Commission (FTC) and gave it the authority to issue cease and desist orders. A **cease and desist order** is an FTC ruling requiring a company to stop an unfair business practice, such as price-fixing, that reduces or limits competition among firms.

CHAPTER 7: *Competition, Market Structures, and the Role of Government* **169**

169

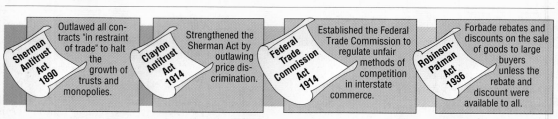

Figure 7.4
Anti-Monopoly Legislation

Sherman Antitrust Act 1890 — Outlawed all contracts "in restraint of trade" to halt the growth of trusts and monopolies.

Clayton Antitrust Act 1914 — Strengthened the Sherman Act by outlawing price discrimination.

Federal Trade Commission Act 1914 — Established the Federal Trade Commission to regulate unfair methods of competition in interstate commerce.

Robinson-Patman Act 1936 — Forbade rebates and discounts on the sale of goods to large buyers unless the rebate and discount were available to all.

Because of past monopolistic practices by some companies, the government enacted four major legislative acts. These laws prohibit monopolies and other types of behavior that restrain competition. **Which act allows government to issue cease and desist orders?**

Robinson-Patman Act

In 1936 Congress passed the Robinson-Patman Act in an effort to strengthen the Clayton Act, particularly the provisions that dealt with price discrimination. Under this act, companies could no longer offer special discount prices only to certain customers. The new law chiefly affected national organizations and chain stores, which were offering goods and services at lower prices than those paid by small independent businesses.

Government Regulation

Government maintains competition mainly by regulating some monopolists' prices and directing the quality of some services offered to the public. The goal is for the government to set the same prices that might exist if there were competition.

Local and state governments regulate many monopolies, such as cable television companies, electric utilities, and even telephone companies. A public commission or other government agency usually approves prices for their services. If the company wants to raise rates, it must argue its case before the commission. If the company wins, prices will go up. If they do not, prices will stay the same.

Agencies of the national government, such as those listed in Figure 7.5, regulate many businesses. Privately owned agencies, such as the Federal Reserve System, have certain regulatory powers such as the power to regulate the money supply, some daily bank operations, and even bank mergers.

Public Disclosure

One of the more potent weapons available to the government is **public disclosure,** or the requirement that businesses reveal information to the public. The Food and Drug Administration, for example, requires content labels on canned goods and other food products. The government also requires that corporations and certain firms disclose financial and operating information.

Any corporation that sells stock to the public and lists its stock on a stock exchange must file periodic reports with the Securities and Exchange Commission. The firms are also required to supply investors with annual reports on the money, securities, and property the investors own, as well as information on sales and profits.

Banks are required to file periodic reports to the Federal Reserve System and other federal agencies. This information is readily available to the firm's competitors as well as to its shareholders and is highly sought after by almost all firms in the industry.

The advantage of public disclosure is that it costs very little to administer and yet provides the market with enough information to prevent market failures. At the same time, businesses are not forced to give away their competitive trade secrets.

Figure 7.5
Federal Regulatory Agencies in the United States

Food and Drug Administration (FDA), 1906	Enforces laws to ensure purity, effectiveness, and truthful labeling of food, drugs, and cosmetics; inspects production and shipment of these products.
Federal Trade Commission (FTC), 1914	Administers antitrust laws forbidding unfair competition, price-fixing, and other deceptive practices.
Federal Communications Commission (FCC), 1934	Licenses and regulates radio and television stations and regulates interstate telephone, telegraph rates and services.
Securities and Exchange Commission (SEC), 1934	Regulates and supervises the sale of listed and unlisted securities and the brokers, dealers, and bankers who sell them.
National Labor Relations Board (NLRB), 1935	Administers federal labor-management relations laws; settles labor disputes; prevents unfair labor practices.
Federal Aviation Administration (FAA), 1958	Regulates air commerce; sets standards for pilot training, aircraft maintenance, and air traffic control; controls U.S. airspace.
Equal Employment Opportunity Commission (EEOC), 1964	Investigates and rules on charges of discrimination by employers and labor unions.
Environmental Protection Agency (EPA), 1970	Coordinates federal environmental programs to fight air and water pollution.
National Highway Traffic Safety Administration (NHTSA), 1970	Sets and enforces laws to promote motor vehicle safety and to protect drivers, passengers, and pedestrians; sets safety and fuel economy standards for new motor vehicles produced or sold in the U.S.
Occupational Safety and Health Administration (OSHA), 1970	Investigates accidents at the workplace; enforces regulations to protect employees at work.
Consumer Product Safety Commission (CPSC), 1972	Sets and enforces safety standards for consumer products.
Nuclear Regulatory Commission (NRC), 1974	Licenses and regulates civilian use of nuclear materials and facilities.
Federal Energy Regulatory Commission (FERC), 1977	Fixes rates and regulates the interstate transportation and sale of electricity, oil, and natural gas; issues permits and licenses for hydroelectric projects and gas pipelines; supervises mergers and stock issues of electric power and natural gas; sets rates for interstate transportation of oil by pipeline.

In order to promote competition and restrict unfair trade policies, the government has created a number of federal regulatory agencies to oversee the economy. Because of government's involvement in the economy, we now say that we have a modified free enterprise system. **With which of the agencies listed above are you familiar? Which affect you directly? Why?**

CHAPTER 7: *Competition, Market Structures, and the Role of Government* **171**

CHAPTER 7
SECTION 3

L2 Constructing a Chart
Have students construct a chart, similar to that in Figure 7.5 on page 171, showing state and local government regulatory agencies.

ASSESS

Check for Understanding

Assign Section 3 Review as homework or an in-class activity.

 Use **Chapter Challenger Interactive Review Software** to review Section 3.

 VISUAL INSTRUCTION

Point out that during the 1970s and 1980s, members of the Carter and Reagan administrations felt that there was too much government interference in the economy, and they sought to limit the regulatory powers of many agencies shown on the chart.

Answer to Caption:

Answers will vary. Some students might mention the FDA, because they have bought food cans with FDA-mandated labels.

$ Free Enterprise Activity $

Select teams of students to debate the following proposition: "Resolved: That the government is too involved in regulating our economy." Before the debate, review Section 3 with the students. Then have them conduct research in the library to obtain additional information on the subject. During the debate, have students not directly involved serve as judges, recording a mark when each side makes a point that supports its position. Have judges tally scores and announce the winner of the debate.

Modified Free Enterprise

Concern over monopolies is one reason for government intervention in the United States economy today. Historically, the freedom to pursue self-interest led some people and businesses to seek economic gain at the expense of others. Acting under the label of competition, some larger firms used their size and power to take advantage of smaller ones. In some markets, monopoly replaced competition.

Because of such conditions, laws to prevent "evil monopolies" and to protect the rights of workers were passed. Labor unions were supported to give workers more bargaining power. Food and drug laws were passed to protect people from false claims and harmful products. Some industries, such as public utilities, became subject to strict government regulation. All these actions led to a modification of free enterprise.

Restrictions on economic freedom are put there not to prevent the benefits of competition, but to bring about a more efficient use of resources. Government takes part in economic affairs for several reasons. One is to promote and encourage competition within the rules of fair play. Another is to prevent and do away with monopolies that do not allow the public to reap the benefits of competition. A third is to regulate industries in which a monopoly is clearly for the public good. As a result, today's modi-

fied private enterprise economy is a mixture of different market structures, different kinds of business organizations, and varying degrees of government regulation.

SECTION 3 REVIEW

**Reviewing
Terms and Facts**

1. **Define** trust, cease and desist order, price discrimination, public disclosure.
2. **Describe** four important antitrust laws.
3. **Provide** at least three examples of limited government regulation in the American economy.
4. **Provide** at least two examples of public disclosure.

5. **Explain** why the United States has a modified free enterprise economy.

**Critical
Thinking**

6. **Synthesizing Information** Identify five examples of how government has intervened in the economy in your community.

**Applying
Economic Concepts**

7. **Public Disclosure** Visit a bank in your community and ask for literature describing the computation of interest and conditions for withdrawal on various savings accounts. Why do you think the bank is so forthcoming on these issues?

Answers to SECTION 3 REVIEW

1. All vocabulary words are defined in the Glossary.
2. Sherman Antitrust Act (1890) outlawed activities in restraint of trade; Clayton Antitrust Act (1914) outlawed price discrimination; Federal Trade Commission Act (1914) established FTC to regulate interstate commerce; Robinson-Patman Act (1936) outlawed rebates and discounts limited to certain customers
3. Examples may include: local and state govern-

ment regulation of monopolies; Fed's regulation of banking operations; and agencies listed in Figure 7.5.
4. Examples may include: FDA requirement of content labels on food products; corporations selling stock required to file reports with SEC.
5. People carry on economic affairs freely but are subject to some government regulation.
6. Examples will vary.

ECONOMICS IN ACTION

Competition and Monopolies

Setting Up the Video

With your classmates, view "Competition and Monopolies" on the videodisc *Economics in Action*. The video focuses on competition in a free enterprise system, using the airline and toy industries as examples. It also discusses how the government sometimes creates monopolies. The U.S. Postal Service, for example, is a monopoly the government allows to control normal first-class delivery of mail.

 Chapter 14
Disc 1, Side 2

View the video by scanning the bar code or by entering the chapter number on your keypad and pressing Search. *(Also available in VHS format.)*

Hands-On Activity

Explore how the government responds to levels of competition. Working in small groups, choose one of the following industries: banking, automobile, telephone and communications, steel, or food processing. Research the level of competition in the industry and predict whether the number of competitors in the industry is likely to increase or decrease and explain why. Conclude by having your group make an oral presentation of your findings to the class.

GLENCOE
TECHNOLOGY

Economics in Action

Chapter 14
Disc 1, Side 2
Title: *Competition and Monopolies*

 If you do not have access to a videodisc player, the **Economics in Action** programs are also available in VHS.

---

computer illustration

SURFING THE "NET"

Government Regulation

Since the late 1800s, the United States government has passed laws to restrict monopolies, combinations, and trusts—legally formed combinations of corporations or companies. Today the government has the power to maintain competition and to regulate certain monopolies that exist for the public welfare. In some cases government has taken over certain economic activities and runs them as government-owned monopolies. Information about recent measures taken by the government to regulate the economy can be found on the Internet.

Getting There

1. Use a search engine. Type in the words *government regulation*.

2. After typing in government regulation, enter words like the following to focus your search: *mergers, antitrust, monopoly*, and *price-fixing*.

3. The search engine will provide you with a number of links to follow. Links are "pointers" to different sites on the Internet and often appear as blue, underlined words.

What to Do When You Are There

Click on the links to navigate through the pages of information. Gather your findings. Using the findings, write several paragraphs describing recent government antitrust regulations. Take a position for or against these regulations and support it with examples from your research.

INTERNET SITES

The following are possible sites for completing the "Net" activities:

Antitrust Policy
http://www.antitrust.org/

Antitrust Policy and Enforcement
http://www.essential.org/antitrust/

U.S. Securities and Exchange Commission
http://www.sec.gov/

Not on the "Net"...

If students have limited or no access to the Internet, have them complete the activity "Government Regulation" by using the *Readers' Guide to Periodical Literature* at the library. Have students look up mergers, antitrust, and price-fixing in the guide. They should then find the listed magazines and other resources they need to complete their research.

173

INTERNET ADDRESS BOOK

Internet addresses that you find useful can be noted in the space below for quick reference.

Answers

Reviewing Key Terms

Paragraphs will vary. Paragraph on pure competition will include *pure competition.* Paragraph on monopolistic competition could include *imperfect competition, monopolistic competition, product differentiation, nonprice competition.* Paragraph on oligopoly will include *collusion, imperfect competition, oligopoly, price leadership, product differentiation, price-fixing, independent pricing, nonprice competition, price war.* Paragraph on monopoly will include *copyright, geographic monopoly, imperfect competition, natural monopoly, technological monopoly, franchise, government monopoly, monopoly, patent.* Monopolistic competition and oligopoly could include *copyright, franchise, patent.*

Reviewing the Facts

1. large number of buyers and sellers, buyers and sellers deal in identical products, buyers and sellers act independently, buyers and sellers are well informed, and ease of entry into the market

2. large number of buyers and sellers, buyers and sellers deal in differentiated products, buyers and sellers act independently, buyers and sellers are well informed, and ease of entry into the market

174

Reviewing Key Terms

Use all the terms below in four paragraphs, with each paragraph about one of the major types of market structures.

collusion
copyright
geographic monopoly
imperfect competition
monopolistic competition
natural monopoly
oligopoly
price leadership
product differentiation
technological monopoly
price-fixing
franchise
government monopoly
independent pricing
monopoly
nonprice competition
patent
price war
pure competition

Reviewing the Facts

SECTION 1 *(pages 152–161)*

1. **Describe** the five characteristics of pure competition.
2. **Explain** the main characteristics of the monopolistic competitor.
3. **Contrast** the oligopolist and the pure competitor.
4. **Describe** the four types of monopolies.

SECTION 2 *(pages 163–167)*

5. **Explain** what happens when markets do not have enough competition.
6. **Provide** two examples of inadequate information in a market.
7. **Explain** what is meant by resource immobility.
8. **Explain** what is meant by positive and negative externalities.
9. **Account** for the reluctance of the private sector to produce public goods.

SECTION 3 *(pages 169–172)*

10. **Identify** four major antitrust laws.
11. **List** 10 major federal government regulatory agencies.
12. **Explain** how public disclosure is used as a tool to prevent market failures.
13. **Describe** a modified free enterprise economy.

Critical Thinking

1. **Making Generalizations** To what extent do you think government should be involved in the free enterprise economy? Defend your answer.
2. **Predicting Consequences** Do you think there would be any advantages to making monopolies or near monopolies break up into smaller, competing firms? If so, what are they? If not, why would there not be?

Applying Economic Concepts

1. **Market Failures** Explain how your newspaper, with its Help Wanted ads and weekly sale prices, helps prevent market failure.
2. **Market Structures** Identify a fast-food product that you consume regularly. Count the number of firms in your community that supply a similar product, and then determine the market structure for that product in your community.

Reinforcing Skills

USING A WORD PROCESSOR

On page 168, you learned some word processing tips. Use those tips to write a report on the Standard Oil Company using the functions listed below.

1. Open a new word processing file.
2. Change the line spacing to double.
3. Type a heading using your own name, your teacher's name, and today's date.
4. Type the title in initial caps, centered.
5. Type the body of the report.
6. Proofread to check for errors.
7. Save your document as STANDARD OIL.
8. Print and then close the document.

3. **Oligopolist:** few large competitors dealing in differentiated products may take actions that can change output, sales, and prices in the industry as a whole; **Pure competitor:** one of many producers dealing in identical products, and the actions he or she may take have no impact on the industry as a whole.

4. Natural monopoly, where costs are minimized by having single producer; geographic monopoly, where business has monopoly because of its geographic location; technological monopoly, where

firm or individual has discovered new manufacturing technique or has created something entirely new; government monopoly, where the government owns and operates business.

5. Without adequate competition, productive resources will not be allocated efficiently.

6. Examples may include a lack of information about wages for the same job in different industries, or lack of information about possible returns on investments in different areas of the country.

nondurable good	large number of buyers and sellers	identical economic products	firms in industry act independently	everyone reasonably well-informed	firms free to enter/exit the market	probable market structure
1.						
2.						
3.						
4.						
5.						

Individual Activity

Draw a table like the one shown above. Then identify five nondurable goods that you recently purchased. In the table, list each item in the first five rows of the first column. Next, fill in columns 2-6 with a yes or no. From these responses, identify the probable market structure (column 7) for each of your five products.

Cooperative Learning Activity

Working in pairs, each pair will research one of the federal regulatory agencies outlined in Figure 7.5. Answer such questions as: What does the agency regulate? What led to the agency being formed? What changes did the agency create? How does the agency personally affect you? After your research is complete, present your research findings to the rest of the class.

Technology Activity

Developing a Multimedia Presentation

In the **Journal Writing** activity on page 151, you were asked to evaluate at least three advertisements for a product. Use your evaluations and a video camera to develop a commercial advertising a product of your choice. Work with a partner or group to describe and show your product in such a way that consumers will want to buy it. Incorporate music, computer graphics if possible, and acting in your video. Present your commercial to the rest of the class. Have other students evaluate your commercial for its effectiveness.

Critical Thinking

1. Answers will vary. Some students may argue that there should be less government involvement, because government regulations add to production costs and, therefore, prices. Other students may suggest that more government involvement is needed to prevent market failures, such as inadequate competition.

2. Answers will vary. Some students will suggest that breaking up the monopolies would be advantageous because it would increase competition. Others might suggest that in the case of natural monopolies it would lead to inefficient use of resources, and there would be no advantage.

Applying Economic Concepts

1. Most students will suggest that the local newspaper helps maintain a competitive economy by providing people with additional information on markets.

2. Answers will vary. In most communities, however, the fast-food market is an oligopoly.

Reinforcing Skills

Students' reports should follow the guidelines given. Students should include information about Standard Oil's monopoly in their reports.

? BONUS TEST QUESTION

Provide examples, other than those mentioned in the chapter, of industries that match, or closely match, each of the four forms of market structure. (*Examples will vary.*)

7. when resources are unable or unwilling to move to markets where returns are highest

8. positive externality: where economic action benefits third party; negative externality: where economic action harms third party

9. The private sector is willing to produce items that can be withheld if people refuse to pay for them.

10. Sherman Antitrust Act (1890), Clayton Antitrust Act (1914), Federal Trade Commission Act (1914), Robinson-Patman Act (1936)

11. See Figure 7.5 for possible entries.

12. Public disclosure requires businesses to provide certain kinds of information that help prevent market failures.

13. one in which people carry on their economic affairs freely, but are subject to government regulation in certain cases

FOCUS

A study by the Economic Policy Institute and Women's Research and Education Institute concluded that differences in pay and benefits between part-time and full-time workers was significant in most workplaces. The study found:

- Women doing regular part-time work earned 20 percent less than full-time women with similar jobs and experience, and male part-time workers made 24 percent less than full-time men. Self-employed women made 25 percent less than full-time women. Self-employed men made 13 percent less than full-time men.
- Large majorities of regular part-time and independently working women, and smaller majorities of men, are working that way because they want to or for family reasons.
- People working only on call or as temps want more work than that. Men with children are the unhappiest temps.

TEACH

L1 *Taking a Poll* Have students poll at least 10 employed adults, asking for their opinions on part-time jobs—Are they fair? Should the government get involved in regulating part-time hours? Should market forces establish worker-employer relations? Have students report the results of their polls to the class.

UNIT 2 CASE STUDY

Issues in Free Enterprise

PART-TIME JOBS

Part-time workers—those without pensions, paid holidays, and sometimes the medical benefits of the average full-time worker—carry a large share of the American workload. Almost one in three workers holds a nonstandard (part-time or temporary) job, according to a study by the Economic Policy Institute and Women's Research and Education Institute. Corporations who hire part-time employees are facing increasing criticism from workers who believe full-time positions are suffering. In 1997 the Teamsters Union even held a 15-day strike against the United Parcel Service (UPS) in an effort to reduce the number of part-time jobs at that company. With UPS being the world's largest package delivery company, the strike drastically reduced trade for several weeks. Did the Teamsters have a case against UPS, or are part-time jobs advantageous to our economy?

Pro

Nearly half of UPS's part-timers are younger than 25; 40 percent are college students. Only 5 percent of part-timers have been with the company more than 10 years. . . . The bulk of these workers prefer part-time work, to help pay college bills, or to provide parents of young kids with flexibility—plus the benefits. Unlike most other companies, UPS has for years offered health coverage and even partial pensions to part-timers. . . .

[T]he Teamsters' broader charge about America's growing part-time economy doesn't square with statistics. Part-time jobs have held steady at 16 to 18 percent of the U.S. workforce for 20 years. . . . Four in five of these workers chose part-time work voluntarily, for family or other reasons. . . .

—MATTHEW MILLER, *U.S. NEWS & WORLD REPORT*, SEPTEMBER 1, 1997

176 UNIT 2: *Microeconomics*

▲ *The Reverend Jesse Jackson, right, and Teamsters President Ron Carey, left, join in the UPS strike against part-time work.*

▼ *Many teenagers would not have jobs if employers did not offer part-time positions.*

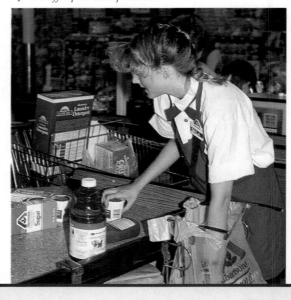

About the Speakers

Pro Matthew Miller is a writer and editor for *U.S. News & World Report*.

Con Eileen Appelbaum is associate director of research at the Economic Policy Institute in Washington, D.C., and co-author of *The New American Workplace*.

Part-time or temporary workers carry a large share of the workload. Many of these temps work part-time hours because they want to or for family reasons.

▼ *How many of these college students are on their way to a part-time job after graduating?*

Con When you go to the deli of your neighborhood super-market on a busy Saturday, you may be surprised to learn that the part-time workers slicing the salami make a lot less than their full-time co-workers. That's because many companies face periods of peak demand and need to hire part-time workers to take care of their customers. But part-time workers are often hired at lower hourly wages than full-time workers doing the same job.

The wage gap between part-time and full-time workers is huge and persistent in our economy. At the median, the hourly pay of the average part-time worker is 64% of full-time pay. That kind of pay difference is a big temptation for companies to employ more part-time workers than can be justified by business needs.

This issue is at the heart of labor's dispute with United Parcel Service and is a prime example of the impact of corporate flexibility on workers. At UPS, for example, there are 10,000 employees who work 35 hours a week but are classified as part-time, are paid the lower wages—nearly 35% less—and receive inferior benefits.

. . . Part-time workers should not suffer a "pay penalty" for working fewer hours, especially when they are providing the much-needed flexibility that companies seek.

—EILEEN APPLEBAUM, *USA TODAY*, AUGUST 7, 1997

Analyzing the Case Study

1. What is the difference between part-time work and full-time work?
2. According to Miller, why are part-time jobs attractive to some workers?
3. What corporate practice toward part-time workers does Appelbaum criticize?
4. With which opinion do you agree? Why?

UNIT 2: *Microeconomics* **177**

ASSESS

Have students answer the questions listed under "Analyzing the Case Study."

CLOSE

After students have read the case study, organize a class discussion on part-time jobs. Encourage students to offer information that supports the position they take.

Answers to Analyzing the Case Study

1. workers without pensions, paid holidays, and sometimes the medical benefits of the average full-time worker

2. Many part-time workers prefer part-time jobs either to help pay college bills or to provide flexibility to parents of young children.

3. the wage gap; that part-time workers are often hired at lower hourly wages than full-time workers doing the same job

4. Students' answers will vary, but they should provide reasons for their responses.

Unit Goals

After studying this unit, students will be able to:

1. **Trace** the development and influence of labor unions.

2. **Explain** how government raises revenues and allocates expenditures.

3. **Describe** the evolution of money and the banking system.

4. **Explain** the organization and role of the Federal Reserve System, other financial institutions, and markets.

Unit Overview

Unit 3 discusses the role of labor, government, and financial institutions in the American economy. **Chapter 8** describes organized labor in the U.S. and examines its influence on employment and wages. **Chapter 9** focuses on how government raises revenue and discusses the nature of taxation, while **Chapter 10** details how government spends revenues. **Chapter 11** discusses the development of the banking system. **Chapter 12** describes the Federal Reserve System and its role as manager of the country's money supply. **Chapter 13** explains the importance of savings to the economy and describes investments in financial assets, equities, and markets.

⌒ If time does not permit teaching the entire unit, use the **Chapter Digests Audiocassettes** to highlight chapter content.

178

UNIT 3
MACRO-ECONOMICS: INSTITUTIONS

It's a billion here and a billion there; the first thing you know it adds up to real money.

—Everett Dirksen,
American politician, 1896–1969

$ Economics and You

In this unit, discover what part economics plays in the following situations:
• Deductions are taken out of your paycheck.
• Your bank account is federally insured.
• Taxes pay for your high school education.
• Your savings account earns less than other investments.

$$ Economics and You

The first example above is an illustration of one way in which government raises revenue. The second example illustrates one step the federal government has taken to ensure a stable banking system.

The third example identifies one program for which government must allocate the revenues it collects. The final example provides an illustration of the risk-return relationship of investment—a savings account is a low-risk investment that, therefore, earns a low return.

Financial investments include buying stocks and bonds.

Connecting with Past Learning

Refer students to Figure 1.8 on page 25. Call on students to explain how labor, government, and such financial institutions as banks are a part of the circular flow of economic activity.

Introducing the Unit

Have each student list what he or she thinks are the three most controversial topics in economics today. Call on volunteers to share their lists with the class, noting new issues on the chalkboard as they are offered. Circle such topics as labor unions, taxes, government spending, deficit, national debt, savings and loan crisis, and so on. Then point out that the circled issues will be discussed at some length in Unit 3.

Unit Project

Have students write an essay titled: "The Life of a Dollar Bill." The essay should trace the dollar from its printing at the Bureau of Engraving and Printing—through the various transactions for which it might be used, including those between businesses and workers, consumers and businesses, consumers and businesses and banks, and government and individuals and businesses—to its fate after it is no longer in a usable condition. Have volunteers read their essays to the class.

Examining the Photograph

Ask students to suggest other forms of financial investments. (*Suggestions might include savings accounts, money market accounts, CDs, IRAs, pension funds, insurance policies, government savings bonds, Treasury bills, antiques, fine art, and so on.*) Then ask students which of the above they would invest in and why. As guidance, ask: What kind of risk are you willing to take with your investment? What kind of return do you expect to gain from your investment? How long are you willing to let your money sit in this particular investment? Point out that these and other investment issues are addressed in Unit 3.

CHAPTER ORGANIZER

Daily Objectives	Reproducible Resources	Multimedia Resources
Section 1 **The Labor Movement** 1. **Explain** why unions are still important today. 2. **Discuss** the development of the labor movement from the late 1700s to the 1930s. 3. **Relate** labor's sucesses during the Great Depression. 4. **State** the major labor developments since World War II.	Reproducible Lesson Plan 8-1 Guided Reading Activity 8-1 Cooperative Learning Activity 13 Consumer Application Activities 13, 19 Math Practice for Economics 13 Free Enterprise Activity 13 Primary and Secondary Source Reading 13 Performance Assessment Activity 13 Section Quiz 8-1*	Focus Activity Transparency 49 Vocabulary PuzzleMaker Chapter Challenger Interactive Review Software Testmaker MindJogger Videoquiz NBR's Economics in Action Video Program
Section 2 **Resolving Union and Management Differences** 1. **Explain** the differences between four kinds of union arrangements. 2. **Describe** several ways to resolve labor and management differences when collective bargaining fails.	Reproducible Lesson Plan 8-2 Guided Reading Activity 8-2 Reinforcing Economic Skill 8 Section Quiz 8-2*	Focus Activity Transparency 50 Vocabulary PuzzleMaker Chapter Challenger Interactive Review Software Testmaker NBR's Economics in Action Video Program
Section 3 **Labor and Wages** 1. **Identify** four main catagories of labor. 2. **Explain** the importance of noncompeting labor grades. 3. **Describe** two different approaches to wage determination.	Reproducible Lesson Plan 8-3 Guided Reading Activity 8-3 Section Quiz 8-3*	Focus Activity Transparency 51 Vocabulary PuzzleMaker Chapter Challenger Interactive Review Software Testmaker
Section 4 **Employment Trends and Issues** 1. **Explain** why union membership is declining. 2. **Describe** reasons for the discrepancy in pay between men and women. 3. **Understand** the minimum wage as it is measured in current and constant dollars.	Reproducible Lesson Plan 8-4 Guided Reading Activity 8-4 Section Quiz 8-4*	Focus Activity Transparency 52 Vocabulary PuzzleMaker Chapter Challenger Interactive Review Software Testmaker NBR's Economics in Action Video Program
Chapter Review and Evaluation	Enrichment Activity 8 Reteaching Activity 8* Economic Vocabulary Activity 8* Chapter 8 Test, Forms A and B	Chapter Digests Audiocassette Activities and Tests* Testmaker MindJogger Videoquiz

*Also available in Spanish

 Blackline Master   Transparency   CD-ROM   Software   Videodisc   Audiocassette

OUT OF TIME? Assign the Chapter 8 Digest Audiocassette and the corresponding Chapter Digest activities and tests.

National Council on Economic Education

THE **Economics** America AND **Economics** International PROGRAMS

VOLUNTARY NATIONAL CONTENT STANDARDS IN ECONOMICS
Emphasized in Chapter 8

Content Standard 10 *Students will understand that:* Institutions evolve in market economies to help individuals and groups accomplish their goals. Banks, labor unions, corporations, legal systems, and not-for-profit organizations are examples of important institutions. A different kind of institution, clearly defined and well enforced property rights, is essential to a market economy.

Content Standard 13 *Students will understand that:* Income for most people is determined by the market value of the productive resources they sell. What workers earn depends, primarily, on the market value of what they produce and how productive they are.

EconomicsAmerica *Resources Available From NCEE*

- *Capstone: The Nation's High School Economics Course*
- *Civics and Government: Focus on Economics*
- *MCG: Economics and Entrepreneurship*
- *Focus: High School Economics*
- *Personal Decision Making: Focus on Economics*
- *Personal Finance Economics: Wallet Wisdom*
- *United States History: Eyes on the Economy, Vol. II*

To order these materials, or to contact your state Council on Economic Education about workshops and programs, call 1-800-338-1192 or visit http://www.nationalcouncil.org**.**

PERFORMANCE ASSESSMENT

The following chapter projects may be assigned at the beginning of the chapter and used for performance assessment.

Multicultural Heritage Have students work in pairs to develop research projects documenting the contributions of various groups to the American labor movement. Topics that pairs might select include the role of women in the labor movement; Isaac Myers and the Colored National Labor Union; César Chavez and the United Farm Workers; A. Philip Randolph and the Brotherhood of Sleeping Car Porters; or a particular union, such as the International Ladies Garment Workers Union. Encourage pairs to use library resources or to write to the headquarters of various unions to obtain information about their selected topics. Have pairs present their completed projects to the class.

Cooperative Learning Organize students into groups of four and tell them they are to undertake a survey of employed people to find out why they work, what they like about working and their particular jobs, and what they do not like about working. Instruct groups to develop 5 to 10 questions for the survey. Have groups compare their questions, and allow groups an opportunity to make revisions to their surveys. To avoid duplication, assign certain areas or neighborhoods for each group to survey. After the data is collected, ask groups to summarize their findings and share the results with the rest of the class. In their presentations, students should comment about how the results were consistent with what they expected or how the results were surprising.

ADDITIONAL RESOURCES

Readings for the Student

Economics in America: Opposing Viewpoints. St. Paul, MN: Greenhaven Press, 1992. Presents pro and con viewpoints on several different issues. The labor issue is "What is the Future of American Labor?"

Taking Sides: Clashing Views on Controversial Economic Issues, Seventh Edition. Guilford: Dushkin, 1995. A broad collection of opposing viewpoints on 20 controversial issues in economics.

Readings for the Teacher

Kaufman, Bruce E. *The Economics of Labor Markets and Labor Relations.* Hinsdale, IL: Dryden Press, 1986. Includes a number of chapters that view labor unions from the economist's perspective.

Schor, Juliet B. *The Overworked American: The Unexpected Decline of Leisure.* New York: Basic Books, 1993. Examines a new phenomenon in the world of work—the decline of leisure time.

Multimedia

America Lost and Found: The Depression Decade. Direct Cinema Education/Social Studies School Service, 10200 Jefferson Boulevard, P.O. Box 802, Culver City, CA 90232–0802. Videocassette, 58 minutes. PBS compilation of rare newsreel footage chronicles events of the 1930s.

Organizing America: A History of Trade Unions in the U.S. Cambridge/Social Studies School Service, 10200 Jefferson Boulevard, P.O. Box 802, Culver City, CA 90232–0802. Videocassette, 40 minutes. Archival footage, personal accounts, and commentary trace the history of American labor.

Chapter Overview

Chapter 8 explains the labor movement and its influence on employment and wages. **Section 1** covers the history of the organized labor movement in the United States from its beginning to the present. **Section 2** explains ways of resolving disputes between unions and management. **Section 3** identifies the four categories of labor, explains the theories of wage determination, and accounts for regional wage differences. **Section 4** discusses three current employment issues—union decline, pay for women, and the minimum wage.

GLENCOE
TECHNOLOGY

VIDEODISC
MindJogger Videoquiz

Use MindJogger to preview the Chapter 8 content.

 Chapter 8
Disc 1, Side B

 Also available in VHS.

inter**NET**
CONNECTION

Resources for Chapter 8 on the World Wide Web*

National Council on Economic Education
http://www.nationalcouncil.org/

Bureau of Labor Statistics
http://stats.bls.gov/

AFL-CIO Home Page
http://www.aflcio.org/

*Sites subject to change.

Union members march to gain public support for their position on labor.

✚ EXTRA CREDIT PROJECT

Have students use library resources to develop a statistical report on labor in the United States. Suggest that they use charts and graphs to illustrate such topics as changes in the labor force, average wages over the years, union membership, and so on.

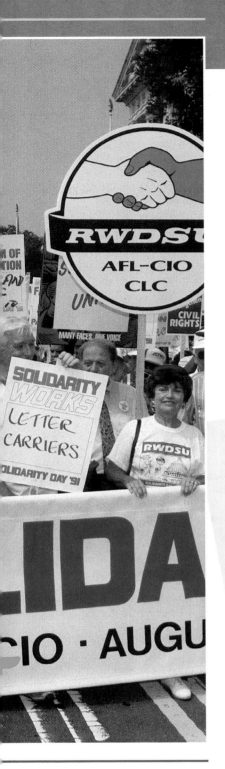

CHAPTER 8

Employment, Labor, and Wages

SECTION 1
The Labor Movement

SECTION 2
Resolving Union and Management Differences

SECTION 3
Labor and Wages

SECTION 4
Employment Trends and Issues

CHAPTER PREVIEW

People to Know

• John L. Lewis
• Labor Relations Specialist

Applying Economic Concepts to Your Life

Opportunity Cost What kind of income do you want to earn after you graduate from high school? Will your current training and skills allow you to reach your income goal? The opportunity costs of your post-high school decisions may remain with you for a long time, so it is important to plan wisely.

Journal Writing

For one week, scan the Help Wanted section of your local newspaper. In your journal, summarize the job titles and job descriptions that you are interested in learning more about. Keep track of the salary ranges for those jobs that you summarize.

CHAPTER 8: *Employment, Labor, and Wages* **181**

Economic Portfolio

In their **Journal Writing** summaries, suggest that students also consider the types of education, training, and experience that might be needed for various jobs and the relationship that exists between these factors and salary levels. Mention that this will help them to complete a persuasive writing activity in the Chapter Review. Refer students to the **Technology Activity** in the Chapter 8 Review on page 207.

Key to Ability Levels — Teaching strategies have been coded for varying learning styles and abilities:
L1 - Basic (activities for all students) **L2 - Average** (activities for average to above-average students)
L3 - Challenging (activities for above-average students) **LEP - Limited English Proficiency**

Connecting to Past Learning

Remind students that prices of consumer goods and services have a parallel in the price of labor. Ask students to list factors that might affect how much a worker is paid. (*Factors mentioned might include workers' skills, education, experience, supply of workers for a particular job, and demand for workers in a particular job.*) As students work through the chapter, have them review and adjust their lists.

Applying Economics

Have students survey family members, friends, and neighbors to find out if they are union members. Suggest that students ask questions about the perceived benefits or disadvantages of union membership. Encourage students to share their findings with the class. Then ask students to write a sentence that makes a generalization about the role of labor unions in the American economy. Encourage students to retain their generalizations.

PERFORMANCE ASSESSMENT

Refer to page **180B** for a Performance Assessment activity for this chapter. Also see the **Performance Assessment Activities** booklet for additional suggestions.

VISUAL INSTRUCTION

Have students discuss the following: How effective do you think marches and demonstrations are in gaining public support for a cause or an issue?

181

FOCUS

Section Objectives

1. Explain why unions are still important today.

2. Discuss the development of the labor movement from the late 1700s to the 1930s.

3. Relate labor's successes during the Great Depression.

4. State the major labor developments since World War II.

Bellringer

Prior to taking roll at the beginning of the class period, display Focus Activity Transparency 49 on the overhead projector and assign the accompanying Student Activity 49.

Motivational Activity

Discuss students' responses to the activity sheet that accompanies Focus Activity Transparency 49.

Preteaching Vocabulary

Ask students to skim the section to locate the key terms listed in the Section Preview. Have students write sentences using each term in context. **LEP**

Use the **Vocabulary PuzzleMaker** to create crossword and word search puzzles.

Section Preview

Objectives

After studying this section, you will be able to:

1. **Explain** why unions are still important today.

2. **Discuss** the development of the labor movement from the late 1700s to the 1930s.

3. **Relate** labor's successes during the Great Depression.

4. **State** the major labor developments since World War II.

Key Terms

macroeconomics, civilian labor force, craft or trade union, industrial union, strike, picket, boycott, lockout, company union, Great Depression, right-to-work law, jurisdictional dispute, independent union

Applying Economic Concepts

Civilian Labor Force Do you work, or are you actively looking for a job? If so, and if you are at least 16 years old, you probably belong to a group that economists call the *civilian labor force*.

This chapter and those that follow deal with **macroeconomics,** the part of economics that deals with the economy as a whole, and with the behavior and decision making by large units, such as labor unions and governments. One of these macro units is the **civilian labor force**—civilian men and women 16 years old and over who are either working or actively looking for a job. The *civilian* classification excludes members of the armed forces, the prison population, and other institutionalized persons. **1**

In 1997 the population of the United States was 267 million. Of this number, slightly more than half were members of the civilian labor force. As can be seen in **Figure 8.1**, this percentage has increased slowly since the end of World War II.

Unions and the Labor Force

Figure 8.1 also shows that a large majority of employed wage and salary workers have no connection with unions. According to the figure, 14.5 percent of employed wage and salary workers belong to unions, with an additional 1.7 percent of nonunion members being represented by unions.

Although the number of unionized workers may seem small, labor unions are important for a number of reasons. First, they have played a significant role in America's history, and they were responsible for much of the legislation that affects current pay levels and working conditions. Second, unions still have a substantial presence in a number of vital industries. Third, they represented nearly 18.1 million workers as recently as 1997.

Historically, unions tended to be concentrated in heavy manufacturing industries. More recently, unions have made major inroads in the service sector, especially among government workers. As **Figure 8.2** shows, 43.0 percent of all government workers were either unionized or represented by a union. ▼

Early Union Development

In 1778 printers in New York City joined together to demand higher pay. This protest was the first time anyone had tried to organize labor in America. Before long, unions of shoemakers, carpenters, and tailors sprang up, each hoping to negotiate agreements covering hours, pay, and working conditions. Only a small percentage of workers belonged to these unions. Of these, most were skilled and already had strong bargaining power.

Until about 1820, most of America's workforce was made up of farmers, small business owners, and

---

Classroom Resources for SECTION 1

- Reproducible Lesson Plan 8-1
- Guided Reading Activity 8-1
- Cooperative Learning Activity 13
- Consumer Application Activities 13, 19
- Math Practice for Economics 13
- Free Enterprise Activity 13
- Primary and Secondary Source Reading 13
- Performance Assessment Activity 13
- Section Quiz 8-1

- Spanish Section Quiz 8-1
- Focus Activity Transparency 49
- NBR's Economics in Action Video Program
- Testmaker
- Vocabulary PuzzleMaker
- Chapter Challenger Interactive Review Software
- MindJogger Videoquiz

Figure 8.1
Population, the Civilian Labor Force, and Employed Wage & Salary Earners

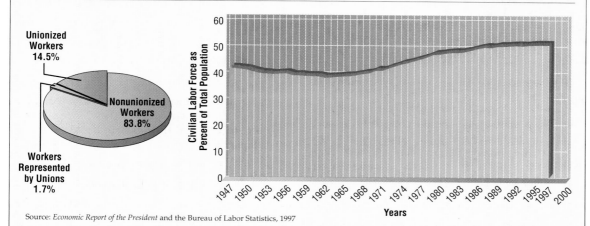

Source: *Economic Report of the President* and the Bureau of Labor Statistics, 1997

In 1997 more than half the population of the United States belonged to the civilian labor force. Of those in the labor force who were employed, fully 83.8 percent had no union affiliation, 14.5 percent were unionized, and another 1.7 percent were represented by unions even though the workers did not belong to a union. **Why do you think the labor force percentages have been increasing since World War II?**

people who were self-employed. Shortly after, however, immigrants began to enter the country in great numbers. Most were willing to work at any pay and under any conditions. They often posed a threat to existing wage and labor standards because they provided a supply of cheap, unskilled labor. **2**

At that time, public opinion was against union activity, and in some parts of the country, the law forbade labor unions. Labor organizers often were viewed as troublemakers, and many workers believed they could better negotiate with their employers on a one-to-one basis.

Civil War to the 1930s

During and after the Civil War, attitudes toward unions began to change. The Civil War led to higher prices, a greater demand for goods and services, and a growing shortage of workers. Industry expanded, and the farm population declined. Hourly workers in industrial jobs made up about one-fourth of the country's working population. Many of the cultural and linguistic differences between immigrants and American-born workers began to fade, and the labor force became more unified.

Checking Understanding

1. Who is included in the civilian labor force?
2. Why were immigrants viewed as a threat in the mid-1800s?

Applying Economic Concepts

☑ **Working Conditions** In 1800 it was common to work from sunup to sundown. Skilled artisans in the cities managed to obtain 10-hour workdays, but the factory workers often labored 12 to 13 hours a day, 6 days a week. By 1860 the average workweek was just under 70 hours.

CHAPTER 8: *Employment, Labor, and Wages* **183**

Guided Practice

L3 *Defending a Position*
Write the following question on the chalkboard: Were better working conditions and wages for the American labor force the result of labor unions or the result of increased demand for skilled labor? Call on volunteers to offer information supporting either side of the question. Then ask students to write a paragraph arguing their position.

VISUAL INSTRUCTION

Ask: In which decades was the civilian labor force less than 40 percent of the population? *(1950s, 1960s)* Point out to students that the 1.7% of workers represented by unions in Figure 8.1 work at firms that have modified union shops or agency shops.

Answer to Caption:

entry of female baby boomers (those who were born in the high birthrate years from 1946 to 1964) and married women into workforce

ANSWERS

1. civilian men and women aged 16 and on either working or actively seeking work

2. They posed a threat to wage and labor standards because they provided a supply of cheap, unskilled labor.

📁 *Cooperative Learning*
Assign Cooperative Learning Activity 13.

Language Disability Restating is difficult for students with language problems. They often have trouble finding synonyms for words in the text. Explain that the point of this procedure is for them to use common language and not to make it sound like the textbook. In the subsection "Civil War to the 1930s," have students look for words that might be somewhat complex and replace them with synonyms.

Independent Practice

 Guided Reading Assign Guided Reading Activity for Section 1. **LEP**

L1 *Constructing a Time Line*
Ask students to construct an annotated time line of the American labor movement from its beginnings to the present day. Suggest that students limit their time lines to 12 entries. Have volunteers discuss their time lines. **LEP**

VISUAL INSTRUCTION

Ask: Which industry do you think was most heavily unionized in the late 1800s? *(manufacturing)*

Answer to Caption:

They were responsible for much of legislation affecting current pay levels and working conditions, and they still have a substantial presence in vital industries.

Types of Unions

By the end of the Civil War, two main types of labor unions existed. One was the **craft** or **trade union**—an association of skilled workers who perform the same kind of work. The Cigar Makers' Union, begun by union leader Samuel Gompers, is an example of this type of union. Other, more recent examples are shown in **Figure 8.3**.

The second type of union was the **industrial union**—an association of all workers in a given industry, regardless of the job each person performs. The growth of basic mass-production industries such as steel and textiles provided the opportunity to organize this kind of union. Because many of the workers in these industries were unskilled and could not join trade unions, they organized as industrial unions instead. **1**

Union Activities

Although unions were making headway, American workers still faced many hardships. Workers had little

---

Figure 8.2
Union Membership and Representation by Industry

Industry	Percent of Employed Workers That Are:	
	Members of Unions	Represented by Unions
Government workers	37.7	43.0
Transportation	27.0	28.4
Communications & Public Utilities	25.9	28.2
Construction	18.5	19.2
Manufacturing	17.2	18.3
Mining	14.1	15.0
Wholesale Trade	6.2	6.7
Services (general)	5.7	6.9
Retail Trade	5.5	6.1
Agricultural Wage & Salary workers	1.9	2.2

Source: Bureau of Labor Statistics, 1997

Labor unions have the most influence in the service industries, which include government, communications, public utilities, and transportation. Agriculture has the least amount of unionization, with manufacturing and mining in the middle. **Why is it still important to study labor unions?**

---

job security and were often replaced by new equipment and mass-production techniques. Tasks once performed by those in skilled crafts could be performed by less skilled workers. With millions of unskilled immigrants arriving every year, and with many others leaving rural America for jobs in cities, high-paid or rebellious workers could be easily replaced.

Unions tried to help workers by negotiating for higher pay, better working conditions, and job security. If an agreement could not be reached, workers could **strike,** or refuse to work until certain demands were met. Unions also pressured employers by having the striking workers **picket,** or parade in front of the employer's business carrying signs about the dispute. The signs might ask other workers not to seek jobs with the company, or they might ask customers and suppliers to take their business elsewhere.

If a strike and picketing did not settle the dispute, a union could organize a **boycott**—a mass refusal to buy products from targeted employers or companies. If a boycott was effective, it hurt the company's business and reduced the employer's income.

Employer Resistance

Employers fought unions in a number of ways. Sometimes the owners called for a **lockout,** or a refusal to let the employees work until management demands were met. Violence often erupted when lockouts were used, and troops were sometimes brought in to keep peace.

At other times, management responded to a strike, or the threat of a strike, by hiring all new workers. Some owners even set up **company unions**—unions organized, supported, or run by employers—to head off efforts by others to organize workers.

Attitude of the Courts

Historically, the courts had an unfavorable attitude toward unions. Under English common law, unions were considered to be conspiracies against business and were prosecuted as such in the United States. This attitude lasted well into the 1800s. Even the Sherman Antitrust Act of 1890—aimed mainly at curbing monopolies—was used to keep labor in line.

In 1902 the United Hatters Union called a strike against a Danbury, Connecticut, hat manufacturer that

---

$ Free Enterprise Activity $

Inform students that, if they have not done so already, at some time they will have to complete a job application. Tell them a completed job application should contain clear and accurate information; should be completed carefully; and should be typed or printed, using a pen with blue or black ink. Point out that, along with an application form, they will have to provide several pieces of information, including their social security number, references, and a list of former employers with dates of employment. Have students prepare to fill out a job application by bringing the above information to class. Distribute sample job applications to students, asking each to fill them in as completely and accurately as possible. You may also refer students to **Preparing a Resume** on page 554.

Figure 8.3
Trade (Craft) and Industrial Unions

TRADE (CRAFT) UNIONS

Printers' Union

Plumbers' Union

Machinists' Union

Electricians' Union

Carpenters' Union

INDUSTRIAL UNIONS

Trade union members are workers who perform a particular kind of work.

Members of an industrial union include all the workers in a particular industry, no matter what kind of work they perform. **What led to the growth of industrial unions?**

had turned down a union demand. The union applied pressure on stores not to stock hats made by the Danbury firm. The hat manufacturer took the union to court under the Sherman Antitrust Act. The Supreme Court ruled that the union was in restraint of trade, thereby dealing a severe blow to organized labor.

The Danbury Hatters case, and several others that followed it, encouraged organized labor to push for relief from the Sherman Antitrust Act. Relief came in 1914 when Congress passed the Clayton Antitrust Act. The Clayton Act stated that a person's labor was not a "commodity or article of commerce." It further stated that labor unions should not be looked upon as "illegal combinations or conspiracies in restraint of trade under the antitrust laws."

The courts, however, tended to disregard the Clayton Act. In 1921 the Supreme Court ruled that the Machinists' Union in New York violated the Sherman Antitrust Act. The union had tried to stop the sale and installation of newspaper printing presses made by a nonunion company in Michigan.

Labor During the Great Depression

The **Great Depression**—the greatest period of economic decline and stagnation in the history of the United States—began with the collapse of the stock market in October 1929, and reached bottom in 1933. It then took until 1939 for the economy to recover to the same level as it had been in 1929.

Unemployment and Wages

Joblessness often stayed above 15 percent throughout the 1930s. During the depths of the Depression, one in four workers was without a job. Of those who did work, most received very little wages. In 1929 the average manufacturing wage had climbed to 55 cents per hour. By 1933, wages had plummeted to 5 cents per hour. **2**

The Great Depression brought misery to millions, but it also brought a change in attitude toward the

QUICK CHECK

Checking Understanding

1. How does an industrial union differ from a trade union?
2. What percentage of workers were unemployed during the Great Depression?

Applying Economic Concepts

 Stock Market During the last week of October 1929, $30 billion in stock value—about the same amount of money the United States spent in World War I—evaporated along with people's dreams of prosperity.

Extending the Content

The AFL-CIO The merger of the AFL with the CIO in 1955 brought together some 16 million workers—more than 85 percent of all union members. Some major unions, however, refused to affiliate with the AFL-CIO. The United Mine Workers of America (UMW) was one of the most prominent of those unions that chose to remain independent.

This decision, in large part, was due to disagreements UMW president John L. Lewis had with the leadership of the AFL. Even so, the UMW remained unaffiliated long after Lewis resigned his post. The UMW did not join the AFL-CIO until 1989.

ASSESS

Check for Understanding

Assign Section 1 Review as homework or an in-class activity.

MEETING LESSON OBJECTIVES

Each objective below is tested by the questions that follow it in parentheses.

1. **Explain** why unions are still important today. **(2)**

2. **Discuss** the development of the labor movement from the late 1700s to the 1930s. **(1, 3)**

3. **Relate** labor's successes during the Great Depression. **(1, 4, 6)**

4. **State** the major labor developments since World War II. **(1, 5, 6)**

Evaluate

📁 📁 🖥 Assign the Section 1 Quiz in the TCR or use the *Economics: Principles and Practices* Testmaker.

VISUAL INSTRUCTION

Ask: What led to the passage of the Taft-Hartley Act? *(antiunion feeling among the American people)*

Answer to Caption:

It limited union power and restricted unions in labor-management disputes.

---

labor movement. Common problems united factory workers. As a result, union organizers renewed efforts to organize workers.

Prounion Legislation

Federal legislation began to help labor during the Depression. The Norris-LaGuardia Act of 1932 prevented federal courts from issuing rulings against unions that were engaged in peaceful strikes, picketing, or boycotts. Companies, therefore, had to negotiate directly with their unions, rather than take the unions to court.

The National Labor Relations Act (NLRA), or Wagner Act, of 1935 gave workers the right to join unions and to bargain collectively through their own chosen representatives. In addition, certain employer activities were defined as unfair labor practices. These practices included interfering with efforts to organize a union and discriminating against employees who engaged in union activities.

The NLRA also set up the National Labor Relations Board (NLRB). The Board was responsible for investigating workers' complaints concerning unfair labor practices. It also had the power to oversee union elections and to certify the results. If a fair election resulted in a union becoming the employees' bargaining agent, employers were required to recognize and negotiate with it.

Finally, in 1938 the Fair Labor Standards Act was passed. It applied to businesses that took part in or affected interstate commerce. The act set a minimum wage to begin in 1939 and called for time-and-a-half pay for overtime, which is now defined as over 40 hours per week. It also forbade labor by children under 16 years old and the holding of hazardous jobs by anyone under 18 years old.

Labor Since World War II

Organized labor was viewed favorably in the 1930s. By the end of World War II, however, public opinion had shifted again. Some people felt that Communists had infiltrated the unions. Others were upset by the loss of production because of strikes. In 1946 alone, more than 116 million workdays were lost because of work stoppages. People began to feel that management, not labor, was the victim.

Antiunion Legislation *Workers urge President Truman to veto the Taft-Hartley Act, which he did. Congress passed the act over Truman's veto.* **What did the act do?**

Antiunion Legislation

Antiunion feelings led to the Labor-Management Relations Act, or Taft-Hartley Act, of 1947. The act put limits on what unions could do in labor-management disputes. Among other things, it gave employers the right to sue unions for breaking contracts and prohibited unions from making union membership a condition for hiring. The act also made it illegal for unions to give money to political campaigns and ordered them to give 60 days' notice before going on strike.

The Taft-Hartley Act had two other provisions that worked against labor. The first was a controversial 80-day "cooling off" period that federal courts could use to delay a strike in the case of a national emergency.

The second was a tough antiunion provision contained in Section 14(b), which allowed individual states to pass right-to-work laws. A **right-to-work law** is a state law making it illegal to require a worker to join a union. If a state has such a law, workers can-

---

Cultural Diversity and Economics

The Knights of Labor The Noble Order of the Knights of Labor, founded in 1869, sought to bring "men and women of every craft, creed, and color" into one big union. The Knights not only welcomed women members but also gave them leadership opportunities. For example, Elizabeth Rodgers led a Chicago division of the Knights that represented some 50,000 male and female workers. Married

with a family, Rodgers registered her occupation as "housewife." To underscore their feelings about race, leaders of the Knights decided to hold the 1886 General Assembly in Richmond, Virginia—which had served as the capital of the Confederacy—and gave African Americans a prominent role in the proceedings.

not be forced to join a union even after they are hired. If a state does not have a right-to-work law, workers can be forced to join the union after they are hired.

In addition, the government tried to stop the criminal influences that had begun to emerge in the labor movement. The Labor-Management Reporting and Disclosure Act, or Landrum-Griffin Act, of 1959 tried to protect individual union members from unfair actions of unions and union officials. The act required unions to file regular financial reports with the government, and it limited the amount of money officials could borrow from the union. The act also required the election of union officials by secret ballot, and that they be held accountable for union funds.

AFL-CIO

The American Federation of Labor (AFL) began in 1886 as an organization of craft unions. It later added several industrial unions. The trade and industrial unions, however, did not always agree about the future of the union movement. In 1935 eight industrial unions in the AFL formed the Committee for Industrial Organization. Headed by John L. Lewis, president of the United Mine Workers of America, its goal was to bring about greater unionization in industry.

The AFL and Lewis, however, did not get along. In 1937 the AFL expelled the unions that made up the Committee for Industrial Organization. Those unions then formed the Congress of Industrial Organizations (CIO). The CIO quickly set up unions in industries that had not been unionized before, such as steel and automobiles. By the 1940s, the CIO had nearly 7 million members.

As the CIO grew stronger, it began to challenge the dominance of the AFL. Before long, the two were in a struggle for control of the labor movement. Each was trying to form unions in areas already organized by the other. In 1955, after almost 20 years of disagreement, the AFL and the CIO finally settled most of their differences and joined to form the American Federation of Labor and Congress of Industrial Organizations (AFL-CIO).

The merger settled many, but not all, of the basic differences between trade and industrial unions. Even today, the two may have a **jurisdictional dispute,** or a disagreement over which union should perform a certain job. Metal workers from an industrial union and pipe fitters from a trade union may not agree on who should install metal pipe.

Independent Unions

Although the AFL-CIO is a major force, other unions are also important in the labor movement. Many are **independent unions**—unions that do not belong to the AFL-CIO, such as the Brotherhood of Locomotive Engineers.

Use **Chapter Challenger Interactive Review Software** to review Section 1.

Reteach

Have students use the key terms listed in the Section Preview to write a summary of the section.

Enrich

Have students research to learn how one of the pieces of legislation mentioned in the section affected the development of organized labor.

CLOSE

In a class discussion, have students compare the role of the labor movement in the late 1800s to its present-day role.

SECTION 1 REVIEW

Reviewing Terms and Facts

1. **Define** macroeconomics, civilian labor force, craft or trade union, industrial union, strike, picket, boycott, lockout, company union, Great Depression, right-to-work law, jurisdictional dispute, independent union.
2. **Explain** why unions are important today.
3. **Describe** several reasons for the rise of unions prior to 1930.

4. **State** why unions became successful during the Great Depression.
5. **Describe** the development of the AFL-CIO.

Critical Thinking

6. **Making Generalizations** How did the five major legislative acts passed between 1932 and 1959 reflect the rise and decline of the labor movement?

Applying Economic Concepts

7. **Civilian Labor Force** How would your participation in the civilian labor force be affected if you joined the armed services?

pelled a number of industrial unions. These expelled unions formed the Congress of Industrial Organizations (CIO) and began to organize industries that had not been unionized before. As the CIO grew in power, it often conflicted with AFL. In 1955, the two unions overcame their differences and joined to form AFL-CIO.

6. The three pieces of legislation passed prior to World War II were prounion, giving organized labor increased powers. The two pieces of legislation passed after the war were antiunion and limited organized labor's power.

7. A person joining the armed services ceases to be a part of the civilian labor force.

187

Answers to SECTION 1 REVIEW

1. All vocabulary words are defined in the Glossary.

2. because they were responsible for much of legislation affecting current pay levels and working conditions; still have a substantial presence in vital industries

3. Civil War brought greater demand for goods and services and shortage of workers. Industry expanded, and hourly workers in industrial jobs made up about 25 percent of working population.

As differences between immigrant and native-born American workers began to fade, the workforce became more unified.

4. Common problems during Great Depression united workers, and union organizers renewed efforts to organize. Federal legislation helped to increase power of unions.

5. AFL started as craft union, but later added a number of industrial unions. Craft and industrial unions did not always agree, and in 1937 AFL ex-

Point out that Lewis strongly supported the use of a new tactic—the sit-down strike—in the struggle to unionize various industries. This tactic, which involved workers occupying their factories, proved particularly effective. Employers could not replace striking workers, nor could they evict the strikers by force for fear that violence might break out. The first sit-down strikes, at a number of General Motors plants in 1936, ended with GM agreeing to recognize the United Auto Workers (UAW).

TEACH

Have students note points in the profile that might support the following statement about John L. Lewis: His greatest strengths and successes highlighted his weaknesses and failures. *(Students might note that while Lewis represented some of the country's poorest workers, he lived in relative luxury, or that while he struggled to establish democracy in the workplace, he ran the UMW with an iron hand.)*

PROFILES IN ECONOMICS

JOHN L. LEWIS
(1880–1969)

For more than 40 years, John L. Lewis was a central figure in the American labor movement. His strong leadership and dynamic style made him a powerful, as well as controversial, labor organizer. As president of the United Mine Workers of America (UMW), Lewis left a lasting influence on twentieth century American labor history.

BEGINNINGS Lewis, the son of Welsh immigrants, had a limited education. He grew up in small midwestern towns, where his father worked as a miner. As a young man, Lewis also worked in the

Lewis addresses textile workers in Lawrence, Massachusetts.

mines, earning a living by his physical strength and ingenuity. He later told a convention of miners, "I have always found that if I

could not make a living in one place, I could in another. . . ."

Lewis became active in his local union and moved rapidly through the ranks. Within a decade, John L. Lewis had become president of the nation's largest labor union. Beginning in 1920, Lewis led the UMW for 4 decades when the labor movement was a dominant force in American life.

LABOR LEADER Lewis challenged the organizing principle of the American Federation of Labor (AFL), which separated unions on the basis of a single craft or trade. Although he respected AFL

leader Samuel Gompers, Lewis believed that unions should be made up of all unskilled workers in a mass-production industry. As a result of this conflict, Lewis split with the AFL and formed the Congress of Industrial Organizations (CIO).

Through strikes and negotiations, Lewis succeeded in raising wages and protecting union workers from unfair labor practices and unsafe conditions. His concern for the safety and well-being of miners was a hallmark of his leadership. The UMW's health and retirement fund resulted from Lewis's confrontations with government officials.

CONTRIBUTIONS AND CONTROVERSY As a person and as a labor leader, John L. Lewis sparked great controversy. He represented millions of poorly paid workers, while he lived in luxury. He upheld democratic ideals, while he ruled his own union with an iron hand. He helped establish a pattern of collective bargaining by defying the federal government.

Examining the Profile

1. **Making Comparisons** How did John L. Lewis's ideas about unions differ from those of the AFL?

2. **For Further Research** Find out how a clash between John L. Lewis and President Harry Truman led to government seizure of mines in 1946. Write a newspaper article about the event.

Answers to Examining the Profile

1. The AFL separated unions on the basis of a single craft or trade. Lewis, however, believed unions should be made up of all unskilled workers in a particular mass-production industry.

2. Newspaper articles will vary. Suggest that students present their articles as front pages of a newspaper and display them on the bulletin board.

Section Preview

Objectives

After studying this section, you will be able to:

1. **Explain** the differences between four kinds of union arrangements.

2. **Describe** several ways to resolve labor and management differences when collective bargaining fails.

Key Terms

closed shop, union shop, modified union shop, agency shop, grievance procedure, mediation, voluntary arbitration, compulsory arbitration, fact-finding, injunction, seizure

Applying Economic Concepts

Union Arrangements Does the company that you or your parents work for have a union? If so, are you or your parents required to join? Four different types of *union arrangements* exist, and one will apply to your situation.

FOCUS

Section Objectives

1. Explain the differences between four kinds of union arrangements.

2. Describe several ways to resolve labor and management differences when collective bargaining fails.

Bellringer

Prior to taking roll at the beginning of the class period, display Focus Activity Transparency 50.

Motivational Activity

Discuss students' responses to the activity sheet that accompanies Transparency 50.

TEACH

Guided Practice

L1 Constructing a Chart Have students construct a continuum of the four union arrangements discussed in Section 2, from the least restrictive to the most restrictive. (*agency shop, modified union shop, union shop, and closed shop*) Have students annotate the continuum by writing a brief explanation of each arrangement. **LEP**

Over the years, many differences have arisen between labor and management. Some, such as the 1981 air traffic controllers' strike, the 1994 professional baseball strike, or the 1997 American Airlines pilot's strike, make headlines. Others do not. In either case, labor and management generally manage to settle their differences without resorting to extreme measures.

Kinds of Union Arrangements

The labor movement has tried to organize workers in ways designed to help them deal more effectively with management. The ways in which workers are organized and settlements are reached have an important impact on the entire economy. Four general kinds of union arrangements have been identified.

Members of the Amalgamated Clothing Workers union march to promote the closed shop in the early 1920s. **How did the passage of the Taft-Hartley Act affect closed shops?**

VISUAL INSTRUCTION

Ask: What, from the union's standpoint, are the benefits of a closed shop? (*guaranteed membership and, therefore, dues; able to bargain with management from a position of strength*)

Answer to Caption:

It made closed shops illegal for companies involved in interstate commerce.

Classroom Resources for SECTION 2

 Reproducible Lesson Plan 8-2
Guided Reading Activity 8-2
Reinforcing Economic Skill 8
Section Quiz 8-2
Spanish Section Quiz 8-2

 Focus Activity Transparency 50
 NBR's Economics in Action Video Program
Testmaker
Vocabulary PuzzleMaker
Chapter Challenger Interactive Review Software

Figure 8.4
Right-To-Work Law States

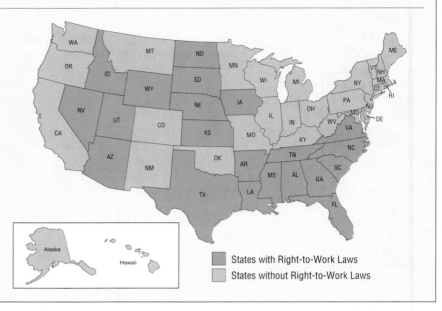

Today, 21 states have right-to-work laws that limit the power of unions. If a state has such a law, unions cannot force workers to join the union as a condition of continued employment. If a state does not have a right-to-work law, workers can be forced to join the union shortly after they are hired, even if they do not want to. **How do union shops and modified union shops differ?**

Source: National Right to Work Committee, 1993

■ States with Right-to-Work Laws
□ States without Right-to-Work Laws

Closed Shops

The most restrictive arrangement is the **closed shop**—an arrangement in which the employer agrees to hire only union members. In effect, the union can determine who is hired by giving or denying a person union membership.

Although this kind of union arrangement was common in the 1930s and early 1940s, the Taft-Hartley Act of 1947 made the closed shop illegal for companies involved in interstate commerce. Because most firms in the United States today are directly or indirectly engaged in interstate commerce, few, if any, closed shops exist.

Union Shops

The second kind of arrangement is the **union shop.** Workers do not have to belong to the union to be hired, but they must join one soon after and remain a member for as long as they keep their jobs. No union shops, however, can require membership sooner than

30 days after employment. The only exception is the construction industry, in which the period is 7 days.

Today, 21 states have taken advantage of Section 14(b) and have passed right-to-work laws that prohibit mandatory union membership. These states are shown in **Figure 8.4.**

Modified Union Shops

The third kind of arrangement is a **modified union shop.** Under this arrangement, workers do not have to belong to a union to be hired and cannot be made to join one to keep their jobs. If workers voluntarily join the union, however, they must remain members for as long as they hold their jobs.

Agency Shops

The final arrangement is the **agency shop.** Under this kind of union arrangement, workers need not be union members to be hired or to keep their jobs. They must pay dues to the union, however, to help pay the

---

costs of collective bargaining. Nonunion workers are subject to the contract negotiated by the union, whether or not they agree with it. Agency shops are primarily responsible for the 1.7 percent of employed wage and salary workers represented by unions in **Figure 8.1.**

Collective Bargaining

When labor and management take part in collective bargaining, a meeting occurs between representatives of both groups. A group of elected union officials represents workers, and company officials in charge of labor relations represent management. Collective bargaining requires compromise from both parties, and the discussions may go on for months. **1**

If the negotiations are successful, both parties agree on basic issues such as pay, working conditions, and fringe benefits. Because it is so difficult to anticipate future problems, however, a **grievance procedure**—a provision for resolving issues that may come up later—may also be included in the final contract.

Normally, union and management are able to reach an agreement. If the disputing parties cannot agree on certain points, other methods are available to resolve the differences.

Mediation

One way to resolve differences is through **mediation**—the process of bringing in a third person or persons to help settle a dispute. The mediator's primary goal is to find a solution that both parties will accept. A mediator must be absolutely neutral so that one party does not benefit at the expense of the other. If the mediator has the confidence and trust of both parties, he or she will be able to learn what concessions each side is willing to make.

In the end, the mediator recommends a compromise to both sides. Neither side has to accept a mediator's decision, although it often helps break the deadlock.

Arbitration

Another way differences can be cleared up is through arbitration. In the case of **voluntary arbitration**, both sides agree to place their differences before a third party whose decision will be accepted as final and binding. The arbitration is voluntary in that both sides agree to its use. It is different from mediation in that both sides agree in advance to abide by the decision of the third-party arbitrator. **2**

In some cases, such as the 1967 railroad strike, labor and management are forced to turn an unsettled dispute over to a third party for a binding decision. This is called **compulsory arbitration** and is seldom used in the United States.

Professional baseball has its own form of salary arbitration. When a player goes to arbitration, his agent and his team's owner submit salary recommendations. The arbitrator examines both in light of the player's performance and the salaries paid to other league players, and then selects one of the two recommendations.

Fact-Finding

A third way to resolve a dispute that collective bargaining cannot settle is through **fact-finding.** Labor and management agree to have an independent third party investigate the issues and recommend possible settlements. This process can be especially useful in situations where each side has deliberately distorted the issues to win public support, or when one side simply does not believe the claims made by the other side. Neither labor nor management has to accept the recommendations the fact-finding committee makes.

Checking Understanding	Applying Economic Concepts
1. What is collective bargaining? 2. How does voluntary arbitration differ from mediation?	☑ **Collective Bargaining** Failing to settle labor disputes quickly can be enormously costly. During the 1994 baseball strike, owners and players each lost about $1 billion. A 15-day United Parcel Service strike in 1997 cost that company about $600 million.

CHAPTER 8: *Employment, Labor, and Wages* **191**

$ Free Enterprise Activity $

Select a recent labor-management dispute covered in the local newspaper to present to the class. After students have reviewed all the information on both sides of the dispute, ask for volunteers to represent labor and management at a collective bargaining session to resolve the differences and negotiate a new contract. Have the remaining members of the class act as government mediators who help resolve the conflict. After the session, ask students to identify the type of union arrangement that was part of this conflict.

Independent Practice

📓 **Guided Reading** Assign Guided Reading Activity for Section 2. **LEP**

L3 *Writing Editorials* Organize the class into two groups. Have one group write editorials supporting government's use of injunctions and seizures in labor disputes. Ask the other group to write editorials opposing the use of these methods. Call on volunteers to read their editorials to the class.

ASSESS

Check for Understanding

Assign Section 2 Review as homework or an in-class activity.

MEETING LESSON OBJECTIVES

Each objective below is tested by the questions on page 192 that follow it in parentheses.

1. **Explain** the differences between four kinds of union arrangements. **(1, 2, 5)**

2. **Describe** several ways to resolve labor and management differences when collective bargaining fails. **(1, 3, 4)**

ANSWERS

1. negotiations between representatives of labor and management

2. Parties do not have to accept results of mediation. With voluntary arbitration, the decision is final and binding.

☑ Use **Chapter Challenger Interactive Review Software** to review Section 2.

Evaluate

🗁 🗁 ☑ Assign the Section 2 Quiz in the TCR or use the *Economics: Principles and Practices* Testmaker to create a customized quiz. Spanish Section Quizzes also are available in the Spanish Resources Binder.

Reteach

Organize students into four groups and assign each group one of the union arrangements. Ask groups to decide who benefits the most from its assigned arrangement—the employee, the employer, the union member, or the union— citing reasons for the answer. Have representatives present answers to the class.

Enrich

Ask students to write a research paper on a recent strike, noting the reasons for the work stoppage, the procedures used to end the dispute, and the final resolution.

CLOSE

Have students speculate how arrangements between employees and employers might be handled other than through collective bargaining.

Injunction and Seizure

A fourth way to settle labor-management disputes is through injunction or seizure. During a dispute, one of the parties may resort to an **injunction**—a court order not to act. If issued against a union, it directs the union not to strike. If issued against a company, it directs the company not to lock out its workers. In 1995, after professional baseball players ended their strike and went back to work, the owners promptly called a lockout. The players then got an injunction against the owners, and the 1995 baseball season began—without a labor agreement.

Under extreme circumstances, the government may resort to **seizure**—a temporary takeover of operations. The purpose of seizure is to allow the government to negotiate with the union. This occurred in 1946 when the government seized the bituminous coal industry. While operating the mines, officials worked out a settlement with the miners' union.

Presidential Intervention

The President of the United States may enter a labor-management dispute by publicly appealing to both parties to resolve their differences. This can be effective if the appeal has public support. The President also can fire federal workers. In 1981 President Ronald Reagan fired striking air traffic controllers because they were federal employees who had gone on strike despite having taken an oath not to do so.

The President also has emergency powers that can be used to end some strikes. When pilots from American Airlines went on strike in 1997 during a peak travel weekend, President Clinton ordered an end to the strike less than 30 minutes after it began.

HELP WANTED

Labor Relations Specialist
▼

Are you a people person? Are you patient, fair-minded, and persuasive? Can you function under pressure? Our firm needs someone like you to formulate labor policy, oversee industrial labor relations, negotiate collective bargaining agreements, and coordinate grievance procedures to handle complaints resulting from contract disputes. You must be knowledgeable about wages and salaries, benefits, pensions, and union and management practices. Courses in labor law, collective bargaining, labor economics, labor history, and industrial psychology are a must.

▼

Education: Degree in labor relations
Median salary: $39,000

SECTION 2 REVIEW

Reviewing Terms and Facts

1. **Define** closed shop, union shop, modified union shop, agency shop, grievance procedure, mediation, voluntary arbitration, compulsory arbitration, fact-finding, injunction, seizure.
2. **List** four kinds of union arrangements.
3. **Describe** six ways to resolve union and management differences when collective bargaining fails.

Critical Thinking

4. **Making Comparisons** If you represented a company during a collective bargaining session, and if negotiations were deadlocked, what course of action would you recommend? Why?

Applying Economic Concepts

5. **Union Arrangements** Contact a firm that has a union in your community. Ask if all workers in the company are required to join, or if only some are. Based on your information, determine if the union arrangement is a closed shop, a union shop, a modified union shop, or an agency shop.

Answers to SECTION 2 REVIEW

1. All vocabulary words are defined in the Glossary.

2. closed shop, union shop, modified union shop, agency shop

3. mediation—a third party is brought in to settle dispute, but the decision is nonbinding; arbitration—a third party decides the dispute and both sides agree to accept decision as final; fact-finding—a third party investigates dispute and recommends possible settlements; injunction—the government obtains court order preventing unions or management from taking action; seizure—the government temporarily takes over business operations; presidential intervention

4. Answers will vary. Some students might choose fact-finding, because this would provide a number of possible solutions to the problem. Others might select arbitration so that the problem could be quickly resolved.

5. Answers will vary.

CRITICAL THINKING SKILL

Analyzing Information

On the day of an earthquake, you see a television interview of an excited eyewitness to the event. Two weeks later, you see a televised interview with a scientist who studies earthquakes but who was not an eyewitness to this particular earthquake. One account is probably more accurate than the other.

Explanation

In studying economics, you will encounter many different kinds of information. Analyzing information helps you see how each kind of information can contribute to your understanding of economics.

Most information falls into two broad categories—primary and secondary sources. Primary sources are documents created at the time the event occurred. Letters, journals, newspaper articles, and photographs are examples of primary sources. Secondary sources are documents created after an event occurred. Secondary sources often pull together information from many sources and provide an overview of events.

Information also takes the following forms: written evidence, visual evidence, and artifacts. Written evidence includes books, periodicals, letters, diaries, and government records and documents. Visual evidence includes charts and graphs, paintings, cartoons, photographs, and films. Artifacts are objects that humans made and used, such as tools, buildings, and toys.

Follow these steps to help you analyze information:
- identify the kind of information
- identify who created it and when
- examine the information and try to answer the "five W" questions: Who is it about? What is it about? When did it happen? Where did it happen? Why did it happen?
- summarize the key ideas

Practice

Read the passages highlighted below. Use the listed steps to help you analyze the information, then answer the questions below.

1. Is the first paragraph a primary or secondary source? How can you tell?
2. Is the second paragraph a primary or secondary source? How can you tell?
3. What events are described in the paragraphs?
4. Who was affected by these events?
5. When did these events take place?
6. Where did these events take place?
7. What are the key ideas?

Throughout the Depression, families who could not pay their rent or make their mortgage payments were evicted from their homes. Some moved in with relatives if they could. The less fortunate ended up in makeshift communities dubbed "Hoovervilles" on the outskirts of cities. One woman later described a Hooverville:

Here were all these people living in old, rusted-out car bodies. I mean that was their home. There were people living in shacks made of orange crates. One family with a whole lot of kids were living in a piano box. This wasn't just a little section, this was maybe ten-miles wide and ten-miles long. People living in whatever they could junk together.
—Peggy Terry, in *Hard Times*, by Studs Terkel

Additional Practice

For further practice in analyzing information, complete the Reinforcing Skills exercise in the Chapter 8 Review on page 207.

TEACHING SKILLS

TEACH

Review the steps provided in the *Explanation*. Working with students, apply the steps to the photograph on page 189. Point out that not all of the "five W" questions will apply to every piece of information that students will be asked to analyze. To conclude, ask students to apply the analyzing information steps to Figure 8.4 on page 190.

Skills Practice For additional practice, have students complete Reinforcing Economic Skill 8.

Answers to SKILL

1. secondary source, because it provides an overview of the Depression
2. primary source, because it is an eyewitness account
3. the experiences of people during the Depression
4. families who were unable to pay their rent or make mortgage payments
5. during the Depression
6. on the outskirts of cities
7. In the Depression, families who were unable to pay their rent or make mortgage payments were evicted from their homes. The unlucky ones ended up in "Hoovervilles" on the outskirts of cities, where they lived as best they could.

FOCUS

Section Objectives

1. Identify four main categories of labor.
2. Explain the importance of noncompeting labor grades.
3. Describe two different approaches to wage determination.

Bellringer

Prior to taking roll at the beginning of the class period, display Focus Activity Transparency 51.

Motivational Activity

Discuss students' responses to the activity sheet that accompanies Transparency 51.

Preteaching Vocabulary

Have students explain the differences between unskilled labor, semiskilled labor, skilled labor, and professional labor and give examples of each. **LEP**

TEACH

Guided Practice

L1 *Advertising* List the four categories of labor on the chalkboard. Ask students to write classified advertisements for a job in each category. Remind students that classified advertisements are usually very brief. Have students compare and discuss their advertisements. **LEP**

Use the **Vocabulary PuzzleMaker** to create crossword and word search puzzles.

Section Preview

Objectives	Key Terms	Applying Economic Concepts
After studying this section, you will be able to: 1. **Identify** four main categories of labor. 2. **Explain** the importance of noncompeting labor grades. 3. **Describe** two different approaches to wage determination.	unskilled labor, semiskilled labor, skilled labor, professional labor, noncompeting labor grades, wage rate, traditional theory of wage determination, equilibrium wage rate, theory of negotiated wages, seniority, labor mobility	**Semiskilled Labor** Have you ever mowed a lawn? Used a drill? Operated a washing machine? If so, your mechanical abilities might classify you as *semiskilled labor*. Semiskilled workers rarely earn a high salary, however, so you may want to think about how you can change your classification.

Many different occupations exist in the United States, and wages usually differ from one occupation to the next. To understand why wages differ, it helps to place workers into broad groups so that we can study the characteristics of each.

Categories of Labor

The four major categories of labor are based on the general level of skills needed to do a particular kind of job. These categories are unskilled, semiskilled, skilled, and professional or managerial.

Workers who lack the training to operate specialized machines and equipment make up the category of **unskilled labor.** Most of these people work mainly with their hands at such jobs as food serving, digging ditches, picking fruit, and mopping floors.

Workers with mechanical abilities are in the **semiskilled labor** category. They may operate electric floor polishers, dishwashers, and other machines that call for a minimal amount of training. **1**

Workers who are able to operate complex equipment and who can do their tasks with little supervision belong to the category of **skilled labor.** Examples are carpenters, typists, tool and die makers, computer technicians, chefs, and computer programmers.

Workers with higher-level skills, such as doctors, teachers, lawyers, and executives of large companies, comprise the category of **professional labor.**

Noncompeting Labor Grades

Workers in one labor category generally do not compete with those in another category. Semiskilled workers do not compete with skilled laborers, and skilled laborers do not compete directly with professional workers. Economists, therefore, say that labor can be grouped into **noncompeting labor grades.**

For the most part, members of one group find it difficult to qualify for occupations open to a higher group. Several reasons explain why the workers in one group tend to stay in that group—cost, opportunity, and initiative.

Cost of Education and Training

Cost is one of the more difficult barriers to advancement. Some individuals have the ability and initiative to obtain additional technical skills, but they may not have the money to pay for the training. Many students have the aptitude to become college professors, but they lack the resources needed for four to six years of post-college study.

Lack of Opportunity

A lack of opportunity poses another barrier, even when people have the ability and the money to finance the additional education. Some people may live in areas where additional training and education

---

Classroom Resources for SECTION 3

- Reproducible Lesson Plan 8-3
- Guided Reading Activity 8-3
- Section Quiz 8-3
- Spanish Section Quiz 8-3
- Focus Activity Transparency 51

- Testmaker
- Vocabulary PuzzleMaker
- Chapter Challenger Interactive Review Software

are not available. Others may have the resources and grades to get into a specialized program such as medical school, but still may not be able to enter because the nearby schools have limited openings.

Lack of Initiative

Although they know that more skills are needed to get a better job, other individuals lack the initiative to get ahead. These people may never acquire additional training or education because they are not willing to put forth the extra effort.

Wage Determination

Most occupations have a **wage rate**—a standard amount of pay given for work performed. Differences in wage rates can be explained in two ways. The first uses the traditional tools of supply and demand. The second recognizes the influence of unions in the bargaining process.

Traditional Theory of Wages

The theory that uses the tools of supply and demand to explain differences in wage rates is called the **traditional theory of wage determination.** Professional managers and athletes, for example, are generally more scarce than ditchdiggers or fruit pickers and are more valuable to their employers.

The concepts of supply and demand can be used to illustrate the traditional approach. In **Figure 8.5,** Graph **A** shows what happens when a relatively large supply of ditchdiggers is coupled with a relatively low level of demand. In Graph **B**, a relatively small supply of professional athletes is paired with a relatively high level of demand. The intersection of supply and demand determines the **equilibrium wage**

rate—the wage rate that leaves neither a surplus nor a shortage in the labor market.

In most cases, the higher the level of skills or grade of labor, the higher the average annual wage rate, although wide salary variations exist within each group. Semiskilled workers will generally receive more than unskilled workers and skilled workers will receive more than semiskilled or unskilled workers. Professional workers generally earn more than any of the others. This relationship is readily evident

Categories of Labor *Each worker above has different skills and, as a result, receives different wages.* **Into which category of labor does each worker fall?**

Checking Understanding

1. How does the category of semiskilled labor differ from unskilled labor?

Applying Economic Concepts

☑ **Barriers to Advancement** Four years at a top private university costs more than $100,000. Four years at an in-state public university averages more than $45,000.

L2 *Classifying Information*
Direct students to draw a chart with three columns headed *Jobs, Category of Labor,* and *Wage Determination.* In the first column, have them list the jobs or occupations of 10 people they know. In the second column, have them note the category of labor into which the corresponding position falls. In the third column, have them hypothesize as to how the wage or salary for the position is determined. Encourage students to compare and discuss their results with other class members.

Independent Practice

◤ ***Guided Reading*** Assign Guided Reading Activity for Section 3. **LEP**

 ### VISUAL INSTRUCTION

Have students suggest how other categories of labor might be illustrated. (*Examples: semiskilled— cleaner using floor polisher; professional—doctor examining patient.*)

Answer to Caption:

chef: skilled labor; food server: unskilled labor

 ### ANSWERS

1. Semiskilled labor requires mechanical ability; unskilled labor requires no such ability.

Meeting Special Needs

Mixed Learners Some students learn best visually. Others are auditory learners. Many are "mixed" learners who use a combination of auditory and visual materials in order to learn. Ask students to look at and then think about the information they get from the right side of Figure 8.6 on page 197. Then ask them to read the caption on the left side of Figure 8.6. Ask students if the graphic listing of information or the written caption provided them with more information. Then ask what the difference is between the kinds of information they can get from graphs and from the text.

ASSESS

Check for Understanding

Assign Section 3 Review as homework or an in-class activity.

 Use **Chapter Challenger Interactive Review Software** to review Section 3.

MEETING LESSON OBJECTIVES

Each objective below is tested by the questions that follow it in parentheses.

1. **Identify** four main categories of labor. **(1, 2, 5)**
2. **Explain** the importance of noncompeting labor grades. **(1, 2, 5, 6)**
3. **Describe** two different approaches to wage determination. **(1, 3, 4)**

VISUAL INSTRUCTION

Ask: If demand for ditchdiggers increased, what would happen to the demand curve and annual salary? *(Demand curve would move to the right, and salary would increase.)*

Answer to Caption:

Traditional theory uses forces of supply and demand to explain wage differences. The theory of negotiated wages points to union strength and collective bargaining process to explain wage rates.

---

in **Figure 8.6**. The occupations are arranged in descending order, with those having the highest level of skills and training at the top.

Several exceptions to the traditional theory exist. Some unproductive workers may receive high wages because of family ties or political influence. Other highly skilled workers receive low wages because of discrimination based on their race, gender, or location.

In addition, workers and employers do not always know what the market wage rate is or should be. A worker may accept a job that pays $6.15 an hour because he or she does not know that the firm next door is paying $7.00 for the same job. An employer may offer to hire someone for $375 a week without knowing that the same service can be obtained for $300. If the forces of supply and demand operate freely, however, wages and the market for labor will operate as the theory suggests.

Theory of Negotiated Wages

At times, the relative strength of organized labor and the collective bargaining process, rather than the forces of supply and demand, determine wages. Economists use the **theory of negotiated wages** to explain wage rates in these cases.

Unions, for example, may get higher wages for their members, but not always because labor is in short supply relative to the demand. Instead, strong union representatives may outnegotiate relatively weaker management representatives regardless of market conditions. **Figure 8.6** helps validate the the-

ory of negotiated wages. The table shows that when workers are either unionized or represented by unions, median weekly salaries are significantly higher than for nonunion workers. This situation applies to all occupations except for the "managerial and professional specialty" category, whose members are seldom unionized.

Another factor that becomes important when unions and collective bargaining enter the picture is **seniority**—the length of time a person has been on the job. Because of their seniority, some workers receive higher wages than others who perform similar tasks. In many cases, senior workers are laid off last when a company cuts back on production.

Regional Wage Differences

Regardless of how wage rates are determined, they can still be different for the same job from one part of the country to another. Supply and demand, labor mobility, cost of living, and attractiveness of location all can make a difference in wage rates.

Labor Mobility

Skilled workers are scarce in some parts of the country and abundant in others. The extent of scarcity causes differences in wage rates. These differences, however, can be narrowed by **labor mobility**—the ability and willingness of workers to relocate in markets where wages are higher.

Figure 8.5
The Traditional Theory of Wage Determination

The market forces of supply and demand explain the equilibrium wage rate for the traditional theory of wage determination. When the supply of workers is large and the demand low, as in Graph A, annual salaries are low. When supply is limited and demand is high, as in Graph B, annual salaries are much higher.

How does the traditional theory of wage determination differ from the theory of negotiated wages?

A. Ditchdiggers — $18,000

B. Professional Athletes — $1,000,000

$ Free Enterprise Activity $

Have students work in small groups to investigate job opportunities in the country. Encourage groups to note the education and training required for each position, starting wage or salary, chances for advancement, and so on, for each position they

list. Have groups present their findings to the class. Use these presentations as the starting point for a discussion on the kinds of positions students might seek in the future.

Figure 8.6
Median Weekly Earnings by Occupation and Union Affiliation

According to the Bureau of Labor Statistics, weekly earnings are significantly higher for the highly skilled occupations. The table also shows that workers who are represented by unions have substantially higher earnings than their nonunion counterparts. **What can you infer about the theory of negotiated wages from this figure?**

Occupation	Represented by Unions	Nonunion Workers
Managerial and Professional Specialty Includes executive, administrative, managerial, professional specialty	$749	$708
Precision Production, Craft, and Repair	698	494
Government Workers	651	519
Technical, Sales, and Administrative Support	524	427
Operators, Fabricators, and Laborers Includes machine operators, assemblers, inspectors, transportation and material moving occupations, helpers and laborers	522	353
Farming, Forestry, and Fishing	423	288

Source: Bureau of Labor Statistics, 1997

Not all workers are equally mobile. Some are reluctant to move away from relatives and friends. Some may want to move, but they find that the cost is too high. Others do not want the inconvenience of buying a new house or renting a new apartment. As a result, the demand for certain skills remains high in some areas and low in others, and wages tend to vary.

Cost of Living

Another factor that affects wages is the cost of living. In Hawaii and many southern states, fresh fruits and vegetables are readily available. In addition, little money is spent on heavy clothing or on heating a home. In Alaska, however, food must be shipped in from thousands of miles away, people must have warm clothing, and every home must be well heated. The cost of living is obviously higher in Alaska than in most southern states. Wages, then, tend to be higher in Alaska than in most southern states.

Location

Location can also make a difference in wages. Some locations are thought to be so attractive that lower wages can be offered there. A person who likes to hunt and fish may be willing to work for less pay in Colorado or Montana than in New York City.

SECTION 3 REVIEW

Reviewing Terms and Facts

1. **Define** unskilled labor, semi-skilled labor, skilled labor, professional labor, noncompeting labor grades, wage rate, traditional theory of wage determination, equilibrium wage rate, theory of negotiated wages, seniority, labor mobility.
2. **List** the four grades or categories of noncompeting labor.

3. **Explain** the two theories of wage determination.
4. **Describe** how climate and location can affect wages in different parts of the country.

Critical Thinking

5. **Evaluating Information** Randomly select three Help Wanted ads from your local paper. Read the skills required for each, and then classify each according to the four noncompeting labor groups.

Applying Economic Concepts

6. **Semiskilled Labor** If you were a semiskilled worker, what could you do to move into a higher category of noncompeting labor?

CHAPTER 8: *Employment, Labor, and Wages* **197**

Evaluate

Assign the Section 3 Quiz in the TCR or use the *Economics: Principles and Practices* Testmaker. Spanish Section Quizzes also are available.

Reteach

Have students write questions to which the key terms listed in the Section Preview are the answers. Call on volunteers to quiz the class with their questions.

Enrich

Point out that wages often include fringe benefits such as paid vacation and health insurance. Have students interview personnel officers at local firms to see what fringe benefits those firms offer. Have students share their findings with the class.

CLOSE

Have students discuss the following: The forces of supply and demand should be the only factors to determine wages.

VISUAL INSTRUCTION

Ask: In which occupation category is the dollar differential between unionized and nonunionized workers greatest? (*Precision Production, Craft, and Repair*)

Answer to Caption:

That they are often successful in winning higher wages for union members.

Employment Trends and Issues

FOCUS

Section Objectives

1. Explain why union membership is declining.
2. Describe reasons for the discrepancy in pay between men and women.
3. Understand the minimum wage as it is measured in current and constant dollars.

Bellringer

 Prior to taking roll at the beginning of the class period, display Focus Activity Transparency 52.

Motivational Activity

Discuss students' responses to the activity sheet that accompanies Transparency 52.

Preteaching Vocabulary

Call on students to use each key term in a sentence. **LEP**

Use the **Vocabulary PuzzleMaker** to create crossword and word search puzzles.

VISUAL INSTRUCTION

Have students identify reasons for the rapid growth in union membership during the 1930s. (*prounion legislation of the New Deal years*)

Answer to Caption:

Unions are the victims of their own success. Higher wages won by unions have led to higher production costs and accompanying loss of sales. This has led to cutbacks in production, job losses, and declining union membership.

Section Preview

Objectives

After studying this section, you will be able to:

1. **Explain** why union membership is declining.
2. **Describe** reasons for the discrepancy in pay between men and women.
3. **Understand** the minimum wage as it is measured in current and constant dollars.

Key Terms

giveback, two-tier wage system, glass ceiling, comparable worth, set-aside contract, current dollars, real or constant dollars, base year

Applying Economic Concepts

Minimum Wage Have you ever held a job at which you earned exactly $5.15 per hour? Do you know others who received the same wage? Is this an incredible coincidence, or is everyone equally skilled at their jobs? More than likely, everyone is receiving the federal *minimum wage* that was raised to $5.15 in 1997.

Several trends and issues have been observed in today's labor movement. These include the decline of union membership, the discrepancy in pay between men and women, and the minimum wage.

Decline of Union Influence

A significant trend in today's economy is the decline in both union membership and influence. As **Figure 8.7** shows, 35.5 percent of nonagricultural workers were members of unions in 1945. This number fell to 21.9 percent by 1980, and then dropped to under 14.5 percent by 1997.

Reasons for Decline

Several reasons are given for the decline in union membership and influence. The first is that many employers made a determined effort to keep unions out of their businesses. Some were active in their opposition and even hired consultants to map out legal strategies to fight unions. Other employers

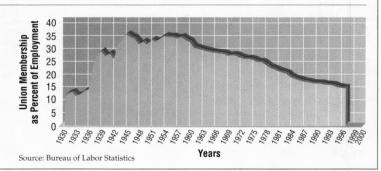

Figure 8.7
Union Membership

Union membership grew rapidly after 1933 and peaked at 35.5 percent in 1945. Since then, it has declined gradually until accounting for less than 14.5 percent of the employed wage and salary workers in 1997. **What is perhaps the most important reason for the decline of unions?**

Source: Bureau of Labor Statistics

Classroom Resources for SECTION 4

- Reproducible Lesson Plan 8-4
- Guided Reading Activity 8-4
- Section Quiz 8-4
- Spanish Section Quiz 8-4
- Focus Activity Transparency 52
- NBR's Economics in Action Video Program
- Enrichment Activity 8
- Reteaching Activity 8
- Spanish Reteaching Activity 8

- Economic Vocabulary Activity 8
- Spanish Economic Vocabulary Activity 8
- Chapter 8 Test, Form A and Form B
- English and Spanish Audiocassettes
- Testmaker
- Vocabulary PuzzleMaker
- Chapter Challenger Interactive Review Software
- MindJogger Videoquiz

made workers part of the management team, adding employees to the board of directors or setting up profit-sharing plans to reward employees.

A second reason for union decline is that new additions to the labor force—especially women and teenagers—traditionally had little loyalty to organized labor. Because many of these workers represent second incomes to families, they have a tendency to accept lower wages. 1

The third and perhaps most important reason for the decline is that unions are the victims of their own success. Unions raised their wages substantially above the wages paid to nonunion workers. As a result, many union-made products, especially in the automobile and steel industries, became so expensive that sales were lost to less expensive foreign competitors and nonunion producers. The loss in sales forced companies to cut back on production, which caused some workers to lose their jobs, and unions to lose some of their members.

Renegotiating Union Wages

Because unions have generally kept their wages above those of their nonunion counterparts, union wages have been under pressure. In some cases, unions agreed to lower their wages because foreign competition threatened industries. In other cases, industries were not profitable and, therefore, could not afford expensive union contracts.

One way employers have been able to reduce union wages is by asking for givebacks from union workers. A **giveback** is a wage, fringe benefit, or work rule given up when labor contracts are renegotiated. 2 When Chrysler faced stiff competition from domestic producers and foreign imports in 1981, workers agreed to give up more than $1 billion in

wages and fringe benefits to keep the company open. In 1986 the United Steel Workers took a pay cut and agreed to a 10-year freeze on pension plan increases to help the LTV Corporation.

Some companies have been able to get rid of labor contracts by claiming bankruptcy. If a company can show the court that wages and fringe benefits contributed significantly to its problems, federal bankruptcy courts usually allow a company to terminate its union contract and establish lower wage scales. LTV threatened to use this tactic against the United Steel Workers in 1992, despite the union givebacks in 1986.

Another way of reducing union salary scales is with a **two-tier wage system.** This system keeps the high wage for current workers, but has a much lower wage for newly hired workers, a practice that is becoming widespread in industry.

In 1997, for example, 2,300 workers at a Kelly-Springfield tire plant in North Carolina struck over company plans to add a new shift at a much lower starting wage, a plan that also reduced overtime pay. In Ohio, locals of the International Union of Electronic Workers have multi-tiered contracts with General Motors, Ford, and Chrysler. One contract even pays starting workers 55 percent of base pay—and requires 17 years before a worker can reach the top scales.

Lower Pay for Women

Overall, women face a considerable gap between their income and that received by men. As **Figure 8.8** shows, female income has been only a fraction of male income over a 40-year period. At least two causes explain this inequality, and several potential solutions exist.

Checking Understanding

1. Why do women and teenagers traditionally have little loyalty to labor unions?
2. What is a giveback?

Applying Economic Concepts

 Cultural Influences Child development experts claim sex stereotyping influences job choices. Girls are praised for being polite and compliant, behaviors that work against them in the labor force. Boys are encouraged to be assertive, which helps them succeed in demanding careers.

CHAPTER 8: *Employment, Labor, and Wages* **199**

TEACH

Guided Practice

L2 *Television News Report*
Have students work in groups of five to prepare a two- or three-minute television newscast on one of the issues discussed in the section. Some students might act as reporters, others might play experts or "people in the street," and still others might take the role of news anchors. Have groups "broadcast" the news programs to the rest of the class.

LINKING PAST AND PRESENT

In 1952, leading economist John Kenneth Galbraith published the ground-breaking study *American Capitalism.* In it, he developed a theory of countervailing power, seeing three major forces in balance in the U.S. economy. These forces were big government, big business, and big labor. Have students consider if this theory is still applicable today.

ANSWERS

1. Many of these workers represent second incomes to families and are willing to take lower wages.
2. wage, fringe benefit, or work rule given up when labor contracts are renegotiated

Meeting Special Needs

Learning Disability To help learning disabled students, illustrate the importance of headings and subheads for understanding the framework for each section. Model student use by asking a question such as: "What would I do if I wanted to know what each section was about?" For Section 4 read:

Decline of Union Influence, Reasons for Decline, Renegotiating Union Wages, Lower Pay for Women, Gender and Occupation, Discrimination, Comparable Worth, Set-Aside Contracts, and so on. Ask students to rephrase the headings using complete sentences.

L2 *Debate* Poll the class to find students who work at minimum wage jobs. Have these students briefly discuss whether or not they think the wage they receive is fair. Then select two teams of students to debate the following: It is time for the minimum wage to be increased. Have students not directly involved in the debate act as judges. At the end of the debate, have the judges declare which team is the winner.

CURRICULUM CONNECTIONS

History The Equal Pay Act of 1963 was a response to a report issued by the President's Commission on the Status of Women. The commission found that, while women made up about one-third of the labor force, very few worked in the professions or held management positions. Further, the commission pointed out that average wages for women were only 60 percent of those for men.

VISUAL INSTRUCTION

Ask: What percentage of male income did females make in 1991? *(about 70 percent)*

Answer to Caption:

Women tend to fill lower-paid positions; discrimination prevents them from getting promotions; career interruptions for childbearing affect women's seniority.

Figure 8.8
Median Female Income as a Percentage of Male Income

Over the years, the income earned by females has been only a fraction of that earned by males. The low point was in 1973 when female income was only 56.6% of male income. The high was in 1996 when the figure was 73.8%. **What explains the income gap between men and women?**

Source: Bureau of Labor Statistics

Gender and Occupation

One reason for the income inequality is that men and women are not evenly distributed among the various occupations. Men have tended to gravitate toward higher-paid occupations, and women have been crowded into a few, lower-paid occupations. The average pay men and women receive will not be equal if the pay is different for the two occupations.

Figure 8.9 shows that, historically, more men enter construction and engineering trades than do women. Likewise, women enter the private household service and office worker occupations in relatively greater numbers than men. As long as construction and engineering wages are higher than private household and office worker wages, men—on average—will earn more than women.

Many women's careers are also interrupted by childbearing, which affects their seniority. Even so, these reasons do not explain why the pay for men and women within the same occupation is often different.

Discrimination

Discrimination is often a major cause of income discrepancy between men and women. Women and minorities feel that their difficulties in getting raises and promotions are like encountering a **glass ceiling,** an invisible barrier that hinders their advancement up the white male-dominated corporate ladder.

Congress passed two major laws to prevent discrimination. The first was the Equal Pay Act of 1963, which prohibits wage and salary discrimination for jobs that require equivalent skills and responsibilities. This act applies only to men and women who work at the same job in the same business establishment.

The second law was the Civil Rights Act of 1964. Title VII of this act prohibits discrimination in all areas of employment on the basis of sex, race, color, religion, and national origin. The law applies to employers with 15 or more workers, and it specifically excludes religious associations and their educational institutions.

The Civil Rights Act of 1964 also set up the Equal Employment Opportunity Commission (EEOC). The EEOC investigates charges of discrimination, issues guidelines and regulations, conducts hearings, and collects statistics. If a pattern of discrimination is discovered, the government can bring suit against a company and force it to remedy the discrimination.

Comparable Worth

One of the corrective measures used to close the income gap between men and women takes the form of **comparable worth.** This principle means that people should receive equal pay for work that is different from, but just as demanding as, other types of work. It has been applied mainly to salary discrimination cases between men and women, although it can be applied to race and age as well. As such, comparable worth goes beyond the concept of equal pay for equal work.

$ *Free Enterprise Activity* $

Have students write a one-page summary of what they have learned in the chapter that will be helpful to a person thinking about entering the labor force in a full-time job. As guidance, write the following issues on the chalkboard and ask students to focus their summaries on any three: Pay, Education or Training, the Role of Unions, Two-Tier Wage System, Discrimination, Comparable Worth. Call on volunteers to present and discuss their summaries.

In the state of Washington, a federal judge ruled that work performed by social service workers—most of whom were female—was just as demanding as some traditionally male occupations. The judge ordered the state to raise wages and give workers several years' back pay. In Illinois, job evaluators determined that the work done by highway workers was roughly equivalent to that done by nurses. In Minnesota, the work of delivery drivers was determined roughly comparable to that of pharmacy assistants.

Comparable worth decisions are not easy to make. Many factors, such as education requirements, occupational hazards, and degree of physical difficulty, must be considered. Some people believe that fair and unbiased comparisons of occupations are almost impossible and violate free-market principles. These people also argue that comparable worth is not needed as long as people are free to enter any profession they desire. Others argue that comparable worth is necessary to remove sex discrimination in the marketplace.

These issues, along with a lack of federal legislation and the reluctance of the courts to interfere with the market, have contributed to a recent decline of comparable worth in the United States. Even so, comparable worth is still widely used in Europe and Canada.

Set-Aside Contracts

Another corrective measure is the government **set-aside contract,** or a guaranteed contract reserved exclusively for a targeted group. The federal government, for

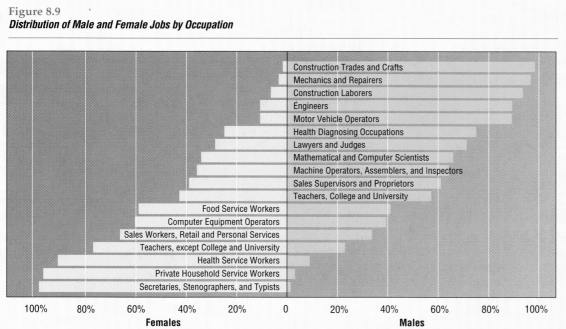

Figure 8.9
Distribution of Male and Female Jobs by Occupation

Construction Trades and Crafts
Mechanics and Repairers
Construction Laborers
Engineers
Motor Vehicle Operators
Health Diagnosing Occupations
Lawyers and Judges
Mathematical and Computer Scientists
Machine Operators, Assemblers, and Inspectors
Sales Supervisors and Proprietors
Teachers, College and University
Food Service Workers
Computer Equipment Operators
Sales Workers, Retail and Personal Services
Teachers, except College and University
Health Service Workers
Private Household Service Workers
Secretaries, Stenographers, and Typists

100%   80%   60%   40%   20%   0   20%   40%   60%   80%   100%
Females   **Males**

Source: *Employment and Earnings,* 1997

One of the reasons for the pay differential between the sexes is that men and women are not evenly distributed among occupations. If men tend to cluster in higher-paid occupations, and if women tend to cluster in lower-paid occupations, the average pay for men and women will differ. **What corrective measures may be used to close the income gap between men and women?**

GLENCOE
TECHNOLOGY

NIGHTLY BUSINESS REPORT
Economics in Action

Chapter 18
Disc 2, Side 1
Title: *The American Labor Force*
Subject: Labor Unions
Ask: What are some reasons for the decline in union membership?
(Many benefits are now widely offered, and many workers see little to gain from joining a union. Also, many unionized jobs have disappeared due to foreign competition.)

 Also available in VHS.

Independent Practice

Guided Reading Assign Guided Reading Activity for Section 4. **LEP**

L3 Applying Economics
Organize students into four groups, assigning each group one of the following topics to research: union decline, comparable worth, renegotiated union agreements, or the minimum wage. When the research is complete, select a student from each group to serve as members of a panel that will discuss the listed topics. Have the rest of the class prepare questions to ask panel members.

VISUAL INSTRUCTION

Answer to Caption:
comparable worth, set-aside contracts

Extending the Content

Comparable Worth and Job Segregation One argument used to justify the application of comparable worth is job segregation. Establishing a system of comparable worth would alleviate the existing situation of job segregation—where women are clustered in the lower-paying occupations. Some economists, however, argue that comparable worth will tend to increase job segregation. These economists suggest that if traditionally female jobs, through the application of comparable worth, receive equal wages to traditionally male jobs, women will lose the incentive to try to break into higher-paid occupations dominated by males.

Comparable Worth *Comparable worth tries to close the income gap between men and women by requiring equal pay for equally demanding types of work.* **Why are comparable worth decisions difficult?**

example, requires a certain percentage of defense contracts be reserved exclusively for minority-owned businesses.

In 1988 the state of California passed a law requiring that 5 percent of the state's bond contracts be set aside exclusively for women lawyers, bankers, and other females who help place the bonds in the hands of investors. Laws such as this are enacted to ensure that the state does not give all of its business to males in a male-dominated profession.

The Minimum Wage

The minimum wage—the lowest wage that can be paid by law to workers in a certain job—was first set in 1939 at $.25 per hour. As Graph **A** in Figure 8.10 shows, the minimum wage increased over time until it reached $5.15 in 1997.

Debate Over the Minimum Wage

The minimum wage has always been controversial. The original intent of the law was to prevent the outright exploitation of workers and to provide some degree of equity and security to those who lacked the skills needed to earn a decent income.

Supporters of the minimum wage argue that these objectives—equity and security—are consistent with America's economic goals. Besides, they say, the wage is not very high in the first place. Others agree with the principle of the minimum wage but think the wage is too high.

Opponents of the minimum wage object to it on the grounds of economic freedom—also one of America's economic goals. They argue that employers should be free to pay whatever wage they want, or whatever wage the market will bear. This group feels that the wage discriminates against young people and is one of the reasons that many teenagers cannot find jobs.

Measured in Current Dollars

Graph **A** in Figure 8.10 shows the minimum wage in **current dollars,** or in dollars that are not adjusted for inflation. The minimum wage is recorded exactly as it was from 1939 to 1998.

When viewed in this manner, it seems as if the minimum wage increased dramatically over time. The graph, however, does not take inflation into account. Because prices tend to increase over time, the purchasing power of the minimum wage is constantly being eroded.

Cultural Diversity and Economics

Civil Rights Act of 1964 In its proposed form, Title VII of the Civil Rights Act of 1964 prohibited job discrimination on the basis of race, color, religion, or national origin. During the House debate on this provision, a southern representative introduced an amendment forbidding discrimination based on gender. The aim of this action was to ridicule the whole idea of discrimination in the workplace and, thus, defeat the provision. The result, however, was very different. Women representatives rallied support for the amendment, and it—and the act as a whole—passed.

Figure 8.10
The Minimum Wage

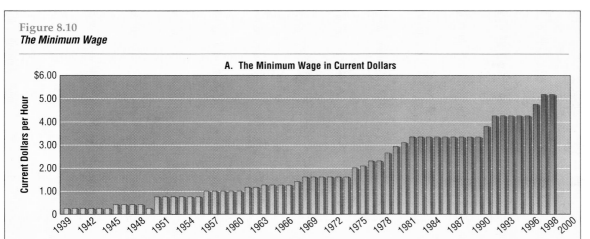

A. The Minimum Wage in Current Dollars

B. The Minimum Wage Adjusted for Inflation

C. The Minimum Wage as a Percent of the Average Manufacturing Wage

Sources: *Statistical Abstract of the United States, Economic Report of the President,* various issues

When the minimum wage is expressed in current dollars, as in Graph A, it appears to have increased dramatically since it was established in 1939. When the minimum wage is adjusted for inflation, as in Graph B, or is viewed as a percentage of the average manufacturing wage, as in Graph C, the minimum wage has lost some ground since 1968. **What arguments do supporters and opponents of the minimum wage use to defend their positions?**

CHAPTER 8: *Employment, Labor, and Wages* **203**

ASSESS

Check for Understanding

Assign Section 4 Review as homework or an in-class activity.

 Use **Chapter Challenger Interactive Review Software** to review Section 4.

MEETING LESSON OBJECTIVES

Each objective below is tested by the questions that follow it in parentheses.

1. **Explain** why union membership is declining. **(2)**
2. **Describe** reasons for the discrepancy in pay between men and women. **(1, 3, 5)**
3. **Understand** the minimum wage as it is measured in current and constant dollars. **(4, 6)**

VISUAL INSTRUCTION

Have students make a generalization about the minimum wage based on the graphs in Figure 8.10. *(Possible response: While minimum wage has steadily increased, its buying power has declined since 1968.)*

Answer to Caption:

Supporters argue that minimum wage provides a degree of equity and security to those who lack skills needed to earn a decent living. Opponents argue that employers should be free to pay whatever they want.

Extending the Content

Minimum Wage and Productivity Some economists suggest that raising the minimum wage may have a positive impact on productivity. First, employers of low-wage workers often are inefficient in the way they use labor. Having to pay higher wages through an increased minimum wage rate might force the employers to use labor more efficiently and, thus, improve productivity. In addition, higher wages will increase real income of workers, and this, in turn, might increase worker motivation, which could translate into increased productivity.

Evaluate

📁 📁 💻 Assign the Section 4 Quiz in the TCR or use the *Economics: Principles and Practices* Testmaker to create a customized quiz. Spanish Section Quizzes also are available in the Spanish Resources Binder.

Reteach

Ask students to write the main ideas of each section subhead in the form of newspaper headlines. Have students compare and discuss their headlines.

📁 📁 Have students complete Reteaching Activity 8. Spanish Reteaching Activities also are available in the Spanish Resources Binder.

Enrich

Have students research and write a report on a state comparable worth law.

📁 Have students complete Enrichment Activity 8.

CLOSE

In a class discussion, have students speculate on what the major employment trends and issues in the next century might be.

DID YOU KNOW?

Escaping Poverty A minimum wage worker who earns $5.15 per hour, and works 40 hours a week for 50 weeks a year, earns $10,300. This is not enough to keep a family of two above the official poverty threshold.

Adjusted for Inflation

To see how the minimum wage looks without the effects of inflation, economists like to measure it in terms of **real** or **constant dollars**—dollars that are adjusted in a way that removes the distortion of inflation. This involves the use of a **base year**—a year that serves as a comparison for all other years.

Although the computations are complex, the results are not. Graph **B**, using a base year of 1992, shows that the minimum wage had relatively more purchasing power in 1968 than in any other year. As long as the base year serves as a "common denominator" for comparison purposes, the results would be the same regardless of the base year used.

Graph **B** also shows that the purchasing power of the minimum wage goes up whenever it increases faster than inflation, as it did in 1997 when the wage went to $5.15. However, the minimum wage remained the same in 1998 whereas prices went up—so the wage actually purchased a little less than it did the year before. As long as the minimum wage remains unchanged, and as long as inflation continues, its purchasing power will continue to decline over time.

Compared to Manufacturing Wages

In Graph **C**, the minimum wage is shown as a percent of the average manufacturing wage. In 1968, for example, the minimum wage was $1.60 and the average manufacturing wage was $3.01. If we divide the two, the minimum wage works out to be 53.2 percent of the manufacturing wage for that year.

1968 was the peak year when measured in this manner. After 1968 the ratio slowly declined to approximately 38 percent by 1998. As long as the minimum wage stays at $5.15, and as long as manufacturing wages continue to go up, this ratio will also continue to decline.

The minimum wage will certainly be raised again. What is not certain is when this will happen. When the minimum wage becomes unacceptably low to voters and their elected officials, Congress will increase it. Some people even want to link the minimum wage to inflation, so that the wage will rise when prices increase.

SECTION 4 REVIEW

Reviewing Terms and Facts

1. **Define** giveback, two-tier wage system, glass ceiling, comparable worth, set-aside contract, current dollars, real or constant dollars, base year.
2. **List** three reasons for the decline of unions.
3. **Describe** two reasons for the income gap between men and women.

4. **Explain** why it is necessary to consider inflation when examining the minimum wage.

Critical Thinking

5. **Demonstrating Reasoned Judgment** In your opinion, how have cultural stereotypes influenced the income gap between men and women?

Applying Economic Concepts

6. **Minimum Wage** A number of arguments exist both for and against the minimum wage. With which side do you agree? Why?

Answers to SECTION 4 REVIEW

1. All vocabulary words are defined in the Glossary.

2. Many employers have made determined efforts to keep unions out of their businesses; new additions to labor force have little loyalty to organized labor; unions are victims of their own success.

3. Women tend to fill lower-paid positions; discrimination prevents them from getting promotions; career interruptions for childbearing affect women's seniority.

4. because prices tend to increase over time, and this erodes the purchasing power of minimum wage

5. Answers may vary. Refer students to the Quick Check on page 199.

6. Answers will vary. Some students might support the minimum wage, arguing that it provides a degree of equity and security to those who lack skills needed to earn a decent living.

ECONOMICS IN ACTION

The American Labor Force

Setting Up the Video

With your classmates, view "The American Labor Force" on the videodisc *Economics in Action*. The video describes the major categories of the American labor force and explains that wages are often determined by the types of skills workers have. A news report describes the history of labor unions and their role today in an era of declining union membership. Particular attention is focused on the rise of unions in retail businesses.

Chapter 18
Disc 2, Side 1

View the video by scanning the bar code or by entering the chapter number on your keypad and pressing Search. *(Also available in VHS format.)*

Hands-On Activity

List the jobs that you, your parents, family members, and friends have. For each job listed, write the classification of labor it falls under—unskilled, semi-skilled, skilled, or professional. Then describe at least one skill or qualification a person would need in order to be a success at that job.

SURFING THE "NET"

Comparable Worth

This chapter notes that women face a considerable gap between their income and that received by men. Several potential solutions exist for closing this income discrepancy, such as comparable worth and set-aside contracts. Use the Internet to find the advantages and disadvantages of comparable worth and/or set-aside contracts.

Getting There

1. Use a search engine. Type in the words *comparable worth* or *set-aside contracts*.

2. Next, enter words like the following to focus your search: *female wages* and *wage discrimination*.

3. The search engine will provide you with a number of links to follow. Links are "pointers" to different sites on the Internet and often appear as blue, underlined words.

What to Do When You Are There

Click on the links to navigate through the pages of information. Gather your findings. Using the findings, take a position either for or against the use of comparable worth, or summarize your findings on set-aside contracts. Write several paragraphs supporting your position with information found on the Internet.

205

INTERNET ADDRESS BOOK

Internet addresses that you find useful can be noted in the space below for quick reference.

GLENCOE TECHNOLOGY

Economics in Action

Chapter 18
Disc 2, Side 1

Title: *The American Labor Force*

 If you do not have access to a videodisc player, the **Economics in Action** programs are available in VHS.

INTERNET SITES

The following are possible sites for completing the "Net" activities:

U.S. Department of Labor, Women's Bureau
http://www.dol.gov/dol/wb/

Workers of America
http://www.woa.org/

Not on the "Net"...

If students have limited or no access to the Internet, have them complete the activity "Comparable Worth" by using the computerized card catalog at the school or local library. At the *s:* prompt, students should type in *labor unions, female workers,* and/or *comparable worth*. They should then use the call numbers to find the books and other resources they need to complete their research.

GLENCOE
TECHNOLOGY

VIDEODISC
MindJogger Videoquiz

Use MindJogger to review
the Chapter 8 content.

Chapter 8
Disc 1, Side B

Also available in VHS.

Answers

Reviewing Key Terms

All definitions can be found in the Glossary.

1. **boycott** (prounion)
2. **closed shop** (prounion)
3. **company union** (anti-union)
4. **compulsory arbitration** (neither)
5. **fact-finding** (neither)
6. **giveback** (antiunion)
7. **grievance procedure** (neither)
8. **lockout** (antiunion)
9. **modified union shop** (neither)
10. **seizure** (neither)
11. **jurisdictional dispute** (neither)
12. **picket** (prounion)
13. **right-to-work law** (antiunion)
14. **agency shop** (neither)
15. **strike** (prounion)
16. **two-tier wage system** (antiunion)
17. **voluntary arbitration** (neither)
18. **mediation** (neither)

Reviewing the Facts

1. Less than 14.5 percent of employed wage and salary workers belong to unions, and a further 1.7 percent of nonunion members are represented in collective bargaining. This amounts to nearly 18.1 million workers.

2. Industrial unions represented all workers in an

Reviewing Key Terms

Define each of the terms below and then classify them as prounion, antiunion, or neither.

1. boycott
2. closed shop
3. company union
4. compulsory arbitration
5. fact-finding
6. giveback
7. grievance procedure
8. lockout
9. modified union shop
10. seizure
11. jurisdictional dispute
12. picket
13. right-to-work law
14. agency shop
15. strike
16. two-tier wage system
17. voluntary arbitration
18. mediation

Reviewing the Facts

SECTION 1 (pages 182–187)

1. **Describe** current union influence in terms of membership and workers represented by unions.
2. **Compare** the two types of unions in the post-Civil War period.
3. **Describe** the advances made by unions during the Great Depression.
4. **Outline** the progress of unions since World War II ended.

SECTION 2 (pages 189–192)

5. **Describe** the four types of union arrangements.
6. **Explain** five approaches to resolving a deadlock that may occur between a union and a company's management.

SECTION 3 (pages 194–197)

7. **Explain** the differences between the four major categories of noncompeting labor.
8. **Explain** why it is so difficult for workers to move from one category of labor to another.
9. **Compare** the two theories of wage determination.
10. **Discuss** the reasons for regional wage differences.

SECTION 4 (pages 198–204)

11. **Explain** why unions have lost members as well as influence in recent years.
12. **Describe** two corrective measures being taken to close the income gap between men and women workers.
13. **Identify** three ways to examine the minimum wage.

Critical Thinking

1. **Making Generalizations** Unions generally argue that the best interests of workers can be served when employees are members of a union. Do you agree or disagree with this argument? Defend your answer.
2. **Analyzing Information** Some people believe that in today's economy, the theory of negotiated wages is more useful than the traditional theory of wage determination. Explain why you agree or disagree.

Applying Economic Concepts

1. **Civilian Labor Force** As you go to and from school, be aware of the various occupations around you. List at least 20 occupations, then classify them according to the four major categories of labor.
2. **Minimum Wage** Poll at least 10 people of various ages, asking for their opinions on the following statement: There should be no minimum wage. Compile the responses and present your findings to the class.

industry, whereas trade or craft unions represented skilled workers who performed same kind of job.

3. Great Depression united workers, and union organizers renewed efforts to organize. Federal legislation helped to increase power of unions.

4. Unions have made limited progress and membership has dwindled.

5. closed shop: employer agrees to hire only union members; union shop: workers must join union after being hired; modified union shop: workers do not have to belong to union, but if they do join, must remain members; agency shop: workers need not be union members but must pay dues

6. mediation, where third person is brought in to help settle dispute; arbitration, where dispute decided by a third party; fact-finding, where third party investigates dispute and recommends possible settlements; injunction, where court order issued to stop union or management actions; seizure, where government takes over company's operations

Reinforcing Skills

ANALYZING INFORMATION

Read the passage, then answer the questions that follow.

It ought to be the employer's ambition, as leader, to pay better wages than any similar line of business, and it ought to be the workers' ambition to make this possible. Of course, there are workers in all factories who seem to believe that if they do their best, it will be only for the employer's benefit—and not at all for their own. It is a pity that such a feeling should exist. But it does exist and perhaps it has some justification. If an employer encourages workers to do their best, and the workers learn after a while that their best does not bring any reward, then they naturally drop back into "getting by." But if they see the profit of hard work in their pay envelope—proof that harder work means higher pay—they also begin to learn that they are a part of the business, and that its success depends on them and their success depends on it.

—Adapted from *My Life and Work* by Henry Ford and Samuel Crowther, 1922.

1. Is this a primary or secondary source? How can you tell?
2. Who is the author?
3. When was it written?
4. What is the passage about?
5. What emotions does the author express about the situation?
6. What are the key ideas?

Individual Activity

Randomly select 10 Help Wanted ads from your local newspaper and rank the ads in order of salary, putting the lowest-paid jobs first and the highest-paid jobs last. Examine the level of skills, training, and/or education required for each. Then explain how the wages and salaries are related to the level of skills, training, and education.

Cooperative Learning Activity

Organize into four groups, with each group being responsible for one of the following topics: union decline, renegotiated union agreements, the minimum wage, and pay discrepancies between men and women. Each group should prepare a three-minute radio or television newscast on their topic to be delivered to the remainder of the class. Each news report should briefly explain the controversies surrounding the issue and update the class with any current information on the topic. You will need to research the issue, using current magazine and newspaper sources as well as current statistical references.

Technology Activity

Using a Word Processor

In the **Journal Writing** activity on page 181, you were asked to scan the Help Wanted section of your local newspaper, summarizing job titles and descriptions that you would like to learn more about. With this information, use a word processor to prepare a "Jobs Outlook" newsletter convincing your peers that higher-paid jobs go to those with more training and skills.

Title your newsletter. Implement various fonts and formatting to make the newsletter visually appealing. Use a persuasive writing style to present your ideas. In this writing style, you state the problem clearly and give your position on the issue. Then present the evidence you have gathered to support your position and to refute any opposing positions. Conclude your newsletter by restating your position and summing up the evidence. Print copies of your newsletter for your class.

CHAPTER 8: *Employment, Labor, and Wages* **207**

from, but just as demanding as, other work; set-aside contracts, for minority-owned businesses

13. in current dollars, in constant dollars, and as a percentage of average manufacturing wage

Critical Thinking

1. Answers may vary.
2. Answers may vary.

Applying Economics

1. Occupations will vary.
2. Responses will vary.

Reinforcing Skills

1. Secondary source—it offers an overview.
2. Henry Ford and Samuel Crowther
3. 1922
4. the importance of the worker
5. understanding, conviction, pity
6. Employers should strive to pay their workers the best wages possible, and workers should take steps to make it possible. If extra effort is rewarded with higher wages, workers begin to feel part of the business.

BONUS TEST QUESTION

Identify the methods used to end union-management disputes.

1. Government goes to court to get order to call off a strike. (*injunction*)
2. A third party reviews all materials provided by both sides, then makes a number of recommendations. (*fact-finding*)

7. Unskilled labor includes workers who lack training to operate specialized equipment; semiskilled labor includes workers with mechanical abilities; skilled labor includes workers who can operate complex machinery with little supervision; professional labor includes workers with higher-level skills.

8. because of cost of training and education, lack of opportunity, and lack of initiative on worker's part

9. Traditional theory uses the forces of supply and demand to explain wage rates; theory of negotiated wages argues that the relative strength of the union and the collective bargaining process are also factors in determining wages.

10. labor mobility, cost of living, and location

11. Many employers have made determined effort to keep unions out of their businesses; new additions to labor force have little loyalty to organized labor; unions are victims of their own success.

12. comparable worth, the principle that people should receive equal pay for work that is different

CHAPTER ORGANIZER

Daily Objectives	Reproducible Resources	Multimedia Resources
Section 1 **The Economics of Taxation** 1. **Explain** the economic impact of taxes. 2. **List** three criteria for effective taxes. 3. **Understand** the two primary principles of taxation. 4. **Understand** how taxes are classified.	🗀 Reproducible Lesson Plan 9-1 🗀 Guided Reading Activity 9-1 🗀 Cooperative Learning Activity 23 🗀 Math Practice for Economics 14 🗀 Primary and Secondary Source Reading 23 🗀 Performance Assessment Activity 14 🗀 Section Quiz 9-1*	🖊 Focus Activity Transparency 69 💿 Vocabulary PuzzleMaker 💿 Chapter Challenger Interactive Review Software 💿 Testmaker ⬤ MindJogger Videoquiz ⬤ NBR's Economics in Action Video Program
Section 2 **The Federal Tax System** 1. **Explain** the progressive nature of the individual income tax. 2. **Explain** the nature of FICA taxes. 3. **Describe** the importance of the corporate tax structure. 4. **Identify** other major sources of federal revenue.	🗀 Reproducible Lesson Plan 9-2 🗀 Guided Reading Activity 9-2 🗀 Section Quiz 9-2*	🖊 Focus Activity Transparency 71 💿 Vocabulary PuzzleMaker 💿 Chapter Challenger Interactive Review Software 💿 Testmaker ⬤ NBR's Economics in Action Video Program
Section 3 **State and Local Tax Systems** 1. **Explain** how state governments collect taxes and other revenues. 2. **Differentiate** between state and local revenue systems. 3. **Interpret** paycheck deductions.	🗀 Reproducible Lesson Plan 9-3 🗀 Guided Reading Activity 9-3 🗀 Reinforcing Economic Skill 9 🗀 Section Quiz 9-3*	🖊 Focus Activity Transparency 72 💿 Vocabulary PuzzleMaker 💿 Chapter Challenger Interactive Review Software 💿 Testmaker ⬤ NBR's Economics in Action Video Program
Section 4 **Current Tax Issues** 1. **Explain** what is meant by the incidence of a tax. 2. **Debate** the advantages and disadvantages of the value added tax. 3. **Describe** the major tax reforms since 1980.	🗀 Reproducible Lesson Plan 9-4 🗀 Guided Reading Activity 9-4 🗀 Section Quiz 9-4*	🖊 Focus Activity Transparency 73 💿 Vocabulary PuzzleMaker 💿 Chapter Challenger Interactive Review Software 💿 Testmaker ⬤ NBR's Economics in Action Video Program
Chapter Review and Evaluation	🗀 Enrichment Activity 9 🗀 Reteaching Activity 9* 🗀 Economic Vocabulary Activity 9* 🗀 Chapter 9 Test, Forms A and B	🎧 Chapter Digests Audiocassette Activities and Tests* 💿 Testmaker ⬤ MindJogger Videoquiz

Also available in Spanish

 Blackline Master   Transparency   CD-ROM   Software   Videodisc   Audiocassette

[00:00] OUT OF TIME? Assign the Chapter 9 Digest Audiocassette and the corresponding Chapter Digest activities and tests.

National Council on Economic Education

The **Economics** America AND **Economics** International PROGRAMS

VOLUNTARY NATIONAL CONTENT STANDARDS IN ECONOMICS
Emphasized in Chapter 9

Content Standard 4 *Students will understand that:*
People respond predictably to positive and negative incentives.

Content Standard 16 *Students will understand that:*
There is an economic role for government to play in a market economy whenever the benefits of a government policy outweigh its costs. Governments often provide for national defense, address environmental concerns, define and protect property rights, and attempt to make markets more competitive. Most government policies also redistribute income.

EconomicsAmerica *Resources Available From NCEE*

- *Capstone: The Nation's High School Economics Course*
- *Civics and Government: Focus on Economics*
- *Personal Decision Making: Focus on Economics*

To order these materials, or to contact your state Council on Economic Education about workshops and programs, call 1-800-338-1192 or visit http://www.nationalcouncil.org.

PERFORMANCE ASSESSMENT

The following chapter projects may be assigned at the beginning of the chapter and used for performance assessment.

Multicultural Heritage Point out that an act of Congress passed in 1917 gave the people of Puerto Rico United States citizenship. As a result, Puerto Ricans use the same currency as the U.S., adhere to the same trade policies and regulations, and share many public goods with other U.S. citizens. At the same time, inhabitants of Puerto Rico have only nonvoting representation in Congress, and they cannot vote in presidential elections. They also do not have to pay federal income taxes.

Ask students to study the Puerto Rican economy, paying particular attention to how the commonwealth raises revenues and what other sources it draws on for funds for public programs. Then select teams of students to take opposing sides and debate the following issue: Puerto Ricans should pay federal taxes just as other U.S. citizens do. Those students not debating should act as judges and declare a winner when the debate is concluded.

Cooperative Learning Organize the class into several groups and ask each group to develop the "ideal" tax and write a report describing it. Instruct the groups to consider the following as they come up with their tax: the three criteria for taxes—equitable, simple, and efficient—and the two principles of taxation—benefit received and ability-to-pay. In completing this task, some students might conduct research on tax systems, others might write the report, and still others might construct graphs, charts, and diagrams providing illustrations of how the tax will be applied and how much revenue it might raise. Have groups present and defend their reports on the ideal tax.

ADDITIONAL RESOURCES

Readings for the Student

A Citizen's Guide to the Federal Budget. U.S. Government Publication, published annually. Superb explanation of the budget process.

Beyle, Thad. *State Government: CQ's Guide to Current Issues and Activities.* Washington, DC: Congressional Quarterly, Inc., 1992. Covers state governments' efforts to raise revenues, including such controversial revenue sources as lotteries.

Readings for the Teacher

Economic Report of the President. Washington, DC: Government Printing Office, published annually. Contains information on sources of revenue, spending programs, and the economic goals of the President.

Multimedia

Road to Wise Money Management: Planning Credit, and Your First Paycheck. Cambridge Career Products. Video, 30 min. Detailed breakdown of taxes.

Government: How It Taxes. Instructional Video, P.O. Box 21, Maumee, OH 43537. Video, 30 min. Discusses and corrects some misconceptions about taxation.

Understanding Taxes. Internal Revenue Service, P.O. Box 458, Wayland, NY 14572. Video, software, transparencies. Materials designed to help high school students better understand the American tax system.

Chapter Overview

This chapter focuses on taxes and other revenues raised by all levels of government. **Section 1** discusses the nature and impact of taxes. **Section 2** describes types of federal taxes and other sources of federal revenue. **Section 3** discusses taxes and other sources of revenue for state and local government. **Section 4** deals with tax issues and reform.

GLENCOE
TECHNOLOGY

VIDEODISC
MindJogger Videoquiz

Use MindJogger to preview the Chapter 9 content.

 | Chapter 9
Disc 2, Side A

Also available in VHS.

interNET
CONNECTION

Resources for Chapter 9 on the World Wide Web*

National Council on Economic Education

http://www.nationalcouncil.org/

OMB Watch—Budget News (Tax Policy)

http://ombwatch.org/ombwatch.html

U.S. Business Advisor

http://www.business.gov/

Sites subject to change.

 VISUAL INSTRUCTION

Ask students who have filed a federal income tax return to describe the process to the class.

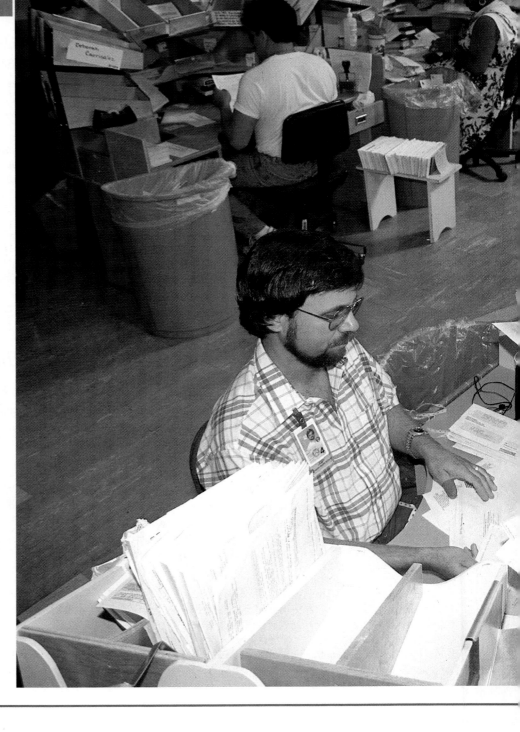

Workers at the Internal Revenue Service process income tax returns.

 Extra Credit Project

Have students create a television-viewing log for news items concerning government and the economy—with specific reference to taxation. Students should record the date, the subject of the item, and the length of time given to the item. When study of the chapter is completed, have students compare and discuss their logs.

CHAPTER 9

Sources of Government Revenue

SECTION 1
The Economics of Taxation

SECTION 2
The Federal Tax System

SECTION 3
State and Local Tax Systems

SECTION 4
Current Tax Issues

CHAPTER PREVIEW

People to Know

- Alice Rivlin
- Accountant

Applying Economic Concepts to Your Life

Payroll Withholding Have you ever questioned why your paycheck has so many deductions? If so, you're not alone! The deductions can be confusing—especially with the *payroll withholding* for federal, state, county, city, and Social Security taxes. If 10 to 30 percent of your income is being withheld, you might want to find out more about it.

Journal Writing

For one week, keep a journal of all taxes you hear about on television or read about in the newspaper. Classify your journal entries into three categories: Federal, State, and Local Taxes.

Connecting to Past Learning

Call on volunteers to review what they have learned about government's role in the economy. Note responses on the chalkboard. Then point out that regulating markets and supplying public goods require money, and government raises this money, for the most part, through taxation—the subject of this chapter.

Applying Economics

Secure current federal income tax materials, including tax booklets and forms, and distribute them to the class. Familiarize students with some of the terms used on the forms, such as *schedule, exemptions, adjusted gross income, taxable income,* and *deductions.* Then present the following hypothetical situation: Don and Jane Smith have a combined adjusted gross taxable income of $35,416. They have two children, aged 12 and 10. They have no additional income or deductions to claim. During the course of the year, Don and Jane had $5,312 withheld from their income for federal taxes.

Have students fill out a current income tax form for Don and Jane Smith. Then ask students if Don and Jane are entitled to a tax refund or if they have to pay more. Invite a professional tax preparer to class to evaluate students' answers.

 PERFORMANCE ASSESSMENT

Refer to page **208B** for a Performance Assessment activity for this chapter. Also see the **Performance Assessment Activities** booklet for additional suggestions.

Economic Portfolio

Before students undertake the **Journal Writing** activity above, suggest that they read the text concerning criteria for taxes on page 212. Point out that considering these criteria as they make their journal entries will help them to complete the **Technology Activity** in the Chapter 9 Review on page 235.

Key to Ability Levels — Teaching strategies have been coded for varying learning styles and abilities:
L1 - Basic (activities for all students)   **L2 - Average** (activities for average to above-average students)
L3 - Challenging (activities for above-average students)   **LEP - Limited English Proficiency**

FOCUS

Section Objectives

1. Explain the economic impact of taxes.
2. List three criteria for effective taxes.
3. Understand the two primary principles of taxation.
4. Understand how taxes are classified.

Bellringer

Prior to taking roll at the beginning of the class period, display Focus Activity Transparency 69 on the overhead projector and assign the accompanying Student Activity 69.

Motivational Activity

Discuss students' responses to the activity sheet that accompanies Focus Activity Transparency 69.

Preteaching Vocabulary

Call on volunteers to tell what they think each key term in the Section Preview means. Have students check the accuracy of their definitions in the Glossary. **LEP**

Use the **Vocabulary PuzzleMaker** to create crossword and word search puzzles.

Section Preview

Objectives

After studying this section, you will be able to:

1. **Explain** the economic impact of taxes.
2. **List** three criteria for effective taxes.
3. **Understand** the two primary principles of taxation.
4. **Understand** how taxes are classified.

Key Terms

sin tax, tax loophole, benefit principle of taxation, ability-to-pay principle of taxation, proportional tax, average tax rate, progressive tax, marginal tax rate, regressive tax

Applying Economic Concepts

Equity Taxes usually are not a pleasant topic. If you are like most people, however, you are willing to pay your fair share. Fairness, or *equity*, one of the main economic goals discussed in Chapter 2, is important to most Americans—especially when it comes to paying taxes.

An enormous amount of money is required to run the federal, state, and local governments of the United States. In 1997, all three levels of government collected approximately $2.5 trillion—or $9,500 for every man, woman, and child in the United States.

To keep up with the tremendous demand for government services, total revenue collections by all levels of government have grown dramatically over the years. Figure 9.1 shows that total collections, even when adjusted for inflation and population growth, increased nearly 700 percent since 1940. The figure also shows that the federal government collects the largest portion of revenues, although its share is declining.

The single most important way governments raise revenue is through taxes on income, sales, and property. Governments also collect revenue in the form of college tuitions, Social Security contributions, unemployment insurance contributions, and even driver's license fees. These revenues have an enormous impact on the economy.

Economic Impact of Taxes

Although taxes and other revenue-raising measures are necessary to support the operations of government, they reduce the income of individuals and businesses. Lower income affects the allocation of pro-

ductive resources, consumer buying and saving habits, and the productivity and growth of the economy.

Resource Allocation

When a tax is placed on a good or service at the factory, the cost of production rises, which shifts the supply curve to the left. The decrease in supply, if demand remains unchanged, raises the price of the product.

People react to the higher price in the manner predicted by the downward-sloping demand curve—they buy less of the product. When sales fall, some manufacturers cut back on production and some workers may lose their jobs. The productive resources—land, capital, labor, and entrepreneurship—are allocated to another industry, or go unused.

Behavior Adjustment

Sometimes taxes are used specifically to change people's behavior. The so-called **sin tax** is a relatively high tax designed to raise revenue as well as reduce consumption of a socially undesirable product, such as liquor or tobacco. Canada used a sin tax in the 1980s when it quadrupled the tobacco tax, pushing the price of a pack of cigarettes to more than $4.00. The government raised considerable revenue from this source during that period. It also reduced per capita cigarette consumption by about one-third.

210 UNIT 3: *Macroeconomics: Institutions*

Classroom Resources for SECTION 1

- Reproducible Lesson Plan 9-1
- Guided Reading Activity 9-1
- Cooperative Learning Activity 23
- Math Practice for Economics 14
- Primary and Secondary Source Reading 23
- Performance Assessment Activity 14
- Section Quiz 9-1
- Spanish Section Quiz 9-1

- Focus Activity Transparency 69
- NBR's Economics in Action Video Program
- Testmaker
- Vocabulary PuzzleMaker
- Chapter Challenger Interactive Review Software
- MindJogger Videoquiz

Figure 9.1
Total Receipts by All Levels of Government

A. Breakdown by Level of Government

	1965	1980	1997
Local	18.9%	16.7%	19.0%
State	19.0%	22.8%	26.0%
Federal	62.1%	60.5%	55.0%

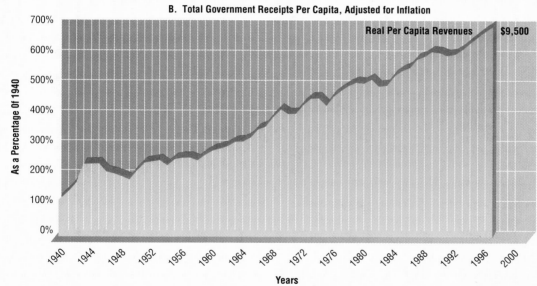

B. Total Government Receipts Per Capita, Adjusted for Inflation

Real Per Capita Revenues $9,500

As a Percentage Of 1940: 700%, 600%, 500%, 400%, 300%, 200%, 100%, 0%

Years: 1940, 1944, 1948, 1952, 1956, 1960, 1964, 1968, 1972, 1976, 1980, 1984, 1988, 1992, 1996, 2000

Source: Bureau of Economic Analysis and the Department of the Census, various years

The composition of revenues collected by all levels of government is changing. The federal government's share, shown in the top of the figure, has declined while state and local government shares have increased. The lower part of the figure shows revenues for all levels of government after being adjusted for inflation and population growth. **In what forms do governments collect revenue?**

TEACH

Guided Practice

L2 Applying Ideas Have students review the discussion of the three criteria for effective taxes on page 212 and the two principles of taxation on pages 212–214. Then organize the class into five groups, assigning each group one criterion or principle. Have groups analyze the property, state sales, and income taxes to see which tax best fits their assigned principle or criterion. Have group representatives present their findings, and then have students vote on which taxes they prefer. **LEP**

L1 Developing Graphs Direct students' attention to the discussion of the economic impact of taxes on pages 210 and 212. Ask students to draw demand and supply curves to graphically illustrate the situations considered in the discussion. **LEP**

VISUAL INSTRUCTION

Have students make a generalization about revenues adjusted for inflation and population growth. *(Total revenues have risen dramatically since the 1950s.)*

Answer to Caption:
taxes on incomes, sales, property; Social Security contributions; college tuition; unemployment insurance contributions; driver's license fees

---

Meeting Special Needs

Memory Disability Note taking is an important skill for all students but essential for students with organization or memory problems. Explain that students will be practicing taking notes. First, discuss the uses of good notes: to help students focus on the important information in the text, to organize the information into readily understandable formats, to aid memory, and to help review for tests. In Section 1, have students take notes in the ways they have in the past. Then talk about the note-taking procedures. What works for them?

Productivity and Growth

Taxes can also hinder productivity and economic growth. If people think that income taxes are too high, they may lose the incentive to work. Why, they argue, should a person earn additional income if much of it will be paid out in taxes? Many businesses feel the same way. If business taxes get too high, there is less incentive to expand production, which in turn slows economic growth. High taxes may also affect the amount of money people save, further reducing the funds available for businesses to borrow and invest. **1**

Criteria for Taxes

To be effective, taxes must meet three criteria: they must be equitable, simple, and efficient.

Equity

The first criterion is equity or fairness. Most Americans feel that taxes should be impartial and just. Problems arise, however, when we try to define *fair*. Some people feel that a tax is fair only if everyone pays the same amount. Others feel it is fair only if wealthier people pay more than those with lower incomes. Still others feel that the only fair tax is a tax on someone else. ☑

We often hear complaints about **tax loopholes**— exceptions or oversights in the tax law that allow some people and businesses to avoid paying certain taxes. Loopholes are a fairness issue, and most people oppose them on the grounds of equity.

Simplicity

A second criterion is simplicity. Tax laws should be written so that both the taxpayer and the tax collector can understand them. This task is not always easy, but people seem more willing to pay taxes when they understand them. Unfortunate consequences may arise if tax laws are too complex or unclear.

Before 1993, for example, most Americans did not know they were required to make Social Security payments on behalf of their household workers if they paid the workers more than $50 during a 3-month period. In 1994 Congress raised and simplified the $50 per quarter threshold to $1,000 annually. After 1995, the threshold was indexed to keep pace with inflation.

Efficiency

A third criterion of an effective tax is efficiency. A tax should be relatively easy to administer and reasonably successful as a revenue-generating device.

The income tax satisfies this requirement fairly well. An employer simply withholds a portion of each employee's pay, then sends a single check to the government on a regular basis. At the end of the year, the employer notifies each employee of the amount of tax withheld. Because most payroll records are now computerized, neither the employer nor the employee is unduly burdened by this withholding system.

Other taxes, especially those collected in toll booths on state highways, are considerably less efficient. The state invests millions of dollars in heavily reinforced booths that span the highway. The cost to commuters, besides the toll, is the wear and tear on their automobiles—including occasional collisions—as drivers simultaneously brake for the booth and jockey for position in the shortest line. After giving a few quarters and dimes to the attendant, each driver takes off again to repeat the process a few miles down the road.

Efficiency also means that the tax should raise enough revenue to be worthwhile. If it does not, or if it harms the economy in other ways, the tax has little value. One interesting case is the luxury tax Congress placed on small private aircraft in 1991. According to IRS records, only $53,000 in revenues were collected that year from this tax. At the same time, the tax raised the price of the aircraft, causing lower sales and layoffs in the private aircraft industry. In the end, unemployment benefits paid out were many times larger than the taxes brought in. This tax has now been repealed.

Two Principles of Taxation

The three criteria above provide some broad guidelines for evaluating various taxes. They do not, however, indicate how to select the persons or groups on whom the taxes will be imposed, or say how much each will pay. Because everyone is a potential taxpayer, "who pays what" is very important.

In general, taxes are based on two principles that have evolved over the years. These principles are the benefit principle and the ability-to-pay principle.

$ Free Enterprise Activity $

Direct students to raise their hands if they pay taxes. Ask a student whose hand was not raised if he or she buys clothing, gasoline, food, or magazines, and point out that in almost all states such articles are taxed when they are purchased. Ask another student whose hand was not raised if he or she attends music concerts or sporting events, and point out that the cost of the ticket probably includes a special entertainment tax. Then have students make a list of goods or services they may have purchased in the last week on which they paid a tax. Ask students to compare and discuss their lists.

Taxation *The daycare worker in the left photograph and the professional city planner in the right photograph both have to pay taxes.* **According to the ability-to-pay principle, how is the amount each person has to pay determined?**

Benefit Principle

The **benefit principle of taxation** is based on two ideas. First, those who benefit from government services should be the ones to pay for them. Second, people should pay taxes in proportion to the amount of services or benefits they receive. **2**

Gasoline taxes are based on the benefit principle. Motorists who buy gasoline benefit from gas taxes because the taxes are used to build streets and highways. Those who drive more than others—and hence use streets and highways more than others—generally pay more taxes because the tax is included in the price of the gasoline.

The benefit principle has two limitations. The first is that many government services provide the greatest benefit to those who can least afford to pay for them. People who receive welfare payments or live in subsidized housing, for example, usually have the lowest incomes. Even if they could pay something, they would not be able to pay in proportion to the benefits received.

The second limitation is that the benefits often are hard to measure. Are people who pay for gasoline the only ones who benefit from the roads built with gasoline taxes? What about the property owners whose property increases in value because of the improved access? What about the hotel and restaurant owners

Checking Understanding
1. How can taxes hinder productivity and economic growth?
2. What is the benefit principle of taxation?

Applying Economic Concepts
 Taxation A key component of President Clinton's health-care reform proposal of 1993 was a hefty hike in tobacco taxes. The rationale was that tobacco caused so many health problems that users should pay a higher portion of health-care costs.

Extending the Content

Tax Equity Although the tax system has been modified to make it more equitable, it is impossible to have a system that is fair for everyone and that is seen by everyone as fair. An analysis of the benefit and ability-to-pay principles of taxation illustrates this point. As is noted in the text on page 213, it is often hard to measure exactly who benefits from a particular government service and even harder to assess how much benefit each person receives. In addition, although two families may have equal incomes, because of different circumstances they may not have the same ability to pay. This difficulty in determining equity is one reason why there are several different kinds of taxes at the federal, state, and local levels.

Performance Assessment Assign Performance Assessment Activity 14.

L2 Journalism Encourage students to imagine they are writers for a current affairs magazine whose readers are mostly junior high students. Ask them to write a 250- to 300-word article titled "The Economics of Taxation" suitable for their readership.

 VISUAL INSTRUCTION

Have students identify the types of taxes the daycare worker and the city planner might pay. (*Answers might include taxes on incomes, sales, property; Social Security contributions; or driver's license fees.*)

Answer to Caption:
by their ability to pay—the higher a person's income, the greater the amount of tax to be paid

ANSWERS
1. High taxes may cause people to lose the incentive to work and businesses the incentive to produce. They may reduce the amount of money people save and, thus, funds available to borrow and invest.
2. Those who benefit from government services should pay for them; people should pay taxes in proportion to the amount of benefits they receive.

ASSESS

Check for Understanding

Assign Section 1 Review as homework or an in-class activity.

 Use **Chapter Challenger Interactive Review Software** to review Section 1.

MEETING LESSON OBJECTIVES

Each objective below is tested by the questions that follow it in parentheses.

1. **Explain** the economic impact of taxes. **(2)**

2. **List** three criteria for effective taxes. **(3)**

3. **Understand** the two primary principles of taxation. **(1, 4, 7)**

4. **Understand** how taxes are classified. **(1, 5, 6)**

Evaluate

👉 👉 💿 Assign the Section 1 Quiz in the TCR or use the *Economics: Principles and Practices* Testmaker to create a customized quiz. Spanish Section Quizzes also are available in the Spanish Resources Binder.

◉ VISUAL INSTRUCTION

Have students discuss which type of tax in Figure 9.2 they think is the most equitable.

Answer to Caption:

Taxes may affect allocation of productive resources, consumer buying and saving habits, and productivity and economic growth.

Figure 9.2
Three Types of Taxes

Type of Tax	Income of $10,000	Income of $100,000	Summary
Proportional	*City Occupational Tax* $97.50, or .975% of income	*City Occupational Tax* $975.00, or .975% of income	As income goes up, the percent of income paid in taxes *stays the same.*
Progressive	*Federal Income Tax* $1,000 paid in taxes, or 10% of total income	*Federal Income Tax* $25,000 paid in taxes, or 25% of total income	As income goes up, the percent of income paid in taxes *goes up.*
Regressive	*State Sales Tax* $5,000 of food and clothing, taxed at 4% for a total tax of $200—or 2% of income	*State Sales Tax* $20,000 of food and clothing, taxed at 4% for a total tax of $800—or .8% of income	As income goes up, the percent of income paid in taxes *goes down.*

Proportional, progressive, and regressive are the three main types of taxes. The key to each is to see what happens to the percent of total income that goes to pay the tax when income goes up. **What impact on the economy do taxes have?**

who profit from tourists arriving by car or bus? These people may buy very little gasoline, but they still benefit from facilities that the gasoline tax helps provide.

Ability-to-Pay Principle

The second approach to taxation is the **ability-to-pay principle of taxation**, which is based on the con-

---

DID YOU KNOW?

Taxes and Revolution The issue of taxes has toppled governments. Rallying under the cry "No taxation without representation!" the American colonists fought for their independence from Great Britain. The lopsided tax structure of French society in the late 1700s—with 97 percent of the population supporting the lavish lifestyles of the aristocracy—was a major cause of the French Revolution.

---

cept that people should be taxed according to their ability to pay, regardless of the benefits they receive. The ability-to-pay principle is based on two factors. First, it recognizes that societies are not always able to measure the benefits derived from government spending. Second, it assumes that persons with higher incomes suffer less discomfort paying taxes than persons with lower incomes.

For example, a family of four with an annual taxable income of $10,000 needs every cent to pay for necessities. If the tax rate was 14 percent, this family would have to pay $1,400—a huge amount for them. On the other hand, a couple with no children and a taxable income of $80,000 could afford to pay a higher tax rate.

Types of Taxes

Three general types of taxes exist in the United States today—proportional, progressive, and regressive. Each is classified according to the way in which the tax burden changes as income changes.

Cultural Diversity and Economics

Taxes Around the World If each student were to ask 10 people the question, Do you pay too much in taxes?, the vast majority of responses would be in the affirmative. A recent study suggests, however, that Americans are among the least taxed people in the industrialized world. In the U.S., all taxes account for about 30 percent of gross domestic prod-

uct (GDP). Of the world's 24 wealthiest nations, only Turkey and Australia collect a smaller percentage of GDP in taxes. Most leading industrialized nations pay close to 40 percent. The study concluded that taxes in the U.S. could be raised substantially and the country would still remain among the least taxed nations.

Proportional Tax

A **proportional tax** imposes the same percentage rate of taxation on everyone, regardless of income. If the income tax rate was 20 percent of all taxable income, a person with $10,000 in taxable income would pay $2,000 in taxes. A person with $20,000 in taxable income would pay $4,000.

If the percentage tax rate is constant, the **average tax rate**—total taxes paid divided by the total income—is constant, regardless of income. If a person's income goes up, the *percentage* of total income paid in taxes does not change.

Progressive Tax

A **progressive tax** is one that imposes a higher percentage rate of taxation on persons with high incomes than on those with low incomes. Progressive taxes use a **marginal tax rate**, the tax rate that applies to the next dollar of taxable income, that increases as the amount of taxable income increases. Therefore, the *percentage* of income paid in taxes increases as income goes up.

Suppose the tax system requires a person to pay $1,000 on $10,000 of taxable income, $4,000 on $20,000 of taxable income, or $20,000 on $60,000 of taxable income. The tax is progressive over this range because the percent of income paid in taxes—10, 20, and 30 percent respectively—rises as income rises.

Regressive Tax

A **regressive tax** is one that imposes a higher *percentage* rate of taxation on low incomes than on high incomes. For example, a person with an annual income of $10,000 may spend $5,000 on food and clothing, while another person with an annual income of $100,000 may spend $20,000 on the same essentials. If the state sales tax was 4 percent, the person with the lower income would pay a higher percentage of total income in taxes.

SECTION 1 REVIEW

Reviewing Terms and Facts

1. **Define** sin tax, tax loophole, benefit principle of taxation, ability-to-pay principle of taxation, proportional tax, average tax rate, progressive tax, marginal tax rate, regressive tax.
2. **Describe** how taxes affect the allocation of resources and productivity.
3. **List** three criteria used to evaluate taxes.
4. **Summarize** the two main principles of taxation.
5. **Explain** the three types of taxes.

Critical Thinking

6. **Analyzing Information** Think of the last tax that you paid. Using the criteria for progressive, proportional, and regressive taxes, determine which type of tax you think it is and explain why.

Applying Economic Concepts

7. **Equity** Which of the two principles of taxation—the benefit principle or the ability-to-pay principle—do you feel is the most equitable? Explain your answer.

CHAPTER 9: *Sources of Government Revenue* **215**

Answers to SECTION 1 REVIEW

1. All vocabulary words are defined in the Glossary.
2. High taxes on a product at the factory raise production costs, which lead to higher prices. Taxes at the point of sale also raise prices. Both cause people to buy less, forcing producers to cut back on production, causing resources to be used elsewhere, or not to be used at all. High taxes may cause people to lose incentive to work and businesses incentive to produce. High taxes may reduce amount of money people save and, thus, funds available to borrow and invest.
3. equity, simplicity, efficiency
4. benefit principle: those who benefit from government services should pay for them, and amount paid should be in proportion to benefit received; ability-to-pay principle: people should be taxed according to their ability to pay
5. proportional tax imposes same tax rate on everyone, regardless of income; progressive tax imposes

FOCUS

Section Objectives

1. Explain the progressive nature of the individual income tax.
2. Explain the nature of FICA taxes.
3. Describe the importance of the corporate tax structure.
4. Identify other major sources of federal revenue.

Bellringer

Prior to taking roll at the beginning of the class period, display Focus Activity Transparency 71.

Motivational Activity

Discuss students' responses to the activity sheet that accompanies Transparency 71.

Preteaching Vocabulary

Ask students to use key terms they know in written sentences. **LEP**

Use the **Vocabulary PuzzleMaker** to create crossword and word search puzzles.

MATH PRACTICE

Have students determine what would be withheld for Social Security and medicare from the paycheck of an individual who worked 40 hours at $6.50 per hour. *(40 × $6.50 = $260, total pay; 6.2 percent of $260 = $16.12 for Social Security tax; 1.45 percent of $260 = $3.77 for medicare)*

Section Preview

Objectives

After studying this section, you will be able to:

1. **Explain** the progressive nature of the individual income tax.
2. **Explain** the nature of FICA taxes.
3. **Describe** the importance of the corporate tax structure.
4. **Identify** other major sources of federal revenue.

Key Terms

individual income tax, payroll withholding system, Internal Revenue Service, tax return, indexing, FICA, medicare, corporate income tax, excise tax, luxury good, estate tax, gift tax, customs duty, user fee

Applying Economic Concepts

User Fees You dislike paying taxes, and politicians dislike talking about them—so they sometimes call taxes by a different name, *user fees*. When ranchers pay the government to graze their animals on federal land, or you pay a charge to enter a national park, remember that these are user fees. It sounds better that way.

The federal government collects taxes from a number of sources. As shown in **Figure 9.3**, the most important revenue sources are individual income taxes, Social Security taxes, and corporate income taxes.

Individual Income Taxes

In 1913 the Sixteenth Amendment to the United States Constitution was ratified. The amendment states that:

The Congress shall have power to lay and collect taxes on incomes, from whatever source derived, without apportionment among the several States, and without regard to any census or enumeration.

Since the amendment was ratified, the federal government has relied heavily on the **individual income tax**—the tax on people's earnings—to finance its operations. In 1998 the federal government collected about 41 percent of its total revenue from this source.

Payroll Deductions

In most cases, the individual income tax is paid over time through a **payroll withholding system**. Under this procedure, an employer uses federal tax tables to estimate the amount of taxes a worker would pay on a given paycheck, and then sends it directly to the government. The agency that receives the tax payment is the **Internal Revenue Service** (IRS), the branch of the Treasury Department in charge of collecting taxes.

After the close of the tax year on December 31, and before April 15 of the following year, the employee files a **tax return**—an annual report to the IRS summarizing total income, deductions, and the taxes withheld by employers. Any difference between the amount already paid and the amount actually owed, as determined by official tax tables like those shown in **Figure 9.4**, is settled when the return is filed. Most differences are usually caused by deductions and expenses that lower the amount of taxes owed, as well as by additional income received that was not subject to tax withholding. **1**

People who are self-employed do not have money withheld from their paychecks. Instead, they are required to send quarterly estimates of their taxes to the Internal Revenue Service. Self-employed individuals also must make a final settlement for the previous year sometime before April 15.

A Progressive Income Tax

The individual income tax is a progressive tax. According to the individual tax tables shown in **Figure 9.4**, single individuals paid a flat 15 percent on all income up to $24,650. After that, the marginal tax

---

Classroom Resources for SECTION 2

- Reproducible Lesson Plan 9-2
- Guided Reading Activity 9-2
- Section Quiz 9-2
- Spanish Section Quiz 9-2

- Focus Activity Transparency 71
- NBR's Economics in Action Video Program
- Testmaker
- Vocabulary PuzzleMaker
- Chapter Challenger Interactive Review Software

Figure 9.3
Federal Government Revenues by Source

In the 1990s, individual income taxes were made more progressive, Social Security taxes were raised on the wealthiest recipients, and strong economic growth generated higher corporate tax collections. All of these occurances reduced the government's need to borrow. **How did government borrowing change between 1990 and 1998?**

Source: *Economic Report of the President,* various years

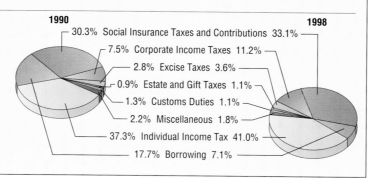

1990   1998

30.3% Social Insurance Taxes and Contributions 33.1%
7.5% Corporate Income Taxes 11.2%
2.8% Excise Taxes 3.6%
0.9% Estate and Gift Taxes 1.1%
1.3% Customs Duties 1.1%
2.2% Miscellaneous 1.8%
37.3% Individual Income Tax 41.0%
17.7% Borrowing 7.1%

rate jumps to 28 percent, 31 percent, 36 percent, and 39.6 percent, depending on the amount of taxable income. The tax schedule is similar for married individuals, with rates scaled so that couples earning higher incomes pay a larger percentage of their income in taxes.

When a tax is progressive, the average tax rate—the total tax paid divided by taxable income—goes up when income goes up. Graph **A** of **Figure 9.5** illustrates this point. The single individual with $10,000 of taxable income pays an average of 15 cents for every dollar earned. If the individual has $35,000 of taxable income, the marginal tax rate is higher (at 28 percent), which raises the average tax on every dollar to 18.8 cents. Likewise, the individual with $145,000 of taxable income pays an average of 28.3 cents on every dollar.

Indexing

Suppose a worker receives a small raise, just enough to offset the rate of inflation. Although that worker is no better off, the raise may still push the worker into a higher tax bracket. Because of this possibility, the individual income tax has a provision for **indexing**—an upward revision of the tax brackets to keep workers from paying higher taxes just because of inflation. **2**

A single individual with no dependents may have exactly $24,650 of taxable income in 1997. If the person receives a 5 percent raise the following year to offset inflation, the $1,233 raise would be taxed at the next marginal tax bracket of 28 percent. The result is that the individual gets pushed into a higher tax bracket simply because of inflation. If the bracket is indexed, or adjusted upward by 5 percent, the 28 percent marginal rate for 1998 would not apply until $25,883 is earned.

Indexing first took effect in 1985 and has been very popular with taxpayers, although some government officials argued against it. They opposed indexing because it reduced the amount of tax revenue the federal government could collect—revenue that could

---

QUICK CHECK

Checking Understanding

1. What is the deadline for filing federal income tax returns?
2. What is the purpose of indexing?

Applying Economic Concepts

 Comparative Economic Systems The United States has one of the lowest top tax rates of industrialized nations. The Netherlands' tax rate is 70 percent compared to France's 57 percent, Germany's 53 percent, Japan's 50 percent, and Sweden's 42 percent.

TEACH

Guided Practice

L1 Constructing a Chart
Draw a two-column chart on the chalkboard using *Federal Taxes* and *Type of Tax* as headings. Ask students to copy the chart in their notebooks. Have students complete the chart by listing the federal taxes described in the section in the first column, and classifying each as proportional, progressive, or regressive in the second column. Call on students to present their charts and explain why they chose the various classifications. **LEP**

VISUAL INSTRUCTION

Ask: Which sources of revenue showed little or no change in terms of percentage of total revenue? (*excise taxes, estate and gift taxes, customs duties, miscellaneous*)

Answer to Caption:
It fell from 17.7 percent to 7.1 percent.

QUICK CHECK

ANSWERS

1. April 15
2. to keep workers from paying higher taxes simply because of inflation

---

Meeting Special Needs

Reading Disability Many students who are not good readers are good at locating information in a text when their attention is directed to it. Without direction, they often cannot make decisions between important facts and elaboration. The notes they take may be filled with nonessential information. Have students read the subsection "Payroll Deductions." Tell students to find one sentence in each paragraph that best states the main idea. Have them defend their choices.

Independent Practice

📁 **Guided Reading** Assign Guided Reading Activity for Section 2. **LEP**

L2 Debate Lead the class in a debate of the following proposition: The only equitable type of tax is the individual income tax. Encourage students to take notes during the debate. Have them use these notes to write a paragraph supporting or challenging the proposition.

L3 Research Have students undertake research on the Social Security tax. Topics they might cover include its history, original purpose, changes in collections and payments, or problems with the system. Suggest that students present their findings in a written report.

VISUAL INSTRUCTION

Answer to Caption:

progressive tax

Figure 9.4
Individual Income Tax Rates for 1997

A. Single Individuals[1]

If taxable income is:	The tax is:
Not over $24,650	15% of taxable income
Over $24,650, but not over $59,750	$3,698, plus 28% of the amount up to $59,750
Over $59,750, but not over $124,650	$13,526, plus 31% of the amount up to $124,650
Over $124,650, but not over $271,050	$33,645, plus 36% of the amount up to $271,050
Over $271,050	$86,349, plus 39.6% of all income over $271,050

B. Married Filing Joint Returns[1]

If taxable income is:	The tax is:
Not over $41,200	15% of taxable income
Over $41,200, but not over $99,600	$6,180, plus 28% of the amount up to $99,600
Over $99,600, but not over $151,750	$22,532, plus 31% of the amount up to $151,750
Over $151,750, but not over $271,050	$38,699, plus 36% of the amount up to $271,050
Over $271,050	$81,647, plus 39.6% of all income over $271,050

[1]Prior to the Omnibus Budget Reconciliation Act of 1993, the highest marginal tax bracket for both single and married filing jointly was 31%.

According to the individual income tax tables above, a single individual with $20,000 of taxable income would pay $20,000 × .15, or $3,000 in taxes. If that same individual made $30,000, taxes would amount to $5,198, or $3,698 plus $1,498 (where $1,498 is .28 × $5,350). Since 1985, individual tax brackets have been indexed, or adjusted upward to off-set the impact of inflation. As a result, the brackets for 1998 and thereafter will be higher than those shown in this figure.
What type of tax is the individual income tax?

---

be used to provide additional services or to reduce the deficit.

FICA Taxes

The second most important federal tax is **FICA**. FICA stands for Federal Insurance Contributions Act and is levied on both employers and employees for Social Security and medicare. **Medicare** is a federal health-care program available to all senior citizens, regardless of income. The two components of FICA are taxed differently.

Social Security Taxes

In 1997 the Social Security component of FICA was 6.2 percent of wages and salaries up to $65,400. After that amount, Social Security taxes are not collected, regardless of income. A person whose income is $65,400 pays a Social Security tax of $4,055, the same amount a person who earns $1,000,000 pays.

218 UNIT 3: *Macroeconomics: Institutions*

Because the Social Security tax is capped, it is proportional up to $65,400, and regressive thereafter. For example, a single individual in 1997 with $35,000 of taxable income would pay an average of 6.2 cents of Social Security taxes on every dollar earned. If that same individual made $135,000, the average tax per dollar would drop to 3.0 cents.

Medicare

Until 1993 the medicare component of FICA was set at a flat 1.45 percent of the first $135,000 of wages and salaries, with nothing additional paid thereafter. This cap was removed January 1, 1994, which makes the tax proportional at all levels of income.

When medicare and Social Security are considered together, as in Graph **B** of Figure 9.5, we can see the overall regressive nature of the FICA tax. For single individuals in 1997, the tax was level at 7.65 percent up to $65,400, and then declined. A single individual earning $35,000 in 1997 paid an average FICA tax of 7.65 cents per dollar. If that same individual made

---

$ Free Enterprise Activity $

To learn more about how taxes affect the behavior of taxpayers, ask pairs of students to interview a variety of taxpayers in your community, including small-business owners, high school students with part-time jobs, large-business managers, and retired persons. Instruct students to ask their subjects to name the taxes they pay and then how paying

taxes affects their economic behavior—hiring new workers, expanding the business, buying products, saving, and so on. Have pairs of students summarize their findings, making special note of any differences among the four groups of taxpayers interviewed.

$135,000, the average FICA tax paid dropped to 4.45 cents per dollar.

Corporate Income Taxes

The third largest category of taxes the federal government collects is the **corporate income tax**—the tax a corporation pays on its profits. The corporation is taxed separately from individuals because the corporation is recognized as a separate legal entity.

Several marginal tax brackets, which are slightly progressive, are placed on corporations. The first is at 15 percent on all income under $50,000. The second is at 25 percent on income from $50,000 to $75,000. The third tax bracket is at 34 percent on income starting at $75,000. Eventually, a 35 percent marginal tax applies to all profits in excess of $18.3 million.

Other Federal Taxes

In addition to income, FICA, and corporate taxes, the federal government receives revenue in the form of excise taxes, estate and gift taxes, and customs duties.

Excise Taxes

An **excise tax** is a tax on the manufacture or sale of certain items, such as gasoline and liquor. Federal excise taxes also are found on telephone services, tires, legal betting, and coal. Because low-income families spend larger portions of their incomes on these goods than do high-income families, excise taxes tend to be regressive.

In 1991 Congress expanded the excise tax to include certain luxury goods. An economic product is called a

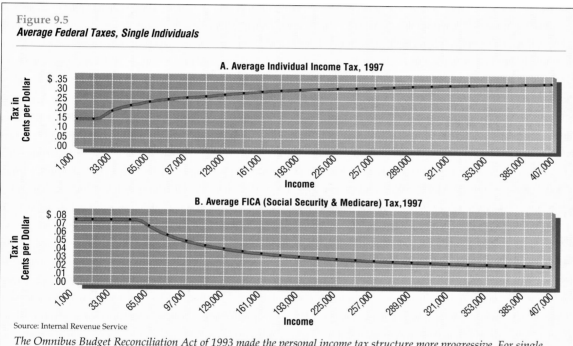

Figure 9.5
Average Federal Taxes, Single Individuals

A. Average Individual Income Tax, 1997

B. Average FICA (Social Security & Medicare) Tax, 1997

Source: Internal Revenue Service

The Omnibus Budget Reconciliation Act of 1993 made the personal income tax structure more progressive. For single individuals in 1997, the average income tax per dollar of taxable income was level at $.15 up to $24,650. After that, the marginal rate rose in stages to 28%, 31%, 36%, and finally 39.6%, which causes the average tax per dollar to increase as taxable income increases. FICA taxes remain proportional up to a point and regressive thereafter, as indicated by the declining average tax paid per dollar of income as income rises. **Why is the FICA tax a regressive tax?**

ASSESS

Check for Understanding

Assign Section 2 Review as homework or an in-class activity.

 Use **Chapter Challenger Interactive Review Software** to review Section 2.

MEETING LESSON OBJECTIVES

Each objective below is tested by the questions that follow it in parentheses.

1. **Explain** the progressive nature of the individual income tax. **(2)**
2. **Explain** the nature of FICA taxes. **(1, 2, 5)**
3. **Describe** the importance of the corporate tax structure. **(2, 3)**
4. **Identify** other major sources of federal revenue. **(1, 4, 6)**

VISUAL INSTRUCTION

Have students write a generalization based on information provided by Figure 9.5. (*Average personal income tax increases at higher incomes, while average FICA tax decreases at higher incomes.*)

Answer to Caption:

because the Social Security portion of FICA is capped at a certain income level—the higher the income, the lower the average FICA tax

---

Extending the Content

The IRS and Tax Returns Taxpayers send their income tax returns to one of the IRS's 10 tax-processing centers. These centers receive and process some 200 million returns and other related documents each year. Using computers, IRS staff members quickly check each return. A small percentage of each year's returns are selected for audit—a more thorough examination. The IRS also investigates suspected violations of the tax laws.

Customs Duties *Government officials inspect goods entering the United States.* **What is a customs duty?**

luxury good (or service) if the demand for the good rises faster than income when income grows. At first the 19 percent luxury tax was indexed to keep up with inflation and applied to many goods, including passenger vehicles in excess of $30,000. The tax was unpopular, however, so boats, aircraft, jewelry, and furs were dropped in 1993. Congress then decided to roll back the luxury tax, lowering it by one percent per year beginning in 1997 and ending in the year 2002, when it reaches 3 percent.

Estate and Gift Taxes

The **estate tax** is the tax the government levies on the transfer of property when a person dies. Estate taxes can range from 18 to 55 percent of the value of the estate. Estates worth less than $600,000 are exempt.

The **gift tax** is a tax on donations of money or wealth and is paid by the person who makes the gift. The gift tax is used to make sure that wealthy people do not try to avoid taxes by giving away their estates before their deaths.

Customs Duties

A **customs duty** is a charge levied on goods brought in from other countries. Many types of goods are covered, ranging from automobiles to silver ore. The duties are relatively low, and they produce little federal revenue.

Miscellaneous Fees

About 1.8 percent of federal revenue is collected through various miscellaneous fees. Because taxes are generally so unpopular, **user fees**—charges levied for the use of a good or service—have been suggested with increasing frequency. President Ronald Reagan was one of the first Presidents to aggressively push for user fees instead of taxes. He proposed many user fees in his 1987 budget, including those paid by visitors to national parks as a means of providing additional funds for upkeep and maintenance.

SECTION 2 REVIEW

Reviewing Terms and Facts

1. **Define** individual income tax, payroll withholding system, Internal Revenue Service, tax return, indexing, FICA, medicare, corporate income tax, excise tax, luxury good, estate tax, gift tax, customs duty, user fee.
2. **Describe** the three largest components of federal revenues.
3. **Identify** the main marginal tax brackets in the corporate income tax structure.
4. **Describe** four other sources of government revenue.

Critical Thinking

5. **Demonstrating Reasoned Judgment** Defend or support the regressive nature of the current FICA tax.

Applying Economic Concepts

6. **User Fees** User fees have been compared to taxes based on the benefit principle of taxation. What are the pros and cons of having user fees as a way to charge admission to national parks?

PROFILES IN ECONOMICS

ALICE RIVLIN
(1931–   )

Alice Rivlin, founding director of the Congressional Budget Office (CBO), former Director of the Office of Management and Budget (OMB) in the Clinton administration, and now Vice Chair of the Fed's Board of Governors, is one of the most respected economists in Washington. As a seasoned professional with a wealth of experience, her knowledge of government finance is virtually unparalleled.

EDUCATION Dr. Rivlin received her Bachelor's degree from Bryn Mawr College in 1952 and her

Rivlin notes that the skills needed to succeed in college are the same skills that make workers more productive in the workplace.

Ph.D. from Radcliffe College in 1958. She joined the prestigious Brookings Institution in 1957, but

left to become Director of the Congressional Budget Office between 1975 and 1983. In 1992 Rivlin took a professorship at George Mason University.

She has written extensively and is known for straightforward and searing views put forth in her many writings. Her most important books include *The Role of the Federal Government in Financing Higher Education* (1961), *Systematic Thinking for Social Action* (1971), *Economic Choices* (1987), *Caring for the Disabled Elderly: Who Will Pay?* (1988), and *Reviving the American Dream* (1992).

BELIEFS Not afraid to be different, Rivlin often questions the status quo in provocative ways. She objects, for example, to the belief that education alone is the reason that some workers, on average, earn more than others. In a paper published in the *American Economic Review*, she argued that:

> . . . the only reason that education is correlated with income is that the combination of ability, motivation, and personal habits that it takes to succeed in education happens to be the same combination that it takes to be a productive worker.
> —"Income Distribution— Can Economists Help?" May, 1975

Dr. Rivlin is a blunt and outspoken opponent of budget deficits, and argues that spending cannot be brought under control until Congress is willing to reform the pension system, subsidies, and other types of transfer payments. Now that she is second-in-command at the Fed, she has yet another opportunity to address the issues that affect the performance of our nation's economy.

Examining the Profile

1. **Analyzing Information** What relationship does Rivlin see between education and income?

2. **For Further Research** Research the work that Rivlin did for President Clinton in the mid-1990s.

Background

Mention that the Congressional Budget Office (CBO) was created in 1974 to refine and improve the process through which Congress reviewed federal spending. To make certain that operations remained as nonpartisan as possible, it was decided that the Democrats and the Republicans would alternate in naming the director of the CBO. Rivlin, a Democratic appointee, created an operation respected by both parties for its thoughtful, thorough, and evenhanded analysis of budgetary matters.

TEACH

Review the profile with students. Then ask them to identify the qualities that have helped Rivlin to become one of the most respected economists in government. (*possible suggestions: straightforward in expressing opinions, not afraid to be different, ready to challenge the status quo, puts forward provocative ideas*)

Answers to Examining the Profile

1. The qualities needed to succeed in education are the same as those needed to succeed in the working world.

2. Findings may vary. Suggest that students present the results of their research in a written report.

SECTION 3
State and Local Tax Systems

FOCUS

Section Objectives

1. Explain how state governments collect taxes and other revenues.
2. Differentiate between state and local revenue systems.
3. Interpret paycheck deductions.

Bellringer

Prior to taking roll at the beginning of the class period, display Focus Activity Transparency 72 on the overhead projector and assign the accompanying Student Activity 72.

Motivational Activity

Discuss students' responses to the activity sheet that accompanies Focus Activity Transparency 72.

Preteaching Vocabulary

Have students read the Glossary definition of each key term listed in the Section Preview. Then ask them to restate each definition in their own words. **LEP**

Use the **Vocabulary PuzzleMaker** to create crossword and word search puzzles.

SECTION 3
State and Local Tax Systems

Section Preview

Objectives

After studying this section, you will be able to:

1. **Explain** how state governments collect taxes and other revenues.
2. **Differentiate** between state and local revenue systems.
3. **Interpret** paycheck deductions.

Key Terms

intergovernmental revenue, sales tax, property tax, real property, tangible personal property, intangible personal property, tax assessor, payroll withholding statement

Applying Economic Concepts

Sales Tax When you purchase an item in most states, you will pay an additional 3 to 6 cents in the form of a *sales tax*. The state sales tax is the tax paid most often, and it is the second largest source of revenue for state governments.

State and local governments, like the federal government, raise revenue in many ways. They receive funds from sales taxes, utility revenues, college and university tuitions, license taxes, property taxes, insurance taxes, and taxes on tickets to theaters, sporting events, and other activities. They also receive **intergovernmental revenues**—funds collected by one level of government that are distributed to another level of government for expenditures.

State and local governments also use many of the same devices as the federal government to raise revenue. Most state and local governments impose income taxes, estate taxes, and gift taxes. Most impose taxes similar to the excise taxes on gasoline and cigarettes. As shown in **Figure 9.1**, state and local governments accounted for about 45 percent of all government revenues.

State Government Revenue Sources

State governments collect their revenues from several sources. **Figure 9.6** shows the relative proportions of each source, the largest of which are examined below.

Intergovernmental Revenues

The funds that states receive from the federal government are the largest source of state government revenues. These funds—for the most part—help finance state expenditures on welfare, education, highways, health, and hospitals.

Sales Taxes

A **sales tax** is a general tax levied on consumer purchases of nearly all products. It is added to the final price the consumer pays, and merchants collect the tax at the time of sale. The taxes are then turned over to the proper state government agency on a weekly or monthly basis. Most states allow merchants to keep a small portion of what they collect to compensate for their time and bookkeeping costs.

The sales tax is the second largest source of revenue for states, accounting for approximately 22.1 percent of total revenues collected. Only five states—Alaska, Delaware, Montana, New Hampshire, and Oregon—do not have a general sales tax. Sales tax rates vary widely for each of the other states, as **Figure 9.7** shows.

The sales tax is a very effective way for states and cities to raise revenue. The tax is difficult to avoid and, because it affects large numbers of consumers, it raises huge sums of money. The sales tax also is relatively easy to administer because the merchant collects it at the point of sale.

A sales tax, however, is a regressive tax because the percentage of income paid in sales tax goes down as income goes up. To counter this regressive feature, many states do not tax such necessities as food and drugs.

222 UNIT 3: *Macroeconomics: Institutions*

Employee Retirement Contributions

Many states levy taxes, fees, or other assessments on their employees to cover the cost of state retirement funds and pension plans. According to Figure 9.6, employee retirement contributions by these workers were the third largest source of state revenue.

Individual Income Taxes

On average, the fourth largest source of state revenues is the individual income tax. Overall, individual income tax revenues are about five times as large as the income tax collected from corporations.

Other Revenues

The remaining revenues that state governments collect are interest earnings on surplus funds; tuition and other fees collected from state-owned colleges, universities, and technical schools; corporate income taxes; and hospital fees.

Local Government Revenue Sources

The major sources of local government revenue are also shown in Figure 9.6. The main categories are discussed below.

Intergovernmental Revenues

Local governments receive the largest part of their revenues in the form of intergovernmental transfers from state governments. These funds are generally

Guided Practice

L1 *Constructing a Chart* On the chalkboard draw a chart similar to that used for the Guided Practice activity in Section 2, but label the columns *State/Local Taxes* and *Type of Tax.* Have students copy and complete the chart by listing the various kinds of state and local taxes in the first column and classifying each tax as proportional, progressive, or regressive in the second column. **LEP**

GLENCOE
TECHNOLOGY

NIGHTLY BUSINESS REPORT

Economics in Action

Chapter 13
Disc 1, Side 2
Title: *The American Tax System*
Subject: Types of taxes
Ask: What level of government levies sales taxes? *(state level of government)*

   Also available in VHS.

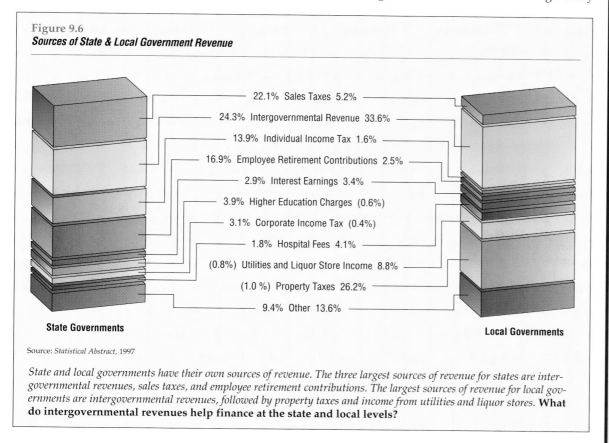

Figure 9.6
Sources of State & Local Government Revenue

22.1% Sales Taxes 5.2%
24.3% Intergovernmental Revenue 33.6%
13.9% Individual Income Tax 1.6%
16.9% Employee Retirement Contributions 2.5%
2.9% Interest Earnings 3.4%
3.9% Higher Education Charges (0.6%)
3.1% Corporate Income Tax (0.4%)
1.8% Hospital Fees 4.1%
(0.8%) Utilities and Liquor Store Income 8.8%
(1.0 %) Property Taxes 26.2%
9.4% Other 13.6%

State Governments

Local Governments

Source: *Statistical Abstract, 1997*

State and local governments have their own sources of revenue. The three largest sources of revenue for states are intergovernmental revenues, sales taxes, and employee retirement contributions. The largest sources of revenue for local governments are intergovernmental revenues, followed by property taxes and income from utilities and liquor stores. **What do intergovernmental revenues help finance at the state and local levels?**

CHAPTER 9: *Sources of Government Revenue* **223**

  VISUAL INSTRUCTION

Mention that lotteries—included in the "Other" category—are a growing source of revenue for more than half the states.

Answer to Caption:
welfare, education, highways, health, and hospitals

Meeting Special Needs

Learning Disability Students with learning disabilities often have difficulty organizing information. Using Section 3, teach students to make comparisons. First, make a two-column chart titled "State and Local Tax Systems." Label the columns "Similarities" and "Differences." Then have students list some of the similarities and differences between the two and write each item in the appropriate column.

L2 *Identifying Ideas* Have students identify the state and local taxes they pay. (*Responses might include sales tax, individual income tax, and various license and user fees.*) Then have them consider the state and local taxes they might pay if they were business owners. (*Responses might include corporate income tax, property tax, and various license and user fees.*)

Independent Practice

 Guided Reading Assign Guided Reading Activity for Section 3. **LEP**

L1 *Applying Ideas* Ask students to keep a record of the total amount of sales taxes they pay during a week. Then have them discuss the following questions: Did sales taxes play a role in your purchasing decisions? How would your spending behavior have differed if there were no sales tax?

L2 *Writing a Report* Have students research and write a report on the major sources of revenue for their state, county, and municipal governments.

VISUAL INSTRUCTION

Point out that because local governments may also collect sales tax, the rate people pay is higher than the state rate.

Answer to Caption:

Mississippi, Rhode Island at 7 percent; Colorado at 3 percent (also accept Alaska, Delaware, Montana, New Hampshire, Oregon at 0 percent)

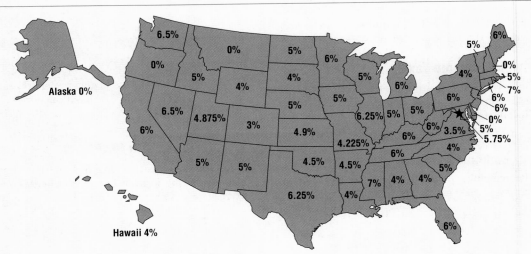

Figure 9.7
State Sales Taxes

In general, the sales tax is the major source of revenue for the states. Income taxes and gasoline taxes are also used, although all taxes vary considerably from one state to another. **What states have the highest sales tax? The lowest?**

---

intended for education and public welfare. A much smaller amount comes directly from the federal government, mostly for urban renewal. **1**

Property Taxes

The second largest source of revenue for local governments is the **property tax**—a tax on real property and tangible and intangible personal property. **Real property** includes real estate, buildings, and anything permanently attached, such as elevators and central air conditioners. **Tangible personal property** includes all tangible items of wealth not permanently attached to land or buildings, such as furniture, automobiles, farm animals, the stock of goods in retail stores, and clothing. **Intangible personal property** is property with an invisible value and is represented by paper documents such as a stock, bond, patent, or check.

The property tax that raises the most revenue is the tax on real estate. Taxes on other personal property, with the exception of automobiles, is seldom collected because of the problem of valuation. Tangible personal

property, for example, is not always brought to the attention of the **tax assessor**—the person who places value on property for tax purposes. As a result, many items that could be taxed never are.

In addition, some property would be difficult or expensive to evaluate fairly. How would tax assessors know the reasonable value of everyone's wedding silver, furniture, baseball card collections, computers, clothing, and other tangible property items? How many thousands of assessors would be needed to assess all these items in the first place? Therefore, those communities that do tax tangible and intangible property use very low rates and receive very little in revenues for their efforts. ✔

Utility and Liquor Store Income

The third largest source of local revenue is derived from the earnings of public utilities and state-owned liquor stores. Figure 9.6 shows that local governments acquired 8.8 percent of their revenues from these sources.

$ Free Enterprise Activity $

Ask students who work to bring paycheck stubs to class. Then have students turn to page 225 and study the paycheck and withholding statement in Figure 9.8. Review the categories on the statement, pointing out that while paycheck stubs may differ in appearance, most contain similar information, such as pay period, hours worked, gross and net pay, and tax figures. Have students locate where

the federal, state, city, and Social Security tax amounts are noted on the paycheck stub, and ask which of these taxes are federal taxes. (*federal income, FICA*) Conclude the activity by having students who brought paycheck stubs locate the various categories on their withholding statements.

Figure 9.8
Biweekly Paycheck and Withholding Statement

The withholding statement attached to your paycheck summarizes many of the federal, state, and local taxes. Federal and state income tax withholdings are almost always shown, as is the FICA (Social Security and medicare) tax. Others withheld may include city income taxes and a number of voluntary deductions, such as health insurance payments and savings plans. **What percentage of this man's pay has been deducted from his paycheck?**

SMITH, SMITH, AND SMITH
ATTORNEYS AT LAW

21-2/000

Number 2,195,903

Date JUNE 25 19 97

Pay to the
Order of: _____ SAM YAMAGUCHI _____ $ 586.89

_____ Five Hundred Eighty-Six Dollars and 89/100 _____ Dollars

THE CENTRAL BANK   NON NEGOTIABLE

Memo _____

⑈0314 ⑉0665⑈ 1 4785927   Treasurer

- -

PLEASE DETACH AND RETAIN THIS PORTION
AS YOUR RECORD OF EARNINGS AND DEDUCTIONS

DATE	PAY END	VO.NO.	EMP. NO.	HRS.	MISC.	CR.UN.	INS.	GROSS
6/16/97	6/27/97		1376	80	3.20			800 00
104 70	40 01	4 00	61 20					586 89
FEDERAL	STATE	CITY	FICA	RET.	BONDS	OTHER		NET

Sales Taxes

Many towns and cities have their own sales taxes. Merchants collect these taxes right along with the state sales tax, at the point of sale. According to Figure 9.6, sales taxes were the fourth most important source of local government revenues. 2

Other Sources

Local governments also collect a portion of funds in the form of hospital fees and personal income taxes. In general, the revenue sources available to local governments are much more limited than those available to the state and federal levels of government.

Examining Your Paycheck

Many of the taxes you pay to federal, state, and local governments are deducted directly from your paycheck. By examining the sample paycheck and **payroll withholding statement** in Figure 9.8, we can identify many of the revenue sources discussed in this chapter.

The worker to whom the check belongs makes $10 an hour and receives a check every two weeks. If the

Checking Understanding

1. What is intergovernmental revenue?
2. How are state and local sales taxes collected?

Applying Economic Concepts

 Taxation Property taxes became extremely unpopular as real estate values rose and taxes skyrocketed during the past two decades. Taxpayers in several states, such as Massachusetts and California, voted to limit the amounts that could be levied.

CHAPTER 9: *Sources of Government Revenue* **225**

ASSESS

Check for Understanding

Assign Section 3 Review as homework or an in-class activity.

 Use **Chapter Challenger Interactive Review Software** to review Section 3.

MEETING LESSON OBJECTIVES

Each objective below is tested by the questions that follow it in parentheses.

1. **Explain** how state governments collect taxes and other revenues. **(1, 2, 6)**
2. **Differentiate** between state and local revenue systems. **(1, 2, 3, 5)**
3. **Interpret** paycheck deductions. **(4)**

VISUAL INSTRUCTION

Ask: What is the largest deduction from the check? *(federal income tax)* The second largest? *(FICA taxes)*

Answer to Caption:
about 27 percent
($800 – $586.89) ÷ $800

ANSWERS

1. funds that states receive from federal government
2. Merchants collect sales taxes at point of sale.

Extending the Content

Direct and Indirect Taxes Taxes can be classified as direct or indirect. Direct taxes are based directly on a person's income or net wealth. The individual income tax and inheritance tax are direct taxes. Indirect taxes are taxes on goods and services that are passed on to the consumer. The sales tax, levied on most purchases, is an indirect tax. The government collects sales taxes from retailers, based on their sales volume. In turn, retailers collect the tax from the consumers who purchase their goods. In this way, consumers are paying the tax indirectly. Excise taxes, custom duties, and taxes on legal transactions also are indirect taxes. Some taxes can be classified as either direct or indirect, depending on the circumstances. For example, a property tax is a direct tax when it is placed on an owner's residence. It is considered an indirect tax when it is placed on an owner's rental property, because the owner can set the rent so that it includes the amount of the property tax.

length of the workweek is 40 hours, the worker's gross pay amounts to $800. The worker is single, has no deductions, and lives and works in Kentucky.

According to withholding tables the federal government supplied for 1997, biweekly workers making at least $800, but less than $820, have $104.70 withheld from their paychecks. Similar tables the state of Kentucky prepared specify that $40.01 is withheld for state income taxes. Because these are both estimates, and because even minor differences between the amounts withheld and the amount actually owed at the end of the year can grow, the worker will file state and federal tax returns between January 1 and April 15 of 1998 to settle the differences.

A half-percent city income tax amounts to $4 and is also deducted from the paycheck. Because the amount is relatively small, cities seldom require workers to file separate year-end tax forms such as those filed for federal and state income taxes.

The federal FICA tax amounts to 7.65 percent (6.20 percent for Social Security and 1.45 percent for medicare) of $800, or $61.20. The FICA is deducted from the gross pay, along with $3.20 in miscellaneous deductions, which leaves the worker with a net pay of $586.89.

If the worker has insurance payments or retirement contributions, purchases savings bonds, or puts money into a credit union, even more deductions will appear on the paycheck although they are not taxes. About the only major taxes that do not appear on the

Property Tax *This historical area of Boston, Massachusetts, has high property taxes.* **How do tangible and intangible personal property differ?**

paycheck are state sales taxes, local property taxes, and federal excise taxes—which are already built into the price of the products by the time they are bought.

SECTION 3 REVIEW

Reviewing Terms and Facts

1. **Define** intergovernmental revenue, sales tax, property tax, real property, tangible personal property, intangible personal property, tax assessor, payroll withholding statement.
2. **Explain** the four major sources of state tax revenues.
3. **Describe** the three major sources of local government revenues.

4. **List** the major types of state, local, and federal taxes reflected on a payroll withholding statement.

Critical Thinking

5. **Analyzing Information** State and local governments receive revenue from various sources. Which source do you think best satisfies the tax criteria listed in the chapter? Defend your answer.

Applying Economic Concepts

6. **Sales Taxes** Why do you think sales taxes are applied to food and beverages purchased at restaurants but not to food and beverages bought at grocery stores?

Answers to SECTION 3 REVIEW

1. All vocabulary words are defined in the Glossary.

2. sales tax—a general tax levied on consumer purchases of nearly all products; intergovernmental revenues that states receive from the federal government; individual income taxes based on people's earnings; employee retirement contributions, taxes, fees or other assessments levied on state employees for retirement and pension plans

3. intergovernmental revenues received from states; property taxes levied on real property, tangible personal property, and intangible personal property; utility and liquor store income, derived from the earnings of public utilities and state-owned liquor stores

4. federal income tax, state income tax, city income tax, FICA taxes

5. Answers will vary.

6. Answers will vary.

CRITICAL THINKING SKILL

Distinguishing Fact From Opinion

Imagine that it is a presidential election year and your economics teacher has asked you to watch a televised debate between the two principal candidates. After watching the debate, you are asked to decide for whom to vote and to give a list of reasons for your decision. To decide, you must be able to distinguish between the facts and the opinions the candidates used during the debate.

Explanation

A fact is a statement or piece of information that can be proved or verified by evidence. An opinion presents a personal viewpoint that cannot be proved true or false. If you can distinguish fact from opinion, you will be better able to make judgments based on a combination of factual information and your own personal values and beliefs.

Use the following steps to help distinguish between fact and opinion in written material and visual media presentations.

- Look for words and phrases that indicate opinion, such as *I think, I believe, probably, seems to me, may, might, could, ought, in my judgment,* or *in my view.*
- Examine the material for expressions of approval and disapproval, such as *good, bad, poor,* and *satisfactory.*
- Be aware of such superlatives as *greatest, worst, finest,* and *best.*
- Look for words that have negative meanings, such as *squander, contemptible,* and *disgrace.*
- Note the use of generalizations that include words such as *none, every,* and *always.*
- Identify facts by looking for statements that can be checked for accuracy, such as names, dates, numbers, and specific actions. Facts often answer the *who, what, when,* and *where* questions.
- Determine whether the information is fact or opinion.

Practice

Use the steps to identify the following statements as either facts or opinions. Give reasons for your choices.

1. Taxes, especially federal taxes, waste consumers' incomes.
2. Taxes, including both taxes on income and sales taxes, reduce consumers' incomes.
3. The individual income tax went into effect in 1913 after Congress proposed and the states ratified the Sixteenth Amendment.
4. All major corporations use loopholes to avoid paying taxes.
5. All levels of government—federal, state, and local—collected about $2.1 trillion in taxes in the early 1990s.
6. The federal government squanders most of the tax money it collects.
7. Taxes should be equitable, simple, and efficient for all taxpayers.
8. The benefit principle of taxation is more fair than the ability-to-pay principle.
9. Lower-income families find it more difficult to pay for the benefits they receive directly from the government.
10. The Omnibus Budget Reconciliation Act of 1993 shifted some of the tax burden to the wealthy to help reduce the deficit.

Additional Practice

For further practice in distinguishing fact from opinion, complete the Reinforcing Skills exercise in the Chapter 9 Review on page 235.

CHAPTER 9: *Sources of Government Revenue* **227**

Answers to SKILL

1. opinion
2. fact
3. fact
4. opinion
5. fact
6. opinion
7. opinion
8. opinion
9. fact
10. fact

SECTION 4
Current Tax Issues

FOCUS

Section Objectives

1. Explain what is meant by the incidence of a tax.

2. Debate the advantages and disadvantages of the value added tax.

3. Describe the major tax reforms since 1980.

Bellringer

Prior to taking roll at the beginning of the class period, display Focus Activity Transparency 73.

Motivational Activity

Discuss students' responses to the activity sheet that accompanies Transparency 73.

Preteaching Vocabulary

Ask students to suggest definitions for the key terms. Have them check the accuracy of the suggestions as they work through the section. **LEP**

Use the **Vocabulary PuzzleMaker** to create crossword and word search puzzles.

TEACH

Guided Practice

L2 **Debate** Select students to debate the following: The federal income tax on corporations and individuals should be replaced with the value added tax. Have students note pro and con points on the issue as the debate takes place. Have them use these notes to write a brief essay supporting or challenging the proposition.

Section Preview

Objectives

After studying this section, you will be able to:

1. **Explain** what is meant by the incidence of a tax.

2. **Debate** the advantages and disadvantages of the value added tax.

3. **Describe** the major tax reforms since 1980.

Key Terms

incidence of a tax, value added tax (VAT), accelerated depreciation, investment tax credit, surcharge, alternative minimum tax

Applying Economic Concepts

Value Added Tax Have you ever not purchased an item because you lacked the extra cash to pay the sales tax? A sales tax is highly visible, in some places adding 7 percent or more to the cost of the product. You are less likely to react directly to a *value added tax*, however, because you may not even know it is there.

Most people feel that they already pay enough taxes. Federal, state, and local governments, however, never seem to have enough revenue to satisfy everyone's needs. For these and other reasons, three tax issues usually are of interest: the incidence of a tax, the value added tax, and tax reform.

Incidence of a Tax

Suppose a city wants to tax a local utility company to raise revenue. Who actually bears the burden of the tax? If the utility is able to raise its rates, consumers will likely bear most of the burden in the form of higher utility bills. If the company's rates are regulated, and if the company's profits are not large enough to absorb the tax increase, shareholders may receive smaller dividends—placing the burden of the tax on the owners. Another alternative is that the company may postpone a pay raise—shifting the burden of the tax to its employees.

This example illustrates the **incidence of a tax**—or the final burden of the tax. This issue is important because the incidence of a tax often can be shifted from one group to another. Although the incidence is usually different in each case, some outcomes can be predicted with the help of supply and demand analysis.

In general, the more elastic the demand for the product, the less likely the burden of the tax can be

shifted from the producer to the consumer. This example is illustrated with the supply and demand curves in Figure 9.9. Before the tax is passed, each market is in equilibrium with five units being sold at $4 each. If the government passes a tax of $1, the cost of production rises, causing producers to supply less output at each and every price. This causes the supply curve to shift from SS to S_1S_1. After the supply curve has shifted, the market must find a new equilibrium price and quantity.

Because consumers purchase fewer goods and services at higher prices, less should be demanded. Just how much less depends on the elasticity of demand for the product. If the demand is very inelastic, as in Graph **A**, the producer will be able to shift most of the tax, or about 90 cents, to the consumer. If the demand is very elastic, as in Graph **B**, the producer will be able to shift only some of the tax, or 50 cents, to the consumer. In both cases, the producer will have to absorb the rest of the tax.

The demand for products such as alcohol, tobacco, medicine, and low-cost housing tends to be inelastic. Because of this inelastic demand, much of the tax placed on the producer, seller, or supplier can be shifted directly to the consumer. If consumer demand is elastic, as in the case of new automobiles, luxurious yachts, upscale homes, and other items that consume a large portion of income, less of the tax is shifted to the consumer. In this case, more of the tax is absorbed by the producer.

228 UNIT 3: *Macroeconomics: Institutions*

Classroom Resources for SECTION 4

Reproducible Lesson Plan 9-4
Guided Reading Activity 9-4
Section Quiz 9-4
Spanish Section Quiz 9-4
Focus Activity Transparency 73
NBR's Economics in Action Video Program
Enrichment Activity 9
Reteaching Activity 9
Spanish Reteaching Activity 9

Economic Vocabulary Activity 9
Spanish Economic Vocabulary Activity 9
Chapter 9 Test, Form A and Form B
English and Spanish Audiocassettes
Testmaker
Vocabulary PuzzleMaker
Chapter Challenger Interactive Review
    Software
MindJogger Videoquiz

The Value Added Tax

One of the more controversial taxes is the **value added tax** (VAT), a tax placed on the value that manufacturers add at each stage of production. It is similar to a national sales tax, and it has the potential to raise enormous amounts of revenues for the federal government. As such, it is a tax on consumption instead of income.

The Concept of Value Added

The production of almost any good or service involves numerous steps. Consider a hypothetical example concerning wooden baseball bats. First, loggers cut the trees and sell the timber to lumber mills. Second, the mills process the logs into smaller units for sale to bat manufacturers. The manufacturers then shape the wood into baseball bats.

After the bats are painted or varnished, they are sold to a wholesaler. The wholesaler sells them to retailers, and retailers sell them to consumers. The whole process is illustrated in Figure 9.10. The first column of numbers shows the value added at each stage of production. Without the VAT, the consumer ends up paying $10 for each bat.

Adding the VAT

If a 10 percent VAT is added at each stage of production, the cumulative value of the bat is 10 percent higher, and the consumer pays $11 instead of $10.

The VAT is very similar to a national sales tax, except that the 10 percent is levied on producers at every step of the production process, rather than simply added at the end. The size of the tax at each stage of production is small, hardly noticeable in some instances, but it still increases the price of the product by 10 percent.

Advantages of a VAT

As a way of raising revenue, the VAT has several advantages. First, it is hard to avoid because the tax collector simply levies it on the total amount of sales less the cost of inputs.

Second, the incidence of the tax is widely spread, which makes it harder for a single firm to shift the burden of the tax to one group or another. Third, the tax is not visible to the final consumer because it has been built into the price before the purchase is made. Because the consumer does not know the actual amount of tax paid, he or she is less likely to become angry about it. Fourth, the VAT is easy to collect because businesses would simply make their VAT payments to the government along with their regular tax payments. Finally, even a relatively small VAT can raise a tremendous amount of revenue, especially when it is applied to a broad range of products.

Disadvantages of a VAT

The main disadvantage of the VAT is that it tends to be invisible to consumers. In the example of the

---

Figure 9.9
Shifting the Incidence of a Tax

If consumer demand for a product is inelastic, as in Graph A, the $1 tax drives the price up substantially for consumers. If consumer demand is more elastic, as in Graph B, consumers still pay a higher price for the product, but more of the $1 tax remains with the producer. **Who bears the burden—the producer or the consumer—when a tax is placed on medicine?**

A. Inelastic Demand

B. Elastic Demand

L1 *Constructing a Chart*
Draw on the chalkboard a three-column chart with the headings *Element of Act*, *Criterion*, and *Principle*. Direct students to review the discussion of the Omnibus Budget Reconciliation Act of 1993 and the Taxpayer Relief Act of 1997 on pages 231–232. Then have them copy and complete the chart by noting the various parts of the acts in the first column, and the criterion and principle of taxation that applies to each part in the second and third columns. **LEP**

GLENCOE
TECHNOLOGY

NIGHTLY BUSINESS REPORT

Economics in Action

Chapter 13
Disc 1, Side 2

Title: *The American Tax System*

Subject: Value added tax

Ask: What is the difference between sales tax and value added tax? *(Sales tax is a percentage of a product's price that is added when a consumer purchases a product. Value added tax is a tax placed on the value that manufacturers add at each stage of production.)*

 Also available in VHS.

VISUAL INSTRUCTION

Have students suggest types of products to which Graph A might apply. *(medicine, tobacco, alcohol)*

Answer to Caption:
consumer pays most of tax

Independent Practice

 Guided Reading Assign Guided Reading Activity for Section 4. **LEP**

L2 *Writing a Letter* Have students assume the role of a worker or a head of a business. Direct them to write a letter to the editor or to one of their congressional representatives explaining why they support or oppose tax reform. Suggest that they focus on the introduction of the VAT or on one of the tax reform acts discussed in the section. Encourage students to refer to the criteria and principles of taxation to support their positions. Select students to share their letters with the class.

L3 *Research* Have students conduct research to find instances in U.S. history of tax reform. Direct students to present their findings in written reports that note why tax reform was proposed, how the tax laws were changed, and whether or not the legislation achieved its aims.

◎ VISUAL INSTRUCTION

Mention that European countries have a standard VAT rate of at least 15 percent, with lower rates for essentials such as food and medicine.

Answer to Caption:

hard to avoid, incidence of tax widely spread, not visible to final consumer, easy to collect, small tax can raise large amount of revenue

---

Figure 9.10
The Value Added Tax

		No Taxes		With a 10% Value Added Tax	
		Value Added	Cumulative Value	Value Added with a 10% VAT	Cumulative Value with VAT
Step 1	Loggers fell trees and sell the timber to the mills for processing.	$1	$1	$1 + $.10 = $1.10	$1.10
Step 2	The mills cut the timber into blanks that will be used to make bats.	$1	$2	$1 + $.10 = $1.10	$2.20
Step 3	Bat manufacturers shape, paint, or varnish the bats and sell them to wholesalers.	$5	$7	$5 + $.50 = $5.50	$7.70
Step 4	The wholesalers sell the bats to retail outlets where consumers can buy them.	$1	$8	$1 + $.10 = $1.10	$8.80
Step 5	The retailers put the bats on the shelves and wait for the consumers.	$2	$10	$2 + $.20 = $2.20	$11.00
Step 6	The consumer buys the bat for:		$10.00		$11.00

The VAT tax is like a national sales tax added to each stage of production. As a result, it is built into the final price of a product and is less visible to consumers. It is widely used in Europe and is popular because even very low rates can raise very large amounts of revenue. **What are the advantages of a VAT?**

---

baseball bat, consumers may be vaguely aware that bat prices went from $10 to $11, but they might attribute this to a shortage of good wood, higher wages because of new union contracts, or some other increased cost of production. In short, consumers cannot be as vigilant about higher taxes when they cannot see them.

Another difficulty with the VAT is that it would compete with state sales taxes. Because the VAT is a federal tax, adding a VAT is like adding a federal sales tax to already-existing state taxes. If some of these bats were sold in Florida, would that state want to forgo its sales tax simply because a federal VAT was in place? Or would it want to impose its own state sales tax of 6 percent, raising the $11 price to $11.66?

The United States currently does not have a VAT, although it is widely used in Europe. Even so, a VAT will always be tempting because it can raise enormous sums of money. As long as the federal government is looking for additional sources of revenue, the VAT will be a likely choice. ☑

Tax Reform in the 1980s and 1990s

Tax reform has received much attention in recent years. The desire to lessen the tax burden on both individuals and businesses drove tax reforms in 1981 and 1986. In 1993 the need for additional government revenue drove tax reform.

Tax Reform in 1981

When President Reagan was elected in 1980, he believed that high taxes were the main deterrent to growth and prosperity. Accordingly, the Economic Recovery Tax Act of 1981 substantially reduced personal and business taxes. **1**

Before the Recovery Act, the individual tax code had 16 marginal tax brackets ranging from a low of 14 percent to a high of 70 percent. Compare this to the five brackets in **Figure 9.4**. The 1981 act lowered the marginal rates in all brackets, and capped the highest marginal tax wealthy individuals paid at 50 percent.

$ Free Enterprise Activity $

Tell students they are going to determine the economic impact of a tax in their community. Have each student choose a product and determine demand elasticity for that product. (Refer students to the three determinants of elasticity in Chapter 4, pages 96–98.)

Next, have students draw, on a single graph, a hypothetical supply and demand curve for their chosen product. Then have students assume a 10 percent tax has been placed on their product.

Finally, have students use their supply and demand curve to determine where the incidence of tax will fall. (*If demand is inelastic, burden of tax will fall on consumers; if demand is elastic, burden will be shared by producers and consumers.*) Conclude by pointing out that when a community decides to place a tax on a product, it must consider the elasticity of the product and who will ultimately pay the tax.

Businesses also got relief. One section of the act provided for **accelerated depreciation**, which allows companies to speed up the depreciation of their plants and equipment by taking larger depreciation charges right away. Because these charges are treated like a cost that is deducted from a firm's income before taxes are paid, accelerated depreciation saved corporations billions of dollars in taxes.

Another section of the act introduced the **investment tax credit** (ITC), which allowed a company to purchase tools and equipment and then receive a tax credit based on the amount spent. A company might purchase a $50,000 machine that qualified for a 10 percent, or $5,000, ITC credit. If the firm owed $12,000 in taxes, the credit reduced this amount to $7,000. ITCs were very popular because they gave businesses a way to directly reduce their tax bills.

Tax Reform in 1986

By the mid-1980s, people started feeling that the tax code favored the rich and powerful. In 1983 more than 3,000 millionaires paid no income taxes. In addition, tens of thousands of others had substantial incomes yet were not required to pay taxes.

Not only the wealthy legally avoided paying taxes. Many corporations did the same. Boeing, ITT, General Dynamics, Transamerica, First Executive Corporation, and Greyhound were profitable from 1981 to 1984. Instead of paying corporate income taxes, however, these companies applied tax losses in earlier years to current profits—and then collected tax refunds during each of those four years.

In 1986 Congress passed the most sweeping tax reform act since income taxes were enacted in 1913. First, it ended the traditionally progressive individual income tax structure by reducing the 16 marginal tax brackets to two brackets (essentially the 15 percent and

28 percent brackets in Figure 9.4). The law also added a 5 percent **surcharge**—or additional tax above and beyond the base rate.

The law also made it difficult for the very rich to avoid taxes altogether. The **alternative minimum tax**, the personal income rate that applies whenever the amount of taxes paid falls below some designated level, was strengthened. Under this provision, people had to pay a minimum tax of 20 percent, regardless of other circumstances or loopholes in the tax code. Finally, the reform act shifted about $120 billion of taxes from individuals to corporations over a 5-year period by removing a number of tax breaks for business.

Tax Reform in 1993

As the United States entered the 1990s, the impact of 10 years of tax cuts was beginning to show. Government spending was growing faster than revenues, and the government had borrow more.

The Omnibus Budget Reconciliation Act of 1993 was driven more by the need for the government to balance its budget than to overhaul the tax brackets. It combined future spending cuts with tax hikes and affected government revenue in several ways. 2

The law added the two top marginal tax brackets of 36 and 39.6 percent shown in Figure 9.4. The law also removed the $135,000 cap on medicare taxes. Those individuals with more than $135,000 had paid no additional medicare taxes, making it very regressive. The medicare tax is now proportional.

The tax provisions of the Omnibus Budget Reconciliation Act were loosely modeled on the ability-to-pay principle of taxation. Except for an increase in the gasoline tax and the way some Social Security receipts were taxed, the law had almost no direct impact on single individuals earning less than $115,000 or couples earning less than $140,000.

Checking Understanding

1. Why were taxes lowered in 1981?
2. Why did government leaders think more taxes were needed in 1993?

Applying Economic Concepts

☑ **Taxation** Many economists who favor a VAT point out that it taxes consumption rather than income. They believe the VAT would encourage Americans to save—and thus avoid the tax. More saving would free money for capital investment.

ASSESS

Check for Understanding

Assign Section 4 Review as homework or an in-class activity.

 Use **Chapter Challenger Interactive Review Software** to review Section 4.

MEETING LESSON OBJECTIVES

Each objective below is tested by the questions that follow it in parentheses.

1. **Explain** what is meant by the incidence of a tax. **(1, 2)**
2. **Debate** the advantages and disadvantages of the value added tax. **(3, 6)**
3. **Describe** the major tax reforms since 1980. **(4, 5)**

Evaluate

🗀 🗀 Assign the Section 4 Quiz in the TCR or use the *Economics: Principles and Practices* Testmaker.

❓ DID YOU KNOW

Jean-Baptiste Colbert described taxation as "the art of [plucking] the goose without making it squawk."

ANSWERS

1. Reagan believed that high taxes were the main deterrent to growth and prosperity.
2. The government needed to balance its budget.

Extending the Content

Tax Reform Has Its Consequences Until 1989 local governments in Great Britain had only one source of revenue—the ability-to-pay-based property tax on residential and business property. The Conservative Party government under the leadership of Prime Minister Margaret Thatcher objected to the property tax and replaced it with a flat rate community charge—or poll tax—which was levied on all adults, regardless of income or wealth. The poll tax, which averaged £ 363 (nearly $700) in its first year alone, was a public relations disaster that ultimately contributed to Margaret Thatcher's downfall.

232

Reteach

Direct students to write sentences that summarize the main ideas of each subsection in Section 4. Have students read and compare their sentences.

📁 📁 Have students complete Reteaching Activity 9. Spanish Reteaching Activities also are available in the Spanish Resources Binder.

Enrich

Have students poll family members, neighbors, and friends on what they think are the major tax issues of the day. Ask students to present their findings and collate the poll results in a class report.

📁 Have students complete Enrichment Activity 9.

CLOSE

Have students discuss the following: If there was one thing you could change in the tax laws, what would it be? Why?

 VISUAL INSTRUCTION

To what colonial battle cry is this taxpayer referring? *(no taxation without representation)*

Answer to Caption:
the wealthiest Americans

Taxation *Some people think any tax is too high, but this viewpoint is not very realistic.* **Who was affected most by tax reform in 1993?**

Tax Reform in 1997

In 1997 the largest tax reduction since the Economic Recovery Tax Act of 1981 was passed. The law was known as the Taxpayer Relief Act of 1997, and the forces that created it were both economic and political.

On the economic side, the government found itself with unexpectedly high tax revenues in 1997. The higher marginal tax brackets introduced in 1993, along with the closure of some tax loopholes, meant that individuals and corporations paid more taxes than before. In addition, unexpectedly strong economic growth resulted in an increased number of people and businesses paying taxes.

On the political side, the balance of power had dramatically shifted in the 1996 elections. Both political parties felt they had commitments to fulfill to the people who voted them into office. For many Republicans, this meant a tax break for individuals with long-term investments in stocks, bonds, and other assets. The tax on capital gains—profits made from the sale of an asset held for 18 months—was reduced

from 28 to 20 percent. Also, profits up to $500,000 from the sale of a home for married couples, or $250,000 for a single individual, were exempt from taxes. Some inheritance taxes were also lowered, which tended to favor the well-to-do.

The tax reductions reflected the "family-friendly" theme of the 1996 elections. Specifically, tax credits of $500 per child and other deductions for educational expenses were included in the legislation. The marginal tax brackets in Figure 9.4 remained unchanged, however, which resulted in a decidedly unbalanced distribution of tax cuts. For example, individuals who had neither children nor valuable assets such as houses, stocks, or bonds received virtually no benefit from the tax reductions.

In the end, an analysis by the Treasury Department determined that nearly half of the benefits went to the top 20 percent of wage earners. The lowest 20 percent of wage earners received less than 1 percent of the tax reductions. With all its categories, the 1997 federal tax law became the most complicated in years.

SECTION 4 REVIEW

Reviewing Terms and Facts

1. **Define** incidence of a tax, value added tax, accelerated depreciation, investment tax credit, surcharge, alternative minimum tax.
2. **Provide** an example of how the incidence of a tax can be shifted.
3. **Explain** the main difference between the VAT and a national sales tax.

4. **Describe** three major tax reform bills since 1980.

Critical Thinking

5. **Identifying Alternatives** Explain how you would recommend changes in the federal tax code if it were to be revised again in the near future.

Applying Economic Concepts

6. **Value Added Tax** Most people do not object to excise taxes—but mostly because they know little about them. How does this assertion apply to characteristics of the VAT?

Answers to SECTION 4 REVIEW

1. Vocabulary are defined in the Glossary.

2. Examples will vary. Possible example: City imposes tax on utility company; utility company raises rates, thus passing on tax to consumers.

3. VAT levied on producers at every stage of production process; sales tax added at point of sale.

4. Economic Recovery Tax Act of 1981, which substantially reduced business and personal taxes; tax reform act of 1986, which made sweeping changes in the tax structure, especially the re-

duction of number of marginal tax brackets from 15 to 2; Omnibus Budget Reconciliation Act of 1993, which raised taxes, especially on the wealthy; Taxpayer Relief Act of 1997, which reduced taxes on the wealthy

5. Answers will vary.

6. Most students will agree that the assertion applies to VAT, pointing out that because VAT is added at each stage of production, it is largely "invisible" to consumers.

ECONOMICS IN ACTION

The American Tax System

Setting Up the Video

With your classmates, view "The American Tax System" on the videodisc *Economics in Action.* The video focuses on different types of taxes collected by state and federal governments. It explains that taxes may be progressive, proportional, or regressive. News segments describe President Clinton's 1993 economic package, discuss user taxes, and differentiate between value added taxes and sales taxes.

Chapter 13
Disc 1, Side 2

View the video by scanning the bar code or by entering the chapter number on your keypad and pressing Search. (Also available in VHS format.)

Hands-On Activity

Contact your local government to obtain a copy of your community's budget. Analyze the amount and types of revenues received from citizens in your county, city, or town. Classify each type of revenue as progressive, proportional, or regressive. Place your findings in a chart entitled "Local Revenues." Share your chart with the rest of the class.

SURFING THE "NET"

Tax Reform

Major tax revision laws have gone into effect since 1980. The Economic Recovery Tax Act of 1981 provided for a substantial reduction in individual and corporate tax rates. The 1986 tax reform law closed some loopholes opened in 1981 and made the individual tax code more proportional. The Omnibus Budget Reconciliation Act of 1993 added marginal tax brackets to the individual tax code, thereby restoring the progressive nature of the tax. Use the Internet to see how tax reform has been addressed since 1993.

Getting There

1. Use a search engine. Type in the words *tax reform*.
2. Next, enter words like the following to focus your search: *individual tax code, capital gains, inheritance tax,* and *sales tax*.
3. The search engine will provide you with a number of links to follow. Links are "pointers" to different sites on the Internet and often appear as blue, underlined words.

What to Do When You Are There

Click on the links to navigate through the pages of information. Gather your findings. Using the findings, create a brochure describing recent tax reforms. Include information from your research, sources for further readings, and graphics to illustrate the brochure.

233

MULTIMEDIA ACTIVITIES

GLENCOE TECHNOLOGY

NIGHTLY BUSINESS REPORT

Economics in Action

Chapter 13
Disc 1, Side 2
Title: *The American Tax System*

If you do not have access to a videodisc player, the **Economic in Action** programs are also available in VHS.

INTERNET SITES

The following are possible sites for completing the "Net" activities:

This Week Online (Tax News & Views)
http://www.dtonline.com/index.htm

Joint Economic Committee
http://www.senate.gov/~jec/

Not on the "Net"...

If students have limited or no access to the Internet, have them complete the activity "Tax Reform" by using the computerized card catalog at the school or local library. At the s: prompt, students should type in *tax code* or *The Federal Budget*. They should then use the call numbers to find the books and other resources they need to complete their research.

INTERNET ADDRESS BOOK

Internet addresses that you find useful can be noted in the space below for quick reference.

_____   _____
_____   _____
_____   _____
_____   _____
_____   _____

Answers

Reviewing Key Terms

1. f	8. k
2. j	9. m
3. h	10. e
4. i	11. c
5. l	12. a
6. d	13. b
7. g	

Reviewing the Facts

1. A heavy tax can be imposed on a product to limit consumption of that product.

2. equity—taxes should be just and impartial; simplicity—tax laws should be easily understood; efficiency—taxes should be relatively easy to administer

3. benefit principle, ability-to-pay principle

4. proportional tax—imposes same tax rate on everyone, regardless of income; progressive tax—imposes higher tax rate on those with higher incomes; regressive tax—imposes a higher tax rate on low incomes

5. Individual income tax is a progressive tax on people's earnings. It is usually collected through payroll withholding system and sent directly to government.

6. Social Security taxes, medicare

7. Corporate income tax is tax corporation pays on its profits.

234

Reviewing Key Terms

Write the letter of the key term that best matches each definition below.

a. ability-to-pay principle
b. corporate income tax
c. estate tax
d. excise tax
e. FICA
f. indexing
g. individual income tax
h. progressive tax
i. proportional tax
j. regressive tax
k. sales tax
l. sin tax
m. VAT

1. annual adjustment of tax brackets to keep pace with inflation
2. average tax per dollar decreases as taxable income increases
3. average tax per dollar increases as taxable income increases
4. average tax per dollar unchanged as taxable income rises
5. designed to discourage consumption of socially undesirable goods or services
6. tax on the manufacture or sale of certain items
7. largest source of revenue for the federal government
8. large source of revenue for state governments
9. national sales tax on value added at each stage of production
10. Social Security and medicare taxes
11. tax on the transfer of property when a person dies
12. tax paid by those who can most afford to pay
13. third largest source of income for the federal government

Reviewing the Facts

SECTION 1 (*pages 210–215*)
1. **Describe** how taxes can be used to affect people's behavior.
2. **Explain** the three criteria used to evaluate taxes.
3. **Name** the two principles of taxation.
4. **Compare** the three types of taxes.

SECTION 2 (*pages 216–220*)
5. **Describe** the main features of the individual income tax.
6. **Identify** the two components of FICA.
7. **Describe** the corporate income tax.
8. **Distinguish** between excise taxes, estate and gift taxes, and customs duties.

SECTION 3 (*pages 222–226*)
9. **Identify** the main sources of revenue for state governments.
10. **List** the main sources of revenue for local governments.
11. **Identify** the main types of taxes that are normally withheld from a worker's paycheck.

SECTION 4 (*pages 228–232*)
12. **Illustrate**, using supply and demand curves, how the incidence of a tax can be shifted.
13. **List** the advantages and disadvantages of a VAT.
14. **Identify** the four major tax reform bills enacted since 1980.

Critical Thinking

1. **Evaluating Information** Explain how the federal income tax does or does not satisfy each of the three criteria for taxes. Give examples to support your explanations.
2. **Synthesizing Information** If you were an elected official who wanted to increase tax revenues, which of the following would you prefer to use—individual income, sales, property, corporate income, user fees, or a VAT? Provide reasons for your decision.

Applying Economic Concepts

1. **User Fees** The following quote appeared in President George Bush's *1990 Budget of the United States:*

   A fee on recreational boaters who use the navigable waters of the United States is proposed. This largely high-income group receives substantial benefit

---

8. excise taxes—taxes on manufacture or sale of certain items; estate taxes—levied on transfer of property when person dies; gift taxes—levied on donations of money or wealth; customs duties—levied on goods brought in from other countries

9. sales taxes, intergovernmental revenues, individual income taxes, employee retirement contributions

10. intergovernmental revenues, property taxes, utilities and liquor stores, sales taxes

11. federal income tax, state income tax, city income

tax, FICA taxes

12. Refer students to Figure 9.9 before they answer this question.

13. Advantages: hard to avoid, incidence of tax widely spread, not visible to final consumer, easy to collect, small tax can raise large amount of revenue; disadvantages: invisible to consumers, might compete with state sales taxes.

14. Economic Recovery Tax Act of 1981, tax reform law of 1986, Omnibus Budget Reconciliation Act of 1993, Taxpayer Relief Act of 1997

from Coast Guard activities. Commercial boaters would be assessed similar fees and major shipping companies would share licensing and inspection costs.

In your own words, prepare a rationale for a user fee that you think should be enacted.

2. **Sales Taxes** Some people object to state and local governments imposing sales and property taxes. What would you say to these people in defense of the two taxes?

Reinforcing Skills

DISTINGUISHING FACT FROM OPINION

Read the following account of the effects of President Clinton's 1993 tax package. Then write three statements of fact and three statements of opinion that are found in this passage.

President Clinton's income-tax increase will squeeze only the wealthiest taxpayers. But the unlucky few will find it hard to escape the higher taxes. That won't stop them from trying. Wealthy taxpayers—those with $250,000 or more in taxable income—will be taxed at a top rate of 39.6%, up from 31% in 1992. So they are frantically looking for ways to shelter income.

"I've never seen people so frightened," said a financial adviser. "They want whatever will help them avoid taxes." Most of the once-loved loopholes that sheltered earned income are gone, erased by the 1986 tax-reform law.

So what's a high-salary executive to do? Anything that will defer salary or bonuses into the future when he or she might be in a lower tax bracket at retirement or tax rates might be lower.

—Janet L. Fix, *USA TODAY*, August 16, 1993

	Ability-to-Pay Principle	**Benefit Principle**
Regressive		
Proportional		
Progressive		

Individual Activity

Make a list of five taxes, charges, or user fees that you pay in your community. Draw a matrix like the one below and classify each of your five taxes in the appropriate places.

Cooperative Learning Activity

Working in groups of three, prepare three questions to be included on a survey about tax issues. Each question should be worded so that it can be answered by *yes*, *no*, or *no comment*. Evaluate the questions as a class, then poll community members about the issues. Discuss the responses you received.

Technology Activity
Building a Database

In the **Journal Writing** activity on page 209, you were asked to classify taxes you read or heard about into three categories: Federal, State, and Local Taxes. Create a database that has a record for each of the articles you used to find your information. Each record should have a separate field for the following: title, author, publication source, year of publication, tax category (Federal, State, Local), criteria of taxation (equity, simplicity, efficiency), and a brief article summary.

Using your computer's software, sort the records by tax category (Federal, State, Local). Create a hard copy of this report. Share your database with the rest of the class.

Critical Thinking

1. Answers may vary. Some students might argue that the tax is equitable because it is progressive. Others may argue that it is not equitable because there are so many exemptions and other loopholes. Some may argue that it is relatively simple for most people because the tax is withheld from the paychecks and they have to file tax documents once a year. Others may say that because people need booklets and instructions from the IRS to fill out tax forms, it is hardly simple. Some might argue that it is efficient because it is relatively simple to administer and raises considerable revenue. Others may assert that a host of bureaucrats needed to review tax forms makes the tax inefficient.

2. Answers will vary. Suggest that students consider the criteria and principles of taxation when developing their answers.

Applying Economic Concepts

1. Answers may vary. User fees students might suggest include entry fees to national parks and auto sticker and license fees for road repairs.

2. Answers may vary. Students might point out that the sales tax is relatively cheap to administer and, because it applies to so many consumers, raises huge amounts of revenue. They may also point out that many public services enable people to maintain and improve the value of their property, so the value of that property should be subject to tax.

Reinforcing Skills

Fact: (1) President Clinton's income-tax increase will squeeze only the wealthiest taxpayers. (2) Wealthy taxpayers will be taxed at a top rate of 39.6%. (3) Most of the once-loved loopholes that sheltered income are gone. **Opinion:** (1) That won't stop them from trying. (2) I've never seen people so frightened. (3) Anything that will defer salary or bonuses into the future. . . .

BONUS TEST QUESTION

Ask students to explain how the user fee illustrates the benefit principle of taxation. *(Those who benefit from the goods and services provided pay for those goods and services. Also, the greater the benefit received—or the greater the amount of goods and services consumed—the greater the contribution in fees.)*

CHAPTER ORGANIZER

Daily Objectives	Reproducible Resources	Multimedia Resources
Section 1 **The Economics of Government Spending** 1. **Explain** why and how government expenditures have grown since the 1940s. 2. **Describe** two kinds of government expenditures. 3. **Describe** how government spending impacts the economy.	📁 Reproducible Lesson Plan 10-1 📁 Guided Reading Activity 10-1 📁 Cooperative Learning Activity 17 📁 Consumer Application Activities 4, 17, 18 📁 Math Practice for Economics 15 📁 Free Enterprise Activity 17 📁 Primary and Secondary Source Reading 17 📁 Performance Assessment Activity 15 📁 Section Quiz 10-1*	🔦 Focus Activity Transparency 67 💿 Vocabulary PuzzleMaker 💿 Chapter Challenger Interactive Review Software 💿 Testmaker 📀 MindJogger Videoquiz
Section 2 **Federal Government Expenditures** 1. **Explain** how the federal budget is established. 2. **Describe** the major components of the federal budget.	📁 Reproducible Lesson Plan 10-2 📁 Guided Reading Activity 10-2 📁 Reinforcing Economic Skill 10 📁 Section Quiz 10-2*	🔦 Focus Activity Transparency 74 💿 Vocabulary PuzzleMaker 💿 Chapter Challenger Interactive Review Software 💿 Testmaker 📀 NBR's Economics in Action Video Program
Section 3 **State and Local Government Expenditures** 1. **Explain** how state and local governments approve spending. 2. **Identify** the major categories of state government expenditures. 3. **Identify** the major categories of local government expenditures.	📁 Reproducible Lesson Plan 10-3 📁 Guided Reading Activity 10-3 📁 Section Quiz 10-3*	🔦 Focus Activity Transparency 75 💿 Vocabulary PuzzleMaker 💿 Chapter Challenger Interactive Review Software 💿 Testmaker 📀 NBR's Economics in Action Video Program
Section 4 **Federal Deficits and the National Debt** 1. **Explain** how the federal deficit is related to the federal debt. 2. **Relate** the impact of the federal debt on the economy. 3. **Describe** recent attempts to control the federal deficit.	📁 Reproducible Lesson Plan 10-4 📁 Guided Reading Activity 10-4 📁 Section Quiz 10-4*	🔦 Focus Activity Transparency 70 💿 Vocabulary PuzzleMaker 💿 Chapter Challenger Interactive Review Software 💿 Testmaker 📀 NBR's Economics in Action Video Program
Chapter Review and Evaluation	📁 Enrichment Activity 10 📁 Reteaching Activity 10* 📁 Economic Vocabulary Activity 10* 📁 Chapter 10 Test, Forms A and B	🎧 Chapter Digests Audiocassette Activities and Tests* 💿 Testmaker 📀 MindJogger Videoquiz

Also available in Spanish

 Blackline Master   Transparency   CD-ROM   Software   Videodisc   Audiocassette

🕐 OUT OF TIME? Assign the Chapter 10 Digest Audiocassette and the corresponding Chapter Digest activities and tests.

National Council
on Economic Education

THE **Economics** America AND **Economics** International PROGRAMS

VOLUNTARY NATIONAL CONTENT STANDARDS IN ECONOMICS
Emphasized in Chapter 10

Content Standard 16 *Students will understand that:*
There is an economic role for government to play in a market economy whenever the benefits of a government policy outweigh its costs. Governments often provide for national defense, address environmental concerns, define and protect property rights, and attempt to make markets more competitive. Most government policies also redistribute income.

Content Standard 20 *Students will understand that:*
Federal government budgetary policy and the Federal Reserve System's monetary policy influence the overall levels of employment, output, and prices.

Economics America *Resources Available From NCEE*

- *Capstone: The Nation's High School Economics Course*
- *Civics and Government: Focus on Economics*
- *Focus: High School Economics*
- *Personal Decision Making: Focus on Economics*
- *United States History: Eyes on the Economy, Vol. II*

To order these materials, or to contact your state Council on Economic Education about workshops and programs, call 1-800-338-1192 or visit http://www.nationalcouncil.org.

PERFORMANCE ASSESSMENT

The following chapter projects may be assigned at the beginning of the chapter and used for performance assessment.

Multicultural Heritage Point out that mandatory spending and entitlements—government benefits to which recipients have legally enforceable rights—make up about two-thirds of government spending. More than 300 Native American groups in 48 contiguous states and a number of Inuit communities in Alaska are among the recipients of these entitlements. The funds are used to provide such services as health, education, and welfare. These benefits, in part, are a form of compensation for past treaty violations and land seizures. Some benefits, however, were mandated by the Indian Self-Determination Act of 1975. Direct one group of students to investigate the specific benefits this measure provides. Direct a second group to research additional entitlements that are targeted to benefit other racial or ethnic groups. Have students present their findings.

Cooperative Learning Organize students into three groups and assign one of the levels of government—federal, state, or local—to each group. Tell groups that their task is to develop a special 10–page edition of a current affairs magazine titled: "How Government Spends Its Revenues." Suggest that they include in their magazines a "message from the editor," a table of contents, and several 2–page articles on important programs or funding issues for their assigned level of government. They should also create an eye-catching cover design that illustrates the main theme of the articles in the magazine. Encourage students to share among themselves the various tasks involved in developing the magazine. Have groups display their magazines.

ADDITIONAL RESOURCES

Readings for the Student

Opposing Viewpoints: Economics in America. San Diego, CA: Greenhaven Press, 1992. Includes a debate on the seriousness of the budget deficit.

Dushkin Annual Editions: Economics. Guilford, CT: Dushkin Publishing Group, 1996. Anthology of articles about current state and local government issues, including finances and funding.

Readings for the Teacher

Economic Report of the President. Washington, DC: Government Printing Office, published annually. Contains information on sources of revenue, spending programs, and the economic goals of the President.

Multimedia

Decisions Decisions: The Budget Process. Tom Snyder Productions, Inc., 80 Coolidge Hill Road, Watertown, MA 02172. MacIntosh, DOS. Students take part in congressional efforts to produce a balanced budget.

Government: How It Spends. Instructional Video, P.O. Box 21, Maumee, OH 43537. Video, 30 min. Explores how the various levels of government get and spend revenues.

The Deficit Game: Money and Society—The MacNeil/Lehrer Economic Reports. Cambridge Studies/Social Studies School Service. VHS video, simulation, guide, 13 min. Long-term effects of budget deficit are explored.

Uncle Sam's Budget Balancer. Banner Blue/Social Studies School Service, 10200 Jefferson Boulevard, P.O. Box 802, Culver City, CA 90232–0802. DOS. Computer program that allows students to explore their own ideas for reducing the federal deficit.

Chapter Overview

Chapter 10 presents the ways in which government spends revenues. **Section 1** gives background information on the growth of government spending and discusses the impact of government expenditures on the economy. **Section 2** describes the process for establishing the federal budget and the major spending categories. **Section 3** outlines state and local government spending. **Section 4** analyzes the relationship between the federal deficit and federal debt and the economic impact of the federal debt.

GLENCOE TECHNOLOGY

VIDEODISC
MindJogger Videoquiz

Use MindJogger to preview the Chapter 10 content.

 Chapter 10
Disc 2, Side A

Also available in VHS.

interNET CONNECTION

Resources for Chapter 10 on the World Wide Web*

National Council on Economic Education
http://www.nationalcouncil.org/

Office of Management and Budget
http://www.access.gpo.gov/omb/

The National Budget Simulation
http://garnet.berkeley.edu:3333/budget.html

National Priorities Project
http://www.natprior.org/

*Sites subject to change.

The construction of interstate highways is a joint federal-state government expenditure.

Extra Credit Project

Ask students to make a weekly budget, noting expected income, categories into which these funds should be divided, the proposed spending on each category, and the actual spending. Have them report if they ran a deficit or surplus, and how they plan to adjust spending in the future.

CHAPTER 10

Government Spending

SECTION 1
The Economics of Government Spending

SECTION 2
Federal Government Expenditures

SECTION 3
State and Local Government Expenditures

SECTION 4
Federal Deficits and the National Debt

CHAPTER PREVIEW

People to Know

• Janet Yellen
• Law Enforcement Officer

Applying Economic Concepts to Your Life

Budget Deficit If you borrow money so that you can spend more than you earn, you run a deficit. When the government spends more than it collects, we say that a *budget deficit* has occurred.

> **Journal Writing**
>
> For one week, write in your journal all government expenditures that you hear about on television or read about in the newspaper. Classify your journal entries into three categories: Federal, State, and Local Government Expenditures.

Economic Portfolio

Suggest that, as students make their **Journal Writing** entries, they note if the expenditures represent transfer payments or the purchase of goods or services.

Key to Ability Levels — Teaching strategies have been coded for varying learning styles and abilities:
L1 - Basic (activities for all students)   **L2 - Average** (activities for average to above-average students)
L3 - Challenging (activities for above-average students)   **LEP - Limited English Proficiency**

237

FOCUS

Section Objectives

1. Explain why and how government expenditures have grown since the 1940s.

2. Describe two kinds of government expenditures.

3. Describe how government spending impacts the economy.

Bellringer

Prior to taking roll at the beginning of the class period, display Focus Activity Transparency 67.

Motivational Activity

Discuss students' responses to the activity sheet that accompanies Transparency 67.

Preteaching Vocabulary

Ask students to write in their own words definitions of the key terms. **LEP**

Use the **Vocabulary PuzzleMaker** to create crossword and word search puzzles.

TEACH

Guided Practice

L2 **Applying Ideas** Write the following headings on the chalkboard: *Allocation of Resources, Distribution of Income,* and *Competition with the Private Sector.* Call on volunteers to provide examples of how government spending produces each of the effects listed on the board. Note their responses on the chalkboard. Have students use this information to write a paragraph on the impact of government spending on the economy.

The Economics of Government Spending

Section Preview

Objectives

After studying this section, you will be able to:

1. **Explain** why and how government expenditures have grown since the 1940s.

2. **Describe** two kinds of government expenditures.

3. **Describe** how government spending impacts the economy.

Key Terms

per capita, public sector, private sector, transfer payment, grant-in-aid, distribution of income

Applying Economic Concepts

Transfer Payments If someone you know has been unemployed, this person may have received a *transfer payment*—a payment for which the government receives neither goods nor services in return. In this case, the transfer payment is an unemployment check. Transfer payments are one of the tools used to promote the goal of economic security.

If all levels of government and all tasks assigned to them are considered, it becomes clear that governments spend huge sums on goods, services, transfer payments, and other programs.

Government Spending in Perspective

In 1997, total expenditures by federal, state, and local governments collectively amounted to nearly $2.6 trillion—a number almost beyond comprehension! On a **per capita**, or per person, basis, this equaled a combined government expenditure of $9,610 for every man, woman, and child in the United States. Because American taxpayers fund these expenditures, the growth of government spending concerns everyone.

Historical Growth

Spending in the public sector did not begin to rise significantly until the 1940s. This increase occurred for two major reasons. The first was the huge amount of spending required because of World War II. The second was the change in public opinion that gave government a larger role in everyday economic affairs.

As the United States emerged from the Great Depression, government was called upon to regulate banks, public utilities, and many other activities. It also became involved with its citizens' economic welfare. Minimum wage laws, Social Security, welfare programs, education, highways, and transportation all began to receive greater attention.

Figure 10.1 shows the historical growth of government expenditures for all three levels of government. The spending has been adjusted for inflation by using constant dollars, and it is shown on a per capita basis to compensate for the growth in population during that period.

How Much Is Too Much?

Over time, many Americans accepted these increased government expenditures as the inevitable consequence of social and cultural change. Still, some people question how many goods and services government should provide—and, therefore, how many expenditures it should assume. Some people want more roads, schools, and welfare programs, while others want fewer. People also disagree on which services the federal government should provide and which state and local governments should provide.

People will always debate the role of government in society. However, we should remember that one of the purposes of government is to promote the broad social and economic goals of its people. In so doing, we also need to recognize that it is important for the benefits of a government policy to outweigh its costs.

Classroom Resources for SECTION 1

- Reproducible Lesson Plan 10-1
- Guided Reading Activity 10-1
- Cooperative Learning Activity 17
- Consumer Application Activities 4, 17, 18
- Math Practice for Economics 15
- Free Enterprise Activity 17
- Primary and Secondary Source Reading 17
- Performance Assessment Activity 15

- Section Quiz 10-1
- Spanish Section Quiz 10-1
- Focus Activity Transparency 67
- Testmaker
- Vocabulary PuzzleMaker
- Chapter Challenger Interactive Review Software
- MindJogger Videoquiz

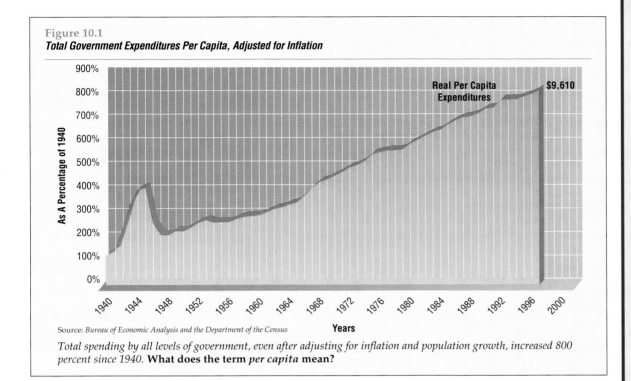

Figure 10.1
Total Government Expenditures Per Capita, Adjusted for Inflation

Real Per Capita Expenditures $9,610

As A Percentage of 1940

Years

Source: *Bureau of Economic Analysis and the Department of the Census*

Total spending by all levels of government, even after adjusting for inflation and population growth, increased 800 percent since 1940. **What does the term *per capita* mean?**

📋 **Cooperative Learning**
Assign Cooperative Learning Activity 17.

Independent Practice

📋 **Guided Reading** Assign Guided Reading Activity for Section 1. **LEP**

L1 Constructing a Graph
Have students look up the total amounts of government spending from 1965 to the present in the *Economic Report of the President*. Have them make a line graph of the information and compare their graphs to Figure 10.1. **LEP**

📋 **Consumer Application**
Assign Consumer Application Activities 4, 17, and 18.

📋 **Math Practice** Assign Math Practice for Economics 15.

VISUAL INSTRUCTION

Point out that the small "bump" in government expenditures in the early 1950s was the result of increased spending on the Korean War.

Answer to Caption:
public: federal, state, and local governments; private: private individuals and businesses

Two Kinds of Spending

Federal, state, and local governments make up the **public sector** of the economy. This sector buys its goods and services from private individuals and businesses, which make up the **private sector** of the economy.

In general, government makes two broad kinds of expenditures. The first is for the purchase of goods and services. The second is in the form of payments to disadvantaged Americans and other designated groups. Public sector spending is very much like that of individuals and businesses. In both cases, resources are scarce and must be used efficiently.

Goods and Services

The government buys many goods, such as tanks for the army, planes for the air force, ships for the navy, and space shuttles. The government also needs office buildings, land for parks, and capital goods for schools and laboratories. In addition, it buys paper

clips and paper, computers, desks, filing cabinets, chairs, soap, and gasoline.

Government also hires people to work in its agencies and staff the military. Payments for these services include the wages and salaries paid to all government employees, including the President, governors, public school teachers, and mayors.

Many of the goods and services government provides are public goods—items consumed collectively rather than by single individuals. Public goods include such items as highways, national defense, schools, and police and fire protection.

Transfer Payments

The second kind of government expenditure is a **transfer payment**—a payment for which the government receives neither goods nor services in return. Transfer payments to individuals include Social Security, welfare, unemployment compensation, and aid to

CHAPTER 10: *Government Spending* **239**

Meeting Special Needs

Reading Disability Occasionally, despite all efforts by a student to learn decoding skills, significant problems remain. Reading comprehension is greatly influenced by these weaker skills. The effort needed to comprehend is overshadowed by the energy expended in decoding. By the time the student finishes a paragraph, he or she may have

forgotten the beginning. For these students who have very poor reading skills, have a good reader tape-record Section 1 so the student can listen while he or she follows along in the text. Remind students to look at all the photos and graphs in the section.

📁 **Free Enterprise** Assign Free Enterprise Activity 17.

📁 **Readings** Assign Primary and Secondary Source Reading 17.

📁 **Performance Assessment** Assign Performance Assessment Activity 15.

ASSESS

Check for Understanding

Assign Section 1 Review as homework or an in-class activity.

MEETING LESSON OBJECTIVES

Each objective below is tested by the questions that follow it in parentheses.

1. **Explain** why and how government expenditures have grown since the 1940s. **(2, 5)**

2. **Describe** two kinds of government expenditures. **(1, 3, 6)**

3. **Describe** how government spending impacts the economy. **(4)**

VISUAL INSTRUCTION

Have students express in the terms of opportunity costs a recent government expenditure in the community.

Answer to Caption:

Transfer payments directly affect low-income people. A factory winning or losing a government contract can affect the incomes of workers throughout the community where the factory is located.

---

people with handicapping conditions. People receive these payments solely because they need assistance.

A transfer payment one level of government makes to another is known as a **grant-in-aid**. Interstate highway construction programs are an example. The federal government grants money to cover the major part of the cost, while the states through which the highways will be built pay the rest. The construction of new public schools also can be financed through grants-in-aid.

Transfer payments also include subsidies—payments made to individuals or entire industries to encourage or protect a certain economic activity. Farmers, for example, often are paid subsidies to stabilize their incomes. In the past, airlines also received subsidies.

Impact of Government Spending

The issue of government spending is complex. The size of the public sector gives it the potential to impact people's daily lives in many ways. Several important effects of government spending are examined below.

Allocation of Resources

Government spending decisions directly affect the allocation of resources. If the government decides to spend its revenues on missile systems in rural areas rather than on social welfare programs in urban areas, economic activity is stimulated in rural areas as resources are shifted there.

The allocation of resources can be affected indirectly, too. In agriculture, the decision to support the prices of milk, grains, tobacco, or peanuts keeps the factors of production working in those industries.

Resource Allocation
The opportunity cost of the government's funding of road construction is the schools, parks, and other facilities that do not receive the funds. **How does government spending affect the distribution of income?**

FRANK AND ERNEST ©by Bob Thaves

YOUR TAX DOLLARS AND A WHOLE LOT OF BORROWED MONEY AT WORK

THAVES 9-14

Without government support, some land would become idle, some workers would have to find new jobs, and some capital would have to be used for other purposes.

Distribution of Income

Government spending also impacts the economy by affecting the **distribution of income**, or the way in which income is allocated to families, individuals, or other designated groups in the economy. The incomes

---

💲 Free Enterprise Activity 💲

Government spending is a frequent and critical target of conversation on the street and in the classroom. Ask students to write down three public goods and/or services for which they believe taxes should *not* be used. In a follow-up discussion, have students present and explain their choices. Note on the chalkboard the items most often selected. Then have students discuss the following: Would the items listed be better produced by the private sector? Why or why not?

Grants-in-Aid *Although public education is primarily a local government expenditure, grants-in-aid often help finance the construction of new public schools.* **What is a grant-in-aid?**

Use **Chapter Challenger Interactive Review Software** to review Section 1.

Evaluate

Assign the Section 1 Quiz in the TCR or use the *Economics: Principles and Practices* Testmaker to create a customized quiz. Spanish Section Quizzes also are available in the Spanish Resources Binder.

Reteach

Have students outline the section by noting the main ideas of each subsection. Encourage students to present and compare their outlines.

Enrich

Have students investigate and write a report on the changes in society—population growth, changes in employment, transportation, and communications, for example—that have led to increased government spending.

CLOSE

Ask students to discuss the economic impact of government spending in their community. For example, how has spending by the school board affected their school?

 VISUAL INSTRUCTION

Ask students to identify another example of a grant-in-aid. *(construction of interstate highways)*

Answer to Caption:

grant by federal government to cover part of cost of project; rest of cost covered by other levels of government

of poor people, for example, can be directly affected by increasing or decreasing transfer payments.

Incomes are also indirectly affected when the government decides where to make expenditures. The decision to buy fighter planes from one factory rather than from another impacts the communities near both factories. Many businesses not linked to either company will feel the effects when workers are laid off or get new jobs and alter their spending habits.

The military base closings in the 1990s had serious implications for income distribution. Communities around the military installations faced devastating short-term reductions in incomes.

Competition With the Private Sector

When the government produces goods and services, it often competes with producers in the private sector. When the government provides national defense or a system of justice, it faces no competition. This is not always the case, however.

In regard to health care, the government runs a system of hospitals for military veterans. Taxpayer dollars fund these facilities, which compete with private-sector hospitals that offer similar services. Many county and city health departments offer free inoculations and other services to their citizens. These also compete with private physicians and health clinics.

SECTION 1 REVIEW

Reviewing Terms and Facts

1. **Define** per capita, public sector, private sector, transfer payment, grant-in-aid, distribution of income.
2. **Describe** the per capita growth in government spending since 1940.
3. **List** two kinds of government spending.
4. **Identify** three ways that government spending may impact the economy.

Critical Thinking

5. **Checking Consistency** The text states that most people agree that government is getting too expensive. Interview five people to see if they agree with this statement.

Applying Economic Concepts

6. **Transfer Payments** Do you think that transfer payments, such as unemployment compensation, are a successful or unsuccessful way to accomplish the goal of economic security? Defend your answer.

Answers to SECTION 1 REVIEW

1. All vocabulary words are defined in the Glossary.

2. Per capita government spending grew dramatically during World War II and then fell back after the war. Since that time it has grown significantly. Even when adjusted for inflation, in 1997 it was 800 percent higher than in 1940.

3. purchase of goods and services, transfer payments to support incomes of disadvantaged Americans

4. It can affect the allocation of resources and the distribution of income, and cause the government to compete with producers in the private sector.

5. Answers will vary. Remind students to ask interview subjects to explain their opinions.

6. Answers will vary. Some students will suggest that transfer payments are successful in accomplishing the goal of economic security because they provide a minimum income for the poorest Americans.

Background

Janet Yellen and her husband, George Akerlof, are a famous economist team. They do much of their work together. Regarding wages and unemployment, Yellen states, "We've also focused a great deal on unemployment. Unemployment is a puzzle for any economist. Why is it that firms don't cut the wages of their current employees when there are people outside their gates lining up to fill out applications, offering to work and willing to accept wages that are lower than the going pay of the current employees? We're associated with a school of thought known as "efficiency wage theory," which takes seriously the idea that firms' wage policies impact the productivity and morale of workers and that firms constantly take those impacts into account in setting and changing wages. Firms don't just try to pay as little as possible to get the needed bodies on board; when there is unemployment, they ask themselves how wage cuts would affect the behavior of the employees. Would they quit or feel dissatisfied and work less hard on the firm's behalf if they feel that wage policies are unfair?" Ask students for their answers to Yellen's question.

TEACH

Have students search the Internet for more information about Janet Yellen. Students should summarize her role and approachability as a Fed governor and Chair of the CEA, as well as her theories concerning wage and price rigidity, crime and the breakdown of the family in the United States, the Community Reinvestment Act, and exchange rates.

PROFILES IN ECONOMICS

JANET YELLEN
(1946–   )

Janet Yellen, Chair of the President's Council of Economic Advisers (CEA), has a knack for explaining things. When she was a student—studying for her Ph.D. in economics in the early 1970s—the lecture notes she took in class became a legend in their own time. The "Yellen Notes," as they were known, were passed around and became the unofficial textbook for several generations of graduate students.

After graduation, Yellen married another economist. Together they studied and wrote about issues ranging from wage and price flexibility to gang behavior and community values.

As Chair of the President's Council of Economic Advisers, Yellen was responsible for developing and explaining President Clinton's economic policy.

UNDERSTANDING COMPLEXITY
Yellen's ability to understand and explain complex economic concepts has helped her career. She served as a respected research economist at the Federal Reserve System, and later became a popular professor at Berkeley. In 1994 she returned to the Fed but this time as a member of its prestigious Board of Governors. In this capacity she frequently briefed the White House on labor markets and welfare reform. As a result of these encounters, President Clinton knew just where to look when he needed a new Chair for the CEA in early 1997.

THE PRESIDENT'S ADVISER As Chair of the CEA, Yellen's biggest challenge is to develop and explain the administration's economic policy—a difficult task given the wide range of issues that need to be addressed. Her top priorities include a balanced federal budget and welfare reform, including measures that would punish fathers who do not support their children. The distribution of income is another priority. "I'm concerned about rising inequality of earnings and its long-term social implications. . . . Education is the answer," claims Dr. Yellen.

These issues, along with many others, are guaranteed to keep the CEA busy. But who better to tackle the job than the person experts call the "economist who explains it all" with analytical talents that are "second to none."

Examining the Profile

1. **Analyzing Information** What is the responsibility of the Chair of the CEA?

2. **Evaluating Information** What are Yellen's top priorities? Do you agree or disagree with any of her priorities? Explain.

Answers to Examining the Profile

1. to develop and explain the administration's economic policy
2. a balanced federal budget, welfare reform, and the distribution of income; Students should provide reasons for their agreement or disagreement with Yellen's priorities.

Federal Government Expenditures

Section Preview

Objectives

After studying this section, you will be able to:

1. **Explain** how the federal budget is established.

2. **Describe** the major components of the federal budget.

Key Terms

federal budget, fiscal year, federal budget deficit, appropriations bill, medicaid

Applying Economic Concepts

Social Security Remember those FICA taxes deducted from your paycheck? The government does not save your FICA taxes until you retire. As soon as this money is collected from you, the government spends it as *Social Security* payments to others—that's why they are called transfer payments.

Before the federal government can spend anything, Congress must establish the **federal budget**—an annual plan outlining proposed revenues and expenditures for the coming year. The federal budget is prepared for a **fiscal year**—a 12-month financial planning period that may or may not coincide with the calendar year.

Establishing the Federal Budget

The federal budget is developed and approved in two main phases. First, the President prepares and submits a budget to Congress. Second, Congress approves the budget.

Executive Formulation

The federal budget sets forth the President's financial plan and indicates the government's priorities. The budget is prepared for a multiyear period, but the primary focus is the upcoming fiscal year.

The government's fiscal year starts on October 1 of every calendar year and expires on September 30 of the following year. Normally, the budget is required to be transmitted to Congress on or before the first Monday following January 3, although it usually takes a little longer when a new President takes office.

President Clinton, for example, was first inaugurated on January 20, 1993. He sent his budget to Con-

gress on April 8, 1993, for the fiscal year beginning on October 1, 1993, and ending on September 30, 1994. Because most of the budget expenditures actually take place in 1994, it is called the 1994 budget.

As the budget is prepared, the President confers with various government agencies, other Executive Office units, and the Office of Management and Budget (OMB). The OMB is the division of the executive branch primarily responsible for assembling the budget under presidential guidelines.

President Clinton's budget for fiscal year 1997, shown in **Figure 10.2**, projected $1,566.8 billion of revenues and $1,687.5 billion of expenditures. Because expenditures were larger than revenues, the budget projected a **federal budget deficit** of $120.7 billion. Whether the numbers in a budget turn out to be accurate depends on a number of factors, including the health of the economy and, more importantly, the will of Congress.

Congressional Action

Congress has the power to approve, modify, or disapprove the President's proposed budget. First, the budget goes to the House of Representatives, which must set initial budget targets by May 15. Between this date and September 15, when the budget targets are to be finalized, the House assigns appropriations bills to various House appropriations subcommittees. An **appropriations bill** is a law that sets federal money aside for a specific purpose.

CHAPTER 10: *Government Spending* **243**

FOCUS

Section Objectives

1. Explain how the federal budget is established.

2. Describe the major components of the federal budget.

Bellringer

 Prior to taking roll at the beginning of the class period, display Focus Activity Transparency 74 on the overhead projector and assign the accompanying Student Activity 74.

Motivational Activity

Discuss students' responses to the activity sheet that accompanies Focus Activity Transparency 74.

Preteaching Vocabulary

Call on students to read aloud the definitions of this section's key terms from the Glossary. Then have volunteers use each term in a sentence.
LEP

Use the **Vocabulary Puzzle-Maker** to create crossword and word search puzzles.

CURRICULUM CONNECTIONS

Language Arts The term *budget* derives from an ancient French word for a kind of leather bag. The term *fiscal* derives from a Latin word meaning "purse" or "basket."

Classroom Resources for SECTION 2

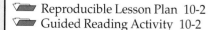 Reproducible Lesson Plan 10-2
Guided Reading Activity 10-2
Reinforcing Economic Skill 10
Section Quiz 10-2
Spanish Section Quiz 10-2

 Focus Activity Transparency 74
NBR's Economics in Action Video Program
Testmaker
Vocabulary PuzzleMaker
Chapter Challenger Interactive Review Software

TEACH

Guided Practice

L1 **The Budget Process** Call on a volunteer to read aloud the description of the process of federal budget making. Note the following on the chalk-board as each is mentioned: the President, OMB, House Appropriations subcommittees, House Appropriations Committee, joint conference committees, Congressional Budget Office. Have students use the items listed to construct a flow chart of the budget process. **LEP**

GLENCOE
TECHNOLOGY

NIGHTLY BUSINESS REPORT

Economics in Action

Chapter 15
Disc 1, Side 2

Title: *Government Spending*

Subject: The federal budget

Ask: How is the federal budget prepared every year? *(Every year the President proposes a federal budget, and Congress accepts it or modifies it.)*

Also available in VHS.

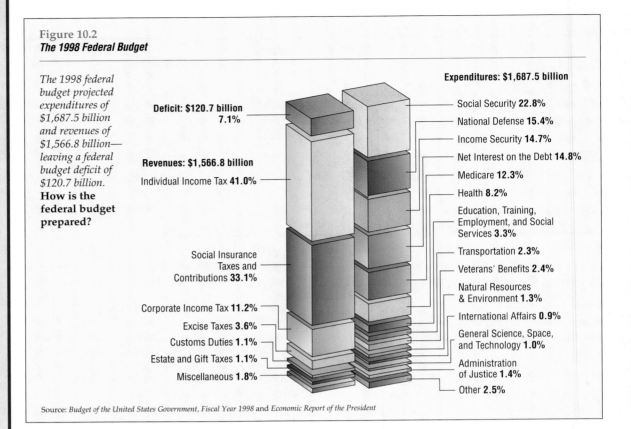

Figure 10.2
The 1998 Federal Budget

The 1998 federal budget projected expenditures of $1,687.5 billion and revenues of $1,566.8 billion— leaving a federal budget deficit of $120.7 billion. **How is the federal budget prepared?**

Deficit: $120.7 billion 7.1%

Revenues: $1,566.8 billion

Individual Income Tax **41.0%**

Social Insurance Taxes and Contributions **33.1%**

Corporate Income Tax **11.2%**

Excise Taxes **3.6%**

Customs Duties **1.1%**

Estate and Gift Taxes **1.1%**

Miscellaneous **1.8%**

Expenditures: $1,687.5 billion

Social Security **22.8%**
National Defense **15.4%**
Income Security **14.7%**
Net Interest on the Debt **14.8%**
Medicare **12.3%**
Health **8.2%**
Education, Training, Employment, and Social Services **3.3%**
Transportation **2.3%**
Veterans' Benefits **2.4%**
Natural Resources & Environment **1.3%**
International Affairs **0.9%**
General Science, Space, and Technology **1.0%**
Administration of Justice **1.4%**
Other **2.5%**

Source: *Budget of the United States Government, Fiscal Year 1998* and *Economic Report of the President*

House subcommittees hold hearings on each bill and debate the measure. If the bill is approved, it is sent to the full House Appropriations Committee. If it passes there, the bill is sent to the entire House for all representatives to vote on it. After the House approves the final bill, it goes to the Senate. The Senate may approve the bill as sent by the House, or it may draft its own version. If any differences exist between the House and the Senate versions, a joint House-Senate conference committee tries to work out a compromise bill.

During this process, the House and the Senate often seek advice from several government bureaus and offices, including the Congressional Budget Office (CBO). The CBO is a congressional agency that evaluates the impact of legislation and projects future revenues and/or expenditures that will result from the legislation.

After the House and Senate both approve the compromise bill, it is sent to the President for signature. Because Congress literally took apart, rewrote, and put back together the President's budget, the final version may or may not resemble the original proposal. If the budget was altered too much, the President can veto the bill and force Congress to come up with a budget closer to the President's original version.

Major Spending Categories

The thousands of individual expenditures in the federal budget can be grouped into the broad categories shown in both Figure 10.2 and Figure 10.3. The most important categories, historically accounting for more than 95 percent of all federal government expenditures, are described on page 246.

VISUAL INSTRUCTION

Ask: What percentage of planned budget expenditures was covered by deficit spending? *(7.1 percent)*

Answer to Caption:

President prepares and submits budget to Congress; Congress approves the budget.

Meeting Special Needs

Reading Disability Students with limited vocabularies often try to use the context of the sentence to determine the meaning of an unfamiliar word. Good readers do this effectively. Poor readers may continue reading even if they cannot determine the meaning. In Section 2, several new words appear whose meanings are expressed in the sentences. Present the following words and ask students to guess at their meanings: *subsidized, outpatient, occupational, vocational,* and *transit.* Have students find these words in the text and see if context helps them define the words.

Figure 10.3
Federal Government Expenditures, 1980-1998

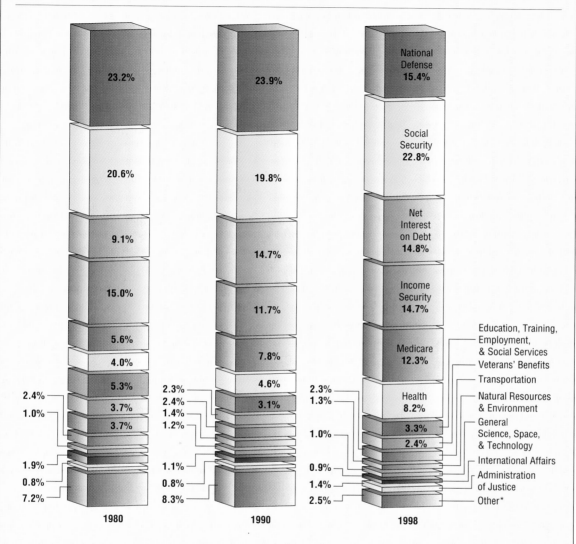

1980
- 23.2%
- 20.6%
- 9.1%
- 15.0%
- 5.6%
- 4.0%
- 5.3%
- 2.4%
- 3.7%
- 1.0%
- 3.7%
- 1.9%
- 0.8%
- 7.2%

1990
- 23.9%
- 19.8%
- 14.7%
- 11.7%
- 7.8%
- 4.6%
- 2.3%
- 3.1%
- 2.4%
- 1.4%
- 1.2%
- 1.1%
- 0.8%
- 8.3%

1998
- National Defense 15.4%
- Social Security 22.8%
- Net Interest on Debt 14.8%
- Income Security 14.7%
- Medicare 12.3%
- Health 8.2%
- 2.3%
- 1.3%
- 3.3%
- 1.0%
- 2.4%
- 0.9%
- 1.4%
- 2.5%

- Education, Training, Employment, & Social Services
- Veterans' Benefits
- Transportation
- Natural Resources & Environment
- General Science, Space, & Technology
- International Affairs
- Administration of Justice
- Other*

Source: *Economic Report of the President*, various years

The major categories of federal government expenditures show some change from 1980 to 1998. National defense expenditures are down, while net interest payments on the debt, medicare, and health expenditures are up. Comparing actual expenditures in 1998 with the most recent budget proposal of the President reveals how the administration would like to shift future spending priorities. **What were the three largest federal spending categories in 1998?**

*"Other" includes Agriculture, General Government, Commerce and Housing, Community and Regional Development, and Energy.

$ Free Enterprise Activity $

Organize the class into five groups and explain that each group is a congressional subcommittee reviewing budget priorities. Ask subcommittees to discuss and rank the programs listed below in descending order with the highest priority first. Encourage subcommittee members to try to reach consensus, although it is not absolutely necessary. After discussion is completed, ask representatives from each subcommittee to share their lists with the class and explain why certain rankings were made.

1. national defense; 2. health care; 3. food for starving people in a nation with civil war; 4. research on the environment; 5. space exploration; 6. homes for the U.S. homeless; 7. Food Stamps; 8. scholarships for needy students to attend college

---

CHAPTER 10
SECTION 2

L2 *Constitutional Principles*
Call on volunteers to explain how the budget process demonstrates the constitutional principle of checks and balances.

Independent Practice

◤ *Guided Reading* Assign Guided Reading Activity for Section 2. **LEP**

L2 *Writing Letters* Direct students to identify a category discussed on pages 244–247 on which they think too much or too little is spent. Then have students write letters to their U.S. representative or one of their senators challenging the spending of so much or so little on that particular category. Make certain students explain the reasons for their challenge. Call on volunteers to read their letters to the class.

L3 *Research* Have students research and write a report on the present year's federal budget. Suggest that they conclude their reports with a general discussion of the spending philosophy represented in the budget.

? DID YOU KNOW

On average, the federal government spends about $3.2 million per minute.

 VISUAL INSTRUCTION

Ask students what in the chart suggests that the debt is a growing problem. (*Net interest on debt has grown from 9.1 percent of total expenditures to 14.8 percent.*)

Answer to Caption:
Social Security, National Defense, Net Interest on Debt

ASSESS

Check for Understanding

Assign Section 2 Review as homework or an in-class activity.

 Use **Chapter Challenger Interactive Review Software** to review Section 2.

MEETING LESSON OBJECTIVES

Each objective below is tested by the questions that follow it in parentheses.

1. **Explain** how the federal budget is established. **(1, 2)**

2. **Describe** the major components of the federal budget. **(3, 4, 5)**

Evaluate

📁 📁 💻 Assign the Section 2 Quiz in the TCR or use the *Economics: Principles and Practices* Testmaker to create a customized quiz. Spanish Section Quizzes also are available in the Spanish Resources Binder.

LINKING PAST AND PRESENT

Congress established the National Aeronautics and Space Administration (NASA) in 1958 to oversee U.S. space flights. Congress took this action largely in response to the Soviet Union's launching of the satellite *Sputnik* the previous year.

Social Security

A growing category, payments to aged and disabled Americans through the Social Security program make up the largest category of federal spending. Retired persons receive benefits from the Old-Age and Survivors Insurance (OASI) program. Others unable to work receive payments from disability insurance (DI) programs.

National Defense

Historically, the largest category of spending was national defense, although it now is in second place. This category includes military spending by the Department of Defense and defense-related atomic energy activities, such as the development of nuclear weapons and the disposal of nuclear wastes.

Interest on the Federal Debt

When the federal government spends more that it collects in taxes and other revenues, it borrows money to make up the difference. Interest on the federal debt made up the third largest category of federal spending in 1990 and 1998. The amount of interest paid varies with changes in interest rates and the amount of money borrowed.

Income Security

This category includes expenditures for retirement benefits to railroad workers, disabled coal miners, civil service retirement and disability programs, and retirement benefits for the military. Subsidized housing, child nutrition, and food programs for low-income families also fall under this category.

Medicare

Medicare, a health-care program available to all senior citizens regardless of income, began in 1966. The program provides an insurance plan that covers major hospital costs. It also offers optional insurance that provides additional coverage for doctor and laboratory fees, outpatient services, and certain equipment costs.

Health

Health-care services for low-income people, disease prevention, and consumer safety usually account for a large percentage of the federal budget. Federal spending for **medicaid**—a joint federal-state medical insurance program for low-income persons—makes up the largest part of health spending. The Occupational Safety and Health Administration (OSHA)—a federal agency that monitors occupational safety and health in the workplace—is also included in this category. So is AIDS and breast cancer research, as well as substance abuse and mental health service programs.

Education, Training, Employment, and Social Services

This budget category includes block grants for elementary, secondary, vocational, and adult education, as well as education for those with handicapping conditions. Other services, such as guaranteed student loans, youth summer employment programs, daycare, foster care, legal services, and care of neglected or homeless children, are also part of this category.

Veterans' Benefits

Federal spending for veterans amounted to a small percentage of the total budget. Among other goods and services, veterans receive education and training, guaranteed home loans, pensions, and hospital and medical care from these funds.

Transportation

This category includes federal expenditures on highways, highway safety, mass transit, railroads, airports, and air traffic regulation. It also includes ocean shipping and other marine safety and transportation expenditures.

Natural Resources and Environment

Money in this category is spent on water resources, conservation, and land management. Pollution control and federal land acquisition for recreational parks are also included.

Extending the Content

Foreign Aid Although foreign aid accounts for only a small percentage of federal expenditures, it is often the subject of heated congressional debate. Some critics say that aid makes the recipient nation dependent on the U.S. to such a degree that its own economic development is stifled. Others contend that foreign aid is a form of bribery, used to gain the support of potentially unfriendly nations. Supporters of foreign aid say a developing nation needs capital equipment in order to develop its economy and raise its standard of living. Foreign aid can help provide this equipment. Supporters also point out that foreign aid is humanitarian, because it provides help for countries and regions of the world troubled by war, famine, and disease. See page 508, Figure 20.3, for international comparisons.

Federal Expenditures *The space shuttle* Challenger *conducts tests for the National Aeronautics and Space Administration.* **What percentage of 1998 federal expenditures went to General Science, Space, and Technology?**

General Science, Space, and Technology

This category includes expenditures for National Science Foundation programs and other general science programs for the Department of Energy and the Department of Defense. Space flight and space flight research are also supported with federal funds.

Administration of Justice

This category includes Justice Department and federal law-enforcement expenditures by the Federal Bureau of Investigation (FBI), Drug Enforcement Administration (DEA), and Immigration and Naturalization Service (INS). It also covers spending on federal prisons and state and local law-enforcement grants.

The administration of justice has been the fastest growing category of federal expenditures since 1980. This growth is the result of the federal government's intensified war on crime and drugs—as well as a federal prison inmate population that nearly doubled during the 1990s.

Other Spending

The remaining categories of government spending include general government, agriculture, commerce and housing, community and regional development, and energy. Each accounted for less than 1 percent of federal government expenditures in 1998.

Reteach

Have each student write three questions about the budget process on index cards. Collect and shuffle the index cards and go through them, selecting students at random to answer questions.

Enrich

Have students answer the question—What do the American people get from federal spending?—by writing a research paper on one of the categories of government expenditures discussed on pages 244–247. Papers should focus on total expenditures, programs provided, and important outcomes of programs.

CLOSE

Ask students to identify the category of federal spending they believe is most important and have them explain their choice.

 VISUAL INSTRUCTION

Some people argue that part of General Science, Space, and Technology spending should be classified under National Defense. Ask students to suggest why this argument might be made. *(General Science, Space, and Technology includes expenditures for general science programs for Department of Defense.)*

Answer to Caption:

1.0 percent

SECTION 2 REVIEW

Reviewing Terms and Facts

1. **Define** federal budget, fiscal year, federal budget deficit, appropriations bill, medicaid.
2. **Describe** the two stages required to establish the federal budget.
3. **List** the largest components of federal government spending.

Critical Thinking

4. **Determining Cause and Effect** In recent decades, people have been living longer and families have been having fewer children. How will the combination of these two factors affect transfer payments, such as Social Security, in the future?

Applying Economic Concepts

5. **Social Security** Contact your local Social Security office to find out about a person's eligibility to receive Social Security payments. Ask about the age, eligibility requirements, the size of the Social Security payments, and other requirements that may apply.

CHAPTER 10: *Government Spending* **247**

Answers to SECTION 2 REVIEW

1. All vocabulary words are defined in the Glossary.

2. executive formulation, in which the President prepares a budget and submits it to Congress; congressional action, during which Congress reviews, modifies, and approves budget

3. Social Security; National Defense; Interest on Federal Debt; Income Security; Medicare; Health; Education, Training, Employment, and Social Services; Veterans' Benefits; Transportation;

Natural Resources and Environment; General Science, Space, and Technology; Administration of Justice; or International Affairs

4. Most students will note that there will be more older people receiving Social Security but fewer people making contributions. The resulting shortfall will have to be addressed by cuts in benefits or increases in contributions.

5. Have students present the results of their inquiries in a written report.

Point out that statistical tables are especially useful when students need to make comparisons. In addition, when information is presented over time, as it is in this example, trends can be quickly noted. Finally, analyzing the information in a table often helps to provide the answers to the How? and Why? of an issue.

📁 *Skills Practice* For additional practice, have students complete Reinforcing Economic Skill 10.

ECONOMIC SKILL

Reading Statistical Tables

How many RBIs did your favorite shortstop drive in? How many touchdowns did your favorite wide receiver score? If you are a baseball or football fan, you probably love to keep records of statistics. Such information can be presented in a table.

Explanation

Economists also research and gather many facts and statistics. These facts can be placed in a table. Tabular data can help you analyze information because tables summarize a large amount of information in a small space. Tabular information is presented in rows and columns, which make it easy to read. Follow the steps below to learn how to read statistical tables.

- Read the title of the table to learn what content is being presented.

- Read any headings, or boxed heads, which may group information into subcategories.
- Read the information in the left-hand column, which often is organized alphabetically, chronologically, or geographically.
- The vertical columns to the right of the left-hand column are the body of the table. Compare the data presented in these columns.

Practice

Analyze the table on this page. Then use the steps outlined above to answer the following questions.
1. What is the title of the table?
2. What subheads are found in the table?
3. What information is being compared?
4. In which years was national defense the highest percentage of expenditures?
5. Which expenditures increased from 1980 to 1998?
6. Which expenditures decreased from 1980 to 1998?

Figure 10.4
Federal Government Expenditures, 1980-1998

Major Categories	1980	1990	1998	Major Categories	1980	1990	1998
National Defense	23.2%	23.9%	15.4%	Transportation	3.7%	2.4%	2.3%
Social Security	20.6%	19.8%	22.8%	Natural Resources & Environment	2.4%	1.4%	1.3%
Net Interest on Debt	9.1%	14.7%	14.8%	General Science, Space, & Technology	1.0%	1.2%	1.0%
Income Security	15.0%	11.7%	14.7%	International Affairs	1.9%	1.1%	0.9%
Medicare	5.6%	7.8%	12.3%	Administration of Justice	0.8%	0.8%	1.4%
Health	4.0%	4.6%	8.2%	Other	7.2%	8.3%	2.5%
Education, Training, & Social Services	5.3%	3.1%	3.3%	Undistributed Receipts	-3.5%	-2.9%	-3.3%
Veterans' Benefits	3.7%	2.3%	2.4%	Total	100%	100%	100%

Additional Practice

For further practice in reading statistical tables, complete the Reinforcing Skills exercise in the Chapter 10 Review on page 263.

Answers to SKILL

1. Federal Government Expenditures, 1980–1998
2. National Defense; Social Security; Net Interest on Debt; Income Security; Medicare; Health; Education, Training, Social Services; Veterans' Benefits; Transportation; Natural Resources and Environment; General Science, Space, and Technology; International Affairs; Administration of Justice; Other; Undistributed Receipts; Total
3. the percentage of total government expenditures for each category for the years 1980, 1990, and 1998
4. 1980 and 1990
5. Social Security; Net Interest on Debt; Medicare; Health; Administration of Justice
6. National Defense; Income Security; Education, Training, and Social Services; Veterans' Benefits; Transportation; Natural Resources and Environment; International Affairs; Other

State and Local Government Expenditures

Section Preview

Objectives

After studying this section, you will be able to:

1. **Explain** how state and local governments approve spending.
2. **Identify** the major categories of state government expenditures.
3. **Identify** the major categories of local government expenditures.

Key Terms

balanced budget amendment

Applying Economic Concepts

Human Capital Local governments spend about 34 percent of their direct expenditures on elementary and secondary education. These expenditures are an investment in *human capital*, which eventually result in more productive citizens and a higher standard of living for everyone. You are getting something in return for paying taxes!

FOCUS

Section Objectives

1. Explain how state and local governments approve spending.
2. Identify the major categories of state government expenditures.
3. Identify the major categories of local government expenditures.

Bellringer

Prior to taking roll at the beginning of the class period, display Focus Activity Transparency 75.

Motivational Activity

Discuss students' responses to the activity sheet that accompanies Transparency 75.

Preteaching Vocabulary

Ask students to explain what they think the term *balanced budget amendment* means. Have them check the meaning by finding the term in the Glossary. **LEP**

Use the **Vocabulary Puzzle-Maker** to create crossword and word search puzzles.

TEACH

Guided Practice

L1 Statistical Table Have students examine Figure 10.4 on page 248 and Figure 10.5 on page 250. Then direct students to use the information in Figure 10.5 to construct a statistical table comparing spending at the state and local levels. **LEP**

The federal government is not the only level of government that has expenditures. State and local levels of government also have expenditures. Like the federal government, these governments must approve spending before revenue dollars can be released.

Approving Spending

At the state level, there are almost as many ways to approve spending as there are states. In most states, however, the process is loosely modeled after that of the federal government.

Some states have enacted a **balanced budget amendment** to their state constitution, which requires them to hold spending in line with revenues. Under these conditions, states are forced to cut spending when state revenues drop. A reduction in revenues may occur if sales taxes or state income taxes fall because of a decline in the general level of economic activity.

At the local level, the approval for spending often rests with the mayor, the city council, the county judge, or some other elected representative or body. Generally, the amount of revenues collected from property taxes and other local sources limits the spending of local agencies. If state and local governments are unable to raise the revenue they need, they face the problem of not having enough financial resources to hire teachers, police officers, or other local and state workers.

State Government Expenditures

The major types of state government expenditures are shown in Figure 10.5. Six of the most important categories, accounting for approximately 73 percent of all state spending, are public welfare, higher education, insurance trust funds, highways, hospitals, and interest on state debt.

Public Welfare

The largest category of expenditures for state governments usually is public welfare. These payments take the form of cash assistance, payments for medical care, expenditures to maintain welfare institutions, and other miscellaneous welfare expenditures.

Higher Education

Generally a large category, higher education is a traditional responsibility of state governments with their networks of state colleges and universities. Local governments spend less in this area, usually to support community colleges and universities.

CHAPTER 10: *Government Spending* **249**

Classroom Resources for SECTION 3

 Reproducible Lesson Plan 10-3
 Guided Reading Activity 10-3
Section Quiz 10-3
Spanish Section Quiz 10-3
 Focus Activity Transparency 75

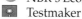 NBR's Economics in Action Video Program
Testmaker
Vocabulary PuzzleMaker
Chapter Challenger Interactive Review Software

GLENCOE
TECHNOLOGY

NIGHTLY
BUSINESS
REPORT

Economics in Action

Chapter 15
Disc 1, Side 2

Title: *Government Spending*

Subject: The federal budget

Ask: What are transfer payments? *(payments, such as Social Security and welfare, made by the government to people who are not producing goods and services for the government)*

Also available in VHS.

Independent Practice

☞ **Guided Reading** Assign Guided Reading Activity for Section 3. **LEP**

 VISUAL INSTRUCTION

Ask: What is the approximate dollar amount that local government spends on all levels of education? *[(1.9% + 34.4%) × $710,366 = $257,863 million]*

Answer to Caption:

State: Public Welfare, Higher Education, Insurance Trust Funds; Local: Elementary and Secondary Education, Public Utilities, Hospitals; Also accept "Other" for both governments.

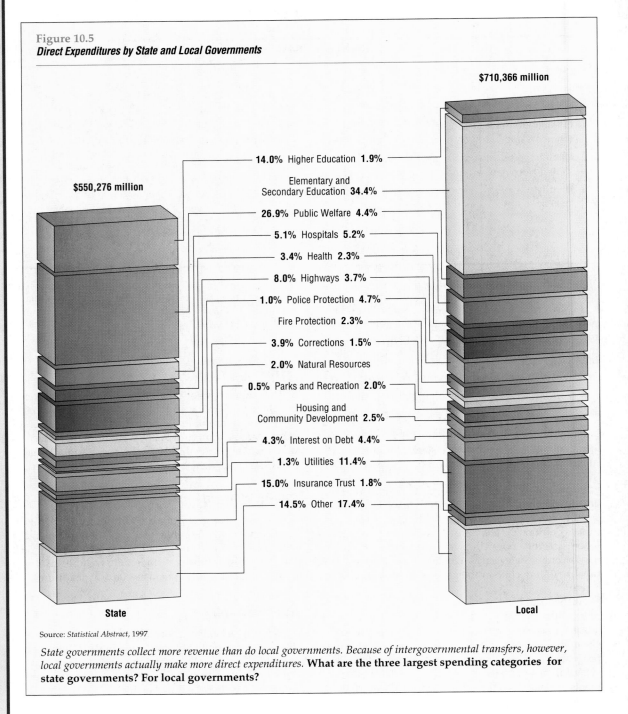

Figure 10.5
Direct Expenditures by State and Local Governments

$710,366 million

$550,276 million

State		Local
14.0%	Higher Education	1.9%
	Elementary and Secondary Education	34.4%
26.9%	Public Welfare	4.4%
5.1%	Hospitals	5.2%
3.4%	Health	2.3%
8.0%	Highways	3.7%
1.0%	Police Protection	4.7%
	Fire Protection	2.3%
3.9%	Corrections	1.5%
2.0%	Natural Resources	
0.5%	Parks and Recreation	2.0%
	Housing and Community Development	2.5%
4.3%	Interest on Debt	4.4%
1.3%	Utilities	11.4%
15.0%	Insurance Trust	1.8%
14.5%	Other	17.4%

State   **Local**

Source: *Statistical Abstract,* 1997

State governments collect more revenue than do local governments. Because of intergovernmental transfers, however, local governments actually make more direct expenditures. **What are the three largest spending categories for state governments? For local governments?**

Meeting Special Needs

Study Strategy Integration of new ideas into the framework of our thinking is an essential component of learning. It requires the application and evaluation of new concepts. Section 3 is ideal for such tasks. Ask students to imagine their world without state and local government expenditures. How would their lives be directly affected? Have students list three positive and three negative effects.

Insurance Trust Funds

Many states have their own retirement funds and insurance funds for state employees. These funds are invested until such time as people retire, become unemployed, or are injured on the job.

Highways

Highway construction and road improvement expenditures are a large category of state expenditures. The federal government builds and maintains much of the interstate highway system, but states maintain state roads and other highways that generally link smaller communities with larger ones.

Hospitals

Because most hospitals do not charge enough in fees to fully recover their costs, they often turn to state and local governments for help. As a result, hospital expenditures are a significant expense for both state and local governments.

Interest on Debt

Interest on state debt, generally in the form of bonds, is the sixth largest category of state government expenditure. In recent years, states have issued bonds to cover everything from general revenue to highways to university dormitories. The size of this component can increase significantly if interest rates rise.

Other Spending

The remaining 27 percent of direct state government expenditures consist of a variety of expenditures. The most important are in the areas of corrections, health, natural resources, and utilities.

Local Government Expenditures

Local governments include counties, municipalities, townships, school districts, and other special districts. The largest categories of spending by local governments make up approximately two-thirds of their total expenditures. These categories include elementary and secondary education, utilities, hospitals, interest on debt, police protection, public welfare, and highways.

Elementary and Secondary Education

Local governments have primary responsibility for elementary and secondary education. Expenditures in this category include teachers' and administrators' salaries, textbooks, and construction and maintenance of school buildings. 1 ✓

Public Utilities

Many public utilities, such as water and electricity, serve local needs. For most local governments, spending on utilities amounts to the second most important expenditure. Because fewer utilities serve people on a statewide basis, state governments spend a much smaller percentage of their budgets on public utilities.

Hospitals

Hospitals receive a large amount from local governments. Many hospitals are city- or municipal-owned, which makes them a large budget item for local governments.

Interest on Debt

State and local governments, like the federal government, sometimes borrow money to cover operating costs or capital spending. Interest payments in this

---

QUICK CHECK

Checking Understanding

1. Which level of government has the major responsibility for primary and secondary education?

Applying Economic Concepts

✓ **The Role of Government** In recent decades, the number of school districts has declined. Better transportation has allowed many school districts to consolidate, thus saving money. The United States has about 15,000 school districts. It had 108,579 in 1942.

L2 Journalism Have students work in pairs to interview family members and friends about how changes in state and local government expenditures have affected them in the last few years. After students have interviewed several people, have them write a brief news article summarizing the impact of changes in government spending at the state and local levels.

ASSESS

Check for Understanding

Assign Section 3 Review as homework or an in-class activity.

🔲 Use **Chapter Challenger Interactive Review Software** to review Section 3.

MEETING LESSON OBJECTIVES

Each objective below is tested by the questions that follow it in parentheses.

1. **Explain** how state and local governments approve spending. **(1, 2)**
2. **Identify** the major categories of state government expenditures. **(3, 5)**
3. **Identify** the major categories of local government expenditures. **(4, 5)**

QUICK CHECK — ANSWERS

1. local government

$ Free Enterprise Activity $

Ask students to assume they are members of the city council in a community with high unemployment and few jobs for recent high school graduates. At a city council meeting, members are notified that a company wants to locate a new manufacturing plant in the community. This would create 300 new jobs, but would also require additional spending for infrastructure repairs and construction and for increased police and fire protection. In return for locating in the community, the company wants some special tax advantages, including no property taxes or utility taxes for 12 years. Have students, as city council members, write a letter to the president of the company either agreeing or not agreeing to the relocation plan and explaining why.

Local Government Expenditures *Spending on utilities, such as electricity, is a local government expenditure.* **What is the largest expenditure of local governments?**

category were nearly the same for both local and state governments. Like the federal government, interest expenses vary as interest rates go up and down.

Police Protection

Most localities have a full-time, paid police force to protect their community. As a result, police protection is a significant cost for local governments. Because there are far fewer state than local police forces, state spending for police protection is much lower.

Public Welfare

Local governments, like state governments, face public welfare expenditures. Unlike state governments, however, local governments spend much less on this category.

Highways

Local governments also spend a significant amount on highways, roads, and street repairs. This expenditure includes the repair of potholes, street signs, and other street-related items.

Other Expenditures

The remaining local government expenditures, approximately one-third of the total, are spread over a wide range of categories. Among the most important are housing and community development, fire protection, and parks and recreation.

SECTION 3 REVIEW

Reviewing Terms and Facts

1. **Define** balanced budget amendment.
2. **Describe** how state governments handle the spending approval process.
3. **List** the six major categories of state spending.
4. **Identify** the seven major categories of local government spending.

Critical Thinking

5. **Making Generalizations** If you were to argue for reduced spending at the state and local levels, which categories shown in **Figure 10.5** would you pick? Explain the reasons for your choice(s).

Applying Economic Concepts

6. **Human Capital** How does the market reward those who have invested in human capital? Cite specific examples from your community.

Answers to SECTION 3 REVIEW

1. All vocabulary words are defined in the Glossary.

2. There are many different methods, but in most states the process is loosely modeled after that of the federal government.

3. Public Welfare, Higher Education, Insurance Trust Funds, Highways, Hospitals, Interest on Debt

4. Elementary and Secondary Education, Public Utilities, Hospitals, Interest on Debt, Police

Protection, Public Welfare, Highways

5. Answers will vary. Students should offer explanations for their choices.

6. Investment in human capital results in more productive workers; greater productivity usually leads to increased profits and higher pay for workers. Examples will vary.

Section Preview

Objectives

After studying this section, you will be able to:

1. **Explain** how the federal deficit is related to the federal debt.
2. **Relate** the impact of the federal debt on the economy.
3. **Describe** recent attempts to control the federal deficit.

Key Terms

deficit spending, federal debt, trust fund, Gross Domestic Product, crowding-out effect, balanced budget, entitlement

Applying Economic Concepts

Deficit Spending According to the 1998 *Budget of the United States Government*, approximately 7 cents of every federal dollar was spent on interest payments on the federal debt. When the government must borrow money to spend it, *deficit spending* occurs. American taxpayers—including you—must pay the interest on that borrowed money.

FOCUS

Section Objectives

1. Explain how the federal deficit is related to the federal debt.
2. Relate the impact of the federal debt on the economy.
3. Describe recent attempts to control the federal deficit.

Bellringer

 Prior to taking roll at the beginning of the class period, display Focus Activity Transparency 70 on the overhead projector and assign the accompanying Student Activity 70.

Motivational Activity

Discuss students' responses to the activity sheet that accompanies Focus Activity Transparency 70.

VISUAL INSTRUCTION

Have students examine Figure 10.8 on page 256 to see how far the $4 trillion public debt has "boldly gone."

Answer to Caption:

It may reduce purchasing power of economy, affect the distribution of income, transfer purchasing power from private to public sector, cut down individual incentive to work, and cause a rise in interest rates.

The amount of **deficit spending**—spending more than is collected in revenues—in recent years by the federal government has been staggering. Sometimes the government plans deficit spending. At other times, a deficit occurs because factors in the economy have reduced the amount of revenues or increased the amount of expenditures.

From the Deficit to the Debt

Figure 10.2 showed that the government projected a $120.7 billion federal deficit for 1998. This projection is based on a number of assumptions about the economy for the coming year. If the economy turns out to be stronger than expected, federal government revenues would go up and expenditures, such as unemployment compensation, would go down. In a very strong economy, the deficit may be cut by 100 percent or more.

In contrast, if the economy turns out to be weaker than expected, tax collections could go down. People might lose their jobs, and unemployment compensation might rise. In that case, the deficit might be 100 percent larger than the one planned.

A History of Deficits

Recent history shows that deficits tend to appear more often than surpluses in the American economy. Figure 10.6 shows the history of federal budget deficits and surpluses since 1940. The numbers in the figure have been converted to constant dollars so that inflation does not distort the deficits.

Federal Debt *In 1998 the federal debt reached $5.7 trillion.* **How does the federal debt impact the economy?**

CHAPTER 10: *Government Spending* **253**

Classroom Resources for SECTION 4

- Reproducible Lesson Plan 10-4
- Guided Reading Activity 10-4
- Section Quiz 10-4
- Spanish Section Quiz 10-4
- Focus Activity Transparency 70
- NBR's Economics in Action Video Program
- Enrichment Activity 10
- Reteaching Activity 10
- Spanish Reteaching Activity 10

- Economic Vocabulary Activity 10
- Spanish Economic Vocabulary Activity 10
- Chapter 10 Test, Form A and Form B
- English and Spanish Audiocassettes
- Testmaker
- Vocabulary PuzzleMaker
- Chapter Challenger Interactive Review Software
- MindJogger Videoquiz

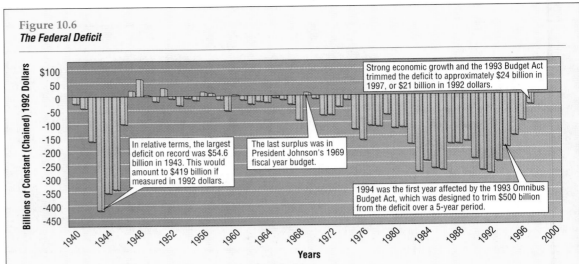

Figure 10.6
The Federal Deficit

Strong economic growth and the 1993 Budget Act trimmed the deficit to approximately $24 billion in 1997, or $21 billion in 1992 dollars.

In relative terms, the largest deficit on record was $54.6 billion in 1943. This would amount to $419 billion if measured in 1992 dollars.

The last surplus was in President Johnson's 1969 fiscal year budget.

1994 was the first year affected by the 1993 Omnibus Budget Act, which was designed to trim $500 billion from the deficit over a 5-year period.

Source: *Economic Report of the President* and *Budget of the United States Government,* various years.

The federal budget has shown a deficit every year since 1970. Deficits add to the federal debt, and interest on the federal debt has become one of the largest categories of federal expenditures. **What is the difference between the federal debt and the federal deficit?**

According to the figure, the largest deficits on record, in relative terms, occurred during World War II. The government quickly recovered, however, and the budget was in balance by 1947.

The huge deficits of the 1980s were a result of two things. First, spending on national defense increased substantially under President Reagan, going from $157 billion in 1981 to $304 billion in 1989. Second, President Reagan's 1981 Economic Recovery Tax dramatically lowered taxes on individuals and businesses, allowing the deficits to persist.

Huge deficits continued under President Bush. Little progress was made until President Clinton's Omnibus Budget Reconciliation Act passed in 1993.

Deficits Add to the Debt

When the federal government runs a deficit, it must finance the shortage of revenue by borrowing from others. It generally does this by having the Department of the Treasury sell bonds and other forms of government debt to the public. If we add up all federal bonds and other debt obligations, we

have a measure of the **federal debt**—the total amount borrowed from investors to finance deficit spending by the federal government.

This debt grows whenever the government sells more bonds to finance deficit spending in any given year. For example, the amount of debt the public held at the end of 1996 amounted to $5,225 billion. After adding the deficit for 1997 to this figure, plus some other government borrowing, the amount of public debt at the end of 1997 totaled about $5,450 billion.

The debt will continue to grow as long as the government spends more than it collects in revenues. Therefore, a zero budget deficit in any given year does not mean that the debt will go away. A zero deficit only means that the debt will not get any larger.

How Big Is the Debt?

The national debt has grown almost continuously since 1900. That year the debt was $1.3 billion. By 1929 it had reached $16.9 billion, and by 1940 it was $50.7 billion. The debt increased to $290.5 billion by 1960,

Figure 10.7
Three Views of the Federal Debt

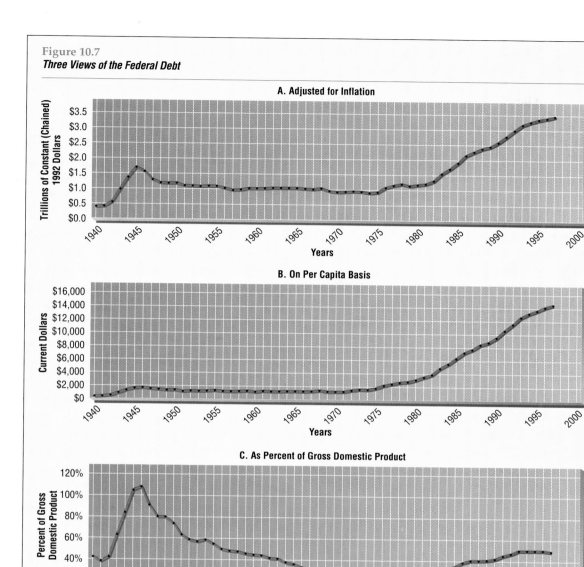

A. Adjusted for Inflation

B. On Per Capita Basis

C. As Percent of Gross Domestic Product

Source: *Economic Report of the President* and *Budget of the United States Government*, various years

The gross federal debt held by the public is huge. Graph A shows that from 1980 to 1997, the federal debt nearly tripled, even when constant dollars were used to remove the effects of inflation. When measured on a per capita basis, as in Graph B, expenditures more than quadrupled to reach about $14,460 for every man, woman, and child in the United States. Finally, as shown in Graph C, the federal debt went from 25.5 percent of the Gross Domestic Product to 49.2 percent. **In what ways does the federal debt impact the American economy?**

CHAPTER 10: *Government Spending* **255**

GLENCOE
TECHNOLOGY

NIGHTLY BUSINESS REPORT

Economics in Action

Chapter 23
Disc 2, Side 1

Title: *How Government Spends, Collects, and Owes*

Subject: Federal Spending and Deficit

Ask: What is the federal budget deficit, and what does the government do to finance it? *(The federal deficit is the difference between the amount of money the government spends and what it receives in taxes. The government makes up the difference by borrowing money; i.e., by selling bonds.)*

 Also available in VHS.

L3 **Debate** Refer students to the definition of the term *balanced budget amendment* on page 249. Then point out that some people strongly recommend the adoption of a federal balanced budget amendment. Select students to debate this issue.

 VISUAL INSTRUCTION

Have students identify the trend shown in all three graphs. *(The federal debt has increased considerably since 1980.)*

Answer to Caption:

may reduce purchasing power of economy, affect distribution of income, transfer purchasing power from private to public sector, reduce individual incentive to work, cause interest rates to rise

---

$ Free Enterprise Activity $

Organize students into groups of five and have groups review Figure 10.2 on page 244 detailing the 1998 federal budget and the discussion of federal government expenditure categories on pages 244–247. Then ask group members to discuss how they will balance the budget by considering such questions as: Should there be caps on the amount of spending for each category? Should expenditures be reduced? If so, should cuts be across the board or in certain categories only? Should taxes be increased? If so, which taxes should be raised? Instruct groups to thoroughly analyze the economic impacts of their recommendations. Have representatives report their recommendations to the class.

Independent Practice

📁 **Guided Reading** Assign Guided Reading Activity for Section 4. **LEP**

L2 Journalism Have students work individually or in small groups to develop a news magazine story titled: The National Debt—Major Threat or False Alarm? Stories should include such topics as the relationship between deficits and the debt, the impact of the debt on the economy, efforts to reduce the deficit and overall debt. Suggest that students illustrate their stories with information like that contained in Figure 10.8. Call on students or groups to present their stories to the class.

DID YOU KNOW

Thomas Jefferson feared that a growing government debt could pose a threat to liberty. "To preserve our independence, we must not let our rulers load us with perpetual debt," he said. "We must make our election between economy and liberty, or provision and servitude."

VISUAL INSTRUCTION

When the 5th edition of this textbook appeared in 1988, the federal debt stretched only once to the sun and back.

Answer to Caption:

The rest of the debt represents money that the government owes to itself; the public portion is the amount the government owes to others.

---

and to $909.1 billion by 1980. By 1997 the gross total federal debt exceeded $5,450 billion—or $5.4 trillion.

Some of this debt, however, is money that the government owes to itself. In 1997 almost $1.5 trillion of this debt was held in government trust funds. A **trust fund** is a special account used to fund specific types of expenditures, such as Social Security and medicare. When the government collects the FICA tax, it puts the revenues in these trust accounts. The money is then invested in government securities until it is paid out.

Because trust fund balances represent money the government owes to itself, most economists tend to disregard this portion of the debt. Instead, they view the public portion of the debt as the economically relevant part of the debt. The total debt is about $1.5 billion larger than the public debt.

Figure 10.7 presents three views of the total federal debt that the public held. Graph **A**, which is adjusted for inflation, shows that the debt did not increase dramatically until the 1980s. Graph **B**, computed on a per capita basis, also shows a dramatic increase in the 1980s. According to this view, the debt

on a per capita basis was approximately $14,500 by the end of 1997.

Graph **C** in the figure shows the debt as a percentage of **Gross Domestic Product** (GDP)—the dollar value of all final goods, services, and structures (houses and commercial buildings) produced within a country during any one year. The debt peaked at 49.6 percent of GDP in 1993, and has remained relatively stable since then. **1**

During the 1970s, many people thought that the debt was not a major problem. During the 1990s, however, many people became alarmed at the sudden increase in the size of the annual deficit and the growth of the federal debt.

Impact of the National Debt

The size of the federal debt has led some people to believe that the United States will go bankrupt if the debt ever gets too large. This, however, cannot happen because public debt is different from private debt.

Figure 10.8
How Big Is the Public Debt?

A $1 bill is about 6 inches (15.2 cm) long. If 4 trillion of these bills were laid end to end, they would form a chain 378.8 million miles (611.0 km) long—more than enough to stretch from the surface of the Earth to the surface of the sun and back—*twice!*

Or,
Suppose you had $4 trillion. If each $1 bill were counted 24 hours a day at the rate of one per second, it would take more than 126,800 years to count them all. At an average life expectancy of 70 years, that is about 1,812 lifetimes!

Or,
A stack of $1,000 bills 4 inches (10 cm) high would make you a millionaire. A $4 trillion national debt represents a stack of $1000 bills 252.5 miles (407.3 km) high!

The publicly held portion of the federal debt reached $4 trillion in 1998. The total federal debt in that year was even higher—at about $5.6 trillion. **Why do economists regard the public portion of the federal debt as the economically relevant part of the debt?**

Extending the Content

Government Securities The U.S. Treasury Department sells government securities (bonds, notes, and bills) to make up the difference between what the federal government takes in every year and what it spends. Government securities are also sold to refinance the debt as other securities mature. Securities may be purchased by individuals or organizations, such as banks and insurance companies. Government agencies also are permitted to purchase securities. An individual can purchase securities through a bank, but he or she must pay a small service charge. Federal Reserve banks (see Chapter 11) are another source for purchasing securities.

Public vs. Private Debt

The key difference between public and private debt is that we owe most of the federal debt to ourselves, whereas private debt is owed to others. This difference is important for two reasons.

The first reason relates to the repayment of the debt. When private citizens borrow money, they usually make plans to repay the debt at some time in the future. When the federal government borrows, it gives little thought to eventual repayment. The government has no real reason to ever pay off the federal debt. When it is time to pay off old bonds, the government simply issues new ones—and then uses the proceeds to pay off the old bonds.

The second reason relates to the loss of purchasing power. When private individuals repay a debt, they give up purchasing power because the money is gone and cannot be used to buy more goods and services. When the federal government repays a debt, there is no loss of purchasing power because the taxes and revenue collected from some groups are simply transferred to others.

The exception is that foreign investors historically have owned 15 to 20 percent of the public debt. When payments are made to investors outside the United States, some purchasing power is temporarily diverted from the American economy.

The Distribution of Income

The federal debt can have a significant impact on the distribution of income within the economy. If the government borrows money from the wealthy, and if the burden of taxes falls on the middle class and the poor, taxes would be transferred to the rich in the form of interest payments on the debt.

If the government borrows money from the middle class, and if the burden of taxes falls on the rich, those taxes would be used to make interest payments to the middle class. The federal tax structure, as much as the size of the debt itself, determines the distribution effects.

A Transfer of Purchasing Power

Another important impact of the federal debt is that it causes a transfer of purchasing power from the private sector to the public sector. In general, the larger the public debt, the larger the interest payments and, therefore, the more taxes needed to pay them. When people have to pay more taxes to the government, they have less money to spend on their own needs.

If the federal government decides to significantly increase spending in areas such as national defense or health care, private individuals will have less to spend on cars, consumer goods, and vacations. If the government decides to fund this spending by borrowing, the transfer of purchasing power will continue for years as the interest payments are spread into the future.

Individual Incentives

A third impact of the federal debt is that the taxes needed to pay the interest can cut down the incentives to work, save, and invest. Individuals and businesses might feel less inclined to work harder and earn extra income if higher taxes will be placed on them. 2

Many people also feel that the government spends taxpayers' money in a careless manner. A community, for example, may secure a federal grant and use the

Checking Understanding	Applying Economic Concepts
1. What does GDP include? 2. How can the federal debt affect worker incentive?	☑ **Federal Spending** When Congress appropriates money for local federal projects, it is often called *pork-barrel legislation.* Although such projects may bring jobs and money into a state, taxpayers often view pork-barrel projects as a waste of their money.

Cultural Diversity and Economics

Sweden Until the early 1990s, Sweden had a "welfare state" philosophy, where Swedes counted on the state to provide for them. "In the past 50 years, we created in this country about the biggest welfare state ever seen. But it was done at the expense of the economic awareness of every citizen. People really had no idea of the cost of everything.

Government subsidies paid 60 percent of housing costs, leaving Swedes used to artificially low rents. The . . . government is gradually reducing

housing subsidies, which are to be halted by 1999. A tax code that routinely claimed half of people's income . . . made it pointless for entrepreneurs to expand businesses. . . ." —Marc Fisher, "Sweden's Reagan Revolution" in *The Washington Post,* June 8–14, 1992. Sweden is discussed further on page 492.

Check for Understanding

Assign Section 4 Review as homework or an in-class activity.

Use **Chapter Challenger Interactive Review Software** to review Section 4.

MEETING LESSON OBJECTIVES

Each objective below is tested by the questions on page 260 that follow it in parentheses.

1. **Explain** how the federal deficit is related to the federal debt. **(1, 2)**

2. **Relate** the impact of the federal debt on the economy. **(3)**

3. **Describe** recent attempts to control the federal deficit. **(4, 6)**

VISUAL INSTRUCTION

Point out that the graph shows an increase in demand due to the willingness of the government to borrow more at each and every price. This causes the interest rate—the price of borrowing—to go up.

Answer to Caption:

It shifts resources—money capital—from the private sector to the public sector.

Figure 10.9
The Crowding-Out Effect Caused by Federal Spending

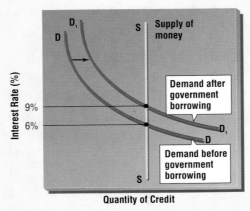

When the government runs a deficit, the additional borrowing causes the demand for credit to increase. This drives the interest rate up and "crowds out" other investors. **How does crowding-out affect the allocation of resources in the economy?**

---

funds to purchase expensive equipment that taxpayers in the community would never have approved. If people feel that their taxes are being squandered, they are less likely to save and invest.

Higher Interest Rates

When the government sells bonds to finance the deficit, it competes with the private sector for scarce resources. An example of this competition is the

---

DID YOU KNOW?

All Those Pages! George Washington was able to put all the figures for the national government's first budget on one large piece of paper. Today, the federal budget is printed in several volumes, with separate perspectives, appendices, and historical tables accounting for well over 2,000 pages.

---

crowding-out effect—the higher-than-normal interest rates that heavy government borrowing causes. Private borrowers are forced to pay the higher rates or leave the market. This effect is illustrated in Figure 10.9. **1**

In the graph, the demand curve for credit in the money market is represented by **DD** and the supply of money by **SS**. If the government runs a deficit and tries to raise funds by selling bonds, it will cause the demand curve to shift to **D₁D₁**. The increased demand for money causes the interest rate to go up. This increase forces other borrowers to pay higher rates or to stay out of the market.

Dealing With the Deficit

Concern over the size of the federal deficit and the debt has led to a number of attempts to control it. Several of the more important attempts are described below.

Gramm-Rudman-Hollings

One of the first significant attempts to control the federal deficit took place when Congress tried to mandate a **balanced budget**, a budget with neither a surplus nor a deficit, by 1991. The legislation was formally called the Balanced Budget and Emergency Deficit Control Act of 1985, or Gramm-Rudman-Hollings (GRH) after its sponsors. At the time, both critics and supporters called the act one of the most important pieces of legislation passed since the Great Depression. ☑

The key to GRH was a set of federal deficit targets for Congress and the President to meet over a six-year period. The federal deficit was to decrease each year until it reached zero in 1991. If Congress and the President could not agree on a budget that met the target in any given year, the automatic reductions would take over and reduce spending, splitting reductions equally between defense and nondefense expenditures. Legislators liked the law because it reduced spending without forcing Congress to vote against popular programs.

Despite the high hopes for GRH, the legislation was a shambles six years later. Instead of having reduced the deficit to zero in 1991, the country had its largest deficit ever of $269.5 billion.

Extending the Content

Downsizing The process of downsizing has reached the federal government. Between 1992 and 1997, the Clinton administration cut the federal workforce by more than 250,000 employees. This was the smallest workforce in 30 years and, as a share of total civilian employment, the smallest

since 1931. Thirteen of the 14 cabinet departments cut their permanent workforces between 1993 and 1996. Only the Justice Department, responsible for controlling crime and drugs, expanded its workforce.

Tax Reform *Tax reform is a popular issue, especially during election years. However, because it is easier for our elected officials to reduce taxes rather than to reduce spending, large federal deficits are difficult to avoid.* **What point is the cartoonist trying to make?**

Gramm-Rudman-Hollings failed for two reasons. First, Congress discovered that it could get around the law by passing spending bills that took effect two or three years later. Because GRH only set the deficit estimate for one year at a time, these bills did not conflict with GRH.

Second, the economy started to decline in July 1990. This decline triggered a safety valve in the law that suspended automatic cuts when the economy was weak. The combination of spending bills that circumvented GRH, the suspension of automatic budget cuts, and the lower federal revenues caused by the declining economy all added to the enormous budget deficit. As a result, the much-anticipated arrival of the balanced budget never materialized. 2

Budget Enforcement Act of 1990

In 1990 Congress passed the Budget Enforcement Act (BEA). The main features of the act combined spending caps with a "pay-as-you-go" provision designed to limit discretionary spending. Under this provision, reductions somewhere in the budget—or a tax increase—had to offset any new program that required additional spending. In addition, the BEA required that five-year revenue estimates be prepared for each new legislative act. If offsetting cost reductions could not be found, then mandatory, across-the-board spending cuts would be made to offset the extra costs.

BEA is much more difficult to circumvent than GRH, but it also has limitations. For one, it applies

Checking Understanding

1. What is the crowding-out effect?
2. Why did the Gramm-Rudman-Hollings Act fail?

Applying Economic Concepts

☑ **Overlooked Revenue** Inefficiencies at the Internal Revenue Service (IRS) are costly. Despite efforts to modernize, it is estimated that the IRS fails to collect about $200 billion of taxes every year— more than enough to balance the federal budget!

CHAPTER 10: *Government Spending* **259**

Evaluate

  🖼 Assign the Section 4 Quiz in the TCR or use the *Economics: Principles and Practices* Testmaker to create a customized quiz. Spanish Section Quizzes also are available in the Spanish Resources Binder.

🔘 VISUAL INSTRUCTION

Remind students that taxes redistribute wealth— which is one reason they are such an emotional issue.

Answer to Caption:
that the federal government has a hard time recognizing the problem of the federal debt

ANSWERS

1. higher-than-normal interest rates that heavy government borrowing causes
2. Congress discovered that the law could be circumvented; a decline in the economy triggered a safety valve in the law that suspended automatic spending cuts.

Extending the Content

Who Owns the National Debt? State and local governments hold about 6.6 percent of the total federal debt. Foreign investors have 23 percent, while the Federal Reserve System has 7.9 percent. Individuals hold 6.6 percent, commercial banks hold 5.4 percent, insurance companies have 4.4 percent, and corporations own 4.8 percent. The remaining debt is owned by other groups and institutions.

Reteach

Write the following on the chalkboard: Nature of the Debt, Impact of the Debt on the Economy, Dealing With the Deficit. Ask students to write summary paragraphs for each of these headings.

👉 👉 Have students complete Reteaching Activity 10. Spanish Reteaching Activities also are available in the Spanish Resources Binder.

Enrich

Have students clip magazine and newspaper articles about specific entitlements and use them to prepare a bulletin board display. In class discussion, review why entitlements have grown over the years.

👉 Have students complete Enrichment Activity 10.

CLOSE

Refer students to the government expenditures list that they made in the Connecting to Past Learning activity at the beginning of the chapter. Ask how their lists compare with the expenditures discussed in the chapter. Then ask students if they were to change the list after studying the chapter, how would it change? Encourage students to discuss any preconceptions that were changed after studying the chapter and what changed them.

only to discretionary spending, not programs like Social Security and medicare that increase automatically. For another, it includes a safety provision that allows for suspension of the act if the economy enters a low-growth phase, or if the President declares an emergency.

Omnibus Budget Reconciliation Act of 1993

President Clinton's Omnibus Reconciliation Act of 1993 was an attempt to trim approximately $500 billion from the deficit over a five-year period. By 1993 the federal deficit had reached such enormous proportions that the act was intended to reduce only the rate of growth of the deficit, not the deficit itself. The act featured a combination of spending reductions and tax increases that made the individual income tax more progressive—especially for the wealthiest 1.2 percent of taxpayers.

This act, along with a period of strong economic growth that raised tax revenues, accounted for much of the budget deficit reduction visible in Figure 10.6.

Line-Item Veto of 1996

In 1996 Congress gave the President the *line-item veto*—the power to cancel specific budget items. The President can veto appropriations, narrowly targeted tax breaks, and new or expanded entitlements *after* the federal budget is approved by both the House and

the Senate. The law took effect in 1997 and was important because it altered the requirement that the President approve or reject the budget in its entirety.

The line-item veto will reduce some spending, but it is unlikely to have a major impact on the total budget because the President can reject only small portions of the budget at a time. Also, Congress has the right to override any presidential veto with a two-thirds majority vote.

Growth of Entitlements

Some of the fastest-growing programs in the federal budget are **entitlements**, broad social programs designed to provide minimum health, nutritional, and income levels for eligible individuals. Entitlements include Social Security, medicaid, medicare, agricultural price supports, federal employee retirement and health benefits, some unemployment compensation, and aid to the poor. These programs are called entitlements because individuals are entitled to draw on these programs if they meet the eligibility requirements.

The problem for deficit reduction is that entitlements represent some of the largest and fastest-growing programs in the federal budget. They are so large that meaningful deficit reduction cannot be accomplished unless these programs are altered. Because these programs support millions of Americans, however, deficit reduction in the future is likely to be as difficult as it has been in the past.

SECTION 4 REVIEW

Reviewing Terms and Facts

1. **Define** deficit spending, federal debt, trust fund, Gross Domestic Product, crowding-out effect, balanced budget, entitlement.
2. **Describe** how the federal deficit affects the debt.
3. **List** five ways the national debt can affect the economy.

4. **Identify** four recent attempts to bring the federal deficit under control.

Critical Thinking

5. **Making Generalizations** Make a list of five ways that you or your family directly benefit from federal government expenditures.

Applying Economic Concepts

6. **Deficit Spending** Identify those benefits that are directly related to entitlement programs. If you were given the task of reducing entitlement programs, which would you choose to reduce or alter? Provide reasons for your choices.

Answers to SECTION 4 REVIEW

1. All vocabulary words are defined in the Glossary.

2. When the federal government runs a deficit, it must borrow to cover the shortage of revenue. This adds to the total debt the government owes.

3. may reduce purchasing power of economy, affect the distribution of income, transfer purchasing power from private to public sector, cut down incentive to work, cause rise in interest rates

4. Balanced Budget and Emergency Deficit Control

Act of 1985 (Gramm-Rudman-Hollings), Budget Enforcement Act of 1990, Omnibus Budget Reconciliation Act of 1993 , line-item veto, 1996

5. Lists will vary, but most will include better education, health, and so on.

6. Social Security, medicaid, medicare, agricultural price supports, federal employee retirement and health benefits, unemployment compensation, aid to the poor; Answers will vary. Students should provide reasons for their choices.

ECONOMICS IN ACTION

How Government Spends, Collects, and Owes

Setting Up the Video

With your classmates, view "How Government Spends, Collects, and Owes" on the videodisc *Economics in Action*. The video focuses on the causes and effects of the federal budget deficit. It describes the deficit and explains that the federal government covers the deficit by selling bonds. A news segment reports on the 1997 efforts to balance the budget, which led to historic changes.

**Chapter 23
Disc 2, Side 1**

View the video by scanning the bar code or by entering the chapter number on your keypad and pressing Search. *(Also available in VHS format.)*

Hands-On Activity

Study **Figure 10.6**, *The Federal Deficit*, on page 254. Note that the deficit has been decreasing in recent years. Locate a copy of the *Statistical Abstract of the United States* or the *Economic Report of the President*, or use the Internet to update the deficit figures. Draw your own graph with the updated figures and share it with the rest of the class.

SURFING THE "NET"

Federal Budgets

The President is responsible for developing the federal budget for the fiscal year, which begins every October 1. The four largest components of the United States federal budget, normally accounting for two-thirds of all federal expenditures, are Social Security, national defense, interest on the federal debt, and income security. Find out how the federal budget of the United States compares to current federal budgets of other nations by surfing the Internet.

Getting There

1. Use a search engine. Type in the words *federal budget*.

2. Next, enter the names of the countries whose federal budgets you would like to compare against the federal budget categories of the United States.

3. The search engine will provide you with a number of links to follow. Links are "pointers" to different sites on the Internet and often appear as blue, underlined words.

What to Do When You Are There

Click on the links to navigate through the pages of information. Gather your findings. Using the findings, create a chart that compares other countries' expenditures in various categories to the United States budget categories and expenditures. Share your charts with the rest of the class. Then discuss what other countries' expenditures reveal about their national priorities.

261

MULTIMEDIA ACTIVITIES

GLENCOE TECHNOLOGY

Economics in Action

Chapter 23
Disc 2, Side 1

Title: *How Government Spends, Collects, and Owes*

If you do not have access to a videodisc player, the **Economics in Action** programs are also available in VHS.

INTERNET SITES

The following are possible sites for completing the "Net" activities:

Commonwealth of Australia—Budget
http://www.finance.gov.au/budget/budget_main.htm

Canadian Department of Finance
http://www.fin.gc.ca/fin-eng.html

Not on the "Net"...

If students have limited or no access to the Internet, have them complete the activity "Federal Budgets" by using the computerized card catalog at the school or local library. At the *s:* prompt, students should type the name of the country(ies) they wish to research. They should then use the call numbers to find the books and other resources they need to complete their research.

INTERNET ADDRESS BOOK

Internet addresses that you find useful can be noted in the space below for quick reference.

GLENCOE
TECHNOLOGY

VIDEODISC
MindJogger Videoquiz

Use MindJogger to review
the Chapter 10 content.

Chapter 10
Disc 2, Side A

Also available in VHS.

Answers

Reviewing Key Terms

Sentences may include:

1. Governments, or the public sector, buy goods and services from the private sector.

2. The grant-in-aid is one form of transfer payment.

3. Deficit spending has to be covered by borrowing, and this may affect the distribution of income.

4. The federal budget outlines proposed revenues and expenditures for the fiscal year.

5. A balanced budget amendment would limit the amount set aside through appropriations bills.

6. The federal debt is the total amount borrowed from investors to finance government deficit spending.

7. To cover deficit spending, the government has to borrow, which may lead to the crowding-out effect.

8. Fast-growing entitlement programs make the establishment of a balanced budget very difficult.

Reviewing the Facts

1. beyond comprehension

2. purchase of goods and services, transfer payments

3. It can affect the allocation of resources and the distribu-

262

Reviewing Key Terms

Write a sentence about each pair of terms below. The sentences should show how the terms are related.

1. public sector, private sector
2. transfer payment, grant-in-aid
3. distribution of income, deficit spending
4. federal budget, fiscal year
5. appropriations bill, balanced budget amendment
6. deficit spending, federal debt
7. deficit spending, crowding-out effect
8. entitlement, balanced budget

Reviewing the Facts

SECTION 1 *(pages 238–241)*

1. **Describe** the magnitude of government spending since 1940.
2. **Identify** two kinds of government spending.
3. **Explain** three ways that government spending can impact the economy.

SECTION 2 *(pages 243–247)*

4. **Identify** the two stages of approval required to establish the federal budget.
5. **Identify** the 10 most important budget categories in the federal budget.

SECTION 3 *(pages 249–252)*

6. **Explain** how states model their budget approval process.
7. **Describe** the major categories of state and local spending.

SECTION 4 *(pages 253–260)*

8. **Discuss** the relationship of the federal deficit to the federal debt.
9. **Identify** how the debt can affect the economy.
10. **List** three legislative attempts to deal with the problem of federal budget deficits.
11. **Cite** at least six examples of entitlement programs.
12. **Explain** why entitlements are so named.

Critical Thinking

1. **Analyzing Information** Examine the major types of federal expenditures in Figure 10.2 on page 244. Classify each as to whether they are entitlement or non-entitlement programs.
2. **Making Comparisons** Compare the federal expenditures for the three years included in Figure 10.3. Identify at least three major differences in the expenditures. How do changes in spending reflect the priorities of the administration that develops the budget?

Applying Economic Concepts

1. **Human Capital** Which of the categories in Figure 10.3 reflect an investment in human capital?
2. **Deficit Spending** If you were a presidential adviser, what spending cuts would you suggest to balance the budget? Explain your reasoning.
3. **Budget Deficits** The federal government has made several attempts to deal with the problem of federal budget deficits. Identify the four important pieces of legislation discussed in the chapter, and outline their main features and weaknesses in a chart similar to the one below.

A. _____
   1. Features:
   2. Weaknesses:

B. _____
   1. Features:
   2. Weaknesses:

C. _____
   1. Features:
   2. Weaknesses:

D. _____
   1. Features:
   2. Weaknesses:

---

tion of income, and cause the government to compete with producers in the private sector.

4. executive formulation, congressional action

5. Social Security; National Defense; Interest on Federal Debt; Income Security; Medicare; Health; Education, Training, Employment, and Social Services; Veterans' Benefits; Transportation; Natural Resources and Environment

6. modeled on that of the federal government

7. states: public welfare, higher education, insurance trust funds, highways, hospitals, and interest on the debt; local governments: elementary and secondary education, public utilities, hospitals, interest on the debt, police protection, public welfare, and highways

8. When the federal government runs a deficit, it must borrow to cover the shortage of revenue. This adds to the total debt the federal government owes.

9. The debt may reduce purchasing power of economy, affect the distribution of income, transfer

Reinforcing Skills

READING STATISTICAL TABLES

Use the table below to answer the following questions.
1. What is the title of the table?
2. What subheads are found in the table?
3. What information is being compared?
4. Which company's product has the most calories? The most salt?

Individual Activity

Examine the list of spending categories in **Figure 10.5** on page 250, and note that each category represents one group of services provided at the state and local levels of government. Make a list of those services you or your family have directly used.

Then examine **Figure 10.2**, which categorizes federal expenditures. Make a list of federal services that you or your family have directly used or from which you have benefited.

Review the amount of revenue each level of government receives in the form of taxes you and your family pay. This information was shown graphically in **Figure 9.1** on page 211. Finally, in a paragraph, summarize which level of government services you use the most and which level of government receives the most revenue for their services.

Cooperative Learning Activity

Organize into groups of five. Using the list of federal government spending categories in this chapter, identify at least six categories that should be targeted for reduced spending. All members of the group should come to a consensus on which categories to cut. Provide reasons for your choices, then compare your results to the other groups in the class.

Figure 10.11
Nutrition of Cheeseburgers and Colas

PRODUCT	CALORIES	CHOLESTEROL (g)	SALT (mg)
Burger King			
Cheeseburger	318	50	661
Double cheeseburger	483	100	851
Whopper with cheese	935	194	1,245
Cola (27 oz.)	324	0	0
McDonald's			
Cheeseburger	305	0	210
Quarter Pounder with cheese	510	115	1,090
Big Mac	500	100	890
Cola (32 oz.)	380	0	0
Wendy's			
Cheeseburger	410	80	760
Big Classic with cheese	640	105	1,345
Big Classic Double with cheese	820	170	1,555
Cola (28 oz.)	350	0	0

Source: Adapted from Michael F. Jacobson's and Sarah Fritschner's *Fast-Food Guide*

Technology Activity

Using a Spreadsheet

Using the Internet, select five states and download or print their state budgets. Using this information, create a spreadsheet to record and analyze the following categories: name of state, budget total, public welfare, higher education, insurance contributions, highways, hospitals, and interest on state debt. Enter the information from each state's budget into the spreadsheet.

After entering the information, create a graph for each state's expenditures. What conclusions can you draw from your data? Where is the most money allocated? What are the differences found in various regions of the United States? Using a word processor, create a brief summary of your findings. Import your spreadsheet and graphs into the document. Print your results and share them with the class.

CHAPTER 10: *Government Spending* **263**

for net interest on the debt, medicare, and health have all risen. An increase indicates that particular category is a priority.

Applying Economic Concepts

1. education, etc.; medicare; health; veterans' benefits

2. Encourage students to offer reasons for their answers.

3. A. GRH; 1. set federal deficit targets over a six year period; automatic spending cuts went into effect; 2. could be circumvented by Congress; weak economy triggered blocks

   B. BEA of 1990; 1. combined spending cuts with "pay-as-you-go" provision; 2. applied only to discretionary spending; suspended during low economic growth

   C. Omnibus Act; 1. mixture of tax increases and spending cuts; 2. failed to stem growth of entitlements

   D. Line-item veto; 1. gives President power to cut budget items; 2. can reject only small portions; Congress can override veto

Reinforcing Skills

1. Nutrition of Cheeseburgers and Colas

2. Product, Calories, Cholesterol (g), Salt (mg)

3. nutrition of products by Burger King, McDonald's, and Wendy's

4. Burger King's Whopper with cheese; Wendy's Big Classic Double with cheese

purchasing power from private to public sector, cut down individual incentive to work, and cause interest rates to rise.

10. Balanced Budget and Emergency Deficit Control Act of 1985, Budget Enforcement Act of 1990, Omnibus Budget Reconciliation Act of 1993, Line-item veto of 1996

11. Social Security, medicaid, medicare, federal employee retirement and health benefits, unemployment compensation, welfare

12. because individuals are entitled to draw on these programs if they meet eligibility requirements

Critical Thinking

1. Entitlements: Social Security, Income Security, Medicare, Veterans' Benefits; Non-entitlements: National Defense, Interest on Federal Debt, Health, Education, Training, Transportation, Natural Resources and Environment, General Science, Administration of Justice, International Affairs

2. National defense has declined, whereas the shares

CHAPTER ORGANIZER

Daily Objectives	Reproducible Resources	Multimedia Resources
Section 1 **The Evolution of Money** 1. **Explain** the three functions of money. 2. **Identify** four major types of money used in early societies. 3. **Trace** the origins of the United States dollar. 4. **Describe** the four characteristics of money.	Reproducible Lesson Plan 11-1 Guided Reading Activity 11-1 Cooperative Learning Activity 15 Consumer Application Activities 12, 15 Math Practice for Economics 16 Free Enterprise Activities 4, 15 Primary and Secondary Source Reading 15 Performance Assessment Activity 16 Reinforcing Economic Skill 11 Section Quiz 11-1*	Focus Activity Transparency 58 Vocabulary PuzzleMaker Chapter Challenger Interactive Review Software Testmaker MindJogger Videoquiz
Section 2 **Early Banking and Monetary Standards** 1. **Explain** the history of privately issued bank notes. 2. **List** five major types of currencies introduced after the Civil War. 3. **State** two advantages and two disadvantages of a gold standard. 4. **Understand** why the United States has an inconvertible money standard.	Reproducible Lesson Plan 11-2 Guided Reading Activity 11-2 Section Quiz 11-2*	Focus Activity Transparency 59 Economic Concepts Transparency 6 Vocabulary PuzzleMaker Chapter Challenger Interactive Review Software Testmaker NBR's Economics in Action Video Program
Section 3 **The Development of Modern Banking** 1. **Explain** the development of the National Banking System. 2. **Relate** the effects of Depression-era bank failures on deposit insurance creation. 3.. **Identify** three other forms of depository institutions.	Reproducible Lesson Plan 11-3 Guided Reading Activity 11-3 Section Quiz 11-3*	Focus Activity Transparency 61 Vocabulary PuzzleMaker Chapter Challenger Interactive Review Software Testmaker NBR's Economics in Action Video Program
Section 4 **Crisis, Reform, and Evolution in the 1980s** 1. **Explain** the forces leading to deregulation of financial institutions in the 1980s. 2. **Relate** the history of the savings and loan crisis.	Reproducible Lesson Plan 11-4 Guided Reading Activity 11-4 Section Quiz 11-4*	Focus Activity Transparency 62 Vocabulary PuzzleMaker Chapter Challenger Interactive Review Software Testmaker NBR's Economics in Action Video Program
Chapter Review and Evaluation	Enrichment Activity 11 Reteaching Activity 11* Economic Vocabulary Activity 11* Chapter 11 Test, Forms A and B	Chapter Digests Audiocassette Activities and Tests* Testmaker MindJogger Videoquiz

Also available in Spanish

 Blackline Master　　 Transparency　　 CD-ROM　　 Software　　 Videodisc　　 Audiocassette

00:00　OUT OF TIME? Assign the Chapter 11 Digest Audiocassette and the corresponding Chapter Digest activities and tests.

PERFORMANCE ASSESSMENT

The following chapter projects may be assigned at the beginning of the chapter and used for performance assessment.

Multicultural Heritage Have students work in small groups to prepare research reports on the money of a selected country. Suggest that groups focus their research on the following topics: (1) The historical evolution of money in the country selected; (2) How the historical development of money, and the money the country uses today, reflects the country's culture; (3) How successfully the country's money performs the three functions of money—medium of exchange, measure of value, and store of value; (4) How the country's money measures up to the four characteristics of money—portability, durability, divisibility, and limited availability. Encourage groups to illustrate their reports with examples of past and present coin and paper money. Have groups present their completed reports to the class.

Cooperative Learning Organize students into four groups and assign one of the following topics to each group: Money from Colonial Times to the Present, Monetary Standards, The Development of Modern Banking, Reforming the Thrift Industry. Suggest that groups break their topics into subtopics and assign subtopics to one or two group members. Explain that each subtopic will become a short article to be published in a class magazine on money and banking in the U.S. Have students conduct research and write a draft of the article on their subtopic. Next, instruct other group members to edit the articles and prepare final drafts. Finally, have groups assemble final drafts into a magazine. Make enough copies of the magazine for distribution to the class.

ADDITIONAL RESOURCES

Readings for the Student

From Rocks to Riches: An Illustrated History of Coins & Currency. New York: Federal Reserve Bank of New York. Packed with interesting and off-beat information about the history of money.

The Story of Banks. New York: Federal Reserve Bank of New York. Comic-book style publication about the development of the banking system.

Readings for the Teacher

Federal Reserve System. Gainesville, FL: University of Florida Center for Economic Education, 1991. Lesson plans and reproducible worksheets on the history, structure, and function of the Federal Reserve System.

Multimedia

Economics U$A: Inflation/The Banking System. The Annenberg/CPB Collection, 19 Gregory Drive, South Burlington, VT 05407–2345. Color video, 60 mins. Second 30-minute segment of video shows how banks operate and how the FDIC tries to prevent bank failures from becoming crises.

Economics in a Changing World: Where Do I Fit In?, Money, Banks & the Role of Government. Churchill Media. 1995. Videocassette, 30 mins. Informative segment focuses on the role of money and banking in today's interdependent world.

Money. Guidance Associates, 150 Clearbrook Road, Elmsford, NY 10523. Color video, 15 mins. Shows the development of money throughout history, from the use of cowrie shells to today's computerized monetary system.

Chapter Overview

Chapter 11 discusses the development of money and the vehicle for its exchange—the banking system. **Section 1** describes the development of money over time and the characteristics that make an object money. **Section 2** tracks the history of banking and the development of monetary standards. **Section 3** focuses on the development of modern banking. **Section 4** explains deregulation of financial institutions.

GLENCOE
TECHNOLOGY

VIDEODISC
MindJogger Videoquiz

Use MindJogger to preview the Chapter 11 content.

 Chapter 11
Disc 2, Side A

 Also available in VHS.

interNET
CONNECTION

Resources for Chapter 11 on the World Wide Web*

National Council on Economic Education

http://www.nationalcouncil.org/

Federal Reserve Bank of Minneapolis

http://woodrow.mpls.frb.fed.us/

Central Banking Resource Center

http://patriot.net/~bernkopf/

FDIC

http://www.fdic.gov/

Sites subject to change.

To successfully perform the functions of money, coins and currencies must be portable, durable, divisible, and limited in supply.

Extra Credit Project

Have students write a research paper on the role that banks—or a particular bank—play in the local economy. Encourage students to illustrate their paper with charts and graphs. Call on volunteers to read their papers to the class.

CHAPTER 11
Money and Banking

SECTION 1
The Evolution of Money

SECTION 2
Early Banking and Monetary Standards

SECTION 3
The Development of Modern Banking

SECTION 4
Crisis, Reform, and Evolution in the 1980s

CHAPTER PREVIEW

People to Know

• Oprah Winfrey
• Bank Teller

Applying Economic Concepts to Your Life

Money Why do you accept money in exchange for a good or service? Why are so many different kinds of money used around the world? *Money* is harder to define than you might think. We usually think of money in terms of what it can do for us, rather than in terms of its nationality, shape, or color.

Journal Writing

For one week, write in your journal the advertising claims you read or hear about from the financial institutions in your area.

Connecting to Past Learning

Students have studied the roles of the federal government in regulating business operations, taxing, and spending. Now they will learn the federal government's role in monetary and banking systems.

Applying Economics

Hold up a ballpoint pen and ask students what they would be willing to trade for it—2 pencils, a candy bar, 20 rubber bands? Note that there is no consensus among students as to the value that should be attached to this item. Have students apply this situation to their everyday lives. Ask what goods or services they would be willing to offer for a pair of jeans or a CD. What goods and services would they accept if they were selling these items? Conclude by pointing out that a medium of exchange that everyone is willing to accept—money—makes the trading of goods and services a much simpler activity.

 PERFORMANCE ASSESSMENT

Refer to page **264B** for a Performance Assessment activity for this chapter. Also see the **Performance Assessment Activities** booklet for additional suggestions.

 VISUAL INSTRUCTION

France, Germany, Great Britain, and Canada have coins for their basic monetary unit. Have students identify the characteristic of money that this focuses on. *(durability)*

Economic Portfolio

Suggest that for each **Journal Writing** entry above, students note the type of financial institution, the services it offers, and the cost of these services. Mention that this will help them to complete a writing activity that asks them to make a comparison of the advertising claims. Refer students to the **Technology Activity** in the Chapter 11 Review on page 291.

Key to Ability Levels — Teaching strategies have been coded for varying learning styles and abilities:
L1 - Basic (activities for all students)   **L2 - Average** (activities for average to above-average students)
L3 - Challenging (activities for above-average students)   **LEP - Limited English Proficiency**

SECTION 1
The Evolution of Money

FOCUS

Section Objectives

1. Explain the three functions of money.
2. Identify four major types of money used in early societies.
3. Trace the origins of the United States dollar.
4. Describe the four characteristics of money.

Bellringer

Prior to taking roll at the beginning of the class period, display Focus Activity Transparency 58.

Motivational Activity

Discuss students' responses to the activity sheet that accompanies Transparency 58.

Preteaching Vocabulary

Direct students to the list of key terms in the Section Preview. Have them use the words they know in sentences.
LEP

Use the **Vocabulary PuzzleMaker** to create crossword and word search puzzles.

LINKING PAST AND PRESENT

In the past, complex exchange arrangements among businesses allowed them to trade barter credits for goods and services. For example, a hotel might have paid a construction company "vacation time" for building work. Bartering helped companies stay busy even when they had uncertain cash flows from their regular operations.

SECTION 1 — The Evolution of Money

Section Preview

Objectives

After studying this section, you will be able to:
1. **Explain** the three functions of money.
2. **Identify** four major types of money used in early societies.
3. **Trace** the origins of the United States dollar.
4. **Describe** the four characteristics of money.

Key Terms

barter economy, money, medium of exchange, measure of value, store of value, commodity money, fiat money, wampum, specie, bullion, monetary unit

Applying Economic Concepts

Barter Did you trade items when you were younger? Did you ever have trouble finding someone who would agree with your terms of the exchange? Trade, or *barter*, is one way to do business, but it is often tedious and time-consuming. That is why most societies use some form of money in their transactions.

Money is something that most people take for granted. Think what the world would be like without it, however. If we lived in a **barter economy,** a moneyless economy that relies on trade, life would be quite different. Without money, the exchange of goods and services would be greatly hindered, because the products some people have to offer are not always acceptable or easy to divide for payment. Money makes life easier for everybody in ways we may not have thought about. ✔️

What Is Money?

Basically, money is what money does. **Money** can be any substance that functions as a medium of exchange, a measure of value, and a store of value.

Medium of Exchange

As a **medium of exchange,** money is something generally accepted as payment for goods and services. In a barter society, trade may occur without a medium of exchange. In colonial times, for example, a merchant might have accepted a chicken in exchange for cloth, or a doctor might have exchanged medical services for potatoes. As societies become more complex, however, trading goods for other goods or services becomes difficult.

Measure of Value

As a **measure of value,** money expresses worth in terms that most individuals understand. To say that a bicycle is worth a television set or 50 bags of onions would be confusing. If a price tag in terms of dollars is put on the bicycle, however, most people can assess its value. They see the dollar price of one object in relation to the dollar price of others. Because one single measurement of value exists, consumers can trade with each other using the common denominator of money.

Store of Value

Money also serves as a **store of value.** Goods or services can be converted into money, which is easily stored until some future time. Money enables a period of time to pass between earning and spending an income.

Money in Early Societies

Money has evolved to make life easier for people. This evolution took place in societies that had virtually no contact with one another and that developed at different times. The result is money that comes in an incredible variety of forms, shapes, and sizes.

Classroom Resources for SECTION 1

- Reproducible Lesson Plan 11-1
- Guided Reading Activity 11-1
- Cooperative Learning Activity 15
- Consumer Application Activities 12, 15
- Math Practice for Economics 16
- Free Enterprise Activities 4, 15
- Primary and Secondary Source Reading 15
- Performance Assessment Activity 16
- Reinforcing Economic Skill 11

- Section Quiz 11-1
- Spanish Section Quiz 11-1
- Focus Activity Transparency 58
- Testmaker
- Vocabulary PuzzleMaker
- Chapter Challenger Interactive Review Software
- MindJogger Videoquiz

Barter Economy *As the cartoon shows, a barter economy can cause problems for those wanting to exchange goods for products they may use.* **How does money function as a medium of exchange?**

TEACH

Guided Practice

L2 Illustrating Ideas On the chalkboard, write the three functions and the four characteristics of money. Have students look at a dollar bill, and call on volunteers to explain how it fulfills each function and exhibits each characteristic. Have students write a paragraph on the following: How and Why the Dollar Bill Qualifies As Money.

Cooperative Learning
Assign Cooperative Learning Activity 15.

VISUAL INSTRUCTION

Call on students to explain why the loaf of bread or the 12 oranges would not work as a measure of value or a store of value. *(People may not accept the value—1 loaf = 12 oranges—of the goods; both goods are perishable and are consumed soon after purchase.)*

Answer to Caption:

It is generally accepted as payment for goods and services.

One of the earliest forms of money was the brightly colored cowrie shells found in parts of the South Pacific and Africa. In New Guinea, dog teeth served as a form of currency, while fishhooks often were used in the Marshall Islands. At Santa Cruz in the South Seas, the feathers of hundreds of honey-eating birds were attached to short sticks to make feather-stick money. Tea leaves compressed into "bricks" comprised money in ancient China, and compressed cheese was used in early Russian trade. The East African Masai used a currency made of miniature iron spears fastened together to form a necklace.

Today, some of this money would be classified as **commodity money**—money that has an alternative use as a commodity. The compressed tea leaves could be made into tea when not needed for trade. Other items became **fiat money**—money by government decree. Other early moneys included the tiny coins used in Asia Minor in the seventh century B.C. These coins had little use as a commodity, but served as money largely because the government said they were money. **1**

The use of money became accepted because it served everyone's best interests to do so. In this sense, money was then—and is now—a social convention, much like the general acceptance of laws and government.

Money in Colonial America

The money early settlers in America used was similar to the money found in earlier societies. Some of it was commodity money, and some was fiat money.

Commodity Money

Many products—gunpowder, musket balls, corn, and hemp—served as commodity money. Perhaps the most famous colonial money was tobacco. In 1618 the governor of colonial Virginia gave it a monetary value of three English shillings, or 36 English pennies, per pound. **2**

Wampum

Other colonies established fiat monies. In 1645 Connecticut set a monetary value for **wampum**—a

---

Checking Understanding

1. How does commodity money differ from fiat money?
2. What products in colonial America served as commodity money?

Applying Economic Concepts

☑ **Barter** Barter still has its uses. In some countries with very high tax rates, people sometimes prefer to be paid in goods and services rather than money. The reason? Income in the form of goods and services is less likely to come to the attention of the tax collector.

ANSWERS

1. Commodity money has an alternative use as a commodity. Fiat money has no other use except as money.
2. gunpowder, musket balls, corn, hemp, tobacco

CHAPTER 11: *Money and Banking* **267**

Meeting Special Needs

Attention Deficiency Students with attention problems are often distracted by movement and noise in the classroom. Have students make a self-evaluation checklist of their classroom attending behaviors by dividing a sheet of paper into two columns, one titled "On-task" and the other "Off-task." As they silently read any part of Section 1 (assign about 10 minutes of reading), call out "check" at intervals. They should put a check in the proper column depending on whether they were paying attention to their reading or whether their minds were "wandering." If they were "off-task," ask them if they know what interfered with their attention.

L1 *Applying Ideas* Call on students to name objects that might be used as money today if there were no dollar bills or coins. List about 10 responses on the chalkboard. Then organize students into groups of five and direct groups to apply the characteristics of money to the listed objects. Have groups select the object that would best serve as money based on their analysis. **LEP**

Independent Practice

📁 *Guided Reading* Assign Guided Reading Activity for Section 1. **LEP**

L3 *Pictorial Essay* Have students develop a four-page pictorial essay on the history of money from colonial times to the present day.

📁 *Consumer Application* Assign Consumer Application Activities 12 and 15.

📁 *Math Practice* Assign Math Practice for Economics 16.

📁 *Free Enterprise* Assign Free Enterprise Activities 4 and 15.

📁 *Readings* Assign Primary and Secondary Source Reading 15.

VISUAL INSTRUCTION

Yap money is not divisible. Small transactions on Yap take place with other units of money, which include smaller stones and beads.

Answer to Caption:
fiat money

form of currency the Narraganset Native Americans made out of white conch and black mussel shells. Because the Narraganset and the settlers used wampum in trade, 6 white or 3 black shells were made equal to 1 English penny. In 1648 the General Court of Massachusetts passed a law ordering the wampum to be "suitably strung" in lengths of 1, 3, and 12 pennies.

Paper Currency

As time went on, other forms of money were used. In some cases, state laws allowed individuals to print their own paper currency. Backed by gold and silver deposits in banks, it served as currency for the immediate area.

Some states passed tax-anticipation notes that could be redeemed with interest at the end of the year. The governments printed the notes, which were used to pay salaries, buy supplies, and meet other expenditures until taxes were received and the notes redeemed. The taxes, however, were collected in coins whenever possible.

Paper money was issued to finance the Revolutionary War. In 1775 the Continental Congress authorized the printing of Continental Currency, or Continental dollars—a form of fiat paper currency with no gold or silver backing. By the end of the war, nearly $250 million had been printed and spent to pay soldiers and to buy materials. **1**

Money *Stone money is still used on the Yap Islands.*
Would this form of money be considered commodity money or fiat money?

Specie

Specie is money in the form of coins, usually made from silver or gold. In the American colonies, some coins were English shillings used to pay government officials. Other coins included Spanish *pesos*, Austrian *talers*, and various European coins that immigrants brought to the colonies.

Coins were the most desirable form of money because most contained silver. Coins, however, were in short supply. By 1776, only $12 million in specie circulated in the colonies. Nearly $500 million in paper currency was in circulation, about one-half of which private individuals and states issued. **2**

Origins of the Dollar

When George Washington became President, one of his first challenges was to set up a new money supply. Benjamin Franklin and Secretary of the Treasury Alexander Hamilton were asked to design the new money, which they based on the Spanish peso.

Pesos

By the late 1700s, the most plentiful coin in circulation was the Spanish peso, which had come to America through piracy and trade. Long before the American Revolution had begun, the Spanish were mining silver in Mexico. They melted the silver into **bullion**—ingots or bars of precious metals—or minted it into coins for shipment to Spain. When the Spanish treasure ships stopped in the West Indies for fresh provisions, they often became victims of Caribbean pirates who spent their stolen treasure in America's southern colonies. ☑

The colonies engaged in a profitable trade known as the triangular trade, which exported rum and imported enslaved Africans. As shown in **Figure 11.1**, molasses from the West Indies was shipped to New England, where much of it was made into rum. The rum was shipped across the Atlantic Ocean to Africa, where it was exchanged for enslaved Africans, who were packed into ships and taken across the Atlantic to the West Indies. There, they would be sold for molasses and for pesos. Part of the income was used to buy more molasses, which, along with pesos, was taken to New England to begin the triangle again.

$ Free Enterprise Activity $

Reviewing the history of money in the United States is a good way to develop appreciation of the importance of stability as a necessary characteristic of money. Organize the class into several groups and assign each a period in U.S. history—the country under the Articles of Confederation, the post- Civil War period, the 1970s, for example. Have groups conduct research on the problems of monetary stability during their assigned periods. Then have groups prepare posters illustrating these problems. Direct groups to display posters on the bulletin board.

Figure 11.1

The triangular trade with Africa and the West Indies brought molasses, enslaved Africans, and Spanish pesos to the colonies. Pesos were also called dollars by the colonists because of their resemblance to the Austrian taler. Eventually, the dollar became the basic monetary unit of the United States. **What characteristics must money have to be a successful medium of exchange?**

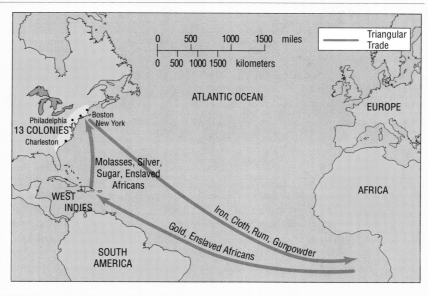

Talers

Pesos were known as pieces of eight, because they were divided into eight sub-parts known as *bits*. Because the pesos resembled the Austrian taler, they were nicknamed talers, which sounded like *dollars*. This term became so popular that Franklin and Hamilton decided to make the dollar the basic **monetary unit,** or standard unit of currency in a country's money system.

Rather than divide the dollar into eighths as the Spanish had done with the peso, Franklin and Hamilton

decided to divide it into tenths, which was easier to understand. Even today, some of the terminology associated with the Spanish peso remains. Many people call a 25-cent coin—one quarter of a dollar—"two bits."

Characteristics of Money

The study of early money is useful because it helps determine the characteristics that give money its value. To be a successful medium of exchange, money must be portable, durable, divisible, and limited in supply.

QUICK CHECK

Checking Understanding

1. What was used to finance the Revolutionary War?
2. Why were coins a more desirable form of money than paper?

Applying Economic Concepts

☑ **Inflation** The silver mined by the Spanish in the 1500s and 1600s led to massive inflation in Spain after the silver was shipped there. The oversupply of money caused prices to go up and the value of money to fall.

CHAPTER 11: *Money and Banking* **269**

Have You Got a Buck? In the frontier areas during the colonial period, hunters often left their deerskins at trading posts until they could pick them up at a later date. As proof of ownership, the frontiersmen would obtain a receipt, which they

could exchange among themselves or use at the trading post for supplies. The receipts, worth about a dollar because of the value of the hides, were called "bucks"—and hence the common name for the dollar.

Performance Assessment
Assign Performance Assessment Activity 16.

ASSESS

Check for Understanding

Assign Section 1 Review as homework or an in-class activity.

 Use **Chapter Challenger Interactive Review Software** to review Section 1.

MEETING LESSON OBJECTIVES

Each objective below is tested by the questions that follow it in parentheses.

1. **Explain** the three functions of money. **(1, 2, 6, 7)**
2. **Identify** four major types of money used in early societies. **(3)**
3. **Trace** the origins of the United States dollar. **(4)**
4. **Describe** four characteristics of money. **(5, 6)**

VISUAL INSTRUCTION

Ask: Based on information from the map, of what metal were pesos made? *(silver)*

Answer to Caption:

portability, durability, divisibility, limited availability

QUICK CHECK ANSWERS

1. Continental Currency, fiat paper currency with no gold or silver backing
2. because most coins contained silver

Evaluate

📁 📁 💻 Assign the Section 1 Quiz in the TCR or use the *Economics: Principles and Practices* Testmaker.

Reteach

Have students explain the relationship of the following to money: medium of exchange, measure of value, store of value, portability, durability, divisibility, limited availability.

Enrich

Have students investigate the steps taken by various countries to combat the counterfeiting of money. Have them present their findings in a written report.

CLOSE

Have students comment on the following statement: The American economy could not function without the dollar bill.

DID YOU KNOW?

What a Salary! Because of the shortage of gold and silver coins and the over-issue of paper currency, people continued to use commodity money after the American Revolution. In 1789 the region of Franklin, which is now part of Tennessee, passed an act that paid the governor a yearly salary of 1,000 deer skins and the Secretary of State 500 raccoon skins.

Portability

Money must be portable, or easily transferred from one person to another. Most money of early societies was very portable—including dog teeth, feather-stick money, and compressed blocks of tea and cheese.

Durability

If money was not reasonably durable, it would not last when handled. Most colonial money was quite durable. Wampum did not require special care when being handled, and it lasted a long time. The fiat paper money of the colonial period had a type of durability in that it could be easily replaced by issuing new bills when old ones became worn.

Divisibility

Money should be easily divisible into smaller units, so that people use only as much as needed for any transaction. Most early money was highly divisible. In the case of the Masai's iron spear currency, the necklace was untied and some of the spears removed. The blocks of tea or cheese were cut with a knife. Bundles of tobacco leaves were broken apart.

Limited Availability

Finally, if something is to serve as money, it must be available, but in limited supply. The dog teeth of New Guinea, for example, were extracted from packs of wild dogs. Because the islanders hunted the dogs for their teeth, the wild dog population never grew too large. Stones used as money on the Yap Islands were carried in open canoes from other islands 400 miles away. Because navigation was uncertain and the weather unpredictable, only 1 canoe in 20 made the round-trip. This ratio kept the supply of stone money from growing too fast.

Money, like almost everything else, loses its value whenever there is too much of it—a major problem for most types of commodity money. In Virginia, for example, the price of tobacco went from 36 pennies a pound to 1 penny a pound after everyone started growing their own money. Wampum even lost its value when settlers used industrial dyes to turn the white shells into black—hoping to double its value.

SECTION 1 REVIEW

Reviewing Terms and Facts

1. **Define** barter economy, money, medium of exchange, measure of value, store of value, commodity money, fiat money, wampum, specie, bullion, monetary unit.
2. **Describe** three functions of money.
3. **Name** five types of early money.
4. **Explain** how the dollar was adopted as the basic monetary unit.

5. **Identify** the four characteristics of money.

Critical Thinking

6. **Determining Cause and Effect** We sometimes hear rumors about changing our currency or specie to a different color, shape, or size. Explain how these changes would or would not affect the role money played.

Applying Economic Concepts

7. **Money** Write a brief critique of the following statement: "Money was invented to make our lives easier. As such, it is our servant, not our master. Those who treat money as the master rather than the servant do not really understand money."

---

1. All vocabulary words are defined in the Glossary.
2. Money acts as a medium of exchange, meaning that it is generally accepted as payment for goods and services; as a measure of value, meaning that it expresses worth in easily understandable terms; and as a store of value, meaning that goods and services can be converted into money, which is easy to store.
3. Any five of the following: cowrie shells, dog teeth, fish

Answers to SECTION 1 REVIEW

hooks, bird feathers attached to sticks, tea leaves compressed into "bricks," compressed cheese, miniature iron spears attached to form necklaces, stones

4. Benjamin Franklin and Alexander Hamilton were asked to design new money for the U.S. They based the design on the Spanish peso, which was nicknamed the *taler,* after an Austrian coin. Taler sounded like *dollar,* and the dollar was divided into tenths rather than eighths.

5. portable, durable, divisible, limited availability
6. Most students will note that as long as the new currency possesses the four characteristics of money and is readily accepted by all as a medium of exchange, its function would not be changed.
7. Most students will note that money is simply a tool that enables the economy to run smoothly.

TECHNOLOGY SKILL

Developing Multimedia Presentations

Your teacher has assigned you to make a classroom presentation. How do you make it interesting enough to hold everyone's attention? Your presentations can be exciting, especially if you use various media.

Explanation

At its most basic, a multimedia presentation involves using several types of media to present your information. To discuss the evolution of money, for example, you might show photographs of various currencies. In a multimedia presentation, you may also show computer graphics that update a historical time line about the development of money, and then present a video showing people using money, credit cards, and/or checks in various ways.

Multimedia as it relates to computer technology is the combination of text, video, audio, and animation in an interactive computer program. You merge computer as well as video images, combining such traditional computer creations as word processing and graphics with television, sound, and video.

In order to create multimedia presentations on a computer, you need to have certain tools. These may include graphic tools and draw programs, animation programs that make still images move, and authoring systems that tie everything together. Your computer manual will tell you which tools your computer can support.

Practice

Ask questions like the following to develop a multimedia presentation on the development of modern banking practices:
1. Which forms of media do I want to include? Video? Sound? Animation? Photographs? Graphics? Other?
2. Which of these media forms does my computer support?
3. What kind of software programs or systems do I need? A paint program? A draw program? An animation program? A program to create interactive, or two-way, communication? An authoring system that will allow me to change images, sound, and motion?
4. Is there a "do-it-all" program I can use to develop the kind of presentation I want?
   Keeping in mind the four guidelines given above, write a plan describing a multimedia presentation you would like to develop. Indicate what tools you will need and what steps you must take to make the presentation a reality.

Additional Practice

For further practice in developing multimedia presentations, complete the Reinforcing Skills exercise in the Chapter 11 Review on page 291.

TEACHING SKILLS

TEACH

This skill helps students develop the ability to create multimedia presentations. Encourage students to look at this skill as an adventure rather than as homework. Point out that this ability will do more than make for interesting classes. It might also prove helpful to them as they enter the workplace.

Have students brainstorm a list of possible forms of media that could be used in a multimedia presentation. Discuss the technologies pictured in the photograph, and also be prepared to demonstrate some of the media appliances. You may want to bring in a team teacher or guest speaker to discuss and demonstrate the development of multimedia presentations on a computer. If necessary, try to schedule computer lab time so that students can sample software and begin to build their own presentations.

📁 **Skills Practice** For additional practice, have students complete Reinforcing Economic Skill 11.

❓ DID YOU KNOW

A 1993 survey found that 7 out of 10 Americans favor putting new faces on their paper currency. First choice was the eagle; second, the Statue of Liberty; and third, President John F. Kennedy.

Answers to SKILL

Answers will vary, depending on students' imaginations, the aspects of the topic they want to present, and the hardware and software available. Make sure that students have checked their computers' capabilities and the available software. You might give students the option of working in groups.

Presentations should be related to modern banking practices. Be sure to arrange class time for the multimedia presentations that result.

FOCUS

Section Objectives

1. Explain the history of privately issued bank notes.

2. List five major types of currencies introduced after the Civil War.

3. State two advantages and two disadvantages of a gold standard.

4. Understand why the United States has an inconvertible money standard.

Bellringer

Prior to taking roll at the beginning of the class period, display Focus Activity Transparency 59 on the overhead projector and assign the accompanying Student Activity 59.

Motivational Activity

Discuss students' responses to the activity sheet that accompanies Focus Activity Transparency 59.

Preteaching Vocabulary

Call on students to explain the meanings of the key terms in their own words. Have students check the accuracy of these definitions by locating the terms in the text. **LEP**

Use the **Vocabulary PuzzleMaker** to create crossword and word search puzzles.

Early Banking and Monetary Standards

Section Preview

Objectives

After studying this section, you will be able to:

1. **Explain** the history of privately issued bank notes.

2. **List** five major types of currencies introduced after the Civil War.

3. **State** two advantages and two disadvantages of a gold standard.

4. **Understand** why the United States has an inconvertible money standard.

Key Terms

monetary standard, state bank, wildcat bank, legal tender, greenback, United States note, National Banking System, national bank, National Bank note, national currency, gold certificate, silver certificate, Treasury coin note, gold standard, inconvertible fiat money standard

Applying Economic Concepts

Legal Tender The currency in your possession states "This note is legal tender for all debts, public and private." This statement is the government's way of establishing paper currency as a uniform money supply, sometimes called *legal tender*. Having a uniform money supply frees you from bartering so you have time for other activities.

Money does more than make it easy to buy and sell goods and services. It also frees time and other resources so that people—and the economy—are productive. In order for a complex economy like that of the United States to run smoothly, it needs a reliable money supply. A **monetary standard**—the mechanism designed to keep the money supply portable, durable, divisible, and limited in supply—helps keep the money supply reliable. The United States has had several monetary standards.

Privately Issued Bank Notes

During the Revolutionary War, nearly $250 million worth of Continental Currency was printed. After the Revolution, Continental Currency was worthless, and people did not trust the government to issue anything except coin. Accordingly, Article 1, Section 8, of the United States Constitution states:

The Congress shall have the power
To coin money, regulate the value thereof, and of foreign coin, and fix the standard of weights and measures;
To provide for the punishment of counterfeiting the securities and current coin of the United States; . . .

To make all laws which shall be necessary and proper for carrying into execution the foregoing powers, and all other powers vested by this Constitution in the government of the United States, or in any department or officer thereof.

Article 1, Section 10, further states:
No State shall . . . coin money; emit bills of credit; make anything but gold and silver coin a tender in payment of debts. . . .

The Constitution, then, gave the federal government the power to mint coins. Section 8 was also widely interpreted to mean that the government could not print paper currency.

Growth of State Banking

By the late 1780s, only four banks existed in the United States. Each bank was allowed to issue its own money during the colonial period, and the new Constitution did not prohibit this practice. As a result, banks began to grow. By 1811 the country had about 100 banks, all but one of which was a **state bank**—a bank that receives its charter to operate from a state government.

The exception was the Bank of the United States which, like the state banks, was privately owned and

---

Classroom Resources for SECTION 2

- Reproducible Lesson Plan 11-2
- Guided Reading Activity 11-2
- Section Quiz 11-2
- Spanish Section Quiz 11-2

- Focus Activity Transparency 59
- Economic Concepts Transparency 6
- NBR's Economics in Action Video Program
- Testmaker
- Vocabulary PuzzleMaker
- Chapter Challenger Interactive Review Software

operated. The Bank of the United States, however, was much larger than any of the state banks and had a federal rather than a state charter. The Bank acted much like the current Department of the Treasury in that it collected fees and made payments on behalf of the federal government.

State banks issued their own currency by printing their notes at local printing shops. People who wanted loans borrowed these notes and paid them back with interest. Because the federal government did not print paper currency until the Civil War, most of the money supply was paper currency that privately owned, state-chartered banks issued.

Abuses in Banking

Most banks printed only the amount of currency they could back with their gold and silver reserves so that people could redeem their notes for gold or silver. Others, however, printed large amounts of currency, and then spent it in distant cities. These banks, often

located in remote areas, hoped it would take a long time for the notes to return to them for redemption. Banks that over-printed their currencies were called **wildcat banks** because people claimed a person had to be a wildcat to get to them.

Problems With Currency

Even when banks were honest, two problems with currency arose. First, each bank issued a different currency. Hundreds of different kinds of notes could be in circulation in any given city. Second, because a bank could print more money whenever it wanted, the temptation to issue too many notes always existed.

By the Civil War, the United States had more than 1,600 banks issuing more than 10,000 kinds of paper currency. Each bank was supposed to have backing in the form of gold or silver, but this was seldom the case. As a result, when people tried to buy something, their notes were often checked against the latest listing of good and bad bank notes.

Figure 11.2
The Metallic Content of United States Coins

	OLD PENNY	NEW PENNY	NICKEL	DIME	QUARTER	HALF DOLLAR	SUSAN B. ANTHONY DOLLAR
	95% copper 5% zinc	97.5% zinc 2.5% nickel	75% copper 25% nickel	91.7% copper 8.3% nickel	91.7% copper 8.3% nickel	91.7% copper 8.3% nickel	87.5% copper 12.5% nickel
Value*	4/10 of one cent	2/10 of one cent	One cent	4/10 of one cent	One cent	Two cents	One cent

*value varies with the price of metal

Source: Bureau of the Mint

The metallic content of coins is selected for both function and value. Metallic alloys that are durable and do not tarnish easily are used whenever possible. The metallic content of coins must also have very low value so that people do not melt them down for their specie content. **What types of currencies did the United States use between 1861 and 1900?**

TEACH

Guided Practice

L1 Constructing a Time Line
Review with students the steps in the development of our modern monetary standard. Then ask students to prepare an illustrated time line on this development. Organize students into small groups and assign each group a time period from colonial times to the present. Have groups assemble pictures or create drawings to illustrate important stages in the development of the monetary standard during their assigned periods. Have groups display their section, in correct chronological order, on the bulletin board. **LEP**

Using Transparencies
Display Economic Concepts Transparency 6. Spanish Transparencies also are available.

 VISUAL INSTRUCTION

Have students use information in Figure 11.2 to demonstrate that the value of the metallic content of a coin has nothing to do with its face value. *(Face value of coins varies from one cent to a dollar, yet content value is never above two cents.)*

Answer to Caption:

There were numerous currencies in use, but five major ones were greenbacks, national currency, gold certificates, silver certificates, Treasury coin notes.

Meeting Special Needs

Attention Deficiency Presenting information in small segments greatly aids many students with attention problems. Ask students to read Section 2 and self-monitor their attention to the task. Ask them whether they think it is easier to read through the whole section and then take notes or if it is better for them to break the reading into briefer units and vary the activity with writing. Point out that there is not a "correct way." The best approach will be the one that works for them.

Greenbacks *This turn-of-the-century greenback was officially backed by gold after 1900.* **What is legal tender?**

The Greenback Standard

Numerous currencies were in use in the United States between 1861 and 1900. One currency, however, dominated during these four decades and became the main monetary standard of the time.

Greenbacks

When the Civil War erupted, both the North and the South needed to raise enormous sums to finance the war. Congress tried to borrow money by selling bonds, but bond sales did not raise as much money as the government needed, so Congress decided to print money.

In 1861 Congress authorized the printing of $60 million of notes called demand notes. Each note, like the state bank notes in existence at the time, was signed by hand—a practice that required many clerks. Although these notes had no gold or silver backing, they were declared **legal tender**—a fiat currency that must be accepted in payment for debts. Because both sides of the notes were printed with green ink to distinguish them from the state notes already in circulation, the new notes were soon dubbed **greenbacks.**

Greenbacks were used mostly in the North, but more money was soon needed. In 1862 Congress passed the Legal Tender Act, which gave the national government the right to print $150 million of **United States notes,** a new currency that had no gold or silver backing. Almost one-half of the currency in circulation in 1863 was United States notes, also called greenbacks.

National Currency

As the war dragged on, and as the amount of greenbacks grew, people feared that the currency might become worthless. They avoided the greenback, and the government was forced to find another way to finance the war.

The answer was to create a **National Banking System** (NBS), which was to consist of financially sound and rigorously inspected private banks. These banks received their charters from the national government and were known as **national banks.** The government hoped the high standards for member banks would give people confidence in the system and its currency. Each bank would issue **National Bank notes** or **national currency,** which were to be uniform in appearance and backed by United States government bonds.

This backing made the currency seem more secure to the public. It also generated a demand for the bonds that the government sold at the outbreak of the Civil War. If a group wanted to set up a national bank, it had to first purchase government bonds as part of the requirement to get the national charter. The bonds were then put on deposit with the United States Treasury as backing against the currency. ☑

Initially, few state-chartered banks joined the system. It was easier for them to have money printed at a local printer than to buy bonds, secure a charter, and then exchange the bonds for national currency. In 1865 the federal government tried to force state banks into the National Banking System by placing a 10 percent tax on all privately issued bank notes. Because state-chartered banks could not afford the tax, they

---

$ Free Enterprise Activity $

Have students experience monetary expansion, such as that which occurred with the issue of Continental Currency or the issue of currency by state banks. Distribute play money of various denominations to the class. Place a number of items, such as a meal ticket, a candy bar, or a pen on the desk and sell a few of the items for the play money. Next, give students twice as much money as they received in the first distribution. Ask them if they are any better off now than they were when they received the first batch of money. Then sell the rest of the items, but at double the original price. Conclude by pointing out that increasing the supply of money means each dollar is actually worth less and will buy less. Although students had more money, they were not better off because their purchasing power had not increased.

withdrew their notes from circulation, leaving only the greenbacks and national currency in circulation. **1**

Gold Certificates

The removal of more than 10,000 different sizes and denominations of state bank notes simplified the currency system for everyone. Before long, however, new types of federal currency appeared.

In 1863 the government issued **gold certificates**— paper currency backed by gold on deposit with the United States Treasury. At first, these yellowbacks, so-called because of the bright yellow ink used on both sides of the bill, were printed in large denominations for banks to use in settling differences with each other at the end of the business day. By 1882, however, the government began printing gold certificates in $20 denominations for the public's general use.

Silver Certificates

In 1886 the federal government issued another kind of paper currency called a silver certificate. **Silver certificates** were modeled after the gold certificates and were backed by silver coins placed on deposit with the Treasury.

Silver certificates were printed as part of a program to support silver prices for miners in the West. The Bland-Allison Act, passed in 1878, required the federal government to buy large amounts of silver and then mint the ore into silver dollars.

Silver dollars were bulky and inconvenient to use, however, so the Bland-Allison Act was amended in 1886 to provide for the printing of silver certificates. Under the amendment, the government agreed to buy silver and hold it in reserve against the silver certificates—thereby pleasing the silver miners while giving the public an alternative to the generally unwanted silver dollars.

Treasury Coin Notes

In 1890 the federal government printed the fifth, and last, type of paper currency issued before the banking system was overhauled in 1913. The currency came in the form of **Treasury coin notes**— paper currency redeemable in both gold and silver. The law was repealed in 1893, and further issues of Treasury coin notes were ended. Because so many were issued in such a short period, however, Treasury coin notes remained in circulation until the 1930s.

The Gold Standard

In 1900 Congress passed the Gold Standard Act, which defined the dollar as being worth 1/20.67 ounce of gold. Congress thus put the country on a **gold standard**—a monetary standard under which the basic unit of currency is equivalent to, and can be exchanged for, a set amount of gold.

Going on the Gold Standard

The Gold Standard Act did not affect the type of currency people used. People continued to use gold certificates, silver certificates, United States notes, National Bank notes, and Treasury coin notes. The only difference was that they could exchange these notes for gold at the Treasury whenever they wanted.

Advantages of a Gold Standard

In general, a gold standard has two major advantages. First, people feel more secure about their money because they know they can always convert it into gold. Second, it prevents the government from printing too much paper currency. The theory is that as long as the government has promised to redeem its

---

QUICK CHECK

Checking Understanding

1. Why did the National Banking System place a 10-percent tax on privately issued bank notes?

Applying Economic Concepts

 Greenback Party The Greenback Party was formed in 1874 to promote the printing of money not backed by gold. Made up mostly of farmers, the Greenbackers believed the issuance of more currency would enable them to pay off their debts.

CHAPTER 11: *Money and Banking* **275**

L2 *Creating Designs* Have students look at any coins and paper currency they have with them. Ask them if the money looks "modern." Tell them that the government has decided to update the currency and give it the "look of the 21st century." Have students draw designs for at least two coins and two notes of this new money. Call on volunteers to present and explain their designs.

L3 *Research* Have students write a research paper on either the monetary issues that dominated American politics in the second half of the 1800s or the operation of the gold standard in the United States. Select students to read their papers to the class.

ASSESS

Check for Understanding

Assign Section 2 Review as homework or an in-class activity.

 Use **Chapter Challenger Interactive Review Software** to review Section 2.

CURRICULUM CONNECTIONS

History The move to the gold standard was made possible by the discovery of huge deposits of gold in South Africa and in the Klondike region of Canada.

QUICK CHECK

ANSWERS

1. to force state banks into the system

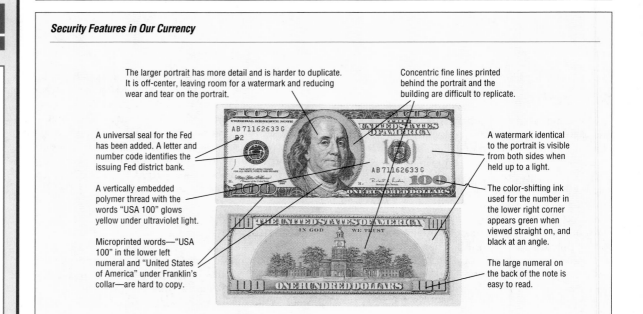

Security Features in Our Currency

The larger portrait has more detail and is harder to duplicate. It is off-center, leaving room for a watermark and reducing wear and tear on the portrait.

Concentric fine lines printed behind the portrait and the building are difficult to replicate.

A universal seal for the Fed has been added. A letter and number code identifies the issuing Fed district bank.

A vertically embedded polymer thread with the words "USA 100" glows yellow under ultraviolet light.

Microprinted words—"USA 100" in the lower left numeral and "United States of America" under Franklin's collar—are hard to copy.

A watermark identical to the portrait is visible from both sides when held up to a light.

The color-shifting ink used for the number in the lower right corner appears green when viewed straight on, and black at an angle.

The large numeral on the back of the note is easy to read.

paper currency in gold, it will print only that amount of money that can be backed by gold. The currency will remain relatively scarce and, therefore, will be more likely to keep its value.

When the United States went on the gold standard, it did not have enough gold to back all paper currency in circulation. This is usually the case for any country that goes on a gold standard, because a country only needs to have the appearance that its currency can be redeemed for gold. It is unlikely that all notes will be redeemed at one time.

Disadvantages of a Gold Standard

One disadvantage of a gold standard is that a growing economy needs a growing money supply, which requires a growing gold stock to back it. If new gold supplies cannot be found, the growth of the money supply eventually begins to slow and perhaps stop, restricting economic growth. Another disadvantage is that people may decide to convert their currency into gold, thereby draining the government of its gold reserves.

Abandoning the Gold Standard

The gold standard remained in force until the Depression years of the 1930s. By that time, banks

began to fail, and many people could not find jobs. Because people felt safer holding gold rather than paper currency, they began to cash in their dollars for gold. Foreign governments with large holdings of dollars began to do the same thing.

The federal government feared it could not continue to back the money supply with gold. On August 28, 1933, President Franklin D. Roosevelt declared a national emergency and decreed that anyone holding more than $100 worth of gold or gold certificates file a disclosure form with the United States Treasury.

Several months later, the Gold Reserve Act of 1934 was passed. It required citizens, banks, and businesses to turn their gold and gold certificates over to the United States government. Those who had filed a disclosure had no choice but to surrender their gold holdings. Others simply ignored the government and kept their gold. Regardless, the United States went off the gold standard in 1934.

The Inconvertible Fiat Money Standard

Since 1934 the United States has been on the **inconvertible fiat money standard.** Under this standard, the money supply is *inconvertible* because it

---

Cultural Diversity and Economics

Some countries—India, for example—operated not on the gold standard, but on the *gold exchange standard.* In this system, people could not exchange their paper notes for gold on demand. Rather, they could get on demand the currency of a country that was on the gold standard. Thus, in the early 1900s, Indians might have gotten American dollars or English pounds sterling—currencies on the gold standard—in exchange for their paper money.

cannot be converted into gold or silver by United States citizens. It is a *fiat* money standard because government decree declared dollars legal money. Since 1975, however, American citizens have been allowed to own gold.

A Managed Money Supply

The money supply of the United States, much like those of other major industrialized countries, is a managed money supply. The government or its designated agent tries to control the quantity, composition, and even the quality of the money supply.

This task is somewhat easier now that a single currency has replaced the early forms of currency. National currency and Treasury coin notes were withdrawn from circulation in the 1930s, and gold certificates were confiscated in 1934. The last issue of United States notes (greenbacks) took place in 1968, and some were still in circulation in the early 1970s. Silver certificates also circulated in the early 1970s, but the government stopped redeeming them for silver dollars in 1968.

Modern money consists largely of checking accounts, coins, and a single currency issued by the Federal Reserve System. How well the money functions depends in part on how well it satisfies the four characteristics of money examined earlier.

Characteristics of Modern Money

Although money has changed in shape, kind, and size over the years, modern money still shares many of the same characteristics of early money. As a medium of exchange, modern money satisfies the four characteristics of money.

Modern money is portable. When people carry checkbooks, they really are carrying very large sums of money, because checks can be written in almost any amount.

Modern money is also durable. Metallic coins last a long time under normal use, and they generally do not go out of circulation unless they are lost. Paper currency also is reasonably durable, with a $1 bill lasting about 18 months in circulation. Checks and checking accounts never wear out.

Modern money rates high on divisibility. The penny, which is the smallest denomination of coin, is small enough for almost any purchase. In addition, checks can be written for the exact amount.

Modern money has an uneven track record when it comes to limited availability and stability in value. The high rates of inflation in the late 1970s and early 1980s tell us that money was not as scarce as it could have been. The money supply, which often grew at a rate of 10 to 12 percent a year during that period, was considered a major cause of inflation.

Reteach

Have students outline the material in the section using the following framework:
Early Banking and Monetary Standards
I. Privately Issued Bank Notes
II. The Greenback Standard
III. The Gold Standard
IV. The Inconvertible Fiat Money Standard

Enrich

Have students prepare an illustrated report on the operations of one of the two agencies that make American currency—the Bureau of the Mint and the Bureau of Engraving and Printing.

CLOSE

Ask students to speculate about what our modern money system would be like if the U.S. were still on the gold standard. Have students give specific illustrations in short essays.

SECTION 2 REVIEW

Reviewing Terms and Facts

1. **Define** monetary standard, state bank, wildcat bank, legal tender, greenback, United States note, National Banking System, national bank, National Bank note, national currency, gold certificate, silver certificate, Treasury coin note, gold standard, inconvertible fiat money standard.
2. **Explain** how privately issued bank notes became part of the money supply.

3. **List** the five major currencies in use after the Civil War.
4. **Explain** why the United States went off the gold standard.
5. **Identify** the characteristics of an inconvertible fiat money standard.

Critical Thinking

6. **Making Comparisons** Some experts have proposed a return to the gold standard. Explain why you think this may or may not be a good idea.

Applying Economic Concepts

7. **Legal Tender** Suppose that Federal Reserve notes did not exist to serve as "legal tender." What else could be done to establish a suitable money supply?

Answers to SECTION 2 REVIEW

1. All vocabulary words are defined in the Glossary.

2. Because the federal government did not print currency until the Civil War, most of the money supply was paper currency issued by privately owned state-chartered banks.

3. greenbacks, national currency, gold certificates, silver certificates, Treasury coin notes

4. During the Depression, many banks failed. People cashed in their dollars for gold, because

they felt safer holding gold rather than paper currency. As a result, the federal government felt it could no longer back the money supply with gold, and it went off the gold standard.

5. Money is not convertible into gold or silver, but it is legal tender because of government decree.

6. Answers may vary. Some students may argue that it is a bad idea, because the money supply would be tied to the amount of gold the country possessed, and a restricted money supply could

impede economic growth. Others might state that it is a good idea, because it would make certain that the value of money remained stable.

7. Answers will vary. As guidance, suggest that students review the development of the monetary standard in the U.S.

Background

Winfrey's father believed that education was the key to success, and he made certain that she had every opportunity to learn. Following her father's beliefs, Winfrey established a $750,000 scholarship fund at Tennessee State University in 1987. "My mission is to use [my] position, power and money to create opportunities for other people," she said.

TEACH

Review the profile with students. Then ask them to note what brought about Winfrey's rise to prominence. *(her ambition and hard work, experience in the television talk-show field, wise business moves)*

School to WORK

Journalist Have students learn more about journalism by volunteering to work on your school newspaper or yearbook staff. Or plan a visit to a local newspaper office. Ask a journalist to discuss his or her job qualifications and responsibilities. Have students prepare questions in advance of the visit.

OPRAH WINFREY
(1954–)

Oprah Winfrey is one of the richest and most powerful women in America. Most people know her as an experienced talk show host, but she has other talents as well. As an actress, she received an Oscar nomination for Best Supporting Actress in *The Color Purple*. As a businessperson, she is the third woman in history (after Mary Pickford and Lucille Ball) to own a major television and film studio. With an annual income of about $100 million, she is poised to become the country's first African American billionaire.

AGAINST ALL ODDS Winfrey's beginnings were humble. She was born to unwed teenage parents in rural Mississippi and grew up in poverty. A troubled childhood followed. Eventually, the teenager went to live with her father, whose insistence on discipline and education soon turned her life around.

At the age of 17, Winfrey became a part-time radio newscaster on Nashville's WVOL. Two years later, while she was attending Tennessee State University, she was hired as a reporter and anchor on WTVF-TV.

In 1976 Winfrey moved to Baltimore, where she found her niche in television as cohost of a Baltimore morning show called "People Are Talking." Winfrey's successful experience in Baltimore paved the way for her to become the undisputed "Queen of Talk" in Chicago.

In 1984 Winfrey took over the ailing "AM Chicago" on WLS-TV. She turned it into a smash hit, driving the successful "Phil Donahue Show" to another city and another time slot. In 1986 the "Oprah Winfrey Show" became nationally syndicated. Within months, it was the third highest rated show in syndication. It became the number one talk show, reaching between 9 and 10 million people daily in more than 190 cities and 12 foreign countries.

Winfrey became the first African American woman to own her own television and film production complex— Harpo Productions, Inc. (Harpo is Oprah spelled backwards).

MAKING A DIFFERENCE Winfrey uses her wealth and influence to make a difference in the lives of others. Under her guidance, *The Oprah Winfrey Show* avoids sensationalism, focusing instead on issues such as drug dependency, weight control, and upbeat topics such as poetry and book clubs.

Winfrey is also a staunch children's rights activist. She proposed a bill to create a national database of convicted child abusers, which President Clinton signed into law in 1994.

Winfrey hosts her talk show.

Examining the Profile

1. **Drawing Conclusions** Why is Oprah Winfrey considered one of the most powerful women in America?

2. **For Further Research** Find out about the many awards Oprah Winfrey has won. Make a time line of her career, showing major achievements.

Answers to Examining the Profile

1. because of her position as one of the richest entertainers in the U.S., her ownership of a television and film production complex, the far reach of her syndicated talk show

2. Time lines may vary. Call on volunteers to display and discuss their time lines.

Section Preview

Objectives

After studying this section, you will be able to:

1. **Explain** the development of the National Banking System.
2. **Relate** the effects of Depression-era bank failures on deposit insurance creation.
3. **Identify** three other forms of depository institutions.

Key Terms

dual banking system, Federal Reserve System, central bank, Federal Reserve note, run on the bank, bank holiday, commercial bank, demand deposit account, thrift institution, mutual savings bank, savings bank, Negotiable Order of Withdrawal, savings and loan association, share draft

Applying Economic Concepts

Demand Deposit Accounts You probably think that checking accounts are pretty useful. A number of post-Civil War bankers thought so, too. They developed *demand deposit accounts* as a way to avoid federal regulation of their activities, not to make life easier for their customers.

anks fulfill two distinct needs in a community. They provide a safe place for people to deposit their money, and they lend excess funds to individuals and businesses temporarily in need of cash. In effect, banks act as economic institutions that bring savers and borrowers together.

The National Banking System

In 1863 the federal government tried to bring the state banks under control by passing the National Banking Act. It set up a system of nationally chartered and inspected banks known as the National Banking System. State banks were invited to become national banks by surrendering their state charters for federal ones.

National Bank Requirements

Those banks that joined the system had to fulfill certain requirements. One was to use *National* or *N.A.*, which stood for National Association, in their titles. The first bank in a community to join the system was generally called the First National Bank; the second, the Second National Bank; and so on. After a number of national banks existed in the community, new members used such titles as the People's National Bank of Commerce, Citizens' National Bank, and the Farmer's and Merchant's Trade Bank, N.A.

A second requirement was to pass stiff inspections by the Comptroller of the Currency, a Treasury Department official appointed by the President to supervise national banks. Because the inspections were rigorous, people knew that national banks, as a group, were relatively safe places to keep their deposits.

A third requirement was for banks to purchase government bonds, which were then used to back the national currency. This final requirement created a new demand for the war bonds that the government was trying to sell during the Civil War.

Dual Banking

Not all banks wanted to join the National Banking System. Some banks managed to remain independent even after the 10 percent tax was placed on privately issued bank notes. They decided to make loans by issuing checking accounts instead of currency.

Use of checking accounts was a relatively new idea. After several years of experimentation, however, many people discovered that checking accounts could be used effectively in place of currency. As a result, the number of state-chartered banks began to grow again after 1880. As shown in **Figure 11.3**, the number of state banks exceeded national banks by 1887.

By then the country had a well-established **dual banking system**—a system that allows banks to obtain charters from either the state or the federal government. Dual banking is a feature of banking

TEACH

Guided Practice

L2 Preparing Lesson Plans
Organize the class into three sections and assign each section one of the following topics: The National Banking System, Banking During the Depression, Other Depository Institutions. Have students in each section work individually to develop a lesson plan to teach their assigned topic to the class. Encourage them to include illustrations where appropriate. Select students from each section to present their lesson plans to the class.

VISUAL INSTRUCTION

Ask: Why did the number of state banks grow markedly after 1880? *(More and more people discovered that checking accounts could be used in place of currency.)*

Answer to Caption:

At present, there are about twice as many state banks as there are national banks.

CURRICULUM CONNECTIONS

History During the Great Depression, the money supply fell by about one-third, causing a nationwide shortage of currency. As a result, towns, counties, and even civic organizations printed their own private currency—known as depression-era script. Some estimates put the amount of script in circulation as high as $1 billion.

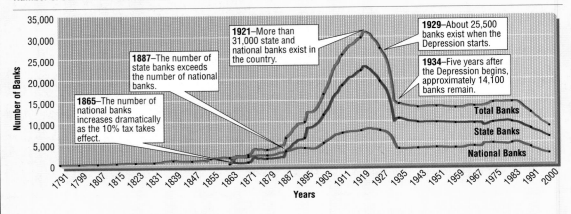

Figure 11.3
Number of State and National Banks

1865—The number of national banks increases dramatically as the 10% tax takes effect.

1887—The number of state banks exceeds the number of national banks.

1921—More than 31,000 state and national banks exist in the country.

1929—About 25,500 banks exist when the Depression starts.

1934—Five years after the Depression begins, approximately 14,100 banks remain.

Total Banks
State Banks
National Banks

Source: Federal Deposit Insurance Corporation and *Historical Statistics of the United States, Colonial Times to 1970.*

The number of banks in the United States grew rapidly after 1880 and peaked in 1921. A period of mergers and consolidations took place from 1921 to 1929, after which the Great Depression took its toll. The number of banks remained relatively constant from 1933 to the 1980s, when another wave of mergers took place. **What can you infer about the state bank–national bank ratio from this graph?**

today, but a choice of charters was never the intent of the National Banking legislation when it was first enacted. Nor was it the intent of Congress when the 10 percent banknote tax was passed. Federal authorities just never thought that checking accounts would become so important.

Need for Further Reform

By 1910 banking reform again was needed. One major reason was that the National Banking System was not designed to deal with the unusually large number of checks being written. Checks written in one bank and deposited in another often took weeks to clear, even when the banks were in the same city.

Another reason for reform was that currency backed by government bonds was difficult to maintain. When the government started to run federal budget surpluses in the 1890s, it decided to reduce the public debt by buying back some of the bonds. Therefore, fewer bonds were available as reserves against the national bank notes.

A final problem was that banks had no place to go for help in times of need. When people needed to borrow money, they could go to a bank. When a national bank needed to borrow funds, however, it could only go to its competitors.

The Federal Reserve System

Reform came in 1913, when Congress created the **Federal Reserve System,** or Fed, to serve as the nation's first true **central bank**—a bank that can lend to other banks in times of need. All national banks were required to join the Fed, and all state-chartered banks were eligible to do so.

The member banks own the Federal Reserve System, although the President of the United States appoints its managers with the approval of Congress. The Fed also has its own currency, called **Federal Reserve notes,** that eventually replaced all other types of federal currency. Federal Reserve notes were backed by gold when first issued in 1914, but became inconvertible fiat money after 1934.

Meeting Special Needs

Learning Disability Students with learning disabilities in reading or with other reading comprehension problems often do not practice or use good self-appraisal and self-management skills while they read. Encourage these skills by making students aware of the need for these unconscious activities. As students read Section 3, tell them to be aware of processes they use to help them understand the material. Have them note the number of times they reread phrases or sentences. Explain that rereading is important for understanding.

Banking During the Great Depression

Although the National Banking System and the Federal Reserve System were operational, many banks were only marginally sound during the 1920s. Part of the reason was the overabundance of banks, a result of the heated expansion that took place between 1880 and 1921. Although some consolidation occurred between 1921 and 1929, the banking industry was overextended when the Great Depression began in 1929.

Bank Failures

The number of bank failures during the 1930s was staggering! At the start of the Depression, about 25,500 banks existed—none of which had any deposit insurance for their customers. As a result, concern about the safety of the deposits often caused a **run on the bank**—a rush by depositors to withdraw their funds from a bank before it failed.

Panic was so widespread that on March 5, 1933, President Roosevelt announced a **bank holiday**—a brief period during which every bank in the country was required to close. Several days later, after Congress passed legislation that strengthened banking, most banks were allowed to reopen. By 1934 more than 10,000 banks had closed or merged with stronger partners.

Federal Deposit Insurance

When banks failed during the Depression, people lost almost everything they had deposited. The Banking Act of 1933, sometimes known as the Glass-Steagall Act, was passed to strengthen the banking industry. Among other changes, the act created the Federal Deposit Insurance Corporation (FDIC) to insure customer deposits in the event of a bank failure. The initial coverage was only $2,500 per account, but it has since been increased to a maximum of $100,000. **1**

The insurance did little for those who lost their savings, but it has provided a sense of security in banking ever since. After the FDIC was created, people worried less about the safety of their deposits, reducing the number of runs on a bank.

Other Depository Institutions

Banks chartered by states or the National Banking System were generally known as **commercial banks** and were distinguished by two primary characteristics. First, they catered to the interests of business and commerce. Second, until the mid-1970s, they were the only financial institutions that issued **demand deposit accounts** (DDAs)—accounts whose funds could be removed by simply writing a check without prior approval from the depository institution. **2**

Other financial institutions accepted the deposits of small investors and, until the mid-1970s, generally did not have demand deposit accounts. These institutions included savings banks as well as savings and loan associations. Historically, they were called **thrift institutions,** or thrifts, because they generally paid higher rates of interest on savings accounts.

Savings Banks

One of the oldest savings institutions in the United States is the **mutual savings bank** (MSB), a depositor-owned financial organization operated only for the benefit of its depositors. Because they had no stockholders, boards of trustees made up of

Checking Understanding

1. What is the purpose of the Federal Deposit Insurance Corporation?
2. What is a demand deposit account?

Applying Economic Concepts

☑ **Bank Failures** From March 5 to March 9, Secretary of the Treasury William Woodin and his advisers worked around the clock to hammer out legislation that would end the banking crisis.

CHAPTER 11
SECTION 3

GLENCOE
TECHNOLOGY

NIGHTLY BUSINESS REPORT

Economics in Action

Chapter 20
Disc 2, Side 1
Title: *Money and Banking*
Subject: Role of banks
Ask: Why were people reluctant to place their money in banks during the early 1900s? *(because banks failed frequently, taking their depositors' money with them)*

Also available in VHS.

Independent Practice

📂 **Guided Reading** Assign Guided Reading Activity for Section 3. **LEP**

L2 **Research** Have students research the Banking Act of 1933. Suggest that students focus their research on the particular conditions during the Great Depression that made the Banking Act necessary. Have students present their findings in a written report.

QUICK CHECK

ANSWERS

1. to insure customer deposits in event of bank failure
2. account in which funds could be removed by simply writing check without prior approval from depository institution

businesspeople who served without pay managed MSBs. Later, many MSBs decided to sell stock to raise additional financial capital. These institutions became **savings banks** (SBs) because depositors do not mutually own them.

Mutual savings banks got their start in the early 1800s. At that time, commercial banks catered primarily to the needs of business and were not interested in the accounts of small wage earners. Savings banks emerged to fill that need. They were popular with consumers and began to spread west following the industrial growth of the large cities.

By the mid-1800s, commercial banks began to notice the savings accounts of factory workers and other wage earners. Commercial banks, along with the savings and loan associations of the period, began to compete more heavily with the savings banks. As a result, savings banks did not spread beyond their foothold in the industrial northeast and those states shown in Figure 11.4.

Even so, savings banks are a powerful influence in the economy. In 1972 the Consumer's Savings Bank of Worcester, Massachusetts, introduced a **Negotiable**

Order of Withdrawal (NOW) account, a type of checking account that pays interest. Because commercial banks had a virtual monopoly on checking accounts at the time, they strongly opposed NOW accounts.

Despite the opposition, the savings banks had political power at the state level, and NOW accounts were allowed to remain in New England. At the national level, however, commercial bankers pushed for federal legislation that temporarily prevented NOW accounts from spreading outside New England. NOW accounts were not available to depository institutions nationwide until 1980.

Savings and Loan Associations

Another type of financial institution was the **savings and loan association** (S&L)—a financial institution that invested the majority of its funds in home mortgages. S&Ls began as cooperative clubs for home-builders in the 1800s. The association's members promised to deposit a certain sum regularly into the association. Members then took turns borrowing money to build a home. By doing this, people had an arrangement that

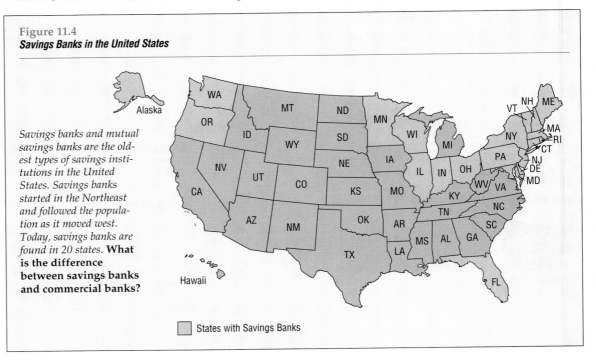

Figure 11.4
Savings Banks in the United States

Savings banks and mutual savings banks are the oldest types of savings institutions in the United States. Savings banks started in the Northeast and followed the population as it moved west. Today, savings banks are found in 20 states. **What is the difference between savings banks and commercial banks?**

☐ States with Savings Banks

Extending the Content

Secondary Bank Functions In recent years, banking and financial institutions have taken on many secondary functions. One is issuing credit cards, such as Mastercard or Visa, which, in a sense, are short-term loans. Some larger banks process credit card payments for major credit card issuers, such as oil companies and large retail operations. In addition, a number of institutions accept utility payments as a convenience for their customers. Many banks provide trust services and investment and business counseling. Furthermore, many banks sell traveler's checks and money orders, rent safety deposit boxes, and provide foreign currency exchange. Banking officials believe that institutions must offer a variety of financial services in order to compete in the marketplace.

individual savings and loan associations. The Board was modeled after components of the Federal Reserve System, which regulated commercial banks. The Federal Savings and Loan Insurance Corporation (FSLIC), a federal government agency much like the FDIC that serves commercial bankers, insured savings and loan deposits.

Credit Unions

A fourth type of depository institution is the credit union. Credit unions are owned and operated by and for their members. Costs are generally low because a sponsor, which may be the members' union or place of employment, often provides management, help, and office facilities.

Because most credit unions are organized around an employer, contributions generally are deducted directly from a worker's paycheck. In recent years, some credit unions followed the commercial and mutual savings banks by offering checking deposits. Known as **share drafts,** they look like any other check or NOW account and provide members with a way to earn interest on deposits that are also available on demand.

Credit union assets are the loans they make to members. Although these assets generally are relatively small, credit unions outnumber commercial banks, S&Ls, or mutual savings banks.

supplied funds for home-building in areas where other sources of financing were not available.

Later, in the 1930s, the Federal Home Loan Bank Board was created to supervise and regulate the

Evaluate

📁 📁 💻 Assign the Section 3 Quiz in the TCR or use the *Economics: Principles and Practices* Testmaker to create a customized quiz. Spanish Section Quizzes also are available in the Spanish Resources Binder.

Reteach

Have students use the key terms listed in the Section Preview to write a summary of the section.

Enrich

Have students research the history and development of banking, or the history of a particular bank, in the community. Suggest that students use the local library, historical society, or banks as sources of information. Encourage students to present their findings in an illustrated time line.

CLOSE

Have students interview a local banker and ask the following questions: Do you ever fear a "run on the bank"? Why or why not? Have students share the results of their interviews.

SECTION 3 REVIEW

Reviewing Terms and Facts

1. **Define** dual banking system, Federal Reserve System, central bank, Federal Reserve note, run on the bank, bank holiday, commercial bank, demand deposit account, thrift institution, mutual savings bank, savings bank, Negotiable Order of Withdrawal, savings and loan association, share draft.
2. **Explain** why the National

Banking System was created.
3. **Explain** why deposit insurance developed in the 1930s.
4. **Identify** three depository institutions.

Critical Thinking

5. **Identifying Alternatives** The FDIC insures deposits up to $100,000. What would you do if you had $400,000 you wanted to deposit and insure?

Applying Economic Concepts

6. **Demand Deposit Accounts** When Adam Smith wrote *An Inquiry into the Nature and Causes of the Wealth of Nations,* he argued that a competitive economy functioned best when everyone pursued their own best interests. Explain how the self-interest of state-chartered banks in 1865 led to the development of demand deposit accounts.

Answers to SECTION 3 REVIEW

1. All vocabulary words are defined in the Glossary.

2. The National Banking System was created to bring the state banks under control and to help finance the Civil War.

3. When banks failed during the Depression, depositors lost all their money. Deposit insurance was established to prevent this situation from happening again.

4. savings banks, savings and loan associations,

credit unions

5. Answers may vary, but most students probably will suggest that they would deposit $100,000 each in four different institutions to make certain all their investments were insured.

6. Banks that wanted to remain independent of the National Banking System could not issue their own currency without paying the 10 percent tax, so they developed checking accounts that were not subject to taxation.

SECTION 4
Crisis, Reform, and Evolution in the 1980s

FOCUS

Section Objectives

1. Explain the forces leading to deregulation of financial institutions in the 1980s.

2. Relate the history of the savings and loan crisis.

Bellringer

 Prior to taking roll at the beginning of the class period, display Focus Activity Transparency 62 on the overhead projector and assign the accompanying Student Activity 62.

Motivational Activity

Discuss students' responses to the activity sheet that accompanies Focus Activity Transparency 62.

Preteaching Vocabulary

Call on a volunteer to define the term *deregulation.* Then have students identify examples of government deregulation in recent years. **LEP**

Use the **Vocabulary PuzzleMaker** to create crossword and word search puzzles.

VISUAL INSTRUCTION

Some futurists believe that visits to the bank will become obsolete as direct deposit, credit cards, and banking over the Internet take the place of cash and checks.

Answer to Caption:

Each type of financial institution seemed convinced that the others had an unfair advantage.

Section Preview

Objectives

After studying this section, you will be able to:

1. **Explain** the forces leading to deregulation of financial institutions in the 1980s.

2. **Relate** the history of the savings and loan crisis.

Key Terms

deregulation, Regulation Q

Applying Economic Concepts

Deregulation Has your school ever relaxed the dress code for a day? Do you know someone who took advantage of the *deregulation,* or the relaxation of rules, by wearing something inappropriate? The government deregulated the savings and loan industry in the 1980s. Some of those institutions did exactly the same thing—they acted inappropriately.

B ecause of the massive banking failures during the Great Depression, financial institutions were closely regulated from 1933 through the 1970s. The regulations even applied to maximum rates of interest that could be paid on various accounts, as well as to restrictions on how and to whom the institutions could lend their funds. **1**

By the late 1970s, almost all financial institutions—commercial banks, savings banks, and savings and loan associations—were begging for relief from federal regulations. When President Ronald Reagan was elected in 1980, the political climate changed, allowing **deregulation,** the removal or relaxation of government restrictions on business. ✓

A Decade of Deregulation

Commercial bankers and the savings and loan associations were the two main groups demanding deregulation. As a result of their lobbying, Congress relaxed restrictions on their activities. A closer look at the historical differences between the various types of financial institutions explains the desire for deregulation.

A Level Playing Field

Before 1980, Congress allowed savings banks and savings and loan associations to pay more interest on

Banking Practices *Most banks offer some form of electronic banking, including services for handicapped people.* **Why did financial institutions want deregulation?**

savings accounts than commercial banks paid. Commercial bankers, who felt at a competitive disadvantage, wanted legislation allowing them to pay the same interest rates as savings banks and S&Ls. The S&Ls were upset, however, because commercial banks and the New England savings banks could issue checking accounts, while they could not.

The savings and loans favored legislation that would allow them to have demand deposit accounts.

Classroom Resources for SECTION 4

- Reproducible Lesson Plan 11-4
- Guided Reading Activity 11-4
- Section Quiz 11-4
- Spanish Section Quiz 11-4
- Focus Activity Transparency 62
- NBR's Economics in Action Video Program
- Enrichment Activity 11
- Reteaching Activity 11
- Spanish Reteaching Activity 11
- Economic Vocabulary Activity 11
- Spanish Economic Vocabulary Activity 11
- Chapter 11 Test, Form A and Form B
- English and Spanish Audiocassettes
- Testmaker
- Vocabulary PuzzleMaker
- Chapter Challenger Interactive Review Software
- MindJogger Videoquiz

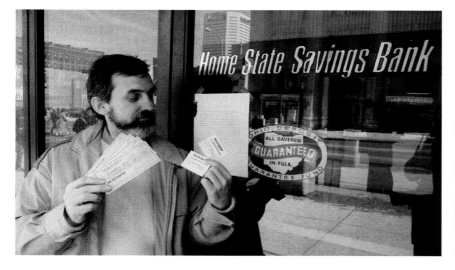

The Ohio S&L Crisis *Prior to 1985, all state-chartered savings institutions in Ohio were insured by a single, privately owned insurance company. The collapse of Home State Savings in March of that year triggered runs by depositors, which forced the governor to close every state-chartered thrift in the state.* **How did inadequate insurance contribute to the crisis in Ohio?**

Guided Practice

L2 *Analyzing Ideas* Have students write a brief paragraph explaining how the phase-out of Regulation Q, new rules on NOW accounts, new rules on borrowing from the Fed, and the Garn-St. Germain Act helped create "a level playing field" for financial institutions.

L3 *Journalism* Write the four main headings of the section on the chalkboard, and tell students these are minor headlines of a news story on banking in the 1980s. Then have students use information on the chalkboard to write the news story.

 VISUAL INSTRUCTION

Call on volunteers to identify the four main problem areas for S&Ls. (*deregulation, high interest rates, inadequate capital, fraud*)

Answer to Caption:

The single, privately owned insurance company was too small to absorb losses resulting from S&L failures.

They also wanted to make short-term, high-interest-rate loans on automobiles and other personal items that commercial banks made. At the same time, commercial banks wanted to make long-term, very stable, home-ownership loans dominated by the S&Ls. Because federal regulations governed their loans, none of the institutions could change the types of loans they were making without further legislation.

By the end of the 1970s, each type of financial institution seemed convinced that the others had an unfair advantage. By 1979 everyone was calling for a "level playing field" that would treat all financial institutions the same.

Deregulation Legislation

Sweeping deregulation took place in 1980 with the passage of the Depository Institutions Deregulation and Monetary Control Act (DIDMCA). The law had several provisions that reduced the differences between competing institutions.

First, **Regulation Q,** the federal requirement that set maximum interest rates on savings accounts, was to be phased out. This action eliminated the advantage that savings banks and S&Ls had over commercial banks when it came to paying higher interest rates on savings accounts. **2**

Second, NOW accounts could be offered on a nationwide basis by any type of financial institution. This provision eliminated the historical advantage that commercial banks had with their check issuing powers, and it eliminated the more recent advantage gained by the New England savings banks with their NOW accounts in 1972.

Third, all depository institutions could borrow from the Federal Reserve System in times of need, a privilege previously reserved for commercial banks. In return, all depository institutions were to set aside

 ANSWERS

1. because of the massive banking failures during the Great Depression
2. federal requirement that set maximum interest rates on savings accounts

---

QUICK CHECK

Checking Understanding

1. Why were financial institutions closely regulated until the 1970s?
2. What was Regulation Q?

Applying Economic Concepts

☑ **Deregulation** In President Reagan's view, business and industry were hamstrung by government red tape. He believed this kept companies less profitable than they might otherwise be and accounted for some of the weaknesses in the American economy.

CHAPTER 11: *Money and Banking* **285**

Independent Practice

📁 *Guided Reading* Assign Guided Reading Activity for Section 4. **LEP**

Meeting Special Needs

Learning Disability Students have difficulty remembering information for many reasons. Point out that Section 4 requires identification of several laws and acts. Have students think about the techniques they can use to remember this information. Can they categorize the laws? Can they write them in alphabetical order? What other strategies can they use?

GLENCOE TECHNOLOGY

NIGHTLY BUSINESS REPORT

Economics in Action

Chapter 20
Disc 2, Side 1
Title: *Money and Banking*
Subject: Bank functions
Ask: What new nontraditional functions have banks taken on? *(selling stocks, insurance, mutual funds)*

Also available in VHS.

L1 *Applying Ideas* Ask students to visit a local bank and note any signs detailing regulations—for example, the FDIC emblem. Have students compare their lists in class. Then lead students in a discussion on the purpose of these regulations. **LEP**

L2 *Identifying Trends* Have students write summaries of five recent magazine or newspaper articles on current banking issues. Use these as the starting point for a class discussion on the most pressing issues in banking today. Have students speculate on how these issues might be resolved.

VISUAL INSTRUCTION

Ask students: Is the situation in the cartoon also consistent with the information in Figure 11.3 on page 280? *(yes, the total number of banks dropped by one-third during the same period)*

Answer to Caption:
The number of S&Ls fell from 4,600 to about 2,000.

---

a certain percent of their customer's deposits in the form of a reserve. The primary purpose of this provision was to give the Fed more control over the money supply.

The Garn-St. Germain Act of 1982 accelerated deregulation by allowing S&Ls and savings banks to enter activities traditionally reserved for commercial banks. These activities included issuing credit cards, non-residential real estate loans, and commercial loans. By the mid-1980s, however, the effects of deregulation would precipitate a crisis in the savings and loan industry.

The Savings and Loan Crisis

The S&L crisis unfolded slowly during the 1980s. In 1980 the United States had 4,600 S&Ls. By mid-1988 bankruptcies and mergers reduced the number to about 3,000. By the mid-1990s fewer than 2,000 institutions survived. These failures and mergers can be traced to four major problem areas: deregulation of

THE WALL STREET JOURNAL

"For credit-card information, press one; for a current statement, press two; for the bank's present owner, press three."

financial institutions, high interest rates, inadequate capital, and outright fraudulent behavior.

Deregulation

One cause of the S&L crisis was deregulation itself. S&L executives hoped to compete in new markets, but they often found themselves in unfamiliar territory. After all, savings and loan institutions were used to having the government tell them how much interest they had to pay, and what types of loans they could and could not make. Most S&Ls, therefore, were not well prepared to face real competition in the marketplace.

High Interest Rates

Another major problem the S&L industry faced was the losses brought on by high interest rates in the mid-1970s and early 1980s. The institutions had made a number of long-term loans to homeowners and builders at low rates, often less than 10 percent, in the 1970s. By 1980, however, some interest rates had increased to more than 15 percent. S&Ls were in an unprofitable situation because they paid depositors more than 10 percent interest on short-term deposits but received less than 10 percent on money loaned out several years before. **1**

Financial Institutions
Mergers are a fact of life for financial institutions. Some institutions merge because they want to become larger. Others merge to avoid failure. During the S&L crisis, floundering thrifts were allowed to merge with commercial banks rather than face bankruptcy. **How did the S&L crisis affect the number of savings institutions from 1980 to the mid-1990s?**

$ *Free Enterprise Activity* $

Have students suggest what they would do if there were no financial institutions and they (1) had a great deal of money that they wanted to keep safe; or (2) owned a business that they wanted to expand but did not have enough money to do so. After several responses, ask students to write a paragraph explaining the relationship between money and banking. Call on volunteers to read

their paragraphs aloud. Conclude by pointing out that while a bank is a business established to make a profit just like any other business, it also plays an important role in the American economy. Banks not only enable complex economic transactions to take place, but they also stimulate economic growth by making loans.

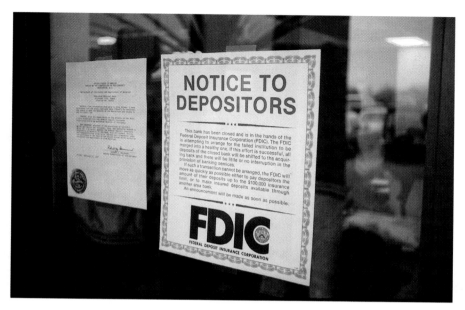

Financial Reform *The FDIC insures banks like the one shown here. After the S&L crisis, the FDIC assumed insurance responsibilities for the thrift industry.* **What agency supervises S&Ls today?**

CHAPTER 11
SECTION 4

ASSESS

Check for Understanding

Assign Section 4 Review as homework or an in-class activity.

Use **Chapter Challenger Interactive Review Software** to review Section 4.

MEETING LESSON OBJECTIVES

Each objective below is tested by the questions that follow it in parentheses.

1. **Explain** the forces leading to deregulation of financial institutions in the 1980s. **(1, 2, 5)**
2. **Relate** the history of the savings and loan crisis. **(3, 4)**

VISUAL INSTRUCTION

Ask: Why was it necessary for FDIC to assume insurance responsibilities? *(Many S&L failures put strain on funds of FSLIC, the agency that insured S&Ls.)*

Answer to Caption:
Office of Thrift Supervision

Inadequate Capital

Most financial institutions have capital reserves that can be used as a cushion to absorb losses when loans fail. Congress, however, gave the savings and loan industry permission to operate with low capital reserves—reserves that were approximately one-half the amount of those commercial banks kept. Bad loans made in the early 1980s hit the S&L industry especially hard, forcing many out of business.

Fraud

One of the consequences of deregulation was a reduced number of inspectors that verified compliance with all of the rules and regulations. As a result,

a few institutions were able to engage in fraud on a scale seldom seen before.

Although the number of fraudulent institutions was small, they handled relatively large amounts of money. When they failed, a tremendous drain was put on the reserves of the FSLIC, the federal agency that insured S&Ls.

Reforming the Thrift Industry

The Financial Institutions Reform, Recovery, and Enforcement Act (FIRREA) was passed in 1989. This act effectively abolished the independence of the savings and loan industry and is regarded by many as

 QUICK CHECK

Checking Understanding

1. How did high interest rates affect the S&L industry?

Applying Economic Concepts

 Fraud Officers in institutions such as Lincoln Savings and Loan in California made large loans to businesses that had little chance of succeeding. Often, the bankers knew—or even chose from their own circle of friends—the business's top executives.

CHAPTER 11: *Money and Banking* **287**

QUICK CHECK

ANSWERS

1. During the 1970s, many S&Ls had made long-term loans at low interest rates. By 1980 interest rates had risen, and S&Ls had to pay high rates on deposits but continued to receive low interest on money loaned earlier.

Extending the Content

Deposit Insurance Many people mistakenly believe that *each* account in a single bank is insured to the $100,000 maximum. This is not true. Point out to students that a person with separate checking and savings accounts in a single bank will only be insured for a maximum of $100,000, regardless of the balance in each account.

287

the most significant financial legislation since the Depression that forced major changes on the industry.

Abolishing the FHLBB

First, the Federal Home Loan Bank Board—the supervisory agency in charge of the S&L industry—was abolished. Its regulatory functions were transferred to a new agency, the Office of Thrift Supervision (OTS), which was part of the United States Treasury. This meant that the surviving S&Ls were to be supervised by the executive branch of the government rather than by an independent agency.

Changing Federal Deposit Insurance

The FSLIC was dissolved and its insurance responsibilities were transferred to the Federal Deposit Insurance Corporation. The FDIC then set up two insurance funds: the Savings Association Insurance Fund (SAIF) to cover the S&Ls, and the Bank Insurance Fund (BIF) to cover commercial banks.

Disposing of Failed Thrifts

Third, a temporary agency called the Resolution Trust Corporation (RTC) was set up to dispose of hundreds of failed thrifts. Because so many depositors had accounts insured to the legal maximum of $100,000, Congress had to appropriate billions of dollars for the bailout. Ultimately, the total bailout cost taxpayers about $300 billion.

Allowing Sound Thrifts to Continue

Many S&Ls were profitable during the crisis. These institutions were allowed to continue operations, and many even kept the words *savings and loan association* in their titles. Others, however, chose to change their name to distance themselves from the crisis that had tarnished so many reputations.

Evolution in the 1990s

The 1980s were so turbulent that *caution* became the watchword of the 1990s. The thrift crisis, with the exception of the lingering clean-up costs, was largely over. The surviving financial institutions adopted more conservative lending policies and became more profitable. Stronger federal regulations were put in place, and both thrifts and commercial banks were required to build up their FDIC insurance.

Banks were allowed to expand their securities businesses, and billions of dollars were spent on mergers to purchase stock and security brokerage firms. Banks also expanded the range of products they offered to include foreign stocks and currencies. Even the thrifts learned how to compete effectively and profitably.

Ultimately, the 1990s saw the development of two major trends. One was the improving health of all financial institutions. The second was the continued erosion of historical differences between the commercial banks, savings banks, and S&Ls.

SECTION 4 REVIEW

Reviewing Terms and Facts

1. **Define** deregulation, Regulation Q.
2. **Describe** the forces that led to deregulation.
3. **Explain** four causes of the savings and loan industry crisis.

Critical Thinking

4. **Identifying Central Issues** Which of the four causes of the S&L crisis do you think played the central role? Explain your answer.

Applying Economic Concepts

5. **Deregulation** List at least two other major industries in the United States economy that have been deregulated. How has deregulation affected these industries?

Answers to SECTION 4 REVIEW

1. All vocabulary words are defined in the Glossary.

2. Each type of financial institution thought that others had an unfair advantage because: savings institutions could pay higher interest on savings accounts than could commercial banks; some savings institutions could not issue checking accounts, nor could they make certain kinds of loans that commercial banks could; commercial banks wanted to offer home mortgages.

3. deregulation—put S&Ls on unfamiliar ground, brought new competition; higher interest rates—S&Ls paying out higher interest rates on deposits than receiving from long-term loans made earlier; inadequate capital—S&Ls operated with low capital reserves, could not absorb losses of failed loans; fraud—reduced inspection led to fraud

4. Have students offer reasons.

5. Answers will vary. Most students will mention the airline and trucking industries.

ECONOMICS IN ACTION

Money and Banking

Setting Up the Video

With your classmates, view "Money and Banking" on the videodisc *Economics in Action*. The video describes our money as fiat money, which means it has value because the government requires us to accept it in exchange for goods and services. A news segment discusses the changes that banking is undergoing as a result of technology and market forces.

Chapter 20
Disc 2, Side 1

View the video by scanning the bar code or by entering the chapter number on your keypad and pressing Search. *(Also Available in VHS format.)*

Hands-On Activity

Working individually or in a group, visit three local banks and obtain brochures or advertisements describing their services. After studying the brochures, create a table that compares available banking services. Then select the bank that best suits your needs and explain why.

SURFING THE "NET"

Manufacturing Money

The money supply of the United States, much like that of the major industrialized countries, is a managed money supply. The government or its designated agent tries to control the quantity, composition, and even the quality of the money supply. The two agencies that make United States currency are the Bureau of the Mint and the Bureau of Engraving and Printing.

What are the roles of these two agencies? Use the Internet to find out about the operations of one of these two currency-making institutions.

Getting There

1. Use a search engine. Type in the words *Bureau of the Mint* and *Bureau of Engraving and Printing*.

2. Next, enter words like the following to focus your search: *currency, United States Mint*, and *counterfeiting*.

3. The search engine will provide you with a number of links to follow. Links are "pointers" to different sites on the Internet and often appear as blue, underlined words.

What to Do When You Are There

Click on the links to navigate through the pages of information. Gather your findings. Using the findings, create a pamphlet that could be distributed by either bureau to describe its role in the creation of American currency.

289

MULTIMEDIA ACTIVITIES

GLENCOE TECHNOLOGY

Economics in Action

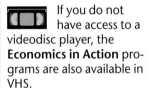

Chapter 20
Disc 2, Side 1

Title: *Money and Banking*

If you do not have access to a videodisc player, the **Economics in Action** programs are also available in VHS.

INTERNET SITES

The following are possible sites for completing the "Net" activities:

Bureau of the Mint
http://www.treas.gov/mint/

Bureau of Engraving and Printing
http://www.bep.treas.gov/

Not on the "Net"...
If students have limited or no access to the Internet, have them complete the activity "Manufacturing Money" by using the computerized card catalog at the school or local library. At the *s:* prompt, students should type in *money, government agencies*, and/or *counterfeiting*. They should then use the call numbers to find the books and other resources they need to complete their research.

INTERNET ADDRESS BOOK

Internet addresses that you find useful can be noted in the space below for quick reference.

_____   _____

_____   _____

_____   _____

_____   _____

_____   _____

GLENCOE
TECHNOLOGY

VIDEODISC
MindJogger Videoquiz

Use MindJogger to review
the Chapter 11 content.

 | Chapter 11
Disc 2, Side A

Also available in VHS.

Answers

Reviewing Key Terms

1. c-e	**12.** b-f
2. b-f	**13.** c-f
3. a	**14.** b
4. e	**15.** e, f
5. c-f	**16.** d
6. c-f	**17.** b-f
7. c, d	**18.** c-e
8. c, d	**19.** a-f
9. c-e	**20.** b-f
10. d-f	**21.** c
11. c-f	

Reviewing the Facts

1. medium of exchange, measure of value, store of value

2. cowrie shells, dog teeth, fish hooks, bird feathers attached to sticks, tea leaves compressed into "bricks," compressed cheese, miniature iron spears attached to form necklaces, stones

3. commodity money, such as musket balls, gunpowder, corn, hemp, tobacco; fiat money, such as wampum; paper money backed by gold and silver deposits; Continental Currency, paper money not backed by gold or silver deposits; specie, including English shillings, Spanish pesos, Austrian talers

4. Franklin and Hamilton were asked to design new money for U.S. Design was based on Spanish peso, nicknamed

290

Reviewing Key Terms

Place each of the vocabulary terms in its correct historical period(s).

Historical Periods:
a. Colonial: 1607–1776
b. Pre-Civil War: 1789–1861
c. Civil War–Pre-Depression: 1861–1929
d. Depression: 1929–1939
e. World War II–FIRREA: 1940–1989
f. 1989–today

1. United States note _____
2. commercial bank _____
3. Continental dollar _____
4. deregulation _____
5. dual banking system _____
6. Federal Reserve System _____
7. gold certificate _____
8. gold standard _____
9. greenback _____
10. inconvertible fiat money standard _____
11. legal tender _____
12. mutual savings bank _____
13. national bank _____
14. wildcat bank _____
15. Negotiable Order of Withdrawal _____
16. run on the bank _____
17. savings and loan association _____
18. silver certificate _____
19. specie _____
20. state bank _____
21. Treasury coin note _____

Reviewing the Facts

SECTION 1 *(pages 266–270)*
1. **List** the three functions of money.
2. **Describe** five types of early money.

---

3. **Discuss** the major forms of money used in the colonial period of United States history—1607–1776.
4. **Explain** the relationship between the Spanish peso, the Austrian taler, and the United States dollar.
5. **List** the four characteristics that give money its value.

SECTION 2 *(pages 272–277)*
6. **Describe** the paper currencies used from the period of the American Revolution to the time of the Civil War.
7. **Explain** the importance of the greenback during the Civil War.
8. **Describe** two advantages and two disadvantages of a gold standard.
9. **Evaluate** modern money as a medium of exchange.

SECTION 3 *(pages 279–283)*
10. **List** three requirements for joining the National Banking System.
11. **Describe** the main difference between the Federal Reserve System and the National Banking System.
12. **Explain** why many banks failed during the Great Depression.
13. **List** three other depository institutions in addition to commercial banks.

SECTION 4 *(pages 284–288)*
14. **Identify** the financial institutions clamoring for deregulation in the 1970s.
15. **Explain** why many savings and loan institutions were not strong enough to absorb the shocks of high interest rates and deregulation.
16. **Describe** the status of the savings and loan industry today.

---

taler after an Austrian coin. Dollar was based on tenths rather than eighths.

5. portability, durability, divisibility, limited availability

6. For the most part, state banks issued their own paper currency. By the Civil War, the U.S. had more than 1,600 banks issuing more than 10,000 different kinds of paper currency.

7. The greenback was issued to help finance the North's war effort. As the war drew to a close, the amount of greenbacks in circulation grew, and

many people feared that the currency would become worthless.

8. Advantages: people feel secure about paper money because they can convert it to gold; prevents government from printing too much paper money. Disadvantages: growing economy needs growing money supply; people may decide to convert their paper money to gold, thereby draining government's gold reserves.

9. portable because coins, currency, and checks are

Critical Thinking

1. **Drawing Conclusions** Do you think the savings and loan crisis and the subsequent provisions of FIRREA characterized a revolution or an evolution of the banking system? Explain your answer.
2. **Expressing Problems Clearly** Design a chart you would use to test the stability of a depository institution.

Applying Economic Concepts

1. **Money** Ask your friends, parents, and neighbors if they have any examples of old currency. If so, make a note of (a) the name of the currency (gold certificate, silver certificate, United States note, etc.); (b) the date on the currency; (c) any mention of backing (silver certificates backed by silver dollars).
2. **Barter** Assume that you live in a bartering society. Organize a list of 10 items that you use frequently, and then identify alternate goods of comparable worth that you would be willing to trade for them.

Reinforcing Skills

DEVELOPING MULTIMEDIA PRESENTATIONS

Study the list of topics below. Choose one of the topics and explain how you would use at least three types of media in a presentation to best teach the topic to your class.

1. Trade in colonial America
2. Origins of the dollar
3. Establishment of a national bank—Alexander Hamilton's view and Thomas Jefferson's view
4. Currencies around the world
5. Banking during the Civil War
6. Roosevelt's bank holiday during the Great Depression

Individual Activity

Assume that the country is returning to privately issued bank notes such as those used before the Civil War. Design the currency you would like to see in circulation.

Cooperative Learning Activity

Working in groups of four, have each member survey one of the following financial institutions: a commercial bank, a savings and loan association, a savings bank (if one exists in your community), and a credit union. List the services that each offers. Compare your lists as a group, and then discuss the differences with the entire class.

Technology Activity

Developing a Multimedia Presentation

In the **Journal Writing** activity on page 265, you were asked to write the advertising claims you read or hear about from the financial institutions in your area. Group the advertising claims into four categories: commercial banks, savings banks, savings and loan institutions, and credit unions. Then develop a videotaped guide to compare the advertisements of each group.

Differentiate the services provided and the costs charged by each type of institution. Combine music, still and moving images, and text within your video production. Using an informative approach, present facts about each category of financial institution in an objective way (without displaying emotion or injecting your opinion). Be careful not to show approval or disapproval. Share your production with the members of the class and with your local Chamber of Commerce.

CHAPTER 11: *Money and Banking* **291**

14. commercial banks, savings and loan associations
15. Congress had given savings and loan industry permission to operate with low capital reserves. These reserves were inadequate to absorb losses resulting from bad loans.
16. The industry is now supervised by a federal agency, the Office of Thrift Supervision, rather than an independent body. Deposit insurance is handled by FDIC rather than FSLIC.

Critical Thinking

1. Most students will suggest that a revolution occurred because the system of deposit insurance changed.
2. Charts will vary but will include such points as interest charged on loans, diversity of investments, reserves available, and so on.

Applying Economic Concepts

1. Examples will vary.
2. Lists will vary.

Reinforcing Skills

Answers will vary but may include animated reenactments, charts and graphs, videos, musical recordings, photographs, animated time lines, readings of newspaper accounts, newsreel footage, map overlays on transparencies, and so on.

? BONUS TEST QUESTION

How is a commercial bank like other businesses? How is it different? (*Like other businesses, its aim is to make a profit. However, it makes that profit by lending other people's money. In doing this, it is closely supervised by state and federal government agencies.*)

---

easy to transport; durable because metallic coins last a long time, paper notes last at least a year, and checking accounts never wear out; divisible because the penny—the smallest coin—is small enough for any purchase, and checks can be written in any amount; mixed record with respect to limited availability

10. use *National* or *N.A.* in title; pass inspection of Comptroller of the Currency; purchase government bonds

11. The Federal Reserve System acted as a central bank, lending to other banks in times of need. The National Banking System was not a central bank.

12. There was an overabundance of banks, none of which had deposit insurance. Customers rushed to remove their deposits before their banks failed. This turned into a panic, and many banks did, indeed, fail.

13. savings banks, savings and loan associations, credit unions

CHAPTER 12 PLANNING GUIDE

CHAPTER ORGANIZER

Daily Objectives	Reproducible Resources	Multimedia Resources
Section 1 **The Federal Reserve System** 1. **Identify** the unique features of the Fed. 2. **Describe** the structure of the Federal Reserve System. 3. **Explain** the major regulatory responsibilities of the Fed.	Reproducible Lesson Plan 12-1 Guided Reading Activity 12-1 Cooperative Learning Activity 16 Consumer Application Activity 16 Math Practice for Economics 17 Free Enterprise Activity 16 Primary and Secondary Source Reading 16 Performance Assessment Activity 17 Section Quiz 12-1*	Focus Activity Transparency 64 Vocabulary PuzzleMaker Chapter Challenger Interactive Review Software Testmaker MindJogger Videoquiz NBR's Economics in Action Video Program Interactive Economics!
Section 2 **Monetary Policy** 1. **Describe** how banks use fractional reserves in their operations. 2. **Apply** fractional reserves to the process of monetary expansion. 3. **Understand** the tools used to conduct monetary policy.	Reproducible Lesson Plan 12-2 Guided Reading Activity 12-2 Section Quiz 12-2*	Focus Activity Transparency 65 Economic Concepts Transparency 18 Vocabulary PuzzleMaker Chapter Challenger Interactive Review Software Testmaker NBR's Economics in Action Video Program Interactive Economics!
Section 3 **Monetary Policy, Banking, and the Economy** 1. **Explain** how monetary policy affects interest rates in the short run. 2. **Relate** monetary expansion to inflation in the long run. 3. **Identify** the two major definitions of money. 4. **Describe** various steps taken to protect the safety of the banking system.	Reproducible Lesson Plan 12-3 Guided Reading Activity 12-3 Reinforcing Economic Skill 12 Section Quiz 12-3*	Focus Activity Transparency 66 Vocabulary PuzzleMaker Chapter Challenger Interactive Review Software Testmaker NBR's Economics in Action Video Program Interactive Economics!
Chapter Review and Evaluation	Enrichment Activity 12 Reteaching Activity 12* Economic Vocabulary Activity 12* Chapter 12 Test, Forms A and B	Chapter Digests Audiocassette Activities and Tests* Testmaker MindJogger Videoquiz

*Also available in Spanish

 Blackline Master   Transparency   CD-ROM   Software   Videodisc   Audiocassette

OUT OF TIME? Assign the Chapter 12 Digest Audiocassette and the corresponding Chapter Digest activities and tests.

National Council on Economic Education

THE **Economics** America AND **Economics** International PROGRAMS

VOLUNTARY NATIONAL CONTENT STANDARDS IN ECONOMICS
Emphasized in Chapter 12

Content Standard 12 *Students will understand that:*
Interest rates, adjusted for inflation, rise and fall to balance the amount saved with the amount borrowed, thus affecting the allocation of scarce resources between present and future uses.

Content Standard 20 *Students will understand that:*
Federal government budgetary policy and the Federal Reserve System's monetary policy influence the overall levels of employment, output, and prices.

Economics America *Resources Available From NCEE*

- *Capstone: The Nation's High School Economics Course*
- *Civics and Government: Focus on Economics*
- *Economies in Transition: Command to Market*
- *Focus: High School Economics*
- *Personal Decision Making: Focus on Economics*
- *Personal Finance Economics: Wallet Wisdom*
- *United States History: Eyes on the Economy, Vol. II*

To order these materials, or to contact your state Council on Economic Education about workshops and programs, call 1-800-338-1192 or visit http://www.nationalcouncil.org**.**

PERFORMANCE ASSESSMENT

The following chapter projects may be assigned at the beginning of the chapter and used for performance assessment.

Multicultural Heritage The 12 Federal Reserve District Banks are located in 12 major U.S. cities. This chapter provides an opportunity for students to do more in-depth study about the cultural diversity of these cities. For example, Atlanta is a multicultural city with a strong African American history. There is also a strong Latino and Asian presence in the city. Have students select 1 of the 12 Federal Reserve District cities and conduct research on the cultural background of that city. Suggest that as students conduct their research, they should consider some of the implications of multiculturalism for doing business. To illustrate, point out that at one commercial bank in Atlanta, tellers speak Japanese, Korean, Vietnamese, and at least two Chinese dialects. Encourage students to use the *Readers' Guide to Periodical Literature* or a computer-search system to locate articles relevant to their topic. Recommend that students present their findings in a promotional brochure encouraging businesses to move to their selected cities.

Cooperative Learning Organize students into five groups of equal size and assign one of the following tools of monetary policy to each group: reserve requirement, open market operations, discount rate, moral suasion, and selective credit controls. Have groups develop methods for teaching the rest of the class about their assigned topic. Encourage groups to think of creative ways to teach the material. For example, the group assigned to present moral suasion might write a scenario in which commercial bankers discuss how moral suasion affects their attitude toward monetary policy. Call on groups to present their "lessons" to the class.

ADDITIONAL RESOURCES

Readings for the Student

I Bet You Thought. . . . New York: Federal Reserve Bank of New York. Corrects misconceptions about money and monetary policy using nontechnical explanations.

Putting it Simply . . . The Federal Reserve. Boston: Federal Reserve Bank of Boston. Booklet presenting basic information about money and monetary policy.

Who We Are and What We Do. St. Louis, MO: Federal Reserve Bank of St. Louis. Pamphlet describing the role and functions of the Federal Reserve.

Readings for the Teacher

Board of Governors, Federal Reserve System. *The Federal Reserve: Purposes and Functions.* Washington, D.C.: Federal Reserve System, regularly revised. Covers structure and functions of the Fed, monetary policy, and the international role of the Fed.

Federal Reserve System. Gainesville, FL: University of Florida Center for Economic Education, 1991. Lesson plans and reproducible worksheets on the history, structure, and function of the Federal Reserve System.

Multimedia

Economics U$A: The Federal Reserve/Stagflation. The Annenberg/CPB Collection, 19 Gregory Drive, South Burlington, VT 05407-2345. Color video, 60 mins. First 30-minute segment of video details the operations of the Fed.

Chapter Overview

Chapter 12 focuses on the Federal Reserve System and the nature and impact of its monetary policy. **Section 1** describes the Federal Reserve System structure and its regulatory functions. **Section 2** explains fractional reserves, how fractional reserves are used in monetary expansion, and how commercial banks operate. This section also discusses the tools of monetary policy. **Section 3** discusses monetary policy in the short run and the long run, and defines money.

GLENCOE
TECHNOLOGY

VIDEODISC
MindJogger Videoquiz

Use MindJogger to preview the Chapter 12 content.

 Chapter 12
Disc 2, Side A

Also available in VHS.

interNET
CONNECTION

Resources for Chapter 12 on the World Wide Web*

National Council on Economic Education

http://www.nationalcouncil.org/

Board of Governors of the Federal Reserve System
http://www.bog.frb.fed.us/

St. Louis Federal Reserve Data Base
http://www.stls.frb.org/fred

Federal Reserve Bank of Minneapolis, Woodrow
http://woodrow.mpls.frb.fed.us/

Sites subject to change.

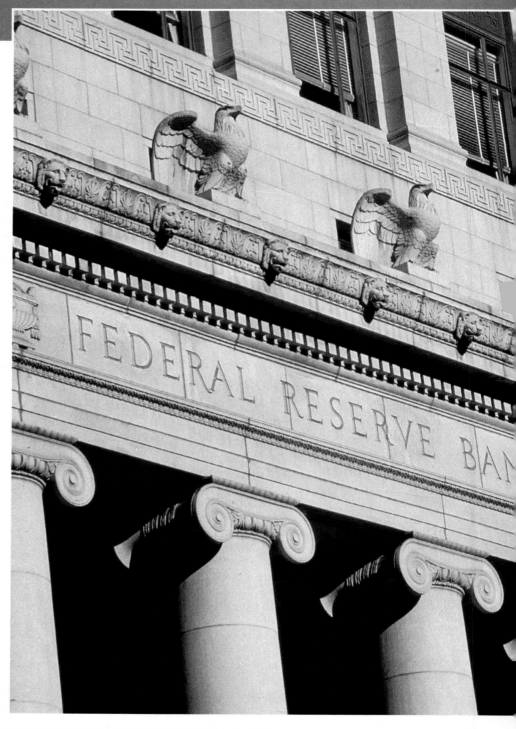

The Federal Reserve Bank for the 12th Federal District is located in San Francisco, California.

Extra Credit Project

Direct students to prepare a four-page, illustrated report on the Federal Reserve System, focusing on the Fed's structure and the major services it provides to the banking industry and to the government. Call on students to present and discuss their reports.

CHAPTER 12

The Federal Reserve System and Monetary Policy

SECTION 1
The Federal Reserve System

SECTION 2
Monetary Policy

SECTION 3
Monetary Policy, Banking, and the Economy

CHAPTER PREVIEW

People to Know

- Alan Greenspan
- Actuary

Applying Economic Concepts to Your Life

Stability in Value One feature of money that you rely on is that it is worth about the same amount from one year to the next. Money must have *stability in value* to function as it should—and many factors ensure that money has this feature.

Journal Writing

For one week, analyze the currency that comes into your possession. In your journal, keep track of the features that appear on the front and back of each bill, noting the similarities and differences between the various currencies.

INTRODUCING CHAPTER 12

Connecting to Past Learning

Call on volunteers to tell when the Federal Reserve System was established and what purpose it served. *(legislation passed by Congress in December 1913 to serve as the nation's central bank)* Point out that the Fed's major role is to strengthen and stabilize the nation's banking and monetary system. Then mention that the way in which the Fed carries out this function is the focus of Chapter 12.

Applying Economics

Ask students to raise their hands if they have a Federal Reserve Note. Call on a student with a raised hand to show his or her note to the class. Then ask the student how he or she knows the bill is a Federal Reserve Note. The student should indicate the words at the top of the bill. Conclude by pointing out that the Federal Reserve System is the nation's central bank and, as such, has a number of responsibilities, one of the most important of which is managing the amount and condition of money in circulation.

 PERFORMANCE ASSESSMENT

Refer to page **292B** for a Performance Assessment activity for this chapter. Also see the **Performance Assessment Activities** booklet for additional suggestions.

Economic Portfolio

Suggest that as students make their **Journal Writing** entries, they consider how they would describe the currency and its functions to a foreign visitor. Point out that this will help them to complete an assignment at the end of the chapter. Refer students to the **Technology Activity** in the Chapter 12 Review on page 317.

 VISUAL INSTRUCTION

Have students find the location of the Federal Reserve Bank for their Federal Reserve district.

Key to Ability Levels — Teaching strategies have been coded for varying learning styles and abilities:
L1 - Basic (activities for all students) **L2 - Average** (activities for average to above-average students)
L3 - Challenging (activities for above-average students) **LEP - Limited English Proficiency**

SECTION 1
The Federal Reserve System

FOCUS

Section Objectives

1. Identify the unique features of the Fed.

2. Describe the structure of the Federal Reserve System.

3. Explain the major regulatory responsibilities of the Fed.

Bellringer

Prior to taking roll at the beginning of the class period, display Focus Activity Transparency 64 on the overhead projector and assign the accompanying Student Activity 64.

Motivational Activity

Discuss students' responses to the activity sheet that accompanies Focus Activity Transparency 64.

Preteaching Vocabulary

Ask students to find each of the key terms in Section 1 and read the term in context. Then call on students to define the term in their own words. **LEP**

Use the **Vocabulary PuzzleMaker** to create crossword and word search puzzles.

SECTION 1
The Federal Reserve System

Section Preview

Objectives

After studying this section, you will be able to:

1. **Identify** the unique features of the Fed.

2. **Describe** the structure of the Federal Reserve System.

3. **Explain** the major regulatory responsibilities of the Fed.

Key Terms

member bank, bank holding company, truth-in-lending laws, Regulation Z, currency, coins, margin requirement

Applying Economic Concepts

Truth-in-Lending Laws Have you or your parents ever bought anything on credit? Have you ever had the salesperson explain the terms of the loan, and then ask you to sign forms saying that everything has been explained to you? All of this was done because of *truth-in-lending laws* that were designed to protect you, the consumer.

On December 23, 1913, Congress passed legislation creating the Federal Reserve System, or Fed, as America's central bank. Today the Fed provides financial services to the government, regulates financial institutions, maintains the payments system, enforces consumer protection laws, and conducts monetary policy. Because everyone uses money, the Fed's activities affect us all.

Unique Features of the Fed

The Fed has an unusual history. It started out as a decentralized banking system. In addition, the Fed is owned by private banks, not the government.

Regional Structure

Congress organized the Fed into the 12 districts shown in **Figure 12.1**. The 12 central Fed banks were to operate independently of one another. These banks were to be only loosely coordinated by a board in Washington, D.C.

This decentralized structure was desired for two reasons. First, Congress wanted to limit the power of each individual bank. More district banks meant smaller banks, and smaller banks were less likely to be powerful. Second, Congress thought that a regional structure would be more responsive to local needs.

Initially each Fed bank was to manage the credit conditions in its particular district. Each bank even issued currency with its own seal as a symbol of equal status. After the bank failures during the Great Depression, however, Congress stripped the district banks of their independence and transferred power to the Federal Reserve Board in Washington, D.C. The Fed has functioned as a single, unified central bank ever since.

Private Ownership

Another unique feature of the Fed is that it is owned by its **member banks**—banks that belong to the Federal Reserve System. The government does not own the Fed. The reason for this is that Congress did not have enough money to create the Fed in 1913, so it required banks to contribute a small amount of financial capital when they joined. In return, member banks received stock in the Fed. To make sure that enough banks became members, Congress required all national banks to join.

The Fed's stock is like any other corporate stock. The Fed pays dividends to its stockholders—the Fed member banks. This gives the privately-owned member banks the right to elect the majority of directors. The directors, in turn, appoint the presidents of the 12 district banks. However, because the Fed's activities are so important to everyone in the country, the top Fed officials are appointed by the United States President and approved by Congress.

Classroom Resources for SECTION 1

- Reproducible Lesson Plan 12-1
- Guided Reading Activity 12-1
- Cooperative Learning Activity 16
- Consumer Application Activity 16
- Math Practice for Economics 17
- Free Enterprise Activity 16
- Primary and Secondary Source Reading 16
- Performance Assessment Activity 17
- Section Quiz 12-1
- Spanish Section Quiz 12-1

- Focus Activity Transparency 64
- NBR's Economics in Action Video Program
- Testmaker
- Vocabulary PuzzleMaker
- Chapter Challenger Interactive Review Software
- MindJogger Videoquiz
- Interactive Economics!

Structure of the Fed

Figure 12.2 outlines the organizational structure of the Federal Reserve System. The Fed's main components have remained virtually unchanged since the Great Depression of the 1930s.

Board of Governors

The President of the United States appoints the 7–member Federal Reserve Board of Governors to 14–year terms. Working out of Washington, D.C., the Board of Governors directs and controls the activities of the Fed. The Senate must confirm each appointment, and the appointments are staggered so that 1 vacancy must be filled every 2 years. One of the Board members serves as chairperson.

The Board is primarily a regulatory and supervisory agency. It sets general policies for Federal Reserve and member banks to follow, regulates certain operations of state-chartered member commercial banks, and conducts some aspects of monetary policy. It also makes a report each year to Congress and puts out a monthly bulletin that reports on national and international monetary matters.

Federal Open Market Committee

The Federal Open Market Committee (FOMC) makes decisions about the growth of the money supply and the level of interest rates. It includes the 7 members of the Board of Governors and 5 district Reserve bank presidents who serve 1-year rotating terms.

The committee meets about 8 times a year in Washington, D.C., to review the country's economy and make decisions about the cost and availability of credit. Most decisions are made in private but are announced almost immediately.

Federal Advisory Council

The 12 district banks provide feedback to the Federal Reserve Board on matters concerning the overall health of the economy. This advice is offered through the Federal Advisory Council (FAC). It is made up of 12 members, each of whom is appointed by the

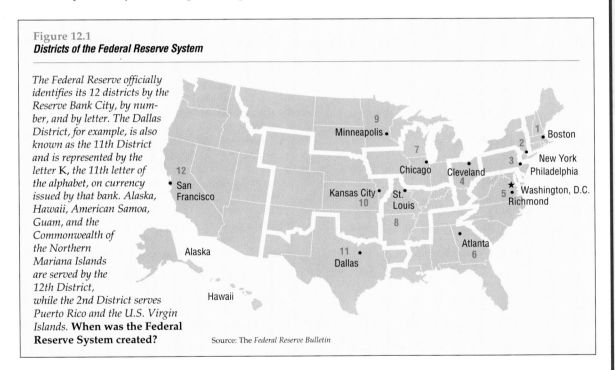

Figure 12.1
Districts of the Federal Reserve System

The Federal Reserve officially identifies its 12 districts by the Reserve Bank City, by number, and by letter. The Dallas District, for example, is also known as the 11th District and is represented by the letter K, the 11th letter of the alphabet, on currency issued by that bank. Alaska, Hawaii, American Samoa, Guam, and the Commonwealth of the Northern Mariana Islands are served by the 12th District, while the 2nd District serves Puerto Rico and the U.S. Virgin Islands. **When was the Federal Reserve System created?**

Source: The *Federal Reserve Bulletin*

TEACH

Guided Practice

L1 Understanding Ideas
Make a number of flash cards that detail some aspect of the Federal Reserve System. Next, review with students the discussion on the structure of the Fed on pages 294–296 and have students study Figure 12.2 on page 297. Then hold up the flash cards, one at a time, and call on students to identify what aspect of the Fed is being described. **LEP**

Cooperative Learning
Assign Cooperative Learning Activity 16.

GLENCOE
TECHNOLOGY

Economics in Action

Chapter 21
Disc 2, Side 1

Title: *The Federal Reserve and Monetary Policy*

Subject: The Fed's responsibilities

Ask: What analogy is made about the American economy and the Fed? *(The American economy is likened to a car—and the Fed as the driver.)*

 Also available in VHS.

 VISUAL INSTRUCTION

Ask: In which city is the Federal Reserve Bank that serves Hawaii? *(San Francisco)*

Answer to Caption:
December 23, 1913

Managed Money *Because countries no longer back their money with gold, they rely on central banks, like the Fed, to manage the amount of money in circulation.* **What are other responsibilities of the Fed?**

member banks in the region. The Federal Advisory Council has little impact on the daily operations of the Fed, and meets with the Board only 4 times a year.

Responsibilities of the Fed

The Federal Reserve System has a broad range of responsibilities. These range from supervising banks to clearing checks to maintaining the money supply and enforcing consumer legislation. All of these responsibilities are discussed below.

In addition, the Fed is responsible for conducting monetary policy, which involves controlling the cost and availability of credit. Monetary policy is discussed in Section 2 of this chapter.

State Member Bank Supervision

All depository institutions—including commercial banks, savings banks, savings institutions, and credit unions—must maintain reserves against their customers' deposits. The Fed is responsible for monitoring the reserves of its state-chartered member banks, while other federal agencies monitor the reserves of nonmember banks and other depository institutions.

Originally, reserves were a matter of prudent banking practice, but today reserves fulfill two key roles. First, the banks use them to clear checks. Second, the Fed uses reserves to control the size of the money supply.

Holding Companies

The Fed also has broad legislative authority over **bank holding companies**—a form of corporation that owns one or more banks. Holding companies, unlike banks, do not accept deposits or make loans. They are simply corporate structures that own other banks. As a result, when people buy stock in a bank today, they generally purchase the stock of the holding company, which in turn owns one or more individual banks.

This arrangement may seem unusual, but the reasons for it are historical. Because of the bank failures during the Great Depression, many restrictions were put on banks. Bankers, in turn, tried to get around the restrictions by setting up holding companies that would not be subject to banking laws because they were not banks in the traditional sense. Later, Congress gave the Fed the power to regulate the activities of the holding companies so that they could not evade restrictions. **1**

Today about 6,000 holding companies control approximately 7,200 commercial banks. In many cases, the holding company structure has resulted in even more regulation and supervision. For example, the FDIC may inspect and regulate 3 nonmember state banks that a single holding company owns, while the Fed regulates the holding company itself.

International Operations

Foreign banks have a large presence in the economy. Banks from 60 different countries operate about 500

$ Free Enterprise Activity $

Refer students to Figure 12.1 on page 295 and remind them that legislation establishing the Federal Reserve System with its 12 Federal Reserve District Banks was passed in 1913. Ask them to study the map and decide how they would change the 12 districts and in which cities they would recommend locating the Federal Reserve District Banks today. Call on volunteers to present and explain their changes to the class.

Lesson 8 of Interactive Economics! and click on "An Introduction to Monetary Policy."

Figure 12.2
Structure of the Federal Reserve System

The Fed has a fairly simple organizational structure. The system is supervised by a 7-member Board of Governors appointed by the President and confirmed by the Senate. The Board also dominates the FOMC, which has primary responsibility for monetary policy. The member banks contribute a small amount of funds to the Fed and receive stock ownership shares in return. The member banks also provide advice to the Board through the Federal Advisory Council, which has one representative for every district bank. **What functions does the Board of Governors perform?**

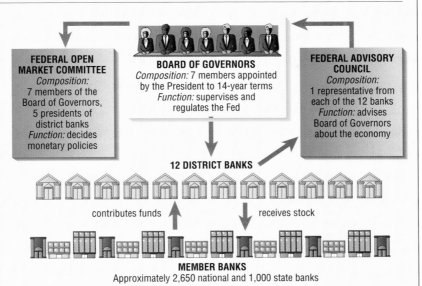

FEDERAL OPEN MARKET COMMITTEE
Composition: 7 members of the Board of Governors, 5 presidents of district banks
Function: decides monetary policies

BOARD OF GOVERNORS
Composition: 7 members appointed by the President to 14-year terms
Function: supervises and regulates the Fed

FEDERAL ADVISORY COUNCIL
Composition: 1 representative from each of the 12 banks
Function: advises Board of Governors about the economy

12 DISTRICT BANKS

contributes funds   receives stock

MEMBER BANKS
Approximately 2,650 national and 1,000 state banks

branches and agencies in the United States. In addition, foreign banks own shares of many large United States banks. In all, foreign banks control about 20 percent of all banking assets in the United States. ☑

The Fed has broad authority to supervise and regulate these foreign banks. Branches and agencies of these banks are examined annually, and the Fed even has the power to terminate the domestic operations of foreign banks. **2**

In addition, the Fed authorizes and supervises the international operations of United States member banks and holding companies. Currently, member banks operate about 800 branches in foreign countries.

Mergers

A merger of two or more banks requires the approval of the appropriate federal banking authority. If the surviving bank is a state member bank, the Fed must approve the merger.

Banking authorities also approve other mergers. If two national banks merge, the Comptroller of the Currency must approve the merger. If two nonmember state banks merge, the appropriate federal agency for approval is the FDIC.

Figure 11.3 on page 280 shows the effect of mergers since 1980. The numerous mergers during this period substantially reduced the number of banks.

QUICK CHECK

Checking Understanding

1. Why did bankers set up holding companies?
2. Who regulates foreign banks that do business in the United States?

Applying Economic Concepts

☑ **Money Supply** About $1,038 worth of currency is in circulation for each of the more than 275 million Americans, yet the Fed can account for only about $260 per person. Officials think people in other countries hold the rest.

Independent Practice

📁 **Guided Reading** Assign Guided Reading Activity for Section 1. **LEP**

L1 *Writing Letters* Obtain the addresses of the 12 Federal Reserve Banks and their 24 branch banks (see *Federal Reserve Bulletin* at your local library) and assign one address to each student. Have students write letters to their assigned bank requesting information on the Fed, its structure, and its functions. When all students have received replies, have them share their information with the class.

📁 **Consumer Application**
Assign Consumer Application Activity 16.

 VISUAL INSTRUCTION

Ask: Which part of the Fed decides monetary policy? Who is involved in making these decisions? *(Federal Open Market Committee; members of Board of Governors, 5 district bank presidents)*

Answer to Caption:

supervises and regulates the Fed

QUICK CHECK

ANSWERS

1. to avoid legislation that regulated banks
2. the Fed

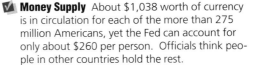

Extending the Content

Truth-in-Savings On June 21, 1993, the Truth-in-Savings Act became law. This legislation makes it possible for savers to compare interest rates in much the same way borrowers have been able to compare interest rates. Banks are required to disclose the Annual Percentage Yield—or APY—which, in effect, means all banks must standardize the way they compute interest on savings accounts,

NOW accounts, and certificates of deposit (CDs). Prior to this act, one bank might use the term *effective yield*, and another *annualized yield.* These terms confused customers. Further, some banks paid interest quarterly, others semi-annually, and still others annually; yet all might have reported the same interest rate. The APY is the interest percentage that all banks must use.

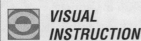 **Math Practice** Assign Math Practice for Economics 17.

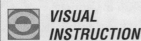 **Free Enterprise** Assign Free Enterprise Activity 16.

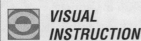 **Readings** Assign Primary and Secondary Source Reading 16.

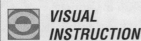 **Performance Assessment** Assign Performance Assessment Activity 17.

L2 **Drawing a Cartoon**
Direct students to draw a cartoon illustrating one of the responsibilities of the Federal Reserve System. Suggest that students make an editorial point with their cartoons—for example, indicating whether or not they think the selected responsibility is one the Fed should fulfill. Call on volunteers to display and explain their cartoons.

L3 **Research** Have students research and prepare an illustrated report on the operations of one of the two agencies that make American money—the Bureau of the Mint and the Bureau of Engraving and Printing.

⊙ **VISUAL INSTRUCTION**

Point out that most checks are cleared in two days. This is a remarkably short period of time considering that the Fed deals with about 20 billion checks each year.

Figure 12.3
Clearing a Check

The process begins with Ruth, who has a $100 demand deposit account (DDA) with Bank X. Ruth writes a check for $5, which she gives to Ed. At the same time, she records the amount in her checkbook to show a new balance of $95. (Note that only the accounts affected by the $5 check are shown in this figure.)

RUTH

| DDA $~~100~~ |
| 95 |

The check is returned to Ruth

BANK X

Bank X then returns Ruth's check to her at the end of the month, along with any others she wrote during the same period. When Ruth gets the canceled checks, she balances her checkbook to make sure her records agree with the bank's.

Bank X learns of Ruth's check only when it arrives from the Fed. The bank then makes up for the loss of the $5 in its MBR account by reducing Ruth's DDA by $5.

BANK X	
MBR $~~10~~	RUTH'S DDA $~~100~~
5	95

Bank X has its MBR reduced, and receives Ruth's check

ED

| DDA $~~100~~ |
| 105 |

Ed deposits check

BANK Y

Ed, who banks at Bank Y, now has the check. If he decides to cash it, he will have $5 in currency in addition to his DDA of $100. If he decides to make a deposit, his DDA will rise to $105. Either way, Bank Y ends up with the check written by Ruth.

Because the check is drawn on Bank X, Bank Y gets payment for it by sending the check to the district Federal Reserve Bank. The Fed then processes the check by transferring $5 from Bank X's MBR account to Bank Y's MBR account. The Fed then sends Ruth's check to Bank X.

BANK Y	
MBR $~~10~~	ED'S DDA $~~100~~
15	105

Bank Y sends check to the Fed district bank for payment

DISTRICT FEDERAL RESERVE SYSTEM BANK

| MBR BANK X $~~10~~ |
| 5 |
| MBR BANK Y $~~10~~ |
| 15 |

Cultural Diversity and Economics

Counterfeiting Made Easy Currency from the Fed is one of the easiest currencies to counterfeit. Other countries use a variety of colors, larger portraits on the bills, and watermarks that are visible when the bill is held to the light. All these features thwart counterfeiters.

Check Clearing

One major service the Fed performs is clearing checks, a process that makes extensive use of the reserves in the banking system. In general, reserves in the system are shifted from one bank to another, depending on the way checks are written on the member banks.

Figure 12.3 illustrates the check-clearing process. The person in the example writes a $5 check. As the check is processed through the banking system, funds are moved from one member bank's account to another until the check returns to the issuer. The money is then removed from the issuer's checking account.

The Fed clears millions of checks at any given time. To accomplish this task, it uses the latest high-speed, check-sorting equipment available. In some cases banks gather information from a check when it is deposited, and then transfer the information to computer files. These files are sent to the Fed, which uses the information to adjust member banks' accounts. In this way, the member bank's balance can be adjusted without the check having to go through the entire system.

Consumer Legislation

The Fed is responsible for some consumer legislation, primarily **truth-in-lending laws** that require sellers to make complete and accurate disclosures to people who buy on credit. Under a provision called **Regulation Z**, truth-in-lending disclosures are extended to millions of individuals by corporations, retail stores, automobile dealers, banks, and lending institutions.

If you buy furniture or a car on credit, you will discover that the seller must explain several items before

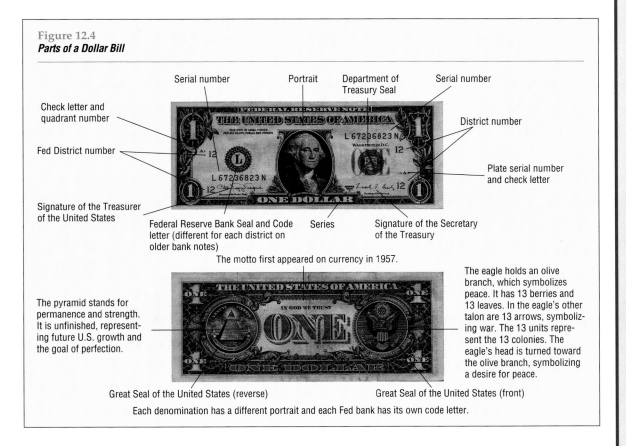

Figure 12.4
Parts of a Dollar Bill

Serial number
Portrait
Department of Treasury Seal
Serial number
Check letter and quadrant number
THE UNITED STATES OF AMERICA
District number
Fed District number
L 67236823 N
Plate serial number and check letter
L 67236823 N
ONE DOLLAR
Signature of the Treasurer of the United States
Federal Reserve Bank Seal and Code letter (different for each district on older bank notes)
Series
Signature of the Secretary of the Treasury

The motto first appeared on currency in 1957.

The pyramid stands for permanence and strength. It is unfinished, representing future U.S. growth and the goal of perfection.

The eagle holds an olive branch, which symbolizes peace. It has 13 berries and 13 leaves. In the eagle's other talon are 13 arrows, symbolizing war. The 13 units represent the 13 colonies. The eagle's head is turned toward the olive branch, symbolizing a desire for peace.

Great Seal of the United States (reverse)
Great Seal of the United States (front)

Each denomination has a different portrait and each Fed bank has its own code letter.

ASSESS

Check for Understanding

Assign Section 1 Review as homework or an in-class activity.

 Use the **Chapter Challenger Interactive Review Software** to review Section 1.

MEETING LESSON OBJECTIVES

Each objective below is tested by the questions that follow it in parentheses.

1. **Identify** the unique features of the Fed. **(3)**
2. **Describe** the structure of the Federal Reserve System. **(2)**
3. **Explain** the major regulatory responsibilities of the Fed. **(1, 3, 4, 5)**

Evaluate

Assign the Section 1 Quiz in the TCR or use the *Economics: Principles and Practices* Testmaker to create a customized quiz. Spanish Section Quizzes also are available in the Spanish Resources Binder.

VISUAL INSTRUCTION

Have students study any currency they have on them. Ask them to identify the Federal Reserve Bank that issued each note. Record which banks are represented and which are not.

$ Free Enterprise Activity $

On the chalkboard, write the following responsibilities of the Fed: *State Member Bank Supervision, Holding Companies, International Operations, Mergers, Check Clearing, Consumer Legislation, Currency,* and *Margin Requirements.* (Call Federal Reserve Board in Washington, D.C., to obtain list of stocks eligible for margin loans.) Ask students to give an example of each Fed responsibility, and note responses on the chalkboard under the appropriate heading. Then organize the class into a number of groups of equal size and have group members discuss which of the Fed's responsibilities they believe is most important to the U.S. economy and why. Call on group representatives to report and explain their group's decision.

you make the purchase. These items include the size of the down payment, the number and size of the monthly payments, and the total amount of interest over the life of the loan. In general terms, Congress mandates that appropriate disclosures be made. The Fed then decides on the specific type of information that would be of the most value to consumers.

Currency

Today's **currency,** the paper component of the money supply, is made up of Federal Reserve notes—fiat paper money issued by Federal Reserve banks and printed at the Bureau of Engraving and Printing. This currency, issued in amounts of $1, $2, $5, $10, $20, $50, and $100, is distributed to the Fed district banks for storage. These banks send it to member banks on request.

When tellers in banks come across currency that is mutilated or cannot be used for other reasons, they ship it to the Fed to be replaced. The Fed then destroys the old currency so that it cannot be put back into circulation. **Figure 12.4** illustrates some of the features of Federal Reserve notes.

The Bureau of the Mint produces **coins,** metallic forms of money, such as pennies, nickels, and dimes. After the coins are minted, they are shipped to the Fed district banks for storage until member banks need them.

Margin Requirements

Before the Great Depression, people speculated wildly on stocks. Easy credit in the form of **margin requirements,** minimum deposits left with a stockbroker to be used as down payments to buy other securities, made much of the speculation possible. For example, with a margin requirement as low as 10 percent, a person had to deposit only $100 with a stockbroker to purchase $1,000 worth of stocks. The stockbroker would supply the remaining $900.

If the stock rose to $1,300, it could be sold and the investor would net $400 after repaying the $900. If, however, the stock dropped to $900, the broker would sell the stock to protect his or her own loan if the investor could not come up with additional margin. Because credit was so easy to get and the margins were so easy to forfeit with even small drops in stock prices, many investors lost everything they had when stock prices crashed in 1929.

Today margin requirements are set at 50 percent for most stocks and bonds, meaning an investor has to put up at least half the money needed to buy eligible stocks and bonds. This requirement has been as high as 80 percent in the past, and is at the discretion of the Fed. The Fed also monitors stock market activity and publishes a list of stocks that are eligible for margin loans.

SECTION 1
REVIEW

Reviewing Terms and Facts

1. **Define** member bank, bank holding company, truth-in-lending law, Regulation Z, currency, coins, margin requirement.
2. **Describe** the structure of the Fed.
3. **Identify** the number of commercial banks that the Fed directly regulates.
4. **List** eight areas in which the Fed has legal responsibility.

Critical Thinking

5. **Synthesizing Information** One of the responsibilities of the Fed is to approve or disapprove of mergers between state member banks. Explain how the mergers of two such banks would be classified according to the discussion of mergers in Chapter 3.

Applying Economic Concepts

6. **Truth-in-Lending Laws** Visit any local store that sells goods on credit—appliances, cars, or furniture, for example. Ask the owner or manager about the type of information that the store is required to disclose when the sale is made. Obtain copies of the disclosure forms and share them with your classmates.

Answers to SECTION 1 REVIEW

1. All words are defined in the Glossary.
2. Member banks contribute a small amount of funds to the Fed, for which they receive ownership shares in return. Member banks also select directors for each of the 12 district banks. Overall supervision of Fed is in hands of seven-member Board of Governors appointed by President and confirmed by Senate. Board also dominates Federal Open Market Committee, which makes monetary policy. Member banks can advise the Board through

Federal Advisory Council, which has one representative for each district bank.
3. about 6,000
4. state member bank supervision, holding companies, international operations, mergers, check clearing, consumer legislation, currency, margin requirements
5. horizontal merger, because both produce banking services
6. Materials gathered by students will differ.

PROFILES IN ECONOMICS

ALAN GREENSPAN
(1926–)

In some ways, Alan Greenspan is like many other people in government today—a long-time public servant, a respected administrator, and a fiscally conservative theorist with a Ph.D. in economics. What sets him apart from everyone else, however, is that he is widely regarded as being the *second* most powerful person in America.

Greenspan is Chairman of the Federal Reserve System's Board of Governors. As such, his views on the economy and the cost and availability of credit are closely watched by almost everyone in the business community.

MOVING MARKETS In late 1996, when stocks were setting record highs during the bull

market of that year, Greenspan asked if prices weren't being propelled by the "irrational exuberance" of investors. The reaction to this seemingly innocent question was almost instantaneous. Investors, fearing that the Fed chairman was about to implement restrictive monetary policies, tried to sell some of their shares before the Fed drove prices down. The result was almost predictable— within hours, stock exchanges around the world lost 2 percent of their value, and the Dow-Jones Industrial Average fell 145 points in the first half-hour of trading!

As president of the Fed's Board of Governors, Greenspan's opinions have the power to affect trading on the stock exchange.

Markets quickly recovered, however, and 1996 and 1997 turned out to be good years for investors. Much of the strong market was due to the Fed's stable monetary policies that kept inflation at near record-level lows.

FISCAL CONSERVATISM Greenspan is a long-time conservative. Early in his career, he was even a staunch advocate of the gold standard, which he saw as a way to assure monetary stability and fiscal responsibility by government. Throughout his career he worked as an economic consultant to private industry, served on a number of corporate and industry boards, chaired President Ford's Council of Economic Advisers, and chaired the National Commission on Social Security Reform under President Reagan.

Greenspan joined the Fed in 1987 and was appointed Chair of the Fed's Board of Governors by Presidents Reagan, Bush, and Clinton. As the second most powerful person in America, people will scrutinize every statement he makes until his third four-year term as Chair ends in June 2000.

Examining the Profile

1. **Drawing Conclusions** What examples in the profile reveal that Greenspan is fiscally conservative?

2. **For Further Research** Research and report on Greenspan's monetary policies from the late 1980s to the late 1990s.

FOCUS

Section Objectives

1. Describe how banks use fractional reserves in their operations.
2. Apply fractional reserves to the process of monetary expansion.
3. Understand the tools used to conduct monetary policy.

Bellringer

Prior to taking roll at the beginning of the class period, display Focus Activity Transparency 65 on the overhead projector and assign the accompanying Student Activity 65.

Motivational Activity

Discuss students' responses to the activity sheet that accompanies Focus Activity Transparency 65.

Preteaching Vocabulary

Call on volunteers to define the key terms listed in the Section Preview. Encourage students to check the accuracy of these definitions in the Glossary. **LEP**

Use the **Vocabulary PuzzleMaker** to create crossword and word search puzzles.

Section Preview

Objectives

After studying this section, you will be able to:
1. **Describe** how banks use fractional reserves in their operations.
2. **Apply** fractional reserves to the process of monetary expansion.
3. **Understand** the tools used to conduct monetary policy.

Key Terms

monetary policy, fractional reserve system, reserve requirement, legal reserves, member bank reserves, liabilities, assets, balance sheet, net worth, excess reserves, liquidity, certificate of deposit, savings account, time deposit, easy money policy, tight money policy, open market operations, trading desk, discount rate, discount window, collateral, moral suasion, selective credit controls

Applying Economic Concepts

Legal Reserves When you cash a check at a bank, you may have noticed the stacks of currency in the teller's drawer. These funds are kept on hand for check-cashing consumers like yourself, but the bank also keeps them for another reason. Coins and currency are part of the bank's *legal reserves,* or funds kept on hand because of legal requirements imposed on the banking system.

One of the Federal Reserve System's most important responsibilities is that of monetary policy. **Monetary policy** involves controlling the expansion and/or contraction of the money supply to influence the cost and availability of credit, thereby influencing economic activity.

Implementing monetary policy is a complex and highly structured process. In order to understand it better, it helps to understand the fractional reserve system upon which our banking system is based.

Fractional Bank Reserves

In the United States, banks operate under a **fractional reserve system,** which requires banks and other depository institutions to keep only a fraction of their deposits in the form of reserves. The formula used to compute the amount of reserves an institution must have is called the **reserve requirement.** The Fed, for example, may require depository institutions to keep 3 percent of their deposits as reserves. The Fed can change the reserve requirement as it sees fit.

The coins, currency, and deposits used to fulfill this requirement are the **legal reserves.** These normally take the form of currency that institutions hold in their vaults, plus deposits with the Federal Reserve

district banks or other locations approved by the regulatory agencies.

The portion of the legal reserves the member banks keep at the Fed district banks is called **member bank reserves** (MBRs). Nonmember banks can hold their reserves at a Fed member bank, or they can obtain permission from their primary regulators to keep their reserves in another location.

How Banks Operate

To understand how a bank operates, it helps to examine the bank's liabilities and assets. Its **liabilities** are the debts and obligations to others. Its **assets** are the properties, possessions, and claims on others. Liabilities and assets generally are put together in the form of a **balance sheet**—a condensed statement showing all assets and liabilities at a given time. The balance sheet also reflects **net worth**—the excess of assets over liabilities, which is a measure of the value of a business.

Organizing a Bank

First, suppose someone obtains a charter to organize the hypothetical State Bank of Highland Heights.

Classroom Resources for SECTION 2

- Reproducible Lesson Plan 12-2
- Guided Reading Activity 12-2
- Section Quiz 12-2
- Spanish Section Quiz 12-2
- Focus Activity Transparency 65
- Economic Concepts Transparency 18
- NBR's Economics in Action Video Program
- Testmaker
- Vocabulary PuzzleMaker
- Chapter Challenger Interactive Review Software
- Interactive Economics!

The bank will have a corporate structure, and the organizers will supply $20 so that the bank can obtain buildings and furniture before it opens for business. In return for this investment, the owners receive stock, which shows as net worth. Panel **A** in Figure 12.5 shows how the balance sheet of a hypothetical commercial bank might look as soon as it is organized.

The balance sheet shows the assets on the left and the liabilities and net worth on the right. To see why net worth is placed on the right side of the balance sheet, rearrange the definition of net worth from

Assets – Liabilities = Net Worth

to

Assets = Liabilities + Net Worth.

The balance sheet in the figure is sometimes called a *T-account* because of its appearance, and it merely separates the assets from the liabilities and net worth the same way as the equal sign does in the above equation. The T-account also works like the equal sign in that the entries on the left must always equal the entries on the right.

Accepting Deposits

Suppose that now a customer walks in and opens a checking account with $100 in currency. This transaction, shown in Panel **B** of Figure 12.5, is reflected on the balance sheet in two ways. First, to indicate that the money is owed to the depositor, the $100 checking account (or demand deposit) is carried as a liability. Second, to indicate that the cash is the property of the bank, it also appears as an asset on the balance sheet.

Actually, the $100 appears in two places on the asset side. $90 appears as cash, and $10 appears as required reserves—the amount that banks set aside according to law as a protection for depositors. The size of the reserve is determined by the reserve requirement, which is 10 percent in this example. If the requirement was 15 percent, $15 would be set aside.

Making Loans

Now that the bank has some cash in hand, it can make loans. In particular, it is free to loan out its **excess reserves,** the cash and currency not needed to

Lesson 8 of Interactive Economics! to learn more about "Fractional Reserves and Monetary Policy."

Figure 12.5

Balance Sheet Entries for a Hypothetical Commercial Bank

A. When a bank is organized as a corporation, the owners contribute cash used to buy buildings and furniture. In return, the owners receive stock.

Assets		Liabilities + NW	
Required Reserves:		Demand Deposits:	
Cash:		Net Worth	
Loans:		Equity:	$20
Bonds:			
Buildings and Furniture:	$20		
	$20		**$20**

B. When a customer opens an account, some of the deposit is set aside as a reserve, while the excess can be loaned out. Note that Net Worth (NW) remains unchanged.

Assets		Liabilities + NW	
Required Reserves:	$10	Demand Deposits:	$100
Cash:	$90	Net Worth	
Loans:		Equity:	$20
Bonds:			
Buildings and Furniture:	$20		
	$120		**$120**

C. When another person wants to borrow money, the bank can lend all cash in excess of its required reserves. The bank actually swaps one asset (cash) for another (the loan or account receivable).

Assets		Liabilities + NW	
Required Reserves:	$10	Demand Deposits:	$100
Cash:		Net Worth	
Securities:		Equity:	$20
Loans:	$90		
Bonds:			
Buildings and Furniture:	$20		
	$120		**$120**

The T-accounts for the hypothetical bank trace the receipt of deposits through the loan-generating process. When the bank finally reaches maturity, it will have a number of assets in the form of loans, reserves, cash, and even government securities. Demand deposits for each of the bank's depositors, along with CDs, savings accounts, and net worth, will appear on the opposite side of the ledger. **If the reserve requirement was 20%, how much could the bank lend?**

TEACH

Guided Practice

L1 Monetary Expansion
Draw a two-column chart on the chalkboard, using *Reserve Requirement* and *Money Created* as headings. Tell students that a deposit of $100 has been made in a federal member bank and that the reserve requirement is 20 percent. Ask students to determine how much must be held in reserve (*$20*) and how much the bank has available for loans (*$80*). Record responses in the appropriate column. Have students copy the chart into their notebooks and record the loans that could be made until the initial $100 is depleted. Ask students to note how much remains in reserve and how much money has been created. (*$100 in reserve, $500 created*) Have students construct a similar chart based on a $500 deposit and a 25 percent reserve requirement. **LEP**

> **VISUAL INSTRUCTION**
>
> Ask: Why is the bank balance sheet sometimes called a T-account? (*because of its appearance*)
>
> **Answer to Caption:**
> *$80*

Meeting Special Needs

Physical Disability Students who have difficulty with fine motor skills are often slow and inefficient writers. Because many assignments require some measure of writing, these students are at a tremendous disadvantage. Teach these students to read short pieces of text and to use an abridged note-taking system of writing only single words and associated facts.

304

---

fulfill the reserve requirement. The excess reserves amount to $90 at this stage of the process.

If another person enters the bank and borrows the amount equal to the excess reserves, the $90 is moved from the cash line to the loans, or accounts receivable, line in the balance sheet. These changes appear in Panel **C**. Note that there is no change in total assets, only in their mix—a change from a non-interest-earning asset (cash) to an interest-earning one (a consumer loan).

If the bank charged 12 percent interest, it would earn $90 × .12, or $10.80 annually. This income, along with income earned on other loans, would then be used to pay its officers and employees, utility bills, taxes, other business expenses, and stock dividends.

Reaching Maturity

In time, the bank would grow and prosper, diversifying its assets and liabilities in the process. Most of a bank's deposits eventually return to the community in the form of loans, and some of those loans will return to the bank in the form of new deposits. **1**

The bank might even use some of its excess reserves to buy federal, state, or local bonds and other securities. The bonds and securities are helpful for two reasons. They earn interest and, therefore, are more attractive than cash. They also have a high degree of **liquidity**—they can be converted into cash in a very short time. Liquidity adds to the bank's ability to serve its customers. When the demand for loans

increases, the bank can sell its bonds and loan the cash to customers.

The bank also might try to attract additional funds by introducing different kinds of products. One product is a **certificate of deposit,** a receipt showing that an investor has made an interest-bearing loan to a bank. Most banks also offer **savings accounts** and **time deposits,** interest-bearing deposits that cannot be withdrawn by check. The two accounts are similar, except that prior notice must be given to withdraw time deposits, while no prior notice is needed to withdraw savings. ✓

Unless costs are extremely high, the bank should be able to make a profit if it can maintain a 2-3 percent "spread" between the rate it charges on its loans, and the rate it pays for funds it borrows in the form of CDs, savings accounts, and time deposits. If a bank pays 6 percent interest on money it receives, for example, it must loan money at a minimum of 8 or 9 percent to make enough income to pay expenses.

Fractional Reserves and Monetary Expansion

The fractional reserve system allows the money supply to grow to several times the size of the reserves the banking system keeps. Figure 12.6 shows how this can happen, but this time uses a reserve requirement of 20 percent.

GO TO Lesson 8 of Interactive Economics! to learn more about "Fractional Reserves and Monetary Policy."

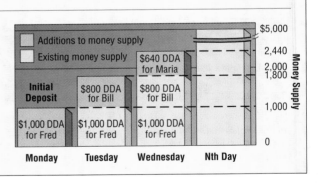

Figure 12.6
Fractional Reserves and the Money Supply

With a 20 percent reserve requirement, a $1,000 cash deposit will result in a fivefold expansion of the money supply. To compute the eventual size of the money supply, the following formula is used:

Total Reserves ÷ Reserve Requirement = Money Supply
or: $1,000 ÷ .20 = $5,000

Because there were no reserves before the $1,000 deposit was made, the deposit will be the reserves in the banking system. **If the initial reserves were $2,000, how large could the money supply get?**

💲 Free Enterprise Activity 💲

Conduct the following simulation of open market operations. Organize students into two groups to represent the public and the Fed. Give 10 slips of paper, each representing $1,000, to each member of the public. Count and record on the chalkboard the total amount of money in circulation. Next, give 10 whole sheets of paper, each one depicting bonds that cost $1,000 each, to each person representing the Fed. Announce that a new issue of bonds is

available for purchase at a good interest rate from the Fed, and have the public buy some. Count and record the money in circulation. Ask the class what happened to the money supply. (*decreased*) Next, have the Fed buy back some of the bonds. Count and record the money now in circulation among buyers. Ask students what has happened to the money supply. (*increased*)

Loans and Monetary Growth

In the figure, a depositor named Fred opens a demand deposit account (DDA) on Monday by depositing $1,000 cash in a national bank. By law, $200 of Fred's deposit must be set aside as a reserve in the form of vault cash or in an MBR with the Fed. The remaining $800 of excess reserves represents the bank's lending power. **2**

On Tuesday, the bank lends its excess reserves of $800 to Bill. Bill can take the loan either in cash or in the form of a DDA with the bank. If he decides to take the DDA, the money never leaves the bank. Instead, it is treated as a new deposit, and 20 percent, or $160, is set aside as a reserve. The remaining $640 are excess reserves that can be lent to someone else.

On Wednesday, Maria enters the bank and borrows $640. She, too, can take the loan in cash or a DDA. If she elects to do the latter, the bank has a new $640 deposit, 20 percent of which must be set aside as a required reserve, leaving $512 of excess reserves.

By Wednesday, Fred has a $1,000 DDA, Bill has an $800 DDA, and Maria has either $640 in cash or a $640 DDA. This amounts to $2,440 in the hands of the non-bank public by the end of the business day—a process that began on Monday with the deposit of $1,000. As long as the bank continues to have excess reserves, the lending process can continue.

Reserves and the Money Supply

Because each new loan is smaller than the one before, the money supply will stop growing at some point. A mathematical relationship exists between the dollar amount of reserves, the reserve requirement, and the size of the money supply. For example, if the dollar amount of reserves equals 20 percent of the money supply, we could write:

$$\text{Total Reserves} = .20 \times \text{Money Supply}$$
$$\text{or,}$$
$$\text{Total Reserves} \div .20 = \text{Money Supply}$$
$$\text{Therefore, } \$1,000 \div .20 = \$5,000$$

This formula shows that $1,000 of total reserves, given a 20 percent reserve requirement, will result in a money supply of $5,000. This amount is the final outcome of the example above when Fred makes his initial deposit.

If Maria takes the loan in cash, however, the monetary expansion process temporarily stops. Before long, though, she will spend the money and it will show up in another bank, enabling the expansion process to resume. Because most bank loans are in the form of DDAs or other accounts rather than cash, the interruption to the expansion process is not that significant.

After the money supply has reached its full size, further changes in the amount of reserves can still affect it. Using the symbol Δ, meaning *change in,* we see that:

$$\Delta \text{ Reserves} = .20 \times \Delta \text{ Money Supply}$$
$$\text{or,}$$
$$\Delta \text{ Reserves} \div .20 = \Delta \text{ Money Supply}$$

Someone, for example, might withdraw $5 from the bank and keep it permanently in a wallet. The money supply would then change by:

$$\Delta \text{ Reserves} \div .20 = \Delta \text{ Money Supply}$$
$$\text{or,}$$
$$-\$5 \div .20 = -\$25.$$

In other words, the money supply would shrink by $25, from $5,000 to $4,975.

Tools of Monetary Policy

The Fed has three major and two minor tools it can use to conduct monetary policy. Each tool affects the

---

QUICK CHECK	**Checking Understanding**	**Applying Economic Concepts**
	1. How are bank deposits funneled back into the community? 2. What would the bank's lending power be if Fred deposited $1,500 rather than $1,000?	**Deposit Insurance** The FDIC currently covers losses up to $100,000. If you have several accounts under one name—$90,000 in a CD, $50,000 in a savings account, and $35,000 in a checking account—the maximum you can collect is $100,000.

Extending the Content

Buying Treasury Securities Some individual investors in Treasury securities prefer to buy through their own commercial banks; however, other investors, in order to avoid the fee that banks charge, deal directly with a regional Federal Reserve Bank or one of its branches. Interested investors must make an offer for the amount of securities they wish to purchase. This offer must be submitted on the appropriate forms and accompanied by payment, either currency or a certified personal check. Investors consider Treasury securities an attractive investment. These securities are safe because they are backed by the federal government and can be sold prior to the maturity date on the Treasury securities market. Buying securities is covered in Chapter 13.

GLENCOE TECHNOLOGY

NIGHTLY BUSINESS REPORT

Economics in Action

Chapter 21
Disc 2, Side 1

Title: *The Federal Reserve and Monetary Policy*

Subject: Monetary policy

Ask: What technique does the Fed use to slow down the economy, and how does it work? *(The Fed attempts to slow down the economy by raising interest rates. This makes money expensive to borrow and encourages consumers and businesses to postpone purchases.)*

Also available in VHS.

L3 *Illustrating Ideas*
Encourage students to draw cartoons or other forms of visual images that illustrate easy money policy and tight money policy. Offer the following examples: for tight money policy—an accordion player (the Fed) squeezing an accordion (money supply); for easy money policy—an accordion player easing pressure on an accordion.

QUICK CHECK

ANSWERS

1. in the form of loans
2. $1,500 × .2 = $300 is set aside, $1,200 to be loaned

ASSESS

Check for Understanding

Assign Section 2 Review as homework or an in-class activity.

Use **Chapter Challenger Interactive Review Software** to review Section 2.

MEETING LESSON OBJECTIVES

Each objective below is tested by the questions that follow it in parentheses.

1. **Describe** how banks use fractional reserves in their operations. **(2, 4, 5)**

2. **Apply** fractional reserves to the process of monetary expansion. **(2)**

3. **Understand** the tools used to conduct monetary policy. **(1, 3)**

VISUAL INSTRUCTION

Have students indicate what action the Fed would take on the reserve requirement if it were following a tight money policy. *(set a higher reserve requirement)*

Answer to Caption:

because other, more flexible tools are available

 Lesson 8 of Interactive Economics! to learn more about "The Reserve Requirement."

Figure 12.7
The Reserve Requirement as a Tool of Monetary Policy

If the Fed wants to control the size of the money supply, it can change the reserve requirement. A low requirement, such as 10 percent, can be used to expand the money supply. A higher requirement, such as 40 percent, has the opposite effect:

Low reserve requirement:
$1,000 ÷ .10 = $10,000

High reserve requirement:
$1,000 ÷ .40 = $ 2,500

The Fed has been reluctant to use the reserve requirement as a policy tool in recent years, even though it has the potential to do so. **Why is the Fed reluctant to use the reserve requirement as a monetary policy tool?**

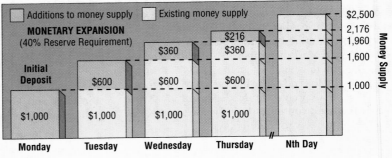

amount of excess reserves in the system, which in turn affects the monetary expansion process described above. The outcome of monetary policy is to influence the cost and availability of credit. The direction of change depends on the objectives of the Federal Reserve System.

Under an **easy money policy,** the Fed allows the money supply to grow and interest rates to fall, which normally stimulates the economy. When interest rates are low, people tend to buy on credit. This encourages sales at stores and production at factories. Businesses also tend to borrow and then invest in new plants and equipment when money is cheap. Under a **tight money policy,** the Fed restricts the growth of the money supply, which drives interest rates up. When interest rates are high, consumers and businesses borrow and spend less, which slows economic growth.

Reserve Requirement

The first tool of monetary policy is the reserve requirement. Within limits that Congress sets, the Fed can change this requirement for all checking, time, or savings accounts in the country.

This tool gives the Fed considerable control over the money supply. Suppose the Fed lowers the reserve requirement in the previous example from 20 to 10 percent. More money could be loaned to Bill, Maria, and others, and the money supply could reach $10,000. If the Fed raises the reserve requirement to 40 percent, however, less money would be loaned, and the money supply would be smaller. The effect of different reserve requirements is shown in Figure 12.7.

Historically, the Fed has been reluctant to use the reserve requirement as a policy tool, in part because

---

Cultural Diversity and Economics

Hawaiian Money To prepare for the possible invasion of Hawaii during World War II, special silver certificates and Federal Reserve Notes were issued. These carried a brown seal and the word *Hawaii* stamped in large letters on both sides of the bill. If Hawaii were captured by the Japanese, the government could simply declare these notes to be obsolete, and therefore not part of the United States money supply.

other monetary policy tools work better. Even so, the reserve requirement can be a very powerful tool should the Fed decide to use it. Figure 12.8 summarizes the impact of a change in the reserve requirement on the money supply in the manner just described, along with the impact of the other monetary tools described below.

Open Market Operations

The second and most popular tool of monetary policy is **open market operations**—the buying and selling of government securities in financial markets. Open market operations affect the amount of excess reserves in the banking system and, therefore, the ability of banks to support new loans.

Suppose the Fed decides to increase the money supply. To do so, it buys government securities from a dealer who specializes in large-volume transactions of those securities. The Fed pays for the securities by writing a check. The dealer then deposits the check with his or her bank. The bank forwards the check to the Fed for payment. At this point, the Fed "pays" the check by increasing the bank's MBR with the Fed. The result is that whenever the Fed writes a check, more reserves are pumped into the banking system. Because only some reserves are needed to back existing deposits, the excess reserves can be loaned out, thus increasing the money supply.

If the Fed wants to contract the money supply and drive up interest rates, it can sell billions of dollars of government securities back to dealers. Dealers pay for

the purchase of securities with checks drawn on their own banks. The Fed then processes the checks by reducing the MBRs of dealers' banks. With fewer reserves in the banking system, fewer loans are made and the money supply contracts.

The Federal Open Market Committee, which reviews and recommends changes in monetary policy, conducts open market operations. Normally the FOMC tries to decide if the current level of interest rates and monetary growth is too high, too low, or just right. After the committee votes to set targets, officials at the trading desk take over. The **trading desk** is the physical location at the Fed's New York district bank where the buying and selling actually takes place. The officials at the desk buy and sell bonds daily to maintain the targets set by the FOMC. The desk is permanently located in New York to be close to the nation's financial markets.

Discount Rate

As a central bank, the Fed makes loans to other depository institutions. The **discount rate**—the interest the Fed charges on loans to financial institutions—is the third major tool of monetary policy.

A bank might obtain a loan from the Fed for two reasons. First, it could have an unexpected drop in its member bank reserves, which would shrink its excess reserves. In this case, the bank would go to the Fed and arrange a short-term loan to cover the shortfall. Second, a bank could be faced with seasonal demands for loans. A bank in an agricultural area, for example,

Lesson 8 of Interactive Economics! to learn more about "Open Market Operations" and "The Federal Discount Rate."

Figure 12.8
Summary of Monetary Policy Tools

Tool	Fed Action	Effect on Excess Reserves	Money Supply
Reserve Requirement	Lower	Frees excess reserves because fewer are needed to back existing deposits in the system.	Expands
	Raise	More reserves are required to back existing deposits, excess reserves contract.	Contracts
Open Market Operations	Buy bonds	Checks written by the Fed add to excess reserves in the system.	Expands
	Sell bonds	Checks written by buyers are subtracted from reserves, excess reserves in the system contract.	Contracts
Discount Rate	Lower	Additional reserves can be obtained at lower cost, excess reserves expand.	Expands
	Raise	Additional reserves through borrowing now more expensive, excess reserves not added.	Contracts

The key to monetary policy is to see how the excess reserves in the system are affected. **What happens to the money supply when the Fed increases excess reserves? Decreases excess reserves?**

Evaluate

 Assign the Section 2 Quiz in the TCR or use the *Economics: Principles and Practices* Testmaker to create a customized quiz. Spanish Section Quizzes also are available in the Spanish Resources Binder.

DID YOU KNOW

The limits within which the Fed can adjust the reserve requirement were set by the Depository Institutions Deregulation and Monetary Control Act of 1980. The present reserve requirement can be found in the current edition of the *Federal Reserve Bulletin*.

VISUAL INSTRUCTION

After students have answered the caption question, offer the following formula: increasing excess reserves = expanding money supply; decreasing excess reserves = contracting money supply.

Answers to Caption:
expands; contracts

Extending the Content

The Fed and Consumer Credit In 1980 the Fed imposed restraints on consumer borrowing in an effort to restrict the money supply. Banks were required to make a deposit with Federal Reserve Banks equal to 15 percent of any increase in total outstanding credit in the form of credit card purchases or unsecured personal loans. Because this special deposit earned no interest, it would increase the cost of making loans and, therefore, discourage the expansion of credit and the money supply.

Reteach

Ask students to write two paragraphs; one explaining how banks can create money, the other explaining the steps the Fed can take to adjust the money supply.

Enrich

Have students investigate the most recent action taken by the Fed on monetary policy. Encourage them to report their findings to the class.

CLOSE

Have students state which of the tools of monetary policy is the most effective in controlling the money supply. Ask them to offer explanations for their selections.

might face a heavy demand for loans during the planting season. In that case, it would need additional MBRs to support the loans made in the spring.

The **discount window** is a teller's window at the Fed that depository institutions use to borrow member bank reserves. Before a bank actually borrows money, however, the terms of the loan are arranged in advance. Next, the depository institution delivers collateral to the window. **Collateral** is the property or other security used to guarantee payment of a loan. Then, when everything is complete, the loan is granted and appears as an increase in the institution's MBR account.

Changes in the discount rate affect the cost of borrowed MBRs. If the Fed wants an easy money policy, it may lower the rate and/or allow more borrowing than before. When this happens, it is sometimes said that the Fed is "opening" the window. The reverse is true if the Fed wants to follow a tight money policy. Then, it discourages borrowing by raising the rate or by making it more difficult to borrow. When this happens, the Fed is "closing" the window.

Most institutions can borrow from the Fed, including member and nonmember banks, savings institutions, and even credit unions. The Fed, however, views access to the window as a privilege rather than a right. As a result, the Fed may limit the number of times a borrower can go to the window.

Other Tools

The Fed may also use two other methods to control the money supply. These are moral suasion and selective credit controls.

Moral suasion is the use of persuasion such as announcements, press releases, articles in newspapers and magazines, and testimony before Congress. Moral suasion works because bankers often try to anticipate changes in monetary policy.

Suppose that the chairperson of the Fed is called before Congress to give his or her view on the state of the economy. Assume also that the chair states that interest rates are somewhat low, and that it would not hurt the economy if they should rise. Bankers might well expect a tighter money policy in the next few weeks. As a result, they might be less willing to loan their excess reserves, and they might even raise their interest rates by a small amount. In the end, the money supply might contract just slightly, even if the Fed did no more than offer its views.

A second method is **selective credit controls**—rules pertaining to loans for specific commodities or purposes. These controls took the form of minimum down payments on cars and other consumer goods during World War II and the Korean War. Selective credit controls during those periods were imposed to free factories to produce war materials. Selective credit controls are seldom used today.

SECTION 2 REVIEW

Reviewing Terms and Facts

1. **Define** monetary policy, fractional reserve system, reserve requirement, legal reserves, member bank reserves, liabilities, assets, balance sheet, net worth, excess reserves, liquidity, certificate of deposit, savings account, time deposit, easy money policy, tight money policy, open market operations, trading desk, discount rate, discount window, collateral, moral suasion, selective credit controls.

2. **Explain** how the availability of excess reserves determines whether a bank can make new loans.

3. **Describe** the three major tools of monetary policy.

Critical Thinking

4. **Drawing Conclusions** At times, someone with a good credit rating may not be able to get a loan. When this happens, the potential customer may be told to "come back next week" to try again. What does this tell you about the bank's reserves? How should the customer react to a situation like this?

Applying Economic Concepts

5. **Legal Reserves** Your local national bank is required to keep its reserves in the form of vault cash and member deposits with the Fed. Why do you suppose that other assets, such as common stocks or real estate, are not suitable reserves?

Answers to SECTION 2 REVIEW

1. All vocabulary words are defined in the Glossary.

2. The bank is required to keep a percentage of its deposits in reserve. What is left is referred to as excess reserves and may be used to make loans.

3. The reserve requirement—by requiring banks to hold more in reserve, Fed can restrict money supply; by requiring less, it can increase money supply. Open market operations—by buying or selling government securities, Fed can restrict or increase

money supply. Discount rate—by raising or reducing interest rate it charges on loans to financial institutions, Fed affects cost of borrowing, thus restricting or increasing money supply.

4. The bank is fully loaned out (temporarily has no excess reserves). This is not unusual; customers should not be offended.

5. because they are not liquid assets that can be used to meet demands on the bank

Section Preview

Objectives

After studying this section, you will be able to:

1. **Explain** how monetary policy affects interest rates in the short run.
2. **Relate** monetary expansion to inflation in the long run.
3. **Identify** the two major definitions of money.
4. **Describe** various steps taken to protect the safety of the banking system.

Key Terms

prime rate, quantity theory of money, monetizing the debt, M1, M2, problem bank list, creditor, agricultural bank, energy bank

Applying Economic Concepts

Money Where do you keep your money? On your person? In a savings or checking account? In the form of traveler's checks or NOW accounts? You, and millions of others, make *money* difficult to define. There are too many ways to hold your money—just ask the Fed!

The impact of monetary policy on the economy is complex. In the short run, monetary policy affects interest rates and the availability of credit. In the long run, it affects inflation. In addition, no one can be sure how long it will take for the effects of monetary policy to impact the economy.

Short-Run Impact

In the short run, an increase or a decrease in the supply of money affects the interest rate, or the price of credit. When the Fed expands the money supply, the cost of credit goes down. When the Fed contracts the money supply, the cost of credit goes up.

This short-run relationship between money and interest rates is shown in Figure 12.9. The demand curve for money has the usual shape, which shows that more money will be demanded when the price of money is low. The supply curve, however, does not have its usual shape. Instead, it is vertical, indicating that the supply of money is fixed at any given time.

Before the market is disturbed, the interest rate, as shown in Graph **A,** is at 12 percent. If the Fed expands the money supply to $\mathbf{S_1S_1}$, the interest rate falls to 10 percent. A contraction of the money supply, as shown in Graph **B,** increases the rate from 12 to 14 percent.

Although the Fed tries to do what is best for the economy, people do not always agree with its decisions. In 1981, for example, the Fed was criticized for allowing interest rates to get too high. That year, the **prime rate**—the best or lowest interest rate commercial bankers charge their customers—reached 21.5 percent. Critics felt that the economy would have been better off if the Fed had expanded the money supply, thus lowering interest rates. Supporters, however, felt these policies reduced inflation.

Long-Run Impact

In the long run, changes in the supply of money affect the general level of prices. This relationship, formally known as the **quantity theory of money,** has been demonstrated repeatedly in history.

Historical Precedents

When the Spanish brought gold and silver back to Spain from the Americas, the increase in the money supply started inflation that lasted for 100 years. When the Continental Congress issued $250 million of currency during the Revolutionary War, the economy suffered severe inflation. A similar thing happened

CHAPTER 12: *The Federal Reserve System and Monetary Policy* **309**

Lesson 8 of Interactive Economics! and click on "An Introduction to Monetary Policy."

Figure 12.9
Short-Run Impact of Monetary Policy

In the short run, the impact of monetary policy is on interest rates, or the price of credit. When the money supply expands, the price of credit goes down. When the money supply is contracted, the price of credit goes up. **Why is the supply of money, SS, shown as a vertical line?**

during the Civil War, when nearly $500 million of greenbacks were printed.

Monetizing the Debt

When the federal government financed the Vietnam War with deficit spending in the 1960s, the crowding-out effect threatened. To keep interest rates from going up, the Fed decided to **monetize the debt**—create enough extra money to offset the deficit spending.

The process of monetizing the debt is illustrated in Figure 12.10. **DD** and **SS** represent the initial demand and supply of money. Suppose, however, that the government borrows $25 billion, shifting the demand curve for money to D_1D_1. If the Fed does not take any action, the interest rate would rise from 10 to 12 percent and crowd out some investors. If the Fed wants to keep the interest rate from rising, it could increase the money supply to S_1S_1 and push interest rates back down to their original level.

In the short run, then, the Fed can increase the money supply just enough to keep the interest rate from rising. This procedure is effective if done infrequently. Repeated short-run attempts to keep rates low, however, result in a long-term expansion of the money supply, making inflation even worse.

Taming Inflation

Much of the federal debt was monetized from the late 1960s until the late 1970s. During this period, the money supply grew at rates of 12 percent or more for

several years in a row. As inflation got worse, the price of most goods and services—including interest rates—also went up. Attempts by the Fed to keep interest rates low by increasing the supply of money worked at first, but eventually inflation was aggravated.

By 1980 the Fed realized that it had to choose between interest rates and inflation. It chose to control inflation. When this happened, the prime rate in 1981 reached 21.5 percent. Most people did not like the high interest rates at the time, but today they recognize that the tight money policies were necessary to bring down inflation.

Other Monetary Policy Issues

When the Fed conducts monetary policy, it has several other issues to consider. The first involves timing and burden.

Timing and Burden

Sometimes a tight money policy might show results in six months. At other times, the impact might not be felt for two years. The same happens when the Fed follows an easy money policy. Such variations in timing make it difficult to use monetary policy to fine-tune the economy. 1

A second problem is that monetary policy has an uneven impact on the economy. If the Fed follows a tight money policy to control inflation, interest rates may increase. Higher rates hurt home-building and automobile sales, because the cost of borrowing goes

---

Meeting Special Needs

Writing Disability A few students who have significant difficulties with written expression require substantial modification to instructional and evaluative procedures used in class. They may find taking notes virtually impossible. Appoint three or four students to be "scribes" in the class

and provide them with either carbon paper or carbonless copy paper. As the class discusses Section 3, have the scribes take complete notes, which they can later share with those who need them. Have poorer note takers write only key words.

Figure 12.10
Monetizing the Debt

When (1) the government borrows to cover a deficit in the federal budget, interest rates tend to rise because of the increased demand for credit, raising the possibility of crowding out. If (2) the Fed expands the money supply just enough to offset the borrowing, interest rates may remain unchanged. **What are the long-run effects of monetizing the debt?**

up. If the Fed follows a loose monetary policy, interest rates may go down. Home-building and automobile sales will then benefit more than other industries.

Present vs. Future Allocation

The Fed must also keep in mind that interest rates and inflation affect the allocation of scarce resources between present and future uses. When interest rates are low, people find it easier to finance the purchase of a car, house, or college education right now. When people spend more today, however, they end up saving less—and therefore consume less in the future.

High interest rates have the opposite effect. When rates are high, some purchases are delayed until rates come down or until people have saved enough to buy the products they desire. As a result, people have more money to spend in the future, and so the use of some resources shifts from the present to the future.

Interest rates do influence people's decisions to either spend or save, but inflation also makes a difference in investment decisions. The Fed considers the *real rate of interest*—the market rate of interest minus the rate of inflation—when conducting monetary policy. To illustrate, the 21.5 percent interest rate in 1981 was not as bad as it sounds when you consider that the inflation rate was 10.5 percent. Subtracting the inflation rate from the interest rate results in only an 11.0 percent real rate of interest.

The Politics of Interest Rates

Because of the way it can control the interest rate, the Fed often comes under a great deal of political pressure. A President, for example, can gain some say over monetary policy by appointing certain people to the Federal Reserve Board of Governors. After these appointments are made, however, the governors can conduct monetary policy as they wish. Some Presidents have tried to increase control by criticizing the Fed. Others have threatened to introduce legislation to make the Fed less independent.

No such laws have been passed recently, although the threats do get the Fed's attention. Even so, the Fed often is reluctant to accommodate demands for lower interest rates because of the fear of inflation. Unlike many politicians, who often insist on lower interest rates during an election year, the Fed is more concerned about the health of the economy in the long run.

People tend to use the interest rate as a measure of the overall health of the economy. In particular, they

QUICK CHECK

Checking Understanding	*Applying Economic Concepts*
1. Why is it difficult to use monetary policy to fine-tune the economy?	☑ **Inflation** Inflation peaked in 1980. Since then it has been significantly lower, with rates in the early 1990s hovering near 4 percent.

$ Free Enterprise Activity $

Invite a local bank official to visit the class to make a presentation on the status of the banking industry today. Suggest that the speaker cover such topics as the reasons banks fail, the steps government agencies take to deal with failed banks, and the safeguards the industry and the federal government have put in place to prevent further failures. After the presentation, have students write short essays summarizing the major points made by the guest speaker.

Independent Practice

📂 **Guided Reading** Assign Guided Reading Activity for Section 3. **LEP**

L3 Debate Have students review the discussion of the politics of interest rates on page 311. Next, have them conduct a class debate on the following: The Federal Reserve System's Board of Governors should be nationally elected officials. Encourage students to write down the major points raised in the debate. Then have them use their notes to write an essay supporting or challenging the resolution.

 VISUAL INSTRUCTION

Have students explain the crowding-out effect. *(higher-than-normal interest rates that result from heavy government borrowing)*

Answer to Caption:
inflation

 ANSWERS

1. because of timing: sometimes policy will show results in six months; sometimes it may take two years for impact to be felt

INTERACTIVE ECONOMICS!

 CD-ROM Monetary Policy

Have students click on the Advanced Topic "The Federal Discount Rate." Then have them apply what they learned about the federal discount rate to the graphs shown on page 310.

💾 *Supplied in both CD-ROM and diskette formats.*

311

L1 Class Project Most Fed district banks shred old money when they take it out of circulation. Have volunteers call your local Fed bank and ask if your class can have some shredded money for a class project or fund-raiser. The shredded money is usually free if you can specify the use of the currency—filler for a paperweight, bookmarks, etc.

ASSESS

Check for Understanding

Assign Section 3 Review as homework or an in-class activity.

◉ Use **Chapter Challenger Interactive Review Software** to review Section 3.

MEETING LESSON OBJECTIVES

Each objective below is tested by the questions that follow it in parentheses.

1. **Explain** how monetary policy affects interest rates in the short run. **(2, 4)**

2. **Relate** monetary expansion to inflation in the long run. **(3, 4, 6)**

3. **Identify** the two major definitions of money. **(1, 7)**

4. **Describe** various steps taken to protect the safety of the banking system. **(5)**

Evaluate

🗁 🗁 ◉ Assign the Section 3 Quiz in the TCR or use the *Economics: Principles and Practices* Testmaker to create a customized quiz. Spanish Section Quizzes also are available in the Spanish Resources Binder.

312

---

think the economy is healthy when interest rates are low. This makes it difficult for elected officials when the Fed allows interest rates to rise.

Defining Money

With so many financial institutions offering various ways to deposit or hold one's money, the Fed has had to develop some new definitions of money to keep track of it.

Figure 12.11 on page 314 lists a number of components of the money supply, or ways that people have chosen to keep money. The Fed groups these together according to function and gives them names. The first is **M1**, which represents the transactional components of the money supply, or the components of the money supply that most closely match money's role as a medium of exchange. This definition of money includes traveler's checks, coins, currency, demand deposits, and other checkable deposits such as NOW accounts and credit union share drafts.

M2 is a measure of money that includes those components most closely conforming to money's role as a store of value. M2 includes M1, small denomination time deposits, savings deposits, and money market funds.

Bank Failures

Bank failures, like the savings and loans, were a serious problem in the 1980s. Bank failures are a problem for three main reasons. First, owners lose whatever investment they might have in a bank. This loss is a personal hardship for them just as the failure of any other business hurts its owners.

Second, publicity surrounding a bank failure strains the credibility of the banking system as a whole. Some depositors might try to withdraw funds or cancel dealings they have with sound banks.

Third, the FDIC has to recover those losses by charging higher rates for deposit insurance on all banks. This raises the cost of banking to depositors.

If a bank is in jeopardy, the FDIC adds the bank's name to a confidential **problem bank list,** which is closely watched. If the problems get worse, the FDIC takes control of the bank. It can then either sell the problem bank to a stronger one, or it can liquidate the bank and pay off the depositors.

Disposing of Failed Banks

When the FDIC takes over a bank, the shareholders know nothing of the FDIC's actions. The sale of one bank to another takes only a few weeks or days, and services are seldom interrupted. People usually find out about the sale when the bank opens for business under a new name. The FDIC uses such secrecy to prevent panic withdrawals and to prevent shareholders from selling their worthless stock to unsuspecting investors.

When the FDIC cannot find a buyer for a failed bank, it may declare the bank insolvent and close its doors. Within a few days, the FDIC begins to pay off depositors directly. This is generally a speedy process, but in some cases depositors do not recover their money for several months.

Depositors, of course, are only covered up to the $100,000 insurance limit. If an account has more than this, the depositor may go to court as a **creditor**—a person or institution to whom money is owed. There, a

---

Extending the Content

Disposable Credit Credit cards are not included in the money supply because, although many people use them to make purchases, they are not really money. Rather, they are an easy method of obtaining a short-term loan from the institution that issued the card. A variation of the credit card, however, may cause the Fed to reassess its definitions of the money supply once again. This card is prepaid and disposable. In other words, the con-

sumer decides how much he or she wants to spend and then buys a card for that amount. As the card is used, value is reduced until the card is used up. The consumer then simply throws the card away. The card is designed to be used at automatic teller machines (ATMs) to draw cash. In the future, however, consumers will be able to make purchases at retail stores, as they can do now with regular credit cards.

suit is filed to recover the rest of the deposit. If the bank happens to be uninsured, depositors and others who have valuables stored in safe deposit boxes are simply out of luck. The chance is slim that a depositor will go to court and recover much, if anything, from the owners of an uninsured, failed bank.

Reasons for Failure

Banks fail for many reasons, but poor management is the main one. Some banks, for example, make loans without adequate collateral. Others fail to keep expenses in line with revenues. Even others are victims of a weak economy.

Many **agricultural banks**—banks with more than 25 percent of their loans in agriculture—have been hit hard because of falling land values and low prices for farm products. **Energy banks**—banks with more than 25 percent of their loans in gas, oil, and other energy areas—were also hit hard when oil prices declined sharply in 1985 and 1986. Many of these banks failed because too many of their loans were concentrated in a weak industry.

In the late 1980s, speculation in real estate was a major problem. Many borrowers used real estate for collateral, and then went out of business. When the banks took control of the property, they discovered that the property had lost its value and could be sold only for a loss. This situation was especially troublesome in the Northeast and the Southwest.

Finally, natural disasters may have an impact on banks. Many of the small commercial banks along the Mississippi River had a difficult time surviving the record floods of 1993, especially because some borrowers could not repay their loans.

New Capital Requirements

During the 1980s, banking authorities took steps to increase the amount of financial capital their owners must put in the bank. This capital is used as a cushion to absorb loan losses and, because it is the property of the bank's owners, the expectation is that the owners will be more careful when they make future loans.

Finally, the FDIC and other federal regulatory agencies are working to better coordinate and improve the quality of their standards and inspections. The 1980s was a difficult decade for the banking industry. Unlike the savings and loan industry, however, the banking industry emerged intact in the 1990s.

SECTION 3 REVIEW

Reviewing Terms and Facts

1. **Define** prime rate, quantity theory of money, monetizing the debt, M1, M2, problem bank list, creditor, agricultural bank, energy bank.
2. **Describe** the short-run impact of monetary policy.
3. **Explain** the long-run impact of monetary policy.
4. **Identify** the problems associated with the timing and burden of monetary policy.
5. **Describe** the recent history of bank failures.

Critical Thinking

6. **Making Generalizations** Historically, expansions in the money supply have set off inflation. Something similar might have happened to you. Identify a period in your life when you had a little more money than usual. How did you spend the extra cash? Were prices as important to you then as they were at other times when you did not have as much to spend? Why do prices tend to increase faster when more money is available?

Applying Economic Concepts

7. **Money** Our money supply, as well as the different forms or ways to hold it, has changed considerably over the years. Describe one or two ways you think United States money might change even more in the future.

Reteach

Ask students to write a paragraph comparing the short-run and long-run effects of monetary policy.

📁 📁 Have students complete Reteaching Activity 12. Spanish Reteaching Activities also are available in the Spanish Resources Binder.

Enrich

Have students select a past monetary policy action taken by the Fed. Ask them to describe the short-run and long-run impact of this action.

📁 Have students complete Enrichment Activity 12.

CLOSE

Have students discuss the following statement: The answer to the nation's debt problem is simply to monetize future deficit spending.

late 1980s. Some small commercial banks whose borrowers were hit by natural disasters also faced problems.

6. Answers may vary, but most students will note that price seems less of an issue when they have more money than usual. They may also point out that as the supply of money increases, the value, or buying power, of each dollar decreases.

7. Answers will vary. As guidance, remind students of the point made in the Extending the Content feature on page 312.

Answers to SECTION 3 REVIEW

1. All vocabulary words are defined in the Glossary.

2. It affects interest rates and the availability of credit. Tight money policies cause interest rates to rise and reduces availability of credit. Easy money policies have opposite effect.

3. It affects inflation. Tight money policies usually bring inflation down, whereas easy money policies cause inflation to rise.

4. It is difficult to predict exactly how long monetary policy will take to produce results. Monetary policy has uneven impact on economy. Tight monetary policy will hurt home-building sales, because cost of borrowing will go up.

5. Agricultural banks have been hard hit in recent years because of falling land values and low prices for farm products. The weakness in the oil industry in the mid–1980s caused problems for energy banks. Speculation in real estate proved a problem for some banks in the Northeast and Southwest in the

313

TEACH

Have students sit in five rows. Direct each row of students to total the amount of money they have in their pockets. Note totals on the chalkboard. Then have students present the information on the chalkboard in the form of a bar graph. Call on a student to analyze the completed bar graph by following the steps in the *Explanation*.

📂 ***Skills Practice*** For additional practice, have students complete Reinforcing Economic Skill 12.

ECONOMIC SKILL

Reading a Bar Graph

You just timed yourself running the 100-yard dash. Now you would like to compare your time to that of the other sprinters on your team. Organizing your times in a bar graph would allow you to visually compare all your times at once.

Explanation

Like line graphs, bar graphs are used to compare facts involving numbers. Bars, or columns, of different lengths are used to represent quantities or totals. Some bar graphs show changes over time, but most are used to compare quantities during the same time period. A bar graph might compare the number of students attending 5 different schools during the same year. A bar graph might also compare the 100-yard dash times of 5 students.

Bar graphs have horizontal and vertical axes that describe the information presented in the graph. Sometimes more than one set of facts are compared on a bar graph. The steps involved in reading a bar graph are:

- Read the title to learn the subject of the graph.
- Look at the horizontal and vertical axes to find out what information the graph presents.
- If the bars are color-coded, read the key indicating what the colors represent.
- Compare the lengths of the bars on the graphs.
- Use the information you have learned from the graph to draw conclusions about the subject.

Practice

Study the bar graph, then answer the questions below.
1. What is the subject of the graph?
2. What information is found along the horizontal axis?
3. What is being compared along the vertical axis?
4. What does the color red represent?
5. What do the striped bars represent?
6. Which component makes up the largest part of the money supply? The smallest part?
7. Which components make up M1?
8. Which components are included in M2?
9. What aspect of Figure 12.11 surprised you the most? Why?

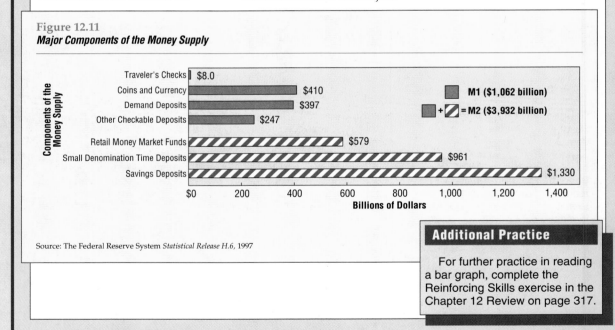

Figure 12.11
Major Components of the Money Supply

Components of the Money Supply:
- Traveler's Checks — $8.0
- Coins and Currency — $410
- Demand Deposits — $397
- Other Checkable Deposits — $247
- Retail Money Market Funds — $579
- Small Denomination Time Deposits — $961
- Savings Deposits — $1,330

Billions of Dollars: $0, 200, 400, 600, 800, 1,000, 1,200, 1,400

■ M1 ($1,062 billion)
■ + ▨ = M2 ($3,932 billion)

Source: The Federal Reserve System *Statistical Release H.6*, 1997

Additional Practice

For further practice in reading a bar graph, complete the Reinforcing Skills exercise in the Chapter 12 Review on page 317.

314 UNIT 3: *Macroeconomics: Institutions*

Answers to SKILL

1. major components of the money supply
2. dollar amounts in billions
3. different components of the money supply
4. M1
5. money supply components that have to be added to M1 to get M2
6. savings deposits; traveler's checks
7. Traveler's checks, coins and currency, demand deposits, other checkable deposits
8. all M1 components plus retail money market funds, small denomination time deposits, savings deposits
9. Answers will vary.

ECONOMICS IN ACTION

The Federal Reserve and Monetary Policy

Setting Up the Video

With your classmates, view "The Federal Reserve and Monetary Policy" on the videodisc *Economics in Action*. The video focuses on how the Federal Reserve System (the Fed) controls the money supply to regulate the nation's economy.

Chapter 21
Disc 2, Side 1

View the video by scanning the bar code or by entering the chapter number on your keypad and pressing Search. *(Also available in VHS format.)*

Hands-On Activity

Most credit card interest rates are tied to the prime rate—the best (or lowest) interest rate that banks charge to their customers. Consumers feel the effects of a rate hike almost immediately. Assume that you have credit-card debt of $12,700. Your current interest rate, tied to the prime rate, is 16.9 percent. What is your annual interest payment? If the prime rate increases by 1 percent, what would your new interest payment be? How much more per year does your credit card now cost you? Prepare a table showing the increasing payments that a 2 percent, 3 percent, and 4 percent hike would cost you. Share your table with the class.

INTERACTIVE ECONOMICS!

Monetary Policy

Introduction

Lesson 8 of *Interactive Economics!* introduces you to monetary policy. Monetary policy involves actions by the Federal Reserve System that affect the availability and cost of credit (interest rates).

Monetary policy is possible because of the fractional reserve system in use today, and because of the Fed's ability to expand and contract the money supply. Why would the Fed want to change the supply of money? The Fed executes monetary policy in order to keep interest rates stable and inflation low.

Using the Software

1. Select "Monetary Policy" from the Main Menu.

2. Click on "An Introduction to Monetary Policy," then click on "Fractional Reserves and Monetary Expansion." Read these tutorials.

3. Go back to the Monetary Policy menu and click on the Advanced Topics Menu, which includes "Open Market Operations," "The Reserve Requirement," and "The Federal Discount Rate."

4. Study the information given, then click on "Economics Lab." Complete the lab by clicking and dragging the glossary terms to the appropriate sentence.

5. Print your completed lab.

315

_____
_____
_____
_____
_____
_____
_____
_____

GLENCOE TECHNOLOGY

NIGHTLY BUSINESS REPORT

Economics in Action

Chapter 21

Disc 2, Side 1

Title: *The Federal Reserve and Monetary Policy*

If you do not have access to a videodisc player, the **Economics in Action** programs are also available in VHS.

INTERACTIVE ECONOMICS!

Before students complete the "Economics Lab" in Lesson 8, ask them the following questions:

1. What is an *interest rate*? (*the price of credit*)

2. How does the Fed keep interest rates stable? (*In order to keep interest rates stable, the Fed must change the supply of money, an action known as monetary policy.*)

3. What three main tools does the Fed use to change the size of the money supply? (*open market operations, changes in the reserve requirement, changes in the discount rate*)

4. What does the existence of a fractional reserve system allow banks to do? (*loan more money than they actually hold, thus increasing the supply of money larger than the amount of legal reserves kept in the banking system*)

CHAPTER 12 REVIEW

GLENCOE
TECHNOLOGY

VIDEODISC
MindJogger Videoquiz

Use MindJogger to review the Chapter 12 content.

 Chapter 12
Disc 2, Side A

Also available in VHS.

Answers

Reviewing Key Terms

1. Board of Governors
2. easy money policy
3. legal reserves
4. excess reserves
5. open market operations
6. monetizing the debt
7. M1
8. monetary policy
9. FOMC
10. discount window

Reviewing the Facts

1. The Fed had a regional structure before the 1930s and a centralized structure after. Privately owned member banks, not the government, own the Fed.

2. Board of Governors: 7 members appointed by President to 14–year terms; FOMC: 7 Board members and 5 district bank presidents; FAC: 1 representative from each of 12 district banks

3. state member bank supervision, holding companies, international operations, mergers, check clearing, consumer legislation, currency, margin requirements

4. The fractional reserve system requires banks to keep only a fraction of their deposits on reserve. They are free, within legal limits, to use the rest as they see fit.

Reviewing Key Terms

Write the key term that best completes the following sentences.

balance sheet
holding company
certificate of deposit
discount window
easy money policy
excess reserves
legal reserves
M1

M2
monetary policy
monetizing the debt
moral suasion
open market operations
FOMC
selective credit controls
Board of Governors

1. The main governing body of the Fed is the _____.
2. A(n) _____ would expand the money supply and tend to lower interest rates.
3. _____ are the funds that banks use to satisfy the reserve requirement.
4. If a bank has _____, it is able to make additional loans to customers.
5. The most popular and effective tool of monetary policy is that of _____.
6. When the Fed increases the money supply to offset the effects of government borrowing, it is _____.
7. The transactional component of the money supply is _____.
8. One of the most important responsibilities of the Fed is _____.
9. The part of the Fed that buys and sells government bonds as part of monetary policy is the _____.
10. A depository institution would go to the _____ if it wanted to borrow reserves from the Fed.

Reviewing the Facts

SECTION 1 *(pages 294–300)*
1. **Describe** two features that distinguish the Fed from other central banks.
2. **Identify** the membership of the Board of Governors, the FOMC, and the FAC.
3. **Identify** the most important regulatory responsibilities of the Fed.

SECTION 2 *(pages 302–308)*
4. **Explain** how banks operate under a fractional reserve system of banking.
5. **Identify** the conditions that enable a bank to make new loans.
6. **Explain** how the total reserves and the reserve requirement can be used to compute the size of the money supply.
7. **Describe** the three major tools of monetary policy.

SECTION 3 *(pages 309–313)*
8. **Identify** the major short-run impact of monetary policy.
9. **Explain** how the long-run impact of monetary policy differs from its short-run impact.
10. **Explain** why the level of interest rates is politically sensitive.
11. **Describe** the steps taken to increase the safety of the commercial banking system.

Critical Thinking

1. **Making Comparisons** If you were on the Federal Reserve Board of Governors and could use only one method to control the money supply, which policy tool would you choose? Why?
2. **Drawing Conclusions** Defend or refute the following statement: The independence of the Federal Reserve System is essential to the health of the economy.

Applying Economic Concepts

1. **Money** Survey your parents to find out how they keep their money (CDs, traveler's checks, savings accounts, time deposits, banks, etc.). How many categories mentioned in this chapter do they use?
2. **Stability in Value** If you were to apply for a loan, how would the lending institution view you as a credit risk? Determine your net worth as a potential borrower by listing your assets and liabilities in a T-account, similar to the one shown in **Figure 12.5**. Refer to page 302 for the definition of *net worth*.

5. When a customer opens an account, the bank must keep a required percentage of the deposit in reserve. The remaining amount of money is free to be used as loans.

6. Dividing the total reserves by the reserve requirement gives the eventual size of the money supply.

7. The reserve requirement—by requiring banks to hold more in reserve, Fed can restrict money supply; by requiring less, it can increase money supply.

Open market operations—by buying or selling government securities, Fed can restrict or increase money supply. Discount rate—by raising or reducing interest rate it charges on loans to financial institutions, Fed affects cost of borrowing, thus restricting or increasing money supply.

8. Short-run impact affects interest rates and the availability of credit. Tight money policy causes interest rates to rise and reduces availability of credit. Easy money policy has opposite effect.

Reinforcing Skills

READING A BAR GRAPH

Use the bar graph below to answer the following questions.

1. What is the subject of this bar graph?
2. What time span is covered?
3. What do the numbers along the vertical axis represent?
4. Which year saw the highest number of bank failures?
5. What does the trend seem to be since then?
6. Why was the number of bank failures high in the 1930s?

Individual Activity

Interview a person who works in a financial institution. A manager of a commercial bank may be interviewed about the bank's primary regulatory agencies, the cost of deposit insurance, and/or the origins of the bank's charter. A loan officer may be interviewed to explain how loans are made and what requirements must be met. A stockbroker may explain the use of margin requirements. After your interviews are completed, share your findings with the class.

Cooperative Learning Activity

Working in groups of four, draw the boundaries of the Federal Reserve districts on a map of the United States. Each group member should then survey three friends, asking them to list the Federal Reserve number that appears on their currency. Tabulate the number of times each district is named. As a group, compare your findings and write your group's district totals in their proper section on the map. Then compare your group's findings with the rest of the class, placing the new totals on a classroom map of Federal Reserve districts. From which district did most currency originate? Why?

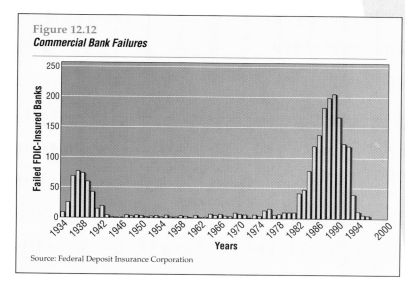

Figure 12.12
Commercial Bank Failures

Source: Federal Deposit Insurance Corporation

Technology Activity

Building a Database

In the **Journal Writing** activity on page 293, you were asked to analyze currency. Create a database for foreign visitors that describes the specific features and purposes of each United States bill and coin. Create fields such as the following: portrait, paper/coin, value, Federal Reserve Bank, watermarks, and so on. Arrange the fields and text in an appealing way, including clip art, decorative fonts, and color. Use words that will easily be understood by someone with limited knowledge of the English language, or translate the database into several languages if possible. Distribute a copy of your database to your local visitor's center or Chamber of Commerce.

Critical Thinking

1. Answers may vary. Students may suggest open market operations because it provides the most flexibility on a day-to-day basis.

2. Answers may vary. As guidance, point out that some politicians disagree on this issue, but the vast majority of economists would argue strongly for the independence of the Fed.

Applying Economic Concepts

1. Answers will vary. Suggest that students present their findings in chart form.

2. T-accounts will vary. Have students compare their balance sheets.

Reinforcing Skills

1. commercial bank failures
2. from 1934 to 1997
3. number of failed FDIC-insured banks
4. 1989
5. marked reduction in the number of failures
6. because of the Great Depression

? BONUS TEST QUESTION

Have students classify the following as easy money policy actions or tight money policy actions.

1. Fed raises reserve requirement. *(tight money policy)*
2. Fed buys government securities. *(easy money policy)*
3. Fed lowers the discount rate. *(easy money policy)*
4. Fed sells government securities. *(tight money policy)*

9. Long-run impact affects inflation rather than interest rates. Tight money policy usually brings inflation down, whereas interest rates rise with a tight money policy.

10. Because people use low interest rates as an indicator of economic health, many politicians want Fed to lower interest rates in election years. The Fed, however, may want interest rates to rise because it is concerned with the long-run health of the economy.

11. Banking authorities increased the amount of financial capital owners must put into the bank. Increased capital is designed to absorb loan losses. FDIC and other regulatory agencies work to better coordinate and improve quality of standards and inspections.

CHAPTER ORGANIZER

Daily Objectives	Reproducible Resources	Multimedia Resources
Section 1 **Savings and the Financial System** 1. **Explain** why saving is important for capital formation. 2. **Explain** how the financial system works to transfer funds from savers to borrowers. 3. **Understand** the role of the major nondepository financial institutions in the financial system.	▱ Reproducible Lesson Plan 13-1 ▱ Guided Reading Activity 13-1 ▱ Cooperative Learning Activity 7 ▱ Consumer Application Activities 7, 9 ▱ Math Practice for Economics 19 ▱ Free Enterprise Activity 7 ▱ Primary and Secondary Source Reading 11 ▱ Performance Assessment Activity 18 ▱ Economic Simulation 4 ▱ Economic Laboratory 4 ▱ Economic Survival: A Financial Simulation ▱ Section Quiz 13-1*	⬛ Focus Activity Transparency 20 ⬛ Vocabulary PuzzleMaker ⬛ Chapter Challenger Interactive Review Software ⬛ Testmaker ◉ MindJogger Videoquiz
Section 2 **Investing in Financial Assets** 1. **Identify** four important investment considerations. 2. **Describe** the three characteristics of bonds. 3. **Describe** the characteristics of major financial assets. 4. **Understand** four views of markets for financial assets.	▱ Reproducible Lesson Plan 13-2 ▱ Guided Reading Activity 13-2 ▱ Reinforcing Economic Skill 13 ▱ Section Quiz 13-2*	⬛ Focus Activity Transparency 42 ⬛ Vocabulary PuzzleMaker ⬛ Chapter Challenger Interactive Review Software ⬛ Testmaker ⬛ Stocktracker Software ◉ NBR's Economics in Action Video Program ◉ Interactive Economics!
Section 3 **Investing in Equities, Futures, and Options** 1. **Recognize** the characteristics of the major stock exchanges. 2. **Explain** how stock market performance is measured. 3. **Understand** how financial assets and equities can be traded in the future.	▱ Reproducible Lesson Plan 13-3 ▱ Guided Reading Activity 13-3 ▱ Section Quiz 13-3*	⬛ Focus Activity Transparency 43 ⬛ Vocabulary PuzzleMaker ⬛ Chapter Challenger Interactive Review Software ⬛ Testmaker ⬛ Stocktracker Software ◉ NBR's Economics in Action Video Program ◉ Interactive Economics!
Chapter Review and Evaluation	▱ Enrichment Activity 13 ▱ Reteaching Activity 13* ▱ Economic Vocabulary Activity 13* ▱ Chapter 13 Test, Forms A and B	🎧 Chapter Digests Audiocassette Activities and Tests* ⬛ Testmaker ◉ MindJogger Videoquiz

Also available in Spanish

 Blackline Master   Transparency   CD-ROM   Software   Videodisc   Audiocassette

⏱ OUT OF TIME? Assign the Chapter 13 Digest Audiocassette and the corresponding Chapter Digest activities and tests.

National Council on Economic Education

THE **Economics** America AND **Economics** International PROGRAMS

VOLUNTARY NATIONAL CONTENT STANDARDS IN ECONOMICS

Emphasized in Chapter 13

Content Standard 10 *Students will understand that:* Institutions evolve in market economies to help individuals and groups accomplish their goals. Banks, labor unions, corporations, legal systems, and not-for-profit organizations are examples of important institutions. A different kind of institution, clearly defined and well enforced property rights, is essential to a market economy.

Economics America *Resources Available From NCEE*

- MCG: *Economics and Entrepreneurship*
- *Learning from the Market: Integrating the Stock Market Game™ across the Curriculum*
- *Personal Decision Making: Focus on Economics*
- *Personal Finance Economics: Wallet Wisdom*

To order these materials, or to contact your state Council on Economic Education about workshops and programs, call 1-800-338-1192 or visit http://www.nationalcouncil.org.

PERFORMANCE ASSESSMENT

The following chapter projects may be assigned at the beginning of the chapter and used for performance assessment.

Multicultural Heritage Point out that an increasing number of foreign corporations are listing their stock on American stock exchanges. Today, for example, hundreds of major foreign corporations are listed on the New York Stock Exchange. These corporations include Daimler-Benz AG, the German manufacturer of the Mercedes car, Pan American Beverages of Panama, and Grupo Tribasa SA, a Mexican construction company. Organize students into a number of small groups and have each group select one of the foreign corporations listed on the New York Stock Exchange. Direct groups to research the culture of the home country of their chosen corporation, making special note of similarities to and differences from U.S. culture. Suggest that groups consider such topics as political system, economic system, language, currency, dress styles, and so on. Have groups present their findings in an illustrated wall display, a museum exhibit, or an illustrated insert for a current affairs magazine.

Cooperative Learning Organize students into five groups and assign one of the following to each group: finance companies, life insurance companies, mutual funds, pension funds, and real estate investment trusts. Have groups develop a brief presentation detailing the history of these institutions and the services they provide. Presentations might take the form of a promotional brochure, a 5- to 10-minute illustrated lecture, or a video presentation. Encourage students to use charts, graphs, and other illustrations in their presentations. Call on groups to make their presentations to the class.

ADDITIONAL RESOURCES

Readings for the Student

Dowd, Merle E. *Wall Street Made Simple.* Garden City, NY: Doubleday and Company, 1992. A thorough explanation of how the stock market works. Suitable for advanced students.

Dowd, Merle E. *Money, Banking, and Credit Made Simple.* Garden City, NY: Doubleday and Company, 1994. Explains how to manage personal resources, including consumer credit, interest rates, bank services, and the uses and abuses of debt.

Readings for the Teacher

Malkiel, Burton G. *A Random Walk Down Wall Street.* New York: W.W. Norton, 1996. A guide written for investors.

Wurman, Richard S., Alan Siegel, and Kenneth M. Morris. *The Wall Street Journal Guide to Understanding Money and Investing.* New York: Access Press, 1990. Provides illustrations to assist interpretation of financial market information.

Multimedia

A History of the Dow: A Century of American Investing. Wall Street Journal Video/Social Studies School Service, 10200 Jefferson Blvd., P.O. Box 802, Culver City, CA 90232-0802. 1996. VHS video, 55 mins. Survey of 100 years of social, cultural, and economic history through the lens of Wall Street and DJIA.

Wall Street On-line: An Investment Simulation for the Classroom. J. Weston Walch/Social Studies School Service. 1993. DOS, masters. Simulation offering hands-on experience researching and developing stock investment strategies.

Wall $treet Week with Louis Rukeyser: An Investment Primer. PBS/Social Studies School Service. VHS video, 60 mins. Explains the basics of the stock market and investing.

Chapter Overview

Chapter 13 discusses the role of savings in the economy and introduces the many types of nonbank financial institutions that play a part in everyday economic life. **Section 1** describes the relationship between savings and the financial system. **Section 2** discusses investment considerations, the major types of financial assets, and markets for financial assets. **Section 3** explains the stock exchanges and futures markets.

GLENCOE
TECHNOLOGY

VIDEODISC
MindJogger Videoquiz

Use MindJogger to preview the Chapter 13 content.

Chapter 13
Disc 2, Side B

Also available in VHS.

interNET
CONNECTION

Resources for Chapter 13 on the World Wide Web*

National Council on Economic Education

http://www.nationalcouncil.org/

SMG2000, The Stock Market Game™
http://www.smg2000.org/

Invest Smart (stock market game, investment lessons)
http://library.advanced.org/10326/

U.S. Securities and Exchange Commission
http://www.sec.gov/

Sites subject to change.

Wall Street is synonymous with money, investors, and the New York Stock Exchange.

Extra Credit Project

Have students create a television-viewing log for news items about the stock market presented on the nightly news. Suggest that some students watch national newscasts and others watch local newscasts. They should record the date, the subject of the item, and the length of time given to the item. When study of the chapter is completed, have students compare and discuss their logs.

CHAPTER 13

Financial Investments, Markets, and Equities

SECTION 1
Savings and the Financial System

SECTION 2
Investing in Financial Assets

SECTION 3
Investing in Equities, Futures, and Options

CHAPTER PREVIEW

People to Know

- Edward T. Lewis
- Stockbroker

Applying Economic Concepts to Your Life

Savings and Growth Do you have a car loan? Do your parents have a mortgage? Whose money enabled you to buy the car and home? It does not matter from whom you borrowed the money. What is important is that someone saved, which allowed you and your parents to borrow and, thus, experience economic growth.

> **Journal Writing**
>
> Scan the stock market listings in the business section of your local newspaper. Assume that you have $50,000 to invest in a stock portfolio, and select one or more stocks in which to invest. Read the economic skill—How to Read Stock Market Reports—on page 333. Then, in your journal, track the progress of your stock(s) for one week or more.

Economic Portfolio

At the end of the **Journal Writing** tracking period, have students list the following information: those stocks that fell in price and those that rose in price, how much each stock changed in price, and the total gains or losses made by the student.

Key to Ability Levels — **Teaching strategies have been coded for varying learning styles and abilities:**
L1 - Basic (activities for all students) **L2 - Average** (activities for average to above-average students)
L3 - Challenging (activities for above-average students) **LEP - Limited English Proficiency**

FOCUS

Section Objectives

1. Explain why saving is important for capital formation.
2. Explain how the financial system works to transfer funds from savers to borrowers.
3. Understand the role of the major nondepository financial institutions in the financial system.

Bellringer

Prior to taking roll at the beginning of the class period, display Focus Activity Transparency 20.

Motivational Activity

Discuss students' responses to the activity sheet that accompanies Transparency 20.

Preteaching Vocabulary

Call on students to define the key terms in their own words. **LEP**

Use the **Vocabulary PuzzleMaker** to create crossword and word search puzzles.

TEACH

Guided Practice

L1 Understanding Ideas
Write the following terms on the chalkboard: *savings, borrowing, growth.* Ask students to imagine they have borrowed money to build a new home. Have students name others who would benefit from building the house. *(building contractors, suppliers, architects, and so on)* Mention that the money they borrowed benefited the

---

SECTION 1
Savings and the Financial System

Section Preview

Objectives

After studying this section, you will be able to:

1. **Explain** why saving is important for capital formation.
2. **Explain** how the financial system works to transfer funds from savers to borrowers.
3. **Understand** the role of the major nondepository financial institutions in the financial system.

Key Terms

saving, savings, financial system, financial asset, financial intermediary, nonbank financial institution, finance company, bill consolidation loan, premium, mutual fund, pension, pension fund, real estate investment trust

Applying Economic Concepts

Financial Assets Do you have a checking account, savings account, or government savings bond? If so, you are a participant in the financial system. You have one or more *financial assets* that represent the transfer of funds from a saver to a borrower.

An economic system must be able to produce capital if it is to satisfy the wants and needs of its people. To produce capital, people must be willing to save, which releases resources for use elsewhere. To the economist, **saving** means the absence of spending, while **savings** refers to the dollars that become available in the absence of consumption. Both are vital to the American economy.

Saving and Capital Formation

When people save, they make funds available to others. When businesses borrow these savings, new goods and services are created, new plants and equipment are produced, and new jobs become available. Saving makes economic growth possible.

Suppose an entrepreneur wants to set up a business. He or she might save some income until he or she is ready to begin, keeping this money in a wallet or in a bank to earn interest. When enough funds have been saved to invest, the entrepreneur sets up shop.

Another entrepreneur might borrow funds from a bank to start a business immediately. If other people have been saving some of their income, the bank should have funds to lend. If people have been spending all of their income, however, the bank may not be able to make the loan even if it wanted to.

For investment to take place, someone in the economy must save. An individual can save as well as invest, as noted in the first example. Another person may save while someone else invests, as described in the second example. When people save, they are abstaining from consumption, which frees resources for others to borrow and use. These resources also make investments possible. **1**

Financial Assets and the Financial System

For people to use the savings of others, the economy must have a **financial system**—a way to transfer savers' dollars to investors.

Financial Assets

When people save, they usually do so in a number of ways. They may put money in a savings account, a commercial bank, or a thrift. They may purchase a certificate of deposit at a depository institution or purchase a government or corporate bond. In each case, the savers obtain receipts for the funds they save.

For a savings account, a savings book or monthly computer statement is the saver's receipt. The receipt for a certificate of deposit (CD) often takes the form of

---

Classroom Resources for SECTION 1

Reproducible Lesson Plan 13-1
Guided Reading Activity 13-1
Cooperative Learning Activity 7
Consumer Application Activities 7, 9
Math Practice for Economics 19
Free Enterprise Activity 7
Primary and Secondary Source Reading 11
Economic Survival: A Financial Simulation
Economic Simulation 4
Economic Laboratory 4

Performance Assessment Activity 18
Section Quiz 13-1
Spanish Section Quiz 13-1
Focus Activity Transparency 20
Testmaker
Vocabulary PuzzleMaker
Chapter Challenger Interactive Review Software
MindJogger Videoquiz

Figure 13.1
Overview of the Financial System

Financial intermediaries help channel surplus funds from savers to borrowers who put the money to work. In return for their funds, lenders receive financial assets—mortgages, DDAs, Treasury bills, Treasury bonds, CDs, savings deposits, mutual fund shares. **What do financial assets represent?**

Surplus Funds

Savers
Households
Businesses

Financial Intermediaries
Commercial Banks
Savings & Loan Associations
Savings Banks
Mutual Savings Banks
Credit Unions
Life Insurance Companies
Mutual Funds
Pension Funds
Real Estate Investment Trusts
Finance Companies

Borrowers
Governments
Businesses

Financial Assets

a passbook, computer printout, or other document. Some government and most corporate bonds are printed on high-quality paper and are designed to convey a sense of value and worth.

Economists have another name for these receipts. They are **financial assets**, or claims on the property and the income of the borrower. These receipts are assets because they are property that has value. They represent claims on the borrower because they specify the amount loaned and the terms at which the loan was made. If the borrower defaults, the lender can use the financial asset as proof in court that funds were borrowed and that repayment is expected.

When funds are lent from one individual or business to another, a financial asset is generated. These assets are a critical part of our financial system.

The Financial System

Two of the main components of the financial system have already been described. The first component was the funds that the saver transferred to the borrower. The second was the financial assets or receipts that

certify the loans were made. The other three components of the financial system, illustrated in Figure 13.1, are the savers, borrowers, and institutions that bring the surplus funds and financial assets together. **2**

Any sector of the economy can supply savings, but the most important sectors are households and businesses. State and local governments provide some savings, but the government sector overall is a net borrower of funds. In Figure 13.1 the savers provide some funds directly to the borrowers, as when households or businesses purchase bonds directly from the government or from the business sector. Other surplus funds, usually in much smaller amounts, are placed with a group of financial institutions that pool the funds and lend them to others.

These institutions are known as **financial intermediaries** and include the depository institutions, life insurance companies, pension funds, and other groups that channel savings from savers to borrowers. These institutions are especially helpful to the many small savers who have only limited savings to deposit.

The last major component of the financial system consists of the borrowers who generate financial assets

economy as a whole, because it generated economic activity. Then point out that all this was made possible by others' savings. Conclude by asking students to write a generalization about the relationship between the three terms on the chalkboard. **LEP**

☞ **Cooperative Learning**
Assign Cooperative Learning Activity 7.

 VISUAL INSTRUCTION

Ask: Do you play a role in the financial system? If so, how? *(Students who have financial assets—checking or savings accounts, savings bonds, and so on—play a role in the financial system.)*

Answer to Caption:
proof of lenders' claim on borrowers' income and assets

 ANSWERS

1. Someone in the economy must save.

2. savers; borrowers; funds that the saver transferred to the borrower; financial assets or receipts that certify loan was made; institutions that bring savers and investors together

---

 QUICK CHECK

Checking Understanding

1. What is necessary before investment can take place?
2. What are the components of the financial system?

Applying Economic Concepts

☑ **Saving** Americans save a much smaller percentage of their income than the Japanese do. As a result, the Japanese have a larger pool of financial capital that can be used to fuel economic growth.

CHAPTER 13: *Financial Investments, Markets, and Equities* **321**

ECONOMIC SURVIVAL ⊛

A FINANCIAL SIMULATION
To help students learn to manage their own finances, have the class play the game **Economic Survival: A Financial Simulation** in which each student enters the workforce, rents an apartment, and deals with everyday events.

Meeting Special Needs

Writing Disability Help students with writing problems glean essential information from the text by providing the standard headings of Who, What, Where, When, and Why (or what happened) to

structure answers. Ask students to read the subsection "Financial Assets and the Financial System" and to write brief responses for each of the five questions.

Independent Practice

📁 **Guided Reading** Assign Guided Reading Activity for Section 1. **LEP**

L2 *Writing a Letter*
Encourage students to imagine they live in a country where people save very little. Have them write a letter to a friend detailing the economic problems the country faces because of the low level of savings.

📁 **Consumer Application** Assign Consumer Application Activities 7 and 9.

📁 **Math Practice** Assign Math Practice for Economics 19.

📁 **Free Enterprise** Assign Free Enterprise Activity 7.

📁 **Readings** Assign Primary and Secondary Source Reading 11.

📁 **Simulation** Assign Economic Simulation 4.

📁 **Laboratory** Assign Economic Laboratory 4.

📁 **Performance Assessment** Assign Performance Assessment Activity 18.

ASSESS

Check for Understanding

Assign Section 1 Review as homework or an in-class activity.

🖥 Use **Chapter Challenger Interactive Review Software** to review Section 1.

Evaluate

📁 📁 🖥 Assign the Section 1 Quiz in the TCR or use the *Economics: Principles and Practices* Testmaker.

when they borrow funds. If a corporation borrows directly from savers, or indirectly from savers through financial intermediaries, the corporation will issue a bond or other financial asset to the lender. Likewise, when the government borrows, it issues government bonds and/or other financial assets to the lender.

As a result, almost everyone participates in the financial system. The smooth flow of funds through the system helps ensure that savers will have an outlet for their savings. Borrowers, in turn, will have a source of financial capital.

Investments

Many businesses and individuals watch for profitable investment opportunities. Among other things, they are looking for financial assets—corporate bonds, government bonds, certificates of deposit, and even savings accounts—in which they can invest.

Nonbank Financial Intermediaries

Savings banks, credit unions, commercial banks, and savings associations obtain funds when their customers or members make regular deposits. Another important group of financial intermediaries includes **nonbank financial institutions**. This group obtains funds in a different manner, and includes finance companies, life insurance companies, pension funds, and real estate investment trusts.

Finance Companies

One nonbank institution is a **finance company**, which makes loans directly to consumers and specializes in buying installment contracts from merchants who sell goods on credit. Without the help of finance companies, many small merchants would find it difficult to do business. Many merchants, for example, cannot afford to wait years for their customers to pay off high-cost items on the installment plan. Instead, the merchant sells the customer's installment contract to a finance company for a lump sum. Utilizing a finance company enables the merchant to advertise instant credit or easy terms without actually carrying the loan full term, absorbing losses for an unpaid

account, or taking customers to court for nonpayment of the loan.

Some finance companies make loans directly to consumers. These companies generally check a consumer's credit rating and will make a loan only if the individual qualifies. Because they make loans to some people considered "high risks," and because they pay more for the funds they borrow, finance companies charge more than commercial banks for loans.

One popular loan many consumer finance companies offer is a **bill consolidation loan**—a loan consumers use to pay off all other bills. The consumer then agrees to repay the finance company over a period of one or more years.

Life Insurance Companies

One of the major financial institutions that does not get its funds through deposits is the life insurance company. Although its primary function is to provide financial protection for survivors of the insured, it also collects a great deal of cash.

The head of a family, for example, may want to leave money for a spouse and children in case of

---

$ *Free Enterprise Activity* **$**

Invite a local business entrepreneur to visit the class. Ask the entrepreneur to explain to students how he or she started the business, paying special attention to the procedures he or she followed to borrow money. Encourage students to ask questions about the role that borrowing plays in business start-ups and operations. Suggest that the entrepreneur conclude by discussing how savings and borrowing have played a role in his or her success in business.

322

death. To do this, he or she may buy a life insurance policy. The price paid for this policy is known as a **premium**, and it must be paid at specified times for the length of the protection.

Because insurance companies collect cash on a regular basis, they often lend surplus funds to others. They may make loans to banks in the form of large certificates of deposit. They also may negotiate other arrangements with smaller consumer finance companies.

Mutual Funds

A **mutual fund** is a company that sells stock in itself to individual investors and then invests the money it receives in stocks and bonds issued by other corporations. Mutual fund stockholders receive dividends earned from the mutual fund's investments. Stockholders can also sell their mutual fund shares for a profit, just like other stocks.

Mutual funds allow people to play the market without risking all they have in one or a few companies. The large size of the mutual fund makes it possible to hire a staff of experts to analyze the securities market before buying and selling securities.

The large size of most funds also allows them to buy many different stocks and bonds and build up a more diversified portfolio than most individual investors could. If the value of one investment fell sharply, the impact on the overall fund would be almost insignificant.

Pension Funds

Another nonbank or nondepository financial institution is the pension fund. A **pension** is a regular allowance intended to provide income security to someone who has worked a certain number of years, reached a certain age, or suffered a certain kind of injury. A **pension fund** is a fund set up to collect income and disburse payments to those persons eligible for retirement, old-age, or disability benefits.

In the case of private pension funds, employers regularly withhold a percentage of workers' salaries to deposit in the fund. During the 30-to-40-year lag between the time the savings are deposited and the time the workers generally use them, the money is usually invested in corporate stocks and bonds. Government pension funds are similar to private ones in that the government makes regular contributions to the fund that will pay benefits later.

Real Estate Investment Trusts

Still another nonbank financial institution is the **real estate investment trust** (REIT)—a company organized chiefly to make loans to construction companies that build homes. Although REITs are not widely known as financial institutions, they help provide billions annually for home construction.

REITs borrow most of their funds from banks and get their income from the rents and mortgage payments of the people who use their money. This income is then used to pay interest on the money borrowed.

SECTION 1 REVIEW

Reviewing Terms and Facts

1. **Define** saving, savings, financial system, financial asset, financial intermediary, nonbank financial institution, finance company, bill consolidation loan, premium, mutual fund, pension, pension fund, real estate investment trust.

2. **Explain** why saving is required for capital formation.
3. **List** four financial assets.
4. **Name** five nonbank financial intermediaries.

Critical Thinking

5. **Making Generalizations** Why might a person choose to borrow money from a finance company that charges higher interest rates than commercial banks do?

Applying Economic Concepts

6. **Financial Assets** An I.O.U. that you draft and give to a friend in payment of a debt is an example of a financial asset. Explain why this is so.

MEETING LESSON OBJECTIVES

Each objective below is tested by the questions that follow it in parentheses.

1. **Explain** why saving is important for capital formation. **(1, 2)**
2. **Explain** how the financial system works to transfer funds from savers to borrowers. **(3, 5, 6)**
3. **Understand** the role of the major nondepository financial institutions in the financial system. **(4, 5)**

Reteach

Have students create a chart that compares the major characteristics of the nonbank financial institutions discussed in the section.

Enrich

Have students conduct an informal poll among family members, neighbors, and friends to discover how many save and for what reasons. Suggest that students collate their results and combine them on a wall chart.

CLOSE

Have students design a symbol or logo that illustrates the relationship between savings and borrowing.

Note: A complete mutual fund quotation appears on page 337.

Answers to SECTION 1 REVIEW

1. All vocabulary words are defined in the Glossary.

2. Saving makes funds available for others to use. When businesses borrow these funds, they create new equipment and plants, employ more workers, and produce new goods and services.

3. mortgages, Treasury bills, Treasury bonds, corporate bonds, CDs, savings deposits, mutual fund shares

4. finance companies, life insurance companies, mutual funds, pension funds, real estate investment trusts

5. These people might be considered "high risk" borrowers who are unable to get loans from commercial banks.

6. It certifies that your friend made you a loan, and it indicates that the friend has a claim on your property or income.

Background

Although *Essence* was exciting and different, it struggled initially. Only 50,000 of the first 200,000 issues sold. A number of advertisers were wary of the magazine's editorial tone of black activism. Lewis took command as publisher of the magazine and, through hard work and sheer determination, made it a success. In its fourth year of publication, *Essence* showed a 40 percent gain in circulation—a larger increase than any other women's magazine.

TEACH

Have students list the various factors that might account for Lewis's success. *(his determination and entrepreneurial skill, having an initial product that was exciting and different, diversification into other areas of communications industry)*

PROFILES IN ECONOMICS

EDWARD T. LEWIS
(1940–   )

As chairman and CEO of Essence Communications, Inc. (ECI), Edward T. Lewis heads one of the largest African American businesses in the United States. His struggle to make *Essence* magazine a success shows determination and entrepreneurial skill.

A NEW IDEA In the late 1960s, Shearson, Hammill & Company (now Shearson-Lehman, American Express) sponsored a conference to encourage initiative in African American capitalism. Edward Lewis, a financial analyst for the First National City Bank, was among those invited to attend. Lewis became interested in one of the ideas discussed at the

Essence magazine currently has a monthly circulation of 950,000 and a readership of 5.1 million.

conference: a slick new magazine to appeal especially to African American women. He and three other young men began planning

their new publication in the evenings after their regular jobs.

After two years, the group had raised $130,000. That was enough to launch the first issue of *Essence* in May 1970. The stylish magazine, which featured full-page color photos of African American models and cutting-edge articles, was exciting and different. After Lewis became publisher of *Essence,* the magazine became a success.

NEW VENTURES Recognizing the need to develop into a broad-

based communications company, Lewis and his partner, Clarence O. Smith, began to diversify ECI. Beginning in 1984, ECI branched out into direct-mail marketing, licensing, art reproduction, book publishing, and television production.

Essence-By-Mail is a mail-order catalog featuring moderately priced merchandise. Essence Licensing markets eyewear, sewing patterns, and hosiery for women of color. Utilizing the *Essence* magazine format, Essence Television Productions, Inc., produced the award-winning "Essence," a weekly syndicated news show that aired from 1984 to 1988. Currently, Essence Television Productions, Inc., produces the "Essence Awards Show," the nation's most prestigious tribute to African American women.

ECI is also a major investor in Amistad Press, a minority book publishing company. Essence Art Reproductions markets reproductions of fine art created by African American artists. In addition, in 1992 ECI acquired a monthly, nonethnic business magazine, *Income Opportunities*.

Examining the Profile

1. **Analyzing Information** Why do you think publishing a fashion magazine for African American women was an innovative idea in the late 1960s?

2. **For Further Research** Examine several issues of *Essence* magazine. Based on the kinds of articles it publishes, write an analysis of the magazine's editorial policy.

Answers to Examining the Profile

1. It was a market that had not been tapped before.
2. Analyses will vary.

Section Preview

Objectives

After studying this section, you will be able to:

1. **Identify** four important investment considerations.
2. **Describe** the three characteristics of bonds.
3. **Describe** the characteristics of major financial assets.
4. **Understand** four views of markets for financial assets.

Key Terms

risk, coupon, maturity, par value, current yield, jumbo CD, junk bond, municipal bond, tax-exempt, savings bond, money market mutual fund, Treasury note, Treasury bond, Treasury bill, Individual Retirement Account, capital market, money market, primary market, secondary market

Applying Economic Concepts

Risk-Return Relationship How can you get the highest return for your money? Someone almost always has an idea for making a fast buck, but these ideas are often risky. Even so, this summarizes the *risk-return relationship* of investing—riskier projects must offer higher returns to be attractive, while less risky investments offer lower returns.

Before people invest in financial assets, they need certain information. Such information includes a basic understanding of investment considerations, the nature of bonds as financial assets, specific characteristics of other financial assets, and the markets for financial assets.

Basic Investment Considerations

When investors buy financial assets, they should keep several factors in mind. The first concerns the relationship between risk and return. The second has to do with the investor's personal investment goals. The third deals with the consistency of investing, and the last deals with avoiding some types of investments.

The Relationship Between Risk and Return

One of the most important relationships in the market is the relationship between risk and return. **Risk**, in an economic sense, is a situation in which the outcome is not certain, but the probabilities can be estimated.

Investors realize that financial assets are risky. Assets may go up or down in price, or the agency that issued the asset may even fail to redeem it, leaving the lender with a loss. As a result, investors demand a higher return to compensate for higher risk.

This relationship between risk and return is illustrated in **Figure 13.2**, which shows that riskier assets must offer higher returns to attract investors. As a result, the first consideration for any investor is the level of risk he or she can tolerate. If the investor is not comfortable with the riskiest assets, he or she should consider others.

Investment Objectives

Another factor an investor considers is the reason for investing. If the goal is to accumulate wealth for retirement, the investor might want to purchase assets that simply appreciate rather than generate income. If the purpose is to accumulate reserves to fund a vacation or to cover living expenses during periods of unemployment, a strategy that focuses on the accumulation of assets that are highly liquid, or easily sold, might be better. Some investors may prefer to accumulate assets that generate a steady stream of income like bonds. Others may already be in a high marginal tax bracket and may prefer to avoid assets that generate taxable income.

The source of income used for investment may help determine which assets are purchased. If the investor receives a steady salary and almost no other income, a payroll deduction plan that puts money in a special retirement fund or purchases government bonds might be best. If the investor receives periodic

CHAPTER 13: *Financial Investments, Markets, and Equities* **325**

FOCUS

Section Objectives

1. Identify four important investment considerations.
2. Describe the three characteristics of bonds.
3. Describe the characteristics of major financial assets.
4. Understand four views of markets for financial assets.

Bellringer

Prior to taking roll at the beginning of the class period, display Focus Activity Transparency 42 on the overhead projector and assign the accompanying Student Activity 42.

Motivational Activity

Discuss students' responses to the activity sheet that accompanies Focus Activity Transparency 42.

Preteaching Vocabulary

Inform students that financial assets are not the same as stocks. The discussion of stocks and stock markets appears in Section 3. Call on volunteers to tell what they think each key term in the Section Preview means. Have other students check the accuracy of these definitions by finding the terms in the text. **LEP**

Use the **Vocabulary PuzzleMaker** to create crossword and word search puzzles.

Classroom Resources for SECTION 2

- Reproducible Lesson Plan 13-2
- Guided Reading Activity 13-2
- Reinforcing Economic Skill 13
- Section Quiz 13-2
- Spanish Section Quiz 13-2

- Focus Activity Transparency 42
- NBR's Economics in Action Video Program
- Stocktracker Software
- Testmaker
- Vocabulary PuzzleMaker
- Chapter Challenger Interactive Review Software
- Intractive Economics!

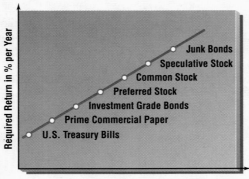

Figure 13.2
The Relationship Between Risk and Return

Junk Bonds
Speculative Stock
Common Stock
Preferred Stock
Investment Grade Bonds
Prime Commercial Paper
U.S. Treasury Bills

Required Return in % per Year

Increasing Degrees of Risk

United States Treasury bills are generally regarded as the safest of all possible investments, and they carry the lowest return. Junk bonds are regarded as the riskiest, which accounts for their high returns. **Why do investors generally require higher returns for some investments?**

bonuses, royalty payments, or other payments on a variable basis, the investor might consider corporate bonds or some other large-denomination financial asset.

In the end, each investor must consider his or her own circumstances and personal investment goals. Investors have a large number of financial assets, equities, and other investments from which to choose. The investor's knowledge of his or her own needs helps narrow the selection.

Consistency

Successful investors generally invest consistently over long periods of time. In most cases, the amount invested is not as important as investing on a regular basis.

Figure 13.3 shows how a very small deposit of $10 per month would grow over a 5-to-30-year period at various interest rates. The balance in the account accumulates fairly quickly, even at modest interest rates. Because $10 is a small amount, imagine how the account would grow if the deposit was for $25, $50, or

even $100 a month! Many investment advisers tell people to save something every month, even if it is not very much.

Avoiding Complexity

Most investors advise others to stick with what they know. Thousands of different investments are available, and many are fairly complicated. Although a person does not have to understand them all to be a good investor, knowing a few fundamentals is important.

One rule that many investors follow is this: if an investment seems too complicated, let it go. Similarly, an investment that promises fantastic returns or seems too good to be true probably is. A few investors do get lucky, but most investors build wealth because they invest regularly, and they try to avoid the investments that seem too far out of the ordinary. **1**

Bonds as Financial Assets

When an agency needs to borrow funds for long periods, it often issues bonds. Bonds are long-term obligations that pay a stated rate of interest for a specified number of years.

Bond Components

A bond has three main components: the **coupon**, or the stated interest on the debt; the **maturity**, or the life of the bond; and the principal, the amount that will be repaid to the lender at maturity. The principal is usually assigned a dollar value that is called the **par value** of the bond. As a result, the terms *par value* and *principal* are often used interchangeably.

Suppose, for example, a corporation sells a 6 percent, 20-year, $1,000 par value bond that pays interest semiannually. The coupon payment to the holder would be $30 semiannually (.06 times $1,000 divided by 2). When the bond reaches maturity, the company would retire the debt by paying the holder the par value of $1,000.

Bond Prices

The investor views the bond as a financial asset that will pay $30 twice a year for 20 years, plus a final

Lesson 10 of Interactive Economics! to learn more about "Basic Investment Considerations."

Figure 13.3
The Power of Compound Interest

This table shows what the balance in an account would look like if monthly deposits of $10 were compounded monthly. **What investment strategy is the key to future financial wealth?**

Annual Interest (in %)	Value at End of Year					
	5	10	15	20	25	30
0	$600	$1,200	$1,800	$2,000	$2,500	$3,600
2	$630	$1,327	$2,097	$2,948	$3,888	$4,927
4	$663	$1,472	$2,461	$3,668	$5,141	$6,940
6	$698	$1,639	$2,908	$4,620	$6,930	$10,045
8	$735	$1,829	$3,460	$5,890	$9,510	$14,904
10	$774	$2,048	$4,145	$7,594	$13,268	$22,605
12	$817	$2,300	$4,996	$9,893	$18,788	$34,950

par value payment of $1,000. Investors can offer $950, $1,000, $1,100, or any other amount for this future payment stream. Investors consider changes in future interest rates, the risk that the company will default, and other factors before they decide what to offer. Supply and demand will then establish the final price.

Bond Yields

In order to compare bonds, investors usually compute the bond's **current yield**, which is the annual interest divided by the purchase price. If an investor paid $950 for the bond described above, the current yield would be $60 divided by $950, or 6.32 percent. If the investor paid $1,100 for the bond, the current yield would be $60 divided by $1,100, or 5.45 percent. Although it may appear as if the issuer fixes the return on a bond when the bond is first issued, the interest received and the price paid determine the actual yield on the bond.

Because the creditworthiness of corporations and governments differ, all 6 percent, 20-year, $1,000 bonds

will not cost the same. Bonds are not insured, and there are no guarantees that the issuer will be around in 20 years to redeem the bond. Therefore, investors will pay more for bonds issued by an agency with an impeccable credit rating. Investors will pay less for a similar bond if it is issued by a corporation with a low credit rating.

Bond Ratings

Fortunately, investors have a way to check the quality of bonds. Two major corporations, Standard & Poor's and Moody's, publish bond ratings. They rate bonds on a number of factors, including the basic financial health of the issuer, the ability to make the future coupon and par value payments, and the issuer's past credit history.

The bond ratings, shown in Figure 13.4, use letters scaled from AAA, which represents the highest investment grade, to D, which generally stands for default. If a bond is in default, the issuer has not kept up with the interest or the par value payments. These

QUICK CHECK

Checking Understanding
1. What rules do many investors follow in regard to investment goals?

Applying Economic Concepts
☑ **Investment Objectives** Your investment objectives will probably change as you grow older. People in their 20s and 30s usually are not concerned about retirement, so they invest to accumulate wealth for other reasons, such as vacations or their children's college education.

CHAPTER 13: *Financial Investments, Markets, and Equities* **327**

$ Free Enterprise Activity $

Organize students into four groups to undertake further study of bonds. Ask one group to interview the school superintendent or another administrator to learn about bonds for schools. The second group could interview a finance official in city, county, or state government to ask about municipal bonds. The third group could interview the controller or president of a local corporation to find out about

corporate bonds. The fourth group might interview a member of Congress or a staff employee of a member of Congress to learn about U.S. Treasury bonds. Have each group present its interview results to the class. Then have students discuss the similarities and differences among the various bonds.

Figure 13.4
Bond Classifications

Standard & Poor's Corporation and Moody's publish similar bond ratings. Junk bonds, those with ratings of BB or Ba and lower, are generally the riskiest types of bonds. **How do bond ratings affect the price of bonds?**

Source: Standard & Poor's Corporation, Moody's

	Standard & Poor's		Moody's	
Highest Investment Grade	AAA	Aaa	Best Quality	
High Grade	AA	Aa	High Quality	
Upper Medium Grade	A	A	Upper Medium Grade	
Medium Grade	BBB	Baa	Medium Grade	
Lower Medium Grade	BB	Ba	Possesses Speculative Elements	
Speculative	B	B	Generally not Desirable	
Vulnerable to Default	CCC	Caa	Poor, Possibly in Default	
Subordinated to Other Debt Rated CCC	CC	Ca	Highly Speculative, often in Default	
Subordinated to CC Debt	C	C	Income Bonds not paying Income	
Bond in Default	D	D	Interest and Principal Payments in Default	

ratings are widely publicized, and investors merely have to ask to find out the rating of any bond they plan to purchase.

Bonds with high ratings sell at higher prices than do bonds with lower ratings. A 6 percent, 20-year, $1,000 par value bond with an AAA grade rating may sell for $1,100 and have a current yield of 5.45 percent. Another 6 percent, 20-year, $1,000 par value bond issued by a different company may have a BBB rating, and may therefore only sell for $950 because of the higher risk. The second bond, however, has a higher current yield of 6.32 percent. This point is the essence of the risk-return relationship—riskier investments require higher returns to compensate for the risk.

Financial Assets and Their Characteristics

The modern investor has a wide range of financial assets from which to choose. They vary in cost, maturity, and safety.

Certificates of Deposit

Certificates of deposit are one of the most common forms of investments available. Many people think of them as just another type of account with a depository institution, but they are really loans investors make to financial institutions. Because banks and others count on the use of these funds for a certain time period, they usually impose penalties when people try to cash in their CDs early.

Certificates of deposit are attractive to small investors because they cost as little as $100. Investors can also select the length of maturity, giving them an opportunity to tailor the expiration date to future expenditures such as college tuition, a vacation, or some other expense.

Finally, CDs issued by commercial banks, savings banks, and savings associations are included in the $100,000 FDIC insurance limit. The National Credit Union Association insures most CDs issued by credit unions. **Jumbo CDs**, or CDs in denominations of more than $100,000, are covered only to the $100,000 limit.

Corporate Bonds

Corporate bonds are perhaps the second most important source of corporate funds, the first being the sale of stock. Some individual corporate bonds have par values as low as $1,000, but par values of $10,000 are more common. The actual prices of the bonds are usually different from the par values because supply and demand for the bonds determines the price. Figure 13.5 shows how to read a listing for corporate bonds.

Investors usually decide on the highest level of risk they are willing to accept, and then try to find a bond that has the best current yield. Exceptionally risky bonds, those that carry a Standard & Poor's rating of BB or lower, or a Moody's rating of Ba or lower, are also called **junk bond**s. These bonds carry a high rate of return as compensation for the possibility of default.

Investors usually purchase corporate bonds as long-term investments, but they can also be liquidated,

---

Extending the Content

Corporate Bonds When buying corporate bonds, you have to consider a number of possible risks. If the corporation experiences economic setbacks, the market value of your bonds may decline. If, after you purchase bonds, there is a rise in interest rates, you will have difficulty reselling those bonds for the price you paid for them. For example, few investors would be willing to pay $10,000 for a bond that pays 8 percent interest annually when, for the same price, they can buy a bond with a 10 percent yearly return. Inflation is another concern. If the rate of inflation is high over the life of the bond, the repayment you receive at maturity will have less buying power than the sum you loaned the corporation initially.

or sold, quickly if the investor needs cash for other purposes. The Internal Revenue Service considers the interest, or coupon, payments on corporate bonds as taxable income, a fact investors must consider when they invest in bonds.

Municipal Bonds

Municipal bonds, or "munis," are bonds issued by state and local government units. States issue bonds to finance highways, state buildings, and some public works. Cities issue bonds to finance baseball and football stadiums or to finance libraries, parks, and other civic improvements.

Municipal bonds are attractive to investors for several reasons. First, they are generally regarded as safe because state and local governments do not go out of business. Because governments have the power to tax, it is generally presumed that they will be able to pay interest and principal in the future.

Most important, however, is that municipal bonds are generally **tax-exempt**—meaning that the federal government does not tax the interest paid to investors. In some cases, the states issuing the bonds also exempt the interest payments from state taxes, which makes them very attractive to investors. The tax-exempt feature also allows the governmental units to pay a lower rate of interest on the bonds, thereby lowering their cost of borrowing.

Government Savings Bonds

The federal government generates financial assets when it sells savings bonds. **Savings bonds** are low-denomination, nontransferable bonds issued by the United States government, usually through payroll-savings plans.

These bonds are usually available in denominations ranging from $50 to $10,000, and they are purchased at a discount from their redemption amount. For example, a new $50 savings bond may be obtained today for $25, but it could take up to 18 years before it could be redeemed for the full $50, depending on the interest rate. The government pays interest on these bonds,

 GO TO Lesson 10 of *Interactive Economics!* to learn more about "Fixed-Income Investments."

Figure 13.5
Typical New York Exchange Bond Listing

Source: *Wall Street Journal*

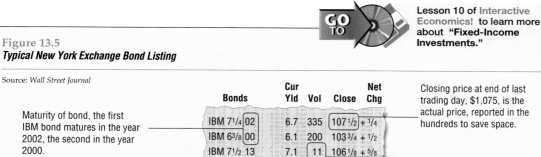

Bonds	Cur Yld	Vol	Close	Net Chg
IBM 7¼ 02	6.7	335	107½	+ ¼
IBM 6⅜ 00	6.1	200	103¾	+ ½
IBM 7½ 13	7.1	11	106⅛	+ ⅝
IntShip 03	...	20	99⅝	− ⅜
IntTch 9⅜ 96	9.4	9	100	....
K mart 8⅜ 17	7.9	80	106	− ⅛

Maturity of bond, the first IBM bond matures in the year 2002, the second in the year 2000.

Abbreviated company name: International Shipholding Corp.

Interest rate as a percent of par value. K-Mart pays 8 ³/₈% per $1,000 of par value.

Annual interest divided by the price you would pay for the bond today. For K-Mart, $8.375/$106 = 7.9%. Note that IntShip pays no interest, so has no current yield. The bond with the higher current yield is riskier, indicating a lower bond rating.

Closing price at end of last trading day, $1,075, is the actual price, reported in the hundreds to save space.

Only 11 bonds were sold during the trading day.

Net change from previous day. If the bond was down ⅛ of $10, it was down $1.25, meaning that it closed at 106 ⅛ the previous day.

The par value of most corporate bonds is reported in units of $1,000. To save space, one of the zeros is dropped from the listing, meaning that ½ is half of $10, or $5. Bonds with higher current yields are riskier bonds, and those with lower yields are generally safer, or higher rated, bonds. **What is the par value of most corporate bonds?**

Independent Practice

 Guided Reading Assign Guided Reading Activity for Section 2. **LEP**

L1 Understanding Ideas
Direct students to carefully study Figure 13.5 on page 329. Then have them select a block of five corporate bonds from the bond listings in *The Wall Street Journal* or in the business section of the local newspaper. Ask students to construct a chart similar to that in Figure 13.5, complete with explanation and analysis. Point out that they may need to consult other sources to find full company names. Encourage students to display and discuss their completed charts. **LEP**

? DID YOU KNOW

Stocks and bonds were traded in the U.S. before the dollar was adopted as the basic monetary unit. The "eighths" reflect the heritage of the Spanish peso.

VISUAL INSTRUCTION

Ask: Which is the riskiest investment shown in the chart? Why? (*IntTch, because it has the highest current yield; the higher the current yield, the riskier the investment*)

Answer to Caption:

$10,000 is the most common par value. However, bond listings are usually reported in units of $1,000 to save space.

Cultural Diversity and Economics

"Foreign" Mutual Funds A financial instrument gaining in popularity among American investors is the mutual fund with assets that are largely foreign. These assets usually are in the emerging areas of the world—Latin America and Asia, for example. The fast-growing economies of these areas usually mean high returns for investors.

LINKING PAST AND PRESENT

War Bonds After the attack on Pearl Harbor, the government introduced savings bonds called war bonds to increase public funding for the war effort. Radio shows sponsored by the Treasury promoted the bonds. Department stores set up window displays with war bond themes and encouraged customers to accept war stamps in place of change. Even movie stars urged the public to buy more bonds.

? DID YOU KNOW

Treasury bonds, notes, and bills are considered part of the national debt.

VISUAL INSTRUCTION

Have students explain how yields for Treasury bonds and notes are equalized. (*Investors pay more for assets with higher rates, less for those with lower rates.*)

Answer to Caption:

because they are regarded as the safest of financial assets

---

but it builds the interest into the redemption price rather than sending checks to millions of investors on a regular basis.

Savings bonds are attractive because they are easy to obtain and there is virtually no risk of default. They cannot be sold to someone else if the investor needs cash, but they can be redeemed early, with some loss of interest, if the investor must raise cash for other purposes. Most investors tend to hold long-term savings bonds, treating them as a form of automatic savings.

International Bonds

The United States government is not the only government to sell bonds. A number of countries issue bonds, although they are generally available only in large denominations usually starting at $1 million. **1**

Pension funds, insurance companies, and even large corporations with large cash reserves purchase these bonds. The risk of international bonds is harder to determine than other types of bonds, so investors have to choose carefully.

International bonds also have one other feature that makes them unique—they often make coupon and principal payments in another currency. The investor does not know if that currency will be stronger or weaker than the dollar when the payments are received in the future.

Money Market Mutual Funds

A special type of mutual fund is a **money market mutual fund**, a business that collects funds from small investors and then makes loans, usually in the form of large CDs, to other borrowers.

Investors like the money market funds because they receive higher interest than they would receive from dealing directly with the banks. The drawback to the arrangement is that FDIC insurance covers neither the jumbo CDs nor the contributions to the funds. The money market mutual funds are slightly riskier than regular CDs, and so pay a higher return.

Treasury Notes and Bonds

When the federal government borrows funds for periods longer than 1 year, it issues Treasury notes and bonds. **Treasury notes** are United States government obligations with maturities of 2 to 10 years, while **Treasury bonds** have maturities ranging from

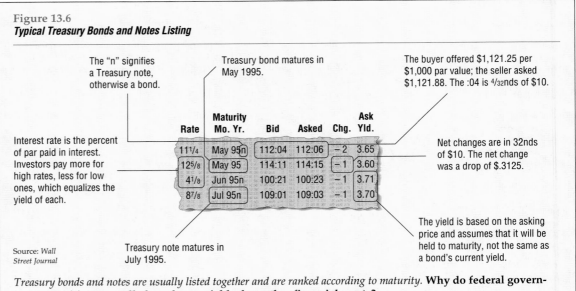

Figure 13.6
Typical Treasury Bonds and Notes Listing

The "n" signifies a Treasury note, otherwise a bond.

Treasury bond matures in May 1995.

The buyer offered $1,121.25 per $1,000 par value; the seller asked $1,121.88. The :04 is 4/32nds of $10.

Interest rate is the percent of par paid in interest. Investors pay more for high rates, less for low ones, which equalizes the yield of each.

Rate	Maturity Mo. Yr.	Bid	Asked	Chg.	Ask Yld.
11¼	May 95n	112:04	112:06	−2	3.65
12⅝	May 95	114:11	114:15	−1	3.60
4⅛	Jun 95n	100:21	100:23	−1	3.71
8⅞	Jul 95n	109:01	109:03	−1	3.70

Net changes are in 32nds of $10. The net change was a drop of $.3125.

The yield is based on the asking price and assumes that it will be held to maturity, not the same as a bond's current yield.

Source: *Wall Street Journal*

Treasury note matures in July 1995.

Treasury bonds and notes are usually listed together and are ranked according to maturity. **Why do federal government securities generally have lower yields than other financial assets?**

$ Free Enterprise Activity $

Have students select a goal, such as saving for a college education or saving to buy a car. Then ask them to select one of the financial assets described in Section 2 as the best choice to reach their goal.

Instruct students to write an essay explaining why they chose that asset, detailing the risk and return. Call on volunteers to read their essays to the class.

Figure 13.7
Financial Assets and Their Markets

Markets are frequently described by the characteristics of the financial assets being traded. If the length of maturity is important, the market is sometimes called a money or capital market. If the ability to sell the asset to someone other than the original issuer is important, the market may be described as being a primary or secondary market. **Why do some financial assets, like CDs, appear in more than one market?**

	Money Market (less than 1 year)	Capital Market (more than 1 year)
Primary Market	Money market mutual funds Small CDs	Government savings bonds IRAs Money market mutual funds Small CDs
Secondary Market	Jumbo CDs Treasury bills	Corporate bonds International bonds Jumbo CDs, Municipal bonds Treasury bonds, Treasury notes

more than 10 to as many as 30 years. The only collateral that secures both is the faith and credit of the United States government. **Figure 13.6** shows how to read a listing for Treasury notes and bonds.

Treasury notes and bonds come in denominations of $5,000 for maturities of 2 to 3 years, and denominations of $1,000 for maturities longer than 4 years. The government also maintains computerized records of its debt holders, so that it can make periodic interest payments to those individuals. **2**

Although these financial assets have no collateral or backing, they are popular with investors because they are generally regarded as the safest of all financial assets. Because of the trade-off between risk and return, however, these assets also have the lowest returns of all financial assets.

Treasury Bills

Federal government borrowing generates other financial assets known as Treasury bills. A **Treasury bill**, also known as a T-bill, is a short-term obligation with a maturity of 13, 26, or 52 weeks in a minimum denomination of $10,000.

The bills do not pay interest directly, but instead are sold on a discount basis, much like government savings bonds. For example, an investor may pay the auction price of $9,300 for a 52-week bill that matures at $10,000. The $700 difference between the amount paid and the amount received is the lender's return. The lender is receiving $700 on a $9,300 investment, for a return of $700 divided by $9,300, or 7.5 percent.

Individual Retirement Accounts

Individual Retirement Accounts (IRAs) are long-term, tax-sheltered time deposits that an employee can set up as part of a retirement plan. If the worker's spouse also works, up to $2,000 per year can be deposited. Up to $2,250 can be deposited if the spouse is not working.

The worker deducts the deposit from his or her taxable income at the end of the year, thereby sheltering the $2,000 from income taxes. Taxes on the interest

Checking Understanding

1. Why are few Americans able to buy international bonds?
2. In what denominations are Treasury notes and bonds sold?

Applying Economic Concepts

 Money Market Mutual Funds Money market mutual funds were introduced in the 1970s when Regulation Q limited the interest that depository institutions could pay. The funds purchased jumbo CDs that were exempt from Regulation Q's limits.

Extending the Content

Money Market Mutual Funds Money market mutual funds are in competition with commercial banks and savings institutions for the small investor. Therefore, they offer services similar to those provided by their competitors—checkbooks, for example. However, there often is a minimum amount for each check, usually about $500.

ASSESS

Check for Understanding

Assign Section 2 Review as homework or an in-class activity.

 VISUAL INSTRUCTION

Ask students to identify the characteristic that determines whether a financial asset is in a primary or a secondary market. (*liquidity*)

Answer to Caption:

because they may have various long-term and short-term maturities

ANSWERS

1. They are available only in large denominations, usually starting at $1 million.
2. $5,000 for maturities of 2 to 3 years, $1,000 for maturities longer than 4 years

331

MEETING LESSON OBJECTIVES

Each objective below is tested by the questions that follow it in parentheses.

1. **Identify** four important investment considerations. (2, 6, 7)

2. **Describe** the four characteristics of bonds. (3)

3. **Describe** the characteristics of major financial assets. (1, 4)

4. **Understand** four views of markets for financial assets. (1, 5)

Evaluate

Assign the Section 2 Quiz in the TCR or use the *Economics: Principles and Practices* Testmaker to create a customized quiz. Spanish Section Quizzes also are available in the Spanish Resources Binder.

Reteach

Have students construct a chart showing the major characteristics of the financial assets discussed in the section.

Enrich

Invite representatives of a bank and a brokerage firm to visit with the class and discuss the advantages and disadvantages of different types of financial assets, such as CDs, IRAs, money market mutual funds, and various kinds of bonds.

CLOSE

Have students discuss the following: If you could give only one piece of advice on investing, what would it be?

332

and the principal will eventually have to be paid, but it gives the worker an incentive to save today, postponing the taxes until the worker is retired and in a lower tax bracket. IRAs are not transferable, and penalties exist if they are liquidated early.

Markets for Financial Assets

Investors often refer to markets according to the characteristics of the financial assets traded in them. These markets are not really separate entities, and many overlap to a considerable degree.

Capital Markets

When investors speak of the **capital market**, they mean a market where money is loaned for periods of more than one year. Long-term CDs and corporate and government bonds that have more than a year to mature all belong to this category. Capital market instruments are shown in the right-hand column of **Figure 13.7.**

Money Markets

When investors speak of the **money market**, they mean a market where money is loaned for periods of less than one year. The financial assets that belong to the money market are shown in the left-hand column of **Figure 13.7.** Note that a person who owns a CD with a maturity of one year or less takes part in the money market. If the CD has a maturity of more than one year, the person takes part in the capital market as a supplier of funds.

Primary Markets

Another way to view financial markets is to focus on the liquidity of a newly created financial asset. If the original issuer is the only one that would redeem it, the financial asset is said to be in the **primary market**.

Government savings bonds and IRAs are in this market because they are both nontransferable. Small CDs are in the primary market because investors tend to cash them in early, rather than try to sell them to someone else, if they need cash.

Secondary Markets

Suppose that a financial asset can be sold to someone other than the original issuer. It then becomes part of the **secondary market**, the market in which existing securities can be resold to new owners. Issuers of financial assets value secondary markets because the investor will not redeem the asset until it reaches maturity.

The major significance of the secondary market is the liquidity it provides to investors. If a strong secondary market exists for a financial asset, the investor knows that the asset can be liquidated fairly quickly and without penalty other than the fees paid to handle the transaction.

SECTION 2 REVIEW

Reviewing Terms and Facts

1. **Define** risk, coupon, maturity, par value, current yield, jumbo CD, junk bond, municipal bond, tax-exempt, savings bond, money market mutual fund, Treasury note, Treasury bond, Treasury bill, Individual Retirement Account, capital market, money market, primary market, secondary market.

2. **Describe** what is meant by the risk-return relationship.

3. **Identify** the three main characteristics of bonds.

4. **List** nine popular financial assets.

5. **Identify** four markets of financial assets.

Critical Thinking

6. **Evaluating Information** Of the four basic investment con-

siderations described, which do you think is the most important? Explain your answer.

Applying Economic Concepts

7. **Risk-Return Relationship** If you had money to invest, in which financial asset(s) would you invest? Why?

Answers to SECTION 2 REVIEW

1. All vocabulary words are defined in the Glossary.

2. the greater the risk of the investment, the higher the required return

3. coupon, maturity, par value

4. certificate of deposit (CD), corporate bond, municipal bond, government savings bond, international bond, money market mutual fund, Treasury note and bond, Treasury bill, Individual Retirement Account

5. capital, money, primary, secondary

6. Answers will vary. Some students may select the risk-return relationship, pointing out that people should feel comfortable about their investment decisions. Others might suggest consistency, pointing out that stable investing practices will almost certainly guarantee success.

7. Answers will vary. Suggest that students take all investment considerations into account before making a decision.

ECONOMIC SKILL

How to Read Stock Market Reports

Open up the financial page of almost any newspaper, and you will see hundreds of rows of what almost appears to be a foreign language. Numbers, codes, prices, and percentages all seem to run together. What you are looking at is the stock market report.

Explanation

Stock prices are listed alphabetically each business day in the financial section of most newspapers. As each trading day begins, stocks usually open at the same price they closed at the day before. The price of a share of stock generally goes up and down throughout the day as the conditions of supply and demand change. At the end of the business day, each stock has a closing price. As a result, three prices generally are available each day for a share of stock—the high, the low, and the closing price. In many cases, the listing also gives such information as the yearly high and low prices, the annual dividend payment and yield, the number of shares sold on that day, and the net change in the price of the stock.

Practice

Figure 13.8 shows examples of stocks traded on the New York Stock Exchange. Read the descriptions of the information presented in the columns, then answer the questions that follow.
1. What was the highest price paid for Reebok during the 52-week period?
2. What was the closing price for Reebok on this particular day?
3. Of the stocks shown, which showed the greatest loss on this particular day?
4. Which stock made the biggest gain on this particular day?
5. Which stock paid the highest dividend?
6. Which stock had the lowest PE ratio?
7. Which stock had the highest PE ratio?
8. How many shares of Reebok were traded on this particular day?
9. If you had purchased 100 shares of Reebok at the year's lowest price, how would you be doing on this particular day?

Figure 13.8
The New York Stock Exchange

The annual dividend is $.80, which is paid in 4 equal installments of $.20 each.

NKE is the ticker symbol, or computer code, for the stock.

The stock hit a high of $49.50, a low of $48.50, and closed at $48.75.

During the day, 845,900 shares were traded.

Nike closed $1.25 lower than the day before. The previous listing would have shown a closing price of $48.75 plus $1.25, or $50.00.

| 52 Weeks | | Stock | Sym | Div | Yld % | PE | Vol 100s | Hi | Lo | Close | Net Chg |
Hi	Lo										
31⁵/₈	22¹/₈	NICOR	GAS	1.22	4.0	15	799	30³/₄	30¹/₄	30¹/₂	− ¹/₄
90¹/₄	49³/₈	Nike B	NKE	.80	1.6	10	8459	49¹/₂	48¹/₂	48³/₄	− 1¹/₄
29⁷/₈	17³/₄	NineWest	NIN	...	...	...	799	26¹/₄	25³/₄	25³/₄	− ³/₈
38⁵/₈	23	Reebok	RBK	.30	1.2	20	1514	24⁷/₈	24³/₈	24⁷/₈	+ ³/₈

During the last 12 months, Nike shares traded for as much as $90.25 and as little as $49.37 a share.

The yield is the dividend divided by the closing price. If you purchased one share at $48.75, and the share paid an annual dividend of $.80, your return would be $.80 ÷ $48.75 = .016, or 1.6%.

The price of today's closing stock, $48.75, divided by the company's earnings on a per share basis is 10. Conversely, $48.75 ÷ 10 = $4.88 per share. Lower price/earnings ratios generally mean more earnings per share; higher price/earnings ratios generally mean smaller earnings per share.

Additional Practice

For further practice in reading stock market reports, complete the Reinforcing Skills exercise in the Chapter 13 Review on page 341.

CHAPTER 13: *Financial Investments, Markets, and Equities* **333**

Answers to SKILL

1. $38.63
2. $24.88
3. Nike B
4. Reebok
5. NICOR
6. Nike B
7. Reebok
8. 151,400
9. You would be $188 up on your original investment. $(24⁷/₈ − 23) \times 100 = 188

TEACHING SKILLS

TEACH

Because so much information is provided in Figure 13.8, it might be useful to have students read aloud the explanations for each entry. To show students how this format is used in the everyday financial world, display the New York Stock Exchange list from a current newspaper. A stock market report from *The Wall Street Journal*, like the one shown here, provides a complete listing of information. Your local newspaper may delete some of the information to save space, but the remaining columns of data will be in the same order. Conclude by assigning the *Practice* activity.

Skills Practice For additional practice, have students complete Reinforcing Economic Skills 13.

? DID YOU KNOW

The 30 stocks in the DJIA are: Allied Signal, Alcoa, American Express, AT&T, Boeing, Caterpillar, Chevron, Coca-Cola, Disney, DuPont, Exxon, Eastman Kodak, General Electric, General Motors, Goodyear, Hewlett Packard, IBM, McDonalds, International Paper, Johnson & Johnson, Merck, Minn. Mining and Manufacturing, J.P. Morgan, Phillip Morris, Procter and Gamble, Sears, Travelers Insurance, Union Carbide, United Technologies, WalMart.

SECTION 3
Investing in Equities, Futures, and Options

Section Objectives

1. Recognize the characteristics of the major stock exchanges.
2. Explain how stock market performance is measured.
3. Understand how financial assets and equities can be traded in the future.

Bellringer

 Prior to taking roll at the beginning of the class period, display Focus Activity Transparency 43.

Motivational Activity

Discuss students' responses to the activity sheet that accompanies Transparency 43.

Preteaching Vocabulary

Have students speculate on the differences among spot markets, futures markets, and options markets. Suggest that they check the accuracy of their ideas by finding these terms in the text. **LEP**

🔲 Use the **Vocabulary PuzzleMaker** to create crossword and word search puzzles.

CURRICULUM CONNECTIONS

Language Arts The term *stock exchange* comes from the old meat and fish market in London called the Stock Exchange. Some sources suggest that this market got its name because it was built where a set of stocks—a device for punishing criminals—once stood.

334

Section Preview

Objectives

After studying this section, you will be able to:

1. **Recognize** the characteristics of the major stock exchanges.
2. **Explain** how stock market performance is measured.
3. **Understand** how financial assets and equities can be traded in the future.

Key Terms

equities, Efficient Market Hypothesis, portfolio diversification, stockbroker, securities exchange, seat, Over-The-Counter market, DJIA, S&P 500, spot market, futures, futures market, option, call option, put option, options market

Applying Economic Concepts

Futures Markets Have you ever negotiated to receive your allowance early, or asked to be paid right away for a service to be completed later? This is the nature of a *futures market*. A contract is issued and payment is rendered for some future activity. Now you can tell your parents that you are not procrastinating; you are getting ready for a future in the world of finance!

In addition to financial assets, investors may buy **equities**, or stocks that represent ownership shares in corporations.

When a market has identical products, large numbers of buyers and sellers, and reasonably good information, prices tend to be about the same from one supplier to the next. This concept explains why the majority of commercial banks, savings banks, and savings institutions pay about the same interest for certificates of deposit with a given maturity.

Market Efficiency

The markets for equities are similar in several respects. Large numbers of buyers and sellers exist, and information about the stocks and the companies that issue them is reasonably good. About the only difference is that some stocks cost more than others.

A number of factors influence the price of a share of stock. A large, profitable company may have a relatively small number of shares outstanding, which generally makes its shares worth more than those of a smaller and less profitable company. Expectations about the future also affect stock prices. For example, two companies may be equal in all respects, but one may have far better growth prospects.

The **Efficient Market Hypothesis** (EMH) is often used to help explain the pricing of equities. The hypothesis argues that stocks are always priced about right, and that bargains are hard to find. A leading expert on the topic explains how this might happen:

Essentially, the EMH states that there are some 100,000 or so full-time, highly trained, professional analysts and traders operating in the market and following some 3,000 major stocks. If each analyst followed only 30 stocks, there would still be 1,000 analysts following each stock. Further, these analysts work for organizations such as Merrill Lynch and Prudential Insurance, which have billions of dollars available with which to take advantage of bargains. As new information about a stock becomes available, these 1,000 analysts all receive and evaluate it at approximately the same time, so the price of the stock adjusts almost immediately to reflect new developments.
—from Eugene F. Brigham's *Fundamentals of Financial Management*

The implication for the investor is that it is almost impossible to "beat the market." If all stocks are priced about right, it does not matter which ones you purchase. The investor may get lucky and pick a stock about to go up, or the investor may get unlucky and pick a stock about to go down. As a result, the best strategy for an investor is **portfolio diversification**, or

---

Classroom Resources for SECTION 3

- 📁 Reproducible Lesson Plan 13-3
- 📁 Guided Reading Activity 13-3
- 📁 Section Quiz 13-3
- 📁 Spanish Section Quiz 13-3
- ✍️ Focus Activity Transparency 43
- 🌀 NBR's Economics in Action Video Program
- 💿 Stocktracker Software
- 📁 Enrichment Activity 13
- 💿 Interactive Economics!

- 📁 Reteaching Activity 13
- 📁 Economic Vocabulary Activity 13
- 📁 Chapter 13 Test, Form A and Form B
- 🎧 English and Spanish Audiocassettes
- 💿 Testmaker
- 💿 Vocabulary PuzzleMaker
- 💿 Chapter Challenger Interactive Review Software
- 🌀 MindJogger Videoquiz

holding a number of stocks, so that increases in some could offset unexpected declines in others.

If an investor wants equities—also known as securities—the investor enlists the assistance of a **stockbroker**—a person who buys or sells securities. The broker arranges to have the stocks purchased at a stock exchange, or supplies the securities from an inventory, or buys them from some other broker.

Organized Stock Exchanges

A number of organized **securities exchanges**—places where buyers and sellers meet to trade securities—exist. An organized exchange gets its name from the way it conducts business. Members pay a fee to join, and trades can only take place on the floor of the exchange. One exchange, shown in **Figure 13.9**, dwarfs all others.

The New York Stock Exchange

The oldest, largest, and most prestigious of the organized stock exchanges in the United States is the New York Stock Exchange (NYSE), located on Wall Street in New York City. This exchange, like most other organized exchanges, has certain rules for both its members and the corporations listed on the exchange.

The NYSE has about 1,400 **seats**, or memberships that allow access to the trading floor. Large brokerage companies, such as Merrill Lynch, may own as many as 20 seats at any given time. The members may

pay well over $1,000,000 for each seat. Members have the right to elect their own directors and vote on the rules and regulations that govern the exchange.

The NYSE lists stocks from approximately 3,000 companies. The companies must meet stringent requirements related to profitability and size, which virtually guarantee that the companies will be among the largest, most profitable, publicly held companies in the country. **Figure 13.8** on page 333 shows how prices are listed on the NYSE.

The American Stock Exchange

Another prestigious national exchange is the American Stock Exchange (AMEX), which is also located in New York City. It has approximately 1,000 listed stocks.

For many years, the AMEX was the second largest organized exchange in the country behind the NYSE. Its growth then slowed, and some of the regional exchanges overtook the AMEX. Today the American is the fourth largest exchange in the country. Overall, the companies represented on the AMEX tend to be smaller and more speculative than those listed on the NYSE.

Regional Stock Exchanges

The regional exchanges include the Chicago, Pacific, Philadelphia, Boston, and Memphis exchanges, along with some smaller exchanges in other cities. Many of these exchanges originally listed corporations that were either too small or too new to be

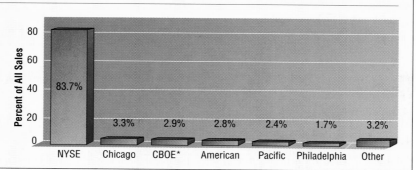

Figure 13.9
Market Value of All Sales on Registered Exchanges

The New York Stock Exchange is the leading market for the sale of stocks and options, having over 80 percent of the sales of all organized exchanges combined. **In addition to the organized exchanges listed here, where else are stocks traded?**

Source: *Statistical Abstract of the United States, 1996*
*Chicago Board Options Exchange

Percent of All Sales

NYSE	Chicago	CBOE*	American	Pacific	Philadelphia	Other
83.7%	3.3%	2.9%	2.8%	2.4%	1.7%	3.2%

CHAPTER 13: *Financial Investments, Markets, and Equities* **335**

Meeting Special Needs

Poor Visual Observers Students with visual-spatial processing problems may have difficulty interpreting the graphs and figures in this chapter. Direct students to Figure 13.8 on page 333 and Figure 13.11 on page 337. Have them note the similarities and differences in the two figures. Then ask them to summarize their findings.

TEACH

Guided Practice

L1 **Stock Listings** Before the lesson, make copies of a section of the NYSE listing and select about 12 companies in the listing. Direct students to study Figure 13.8 on page 333. Then distribute copies of the listing to the class. Announce each company in turn and call on a volunteer to provide an explanation of that company's listing. Direct students to follow one of the 12 companies in the stock exchange listing for a week. Select students to share the results with the class.

 VISUAL INSTRUCTION

Ask: What kinds of corporations were originally listed on the regional exchanges? *(those too small or too new to be listed on the NYSE)*

Answer to Caption:
on the Over-The-Counter market

 INTERACTIVE ECONOMICS!

 CD-ROM
Personal Finance

Have students click on "Stocks, Stock Markets, and Mutual Funds." After students read the tutorial, have them draw a diagram explaining the process of buying and selling stocks. Ask students to share their diagrams with the rest of the class.

Supplied in both CD-ROM and diskette formats.

GLENCOE
TECHNOLOGY

NIGHTLY BUSINESS REPORT

Economics in Action

Chapter 10

Disc 1, Side 2

Title: *Saving and Investing*

Subject: Stocks and mutual funds

Ask: What are the trade-offs involved in investing in stocks or mutual funds? *(These investments may provide high rates of interest, but they are risky.)*

 Also available in VHS.

STOCKTRACKER

A STOCK MARKET SOFTWARE SIMULATION

Use this simulation to help students understand the complex workings of the stock market. The entire simulation can be completed in a few days, or you may wish to extend the game for an entire grading period.

Independent Practice

📂 **Guided Reading** Assign Guided Reading Activity for Section 3. **LEP**

⊙ **VISUAL INSTRUCTION**

Answer to Caption:

Dow-Jones Industrial Average covers just NYSE; Standard & Poor's 500 covers NYSE, AMEX, and OTC markets.

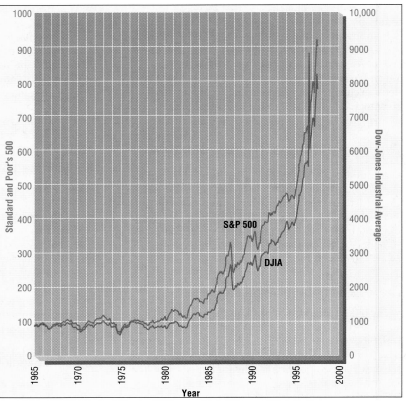

Figure 13.10
Tracking Stock Prices—the DJIA and Standard & Poor's 500

The Dow-Jones Industrial Average and Standard & Poor's 500 are two indices used to track stock prices. **Which index covers just the NYSE, and which index covers the NYSE, the AMEX, and OTC markets?**

listed on the NYSE or the AMEX. Today, however, many stocks are dual listed and can be found on the NYSE or as well as on a regional exchange. The regionals also meet the needs of the smaller and middle-sized corporations in their region.

Global Stock Exchanges

Stock exchanges can be found throughout the world. Exchanges operate in such cities as Sydney, Tokyo, Hong Kong, Singapore, Johannesburg, and Frankfurt. Developments in computer technology and electronic trading have linked these markets so that most major stocks can be traded around the clock, somewhere in the world.

The Over-The-Counter Market

Despite the importance of the organized exchanges, the great majority of stocks in the United States are not traded on exchanges. Instead, they are traded on the **Over-The-Counter market** (OTC)—an electronic marketplace for securities that are not listed or traded on an organized exchange.

Securities traded on this exchange are listed in a sophisticated computer network called the National Market System (NMS). The members of the OTC mar-

DID YOU KNOW?

Breaking Tradition Listing stock quotations in eighths of a dollar—a holdover from the days of the Spanish peso—will end by the year 2000. Major exchanges will adopt a decimal system.

$ Free Enterprise Activity $

Ask students to learn more about the corporation whose stock they followed for a week in the Guided Practice Activity. Have students investigate the goods or services the corporation produces, how many employees it has, where it is located, and what its prospects are for future growth. Instruct students to consult *Standard and Poor's,*

Moody's, or *Value Line,* or contact a stockbroker for information. After students have studied the corporation and have followed the stock, have them write a letter to a friend describing the stock from the viewpoint of a prospective investor interested in possibly buying shares of the corporation. Call on students to read their letters to the class.

Lesson 13 of Interactive Economics! to learn more about "Stocks, Stock Markets, and Mutual Funds."

Figure 13.11
Typical Mutual Fund Quotations

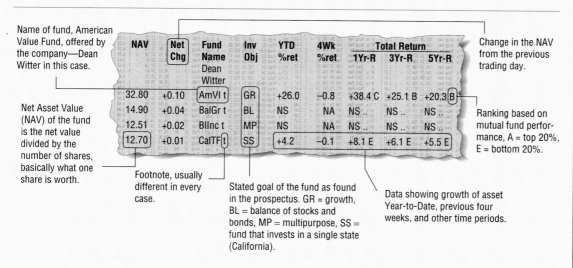

Name of fund, American Value Fund, offered by the company—Dean Witter in this case.

Net Asset Value (NAV) of the fund is the net value divided by the number of shares, basically what one share is worth.

Footnote, usually different in every case.

Stated goal of the fund as found in the prospectus. GR = growth, BL = balance of stocks and bonds, MP = multipurpose, SS = fund that invests in a single state (California).

Data showing growth of asset Year-to-Date, previous four weeks, and other time periods.

Change in the NAV from the previous trading day.

Ranking based on mutual fund performance, A = top 20%, E = bottom 20%.

NAV	Net Chg	Fund Name Dean Witter	Inv Obj	YTD %ret	4Wk %ret	1Yr-R	3Yr-R	5Yr-R
32.80	+0.10	AmVl t	GR	+26.0	–0.8	+38.4 C	+25.1 B	+20.3 B
14.90	+0.04	BalGr t	BL	NS	NA	NS ..	NS ..	NS ..
12.51	+0.02	Bllnc t	MP	NS	NA	NS ..	NS ..	NS ..
12.70	+0.01	CalTF t	SS	+4.2	–0.1	+8.1 E	+6.1 E	+5.5 E

The most comprehensive mutual fund quotations are found in The Wall Street Journal. *The quotations show the growth objectives, total returns on the mutual funds, as well as a ranking. Note how the various mutual funds offered by the same company have different performance ratings.* **Why do investors like to invest in mutual fund shares?**

ket belong to the National Association of Securities Dealers (NASD). NASDAQ, the National Association of Securities Dealers Automated Quotation, is the listing that provides information on stocks that this group trades. The main difference between a NASDAQ listing and the NYSE is that few OTC stocks pay dividends, mostly because they are new companies.

Measures of Stock Performance

Because most investors are concerned about the performance of their stocks, they often consult two popular indicators of the market's performance.

Dow-Jones Industrial Average

The **Dow-Jones Industrial Average (DJIA)**, shown in Figure 13.10, is the most popular and widely publicized measure of stock market performance on the NYSE. In 1884 the Dow-Jones corporation published the average closing price of 11 active stocks. Eventually, the list covered 30 representative stocks.

At one time, a one "point" change in the DJIA meant that an average share of stock changed by $1. However, the evolution of the DJIA over the years has invalidated any such comparison. Consequently, it is better to focus on the percentage change, rather than the number of points.

Standard & Poor's 500

Another popular measure is the **Standard & Poor's 500 (S&P 500)**, a stock performance index that uses the price changes of 500 representative stocks as an indicator of overall market performance. Because the sum of 500 stock prices would be rather large, it is reduced to an index number. Unlike the Dow-Jones, the Standard & Poor's 500 reports on stocks listed on the NYSE, AMEX, and OTC markets.

CHAPTER 13: *Financial Investments, Markets, and Equities* **337**

Extending the Content

Development of the NYSE Before 1792, no organized market for trading securities existed. In May of that year, individuals who wanted to trade in securities met in New York City, only a short walk from the present site of the NYSE. At first, only United States bonds and a few stocks were traded on the NYSE, but trading activity increased as the 1800s progressed, reflecting economic growth and expansion. In 1867 the NYSE introduced the stock ticker, a machine that records purchases and sales of stock. This innovation helped accommodate the growth brought about by the Industrial Revolution. Nearly 100 years later, electronic data processing automated a large part of the transfer of trading information. Today, it is not unusual for more than 500 million shares of stock worth billions of dollars to be traded on the NYSE in a single day.

CHAPTER 13
—SECTION 3—

L3 Research Ask students to select one of the following—NYSE, AMEX, a regional stock exchange, or a global stock exchange—and conduct library research about their selected topic. Students should consider such items as the size of the exchange, its location, the kind of corporations that are listed on the exchange, and how trading operates on the exchange. Encourage students to write reports summarizing their research.

ASSESS

Check for Understanding

Assign Section 3 Review as homework or an in-class activity.

 Use **Chapter Challenger Interactive Review Software** to review Section 3.

 VISUAL INSTRUCTION

Have students recall what a mutual fund is. *(company that sells stock in itself to investors and then invests these funds in other stocks and bonds)*

Answer to Caption:
They can play the market without risking all on one or a few companies.

QUICK CHECK

ANSWERS

1. NYSE and AMEX
2. stock performance measure that uses price changes of 500 representative stocks listed on NYSE, AMEX, and OTC markets

337

Trading in the Future

In Figure 13.7, markets were defined according to the life of the financial asset and whether or not it could be resold. Another attribute of a financial asset is time, which leads to a discussion of spot, futures, and options markets.

Spot Markets

A **spot market** is a market in which a transaction is made immediately at the prevailing price. The spot price of gold in London, for example, is the current price as it exists in that city. The term *spot* means "immediate" and is used to distinguish this market from two other markets that trade in the future.

Futures Markets

Futures are contracts to buy or sell at a specific date in the future, at a price specified today. For example, two parties may agree to buy a specified amount of gold at $450 an ounce three, six, or nine months in the future. The buyer would pay the money today, and the seller would deliver the commodity in the future.

Futures markets are the markets in which futures are bought and sold. Many of these markets are affiliated with the grain and livestock exchanges that originated in the Midwest. The markets include the New York Mercantile Exchange, the Chicago Board of Trade, the Chicago Mercantile Exchange, the New York Cotton Exchange, and the Kansas City Board of Trade.

Options Markets

Options are contracts that give investors the option to buy or sell commodities and/or financial assets at some point in the future at a price agreed upon today. Options are closely related to futures, the main difference being that options give one of the parties the opportunity to back out of the future delivery.

For example, you may pay $5 today for a **call option**—the right to *buy* a share of stock at a specified price some time in the future. If the call option gives you the right to purchase the stock at $70, and if the price of the stock drops to $30, you tear up the option and buy the stock at the going price. If the price should go to $100, however, you could purchase the stock for $70. Either way, the $5 option gives you the right to make the choice in the future.

If you were interested in selling instead of buying, you would have purchased a **put option**—the right to *sell* a share of stock at a specified price in the future. If you pay $3 for the right to sell at $50, and if the price of the stock drops to $40, you can require the buyer to pay the contract price for the stock. You would then net $47 from the sale, the $50 contract price minus the $3 paid for the option. If the price went to $80 instead, you would be better off to tear up the option and sell the stock for $80.

Options markets are the markets in which options are traded. Most of the exchanges that offer futures also sell options.

SECTION 3 REVIEW

Reviewing Terms and Facts

1. **Define** equities, Efficient Market Hypothesis, portfolio diversification, stockbroker, securities exchange, seat, Over-The-Counter market, DJIA, S&P 500, spot market, futures, futures market, options, call option, put option, options markets.

2. **Name** the major organized stock exchanges in the United States.

3. **Discuss** two measures of stock market performance.

4. **Identify** the difference between futures and options contracts.

Critical Thinking

5. **Making Generalizations** Does the Efficient Market Hypothesis support or refute your conceptions of playing the stock market? Explain.

Applying Economic Concepts

6. **Futures Markets** Would you ever invest in a futures contract? Why or why not?

Answers to SECTION 3 REVIEW

1. All vocabulary words are defined in the Glossary.

2. national: NYSE, AMEX; regional: Chicago, CBOE, Pacific, Philadelphia

3. Dow-Jones Industrial Average is most popular and widely publicized measure of stock performance, using 30 representative stocks listed on NYSE as indicator. S&P 500 is stock performance index that uses price changes of 500 representative stocks as performance indicator.

4. Futures are contracts to buy or sell in future at a price set today; options are contracts that give investor option to buy or sell in future at price set today.

5. Answers will vary. Ensure that students offer reasons for their answers.

6. Some students may argue that it is impossible to foretell what would be a fair price in the future. Others may point out that tracking can give the investor an idea of future prices.

ECONOMICS IN ACTION

Saving and Investing

Setting Up the Video

With your classmates, view "Saving and Investing" on the videodisc *Economics in Action*. The video focuses on four investment strategies, including low-risk/low-return savings accounts and bonds, and high-risk/potentially high-return stocks and mutual funds. News segments then consider the effects of inflation on savings goals and the high potential and risk involved in investing in stocks.

**Chapter 10
Disc 1, Side 2**

View the video by scanning the bar code or by entering the chapter number on your keypad and pressing Search. *(Also available in VHS format.)*

Hands-On Activity

Imagine that you invested $1,000 about six months ago in one or more stocks. Use newspaper stock tables to determine how much stock you could have purchased. Then, on a line graph ending with this week's price, chart how your investment has done over the last six months. Compare your investment's performance with the return you would have received if you had invested your $1,000 in a savings account paying 5.5 percent interest. Share your results with the rest of the class.

INTERACTIVE ECONOMICS!

Personal Finance

Introduction

Lesson 10 of *Interactive Economics!* deals with investing in financial assets, an area of increasing interest and importance to most people. Financial assets are legal documents that are claims on the income and property of the borrower. They include CDs, bonds, government securities, home mortgages, and a host of other assets as well. Equities are ownership shares in corporations and are highly sought after by investors. People deal in these assets and equities day in and day out, so it helps to know how to think about them as well as to understand as much about them as we can.

Using the Software

1. Select "Personal Finance" from the Main Menu.

2. Read the Overview to "Personal Finance," then click on "Basic Investment Considerations," and "Stocks, Stock Markets, and Mutual Funds." Read these tutorials.

3. Go back to the Personal Finance Menu and click on the Advanced Topics Menu, which includes "Fixed-Income Investments," and "Loan Amortizations."

4. Study the information given, then click on "Economics Lab." Complete the lab by clicking and dragging the glossary terms to the appropriate sentences.

5. Print your completed lab.

339

GLENCOE
TECHNOLOGY

NIGHTLY BUSINESS REPORT

Economics in Action

Chapter 10
Disc 1, Side 2
Title: *Saving and Investing*

If you do not have access to a videodisc player, the **Economics in Action** programs are also available in VHS.

INTERACTIVE ECONOMICS!

Before students complete the "Economics Lab" in Lesson 10, ask them the following questions:

1. What is the general term for ownership shares in a corporation? (*equities*)

2. What is the first thing that investors must consider before purchasing financial assets? (*the risk-return relationship*)

3. Why should investors who might need to convert their investment to cash on short notice steer away from stocks? (*The stock prices might be at a low point when the investor wants to sell.*)

4. Why is it important to develop a regular investment plan, even if you only invest small amounts? (*The investment grows over time.*)

TEACHER NOTES

_____
_____
_____
_____
_____
_____
_____
_____
_____

GLENCOE
TECHNOLOGY

VIDEODISC
MindJogger Videoquiz

Use MindJogger to review the Chapter 13 content.

 Chapter 13
Disc 2, Side B

Also available in VHS.

Answers

Reviewing Key Terms

Paragraphs will vary. Students should incorporate chapter concepts in their paragraphs.

Reviewing the Facts

1. Saving makes funds available for others to use. When businesses borrow these funds, they create new equipment and plants, employ more workers, and produce new goods and services.

2. People decide to save—by opening a savings account, for example—and receive some form of receipt in return. In this case, the receipt is a savings book. These receipts are financial assets.

3. finance companies, life insurance companies, mutual funds, pension funds, real estate investment trusts

4. relationship between risk and return, investment objectives, consistency of investment, avoiding complex investments

5. Current yields are obtained by dividing annual interest by purchase price.

6. Corporate bonds have common par values of $10,000, but their prices actually are set by supply and demand, and they can be resold.

340

Reviewing Key Terms

For each of the investments below, write a brief paragraph that describes at least three of the term's principal characteristics.

1. Treasury bond
2. Treasury bill
3. equities
4. Treasury note
5. futures
6. Individual Retirement Account
7. jumbo CD
8. junk bond
9. money market mutual fund
10. municipal bond
11. options

Reviewing the Facts

SECTION 1 *(pages 320–323)*
1. **Explain** the relationship between savings and capital formation.
2. **Describe** how financial assets are created in the free enterprise system.
3. **Describe** five nonbank financial intermediaries in the American economy.

SECTION 2 *(pages 325–332)*
4. **Name** four considerations important to investors.
5. **Explain** how current yields are computed.
6. **Compare** five types of bonds that are commonly traded in the United States.
7. **Explain** how capital markets and secondary markets get their names.

SECTION 3 *(pages 334–338)*
8. **Explain** what the Efficient Market Hypothesis means to investors.
9. **Compare** the NYSE with the other organized stock exchanges.

10. **Describe** the nature of the Over-The-Counter market.
11. **Compare** the similarities and differences between the Dow-Jones Industrial Average and the Standard & Poor's 500.
12. **Explain** how options contracts are different from futures contracts.

Critical Thinking

1. **Drawing Conclusions** If you contacted several local banks to get their rates paid on various CDs, you would find that rates vary only slightly from one institution to another. Do you think the similarities are caused by collusion or by efficient markets? Explain.
2. **Identifying Alternatives** The financial assets listed in the chapter are representative of those available in the American economy but are not complete. Research to find other assets, such as commercial paper and banker's acceptances, that could be added to the list.

Applying Economic Concepts

1. **Risk-Return Relationship** List five possible investments a person could make if funds were available. Rank the investments in order of how much risk each entails (from highest to lowest). Then rank the investments according to expected returns (from highest to lowest). What is the significance of the rankings to the risk-return relationship?
2. **Financial Assets** Visit a local bank or a nonbank financial institution and ask for its free brochure that outlines the institution's investment opportunities such as savings accounts, certificates of deposit, money market accounts, and stock brokerage accounts. Write a brief report describing the financial assets the institution generates or trades.

Interest on corporate bonds is taxable income. Municipal bonds are issued by state and local governments and are tax-exempt. Government savings bonds are low-denomination, nontransferable bonds issued by the U.S. government. International bonds are large-denomination bonds issued by foreign governments. Payments on these bonds often are made in foreign currency. Treasury bonds, issued by the federal government, have maturities of 10 to 30 years and come in denominations of $1,000.

7. capital market: market where money is loaned for periods of more than one year; secondary market: market in which existing securities can be resold to new owners

8. that it is almost impossible for the investor to "beat the market"

9. NYSE is the oldest, largest, and most prestigious of all the organized stock exchanges.

Reinforcing Skills

HOW TO READ STOCK MARKET REPORTS

You learned how to read stock market reports in the skill lesson in this chapter. Analyze the stock market listing below, from one of the issues of The Wall Street Journal. *Then answer the questions that follow.*

52 Weeks							Vol				
Hi	**Lo**	**Stock**	**Sym**	**Div**	**Yld%**	**PE**	**100s**	**Hi**	**Lo**	**Close**	**NetChg**
90¼	44	Nike B	NKE	.80	1.5	11	4775	53⅜	51¾	52	−1½
49⅛	33¾	Penney JC	JCP	1.44	3.5	12	7107	41⅞	41¼	41⅝	+⅜
43⅝	34½	PepsiCo	PEP	.64	1.5	24	11641	41⅞	41¼	41½	−⅛
13⅛	8¼	Pier 1	PIR	.10	.9	21	2846	11	10¾	10⅞	+¼
34⅛	23	WalMart	WMT	.13	.5	29	43968	27⅞	27	27⅝	+⅝

1. What was the highest price paid for PepsiCo during the 52-week period?
2. What was the closing price for WalMart on this particular day?
3. Which stock showed the greatest loss on this particular day? What was the loss?
4. How many shares of Penney JC were traded on this particular day?
5. Which stock paid the highest dividend?
6. Which stock cost the most per share on this particular day?
7. How many shares of Nike were traded on this particular day?
8. If you had purchased 100 shares of Pier 1 at the year's lowest price, how would you be doing on this particular day?

Individual Activity

The chapter stated that successful investors tend to avoid complex investments that they do not fully understand. Explain why you might agree or disagree with this advice.

Cooperative Learning Activity

In your local newspaper, find a listing of a stock, a corporate bond, a Treasury note, and a mutual fund. Organize into four groups, and have each group interpret one of the listings. Share your results with the rest of the class.

Technology Activity

Using the Internet

In the **Journal Writing** activity on page 319, you were asked to invest $50,000 in a stock portfolio and to track the progress of your stock(s) for one week or more. To help you track the progress of your stock(s), use the following Internet sites:

The Dow Jones Averages®
http://averages.dowjones.com/about.html

The New York Stock Exchange
http://www.nyse.com/

American Stock Exchange
http://www.amex.com/

Chicago Board of Trade
http://www.cbot.com/

Share your results with the rest of the class.

CHAPTER 13: *Financial Investments, Markets, and Equities* **341**

Applying Economic Concepts

1. Lists will vary. Refer students to Figure 13.2 on page 326 to establish risk and returns. There is a direct relationship between risk and return—the higher the risk, the greater the expected return.

2. Reports will vary.

Reinforcing Skills

1. $43.63
2. $27.63
3. Nike B, $1.50
4. 710,700
5. Penney JC
6. Nike B
7. 477,500
8. Your investment would show a $263 gain. $(10\frac{7}{8} - 8\frac{1}{4}) \times 100 = \$263$

BONUS TEST QUESTION

Identify the market described in each statement below:

1. Where money is loaned for periods of less than one year. (*money market*)
2. Where securities can be resold to new owners. (*secondary market*)
3. Where transactions are made immediately at prevailing prices. (*spot market*)
4. Where money is loaned for periods of more than one year. (*capital market*)

10. The Over-The-Counter market is an electronic marketplace for securities not listed on organized exchanges.

11. Dow-Jones Industrial Average uses 30 representative stocks listed on NYSE as indicator. S&P 500 is stock performance index that uses price changes of 500 representative stocks listed on NYSE, AMEX, and OTC market as performance indicator.

12. Futures contracts are a promise to buy or sell in future at a price set today; options contracts give investor option to buy or sell in future at price set today.

Critical Thinking

1. efficient markets; because interest rates, or the price of money, are set by the forces of supply and demand

2. Assets lists may vary.

FOCUS

Before students read the case study, have volunteers define the terms *welfare* (p. 409) and *workfare* (p. 412). Then ask a student to write on the chalkboard a sentence that compares the two programs. Leave the sentence on the chalkboard throughout the time spent on the case study.

TEACH

L2 Debate Review the case study with students. Then select teams of students to debate the following: "There's no such thing as a free lunch—workfare is the way to go." Have students not directly involved in the debate act as judges and keep a record of points made by each team. At the end of the debate, have judges tally their scores and declare the winning debate team.

L2 Research Organize students into a number of small groups and assign one of the following topics: Origins of the Welfare System; Original Programs; Programs Added in Later Years; Welfare Today; Workfare—How It Works, Where It Operates. Have groups use textbooks and library resources to develop a brief oral presentation on their assigned topic. Have groups select representatives to make their presentations to the class.

UNIT 3

CASE STUDY

Issues in Free Enterprise

REPLACE WELFARE WITH WORKFARE?

After the Great Depression of the 1930s, the United States created a number of welfare programs to help reduce economic instability and insecurity. Over time, however, the cost and effectiveness of welfare programs has been questioned. A growing number of people would like to replace welfare programs with workfare—programs requiring people to exchange some of their labor for benefits. The two views here were voiced at a hearing before a congressional Subcommittee on Trade, Productivity, and Economic Growth.

Pro

Only 15% of welfare mothers work at a given time, according to government surveys, and the rate is still lower among the long-term cases. Workfare is one of the keys to solving poverty and dependency in the United States. If more of the poor worked, many fewer would need support. . . .

Allegedly, [the welfare program Aid to Families with Dependent Children] breaks up families because eligibility is usually limited to single parents with children, and it discourages work because most of what recipients earn is deducted from their welfare grants. . . .

On balance, workfare is certainly worthwhile. The long-term poor are notably unresponsive to the opportunities around them. They have not taken advantage of existing employment, as recent immigration groups have, nor have benefit-oriented social programs done much to help them. Workfare . . . [is] the most promising development in social policy since the Great Society.

—FROM LAWRENCE M. MEAD, ASSOCIATE PROFESSOR OF POLITICS AT NEW YORK UNIVERSITY

▲ Social welfare programs were developed to aid people in need, like this family displaced by a drought in Oklahoma.

▼ Training classes help welfare recipients increase their skills.

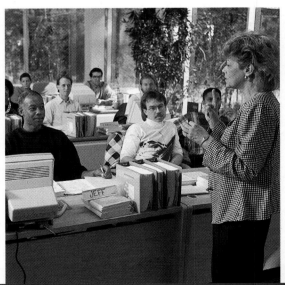

342 UNIT 3: *Macroeconomics: Institutions*

About the Economists

Pro At the time of this opinion, Lawrence M. Mead was an Associate Professor of Politics at New York University. His statements were drawn from his book, *Beyond Entitlement: The Social Obligations of Citizenship*, New York: Free Press, 1986.

Con Morton H. Sklar, at the time of this opinion, was Legal Counsel and Director of Jobs Watch. Jobs Watch is a public interest project that provides information and support services on issues related to unemployment.

The Temporary Aid to Needy Families (TANF) program provides aid to single parents.

▼ Workfare requires people to exchange some of their labor for benefits.

Con

The assumption that the only thing that keeps welfare recipients on the rolls is a lack of motivation to work is a gross misconception. Half of recipients . . . find jobs and leave welfare in their own right after a relatively brief stay in the program. The remainder of employable recipients, who make up only approximately 7% of all those receiving welfare, remain in the program for longer than two year stints. But this is the group that is least likely to benefit from workfare, or be motivated by experience, since they face the types of more serious academic and skill deficiencies that are not affected or improved by short-term work assignments.

Another misconception about what workfare is and is not . . . is the widespread assumption that the program saves money. Recent experiences with workfare in state after state prove the contrary—that in fact the program costs substantially more than it saves through reduced welfare payments.

—MORTON H. SKLAR, LEGAL COUNSEL AND DIRECTOR OF JOBS WATCH

Analyzing the Case Study

1. What is workfare?
2. What evidence does Lawrence Mead cite to explain that workfare should replace welfare?
3. What evidence does Morton Sklar cite to explain that workfare should not replace welfare?
4. With which opinion do you agree? Why?

UNIT 3: *Macroeconomics: Institutions* **343**

Issues in Free Enterprise

ASSESS

Have students answer the questions listed under "Analyzing the Case Study."

CLOSE

Have students consider arguments presented in the case study and in the debate conducted in the activity on page 342 to write a paragraph that represents their own opinions on the issue of welfare vs. workfare. Select students to read and defend their paragraphs.

Answers to Analyzing the Case Study

1. A program requiring people to exchange some of their labor in return for welfare benefits.

2. Welfare causes family breakups and discourages recipients from working. The long-term poor have not taken advantage of job opportunities around them, and benefit-oriented programs have not helped them.

3. Most welfare recipients quickly leave the program for jobs. The remaining few have problems that would not be solved by workfare. Evidence suggests that workfare does not, as claimed, save money.

4. Answers will vary. Have students refer to the paragraphs they wrote for the Close activity before completing this question.

Unit Goals

After studying this unit, students will be able to:

1. **Discuss** the components of national income accounting that measure economic growth.

2. **Describe** the phases of the business cycle and its possible causes.

3. **Explain** the social costs of economic instability caused by inflation, unemployment, and poverty.

4. **Apply** monetary and fiscal policy to promote economic growth and stability.

Unit Overview

This unit explains the measurement of the U.S. economy and policies designed to achieve economic growth and stability. **Chapter 14** focuses on Gross Domestic Product (GDP). **Chapter 15** analyzes economic growth and explains the business cycle. **Chapter 16** discusses unemployment, inflation, and the distribution of poverty and incomes. **Chapter 17** focuses on the goal of economic stability and the policies needed to achieve it.

⌒ If time does not permit teaching the entire unit, use the **Chapter Digests Audiocassettes** to highlight chapter content.

UNIT 4

MACRO-ECONOMICS: POLICIES

CHAPTER 14
Gross Domestic Product

CHAPTER 15
Population, Economic Growth, and Business Cycles

CHAPTER 16
Unemployment, Inflation, and Poverty

CHAPTER 17
Achieving Economic Stability

A recession is when your neighbor is out of work. A depression is when you're out of work.

—Harry S Truman

$ Economics and You

In this unit, discover what part economics plays in the following situations:

• The sale of a used car does not add to the country's total gross domestic product.

• Your dollar bill buys less than 6 cents worth of the goods and services that it bought in 1900.

$$ Economics and You

The first example above is an illustration of how Gross Domestic Product (GDP) is measured. Because transferring the ownership of a used car creates no new wealth, it is not counted as part of GDP.

The second example above illustrates the impact of inflation on the economy. A rise in the general level of prices causes money to lose value and, thus, purchasing power.

In the United States, macroeconomic policies try to stimulate the nation's overall economic growth.

Connecting with Past Learning

Ask students to explain how the economic goals of growth and stability are related to the meaning of economics. Point out that individuals are faced with unlimited wants and limited resources. Economic growth and stability are important to individuals as they try to maximize their satisfaction.

Introducing the Unit

Ask students to summarize magazine and newspaper articles or television news reports on population growth, economic growth and stability, inflation, unemployment, or poverty. Call on students to present and discuss their summaries. Then have students decide which of the situations addressed in the summaries affect them and their community directly. Have students explain their decisions.

Unit Project

Prepare a bulletin board with two sections, one labeled *Monetary Policy* and the other labeled *Fiscal Policy.* As students study the unit, have them bring in and pin to the board articles, illustrations, brochures, and so on that deal with some aspect of monetary policy or fiscal policy. At the conclusion of unit study, have students use materials from the bulletin board to write a paragraph explaining how monetary and fiscal policy promote economic growth and stability.

Examining the Photograph

As students study the photograph, ask them to consider the following questions: How does the photograph illustrate Gross Domestic Product (GDP)? How does the photograph illustrate economic growth? After completing study of the unit, have students return to the photograph and answer these questions. *(New automobiles are counted as part of GDP. Increasing productivity in the automobile industry contributes to economic growth.)*

345

CHAPTER ORGANIZER

Daily Objectives	Reproducible Resources	Multimedia Resources
Section 1 **Measuring the Nation's Output** 1. **Explain** how Gross Domestic Product is measured. 2. **Describe** the limitations of GDP. 3. **Understand** the importance of GDP.	• Reproducible Lesson Plan 14-1 • Guided Reading Activity 14-1 • Cooperative Learning Activity 14 • Consumer Application Activity 14 • Math Practice for Economics 20 • Primary and Secondary Source Reading 14 • Performance Assessment Activity 19 • Section Quiz 14-1*	• Focus Activity Transparency 78 • Economic Concepts Transparency 13* • Vocabulary PuzzleMaker • Chapter Challenger Interactive Review Software • Testmaker • MindJogger Videoquiz • NBR's Economics in Action Video Program
Section 2 **Measuring the Nation's Income** 1. **Explain** why GNP is a better measure of total income than GDP. 2. **Discuss** five measures of the nation's income. 3. **Identify** the three domestic sectors of the United States economy and the income received by each. 4. **State** the four sectors used in an output-expenditure model.	• Reproducible Lesson Plan 14-2 • Guided Reading Activity 14-2 • Reinforcing Economic Skill 14 • Section Quiz 14-2*	• Focus Activity Transparency 79 • Economic Concepts Transparency 13* • Vocabulary PuzzleMaker • Chapter Challenger Interactive Review Software • Testmaker • NBR's Economics in Action Video Program
Section 3 **GDP and Changes in the Price Level** 1. **Explain** how a price index is constructed. 2. **Describe** three price indices. 3. **Understand** the difference between real and current GDP.	• Reproducible Lesson Plan 14-3 • Guided Reading Activity 14-3 • Section Quiz 14-3*	• Focus Activity Transparency 54 • Vocabulary PuzzleMaker • Chapter Challenger Interactive Review Software • Testmaker
Chapter Review and Evaluation	• Enrichment Activity 14 • Reteaching Activity 14* • Economic Vocabulary Activity 14* • Chapter 14 Test, Forms A and B	• Chapter Digests Audiocassette Activities and Tests* • Testmaker • MindJogger Videoquiz

Also available in Spanish

 Blackline Master   Transparency   CD-ROM   Software   Videodisc   Audiocassette

⏱ OUT OF TIME? Assign the Chapter 14 Digest Audiocassette and the corresponding Chapter Digest activities and tests.

National Council on Economic Education

THE **Economics** America AND **Economics** International PROGRAMS

VOLUNTARY NATIONAL CONTENT STANDARDS IN ECONOMICS
Emphasized in Chapter 14

Content Standard 18 *Students will understand that:*
A nation's overall levels of income, employment, and prices are determined by the interaction of spending and production decisions made by all households, firms, government agencies, and others in the economy.

EconomicsAmerica *Resources Available From NCEE*

- *Capstone: The Nation's High School Economics Course*
- *Focus: High School Economics*
- *Geography: Focus on Economics*
- *Learning from the Market: Integrating the Stock Market Game ™ across the Curriculum*

To order these materials, or to contact your state Council on Economic Education about workshops and programs, call 1-800-338-1192 or visit http://www.nationalcouncil.org.

PERFORMANCE ASSESSMENT

The following chapter projects may be assigned at the beginning of the chapter and used for performance assessment.

Multicultural Heritage Assign each student a nation of the world, making certain there is a representative spread across continents and a roughly equal balance of industrialized and developing nations in the assignments. Direct students to use recent encyclopedias, almanacs, and statistical abstracts to find for their assigned nations the various economic measures mentioned in the chapter. Ask students to create an illustrated table of the statistics they are able to gather. Then have them put all the tables together in a display on the bulletin board. Suggest that they place their tables roughly according to geographic location, with the Americas to the left of the bulletin board, Europe and Africa in the center, and Australasia on the right.

Cooperative Learning Organize students into groups of five. Encourage groups to imagine they work for a government information office and have been given the task of educating the public on Gross Domestic Product, national income, and price indices. Direct groups to develop a 10-minute, illustrated presentation on these three topics. Suggest that group members share tasks among themselves— some might undertake research, others might take responsibility for writing, and still others might develop charts, graphs, and other visual materials. Urge group members to work together in making their presentations to the rest of the class. As a further test of the effectiveness of the presentations, have groups make them to other classes not studying economics this semester.

ADDITIONAL RESOURCES

Readings for the Student

Cox, Carol G., and Alice Rivlin. *Understanding Economic Policy: A Citizen's Handbook.* League of Women Voters, 1990. Concise presentation of key concepts and issues related to the American economy.

Frumkin, Norman. *Tracking America's Economy.* New York: M. E. Sharpe, Inc., 1992. Explains basic economic statistics, such as industrial production, unemployment, productivity, and how these statistics are used to analyze economic trends.

Readings for the Teacher

Clayton, Gary E., and Martin Gerhard Giesbrecht. *Everyday Economic Statistics.* New York: McGraw-Hill Publishing Company, 1997. Provides basic information on the meaning and uses of well-known types of economic statistics.

Economic Report of the President. Washington, DC: Government Printing Office, published annually. Useful source of information on GDP, GNP, national income, and other statistics.

Multimedia

Go With the Flow. Instructional Video, P.O. Box 21, Maumee, OH 43537. Video, 30 mins. Follows students as they construct model of circular flow among economic sectors.

Measuring My Success. Instructional Video, P.O. Box 21, Maumee, OH 43537. Video, 30 mins. Reviews GNP and national income accounting.

Chapter Overview

Chapter 14 examines the ways in which the nation's economic performance is measured. **Section 1** explains how Gross Domestic Product is calculated and the problems accompanying those calculations. **Section 2** describes why GDP is a better measure of total output than Gross National Product, or GNP. In addition, five measures of the nation's income are described, and the output-expenditure model is discussed. **Section 3** explains the importance of adjusting for inflation or deflation when calculating GDP.

GLENCOE
TECHNOLOGY

VIDEODISC
MindJogger Videoquiz

Use MindJogger to preview the Chapter 14 content.

Chapter 14
Disc 2, Side B

Also available in VHS.

interNET
CONNECTION

Resources for Chapter 14 on the World Wide Web*

National Council on Economic Education
http://www.nationalcouncil.org/

Bureau of Economic Analysis (Overview of the Economy)
http://www.bea.doc.gov/bea/glance.htm

Business Cycle Indicators (Prices)
http://www.globalexposure.com/07bcilst.html

*Sites subject to change.

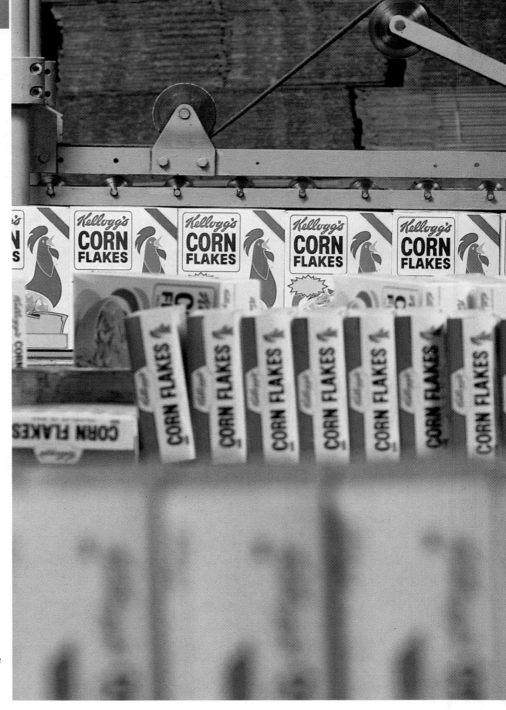

Any final product manufactured within the United States is included in the country's GDP.

Extra Credit Project

Ask students to develop an illustrated report titled "Tracking the Economy," using the following three headings: "Measuring the Nation's Output," "Measuring the Nation's Income," and "Adjusting for Price Changes." Call on volunteers to present their reports to the class.

CHAPTER 14

Gross Domestic Product

SECTION 1
Measuring the Nation's Output

SECTION 2
Measuring the Nation's Income

SECTION 3
GDP and Changes in the Price Level

CHAPTER PREVIEW

People to Know

• John Maynard Keynes
• Restaurant Manager

Applying Economic Concepts to Your Life

Gross Domestic Product As you grow older, you will probably want to have a decent car, a comfortable home, and more leisure time. Others want the same. The total dollar amount of all final output produced in a year's time in the United States is its *Gross Domestic Product* (GDP). GDP is important to you and to others—that is why you hear so much about it.

> **Journal Writing**
>
> For one week, clip articles from the newspaper that refer to one of the following: consumer expenditures, business expenditures, government expenditures, and exports or imports. In your journal, correctly log the expenditures under one of the four headings.

Economic Portfolio

As students clip their articles and log their entries for the **Journal Writing** activity, have them consider who makes up each sector of the economy.

This will help them complete the **Technology Activity** included in the Chapter Review.

Key to Ability Levels — Teaching strategies have been coded for varying learning styles and abilities:
L1 - Basic (activities for all students) **L2 - Average** (activities for average to above-average students)
L3 - Challenging (activities for above-average students) **LEP - Limited English Proficiency**

Connecting to Past Learning

Ask students to review the concept of circular flow as illustrated in Figure 1.8 on page 25 and in Figure 13.1 on page 321. Then refer students to Figure 14.3 on page 358 and explain that it presents another illustration of circular flow, this time among three sectors of the economy—Business, Government, and Consumer.

Applying Economics

Tell students that before starting to work for a business, a new employee must complete several forms that affect his or her disposable personal income. Some of these forms are requested by government for taxes and Social Security; others are required by the business for insurance and retirement plans. Contact the human resources department of several local companies to secure some of these forms. After explaining the information required on the forms, give students a hypothetical salary, then have them complete the forms.

 PERFORMANCE ASSESSMENT

Refer to page **346B** for a Performance Assessment activity for this chapter. Also see the **Performance Assessment Activities** booklet for additional suggestions.

 VISUAL INSTRUCTION

Stress that GDP measures output only within the country's borders. If this American-owned cereal factory were located in Mexico or Canada, its final product would not be counted in U.S. GDP.

FOCUS

Section Objectives

1. Explain how Gross Domestic Product is measured.
2. Describe the limitations of GDP.
3. Understand the importance of GDP.

Bellringer

Prior to taking roll at the beginning of the class period, display Focus Activity Transparency 78.

Motivational Activity

Discuss students' responses to the activity sheet that accompanies Transparency 78.

Preteaching Vocabulary

Write the key terms for this section on the chalkboard. Have volunteers skim the section to find each term, read it in context, and paraphrase its meaning for the class. **LEP**

Use the **Vocabulary PuzzleMaker** to create crossword and word search puzzles.

TEACH

Guided Practice

Cooperative Learning
Assign Cooperative Learning Activity 14.

Using Transparencies
Display Economic Concepts Transparency 13. Spanish Transparencies also are available.

SECTION 1
Measuring the Nation's Output

Section Preview

Objectives

After studying this section, you will be able to:
1. **Explain** how Gross Domestic Product is measured.
2. **Describe** the limitations of GDP.
3. **Understand** the importance of GDP.

Key Terms

national income accounting, structures, intermediate products, secondhand sales, nonmarket transactions, underground economy

Applying Economic Concepts

Nonmarket Transactions Do you contribute to the Gross Domestic Product? You do when you work at a job in the market economy. Your help around the house or mowing your own lawn does not contribute to GDP, however. *Nonmarket transactions* such as chores or lawn mowing may seem like work to you, but they do not count in government statistics.

Just as economists study the amount of goods and services that single producers bring to market, they also study the total amount of goods or services the economy as a whole produces. To study such massive amounts of output, economists use **national income accounting**—a system of statistics and accounts that keeps track of production, consumption, saving, and investment in the economy.

This data then becomes part of the National Income and Product Accounts (NIPA) kept by the United States Department of Commerce. These accounts are used to measure how the economy is doing and to trace long-term trends. The NIPA is like a statistical road map that tells Americans where they are and how they got there.

Gross Domestic Product

The single most important measure of overall economic performance is Gross Domestic Product (GDP)—the dollar amount of all final goods and services produced within a country's national borders in a year. GDP is one of the most comprehensive statistics kept concerning the economy's performance.

Measurement

From a conceptual point of view, the measurement of GDP is fairly easy to understand. Basically, all final

goods and services produced in a 12-month period are multiplied by their prices to get the dollar value of production.

Figure 14.1 shows GDP computed in this way. The first column of the figure contains 3 broad categories of production used in the NIPA: goods, services, and structures. The last category, **structures,** includes residential housing, apartments, and buildings for commercial purposes. The second column lists some of the final goods and services produced in the year. The next two columns contain the quantity produced and the average price of each product. To get GDP, multiply the quantity of each good by its price and then add the results, as done in the last column of the figure.

Sampling and Survey Methods

Because a listing such as that in **Figure 14.1** would be far too long to compile for today's economy, government statisticians generally use sampling techniques and other methods to estimate both the quantity and the respective prices of the individual products. By using sampling techniques, however, the figures become less accurate.

Most of the figures used to compute GDP are based on reliable estimates. A few others are little more than educated guesses. Imagine, for example, how hard it would be to determine the exact value of all the lawns

---

Classroom Resources for SECTION 1

- Reproducible Lesson Plan 14-1
- Guided Reading Activity 14-1
- Cooperative Learning Activity 14
- Consumer Application Activity 14
- Math Practice for Economics 20
- Primary and Secondary Source Reading 14
- Performance Assessment Activity 19
- Section Quiz 14-1
- Spanish Section Quiz 14-1
- Focus Activity Transparency 78

- Economic Concepts Transparency 13
- Spanish Economic Concepts Transparency 13
- NBR's Economics in Action Video Program
- Testmaker
- Vocabulary PuzzleMaker
- Chapter Challenger Interactive Review Software
- MindJogger Videoquiz

Figure 14.1
Estimating Gross Domestic Product

Gross Domestic Product is the dollar value of all final goods, services, and structures produced within a country's borders in a year. Conceptually, GDP can be measured by multiplying the quantity of every product by its price, and then adding the results. In the hypothetical case on the right, GDP amounts to $7 trillion. **What problem arises because the GDP uses sampling techniques?**

	Product	Quantity (millions)	Price (each)	Dollar Value (millions)
Goods	Automobiles	6	$16,000	$96,000
	Replacement Tires	10	$40	$400
	Shoes	55	$40	$2,200
	...*	...*	...*	...*
Services	Haircuts	150	$8	$1,200
	Income Tax Filings	30	$150	$4,500
	Legal Advice	45	$200	$9,000
	...*	...*	...*	...*
Structures	Single Family	3	$75,000	$225,000
	Multifamily	5	$300,000	$1,500,000
	Commercial	1	$1,000,000	$1,000,000
	...*	...*	...*	...*
			Total Gross Domestic Product =	**$7 trillion**

Note: ...*other goods, services, and structures

students mow for neighbors. At best, only a reasonable approximation of the value could be made. GDP figures are accepted as being a reasonably complete, but not a perfect, measure of the total production that occurs in an economy in one year's time.

Intermediate Products

When the Department of Commerce analyzes the tons of data that flow into its offices, it faces several classification decisions concerning what should, and should not, be included in the figures that measure GDP. One such decision involves the exclusion of **intermediate products**—products used in making other products already counted in GDP. Replacement tires for automobiles, for example, can be counted in GDP, but tires for new cars cannot. Some newly produced tires will be placed on new cars, and the value of those tires will be built into the price of the car. If intermediate products are not eliminated from GDP, they would be counted twice, making GDP seem larger than it actually is.

The same problem occurs with other intermediate goods such as flour, sugar, and salt. If these items are bought for final use by the consumer, they should be counted as part of the final output, and therefore as part of GDP. If the products are used in the production of bread or any other bakery good bought by the consumer, they should not be counted.

Secondhand Sales

Another classification decision involves the exclusion of **secondhand sales**—the sales of used goods. When products already produced are transferred from one person or group to another, no new wealth is created. Although the sale of a used car, house, clothes, or compact disc player may give others cash that they can use on new purchases, only the original sale is included in GDP.

Production Within National Borders

The final characteristic of GDP is that it represents total production within the nation's borders, regardless

L2 *Classifying Ideas* Draw a two-column chart on the chalkboard, using *Strengths of GDP* and *Weaknesses of GDP* as column headings. Call on volunteers to identify strengths of the GDP, and enter responses under the appropriate heading. Do the same for weaknesses of the GDP. Then have students use information in the chart to write a paragraph on how the GDP, despite its weaknesses, is a valuable measure of economic performance and economic health.

GLENCOE TECHNOLOGY

NIGHTLY BUSINESS REPORT

Economics in Action

Chapter 19
Disc 2, Side 1

Title: *Measuring the Economy's Performance*

Subject: Gross domestic product

Ask: What is gross domestic product? *(the total dollar value of all final goods and services produced in a country in a single year)*

 Also available in VHS.

VISUAL INSTRUCTION

Point out that GNP—a measure of income—rather than GDP—a measure of output—is a more widely accepted measure for international comparisons.

Answer to Caption:
Figures can be less accurate.

Meeting Special Needs

Study Strategy Many learning disabled students have difficulty knowing when to employ a strategy to help them learn new information. Remind students that they have been practicing components of a study routine that they have learned. Review the strategy steps in sequence. Ask them to write a list of the activities they could use to learn the information in the section "Measuring the Nation's Output." Then ask how each activity is related to a study routine component.

Independent Practice

📁 **Guided Reading** Assign Guided Reading Activity for Section 1. **LEP**

L1 *Nonmarket Transactions* Over a weekend, have students list any nonmarket transactions they observe. Have them explain why they think each listed item is a nonmarket transaction. Call on students to share and discuss their lists and explanations. **LEP**

📁 **Consumer Application** Assign Consumer Application Activity 14.

📁 **Math Practice** Assign Math Practice for Economics 20.

📁 **Readings** Assign Primary and Secondary Source Reading 14.

📁 **Performance Assessment** Assign Performance Assessment Activity 19.

VISUAL INSTRUCTION

Ask: If cash changes hands in a secondhand sale, why is it not included in the GDP? (*because no new wealth is created*)

Answer to Caption:

Intermediate products are used in the making of other products that will be in GDP. Second-hand sales are sales of used goods counted earlier in GDP.

---

of who owns the resources. Japanese automobiles produced in Kentucky, Indiana, Ohio, or Tennessee count in GDP even if the plants are owned by investors who live outside the United States. Conversely, production in United States-owned plants that are located in Mexico or Canada is not counted in GDP.

Other Considerations

Although GDP is the most comprehensive measure of output for the economy, some factors reduce its reliability. These other considerations do not make GDP any less useful as a measure of final output, but they do help keep its importance in perspective.

Reporting Delays

Because of the magnitude of the task, some unavoidable delays occur when final GDP figures are reported. The reporting process includes so much data that GDP estimates are made only quarterly, or every 3 months. The figures are revised for months after that, so it takes a while to discover how the economy actually performed. As a result, a gap exists between actual GDP and reported GDP. To know how the economy is performing today may require a wait of nearly 6 months for revised figures.

Composition of Output

Increases in GDP generally are considered desirable because they imply that people had jobs and earned an income. GDP alone, however, tells nothing about the composition of output. If GDP increases by $10 billion, for example, we know that additional output took place. While the initial increase in production might be viewed positively, people might feel differently if they discover that the extra production took the form of military nerve gas stockpiles rather than schools, libraries, and public parks.

A decline in GDP is usually interpreted to mean that the country is not doing as well as before. Would people be as upset if they knew the decline was caused by a new, inexpensive, miracle drug that reduced the need for medical services and made other drugs on the market obsolete? In the long run, the drug might make people healthier and able to produce more. **1**

Quality of Life

Aggregate figures for total production tell little about the impact of that production on the quality of life. The construction of 10,000 new homes may initially appear to be good for the economy. If the homes threaten a wildlife refuge or destroy the natural beauty of an area, however, the value of the homes may be

Secondhand Sales *The antiques sold in this store do not create new wealth and, therefore, are not counted in the GDP.* **How do secondhand sales differ from intermediate products?**

💲 Free Enterprise Activity 💲

Remind students that the GDP might increase 10 to 15 percent if underground economy transactions were included. Then ask students to brainstorm about ways to decrease the amount of activity in the underground economy. Note responses on the chalkboard. (*Responses may include: lower taxes,*

increased policing of underground economy activities, harsher penalties for those convicted of taking part in underground economy activities) Have students use the information on the chalkboard to write a letter to their member of Congress on ways to tackle the problem of the underground economy.

viewed differently. In practice, GDP does not factor in quality of life issues, but it is helpful to think about such matters to gain a better understanding of GDP.

Some economists have suggested using a Measure of Economic Welfare (MEW), which would be constructed by making certain adjustments to GDP. Factors such as the number of hours lost in traffic jams, the cost of air and water pollution, and the cost of crime would be deducted from GDP. Other factors such as increases in leisure time and healthier lives would be added. 2

Exclusion of Nonmarket Activities

Another feature of GDP is the exclusion of **nonmarket transactions**—transactions that do not take place in the market. Some exclusions are caused by a problem of measurement. GDP does not take into account the value of people's services when they mow their own lawns or perform their own home maintenance. These activities are counted only when they are done for pay outside the home.

Perhaps the largest group of nonmarket transactions excluded from GDP includes the services that homemakers provide. If homemakers received pay for the cooking, cleaning, laundering, child care, and other household chores they usually perform, billions of dollars would be spent every year for these services.

Illegal Activities

Many other activities take place in the market, but they are excluded from GDP because they are illegal and are not reported. A whole range of unreported activities exists, including some gambling, smuggling, prostitution, drugs, and counterfeiting. These unreported illegal activities, plus some legal ones that are not disclosed for tax reasons, are part of the **underground economy**.

Importance of GDP Analysis

Despite the limitations of GDP, most economists agree that it is a fairly good indicator of economic health. When interpreted properly, GDP analysis becomes a useful tool in economic understanding. It is one of the few statistics generally regarded as a measure of both the economy's performance and its general health. ✓

Economic Performance

Generally, Americans want to hear that the United States has a large GDP. Production is valued because it is the primary way of supplying the additional goods and services needed to both satisfy people's wants and to improve the way people live. In

---

Checking Understanding

1. How is a decline in GDP usually interpreted?
2. How would the proposed Measure of Economic Welfare differ from GDP?

Applying Economic Concepts

 Gross Domestic Product A key concept of GDP is that it includes only the goods produced in a given nation. The American GDP, for example, does not include automobiles made at an American-owned plant in Canada, but does include Hondas made in Ohio with Japanese funds.

CHAPTER 14: *Gross Domestic Product* **351**

351

Reteach

Have students write summary paragraphs on the following topics: Strengths of the GDP, Weaknesses of the GDP, Importance of GDP Analysis.

Enrich

Direct students to consult a recent copy of the *Statistical Abstract of the United States* to find a year in which GDP increased or decreased significantly. Have them conduct research to determine why GDP changed significantly and to note what economic policy changes, if any, were enacted. Ask students to present their findings in a brief oral report.

CLOSE

Ask students to list 10 factors not recorded directly in the GDP that affect the quality of life negatively or positively. Select students to share their lists. Then lead the class in a discussion of how these factors might be measured for inclusion in the GDP.

VISUAL INSTRUCTION

Point out that estimates suggest France's underground economy is equal to about one-third of its GDP. In Italy, it probably is as high as 40 percent.

Answer to Caption:

illegal activities, such as gambling and smuggling; some legal activities not reported to avoid taxes

Underground Economy *Although estimates differ, economists generally agree that between 5 and 15 percent of all economic activity is part of the underground economy and is not included in GDP.* **What activities make up the underground economy?**

measuring GDP, Americans keep track of production to know how they are doing and to tell where they have been or might be going.

Economic Health

When GDP grows, people realize that the additional production will help satisfy more of their wants and needs. If GDP does not grow, people become unhappy and dissatisfied with government or its leaders. One way they express this is by voting for a different President or other elected officials. Historically, during periods of economic decline, everyone suffers—especially incumbents.

When GDP does not grow, new economic policies are often proposed and implemented in the belief that they will stimulate the economy. Their success—or lack of success—is measured in terms of how GDP reacts. For these reasons, GDP is the single most important economic statistic compiled today.

SECTION 1 REVIEW

Reviewing Terms and Facts

1. **Define** national income accounting, structures, intermediate products, secondhand sales, nonmarket transactions, underground economy.
2. **Describe** how GDP is measured.
3. **List** five factors to be aware of when considering GDP.

4. **Identify** two other uses of GDP.

Critical Thinking

5. **Making Generalizations** In what situations might society benefit from a low GDP?

Applying Economic Concepts

6. **Gross Domestic Product** Explain why GDP goes down when you quit your job to go to college.

Answers to SECTION 1 REVIEW

1. All vocabulary words are defined in the Glossary.

2. Sampling techniques are used to estimate all the goods, services, and structures produced within national boundaries in a given year. These products are multiplied by their prices to get the dollar value of production.

3. reporting delays, composition of output, quality of life, exclusion of nonmarket activities, illegal activities

4. can be used as a measure of economic performance and a measure of economic health

5. Answers may vary.

6. Most students will note that removal of their labor will reduce production, so there will be fewer final goods to be counted in the GDP. Also, college students who are not working reduce the service sector of the GDP.

PROFILES IN ECONOMICS

JOHN MAYNARD KEYNES
(1883–1946)

John Maynard Keynes, a British economist, is widely regarded as the most important economist of the twentieth century. He wrote numerous books and articles that focused on short-run problems instead of the long-run equilibrium solutions prevalent at the time. Keynes defended his short-run approach on the grounds that "in the long run, we are all dead."

His most famous and influential work was *The General Theory of Employment, Interest, and Money*, which appeared in 1936. The book, written during the depths of the Great Depression, offered new

theories soon took the world by storm.

EDUCATION AND BACKGROUND Keynes was a remarkable person. He first showed his interest in economics at age 5, when he became interested in the theory of interest rates. He attended Eton and Cambridge University to study mathematics, but two of the world's leading economists—A.C. Pigou and Alfred Marshall—finally encouraged him to study economics.

After graduation, Keynes took a civil service position and then returned to Cambridge as a lecturer and editor of the leading economic journal in Great Britain.

Keynesian economics supported hiring artists in the 1930s to paint murals in public buildings. This mural, painted by Maxwell B. Starr, is in the Rockdale, Texas, post office.

insights on the way the economy worked. The policy recommendations derived from his

He served with distinction in a number of government positions. Keynes made a small fortune in stocks and foreign currencies, was a patron of the arts, and married the most popular and beautiful woman of his era.

OUTPUT-EXPENDITURE MODEL
Keynes's *General Theory* divided the economy into the four sectors —consumer, investment, government, and foreign— used in the output-expenditure model. Keynes hypothesized that the instability observed during the Great Depression resulted from a collapse of business spending, which could be offset by increased government spending. The theories were revolutionary, but they quickly gained the support of government and economists alike.

Soon, the label *Keynesian economics* stood for any government taxing and spending policies designed to stimulate the private sector. The national income and product accounts that are used today to track GNP, GDP, National Income, Personal Income, and Disposable Personal Income are all derived from the sector approach outlined in Keynes's *General Theory*.

Examining the Profile

1. **Synthesizing Information** Provide an example of an expenditure that would fall under the heading *Keynesian economics*.

2. **For Further Research** Find out why Keynesian economics is also called *interventionist*.

FOCUS

Section Objectives

1. Explain why GNP is a better measure of total income than GDP.

2. Discuss five measures of the nation's income.

3. Identify the three domestic sectors of the United States economy and the income received by each.

4. State the four sectors used in an output-expenditure model.

Bellringer

Prior to taking roll at the beginning of the class period, display Focus Activity Transparency 79.

Motivational Activity

Discuss students' responses to the activity sheet that accompanies Focus Activity Transparency 79.

Preteaching Vocabulary

Randomly list the five measures of income on the chalkboard. Have students rank them in descending order from the largest to the smallest and explain the meaning of each. **LEP**

Use the **Vocabulary PuzzleMaker** to create crossword and word search puzzles.

Section Preview

Objectives

After studying this section, you will be able to:

1. **Explain** why GNP is a better measure of total income than GDP.

2. **Discuss** five measures of the nation's income.

3. **Identify** the three domestic sectors of the United States economy and the income received by each.

4. **State** the four sectors used in an output-expenditure model.

Key Terms

Gross National Product, net national product, capital consumption allowances, national income, indirect business tax, personal income, retained earnings, undistributed corporate profits, disposable personal income, household, unrelated individual, family, output-expenditure model, personal consumption expenditures, gross private domestic investment, net exports of goods and services

Applying Economic Concepts

Disposable Personal Income Examine your payroll withholding statement carefully to see how much was taken out in the form of taxes and other deductions such as FICA. The net pay that you brought home was part of what economists call *disposable personal income*. It is one of the major measures of the nation's income—and you own a part of it!

The National Income and Product Accounts (NIPA) uses five measures of the nation's total income. This income is paid to different sectors of the economy, which use the income to purchase more output. This is similar to the circular flow concept examined in Chapter 1.

The Concept of Aggregate Income

Whenever anything is produced in the United States economy, and this includes all of the goods, services, and structures listed in **Figure 14.1**, payments are made to the four factors of production—land, capital, labor, and entrepreneurship.

If the United States economy were a closed economy, having no contact with the outside world, GDP would be similar to a two-sided coin. One side would represent the total amount of output produced, while the other side would represent the total payments to all factors of production. GDP would measure income as well as output.

In actuality, GDP includes foreign-owned goods produced in the United States. In addition, GDP

excludes income earned by U.S.-owned resources that are employed outside the national borders. As a result, GDP is not a proper measure of the total income earned by American citizens. GDP can, however, be used to derive five measures of income. **1**

Five Measures of Income

In order to convert total output to total income, two adjustments must be made to GDP. The new measure can then be broken down into component parts, providing five separate measures of the nation's income.

Gross National Product

The largest measure of an economy's total income, shown in **Figure 14.2**, is **Gross National Product** (GNP). GNP is the dollar value of all final goods, services, and structures produced in one year with labor and property supplied by United States residents. ✓

To go from GDP to GNP, it is necessary to add all payments that Americans receive from outside the

---

Classroom Resources for SECTION 2

- Reproducible Lesson Plan 14-2
- Guided Reading Activity 14-2
- Reinforcing Economic Skill 14
- Section Quiz 14-2
- Spanish Section Quiz 14-2
- Focus Activity Transparency 79
- Economic Concepts Transparency 13

- Spanish Economic Concepts Transparency 13
- NBR's Economics in Action Video Program
- Testmaker
- Vocabulary PuzzleMaker
- Chapter Challenger Interactive Review Software

Figure 14.2
The National Income and Product Accounts (in billions of current-dollars)

The National Income and Product Accounts show the relationship between GDP—the aggregate measure of the nation's output—and five measures of the nation's income.

What is the main difference between GDP and GNP?

Source: *Survey of Current Business,* 1997
(Data for first quarter)

Gross Domestic Product (GDP)	**$7,872**
Plus: Payments to American citizens who employ resources outside the U.S.	242
Less: Payments to foreign-owned resources employed inside the U.S.	270
Gross National Product (GNP)	**$7,844**
Less: Capital consumption allowances and adjustments (depreciation)	869
Net National Product (NNP)	**$6,975**
Less: Indirect business taxes and subsidies	549
National Income (NI)	**$6,427**
Plus: Government transfer payments to persons and personal interest income	2,116
Less: Undistributed corporate profits, corporate income taxes, and Social Security payments	1,844
Personal Income (PI)	**$6,698**
Less: Personal taxes and nontax payments	919
Disposable Personal Income (DI)	**$5,780**

United States. Then one must subtract all payments made to foreign-owned resources in the United States. **2**

Figure 14.2 shows that GDP and GNP are approximately the same size. This is merely a coincidence, however, as the two measures are fundamentally different. In this case, the United States merely happened to have approximately the same amount of investment in the rest-of-the-world (ROW) as the ROW had invested in the United States. For many other countries, the difference between GNP and GDP can be much larger.

Net National Product

The second largest measure of the nation's total income is **net national product** (NNP)—GNP minus **capital consumption allowances**, the depreciation and other deterioration of the capital stock that takes place as a result of production.

When the economy produces a given amount of goods, services, and structures in a given year, some of the capital equipment is used up. According to Figure 14.2, GNP amounted to $7,844 billion. If the amount of worn-out and used-up capital goods amounts to

QUICK CHECK

Checking Understanding

1. Why is GDP not a proper measure of the total income earned by American citizens?
2. What calculations are necessary to go from GDP to GNP?

Applying Economic Concepts

 Gross National Product Until recently, the United States reported the GNP rather than the GDP as the principal measure of economic performance. Note that GNP says nothing about production taking place within national boundaries.

TEACH

Guided Practice

L2 Comparing Graphs
Organize students into groups of five and provide groups with copies of data on GDP and the four sectors that make up GDP—consumer, investment, government, and foreign—for a 10-year period. Have each student construct a line graph for one of the five sets of statistics. Then have groups work together to draw up a brief report on trends and similarities and differences among the graphs.

VISUAL INSTRUCTION

Ask: Which sector receives disposable personal income? How does it use this income? (*consumer sector; to save and to purchase goods and services*)

Answer to Caption:
GDP does not count payments Americans receive from outside U.S. but does count payments made to foreign-owned resources employed within U.S.

 ANSWERS

1. It excludes income earned by U.S. resources outside national borders, and includes foreign-owned goods produced in the U.S.
2. Add payments Americans receive from outside U.S.; subtract payments made to foreign-owned resources employed within U.S.

Meeting Special Needs

Study Strategy Model the use of the "Question" component of the study routine for students who are not fluent in asking questions. Explain that this exercise is part of the study routine and should be practiced whenever reading for information in a text. Read aloud the first sentence of each paragraph under the heading "Five Measures of Income." For the first paragraph ask, "What adjustments must be made to GDP to use it for measuring the nation's income?" For the second paragraph ask, "What is the largest measure of an economy's total income?" Have students form other questions.

$869 billion, the net amount of production—the net national product—would be $6,975 billion.

National Income

Another measure of the nation's total income is **national income** (NI), net national product minus all taxes—except the corporate profits tax—that businesses must pay as a cost of doing business. Examples of these taxes, also known as **indirect business taxes**, are excise taxes, property taxes, licensing fees, customs duties, and general sales taxes.

Personal Income

Still another measure of the nation's total income is **personal income** (PI)—the total amount of income going to consumers before individual income taxes are subtracted. To go from national to personal income, four adjustments must be made.

First, income that does not go to the consumer must be subtracted from national income. One such type of income is **retained earnings**, also known as **undistributed corporate profits**. These are the profits that corporations keep to reinvest in new plants and equipment.

The second type of income that must be subtracted consists of the income taxes paid by corporations. This is a form of income to government. The third type of income that must be subtracted is Social Security

payments. After these three types of income have been subtracted from national income, transfer payments in the form of unemployment insurance, Social Security, medicaid, and several other forms of assistance must be added back in. The resulting total is personal income.

Disposable Personal Income

The smallest measure of income is **disposable personal income** (DI)—the total amount of income the consumer sector has at its disposal after personal income taxes. This is an important measure because it reflects the actual amount of money the consumer sector is able to spend. **1**

At the individual level, a person's disposable income is equal to the amount of money received from an employer after taxes and Social Security have been taken out. The $586.89 net pay on the check in **Figure 9.8** on page 225, plus the $3.20 of miscellaneous deductions, is disposable personal income.

The $3.20 is part of disposable income because the deduction was for something other than FICA or taxes. The wage earner could even choose to have more of the salary withheld to cover contributions to a credit union, to a social agency like the United Way, or to buy savings bonds. These contributions would not lower a person's disposable personal income, however. Payroll deductions are merely one way of allocating disposable income.

Economic Sectors and Circular Flows

It is useful to think of the economy as being made up of several different parts, called sectors. These sectors receive various components of the national income, and they use this income to purchase the total output. Sectors, described below and illustrated in **Figure 14.3**, are critical links in the circular flow of economic activity.

Consumer Sector

One sector of the macro economy is the consumer sector. Its basic unit is the **household**, which is made up of all persons who occupy a house, apartment, or

---

$ *Free Enterprise Activity* $

Point out that, in part, the amount of free enterprise in the economy is related to the total expenditures in the government sector. Then organize students into six groups and assign each group an even-numbered, recent year. Have groups discover the size of the government sector in relation to the

other sectors for their particular year. Next, have groups research government activity during that year. Finally, have groups write a brief report about the role of government in the economy for their year, citing government activities and any unusual rise or fall in government expenditures.

room that constitutes separate living quarters. A household includes related family members and all others—such as lodgers, foster children, and employees—who share the living quarters.

As long as the person or persons occupy a separate place of residence, a household also can consist of an **unrelated individual**. This is a person who lives alone or with nonrelatives even though he or she may have family living elsewhere. The concept of a household is somewhat broader than that of a **family**—a group of two or more persons related by blood, marriage, or adoption living together.

All three definitions have value to the United States Bureau of the Census. The definition of the household is especially useful because the demand for durable goods, such as stoves, water heaters, furnaces, and refrigerators, is more closely tied to the number of households than to the number of families. Many households, even when made up of persons not related by blood, marriage, or adoption, tend to behave as a single economic unit.

The consumer sector, shown as *C* in Figure 14.3, receives its income in the form of the disposable personal income described above and illustrated in Figure 14.2. In a sense, the consumer sector receives the income that is left over after all of the depreciation, taxes, and FICA payments are made, plus the income received in transfer payments that are added back in.

Investment Sector

A second sector of the macro economy is the business, or investment, sector. It is made up of proprietorships, partnerships, and corporations. It is the productive sector responsible for bringing the factors of production together to produce output.

The income to the investment sector, labeled *I* in Figure 14.3, is the depreciation, retained earnings, and personal savings borrowed from consumers through the financial system. Depreciation is considered a form of income because businesses are allowed to treat it as an expense and subtract it from their profits before they pay taxes. Because the depreciation never leaves the firm, it is a form of income to that sector.

Government Sector

A third sector in the macro economy is the government, or public, sector. It includes the local, state, and federal levels of government. When speaking of the government sector, the reference is to government in general rather than to a specific level.

The government sector, shown as *G* in Figure 14.3, receives its income from indirect business taxes, corporate income taxes, Social Security contributions, and personal income taxes from the consumer or household sector.

Foreign Sector

A fourth sector of the macro economy is the foreign sector, usually identified as *F,* but not shown in Figure 14.3. This sector includes all consumers and producers outside the United States. This sector, unlike the other sectors, does not have a source of income specific to it. Instead, the sector represents the difference between the dollar value of goods sent abroad and the dollar value of goods purchased from abroad. If the two are reasonably close, the foreign sector appears to be fairly small, even when there are a large number of goods and services being traded in both directions. **2**

QUICK CHECK

Checking Understanding	**Applying Economic Concepts**
1. How is disposable personal income different from personal income? 2. What does the foreign sector include?	☑ **Disposable Personal Income** Employees can choose a variety of payroll deductions. One is contributions to a 401K—a company-sponsored retirement plan. Another is a flexible spending account that sets aside money for medical emergencies. Both deductions are tax-deferred.

Extending the Content

Three Kinds of Consumption National income accounting records three classifications of consumption in the consumer sector. Durable goods are goods with an average life of more than three years—automobiles, furniture, and appliances, for example. Nondurable goods are goods that have an average life of less than three years—shampoo, food products, gasoline, and clothing, for example.

Services, such as financial or legal advice, health care, and haircuts, make up the final classification of consumption. In some instances, such classifications seem arbitrary. A well-made overcoat, for example, may last for 5 to 10 years. Even so, as an item of clothing it would be regarded as a nondurable good.

ASSESS

Check for Understanding

Assign Section 2 Review as homework or an in-class activity.

 Use **Chapter Challenger Interactive Review Software** to review Section 2.

MEETING LESSON OBJECTIVES

Each objective below is tested by the questions that follow it in parentheses.

1. **Explain** why GNP is a better measure of total income than GDP. **(1, 2)**

2. **Discuss** five measures of the nation's income. **(1, 3)**

3. **Identify** the three domestic sectors of the United States economy and the income received by each. **(4, 6)**

4. **State** the four sectors used in an output-expenditure model. **(4, 5)**

VISUAL INSTRUCTION

Have students identify the sources of government's income. *(Corporate income taxes, indirect business taxes, social security contributions, personal taxes)*

Answer to Caption:
Both show how separate sectors of the economy are interrelated.

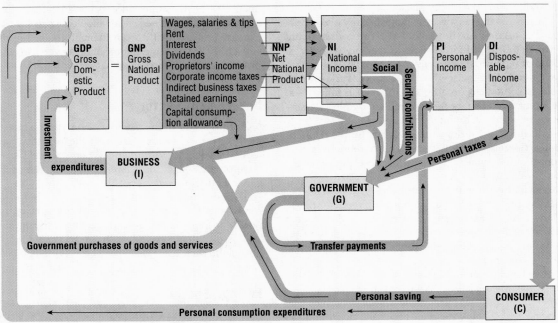

Figure 14.3
The Circular Flow of Economic Activity

In a closed economy such as the one shown here, GDP is the same as GNP. The three sectors of the economy—Business, Government, and Consumer—combine to purchase the nation's total output. This generates income that eventually flows back to the individual sectors. **How does this circular flow relate to the output-expenditure model?**

The Output-Expenditure Model

The circular flow in **Figure 14.3** is complete when the **output-expenditure model** is introduced—a macroeconomic model used to show aggregate demand by the consumer, investment, government, and foreign sectors. When this is written algebraically as

$$GDP = C + I + G + F,$$

the equation becomes the formal output-expenditure model used to explain and analyze the performance of the economy.

The consumer sector spends its income on the goods and services used by households and unrelated individuals. These **personal consumption expenditures** include groceries, rent, books, automobiles, clothes, and almost anything else people buy.

The investment, or business, sector spends its income on plant, equipment, inventories, and other investment goods. These expenditures, known as **gross private domestic investment**, represent the total value of capital goods created in the economy during the year. The term *gross* is used because purchases of all capital goods are included.

The government sector spends its income on many categories, including national defense, income security, interest on the debt, hospital care, roads, and education. The only major government expenditure

---

Cultural Diversity and Economics

When an American tourist visits a foreign country, the money he or she spends there has the same effect on net foreign investment as a U.S. import.

Exports *United States exports make up part of what is considered the foreign sector of the macro economy.* **In addition to exports, what else is included in the foreign sector?**

Evaluate

📁 📁 💿 Assign the Section 2 Quiz in the TCR or use the *Economics: Principles and Practices* Testmaker to create a customized quiz. Spanish Section Quizzes also are available in the Spanish Resources Binder.

Reteach

Have students write 10 questions on the content of the section. Select a number of students to use their questions to quiz the class.

Enrich

Have students write an essay comparing GDP and GNP as measures of economic health and economic performance. Select students to read and discuss their essays.

CLOSE

Have students use information in Figure 14.2 to develop equations for GDP and each of the five measures of income. Call on students to share their equations with the class.

not included in total output is transfer payments, because this money is used by others to buy goods and services that are part of the total GDP.

The foreign sector also buys many goods and services—tractors, computers, airplanes, and farm products—that make up GDP. In addition, it supplies other products—British woolens, Japanese cars, Korean shirts, and Brazilian shoes—to be consumed at home. For this reason, the foreign sector's purchases are called **net exports of goods and services**, a term that refers to the difference between the United States's exports and its imports.

SECTION 2 REVIEW

Reviewing Terms and Facts

1. **Define** Gross National Product, net national product, capital consumption allowances, national income, indirect business tax, personal income, retained earnings, undistributed corporate profits, disposable personal income, household, family, unrelated individuals, output-expenditure model, personal consumption expenditures, gross private domestic investment, net exports of goods and services.

2. **Describe** the difference between GNP and GDP.
3. **List** the five aggregate measures of income.
4. **Identify** the sectors used in the output-expenditure model.

Critical Thinking

5. **Synthesizing Information** Disposable personal income shows up as part of the aggregate expenditures in the output-expenditure model. Write the equation for this model and then indicate where your net pay would fit in.

Applying Economic Concepts

6. **Disposable Personal Income** After the consumer sector gets its disposable personal income, it saves a portion and then spends the rest on goods and services. How does this compare to the way you allocate your disposable income?

VISUAL INSTRUCTION

Have students explain what is meant by the term *net exports of goods and services.* *(difference between U.S. exports and imports)*

Answer to Caption:
foreign products to be consumed in the U.S.

Answers to SECTION 2 REVIEW

1. All vocabulary words are defined in the Glossary.

2. GDP counts production only in U.S., regardless of who owns resources; GNP measures income received by American citizens, regardless of where productive resources are located.

3. Gross National Product, Net National Product, National Income, Personal Income, Disposable Personal Income

4. consumer, investment, government, and foreign sectors

5. GDP = C + I + G + F; in the consumer sector as disposable personal income is used for consumer consumption expenditures

6. Answers will vary. Stress the importance of savings.

Using E-Mail

Why use paper and pen to send a message when a computer can immediately deliver your message 24 hours a day? Why spend $20 to $30 to have a document delivered by a mail service when you can send the mail for the price of a local phone call? Electronic mail, or E-mail, is a substitute for paper, pen, and a post office.

Explanation

E-mail allows you to send and receive electronic mail messages and data worldwide, to and from anyone connected to the Internet. Your computer is ready for communicating electronically after you obtain three things. First, you need a *modem*—a device that enables computers to communicate with each other through telephone lines. Second, you must subscribe to an Internet service provider (ISP)—a company that charges a fee to provide you with easy access to the Internet. Most ISPs will offer you the third item you need—*communications software* to use E-mail easily.

To send or receive a message, you must first start your E-mail software. Then type in the address of the person to whom you are sending the message. An address has two parts separated by the @ (at) symbol. The first part of the address is called a *user name.* This is usually a real name or a given name. The second part of the address identifies your ISP and is called the *domain name.* The last few letters in a domain name give you a clue as to the type of address. *Gov* is a government address. *Edu* is an educational institution address. *Com* is a commercial address.

After typing in your message, click the SEND button. Your ISP receives the message and stores it in an electronic "mailbox." The message is available whenever the recipient chooses to retrieve it and send you a return message.

When you receive E-mail, the sender's address is on the message. You can usually add it to your electronic address book at that time.

Practice

To send an E-mail message, complete the following steps:

1. Select the "prepare message" function from your communications software.

2. Type in the address of the person who will receive your E-mail.

3. Type in your message, practicing *Netiquette*—some basic rules of E-mail etiquette. For example, check for spelling and grammar errors. Do not type in ALL CAPS, which is like shouting. Include a subject line that describes your message clearly.

4. When your message is complete, click on the SEND button.

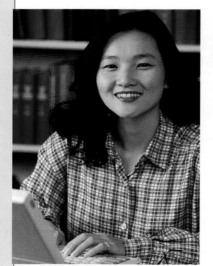

E-mail has changed the way people think about communicating. When you E-mail someone for the first time, add their E-mail address to your address book at the same time.

Additional Practice

For further practice in using E-mail, complete the Reinforcing Skills exercise in the Chapter 14 Review on page 367.

Teacher's Notes

Point out to students that exchanging E-mail messages with someone in another country is a good way to find out about another part of the world. Ask students: If you could send an E-mail message to someone your age in another country, what would you talk about? Compose the E-mail message you would send to introduce yourself to this person.

Section Preview

Objectives

After studying this section, you will be able to:

1. **Explain** how a price index is constructed.
2. **Describe** three price indices.
3. **Understand** the difference between real and current GDP.

Key Terms

price index, market basket, consumer price index, producer price index, wholesale price index, implicit GDP price deflator, current GDP, nominal GDP, real GDP, GDP in constant dollars

Applying Economic Concepts

Market Basket When statisticians construct the consumer price index, they use a *market basket* consisting of items most frequently purchased by consumers. The way you and others spend your income helps determine the products in the market basket.

A major problem with GDP is that it is subject to distortions because of inflation—a rise in the general price level. With inflation, output may appear to grow from one year to the next without actually doing so.

To see how this happens, compare the GDP in Figure 14.1 with the GDP in Figure 14.4. Assume that the second table was compiled one year after the first, and that the inflation rate during that year was 10 percent. The second and third columns in each table show that the composition and quantity of output was the same for both years. In other words, there was no real change in the amount of goods and services produced.

The fourth column in each table, however, is not the same. Neither is the fifth. In these columns, everything costs 10 percent more in the second table than in the first one. This makes GDP rise by 10 percent, or $700 billion, revealing the effects of inflation. The major problem is that the dollar value of the final output went up without any real underlying changes in the quantity of goods and services produced.

Constructing a Price Index

To reduce the distortions of inflation, economists construct a **price index**—a statistical series that can be

Figure 14.4
Estimating Gross Domestic Product

Inflation can distort the value of Gross Domestic Product from one year to the next. The GDP is 10 percent larger in the figure on the right than it was in Figure 14.1. A comparison of the two reveals that all of the increase was caused by higher prices—there were no changes in the actual number of goods, services, and structures produced. **Why is it desirable to remove inflation from GDP?**

	Product	Quantity (millions)	Price (each)	Dollar Value (millions)
Goods	Automobiles	6	$17,600	$105,600
	Replacement Tires	10	$44	$440
	Shoes	55	$44	$2,420
	...*	...*	...*	...*
Services	Haircuts	150	$9	$1,350
	Income Tax Filings	30	$165	$4,950
	Legal Advice	45	$220	$9,900
	...*	...*	...*	...*
Structures	Single Family	3	$82,500	$247,500
	Multifamily	5	$330,000	$1,650,000
	Commercial	1	$1,100,000	$1,100,000
	...*	...*	...*	...*
			Total Gross Domestic Product = $7.7 trillion	

Note: ...*other goods, services, and structures

FOCUS

Section Objectives

1. Explain how a price index is constructed.
2. Describe three price indices.
3. Understand the difference between real and current GDP.

Bellringer

Prior to taking roll at the beginning of the class period, display Focus Activity Transparency 54 on the overhead projector and assign the accompanying Student Activity 54.

Motivational Activity

Discuss students' responses to the activity sheet that accompanies Focus Activity Transparency 54.

Preteaching Vocabulary

Call on volunteers to offer definitions for each of the key terms. Ask other students to check the accuracy of these definitions in the Glossary. **LEP**

 Use the **Vocabulary PuzzleMaker** to create crossword and word search puzzles.

VISUAL INSTRUCTION

Make certain that students understand the meaning of the term *inflation*—a rise in the general price level.

Answer to Caption:
With inflation, it appears that output has grown when, in fact, it has not.

Figure 14.5
Constructing the Consumer Price Index

The Bureau of Labor Statistics measures items in terms of their 1993-95 base-period prices. The total value of the items is assigned a base value of 100 percent. As time goes by, prices change, giving the new market basket a different total value. The new price index is computed by dividing the cost of the new market basket by the old basket. **Why is the market basket the same from one year to the next?**

Item	Description	Price Base Period (1993-95)	Price Second Period (1997)	Price August (1998)
1.	Toothpaste (7 oz.)	$1.40	$1.49	$2.25
2.	Milk (1 gal.)	1.29	1.29	1.79
3.	Peanut butter (2 lb. jar)	2.50	2.65	3.73
4.	Light bulb (60 watt)	.45	.48	.65
::::::	::::::	::::::	::::::	::::::
364.	Automobile engine tune-up	40.00	42.00	64.75
Total Cost of Market Basket:		$1,792.00	$1,895.94	$1,952.81
Index Number:		100%	105.8%	109.0%

used to measure changes in prices over time. It can be compiled for a specific product or for a range of items.

It is not difficult to construct a price index. First, a base year—a year that serves as the basis of comparison for all other years—is chosen. The particular year chosen can vary. The base year is used only in a comparative sense and generally is updated as time goes by.

Second, a **market basket** of goods is selected. These are goods representative of the purchases that will be made over time. Although the number of items in the market basket is a matter of judgment, it must remain fixed after the selection is made. The advantage of this market basket concept is that it captures the overall trend in prices.

Finally, the price of each item in the market basket is recorded and then totaled. The total represents the prices of the market basket in the base year and is assigned a value of 100 percent.

Figure 14.5 shows how a price index can be constructed for a representative market basket with a large number of items. Because 1993-95 is used as the base period, the prices in the base-year column are lower than those today. The total of the market prices—$1,792.00—is assigned a value of 100 percent, which is the index number for that year.

In order to see how prices change from one year to the next, the price for each of the items must be recorded for the base year and then recorded again a year later. Because the total of the items for the second year—$1,895.94—is 5.8 percent higher than the total for the first year, the new index number is 105.8. The prices for each year that follows also must be recorded and

totaled to find the new index number. This procedure is repeated until the price index is finished.

Major Price Indices

Price indices can be constructed for a number of different purposes. Some measure changes in the price of a single item. Some measure the price changes of imported goods, while others do the same for agricultural products. Of all these measures, three are especially important. They are the consumer price index, the producer price index, and the implicit GDP price deflator.

Consumer Price Index

The **consumer price index** (CPI) reports on price changes for about 90,000 items in 364 categories. Prices for the goods and services currently sampled are taken from 85 geographically distributed areas around the country. Some of the items are surveyed in all the areas, while others are sampled in only a few.

The consumer price index is compiled monthly by the Bureau of Labor Statistics and is published for the economy as a whole. There also are separate indices for 28 selected areas around the country.

Producer Price Index

The **producer price index**, formerly called the **wholesale price index**, measures price changes received by domestic producers for their output. It

Figure 14.6
Current vs. Real GDP

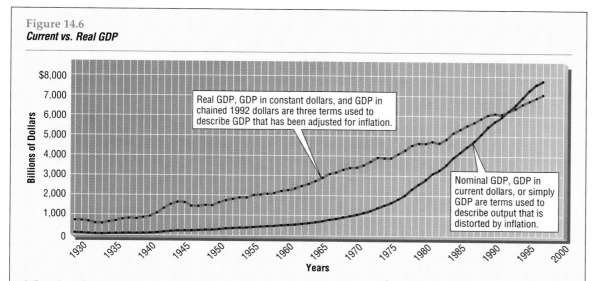

Real GDP, GDP in constant dollars, and GDP in chained 1992 dollars are three terms used to describe GDP that has been adjusted for inflation.

Nominal GDP, GDP in current dollars, or simply GDP are terms used to describe output that is distorted by inflation.

When the inflation is removed to show GDP in terms of constant dollars, we get a better picture of the underlying trends. Notice how declines in GDP are not even evident when a current, or unadjusted, measure is used. Because the Department of Commerce uses 1992 as the base year, GDP is the same for both measures in that year.

Source: *Economic Report of the President*

uses a sample of about 3,000 commodities and has a base year of 1982.

The producer price index also is reported monthly by the Bureau of Labor Statistics. Although it is compiled for all commodities, it also is broken down into subcategories that include farm products, fuels, chemicals, rubber, pulp and paper, and processed foods.

Implicit GDP Price Deflator

The **implicit GDP price deflator** shows the average level of prices for all goods and services in the economy. It is computed quarterly and has a base year of 1992.

Because GDP is a measure of the final output of goods and services and it covers thousands of items instead of hundreds, many economists believe it is a good, long-run indicator of the price changes that consumers face. Because the deflator is compiled quarterly, however, it is not as useful for measuring month-to-month changes in inflation.

Real vs. Current GDP

When GDP is not adjusted for inflation, it is called **current GDP, nominal GDP,** or simply GDP. When the distortions of inflation have been removed, it is called **real GDP, GDP in constant dollars,** or *GDP in chained dollars.*

Converting GDP to Real Dollars

Suppose we want to convert current GDP to GDP in real (inflation-adjusted) dollars. The procedure that allows us to do this is dividing current GDP by the deflator and then multiplying by 100 (since the deflator is really a percent). Or:

$$\text{Real GDP} = \frac{\text{GDP in current dollars}}{\text{GDP deflator}} \times 100$$

To illustrate, GDP for the second quarter of 1997 was $8,035 billion. The GDP deflator for that period was 112.14, meaning that prices were 112.14 percent higher in 1997 than they were in 1992. If we wanted to

CHAPTER 14: *Gross Domestic Product* **363**

ASSESS

Check for Understanding

Assign Section 3 Review as homework or an in-class activity.

 Use **Chapter Challenger Interactive Review Software** to review Section 3.

MEETING LESSON OBJECTIVES

Each objective below is tested by the questions that follow it in parentheses.

1. **Explain** how a price index is constructed. **(2, 5, 6)**
2. **Describe** three price indices. **(1, 3)**
3. **Understand** the difference between real and current GDP. **(4)**

VISUAL INSTRUCTION

Point out that adjusting GDP for inflation is important because economists are more interested in the economy's total output than in the price tag attached to that output.

$ Free Enterprise Activity $

Remind students that economic equity is a major economic goal in the U.S. Then point out that a significant problem associated with increases in the CPI is the inequities that might be created. For example, there might be a rise in grocery prices, but the incomes of people who need to buy groceries may not rise as much. Direct students to research a period in American history when there was a rapid rise in prices. Have them write a report on how people coped with rising prices.

AUDIO - VIDEO

"The price may seem a little high, but you have to remember that's in today's dollars."

As long as we have inflation, we must be careful when comparing today's prices with earlier ones. **How can we compare a price today with a price from an earlier period?**

find GDP in real terms, we divide current GDP by the deflator for that year and multiply by 100:

$$\text{Real GDP} = \frac{\$8{,}035 \text{ billion}}{112.14} \times 100 = \$7{,}165 \text{ billion}$$

The amount of $7,165 billion, then, is the dollar value of all goods and services produced in 1997 if measured in 1992 prices.

Comparing GDP in Different Years

The main reason for converting nominal dollar amounts to real dollars is to make comparisons over time. For example, nominal GDP for the second quarter of 1997 was larger than the nominal GDP for the second quarter of 1996. Was this increase caused by an actual increase in the quantity of goods and services produced? Or was some of the increase in nominal GDP caused by inflation?

We can find out by converting the 1996 second quarter GDP of $7,608 billion to 1992 dollars through the same procedure described above:

$$\text{Real GDP} = \frac{\$7{,}608 \text{ billion}}{109.85} \times 100 = \$6{,}925 \text{ billion}$$

In terms of constant 1992 dollars, real GDP in 1996 amounted to $6,925 billion. Because the 1997 real or constant dollar GDP amount of $7,165 was greater than the 1996 real dollar amount, there was a real increase in GDP that was not due to inflation.

SECTION 3 REVIEW

Reviewing Terms and Facts

1. **Define** price index, market basket, consumer price index, producer price index, wholesale price index, implicit GDP price deflator, current GDP, nominal GDP, real GDP, GDP in constant dollars.
2. **Explain** why a market basket is used whenever a price index is constructed.
3. **List** three major price indices.

4. **Provide** an example in which real GDP would be greater than current GDP.

Critical Thinking

5. **Making Comparisons** One difficulty with using the market basket concept of making comparisons over long periods is that the composition of the market basket changes. What do you think a typical market basket 20 years ago might have had in it that we do not use today? What do you think a future market basket might have that we do not have today?

Applying Economic Concepts

6. **Market Basket** If you were to construct a market basket of goods and services that high school students typically consume, what would you select?

Answers to SECTION 3 REVIEW

1. All vocabulary words are defined in the Glossary.

2. It captures the overall trend in prices.

3. consumer price index, producer price index, implicit GDP price deflator

4. in years prior to the base year; Because base year prices are higher than in earlier years, conversion to current dollars would cause previous years' GDP to be higher. (See Figure 14.6.)

5. Answers will vary. Most students' lists will reflect changes caused by technological developments.

6. Answers will vary. Ask students to explain why they chose particular items.

ECONOMICS IN ACTION

Measuring the Economy's Performance

Setting Up the Video

With your classmates, view "Measuring the Economy's Performance" on the videodisc *Economics in Action*. The video focuses on the statistical measurements used to monitor the economy's performance, including Gross Domestic Product (GDP), consumer price index (CPI), and producer price index (PPI). A news report examines how the CPI is compiled and stresses its importance in monitoring inflation.

 **Chapter 19
Disc 2, Side 1**

View the video by scanning the bar code or by entering the chapter number on your keypad and pressing Search. (Also available in VHS format.)

Hands-On Activity

Construct your own consumer price index. Select 10 categories of expenditures that you and your family spend the most money on, such as hair products, clothing, breakfast cereal, gasoline, fast food, and so on. Identify at least 5 specific items for each category, which will put 50 items in your market basket. Price the items on a per month basis for 6 months to measure the changes in your consumer price index.

SURFING THE "NET"

Measuring the Nation's Output

Just as economists study the amount of goods and services that single producers bring to market, they also study the total amount of goods and services the economy as a whole produces. To study such massive amounts of output, economists use national income accounting—a system of statistics and accounts that keeps track of production, consumption, saving, and investment in the economy.

The data then become part of the National Income and Product Accounts (NIPA) kept by the United States Department of Commerce. Use the Internet to see for yourself how the economy is doing.

Getting There

1. Use a search engine. Type in the words *Department of Commerce*.
2. Next, enter words like the following to focus your search: *Gross Domestic Product*, *personal income*, and *national income*.
3. The search engine will provide you with a number of links to follow. Links are "pointers" to different sites on the Internet and often appear as blue, underlined words.

What to Do When You Are There

Click on the links to navigate through the pages of information. Download and print a report or press release from the Commerce Department. Prepare a brief presentation of the materials to share with your class.

365

GLENCOE TECHNOLOGY

NIGHTLY BUSINESS REPORT

Economics in Action

Chapter 19
Disc 2, Side 1

Title: *Measuring the Economy's Performance*

 If you do not have access to a videodisc player, the **Economics in Action** programs are also available in VHS.

INTERNET SITES

The following are possible sites for completing the "Net" activities:

U.S. Department of Commerce
http://www.doc.gov/

Economic Statistics Briefing Room (Prices)
http://www.whitehouse.gov/fsbr/prices.html

Not on the "Net"...

If students have limited or no access to the Internet, have them complete the activity "Measuring the Nation's Output" by using the computerized card catalog at the school or local library. At the *s:* prompt, students should type in *Gross Domestic Product* or *Department of Commerce*. They should then use the call numbers to find the books and other resources they need to complete their research.

GLENCOE
TECHNOLOGY

 VIDEODISC
MindJogger Videoquiz

Use MindJogger to review
the Chapter 14 content.

 Chapter 14
Disc 2, Side B

Also available in VHS.

Answers
Reviewing Key Terms

Sample sentences:

1. Base year and market basket are both used in con-
structing a price index.

2. Both are treated as income
to the business sector.

3. Both are used as a measure
of the nation's economy.

4. A household may consist of
an unrelated individual.

5. Intermediate products and
secondhand sales are not
counted in GDP.

6. *Nominal GDP* and *current
GDP* are two terms for GDP
not adjusted for inflation.

7. Spending by the consumer
sector is known as personal
consumption expenditures,
while spending on capital
goods by the investment
sector is called gross private domestic investment.

8. *Real GDP* and *GDP in constant dollars* are two terms
for GDP adjusted for
inflation.

9. Retained earnings and
undistributed corporate
profits describe profits that
corporations reinvest in
plant and equipment.

10. The underground economy
and nonmarket transac-
tions are not counted in
GDP.

366

Reviewing Key Terms

*Examine the pairs of words below. Then write a sen-
tence explaining what each of the pairs have in common.*

1. base year
   market basket
2. capital consumption allowances
   undistributed corporate profits
3. Gross National Product
   Net National Product
4. household
   unrelated individuals
5. intermediate products
   secondhand sales
6. nominal GDP
   current GDP
7. personal consumption expenditures
   gross private domestic investment
8. real GDP
   GDP in constant dollars
9. retained earnings
   undistributed corporate profits
10. underground economy
    nonmarket transactions

Reviewing the Facts

SECTION 1 *(pages 348–352)*
1. **Describe** the three categories of products that
   make up GDP.
2. **List** five characteristics of GDP.
3. **Explain** why GDP is an important concept.

SECTION 2 *(pages 354–359)*
4. **Explain** why GDP is not the correct measure of
   total income.
5. **Identify** the five measures of the nation's
   income.

6. **Describe** the three main sectors that make up
   the United States economy.
7. **Describe** the output-expenditure model.

SECTION 3 *(pages 361–364)*
8. **Explain** why price indices are used to measure
   the economy.
9. **Identify** three of the major price indices the federal government calculates.
10. **Explain** how the government uses the implicit
    GDP price deflator to convert nominal GDP to
    real GDP.

Critical Thinking

1. **Predicting Consequences** Suppose that politicians wanted to examine the growth of real output over the last 10 years. What conclusions
   would they reach if they used GDP measured in
   current dollars? How would these conclusions
   be different if they examined GDP measured in
   real dollars?
2. **Expressing Problems Clearly** Write a paragraph
   defending the use of GDP to an individual who
   argues that life should be measured by more
   than GDP. Be certain to address the issue of quality of life in your paragraph.

Applying Economic Concepts

1. **Gross Domestic Product** Defend or refute the
   use of the Measure of Economic Welfare (MEW),
   rather than GDP, to measure the economy's
   overall well-being.
2. **Disposable Personal Income** Some economists
   believe that disposable personal income is
   almost as important a measure of economic performance as GDP. What do you think? Provide
   reasons for your answer.

Reviewing the Facts

1. goods, tangible products; services, products of a
   nonphysical nature; structures, housing, apartment
   buildings, and commercial buildings

2. reporting delays, composition of output, quality of
   life, exclusion of nonmarket transactions, illegal
   activities

3. It is a reliable measure of the country's economic
   performance and health.

4. It includes foreign-owned goods produced in
   the U.S. and excludes income earned by U.S.-
   owned resources employed outside the
   national boundaries.

5. GNP, net national product, national income, personal income, disposable personal income

6. consumer sector, households in the U.S.; investment sector, business organizations; government
   sector, local, state, and federal governments

Reinforcing Skills

USING E-MAIL

In the skill on page 360, you learned the basics of electronic mail, or E-mail. Read the following information to learn more about E-mail, then follow the instructions below.

PARTS OF A MESSAGE

Most messages include a heading, a body, and a signature. The heading includes the captions *To, From, Date,* and *Subject*—similar to a memo. A **CC notation** in the **CC box** is used when you want to send a copy of your message to one or more persons. The headings *From* and *Date* are usually filled in automatically and may not appear on the screen where you compose the message.

The body is the text of your message. You should keep your E-mail messages short. An E-mail message should be no longer than 25 lines—the number of lines that will fit on one screen.

The signature, which usually includes your name and perhaps an address, is at the end of the body. It may be added by the software when the message is sent or perhaps by clicking a button.

---

1. Connect to your Internet service provider.
2. Start the E-mail software.
3. Compose and send an E-mail message to one of your U.S. senators or representatives, requesting information about improving technology in America's classrooms. The front pages of your phone book may have listings for government officials that include an E-mail address.
4. Print a copy of your E-mail message and share it with the rest of the class.

Individual Activity

Construct a "high school price index." Survey students to see how they spend their money, and then identify the largest categories of expenditures.

Identify several specific items in each category, and locations where the items can be purchased in your community. Price the items on a per week basis for one month. Compare your price index with those of the rest of the class.

Cooperative Learning Activity

Working in groups of four, have each member choose one of the four measures of the nation's total income besides GNP. Each person is responsible for answering the following questions about its measure: (a) What does your measure show? (b) What is added or subtracted to find the measure? (c) To whom would this measure be most valuable? (d) Why? Have each member present his or her conclusions to the group. Then have each group compare their conclusions.

Technology Activity
Developing a Multimedia Presentation

In the **Journal Writing** activity on page 347, you were asked to clip and log newspaper articles under one of the following headings: consumer expenditures, business expenditures, government expenditures, and exports or imports. Now imagine that you must teach a younger class the differences among the four sectors that make up our economy. Using a camcorder, videotape examples of consumer expenditures, government expenditures, business or investment expenditures, and foreign expenditures (refer to pages 358-359 for examples). Explain on camera how all four sectors work together. Show your video to the class.

CHAPTER 14: *Gross Domestic Product* **367**

Applying Economic Concepts

1. Some students will suggest that such factors as time lost in traffic jams or the cost of pollution are part of the economic picture and, as such, should be reflected in GDP. Others will point out that GDP measures economic performance, one gauge of quality of life.

2. Some students will point out that one advantage of disposable personal income is that it shows the income the consumer sector has to spend. Others will mention that it has a disadvantage in that it does not take into account the income of other sectors of the economy.

Reinforcing Skills

Have the students share the E-mail messages they composed.

BONUS TEST QUESTION

Write *yes* for items that would be included in the GDP, *no* for those that would not.

1. Automobiles produced by a Japanese-owned factory in Tennessee. *(yes, final product produced in U.S.)*

2. A new football stadium. *(yes, final product)*

3. Leather bought by shoe factory. *(no, intermediate product)*

---

7. a macroeconomic model used to show aggregate demand by four sectors of the economy, GDP = C + I + G + F

8. to reduce the distortions of inflation

9. consumer price index, producer price index, implicit GDP price deflator

10. Nominal GDP is divided by the implicit GDP price deflator and then multiplied by 100.

Critical Thinking

1. By looking at current GDP, they would assume that GDP had shown marked growth. Using real GDP, they would see that while GDP had grown, the rise had not been so striking.

2. Some students might note that GDP is a reliable measure of economic performance, which is closely related to a country's standard of living—one measure of quality of life.

CHAPTER 15 PLANNING GUIDE

CHAPTER ORGANIZER

Daily Objectives	Reproducible Resources	Multimedia Resources
Section 1 **Population** 1. **Explain** how population is estimated in the United States. 2. **Describe** the factors affecting future population growth.	• Reproducible Lesson Plan 15-1 • Guided Reading Activity 15-1 • Cooperative Learning Activity 3 • Consumer Application Activity 6 • Math Practice for Economics 29 • Free Enterprise Activity 14 • Primary and Secondary Source Reading 3 • Performance Assessment Activity 23 • Reinforcing Economic Skill 15 • Section Quiz 15-1*	• Focus Activity Transparency 80 • Vocabulary PuzzleMaker • Chapter Challenger Interactive Review Software • Testmaker • MindJogger Videoquiz
Section 2 **Economic Growth** 1. **Describe** how economists measure the growth of the United States economy. 2. **Explain** the importance of economic growth. 3. **Outline** the factors of economic growth. 4. **Relate** productivity to economic growth.	• Reproducible Lesson Plan 15-2 • Guided Reading Activity 15-2 • Section Quiz 15-2*	• Focus Activity Transparency 81 • Economic Concepts Transparencies 3, 19* • Vocabulary PuzzleMaker • Chapter Challenger Interactive Review Software • Testmaker • NBR's Economics in Action Video Program
Section 3 **Business Cycles and Fluctuations** 1. **Explain** the phases of the business cycle. 2. **Trace** the history of business cycles in the United States. 3. **Identify** five causes of business cycles.	• Reproducible Lesson Plan 15-3 • Guided Reading Activity 15-3 • Section Quiz 15-3*	• Focus Activity Transparency 56 • Vocabulary PuzzleMaker • Chapter Challenger Interactive Review Software • Testmaker • NBR's Economics in Action Video Program
Chapter Review and Evaluation	• Enrichment Activity 15 • Reteaching Activity 15* • Economic Vocabulary Activity 15* • Chapter 15 Test, Forms A and B	• Chapter Digests Audiocassette Activities and Tests* • Testmaker • MindJogger Videoquiz

Also available in Spanish

 Blackline Master   Transparency   CD-ROM   Software   Videodisc   Audiocassette

⏱ OUT OF TIME? Assign the Chapter 15 Digest Audiocassette and the corresponding Chapter Digest activities and tests.

National Council on Economic Education

THE **Economics** America AND **Economics** International PROGRAMS

VOLUNTARY NATIONAL CONTENT STANDARDS IN ECONOMICS
Emphasized in Chapter 15

Content Standard 15 *Students will understand that:*
Investment in factories, machinery, new technology, and the health, education, and training of people can raise future standards of living.

Content Standard 18 *Students will understand that:*
A nation's overall levels of income, employment, and prices are determined by the interaction of spending and production decisions made by all households, firms, government agencies, and others in the economy.

Economics America *Resources Available From NCEE*

- *Capstone: The Nation's High School Economics Course*
- *Economics and the Environment*
- *Focus: High School Economics*
- *Geography: Focus on Economics*
- *MCG: International Trade*
- *United States History: Eyes on the Economy, Vol. II*
- *World History: Focus on Economics*

To order these materials, or to contact your state Council on Economic Education about workshops and programs, call 1-800-338-1192 or visit http://www.nationalcouncil.org.

PERFORMANCE ASSESSMENT

The following chapter projects may be assigned at the beginning of the chapter and used for performance assessment.

Multicultural Heritage Refer students to Figure 15.3 on page 374. Direct them to research the latest figures for the racial and ethnic makeup of the United States, their state, their county, their school district, and their city, town, or village using the same categories as those in Figure 15.3. Mention that a good source of national and state information is the current edition of the *Statistical Abstract of the United States.* Suggest that students consult county and community administrative offices for local population data. Instruct students to use the information they gather to construct a bar graph showing the percentages of population by race and ethnic origin for the United States, the state, the county, the community, and the school district. Call on students to present their graphs. Then discuss the differences in racial and ethnic makeup of the various populations shown in the graph.

Cooperative Learning Select five of the major concepts discussed in the chapter, such as the population pyramid, per capita GDP growth vs. GDP growth, standard of living, productivity, the Great Depression, and the business cycle. Then organize the class into five groups and assign one of the selected concepts to each group. Explain that groups are to study their assigned concept in depth and then teach it to the rest of the class using a creative teaching presentation, such as a mural, a drama, or a bulletin board display. Make certain that various tasks involved in the presentation—research, writing, artwork, role play, and so on—are shared among group members. Have groups make their teaching presentations to the rest of the class.

ADDITIONAL RESOURCES

Readings for the Student

Hildebrand, George. *Business Cycle Indicators and Measures: A Complete Guide to Interpreting the Key Economic Indicators.* Chicago, IL: Probus Publishing Company, 1992. Introduces and discusses important indicators of economic activity.

Schraff, Anne E. *The Great Depression and the New Deal.* New York: Franklin Watts, 1990. Early chapters recount the prosperity of the 1920s, the crash of 1929, and the Great Depression.

Readings for the Teacher

American Demographics. Ithaca, NY: American Demographics, Inc., published monthly. Periodical that includes articles about population and economic trends.

Galbraith, John Kenneth. *The Great Crash: 1929.* Boston: Houghton Mifflin, 1988. Details the stock market crash and its causes and consequences.

Multimedia

Economics U$A: U.S. Economic Growth/Booms & Busts. The Annenberg/CPB Collection, 1992. 19 Gregory Drive, South Burlington, VT 05403. Color video, 60 mins. Describes the history of U.S. economic growth.

What Is a Recession? American School Publishers/Social Studies School Service, 10200 Jefferson Boulevard, P.O. Box 802, Culver City, CA 90232–0802. Color video, 19 mins. Compares America's most recent recession with previous economic downturns.

Chapter Overview

This chapter explores population characteristics and changes, economic growth, and the business cycle. **Section 1** analyzes the U.S. population, how it is counted, and population trends and projections. **Section 2** discusses economic growth, its measurement, its importance, and how it relates to productivity. **Section 3** explains the business cycle and its history and causes.

GLENCOE
TECHNOLOGY

VIDEODISC
MindJogger Videoquiz

Use MindJogger to preview the Chapter 15 content.

 Chapter 15
Disc 2, Side B

Also available in VHS.

*inter*NET
CONNECTION

Resources for Chapter 15 on the World Wide Web*

National Council on Economic Education
http://www.nationalcouncil.org/

Business Cycle Indicators
http://www.globalexposure.com/

FedWorld Information Network
http://www.fedworld.gov/

Fedstats
http://www.fedstats.gov/

*Sites subject to change.

The construction of new houses is perceived as a sign of economic growth.

 Extra Credit Project

Have students write an illustrated report on population changes, economic growth, and business fluctuations in their community over the last 20 years. Call on volunteers to present their reports to the class.

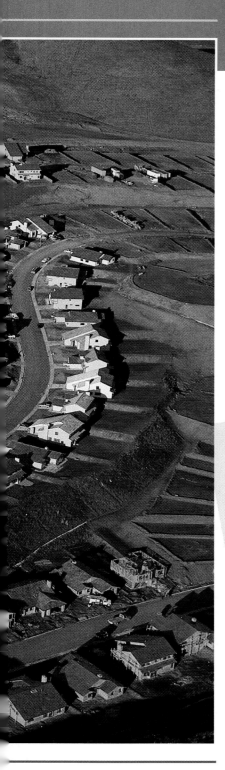

CHAPTER 15

Population, Economic Growth, and Business Cycles

SECTION 1
Population

SECTION 2
Economic Growth

SECTION 3
Business Cycles and Fluctuations

CHAPTER PREVIEW

People to Know

• Walter E. Williams
• Systems Analyst

Applying Economic Concepts to Your Life

Economic Growth Do you want to get ahead in the world? Do you want a quality education, a good job, and all the so-called comforts of life? Do you think other people want the same things? The nation's *economic growth* is everyone's key to a better future. A growing economy means an expanding economy, one that continues to provide more people with what they want or need.

> ### Journal Writing
> For one week, write in your journal all the goods and services your local government provides that you use and that you observe others using.

Connecting to Past Learning

Remind students that the four factors of production were introduced in Chapter 1 and have been mentioned in discussions in several other chapters. Point out that in this chapter, the factors of production are discussed in relation to economic growth. Call on volunteers to identify the four factors, and note their responses on the chalkboard. Then have students indicate how each factor might contribute to economic growth. Suggest that students review and adjust their ideas as they read the chapter.

Applying Economics

Draw two circles on the chalkboard, making one circle twice as large as the other, and tell students these are two pies. Divide each pie into eight equal slices. Ask students from which pie they would rather have a slice. Then write the word *growth* on the chalkboard and explain that economic growth enables people to have bigger slices of the country's "economic pie."

 PERFORMANCE ASSESSMENT

Refer to page **368B** for a Performance Assessment activity for this chapter. Also see the **Performance Assessment Activities** booklet for additional suggestions.

Economic Portfolio

Before students begin to compile their **Journal Writing** entries, have them consider how a growing economy might help to improve or expand the public sector.

Key to Ability Levels — **Teaching strategies have been coded for varying learning styles and abilities:**
L1 - Basic (activities for all students) **L2 - Average** (activities for average to above-average students)
L3 - Challenging (activities for above-average students) **LEP - Limited English Proficiency**

 VISUAL INSTRUCTION

Have students suggest how new housing indicates economic growth. (*New structures will cause a growth in GDP, a reliable measure of economic growth.*)

369

Population

FOCUS

Section Objectives

1. Explain how population is estimated in the United States.

2. Describe the factors affecting future population growth.

Bellringer

 Prior to taking roll at the beginning of the class period, display Focus Activity Transparency 80 on the overhead projector and assign the accompanying Student Activity 80.

Motivational Activity

Discuss students' responses to the activity sheet that accompanies Focus Activity Transparency 80.

Preteaching Vocabulary

Call on students to read aloud the definitions of this section's terms and concepts from the Glossary. Then call on volunteers to use each term in a sentence. **LEP**

Use the **Vocabulary PuzzleMaker** to create crossword and word search puzzles.

DID YOU KNOW

The term *demography*, which means "the study of human populations," is derived from the Greek word *demos*, meaning "people."

Section Preview

Objectives

After studying this section, you will be able to:

1. **Explain** how population is estimated in the United States.

2. **Describe** the factors affecting future population growth.

Key Terms

census, urban population, rural population, center of population, demographer, fertility rate, life expectancy, net immigration, baby boom, population pyramid, dependency ratio

Applying Economic Concepts

Urban vs. Rural You have probably heard the terms *urban* and *rural* so often that you are unaware that they are economic terms. They are, and the term that fits you depends on where you live. If you live in a town with a population of more than 2,500, you are considered an urban resident. If your community's population is less than 2,500, you are a rural resident.

The size and growth of its population is important to every society. Population means people, and people provide labor. Labor, in turn, provides for people's needs and wants.

The rate at which population grows influences economic growth. If a nation's population grows too fast, per capita output may fall. The country could end up with more mouths than it can feed. Conversely, if a nation's population grows too slowly, there may not be enough workers to sustain economic growth.

The United States Population

The Constitution of the United States requires the government to periodically take a **census**, an official count of all people, including their place of residence. Because the official census occurs every 10 years, it is called the *decennial census*. The nation's founders initiated the decennial census to apportion the number of representatives each state elects to Congress. **1**

Counting the Population

The federal government conducted the first census in 1790. Throughout the 1800s, temporary agencies, created each decade, conducted the counts. In 1902 Congress permanently established the Bureau of the

Census. Today, the Bureau works year-round, conducting monthly surveys relating to the size and other characteristics of the population.

When the Bureau of the Census conducts the decennial census, it uses the household as its primary survey unit. About 5 in every 6 households receives a "short form," which takes just a few minutes to fill out. The remaining households receive a "long form," which includes more questions and serves to generate a more detailed profile of the population. Bureau employees use different methods to count special groups, such as homeless persons, who do not normally conform to the household survey unit.

The Census Bureau tabulates and presents its data in a number of ways. One classification denotes the size of the **urban population**. Urban residents are generally those living in incorporated villages or towns with 2,500 or more inhabitants. The contrasting **rural population** makes up the remainder of the total population, including those persons who live in sparsely populated areas along the fringes of cities. **2**

Historical Growth

The population of the United States has grown considerably since colonial times. The rate of growth, however, has steadily declined. Between 1790 and 1860, the population grew at a compound rate of 3.02

Classroom Resources for SECTION 1

- Reproducible Lesson Plan 15-1
- Guided Reading Activity 15-1
- Cooperative Learning Activity 3
- Consumer Application Activity 6
- Math Practice for Economics 29
- Free Enterprise Activity 14
- Primary and Secondary Source Reading 3
- Performance Assessment Activity 23

- Reinforcing Economic Skill 15
- Section Quiz 15-1
- Spanish Section Quiz 15-1
- Focus Activity Transparency 80
- Testmaker
- Vocabulary PuzzleMaker
- Chapter Challenger Interactive Review Software
- MindJogger Videoquiz

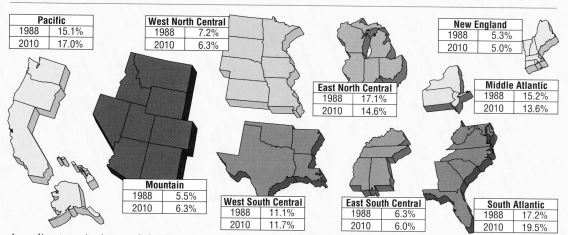

Figure 15.1
Projected Distribution of Population by Region, 1988 to 2010

Pacific	
1988	15.1%
2010	17.0%

West North Central	
1988	7.2%
2010	6.3%

New England	
1988	5.3%
2010	5.0%

East North Central	
1988	17.1%
2010	14.6%

Middle Atlantic	
1988	15.2%
2010	13.6%

Mountain	
1988	5.5%
2010	6.3%

West South Central	
1988	11.1%
2010	11.7%

East South Central	
1988	6.3%
2010	6.0%

South Atlantic	
1988	17.2%
2010	19.5%

According to projections made by the Bureau of the Census, population as a proportion of the overall population is expected to grow in the South Atlantic, West South Central, Mountain, and Pacific regions of the country. **How will this affect the center of population over the next 15 years?**

Source: *Projections of the Population of States by Age, Sex, and Race: 1988 to 2010,* Bureau of the Census

percent a year. From the beginning of the Civil War until 1900, the average fell to 2.23 percent. From 1900 to the beginning of World War II, the rate dropped to 1.38 percent. It declined slowly but steadily after that, and by 1994 the rate of population growth had fallen to below 1 percent—where it remains today.

Historically, the census also shows a steady trend toward smaller households. During colonial times, household size averaged 5.8 people. By 1960 the average had fallen to 3.33 and then to about 2.65 people today. The figures reflect a worldwide trend toward smaller families in industrial countries where couples often view children as a financial liability. The figures also show that more individuals are living alone today than ever before.

Regional Change

Census reports over the years have indicated significant changes in where people live. **Figure 15.1** shows the expected shifts in population distribution. According to the map, the growth of population in the West and South will offset the loss of population in the Northeast and Central Plains regions.

Checking Understanding	**Applying Economic Concepts**
1. Why does the federal government conduct a census every 10 years? 2. What is the difference between an urban population and a rural population?	**Population** How many siblings do you have? How many siblings do your parents have? Your grandparents? Poll adults you know to find out their reasons for limiting their number of children.

TEACH

Guided Practice

L2 Identifying Trends Have students review the section to identify the population trends that are mentioned. Then instruct students to write a brief essay that discusses how these trends will affect their lives in the future.

Cooperative Learning Assign Cooperative Learning Activity 3.

Independent Practice

Guided Reading Assign Guided Reading Activity for Section 1. **LEP**

L1 Writing a Letter Have students write a letter to the Bureau of the Census requesting information on how census information is gathered and analyzed. **LEP**

VISUAL INSTRUCTION

Ask: What share of the total population is your region projected to have in 2010? *(Answers will vary.)*

Answer to Caption:
It will move southward and westward.

QUICK CHECK
ANSWERS

1. to apportion the number of representatives each state elects to Congress
2. urban: people living in incorporated villages or towns of more than 2,500 inhabitants; rural: remainder of total population

---

Meeting Special Needs

Inefficient Readers Scanning a passage before reading can help students develop a time frame for the events or ideas that are presented. Have students scan the subsection "Historical Growth" for time markers such as the words "Between 1790 and 1860." Note that many paragraphs contain these markers. Other examples are: "From the beginning of the Civil War . . ."; "From 1900 . . ."; and "During colonial times. . . ."

371

Figure 15.2
The Center of Population

The center of population is the point where the country would balance if the map were flat and every American weighed the same. The center has moved steadily to the west and south following the growth of population since the first census was conducted in 1790. **Where was the center of population for the 1990 census?**

Source: *1993 Statistical Abstract of the United States.*

Another indicator of distribution shifts is the **center of population**—the point where the country would balance if it could be laid flat and all the people weighed the same. In 1790 the center was 23 miles east of Baltimore, Maryland. Since then, it has moved farther west, as **Figure 15.2** illustrates. By the year of the 1990 decennial census, the center of population had reached a point about 9.7 miles southeast of Steelville, Missouri.

Projected Population Trends

Population trends interest many groups of people. Politicians, for example, closely watch distribution shifts to see how voting patterns may change. Community leaders are interested because increases or decreases in local population impact services such as sanitation, education, crime prevention, and fire protection. Businesses use census data to help determine new plant locations, products and services, and sales territories. **1**

Factors Affecting Growth

In November 1992, the Bureau of the Census released a report called *Population Projections of the United States by Age, Sex, Race, and Hispanic Origin: 1992 to 2050.* The report offered three population growth scenarios—high, middle, and low—that could take place in the United States between 1990 and 2050.

The three scenarios are estimates only. They are based on factors developed by **demographers**—people who study growth, density, and other characteristics of population. According to demographers, the three most important factors affecting population growth are fertility, life expectancy, and net immigration levels. **2**

The first factor, the **fertility rate**, is the number of births that 1,000 women are expected to undergo in their lifetime. A fertility rate of 2,110, for example, translates to 2.11 births per woman. For its middle growth projection, the one most likely to occur, the Bureau of the Census assumed a fertility rate of 2,119 for the United States. That rate is barely above the replacement rate—the rate at which the number of births in a population just offsets the number of deaths.

The second factor, **life expectancy**, is the average remaining life span of people who reach a given age. The Bureau of the Census predicts that life expectancy at birth will go from 75.8 years to 82.1 years by 2050.

The third major factor, **net immigration**, considers the net change in population caused by people moving into and out of the country. The Bureau's report assumes a constant net immigration of about 880,000 per year (1,040,000 immigrants and 160,000 emigrants). It also takes into account changes in the immigration laws made in 1991 and certain other factors, such as undocumented immigration from Mexico and the Caribbean.

Considering the three factors above, and assuming that the Bureau's middle-growth projection holds true, the rate of population growth in the United

---

$ Free Enterprise Activity $

Census information can be valuable to the small, private businesses that are so important to the growth and success of our free enterprise economy. Ask students to choose a particular small business, such as a restaurant. Then have students consult a *Statistical Abstract of the United States* or census data publications and look for trends in their region. Suggest that they do this by looking for answers to the following: Is population increasing? Is the number of businesses increasing? Is disposable personal income increasing? Is the volume of sales increasing? Have students write a paragraph, based on the data they collect, explaining why they would or would not advise a friend to enter their selected business.

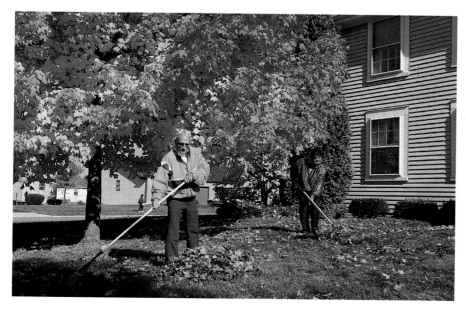

Population Projections
Life expectancy at birth is projected to be 82.1 years in the United States by the year 2050. **What is the projected United States population by 2050?**

States will continue to decline. The growth rate is likely to hold at .90 percent from 1995 to 2000. It will decline to .82 percent between 2000 and 2005, and then continue to decrease until it reaches .49 percent by 2050. At that time, the resident United States population should total about 380 million people.

Projections by Age and Sex

In making its projections, the Bureau of the Census assumed that the aging of the baby boom generation will drive many characteristics of the population. People born during the **baby boom**, the high birthrate years from 1946 to 1964, make up a sizeable portion of the population. As shown in **Figure 15.4** on page 375, people born during the baby boom generation create a pronounced bulge in the **population pyramid**, a type of bar graph that shows the breakdown of population by age and sex.

In the population pyramid for 1990, the baby boomers fall into the age bracket beginning at 25 and ending at 44. As years pass, more births add to the bottom of the pyramid and shift earlier groups upward into higher age brackets. In the population pyramid for the year 2000 on page 391, the baby boomers have aged 10 years and have moved into the 35–54 bracket.

Eventually, the baby boomers will reach their retirement years and want to collect pensions, Social Security, medicare, and medicaid benefits. Because most of these payments are transfer payments, they will place a heavy burden on the younger and

---

QUICK CHECK

Checking Understanding

1. Why are people interested in population trends?
2. What are the most important factors affecting population growth, according to demographers?

Applying Economic Concepts

☑ **Baby Boom** Baby boomers fueled the economy. During the 1950s, school enrollments increased by 13 million, the sale of musical instruments reached $149 million a year, the number of Girl Scouts and Brownies doubled, and the number of Little Leagues reached nearly 6,000.

CHAPTER 15: *Population, Economic Growth, and Business Cycles* **373**

Extending the Content

The Census and Economic Data In addition to counting the number of people, identifying population trends, and making projections, the Bureau of the Census also collects a significant amount of data that is of interest to private businesses. For example, the Census Bureau gathers information on farms, wholesale businesses, service industries, transportation, manufacturing, construction, and retailing. One of the many Bureau of the Census publications is called *Retail Trade: United States*.

Evaluate

 Assign the Section 1 Quiz in the TCR or use the *Economics: Principles and Practices* Testmaker to create a customized quiz. Spanish Section Quizzes also are available in the Spanish Resources Binder.

Reteach

Encourage students to imagine they are to give a 10–minute lecture on the U.S. population to a class of junior-high students. Have students draw up an outline for their lecture.

Enrich

Invite an official from state or local government to visit the class and talk about how population projections affect government plans concerning raising revenue and allocating expenditures.

CLOSE

Have students identify the population trend that they think will have the greatest impact on the nation and on their community in the next 25 years. Ask students to explain their choices.

VISUAL INSTRUCTION

Mention that the graph indicates that our nation will become more culturally diversified as the 21st century progresses.

Answer to Caption:

Asians and Hispanics; Whites

Figure 15.3

Projected Change in U.S. Population by Race and Ethnic Origin, 1990–2050

According to projections made by the United States Bureau of the Census, the distribution of population by race will change dramatically by the middle of the next century. **Which ethnic components of the population are expected to make the largest gains? The largest losses?**

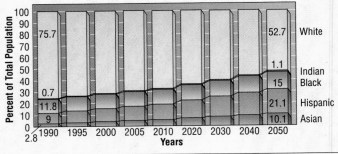

Source: *Population Projections in the United States, by Age, Sex, Race and Hispanic Origin: 1992–2050*, U.S. Bureau of the Census.

relatively smaller working population. The burden becomes evident with changes in the **dependency ratio**—a ratio based on the number of children and elderly for every 100 persons in the working-age bracket of 18 through 64. The dependency ratio in 1998 stood at 63.9. According to Census Bureau projections, it will rise to 67.5 by 2020, to 77.5 in 2030, and to 78.0 by the year 2040.

Notice what the population pyramids indicate about gender. Compare the left sides of the pyramids with the right. The right sides in both pyramids are larger in the older age brackets, showing that women tend to outlive men. Separate population pyramids can also be created for any racial or ethnic group.

Projections by Race and Ethnic Origin

Figure 15.3 shows some projections that the Bureau of the Census makes according to race and ethnic origins of the population. In 1990 whites were the largest component in the total population. The numbers of African Americans, Hispanic Americans, Asian Americans, and Native Americans followed in that order.

Differences in fertility rates, life expectancies, and immigration rates will change racial statistics dramatically in the future. By 2050, the Asian component of the population will increase nearly 5 times, and the Hispanic component will almost double. The number of African Americans will also increase. Whites will retain a bare majority of 52.7 percent.

SECTION 1 REVIEW

Reviewing Terms and Facts

1. **Define** census, urban population, rural population, center of population, demographer, fertility rate, life expectancy, net immigration, baby boom, population pyramid, dependency ratio.

2. **Describe** the recent changes in population growth on a regional basis.

3. **List** the three most important factors that determine future population growth.

Critical Thinking

4. **Predicting Consequences** At some point, the baby boomers will reach their retirement years. How will this development affect your generation? How do you think the baby boomers will feel about the same development?

Applying Economic Concepts

5. **Urban vs. Rural** What could happen to your community that might cause it to be classified as rural instead of urban, or urban instead of rural?

Answers to SECTION 1 REVIEW

1. All vocabulary words are defined in the Glossary.

2. Population growth has increased in the West and South but decreased in the Northeast, Middle Atlantic, and Central Plains regions.

3. fertility, life expectancy, net immigration

4. Answers will vary. Students may point out that the dependency ratio will rise, which will place a burden on the younger generation. The retired generation may be worried that those in the workforce cannot help support the retired; many have already planned for their retirement, however.

5. Answers will vary. Students may list an increase or decrease in population growth; increased or decreased economic development that would affect population; natural disasters or a discovery of resources that would cause people to leave or transfer there.

Interpreting Population Pyramids

Demographers, economists, government officials, businesspeople, and others use population pyramids to study human populations. Population pyramids help demographers see at a glance whether the population of an area is mostly old or young, and whether it is mostly male or female. In addition, it is possible to tell if a change in the growth rate of an area's population is imminent. Such information can help businesspeople and government officials plan for the future. An increase in the percentage of very young children, for example, will probably create a need for more schools.

Explanation

A population pyramid is a type of bar graph that shows how the population of an area, such as a country or a city, is divided by age and by sex.

Look at the pyramid on this page. Note that each bar stands for a certain age group, with the youngest age group at the bottom. A line divides each bar to show the percentage of males and females in each age group. Male percentages are shown on the left side of the graph, female percentages on the right side.

Use the following steps to interpret population pyramids.

- Read the title of the population pyramid to see what area is being analyzed.
- Read the percentages along the horizontal axis.
- Examine the ages along the vertical axis.
- Compare the bars for each age group and sex.

Practice

Study the population pyramid on this page. Then answer the following questions.

1. What does the population pyramid show?
2. Which age group is largest for males? For females?
3. Which age group is smallest for males? For females?
4. Which gender has a larger percentage of people that are 70 years old and over?
5. What percentage of the population is in the 30-to-40 age groups?
6. What percentage of the population is in your age group?

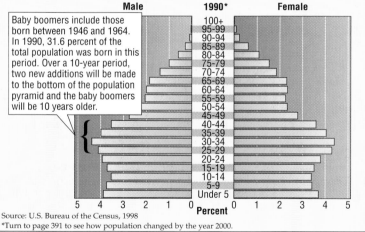

Figure 15.4
Distribution of the U.S. Population by Age and Sex, 1990

Baby boomers include those born between 1946 and 1964. In 1990, 31.6 percent of the total population was born in this period. Over a 10-year period, two new additions will be made to the bottom of the population pyramid and the baby boomers will be 10 years older.

Male | 1990* | Female

Under 5, 5-9, 10-14, 15-19, 20-24, 25-29, 30-34, 35-39, 40-44, 45-49, 50-54, 55-59, 60-64, 65-69, 70-74, 75-79, 80-84, 85-89, 90-94, 95-99, 100+

Percent: 5 4 3 2 1 0 / 0 1 2 3 4 5

Source: U.S. Bureau of the Census, 1998
*Turn to page 391 to see how population changed by the year 2000.

Additional Practice

For further practice in interpreting population pyramids, complete the Reinforcing Skills exercise in the Chapter 15 Review on page 390.

Answers to SKILL

1. the percentage of males and females in each age group for the year 1990
2. 30–34 for both
3. Students may answer 100+ for both or 95–99 for both.
4. female
5. about 16.8 percent
6. a little more than 7.2 percent in the 15–19 age group

SECTION 2
Economic Growth

FOCUS

Section Objectives

1. Describe how economists measure the growth of the United States economy.

2. Explain the importance of economic growth.

3. Outline the factors of economic growth.

4. Relate productivity to economic growth.

Bellringer

Prior to taking roll at the beginning of the class period, display Focus Activity Transparency 81 on the overhead projector and assign the accompanying Student Activity 81.

Motivational Activity

Discuss students' responses to the activity sheet that accompanies Focus Activity Transparency 81.

Preteaching Vocabulary

Have students write questions for which the key terms are answers. Use these questions to quiz students on their understanding of the key terms. **LEP**

Use the **Vocabulary PuzzleMaker** to create crossword and word search puzzles.

SECTION 2
Economic Growth

Section Preview

Objectives

After studying this section, you will be able to:

1. **Describe** how economists measure the growth of the United States economy.

2. **Explain** the importance of economic growth.

3. **Outline** the factors of economic growth.

4. **Relate** productivity to economic growth.

Key Terms

real GDP per capita, growth triangle, standard of living, tax base, renewable resources, capital-to-labor ratio, labor productivity

Applying Economic Concepts

Standard of Living Do your worldly possessions make your life easier? Would more possessions make you even more comfortable? When you think about such questions, you are thinking about your *standard of living*. The standard of living measures only the material side of your life, but it will probably always be important to you.

---

conomic growth, one of the seven major goals of the United States economy, has the potential for improving everyone's lot in life. *Everyone* includes not only every American, but also people living in other countries.

Economic Growth in the United States

In order to see the potential of economic growth, we need to know how to measure it. Two measures are equally important. Both relate to topics already covered in earlier chapters.

Measuring Growth

When we measure economic growth in the short term—for a period of one to five years—real GDP is a fairly satisfactory gauge. Changes in real GDP on a quarterly or annual basis are the statistics we hear about most often in the news.

When it comes to the long run, however, real GDP does not tell the whole story. Because population also grows, **real GDP per capita**—the dollar amount of real GDP produced for every person in the

economy—is a better measure. Most economists feel that it is the single most important measure of long-term growth.

Dividing the real GDP by the population yields the real GDP per capita figure. If the population grows faster than real GDP, the average amount of output produced for each person in the economy falls. If the population grows more slowly than real GDP, there will be more goods and services available for everyone.

The Historical Record

Figure 15.5 compares real GDP with real GDP per capita. In 1997, for example, real GDP in terms of constant dollars was about $7.2 trillion. Because the population in that year was nearly 268 million, the total output for each man, woman, and child in the country amounted to about $26,700 in constant dollars.

Rates of growth become evident in a **growth triangle**—a table that traces annual rates of growth for various periods of time. **Figure 15.6** shows that there was almost no growth in real GDP per capita between 1929 and 1940. From 1940 to 1970, the annual rate was 2.9 percent, and from 1970 to 1980, it fell to 2.0 percent. Between 1980 and 1990, the annual rate of growth fell to 1.9 percent and then to 1.2 percent in the 1990s, one of the lowest rates ever.

Because of low numbers like those above, economists and other experts realize that the United States could be doing better. Recent growth rates are not cause for alarm, but they are cause for concern. As a result, many federal economic policies have been proposed to stimulate long-term economic growth. Many more such policies will undoubtedly be proposed in the future.

Importance of Economic Growth

Economic growth benefits a country in many ways. It raises the standard of living, eases the burden of government, and helps solve domestic problems. It can also boost the economies of foreign trade partners.

Standard of Living

A major feature of a free enterprise economy is its ability to increase real per capita output enough to allow people to raise their standard of living. The **standard** **of living** means the quality of life based on the possession of necessities and luxuries that make life easier. In the end, a free enterprise system also increases people's free time, allowing them to devote more attention to families, hobbies, and recreational activities.

Government Spending

Economic growth benefits government at all levels by enlarging the **tax base**—the incomes and properties that may be taxed. Enlarged tax bases increase government revenues, which can add to the number and quality of public services.

Domestic Problems

Like most countries of the world, the United States faces varying degrees of poverty, inadequate medical care, inequality of opportunity, and economic insecurity. Most of these problems stem from economic need. Economic growth creates more jobs and income for more people, thus helping to alleviate social ills at their source.

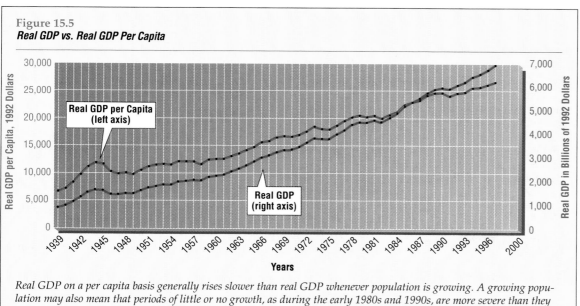

Figure 15.5
Real GDP vs. Real GDP Per Capita

Real GDP per Capita (left axis)

Real GDP (right axis)

Years

Real GDP on a per capita basis generally rises slower than real GDP whenever population is growing. A growing population may also mean that periods of little or no growth, as during the early 1980s and 1990s, are more severe than they appear when measured in terms of real GDP. **How do real GDP and real GDP per capita differ?**

Source: *Economic Report of the President,* various years.

TEACH

Guided Practice

L1 Brainstorming Organize students into several groups. Have groups brainstorm why economic growth is important to a high school student. Have a representative from each group share the results of their brainstorming session. List new reasons on the chalkboard as they are mentioned. Have students use the list to identify some of the signs of economic growth in their community.

GLENCOE
TECHNOLOGY

NIGHTLY BUSINESS REPORT

Economics in Action

Chapter 30
Disc 2, Side 2

Title: *Technological and Social Change and the Economy*

Subject: Impact of change on the American workforce

Ask: How have geographic and population changes affected the United States's economy? *(Many companies have moved to the West and South, taking workers with them.)*

 Also available in VHS.

VISUAL INSTRUCTION

Answer to Caption:
Real GDP is the dollar amount of final output for the whole economy; real GDP per capita is the dollar amount of real GDP produced for each person in the economy.

L2 Constructing a Chart On the chalkboard draw a chart with *Positive Aspects* and *Negative Aspects* as horizontal headings; and *Land, Capital, Labor,* and *Entrepreneurship* as vertical headings. Have students review the discussion on factors influencing economic growth on pages 378–380. Then ask students to offer negative and positive aspects in the use of each of the four factors of production and enter their suggestions under the appropriate column. Finally, have students choose the factor of production they believe has contributed most to economic growth in the U.S. and write a paragraph justifying their choices.

VISUAL INSTRUCTION

Have students note the five-year period that experienced the greatest rate of growth. *(1940–1945, 10.8%)*

Answer to Caption:

because if changes in population are not taken into account, changes in real GDP can be misstated

---

Figure 15.6
Annual Growth Rates of Real GDP Per Capita

If we do not take population growth into account, changes in real GDP can be overstated. To find the annual compound rate between two dates, find the beginning year on the horizontal axis and read up to the ending year row on the vertical axis. **Why is real GDP per capita considered the best measure of long-term economic growth?**

Most of the decline during the Great Depression took place between 1929 and 1933.

To find the annual rate of growth during the 1970s, start with 1970 on the horizontal axis and read up to the 1980 row.

On a per capita basis, the economy grew slower in the 1980s than in the 1970s—and even slower in the 1990s.

Ending Year	1929	1940	1945	1950	1955	1960	1965	1970	1975	1980	1985	1990
1929												
1933	-8.3%											
1939	0.2%											
1940	0.8%											
1945	3.7%	10.3%										
1950	2.4%	4.0%	-1.9%									
1955	2.4%	3.6%	0.4%	2.6%								
1960	2.1%	2.9%	0.5%	1.7%	0.8%							
1965	2.3%	3.0%	1.2%	2.3%	2.1%	3.4%						
1970	2.3%	2.9%	1.4%	2.3%	2.1%	2.8%	2.2%					
1975	2.2%	2.7%	1.5%	2.1%	2.0%	2.4%	1.9%	1.6%				
1980	2.3%	2.6%	1.6%	2.2%	2.1%	2.4%	2.1%	2.0%	2.5%			
1985	2.2%	2.6%	1.6%	2.2%	2.1%	2.3%	2.1%	2.0%	2.2%	2.0%		
1990	2.2%	2.5%	1.7%	2.1%	2.1%	2.3%	2.0%	2.0%	2.1%	1.9%	1.9%	
1997	2.1%	2.3%	1.6%	2.0%	1.9%	2.1%	1.9%	1.8%	1.8%	1.6%	1.5%	1.2%
Starting Year	1929	1940	1945	1950	1955	1960	1965	1970	1975	1980	1985	1990

Source: *Economic Report of the President,* various years.

Helping Other Nations

Economic growth increases American demand for foreign trade products. When the United States purchases the goods of other countries, it helps create jobs and income in those countries. New or increased income enables those people to buy goods and services from the United States, which may also create new jobs here. Consumers in the United States and the countries with which it trades benefit from an increased variety of competitively priced goods and services.

An increase in foreign trade also helps other countries allocate resources to their most efficient uses. When people in the United States purchase foreign products, productive resources in those countries are attracted to the growing export industries. The resources of many nations are put to their most productive use. In the long run, this stimulates world economic growth.

Global Role Model

A number of emerging nations have not yet formed their political and economic ideologies. These nations tend to copy the economic and political systems of established industrial nations. Many people in the United States believe that emerging nations will be best able to help themselves if they adopt a free market system.

In the past, countries of the free world and the communist world each tried to influence the economic development of emerging countries. The competition ended in recent years with the fall of communism in Europe and the breakup of the Soviet Union. Successful economic growth in the United States may help some of these nations select their economic system.

Factors Influencing Economic Growth

The ability of an economy to produce output determines its growth. A number of considerations are involved, including the quantity and quality of the factors of production—land, capital, labor, and entrepreneurship. The availability and organization of these resources determine how the economy grows.

Land

The United States abounds in most natural resources. Unlike such island nations as Great Britain and Japan, it need not depend heavily on international trade for raw materials. Although minerals such as chromium, cobalt, crude oil, and diamonds must be imported, the United States is reasonably self-sufficient in many natural resources.

378 UNIT 4: *Macroeconomics: Policies*

$ Free Enterprise Activity $

Organize students into several groups and have each group brainstorm ways to increase the productivity of the United States. Then have groups select the method for increasing productivity that they agree, by consensus, is the best. Have groups present and explain their methods. In a follow-up class discussion, have students consider which methods would require some kind of government intervention and what the possible consequences of that intervention might be.

Even so, the United States needs to conserve its natural resources. Many of the natural resources most Americans take for granted—clean air and water, forests, and fertile land—are dwindling rapidly. Only some of these resources are **renewable resources**, ones that can be replenished. Reseeding, for example, can restore some but not all forests for use in the foreseeable future. Trees such as California redwoods and giant firs require centuries to grow to full size. **1** ☑

Capital

An increasing supply of high-quality capital stock favors overall economic growth. Today the capital stock in the United States is growing at a rate of about $300 billion a year.

Economists sometimes speak of the **capital-to-labor ratio**, which they obtain by dividing total capital stock by the number of workers in the labor force. The ratio expresses the average amount of capital stock each worker uses in his or her job. In today's civilian workforce, the average worker uses well over $150,000 worth of capital equipment and capital structures. A high capital-to-labor ratio usually encourages economic growth.

Capital goods result from production. Consequently, it is possible to influence their creation. The key is saving, and the key to saving is the consumer. When people cut back on consumption in order to save and invest, they free up factors of production to generate new capital. **2**

Reducing consumption so that more can be saved is not always possible. In some countries, people are so poor and their incomes so low that they must spend everything they earn just to exist. In these countries, there is very little saving and, therefore, low investment in capital goods. Without capital goods, overall output remains low. People are

trapped by circumstances. They are too poor to save, but their incomes can rise only if they have savings to invest in capital goods.

Labor

In order for any country's economy to grow, it must have a skilled and growing labor force. In general, the size of the labor force is related to the size of the population. If the rate of population growth in the United States continues to decline as it has in the past, the labor force growth rate could also decline. Workers from other countries, however, could make up for a labor shortage if it occurs. New additions to the labor force, such as retirees and others who traditionally have stayed at home, could also help offset a labor shortage.

QUICK CHECK

Checking Understanding

1. What are renewable resources?
2. How does saving influence economic growth?

Applying Economic Concepts

 Environment In 1990 the Environmental Protection Agency reported that nearly 150 million Americans lived in areas where the air was considered unhealthy. After much debate, Congress amended the Clean Air Act in 1990, setting standards for factories, oil refiners, and automakers.

CHAPTER 15
—SECTION 2—

Independent Practice

📂 *Guided Reading* Assign Guided Reading Activity for Section 2. **LEP**

L3 *Researching* Have students study everyday life in another time period. Mention that *The Everyday Life in America* series, published by HarperCollins, is a useful source of such information. Then ask students to write an essay comparing life for young people in their selected time period to life for young people today. Suggest that they focus on the standard of living in the two time periods. Call on volunteers to read their essays to the class.

ASSESS

Check for Understanding

Assign Section 2 Review on page 381 as homework or an in-class activity.

🔘 Use **Chapter Challenger Interactive Review Software** to review Section 2.

QUICK CHECK | **ANSWERS**

1. resources that can be replenished
2. Saving frees up factors of production to generate new capital, which leads to overall economic growth.

Extending the Content

Zero GDP Growth Some economists are now expressing the view that economic growth is not necessary. This point of view, first presented in the 1970s when the U.S. was experiencing the effects of the OPEC oil embargo, suggested that the problem of oil shortages should be resolved by learning to live with less. Later, other economists pointed to problems associated with pollution and the deple-

tion of natural resources as reasons for discarding economic growth as a major economic goal. However, critics argue that this viewpoint—often referred to as *zero GDP growth*—is contrary to the basic concept of economics—people's wants are unlimited. Increasing productivity, they suggest, is the only way to address this "economic truth."

Observers consider the American labor force more skilled today than it was in the past. Some have reached their conclusions after measuring the increasing number of school years that workers complete. In 1970, for example, the median number of school years workers had completed was 12.1. By 1991 this number had reached 12.7. By 2000, it will exceed 13. At that point, one-half of the labor force will have a high school education plus at least one year of college or its equivalent.

A number of other factors, such as worker desire and motivation, also affect the quality of the labor force. At present, economists do not have reliable measures for such factors.

Entrepreneurs

The entrepreneur's role as agent of change qualifies him or her as a key to economic growth. A country can have all the other growth potentials, but without entrepreneurs who are willing to innovate and take risks, the economy is apt to lag.

As a group, entrepreneurs require little more than a business climate that allows them to succeed. Such a climate would probably include a minimum of government regulation and an economic system that allows them to keep much of their profits. Accordingly, a tax code with low marginal rates for upper income brackets would be more favorable for entrepreneurs than a code with high marginal rates.

DID YOU KNOW?

Born Elsewhere In many respects, America is still the melting pot of the world. A 1997 study by the U.S. Bureau of the Census found that approximately 9.3 percent of American residents—or nearly 1 in 10—was born in another country. The 10 most common countries of origin are Mexico (6.7 million), Philippines (1.2 million), China (801,000), Cuba (772,000), India (757,000), Vietnam (740,000), El Salvador (740,000), Canada (770,000), Great Britain (579,000), and Korea (550,000).

Productivity and Growth

Productivity refers to the efficient use of productive inputs to create goods and services. Without productivity, economic growth does not occur.

Historical Record

Productivity is measured in terms of labor inputs, even though labor is only one factor of production. Because labor is the variable input, productivity is usually defined as **labor productivity**—the rate of growth of output per unit of labor input.

Figure 15.7 shows the history of labor productivity in the United States economy since 1959. The growth of labor productivity has been somewhat uneven. From 1959 to 1973, the productivity index increased from 54.3 to 80.8, for an annual compound growth rate of 2.36 percent per year. From 1974 to 1998, however, the productivity rate averaged only 1.15 percent per year.

Productivity is still growing, but at a rate slow enough to threaten economic growth and the general standard of living. Declining productivity growth has cost the United States some of its competitive edge. This means that we risk losing jobs and profits to other countries who produce more efficiently.

Effects

If productivity falters, the entire economy suffers. When declining labor productivity in the United States is combined with a rise in the price level, the prices of goods and services become higher than those that other countries charge. Inexpensive imports encourage people and firms to buy foreign-made products instead of American-made ones.

As productivity decreases, companies cut jobs and lay off workers. Only some of the laid-off workers will be able to find jobs in other industries. Some highly-trained workers find they must take jobs in industries that do not utilize all their skills. If workers have to take time to retrain or learn new skills, the economy suffers yet another decline in productivity.

Causes

No one completely understands the dynamics of productivity. Economists can measure it and relate it

Cultural Diversity and Economics

By the year 2000, more people will live in urban areas than in rural ones, and most of this change will take place in developing countries. Cities in developed nations, for the most part, have stopped growing, whereas cities in developing countries continue to grow. If this trend continues, two-thirds of the world's population will live in urban areas by the year 2025.

In 1900 only 11 cities in the world had populations of 1 million. By 2000 there will be approximately 300. In another 20 years there will be nearly 600. Many of these cities will be pushed to the breaking point as they try to accommodate millions of people who flock to urban areas in an effort to flee rural poverty.

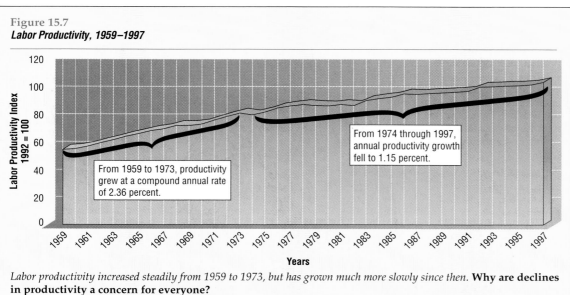

Figure 15.7
Labor Productivity, 1959–1997

Labor Productivity Index 1992 = 100

From 1959 to 1973, productivity grew at a compound annual rate of 2.36 percent.

From 1974 through 1997, annual productivity growth fell to 1.15 percent.

Years

Labor productivity increased steadily from 1959 to 1973, but has grown much more slowly since then. **Why are declines in productivity a concern for everyone?**

Source: *Economic Report of the President,* various years.

to economic growth. What remains unclear, however, is just what drives the overall economic system.

Some people feel that productivity in the United States is down because workers are too lax in their work habits and do not care enough about the companies that employ them. Others say that employers are indifferent and do not care enough about their workers. Still others charge that the tax structure discourages companies from reinvesting earnings in new capital and equipment. Others criticize the educational system.

Each of the views has some truth. The fact remains, however, that the United States has been unable to reverse its declining rate of productivity growth. How to increase productivity is one of the major questions facing the American economy today.

SECTION 2 REVIEW

Reviewing Terms and Facts

1. **Define** real GDP per capita, growth triangle, standard of living, tax base, renewable resources, capital-to-labor ratio, labor productivity.
2. **Describe** two measures of economic growth.
3. **List** five important aspects of economic growth.

4. **Identify** the factors influencing economic growth.
5. **Explain** the consequences of a declining labor productivity rate.

Critical Thinking

6. **Determining Cause and Effect** Why is productivity important to a nation's standard of living?

Applying Economic Concepts

7. **Standard of Living** Identify your most valued material possession. List the ways in which this possession enhances your standard of living.

CHAPTER 15: *Population, Economic Growth, and Business Cycles* **381**

Background

Williams's syndicated column generates a great deal of correspondence, especially from African Americans. Some are very harsh, accusing him, he says, of "giving aid and comfort to racism around the United States," and of "pushing a white man's agenda." Other readers, however, have congratulated him for his "colorblind" and "evenhanded" examination of controversial issues.

TEACH

Write the following on the chalkboard: *Minimum Wage, Economic Freedom, Affirmative Action.* Direct students to review the Profile. Then call on volunteers to paraphrase Williams's ideas of the three topics noted on the chalkboard. Conclude by assigning the *Examining the Profile* activity.

PROFILES IN ECONOMICS

WALTER E. WILLIAMS
(1936–   )

Walter E. Williams is a contemporary American economist, author, and Professor of Economics at George Mason University. Dr. Williams's views are decidedly free market and often controversial. His many publications have opposed the minimum wage, affirmative action, and agricultural price supports.

THE MINIMUM WAGE While many people support the minimum wage as a means to prevent the exploitation of unskilled workers, Dr. Williams would rather see it abolished. His reasons are compelling:

Williams uses South Korea's economy as an example of growth without government interference. Here, a South Korean worker tests fiber optics.

In 1948, black teenage unemployment was less than that of whites. Compare it with today and it's the opposite. You can't explain it by saying there was less racism in 1948 than there is today. You can't explain it by saying that blacks had more education than whites in 1948. You have to explain it by increases in both the level and coverage of the minimum wage law.

ECONOMIC FREEDOM According to Williams, economic freedom is the key to both economic growth and the distribution of wealth. He often points to the rapid economic development of Hong Kong, Korea, Taiwan, and Singapore as evidence of economic growth without government intervention. He even opposes agricultural price supports and affirmative action for minorities on the same grounds.

AFFIRMATIVE ACTION In the case of affirmative action, Williams argues that programs designed to create a special opportunity for one group do more than exclude another group. They tarnish the achievements of the very minorities they sought to protect.

I think many government programs have harmed blacks in making achievements less credible. For example, whatever inspiration Harvard or the University of Virginia has in requiring so many articles in the law journals to be written by women or by minorities reduces the credibility of a black student or a female student having written for the law journal.

Perhaps Williams is controversial, but he likes to challenge his readers and his students with provocative views. Williams is one of the few columnists in the country whose fans have organized an official booster club. Today Williams is the Chair of the Economics Department at George Mason University.

Examining the Profile

1. **Analyzing Information** Why is Williams against affirmative action programs?

2. **For Further Research** Find out why Williams believes that quotas are unconstitutional.

Answers to Examining the Profile

1. He believes they tarnish the achievements of the very minorities they were established to protect.

2. Suggest that students use the library's computer or card catalog to discover works published by Williams, or newspaper indexes to locate his various columns.

Section Preview

Objectives

After studying this section, you will be able to:

1. **Explain** the phases of the business cycle.
2. **Trace** the history of business cycles in the United States.
3. **Identify** five causes of business cycles.

Key Terms

business cycle, business fluctuation, recession, peak, trough, expansion, trend line, depression, depression scrip, econometric model, index of leading indicators

Applying Economic Concepts

Economic Security Do you have a job and a paycheck on which you and/or others depend? When the economy is slow, workers can experience job layoffs—and economic hardship. Among the seven major goals of the United States economy, *economic security* is one goal prized by Americans. To understand how economic security can sometimes suffer, we must understand business cycles.

FOCUS

Section Objectives

1. Explain the phases of the business cycle.
2. Trace the history of business cycles in the United States.
3. Identify five causes of business cycles.

Bellringer

Prior to taking roll at the beginning of the class period, display Focus Activity Transparency 56 on the overhead projector and assign the accompanying Student Activity 56.

Motivational Activity

Discuss students' responses to the activity sheet that accompanies Focus Activity Transparency 56.

Preteaching Vocabulary

Have students create an annotated diagram of the business cycle using the following key terms as labels: *business cycle, business fluctuation, recession, peak, trough, expansion,* and *trend line.* **LEP**

Use the **Vocabulary PuzzleMaker** to create crossword and word search puzzles.

VISUAL INSTRUCTION

Point out that business cycles vary in length as well as severity.

Answer to Caption:

as orange areas; when real GDP makes a downward turn

To economists, **business cycles** are the recurring ups and downs of real GDP. The term *cycles* suggests that the ups and downs occur systematically, perhaps even predictably. Other economists prefer to talk about **business fluctuations** instead. The term *fluctuations* implies that real GDP will go up and down from time to time, but not in a regular and predictable manner.

Phases of the Business Cycle

Figure 15.8 shows the two phases of a business cycle. The first is **recession**, a period of decline in the economy as measured by changes in real GDP. In economic terms, a recession occurs when real GDP declines for two quarters, or six months, in a row. It begins when the economy reaches a **peak**—the point where real GDP stops going up. It ends when the economy reaches a **trough**—the turnaround point where real GDP stops going down.

As soon as the declining real GDP bottoms out, the economy moves into the second phase of the cycle, **expansion**—a period of recovery from a recession. Expansion continues until the economy reaches a new peak. If no periods of recession and expansion occurred, the economy would follow an even growth path

Figure 15.8
Phases of the Business Cycle

The business cycle is marked by alternating phases of recession and expansion. The economy is in recession when real GDP declines for two quarters or more in a row. The trough marks the turning point when real GDP starts to go up again, changing the recession into an expansion. **How are the recessionary periods in this graph illustrated?**

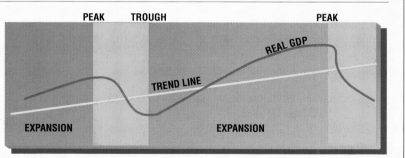

PEAK   TROUGH   PEAK
REAL GDP
TREND LINE
EXPANSION   EXPANSION

Classroom Resources for SECTION 3

- Reproducible Lesson Plan 15-3
- Guided Reading Activity 15-3
- Section Quiz 15-3
- Spanish Section Quiz 15-3
- Focus Activity Transparency 56
- NBR's Economics in Action Video Program
- Enrichment Activity 15
- Reteaching Activity 15

- Spanish Reteaching Activity 15
- Economic Vocabulary Activity 15
- Spanish Economic Vocabulary Activity 15
- Chapter 15 Test, Form A and Form B
- English and Spanish Audiocassettes
- Testmaker
- Vocabulary PuzzleMaker
- Chapter Challenger Interactive Review Software
- MindJogger Videoquiz

TEACH

Guided Practice

L2 *Applying Ideas* Refer students to Figure 15.8 on page 383 and the accompanying discussion on pages 383–384. Then list the following terms on the chalkboard: *employment, income, GDP, investment, interest rates.* Ask students to identify what happens to each of these economic indicators during recession, expansion, peak, and trough phases of the business cycle. As guidance, offer the following example: During an expansion, employment increases, national income increases, GDP grows, investment increases, and interest rates rise.

GLENCOE
TECHNOLOGY

NIGHTLY BUSINESS REPORT
Economics in Action

Chapter 30
Disc 2, Side 2

Title: *Technological and Social Change and the Economy*

Subject: The impact of technology on the economy

Ask: How will changes in technology affect the workplace? *(Lack of experience with new technology leads to low productivity in the short-term.)*

Also available in VHS.

VISUAL INSTRUCTION

Answer to Caption:

It was much longer and more severe than other recessionary periods.

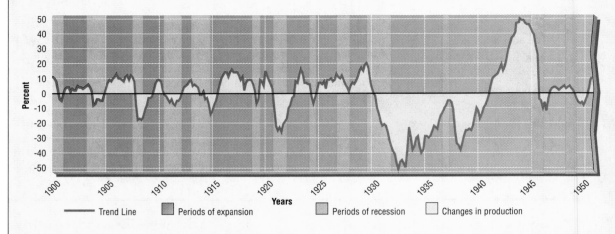

Figure 15.9
History of Business Activity in the United States

Years

— Trend Line   ■ Periods of expansion   ■ Periods of recession   □ Changes in production

The United States has a long history of business cycles or fluctuations. **From examining this graph, how does the Great Depression compare to other recessionary periods in our history?**

called a **trend line**. As **Figure 15.8** shows, the economy departs from and then returns to its trend line as it passes through phases of recession and expansion.

If a recession becomes very severe, it may turn into a **depression**—a state of the economy with large numbers of people out of work, acute shortages, and excess capacity in manufacturing plants. Most experts agree that the Great Depression of the 1930s was the only depression the United States has ever had.

If the economy grows relatively fast during a recovery, it may surpass the trend line enough to raise real GDP to new heights. An occasional decline in real GDP will not change the overall climb. If, however, real GDP declines two quarters in a row, the economy by definition goes back into a recession.

Business Cycles in the United States

As **Figure 15.9** shows, business activity in the United States has followed an irregular course throughout the twentieth century. The worst and most prolonged downturn was the Great Depression. The years since World War II have taken on a special pattern of their own.

The Great Depression

The stock market crash on October 29, 1929, or "Black Tuesday," marks the beginning of the Great Depression. Between 1929 and 1933, GDP fell from approximately $103 to $55 billion—a decline of nearly 50 percent. At the same time, the number of people out of work rose nearly 800 percent—from 1.6 to 12.8 million. During the worst years of the Depression, one out of every four workers was jobless. Even workers who had jobs suffered. The average manufacturing wage, which had reached 55 cents an hour by 1933, plunged to 5 cents an hour in many areas.

Many banks across the country failed. The FDIC did not exist at the time, so depositors were not protected. To prevent panic withdrawals, the federal government declared a "bank holiday" in March 1933. Every bank in the country closed for several days, and many banks never reopened.

Meeting Special Needs

Language Delayed Students with language concept problems will need practice in categorizing information. Direct students' attention to the headings in this section: Phases of the Business Cycle, Business Cycles in the United States, The Great Depression, Causes of the Great Depression, and so on. After reading each subsection, have students think of alternative headings or replace each heading with a statement.

GO TO — Lesson 7 of Interactive Economics! to learn more about "The Role of Government."

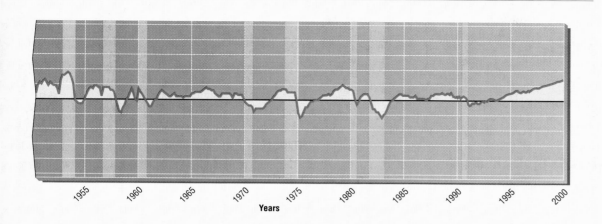

Years

Source: Based on data from the Society Bank, Cleveland, Ohio, and updates by author

The money supply fell by one-third. Currency was in such short supply that towns, counties, chambers of commerce, and other civic bodies resorted to printing their own money, known as **depression scrip**. It amounted to several billion dollars and was used to pay teachers, firefighters, police officers, and other municipal employees. **1**

Causes of the Great Depression

Economists have not pinpointed an exact cause of the Great Depression, but a number of different factors seem to have contributed. One factor was the disparity in the distribution of income. A great number of very poor and very rich people lived in American society. The poor could not stimulate the economy with consumer spending because they had little or no income. The rich had the income, but often used it for such nonproductive activities as stock market speculation. **2**

Easy and plentiful credit appears to have played a role, too. Many people in the late 1920s borrowed heavily. Their debts made them vulnerable to credit contractions, high interest rates, and even minor business fluctuations. When the crunch came, heavily indebted people had nothing to fall back on. ☑

Economic conditions in other parts of the world also played a part. During the 1920s, the United States

Checking Understanding

1. What was depression scrip?
2. How did the distribution of income contribute to the Great Depression?

Applying Economic Concepts

☑ **Buying on Credit** When the automobile was mass-produced, many people had their first debt. By 1927, two out of three cars were bought on credit. In 1928, 85 percent of furniture, 80 percent of phonographs, and 75 percent of radios were also bought on credit.

CHAPTER 15: *Population, Economic Growth, and Business Cycles* **385**

L2 *Illustrating Ideas* To illustrate the impact of a downturn in business activity, point out that one person's spending is someone else's income. When spending does not take place, a chain reaction is set off that affects the whole economy. Then provide students with the following scenario: Joe's Diner is a popular lunch spot with workers from Handmade Steel Products. In fact, Joe could not run the diner at a profit without the business from Handmade's workers. Handmade's management has just announced that the factory will close within weeks.

Have students construct an annotated flow diagram that illustrates the chain reaction set off by the closing of the factory. Call on volunteers to display and discuss their diagrams.

 ANSWERS

1. money printed by towns, counties, chambers of commerce, and other civic bodies
2. The poor had little income to spend to stimulate the economy. The rich had income, but often spent it on such nonproductive activities as stock market speculation.

Free Enterprise Activity

Write the following statement on the chalkboard: *Some economists have suggested that business cycles are the result of the clustering of new inventions and innovation.* Begin a discussion of the statement by asking students how new inventions and innovations stimulate growth of the economy. Ask what happens to the land, labor, and capital when new production methods are employed. Then have students hypothesize about the effects of new production methods on the business cycle. As an example, point out that the economy was stimulated by the introduction of the personal computer in the late 1970s. Investment in the industry increased as the new product was copied, production increased, and employment grew. Conclude by asking students for examples of innovation and invention that have changed production methods in their or their parents' lifetimes.

Independent Practice

✐ **Guided Reading** Assign Guided Reading Activity for Section 3. **LEP**

L3 *Writing a Report* Have students imagine they are economic advisers to the President. Have them write a report noting what phase of the business cycle the economy is presently in and how the various factors that cause business cycles may have contributed to this position. Select students to present and discuss their reports.

L2 *Summarizing* Tell students to locate a magazine or newspaper article that discusses the economy in a recession or an expansion. Have students summarize the main points of the article and present them to the rest of the class in an oral report.

CURRICULUM CONNECTIONS

Journalism Perhaps the most vivid description of the stock market crash appeared on the front page of the October 30 edition of the show-business newspaper, *Variety*. A banner headline blared: "WALL ST. LAYS AN EGG."

---

made many foreign loans, which helped support a high level of international trade. Shortly before the Depression began in the United States, the government had to withdraw many of these loans. Without the loans, some foreign nations could no longer buy American goods, so American exports fell sharply.

At the same time, high American tariffs on imports kept many countries from selling goods to the United States. Some countries depended heavily on their sales to the United States, and before long, they too were faced with economic crises. As the Depression spread from country to country, world trade declined, and American exports dropped even further.

Business Cycles Since World War II

The Great Depression was over by 1940, and the United States economy had returned to its growth trend line. At the same time, massive government spending for wartime goods added a huge stimulant to the economy during most of the early 1940s.

Recession returned in 1945, but it did not last. As soon as the war was over, consumers went on a buying binge that stimulated expansion again. The economy has experienced several more recessions since 1945, but each downturn was short compared with the length of the recovery that followed. The average recession lasted 11 months, the average expansion 43 months.

All the recessions since 1945 have taken place in fairly regular sequence. Two striking exceptions are worth noting, however. The first occurred in the mid-1960s, during the Vietnam War. Again, massive spending on the war effort probably warded off a recession.

The second exception was the mid-1980s. A few economic indicators identified some weakness in 1987, but real GDP never turned down long enough for recession to occur. Many economists believe that the heavy deficit spending of the 1980s stimulated the economy so that a recession could not develop.

Causes of Business Cycles

Over the years, economists have offered a number of different reasons why business cycles occur. Each theory has some validity, but none can claim to be the single explanation. In most cases, several factors work together to cause a cycle.

Capital Expenditures

Changes in capital expenditures are one possible cause of business cycles. When the economy is expanding, businesses expect future sales to be high, so they invest heavily in capital goods. Companies may build new plants or buy new equipment to replace older equipment in their plants.

After a while, businesses may decide they have expanded far enough. They begin to pull back on their capital investments, causing layoffs in the capital goods industries and, eventually, recession.

Inventory Adjustments

Inventory adjustments, or changes in the level of business inventories, are a second possible cause of business cycles. Some businesses cut back their inventories at the first sign of an economic slowdown, and then build them back up again at the first sign of an upturn. Either action causes investment expenditures—and real GDP—to fluctuate.

The influence of inventory adjustments showed up clearly in the business cycle of the late 1940s. Right after World War II, businesses in the United States invested heavily in inventories to fill shelves depleted during the war years. By 1948 consumer demand caught up with the backlog, and people stopped buying. Inventories built up on store and factory shelves, so businesses stopped investing in inventory. The resulting recession of 1949 lasted for about a year.

Innovation and Imitation

A third possible cause of business cycles is innovation. An innovation may be a new product or a new way of performing a task. When a business innovates, it often gains an edge on its competitors because its costs go down or its sales go up. In either case, profits increase, and the business grows.

If other businesses in the same industry want to keep up, they must copy what the innovator has done or come up with something even better. Generally, the imitating companies must invest heavily to do this, and an investment boom follows. After the innovation takes hold in the industry, however, the situation changes. Further investments are unnecessary, and economic activity may slow. Meanwhile, the fluctuation of investments has produced a business cycle.

Extending the Content

Uncertainty and Predictions There is no sure way to predict future economic growth. A careful economic forecaster knows that past data is not necessarily a good predictor of future events. Even though there is an abundance of data about past economic activity, too many unknowns exist to predict the future with any certainty. To begin with, there are too many variables to measure, and the variables affecting economic activity can change from one time period to another. For example, when the automobile was first developed, few people felt that it would have a long-lasting economic impact. It literally became the driving force of the entire economy, however.

Monetary Factors

A fourth possible cause of business cycles are the credit and loan policies of the commercial banking system and the Federal Reserve. When "easy money" policies are in effect, interest rates are low and loans are easy to get. Easy money encourages the private sector to borrow and invest, which stimulates the economy for a short time. Eventually the increased demand for loans causes interest rates to rise, which in turn discourages new borrowers.

As borrowing and spending slow down, the level of economic activity declines. Lenders think twice about making new loans or renewing old ones. Interest rates fall and the business cycle begins again.

External Shocks

A final potential cause of business cycles is external shocks, such as increases in oil prices, wars, and international conflict. Some shocks drive the economy up, as when Great Britain discovered North Sea oil in the 1970s. Other shocks can be negative, as when high oil prices hit the United States in the early 1970s.

Predicting Business Cycles

Because of the huge costs of economic instability, much work has been done to forecast business cycles. Economists use two methods to make their forecasts. One involves macroeconomic modeling, while the other makes use of statistical predictors.

Econometric Models

An **econometric model** is a macroeconomic model that uses algebraic equations to describe how the economy behaves. Most models used today are based on some adaptation of the output-expenditure model we examined earlier on page 358:

$$GDP = C + I + G + F.$$

For example, an economist might use X to stand for exports and M for imports instead of the F for the foreign sector:

$$GDP = C + I + G + (X - M).$$

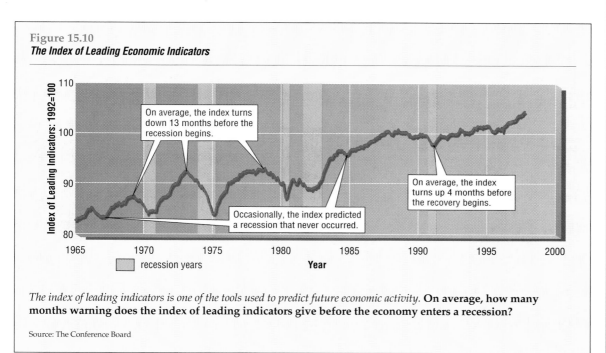

Figure 15.10
The Index of Leading Economic Indicators

On average, the index turns down 13 months before the recession begins.

Occasionally, the index predicted a recession that never occurred.

On average, the index turns up 4 months before the recovery begins.

☐ recession years   **Year**

The index of leading indicators is one of the tools used to predict future economic activity. **On average, how many months warning does the index of leading indicators give before the economy enters a recession?**

Source: The Conference Board

ASSESS

Check for Understanding

Assign Section 3 Review on page 388 as homework or an in-class activity.

 Use **Chapter Challenger Interactive Review Software** to review Section 3.

MEETING LESSON OBJECTIVES

Each objective below is tested by the questions that follow it in parentheses.

1. **Explain** the phases of the business cycle. (**1, 2, 5, 7**)
2. **Trace** the history of business cycles in the United States. (**3**)
3. **Identify** five causes of business cycles. (**4, 6**)

Evaluate

🗁 🗁 ⊙ Assign the Section 3 Quiz in the TCR or use the *Economics: Principles and Practices* Testmaker to create a customized quiz. Spanish Section Quizzes also are available in the Spanish Resources Binder.

VISUAL INSTRUCTION

Have students explain why the 10 indicators are combined into one index. (*No single indicator has proven completely reliable.*)

Answer to Caption:
about 13 months

Reteach

Organize students into groups of four. Assign each group member one of the four subheadings in the section. Then have students create a cartoon, flow chart, or some other form of visual that illustrates the main idea of their assigned subheading. Have groups present and discuss their illustrations.

👝 👝 Have students complete Reteaching Activity 15. Spanish Reteaching Activities also are available in the Spanish Resources Binder.

Enrich

Have students write a research paper on the stock market crash of 1987. Suggest that they compare the 1987 crash to that of 1929.

👝 Have students complete Enrichment Activity 15.

CLOSE

Have students discuss the following questions: Are there any measures you can take to protect yourself from the ups and downs of the business cycle? If so, what are they?

Other equations in the model also may be substituted for some of the variables. Suppose that households annually spend a fixed amount of money, designated as *a*, along with 95 percent of their disposable personal income. In this case, C = a + .95 (DI). If this were substituted for the C in the output-expenditure model, the equation would read:

$$GDP = a + .95 (DI) + I + G + (X - M).$$

The equation can also be broken down into smaller and smaller components. Econometric models such as this can have as few as 20 or as many as 1,000 variables. To get a prediction of GDP for the coming quarter, forecasters put in the latest figures for the money supply, interest rates, the dollar value of exports and imports, and anything else that is needed. Because most econometric models are programmed to be solved by computer, very little time is needed to obtain a solution.

As the quarter unfolds, actual changes in the economy are compared to the predictions of the model. The model is then updated, thus enhancing its accuracy. Some models give reasonably good forecasts for up to 9 months, but accuracy goes down considerably after that. Overall, short-term econometric models have proven their value and are used extensively.

Index of Leading Indicators

A second method used to predict turning points in business cycles is the **index of leading indicators**. The index is a composite of 10 statistical series that usually turns down before real GDP turns down, and turns up before real GDP turns up.

Some statistical indicators, such as the length of the average workweek—which tends to shrink just before a recession begins—are fairly good predictors of change in real GDP. Still, no single series has proven completely reliable. To resolve this problem, 10 individual series are combined into an overall index that closely patterns the behavior of real GDP, making the index of leading indicators a useful tool.

The behavior of this composite index can be seen in Figure 15.10. The orange areas represent recessions and the blue areas expansions. The average time between a dip in the index and the onset of recession is about 13 months. The average time between a rise in the index and expansion is about 4 months.

In general, economists think the index of leading indicators predicts a recession when it turns down 3 months in a row. Since 1965, however, the index has predicted 3 recessions that never occurred. The first was in 1966 during the heavy expenditures of the Vietnam War. The second was during the deficit spending of the 1980s. The last was in early 1995.

The index of leading indicators is a reasonably good, but not completely reliable, indicator of future economic activity. Therefore, the information it supplies is used along with the results that other econometric models generate. Together, the results generally let the forecaster predict how real GDP will behave in the short run.

SECTION 3 REVIEW

Reviewing Terms and Facts

1. **Define** business cycle, business fluctuation, recession, peak, trough, expansion, trend line, depression, depression scrip, econometric model, index of leading indicators.
2. **Identify** the two main phases of a business cycle.

3. **Assess** the severity of the Great Depression.
4. **List** five causes of business cycles.
5. **Identify** two ways to predict business cycles.

Critical Thinking

6. **Demonstrating Reasoned Judgment** Supply evidence to support the following statement: Activities of the federal government can impact the economy.

Applying Economic Concepts

7. **Economic Security** If you were the head of a household, how would you plan your spending if you had an accurate prediction of future business cycles?

Answers to SECTION 3 REVIEW

1. All words are defined in the Glossary.
2. recession, expansion
3. It was the worst economic downturn in U.S. history; GDP fell 50 percent; one out of four workers was jobless; manufacturing wage plunged to 5 cents an hour; many banks failed; many depositors lost everything; money supply fell by one-third.
4. capital expenditures, inventory adjustments, innovation and imitation, monetary factors, external shocks

5. econometric models, index of leading indicators
6. Answers will vary, but students may cite the tax policies of the federal government, international affairs, and military base closings as evidence that actions of the government impact the economy.
7. Answers will vary. Students may note that if they knew a recession was imminent, they might save more of their paychecks.

ECONOMICS IN ACTION

Technological and Social Change and the Economy

Setting Up the Video

With your classmates, view "Technological and Social Change and the Economy" on the videodisc *Economics in Action.* The video focuses on the impact of social and technological changes on the American workforce. A news segment demonstrates that computers and automation will continue to change the way we do business.

Chapter 30
Disc 2, Side 2

View the video by scanning the bar code or by entering the chapter number on your keypad and pressing Search. (Also available in VHS format.)

Hands-On Activity

Evaluate the impact of technology on your life. Create two lists. In the first list, name activities in your life that involve technology. In the second list, name activities that you believe will involve technology in the future. How will new technologies affect the American workforce? Write a paragraph describing the types of skills you will need in your future to adapt to our high-tech society.

SURFING THE "NET"

Population Changes

The Constitution of the United States requires a census of the population every 10 years. The Bureau of the Census conducts the count. It classifies the population in several ways, including a division into urban and rural populations, life expectancies, fertility rates, and dependency ratios. What are some of the specific population changes that are predicted by the Bureau of the Census? How do those changes vary in different areas of the United States? Use the Internet to find out.

Getting There

1. Use a search engine. Type in the words *Bureau of the Census.*

2. Next, enter words like the following to focus your search: *population, ethnic groups, immigration, life expectancy,* and *dependency ratio.*

3. The search engine will provide you with a number of links to follow. Links are "pointers" to different sites on the Internet and often appear as blue, underlined words.

What to Do When You Are There

Click on the links to navigate through the pages of information. Gather your findings. Using the findings and your word processor, write several paragraphs describing the specific population changes that are predicted by the Bureau of the Census. Share your findings with your class.

INTERNET SITES

The following are possible sites for completing the "Net" activities:

U.S. Census Bureau
http://www.census.gov/

Statistical Abstract of the United States
http://www.census.gov/stat_abstract/

Population Reference Bureau
http://www.prb.org/

Not on the "Net"...

If students have limited or no access to the Internet, have them complete the activity "Population Changes" by using the *Statistical Abstract of the United States* to complete their research.

389

INTERNET ADDRESS BOOK

Internet addresses that you find useful can be noted in the space below for quick reference.

_____   _____
_____   _____
_____   _____
_____   _____
_____   _____

CHAPTER 15
REVIEW

CHAPTER 15 REVIEW

VIDEODISC
MindJogger Videoquiz

Use MindJogger to review the Chapter 15 content.

Chapter 15
Disc 2, Side B

Also available in VHS.

Answers

Reviewing Key Terms

Sentences will vary. Sample sentences are provided below.

1. The decennial census counts both urban population and rural population.

2. Demographers study how far the center of population moves.

3. Fertility and life expectancy are two factors that affect population growth.

4. The aging of the baby boom generation will increase the dependency ratio.

5. A high capital-to-labor ratio encourages labor productivity and, therefore, economic growth.

6. To some economists, a business cycle differs from a business fluctuation in that cycles are systematic, while fluctuations are unpredictable.

7. A recession begins after the economy reaches a peak.

8. Economic expansion continues until the economy reaches a peak.

9. A depression has a much deeper trough than a recession.

10. Currency was so scarce during the Great Depression that civic bod-

Reviewing Key Terms

Write a sentence for each pair of terms below.

1. urban population; rural population
2. demographers; center of population
3. fertility rate; life expectancy
4. baby boom; dependency ratio
5. capital-to-labor ratio; labor productivity
6. business cycle; business fluctuation
7. recession; peak
8. peak; expansion
9. trough; depression
10. depression; depression scrip
11. trend line; business cycle

Reviewing the Facts

SECTION 1 *(pages 370–374)*
1. **Describe** the historical growth of population in the United States.
2. **Describe** how the population of the United States is expected to change by the year 2050.

SECTION 2 *(pages 376–381)*
3. **Trace** the record of real economic growth per capita in the United States.
4. **Explain** the importance of economic growth to the United States and other countries.
5. **Name** the factors that are essential for economic growth.
6. **Describe** the relationship between productivity and economic growth.

SECTION 3 *(pages 383–388)*
7. **Identify** the two phases through which a business cycle fluctuates.
8. **List** the factors that contributed to the Great Depression.
9. **Describe** the five probable causes of the business cycle.
10. **Explain** two methods that economists use to predict business cycles.

Critical Thinking

1. **Synthesizing Information** Review the population projections for growth and distribution shown in Figure 15.1 on page 371. Suppose that you are planning to open a new department store. In what region of the country would you locate your store? What special lines of merchandise would you feature? Explain your answers.

2. **Formulating Questions** Assume that you could go back in time and interview Americans living in the 1930s. Prepare a list of questions that you would like to ask about living conditions during the Great Depression.

Applying Economic Concepts

1. **Economic Growth** Obtain from the library a copy of the most recent monthly report of leading economic indicators. Describe recent movements of the index. Explain what you think the movements indicate for future economic growth.

2. **Standard of Living** Under what circumstances, if any, do you think you might prefer economic security to a rise in standard of living?

Reinforcing Skills

INTERPRETING POPULATION PYRAMIDS
Use the population pyramid on page 391 to answer the following questions.
1. What does the population pyramid show?
2. Which age group is largest for males? For females?
3. Which age group is smallest for males? For females?
4. Which gender has a larger percentage of people that are 70 years old and over?
5. What percentage of the population is in the 30-to-40 age groups? How does this compare to the same age groups in Figure 15.4 on page 375?
6. What percentage of the population is in your age group?

---

ies resorted to printing depression scrip.

11. Most business cycles follow a general trend line in their alternating phases of recession and expansion.

Reviewing the Facts

1. Although the population has grown considerably since colonial times, the rate of growth has steadily declined. Between 1790 and 1860, the population grew 3.02 percent a year. It is under 1 percent today.

2. rate of population growth is expected to decline as fertility declines; life expectancy at birth predicted to be 82.1 years

3. Refer students to Figure 15.6 to answer this question. Rates of economic growth have declined from 2.9 percent (1940 to 1970) to 2.0 percent (1970 to 1980) to 1.6 percent between 1980 and 1997.

4. It raises the standard of living, eases the burden of government, helps solve domestic problems, boosts

Individual Activity

Find the most recent real GDP per capita in Figure 15.5 on page 377. Assume that after taxes, the amount equals your annual income. Assume also that you are living alone and must provide for all your wants and needs. Use local newspaper advertisements to get an idea of current prices for rent, food, clothing, and automobiles. Use your findings to list what you might spend for housing, food, clothing, transportation, and entertainment without exceeding your annual income. Explain why you would or would not be content with your standard of living. How do you think society and the economy in your community would change if everyone lived on a net income equal to the real GDP per capita?

Cooperative Learning Activity

Productivity is important wherever goods and services are produced. Compile a class list of suggestions for improving overall educational productivity in your school or school district. (More audiovisual equipment or computers and different class populations are a few possibilities.) Working in groups of four, have each group select a different item from the class list. In your group, make an outline of how and why you think your item would increase productivity. Compare your outline with those of the other groups. Take a class vote to reach consensus on the two suggestions you would most like to submit to the Board of Education.

Technology Activity
Using a Spreadsheet

Use the following information to create a spreadsheet and then a bar graph showing United States real GDP per capita for four years.

Year	Population	Real GDP in $billions
1960	179,323,000	$2,263
1970	203,302,000	$3,398
1980	226,542,000	$4,615
1990	248,710,000	$6,136

Remember to use the following equation to determine real GDP per capita: Real GDP divided by population = Real GDP per capita. You may find your calculations will be easier if you change GDP from billions of dollars to millions. When your calculations are done, input the information onto a spreadsheet, then convert the numbers to a bar graph. Print out your completed graph.

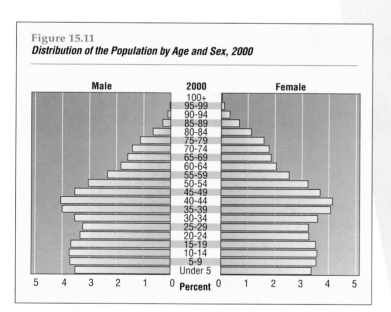

Figure 15.11
Distribution of the Population by Age and Sex, 2000

Applying Economic Concepts

1. Economic indicator movement will vary. Remind students that the index usually turns down before real GDP turns down, and turns up before real GDP turns up.

2. Answers will vary. Students may note that economic security provides a measure of comfort in the short run, but a low standard of living may cause frustration and hopelessness in the long run.

Reinforcing Skills

1. the distribution of the population by age and sex in the year 2000

2. 40–44; 40–44

3. Students may answer 100+ for both or 95–99 for both

4. female

5. about 15.2 percent in the 30–39 range; it is smaller than the 1990 percentage of about 16.8 percent

6. a little under 7.2 percent

? BONUS TEST QUESTION

Have students identify which stage of the business cycle—peak, trough, recession, or expansion—the following statements describe:

1. Economic analysts state that unemployment has "bottomed out." (*trough*)

2. Output and employment are on the decline. (*recession*)

3. Factory employment has increased steadily. (*expansion*)

4. Output and employment are near capacity. (*peak*)

the economies of foreign trade partners, and serves as a global role model.

5. quantity and quality of land, capital, labor, entrepreneurs

6. Productivity fosters economic growth.

7. recession, expansion

8. disparity in the distribution of income, spending on speculative activities, easy and plentiful credit, economic conditions in other parts of the world, high American tariffs on imports

9. capital expenditures, inventory adjustments, innovation and imitation, monetary factors, external shocks

10. Econometric models provide algebraic equations that give fairly accurate short-term predictions. The index of leading indicators uses 10 statistical series to make short-term predictions.

Critical Thinking

1. Answers will vary.

2. Questions will vary.

CHAPTER ORGANIZER

Daily Objectives	Reproducible Resources	Multimedia Resources
Section 1 **Unemployment** 1. **Explain** how the Bureau of Labor Statistics determines if a person is employed. 2. **Describe** five kinds of employment.	Reproducible Lesson Plan 16-1 Guided Reading Activity 16-1 Cooperative Learning Activity 18 Consumer Application Activity 11 Math Practice for Economics 30 Free Enterprise Activity 18 Primary and Secondary Source Reading 18 Performance Assessment Activity 24 Section Quiz 16-1*	Focus Activity Transparency 76 Economic Concepts Transparency 16* Vocabulary PuzzleMaker Chapter Challenger Interactive Review Software Testmaker MindJogger Videoquiz NBR's Economics in Action Video Program
Section 2 **Inflation** 1. **Explain** how inflation is measured. 2. **Discuss** five causes of inflation. 3. **Analyze** the destabilizing consequences of inflation.	Reproducible Lesson Plan 16-2 Guided Reading Activity 16-2 Reinforcing Economic Skill 16 Section Quiz 16-2*	Focus Activity Transparency 82 Economic Concepts Transparency 17* Vocabulary PuzzleMaker Chapter Challenger Interactive Review Software Testmaker NBR's Economics in Action Video Program
Section 3 **Poverty and the Distribution of Income** 1. **Explain** how economists measure the distribution of income. 2. **Discuss** the reasons for the inequality of income. 3. **Describe** how poverty levels are defined and measured. 4. **Discuss** six antipoverty programs.	Reproducible Lesson Plan 16-3 Guided Reading Activity 16-3 Section Quiz 16-3*	Focus Activity Transparency 83 Vocabulary PuzzleMaker Chapter Challenger Interactive Review Software Testmaker NBR's Economics in Action Video Program
Chapter Review and Evaluation	Enrichment Activity 16 Reteaching Activity 16* Economic Vocabulary Activity 16* Chapter 16 Test, Forms A and B	Chapter Digests Audiocassette Activities and Tests* Testmaker MindJogger Videoquiz

Also available in Spanish

 Blackline Master   Transparency   CD-ROM   Software   Videodisc   Audiocassette

⏱ 00:00 OUT OF TIME? Assign the Chapter 16 Digest Audiocassette and the corresponding Chapter Digest activities and tests.

National Council on Economic Education

THE **Economics** America AND **Economics** International PROGRAMS

VOLUNTARY NATIONAL CONTENT STANDARDS IN ECONOMICS
Emphasized in Chapter 16

Content Standard 13 *Students will understand that:*
Income for most people is determined by the market value of the productive resources they sell. What workers earn depends, primarily, on the market value of what they produce and how productive they are.

Content Standard 19 *Students will understand that:*
Unemployment imposes costs on individuals and nations. Unexpected inflation imposes costs on many people and benefits some others because it arbitrarily redistributes purchasing power. Inflation can reduce the rate of growth of national living standards, because individuals and organizations use resources to protect themselves against the uncertainty of future prices.

Economics America *Resources Available From NCEE*

- *Capstone: The Nation's High School Economics Course*
- *Civics and Government: Focus on Economics*
- *Economies in Transition: Command to Market*
- *Focus: High School Economics*
- *United States History: Eyes on the Economy, Vol. II*

To order these materials, or to contact your state Council on Economic Education about workshops and programs, call 1-800-338-1192 or visit http://www.nationalcouncil.org.

PERFORMANCE ASSESSMENT

The following chapter projects may be assigned at the beginning of the chapter and used for performance assessment.

Multicultural Heritage According to an October 1997 report by the Bureau of Labor Statistics, the unemployment rate for African Americans was more than twice the unemployment rate for white Americans for all of 1997. Likewise, the unemployment rate for Hispanics was about 1.5 times higher than the white unemployment rate.

   Organize students into several groups to act as policy think tanks. Direct the think tanks to develop policy recommendations to prevent unemployment falling unduly heavily on one group in society during future recessions. Have group representatives present their policy recommendations in oral reports to the class.

Cooperative Learning Organize students into three groups and assign one of the following topics to each group: Causes of Unemployment, Causes of Inflation,Causes of Poverty. Direct groups to prepare an annotated pictorial wall display that could be used to teach their assigned topic. Group members should share the various tasks involved in the project: design, research, artwork, writing, and construction of the display. A team of three students from each group should use the display to teach their topic to the class.

ADDITIONAL RESOURCES

Readings for the Student

Davis, Bertha. *Poverty in America.* New York: Franklin Watts, 1991. Analyzes causes of poverty and examines government programs designed to combat this serious problem.

Meltzer, Milton. *The American Promise: Voices of a Changing Nation, 1945–Present.* New York: Bantam Books, 1990. A series of essays on such issues as poverty, immigration, and the environment. Provides historical perspective on change in America.

Readings for the Teacher

Buchholz, Todd G. *New Ideas from Dead Economists: An Introduction to Modern Economic Thought.* New York: New American Library, 1990. Applies ideas of some of the best-known economists to problems facing today's economy.

Duncan, Cynthia M., ed. *Rural Poverty in America.* New York: Auburn House, 1992. Analysis of rural poverty and policies designed to solve this problem.

Multimedia

The Inflation File. World Research, Inc. P.O. Box 9359, San Diego, CA 92169. Video, 28 mins. An informative review of the causes, consequences, and possible cures of inflation.

Upstairs, Downstairs. Cambridge Studios/Social Studies School Service, 10200 Jefferson Boulevard, P.O. Box 802, Culver City, CA 90232–0802. Video, 7 mins. Discusses the nature and impact of the widening gap in income inequality. Part of the MacNeil/Lehrer Business Reports series.

Chapter Overview

Chapter 16 focuses on unemployment, inflation, and poverty—their causes and effects and how to measure them. **Section 1** defines the various kinds of unemployment and explains the concept of full employment. **Section 2** considers inflation—its characteristics and probable causes and the destabilizing effect it can have on the economy. **Section 3** explains the Lorenz curve and reasons for income inequality, and discusses poverty and various antipoverty programs.

GLENCOE
TECHNOLOGY

VIDEODISC
MindJogger Videoquiz

Use MindJogger to preview the Chapter 16 content.

 | Chapter 16
Disc 2, Side B

Also available in VHS.

interNET
CONNECTION

Resources for Chapter 16 on the World Wide Web*

National Council on Economic Education

http://www.nationalcouncil.org/

Institute for Research on Poverty

http://www.ssc.wisc.edu/irp

Joint Center for Poverty Research

http://www.spc.uchicago.edu/PovertyCenter/

*Sites subject to change.

At any given time, millions of Americans are unemployed.

Extra Credit Project

Have students monitor television newscasts, newspapers, and current affairs magazines for stories on unemployment, inflation, and poverty.

Ask students to write a report summarizing these stories, paying special attention to the causes and solutions discussed.

CHAPTER 16

Unemployment, Inflation, and Poverty

SECTION 1
Unemployment

SECTION 2
Inflation

SECTION 3
Poverty and the Distribution of Income

CHAPTER PREVIEW

People to Know

- Wilma Mankiller
- Sociologist

Applying Economic Concepts to Your Life

Economic Stability Do you worry about the future? If you are concerned about getting a job, earning a decent income, or keeping up with inflation, you are not alone. Many people do, which is why the concept of *economic stability* is important to everyone.

> ### Journal Writing
>
> For one week, summarize in your journal current trends in inflation and unemployment rates that you read about in newspapers such as *The Wall Street Journal* or your local paper.

CHAPTER 16: *Unemployment, Inflation, and Poverty* **393**

Connecting to Past Learning

List the terms *unemployment*, *inflation*, and *poverty* on the chalkboard. Have students write sentences explaining how each of the listed terms relates to economic stability, one of the seven economic goals discussed in Chapter 2. Call on volunteers to read and discuss their sentences.

Applying Economics

Have students clip current newspaper and magazine articles about the three topics in Chapter 16—unemployment, inflation, and poverty. Select a number of students to summarize their articles. Then have students discuss which of the three problems presents the greatest challenge for the U.S. economy and which presents the greatest challenge for their state and local economies.

PERFORMANCE ASSESSMENT

Refer to page **392B** for a Performance Assessment activity for this chapter. Also see the **Performance Assessment Activities** booklet for additional suggestions.

VISUAL INSTRUCTION

Have students discuss recent business closings in the region and the impact these closings had on people in their community.

Economic Portfolio

Point out that students, in making their **Journal Writing** entries, should consider the requirements of the writing assignment they are asked to complete in the Chapter Review. Refer students to the **Technology Activity** in the Chapter 16 Review on page 415.

Key to Ability Levels — Teaching strategies have been coded for varying learning styles and abilities:
L1 - Basic (activities for all students)   **L2 - Average** (activities for average to above-average students)
L3 - Challenging (activities for above-average students)   **LEP - Limited English Proficiency**

FOCUS

Section Objectives

1. Explain how the Bureau of Labor Statistics determines if a person is employed.

2. Describe five kinds of unemployment.

Bellringer

Prior to taking roll at the beginning of the class period, display Focus Activity Transparency 76 on the overhead projector and assign the accompanying Student Activity 76.

Motivational Activity

Discuss students' responses to the activity sheet that accompanies Focus Activity Transparency 76.

Preteaching Vocabulary

Ask students to write questions for which the key terms are the answers. Have students use their questions to test each others' understanding of the key terms. **LEP**

Use the **Vocabulary PuzzleMaker** to create crossword and word search puzzles.

TEACH

Guided Practice

L1 **Understanding Ideas** List on the chalkboard the five types of unemployment. Ask students to write five sentences, with each sentence providing an example of one type of unemployment. **LEP**

Section Preview

Objectives

After studying this section, you will be able to:

1. **Explain** how the Bureau of Labor Statistics determines if a person is employed.

2. **Describe** five kinds of unemployment.

Key Terms

unemployed, unemployment rate, frictional unemployment, structural unemployment, cyclical unemployment, seasonal unemployment, technological unemployment, automation, full employment

Applying Economic Concepts

Employment Did you work for at least one hour per week for pay or profit last summer? One hour may not sound like much, but it is a significant number to the United States Bureau of Labor Statistics, especially if they are trying to decide whether or not you have *employment*.

Nearly one-half of the population of the United States belongs to the civilian labor force, and at any given time, millions of these people are without jobs. Being without a job is a problem that has affected almost everyone, and it affects some people more than others. The issue is so important that full employment is one of the seven economic and social goals of the American economy.

Measuring Unemployment

To understand the severity of joblessness, we need to know how it is measured, as well as what the measure overlooks. The measure of joblessness is the unemployment rate, one of the most closely watched statistics in the economy.

The Unemployment Rate

During the middle of any given month, thousands of specialists from the Bureau of the Census begin their monthly survey of about 50,000 households in nearly 2,000 counties in all 50 states. Census workers are looking for the **unemployed**—people available for work who made a specific effort to find a job during the past month and who, during the most recent survey week, worked less than 1 hour for pay or profit. People are also classified as unemployed if they worked in a family business without pay for less than 15 hours a week.

After the Census workers collect their data, they turn it over to the Bureau of Labor Statistics for analysis and publication. At any given time, millions of Americans are unemployed.

Unemployment also is expressed in terms of the **unemployment rate**, the number of unemployed individuals divided by the total number of persons in the civilian labor force. As **Figure 16.1** shows, the unemployment rate tends to rise dramatically during recessions and then come down slowly afterward. The unemployment rate is very sensitive to downturns in real GDP and is one of the lingering economic costs of a recession.

Limitations of the Unemployment Rate

It might seem that a measure as extensive and comprehensive as the unemployment rate would summarize the problem. If anything, however, the unemployment rate understates employment conditions for two reasons.

First, the unemployment rate does not count those who have become so frustrated or discouraged that they have stopped looking for work. These labor-force "dropouts" may include nearly 1 million people during recessionary periods. Although they are not working, these people are not classified as unemployed because they did not try to find a job within the past four weeks.

Second, people are considered employed even when they hold part-time jobs. Someone who has lost

Classroom Resources for SECTION 1

- Reproducible Lesson Plan 16-1
- Guided Reading Activity 16-1
- Cooperative Learning Activity 18
- Consumer Application Activity 11
- Math Practice for Economics 30
- Free Enterprise Activity 18
- Primary and Secondary Source Reading 18
- Performance Assessment Activity 24
- Section Quiz 16-1
- Spanish Section Quiz 16-1

- Focus Activity Transparency 76
- Economic Concepts Transparency 16
- NBR's Economics in Action Video Program
- Testmaker
- Vocabulary PuzzleMaker
- Chapter Challenger Interactive Review Software
- MindJogger Videoquiz

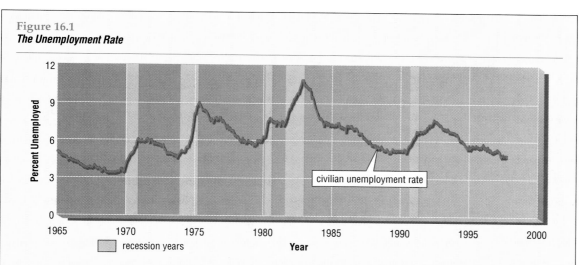

Figure 16.1
The Unemployment Rate

Percent Unemployed

civilian unemployment rate

recession years   **Year**

The unemployment rate goes up sharply during a recession and then comes down slowly thereafter. When the rate moves as little as 0.1 percent, approximately 136,500 workers are affected. **How many hours per week do you have to work for pay or profit in order to be employed?**

Source: Bureau of Labor Statistics, United States Department of Commerce.

CHAPTER 16
SECTION 1

📁 *Cooperative Learning*
Assign Cooperative Learning Activity 18.

GLENCOE
TECHNOLOGY

NIGHTLY BUSINESS REPORT
Economics in Action

Chapter 22
Disc 2, Side 1
Title: *What Are Unemployment and Inflation?*
Subject: Effects of unemployment on the nation's economy
Ask: Why does the video call unemployment a barometer of the economy? *(because unemployment tends to rise during recessions and drop during periods of expansion)*

    Also available in VHS.

a high-paying job, but is working just one hour a week at a minimum wage job, would still be considered employed. As a result, being employed is not the same as being fully employed.

Small movements in the unemployment rate have a tremendous impact on the economy. With a civilian labor force of approximately 136.5 million people, a 0.1 percent rise in the unemployment rate would mean that nearly 136,500 people had lost their jobs. This number is more than the population of cities such as Laredo, Texas; Evansville, Indiana; Boise, Idaho; or Tallahassee, Florida.

Kinds of Unemployment

Economists have identified several different kinds of unemployment. The nature and cause of each affect how much unemployment can be reduced in the economy.

Frictional Unemployment

One kind of unemployment is **frictional unemployment**—unemployment caused by workers who are "between jobs" for one reason or another. If these workers do not work for one week between jobs, they can be classified as unemployed.

The economy always has some workers who have left one job to look for or to take another. As long as workers change jobs, some frictional unemployment will be present.

Structural Unemployment

A second—and more serious—kind of unemployment is **structural unemployment**. Structural unemployment occurs when a fundamental change in the operations of the economy reduces the demand for workers and their skills.

Consumer tastes sometimes change, and certain goods and services no longer are in demand. In the

CHAPTER 16: *Unemployment, Inflation, and Poverty* **395**

 VISUAL INSTRUCTION

Mention that the unemployment survey was redesigned in 1993 after Labor Department researchers discovered that the old survey may have been underestimating the jobless rate by 0.5 percent.

Answer to Caption:
1 hour or more; 15 hours or more in a family business

Meeting Special Needs

Language Delayed Students with difficulty categorizing information will find it helpful to use a framework for comparing the different types of unemployment discussed in this section. Develop categories for these comparisons such as: Who does the unemployment affect? What is the nature of the

unemployment? What is the cause of the unemployment? How does this type of unemployment differ from the other types? How is it similar? Direct students in searching for information that might be included in these categories.

Independent Practice

Guided Reading Assign
Guided Reading Activity for
Section 1. **LEP**

Consumer Application
Assign Consumer Application
Activity 11.

Math Practice Assign
Math Practice for Economics 30.

Free Enterprise Assign
Free Enterprise Activity 18.

Readings Assign
Primary and Secondary Source
Readings 18.

Performance Assessment
Assign Performance Assessment Activity 24.

ASSESS

Check for Understanding

Assign Section 1 Review
as homework or an in-class
activity.

Use **Chapter Challenger
Interactive Review Software** to
review Section 1.

MEETING LESSON OBJECTIVES

Each objective below is
tested by the questions that
follow it in parentheses.

1. **Explain** how the Bureau
of Labor Statistics determines if a person is employed. **(1, 2, 4, 5)**

2. **Describe** five kinds of
unemployment. **(1, 3, 6)**

---

early 1900s, people reduced their demand for horses, buggies, and buggy whips in favor of domestic automobiles. Later, tastes changed in favor of foreign-made automobiles, causing considerable unemployment in Michigan, Ohio, and the industrial Northeast.

Industries may change the way they operate. During the 1990-1991 recession, a series of mergers and cost reductions trimmed the white-collar labor forces in the banking and computer industries. This change was sudden and left millions of highly skilled people out of work. Many of these workers had to develop new skills before they could find employment in other industries.

Sometimes the government contributes to structural unemployment when it changes the way it does business. Congress's decision to close military bases in the 1990s is a prime example. Military bases are much larger than private companies, and the impact of the base closings is concentrated in select regions and communities. Some areas may be able to attract new industry that would employ many of the unemployed workers, but most workers will have to develop new skills or move to other regions.

Cyclical Unemployment

A third kind of unemployment is **cyclical unemployment**—unemployment directly related to swings in the business cycle. During a recession, for example, many people put off buying certain durable goods such as automobiles, refrigerators, washers, dryers, and new homes. As a result, some industries lay off workers until the economy recovers.

DID YOU KNOW?

Stay in School! Approximately 65 percent of the 2.7 million high school graduates in 1996 were attending colleges or universities in the autumn after they graduated. Women were more likely to go to college than men— 68 percent compared to 60 percent. Nearly one-half million people dropped out of high school that same year, however. Of these, only 58 percent were in the labor force, and their unemployment rate was 28 percent.

Cyclical unemployment may be mixed with other kinds of unemployment. In 1991 the economy underwent structural unemployment among the white-collar workforce, along with cyclical unemployment because of the recession.

Even though cyclical unemployment is serious, affected workers generally get their jobs back when the economy improves. Accordingly, many try to wait out the recession by living on savings or by taking temporary jobs.

Seasonal Unemployment

A fourth kind of unemployment is **seasonal unemployment**—unemployment resulting from changes in the weather or changes in the demand for certain products. Many carpenters and builders, for example, have less work during the winter than during the spring and summer because some tasks, such as replacing a roof or digging a foundation, are harder to do when the weather is cold. Other workers, such as cashiers and clerks in retail stores, are especially in demand during holidays when stores register about 25 percent of their annual sales.

The difference between seasonal and cyclical unemployment relates to the period of measurement. Cyclical unemployment takes place over the course of the business cycle, which may last 3 to 5 years. Seasonal unemployment takes place every year, regardless of the general health of the economy.

Technological Unemployment

A fifth kind of unemployment is **technological unemployment**—unemployment caused when workers with less skills, talent, or education are replaced by machines that do their jobs. Technological unemployment happens when workers face the threat of **automation**—production with mechanical or other processes that reduces the need for workers.

In some cases, automation results in massive unemployment. Japan, for example, pioneered the use of large mechanized factories. Entire assembly lines in industries such as automobiles and steel are staffed by one-fifth of the workers needed in similar American plants.

Because technological unemployment results partly from new methods of production, it is similar to structural unemployment. The major difference

---

$ Free Enterprise Activity $

For more than 50 years, the *Occupational Outlook Handbook* has provided information about the world of work. Currently, the *Handbook* presents expected employment changes in nearly 250 occupations between now and the year 2000, including the qualifications that will be needed for them.

Ask your students to list two or three occupations that interest them. Have them research these occupations in the *Handbook* and report to the class the occupations' salaries and qualifications.

THE WALL STREET JOURNAL

PERSONNEL DEPT.

AUTOMATION DEPT.

BURBANK

"Uh-oh."

Technological Unemployment *When technological unemployment occurs, many workers find they have to learn new skills.* **What causes technological unemployment?**

between the two is that other factors totally unrelated to more efficient means of production can cause structural unemployment.

The Concept of Full Employment

Economists and others have long wrestled with the concept of full employment. Full employment does not mean zero unemployment. Instead, **full employment** is the lowest possible unemployment rate with the economy growing and all factors of production being used as efficiently as possible.

Economists have also debated whether or not there is an acceptable level of unemployment. During the 1960s, it was thought that full employment meant an unemployment rate of about 4 percent or below. Most believed that efforts to reduce unemployment below this figure would not be successful.

Although President Lyndon Johnson implemented many programs to try to lower the rate, it remained in the 5 to 6 percent range for most of the early 1960s. The rate finally did drop below 4 percent during the Vietnam War when wartime spending stimulated the economy and the draft thinned the ranks of the unemployed.

Low unemployment is difficult to achieve because of the business cycle. **Figure 16.1** shows that the 1969-1970 recession drove the unemployment rate to 6.1 percent. The 1974 recession drove the rate to 9.0 percent in 1975, and the 1981-1982 recession drove the rate to 10.8 percent. The rate declined thereafter, but the 1991 recession drove it back up to 7.8 percent. It fell below 5.0 percent in mid-1997, but the next recession will undoubtedly make it rise again.

As a result of these experiences, most economists have given up the idea of a 4 percent unemployment rate as a measure of full employment. Today, most argue that full employment is reached when the unemployment rate drops below 5 percent.

SECTION 1 REVIEW

Reviewing Terms and Facts

1. **Define** unemployed, unemployment rate, frictional unemployment, structural unemployment, cyclical unemployment, seasonal unemployment, technological unemployment, automation, full employment.
2. **Describe** how the government collects monthly data on employment.

3. **List** the five major kinds of unemployment.
4. **Identify** the level of employment that most economists today classify as full employment.

Critical Thinking

5. **Analyzing Information** Why may a government statistic about the number of employed people be misleading?

Applying Economic Concepts

6. **Employment** Examine the similarities and differences between structural and technological unemployment. Give an example of each. Why are these kinds of unemployment serious problems for an economy?

Answers to SECTION 1 REVIEW

1. All words are defined in the Glossary.

2. Bureau of the Census surveys about 50,000 households monthly looking for unemployed. Census workers turn their data over to the Bureau of Labor Statistics for analysis and publication.

3. frictional, structural, cyclical, seasonal, technological

4. below 5 percent

5. It does not count those who have stopped looking for work, and people are considered employed even when they hold part-time jobs.

6. Structural unemployment occurs when certain goods and services are no longer in demand or when industries change the way they operate. Mergers in the early 1990s trimmed many white-collar jobs. Technological unemployment results from a change in the means of production, such as when automation replaces human labor. Frictional, cyclical, and seasonal are temporary; structural and technological are long-term.

Background

Mankiller was, in fact, a CEO, because her duties as Principal Chief included running Cherokee Nation Industries. Income from the corporation's various operations—including a motel, a gift shop, a ranch, a lumber company, and a number of factories—accounts for nearly half the Cherokee Nation's annual budget.

TEACH

Review the profile with students. Then ask them to identify the qualities that may have helped Mankiller win a leadership position in the Cherokee Nation. *(She knew firsthand the problems that the Cherokee people faced; she had proved successful as a community organizer.)*

WILMA MANKILLER

(1945–   )

As the first female Principal Chief of the Cherokee Nation, Wilma Mankiller compared her job to "being president of a tiny country, a CEO, and a social worker." Mankiller, whose name comes from an eighteenth-century warrior, led 170,000 Cherokees who made up the second-largest Native American nation after the Navajos.

CHEROKEE HERITAGE
Mankiller's ancestors once lived in the Great Smoky Mountain region. During the winter of 1838-1839, federal troops forced 13,000 to 17,000

Mankiller spearheaded several community projects.

Cherokees to move to Indian Territory, in present-day Oklahoma. Thousands died along the journey known as the "Trail of Tears."

Today, many Cherokees battle poverty, ill health, unemployment, and low self-esteem. Wilma Mankiller, who was born in Tahlequah—the Cherokee capital—experienced firsthand the problems of her people. As chief, Mankiller's goal was to help Cherokees solve their own economic problems. She says, "I always try to emphasize that we can do anything if we set our minds to it."

HANDS-ON LEADERSHIP Mankiller began working with the Cherokee Nation in 1977. She organized the citizens of Bell, a rural Cherokee community near Stillwell, to build a 16-mile water pipeline. The Bell

project had several results. It provided water to a community that had none. It proved that community empowerment can succeed. In addition, it brought Wilma Mankiller into the public eye.

Mankiller was elected Deputy Chief in 1983, and she succeeded Ross Swimmer as Principal Chief when he resigned in 1985. She was then reelected with nearly 83 percent of the vote and served as Principal Chief until 1995.

The Cherokee Nation has an annual budget of more than $50 million. It operates industries, health clinics, and cultural programs that employ nearly 2,000 people. Mankiller's activities after leaving office included teaching at Dartmouth College and coediting the *Reader's Companion to the History of Women in the United States.*

OPTIMISTIC OUTLOOK Chief Mankiller remains optimistic about the future. She says,

I think the most positive thing happening is that people are beginning to understand that they can live and work in a very modern, fast-moving society . . . but also celebrate who they are as Cherokees and maintain a sense of self.

Examining the Profile

1. **Recognizing Ideologies** What was Mankiller's view about solving the economic problems of the Cherokees?

2. **For Further Research** Find out how other Native American nations are using free enterprise to fight poverty.

Answers to Examining the Profile

1. Mankiller felt that the Cherokee people must solve their economic problems themselves.

2. Research results may vary. Suggest that students present their findings in an illustrated report.

Section Preview

Objectives

After studying this section, you will be able to:

1. **Explain** how inflation is measured.
2. **Discuss** five causes of inflation.
3. **Analyze** the destabilizing consequences of inflation.

Key Terms

price level, deflation, creeping inflation, galloping inflation, hyperinflation

Applying Economic Concepts

Inflation Have you ever rushed to a store to purchase an item because you thought its price would rise? Remember all the confusion and anxiety it caused? *Inflation* affects the economy in the same way—it causes economic instability because people change their spending habits and generally act differently when they expect prices to rise.

Inflation is a special kind of economic instability—one that deals with changes in the level of prices rather than the level of employment and output. Even so, changes in prices, employment, and output are linked.

Inflation in the United States

To better understand the concept of inflation, you must examine how it is measured. A variety of terms describe the severity of inflation.

Measuring Inflation

Two terms are often used to describe prices. One is the *price level*; the other is *inflation*. The **price level** refers to the relative magnitude of prices at one point in time and is generally used for comparative purposes. Today's price level may be higher, lower, or about the same as prices five years ago.

To measure the price level, economists select a market basket of goods and construct a price index such as the consumer price index, the producer price index, or the implicit GDP price deflator. Figure 16.2 shows how the consumer price index looks from 1900 to the present. This index uses a base of 1993–95 = 100, and shows that the biggest increase in the price level took place after 1970.

Inflation is a rise in the general price level and is generally reported in terms of annual rates of change. If, for example, the price level at the beginning of one year is 111, and it reaches 115 by the beginning of the next, the inflation would be computed as follows (note that everything is multiplied by 100 at the end to convert the decimal to a percent):

$$\text{inflation rate} = \frac{\Delta \text{ price level}}{\text{beginning price level}} \times 100$$

Or,

$$\text{inflation rate} = \frac{(115-111)}{111} \times 100$$

$$= 3.6\%$$

After the change in the price level is converted to a rate, the rate is shown separately, as in Figure 16.3. The figure also shows that inflation tends to rise near the end of an expansion, and that the unemployment and slack economic conditions during a recession tend to reduce the effect of the inflation somewhat.

From time to time, unusual circumstances may cause **deflation**, or a decrease in the general price level. Only two significant deflations have taken place in the 1900s. One was during the post-World War I recession of the early 1920s. The other was during the Great Depression of the 1930s.

CHAPTER 16: *Unemployment, Inflation, and Poverty* **399**

FOCUS

Section Objectives

1. Explain how inflation is measured.
2. Discuss five causes of inflation.
3. Analyze the destabilizing consequences of inflation.

Bellringer

Prior to taking roll at the beginning of the class period, display Focus Activity Transparency 82 on the overhead projector and assign the accompanying Student Activity 82.

Motivational Activity

Discuss students' responses to the activity sheet that accompanies Focus Activity Transparency 82.

Preteaching Vocabulary

Have students locate the key terms in the text. Then call on volunteers to use each term correctly in a sentence. **LEP**

Use the **Vocabulary PuzzleMaker** to create crossword and word search puzzles.

CURRICULUM CONNECTIONS

Statistics Government researchers report that the CPI may overstate the annual cost of living by as much 1.1 percent. The problem, they report, is that the CPI does not promptly recognize changes in spending patterns.

Classroom Resources for SECTION 2

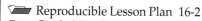

- Reproducible Lesson Plan 16-2
- Guided Reading Activity 16-2
- Reinforcing Economic Skill 16
- Section Quiz 16-2
- Spanish Section Quiz 16-2
- Focus Activity Transparency 82

- Economic Concepts Transparency 17
- Spanish Economic Concepts Transparency 17
- NBR's Economics in Action Video Program
- Testmaker
- Vocabulary PuzzleMaker
- Chapter Challenger Interactive Review Software

Figure 16.2
The Consumer Price Index

The consumer price index is a widely used measure of the price level. The CPI is used to compute the inflation rate, but is not a measure of inflation by itself. **What is the difference between the price level and the rate of inflation?**

Source: Bureau of Economic Analysis, United States Department of Commerce.

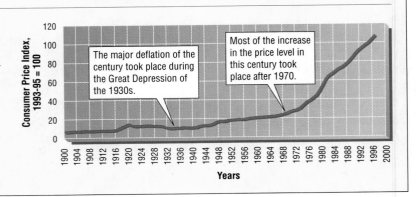

Degrees of Inflation

Several terms describe the severity of inflation. One is **creeping inflation**—inflation in the range of 1 to 3 percent per year. Another is **galloping inflation**, a more intense form of inflation that can go as high as 100 to 300 percent. Many Latin American countries and many countries in the former Communist bloc have experienced rates in this range in recent years. When inflation gets totally out of control—in the range of 500 percent a year and above—it turns into **hyperinflation**. Hyperinflation, however, does not happen very often and generally is the last stage before a total monetary collapse.

The record for hyperinflation was set in Hungary, when huge amounts of currency were printed to pay the government's bills during World War II. By the end of the war, it was claimed that 828 octillion (828,000,000,000,000,000,000,000,000,000) *pengös* equaled one prewar *pengö*. Because all the zeros would not fit on the bills, the larger denomination notes had their amounts spelled out in words rather than numbers.

Other countries such as Argentina, Mexico, Bolivia, and the former Soviet Union have had brief bouts with hyperinflation. Fortunately, inflation in the United States has never reached such proportions. Rates during the 1970s and early 1980s ranged from 5 percent to more than 15 percent as measured by the consumer price index.

Causes of Inflation

Several explanations have been offered for the causes of inflation. These explanations include the demand-pull theory, the government deficit, the cost-push theory, the wage-price spiral, and excessive monetary growth. Because no simple test determines which is better than the others, each has some validity.

Demand-Pull

One explanation is the demand-pull theory. According to this theory, all sectors in the economy try to buy more than the economy can produce.

Consumers, businesses, and governments converge on stores to buy goods and services, which causes shortages. Merchants can afford to lose some customers, so some merchants raise their prices. Others do not offer discounts or run sales. In either case, the result is the same—the price level rises.

Government Deficit

Another approach involves the federal government's deficit. Basically, this explanation is a variant of the demand-pull theory. While demand-pull blames excess demand on all sectors, the government deficit approach blames inflation only on the federal deficit.

Cultural Diversity and Economics

Hyperinflation Another example of hyperinflation occurred in Germany after World War I. Prices soared so high that people had to take wheelbarrows full of money to pay for groceries. Late in 1993, the government of former Yugoslavia issued a bank note with a face value of 50 billion dinars (worth about $12 at the time).

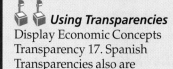
Figure 16.3
The Rate of Inflation

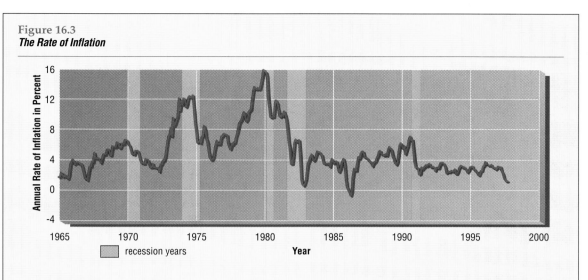

recession years — Year

Inflation tends to increase at the end of expansions, and tends to decrease during periods of recession. **How do economists compute the rate of inflation?**

Source: Bureau of Economic Analysis, United States Department of Commerce.

The federal deficit can contribute to inflation, especially if the Federal Reserve System expands the money supply to keep the interest rate down. If the debt is not monetized, some borrowers will be crowded out as interest rates rise. In such a situation, the federal deficit may have a greater destabilizing impact on output and employment than on the price level.

Cost-Push

A third explanation economists put forth is the cost-push theory. It says that labor groups—as well as others who drive up prices of inputs for manufacturers—cause inflation.

This situation might take place when a strong national union wins a large wage contract, forcing producers to raise prices to consumers to recover the labor costs. An unexpected increase in the cost of nonlabor inputs also could cause the price level to rise. Such a price rise occurred during the 1970s when oil prices went from $5 to $35 a barrel.

Wage-Price Spiral

Still another explanation says that no single group is to blame for inflation. According to this explanation, a self-perpetuating spiral of wages and prices gets started that is difficult to stop.

Higher prices force workers to ask for higher wages. If they get the higher wages, producers try to recover them with higher prices. If either side tries to increase its relative position with a larger price hike than before, the rate of inflation keeps rising.

Excessive Monetary Growth

A final reason given for inflation is excessive monetary growth. The monetary growth becomes excessive when the money supply grows faster than real GDP.

CHAPTER 16: *Unemployment, Inflation, and Poverty* **401**

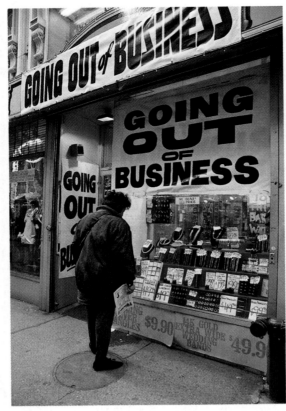

Consequences of Inflation *Inflation can cause consumers to change their spending habits, which may result in business closings.* **Why are people on fixed incomes especially hard-hit during inflationary periods?**

According to this theory, which may be the most popular of all, any extra money that is created will increase some group's purchasing power. When this money is spent, it causes a demand-pull effect that drives up prices.

Those who prefer the excess money theory to demand-pull point out that credit alone cannot keep inflation going. At some point, they say, borrowers will have gotten all the credit they can handle and the effects of demand-pull will taper off. Therefore, for inflation to continue, the money supply must grow faster than the increase in real output.

Consequences of Inflation

The problem of inflation is more severe than most people think and involves more than rising prices. Inflation can have a destabilizing effect on an economy for several reasons.

The Dollar Buys Less

The immediate and most obvious effect of inflation is that the dollar buys less. Because the purchasing power of the dollar falls as prices rise, a dollar loses value over time. For example, today the dollar buys approximately 5 cents worth of the goods and services that it bought in 1900. **Figure 16.4** shows this falling value.

Decreased purchasing power is especially hard on retired people with fixed incomes because their money buys a little less each month. Those not on fixed incomes, such as doctors, lawyers, bankers, plumbers, and accountants, are better able to cope. They can increase their fees to have additional income.

Spending Habits Change

A second destabilizing effect is that inflation can cause consumers and investors to change their spending habits, which disrupts the economy. Prices go up during an inflationary period, and the price of money—the interest rate—is no exception. In the early 1980s, the interest rate in the United States rose so high that consumer spending on durable goods, especially housing, fell dramatically.

During the recession of 1981, the impact of the interest rate on housing was particularly severe. Suppose, for example, that a young couple wanted to borrow $60,000 for 20 years to buy a house. At a 10 percent interest rate, their monthly mortgage payment would be $579.01. At 14 percent, the payment would be $746.11. In 1981 some mortgage rates reached 18 percent, which meant a monthly payment of about $926 for the same loan. As a result, the housing industry almost collapsed.

Businesses also adjusted their spending habits. In 1981, when interest rates on business loans often exceeded 20 percent, many merchants cut back on factory orders to reduce the cost of borrowing.

Extending the Content

Government and Inflation Consumers and businesses are not the only groups that suffer the adverse effects of inflation. Government, too, is affected. As prices rise, state, local, and federal governmental units must pay more for the goods and services they purchase. In order to produce more revenues for these expenditures, taxes must be raised or money must be borrowed. Interest rates, however, are higher during an inflationary period. In addition, higher taxes are especially unpopular during this time because increasing prices have already reduced real disposable income.

Figure 16.4
The Declining Value of the Dollar

When the price level goes up, the purchasing power of the dollar goes down. When the price level goes down, as it did during the Great Depression, the purchasing power of the dollar goes up. Today, the dollar buys about 5 percent of the goods and services it purchased in 1900. **If inflation continues, what will happen to the purchasing power of the dollar?**

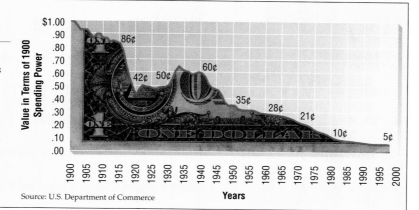

Source: U.S. Department of Commerce

Reteach
Have students summarize the section by writing a paragraph using the key terms.

Enrich
Have students research a country that has experienced hyperinflation.

CLOSE

Ask students to debate the following: "In a free enterprise economy, economic growth automatically means rising prices."

VISUAL INSTRUCTION

Ask: On average, how much value has the dollar lost annually between 1900 and 1998? *(about 1¢ per year)*

Answer to Caption:
It will decrease.

Eventually the factories had to lay off workers because of the decline in orders.

Speculation Increases

A third destabilizing effect of inflation is that it tempts some people to speculate heavily in an attempt to take advantage of a higher price level. People who ordinarily put their money in reasonably safe investments begin buying condominiums, diamonds and gemstones, works of art, and other exotic items that usually increase in price. Because such purchases divert spending from normal channels, some structural unemployment may take place.

The Distribution of Income Is Altered

Finally, inflation alters the distribution of income. During long inflationary periods, lenders are generally hurt more than borrowers. Loans made earlier are repaid later in inflated dollars—or dollars with less purchasing power because they buy less.

Suppose, for example, that a person borrows money to buy bread selling at 50 cents a loaf. If the amount borrowed was $100, it would buy 200 loaves of bread. If inflation sets in, and if the price doubles by the time the loan is paid back, the lender will be able to buy only 100 loaves of bread when the money is returned. Inflation in the long run, then, favors debtors over creditors.

SECTION 2 REVIEW

Reviewing Terms and Facts

1. **Define** price level, deflation, creeping inflation, galloping inflation, hyperinflation.
2. **Describe** how the CPI is used to compute the inflation rate.
3. **List** the five causes of inflation.
4. **Identify** four ways inflation destabilizes the economy.

Critical Thinking

5. **Understanding Cause and Effect** Explain the effect that inflation has on the financial positions of borrowers and lenders. If you managed a bank, what interest rate would you charge to overcome the disadvantage of long-term inflation?

Applying Economic Concepts

6. **Inflation** What does an inflation rate of 4 percent mean?

CHAPTER 16: *Unemployment, Inflation, and Poverty* **403**

TEACH

Write *Texas* and *California* on the chalkboard. Ask students what factors they would consider in making a comparison of these two states and note responses on the chalkboard. *(Responses will include: area, geography, population, economy, government, major cities, and so on.)* Point out that comparing such factors will help establish the similarities and differences between the states. Conclude by pointing out that this is one of the major steps in making comparisons.

Skills Practice For additional practice, have students complete Reinforcing Economic Skills 16.

CRITICAL THINKING SKILL
Making Comparisons

Which brand of hair spray costs less? Which football team has the best record? Which teacher gives the most homework? These questions involve making comparisons. When you make a comparison, you examine two or more examples to identify their similarities and differences.

Explanation

The following steps will aid you in making comparisons:
- Determine the purpose for making the comparison.
- Read or study each item to be compared.
- Identify similarities and differences among the items you are comparing.
- Draw conclusions based on the comparisons you made.

Angela, a corporate communicator who turned down two promotions:

> Job satisfaction is the most important thing to me. . . . In those other jobs, I would have had less responsibility, less of a challenge. The only benefit was more money. . . . I asked the advice of managers who had been around awhile. They said that ten or 20 years ago it would have been a black mark to turn down those jobs. . . . But in this environment, I feel that I can afford to be selective.

Linda, an engineer at the same corporation where her father has worked for 30 years:

> I feel guilty for saying this, but I don't feel the same kind of loyalty his [her father's] generation felt. They stayed through thick and thin. I wouldn't feel bad about going [elsewhere] if that's what was needed to develop my career. . . . Maybe a career isn't all it's cracked up to be. It's still important to me, but it's not the No. 1 thing in my life.

Rick, an investment broker who left a major bank to work for a smaller firm:

> I want to be happy and fulfilled—socially and culturally—and to progress in the work world to the point where I'm happy with myself. I'm not shooting for a title. . . . Our generation is much less political in the workplace than the ones that preceded us. . . . I want to earn my place with grace and style, not to lick someone else's heels for it.

—"What 25-Year-Olds Want," *Fortune*

Practice

In the 1990s, *Fortune* magazine conducted a survey to find out how 25-year-olds felt about their careers. All those interviewed were college graduates who worked for major corporations or professional firms. Read the excerpts below, then answer the questions that follow.
1. What is the purpose for this comparison?
2. What are the similarities among Angela, Linda, and Rick?
3. What are the differences among Angela, Linda, and Rick?
4. According to these three people, how did the attitudes of the previous generation differ from their own?
5. What conclusion can you draw from this comparison?

Additional Practice

For further practice in making comparisons, complete the Reinforcing Skills exercise in the Chapter 16 Review on page 415.

Answers to SKILL

1. to determine whether attitudes toward careers are the same or different among members of this generation and the previous generation's
2. All are the same age, hold good jobs, and have similar attitudes toward work.
3. Angela turned down promotions because they did not advance her career. Linda would ignore her family's strong ties to the company for advancement. Rick prefers social and cultural fulfillment rather than traditional career advancement.
4. Members of the previous generation would feel obliged to accept promotions, had much more company loyalty, and would compete for status. Members of this generation feel that they can be selective, can change jobs, and can balance a career with other interests.
5. Answers will vary. Most students will note that the way young people view career advancement is very different from the way it was viewed even 10 years ago.

Section Preview

Objectives

After studying this section, you will be able to:

1. **Explain** how economists measure the distribution of income.
2. **Discuss** the reasons for the inequality of income.
3. **Describe** how poverty levels are defined and measured.
4. **Discuss** six antipoverty programs.

Key Terms

Lorenz curve, blue-collar worker, white-collar worker, poverty threshold, income-to-poverty ratio, welfare, food stamps, negative income tax, enterprise zone, workfare

Applying Economic Concepts

Distribution of Income Do you compare what you make to the earnings of others? The Department of Commerce does, too. It measures and ranks incomes to examine the *distribution of income.*

FOCUS

Section Objectives

1. Explain how economists measure the distribution of income.
2. Discuss the reasons for the inequality of income.
3. Describe how poverty levels are defined and measured.
4. Discuss six antipoverty programs.

Bellringer

Prior to taking roll at the beginning of the class period, display Focus Activity Transparency 83.

Motivational Activity

Discuss students' responses to the activity sheet that accompanies Transparency 83.

Preteaching Vocabulary

Call on students to find and read aloud the definition of each key term. Ask other students to restate the meaning in their own words. **LEP**

Use the **Vocabulary Puzzlemaker** to create crossword and word search puzzles.

? DID YOU KNOW

Some European countries, worried by rising unemployment rates, have called for the institution of a four-day work week. Although it would mean a cut in workers' wages, many unions support the idea. In Italy, unions are campaigning with the slogan: "Work less, and everyone works."

In the United States, as elsewhere, people do not have the same income. Economists use the term *distribution of income* to describe the way income is distributed among individuals, families, households, and other groups.

The Distribution of Income

Economists analyze the distribution of income in several ways. It can be analyzed by looking at households, families, single individuals, geographic regions, race and ethnic origin, sex, or educational attainment.

A more common method is to use the family as the basic income unit and then rank all families from lowest to highest. After the incomes are ranked, the ranking is divided into quintiles, or fifths, and then examined.

Table **A** in **Figure 16.5** shows quintile data for two different years. This data is then shown as a **Lorenz curve**—a curve that shows how much the actual distribution of income varies from an equal distribution. In Graph **B,** 4.2 percent of the total income is the amount that the lowest quintile receives. This amount is combined with the income the next quintile earns, and then plotted as point **a.** This number is then added to the income that the middle quintile earns and is plotted as point **b**—showing that the poorest 60

percent of the families earned 30.0 percent of the total income. This process continues until the cumulative values of all quintiles are plotted.

If all families received exactly the same income, the Lorenz curve would appear as a diagonal line running from one corner of the graph to the other. Therefore, 20 percent of the families would earn 20 percent of the income, and 80 percent of the families would earn 80 percent of the income. Because all families do not receive the same income, however, the curve showing the actual income distribution is not a diagonal. The area on the graph between the diagonal and the Lorenz curve shows the degree of income inequality. The larger this area, the more unequal the distribution of income.

Reasons for Income Inequality

A number of reasons explain why the incomes of various groups may be different. They include education, wealth, discrimination, ability, and monopoly power.

Education

Some people have higher incomes than others because they have more education. Education puts them in a better position to get higher-paying jobs

---

406

TEACH

Guided Practice

L3   *Writing a News Article*

Write the following on the chalkboard: *education, wealth, discrimination, ability, monopoly power.* Tell students that these factors are the major topics for a newspaper article on income inequality. Call on volunteers to suggest how the listed factors might help to explain income inequality. Note responses under the appropriate factor. Then ask students to use information on the chalkboard to write the news article. Select students to read their articles to the class.

VISUAL INSTRUCTION

Ask: In which direction does the Lorenz Curve move if income distribution becomes more unequal? *(to the right, further from the diagonal)*

Answer to Caption:

education, wealth, discrimination, ability, monopoly power

Figure 16.5
The Distribution of Income by Families

(A) Family Income Ranked by Quintiles

	1980	-------- 1996 --------	
	Quintiles	Quintiles	Cumulative
Lowest Fifth	5.3%	4.2%	4.2%
Second Fifth	11.6%	10.0%	14.2%
Third Fifth	17.6%	15.8%	30.0%
Fourth Fifth	24.4%	23.1%	53.1%
Highest Fifth	41.1%	46.8%	100.0%
Top 5 percent	14.6%	20.3%	

Source: U.S. Bureau of the Census.

The Lorenz curve is often used to show the distribution of income in the United States. Between 1980 and 1996, the distribution of income became more unequal, with each lower quintile earning slightly less than it did in the earlier period.
What five factors help explain why some groups have more income than others?

---

that require a higher level of skills. Although exceptions exist, there generally is a strong relationship between median income and level of education.

Wealth

Income also tends to vary because some people in the United States hold more wealth than others, and the distribution of wealth is even more unequal than the distribution of income. When wealth holders are ranked from highest to lowest, the top fifth has 75 percent of all the wealth in the country. The bottom two-fifths, which is 40 percent of the people in the country, have less than 2 percent of the total wealth.

This inequality clearly has an impact on people's ability to earn income. Wealthy families can send their children to expensive colleges and universities. The wealthy can also afford to set their children up in business so they can earn a better income. Even if the wealthy choose not to work, they can make investments that will bring them tax-free income.

Discrimination

Discrimination is another factor that influences the distribution of income. Women may not be promoted to executive positions in some companies because male executives believe that women cannot handle the pressures of such jobs. Certain unions may deny immigrants or ethnic minorities membership on the grounds that certain ethnic groups "don't belong" in certain professions.

Although discrimination is against the law, it still takes place. When it does occur, discrimination causes women and minority groups to be crowded into other labor markets where oversupply drives down wages.

Ability

Some people earn more income because they have certain natural abilities, such as a professional athlete who earns millions of dollars every year. Such athletes as Barry Bonds, Michael Jordan, Shaquille O'Neal, and Steffi Graf earn high incomes because they have

---

Meeting Special Needs

Study Strategy   To help build discussion skills for gifted students, appoint two or three students to plan and lead a class or panel discussion about the Lorenz curve—how it is constructed, how cumulative percentages are arrived at, and what a "wider" curve means. Be sure students limit the focus of the discussion and take into account the class time allowed.

unique abilities or talents. The same is true of popular performers such as Oprah Winfrey or Harrison Ford.

Monopoly Power

Another important reason for differences in the distribution of income is the degree of monopoly power that certain groups hold. Unions, for example, have considerable power and have been able to obtain higher wages for their members. Union carpenters, electricians, truck drivers, auto workers, and other **blue-collar workers**—industrial or factory workers who receive wages—generally are paid higher wages than those workers who are not in unions. Some **white-collar workers**—clerical, business, or professional workers who generally are salaried—also hold a degree of monopoly power. The American Medical Association, for example, has been successful in limiting the number of people in its profession by limiting enrollments in medical schools.

Poverty

Poverty is a relative measure that depends on prices, the standard of living, and the incomes that others earn. What may seem like poverty to one person may seem like riches to another. Even so, government figures show that more than 13.7 percent of all Americans lived in poverty in 1996. To understand how this happens, the definition of poverty as well as poverty-related issues must be examined.

Defining Poverty

Families and individuals are defined as living in poverty if their incomes fall below a certain level, or threshold. The **poverty threshold** is the annual dollar benchmark used to evaluate the money income that families and unrelated individuals receive. For administrative purposes, the thresholds are converted into the *poverty guidelines* shown in **Figure 16.6**. If families and unrelated individuals have an annual income below this level, they are in poverty. Supplements such as food stamps, subsidized housing, and medicaid do not count in the computation.

In 1964 the Social Security Administration developed poverty measures using two studies the United States Department of Agriculture did in the 1950s. The first study developed four alternative, but nutri-

tionally adequate, food plans for individuals and families of different sizes. The least expensive food plan was then selected as the food budget that would keep people out of poverty.

The second study found that families typically spend one-third of their total income on food. To obtain the poverty limits, the Social Security Administration simply multiplied the least expensive food budget by three. Today, the guidelines are indexed to the inflation rate so they go up just enough every year to offset the increase in the price level.

Income-to-Poverty Ratios

The Lorenz curve ranked family incomes but did not tell anything about the number of people in poverty. The United States Department of Commerce uses a different method to make this comparison.

Figure 16.6
Poverty Guidelines

Size of Family Unit	1996	1997
1 person	$7,740	$7,890
2 persons	10,360	10,610
3 persons	12,980	13,330
4 persons	15,600	16,050
5 persons	18,220	18,770
6 persons	20,840	21,490
7 persons	23,460	24,210
8 persons	26,080	26,930
9 persons	28,700	29,650

Guidelines for Alaska and Hawaii are slightly higher.

Families and unrelated individuals who have incomes below the official poverty levels listed above are defined as being in poverty. Only money income is counted. Other aid such as food stamps, medicaid, and subsidized housing, while helpful, is not counted. These numbers are indexed annually to the rate of inflation. **How were the poverty measures first established?**

Source: *The Federal Register*, various editions.

$ Free Enterprise Activity $

Have students review the discussion of the income-to-poverty ratio on pages 407–408. Then have them calculate the income-to-poverty ratio for the following:

1. A family of four with an income of $25,000 in 1997. ($25,000 ÷ $16,050 = 1.56)

2. An individual with an income of $10,000 in 1997. ($10,000 ÷ $7,890 = 1.27)

3. A family of 3 with an income of $11,500 in 1997. ($11,500 ÷ $13,330 = 0.86)

4. An individual who earned $6,750 in 1997. ($6,750 ÷ $7,890 = 0.86)

5. A family of eight with an income of $38,000 in 1997. ($38,000 ÷ $26,930 = 1.41)

Have students identify which of the families and individuals lived below the poverty threshold. (3, 4)

Independent Practice

📁 **Guided Reading** Assign Guided Reading Activity for Section 3. **LEP**

L2 Conducting an Interview
Have students investigate which local government agencies provide assistance for low-income families in the community. Then have students interview an official at one of these agencies to determine the answers to the following: What assistance programs does the agency oversee? Who is eligible for benefits? How much is given in benefits? Is some form of work required of benefit recipients who are capable of working? Are there any restrictions on those receiving benefits? In your opinion, what are the strengths and weaknesses of your assistance programs? Have students report their findings to the rest of the class.

VISUAL INSTRUCTION

Ask: In what year was the top fifth's income-to-poverty ratio highest? *(1996)*

Answer to Caption:

The lowest fifth has remained at or below the poverty threshold. The highest fifth made considerable gains over time.

DID YOU KNOW

Before the establishment of many antipoverty programs in the 1960s, more than 20 percent of all Americans lived in poverty.

Figure 16.7
Average Income-to-Poverty Ratios

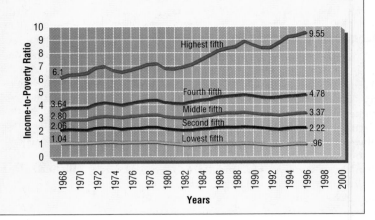

Income-to-poverty ratios are used to adjust for the differences in family sizes. When ranked by quintiles, all groups except for the lowest made some progress between 1968 and 1996. The .96 ratio for the lowest fifth means that the average family income for that group is only 96 percent of the poverty threshold. **What has happened to the lowest and the highest fifths over time?**

Source: U.S. Census Bureau.

The measure is the **income-to-poverty ratio**, which divides family income by the poverty level. This measure, according to the Department of Commerce, has the advantage of compensating for family size:

. . . a four-person family containing two related children under 18 with an income in 1991 of $25,000 would have an income-to-poverty level of 1.81 (i.e. $25,000/$13,812). A two-person family . . . with an income of $25,000 in 1991 would have a much higher ratio of 2.72 ($25,000/$9,120). A ratio under 1.00 indicates that the family was below the poverty level during the calendar year. Income-to-poverty ratios . . . adjust for family size and economies of scale, enabling more reasonable comparisons of economic well-being between families.
—U.S. Department of Commerce, *Money Income of Households, Families, and Persons in the United States: 1991*

These ratios, like family incomes, can be ranked and divided into quintiles. For 1996, **Figure 16.7** shows that, on average, the entire lowest quintile—or 20 percent of American families—have incomes that place them below the poverty threshold.

To see how the distribution of poverty changes over time, one can examine the average income-to-poverty ratio for each quintile to see if it is going up or down. For incomes to become more equal over time, the ratios for the upper quintiles would have to fall and the ratios for the lower quintiles would have to rise. **Figure 16.7** shows exactly the opposite.

What Caused the Gap to Grow?

According to the Bureau of the Census, the growing spread in the distribution of income that took place in the 1980s occurred for several reasons. The first involved a structural change in the economy as industry changed from goods production to service production. Because wages are typically lower in the service industries such as fast-food chains, movie theaters, and entertainment parks, weekly paychecks tend to be lower. ☑️

The second reason for the spread in income distribution was the growing gap between well-educated and poorly educated workers. During the 1990s, wages for the highly skilled soared, while wages for the less skilled tended to remain about the same. The addition of many low-skilled immigrants during this period helped widen the disparity.

A third reason, declining unionism—especially among low-skilled workers—added to the growing differential. Unions have successfully kept the wages of their workers well above the wages paid to nonunion workers. The decline of unions meant that many of the low-skilled workers had to work elsewhere for less pay. **1**

The fourth reason for the income gap concerns the changing structure of the American family. The shift from married-couple families to single-parent families and other nonfamily household living arrangements tends to lower average family income.

Extending the Content

Distribution of Poverty Poverty is not evenly distributed across the country. In 1996, for example, the states with the highest rates of poverty were Washington D.C., Mississippi, Louisiana, and New Mexico. In contrast, the lowest poverty rates were found in New Hampshire, Utah, Indiana, and Alaska. Refer students to Figure 16.8 on page 410 and point out that, in general, there is an inverse relationship between poverty rates and income. In other words, states with high income levels tend to have lower poverty rates.

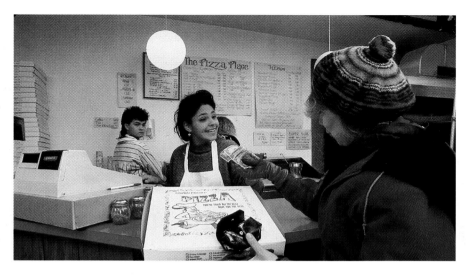

Distribution of Income
One reason for the spread in income distribution is the increasing number of workers in low-paying service jobs, such as fast-food servers. **How has the changing structure of the family contributed to the income distribution disparity?**

Antipoverty Programs

Over the years, the federal government has instituted a number of programs to help the needy. Most come under the general heading of **welfare**—economic and social programs that provide regular assistance from the government or private agencies because of need. These welfare programs provide three basic kinds of help—income assistance, general assistance, and assistance in the form of social service programs. Other antipoverty programs include proposals for a negative income tax, enterprise zones, and workfare.

Income Assistance

Programs that provide direct cash assistance to those in need fall into the category of income assistance. One such program is the Temporary Aid to Needy

Families (TANF), which replaced the Aid to Families with Dependent Children (AFDC) in 1996. States determine whether a family is eligible. Although provisions and benefits vary state to state, many families are able to receive cash payments because of the death, continuous absence, or permanent disability of a parent. The TANF was part of the 1996 welfare reform bill and is designed to expire in 2002. **2**

Another income assistance program is the Supplemental Security Income (SSI), which makes cash payments to blind or disabled persons age 65 and older. Originally, the states administered the program because benefits varied so much from state to state. The federal government took it over in 1979.

General Assistance

Programs that assist poor people but do not provide direct cash assistance fall into the category of

---

Checking Understanding

1. How did the decline of unionism affect the general level of wages?
2. Who determines which families are eligible for TANF?

Applying Economic Concepts

Income While the wages of many workers dropped in the 1980s, the richest Americans accrued even more wealth—until the richest 1 percent owned 36 percent of the country's total wealth.

L3 Writing a Report
Organize students into six groups and assign each group one of the types of antipoverty programs discussed in the section. Have groups prepare a report that outlines the history and development of their assigned program and evaluates its effectiveness in combatting poverty. Direct groups to choose representatives to present their reports to the class.

 VISUAL INSTRUCTION

Before students answer the caption question, have them identify four reasons for the spread in income distribution. (*structural change in economy, growing gap between well-educated and poorly educated workers, declining unionism, changing family structure*)

Answer to Caption:

The shift from married-couple families to single-parent families tended to lower family income.

 ANSWERS

1. Unions had successfully kept their members' wages above those of nonunion members. The decline of unions lessened wage differential between union and nonunion workers.
2. individual states

Cultural Diversity and Economics

Historical Perspective A congressional investigation into poverty, conducted during the early 1960s, found that people from certain racial, ethnic, and social groups were more likely to be poor than others. The report noted that nearly half of all nonwhite Americans lived in poverty. In addition, it found that impoverishment affected almost 50 percent of all families headed by women or senior citizens of either sex. The report also found a correlation between education and poverty; nearly two-thirds of poor families were headed by people who had only an elementary-school education.

ASSESS

Check for Understanding

Assign Section 3 Review on page 412 as homework or an in-class activity.

Use **Chapter Challenger Interactive Review Software** to review Section 3.

MEETING LESSON OBJECTIVES

Each objective below is tested by the questions that follow it in parentheses.

1. **Explain** how economists measure the distribution of income. **(1, 2, 6, 7)**

2. **Discuss** the reasons for the inequality of income. **(3, 6)**

3. **Describe** how poverty levels are defined and measured. **(1, 4)**

4. **Discuss** six antipoverty programs. **(1, 5)**

VISUAL INSTRUCTION

Have students identify any regional patterns in per capita personal income and average annual percentage growth of real per capita personal income.

Answer to Caption:

Answers will vary.

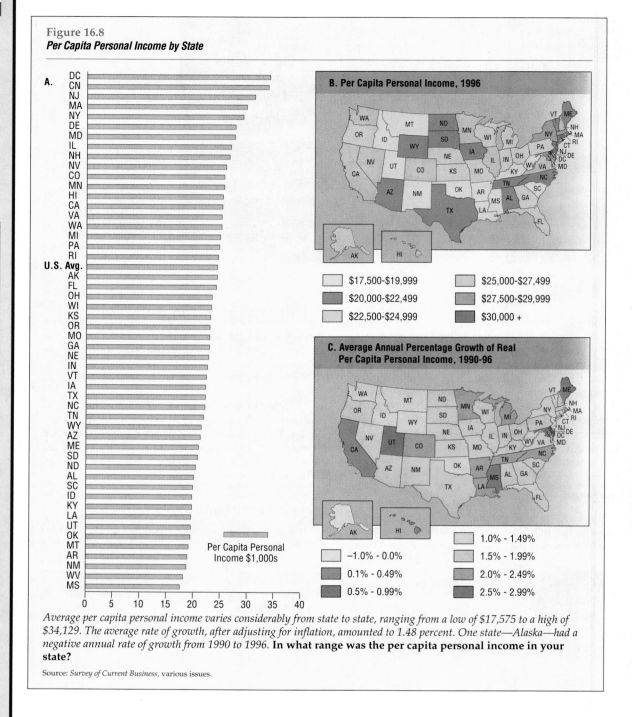

Figure 16.8
Per Capita Personal Income by State

B. Per Capita Personal Income, 1996

- $17,500–$19,999
- $20,000–$22,499
- $22,500–$24,999
- $25,000–$27,499
- $27,500–$29,999
- $30,000 +

C. Average Annual Percentage Growth of Real Per Capita Personal Income, 1990-96

- −1.0% - 0.0%
- 0.1% - 0.49%
- 0.5% - 0.99%
- 1.0% - 1.49%
- 1.5% - 1.99%
- 2.0% - 2.49%
- 2.5% - 2.99%

Per Capita Personal Income $1,000s

Average per capita personal income varies considerably from state to state, ranging from a low of $17,575 to a high of $34,129. The average rate of growth, after adjusting for inflation, amounted to 1.48 percent. One state—Alaska—had a negative annual rate of growth from 1990 to 1996. **In what range was the per capita personal income in your state?**

Source: *Survey of Current Business*, various issues.

410 Unit 4: *Macroeconomics: Policies*

$ Free Enterprise Activity $

Have students write at least three ideas for reducing poverty. Call on students to share their lists with the class and note on the chalkboard the most frequently mentioned solutions. Lead a class discussion on the economic and social costs and benefits of the solutions noted on the chalkboard. Finally, have students select which idea they think is the best and write letters to the editor of the local newspaper proposing this solution to the problem of poverty.

general assistance. One example is the food stamp program that serves millions of Americans. **Food stamps** are government-issued coupons that can be redeemed for food. They may be given or sold to eligible low-income persons. If, for example, a person pays 40 cents for a $1 food coupon, that person is getting a dollar's worth of food for a fraction of its cost. The program, which began in 1961 and became law in 1964, is different from other programs because it is based solely on income. Age, race, and physical condition play no part in determining eligibility. **1**

Another general assistance program is medicaid— a joint federal-state medical insurance program. Under the program, the federal government pays a majority of health-care costs, and the state governments pay the rest. Medicaid serves millions of Americans, including children, the visually impaired, and the disabled. ☑

Social Service Programs

Over the years, the individual states have developed a wide variety of social service programs to help the needy. These include such areas as child abuse prevention, foster care, family planning, job training, child welfare, and day care.

Although the states control the kinds of services the programs provide, the federal government matches part of the cost. To be eligible for matching funds, a state must file an annual service plan. If the plan is approved, the state is free to select the social issues it wishes to address, set the eligibility requirements, and decide how the program is to be carried out.

Negative Income Tax

The **negative income tax** is a proposed type of tax that would make cash payments to certain groups below the poverty line. Called a negative income tax, it is different from the antipoverty programs listed above because it is a market-based program designed to encourage people to work. **2**

Under the negative income tax, the federal government would set an income level below which people do not have to pay taxes. Then, the government would pay a certain amount of money to any person who earned less than that level. A person who earned no income during a year might receive $3,000, making that person's total income for the year $3,000. Someone else who actually earned $3,000 might receive $1,500 from the government, bringing that person's annual income to $4,500. A third person who made $6,000 would receive nothing from the government, but would also not make enough to pay taxes.

Anyone who earned more than $6,000, however, would have to pay some taxes. In addition, as income got higher, so would the taxes. A person with an

QUICK CHECK

Checking Understanding

1. How do food stamps lower recipients' grocery bills?
2. How does the negative income tax differ from other antipoverty programs?

Applying Economic Concepts

☑ **Income Distribution** Large-scale social welfare programs began during the Great Depression. Economic conditions were so bad that private charities could not help everyone who needed financial assistance. Today, charities and the government share the costs of public assistance.

CHAPTER 16: *Unemployment, Inflation, and Poverty* **411**

Extending the Content

War on Poverty In his Inaugural Address, President John F. Kennedy stressed that fighting poverty would be a major priority of his administration. To ease the plight of the poor, Kennedy pushed for an increase in the minimum wage and passed the Area Redevelopment Act, which authorized grants to depressed areas, and the Housing Act of 1961, which was directed toward improving low- and middle-income housing.

After Kennedy's assassination, President Lyndon B. Johnson continued these efforts, declaring an "unconditional war on poverty." As a result, a profusion of legislation poured out of Congress, establishing such antipoverty programs as the Job Corps, a work training scheme for young Americans; Head Start, a program for preschoolers from poor families; Volunteers in Service to America (VISTA), which sent volunteers to work in depressed neighborhoods; and medicaid, which provided free health care for the poor.

CLOSE

Encourage students to imagine they are designing a time capsule to be opened in the year 2100. Have them select 12 items to include in the capsule that would tell people of the future about unemployment, inflation, and poverty in the 1990s.

CURRICULUM CONNECTIONS

Government The antipoverty legislation of the 1960s was stimulated by the publication of Michael Harrington's *The Other America* (1962). In it, Harrington pointed out the irony that in the world's most affluent nation, nearly one-fourth of the population lived in poverty.

VISUAL INSTRUCTION

Have students investigate any enterprise zones in their community.

Answer to Caption:

Unemployed people can find work in their own neighborhoods; run-down areas can begin to grow.

income of $10,000 might pay a tax of $1,500, while a person with an income of $15,000 might pay $3,000.

The negative income tax could be cost-effective because it would eliminate costly welfare programs, yet still allow people to have money to spend as they saw fit. Government would also save because it would have fewer administrative costs. Although the tax is not used, many people believe it would be a reasonable alternative to the existing welfare programs.

Enterprise Zones

Special **enterprise zones** are areas where companies can locate free of certain local, state, and federal tax laws and operating restrictions. The zones benefit businesses and area residents because people can find work without worrying about transportation, and run-down areas can begin to grow.

Nearly everyone agrees that one of the best weapons in the fight against poverty is a healthy and growing economy. The enterprise zone concept is an attempt to focus some of that growth directly in the areas that need it most, making more employment opportunities available.

Workfare Programs

Because of rising welfare costs, many state and local governments require those who receive welfare to provide labor in exchange for benefits. **Workfare** is a program that requires welfare recipients to

Enterprise Zones *Quincy Market in Boston, Massachusetts, has been revitalized with shops, boutiques, and restaurants.* **How do enterprise zones help businesses and area residents?**

exchange some of their labor for benefits. People on workfare often assist law enforcement officials or sanitation and highway crews, or perform other types of community service work.

The work is required of almost everyone except those with very young children, the disabled, and the elderly. Supporters of the program argue that the recipients learn skills on the job.

SECTION 3 REVIEW

Reviewing Terms and Facts

1. **Define** Lorenz curve, blue-collar worker, white-collar worker, poverty threshold, income-to-poverty ratio, welfare, food stamps, negative income tax, enterprise zone, workfare.
2. **Describe** how the distribution of income is measured.
3. **List** the five main reasons for inequality of income.

4. **Explain** how income-to-poverty ratios are used to measure the growing inequality of income.
5. **Identify** the major programs and proposals designed to alleviate the problem of poverty.

Critical Thinking

6. **Analyzing Information** Some people have said that the "rich got richer" in the 1990s. What

factors can you cite to explain that what actually happened was more complex than this simple statement?

Applying Economic Concepts

7. **Distribution of Income** What would happen to the Lorenz curve if aid such as food stamps and medicaid were treated as income?

Answers to SECTION 3 REVIEW

1. All words are defined in the Glossary.
2. Incomes are ranked by families from lowest to highest, then divided into quintiles. Quintile data is then plotted as a Lorenz curve.
3. education, wealth, discrimination, ability, monopoly power
4. Family income is divided by the poverty level. These ratios are then ranked and divided into quintiles. The income-to-poverty ratios for each quintile are spreading farther apart, revealing a growing

inequality of income.
5. TANF; SSI; food stamps; medicaid; social service programs such as child abuse prevention, foster care, family planning; enterprise zones; workfare
6. Students may note the reasons for income inequality and the gap in the income-to-poverty ratio.
7. It would move closer to the 45-degree diagonal, with less area between it and the diagonal line.

ECONOMICS IN ACTION

What Are Unemployment and Inflation?

Setting Up the Video

With your classmates, view "What Are Unemployment and Inflation?" on the videodisc *Economics in Action*. The video focuses on the effects of unemployment and inflation on the nation's economy. Unemployment tends to rise in times of recession and drop during times of expansion. News segments detail unemployment and inflation in 1997.

Chapter 22
Disc 2, Side 1

View the video by scanning the bar code or by entering the chapter number on your keypad and pressing Search. *(Also available in VHS format.)*

Hands-On Activity

The greatest period of unemployment occurred during the Great Depression in the 1930s. Research to see how unemployment affected the country since the year 1900. Use a copy of the *Statistical Abstract of the United States* or the Internet to find data on unemployment from 1900 to today. Use the data to construct a line graph. Share your graph with the class.

SURFING THE "NET"

Measuring Unemployment

The Bureau of the Census identifies unemployed persons in monthly samples of approximately 50,000 households across the country. The number of unemployed is then divided by the civilian labor force to express unemployment as a rate. The unemployment rate is comprehensive but does not count the dropouts, nor does it distinguish between full and part-time employment. Use the Internet to find out the current level of unemployment.

Getting There

1. Use a search engine. Type in the word *unemployment.*
2. Next, enter words like the following to focus your search: *Bureau of the Census, unemployment rate,* and *labor force.*
3. The search engine will provide you with a number of links to follow. Links are "pointers" to different sites on the Internet and often appear as blue, underlined words.

What to Do When You Are There

Click on the links to navigate through the pages of information. Gather your findings. Use the findings to write several paragraphs describing the definition, measurement, and current level of unemployment. Share your paragraphs with the class.

413

GLENCOE TECHNOLOGY

NIGHTLY BUSINESS REPORT

Economics in Action

Chapter 22
Disc 2, Side 1

Title: *What Are Unemployment and Inflation?*

If you do not have access to a videodisc player, the **Economics in Action** programs are also available in VHS.

INTERNET SITES

The following are possible sites for completing the "Net" activities:

Poverty Statistics
http://www.census.gov/hhes/www/poverty.html

Economic Statistics Briefing Room (Unemployment)
http://www.whitehouse.gov/fsbr/employment.html

Not on the "Net"...

If students have limited or no access to the Internet, have them complete the activity "Measuring Unemployment" by using *Readers' Guide to Periodical Literature* at the school or local library. Students should look for articles about unemployment and the labor force. They should then find the articles and other resources they need to complete their research.

INTERNET ADDRESS BOOK

Internet addresses that you find useful can be noted in the space below for quick reference.

GLENCOE
TECHNOLOGY

VIDEODISC
MindJogger Videoquiz

Use MindJogger to review the Chapter 16 content.

Chapter 16
Disc 2, Side B

Also available in VHS.

Answers

Reviewing Key Terms

1. f.	7. e.	13. k.
2. d.	8. p.	14. i.
3. j.	9. n.	15. o.
4. m.	10. a.	16. c.
5. l.	11. h.	
6. b.	12. g.	

Reviewing the Facts

1. It is the number of unemployed individuals divided by the total number of persons in the civilian labor force.

2. frictional, structural, cyclical, seasonal, technological

3. It is reached when the unemployment rate drops below 5 percent.

4. The price level refers to the relative magnitude of prices at one point in time. Inflation is a rise in the general price level and is generally reported in terms of annual rates of change.

5. demand-pull, the government deficit, cost-push, wage-price spiral, and excessive monetary growth

6. The dollar buys less, spending habits change, speculation increases, and the distribution of income is altered.

7. the way income is distributed among individuals, families, households, and

414

CHAPTER 16 REVIEW

Reviewing Key Terms

Write the letter of the key term that best matches each definition below.

a. blue-collar workers
b. cyclical unemployment
c. unemployed
d. food stamps
e. frictional unemployment
f. full employment
g. income-to-poverty ratio
h. inflation
i. Lorenz curve
j. poverty threshold
k. price level
l. seasonal unemployment
m. structural unemployment
n. technological unemployment
o. white-collar workers
p. workfare

1. an unemployment rate below 5 percent
2. an example of a welfare program
3. annual benchmark used to evaluate the money income that families receive
4. caused by a shift in demand or a change in the way the economy operates
5. caused by annual changes in weather, holiday seasons
6. caused by periodic swings in business activity
7. caused by workers who are "between jobs" for short periods
8. describes the requirement that welfare recipients exchange labor for benefits
9. happens when workers face the threat of automation
10. industrial workers who receive wages
11. measured by changes in the CPI
12. measure of income that compensates for family size
13. measured by the CPI
14. shows how much the actual distribution of income differs from an equal distribution

414 UNIT 4: *Macroeconomics: Policies*

---

15. workers who receive salaries
16. works less than one hour per week for pay or profit

Reviewing the Facts

SECTION 1 *(pages 394–397)*
1. **Describe** how the unemployment rate is computed.
2. **Identify** the major types of unemployment.
3. **Explain** what is meant by full employment.

SECTION 2 *(pages 399–403)*
4. **Compare** the difference between the price level and inflation.
5. **Identify** the five causes of inflation.
6. **List** four destabilizing effects of inflation.

SECTION 3 *(pages 405–412)*
7. **Explain** what is meant by the distribution of income.
8. **Identify** five major reasons for inequality in the distribution of income.
9. **Explain** how the Lorenz curve is used to show the inequality of income distribution.
10. **Name** six antipoverty programs.

Critical Thinking

1. **Analyzing Information** Of the reasons for income inequality listed in the chapter, which reason would be most difficult for government to influence or control? Explain.
2. **Synthesizing Information** Explain how the government calculates the rate of inflation.

Applying Economic Concepts

1. **Employment** Explain why full employment does not mean that everyone has a job.
2. **Inflation** List two causes of inflation for which the government may be responsible.

---

other groups

8. education, wealth, discrimination, ability, and monopoly power

9. Family incomes are ranked from lowest to highest, then the ranking is divided into quintiles. This information, plotted as a Lorenz curve, shows how much the actual distribution of income varies from an equal distribution.

10. income assistance, general assistance, social serv-

ice programs, negative income tax, enterprise zones, workfare programs, and any specific programs under these general headings

Critical Thinking

1. Answers will vary. Students may note that discrimination and ability would be difficult for government to influence or control. Although antidiscrimination laws already are in place, it is difficult to control or change people's attitudes.

Reinforcing Skills

MAKING COMPARISONS

Read the excerpts below, then answer the questions that follow.

(1) In Texas, the state's education commissioner has proposed replacing textbooks with laptop computers.

. . . [A]s schools nationwide rush to spend billions of dollars installing computers, a growing body of research questions whether this expensive endeavor is paying off in improved student performance.

The problem is that rosy expectations are crashing against the reality of low budgets. Schools buy computers, then fail to retool teacher training and curricula to take advantage of them.

Without remedial action, the $4 billion being spent annually to wire the nation's schools risks being wasted on well-stocked computer labs that too few educators and students can put to effective use.

(2) One of the great needs of American business today is a workforce skilled in communications and computer technology. To succeed in the 21st century economy, kids need to get their hands on the tools of the 21st century today.

Computers and communications networks create specialized learning for children with disabilities, children who don't use English as a first language and children who want to pursue specialized subjects not taught in their schools. . . .

All studies show that parental involvement is the most important factor in school success. So shouldn't parents be encouraged to be involved by making phone calls and sending e-mail to teachers? That requires connecting every classroom.

—USA Today, October 7, 1997

1. What is the purpose for this comparison?
2. How does the second view differ from the first?
3. What conclusion can you draw from this comparison?

Individual Activity

Unemployment is an experience most people would like to avoid. Review the five kinds of unemployment identified in this chapter. Write a paragraph explaining how you could prepare in order to avoid each kind. Consider such factors as education, type of job, and location you might choose.

Cooperative Learning Activity

Organize into a number of groups corresponding to the categories of job listings in the Help Wanted ads of your local newspaper. Group A, for example, could be assigned the sales ads; Group B, the medical ads; and so on. Each group should count the total number of jobs listed, find the average wage from among those that list salaries, and list the general qualifications for different jobs in each set of ads. After all facts are compiled, compare job categories. Where are the best opportunities?

Technology Activity

Using the Internet

In the **Journal Writing** activity on page 393, you were asked to summarize current trends in inflation and unemployment that you read about in newspapers. Now look for information from the following sites on the Internet: the Census Bureau, the Bureau of Economic Analysis, and the Economic Statistics Briefing Room.

Search for recent articles discussing unemployment, inflation, or poverty. Download at least two recent press releases from each of the above sites. Summarize the articles and share your findings with other members of the class.

integrated into the classroom to enable American students to succeed in the 21st century economy; to create specialized learning for children with disabilities or who do not speak English as a first language; and to encourage parents to be involved in their children's education.

3. People differ on the amount and speed of technology they feel should be integrated into America's classrooms.

? BONUS TEST QUESTION

Have students answer the following problem:

1. What is the unemployment rate under the following circumstances: The civilian labor force numbers 15,000; there are 945 people available and looking for work; 20 of these people worked more than 3 hours last week; another 10 worked more than 15 hours last week in a family business. *(Ans: $(945-20-10) \div 15,000 = 6.10$)*

Ability is difficult to control, but it can be influenced if a person is given the resources to improve his or her skill.

2. The change in the annual price level is divided by the beginning price level. This figure is multiplied by 100 to convert the number to a percentage.

Applying Economic Concepts

1. Full employment does not take into account those people who have stopped looking for a job. Full employment does count workers with part-time jobs as being employed, even if they work only one hour a week.

2. demand-pull, the government deficit

Reinforcing Skills

1. to determine the arguments for and against adding technology to the nation's classrooms

2. The second view argues that technology must be

CHAPTER ORGANIZER

Daily Objectives	Reproducible Resources	Multimedia Resources
Section 1 **The Cost of Economic Instability** 1. **Explain** the economic costs of instability. 2. **Describe** the social costs of instability.	Reproducible Lesson Plan 17-1 Guided Reading Activity 17-1 Cooperative Learning Activity 24 Math Practice for Economics 31 Primary and Secondary Source Reading 24 Economic Simulation 5 Economic Laboratory 5 Performance Assessment Activity 3 Section Quiz 17-1*	Focus Activity Transparency 84 Vocabulary PuzzleMaker Chapter Challenger Interactive Review Software Testmaker MindJogger Videoquiz Interactive Economics!
Section 2 **Macroeconomic Equilibrium** 1. **Explain** the concept of aggregate supply. 2. **Describe** the importance of aggregate demand. 3. **Examine** the nature of macroeconomic equilibrium.	Reproducible Lesson Plan 17-2 Guided Reading Activity 17-2 Reinforcing Economic Skill 17 Section Quiz 17-2*	Focus Activity Transparency 55 Economic Concepts Transparencies 14, 15* Vocabulary PuzzleMaker Chapter Challenger Interactive Review Software Testmaker Interactive Economics!
Section 3 **Stabilization Policies** 1. **Explain** the operations and impact of fiscal policy. 2. **Distinguish** between supply-side economics and fiscal policy. 3. **State** the basic assumptions of monetary policy.	Reproducible Lesson Plan 17-3 Guided Reading Activity 17-3 Section Quiz 17-3*	Focus Activity Transparency 77 Economic Concepts Transparency 19* Vocabulary PuzzleMaker Chapter Challenger Interactive Review Software Testmaker NBR's Economics in Action Video Program Interactive Economics!
Section 4 **Economics and Politics** 1. **Explain** why monetary policy sometimes conflicts with other economic policies. 2. **Recognize** that economists have differing views.	Reproducible Lesson Plan 17-4 Guided Reading Activity 17-4 Section Quiz 17-4*	Focus Activity Transparency 85 Vocabulary PuzzleMaker Chapter Challenger Interactive Review Software Testmaker
Chapter Review and Evaluation	Enrichment Activity 17 Reteaching Activity 17* Economic Vocabulary Activity 17* Chapter 17 Test, Forms A and B	Chapter Digests Audiocassette Activities and Tests* Testmaker MindJogger Videoquiz

Also available in Spanish

 Blackline Master   Transparency   CD-ROM   Software   Videodisc   Audiocassette

00:00 **OUT OF TIME?** Assign the Chapter 17 Digest Audiocassette and the corresponding Chapter Digest activities and tests.

THE **Economics** America AND **Economics** International PROGRAMS

VOLUNTARY NATIONAL CONTENT STANDARDS IN ECONOMICS
Emphasized in Chapter 17

Content Standard 12 *Students will understand that:*
Interest rates, adjusted for inflation, rise and fall to balance the amount saved with the amount borrowed, thus affecting the allocation of scarce resources between present and future uses.

Content Standard 18 *Students will understand that:*
A nation's overall levels of income, employment, and prices are determined by the interaction of spending and production decisions made by all households, firms, government agencies, and others in the economy.

Content Standard 20 *Students will understand that:*
Federal government budgetary policy and the Federal Reserve System's monetary policy influence the overall levels of employment, output, and prices.

Economics America *Resources Available From NCEE*

- *Capstone: The Nation's High School Economics Course*
- *Civics and Government: Focus on Economics*
- *Focus: High School Economics*
- *United States History: Eyes on the Economy, Vol. II*

To order these materials, or to contact your state Council on Economic Education about workshops and programs, call 1-800-338-1192 or visit http://www.nationalcouncil.org.

PERFORMANCE ASSESSMENT

The following chapter projects may be assigned at the beginning of the chapter and used for performance assessment.

Multicultural Heritage Remind students that the GDP gap measures the difference between actual GDP and potential GDP if all resources were fully employed. Therefore, the greater the level of unemployment, the greater the GDP gap. Point out that unemployment is usually higher among males, among all people ages 16–19, and among African Americans. Have students conduct library research to discover the reasons unemployment is higher among these sectors of society. Suggest that students present their findings in a written report.

Cooperative Learning Organize the class into five groups and assign one of the following topics to each group: macroeconomic equilibrium, GDP gap, automatic stabilizers, fiscal policy, and monetary policy. Have groups prepare a pictorial essay that presents information about their assigned topic. Encourage groups to use graphs and other illustrative materials whenever appropriate. Suggest that groups display their essays on the bulletin board following the order in which the topics are listed above. Use the display to review the content of the chapter.

ADDITIONAL RESOURCES

Readings for the Student

The American Economy: Government's Role, Citizen's Choice. Close Up Foundation, 1995. Analysis of how decisions made by government officials have a direct effect on the daily lives of Americans.

Stein, Herbert, and Murray Foss. *An Illustrated Guide to the American Economy.* Washington, DC: American Enterprise Institute, 1995. Uses full-color illustrations to help students visualize key economic concepts.

Readings for the Teacher

Blinder, Alan S. *Growing Together.* Knoxville, TN: Whittle Direct Books, 1991. Addresses economic growth, productivity, capital, and human resources.

Rivlin, Alice. *Reviving the American Dream: The Economy, the States, and the Federal Government.* Washington, DC: The Brookings Institution, 1992. Brings together economics and politics to address important domestic issues.

Multimedia

Economics U$A: John Maynard Keynes/Fiscal Policy. The Annenberg/CPB Collection, 19 Gregory Drive, South Burlington, VT 05407–2345. Color video, 60 mins. Reviews the ideas of Keynes and discusses the nature of fiscal policy.

Economics U$A: Monetary Policy/Stabilization Policy. The Annenberg/CPB Collection, 19 Gregory Drive, South Burlington, VT 05407–2345. Color video, 60 mins. An analysis of the monetarist view of stabilization policies.

Chapter Overview

Chapter 17 focuses on the efforts to create an economic environment conducive to growth and stability. **Section 1** describes the misery index and GDP gap and discusses the social costs of economic instability. **Section 2** illustrates the concept of macroeconomic equilibrium using the aggregate demand curve and the aggregate supply curve. **Section 3** shows how monetary policy and fiscal policy can achieve economic stability and growth. **Section 4** discusses the interrelationship of economics and politics.

GLENCOE
TECHNOLOGY

VIDEODISC
MindJogger Videoquiz

Use MindJogger to preview the Chapter 17 content.

 Chapter 17
Disc 3, Side A

Also available in VHS.

inter**NET**
CONNECTION

Resources for Chapter 17 on the World Wide Web*

Congressional Budget Office Studies & Reports (Macroeconomic Analysis)
http://www.cbo.gov/
reports.cfm

Council of Economic Advisers
http://www.gpo.gov/eop/

Social Statistics Briefing Room (Crime)
http://www.whithouse.gov/
fsbr/crime.html

Sites subject to change.

The mental and social health of society is an important concern for economists.

 Extra Credit Project

Have students write a report outlining the present administration's fiscal policies and the current monetary policies followed by the Fed. Call on volunteers to present and discuss their reports.

CHAPTER 17

Achieving Economic Stability

SECTION 1
The Cost of Economic Instability

SECTION 2
Macroeconomic Equilibrium

SECTION 3
Stabilization Policies

SECTION 4
Economics and Politics

CHAPTER PREVIEW

People to Know

• Milton Friedman
• Urban and Regional Planner

Applying Economic Concepts to Your Life

Monetary Policy Do you have a savings account that pays interest? Has the interest rate ever gone up? If so, your bank might have increased rates because the Fed had raised interest rates to combat inflation and encourage people to save. The Fed's control over interest rates is an example of *monetary policy*.

Journal Writing

For one week, keep a journal of newspaper articles detailing inflation rates and unemployment statistics. Both figures are measures of economic instability.

Economic Portfolio

As students gather their articles for the **Journal Writing** activity, have them write a short report explaining how inflation and unemployment statistics reflect the overall health of the economy.

Key to Ability Levels — Teaching strategies have been coded for varying learning styles and abilities:
L1 - Basic (activities for all students) **L2 - Average** (activities for average to above-average students)
L3 - Challenging (activities for above-average students) **LEP - Limited English Proficiency**

INTRODUCING CHAPTER 17

Connecting to Past Learning

Remind students of how they established the equilibrium price of a product by using supply and demand curves. To illustrate, draw a supply curve and a demand curve on the chalkboard, and mark the point where they intersect as the equilibrium price. Point out that in Chapter 17, students will apply this process to the economy as a whole.

Applying Economics

Write the heading *Life Goals* on the chalkboard. Ask students to suggest some of their life, or long-term, goals, such as buying a house, getting married, and/or having a family. List goals under the heading on the chalkboard as students volunteer them. Ask students to identify the factors that might influence *when* they achieve their goals. If financial security is mentioned, note and circle it on the chalkboard. Point out that financial security can be better achieved when there is economic stability. Conclude by stressing that economic stability affects students' personal goals as well as the goals of the United States.

PERFORMANCE ASSESSMENT

Refer to page **416B** for a Performance Assessment activity for this chapter. Also see the **Performance Assessment Activities** booklet for additional suggestions.

VISUAL INSTRUCTION

Ask students for examples of social ills in their community caused by a weak or an unstable economy.

FOCUS

Section Objectives

1. Explain the economic costs of instability.

2. Describe the social costs of instability.

Bellringer

 Prior to taking roll at the beginning of the class period, display Focus Activity Transparency 84 on the overhead projector and assign the accompanying Student Activity 84.

Motivational Activity

Discuss students' responses to the activity sheet that accompanies Focus Activity Transparency 84.

Preteaching Vocabulary

Have students locate the meanings of the key terms in the Glossary. Call on other students to use each term in a sentence. **LEP**

Use the **Vocabulary PuzzleMaker** to create crossword and word search puzzles.

VISUAL INSTRUCTION

Ask: What is the GDP gap at point c? At point d? *(15 guns and approximately 130 units of butter; 200 units of butter)*

Answer to Caption:

employment declines

SECTION 1
The Cost of Economic Instability

Section Preview

Objectives

After studying this section, you will be able to:

1. **Explain** the economic costs of instability.

2. **Describe** the social costs of instability.

Key Terms

stagflation, GDP gap, misery index, discomfort index

Applying Economic Concepts

Misery Index Do you know someone who has suffered from unemployment and inflation at the same time? If so, you probably understand the frustration and feelings of helplessness that accompany that situation. Millions of others do, too, which is why economists have invented a measure called a *misery index*.

Unemployment and inflation are forms of economic instability closely tied to long-term economic growth. The instability carries an enormous cost—one that can be measured in economic as well as human terms.

The Economic Costs

On one level, unemployment and inflation are simply numbers that are collected, reported in the press, or plotted on a graph. At another level, they represent enormous economic failures that waste the resources of the nation and its people.

Stagflation

In the past, recessions brought inflation under control. Although no one really wanted a recession, it did work to resolve this problem.

By the 1970s, however, inflation was becoming more persistent. Recessions still reduced inflation

---

Figure 17.1
The GDP Gap and the Production Possibilities Frontier

When all resources are fully employed, a country can produce anywhere along its production possibilities frontier. When some resources are idle, or are not employed efficiently, production falls short of its potential. The GDP gap is the difference between the actual production at point **a** and the potential production as indicated by points **b, c,** or **d.** **What happens to employment if GDP declines even a fraction of a percentage?**

The GDP gap can be expressed as 35 guns not produced, or:

As 15 guns and approximately 130 units of butter not produced, or:

As 200 units of butter not produced.

(Quantity of Guns axis: 10 20 30 40 50 60 70 80 90 100 110)
(Quantity of Butter axis: 100 200 300 400 500 600 700 800 900)

 GO TO *Lesson 1 of* Interactive Economics! *to learn more about* **"The Cost of Unemployed and Underemployed Resources."**

418 UNIT 4: *Macroeconomics: Policies*

Classroom Resources for SECTION 1

- Reproducible Lesson Plan 17-1
- Guided Reading Activity 17-1
- Cooperative Learning Activity 24
- Math Practice for Economics 31
- Primary and Secondary Source Reading 24
- Economic Simulation 5
- Economic Laboratory 5
- Performance Assessment Activity 3
- Section Quiz 17-1

- Spanish Section Quiz 17-1
- Focus Activity Transparency 84
- Testmaker
- Vocabulary PuzzleMaker
- Chapter Challenger Interactive Review Software
- Interactive Economics!
- MindJogger Videoquiz

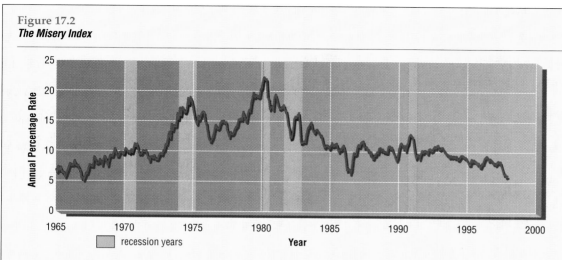

Figure 17.2
The Misery Index

Annual Percentage Rate

25
20
15
10
5
0

1965　1970　1975　1980　1985　1990　1995　2000

□ recession years

Year

Source: Bureau of Economic Analysis, United States Department of Commerce.

The misery index is the sum of the monthly inflation and unemployment rates. It is not an official government statistic, but it is often used as a measure of consumer distress during periods of high unemployment and inflation. **Why is the misery index also called the discomfort index?**

somewhat, but the economy began to encounter **stagflation**—a period of stagnant growth and inflation. Many periods of stagflation have plagued the nation since the beginning of the 1970s, and the problem is likely to recur.

The GDP Gap

The **GDP gap** is the difference between the actual GDP and the potential GDP that could be produced if all resources were fully employed. The gap is a measure of the cost of unemployed resources in terms of output not produced.

The GDP gap, illustrated in **Figure 17.1**, shows the production possibilities curve in the classic guns versus butter example. Note that the output not produced because of resources that lie idle can be measured in either guns, butter, or a combination of the two items.

In a more dynamic sense, business cycles or fluctuations make the size of this gap vary over time. The scale of GDP is also such that if GDP declines even a

fraction of a percentage point, the amount of lost production and income can be enormous.

In 1997, for example, the GDP of the United States economy exceeded $8 trillion. If an $8 trillion economy declines just one-fourth of 1 percentage point, $20 billion of production would be lost. This amount is more than the federal government spent on agriculture or general science, space, and technology during the entire 1997 fiscal budget year. Described in other terms, this amount would be equal to 750,000 workers losing jobs that paid $26,600 each for an entire year. In practice, the effects of a decline in GDP generally are spread out over a large area rather than being concentrated in just one spot, but they are no less severe.

The Misery Index

The **misery index**, sometimes called the **discomfort index**, is the sum of the monthly inflation and unemployment rates. Although it is not an official government statistic, it is a more comprehensive measure of consumer suffering during periods of high

TEACH

Guided Practice

L1 Understanding Ideas On the chalkboard, write *Economic Instability*. Underneath, draw a two-column chart with the headings *Economic Costs* and *Social Costs*. Have students decide the two most important economic and social costs of economic instability. **LEP**

Cooperative Learning
Assign Cooperative Learning Activity 24.

Independent Practice

Guided Reading Assign Guided Reading Activity for Section 1. **LEP**

L2 Drawing a Cartoon
Have students draw cartoons that illustrate one or more of the social costs of economic instability. **LEP**

 VISUAL INSTRUCTION

Answer to Caption:
It indicates discomfort consumers suffer because of high inflation and unemployment.

 INTERACTIVE ECONOMICS!

CD-ROM Opportunity Costs

Have students click on "The Cost of Unemployed Resources." Ask: **What does a point inside the production possibilities frontier show?** *(the opportunity cost measured in terms of output NOT produced because some resources were not working to their fullest potential)*

 Supplied in both CD-ROM and diskette formats.

Meeting Special Needs

Reading Disability Students with reading problems are often helped by having a specific purpose presented by the teacher. Focused reading exercises help in two ways: they help the reader by presenting a limited goal, and they make the reader more

active, requiring judgments to be made about the applicability of the material to the question. Have students read "The Social Costs" on pages 420–421. Ask them to find examples in their daily lives of the various types of social costs listed.

📂 **Math Practice** Assign Math Practice for Economics 31.

📂 **Readings** Assign Primary and Secondary Source Reading 24.

📂 **Simulation** Assign Economic Simulation 5.

📂 **Laboratory** Assign Economic Laboratory 5.

📂 **Performance Assessment** Assign Performance Assessment Activity 3.

ASSESS

Check for Understanding

Assign Section 1 Review as homework or an in-class activity.

💿 Use **Chapter Challenger Interactive Review Software** to review Section 1.

MEETING LESSON OBJECTIVES

Each objective below is tested by the questions that follow it in parentheses.

1. Explain the economic costs of instability. **(1, 2, 4, 5)**

2. Describe the social costs of instability. **(3)**

VISUAL INSTRUCTION

Ask: How does having the ability to provide for their families affect people's attitudes about the future. *(They are more positive.)*

Answer to Caption:
Society can more easily deal with social problems.

---

inflation and unemployment. The index is relevant only over long periods because of the wide month-to-month swings in some of the numbers.

Figure 17.2 shows the misery index for a period beginning in 1965. The index was at its worst from the mid-1970s through the early 1980s.

Uncertainty

When real GDP declines, a great deal of uncertainty exists. A worker may not buy something because of concern over his or her job. This uncertainty usually translates into purchases that are not made, causing some jobs to be lost.

The worker is not the only one the uncertainty affects. The owner of a business producing at capacity may decide against an expansion although new orders are arriving daily. Instead, the producer—aware that the demand for products is greater than the supply—may try to raise prices, which increases inflation. The producer may also try to decrease overtime or even lay off workers in anticipation of a downturn.

The Social Costs

The cost of instability can be measured in dollars rather easily, but it is harder to measure in terms of human suffering. In human terms, the costs are almost beyond comprehension. Because of these social costs, everyone agrees that stability must be achieved. Economists are interested not only in the production of society, but in its mental and social health as well.

Wasted Resources

Human suffering during periods of instability goes beyond not having more goods and services that raise the standard of living. The labor resource is wasted, with people wanting work but not being able

Family Values *A healthy economy means that people will be more certain of their ability to provide for themselves and their families.* **What are some benefits of a healthy economy?**

💲 Free Enterprise Activity 💲

Remind students that the cost of economic instability includes wasted resources, political instability, and crime. Organize students into several groups, and have each group propose and discuss possible ways to reduce the social costs of economic instability. Call on groups to offer their solutions. Classify solutions in two categories—those that require significant government intervention and those that require little or no government intervention. Select a few solutions and discuss their feasibility.

to find it. The economy has failed to satisfy the basic human need to be a useful and productive member of society. This labor situation is particularly acute in inner cities where unemployment rates run high among minority groups.

Wasted resources are not limited to just human resources. Factories with idle capacity are waiting to be utilized. Natural resources may also lie unused or go to waste.

Political Instability

Politicians also suffer from the consequences of economic instability. When times are hard, voters are dissatisfied, and incumbents are often thrown out of office. If too much economic instability exists, as during the Great Depression of the 1930s, voters are often willing to vote for radical change. As a result, economic stability adds to the political stability of our nation.

Crime and Family Values

High crime rates, too few economic and social opportunities for minorities, the loss of individual freedoms, and the lack of stability for many Americans are all grounds for concern. Many people believe that some of these social ills cannot be cured without the help of a strong and stable economy.

When the economy is healthy, society can more easily deal with its social problems. Communities have higher tax collections, which can increase police protection and municipal services. Companies are

more willing to hire disadvantaged persons and provide on-the-job training.

A healthy economy means that people will be more certain of their ability to provide for themselves and their families. When people can do this, they are more positive about the future in general.

Economic instability affects other parts of society, too. When the economy is healthy, families make numerous purchases, many of them on credit. If the economy declines, some debtors may lose income and have to declare bankruptcy to end their debts.

HELP WANTED

Urban and Regional Planner
▼

Expanding suburban community is accepting applications for the position of urban and regional planner. Your job will be to study the needs of our growing population. You will then formulate a plan outlining the best use of land for housing, schools, and shopping areas. The ideal person for this job will be able to balance the needs of the community with a concern for the environment.

▼

Education: Master's degree in city planning
Salary: $38,000

SECTION 1 REVIEW

Reviewing Terms and Facts

1. **Define** stagflation, GDP gap, misery index, discomfort index.
2. **Explain** how economists measure the economic cost of instability.
3. **Describe** the social cost of instability.

Critical Thinking

4. **Making Generalizations** If the GDP gap in a given year rises dramatically, what types of unemployment and inflation data would be present?

Applying Economic Concepts

5. **Misery Index** How might the psychological strains that many people feel in difficult economic times help prolong the economic downturn?

CHAPTER 17: *Achieving Economic Stability* **421**

Evaluate

📁 📁 💻 Assign the Section 1 Quiz in the TCR or use the *Economics: Principles and Practices* Testmaker.

Reteach

Have students identify social costs, such as crime and poverty, that result from economic instability. As students name the costs, ask them to relate each to a specific economic factor. Increased violence in urban areas, for example, might be related to high unemployment.

Enrich

Have students locate unemployment and inflation figures for their state or local area over the last 20 years. Have them use these statistics to construct a state or local misery index.

CLOSE

Have students discuss how economic instability has affected their community.

? DID YOU KNOW

Americans have an 83 percent chance of being victims of a violent crime in their lives.

Answers to SECTION 1 REVIEW

1. All vocabulary words are defined in the Glossary.

2. They measure it in terms of the GDP gap and the misery index.

3. Resources are wasted, political stability is threatened, crime rates increase, and social problems increase.

4. Unemployment will rise and inflation will taper off.

5. Answers will vary. Students may note that workers who have been laid off for long periods of time may be reluctant to spend money on purchases even after they are rehired because they lived with uncertainty for so long. This reluctance keeps manufacturers from producing, which, in turn, keeps some jobs from getting filled.

FOCUS

Section Objectives

1 Explain the concept of aggregate supply.
2. Describe the importance of aggregate demand.
3. Examine the nature of macroeconomic equilibrium.

Bellringer

At the beginning of the class period, display Focus Activity Transparency 55.

Motivational Activity

Discuss students' responses to the activity sheet that accompanies Transparency 55.

Preteaching Vocabulary

Have students use all three key terms in a single sentence in which their relationships to each other are demonstrated.
LEP

Use the **Vocabulary PuzzleMaker** to create crossword and word search puzzles.

TEACH

Guided Practice

L1 Understanding Ideas
Write the following on the chalkboard: *Increase in Aggregate Supply, Decrease in Aggregate Supply, Increase in Aggregate Demand, Decrease in Aggregate Demand.* Call on students to identify factors that would cause these four situations to occur and note their responses under the appropriate heading. Then ask students to select one factor from each heading and illustrate the shift of the curve graphically. **LEP**

422

SECTION 2
Macroeconomic Equilibrium

Section Preview

Objectives

After studying this section, you will be able to:

1. **Explain** the concept of aggregate supply.
2. **Describe** the importance of aggregate demand.
3. **Examine** the nature of macroeconomic equilibrium.

Key Terms

aggregate supply curve, aggregate demand curve, macroeconomic equilibrium

Applying Economic Concepts

Equilibrium Have you ever experienced one of those rare moments when you feel completely satisfied and do not want to change anything that you are doing? The economy behaves like that sometimes. The situation is called *equilibrium*, and variables such as price and quantity will remain unchanged unless something happens to disturb the system.

When we study markets, we often use the tools of supply and demand to show how the equilibrium price and quantity of output are determined. When we study the economy as a whole, we can use the concepts of supply and demand in much the same way.

Aggregate Supply

Individual firms try to maximize their profits by finding the quantity of output at which the marginal cost of producing the next unit of output is equal to the marginal revenue from the sale of that output. If the price that consumers are willing to pay increases, producers would increase their production.

The Aggregate Supply Curve

If, at any given price level, the annual production of all final goods and services within a country's borders were added together, we would have a measure of GDP. At a different level of prices, firms would adjust their profit-maximizing quantities of output, producing a slightly different level of GDP. If it were somehow possible to keep adjusting the price level to see how total output changed, we could then construct an **aggregate supply curve**, which shows the real level of GDP that could be produced at various price levels.

Figure 17.3 shows how an aggregate supply curve for the whole economy might look. It is shown as upward sloping, but with a horizontal as well as vertical range. The horizontal range represents various levels of output that coexist with large amounts of unemployed resources. If the economy is producing at point **a**, output can be expanded to point **b** by putting some of the resources to work without causing any change in the general price level.

Any expansion of real GDP beyond point **b**, which has an output of Q_1, is not possible without some increase in the price level, however. By the time the economy has reached point **c**, the price level has risen to P_1 because firms have been competing for increasingly scarce resources. Point **c** is also the location where all resources are fully employed. When firms try to expand production beyond Q_2, they merely drive up prices.

Increase in Aggregate Supply

The aggregate supply curve, like the supply curve of the individual firm, can increase. Most of the increases in aggregate supply are tied to the cost of production for the individual firm. If the cost goes down for all firms, aggregate supply increases, which shows as a shift to the right.

Factors that might lower the costs of production for all individual firms include the discovery of less

422 UNIT 4: *Macroeconomics: Policies*

Classroom Resources for SECTION 2

Reproducible Lesson Plan 17-2
Guided Reading Activity 17-2
Reinforcing Economic Skill 17
Section Quiz 17-2
Spanish Section Quiz 17-2
Focus Activity Transparency 55
Economic Concepts Transparencies 14, 15

Spanish Economic Concepts Transparencies 14, 15
Testmaker
Vocabulary PuzzleMaker
Chapter Challenger Interactive Review Software
Interactive Economics!

Figure 17.3
The Aggregate Supply Curve

The aggregate supply curve shows the amount of real GDP that could be produced at various price levels. An increase in aggregate supply comes about when production costs for all individual producers fall. **What causes a decrease in aggregate supply?**

CD-ROM
Macroeconomic
Equilibrium

Have students click on "The Aggregate Supply Curve." Ask: What do the vertical and horizontal axes show on the aggregate supply curve? *(The vertical axis shows an overall price level such as the consumer price index. The horizontal axis shows real GDP.)*

 Supplied in both CD-ROM and diskette formats.

Using Transparencies
Display Economic Concepts Transparencies 14 and 15. Spanish Transparencies also are available.

Independent Practice

📂 **Guided Reading** Assign Guided Reading Activity for Section 2. **LEP**

---

expensive natural resources, lower prices for imported oil, and lower interest rates. Increases in labor productivity, new technologies, a liberalization of immigration laws, and lower taxes would also shift the aggregate supply curve to the right. **1** ✓

Decrease in Aggregate Supply

Factors that tend to increase the cost of production for an individual firm tend to decrease aggregate supply. These factors include higher prices for foreign oil, higher interest rates, and lower labor productivity.

Other factors decreasing aggregate supply include higher government taxes and the tightening of immigration laws, which would deny some firms a source of cheap labor. Any increase in cost that causes firms to offer fewer goods and services for sale at each and every price would shift the aggregate supply curve to the left. **2**

Aggregate Demand

Aggregate demand is like aggregate supply in several respects. First, it is an aggregate, or summary,

QUICK CHECK

Checking Understanding	**Applying Economic Concepts**
1. What factors might lower production costs for all firms? 2. How do higher taxes affect aggregate supply?	**Aggregate Supply** During the 1970s the price of imported oil skyrocketed—from about $5 a barrel to about $35. The increase affected many industries because petroleum is used in products as diverse as aspirin, carpets, compact discs, and toothpaste.

VISUAL
INSTRUCTION

Which way would the aggregate supply curve move if the price of imported oil doubled? *(to the left)*

Answer to Caption:
any increase in cost that will cause firms to offer fewer goods

QUICK CHECK
ANSWERS

1. discovery of less expensive natural resources, lower prices for imported oil, lower interest rates, increased labor productivity, new technologies, lower taxes, liberalization of immigration laws
2. They cause it to decrease.

Reading Disability Students with poor reading skills often learn best by having new procedures modeled for them several times. Many reading comprehension strategies require students to restate what they have read. Explain to students that you are going to model a restating strategy for a

sentence. Have students turn to the heading "Aggregate Supply" and read the first sentence. Demonstrate restating: "A business owner can maximize his or her profits by producing that quantity of goods where marginal cost and marginal revenue are equal."

423

GO TO Lesson 6 of *Interactive Economics!* to learn more about "The Aggregate Demand Curve."

Figure 17.4
The Aggregate Demand Curve

*The aggregate demand curve shows the amount of real GDP the economy would demand at all possible price levels. When the price is high, as at P_1, only Q_0 of real GDP can be purchased, leaving the economy at point **a**. At a lower price level, such as P_0, more output can be purchased, leaving the economy at point **b**. **What causes the aggregate demand curve to shift?***

measure of the demand of all economic units in the economy. Second, it can be represented in the form of a graph. Third, aggregate demand can either increase or decrease over time.

The Aggregate Demand Curve

Figure 17.4 illustrates the **aggregate demand curve,** a graph showing the quantity of real GDP that would be purchased at each possible price level in the economy. This curve represents the sum of consumer, business, and government demands at various price levels. It slopes downward and to the right like the demand curve for individuals, but for an entirely different reason.

The reason is based on the underlying assumption that the economy can have only one money supply at a time. The size of this supply is fixed and has a different purchasing power at every possible price level. When prices are very high, a given money supply will purchase a limited amount of output, such as that represented by point **a.** When prices are much lower, everyone will be able to buy relatively more GDP, leaving everyone at point **b.** If the price level

dropped further, even more GDP could be purchased, which is why the curve tends to slope downward and to the right.

Increase in Aggregate Demand

The aggregate demand curve, like the aggregate supply curve, can increase or decrease depending on certain conditions. An important factor is a change in the amount of money that people save. If consumers collectively save less and spend more, the increase in consumer spending would increase aggregate demand, shifting the aggregate demand curve to the right.

Expectations about future economic conditions often affect consumer, business, and government spending. If better economic conditions are forecast, all sectors may spend more, shifting aggregate demand to the right.

Finally, an increase in transfer payments—financed through deficit spending—or a general reduction in taxes could increase the spending of the consumer sector. The effect might be short-lived, but some increased spending would take place.

Decrease in Aggregate Demand

Expectations can also play a major role in decreasing aggregate demand. If any of the sectors anticipate a bleak economic or political climate, they will cut back on spending, which will have the collective impact of purchasing less GDP at every price level.

Higher taxes and lower transfer payments could also reduce aggregate spending. Such decisions shift the aggregate demand curve to the left because all sectors collectively buy less GDP at all levels of prices.

Equilibrium

Figure 17.5 shows the aggregate demand and supply curves put together, indicating macroeconomic equilibrium. **Macroeconomic equilibrium** is determined by the intersection of the aggregate supply and aggregate demand curves and is the level of real GDP consistent with a given price level.

In the figure, **Q** is the level of real GDP that is consistent with the price level **P**. If the economy is growing, with newer levels of output larger than previous ones, the price level may or may not change.

Figure 17.5 points out a dilemma facing economic policymakers. The economy must be allowed to grow to new levels of real GDP, but it must do so without unduly increasing the price level, which causes inflation. A number of economic policies are available, and each affects the aggregate supply and aggregate demand curves in different ways.

 GO TO Lesson 6 of Interactive Economics! to learn more about "Macroeconomic Equilibrium."

Figure 17.5
Macroeconomic Equilibrium

The economy is at equilibrium when the quantity of real GDP demanded is equal to the real GDP supplied at a given price level. The question facing economic policymakers is how to increase real GDP without increasing the price level. **Why is it important to not increase the price level?**

Aggregate supply and demand curves are useful concepts, providing a framework for analyzing a problem. They can be used to give an idea of the way and direction that things will change, but they do not yield exact predictions. Even so, they are becoming increasingly important in analyzing the issue of macroeconomic equilibrium.

SECTION 2 REVIEW

Reviewing Terms and Facts

1. **Define** aggregate supply curve, aggregate demand curve, macroeconomic equilibrium.
2. **Describe** the factors that would cause aggregate supply to increase.
3. **List** the factors that would cause aggregate demand to decrease.

4. **Describe** the policy objectives economic policymakers face.

Critical Thinking

5. **Making Comparisons** How do aggregate supply and demand differ from simple supply and demand?

Applying Economic Concepts

6. **Equilibrium** How would a decrease in business investments affect the macroeconomic equilibrium?

Evaluate

Assign the Section 2 Quiz in the TCR or use the *Economics: Principles and Practices* Testmaker to create a customized quiz. Spanish Section Quizzes also are available in the Spanish Resources Binder.

Reteach

Have students write brief paragraphs explaining aggregate supply, aggregate demand, and macroeconomic equilibrium.

Enrich

Direct students to scan the business pages of the newspaper for stories that detail conditions that might cause a change in aggregate supply or aggregate demand. Have students summarize the articles they find, focusing on how aggregate supply or aggregate demand will change.

CLOSE

Encourage students to write a riddle, poem, or proverb that explains macroeconomic equilibrium.

VISUAL INSTRUCTION

Have students explain why aggregate supply and demand curves are useful economic tools. (*They can be used to indicate the way and direction the economy will change.*)

Answer to Caption:
It will cause inflation.

Answers to SECTION 2 REVIEW

1. Words are defined in the Glossary.
2. Costs of production decrease through the discovery of less expensive natural resources, lower prices for imported oil, lower interest rates, increases in labor productivity, new technologies, liberalized immigration laws, lower tax rates.
3. expectations of a bleak economic or political climate, higher taxes, lower transfer payments, and a decrease in government, consumer, or business spending

4. to stimulate real GDP without increasing inflation
5. Aggregate supply and demand show how price level and total output are determined for the economy as a whole; supply and demand show how price and quantity are determined in an individual market.
6. It would cause workers to lose jobs and spend less. Aggregate demand would decrease, real GDP fall, and price level decline.

TEACH

Students who are familiar with the Internet have an interactive way to learn. The Internet often can provide students with more recent information than would appear in books or magazines.

After students find the information they want, explain to them that they can print or download the file to their computer. When you download from the Internet, you copy information from a Web site to another location. Students can download by using the File menu and Save command. If any of the hypertext words say *download*, you can download by simply clicking on these words.

After students download information from the Internet, they can integrate facts, direct quotes, pictures, or other information into their own documents. Point out that students must carefully read the on-line credits or copyright information provided to avoid violating copyright rules.

Facts cannot be copyrighted, so students do not have to worry about using facts that they download. However, lengthy articles and most images on the Internet are copyrighted and should not be used without the owner's permission.

☞ Skills Practice For additional practice, have students complete Reinforcing Economic Skill 17.

TECHNOLOGY SKILL

Using the Internet

The Internet—often referred to as the "Net"—is composed of a massive number of computers linked together through a worldwide, high-speed, telecommunications network. Originally created by the U.S. Department of Defense in the 1960s, the Internet makes it easy for people to share information and ideas worldwide.

Explanation

To get on the Internet, you will need three items. First you need a personal computer—either an IBM-compatible machine or a Macintosh. Then you need a *modem*—a device that connects your computer to a telephone line. Finally, you need an account with an Internet service provider (ISP) such as America Online, CompuServe, or a local provider. You log on to the Internet through your ISP.

Now you can "surf" the Net—send E-mail, join a newsgroup, subscribe to a mailing list, or explore the World Wide Web (WWW). Of all the segments of the Internet, the WWW is the most popular. Through the use of software called a *Web browser*, you can peruse page after page of information about almost anything you can imagine.

Each page on the WWW is referred to as a *Web site*, which can be a university, a government agency, or a company that maintains Web pages for you to explore. A *home page* is a Web page that functions like the table of contents in a book. It is a good starting point for information.

Each page has its own address or URL (Uniform Resource Locator), which usually begins with a prefix of *http://* If you don't know the address, you can type key words into a *search engine* such as AltaVista or Yahoo to help you find information quickly. Another easy way to gather more information is through *hyperlinks*, which appear on the screen as blue, underlined text. When you click on these links, the browser loads that page quickly.

Practice

Select a search engine and use it to discover the answers to the following questions.
1. Who were the first people to use paper money?
2. What is London's equivalent of Wall Street?
3. Which state has the lowest per capita personal income?
4. What is the WWW address for the White House?
5. What is the WWW address for the World Bank?

Additional Practice

For further practice in using the Internet, complete the Reinforcing Skills exercise in the Chapter 17 Review on page 441.

Save the locations of your favorite Web sites as bookmarks. Through bookmarks, you can quickly locate the site without having to remember a long Web address.

426 UNIT 4: *Macroeconomics Policies*

Answers to SKILL

1. the Chinese
2. "the city"
3. Mississippi
4. http://www.whitehouse.gov/
5. http://www.worldbank.org/

Stabilization Policies

Section Preview

Objectives

After studying this section, you will be able to:

1. **Explain** the operations and impact of fiscal policy.
2. **Distinguish** between supply-side economics and fiscal policy.
3. **State** the basic assumptions of monetary policy.

Key Terms

fiscal policy, Keynesian economics, consumption function, multiplier, accelerator, automatic stabilizer, unemployment insurance, supply-side economics, Laffer curve, monetarism, wage-price controls

Applying Economic Concepts

Fiscal Policy You may know someone who collects unemployment insurance, Social Security, or medicare. These programs stabilize a person's income in the event of a layoff, a retirement, or a medical emergency. They are called automatic stabilizers—one of the tools of *fiscal policy*.

E conomic growth, full employment, and price stability are three of the seven major economic goals of the American people. In order to reach these goals, sound economic policies must be designed and implemented.

Economic stability can be achieved in several ways. Some people favor policies that stimulate aggregate demand, while others favor ones that stimulate aggregate supply. Still others prefer policies that promote the growth of the money supply. Sometimes these policies are consistent with each other. At other times, they are not.

Demand-Side Policies

Demand-side policies are federal policies designed to increase or decrease total demand in the economy by shifting the aggregate demand curve to the right or to the left. One approach is known as **fiscal policy**—the use of government spending and taxing to influence economic activity—and is perhaps the most popular way to influence the economy.

Fiscal policies are derived from **Keynesian economics**, a set of actions designed to lower unemployment by stimulating aggregate demand. John Maynard Keynes put forth these theories in 1936, and they dominated the thinking of economists until the 1970s.

The Keynesian Framework

Keynes provided the basic framework with the output-expenditure model, GDP = C + I + G + F. According to this model, any change in GDP on the left side of the equation could be traced to changes on the right side of the equation. The question was, which of the four components caused the instability?

According to Keynes, the net impact of the foreign sector (F) was so small that it could be ignored. The government sector (G) was not the problem either, because its expenditures were normally stable over time. Spending by the consumer sector (C), stated Keynes, was the most stable of all. It was so stable that it could even be specified in terms of a **consumption function**, a schedule showing relatively constant and predictable levels of spending associated with different levels of disposable income. Ruling out F, G, and C, it then appeared that the business or investment sector (I) was to blame for the instability.

In Keynes's theory, investment sector spending was not only unstable, but had a magnified effect on other spending. If investment spending declined by $50 billion, for example, many workers would lose their jobs. These workers in turn would spend less and pay fewer taxes. Soon, the amount of spending by all sectors in the economy would be down by more than the initial decline in investment. This effect is called the **multiplier**, and says that a change in investment spending will have a magnified effect on total spending.

CHAPTER 17: *Achieving Economic Stability* **427**

Classroom Resources for SECTION 3

Reproducible Lesson Plan 17-3
Guided Reading Activity 17-3
Section Quiz 17-3
Spanish Section Quiz 17-3
Focus Activity Transparency 77
Economic Concepts Transparency 19

Spanish Economic Concepts Transparency 19
NBR's Economics in Action Video Program
Testmaker
Vocabulary PuzzleMaker
Chapter Challenger Interactive Review Software
Interactive Economics!

FOCUS

Section Objectives

1. Explain the operations and impact of fiscal policy.
2. Distinguish between supply-side economics and fiscal policy.
3. State the basic assumptions of monetary policy.

Bellringer

Prior to taking roll at the beginning of the class period, display Focus Activity Transparency 77 on the overhead projector and assign the accompanying Student Activity 77.

Motivational Activity

Discuss students' responses to the activity sheet that accompanies Focus Activity Transparency 77.

Preteaching Vocabulary

Ask students to find each of the key terms in the Glossary and study their meanings. Then call on volunteers to explain in their own words the meaning of the key terms. **LEP**

Use the **Vocabulary PuzzleMaker** to create crossword and word search puzzles.

TEACH

Guided Practice

L2 Debate Have students indicate by a show of hands whether they favor demand-side or supply-side economics. Organize students into two groups according to their votes. Then have the two groups debate the following: To ensure economic stability in the United States, the policy known as supply-side economics must be instituted and maintained.

427

Keynesian Economics
*Keynesian economics
states that economic activity will be stimulated if
the federal government
invests in projects such as
hydroelectric plants.*
**What role do govern-
ment deficits have
according to this
theory?**

The multiplier is believed to be about 2 in today's economy. Therefore, if investment spending goes down by $50 billion, the decline in overall spending could reach $100 billion.

Conditions are likely to be made even worse by the **accelerator**—the change in investment spending caused by a change in total spending. After a decline in overall spending gets started, it causes investment spending to be reduced even further. Before long, the economy is trapped in a downward spiral. The combined multiplier-accelerator effect is important because it adds to the instability of GDP.

The Role of Government

Keynes argued that only the government was able to step in and offset changes in investment sector spending. This action would take the form of fiscal policy in which the government implements spending and/or taxation policies to influence economic activity. **1**

The government could take a direct role and set up its own spending to offset the decline in spending by businesses. It could also play an indirect role by lowering taxes and enacting other measures to encourage businesses and consumers to spend more.

Suppose the government wanted to take direct steps right away to offset a $50 billion decline in business spending. To do this, it could spend $10 billion to build a dam in a rural area, give $20 billion in grants to cities to fix up poor neighborhoods, and spend another $20 billion in several other ways. In this way, the $50 billion that business did not spend would be replaced by the $50 billion the government spends. Thus, the overall sum of C + I + G + F would remain unchanged.

Instead of spending the $50 billion, perhaps the government could reduce tax rates by that amount and give investors and consumers more purchasing power. If the $50 billion not collected in taxes were spent, the initial decline in investment spending would be offset, and the sum for C + I + G + F again would remain the same.

Either way, the government would likely run the risk of a growing federal deficit. In Keynes's view, the deficit was unfortunate, but needed to stop further declines in economic activity. When the economy recovered, tax collections would rise, the government would run a surplus, and the debt could be paid back.

The Keynesian model gave short-term government deficits legitimacy. The justification for temporary federal deficits was one of the lasting contributions of

---

Figure 17.6
Fiscal Policy and the Aggregate Demand Curve

*Fiscal policies are designed to increase aggregate demand. Successive increases in aggregate demand—or moving the economy from **a** to **d**—put increasing pressure on the price level as the unemployed resources in the economy find employment.* **What are two limitations of fiscal policy?**

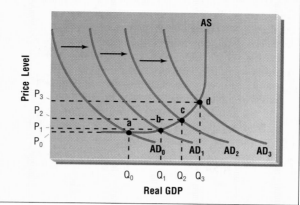

Lesson 6 of Interactive Economics! to learn more about "Fiscal Policy, Monetary Policy, and Macroeconomic Equilibrium."

L2 **Applying Ideas** Have students discuss what they believe are the most important macroeconomic problems today: unemployment, inflation, slow growth in productivity, for example. List problems on the chalkboard as they are identified. Organize students into several small groups, randomly assigning a macroeconomic problem to each group. Encourage groups to imagine they are the President's Council of Economic Advisers or the Fed Board of Governors. Have them develop a policy recommendation to tackle their assigned macroeconomic problem. Have group representatives present and discuss their recommendations.

 VISUAL INSTRUCTION

Ask: What is the ultimate result of increasing aggregate demand past AD_3? *(inflation)*

Answer to Caption:

The federal government has difficulty in controlling spending, and planning government spending to offset changes in investment spending is almost impossible.

Keynesian economics and a major departure from the economic thinking of the time.

Automatic Stabilizers

Another key component of fiscal policy is the role of **automatic stabilizers**, programs that automatically trigger benefits if changes in the economy threaten people's incomes. Two important stabilizers are unemployment insurance and federal entitlement programs. 2

Unemployment insurance is insurance that employers pay for through payroll taxes. Nearly all American workers who lose their jobs through no fault of their own can collect this insurance. Workers who are fired because of misconduct or who quit without good reason generally cannot collect it.

Although workers generally have to wait several weeks to collect benefits, most end up getting payments of about one-third to one-half of their weekly pay. The benefits vary from state to state. Under normal conditions, most states allow workers to collect the insurance for up to 26 weeks. When unemployment is high, however, they may be allowed to collect longer.

Federal entitlement programs, also known as entitlements, are social welfare programs designed to provide minimum health, nutritional, and income levels for selected groups of people. They include such federal programs as welfare, government pensions, medicare, medicaid, and Social Security.

Congress provides guidelines that determine who qualifies for—or is entitled to—these benefits. The availability of these programs is a guarantee that economic instability or some other factor will not cause aggregate demand to fall below a certain level for selected groups of people.

Fiscal Policy and Aggregate Demand

The impact of fiscal policies can be illustrated with the aggregate demand curve. **Figure 17.6** shows a

Checking Understanding

1. What did Keynes believe to be the only way to offset changes in investment sector spending?
2. What are two examples of automatic stabilizers?

Applying Economic Concepts

 Federal Deficit Keynes probably did not foresee the massive federal deficits of the American economy today. He thought that the deficits caused by government spending during downturns would end after prosperity was restored.

QUICK CHECK

ANSWERS

1. for government to step in and counteract declines in investment spending by introducing its own spending and tax cuts

2. unemployment insurance, federal entitlement programs

CHAPTER 17: *Achieving Economic Stability* **429**

$ Free Enterprise Activity $

Provide students with the following scenario: The United States is experiencing a severe recession. Nationwide unemployment is at 10 percent, but in some regions it stands at 25 percent. Inflation, however, is running at an annual rate of 3 percent. Consumer and business spending are down. GDP has fallen 5 percent over the last 3 quarters, and government revenues have declined.

Have students analyze the scenario above and select an economic policy—demand-side, supply-side, or monetarism—to bring the United States out of the recession. Direct students to write a brief report detailing and justifying the actions they would take.

Using Transparencies
Display Economic Concepts Transparency 19 on the overhead projector and use the guidelines given in Teaching Strategy 19. Assign Student Activity 19. Spanish Transparencies are also available in the Spanish Resources Binder.

Independent Practice

📁 **Guided Reading** Assign Guided Reading Activity for Section 3. **LEP**

VISUAL INSTRUCTION

Have students explain why the two polices are so named. *(Supply-side policies are designed to increase output; demand-side policies are designed to increase demand.)*

Answer to Caption:

because demand-side policies did not seem to be controlling the country's growing unemployment and inflation

---

single aggregate supply curve and several aggregate demand curves. When aggregate demand is very low, as during the Great Depression or other periods of severe economic downturns, the economy would be at point **a,** where AD_0 intersects AS. Increases in government spending—public works projects, transfer payments, or even tax reductions—could be used to increase aggregate demand to AD_1. Because many resources are unemployed, the movement of the economy from **a** to **b** causes very little price inflation.

Further attempts to increase aggregate demand, shown in **Figure 17.6** as AD_2 and AD_3, produce successively less output with increasingly higher price levels. Eventually, all attempts the government sector makes to increase aggregate demand would only increase the price level, without increasing the production of real GDP.

Limitations of Fiscal Policy

Keynes envisioned the role of government spending as a counterbalance to changes in investment spending. The ideal situation would be for government to increase spending to offset declines in business spending, and to decrease spending whenever business spending recovered. In practice, however,

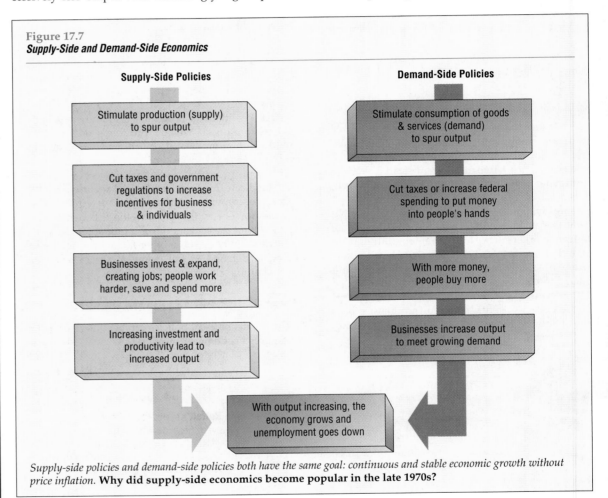

Figure 17.7
Supply-Side and Demand-Side Economics

Supply-Side Policies

Stimulate production (supply) to spur output

Cut taxes and government regulations to increase incentives for business & individuals

Businesses invest & expand, creating jobs; people work harder, save and spend more

Increasing investment and productivity lead to increased output

Demand-Side Policies

Stimulate consumption of goods & services (demand) to spur output

Cut taxes or increase federal spending to put money into people's hands

With more money, people buy more

Businesses increase output to meet growing demand

With output increasing, the economy grows and unemployment goes down

Supply-side policies and demand-side policies both have the same goal: continuous and stable economic growth without price inflation. **Why did supply-side economics become popular in the late 1970s?**

Extending the Content

Demand-Side Policies During a recession, demand-side economics calls for an expansionary fiscal policy. This involves increased government spending, or tax cuts, or a combination of both. This approach would tend to move the government's budget toward a deficit. In times of high inflation, demand-side economics calls for a contractionary fiscal policy. This would mean government spending cuts, or tax increases, or a mix of the two. This approach would tend to move the government's budget toward a surplus.

the federal government seems unable to bring its spending under control, especially when it comes to reducing expenditures or balancing its budget. **1**

In addition, planning federal expenditures to offset changes in investment spending seems almost impossible. Even if Congress knew that investment spending would be down next year, it is highly unlikely that offsetting federal expenditures could be approved in time. Any expenditure bill introduced in Congress would be debated, taken apart, rewritten, and possibly loaded with a host of unrelated amendments before it was ever passed. Even if the bill was passed in record time, the money might not actually be spent for years, especially if the bill authorized the construction of new roads, bridges, or buildings.

As a result, the most effective counter-cyclical fiscal policies used today are the automatic stabilizers. The advantage of the stabilizers is that spending approval is not needed whenever the economy enters a recession, or whenever people lose jobs and need unemployment insurance coverage. **2**

Supply-Side Policies

Economic policies designed to stimulate output and lower unemployment by increasing production in the economy are known as **supply-side economics**. The supply-side views began to interest people in the late 1970s because demand-side policies did not seem to be controlling the country's growing unemployment and inflation. In the 1980s, supply-side policies became the hallmark of President Reagan's administration.

Comparison with Demand-Side Policies

The differences between supply-side economics and demand-side economics are smaller than most people realize. Both policies, which are summarized

in **Figure 17.7**, use national income accounts to measure the economy's performance. Both policies accept the multiplier and the accelerator. Both policies have the same goal in mind—increasing production and decreasing unemployment without increasing inflation.

Supply-side economists believe, however, that the role of government has increased to the point at which individual incentives to work, save, and invest are being destroyed. They want the government to take a smaller role in economic affairs, while letting the free market play a larger role. This approach contrasts with that of the demand-siders, who want to stimulate output by generating demand with increased levels of government spending.

Smaller Role for Government

A key issue for supply-siders is government's role in the economy, which they believe must be reduced. One way to do this is to reduce the number of federal agencies. Another way to make government's role smaller is through deregulation—removing established regulations with which industries must comply. Deregulation is a major objective of supply-siders and is favored by some demand-siders as well.

Under the administration of President Jimmy Carter, major steps were taken to deregulate the energy, airline, and trucking industries to encourage competition. The Reagan administration continued deregulation efforts in the savings and loan industry, hoping to bring about more competition.

Federal Tax Structure

Another target of supply-siders is the federal tax burden on individuals and businesses. They believe that if taxes are too high, people will not want to work, and businesses will not produce as much as

---

Checking Understanding	**Applying Economic Concepts**
1. According to Keynesian theory, how should declines in business spending be offset? 2. What are the most effective counter-cyclical fiscal policies used today?	**Deregulation** Many people believe that certain industries should be subject to more government regulation. These people want the government to reregulate the banking and airline industries, among others.

L3 *Television News Report*
Organize students into two groups, assigning one group the topic "Demand-Side Economic Policies" and the other the topic "Supply-Side Economic Policies." Have each group prepare a five-minute television news report on its assigned topic. Reports should provide answers to the following questions: What is the goal of the policy? How or by whom was the policy developed? When and by whom has the policy been practiced? What is government's role in the policy? What are the immediate and long-term consequences of the policy? Have each group "broadcast" its news report for the rest of the class.

DID YOU KNOW

Before the advent of supply-side economics, demand-side policies were primarily known as Keynesian economics. Remind students that Keynes was the subject of Chapter 14's Profile in Economics (see page 353).

ANSWERS

1. by increased government spending
2. automatic stabilizers such as unemployment insurance and entitlements

---

Cultural Diversity and Economics

When Margaret Thatcher became prime minister of Great Britain in 1979, she inherited an economy beset by stagflation. The rate of inflation had hit double digits and growth of real GDP was one of the lowest in Europe. In response, Thatcher instituted her own form of supply-side economics. Government spending, especially on social programs, was drastically cut, tax rates were slashed, and government regulation of business was re-

duced. Thatcher also sold off many state-owned industries to further stimulate private business. The results were mixed. By the mid-1980s, inflation was under control and the growth of real GDP was one of the highest in Europe. Unemployment, however, reached double-digit numbers as previously state-owned businesses shed excess workers.

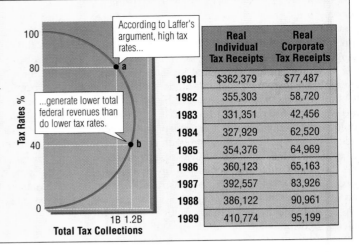

Figure 17.8
The Laffer Curve

The Laffer curve was used to argue that lower tax rates would ultimately generate higher tax revenues as a result of economic growth. In retrospect, it turned out that lower tax rates generated lower federal tax revenues. After adjusting for inflation, federal tax revenues generally declined after taxes were reduced in 1981. Taxes were raised in 1986, and total tax collections increased. **What role did the Laffer curve play in the economic policies of the 1980s?**

	Real Individual Tax Receipts	Real Corporate Tax Receipts
1981	$362,379	$77,487
1982	355,303	58,720
1983	331,351	42,456
1984	327,929	62,520
1985	354,376	64,969
1986	360,123	65,163
1987	392,557	83,926
1988	386,122	90,961
1989	410,774	95,199

they could. Lower tax rates, they argue, allow individuals and businesses to keep more of the money they earn, which encourages them to work harder. This would give workers more money to spend in the long run. Government would also gain as total tax collections go up because of the extra activity.

The **Laffer curve**—a hypothetical relationship between federal tax rates and tax revenues—illustrates the supply-siders' belief. It was the basis for President Reagan's tax cut of 1981, which reduced income taxes 25 percent over a 3-year period. The Laffer curve, along with the inflation-adjusted individual and corporate tax revenues collected between 1981 and 1986, are shown in **Figure 17.8**. **1**

Today, economists feel that either the assumptions or the interpretation of the Laffer curve are invalid. The increased revenue collections as a result of the deep tax cuts simply never materialized. After adjusting for inflation, both individual income tax receipts and corporate tax receipts were lower in 1986 than they were in 1981. Because tax collections never went up, the federal budget showed a deficit instead. Real tax collections did not surpass their 1981 levels until after the 1986 tax revisions took effect in 1987.

Supply-Side Policies and Aggregate Supply

Supply-side policies can be illustrated in terms of the aggregate supply curve. **Figure 17.9** shows a

single aggregate demand curve and several aggregate supply curves.

When aggregate supply is very low, the economy would be at point **a**, where AS_0 intersects AD. If supply-side policies were successfully instituted, the aggregate supply curve would shift to AS_1, moving the point of macroeconomic equilibrium to **b**. Without any corresponding change in aggregate demand, real output would grow, and the price level would come down.

Further attempts to increase aggregate supply to move the economy to **c** has even less impact on the price level. If the aggregate supply curve does have a horizontal range—a matter of conjecture—then the price level could never be reduced below P_0.

Limitations of Supply-Side Policies

Perhaps the main limitation of supply-side policies is a lack of enough experience with them to know how they affect the economy. Even the concepts of aggregate supply and aggregate demand are largely conceptual, making it difficult to predict the exact consequence of any particular supply-side policy based on the shapes of the two curves.

In the case of the Laffer curve, total tax collections, when adjusted for inflation, actually declined after the 1981 tax reductions were implemented. The result is that one of the main foundations of the supply-side school was found to be weak.

432 UNIT 4: *Macroeconomics: Policies*

Extending the Content

The Tax Wedge Supply-side economists argue that increases in taxes—most notably sales, excise, and social security taxes—are eventually incorporated into business costs and, therefore, result in higher prices. Taxes, they continue, act as a "wedge" between the actual costs of productive resources and the prices charged for products. Higher prices lead to a decrease in demand, which, in turn, leads to a cutback in production. The tax wedge, supply-siders conclude, causes a decrease in aggregate supply.

Nevertheless, policies that promote productivity, reduce unnecessary paperwork, or otherwise allow the economy to grow to its maximum potential are certainly worthwhile. Everyone, including demand-siders, favors policies such as these.

Finally, supply-side economic policies are designed more to restore economic growth rather than to remedy economic instability. No matter how fast or slow the economy grows, it seems to have a tendency to fluctuate around its trend line. Supply-side policies during the Reagan presidency tended to weaken the automatic stabilizers by making the federal tax structure less progressive and by reducing many of the "safety net" programs.

Monetary Policies

Both demand-side economics and supply-side economics are concerned about stimulating production and employment. Neither policy assigns much importance to the money supply. A doctrine called **monetarism**, however, places primary importance on the role of money and its growth.

Monetarists believe that fluctuations in the money supply can be a destabilizing element that leads to unemployment and inflation. They favor policies that lead to stable, long-term monetary growth at levels low enough to control inflation. 2

Reviewing the Tools of Monetary Policy

When the Federal Reserve System conducts monetary policy, it generally tries to affect the cost and the availability of credit by expanding and contracting the money supply. The Fed's main tools in this regard are open market operations, the discount rate, and a change in the reserve requirement. ☑

GO TO
Lesson 7 of Interactive Economics! to learn more about "Fiscal Policy and Aggregate Supply."

Figure 17.9
Supply-Side Policies and the Aggregate Supply Curve

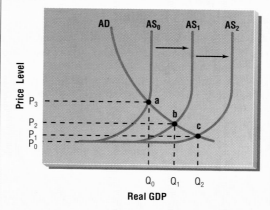

Supply-side policies are designed to increase aggregate supply. When the aggregate supply curve shifts to the right, additional real GDP can be produced at lower price levels. **What are some examples of supply-side policies?**

If the Fed wants to expand the money supply through open market operations, it will buy government securities. This increases the excess reserves in the banking system and makes loan expansion possible. The Fed may also lower the discount rate in an effort to lower the cost of credit for borrowers. Lowering the reserve requirement is a third possibility, but is unlikely to be used as long as the other monetary policy tools work.

If the Fed wants to contract the money supply, it would sell securities in the open market to drain reserves from the banking system. It could also raise

MEETING LESSON OBJECTIVES

Each objective below is tested by the questions that follow it in parentheses.

1. **Explain** the operations and impact of fiscal policy. **(1, 2, 6)**
2. **Distinguish** between supply-side economics and fiscal policy. **(1, 2, 3, 5)**
3. **State** the basic assumptions of monetary policy. **(1, 4)**

VISUAL INSTRUCTION

Ask: What does a shift of the aggregate supply curve to the right indicate? *(an increase in aggregate supply)*

Answer to Caption:

reducing number of federal agencies, deregulation, tax cuts

ANSWERS

1. the Laffer Curve
2. They destabilize the economy, causing unemployment and inflation.

QUICK CHECK

Checking Understanding

1. What graphic illustrates supply-side economics?
2. According to monetarists, how do fluctuations in the money supply affect the economy?

Applying Economic Concepts

 Monetary Policy Although monetary policy and fiscal policy both are designed to stabilize the economy, a different part of the government is responsible for each. The Fed conducts monetary policy. Congress and the President conduct fiscal policy.

$ Free Enterprise Activity $

Invite a local business owner or manager to visit the class and make a presentation on the topic, "How Macroeconomic Policies Affect My Business." In a follow-up class discussion, have students consider the role that government plays in carrying out fiscal and monetary policies.

Evaluate

📁 📁 💻 Assign the
Section 3 Quiz in the TCR or
use the *Economics: Principles and
Practices* Testmaker to create a
customized quiz. Spanish
Section Quizzes also are avail-
able in the Spanish Resources
Binder.

Reteach

Have students outline the
major aspects of demand-side
policies, supply-side policies,
and monetary polices.

Enrich

Have students read about
current macroeconomic issues
and policies in another nation,
such as Canada, Japan, Germany, or Great Britain. Have
students write an essay comparing the current macroeconomic issues and policies of
their selected country with
those of the United States.

CLOSE

Have students discuss
the following statement:
"Economic policymakers are
about as skillful at predicting
outcomes of their policies as
meteorologists are at forecast-
ing the weather."

the discount rate to make borrowing from the Fed more costly. Finally, and as a last resort, it could raise the reserve requirement.

Interest Rates and Inflation

In the short run, expansionist monetary policy can be used to lower interest rates. This action would reduce the cost of consumer and business borrowing and shift the aggregate supply curve to the right. Real GDP would tend to increase, but so would the possibility of future inflation. The money supply can grow over time, but how fast should the money supply be allowed to grow?

Most monetarists believe that if the money supply is allowed to grow at a slow but steady rate, inflation will be controlled. The rates of growth of real GDP and productivity would determine the rate at which the money supply grows.

If the rate of growth of real GDP were 3 percent, and that of productivity 1 percent, the money supply would grow at about 4 percent without causing infla-tion. At this rate, there would be just enough extra money each year to buy the additional goods and ser-vices the economy produces. With less money in cir-culation, inflation would slowly be reduced and, in time, would fade altogether.

This approach to inflation control is in sharp contrast to others tried earlier. In the early 1970s, for example, President Richard Nixon tried to stop inflation by imposing **wage-price controls**—regula-tions that make it illegal for businesses to give work-ers raises or to raise prices without the explicit permission of the government. Most monetarists at the time said the controls would not work. The econ-omy ultimately proved the economists correct; the controls did little to stop inflation.

Monetary Policy and Unemployment

Monetarists argue that attempts to cut unemploy-ment by expanding the money supply provide only temporary relief. They argue that excessive rates of monetary growth eventually drive up prices and interest rates.

Higher interest rates raise the cost of borrowing for businesses, which shifts the aggregate supply curve to the left. The increased cost of borrowing also shifts the aggregate demand curve to the left. The result is that real GDP could fall back to its original level—but at a different and much higher price level. The result would appear almost as if the aggregate supply and demand curves shifted up together, rather than to the left.

An overly expansionist monetary policy, then, will cause long-term inflation. Monetary policy is not a long-term cure for unemployment.

SECTION 3 REVIEW

Reviewing Terms and Facts

1. **Define** fiscal policy, Keynesian economics, consumption func-tion, multiplier, accelerator, auto-matic stabilizer, unemployment insurance, supply-side econom-ics, Laffer curve, monetarism, wage-price controls.
2. **Describe** the objectives of demand-side policies.

3. **Identify** the main assumptions of supply-side policies.
4. **Name** the tools of monetary policy.

Critical Thinking

5. **Making Comparisons** How do demand-side policies and supply-side policies differ?

Applying Economic Concepts

6. **Fiscal Policy** Fiscal policy is one of the tools designed to stabilize the economy. How does it shift the aggregate demand curve?

Answers to SECTION 3 REVIEW

1. All vocabulary words are defined in the Glossary.

2. to achieve steady economic growth and low unemployment by affecting aggregate demand

3. If taxes, government regulations, and government spending are decreased, businesses and individuals will produce and spend more. Increased invest-ment and productivity would lead to increased output.

4. open market operations, the discount rate, and a change in the reserve requirement

5. Supply-side policies want the government to take a smaller role in economic affairs. Demand-side policies want to stimulate output by generat-ing demand with increased levels of government spending.

6. by spending more to offset the decline in invest-ment spending, by lowering taxes and enacting other measures to encourage businesses and con-sumers to spend more

PROFILES IN ECONOMICS

MILTON FRIEDMAN
(1912–   )

Milton Friedman is an influential and conservative American economist closely associated with the school of thought known as monetarism. Dr. Friedman was affiliated with the National Bureau of Economic Research, taught at the University of Chicago from 1946 to 1977, and wrote a popular column for *Newsweek.* He is currently a fellow with the Hoover Institute at Stanford University.

COMPETITIVE CAPITALISM Dr. Friedman's writings have covered an extraordinary variety of topics, many of which were put forth in his early classic, *Capitalism and Freedom,* written in 1962. The major theme of the book was

Friedman believes the freedom to fail in a free enterprise economy is important— failures release resources for use elsewhere.

"the role of competitive capitalism . . . as a system of economic freedom and a necessary condition for

political freedom." This text put forth proposals such as opposition to agricultural subsidies and price controls, the creation of a volunteer army, a system of vouchers for public schools, and opposition to the minimum wage. Although his ideas were radical departures from prevailing thought at the time, the power of his arguments was such that many of his opinions came to fruition.

MONETARISM The general public is probably most familiar with Friedman through his short editorials that appeared in *Newsweek.*

Within the academic community, Friedman has impeccable credentials in the area of monetary history. His writings are the definitive works on the growth of the money supply and its relationship to inflation and real changes in the economy.

Friedman has been most influential with his unwavering support of monetarism—the theory that the quantity of money does matter because of its impact on the overall state of the economy. The key to his argument is that changes in the rate of growth of the money supply have varying and unpredictable lags, which makes fine-tuning the economy virtually impossible. Friedman claims that the Federal Reserve System should let the money supply grow at a constant rate to avoid destabilizing the economy.

Friedman's arguments had an enormous impact on the economics profession. His views attracted a number of adherents and, before long, the school of monetarism grew. For his stabilization policy, Friedman was awarded the Nobel Prize in economics in 1976.

Examining the Profile

1. **Identifying Central Issues** What is the core of Friedman's stabilization policy?

2. **For Further Research** Research and report on Friedman's free market positions in his highly acclaimed book, *Free To Choose: A Personal Statement,* coauthored with Rose Friedman.

FOCUS

Section Objectives

1. Explain why monetary policy sometimes conflicts with other economic policies.

2. Recognize that economists have differing views.

3. Understand the way that politics and economics interact.

Bellringer

Prior to taking roll at the beginning of the class period, display Focus Activity Transparency 85 on the overhead projector and assign the accompanying Student Activity 85.

Motivational Activity

Discuss students' responses to the activity sheet that accompanies Focus Activity Transparency 85.

Preteaching Vocabulary

Have students explain, in their own words, the role and importance of the Council of Economic Advisers. **LEP**

Use the **Vocabulary PuzzleMaker** to create crossword and word search puzzles.

TEACH

Guided Practice

L2 *Making Comparisons*
Call on students to identify similarities and differences between the Fed and the Council of Economic Advisers. Note suggestions on the chalkboard. Then have students use this information to write a comparative essay on these two bodies.

SECTION 4
Economics and Politics

Section Preview

Objectives

After studying this section, you will be able to:

1. **Explain** why monetary policy sometimes conflicts with other economic policies.

2. **Recognize** that economists have differing views.

3. **Understand** the way that politics and economics interact.

Key Terms

Council of Economic Advisers

Applying Economic Concepts

Diversity of Opinion Friends often disagree over how something should be done. Economists behave the same way. They often see the economic problems of the world differently and offer different solutions. Much *diversity of opinion* exists among economists.

Someone looking at the economic history of the United States might decide that economists have not had much success coping with the problems of economic instability and growth. Inflation is sometimes a problem; unemployment goes up and down; recessions come and go. Despite all of this, more progress has been made than most people realize.

A major difficulty with the pursuit of stabilization and growth policies is that the problem goes beyond a simple analysis of aggregate supply and demand curves. Many dynamics are involved.

An Independent Monetary Authority

An interesting feature of the American economy is that fiscal policy is in the hands of elected officials, but monetary policy is not. Monetary policy is the responsibility of the Federal Reserve System (the Fed).

Monetary and fiscal policy can—and often do—operate at cross-purposes. During an election year, for example, a President may want to stimulate GDP and take credit for a growing economy. Politicians can lower taxes, increase Social Security payments, and approve federal spending projects.

The Fed, however, might have different ideas. If inflation is a problem at the time, the Fed might want to follow a tight monetary policy to slow the growth of money and reduce inflation. High interest rates

generally go along with tight money, and they will work against the expansion the President hopes for.

This situation occurred during the presidential campaign of 1992. Because of the threat of inflation, the Fed was pursuing a tighter monetary policy than President Bush wanted. The economy had entered a recession in 1990. The slow economic growth may have convinced many people to vote for other candidates instead. The election was fairly close, leading many people to conclude that the state of the economy was indeed a factor that influenced the election's outcome. **1**

Congress so far has not been willing to make the Fed less independent. Most members of Congress believe that the power to create money should be in the hands of an independent agency rather than in those of elected officials.

Why Economists Differ

Because economists have different backgrounds and experience, their advice can often seem contradictory. One reason for the differences is that most economic explanations and theories are a product of the problems of the times. Demand-side economics, for example, came about during the 1930s when the unemployment rate was at record highs. Because the government sector was so small at the time, supply-side policies designed to make government's role even smaller probably would not have helped much.

Classroom Resources for SECTION 4

Reproducible Lesson Plan 17-4
Guided Reading Activity 17-4
Section Quiz 17-4
Spanish Section Quiz 17-4
Focus Activity Transparency 85
Enrichment Activity 17
Reteaching Activity 17
Spanish Reteaching Activity 17

Economic Vocabulary Activity 17
Spanish Economic Vocabulary Activity 17
Chapter 17 Test, Form A and Form B
English and Spanish Audiocassettes
Testmaker
Vocabulary PuzzleMaker
Chapter Challenger Interactive Review Software
MindJogger Videoquiz

The monetarist point of view emerged in the 1960s and 1970s when inflation soared. Because demand-side economics were not designed to deal with inflation, new solutions were needed. The problem with the monetarist view, however, was that it offered long-term solutions but little short-term relief. **2**

The supply-side explanations eventually grew out of frustration with the economic health of the country and the solutions that the demand-siders and monetarists offered. Again, something new and different seemed to be needed.

For the most part, economists generally do not define their position as purely demand-side, supply-side, or monetarist. Many demand-siders are monetarists when it comes to controlling inflation. Many monetarists are supply-siders when it comes to agreeing on the potential burden of the tax structure. Supply-siders and demand-siders even agree on multiplier-accelerator interactions. Economists often take a middle road that incorporates many points of view.

Change has become a fact of life in the United States. As long as society keeps changing, new problems will continue to arise. From each new set of problems, new theories are bound to emerge.

Economic Politics

In the 1800s, the science of economics was known as "political economics." After a while, however, the economists broke away from the political theorists and tried to establish economics as a science in its own right.

In recent years, the two fields have merged again. This time, however, they have done so in a way best described as "economic politics." Today, politicians are concerned with the economic consequences of what they do.

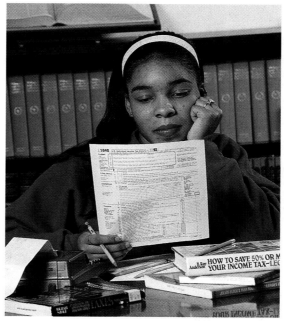

Economic Awareness *Staying informed about the workings of the economy will help in such activities as job searches or tax preparation.* **What is the Council of Economic Advisers?**

The Council of Economic Advisers

Generally, economists and politicians work together fairly closely. The President of the United States, for example, has a three-member **Council of Economic Advisers** to report on economic developments and to propose strategies. The economists basically are the advisers, while the politicians direct or implement the policies.

This system has two weaknesses. The first is that the politicians are not always willing—or able—to

---

QUICK CHECK

Checking Understanding

1. Why might monetary and fiscal policy be at odds during an election year?
2. When did the monetarist point of view emerge?

Applying Economic Concepts

 Role of Government Congress established the Council of Economic Advisers in 1946 to promote growth and stability. The President, with Senate approval, appoints the advisers.

CHAPTER 17
SECTION 4

Independent Practice

☞ *Guided Reading* Assign Guided Reading Activity for Section 4. **LEP**

ASSESS

Check for Understanding

Assign Section 4 Review as homework or an in-class activity.

◉ Use **Chapter Challenger Interactive Review Software** to review Section 4.

VISUAL INSTRUCTION

Stress that being well informed is the keystone of intelligent decision making.

Answer to Caption:

three-member body that reports to President on economy and economic policies

QUICK CHECK

ANSWERS

1. because fiscal policy is controlled by politicians, and monetary policy is controlled by an independent body
2. 1960s and 1970s

$ Free Enterprise Activity $

Have students review business and economics periodicals from previous years for several articles that make predictions about the economy. Ask students to summarize what economists predicted, the extent to which predictions agreed, and the accuracy of the predictions.

MEETING LESSON OBJECTIVES

Each objective below is tested by the questions that follow it in parentheses.

1. **Explain** why monetary policy sometimes conflicts with other economic policies. **(2, 6)**

2. **Recognize** that economists have differing views. **(3)**

3. **Understand** the way that politics and economics interact. **(1, 4, 5)**

Evaluate

📁 📁 💿 Assign the Section 4 Quiz in the TCR or use the *Economics: Principles and Practices* Testmaker.

Reteach

Call on students to explain the nature of economic politics.

📁 📁 Have students complete Reteaching Activity 17. Spanish Reteaching Activities also are available in the Spanish Resources Binder.

Enrich

Have students write a research paper on an election year where fiscal and monetary policy were at odds.

📁 Have students complete Enrichment Activity 17.

CLOSE

Have students discuss playwright George Bernard Shaw's comment that if you laid all the economists end to end, they still would not reach a conclusion.

▶ DID YOU KNOW?

Oops! In 1936 the *Literary Digest*, a national magazine, conducted a public opinion poll to predict the winner of that year's presidential election. On the basis of more than 2 million postcard responses, the magazine predicted that Alfred M. Landon would defeat Franklin D. Roosevelt. Roosevelt, however, won by a landslide. What went wrong? The *Literary Digest* had polled only upper-class and middle-class Americans. The sample was not representative of the majority of Americans, who were suffering the effects of the Great Depression and who reelected Roosevelt.

follow the economists' advice. A President may want a balanced budget, but to achieve this, the economic advisers may recommend raising taxes. If one of the President's campaign pledges was to not raise taxes, the economists' advice may be ignored.

Another problem is that the political system does not always react quickly enough to deal with current economic problems. In 1974, for example, the American economy entered a severe recession. At the time, it was considered the worst recession since the 1930s. Nearly everyone felt that something should be done to stimulate the economy.

After the recession was well underway, Congress approved a $100 refund on income taxes to stimulate the economy. The refunds were mailed during the second quarter of 1975, shortly after the recession ended and too late to stimulate the economy in the way originally intended.

When the 1990 recession began, politicians simply waited for it to go away. Monetary policy was used to give the economy a "soft landing," but the recession was deeper than expected and the subsequent recovery was anemic.

Increased Understanding and Awareness

Despite everything, economists have had some success in the description, analysis, and explanation of economic activity. They have managed to develop many statistical measures of the economy's performance, as well as models that are well suited to economic analysis and explanation. In the process, they have helped the American people become more aware of the workings of the economy. This awareness has benefited everyone, from the student just starting out to the politician who must answer to the voters.

Today, economists know enough about the economy to prevent a depression like the one in the 1930s. It is doubtful that economists know enough—or can convince others that they know enough—to avoid minor recessions. They can, however, devise policies to stimulate growth and to help certain groups when unemployment rises or inflation strikes.

SECTION 4 REVIEW

Reviewing Terms and Facts

1. **Define** Council of Economic Advisers.
2. **Explain** why Congress wants to continue having an independent monetary authority.
3. **List** several reasons economists differ.
4. **Explain** what *economic politics* means.

Critical Thinking

5. **Making Inferences** Suppose that, in an election year, Congress passes a massive tax cut although inflation is at 9 percent. What actions might the Fed take during such economic times?

Applying Economic Concepts

6. **Diversity of Opinion** Why do monetary and fiscal policies often operate at cross-purposes? What impact does this conflict have on the economy?

Answers to SECTION 4 REVIEW

1. **Council of Economic Advisers:** three-member council that reports on economic developments and proposes strategies to the President

2. Most members believe that the power to create money should be in the hands of an independent agency rather than in those of elected officials.

3. because they have different backgrounds and experience

4. Politicians are concerned with the economic consequences of what they do.

5. They may raise interest rates to slow the growth of money and reduce inflation.

6. because fiscal policy is in the hands of elected officials, but monetary policy is the responsibility of the Fed; Fiscal policies can harm the Fed's policies, and vice versa.

ECONOMICS IN ACTION

Economic Growth and Stability

Setting Up the Video

With your classmates, view "Economic Growth and Stability" on the videodisc **Economics in Action**. The video focuses on three theories for controlling economic cycles. The first theory—demand-side economics—argues that the government should take an active role in the economy by providing more jobs. The second theory—supply-side economics—pro-

Chapter 24
Disc 2, Side 2

Scan the bar code or enter the chapter number on your keypad and press Search. *(Also available in VHS format.)*

poses that the government reduce its involvement in the economy. Monetarism, the third theory, believes the economy can be controlled by controlling the money supply.

Hands-On Activity

Imagine that the economy is in a recession. What can the government do to try to improve it? Write your suggestions in a list, then classify the suggestions according to which economic theory they represent. Focusing on demand-side and supply-side actions, discuss the likely consequences of each suggestion.

INTERACTIVE ECONOMICS!

Macroeconomic Equilibrium

Introduction

Lesson 6 of **Interactive Economics!** deals with macroeconomic equilibrium, which is similar in many respects to the equilibrium found in an individual market. The major similarities are the general shapes of the supply and demand curves, the equilibrium at the intersection of the two curves, and that surpluses and shortages push the price level toward equilibrium.

The major differences are that demand and supply are measured in terms of aggregates, and quantity is measured in terms of real GDP. Another difference is that the government has, within limits, the ability to influence the equilibrium with the use of fiscal and monetary policy tools.

Using the Software

1. Select "Macroeconomic Equilibrium" from the Main Menu.
2. Read the introduction to "Macroeconomic Equilibrium," then click on and review "The Aggregate Demand Curve."
3. Now click on and review "The Aggregate Supply Curve."
4. Finally, click on and review the "Advanced Topics."
5. Study the two topics given, then click on "Economics Lab." Complete the lab by clicking and dragging the correct captions to their proper graphs.
6. Print your completed lab.

439

MULTIMEDIA ACTIVITIES

GLENCOE TECHNOLOGY

NIGHTLY BUSINESS REPORT

Economics in Action

Chapter 24
Disc 2, Side 2

Title: *Economic Growth and Stability*

If you do not have access to a videodisc player, the **Economics in Action** programs are also available in VHS.

INTERACTIVE ECONOMICS!

Before students complete the "Economics Lab" in Lesson 6, ask them the following questions:

1. How is macroeconomic equilibrium similar to the equilibrium found in an individual market? *(the general shapes of the supply and demand curves are similar; the equilibrium is found at the intersection of the two curves; and pressures exerted by surpluses and shortages push the price level toward equilibrium)*

2. What are the major differences? *(demand is measured in terms of aggregate demand; supply is measured in terms of aggregate supply; prices are measured in terms of the price level using a measure such as the CPI; quantity is measured in terms of real GDP)*

TEACHER NOTES

GLENCOE
TECHNOLOGY

VIDEODISC
MindJogger Videoquiz

Use MindJogger to review
the Chapter 17 content.

 Chapter 17
Disc 3, Side A

Also available in VHS.

Answers

Reviewing Key Terms

1. B
2. A
3. B
4. B
5. A
6. B
7. B
8. B
9. A
10. C

Reviewing the Facts

1. the GDP gap, the misery index

2. wasted resources, political instability, high crime rates, increase in bankruptcy

3. The supply curve of a firm is upward sloping, with individual prices on the vertical axis. The aggregate supply curve is also upward sloping, but with a horizontal as well as vertical range, and the price level is on the vertical axis.

4. decrease in savings, increase in consumer spending, improved expectations, increase in government spending and transfer payments, and decrease in taxes

5. when the quantity of real GDP demanded is equal to the real GDP supplied at a

Reviewing Key Terms

Classify each of the terms below into one of the following categories:

A. supply-side policies
B. demand-side policies
C. monetarist policies

1. aggregate demand curve
2. aggregate supply curve
3. automatic stabilizer
4. consumption function
5. deregulation
6. entitlements
7. fiscal policy
8. Keynesian economics
9. Laffer curve
10. open market operations

Reviewing the Facts

SECTION 1 *(pages 418–421)*
1. **List** two statistics used to identify the problems of growth and economic instability.
2. **Name** some of the social costs of instability.

SECTION 2 *(pages 422–425)*
3. **Describe** the difference between the supply curve of a firm and the aggregate supply curve.
4. **Identify** the factors that would cause the aggregate demand curve to increase.
5. **Discuss** what is meant by macroeconomic equilibrium.

SECTION 3 *(pages 427–434)*
6. **Identify** the major tools of fiscal policy.
7. **List** the main assumptions of the supply-siders.
8. **Describe** the short-term and long-term impacts of monetary policy.

SECTION 4 *(pages 436–438)*
9. **Explain** why the monetary policies of the Fed are not always consistent with the objectives of fiscal policy.

10. **Explain** why new problems will arise in the economy, even as old ones are solved.
11. **State** an example of how politics sometimes overrides sound economic policies.

Critical Thinking

1. **Drawing Conclusions** Why is the misery index a more personal measure of the social costs of instability than other concepts such as the GDP gap?
2. **Making Predictions** What would happen to the aggregate demand curve—as shown below— if there was a sudden growth in consumer spending fueled by a massive tax cut? How would such a shift affect macroeconomic equilibrium and the general price level?

Macroeconomic Equilibrium

The economy is at equilibrium when the quantity of real GDP demanded is equal to the real GDP supplied at a given price level. The question facing economic policymakers is how to increase real GDP without increasing the price level.

given price level

6. spending and/or taxation policies to influence economic activity, automatic stabilizers such as underemployment insurance, entitlements

7. that deregulation and lower taxes will give businesses and consumers more incentive to produce and spend, thus increasing revenue collections because of the extra activity

8. In the short term, monetary policy can affect inter-

est rates and perhaps unemployment. In the long term, expansionist monetary policy can cause inflation.

9. Elected officials are in charge of fiscal policy and may implement programs to appeal to the public. The Fed, hoping to prevent inflation, may implement policies that work against the government programs.

10. because society keeps changing

Applying Economic Concepts

1. **Monetary Policy** At one time or another, most Presidents have complained about the independence of the Fed. Do you think this independence should be maintained, or that elected officials should have more control over monetary policy? Support your answer.

2. **Diversity of Opinion** Some economists favor policies that stimulate demand, while others favor those that stimulate the supply of goods and services. Still others prefer policies based on the growth of the money supply. With which group do you agree? Support your choice.

Reinforcing Skills

USING THE INTERNET

Log on to the Internet. Then, using a search engine, type in the following key words:

- Keynesian economics
- unemployment
- macroeconomic equilibrium
- inflation
- fiscal policy
- Laffer curve

Print out (or download) any articles or reports on these topics. Using the information you retrieved, prepare a two-paragraph report on each topic listed above—defining the term(s) and summarizing its significance to economic security. Add a list of Web sites and bibliography entries at the end of your report.

Individual Activity

Both demand-side and supply-side policies are designed to ensure stable economic growth. The approaches differ, however, on what should be done to achieve this goal. Assume that real GDP growth was negative during the last quarter. Make a two-column chart. In the left column, list the policies that demand-side economists would follow to help the economy. Place the supply-side solutions in the right column. How do the two approaches differ?

Cooperative Learning Activity

Organize into two groups. One group will represent members of Congress. The other group will represent officials of the Federal Reserve System. You have just been notified of the following economic statistics: Two months ago inflation was at 5 percent; last month it shot up to 8 percent. Meet with the members of your group to determine what fiscal and monetary policies should be followed, bearing in mind that the national elections are four months away.

Technology Activity

Using a Word Processor

Politicians and manufacturers often rely on public opinion polls to collect the information they need. A *public opinion poll* is a scientific way of measuring what people think about a particular topic at a particular time. A group of people, known as a *sample,* are asked the same set of questions. The idea is that this sample will represent the opinions of the whole population. Using a word processor, develop your own public opinion poll following these guidelines.

1. Limit the number of questions to fewer than five.
2. Word your questions carefully, avoiding terms that tend to influence answers.
3. Make sure respondents understand the scoring of the answers. For example, if they can circle any number from 1 through 5, they should understand that "1" means "strongly agree" and "5" means "strongly disagree."
4. Control the way the poll is taken. Have your sample answer the questions alone, not within a group setting.
5. Draw accurate conclusions from your polls, keeping in mind that some answers may not be reliable and that public opinion changes rapidly.

CHAPTER 17: *Achieving Economic Stability* **441**

Have students identify the impact on aggregate supply or aggregate demand of each of the following:

1. OPEC decides to double its output. *(Oil prices fall; aggregate supply will increase.)*

2. Income tax rates are increased 10 percent. *(People have less money to spend; aggregate demand will decline.)*

3. People expect the next set of economic indicators to show a sharp economic decline. *(Unfavorable expectations; aggregate demand will decline.)*

4. Technological developments result in increased labor productivity. *(Increase in productivity; aggregate supply will increase.)*

5. An opinion poll shows rising consumer confidence in the economy. *(Favorable expectations, aggregate demand will increase.)*

11. Answers will vary, but students may cite the refusal of the President and Congress to raise taxes, even when economic advisers recommend it.

Critical Thinking

1. It measures consumer suffering during periods of high inflation and unemployment.

2. The aggregate demand curve would shift to the right, putting increasing pressure on the price level and increasing real GDP.

Applying Economic Concepts

1. Answers will vary. Students should support their answers with sound reasoning.

2. Answers will vary. Students should provide reasons for their choices.

Reinforcing Skills

Lists of Web sites will vary. Have students present the results of their "surfing" to the class.

ARE AMERICANS PRODUCTIVE?

America enters the 21st century in a culture of invention and technology. One estimate states that more than half of all human knowledge has been produced within the past 50 years. More than half of all United States patents have been issued in the past 40 years. Yet with companies offering innovative goods and services at such a furious pace, statistics seem to reveal that American worker productivity is declining. Are Americans productive?

▲ *Technology helps as well as hinders productivity. A network crash, for example, can cripple a company.*

▼ *Many American workers question the statistics showing that U.S. employees work fewer hours and have more leisure time.*

Pro

Many middle-income earners do not have to consult an economist to find out what's been happening to wages. They know from experience that the answer is "not much." They complain that they work just as hard as their parents did, but don't seem to be making comparable gains in living standards. It seems almost un-American for a generation to be worse off than its parents.

Some explain this phenomenon by blaming it on the profligacy of the current generation of wage earners. They don't know how to save, and they don't know what real work—putting your nose to the grindstone—is all about. This explanation is undoubtedly true for certain individuals, but it does not explain the nationwide stagnation of wages at a time when labor productivity is growing.

. . . The more fitting explanation for the divergence of wages and productivity is that, in fact, people are making less than they used to in real terms for doing comparable work, or maybe getting the same amount for doing more.

—ELIA KACAPYR, "TAKING WHAT'S GIVEN—
WORKING FOR A LIVING," *AMERICAN DEMOGRAPHICS*

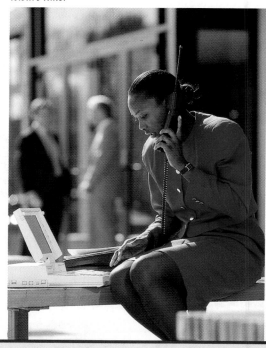

About the Speakers

Pro Elia Kacapyr is a writer and editor for *American Demographics* magazine.

Con W. Michael Cox is vice president and economic adviser for the Federal Reserve Bank of Dallas.

◄ *Productivity statistics do not reflect the time employees spend socializing on the job.*

▼ *Many corporations provide on-site fitness facilities for their employees, believing that a healthy employee is a productive employee.*

Con

Americans today are less willing to bow to the deity of productivity and devote ourselves to churning out as much as possible. We've progressed from narrow productivity concerns to "have a nice day." What working conditions did Americans tolerate decades ago for the sake of productivity? Foul air, bad lighting, hazardous substances, long hours, inadequate sanitation, inflexible schedules, repetitive tasks, the risk of death. Few of today's workers face the on-the-job risks of their grandparents. . . . Hours at work have fallen for decades. Many workers have flexible schedules, including regular breaks. What are workers' concerns in the 1990s? Meaningful work, respect, empowerment, social activities, wellness programs and family benefits.

What's more, there's evidence that workers are using more of their on-the-job time for socializing, running errands, attending colleagues' retirement parties, selling their kids' Girl Scout cookies, exercising in company facilities—a little bit here, a little bit there. It all adds up: time-diary surveys find that the gap between actual weekly work time and what's reported in government statistics rose from one hour in 1965 to six hours today. But neither the GDP nor productivity statistics reflect job time spent on socialization, personal business or relaxation while at work.

—W. MICHAEL COX AND RICHARD ALM,
"THE ECONOMY AT LIGHT SPEED:
TECHNOLOGY AND GROWTH IN THE
INFORMATION AGE—AND BEYOND," FEDERAL
RESERVE BANK OF DALLAS

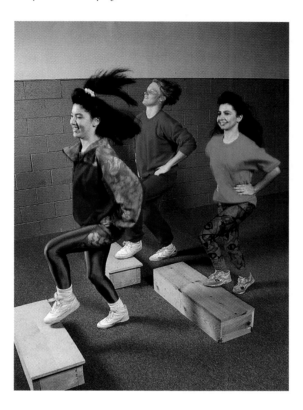

Analyzing the Case Study

1. What information does Kacapyr reveal about Americans' productivity and wages?

2. What evidence do Cox and Alm cite to explain that Americans are not as productive as their grandparents?

3. With which opinion do you agree? Why?

L2 *Role Play* Have students attempt to write the numerals 1 through 300 on a sheet of paper. As they are writing, ask them to recite the alphabet. Then ask them to name their and their family members' birth dates and ages. Finally, have students list the names of as many United States Presidents in order as they can. After the exercise, point out that productivity depends in large part on being able to focus on one activity at a time. Have students discuss times when their productivity decreased due to interruptions or trying to do too many tasks at one time.

ASSESS

Have students answer the questions listed under "Analyzing the Case Study."

CLOSE

Have a number of students read their answers to question 4 in the "Analyzing the Case Study" activity. Use these readings as the starting point for a debate on American productivity.

Answers to Analyzing the Case Study

1. that Americans work just as hard as their parents did but don't seem to be making comparable gains in living standards; that labor productivity is growing whereas wages are stagnant

2. that workers are using more of their on-the-job time for socializing, running errands, and so on; that the gap between actual weekly work time and what's reported in government statistics rose to 6 hours

3. Answers will vary. Have students provide reasons for their answers.

Unit Goals

After studying this unit, students will be able to:

1. **Appreciate** the interdependence among nations and the importance of international trade and foreign exchange.

2. **Compare** major economic systems of the world to capitalism.

3. **Analyze** the problems of economically developing countries.

4. **Show** how market prices help conserve limited resources.

Unit Overview

This unit examines economics from a global perspective. **Chapter 18** examines international trade. **Chapter 19** presents the spectrum of economic systems and traces the rise and fall of the Soviet Union. The problems faced by developing countries are the subject of **Chapter 20. Chapter 21** reviews the economic challenges the world faces.

⏏ If time does not permit teaching the entire unit, use the **Chapter Digests Audicassettes** to highlight chapter content.

Connecting with Past Learning

Point out that in **Unit 5,** students will be asked to apply many of the economic concepts that they learned in earlier chapters—scarcity, opportunity cost, supply and demand, elasticity, the price mechanism, for example—to global economics.

UNIT 5

INTERNATIONAL AND GLOBAL ECONOMICS

CHAPTER 18
International Trade

CHAPTER 19
Comparative Economic Systems

CHAPTER 20
Developing Countries

CHAPTER 21
Global Economic Challenges

Our interest will be to throw open the doors of commerce, and to knock off its shackles, giving freedom to all persons for the vent of whatever they may choose to bring into our ports, and asking the same in theirs.

—Thomas Jefferson

Economics and You

In this unit, discover what part economics plays in the following situations:

• Imported goods sometimes cost more than domestically produced ones.

• Capitalism has triumphed over communism.

• Population growth rates on the other side of the world affect you.

$$ Economics and You

The first example above is an illustration of one aspect of international trade—tariffs. The second example refers to the recent collapse of the communist economic system, largely because of the incredible inefficiency of central planning. The third example provides an illustration of the interdependence of the world's nations. For example, rapid population growth in South American countries might cause a surge of immigration—legal and illegal—to the U.S.

Introducing the Unit

In this unit, students will discover the importance of economic interdependence and examine economic issues on a global scale. Ask students to consider the following questions: Why do nations trade? How do other economic systems differ from our own? What are some of the problems of developing nations, and what can be done to foster their economic development? What types of global economic challenges face all nations? Direct students to write answers in their notebooks. Have them check and adjust their answers as they study the unit.

Unit Project

Have students work cooperatively to develop a questionnaire on the major global economic challenges of a new century. Then organize students into three groups, and have each one administer the questionnaire to one of the following: students, school faculty, adults in the community. Have students collate their findings and display them on the bulletin board.

The many ships filling Hong Kong's harbor symbolize the interdependency among nations in the global economy.

Examining the Photograph

To further this illustration of the concept of interdependency, offer the following scenario: One of the ships moored in the harbor might be flying a Greek flag and carrying a cargo of cotton from Egypt. Another ship, registered in Panama, might be about to leave for the U.S. with a consignment of shirts produced by Hong Kong's thriving textile industry. Then have students investigate exactly how an everyday item they own—a pair of sneakers manufactured in South Korea, for example—made its way to a local store.

445

CHAPTER ORGANIZER

Daily Objectives	Reproducible Resources	Multimedia Resources
Section 1 **Absolute and Comparative Advantage** 1. **Explain** the importance of international trade in today's economy. 2. **Describe** the meaning of absolute advantage. 3. **Relate** the importance of comparative advantage to international trade policies.	Reproducible Lesson Plan 18-1 Guided Reading Activity 18-1 Cooperative Learning Activity 19 Consumer Application Activity 20 Math Practice for Economics 25 Free Enterprise Activities 19, 20 Primary and Secondary Source Reading 19 Performance Assessment Activity 25 Section Quiz 18-1*	Focus Activity Transparency 86 Economic Concepts Transparency 20* Vocabulary PuzzleMaker Chapter Challenger Interactive Review Software Testmaker MindJogger Videoquiz Interactive Economics!
Section 2 **Barriers to International Trade** 1. **Explain** how international trade can be restricted to protect special interests. 2. **Cite** the main argument for protection. 3. **Relate** the history of the free trade movement.	Reproducible Lesson Plan 18-2 Guided Reading Activity 18-2 Reinforcing Economic Skill 18 Section Quiz 18-2*	Focus Activity Transparency 88 Vocabulary PuzzleMaker Chapter Challenger Interactive Review Software Testmaker NBR's Economics in Action Video Program
Section 3 **Financing and Trade Deficits** 1. **Explain** how foreign currency is used in trade. 2. **Describe** the problem of a trade deficit and the main solution to the problem.	Reproducible Lesson Plan 18-3 Guided Reading Activity 18-3 Section Quiz 18-3*	Focus Activity Transparency 87 Economic Concepts Transparency 21* Vocabulary PuzzleMaker Chapter Challenger Interactive Review Software Testmaker NBR's Economics in Action Video Program
Chapter Review and Evaluation	Enrichment Activity 18 Reteaching Activity 18* Economic Vocabulary Activity 18* Chapter 18 Test, Forms A and B	Chapter Digests Audiocassette Activities and Tests* Testmaker MindJogger Videoquiz

Also available in Spanish

 Blackline Master Transparency CD-ROM Software Videodisc Audiocassette

00:00 **OUT OF TIME?** Assign the Chapter 18 Digest Audiocassette and the corresponding Chapter Digest activities and tests.

National Council on Economic Education

THE **Economics** America AND **Economics** International PROGRAMS

VOLUNTARY NATIONAL CONTENT STANDARDS IN ECONOMICS
Emphasized in Chapter 18

Content Standard 5 *Students will understand that:*
Voluntary exchange occurs only when all participating parties expect to gain. This is true for trade among individuals or organizations within a nation, and among individuals or organizations in different nations.

Content Standard 6 *Students will understand that:*
When individuals, regions, and nations specialize in what they can produce at the lowest cost and then trade with others, both production and consumption increase.

Content Standard 7 *Students will understand that:*
Markets exist when buyers and sellers interact. This interaction determines market prices and thereby allocates scarce goods and services.

Economics America *Resources Available From NCEE*

- *Capstone: The Nation's High School Economics Course*
- *MCG: International Trade*
- *Civics and Government: Focus on Economics*
- *Geography: Focus on Economics*
- *United States History: Eyes on the Economy, Vol. II*
- *World History: Focus on Economics*

To order these materials, or to contact your state Council on Economic Education about workshops and programs, call 1-800-338-1192 or visit http://www.nationalcouncil.org.

PERFORMANCE ASSESSMENT

The following chapter projects may be assigned at the beginning of the chapter and used for performance assessment.

Multicultural Heritage On separate pieces of paper, write the names of five important trading partners of the U.S., such as Japan, Canada, Mexico, Germany, and Great Britain. Fold the pieces of paper and place them in a box. Organize the class into five groups and have a representative from each group draw a slip of paper from the box. Tell groups not to share the name on the paper with other groups.

Have groups research the products traded between their country and the U.S. Mention that such information may be found by conducting library research or by writing the country's embassy in the U.S. Encourage groups to develop charades or scenarios that will demonstrate the kinds of trade that take place between their country and the U.S. Have groups perform their charades and scenarios and have the rest of the class try to identify the various trading partners.

Cooperative Learning Organize students into five or six groups and assign each group a topic concerning trade—trade agreements, trading blocs, barriers to trade, foreign exchange and trade, and so on. Have groups prepare a four-page pictorial essay on their assigned topic. Illustrations used may include photographs, cartoons, sketches, maps, charts, graphs, and flow diagrams. Encourage group members to share among themselves the various tasks involved in preparing the essay. Have groups display their completed essays on the bulletin board.

ADDITIONAL RESOURCES

Readings for the Student

Gonnelli, Adam. *The Basics of Foreign Trade and Exchange.* New York: Federal Reserve Bank of New York, 1993. Provides basics of international trade and exchange; includes teacher's guide.

Opposing Viewpoints: Trade. San Diego, CA: Greenhaven Press, 1991. Offers debates on such issues as free trade, unfair trading practices, trade deficits, and the future of world trade.

Readings for the Teacher

Jessup, Jay M., and Maggie L. Jessup. *Doing Business in Mexico.* Rocklin, CA: Prima Publishing, 1993. Provides background information and advice about Mexican culture, industries, and emerging business opportunities.

Hugill, Peter J. *World Trade Since 1431: Geography, Technology, and Capitalism.* Baltimore, MD: Johns Hopkins University Press, 1993. Traces the history of world trade and the development of capitalism.

Multimedia

Return to Mocha. Modern Talking Pictures Service, 5000 Park St. N., St. Petersburg, FL 33709. Video, 27 mins. Demonstrates the advantages of international trade.

Trade Wars. Trade Wars, P.O. Box 147050, Gainesville, FL 32614–7050. Simulation. Game that involves students in global competition, fluctuating currencies, and trade negotiations.

Chapter Overview

Chapter 18 focuses on the topic of international trade. **Section 1** examines the concepts of absolute advantage and comparative advantage. **Section 2** discusses trade barriers, such as tariffs and quotas, and reviews the debate on protectionism and free trade. **Section 3** explains foreign exchange, the difference between fixed and flexible exchange rates, and the trade deficit.

GLENCOE
TECHNOLOGY

VIDEODISC
MindJogger Videoquiz

Use MindJogger to preview the Chapter 18 content.

 Chapter 18
Disc 3, Side A

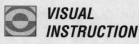 *Also available in VHS.*

inter**NET**
CONNECTION

Resources for Chapter 18 on the World Wide Web*

National Council on Economic Education
http://www.nationalcouncil.org/

World Trade Organization
http://www.wto.org/

U.S. Chamber of Commerce
http://www.uschamber.org/

*Sites subject to change.

VISUAL INSTRUCTION

Have students identify the foreign-made consumer electronics products that they or their families own.

At this international trade show, various countries display their consumer electronics products.

 Extra Credit Project

Have students write essays on the role that international trade plays in the American economy. Suggest that they illustrate their essays with examples, charts, and graphs. Call on volunteers to present and discuss their essays.

CHAPTER 18

International Trade

SECTION 1
Absolute and Comparative Advantage

SECTION 2
Barriers to International Trade

SECTION 3
Financing and Trade Deficits

CHAPTER PREVIEW

People to Know

• Bill Gates
• Customs Inspector

Applying Economic Concepts to Your Life

International Trade Is *international trade* important to you? On average, Americans spend nearly $4,000 per year on imported goods and services. Look at the labels on your clothes, in your shoes, on food products you buy, or even on the car you drive—and you see why international trade is important to everyone.

> ### Journal Writing
>
> For one week, be aware of every manufactured item you handle—from the clothes you put on in the morning to the cafeteria trays used in your school. Analyze each item for its producer. In your journal, log the items you use daily and note whether each is domestically produced or foreign-made.

Connecting to Past Learning

Ask a student to write the equation for the output-expenditure model on the chalkboard. Circle the "F" in the equation and ask students to identify what it represents. *(foreign sector of the economy)* Then have a student explain what role the foreign sector plays in the economy. *(sells products to be consumed by foreign countries, buys foreign products to be consumed in the U.S.)* Point out that the activities of the foreign sector can be called *international trade*—the subject of this chapter.

Applying Economics

Ask students to name articles of clothing, watches, shoes, and other items they have with them that are foreign-made. List these on the chalkboard. Ask those students who responded why they purchased a foreign-made article rather than one made in the U.S. Discuss these reasons with the class. Conclude by asking students if they believe Americans depend too much on foreign trade. Have students keep this question in mind as they study Chapter 18.

✓ PERFORMANCE ASSESSMENT

Refer to page **446B** for a Performance Assessment activity for this chapter. Also see the **Performance Assessment Activities** booklet for additional suggestions.

Economic Portfolio

As students make their **Journal Writing** entries, suggest that they consider such questions as: Should international trade be completely free of restrictions? Should the trading of particular products, or trade with a particular country, be restricted? Should political considerations influence our trade policies? Point out that this will help them to complete a writing activity in the Chapter Review. Refer students to the **Technology Activity** in the Chapter 18 Review on page 469.

Key to Ability Levels — Teaching strategies have been coded for varying learning styles and abilities:
L1 - Basic (activities for all students) **L2 - Average** (activities for average to above-average students)
L3 - Challenging (activities for above-average students) **LEP - Limited English Proficiency**

FOCUS

Section Objectives

1. Explain the importance of international trade in today's economy.

2. Describe the meaning of absolute advantage.

3. Relate the importance of comparative advantage to international trade.

Bellringer

 Prior to taking roll at the beginning of the class period, display Focus Activity Transparency 86.

Motivational Activity

Discuss students' responses to the activity sheet that accompanies Transparency 86.

Preteaching Vocabulary

Have students explain in their own words the difference between absolute and comparative advantage. **LEP**

Use the **Vocabulary Puzzlemaker** to create crossword and word search puzzles.

TEACH

Guided Practice

☞ **Cooperative Learning**
Assign Cooperative Learning Activity 19.

VISUAL INSTRUCTION

What gives Colombia an absolute advantage in emerald production? *(a large supply of emeralds)*

Answer to Caption:

specialization and comparative advantage

448

SECTION 1
Absolute and Comparative Advantage

Section Preview

Objectives

After studying this section, you will be able to:

1. **Explain** the importance of international trade in today's economy.

2. **Describe** the meaning of absolute advantage.

3. **Relate** the importance of comparative advantage to international trade policies.

Key Terms

absolute advantage, comparative advantage

Applying Economic Concepts

Comparative Advantage When you and a friend team up to do something, how do you divide the work? If you want to get the job done quickly, you probably specialize and perform the task that you do best. If this is the way you work, you already know about *comparative advantage*.

The key to trade—whether among people, states, or countries—is specialization. Some people specialize in cutting hair. Others specialize in fixing television sets. These people exchange their services for money, which they then use to buy the specialized talents and services of others.

Different regions of the United States specialize in certain economic activities in much the same way. Pittsburgh, for example, is a center of the steel industry, and Detroit specializes in automobiles. The Midwest and High Plains areas are known for wheat farming. Texas is recognized for oil and cattle, while Florida and California are famous for citrus fruit. All of these states trade with one another so that people in one area can consume the goods and services that workers in other areas offer.

What is true of specialization in the United States is also true in other regions of the world. Each region or country generally produces what it is best suited to do. As a result, international trade allows all countries the opportunity to take advantage of local production efficiencies. ✓

Absolute Advantage *Colombia produces 90 percent of the world's emeralds. This gives the country an absolute advantage over most nations in regard to emerald production.* **What is the key to trade?**

448 UNIT 5: *International and Global Economics*

Figure 18.1
United States Merchandise Trade by Area

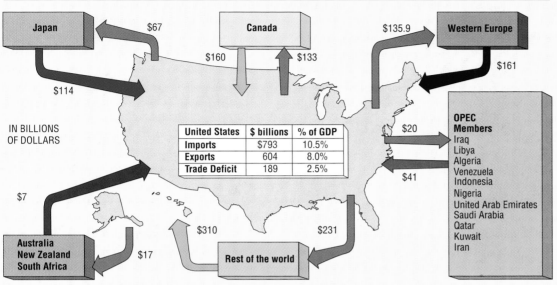

Japan				Canada			Western Europe

$67

$135.9

$160 $133

$161

$114

IN BILLIONS OF DOLLARS

United States	$ billions	% of GDP
Imports	$793	10.5%
Exports	604	8.0%
Trade Deficit	189	2.5%

$20

$41

OPEC Members
Iraq
Libya
Algeria
Venezuela
Indonesia
Nigeria
United Arab Emirates
Saudi Arabia
Qatar
Kuwait
Iran

$7

$310 $231

Australia New Zealand South Africa $17   **Rest of the world**

The United States exports merchandise all over the world. The biggest trade imbalance is with Japan, followed by OPEC members. **Which region of the world trades the most with the United States?**

Source: *Economic Report of the President, 1997.*

The United States and International Trade

In recent years, international trade has become increasingly important to all nations. Most of the products exchanged are goods, although a growing number of services—such as insurance and banking—are also bought and sold.

The Extent of Trade

The United States relies extensively on international trade. By 1998, imports of goods and services amounted to about $1,050 billion. This number corresponds to nearly $4,000 for every person in the country, and has grown steadily over the years. **1**

Figure 18.1 shows the trade patterns for merchandise between the United States and the rest of the

Checking Understanding	**Applying Economic Concepts**
1. By 1998, what was the value of United States imports per person?	☑ **International Trade** International trade is similar to trade between cities, states, or regions within a country. The main difference is that international trade involves different currencies, tariffs, and greater distances.

CHAPTER 18: *International Trade* **449**

L2 Analyzing Information
Refer students to Figure 18.2 and ask: What would happen if the U.S. was no longer able to import these materials? Have students write a paragraph about the importance of international trade to daily life in the U.S.

INTERACTIVE ECONOMICS!

 CD-ROM International Trade
Have students go to the Introduction menu and click on "Finding Comparative Advantage." Ask students to read through the tutorial and find the comparative advantage for both Alpha and Beta.

Supplied in both CD-ROM and diskette formats.

 Using Transparencies
Display Economic Concepts Transparency 20. Spanish Transparencies also are available.

Independent Practice

Guided Reading Assign Guided Reading Activity for Section 1. **LEP**

 VISUAL INSTRUCTION
Ask: What is the total merchandise trade deficit? *($189 billion)* What percentage of the GDP does this represent? *(2.5 percent)*

Answer to Caption:
Western Europe

 ANSWERS
1. approximately $4,000

449

Lesson 9 of Interactive
Economics! to learn more
about "Finding
Comparative Advantage."

L3 *Writing a Report* Ask students to select a major U.S. corporation that has a significant part of its total sales from exports. Have students write a report on where the corporation exports, what it exports, the value of those exports, and whether foreign trade is a growing or declining part of the corporation's business. Suggest that students illustrate their reports with charts.

📁 *Consumer Application* Assign Consumer Application Activity 20.

📁 *Math Practice* Assign Math Practice for Economics 25.

📁 *Free Enterprise* Assign Free Enterprise Activities 19 and 20.

📁 *Readings* Assign Primary and Secondary Source Reading 19.

📁 *Performance Assessment* Assign Performance Assessment Activity 25.

ASSESS

Check for Understanding

Assign Section 1 Review as homework or an in-class activity.

🔲 Use **Chapter Challenger Interactive Review Software** to review Section 1.

VISUAL INSTRUCTION

Have students identify the origins of the raw materials used to make an aluminum can. (*Australia, Guinea, Jamaica*)

Answer to Caption:

Some raw materials are essential to daily life, and trade is the only way to obtain them.

Figure 18.2
American Dependency on Trade: Imports as a Percent of Consumption

Raw Material	Imports as a Percent of Consumption	Primary Foreign Sources	Use of Raw Material
Industrial Diamonds	100	South Africa, Australia, Zaire, Botswana	Industrial cutting tools, oil well drills
Columbium	100	Brazil, Canada, Thailand	Atomic energy reactors, hardened steel
Mica (sheet)	100	India, Belgium, France	Electrical insulation, ceramics
Strontium	100	Mexico, Spain	Flares, fireworks
Manganese	100	South Africa, Gabon, France	Stainless steel, dry cell batteries, industrial dies
Bauxite	99	Australia, Guinea, Jamaica	Anything made of aluminum
Platinum	91	South Africa, United Kingdom, Russia	Electrical components, jewelry, dentistry, electroplating
Tantalum	86	Thailand, Germany, Brazil	Surgical instruments and missile parts
Cobalt	79	Zaire, Zambia, Canada	High-temperature jet fighter engines
Chromium	75	South Africa, Zimbabwe, Turkey	Chrome, ball bearings, trim on appliances and cars
Tungsten	84	China, Bolivia, Canada	High-temperature materials, lamp filaments, instruments

International trade is the primary means by which nations, including the United States, obtain many essential yet scarce materials. **How does the lack of certain raw materials force nations to become interdependent?**

Source: *Statistical Abstract of the United States,* 1996

---

world. The sheer volume of this trade between nations of such different geographic, political, and religious characteristics is proof that trade is beneficial. Nations trade for the same reasons individuals do—because they are free to do so, and they believe they are better off with trade than without it.

The Necessity of Trade

Without international trade, many products would not be available on the world market. Bananas, for example, would not leave Honduras, nor would coffee beans leave Brazil. Some people think of international trade as a way to obtain exotic products and fancy consumer goods, but the issue is more complex than that.

Many imports, for example, are necessities such as oil, clothing, and shoes. We also import minerals, metals, and raw materials that are not available in the

United States. Figure 18.2 lists some essential raw materials that would not be available without trade.

Absolute Advantage

In some cases, it may be cheaper for a country to import a product than to manufacture it. The differences in production costs from one country to another form a basis for international trade. The production costs vary because of differences in natural resources, climate, labor force, and capital. When a country is able to produce more of a given product than another, it has an **absolute advantage**.

Consider, for example, the case of two countries—Alpha and Beta—which are the same size in terms of area, population, and capital stock. Only their climate and soil fertilities differ. In each country, only two crops can be grown—coffee and cashew nuts.

💲 *Free Enterprise Activity* 💲

Point out that geographic factors have an enormous influence on international trade. The climate, weather, topography, soil fertility, and natural resources all affect what a nation is able to produce and export. Have students select a product that a particular nation exports and write a paragraph explaining how geographic factors influence the production of that item.

If both countries devote all of their efforts to producing coffee, Alpha can produce 40 million pounds and Beta 6 million. Alpha has an absolute advantage in the production of coffee. If both countries devote all their efforts to the production of cashew nuts, Alpha can produce 8 million pounds and Beta 6 million. Alpha also has an absolute advantage in the production of cashew nuts.

For years, people thought that absolute advantage was the basis for trade because it enabled a country to produce enough of a good to consume domestically as well as to export. The theory of absolute advantage did not explain how a large country could trade with a small country to the benefit of both.

Comparative Advantage

Even when one country enjoys an absolute advantage in the production of all goods, trade between it and another country is still beneficial if one country can produce a product relatively more efficiently. The more efficient country has a **comparative advantage** in the production of a good if it can produce that good at a relatively lower opportunity cost.

Alpha, for example, has a comparative advantage in the production of coffee. Given a fixed amount of resources, it can produce relatively more coffee than

nuts. If Alpha were to specialize in the production of one good, it would choose coffee beans.

Beta, however, does a relatively better job of producing cashew nuts. Its comparative advantage in cashew nuts would lead Beta to specialize in their production.

The concept of comparative advantage is based on the assumption that everyone will be better off producing the products they produce relatively best. This concept applies to individuals, companies, states, and regions as well as to nations.

When nations specialize in the goods they are most efficient at producing, the total world output is greater. Take, for example, the case of the United States and Brazil. The United States has excellent supplies of iron and coal. It also has the capital and the labor that are needed to produce tractors and farm machinery efficiently. Brazil, in contrast, does not have as much capital or skilled labor. It does have the amount and kind of land, labor, and climate to produce coffee efficiently.

The United States, therefore, has a comparative advantage in the production of tractors and farm machinery. Brazil has a comparative advantage in the production of coffee. Trade between the two countries would be valuable to both. Each country could produce its specialty at a lower cost and enjoy larger total consumption.

SECTION 1 REVIEW

Reviewing Terms and Facts

1. **Define** absolute advantage, comparative advantage.
2. **Explain** why international trade is crucial to the United States today.
3. **Explain** why world output is larger when international trade is based on comparative advantage.

Critical Thinking

4. **Making Generalizations** Are the products that your state produces and sells to others based on absolute advantage or on comparative advantage? Explain your answer.

Applying Economic Concepts

5. **Comparative Advantage** If you were to open a business with two of your best friends, how would you divide the work to be done? Do your decisions regarding who does what reflect comparative advantage? Explain.

CHAPTER 18: *International Trade* **451**

Answers to SECTION 1 REVIEW

1. All vocabulary words are defined in the Glossary.

2. Essential raw materials not available in the United States can be imported.

3. When each nation focuses on the product(s) it can produce relatively more efficiently, total world output goes up.

4. Answers will vary. Students' answers should reflect an awareness of their state's products and an understanding of absolute advantage and comparative advantage.

5. Answers will vary. Students may assign tasks based on each person's relative strengths, which would reflect comparative advantage.

MEETING LESSON OBJECTIVES

Each objective below is tested by the questions that follow it in parentheses.

1. **Explain** the importance of international trade in today's economy. **(2)**
2. **Describe** the meaning of absolute advantage. **(1, 4)**
3. **Relate** the importance of comparative advantage to international trade policies. **(1, 3, 4, 5)**

Evaluate

Assign the Section 1 Quiz in the TCR or use the *Economics: Principles and Practices* Testmaker to create a customized quiz. Spanish Section Quizzes also are available in the Spanish Resources Binder.

Reteach

Have students write two questions for each major heading in the section. Collect questions and use them to test students' understanding of the section.

Enrich

Have students research the products for which the U.S. has a comparative advantage and why.

CLOSE

Have students discuss the following: "International trade is the life-blood of the economy."

PROFILES IN ECONOMICS

BILL GATES
(1955–   )

"Our success," says Bill Gates, "is based on only one thing: good products. It's not very complicated." The success of Microsoft Corporation's products has made Gates—cofounder and CEO—possibly the richest person in the world.

TEENAGE WIZARDRY While in high school, Gates designed a class scheduling program so that he could take courses with the prettiest girls in his school. He also started Traf-O-Data, a computer traffic analysis company.

At age 19, Gates dropped out of pre-law at Harvard University to pursue his interest in computer technol-

The development of Windows® has brought Bill Gates phenomenal wealth.

ogy. Gates and his friend Paul Allen wrote a condensed operating-system language, which they licensed to a computer manufacturer. From this success, Gates and Allen established Microsoft Corporation in 1975.

INTO THE BIG LEAGUES In 1980 IBM—the computer industry leader—asked Gates to develop an operating system for its new personal computer. Gates bought a system from a small company for $50,000. He revamped it and licensed it to IBM for $125,000. The system was called MS-DOS, for Microsoft Disk Operating System. Because Gates retained ownership of MS-DOS, he was in a position to market the system to other companies. In 1981 IBM unveiled its PC, setting off the personal computer boom.

MS-DOS became the dominant operating system in the market.

Microsoft went public in 1986, and the stock did better than expected. Gates, who owned 45 percent of the company, became a millionaire several hundred times over. Smaller investors gained also.

CONTINUING SUCCESS At age 42, Bill Gates had an estimated net worth of about $38 billion. Much of Gates's success came from his unique combination of technological expertise and an understanding of the computer needs of the average user. Windows®, an operating program featuring simplified commands and eye-catching graphics, swept the market. By 1993 Windows® was selling 1 million copies a month, and Microsoft operating systems ran nearly 90 percent of the world's PCs. This was followed by Windows 95® and NT4.0, products that enjoyed even more success. Entrepreneurs such as Bill Gates are the driving force for much of the change in a free enterprise economy.

Examining the Profile

1. **Predicting Consequences** How might the Microsoft story have been different if Gates had sold MS-DOS to IBM rather than retaining ownership?

2. **For Further Research** Find out how Microsoft's success led to antitrust charges in the 1990s. Write a summary of your findings.

Answers to Examining the Profile

1. If Gates had not retained ownership of MS-DOS, he could not have marketed it to other companies. Microsoft might not have become a leader in the operating-system market.

2. Answers will vary. Call on students to present and discuss their summaries.

Section Preview

Objectives

After studying this section, you will be able to:

1. **Explain** how international trade can be restricted to protect special interests.
2. **Cite** the main argument for protection.
3. **Relate** the history of the free trade movement.

Key Terms

tariff, quota, protective tariff, revenue tariff, protectionist, infant industries argument, balance of payments, trade deficit, most favored nation clause, General Agreement on Tariffs and Trade (GATT), North American Free Trade Agreement (NAFTA)

Applying Economic Concepts

Quotas Do you think the prices of some goods are too high? If you do, you are like many other people. Over the years, *quotas* have limited the import of some foreign goods to protect some industries in the United States. The high-priced imports do protect some American workers, but they also affect your pocketbook.

Although international trade can bring many benefits, some people object to it because it can displace selected industries and groups of workers in the United States. It is not unusual to hear workers say they have lost their jobs because of unfair foreign competition. Therefore, while many people support international trade, some strongly oppose it.

Restricting International Trade

Historically, trade has been restricted in two major ways. One is through **tariffs**—taxes placed on imports to increase their price in the domestic market. The other is through **quotas**—limits placed on the quantities of a product that can be imported.

Tariffs

Governments levy two kinds of tariffs—protective and revenue. A **protective tariff** is a tariff high enough to protect less efficient domestic industries. Suppose, for example, that it costs $1 to produce each gadget in the United States. Each gadget made in another country, however, can be imported for 35 cents, including transportation costs. If a tariff of 95 cents is placed on each imported gadget, the cost climbs to $1.30—more than the cost of the American-made gadget. The

domestic industry is protected from being undersold by a foreign industry.

The **revenue tariff** is designed to raise money. It must be high enough to generate funds when imported goods enter the country, yet not so high as to prohibit imports. If the tariff on imported gadgets was 40 cents, the price of the imports would be 75 cents, or 25 cents less than the price of the American-made ones. The tariff would be raising revenue rather than protecting domestic producers from foreign competition.

In practice, all tariffs raise some revenue and offer some protection. Before the Civil War, tariffs were the chief source of revenue for the federal government. From the Civil War to 1913, tariffs provided about one-half of the government's total revenue. In 1913 the federal income tax was passed, which gave the government a new and more lucrative source of revenue.

Quotas

Foreign goods sometimes cost so little that even a high tariff on them may not protect the domestic market. In such cases, the government generally uses a quota to keep foreign goods out of the country.

Quotas can be more powerful than tariffs, and may have more of an impact on international trade. A quota can be set as low as zero to keep a product from entering the country at all. If the total supply of a

FOCUS

Section Objectives

1. Explain how international trade can be restricted to protect special interests.
2. Cite the main argument for protection.
3. Relate the history of the free trade movement.

Bellringer

Prior to taking roll at the beginning of the class period, display Focus Activity Transparency 88 on the overhead projector and assign the accompanying Student Activity 88.

Motivational Activity

Discuss students' responses to the activity sheet that accompanies Focus Activity Transparency 88.

Preteaching Vocabulary

Organize students into pairs. Have one student read aloud a term and its meaning from the text. Then have the other student explain the meaning of the term in his or her own words. Direct students to change tasks after each term.
LEP

Use the **Vocabulary PuzzleMaker** to create crossword and word search puzzles.

Classroom Resources for SECTION 2

- Reproducible Lesson Plan 18-2
- Guided Reading Activity 18-2
- Reinforcing Economic Skill 18
- Section Quiz 18-2
- Spanish Section Quiz 18-2
- Focus Activity Transparency 88
- NBR's Economics in Action Video Program
- Testmaker
- Vocabulary PuzzleMaker
- Chapter Challenger Interactive Review Software

TEACH

Guided Practice

L2 **Applying Ideas** Provide students with the following scenario: You (the students) are the president of a nation with a relatively healthy economy. One of your major industries—widget making—is in decline, however, largely because of foreign competition. Members of your political party who represent districts where widget making is the main industry want a high tariff on imported widgets. In addition, workers in the widget industry have launched a huge publicity campaign in support of a tariff increase. At the same time, many people are calling for no tariff because they want to be able to buy cheap widgets.

Have students explain what they, as leaders, intend to do and why. Have them write their decision in the form of a speech to be made to the nation.

 VISUAL INSTRUCTION

Ask students to suggest how a free trade supporter might answer these demonstrators. *(no real proof that protection saves American jobs; problem may not be foreign competition, but inefficient domestic production)*

Answer to Caption:

national defense reasons, protecting emerging industries, protecting domestic jobs, keeping money at home, helping the balance of payments

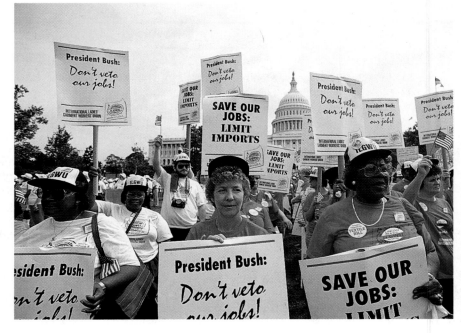

Protectionism *These workers believe that foreign imports cost American workers their jobs. Thus, they want imports restricted.* **What arguments do protectionists use in support of trade restrictions?**

product is restricted, domestic consumers will not be able to consume as much of it and domestic producers can charge higher prices for it.

By 1981, for example, domestic automobile producers faced intense competition from lower-priced Japanese automobiles. Rather than lower their own prices, domestic manufacturers wanted President Reagan to establish automobile import quotas on Japanese cars. The Reagan administration told the Japanese to voluntarily restrict auto exports, and they reluctantly agreed. As a result, Americans had fewer cars from which to choose, and the prices of all cars were higher than they would otherwise have been.

During the Bush administration, "voluntary" import quotas were imposed on steel. The quotas protected jobs in the domestic steel industry, but at the cost of higher steel prices for the rest of the country.

Other Barriers

Tariffs and quotas are not the only barriers to trade. Many imported foods, for example, are subject to health inspections far more rigorous than those given to domestic foods. Another tactic is to require a

license to import. If the government is slow to grant the license, or if the license fees are too high, international trade is restricted. **1**

Arguments For Protection

International trade has been a subject of debate for many years. Some people, known as **protectionists**, favor tariffs, quotas, and other trade barriers. Others, known as free traders, favor fewer trade restrictions.

National Defense

One of the most important arguments for trade barriers centers on national defense. Protectionists argue that without trade barriers, a country could become too specialized and end up too dependent on other countries.

During wartime, a country might not be able to get such critical supplies as food, oil, and weapons. The governments of such countries as Israel and South Africa have developed large armaments industries for such crises. They want to be sure they will have a

---

Meeting Special Needs

Study Strategy Motivation to read sometimes comes from having students predict the information that is going to follow and then evaluating the extent to which they were correct. Ask students to predict what might happen if harsh trade restric-

tions were erected between all nations of the world. Then have students read the section. After students have completed reading, have them review their predictions to see if they were correct.

"You like protectionism as a 'working man.' How about as a consumer?"

Protectionism *Arguments exist both for and against protectionism.* **How might the issue of protectionism differ for a worker and a consumer?**

domestic supply source if hostilities break out or other countries impose economic boycotts.

Free traders admit that national security is a compelling argument for trade barriers. They believe, however, that having a reliable source of domestic supply must be weighed against the reality that the supply will be smaller and possibly less efficient than it would be with free trade. The problem of deciding which industries are critical to national defense must also be considered. The steel, auto, ceramic, and electronic industries all have argued at one time or another that they are critical to national defense.

Infant Industries

The **infant industries argument**—the belief that new or emerging industries should be protected from foreign competition—is also used to justify trade barriers. Protectionists claim that these industries need to gain strength and experience before they can compete against developed industries in other countries. Trade barriers would give them the time they need to develop. If infant industries compete against foreign industries too soon, they might fail. **2**

Many people are willing to accept the infant industries argument only if protection will eventually be removed, allowing the industry to compete on its own. Some Latin American countries have tried using tariffs to protect their infant automobile industries, with tariffs as high as several hundred percent. In some cases, the tariff raised the price of used American-made cars to more than double the cost of new ones in the United States.

Protecting Domestic Jobs

A third argument—the one used most often—is that tariffs and quotas protect domestic jobs from cheap foreign labor. Workers in the shoe industry, for example, have protested the import of lower-cost Italian, Spanish, and Brazilian shoes. Garment workers have opposed the import of lower-cost Korean, Chinese, and Indian clothing. Steelworkers have blocked foreign-made cars from company parking lots to

---

 QUICK CHECK

Checking Understanding

1. How can import licenses restrict international trade?
2. What is the infant industries argument?

Applying Economic Concepts

 National Defense Despite the end of the cold war, the 1998 defense budget was close to $270 billion. Some suggest that the United States support weapons research but put off producing the weapons until a need for them becomes clear, and cost controls are assured.

$ Free Enterprise Activity $

Organize students into three groups. Assign two groups the pro or con position on the following proposition: United States industries should be protected from foreign competition. Have the two groups research and debate the proposition. Have the third group act as judges and keep track of major points and arguments made during the debate.

L3 *Simulation* Have students simulate a congressional subcommittee hearing on a bill to raise tariffs on imported goods, especially automobiles. Select nine students, five to act as subcommittee members and four to act as expert witnesses—a consumer advocate, an auto worker, a CEO of a leading American auto company, and a representative of a foreign auto company with plants in the U.S. Have experts make brief presentations to the subcommittee and have members ask them questions. Direct the rest of the class to act as reporters, summarizing the arguments for and against the tariff.

VISUAL INSTRUCTION

Ask students to prioritize the arguments for protection.

Answer to Caption:

People, as consumers, want to buy products at low prices; therefore they may oppose protectionism. As workers, they want their jobs protected, so they usually support protectionism.

QUICK CHECK

ANSWERS

1. when government is slow to grant licenses, or if license fees are too high
2. that new or emerging industries need to gain strength and experience before they can compete against established industries in other countries

GLENCOE
TECHNOLOGY

NIGHTLY BUSINESS REPORT

Economics in Action

Chapter 27
Disc 2, Side 2

Title: *International Trade*

Subject: Effects of trade wars

Ask: What factors can lead to a trade war?
(A trade imbalance may lead a country to impose tariffs on imported goods. Other nations may respond with trade barriers of their own.)

 Also available in VHS.

 VISUAL INSTRUCTION

Mention that KFC has had more success in China and many other Asian countries than has McDonald's. The reason is that chickens are relatively plentiful and inexpensive in Asia, whereas the beef needed for hamburgers is not.

Answer to Caption:

They use resources that might be used more profitably elsewhere.

International Trade *KFC and other food franchises have expanded worldwide.* **How does the protection of inefficient industries hurt the economy?**

show their displeasure with the foreign-made steel used in producing the cars.

Whether limiting foreign trade preserves American jobs is hard to prove. In the long run, those industries that find it hard to compete are generally inefficient. Many people believe these industries should be allowed to die out to free their resources for use elsewhere. The problem, however, lies in the short run, when unemployment and hardship are likely to occur. Workers want to keep their jobs or live in the communities in which they grew up.

When inefficient industries are protected, the economy produces less and the standard of living goes down. Because of unnecessarily high prices, people buy less of everything, including those goods produced by protected industries. If prices get too high, substitute products will be found.

Free traders argue that the profit-and-loss system is one of the major features of the American economy. Profits reward the efficient and hard-working, while losses eliminate the inefficient and weak.

Keep the Money at Home

Another argument for trade barriers claims that limiting imports will keep American money in the United States instead of allowing it to go abroad.

Free traders, however, point out that the American dollars that go abroad generally come back again. The Japanese, for example, use the dollars they receive for their automobiles to buy American cotton, soybeans, and airplanes. These purchases benefit American workers in those industries.

The same is true of the dollars used to buy oil from the Middle East. The money comes back to the United States when oil-wealthy foreigners buy American-made oil technology, Kentucky horse farms, and Hollywood mansions. Keeping the money home hurts those American industries that depend on exports for their jobs. **1**

Helping the Balance of Payments

Another argument involves the **balance of payments**—the difference between the money paid to and received from other nations. Protectionists argue that restrictions on imports help the balance of payments. When the economy runs a **trade deficit**—a deficit in the "goods" component of the balance of payments—it is spending more on imports than it earns on exports. As a result, money leaves the country, some jobs are lost, and the dollar is threatened. ✔

What protectionists overlook, however, is that the dollars return to the United States to stimulate

---

Extending the Content

The Smoot-Hawley Tariff Act The Smoot-Hawley Tariff Act of 1930 increased duties on raw agricultural materials from 38 to 49 percent and on other goods from 31 to 34 percent. This raised the prices of imported goods so much that tariff revenues represented 45 percent of the total value of all imports. Just 10 years before, this figure had stood at 16 percent. Many experts argue that this tariff made the Great Depression even worse.

Free Trade *Free traders argue that limiting tariffs and quotas allows consumers to choose from a wide variety of both domestic and foreign products.* **What is the purpose of the GATT?**

CHAPTER 18
SECTION 2

Independent Practice

◤ **Guided Reading** Assign Guided Reading Activity for Section 2. **LEP**

L3 *History* Organize students into several groups, and assign each group a particular period in U.S. history. Have groups research international trade during the assigned periods to determine the primary countries with which the U.S. traded, the extent of the trade, any trade restrictions or legislation passed, and the effect of such restrictions on American markets. Have groups report their findings to the rest of the class.

employment in other industries. In the United States economy, the balance of payments adjusts automatically to deficits and surpluses. Most economists do not believe that interfering with free trade can be justified on the grounds of helping the balance of payments.

The Free Trade Movement

Using trade barriers to protect domestic industries and jobs works only if other countries do not use trade barriers. If they do, all countries suffer because they have neither the benefits of efficient production nor access to less costly inputs from other nations.

Tariffs During the Great Depression

In 1930 the United States passed the Smoot-Hawley Tariff, one of the highest in history. It set import duties so high that the price of many imported goods rose nearly 70 percent. When other countries did the same, international trade nearly came to a halt. **2**

Before long, most countries realized that high tariffs hurt more than they helped. As a result, in 1934 the United States passed the Reciprocal Trade

ASSESS

Check for Understanding

Assign Section 2 Review as homework or an in-class activity.

 VISUAL INSTRUCTION

Point out that some people support free trade because it encourages competition.

Answer to Caption:
to reduce barriers to trade

 QUICK CHECK

Checking Understanding

1. Who is hurt when American dollars are kept in the United States?
2. What effect did the Smoot-Hawley Tariff have on international trade?

Applying Economic Concepts

☑ **Trade Deficit** Two measures of the trade deficit are often confused. The most comprehensive includes both goods and services, and is simply called the trade deficit, or the deficit on current account. If services are excluded, it is called the merchandise trade deficit.

 QUICK CHECK

ANSWERS

1. American industries that depend on exports
2. It nearly brought international trade to a standstill.

CHAPTER 18: *International Trade* **457**

Cultural Diversity and Economics

Loss of Culture? Some Mexicans have expressed concern about the cultural impact of NAFTA. The increased exchange between the U.S. and Mexico, they suggest, will result in Mexican tradition being swamped by American technology and culture. The biggest impact will come in rural areas, where traditional Native American culture still flourishes.

Most rural people make a living from farming small plots of land, and they will not be able to compete with American farmers. As a result, many will simply abandon their farms and head for the cities. "We could be looking at the loss of our cultural environment," a Mexican sociologist predicted.

Use **Chapter Challenger Interactive Review Software** to review Section 2.

MEETING LESSON OBJECTIVES

Each objective below is tested by the questions that follow it in parentheses.

1. **Explain** how international trade can be restricted to protect special interests. **(1, 2, 5, 6)**

2. **Cite** the main argument for protection. **(1, 3, 5, 6)**

3. **Relate** the history of the free trade movement. **(4)**

Evaluate

Assign the Section 2 Quiz in the TCR or use the *Economics: Principles and Practices* Testmaker to create a customized quiz.

VISUAL INSTRUCTION

Point out that the written agreement is so detailed that it runs to 5 volumes and weighs 15 pounds!

Answer to Caption:

It stimulates trade by reducing barriers to trade.

Figure 18.3
The North American Free Trade Agreement

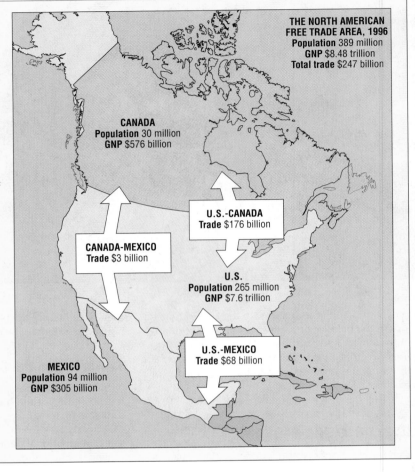

The North American Free Trade Agreement (NAFTA) makes up the second largest free-trade area in the world, after the European Union. After NAFTA was implemented, trade between the three nations began to grow by 10 to 15 percent annually. **How does NAFTA affect the market for goods and services in North America?**

Source: United States Commerce Department, Mexican Commerce Secretariat

THE NORTH AMERICAN FREE TRADE AREA, 1996
Population 389 million
GNP $8.48 trillion
Total trade $247 billion

CANADA
Population 30 million
GNP $576 billion

U.S.-CANADA
Trade $176 billion

CANADA-MEXICO
Trade $3 billion

U.S.
Population 265 million
GNP $7.6 trillion

U.S.-MEXICO
Trade $68 billion

MEXICO
Population 94 million
GNP $305 billion

Agreements Act, which allowed it to reduce tariffs up to 50 percent if the other countries agreed. The act also contained the **most favored nation clause**—a provision allowing a country with such an agreement to receive the same tariff reduction that the United States negotiates with another country.

Suppose, for example, that the United States and China have a trade agreement with a most favored nation clause. If the United States then negotiates a tariff reduction with another country, the reduction would also apply to China. This clause is very important to a foreign country, because its goods will then sell at a lower price in the American market.

Tariffs After World War II

In 1947, 23 countries signed the **General Agreement on Tariffs and Trade** (GATT). The GATT extended tariff concessions and worked to do away with import quotas. Later, the Trade Expansion Act of

---

Extending the Content

Uruguay Round The Uruguay Round of the GATT lasted 7 years and involved more than 100 nations. The final agreement, which ran to 550 pages, touched practically every imaginable trade topic—from subsidies paid to Japanese rice farmers to the number of American television programs and movies that European countries could show. After ratification by the participating nations, the agreement took effect in 1995.

1962 gave the President of the United States the power to negotiate further tariff reductions. As a result of this legislation, tariffs were significantly reduced in 1967 and 1979, with more than 100 countries agreeing to reduce the average level of tariffs.

Most recently, the Uruguay Round—trade negotiations that began in 1986 and concluded in 1994—replaced the GATT with the World Trade Organization (WTO). The purpose of the international agency WTO, headquartered in Geneva, Switzerland, is to promote world trade. It administers previous GATT trade agreements, settles disputes between governments, organizes trade negotiations, and provides technical assistance and training for developing countries.

Because so many countries have been willing to reduce tariffs and quotas under GATT, international trade is flourishing. Tariffs that once nearly doubled the price of many goods now increase the average cost only a small percentage. Tariffs have been dropped altogether on some categories of goods. As a result, stores are able to offer a wide variety of industrial and consumer goods.

NAFTA

The **North American Free Trade Agreement** (NAFTA), which the Bush administration proposed and the Clinton administration concluded, is another attempt to liberalize free trade. Before NAFTA, United States goods entering Mexico faced an average tariff of 10 percent. At the same time, half the goods entering the United States from Mexico were duty-free, while the other half faced an average tax of only 4 percent.

Exceptions did exist, however. A 32 percent tariff on brooms imported from Mexico protected broom makers in southern Illinois. The high tariff barriers protected the jobs of up to 3,000 workers who hand-wired sheaves of broomcorn to wooden handles. NAFTA will reduce the tariff on Mexican brooms to zero over a 15-year period, which will threaten these American jobs.

Free trade is good in general, but it is not painless. Because some workers will always be displaced when nations agree to lower barriers to international trade, NAFTA was controversial. Opponents predicted that high-paid American jobs would be lost to Mexico. Proponents predicted that trade between all three nations would increase dramatically, stimulating growth and bringing a wider variety of lower-cost goods to everyone.

The case for freer trade is a classical case of cost-benefit analysis. Some of the costs and benefits identified during the NAFTA debate actually occurred, but not to the extent originally predicted. In the end, freer trade allowed the NAFTA partners to capitalize on their comparative advantages for everyone's gain.

SECTION 2 REVIEW

Reviewing Terms and Facts

1. **Define** tariff, quota, protective tariff, revenue tariff, protectionist, infant industries argument, balance of payments, trade deficit, most favored nation clause, General Agreement on Tariffs and Trade (GATT), North American Free Trade Agreement (NAFTA).
2. **Describe** three barriers to international trade.
3. **List** five arguments for protection.

4. **Identify** three legislative acts since 1933 that have helped liberalize international trade.

Critical Thinking

5. **Demonstrating Reasoned Judgment** If you were a member of Congress approached by a delegation of autoworkers seeking additional tariff or quota protection, how would you respond? Defend your response.

Applying Economic Concepts

6. **Quotas** Explain how a quota on a good or service produced in your community can protect the jobs in a particular industry. Then explain how the same quota might be harmful to others.

CHAPTER 18
SECTION 2

Reteach

Have students summarize the arguments for protection and for free trade.

Enrich

Have students write to their U.S. senator or representative to request copies of recent testimony about some aspect of international trade given before a congressional subcommittee. Have students share the materials they receive with the rest of the class.

CLOSE

Have students discuss the impact that NAFTA might have on the American way of life.

Answers to SECTION 2 REVIEW

1. All vocabulary words are defined in the Glossary.

2. Answers may include three of the following: tariffs to protect less efficient domestic industries and to raise money, quotas to keep foreign goods out of the country, rigorous health inspections on imported foods, requiring a license to import.

3. national defense, infant industries, protect domestic jobs, keep the money home, help the balance of payments

4. Answers may include three of the following: Reciprocal Trade Agreements Act, General Agreement on Tariffs and Trade (GATT), Trade Expansion Act of 1962, North American Free Trade Agreement (NAFTA)

5. Students should support their positions.

6. Students' explanations should include the idea that quotas favor the producer by restricting competition but that consumers may pay a higher price for the product.

TEACH

Ask students to imagine that the school board has ordered the transfer of funding from arts activities to the football program. Direct students to write a few sentences expressing their feelings on the school board order. Call on students to read their sentences aloud. Have the rest of the class identify words used in the sentences that might indicate bias.

📂 **Skills Practice** For additional practice, have students complete Reinforcing Economic Skills 18.

CRITICAL THINKING SKILL

Recognizing Bias

Two of your friends have just seen a horror movie. You meet them as they are coming out of the theater. One friend says, "That was the scariest movie I've ever seen in my life! I'll never get to sleep tonight." The other friend says, "Are you kidding? That movie was so boring, I almost fell asleep in it." Who is right? How could two people have such different ideas about the same movie?

Explanation

Most people have preconceived feelings and attitudes that affect their point of view. This viewpoint, or *bias*, influences the way they interpret events. A person's writing often reflects his or her bias. Therefore, an idea that is stated as a fact may be only an opinion. Recognizing bias will help you judge the accuracy of what you hear or read.

To recognize bias, follow these steps:
- Identify the author and examine his or her views and reasons for writing the material.
- Look for language that reflects emotion or generalizations.

- Examine the writing for imbalanced presentation—leaning to one viewpoint and failing to provide equal coverage of other viewpoints.
- Identify statements of fact.
- Determine how the author's bias is reflected in the work.

Practice

Read the two excerpts on this page about the North American Free Trade Agreement (NAFTA). Then answer the questions that follow.

1. Based on the excerpt, why does the U.S. Chamber of Commerce favor NAFTA?
2. What evidence of bias do you find in the Chamber of Commerce argument?
3. What language in the AFL-CIO editorial reflects emotion or generalizations?
4. What conclusions might you draw about NAFTA from these excerpts?

NAFTA does provide clear, fair, transparent and predictable trade rules with Mexico—a country that has traditionally discriminated against U.S. products. NAFTA's fair trade rules have helped our exports boom during Mexico's growth years—and . . . protected 200,000 U.S. export jobs during the Mexican economic crisis of 1995.

Our exports to Mexico rose 23% in 1996 and our imports rose 18%. Our exports to Mexico now sustain over 1 million jobs in the United States, and Mexico has moved to become our second largest trading partner. NAFTA's opponents predicted that 6 million U.S. jobs would move to Mexico. They were wrong, there has been a NET increase of over 130,000 jobs thanks to NAFTA.

—U.S. Chamber of Commerce, October 1997

The fast-track NAFTA deal with Mexico and Canada in 1993 is a perfect example of what happens when we rush into agreements that don't take into consideration the concerns of workers and consumers. Ever since the NAFTA deal was struck:

1. *America lost 420,000 jobs as corporations shifted production to Mexico and Canada. According to a Wall Street Journal poll in 1992, 40 percent of corporate executives admitted they were likely to shift production to Mexico because of NAFTA.*
2. *Employers are using the threat of plant closures to drive wages down. People who found new employment after their jobs moved to Mexico took an average pay cut of $4,400.*

—AFL-CIO, October 1997

Additional Practice

For further practice in recognizing bias, complete the Reinforcing Skills exercise in the Chapter 18 Review on page 469.

Answers to SKILL

1. The Chamber of Commerce believes that NAFTA's fair trade rules have helped U.S. exports to Mexico and protected 200,000 U.S. export jobs; and that because of NAFTA, there has been an increase of over 130,000 jobs.

2. The statements present only one positive viewpoint. Words such as "clear, fair, transparent, and

predictable" are meant to sway the reader toward the Chamber of Commerce's opinion.

3. phrases such as "fast-track NAFTA deal," "when we rush into," "don't take into consideration," "employers are using the threat of plant closures"

4. NAFTA is highly controversial and hotly debated.

Financing and Trade Deficits

Section Preview

Objectives

After studying this section, you will be able to:

1. **Explain** how foreign currency is used in trade.
2. **Describe** the problem of a trade deficit and the main solution to the problem.

Key Terms

foreign exchange, foreign exchange market, foreign exchange rate, fixed exchange rate, devaluation, floating exchange rate, flexible exchange rate, foreign exchange futures, trade-weighted value of the dollar

Applying Economic Concepts

Foreign Exchange Do you have souvenir foreign currency—Canadian dollars, Mexican pesos, British pounds, French francs, or perhaps some other currency? If so, you own *foreign exchange*, just as some big investors around the world do.

Trade between nations is similar to exchange between individuals. The major difference is that each country has its own monetary system. Because of the different currencies used, financing world trade is complicated.

Financing International Trade

Scenarios like the following occur every day across the globe. A clothing firm in the United States wants to import business suits from a company in Great Britain. Because the British firm pays its bills in a currency called *pound sterling*, it wants to receive payment in sterling. Therefore, the American firm must exchange its dollars for British pounds.

Foreign Exchange

In the field of international finance, foreign currencies are known as **foreign exchange** and are bought and sold in the **foreign exchange market**. Included in this market are banks that help secure foreign currencies for importers, as well as banks that accept foreign currencies from exporters.

Suppose that one pound sterling, £1, is equal to $1.62. If the business suits are valued at £1,000 in London, the American importer can go to an American bank and buy a £1,000 check for $1,620 plus a small service charge. The American firm then pays the British merchant, and the suits are imported.

American exporters sometimes accept foreign currency or checks written on foreign banks for their goods. They deposit the payments in their own banks, which helps the American banking system build a supply of foreign currency. This currency then can be sold to American firms that want to import goods from other countries. As a result, the importer and the exporter end up with the currency of their own countries.

When the price of one country's currency is described in terms of another country's currency, it is known as the **foreign exchange rate**. The rate can be quoted in terms of the United States dollar equivalent, as in $1.62 = £1, or in terms of foreign currency per United States dollar, £.6173 = $1. Most often, however, the rate is reported in both, as shown in the foreign currency listings in **Figure 18.4**.

Fixed Exchange Rates

In the past, two major kinds of exchange rates existed—fixed and flexible. For most of the 1900s, the world depended on **fixed exchange rates**—a system under which the price of one currency is fixed in terms of another so that the rate does not change.

When the world was on a gold standard, each country defined its currency in terms of a given amount of gold. Before 1971, for example, the United States dollar was worth 1/35 ounce of gold, and the British pound, 1/12.5 ounce of gold. After the gold content was specified, the value of one country's

---

Section Objectives

1. Explain how foreign currency is used in trade.
2. Describe the problem of a trade deficit and the main solution to the problem.

Bellringer

Prior to taking roll at the beginning of the class period, display Focus Activity Transparency 87 on the overhead projector and assign the accompanying Student Activity 87.

Motivational Activity

Discuss students' responses to the activity sheet that accompanies Focus Activity Transparency 87.

Preteaching Vocabulary

Ask students to explain, in their own words, how each of the key terms is related to international trade. **LEP**

Use the **Vocabulary PuzzleMaker** to create crossword and word search puzzles.

Classroom Resources for SECTION 3

- Reproducible Lesson Plan 18-3
- Guided Reading Activity 18-3
- Section Quiz 18-3
- Spanish Section Quiz 18-3
- Focus Activity Transparency 87
- Economic Concepts Transparency 21
- Spanish Economic Concepts Transparency 21
- NBR's Economics in Action Video Program
- Enrichment Activity 18
- Reteaching Activity 18
- Spanish Reteaching Activity 18
- Economic Vocabulary Activity 18
- Spanish Economic Vocabulary Activity 18
- Chapter 18 Test, Form A and Form B
- English and Spanish Audiocassettes
- Testmaker
- Vocabulary PuzzleMaker
- Chapter Challenger Interactive Review
- MindJogger Videoquiz

Guided Practice

L2 *Applying Ideas* Direct students to select a country in which they would like to travel. Have them estimate the length of time they might like to vacation in the country and how much money they would need for the trip. Then inform students that, prior to traveling to a foreign country, visitors should exchange American dollars for that country's currency. Provide students with copies of today's exchange rate listings from *The Wall Street Journal* or the business section of the local newspaper to find their country's current rate of exchange, and convert the amount of estimated travel money to the foreign currency. Then discuss why an exchange rate might be a factor in making vacation plans. **LEP**

Using Transparencies

Display Economic Concepts Transparency 21 on the overhead projector and use the guidelines given in Teaching Strategy 21. Assign Student Activity 21. Spanish Transparencies also are available in the Spanish Resources Binder.

 VISUAL INSTRUCTION

Have students check today's exchange rates to see how they have changed since October 1997.

Answer to Caption:

to provide up-to-date information on foreign exchange rates

---

currency could be measured in terms of the value of another country's currency. The British pound was backed by 2.8 times as much gold as the American dollar. Therefore, the British pound was worth $2.80.

Gold served as the common denominator that allowed comparisons of currencies, and it also kept exchange rates in line. Suppose that a country allowed its money supply to grow too fast and then spent some of the money on imports. Under a gold standard, the other countries holding the currency had the right to demand that it be converted into gold. Because no country wanted to lose its gold, each worked to keep its money supply under control.

This practice did not work in the 1950s and 1960s, however, when the United States developed a huge appetite for imports. During that time, it bought large quantities of foreign goods with dollars. At first, foreign countries willingly held dollars because they were acceptable as an international currency. Year after year, dollars went to other countries to buy imports, but only a small amount of these dollars came back as other countries bought American exports.

As dollars began to pile up in the rest of the world, many countries wondered if the United States could honor its promise that the dollar was "as good as gold." France and several other countries sent their

dollars back to the United States, demanding gold in return at the rate of $35 an ounce.

The United States faced a problem if all countries tried to redeem their dollars for gold. Several solutions to the problem existed. The United States could have limited imported goods. Other countries might have retaliated, however, and limited American products. The United States could have restricted the growth of the money supply, but this action might have led to a recession. The country could have decided on **devaluation**—making currency worth less in terms of gold. Other countries might have followed suit and reduced their gold content by as much or more. Because many American politicians

---

Figure 18.4
A Typical Foreign Exchange Rate Listing

EXCHANGE RATES
Thursday, October 2, 1997

The New York foreign exchange selling rates below apply to trading among banks in amounts of $1 million and more, as quoted at 4 p.m. Eastern time by Dow Jones and other sources. Retail transactions provide fewer units of foreign currency per dollar.

Country	U.S. $ equiv. Thu.	Currency per U.S. $ Thu.
Argentina (Peso)	1.0014	.9986
Australia (Dollar)	.7290	1.3717
Britain (Pound)	1.6159	.6189
Canada (Dollar)	.7274	1.3748
Czech. Rep. (Koruna) Commercial rate	.03066	32.613
Chile (Peso)	.002415	414.15
China (Renminbi)	.1203	8.3149
Finland (Markka)	.1881	5.3161
France (Franc)	.1678	5.9585
Germany (Mark)	.5640	1.7730
Israel (Shekel)	.2852	3.5060
Japan (Yen)	.008224	121.60
Mexico (Peso) Floating rate	.1290	7.7500
South Korea (Won)	.001095	913.45
Taiwan (Dollar)	.03496	28.601

In the first column of the listing, one British pound costs 1.62 American dollars. The second column shows that one United States dollar is worth .6189 British pounds. **Why do many local and financial papers carry daily exchange rate listings such as the one above?**

Source: Adapted from the *Wall Street Journal*, October 2, 1997

Figure 18.5
Flexible Exchange Rates

A. The Foreign Exchange Market for Dollars

B. The Foreign Exchange Market for Marks

The value of foreign exchange, like the value of most other products, is determined by supply and demand. When investors sell one currency to buy another, the value of the currency being sold falls, while the value of the currency being purchased rises. **Who buys and sells foreign exchange?**

viewed devaluation as an admission of failure, they opposed such a move.

Instead, President Richard Nixon solved the problem in August 1971, by announcing that the United States no longer would redeem dollars for gold. This action saved the gold stock for other purposes. At the same time, however, it angered many foreign holders of American dollars who were planning to cash them in for gold. **1** ✔

Flexible Exchange Rates

When the United States went off the gold standard, the world monetary system went to a **floating**

or **flexible exchange rate**. Under this system, the forces of supply and demand establish the value of one country's currency in terms of the value of another country's currency.

The supply and demand graphs in **Figure 18.5** show flexible exchange rates. Before 1971, for example, the price of the German mark (DM) in the United States was 25 cents, and the price of the dollar in Germany was 4 DMs. In the years that followed, however, the United States imported more from Germany than it exported.

As importers in the United States sold dollars for DMs, the supply of dollars in the foreign currency

Checking Understanding

1. Why did President Nixon break the link between gold and the dollar in 1971?

Applying Economic Concepts

✔ **Gold Bullion** Fort Knox, a 109,000-acre complex near Louisville, Kentucky, is the site of the United States Bullion Depository. It holds more than $6 billion in gold bars. The nearly pure gold bars are each slightly smaller than a building brick, yet each weighs 27.5 pounds.

$ Free Enterprise Activity $

Write the following exchange rate problems on the chalkboard and have students solve them:

1. A television set sells for ¥ 52,500 in Tokyo. How much would it cost in U.S. dollars if the exchange rate was ¥ 110 = $1.00? *(52,500 ÷ 110 = $477.27)*

2. A clock in London sells for £200. How much would it cost in U.S. dollars if the exchange rate was £1 = $1.62? *(200 × $1.62 = $324)*

3. A pair of blue jeans costs $29.99 in Los Angeles. How much would this item cost in Canadian dollars if the exchange rate was Canadian $1.00 = U.S. $0.76? *(29.99 ÷ 0.76 = Canadian $39.46)*

GLENCOE
TECHNOLOGY

NIGHTLY BUSINESS REPORT
Economics in Action

Chapter 27
Disc 2, Side 2
Title: *International Trade*
Subject: Exchange rates
Ask: What is a floating exchange rate system? *(The value of each nation's currency changes constantly. Under this mechanism, the market determines the value of goods and services in other nations' currencies.)*

Also available in VHS.

Independent Practice

⮡ **Guided Reading** Assign Guided Reading Activity for Section 3. **LEP**

VISUAL INSTRUCTION

Ask: What happens to the value of the dollar when the supply of dollars in the foreign currency market increases? *(value falls)*

Answer to Caption:
American importers, exporters

ANSWERS

1. The alternative, devaluation, was viewed as an admission of failure by many American politicians.

"Then it's agreed. Until the dollar firms up, we let the clamshell float."

Copyright by: Ed Fisher, ©1971, The New Yorker Magazine, Inc.

Flexible Exchange Rates *Under a system of flexible exchange rates, the value of a currency is determined by supply and demand.* **What is the term given to the currency of other nations that is used in trade?**

market increased. The increased supply drove the value of the dollar down. At the same time, the growing demand for DMs drove up the value of the DM.

In the early 1970s, for example, it cost 12,000 DMs to make a Volkswagen. At 4 DMs per $1, an American importer paid $3,000 to buy the Volkswagen. Even after adding shipping charges and other expenses, the importer still could sell the automobile at a competitive price. As more cars were imported, however, the supply of dollars in the foreign exchange market increased. At the same time, the demand for DMs rose and caused the value of the dollar to drop.

When the dollar reached 2 DMs, the new exchange rate cost the importer more dollars. The importer now had to pay $6,000 for 12,000 DMs. At the higher price, the car no longer was as competitive as before. Excessive imports thus caused the deficit in the balance of payments. The value of the dollar declined, making imports cost more.

Although imports were hurt, the weak dollar caused American exports to rise. A German company that bought American soybeans at $6 a bushel before 1971, for example, would have paid 24 DMs for each bushel. After 1971, however, it had to pay only 12 DMs for each bushel. As a result, soybeans were cheaper, and more could be sold abroad.

When the world first adopted flexible rates, some people feared they might not work because of the fluctuations in exchange rates. The system has worked better than most people thought it would, however. A company can even buy **foreign exchange futures**—currencies on the futures market—to protect against changing exchange rates. A company can agree to buy currency 30, 90, or 180 days in the future at prices agreed upon now. More importantly, the switch to flexible rates did not interrupt the growth in international trade as many people had feared. More countries trade with one another today than ever before.

The Trade Deficit

The United States has a trade deficit. What do these numbers really mean, and how does the deficit affect the economy?

The Problem of a Trade Deficit

A large, long-lasting trade imbalance reduces the value of a country's currency on the foreign exchange markets. Devalued currency causes a chain reaction that affects output and employment in that country's industries. The large deficit in the United States balance of payments in the mid-1980s, for example, flooded the foreign exchange markets with dollars. An increase in the supply of dollars, as illustrated in Figure 18.5, causes the dollar to lose some of its value on the foreign currency markets.

When the dollar gets weaker, Americans have to pay more for imports, and foreigners pay less for American exports. As imports fall and exports rise, unemployment in the import industries results. In time, however, the dollar will get strong again and the process reverses. The economy may adjust slowly to changes in the value of the dollar, but the adjustments do take place. ☑

464 UNIT 5: *International and Global Economics*

Extending the Content

The International Monetary Fund A conference was held in 1944 at Bretton Woods, New Hampshire, to address a number of economic problems, including financial instability. In an attempt to stabilize currencies, the 44 nations in attendance established the International Monetary Fund (IMF). Each nation agreed to fix the value of its currency in relation to the dollar and gold. If the value of a nation's currency fell by more than 1 percent, the nation was to buy its own currency and force the price back up. If the value of the currency went above 1 percent of its stated value, the nation was to increase the supply of its currency by selling it. In addition, the IMF made loans to countries with balance of payments problems to help stabilize their currencies.

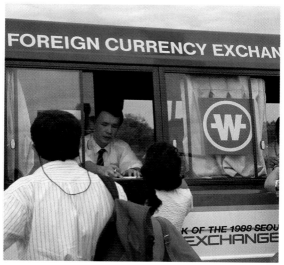

Foreign Exchange *At the 1988 Summer Olympics, foreign tourists exchange their currency for South Korean won.* **What is a foreign exchange rate?**

International Value of the Dollar

Since floating rates became the standard in 1971, the Federal Reserve System has kept a statistic called the **trade-weighted value of the dollar**. This index shows the strength of the dollar against a group of foreign currencies. When the index falls, the dollar is weak in relation to other currencies. When the index rises, the dollar is strong.

Figure 18.6 shows how the trade-weighted value of the dollar has changed from 1973 to 1998. When the dollar reached its strongest level in 1985, foreign goods became less expensive, and American exports became more costly for the rest of the world. As a result, imports rose, exports fell, and the United States suffered record trade deficits in 1986 and 1987.

As the deficits persisted, the value of the dollar fell, making imports more expensive and exports more attractive to the rest of the world. By 1991, the overall deficit in the balance of payments had fallen to just under $4 billion. The trade deficit will continue to rise and fall as the value of the dollar continues to change.

The resulting shift in employment between export and import industries is one of the biggest problems with a trade deficit. In the automobile industry, for example, Japanese cars once undercut the price of cars being produced in Detroit, causing severe unemployment for both domestic autoworkers and domestic car dealerships. As the Japanese yen rose against the dollar in the early 1990s, however, the price of Japanese cars increased, making domestic automobiles more attractive and restoring some of the employment in that industry. As consumers began to demand more American-made cars relative to foreign-made ones, employment generated by foreign-car imports fell. **1**

Correcting Trade Deficits

Under flexible exchange rates, trade deficits automatically correct themselves through the price system. A strong currency, for example, will probably lead to a deficit in the balance of payments. The bigger the deficit, and the longer it lasts, the more likely the value of the currency will fall. Because the time span for the whole process varies, improvement in trade balances cannot be predicted very accurately. **2**

Trade imbalances can sometimes be improved with quotas, tariffs, or other means. Most economists believe that when legislators use these methods, however, threatened industries receive only temporary relief. Past attempts to legislate trade have largely

Checking Understanding

1. What is one of the biggest problems with a trade deficit?
2. How do trade deficits correct themselves under flexible exchange rates?

Applying Economic Concepts

☑ **Trade Deficit** In recent years, the trade deficit has attracted almost as much attention as the federal budget deficit. Unlike the latter, however, the trade deficit has the potential to be self-correcting.

CHAPTER 18: *International Trade* **465**

Cultural Diversity and Economics

With the introduction of market reforms in the Russian economy, the value of the Russian currency, the ruble, tumbled. As a result, many Russians avoided the ruble in economic transactions. Some stores—especially those that sold foreign products—preferred to be paid in dollars, marks, or another stable foreign currency. This

drove down the value of the ruble even further, however. In 1993 alone, the exchange rate for the ruble went from 570 to the dollar to about 1,250 to the dollar. By the beginning of 1998, the rate was approximately 6,000 rubles to the dollar.

 CHAPTER 18 SECTION 3

Evaluate

 Assign the Section 3 Quiz in the TCR or use the *Economics: Principles and Practices* Testmaker to create a customized quiz. Spanish Section Quizzes also are available in the Spanish Resources Binder.

? DID YOU KNOW

Because the ruble fell so much in value during the 1990s, the U.S. dollar became Russia's second currency. The most popular note was the new $100 bill introduced in the United States in 1996. To meet demand, planeloads of currency were flown into Russia, and Russian banks even charged their citizens $2 to exchange old U.S. currency into the new $100 bills.

 VISUAL INSTRUCTION

Ask: If the exchange rates shown in Figure 18.4 on page 462 were in effect, how many *won* would these tourists get for $75? *(913.45 × 75 = 68,508.75 won)*

Answer to Caption:

the value of one country's currency in terms of another country's currency

QUICK CHECK

ANSWERS

1. the shift in employment between import and export industries
2. through the price system

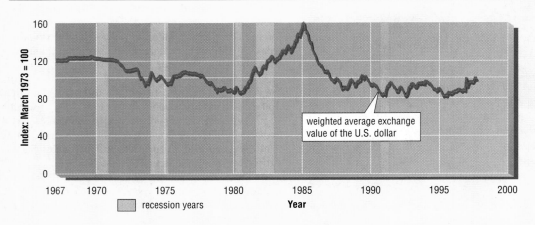

Figure 18.6
The Trade-Weighted Average Value of the Dollar

Index: March 1973 = 100

weighted average exchange value of the U.S. dollar

☐ recession years   Year

When the value of the dollar goes up, American exports go down and imports rise, which causes problems for the balance of payments. When the value of the dollar goes down, imports become more expensive, and the balance of payments tends to improve. **What causes the value of the dollar to fluctuate?**

Source: *The Economic Bulletin Board,* Bureau of Economic Analysis.

failed. As a result, many people believe a country should adjust slowly to change, rather than all at once.

Deficits and surpluses in a country's balance of payments generally tend to be temporary. When the dollar became strong in 1985, people worried about unemployment in export industries. When the dollar weakened in 1991, people worried about unemployment in import industries. As long as deficits and surpluses in a country's balance of payments generally correct themselves, the United States and many other countries no longer need to design economic policies just to improve their balance of payments.

SECTION 3 REVIEW

Reviewing Terms and Facts

1. **Define** foreign exchange, foreign exchange market, foreign exchange rate, fixed exchange rate, devaluation, floating exchange rate, flexible exchange rate, foreign exchange futures, trade-weighted value of the dollar.

2. **Describe** how the value of foreign exchange is determined.

3. **Explain** how trade deficits are corrected.

Critical Thinking

4. **Making Generalizations** How do exchange rates influence international trade?

Applying Economic Concepts

5. **Foreign Exchange** How does a weak American dollar affect you as a consumer? How does a strong dollar affect you?

Answers to SECTION 3 REVIEW

1. All vocabulary words are defined in the Glossary.

2. It is determined by the forces of supply and demand. When one currency is sold to buy another, the value of the currency being sold falls, and the value of the other currency rises.

3. Under flexible exchange rates, trade deficits correct themselves through the price system. Trade imbalances can temporarily be improved with quotas, tariffs, and other means.

4. When a country's currency is weak, other countries will import more of that country's products. When a country's currency is strong, it will export less because the price of the product is less competitive in a foreign market.

5. A weak dollar means consumers will pay more for foreign products. A strong dollar means prices of imports will fall.

ECONOMICS IN ACTION

International Trade

Setting Up the Video

With your classmates, view "International Trade" on the videodisc *Economics in Action*. The video focuses on factors involved in international trade. It explains that since each nation has a different currency, money is exchanged in the foreign exchange market. It also discusses the importance of trade surpluses and deficits to national economies.

Chapter 27
Disc 2, Side 2

Scan the bar code or enter the chapter number on your keypad and press Search. *(Also available in VHS format.)*

Hands-On Activity

Find a table of currencies in the business section of your local newspaper. Imagine that you are visiting Europe on vacation. Use the currency table to figure out the dollar cost of each of the following:

1. A dinner in France costing 288 French francs
2. A sightseeing tour in southern England costing 150 British pounds
3. A castle tour in Germany costing 65 German marks
4. A lunch in Italy costing 7,500 Italian lire.

Share your findings with the class.

INTERACTIVE ECONOMICS!

International Trade

Introduction

Lesson 9 of *Interactive Economics!* deals with international trade, which takes place for the same reasons that exchange takes place between individuals. First, trade—whether it be local, regional, or international—is an important way to acquire goods and services that may simply not be available otherwise. Second, people are generally able to produce more and enjoy a higher level of consumption when they specialize in activities they perform relatively more efficiently.

Using the Software

1. Select "International Trade" from the Main Menu.
2. Read the introduction to "International Trade," then click on and review "Alpha's Opportunity Costs," "Beta's Opportunity Costs," and "Finding Comparative Advantage."
3. Next, go to the "Advanced Topics" menu and study the two topics given.
4. Then click on "Economics Lab." Complete the lab by clicking and dragging the appropriate numbers to the tables that represent production, exports, imports, or consumption.
5. Print your completed lab.

467

TEACHER NOTES

GLENCOE
TECHNOLOGY

VIDEODISC
MindJogger Videoquiz

Use MindJogger to review
the Chapter 18 content.

Chapter 18
Disc 3, Side A

Also available in VHS.

Answers

Reviewing Key Terms

Sentences may vary. Sample
sentences are provided below.

1. The country that can produce the most of a product
has an absolute advantage,
but the country that can
produce that same product
relatively more efficiently
has comparative advantage.

2. A trade deficit is a deficit in
the "goods" component of
the balance of payments.

3. Flexible exchange rates help
countries automatically
correct deficits or surpluses
in their balance of payments.

4. Devaluation lowers the
value of a currency under a
fixed exchange rate.

5. Under a system of flexible
exchange rates, the value of
foreign exchange is meas-
ured in terms of another
country's currency.

6. A protectionist wants infant
industries protected from
foreign competition.

7. A protective tariff and a
revenue tariff are taxes
levied on foreign imports.

8. Tariffs and quotas are barriers to free trade.

9. When the trade-weighted
value of the dollar rises,
the trade deficit increases.

Reviewing Key Terms

*For each of the pairs of terms below, write a sentence or
short paragraph showing how the two are related.*

1. absolute advantage
   comparative advantage
2. balance of payments
   trade deficit
3. balance of payments
   flexible exchange rates
4. devaluation
   fixed exchange rate
5. foreign exchange
   flexible exchange rates
6. protectionist
   infant industries
7. protective tariff
   revenue tariff
8. tariff
   quota
9. trade deficit
   trade-weighted value of the dollar

Reviewing the Facts

SECTION 1 *(pages 448–451)*
1. **Describe** the extent of United States involvement in world trade.
2. **Describe** a case in which the United States might
   have an absolute advantage over another country in the production of a good.
3. **Explain** how comparative advantage can make
   trade between countries of different sizes
   possible.

SECTION 2 *(pages 453–459)*
4. **Name** three barriers to international trade.
5. **Describe** five protectionist arguments.

6. **Describe** the role of GATT in the free trade
   movement.

SECTION 3 *(pages 461–466)*
7. **Differentiate** between fixed and flexible
   exchange rates.
8. **Explain** how deficits can be self-correcting
   when currency values are allowed to be
   flexible.

Critical Thinking

1. **Determining Relevance** Many industries claim
   they are vital to the country's defense. Which
   industries do you think qualify? Explain your
   choices.
2. **Demonstrating Reasoned Judgment** Do you
   favor protection as a national trade policy? Why
   or why not?
3. **Demonstrating Reasoned Judgment** It has been
   announced that the government has to generate
   additional revenue. To do this, it can raise taxes
   or increase tariff rates. Which do you as a consumer prefer? Give reasons to support your
   choice.
4. **Analyzing Information** Some people feel the
   United States should return to a system of fixed
   exchange rates. Defend or oppose this view.

Applying Economic Concepts

1. **Comparative Advantage** Think of a project you
   recently completed with a friend. How could
   you have completed the project more efficiently,
   applying the principle of comparative advantage? Explain.
2. **Quotas** You have just started a business manufacturing toothbrushes. Would you favor a quota
   on imported toothbrushes? Why or why not?

Reviewing the Facts

1. In 1998 imports of goods and services amounted to
   about $1,050 billion, or about $4,000 for every person in the country.

2. The U. S. would have an absolute advantage if it
   could produce more of a product, such as wheat.

3. Because a country has a comparative advantage
   when it can make a product relatively more efficiently, a country can be competitive no matter
   what its size.

4. tariffs, quotas, inspections, licensing requirements

5. A country that becomes too dependent on other
   countries may be unable to get critical supplies
   during wartime. Infant industries should be protected against foreign competition. Domestic jobs
   need to be protected from cheap foreign labor.
   Trade barriers will keep American money at home.
   Help the balance of payments by restricting
   imports.

6. GATT extended tariff concessions and worked to
   do away with import quotas, thus encouraging free
   trade.

Reinforcing Skills

RECOGNIZING BIAS

Read the following excerpt, then answer the questions that follow.

Look at the signs of decline in this country because our democracy has not been allowed to strengthen itself. Because we don't spend enough time as public citizens. Because we have allowed global corporations, with no allegiance to our country, to scour for the dictatorships and the dirt cheap labor, to exploit and export the jobs there. We have allowed them to take over our government, to dominate our economy, to exploit small business, to straitjacket inventors, to shape our very culture— to replace our thought culture with commercial culture, that stresses violence and addiction—to decide what kind of research is done at our universities, to decide that the ordinary people pay the taxes (as someone once said, "Only the little people pay taxes."), to decide that they, the corporations, weren't going to pay any taxes.

And now look at the result. In the 1950s corporate income tax represented between 25 and 30% of the federal outlays. Today it's between 6 and 8%. Record corporate profits, record stock market prices, record executive compensations, and they are paying a shrinking amount. And many of these giant corporations pay 1% federal tax, 2% federal tax.

—From Ralph Nader's Acceptance Speech at the Green Party National Convention, August 1996

1. What evidence of bias do you find in this argument?
2. What language in the excerpt reflects emotion or generalizations?
3. What conclusions might you draw about corporations and their ethics from these excerpts?

Individual Activity

The North American Free Trade Agreement (NAFTA) has been highly controversial. Keeping in mind what you know about tariffs and international trade, where do you stand on this issue? Outline three arguments in support of your position.

Cooperative Learning Activity

Working in groups of four, have each group choose one familiar item that is imported in the United States. Collect information about that item, including where it comes from and how much it costs. Learn why the country produces this item and what it imports from the United States. Compare your information with the rest of the class's.

Technology Activity

Using E-mail

In the **Journal Writing** activity on page 447, you were asked to log items you use daily and to note whether each is domestically produced or foreign-made. Now, using the persuasive writing style, E-mail an editorial explaining your opinion on international trade to your local newspaper.

Note that the persuasive writing style aims to persuade the reader to agree with a certain opinion. In this style, facts and other information may be given. These facts, however, are added to support your point of view and to persuade the reader to agree with you.

In writing a persuasive argument, it is important to state the problem clearly and to give your position on the issue. Then present the evidence you have gathered to support your position and to refute any opposing position. Conclude your argument by restating your position and summing up the evidence.

CHAPTER 18: *International Trade* **469**

Applying Economic Concepts

1. Students may cite strengths and weaknesses to assess how the project could have been completed more efficiently.

2. Students may argue that a quota on imported toothbrushes would lessen foreign competition, or they may argue that quotas will push up the price of their product.

Reinforcing Skills

1. The tone of the speech and the language used indicates that it was written from an anticorporation point of view.

2. phrases and words such as "dirt cheap labor," "exploit," "straitjacket," "stresses violence and addiction," "ordinary people"

3. that corporations, which are not paying their fair share of taxes, are cheating the "ordinary people" who do pay taxes

? BONUS TEST QUESTION

Arcania has the capacity to produce 6,000 widgets or 4,000 wombles per week. Esoterica has the capacity to produce 4,000 widgets and 3,000 wombles per week. Arcania specializes in widgets and Esoterica specializes in wombles. Explain why. (*Arcania has a comparative advantage in widgets because it does a relatively better job of producing widgets. Esoterica has a comparative advantage in wombles because it does a relatively better job of producing wombles.*)

7. Under fixed rates, each country's currency is fixed in terms of gold or another currency. Under flexible exchange rates, the value of a currency is determined by supply and demand.

8. A flexible exchange rate allows for the value of currency to rise and fall. This reverses the process that causes a trade deficit in the first place.

Critical Thinking

1. Answers will vary. Students' choices should include industries that contribute to or are responsible for products critical to a nation's survival during wartime, such as food, oil, and weapons.

2. Students may cite or reject protectionist arguments.

3. Students should explain how tax increases vs. increased tariff rates will affect consumers.

4. Students' answers should reflect an understanding of fixed exchange rates, why the system was changed, and the implications of implementing such a system again.

CHAPTER ORGANIZER

Daily Objectives	Reproducible Resources	Multimedia Resources
Section 1 **The Spectrum of Economic Systems** 1. **Explain** the advantages and disadvantages of capitalism. 2. **Describe** the differences between socialism, capitalism, and communism. 3. **Compare** the features of communism to other types of economic systems.	Reproducible Lesson Plan 19-1 Guided Reading Activity 19-1 Cooperative Learning Activity 20 Consumer Application Activity 21 Math Practice for Economics 26 Free Enterprise Activity 21 Primary and Secondary Source Reading 20 Performance Assessment Activity 26 Section Quiz 19-1*	Focus Activity Transparency 89 Vocabulary PuzzleMaker Chapter Challenger Interactive Review Software Testmaker MindJogger Videoquiz NBR's Economics in Action Video Program
Section 2 **The Rise and Fall of Communism** 1. **Explain** the rise of the Soviet economy under Lenin and Stalin. 2. **Describe** the complexities of a centrally planned economy. 3. **Understand** the forces that brought about the collapse of communism as an economic system.	Reproducible Lesson Plan 19-2 Guided Reading Activity 19-2 Reinforcing Economic Skill 19 Section Quiz 19-2*	Focus Activity Transparency 99 Vocabulary PuzzleMaker Chapter Challenger Interactive Review Software Testmaker NBR's Economics in Action Video Program
Section 3 **The Transition to Capitalism** 1. **List** four problems encountered when an economy makes the transition to capitalism. 2. **Recognize** the major countries and regions that are making the transition to capitalism.	Reproducible Lesson Plan 19-3 Guided Reading Activity 19-3 Section Quiz 19-3*	Focus Activity Transparency 91 Economic Concepts Transparency 22* Vocabulary PuzzleMaker Chapter Challenger Interactive Review Software Testmaker NBR's Economics in Action Video Program
Section 4 **The Various Faces of Capitalism** 1. **Explain** the factors that encouraged economic growth in Japan. 2. **Rank** the "Asian Tigers" according to per capita GNP. 3. **Describe** Sweden's retreat from socialism.	Reproducible Lesson Plan 19-4 Guided Reading Activity 19-4 Section Quiz 19-4*	Focus Activity Transparency 100 Vocabulary PuzzleMaker Chapter Challenger Interactive Review Software Testmaker NBR's Economics in Action Video Program
Chapter Review and Evaluation	Enrichment Activity 19 Reteaching Activity 19* Economic Vocabulary Activity 19* Chapter 19 Test, Forms A and B	Chapter Digests Audiocassette Activities and Tests* Testmaker MindJogger Videoquiz

Also available in Spanish

 Blackline Master   Transparency   CD-ROM   Software   Videodisc   Audiocassette

⏱ OUT OF TIME? Assign the Chapter 19 Digest Audiocassette and the corresponding Chapter Digest activities and tests.

National Council on Economic Education

THE **Economics** America AND **Economics** International PROGRAMS

VOLUNTARY NATIONAL CONTENT STANDARDS IN ECONOMICS
Emphasized in Chapter 19

Content Standard 3 *Students will understand that:*
Different methods can be used to allocate goods and services. People, acting individually or collectively through government, must choose which methods to use to allocate different kinds of goods and services.

Content Standard 16 *Students will understand that:*
There is an economic role for government to play in a market economy whenever the benefits of a government policy outweigh its costs. Governments often provide for national defense, address environmental concerns, define and protect property rights, and attempt to make markets more competitive. Most government policies also redistribute income.

Economics America *Resources Available From NCEE*

- *Capstone: The Nation's High School Economics Course*
- *Civics and Government: Focus on Economics*
- *Economies in Transition: Command to Market*
- *World History: Focus on Economics*

To order these materials, or to contact your state Council on Economic Education about workshops and programs, call 1-800-338-1192 or visit http://www.nationalcouncil.org.

PERFORMANCE ASSESSMENT

The following chapter projects may be assigned at the beginning of the chapter and used for performance assessment.

Multicultural Heritage Have each student select one of the nations mentioned in the chapter. Direct students to gather either current or historical information about the economic system of their selected nation. Then have students investigate their chosen nation's cultural heritage. Finally, ask students to collate their findings in a report, showing direct relationships between the country's culture and characteristics of its economic system. Call on students to present their reports to the class.

Cooperative Learning Organize students into several groups and assign groups the following project: Design a museum exhibit entitled "The Fall of Communism." Suggest that groups focus on the whole Soviet sphere or on one particular country, and that they divide their exhibits into three sections—"Before Communism," "During Communism," and "After Communism." Make sure that group members share the various tasks involved in completing the project. Call on groups to display and discuss their exhibit designs.

ADDITIONAL RESOURCES

Readings for the Student

Heilbroner, Robert L. *The Worldly Philosophers*, 6th ed. New York: Touchstone, 1986. Introduction to the great economic thinkers. Suitable for advanced students.

Economics 97/98: Annual Editions. Dushkin, 1997. Anthology of articles reprinted from prominent publications.

Readings for the Teacher

Nagorski, Andrew. *The Birth of Freedom: Shaping Lives and Societies in the New Eastern Europe.* New York: Simon and Schuster, 1993. Traces recent changes in Eastern Europe, focusing on the introduction of the market economy.

Yergin, Daniel, and Thane Gustafson. *Russia 2010, and What It Means for the World.* New York: Random House, 1994. Develops five scenarios of how Russia might develop over the next few years.

Multimedia

Capitalism, Communism, Socialism: An Introduction. BFA Educational Media, 468 Park Avenue South, New York, NY 10016. Video, 28 mins. Details the distinct political, economic, and social aspects of these three systems.

Getting Out of Business: Privatization and the Modern State. Films for the Humanities and Science, P.O. Box 2053, Princeton, NJ 08543–2053. Video, 59 mins. Presents privatization examples from different nations.

Chapter Overview

Chapter 19 reviews the ways in which the various economic systems function to fulfill economic goals. **Section 1** compares the characteristics of each of the three major economic systems, showing where they fall on an economic spectrum. **Section 2** traces the history of the Soviet Union from the 1917 Revolution to its recent collapse. **Section 3** describes transition problems facing countries as they move toward capitalism. **Section 4** deals with the economies of Japan and Singapore, Taiwan, Hong Kong, and South Korea.

GLENCOE
TECHNOLOGY

VIDEODISC
MindJogger Videoquiz

Use MindJogger to preview the Chapter 19 content.

Chapter 19
Disc 3, Side A

Also available in VHS.

inter**NET**
CONNECTION

Resources for Chapter 19 on the World Wide Web*

National Council on Economic Education
http://www.nationalcouncil.org/

Capitalism
http://www.capitalism.org/index.html

Socialism
http://www.worldsocialism.org/

Asian Studies
http://coombs.anu.edu.au/WWWVL-AsianStudies.html

Sites subject to change.

先进科技引潮流,优质可

Trinitron
单枪三束彩色电视机

1. 采用单电子枪画像更鲜明。
2. 大镜头装置保证了锐利的屏光图像。
3. 荫栅装饰使颜色光彩夺目。
4. 隔离栅格使图像对比分明。
5. 圆柱萤光屏实现画像无重影。

KV-2092CH   KV-1882CH

Betamax
贝特马可思

1.U型装带系统。
2.较大型磁头鼓。
3.小型盒式录象带。

SL-C30CH   SL-P200

一体摄象录象机
BMC-500P

携带式
双卡收录机
CFS-W900   CFS-W600   CFS-W3

音响组合

激光数字式电唱机
D-50

FH-15R   FH-10W   FH-

不
随地

The communist economy of China has recently begun to experiment with capitalism.

Extra Credit Project

Have students work individually or in small groups to create a three-part bulletin board display illustrating the three economic systems discussed in Chapter 19. Suggest that students use photo-graphs, sketches, tables, charts, and graphs—accompanied by captions—to illustrate the three systems.

CHAPTER 19

Comparative Economic Systems

SECTION 1
The Spectrum of Economic Systems

SECTION 2
The Rise and Fall of Communism

SECTION 3
The Transition to Capitalism

SECTION 4
The Various Faces of Capitalism

CHAPTER PREVIEW

People to Know

- Karl Marx
- Statistician

Applying Economic Concepts to Your Life

Capitalism Have you ever used your lawn mower to cut someone else's yard, watched the neighbor's child, or organized a group for a car wash? The freedom to use your own tools and labor in pursuit of profits is one of the main features of capitalism. Capitalism is more than an ideology. It is the way we live and the way the world is headed.

> **Journal Writing**
>
> For one week, summarize in your journal news articles you read about events in eastern Europe and the Commonwealth of Independent States, and other former Soviet bloc nations. Focus on articles that relate to those regions working to convert from a command economy to a market economy.

Connecting to Past Learning

Call on students to define the terms *command economy* and *market economy*. Have students suggest how these terms might be applied to the three economic systems discussed in Chapter 19. Refer them to Figure 19.1 on page 473 for guidance.

Applying Economics

Ask students to suggest words they commonly associate with the communist economic system. Note their suggestions on the chalkboard. Then refer students to the text definition of communism on page 474. Point out, however, that in economic terms, communism has become synonymous with lack of incentive, shoddy quality of products, shortages, and so on. Conclude by mentioning that these factors, in large part, caused the collapse of communism.

 PERFORMANCE ASSESSMENT

Refer to page **470B** for a Performance Assessment activity for this chapter. Also see the **Performance Assessment Activities** booklet for additional suggestions.

 VISUAL INSTRUCTION

Have students speculate on the problems China might face in mixing communism and capitalism.

Economic Portfolio

Suggest that, in their **Journal Writing** entries, students first summarize the developments noted in the news articles, then arrange those developments in chronological order. Point out that this will help them complete the writing activity at the end of the chapter. Refer students to the **Technology Activity** in the Chapter 19 Review on page 495.

Key to Ability Levels — Teaching strategies have been coded for varying learning styles and abilities:
L1 - Basic (activities for all students)   **L2 - Average** (activities for average to above-average students)
L3 - Challenging (activities for above-average students)   **LEP - Limited English Proficiency**

FOCUS

Section Objectives

1. Explain the advantages and disadvantages of capitalism.

2. Describe the differences between socialism, capitalism, and communism.

3. Compare the features of communism to other types of economic systems.

Bellringer

Prior to taking roll at the beginning of the class period, display Focus Activity Transparency 89.

Motivational Activity

Discuss students' responses to the activity sheet that accompanies Transparency 89.

Preteaching Vocabulary

Write the key terms *socialism* and *communism* on the chalkboard. Call on students to explain how these terms differ from each other. **LEP**

Use the **Vocabulary PuzzleMaker** to create crossword and word search puzzles.

TEACH

Guided Practice

L1 *Analyzing Ideas* Conduct a class discussion concerning the ways in which people are motivated to produce goods and services in each of the three types of economic systems. Conclude by asking students what they consider the good and bad aspects of each system. **LEP**

Section Preview

Objectives

After studying this section, you will be able to:

1. **Explain** the advantages and disadvantages of capitalism.

2. **Describe** the differences between socialism, capitalism, and communism.

3. **Compare** the features of communism to other types of economic systems.

Key Terms

socialism, communism

Applying Economic Concepts

Surplus Value Have you ever felt exploited because you thought you were paid less than the value of your labor? If so, you have something in common with Karl Marx, who founded communism and introduced the concept of *surplus value* that is extracted from labor.

To deal with the fundamental problem of scarcity, three types of economic systems exist—traditional, market, and command. Command economies often have a communist form of government. Countries with market economies are called capitalist nations, and socialist countries often have a combination of both command and market economies.

The three forms of organization—communism, socialism, and capitalism—are shown in Figure 19.1. At the far left is communism, in which a strong central government influences almost every economic decision. At the far right is capitalism, in which government has a limited role. As one moves from left to right along the spectrum, both the ownership of resources and the degree of government involvement in the operation of the economy change. No fine line separates communism, socialism, and capitalism. They appear on the spectrum as having a greater or lesser degree of government involvement and private ownership of resources.

Capitalism

Under capitalism, the means of production are privately owned. Supply and demand determines prices, and businesses are free to direct resources into activities that promise the greatest profits.

Advantages of Capitalism

The main advantage of capitalism is efficiency. If there are many buyers and sellers, if resources are reasonably mobile, and if buyers and sellers are reasonably well-informed, then resources will be directed to their most profitable and efficient use. **1**

This efficiency is a result of individual freedom and the operation of the price system. Individuals have the freedom to purchase the goods and services that best satisfy their preferences. Producers have the freedom to direct productive resources into activities that consumers demand most. Prices serve as signals to both consumers and producers.

Capitalism has the flexibility to accommodate change. When consumer preferences change, or when the price of resources changes, signals are sent through the price system and everyone adjusts accordingly. Capitalism has evolved and adapted into a system capable of answering the basic WHAT, HOW, and FOR WHOM questions in a decentralized manner.

Disadvantages of Capitalism

Capitalism has a few weaknesses. Although it is efficient in satisfying the demands of consumers, it does not always satisfy everyone's needs.

Classroom Resources for SECTION 1

- Reproducible Lesson Plan 19-1
- Guided Reading Activity 19-1
- Cooperative Learning Activity 20
- Consumer Application Activity 21
- Math Practice for Economics 26
- Free Enterprise Activity 21
- Primary and Secondary Source Reading 20
- Performance Assessment Activity 26
- Section Quiz 19-1
- Spanish Section Quiz 19-1

- Focus Activity Transparency 89
- NBR's Economics in Action Video Program
- Testmaker
- Vocabulary PuzzleMaker
- Chapter Challenger Interactive Review Software
- MindJogger Videoquiz

Figure 19.1
The Spectrum of Economic Systems

The spectrum of economic systems runs from communism on the left to capitalism on the right. The distinguishing feature is the ownership of the factors of production and the role of government in deciding WHAT, HOW, and FOR WHOM to produce. Since the collapse of the Soviet Union, many countries have shifted more toward capitalism.
What reasons are given for the collapse of the Soviet Union?

COMMUNISM	SOCIALISM	CAPITALISM
Directed by Command		Directed by the Free Market
Ownership of Resources		
All productive resources are government owned and operated.	Basic productive resources are government owned and operated; the rest are privately owned and operated.	Productive resources are privately owned and operated.
Allocation of Resources		
Centralized planning directs all resources.	Government plans ways to allocate resources in key industries.	Capital for production is obtained through the lure of profits in the market.
Role of Government		
Government makes all economic decisions.	Government directs the completion of its economic plans in key industries.	Government may promote competition and provide public goods.

At a collective level, capitalism ignores the production of many public goods such as roads, public schools, a system of justice, and national defense. The market produces private goods and services—items that can be withheld if people refuse to pay for them. At an individual level, capitalism produces only for those who have demand, which means the ability and willingness to pay. A system of pure capitalism would ignore poor people, the unemployed, and less productive members of society. 2

Pure capitalism can also be unstable, as illustrated by the Great Depression. Life under capitalism can be harsh for some people unless the system has been modified by adding safety nets in the form of unemployment insurance, Social Security, and other entitlement programs. ☑

Socialism

Under **socialism**, many of the basic productive resources are government owned and operated, with prices playing a major role in the allocation of resources. Most socialist societies are democracies in which elected officials and, ultimately, the people direct the allocation of resources in key industries.

QUICK CHECK

Checking Understanding
1. What is the main advantage of capitalism?
2. What people does pure capitalism tend to ignore?

Applying Economic Concepts
☑ **Capitalism** Pure capitalism does not exist in the world today. Most countries that are essentially capitalist have some government regulation, making them mixed or modified free enterprise economies.

CHAPTER 19: Comparative Economic Systems **473**

Independent Practice

☞ **Guided Reading** Assign Guided Reading Activity for Section 1. **LEP**

☞ **Consumer Application** Assign Consumer Application Activity 21.

☞ **Math Practice** Assign Math Practice for Economics 26.

☞ **Free Enterprise** Assign Free Enterprise Activity 21.

☞ **Readings** Assign Primary and Secondary Source Reading 20.

☞ **Performance Assessment** Assign Performance Assessment Activity 26.

L2 Comparing Lives Have students research and write a report that compares everyday life in a capitalist country to everyday life in a socialist or communist country. Call on volunteers to share their reports with the class.

ASSESS

Check for Understanding

Assign Section 1 Review as homework or an in-class activity.

MEETING LESSON OBJECTIVES

Each objective below is tested by the questions that follow it in parentheses.

1. **Explain** the advantages and disadvantages of capitalism. **(2, 5)**

2. **Describe** the differences between socialism, capitalism, and communism. **(1, 3, 4, 5, 6)**

3. **Compare** the features of communism to other types of economic systems. **(4, 6)**

474

Advantages of Socialism

Socialism addresses the FOR WHOM question directly. Those who are not fortunate or productive enough to earn a competitive income still share in the benefits of society. These benefits may include free education, health care, welfare, access to the arts and cultural events, and even guaranteed jobs in government-owned industries.

Although the government owns the majority of productive resources in a socialist society, people use their electoral power to influence many of the HOW, WHAT, and FOR WHOM questions. Those who might have been left on the fringes of a capitalist society—the unemployed and the homeless—can benefit more fully from the activities of a socialist society.

Disadvantages of Socialism

Socialism is normally less efficient than capitalism. If workers receive government guarantees of jobs, more workers will be hired than are really necessary, driving up the cost of production.

The price system still plays a vital role, but its efficiency is reduced when the government substitutes its judgment for the discipline of the market. Finally, special interests often become entrenched and have a political influence far in excess of their numbers. When this happens, decisions over WHAT, HOW,

---

DID YOU KNOW?

How Many Statisticians Does It Take?
Predicting the economy is not only more difficult than predicting the weather but sometimes less reliable. Official statistics often are inaccurate. Governments struggle to improve the situation, but hiring more statisticians does not seem to be the solution. A 1993 survey indicated that Germany and France employed the most government statisticians. Canada and Australia ranked highest regarding the accuracy and integrity of their reports, however.

---

and FOR WHOM to produce tend to be waged at the ballot box rather than in the marketplace.

Communism

Under pure **communism**, which is both a political and an economic framework, all property is collectively owned, and labor is organized for the common advantage of the community. Because private property does not exist, the state owns all economic goods, including factories and other means of production.

Theoretically, communism is a selfless society where everyone works to the best of their abilities and consumes according to their needs. Goods and services have no prices, eliminating the need for wages, rents, interest rates, or profits. Theoretical communism has no social classes and no need for a central government authority.

To date, no modern country has achieved the ideal of pure communism. Countries such as China and the former Soviet Union instead developed rigid command-type economies where the state—usually represented by a single authoritarian party—claimed the ideal of pure communism as its eventual goal. The advantages and disadvantages listed below relate to the realities of communism as found in these countries, not to the theoretical ideal.

Advantages of Communism

One of the main advantages of communism, from the worker's point of view, is security. The state directs workers into their jobs, and workers are not fired or dismissed as they could be in other societies.

The state also provides a broad range of public goods such as health care, education, and a military defense system. Because of the guarantee of a steady job, workers seldom face job uncertainty.

Disadvantages of Communism

The disadvantages of communism are numerous. First, individual freedom is lost. People have little or no say in their jobs and are not free to move elsewhere if they are dissatisfied. The bureaucracy determines

---

$ Free Enterprise Activity $

Organize students into three groups and assign each group one of the three economic systems. Direct groups to organize a furniture factory in accordance with their assigned economic system. Have groups consider and answer the following questions: How will you get the money to begin production? From where will the factors of production come? How will workers be paid? How much will be produced? How will production be organized? How will the furniture be distributed? Have group representatives share their responses with the class.

Command Economy
Women workers assemble pocket watches at the 2nd State Watch Factory in Moscow in 1952. **How does a lack of incentives affect job performance?**

pay, and most people receive the same pay regardless of how hard they work.

The lack of incentives can cause frustration on the job, low productivity, and shoddy products. Most communist states place a high priority on military preparedness, resulting in the neglect of consumer goods that are highly prized in other parts of the world.

One of the biggest drawbacks to communism is the inefficiency of centralized planning. The resources needed to execute the planning and the overwhelming obstacles to effective execution are serious problems that communist countries encounter after reaching a certain size. The virtual collapse of the Soviet economy is evidence of these inefficiencies.

SECTION 1 REVIEW

Reviewing Terms and Facts

1. **Define** socialism, communism.
2. **Describe** the main advantages of capitalism.
3. **Describe** one advantage of socialism.
4. **Describe** three disadvantages of communism.

Critical Thinking

5. **Making Comparisons** How does the role of the individual differ under capitalism, socialism, and communism?

Applying Economic Concepts

6. **Surplus Value** According to Karl Marx, employers take advantage of their employees by paying them less than they are worth in order to make a larger profit. Do you think Marx's opinion is valid in the United States today? Why or why not?

Use **Chapter Challenger Interactive Review Software** to review Section 1.

Evaluate
Assign the Section 1 Quiz in the TCR or use the *Economics: Principles and Practices* Testmaker to create a customized quiz. Spanish Section Quizzes also are available in the Spanish Resources Binder.

Reteach
Have students write summary paragraphs noting the characteristics, advantages, and disadvantages of capitalism, socialism, and communism.

Enrich
Have students select one of the countries mentioned in the section and write a paragraph showing how that country's economic system compares to the pure form of capitalism, socialism, or communism.

CLOSE

Have students work individually or in small groups to develop logos or symbols for capitalism, socialism, and communism. Call on volunteers to display and explain their logos or symbols.

VISUAL INSTRUCTION

Ask: Suppose the watch factory produced 5,000 watches a week. How was this level of production arrived at? (*Central planners made the decision.*)

Answer to Caption:
can cause frustration on the job, low productivity, shoddy products

475

Answers to SECTION 1 REVIEW

1. All words are defined in the Glossary.

2. It directs resources to their most profitable and efficient use without government intervention; it provides freedom for consumers and producers; it has flexibility to accommodate change.

3. People who cannot earn a competitive income still share in the benefits of society.

4. Individuals have little or no say in their jobs, and they are not free to move elsewhere if they are dissatisfied; lack of incentives causes frustration, low productivity, and shoddy products; central planning is inefficient and difficult to execute.

5. capitalism: individuals have freedom to make choices and satisfy their preferences; socialism: individuals share in benefits of society, use their voting power to influence government decisions; communism: individuals taken care of by government but have virtually no individual freedom.

6. Answers will vary. Students' answers should be supported by valid examples.

Background

Point out that Marx's theories assumed that communism would first develop in the industrialized world. However, the two great communist revolutions came in Russia and China, both of which had extensive agricultural economies.

TEACH

On the chalkboard draw the following continuum: slavery → feudalism → capitalism → communism. Have students explain how this illustrates Marx's view of history. *(Represents four stages of history as seen by Marx.)* Then call on a student to explain how, according to Marx, the first three stages differ from the final stage. *(first three characterized by class conflict; final stage characterized by equality)*

PROFILES IN ECONOMICS

KARL MARX
(1818–1883)

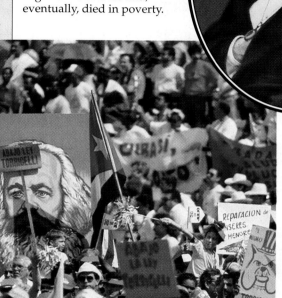

Karl Marx was an economic historian, social scientist, and revolutionary. He earned his doctorate in philosophy and history from the University of Berlin, but because of his radical views, he could not get a teaching position.

Throughout the 1840s, he wandered from Cologne to Paris to Brussels. He joined with socialist and radical groups and edited radical newspapers. Persecuted by Prussian and Parisian authorities, Marx fled to London in 1849 where he began a life of exile and, eventually, died in poverty.

Workers around the world celebrate May 1 as a holiday to honor working people.

THE COMMUNIST MANIFESTO Marx is best known for *The Communist Manifesto*, published in 1848, and *Das Kapital*, the first volume of which was published in 1867. In these works, he argues that all history has been a class struggle. In each era, one class was pitted against another: master against slave, lord against serf, capitalist against worker—the haves against the have-nots.

Marx divided the society of his day into the *proletariat*—people who must work for a living because they have no means of production of their own—and capitalists or *bourgeoisie*—people who own land and capital and hire labor.

LABOR EXPLOITATION Marx argued that labor was exploited in a capitalist society. Marx gave the name *surplus value* to the difference between the wage paid and the market value of the worker's output. He believed this difference became the capitalist's profit.

In Marx's view, the recurring cycles of prosperity and depression were capitalism's greatest defect. With each recurring cycle, workers would suffer more than before, while money and power would fall into the hands of the capitalists. Hostilities would build between the working class and the capitalists until the oppressed workers would rise up in a violent revolution. During the transition, the proletariat would have to depend on its political power through a strong government.

THEORETICAL COMMUNISM After everyone became equal, however, no single class would have power over another. Government no longer would be needed and could be eliminated. In this ideal state of communism, everyone would produce to the best of their abilities, and everyone would consume to the extent of their needs.

Examining the Profile

1. **Analyzing Information** According to Marx, through what stages must society go before it can reach the ideal state of communism?

2. **For Further Research** Find out how the former Soviet Union adapted Marx's philosophies to the Soviet economy.

Answers to Examining the Profile

1. Recurring cycles of prosperity and depression would lead to greater conflict between the proletariate and the bourgeoisie. Eventually, this would lead to a violent revolution and overthrow of the bourgeoisie. After a transition period in which the proletariate rule through a strong government, communism would be established.

2. Encourage students to present their findings in a written report.

The Rise and Fall of Communism

Section Preview

Objectives

After studying this section, you will be able to:

1. **Explain** the rise of the Soviet economy under Lenin and Stalin.

2. **Describe** the complexities of a centrally planned economy.

3. **Understand** the forces that brought about the collapse of communism as an economic system.

Key Terms

Five-Year Plan, collectivization, Gosplan, state farm, collective farm, piecework, storming, perestroika

Applying Economic Concepts

Perestroika Have you ever thought that some aspects of the economy should be changed from top to bottom? Perhaps health care or welfare comes to mind. If so, then you believe in *perestroika*, which is the Russian term for "restructuring."

In the absence of pure communism, the former Soviet Union is the most frequently cited example of a communist economic system. The early Soviet economy showed the main advantage of a command system—that it can mobilize resources and change direction in a short period of time. The sudden disintegration of the Soviet economy in the late 1980s, however, demonstrates the weaknesses of communism.

The Economy Under Lenin and Stalin

In 1917 a revolutionary named Vladimir Ilyich Ulyanov, or Lenin, overthrew the government of Russia. In its place, he set up a communist government. Lenin was a strong believer in theoretical communism, and he quickly took steps to develop a communist society. Large estates were taken from the rich, and the land was divided up and given to the peasants. Lenin also outlawed private property and turned the country's few factories over to the workers.

Forced Industrialization

The workers, however, could not manage the factories. Before long, production fell and the economy began to disintegrate. People lost faith in the money supply, and a system of barter emerged. The government sent armed forces to the farms to confiscate surplus food for the hungry city dwellers and industrial workers. The angry farmers retaliated by reducing their production so there would be no surplus crops.

The government then tried to increase production by assigning workers to the jobs it wanted done. Those who did not obey were sent to prison. Agricultural and industrial production fell even further, and internal strife spread throughout the country.

By 1921, when the situation was at its worst, Lenin introduced his New Economic Policy (NEP) to reintroduce some capitalist methods. Peasants now could lease land and hire labor, and small, privately owned businesses could operate. Many of the *kulaks*, or most prosperous peasants, fared well under the NEP.

Central Planning Under Stalin

By 1927, many changes had taken place. Russia had become the Soviet Union, and the country was under Communist party control. Lenin had died, and Joseph Stalin was the new leader. Stalin feared war with the western democracies and wanted to transform the Soviet economy from an agricultural to an industrial one.

CHAPTER 19: *Comparative Economic Systems* **477**

FOCUS

Section Objectives

1. Explain the rise of the Soviet economy under Lenin and Stalin.

2. Describe the complexities of a centrally planned economy.

3. Understand the forces that brought about the collapse of communism as an economic system.

Bellringer

Prior to taking roll at the beginning of the class period, display Focus Activity Transparency 99 on the overhead projector and assign the accompanying Student Activity 99.

Motivational Activity

Discuss students' responses to the activity sheet that accompanies Focus Activity Transparency 99.

Preteaching Vocabulary

Have students study each of the key terms in the Section Preview. Call on volunteers to explain the key terms in their own words. **LEP**

Use the **Vocabulary PuzzleMaker** to create crossword and word search puzzles.

Classroom Resources for SECTION 2

- Reproducible Lesson Plan 19-2
- Guided Reading Activity 19-2
- Reinforcing Economic Skill 19
- Section Quiz 19-2
- Spanish Section Quiz 19-2

- Focus Activity Transparency 99
- NBR's Economics in Action Video Program
- Testmaker
- Vocabulary PuzzleMaker
- Chapter Challenger Interactive Review Software

TEACH

Guided Practice

L2 Understanding Ideas
Organize students into three groups and assign each group one of the section's main headings—The Economy Under Lenin and Stalin, The Soviet Economy after Stalin, and The Collapse of the Soviet Economy. Have group members identify the most important ideas in their assigned topics. Then have groups team-teach the important ideas to the rest of the class. **LEP**

GLENCOE
TECHNOLOGY

NIGHTLY
BUSINESS
REPORT
Economics in Action

Chapter 26
Disc 2, Side 2

Title: *Comparative Economic Systems*

Subject: Karl Marx as founder of modern socialism and communism

Ask: How did Marx view history? *(as a struggle between workers and bosses)*

  Also available in VHS.

VISUAL INSTRUCTION

Ask: Who fared well under the NEP? *(kulaks, or prosperous peasants)*

Answer to Caption:
capitalist methods

Lenin *In November 1917, Bolshevik party leader Lenin seized control of the Russian government.* **What did Lenin's NEP reintroduce?**

To accomplish this goal, he canceled the NEP and, in 1928, introduced the government's first **Five-Year Plan**—a comprehensive, centralized economic plan designed to achieve rapid industrialization. The plan announced quotas for all industries to fulfill. By 1933, industry was to increase its output 250 percent and agriculture its output 150 percent. **1**

Collective Agriculture

Under Stalin's leadership, the process of **collectivization**—the forced common ownership of all agricultural, industrial, and trading enterprises—began. Not surprisingly, many people who prospered under the NEP opposed the reforms. Peasants even destroyed their livestock and sabotaged their equipment rather than turn their property over to the collective farms.

Stalin's retaliation was brutal. Millions of people were killed or imprisoned. Ukrainian grain stores were seized in the winter of 1932, causing the starvation

of more than 5 million peasants. The suffering in the cities was nearly as harsh. Workers were forced into employment in heavy industry, strikes were forbidden, and the standard of living deteriorated drastically. ☑

Transformation to Industry

Industry fared better than agriculture. Industry grew so fast that many new factories stood idle. New workers could not be trained quickly enough, and unskilled labor ruined much of the usable factory equipment.

Although the first Five-Year Plan did not achieve all of its goals, the government continued with more planning. The second plan proved more successful than the first. World War II interrupted the third plan, and the fourth was devoted largely to rebuilding those industries destroyed during the war. The plans that followed concentrated heavily on defense industries, space exploration, and some consumer goods.

The Soviet Economy After Stalin

Stalin's brutal regime ended in 1953. By then the Soviet economy had successfully completed its transition from a backward agrarian economy to a major industrial power. The Soviet government and its comprehensive system of planning dominated the Soviet economy, but the real force was the ruling Communist party. It decided on economic policy, did the actual planning, and put the plans into effect.

Complexities of Central Planning

In the Soviet economy, the central planning authority, or **Gosplan**, devised the Five-Year Plans and broke them down into one-year periods for implementation. As the Soviet economy grew, this process became increasingly complex.

Consider the difficulties in a single industry such as shoes. First, the planners have to decide how many shoes should be produced in any given year. This amount would depend on the population and the number of pairs that each person, on average, would need. The planners would then have to decide how many pairs to make of each style, including colors, sizes, and widths.

Meeting Special Needs

Reading Strategy On an outline map of the world, have students locate the countries and places mentioned in Chapter 19 as they are introduced.

Next, the various sizes, grades, and amounts of leather, dye, metal eyelets, thread, glue, and other materials needed to produce the shoes must be estimated. After the central planners developed this data, individual factories were given monthly and annual quotas. A factory that produced thread would be told how much thread of every diameter and color to produce for use in other industries.

Similar decisions had to be made for all industries, including clothing, farm implements, stationery, and military goods. The planners detailed everything that would be needed in the economy right down to nails and paper clips. Even these minor items required the planners to make estimates of iron ore, coal, coke, blast furnaces, mining equipment, and even trains and ore cars.

To ensure the growth of the economy from one year to the next, all the planners had to do—or so they thought—was to increase the quotas given to the factories. In short, the central planners determined almost everything beforehand. Plant managers and workers had almost no say in how things were to be done. 2

Agriculture

The situation was similar in agriculture, where food was raised on state, collective, and peasant farms. The state owned and operated the **state farms**. Workers on the state farms were paid for the number of items they produced. All output was turned over to the government at set prices.

Peasant families worked **collective farms**, or small farms collected into a single unit for joint operation. The land, buildings, tools, livestock, and machines belonged to the government, which bought a certain amount of produce per acre. Peasant families were allowed to keep their homes and household goods, a few cattle, and a small plot of land for themselves.

The agricultural sector was one of the major problems for the Soviet economy. One reason was that many of the planners were political appointees who did not understand the industry they supervised. Alexander Solzhenitsyn, Soviet dissident and author of *The Gulag Archipelago*, recounted the story of one bureaucrat who ordered that the crops be planted by broadcasting the seed on top of the late spring snows. The theory was that the snow would melt and nourish the seed at the same time. Instead, birds ate some of the grain. The rest mildewed. When the snows melted, the provinces were out of seed and the ensuing crop was a disaster.

Despite its efforts, the government was not able to make agriculture as efficient as that of many capitalist countries. In the mid-1980s, before the collapse of the Soviet Union, nearly 25 percent of the workforce was in agriculture. In the United States at the time, only 3 percent of the workforce was in agriculture.

The Collapse of the Soviet Economy

The Soviet Union made considerable progress with industrialization, but it never caught up to the United States. Despite its larger population and land area, the Soviet Union's GNP never exceeded two-thirds of that of the United States. The Soviet Union lagged much further behind when measuring such items as automobiles, telephones, televisions, and other consumer goods. A number of factors that could not be overcome eventually led to the collapse of the Soviet economy.

Lack of Effective Incentives

To offset low morale in the factories, a number of incentive programs were attempted. One involved

Checking Understanding	**Applying Economic Concepts**
1. What was the purpose of the Five-Year Plan? 2. What did planners think they had to do to ensure economic growth?	**Communism** Stalin established one of the most brutal dictatorships in history. He demanded complete obedience and used terror to achieve it. People accused of disloyalty were either shot or sent to labor camps in Siberia.

CHAPTER 19: *Comparative Economic Systems* **479**

Independent Practice

Guided Reading Assign Guided Reading Activity for Section 2. **LEP**

L2 *Time Line* Have students research and construct an annotated time line of the Soviet Union's economic policies from 1917 to its collapse. Have them incorporate Lenin's policies, various five-year plans of Lenin's successors, and Gorbachev's efforts at reform under perestroika. Call on students to display and discuss their time lines.

ANSWERS

1. to transform the Soviet economy from an agricultural one to an industrial one
2. to increase the quotas given to factories

CURRICULUM CONNECTIONS

Language Arts The term *bolshevik* comes from the Russian word meaning "greater." The Bolsheviks were the majority—and more radical—faction of the Russian Social Democratic party.

$ Free Enterprise Activity $

Ask students to prepare an outline for a five-year plan for their own lives. Point out that they should address not only where they want to be and what they want to be doing five years from now, but also how they are going to get there. For example, how are they going to get the education and training necessary for the job they choose? Call on volunteers to share their plans. Then have students discuss what problems they faced in drawing up their plans. Conclude by having students compare their problems with those that would face a nation preparing a five-year plan.

ASSESS

Check for Understanding

Assign Section 2 Review as homework or an in-class activity.

🖥 Use **Chapter Challenger Interactive Review Software** to review Section 2.

> **MEETING LESSON OBJECTIVES**
>
> Each objective below is tested by the questions that follow it in parentheses.
>
> 1. **Explain** the rise of the Soviet economy under Lenin and Stalin. **(2)**
> 2. **Describe** the complexities of a centrally planned economy. **(1, 3, 4)**
> 3. **Understand** the forces that brought about the collapse of communism as an economic system. **(4, 5, 6)**

Evaluate

📁 📁 🖥 Assign the Section 2 Quiz in the TCR or use the *Economics: Principles and Practices* Testmaker. Spanish Section Quizzes also are available.

LINKING PAST AND PRESENT

A number of former Czechoslovakian government officials ruefully noted that the reforms under perestroika were similar to those they attempted in the "Prague Spring" of 1968. Back then, however, the Soviet authorities declared such actions as "anticommunist" and sent in tanks to bring them to a halt.

480

---

the use of **piecework**, meaning that workers are paid for each piece of output they produce rather than for the number of hours they work.

Although this system may seem like a good idea, piecework quotas often were set at unrealistically high levels. This led to **storming**, where workers kept a slow pace until the last week of the month, and then sped up just enough to fill the quota. The rush at the end often affected the quality of the products. Because of storming, knowledgeable Soviet shoppers often avoided buying goods made at the end of the month.

Other incentives included patriotic and emotional appeals. Workers who had outstanding records or did something special were awarded hero medals, such as the Order of Lenin and the Hero of Social Labor. Some of these medals brought rewards such as free public housing or vacations.

Yet another approach to incentives was a wage system based on job performance, with skilled and more productive workers receiving higher pay. While this incentive is used extensively in capitalist societies, however, it was never used widely in the former Soviet economy.

Production Quotas

As with incentives, quotas also failed at the factory level. During the 1950s, the Soviet economy had a reputation for producing some of the world's poorest consumer and industrial goods. Shoe factories, for example, were given quotas in terms of millions of pairs of shoes. Because small shoes could be made fastest, more were made than were needed. When the quotas were changed to measure production in the amount of shoe leather consumed, the result was shoes with some of the thickest soles in the world.

Production of Consumer Goods

Another major problem was the inadequate supply of consumer goods. After World War II, the Soviet people were asked to make sacrifices so their children might have a better life. Many willingly did so.

In the 1970s and 1980s, those children were adults. When they were asked to make sacrifices so their children could have a better life, they were not as willing as their parents had been. The new generation had not suffered from the ravages of war. In addition, they

---

were more aware of the standards of living in other parts of the world. As a result, they were impatient for more consumer goods.

Perestroika

When Mikhail Gorbachev assumed power in 1985, the Soviet economy was weaker than anyone imagined. The main cause was the burden imposed by centralized planning. The economy had become too complex and too large to be managed in the traditional manner.

Plant managers were under increasing pressure to meet or exceed quotas. Glitches in planning, however, were creating shortages and other problems that made life difficult for the plant managers. To facilitate the process, "fixers" called *tolkachi* were employed to resolve shortages or dispose of excess inventories. The tolkachi soon became indispensable to producers who wanted to fulfill their quotas. At the same time, they also caused problems for other plants whenever they rerouted a shipment or otherwise interrupted the master plan of the central planners.

Accordingly, Gorbachev introduced a policy of **perestroika**, the fundamental restructuring of the

---

Extending the Content

Collectivism The common ownership of the means of production emphasizes the superiority of the group and the state at the expense of the individual. Individualism in any form was not only discouraged, but denounced as being against the state. In addition, the ideology of collectivism reinforced an uncritical acceptance of and allegiance to the power of the state. This, in turn, resulted in acceptance of economic decisions made by the central authorities, even when these decisions meant a denial of individual needs and wants.

Perestroika Mikhail Gorbachev did more than any other person to end the cold war and lift the iron curtain from Europe. He was unsuccessful, however, in saving the former Soviet Union's faltering economy. Here, Gorbachev is shown at the New York Stock Exchange. **What was perestroika?**

Reteach

Have students outline the section using the following framework:
 I. The Economy Under Lenin and Stalin
 II. The Soviet Economy After Stalin
 III. The Collapse of the Soviet Economy

Enrich

Have students write a biographical sketch of Lenin, Stalin, or Gorbachev that focuses on his economic policies. Call on students to read their sketches to the class.

CLOSE

Have students identify what they feel was the major factor in the collapse of the Soviet economy. Call on volunteers to explain their answers.

economy and government. Under the restructuring, Five-Year Plans were retained, but the various ministries of production were to be converted to efficient, state-owned enterprises that would compete in a market economy. Plant managers were given more freedom to buy and sell in pursuit of profits, and small business was encouraged.

Perestroika represented a halfway point between a market economy and centralized planning. Gorbachev, however, did not remain in power long enough to see his plans realized. Whether perestroika would have worked is a matter of conjecture. Those in industry who opposed Gorbachev's reforms allowed shortages and other problems to persist, and then used these problems as proof that the reforms were failing. Gorbachev's successor, Boris Yeltsin, faced similar opposition. Ultimately, the collapse of the economy, the collapse of the political leadership, and the stresses of ethnic diversity and unrest combined to cause the downfall of the Soviet Union.

SECTION 2 REVIEW

Reviewing Terms and Facts

1. **Define** Five-Year Plan, collectivization, Gosplan, state farm, collective farm, piecework, storming, perestroika.
2. **Explain** why Stalin wanted forced industrialization.
3. **Identify** several complexities of central planning.
4. **Describe** how central planning contributed to the breakdown of the Soviet economy.

Critical Thinking

5. **Making Predictions** Based upon recent changes, is the former Soviet Union moving toward capitalism or away from capitalism? Give evidence to support your conclusions.

Applying Economic Concepts

6. **Perestroika** Since the mid-1980s, the former Soviet Union has undergone tremendous changes, some of which led to hyperinflation. Why would this hyperinflation hinder the movement toward capitalism?

VISUAL INSTRUCTION

Ask students to explain how perestroika changed the Soviet economy. *(Central planning was retained in the form of five-year plans, but elements of market economy were introduced in state-owned businesses, and small business was encouraged.)*

Answer to Caption:

the fundamental restructuring of the Soviet economy and government

CHAPTER 19: *Comparative Economic Systems* **481**

Answers to SECTION 2 REVIEW

1. All vocabulary words are defined in the Glossary.

2. Stalin feared war with western democracies.

3. Planners had to decide how much of a given product would be made in a year. Then they had to decide on sizes, color, and so on. They also had to anticipate all of the inputs that would be needed, again deciding on kinds, colors, and so on. The planners then set monthly and yearly quotas for each individual factory.

4. Central planning on such a massive scale was too complex to be effective. Poor decisions by planners compounded problems.

5. Answers will vary. Students should cite specific changes to support their conclusions.

6. Hyperinflation makes money worthless. The economy reverts to barter, making exchange and other market activities difficult.

Sometimes data is easier to understand by viewing a chart or graph than by looking just at numbers. Spreadsheet programs allow you to create charts and graphs from data in a spreadsheet. A graph may use bars, lines, or other pictures to show the relationships among the values in the spreadsheet. Have students practice creating and editing bar, line, and pie graphs. Make sure they remember to add a title and a legend to the graph, explaining how the colors or lines correspond to the data in the spreadsheet.

Skills Practice For additional practice, have students complete Reinforcing Economic Skill 19.

TECHNOLOGY SKILL

Using a Spreadsheet

People use electronic spreadsheets to manage numbers quickly and easily. Formulas may be used to add, subtract, multiply, and divide the numbers in the spreadsheet. If you make a change to one number, the totals are recalculated automatically for you. The computer will even change your spreadsheet numbers into a graph.

Explanation

A spreadsheet is an electronic worksheet. All spreadsheets follow a basic design of rows and columns. Columns, arranged vertically, are assigned letters—A, B, C, AA, BB, CC, and so on. Rows, arranged horizontally, are assigned numbers—1, 2, 3, and so on. The point where a column and row intersect is called a *cell*. The cell's position on the spreadsheet is labeled according to its corresponding column and row—the cell at the intersection of Column A and Row 1 is labeled A1, for example.

To reach a specific cell, use the cursor keys or a mouse. The computer will indicate which cell you are in by placing a boldface border around it or by highlighting it. The contents of the cell will also appear on a line at the top or on the bottom of the screen, called a *status line* or *formula line*.

Spreadsheets use *standard formulas* to calculate numbers that are in various cells. You create a simple mathematical equation that uses these standard formulas. To create a formula, you begin by selecting the cell where you want to display the formula results. Type an equal sign (=) and then build the formula, step by step. For example, the formula $=B2+B3$ adds the values in cells B2 and B3. The formula $=A5/C2$ divides the value in cell C2 into the value in cell A5. An asterisk (*) signifies multiplication: $=(B2*C3)+D1$ means you want to multiply the value in cell B2 times C3, then add the value in cell D1. Because adding is the most common function of spreadsheets, most have an *AutoSum* key (Σ) that you can click on to place a sum in a highlighted cell.

Practice

1. Open a new spreadsheet file.
2. Type the information in columns A through D as shown below.
3. Type the following formula in cell B9 to calculate total gold medals won by the four countries listed: $=B5+B6+B7+B8$. Observe the formula in the status line before you press *Enter*.
4. In cell E5, use the *AutoSum* function (Σ) to calculate total medals won by the U.S.
5. Click and drag this formula to cells E6 through E8 to find the other nations' sums.
6. Print your results and share them with the class.

	A	B	C	D	E
1	Final Medal Standings				
2	1996 Summer Olympic Games				
3					
4	Nation	Gold	Silver	Bronze	
5	U.S.	44	32	25	
6	Russia	26	21	16	
7	Germany	20	18	27	
8	China	16	22	12	
9					

D3 ▼ =

Additional Practice

For further practice in using a spreadsheet, complete the Reinforcing Skills exercise in the Chapter 19 Review on page 495.

Answers to SKILL

Have students practice inserting new data into a spreadsheet and creating bar and line graphs from this information.

The Transition to Capitalism

Section Preview

Objectives

After studying this section, you will be able to:

1. **List** four problems encountered when an economy makes the transition to capitalism.

2. **Recognize** the major countries and regions that are making the transition to capitalism.

Key Terms

privatization, Solidarity, black market, Great Leap Forward

Applying Economic Concepts

Inflation Have you ever noticed that the prices of goods and services keep rising? Under capitalism, supply and demand interact to set prices, and moderate *inflation* is to be expected. In eastern Europe and the former Soviet Union, however, the move from a command economy to a market economy has resulted in hyper-inflation.

Historically, communism and capitalism have been viewed as two opposing political and economic structures. The collapse of communism, however, does not mean that the transition to capitalism will be smooth, or that it will be made at all. An examination of the problems will show why.

Problems of Transition

An economy will face several major problems when and if it makes the transition to capitalism. These problems are discussed below.

Privatization

The primary feature of capitalism is private property—especially capital, which is sometimes referred to as the means of production. Because most communist governments owned the means of production, a way had to be found to convert state-owned factories to private ownership, a process known as **privatization.**

In Poland, Hungary, and the Czech Republic, this transition was accomplished using vouchers. Vouchers were certificates either given to people or sold at very low prices, depending on the country. As the vouchers were distributed, the government drew up a list of companies to be privatized and then orga-

nized as a corporation. The corporate shares were auctioned, and people would bid for the shares using their vouchers for payment. As people exchanged their vouchers for shares, ownership of the previously state-owned enterprises transferred to private hands.

In other cases, the transition governments simply sold state-owned companies to foreign corporations. The government then used the funds to pay other bills or make other purchases. These transactions bypassed the citizens and transferred ownership to foreign investors.

Loss of Political Power

Under communism, the Communist party was the ruling class. The transition to capitalism stripped this group of its political power and transferred this power to the new class of entrepreneurs and capitalists.

In countries where the Communists were literally thrown out—as in Poland, Czechoslovakia, and Hungary—the Communist leaders lost their power before industry was privatized. In these countries, the voucher system worked reasonably well.

In other countries, former Communist leaders grabbed a large share of vouchers, and thus a large portion of ownership in many privatized companies. In the most blatant cases, some of which occurred in

CHAPTER 19: *Comparative Economic Systems* **483**

At midnight on November 9, 1989, East German officials opened the infamous Berlin Wall that divided East and West Berlin for 28 years. **What problems face former communist countries as they make the transition to capitalism?**

Russia following the collapse of the Soviet Union, the ownership of companies was simply transferred to politicians who were influential during the transition period. Former political leaders converted their political power to economic power in the form of resource ownership.

The Discipline of Capitalism

Many countries that desire a capitalist structure have focused on the benefits to be obtained, but not the costs. The costs can hinder or even discourage a country from making the transition.

The disadvantages of capitalism, made apparent during the Great Depression, included instability, unemployment, and social unrest. At that time, the United States did not have the fiscal policies, the automatic stabilizers, and the social welfare nets needed to lessen the devastation of the Depression. Now that such assistance exists, most economists agree that another Great Depression will never occur in the United States. **1**

The same cannot be said for the nations in transition. They have not yet developed the automatic stabilizers and the social welfare nets that cushion the instabilities of capitalism. During the transition phase, nations will most likely experience the instabilities of early capitalism—the unemployment, the inflation, and the lost production—long before they experience the benefits. ✓

Responding to New Incentives

Finally, countries that make the transition to capitalism have to learn to live with a whole new set of incentives. The government in the former Soviet Union, for example, told its people what to do for decades. Now people must learn how to make decisions on their own. They must learn how to take the initiative, how to interpret prices, and how to fend for themselves because the government no longer guarantees their jobs nor keeps prices artificially low.

These adjustments will be enormous, perhaps even prohibitive, for some people. Many will even long for the past when life was simpler. These people may not want to go through the discipline of capitalism. Attitudes like these will be a major obstacle to the transition.

Countries and Regions in Transition

Despite the transitional problems, the rise of capitalism is one of the most remarkable phenomena of the late twentieth century. Today, nations and regions all over the globe are making the transition.

Russia

Privatization in Russia is well underway, despite the continued resistance of hard-liners. Some privatization took place under Gorbachev, but President Boris Yeltsin accelerated the process when he signed a 1992 decree requiring that state-owned enterprises be converted to privately-owned ones.

Many conversions took place when the government printed and distributed vouchers to the people. The people then used the vouchers to purchase shares of stock in the newly converted companies.

Smaller businesses were also being privatized at a rapid rate. Soon more than half of the restaurants and shops in the major cities were in private hands.

Eventually Russia opened a stock market so that individuals could buy and sell shares of stock. The widespread ownership of the means of production by individuals is now a reality in a country that once preached about the evils of private ownership.

Eastern Europe

The nations of eastern Europe, especially those that were unwilling members of the Soviet bloc, are the newest nations to embrace capitalism. The struggle for freedom began in Poland with **Solidarity**, the independent and sometimes illegal union that Lech Walesa established in 1980. Solidarity was influential in securing a number of political freedoms in Poland.

Figure 19.2
New and Emerging Stock Markets

Country	Number of Listed Companies	Country	Number of Listed Companies
Argentina	147	Morocco	47
Brazil	551	Nigeria	183
Chile	291	Pakistan	782
China	540	Peru	231
Colombia	189	Philippines	216
Egypt	646	Poland	83
Greece	224	Portugal	158
Honduras	111	Russia	73
Hungary	45	South Korea	760
India	8,800	Sri Lanka	235
Indonesia	253	Taiwan	382
Israel	655	Thailand	454
Jamaica	46	Turkey	229
Malaysia	621	Venezuela	88
Mexico	193	Zimbabwe	64

New and emerging stock markets are now found all over the world, and more are still to come. **Why is the corporate form of organization a necessary component of capitalism?**

Source: *Emerging Stock Markets Factbook*, 1997.

Checking Understanding

1. What safeguards ensure that the United States will never again face an economic downturn as severe as the Great Depression?

Applying Economic Concepts

 Market Failures Russia has gone through tough economic times since the collapse of communism. Soaring unemployment and inflation have led some Russians to wish for a return to Soviet rule. Most Russians, however, accept that the transition to capitalism will be difficult.

CHAPTER 19: *Comparative Economic Systems* **485**

Display Economic Concepts Transparency 22 on the overhead projector and use the guidelines given in Teaching Strategy 22. Assign Student Activity 22. Spanish Transparencies also are available in the Spanish Resources Binder.

Independent Practice

Guided Reading Assign Guided Reading Activity for Section 3. **LEP**

L3 Analyzing Ideas
Encourage students to research current news reports about the economies of the countries discussed in the section. Have students use this information to speculate which of these countries will be most successful in the transition to capitalism. Call on volunteers to present and justify their speculations.

 VISUAL INSTRUCTION

Have students check business newspapers and periodicals to find out the latest developments on emerging stock markets.

Answer to Caption:

In free enterprise economies, corporations are responsible for most of the business activity.

ANSWERS

1. fiscal policies, automatic stabilizers, social welfare nets

$ Free Enterprise Activity $

Review with students the four problems associated with the transition to capitalism. Then organize students into several groups. Have group members use their knowledge of the American economic system to brainstorm ways that these problems might be overcome. Direct groups to use these ideas to write an editorial on how this transition might be made successfully. Call on group representatives to read their editorials to the class.

ASSESS

Check for Understanding

Assign Section 3 Review as homework or an in-class activity.

 Use **Chapter Challenger Interactive Review Software** to review Section 3.

MEETING LESSON OBJECTIVES

Each objective below is tested by the questions that follow it in parentheses.

1. **List** four problems encountered when an economy makes the transition to capitalism. **(1, 2, 4, 5)**

2. **Recognize** the major countries and regions that are making the transition to capitalism. **(3)**

◉ VISUAL INSTRUCTION

Point out that, today, most Chinese farmers have government contracts to produce a set amount of crops. Any surplus they have after fulfilling their contracts may be sold at "free markets."

Answer to Caption:

some private business is allowed, managers of state-owned businesses have more authority to make decisions, some incentives offered to promote worker productivity

---

Communes *Although China has recently begun to experiment with capitalism, many communes still harvest crops, such as this one in Shaanxi Province.* **How has capitalism affected business in China?**

Eventually, the Communist party lost power, and interest in capitalism grew. Political reform slowed privatization plans at first, but capitalism finally appeared to be under way again in the wake of progress by Poland's neighbors.

Hungary is another country well on the way to capitalism. Hungary was often regarded as the most Western of the Eastern bloc countries, and it often had a flourishing **black market**—a market in which entrepreneurs and merchants sold goods illegally. Hungary's experience with markets helped ease the transition to capitalism.

The Czech Republic is yet another country in transition. By early 1998, more than 60 percent of the economy was in private hands. Progress accelerated after the separation of the Czech and Slovak Republics, a separation based in part on the Slovakian concern about adopting the capitalist ways of the West. The Czechs, who were strongly influenced by the economic success of the former West Germany, are now more able to pursue reforms.

The Baltic states of Estonia, Latvia, and Lithuania are also making great strides toward capitalism. Latvia and Lithuania have their own stock markets to help facilitate the transition. Estonia has made so much progress that it—along with the Czech Republic, Hungary, and Poland—will be considered for membership in the European Union between 2002 and 2006.

486 UNIT 5: *International and Global Economics*

Latin America

In the past, many Latin American countries followed a path of economic development that combined socialism and isolationism based on the infant industries argument. Mexico accelerated the move to capitalism and open markets in 1989, as it made plans to restructure its economy for the North American Free Trade Agreement (NAFTA). Under President Salinas de Gortari, the government sold thousands of state-owned companies and cut back on the government bureaucracy.

Chile has also taken major steps to foster the growth of capitalism. It has privatized airlines, telephone services, and utilities. Chile even used the billions deposited in its pension funds to supply capital for new entrepreneurs. As a result, the country exports copper, lumber, fruit, and even software to the rest of the world. Chile's markets include the United States, which imports millions of Popsicle sticks, and Japan, which imports chopsticks.

Argentina has similarly embarked on a crash program to remove government from the everyday business of running the economy. The country has sold oil fields, petrochemical plants, and a number of other formerly state-owned businesses. The Argentinian army was even moved out of barracks in Buenos Aires so that the real estate could be sold to private interests.

Cultural Diversity and Economics

Income Distribution in China One of the basic communist economic principles is income egalitarianism—that is, there should be little difference among people's incomes, regardless of their jobs. As Chinese leaders introduced elements of capitalism into their economy, however, they realized that this principle did not fit in with the free enterprise concepts of competition and incentives. Therefore, in late 1993, they announced that they would abandon egalitarianism in favor of "the principle of more pay for more work and [a widening in] the income gap." They did not, however, endorse rampant individualism. The new wealthy class, they continued, "should be encouraged to lead forward and support those lagging behind."

China

The People's Republic of China became a communist economy in 1949. That year, the Chinese Communists, under the leadership of Mao Zedong, gained control of the country. Over the years, China modeled itself after the Soviet Union, adopting a series of Five-Year Plans to manage its growth.

In 1958 the **Great Leap Forward**—the second Five-Year Plan—tried to institute a system of pure communism and an industrial and agricultural revolution almost overnight. Industrialization was pushed and, at the same time, collectivization of agriculture was intensified. Farmers were forced off their land and made to live and work on large, state-owned farms. The Great Leap Forward turned out to be a disaster, however. The agricultural experiment failed, and the economy never came close to achieving the planned degree of industrialization. Even the gains made during the first Five-Year Plan were lost.

Other plans followed, but by the late 1970s, the government decided that the country no longer could follow the growth models of either the Soviet Union or other command-type economies. China and its population were too large for large-scale centralized planning. Industrializing the cities enough to provide jobs for nearly one-fourth of the world's population would be nearly impossible.

By the early 1980s, the influence of other successful market economies in Asia—Taiwan, South Korea, Hong Kong, and Singapore—was too much for China to ignore. One of China's provinces, the Guangdong Province just north of Hong Kong, copied many of the free market practices of the region and was even allowed to officially experiment with capitalism. At one time Guangdong was an embarrassment to the official communist dogma, but it was later touted as a role model for the rest of the nation.

China was also influenced by the eventual reunification with Hong Kong, which took place in 1997. The city of Shanghai, in particular, embarked on a program of reforms and expansion in an attempt to become China's "first city" after the reunification.

Today China is no longer experimenting with capitalism. It is instead privatizing industries, introducing market reforms, and otherwise acting in a decidedly capitalistic manner. China still has a long way to go, and the government still directs most major economic activity. Its economy has evolved, however, into what President Jiang Zemin called "socialism with Chinese characteristics," loosely translated as free market capitalism.

SECTION 3 REVIEW

Reviewing Terms and Facts

1. **Define** privatization, Solidarity, black market, Great Leap Forward.
2. **List** four problems a country is likely to encounter when converting to capitalism.
3. **Identify** two major countries that are making the transition to capitalism.

Critical Thinking

4. **Formulating Questions** Suppose you are visiting one nation in eastern Europe adopting a market economy. What questions would you ask local officials to determine whether they are successfully moving toward capitalism?

Applying Economic Concepts

5. **Inflation** Assume that your salary is 300 rubles per month. The government-controlled price of bread is 5 rubles, and you buy 5 loaves each month. What percentage of your income do you spend on bread? After the government deregulates prices, bread costs 15 rubles. What percentage of your income goes to buy bread? How does the inflation affect your standard of living?

CHAPTER 19: *Comparative Economic Systems* **487**

CHAPTER 19
SECTION 3

Evaluate

Assign the Section 3 Quiz in the TCR or use the *Economics: Principles and Practices* Testmaker to create a customized quiz. Spanish Section Quizzes also are available in the Spanish Resources Binder.

Reteach

Have students write 10 questions on the section's content. Collect the questions and use them to check students' understanding of the section.

Enrich

Have students write a letter to a pen pal in a former communist country explaining how capitalism works, using the American economy as an example.

CLOSE

Have students discuss the following: What is the greatest challenge facing nations making the transition to capitalism? Why?

? DID YOU KNOW

China has one of the fastest-growing economies in the world. The World Bank estimates that from 1980, China's real GDP growth was three times higher than that of the U.S. At this rate China's economy will overtake the U.S. by the year 2010.

Answers to SECTION 3 REVIEW

1. All vocabulary words are defined in the Glossary.
2. privatization, loss of political power, discipline of capitalism, responding to new incentives
3. Answers may vary. Students may choose any two of the following: Russia, Poland, Hungary, the Czech Republic, Mexico, Chile, Argentina, China.
4. Questions will vary but should make reference to elements of capitalism, such as who owns the factors of production, how prices are established, how capital is obtained for production, and what role government plays in the economy.
5. 8.3% or $(5 \times 5) \div 300$; 25% or $(5 \times 15) \div 300$; Inflation lowers the standard of living because the same amount of money cannot buy as much as before.

487

FOCUS

Section Objectives

1. Explain the factors that encouraged economic growth in Japan.

2. Rank the "Asian Tigers" according to per capita GNP.

3. Describe Sweden's retreat from socialism.

Bellringer

Prior to taking roll at the beginning of the class period, display Focus Activity Transparency 100 on the overhead projector and assign the accompanying Student Activity 100.

Motivational Activity

Discuss students' responses to the activity sheet that accompanies Focus Activity Transparency 100.

Preteaching Vocabulary

Ask students to use the terms *capital-intensive* and *keiretsu* in a paragraph describing the Japanese economy. **LEP**

Use the **Vocabulary PuzzleMaker** to create crossword and word search puzzles.

Section Preview

Objectives

After studying this section, you will be able to:

1. **Explain** the factors that encouraged economic growth in Japan.

2. **Rank** the "Asian Tigers" according to per capita GNP.

3. **Describe** Sweden's retreat from socialism.

Key Terms

capital-intensive, *keiretsu*

Applying Economic Concepts

Economic Growth Have you ever looked at the labels inside your clothes? If so, you may have noticed that many of them were made in Korea, Taiwan, China, or Hong Kong. Asian economies have experienced explosive *economic growth* recently. They now compete directly with American enterprises.

Capitalism is a force that is sweeping the world. It is also a force that has many different faces. The common element of capitalism is that the factors of production are privately owned and controlled, but there are many variations on this theme.

Japan

Japan, like the United States, has a capitalist economy. Unlike the United States, however, Japan's government is very involved in the day-to-day activities of the private sector.

At the end of World War II, Japan was a devastated country. Today, it is the second largest industrial nation in the world, with a GNP about 70 percent of that of the United States. Between 1985 and 1995, Japan's growth of real per capita output averaged an impressive 2.9 percent annually.

Worker Attitudes

One of the reasons for Japan's success is the workers' intense loyalty to their employers. Many workers join large companies for life. In return, the company supplies such benefits as wedding halls where marriages can be performed, schools, and vacation resorts.

Japanese workers take great pride in the quality of their work. A company's entire workforce often arrives early to take part in group calisthenics and meditation exercises. Workers often sing company songs to boost their spirits. If a worker is behind in a task, others who can help do so. Those who cannot help stay at their stations and clean their work areas, arrange their tools, and prepare for the next day. No one leaves the work floor or goes home until every worker's tasks have been completed. ☑

Capital Investment

Another reason for Japan's success is the ability and willingness of the Japanese to develop new technology. Because of their relatively small population, they have worked to boost productivity by developing industries that are **capital-intensive**. In such industries, a large amount of capital is used for every person employed in manufacturing. Today, the Japanese are recognized as the world leader in the area of industrial robots. As a result, most factories require only a fraction of the workers that similar factories in other countries need. **1**

Most large Japanese firms also belong to a *keiretsu* (ky • reht • soo)—a tightly knit group of firms governed by an external board of directors. The *keiretsu* are often made up of firms that compete with one another. The role of the governing board is to ensure that competition does not get so fierce that individual firms are threatened. A similar agreement in the United States among competing firms would be illegal under our antitrust laws.

488 UNIT 5: *International and Global Economics*

Classroom Resources for SECTION 4

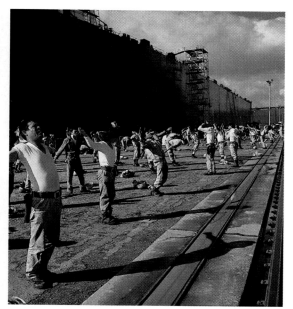

Worker Attitudes *Japan's economic success is a result in part of its workers' loyalty and pride in their products.* **What other factors have contributed to Japan's success?**

The Role of Government

Japan has a relatively small public sector. The government has only a modest military capability and is not burdened with welfare spending. As a result, taxes are low, which allows individuals to save their money or spend it on consumer goods.

The Japanese government works closely with businesses to limit foreign competition in the domestic market. The government provides fewer public goods than do most other capitalist societies, but the government is also more closely allied with businesses than in other countries.

A Closed Economy?

Although the Japanese have been successful, their economy is generally closed to the products of foreign producers. When foreign companies tried to sell their goods in Japan, many encountered numerous obstacles ranging from delayed government permission to huge amounts of paperwork.

Delays in getting permission to sell are so common that many businesses have been completely discouraged from exporting to Japan. Some companies found that, while they were waiting for permission, Japanese companies introduced and sold products similar to theirs. Actions such as these have led to accusations that Japan uses discriminatory policies toward foreign-made products.

Until recently, Japan was even reluctant to import rice, a food staple, in order to protect domestic rice producers. As a result, the cost of rice to the Japanese consumer is several times higher than it would be if Japan imported rice from the world markets.

A High Cost of Living

Protectionism in Japan may help certain segments of the economy such as the rice farmers, but it does not help the consumer. Because foreign competitors supply so few goods, products generally are high-priced. Citrus fruits cost about six times more in Japan than they do in the United States. Clothing costs two to three times as much, and even cameras and electronics cost more in Japan than elsewhere. 2

For years, the Japanese have been making electronic consumer goods and selling them abroad. Recently, Japanese citizens discovered they can purchase their own goods cheaper in Hawaii than they can in their own country. As a result, Japanese cameras, radios, and other electronic equipment are

Checking Understanding	**Applying Economic Concepts**
1. What is a capital-intensive industry? 2. How has protectionism harmed Japanese consumers?	**Worker Attitudes** Some Japanese employers are making efforts to reduce their employees' work hours. Some firms have to halt elevators or shut off the air-conditioning to make sure that employees stick to their official hours.

CHAPTER 19: *Comparative Economic Systems* **489**

CHAPTER 19
SECTION 4

TEACH

Guided Practice

L2 Making Comparisons On the chalkboard, list the six countries discussed in Section 4. Call on volunteers to identify the major characteristics of these countries' economies. Note their responses next to the appropriate country name. Then have students use the information on the chalkboard to write a comparative essay on the economies of Japan, the Asian Tigers, and Sweden.

 VISUAL INSTRUCTION

Have students who want to learn more about Japanese managerial practices read William G. Ouchi's *Theory Z* (Addison-Wesley, 1981).

Answer to Caption:
high level of capital investment, government assistance to business

ANSWERS

1. one in which a large amount of capital is used for every person employed in manufacturing
2. Products generally are higher-priced.

Meeting Special Needs

Reading Disability Many students who are not good readers are good at locating information in a text when their attention is directed to it. Without direction, they often cannot make distinctions between important facts and elaboration. The notes they take may be filled with nonessential informa-

tion. In the subsection "The Asian Tigers," main ideas are obvious but not always stated in the first sentence of the paragraph. Tell students to find one sentence in each paragraph that best states the main idea. Have them defend their choices.

GLENCOE
TECHNOLOGY

NIGHTLY
BUSINESS
R E P O R T

Economics in Action

Chapter 26
Disc 2, Side 2

Title: *Comparative
Economic Systems*

Subject: Hong Kong

Ask: How long was Hong
Kong a British colony?
(156 years)

Also available in VHS.

Independent Practice

Guided Reading Have
students complete Guided
Reading Activity for Section 4.
LEP

L3   Research Paper Have
students conduct research on
one of the countries discussed
in the section. Suggest that
students find information on
social, political, and economic
conditions in their selected
countries. Ask students to
present their findings in short
research papers.

DID YOU KNOW

Each of the four Asian
Tigers has opened textile
and garment plants in
Central America, taking
advantage of cheap labor
and more favorable U.S.
import quotas.

---

among the most popular souvenirs Japanese vaca-
tioners bring back from their trips abroad.

The current Japanese economy benefits the capitalists. The benefits of economic growth have not trick-
led down to the Japanese consumer the way they
have in other countries.

Reliance on Trade

If Japan wants its growth to continue, it must
actively engage in international trade. As an island
nation with few natural resources, it must import most
of its oil as well as a number of other critical materials.
The Japanese are expected to aggressively develop
their export markets so they can buy more imports.

Japan's huge trade imbalances with the rest of the
world, however, have driven up the value of Japanese
currency, the yen. When the value goes too high, the
Japanese economy will export fewer cars, cameras,
and other consumer products. At the same time, current Japanese policies are keeping low-cost rice, clothing, and other imports out of the country and away
from Japanese consumers.

DID YOU KNOW?

China in Charge   On July 1, 1997, China
took charge of Hong Kong, thereby ending
150 years of British rule. The countdown for
the transfer of Hong Kong began in 1984
when British Prime Minister Margaret Thatcher
and Chinese Premier Zhao Ziyang signed the
Sino-British Joint Declaration. The document
established the principle of "one country, two
systems" for Hong Kong, allowing Hong Kong
to keep its capitalist economy within the
socialist system of China for 50 years. At first,
the pending reunification caused hundreds of
thousands of people to leave Hong Kong for
Canada, Australia, and the United States.
Many have returned, however, with the belief
that Hong Kong will change China more than
China will change Hong Kong.

The Asian Tigers

Three other Asian countries—Singapore, Taiwan,
and South Korea—have made striking economic
progress during the last 30 years. The British colony of
Hong Kong also experienced explosive growth before
it was reunified with China. Collectively, the four are
called the "Asian Tigers." Each has based its growth on
capitalism, but each has taken a slightly different path.

Hong Kong

When Hong Kong was still a British colony, it was the
most progressive and successful of the four Asian Tigers.
Hong Kong has a population of about 6.2 million and
was recognized as perhaps the freest market economy in
the world, with virtually no government interference.

Entrepreneurs in Hong Kong developed a manu-
facturing-based economy that uses technology other
countries have already developed. Their major industrial products include textiles, clothing, electronic
games, telephones, radios, watches, electronic components, and toys.

Producers in Hong Kong are exceptionally efficient, and their manufacturing plants are among the
most flexible in the world. Companies that want to
bring products to the market as quickly as possible
often turn to Hong Kong because producers there can
turn a prototype into a finished assembly-line product faster than any other producer.

By the time of unification, Hong Kong's per capita
GNP was 85 percent of that in the United States, and
37 times that of China. China has promised not to
interfere with the markets in Hong Kong for a period
of 50 years, but the impact of unification is difficult to
predict. The impact will also be hard to measure
because economic statistics for Hong Kong will no
longer be reported separately, but will become part of
China's overall statistics.

Singapore

The second Asian Tiger is Singapore, with a per
capita GNP almost as large as Hong Kong's. The population in Singapore is approximately 3 million, and
the approach to economic growth is markedly different from the other Asian Tigers.

More than 1,000 multinationals have been attracted
to Singapore with the help of generous tax breaks,

$ Free Enterprise Activity $

Ask students to list the similarities and differences between the U.S. economic system and the
economic systems of the six countries discussed in
Section 4. Then have students write a paragraph
answering the following: What, in your opinion,
are the most essential characteristics of the U.S.

economic system? Do the six countries' economic
systems have these essential characteristics? Are
there any characteristics of these other countries'
economic systems that you think the U.S. should
adopt? Why or why not?

government subsidies, and government-sponsored training of employees. Unlike Hong Kong, Singapore has made a determined effort to develop its own technologies through extensive spending on research and development.

The government of Singapore is trying to develop a few select industries, including telecommunications services, software, and biotechnology. The government has spent millions on laboratories, attracting top scientists from all over the world. The biotechnology industry has scored some original successes, one of which includes the transfer of firefly genes—which glow in the dark—to orchids.

Taiwan

The Republic of China, also known as Taiwan, is an island about the size of West Virginia located off the coast of the People's Republic of China. Taiwan's population is about 21 million, and the per capita GNP is approximately one-third that of the United States.

Taiwan's economic development called for the Taiwanese government to intervene in various markets to direct the flow of resources. For example, the government would set artificially high rates on savings accounts to attract deposits from consumers. The savings would then be lent to targeted industries at artificially low rates to stimulate growth. The subsidies to both the savers and the borrowers were expensive,

but they also helped direct an enormous amount of funds into capital formation.

Planning continues to be a feature of the Taiwanese economy in the 1990s. The most recent plan identified 10 industries—including telecommunications, consumer electronics, semiconductors, precision machinery, aerospace, pharmaceuticals, and others—for government-assisted intervention.

Taiwan was one of the early economic powers in Asia, but some people wonder if the centralized planning process will hamper future economic growth. Despite its early start, the per capita GNP in Taiwan has fallen far behind those of Hong Kong and Singapore.

South Korea

South Korea has the smallest per capita GNP of the Asian Tigers at 36 percent of that of the United States. South Korea was devastated by civil war in the early 1950s, however, so it had much more to overcome than did the others.

In the past, a group of technocrats governed Korea with the help of the military. The factors of production were privately owned, but a small number of powerful business families dominated the private economy.

These business families were the main source of campaign funds to politicians. Therefore, politicians often granted them favors, allowing them to develop

Figure 19.3
Capitalism in Asia—The Asian Tigers

Because of the dynamic growth and economic progress made by South Korea, Hong Kong, Singapore, and Taiwan since the end of World War II, they are sometimes called the "Asian Tigers." Some observers have even suggested that the Guangdong Province of mainland China could be added to this list. **How have the Asian Tigers relied on capitalism to spur their economic growth?**

ASSESS

Check for Understanding

Assign Section 4 Review as homework or an in-class activity.

○ Use **Chapter Challenger Interactive Review Software** to review Section 4.

MEETING LESSON OBJECTIVES

Each objective below is tested by the questions on page 492 that follow it in parentheses.

1. **Explain** the factors that encouraged economic growth in Japan. **(1, 2, 5)**
2. **Rank** the "Asian Tigers" according to per capita GNP. **(3)**
3. **Describe** Sweden's retreat from socialism. **(4, 6)**

Evaluate

📁 📁 💻 Assign the Section 4 Quiz in the TCR or use the *Economics: Principles and Practices* Testmaker to create a customized quiz. Spanish Section Quizzes also are available in the Spanish Resources Binder.

◎ **VISUAL INSTRUCTION**

Why might Guangdong Province be added to the list of Asian Tigers? (*It has adapted many of the free-market approaches of the Tigers.*)

Answer to Caption:
They have taken different approaches, but all have elements of free enterprise.

Extending the Content

Lifetime Employment in Japan Lifetime employment means that a person will have a job with the same firm for the rest of his or her life. These jobs often go to graduates of the best universities. To gain admission to these institutions, it is necessary to score high on the comprehensive examinations given in high school. In other words, a person's job is directly related to success in educa- tion. With lifetime employment, an individual can move up or down within the same firm depending on his or her success at each level. For example, unproductive workers may be assigned to unimportant jobs. Even when corporations go through tough times, many have tried to avoid layoffs, preferring instead to reassign employees.

Have students write a generalization about each of the six economies discussed in the section.

➲ ➲ Have students complete Reteaching Activity 19. Spanish Reteaching Activities also are available in the Spanish Resources Binder.

Enrich

Invite a guest speaker who has visited or lived in Sweden, Japan, or one of the Asian Tigers to talk to the class about that country's standard of living, its main industries, and how culture influences the economy.

➲ Have students complete Enrichment Activity 19.

CLOSE

Have students use information from the section to comment on the following statement: Capitalist economies have more differences than similarities.

and dominate consumer goods, shipbuilding, steel, and automotive industries. At first, the close-knit relationship between the politicians and the families contributed dramatically to economic growth. Growth slowed somewhat in the 1990s, however, as the political structure became more democratic and feuds arose between the top families and the new politicians. South Korea's further economic growth will depend on whether the private economy adapts to competition and relies less on its relationship with the political sector.

Sweden

Sweden is a mature industrial nation once regarded as the "socialist state that works." The reputation was apt because Sweden provided a broader range of social welfare programs for its citizens than did any other free-world country.

Some of the basic industries were nationalized, but Sweden also had a considerable amount of private enterprise. The country, therefore, was not a model of pure socialism in the traditional sense.

The Welfare State

Many worker benefits were instituted during the 44-year rule of the Socialist party. During this time, wages were high, jobs were easy to find, and unemployment was in the 1 to 3 percent range. The Swedish economy—with its generous maternity, education, disability, and old-age benefits—was thought to be the model of European socialism.

Because government owned some but not all basic industry, it relied on steep taxes to pay for the benefits. In the mid-1980s, tax receipts were about 50 percent of GNP. In some cases, additional income that Swedish citizens earned was taxed at an 80 percent rate, meaning that a person who earned an additional $100 would keep only $20. Some individuals left the country to avoid high taxes. When tennis star Bjorn Borg was at the peak of his career, he resided outside of Sweden to avoid paying high taxes.

Many others devised ways to avoid paying taxes. Some craft workers resorted to barter. A carpenter who built some cabinets for an auto mechanic, for example, might be paid with repair work on the family car.

Restructuring

Eventually, the heavy tax burden and the additional costs of the welfare state began to cut into Sweden's economic growth. Growing inflation added to the problems, as did a massive government deficit. Growing discontent with conditions finally led to the defeat of the Socialist party in 1976.

A free-market government was elected in 1991, and by 1993, the public sector had been reduced to one-third of the jobs in the economy. Taxes on individuals and corporations had likewise been cut to where they were among the lowest in Europe. Many government-owned businesses had been privatized, and more are scheduled to be converted.

SECTION 4 REVIEW

Reviewing Terms and Facts

1. **Define** capital-intensive, *keiretsu*.
2. **Describe** how worker attitudes in Japan contribute to economic growth.
3. **State** which "Asian Tiger" faces the most uncertain future. Give reasons for your choice.

4. **Explain** how Sweden's retreat from socialism affected the nation's tax rates.

Critical Thinking

5. **Making Predictions** How might continued economic growth in Asia affect industries in the United States?

Applying Economic Concepts

6. **Economic Growth** How has Sweden's transition from socialism to capitalism helped promote economic growth?

Answers to SECTION 4 REVIEW

1. All words are defined in the Glossary.

2. Japanese workers feel an intense loyalty to their employers, take great pride in the quality of their work, and are very supportive of their fellow workers, which helps to increase productivity.

3. Hong Kong faces the most uncertain future, because it was returned to China in 1997.

4. The retreat allowed taxes to be cut.

5. Answers may vary. Continued economic growth in Asia could be beneficial to U.S. industries because they may import more American products, or it could be detrimental because Asian industries will create more competition for American industries.

6. The transition to capitalism reduced the heavy tax burden and the high costs of the welfare state. Privatization of government-owned business has enabled the government to eliminate some of its massive debt.

ECONOMICS IN ACTION

Comparative Economic Systems

Setting Up the Video

With your classmates, view "Comparative Economic Systems" on the videodisc *Economics in Action.* The video shows that in a socialist system, the government owns some factors of production. In a capitalist system, factors of production are privately owned. A news report details the apprehension that investors faced as Hong Kong was about to be returned to China.

Chapter 26
Disc 2, Side 2

View the video by scanning the bar code or by entering the chapter number on your keypad and pressing Search. *(Also available in VHS format.)*

Hands-On Activity

Choose a country that interests you, such as Russia, China, Cuba, Germany, Great Britain, the United States, Japan, or Argentina. Use resources in the library or on the Internet to research whether your chosen country's economic system is primarily socialist, capitalist, or a mixture of the two. Detail your findings in a report to the class.

 SURFING THE "NET"

Spectrum of Economic Systems

The world's economic systems can be shown on a spectrum ranging from those systems with almost total government control to those that include very few government regulations. Under capitalism, individuals own the means of production, and the interaction of supply and demand determines prices. Under socialism, the government owns many of the means of production, and elected officials allocate and manage these resources. In contrast, the government owns all means of production under a pure command economy. Use the Internet to see what your life as a consumer would be like under the different economic systems.

Getting There

1. Use a search engine. Type in the words *economic systems.*
2. Next, enter words like the following to focus your search: *capitalism, socialism*, and *command economy.*
3. The search engine will provide you with a number of links to follow. Links are "pointers" to different sites on the Internet and often appear as blue, underlined words.

What to Do When You Are There

Click on the links to navigate through the pages of information. Gather your findings. Use the findings to write several paragraphs describing how your life as a consumer would be different under each of these economic systems. Share your paragraphs with the class.

GLENCOE TECHNOLOGY

Economics in Action

Chapter 26
Disc 2, Side 2

Title: *Comparative Economic Systems*

If you do not have access to a videodisc player, the **Economics in Action** programs are also available in VHS.

INTERNET SITES

The following are possible sites for completing the "Net" activities:

Capitalism — Frequently Asked Questions
http://www.ocf.berkeley.edu/~shadab

Karl Marx
http://swift.eng.ox.ac.uk/jdr/marx.html

Not on the "Net"…

If students have limited or no access to the Internet, have them complete the activity "Spectrum of Economic Systems" by using the computerized card catalog or their school or local library to complete their research. At the s: prompt, students can type in *capitalism, communism,* or *socialism.*

INTERNET ADDRESS BOOK

Internet addresses that you find useful can be noted in the space below for quick reference.

_____   _____
_____   _____
_____   _____
_____   _____
_____   _____

GLENCOE
TECHNOLOGY

VIDEODISC
MindJogger Videoquiz

Use MindJogger to review
the Chapter 19 content.

 Chapter 19
Disc 3, Side A

 Also available in VHS.

Answers

Reviewing Key Terms

1. e.
2. f.
3. h.
4. a.
5. i.
6. g.
7. c.
8. b.
9. d.
10. j.

Reviewing the Facts

1. Government may promote competition and provide public goods.

2. through the price system and the voting process

3. the state as governed by a single authoritarian party

4. Peasants could lease land and hire labor, and small, privately owned businesses could operate.

5. They set unrealistically high quotas, which led to the production of shoddy goods; failed to specify quotas succinctly enough, which led to excesses in some products and shortages in others; and failed to establish effective incentives for workers.

6. Perestroika allowed some industries to compete in a market economy, allowed

494

Reviewing Key Terms

Write the key term that best completes the following sentences.

a. state farm
b. socialism
c. black market
d. capital-intensive
e. privatization
f. Five-Year Plan
g. collective farm
h. communism
i. perestroika
j. storming

1. In most former communist countries, state-owned enterprises are being converted to private ownership, a process known as ___ .
2. To direct production, Soviet planners adopted a ___ .
3. Under ___ the government owns all the means of production.
4. In the Soviet agricultural system, the state owned and operated each ___ .
5. Soviet leader Mikhail Gorbachev introduced a policy of ___ , the fundamental restructuring of the economy and government.
6. In the Soviet Union, groups of peasant families, each of which was allowed to keep its home and household goods, a few cattle, and a small plot of land, worked each ___ .
7. Most nations of Eastern Europe had a flourishing ___ where entrepreneurs and merchants sold goods illegally.
8. Under ___ , the government owns many, but not all, the basic productive resources.
9. In ___ industries, a large amount of capital is used for every person employed in manufacturing.
10. Piecework quotas often led to ___ , in which workers worked slowly until the last week of the month and then sped up just enough to get the quota filled.

Reviewing the Facts

SECTION 1 *(pages 472–475)*
1. **Explain** the role of the government in a capitalist economic system.
2. **Describe** how the people in a socialist economy help allocate the use of resources.
3. **Describe** who answers the basic economic questions in a communist system.

SECTION 2 *(pages 477–481)*
4. **State** what practices the New Economic Policy instituted.
5. **Describe** the problems that central planning caused in the Soviet economy.
6. **Explain** the impact that perestroika had on the Soviet economy.

SECTION 3 *(pages 483–487)*
7. **List** the problems that nations may face as they try to make the transition from communism to capitalism.
8. **Name** the nations that are currently trying to adapt to a market economy and describe the specific problems they are facing in their transition.

SECTION 4 *(pages 488–492)*
9. **Explain** the role the government plays in Japan's economy.
10. **Describe** how the approaches to economic growth differ in the regions of Hong Kong and Singapore.
11. **Trace** Sweden's transition from socialism to capitalism.

Critical Thinking

1. **Evaluating Information** Do you think five-year plans could work in the United States? Why or why not?

plant managers to pursue profits, and encouraged small businesses.

7. privatization, loss of political power, discipline of capitalism, responding to new incentives

8. Answers may include the following: Russia—uncertain nature of the political leadership; Poland—political reform slowed privatization; Hungary—private sector increasing production; the Czech Republic—still making transition to private ownership; Estonia, Latvia, Lithuania—still

developing market economies and privatizing industries; Mexico—gradually opening markets; Chile—still working at privatizing services; Argentina—still removing government from economy.

9. Government keeps taxes low and works closely with businesses to limit foreign competition in the domestic market.

10. Before the unification with China, Hong Kong had virtually no government interference in the econ-

2. **Drawing Conclusions** The Communists promised people that their system would lead to workers' paradises throughout the world. By the early 1990s, however, communist systems and their command economies in most countries had collapsed. Why do you think communism was such a failure?

Applying Economic Concepts

1. **Capitalism** Many nations are attempting to switch from communism or socialism to capitalism. Often, the transition has been quite difficult. What suggestions would you make to the leaders of these nations to help ease the transition to capitalism?
2. **Economic Growth** The "Asian Tigers" have experienced rapid economic growth and development. Do you think they can sustain this growth rate? Why or why not?

Reinforcing Skills

USING A SPREADSHEET

Use a spreadsheet to enter your test scores and homework grades. At the end of the grading period, the spreadsheet will calculate your average grade. The following steps will help you get started.

1. In cells B1 through D1, type *Homework, Quizzes, Tests*.
2. In cells A2 through A31, type in every date for the current six-week grading period.
3. Beginning in cells B2 through D2, enter the point totals you earned for every homework assignment, quiz, and test. Keep repeating this process for every date in the grading period.
4. In cell B32, use the *AutoSum* function (Σ) or a formula such as *=SUM(B2:B31)/30* to calculate your average homework grade for the six weeks. Click and drag this formula to cells C32 and D32 to find your quiz and test averages as well.
5. Insert a new row at the top of your spreadsheet, put a title in cell B1, and print your results.

Individual Activity

Choose one of the nations profiled in this chapter. Go to the library to find information on recent events in the nation's move toward capitalism. Construct a collage of headlines about these developments. Include with the collage a brief assessment of how the nation is working through the transition.

Cooperative Learning Activity

Organize into two groups. One group will represent former communist governments attempting to change to a capitalist system. The other group will represent officials from the United States trying to aid the transition. Each group should meet separately to devise a plan of action. The groups should then meet together to come up with a plan that will ensure a peaceful transition.

Technology Activity

Using a Computerized Card Catalog

In the **Journal Writing** activity on page 471, you were asked to keep track of events in Eastern Europe and the former Soviet Union. Using a computerized card catalog, find other sources describing economic events in these areas. Compose a journal article analyzing current developments in either of those regions of the world. Include quotes from the sources you found using the computerized card catalog.

CHAPTER 19: *Comparative Economic Systems* **495**

2. Answers will vary. Students may argue that the lack of individual freedom undermined the efforts of communism, or that the incompetence and inefficiency of central planning led to the downfall of communism.

Applying Economic Concepts

1. Answers will vary. Students' advice should target the problems most often encountered in such a transition and offer suggestions to counter these problems.
2. Answers will vary. Students' answers should reflect knowledge of the economic growth and development of the "Asian Tigers," as well as an understanding of capitalism.

BONUS TEST QUESTION

Have students write a brief essay explaining why communism collapsed or detailing the problems that face nations making the transition to capitalism. *(Essays will vary.)*

---

omy, but in Singapore, government provides generous tax breaks and subsidies and sponsors training of employees. Singapore has made an effort to develop its own technologies, but Hong Kong uses the technology of other countries. Singapore is trying to develop a few select industries, but Hong Kong produces numerous products for other countries.

11. Sweden was ruled by the Socialist party for 44 years. Eventually, the heavy tax burden, costs of the welfare state, growing inflation, and massive

government deficit caused public discontent that led to the defeat of the Socialist party in 1976. In 1991 a free-market government was elected. Welfare was scaled back, and taxes were lowered to among the lowest in Europe.

Critical Thinking

1. Answers will vary. Students may point out that the extensive role of government in five-year plans would probably ensure that they would not be accepted in the United States.

CHAPTER 20 PLANNING GUIDE

CHAPTER ORGANIZER

Daily Objectives	Reproducible Resources	Multimedia Resources
Section 1 **Economic Development** 1. **State** the concern for the plight of the developing countries. 2. **Identify** the obstacles to economic development	☞ Reproducible Lesson Plan 20-1 ☞ Guided Reading Activity 20-1 ☞ Cooperative Learning Activity 21 ☞ Consumer Application Activity 22 ☞ Math Practice for Economics 27 ☞ Free Enterprise Activity 22 ☞ Primary and Secondary Source Reading 21 ☞ Performance Assessment Activity 22 ☞ Section Quiz 20-1*	🔦 Focus Activity Transparency 92 🔦 Economic Concepts Transparency 22* 💿 Vocabulary PuzzleMaker 💿 Chapter Challenger Interactive Review Software 💿 Testmaker 💿 MindJogger Videoquiz 💿 NBR's Economics in Action Video Program
Section 2 **A Framework for Development** 1. **Explain** the stages of economic development. 2. **Describe** the steps industrialized countries need to take to help developing nations. 3. **Describe** the steps developing countries need to follow to help themselves.	☞ Reproducible Lesson Plan 20-2 ☞ Guided Reading Activity 20-2 ☞ Reinforcing Economic Skill 20 ☞ Section Quiz 20-2*	🔦 Focus Activity Transparency 93 💿 Vocabulary PuzzleMaker 💿 Chapter Challenger Interactive Review Software 💿 Testmaker 💿 NBR's Economics in Action Video Program
Section 3 **Financing Economic Development** 1. **Describe** one internal and two external sources of funds for economic development. 2. **Explain** the role of international lending and developing agencies. 3. **Explain** how regional cooperation can assist economic growth.	☞ Reproducible Lesson Plan 20-3 ☞ Guided Reading Activity 20-3 ☞ Section Quiz 20-3*	🔦 Focus Activity Transparency 95 💿 Vocabulary PuzzleMaker 💿 Chapter Challenger Interactive Review Software 💿 Testmaker 💿 NBR's Economics in Action Video Program
Chapter Review and Evaluation	☞ Enrichment Activity 20 ☞ Reteaching Activity 20* ☞ Economic Vocabulary Activity 20* ☞ Chapter 20 Test, Forms A and B	🎧 Chapter Digests Audiocassette Activities and Tests* 💿 Testmaker 💿 MindJogger Videoquiz

Also available in Spanish

 Blackline Master   Transparency   CD-ROM   Software   Videodisc   Audiocassette

⏱ 00:00 OUT OF TIME? Assign the Chapter 20 Digest Audiocassette and the corresponding Chapter Digest activities and tests.

PERFORMANCE ASSESSMENT

The following chapter projects may be assigned at the beginning of the chapter and used for performance assessment.

Multicultural Heritage Invite a guest speaker to class to discuss the relationship between culture and economic development in one of the developing countries. The speaker might be a former Peace Corps member, the representative of a local international relations club, an exchange student at a nearby university, a banker who is involved in international banking, or a historian with expertise in a developing country. After the presentation, have students write a brief essay in which they address cultural differences and similarities between the developing country and the U.S. and how cultural factors may have impeded or promoted economic development in the developing country.

Cooperative Learning Organize the class into five or six groups and ask all groups to create a special edition of a current affairs magazine on the topic of developing countries. Suggest that groups attempt to answer the following questions in their magazines: What is a developing country? How are limited natural resources and population growth obstacles to economic growth? How are the lack of education and technology obstacles to economic growth? How are foreign debt and capital flight obstacles to economic development? Why should the U.S. and other nations in the international community be concerned about developing countries? Ensure that group members share the various tasks involved in creating the magazine—design, artwork, research, writing, and so on—among themselves. Display completed magazines around the classroom.

ADDITIONAL RESOURCES

Readings for the Student

Elliott, Charles. *Atlas of Economic Issues.* New York: Facts on File, 1992. Uses maps and other visuals to examine a number of basic economic concepts.

Spencer, William. *The Challenge of World Hunger.* Hillside, NJ: Enslow Publishers, 1991. Realistic look at world hunger; provides data on social, economic, environmental, and political causes of hunger.

Readings for the Teacher

Eucken, Walter. *The Foundations of Economics.* New York: Springer-Verlag, 1992. Discusses stages in economic development.

Economist Atlas. New York: Henry Holt & Co., 1992. Provides political and economic data on all nations of the world.

Multimedia

GNP per Capita. The International Bank for Reconstruction and Development/The World Bank, 1818 H Street NW, Washington, DC 20433. Teaching guide and poster kit. Posters showing GNP per capita and industry, agriculture, trade, education, and health care for many countries.

The Developing World. Social Studies School Service, 10200 Jefferson Boulevard, P.O. Box 802, Culver City, CA 90232–0802. Video, 20 mins. Uses visual images and statistics to compare living standards in industrial and developing nations; also shows how developing countries are moving toward economic growth.

Chapter Overview

Chapter 20 focuses on economic development. **Section 1** defines the term *developing country* and explains why the international community is concerned about developing nations. **Section 2** provides a framework for economic development, while **Section 3** discusses the sources of capital for financing economic development.

GLENCOE
TECHNOLOGY

VIDEODISC
MindJogger Videoquiz

Use MindJogger to preview the Chapter 20 content.

Chapter 20
Disc 3, Side A

   Also available in VHS.

inter**NET**
CONNECTION

Resources for Chapter 20 on the World Wide Web*

National Council on Economic Education
http://www.nationalcouncil.org/

European Union
http://europa.eu.int/

OPEC Home Page
http://www.opec.org/

Sites subject to change.

Buyers and sellers engage in voluntary exchange at a market in Peru.

VISUAL INSTRUCTION

Have students compare the voluntary exchange shown in the photograph to the types of voluntary exchange in which they are regularly involved.

   Extra Credit Project

Have students create a two-part data bank on the industrialized world and the developing world. Suggest that they include statistics on such topics as GDP, population growth, natural resources, education and technology, and so on. Have students compare their data banks.

CHAPTER 20

Developing Countries

SECTION 1
Economic Development

SECTION 2
A Framework for Development

SECTION 3
Financing Economic Development

CHAPTER PREVIEW

People to Know

• Sir Arthur Lewis
• Peace Corps Volunteer

Applying Economic Concepts to Your Life

Per Capita GNP How long would it take you to earn $500? Is that a large sum of money? You may be surprised to learn what percentage of the world population has an annual *per capita GNP* of less than $500.

Journal Writing

For one week, keep a journal of all the economic problems of developing nations that you hear reported in the news. List the countries in one column and their problems in a second column.

Connecting to Past Learning

Call on a student to write the meaning of *GNP per capita* on the chalkboard. Then refer students to Figure 20.1 on pages 500–501 and point out that GNP per capita is one measure used to define developing countries. Conclude by mentioning that the way in which poorer nations of the world can achieve economic development is the focus of this chapter.

Applying Economics

Ask students to read the *Applying Economic Concepts to Your Life* paragraph on this page. Next, have students tally their normal weekly expenses to see how many weeks it would take them to spend $500—per capita GNP for the poorest developing countries. Conclude by leading students in a discussion of the types of everyday items and activities they would have to do without if they lived in a developing nation.

PERFORMANCE ASSESSMENT

Refer to page **496B** for a Performance Assessment activity for this chapter. Also see the **Performance Assessment Activities** booklet for additional suggestions.

Economic Portfolio

Suggest that students attempt to categorize the problems they record in their **Journal Writing** entries. Point out that this will help them write the agenda for the writing assignment in the Chapter Review. Refer students to the **Technology Activity** in the Chapter 20 Review on page 517.

Key to Ability Levels — Teaching strategies have been coded for varying learning styles and abilities:
L1 - Basic (activities for all students) **L2 - Average** (activities for average to above-average students)
L3 - Challenging (activities for above-average students) **LEP - Limited English Proficiency**

FOCUS

Section Objectives

1. State the concern for the plight of the developing countries.

2. Identify the obstacles to economic development.

Bellringer

Prior to taking roll at the beginning of the class period, display Focus Activity Transparency 92 on the overhead projector and assign the accompanying Student Activity 92.

Motivational Activity

Discuss students' responses to the activity sheet that accompanies Transparency 92.

Preteaching Vocabulary

Direct students to find definitions of the key terms in the Glossary. Then have students write a paragraph that shows how crude birthrate, zero population growth, external debt, and capital flight are related to developing countries. **LEP**

Use the **Vocabulary PuzzleMaker** to create crossword and word search puzzles.

TEACH

Guided Practice

L2 *Journalism* List the obstacles to economic development on the chalkboard and tell students that the list is the outline for a news story on the struggle of developing nations to achieve economic growth. Then direct students to use information in the list to write the news story.

Economic Development

Section Preview

Objectives

After studying this section, you will be able to:

1. **State** the concern for the plight of the developing countries.

2. **Identify** the obstacles to economic development.

Key Terms

developing country, crude birthrate, zero population growth, external debt, capital flight

Applying Economic Concepts

Life Expectancy Think about what you want to do in life. How long will it take you to do all you want? If you lived in a developing country, your *life expectancy* would be much shorter than it is right now. Your life might even be half over before you reached the age of 25.

Many people are concerned about the economic condition of **developing countries**—countries whose average per capita GNP is a fraction of that in more industrialized countries. Most developing countries are located in Africa, Asia, and Latin America.

Interest in Economic Development

The international community's concern for the developing countries is humanitarian as well as economic and political. In many ways, developing economies are similar to other economies of the world. The major difference is that their problems are much greater.

Concern for Developing Countries

The first concern is humanitarian. Industrialized countries of the world often believe it is their moral responsibility to help those who have less than they do. Many people in developing countries starve to death or die from diseases related to inadequate diets. Under such conditions, countries enjoying abundance find it difficult not to offer help.

The second concern is economic. Assistance to developing countries helps assure the industrial nations of a stable supply of certain raw materials. Developing countries also provide markets for the products of industrial nations. Developing countries buy about one-third of United States exports. This amount is more than the combined purchases of the European

Union, Japan, and Australia. In the long run, helping developing countries increases international trade.

The third concern is political. Despite the increasing failure of communism, various political ideologies wage a continuing struggle for the allegiance of developing countries. These ideological groups, in turn, struggle against industrial nations to gain more allies and greater political strength.

A gap between industrialized and developing countries has long existed, but never has it been so obvious or important as it is today. The growing difference in incomes has led to greater unrest and social disorder in different parts of the world. Many people in developing countries want some of the abundance enjoyed in industrialized countries. When these people do not achieve what they want as quickly as they would like, the result can be revolution, social upheaval, and even war.

Per Capita GNP

Today more than 1.2 billion people exist on an income of less than $1 a day. According to Figure 20.1, the majority of these people are in Africa and Asia. The map contrasts the income of the industrialized nations and the developing nations, scaling each country to show the size of its GNP relative to other countries. Thus, the United States, which has the largest GNP in the world, is the largest area on the map. Countries with smaller GNPs are scaled accordingly.

The map is also color coded to show countries with similar per capita GNPs. When viewed this way, the

---

Classroom Resources for SECTION 1

- Reproducible Lesson Plan 20-1
- Guided Reading Activity 20-1
- Cooperative Learning Activity 21
- Consumer Application Activity 22
- Math Practice for Economics 27
- Free Enterprise Activity 22
- Primary and Secondary Source Reading 21
- Performance Assessment Activity 22
- Section Quiz 20-1
- Spanish Section Quiz 20-1

- Focus Activity Transparency 92
- Economic Concepts Transparency 22
- Spanish Economic Concepts Transparency 22
- NBR's Economics in Action Video Program
- Testmaker
- Vocabulary PuzzleMaker
- Chapter Challenger Interactive Review Software
- MindJogger Videoquiz

contrast is clearly shown between the industrialized economies of North America, western Europe, and Japan, and the developing countries of South America, the Caribbean, Africa, and Asia. The gap between industrialized and developing countries is enormous. In the past few years, it has become even wider because many developing countries have experienced negative rates of growth.

Another reason for the growing gap between industrialized and developing countries is the relatively small total output for so many countries. If a developing country like Vietnam were to expand by 10 percent, only $24 would be added to its annual per capita GNP. In comparison, a 1 percent economic growth in the United States would add more than $300 to its annual per capita GNP.

Obstacles to Economic Development

Before examining some of the possible solutions to the plight of developing countries, we need to take a closer look at some common problems.

Population

One major obstacle to economic development is population growth. The populations of most developing countries grow at a rate much faster than those of industrialized countries. One reason for this growth is the high **crude birthrate**—the number of live births per 1,000 people. **Figure 20.2** shows that the countries with the highest birthrates in the world are developing countries, while the lowest birthrates are found in industrialized countries.

In some developing countries, the population is so large that there is barely enough fertile land and other resources to support it. Many less developed countries depend extensively on agriculture, adding to the problem. In these countries, an incentive to have many children exists. Most farms are worked by families, and children can work in the fields at an early age. More children means more workers. In addition, having many children ensures the parents that someone will look after them in their old age.

Another problem for developing countries is increasing life expectancy—the average remaining lifetime in years for persons who reach a certain age. Better education, international aid, and emphasis on health-care facilities help people live longer. A high life expectancy coupled with a high crude birthrate makes it difficult to increase per capita GNP.

Finally, people have different views on what is the proper rate of population growth. Some feel that the earth is too crowded already and that societies should work for **zero population growth** (ZPG)—the condition in which the average number of births and deaths balance so that a population stops growing. Others feel that population growth is a natural event and that efforts to disrupt it are morally and religiously wrong.

Natural Resources

Another obstacle to economic growth is limited natural resources. No country can develop beyond its resource potential. Unproductive land or a harsh climate can limit economic growth. A shortage or lack of natural resources or energy sources needed for industry also hinders growth. Some countries may be fortunate enough to discover a valuable mineral to finance development, but most focus on agriculture.

International agencies, such as the World Bank, fund agricultural projects. Recently, the World Bank has undertaken projects to control the desert locust in East Africa. It also has funded projects to develop cotton, clove, cashew, tobacco, and tea crops in Tanzania and Ghana, as well as to increase the production of millet and sorghum in northern Nigeria.

Education and Technology

Still another obstacle to economic development is a lack of appropriate education and technology. Many developing countries do not have a highly literate population or the high level of technical skills needed to build an industrial society. In addition, most do not have money to train engineers and scientists.

Many developing countries cannot even afford to provide free public education for school-age children. In those that can, not everyone is able to take advantage of it. In many cases, children must work to help feed their families. As a result, much of the population may not have the basic skills needed to continue with higher education when it is offered.

CHAPTER 20: *Developing Countries* **499**

CHAPTER 20
SECTION 1

📂 *Cooperative Learning*
Assign Cooperative Learning Activity 21.

GLENCOE TECHNOLOGY

NIGHTLY BUSINESS REPORT

Economics in Action

Chapter 28
Disc 2, Side 2
Title: *Developing Countries*
Subject: Economic challenges of developing nations
Ask: On what are most developing economies based? *(agriculture)*

Also available in VHS.

Using Transparencies
Display Economic Concepts Transparency 22 on the overhead projector and use the guidelines given in Teaching Strategy 22. Assign Student Activity 22. Spanish Transparencies also are available in the Spanish Resources Binder.

Independent Practice

📂 *Guided Reading* Assign Guided Reading Activity for Section 1. **LEP**

❓ DID YOU KNOW

Nine of every 10 children born today are born in developing nations. In the last 20 years of the century, the number of people 20 to 40 years of age will have increased by 630 million in developing nations, compared to about 20 million in industrialized nations.

Meeting Special Needs

Visual Learners For visual learners, a diagram is an especially useful tool to help students remember relationships. Have students examine Figure 20.1 on pages 500–501. Point out what the diagram is showing: each country's land area is shown in proportion to its GNP; each country's GNP per capita is shown with the use of various colors in the key.

L2 *Applying Ideas* Refer
students to Figure 20.1 and
have each student select a developing nation. Students
should conduct research to
discover the most problematic
obstacles to economic development for their selected nation.
Suggest that students present
their findings in a brief written
report.

☛ *Consumer Application*
Assign Consumer Application
Activity 22.

☛ *Math Practice* Assign
Math Practice for Economics 27.

☛ *Free Enterprise* Assign
Free Enterprise Activity 22.

☛ *Readings* Assign
Primary and Secondary Source
Reading 21.

CURRICULUM CONNECTIONS

History Initially, the
purpose of the World
Bank was to assist in the
reconstruction of Europe.
This task was handled by
the Marshall Plan, how-
ever, and the World Bank
soon became the leading
development aid agency.

❓ DID YOU KNOW

Capital flight is not
limited to developing
countries. The *Financial
Times* of London estimated
that in 1996, nearly $22
billion left Russia illegally,
or ended up "under mat-
tresses and floor boards."
This is more than 10 times
the amount of direct for-
eign investment that
flowed into the country in
that year.

Foreign Debt

A major problem facing nations today is the size of
their **external debt**—money borrowed from foreign
banks and governments. Some nations have borrowed
so much they may never be able to repay loans.

According to most estimates, the total external debt
for all developing countries is currently more than $1
trillion. At one time in the 1990s, Mexico and Brazil
each owed $100 billion to investors in other countries,
mainly the United States. For Mexico, this figure
equaled about two-thirds of the country's GNP. For
Brazil, the debt owed to others was closer to 40 percent
of its total GNP.

When debts get this large, countries have trouble
even paying interest on the loans. As a result, some
developing nations talk about defaulting, or not
repaying borrowed money. Most people do not
expect this to happen, however, because developing
countries fear that lending nations may retaliate. In
addition, a country that defaults on its loans may
never be able to borrow again.

When countries approach default, borrowers and
lenders often try to revise the repayment schedule.
Some lenders have found creative ways to resolve the
debt crisis. Recently, for example, the Philippines was
unable to repay a major loan to the Bank of America.
The Bank of America accepted an offer of 40 percent
stock ownership in the Bank of the Philippines
instead of the repayment.

Capital Flight

Another problem for developing nations is **capital
flight**—the legal or illegal export of a nation's currency
and foreign exchange. Capital flight may cause countries to face a cash shortage, which prevents them from
paying interest on their foreign debt. At a minimum, it
limits the funds available for capital investment.

For the most part, capital flight takes place when
corrupt officials smuggle money out of the country
and deposit it abroad. A Nigerian investigation found
that corrupt officials were depositing $25 million
abroad daily at the peak of the oil boom in the 1970s.
This may be one reason why Nigeria experienced a
negative per capita rate of growth from 1973 to 1983,
although it was an OPEC nation with rich oil reserves.

At other times, capital flight occurs because people
living in the borrowing countries have no faith in their
government or the future of the country's economy.

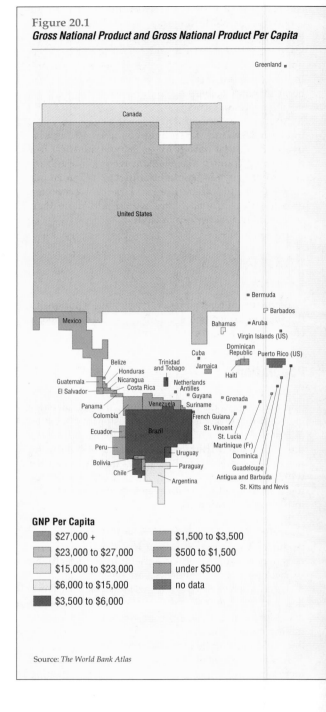

Figure 20.1
Gross National Product and Gross National Product Per Capita

GNP Per Capita

$27,000 +	$1,500 to $3,500
$23,000 to $27,000	$500 to $1,500
$15,000 to $23,000	under $500
$6,000 to $15,000	no data
$3,500 to $6,000	

Source: *The World Bank Atlas*

Free Enterprise Activity $

Have students imagine they are successful entrepreneurs in the U.S., and they wish to expand
and establish a branch of their business in one of
the developing countries. Encourage these entrepreneurs to prepare a business plan that discusses
the opportunities and obstacles presented by opening a business in that developing nation. Select
students to present and explain their plans to the
class.

If every country's land area was proportional to its Gross National Product, the world would look like the map in this figure. When GNP is computed on a per capita basis, we get another view of a country's productivity. **Which countries have a per capita GNP larger than the United States's?**

📁 **Performance Assessment**

Assign Performance Assessment Activity 22.

ASSESS

Check for Understanding

Assign Section 1 Review as homework or an in-class activity.

⊙ Use **Chapter Challenger Interactive Review Software** to review Section 1.

MEETING LESSON OBJECTIVES

Each objective below is tested by the questions that follow it in parentheses.

1. **State** the concern for the plight of the developing countries. **(2)**

2. **Identify** the obstacles to economic development. **(1, 3, 4, 5, 6)**

Evaluate

📁 📁 ⊙ Assign the Section 1 Quiz in the TCR or use the *Economics: Principles and Practices* Testmaker to create a customized quiz. Spanish Section Quizzes also are available in the Spanish Resources Binder.

VISUAL INSTRUCTION

Ask: Which country has the largest GNP? The second-largest GNP? *(U.S.; Japan)*

Answer to Caption:

Norway, Denmark, Germany, Switzerland, Japan, Luxembourg

Extending the Content

Using GNP Instead of GDP For purposes of international comparisons, economists like to use GNP rather than GDP. GNP is a measure of the total *income* earned by all citizens in a country, whereas GDP is a measure of total *output* produced within national boundaries. If GDP were used instead of GNP, then relatively poor countries with large foreign-owned investments would appear to be more prosperous than they really are.

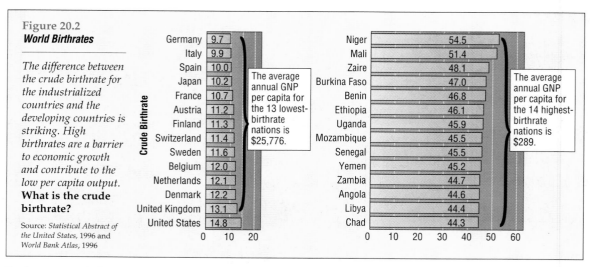

Figure 20.2
World Birthrates

The difference between the crude birthrate for the industrialized countries and the developing countries is striking. High birthrates are a barrier to economic growth and contribute to the low per capita output. **What is the crude birthrate?**

Source: *Statistical Abstract of the United States, 1996* and *World Bank Atlas, 1996*

Country	Crude Birthrate
Germany	9.7
Italy	9.9
Spain	10.0
Japan	10.2
France	10.7
Austria	11.2
Finland	11.3
Switzerland	11.4
Sweden	11.6
Belgium	12.0
Netherlands	12.1
Denmark	12.2
United Kingdom	13.1
United States	14.8

The average annual GNP per capita for the 13 lowest-birthrate nations is $25,776.

Country	Crude Birthrate
Niger	54.5
Mali	51.4
Zaire	48.1
Burkina Faso	47.0
Benin	46.8
Ethiopia	46.1
Uganda	45.9
Mozambique	45.5
Senegal	45.5
Yemen	45.2
Zambia	44.7
Angola	44.6
Libya	44.4
Chad	44.3

The average annual GNP per capita for the 14 highest-birthrate nations is $289.

Business owners, for example, may deposit their profits abroad. When they want to expand or invest, they try to borrow from industrialized nations.

Government

Government also can be an obstacle to economic development. A country whose government often changes will have a hard time developing economically. Such constant changes impede long-term planning. Economic development is made even more difficult if the political changes occur through vio-

lent revolution where industrial facilities may be destroyed.

Economic development also will be slowed if a government is not honest. Corrupt officials can damage the economy in several ways. One way is by depositing the nation's savings in a personal account in a foreign bank. Another way is by spending huge sums meant for the economy on lavish personal living.

In either case, the people see the results of their labor being spent recklessly or enriching someone else while their lives remain the same. This discourages them and reduces their incentive to save or invest.

SECTION 1 REVIEW

Reviewing Terms and Facts

1. **Define** developing country, crude birthrate, zero population growth, external debt, capital flight.
2. **List** three reasons people are concerned about developing countries.
3. **List** six factors that may be obstacles to economic development.

4. **Explain** why it is difficult for some developing countries to slow the rate of population growth.

Critical Thinking

5. **Identifying Alternatives** Suppose you are an official in charge of economic development in a developing country. Choose the first two obstacles to eco-

nomic development that you would address and tell why you would tackle them first.

Applying Economic Concepts

6. **Life Expectancy** Explain why an official of a developing nation would have both positive and negative views of increasing life expectancy.

Answers to SECTION 1 REVIEW

1. All words are defined in the Glossary
2. humanitarian, economic, and political
3. population growth, limited natural resources, lack of appropriate education and technology, overwhelming external debt, capital flight, government that changes often, corrupt government officials
4. More children mean more workers in countries depending extensively on agriculture; some parents have many children to ensure that someone will take care of them when they get old; increasing

life expectancy along with high crude birthrate increases population growth; some people feel any interference to control population is wrong.

5. Students should support their choices.

6. Increasing life expectancy enables people to plan far-reaching goals and may increase productivity. However, increased population requires food, shelter, and clothing; decreases per capita GNP; and costs the government more for health care and social services for the elderly.

PROFILES IN ECONOMICS

W. ARTHUR LEWIS
(1915–1991)

Economist Sir W. Arthur Lewis achieved many firsts. He attended school in his native St. Lucia, and he earned a scholarship to attend the London School of Economics. In 1937 he graduated first in his class. Soon after, while working on a Ph.D. in Economics, he was the first black to receive an assistant lectureship at the same institution. In 1979 he was the first black to win the Nobel Prize in Economics (jointly with Theodore Schultz) for his work on the economic problems of developing nations.

Workers in Sri Lanka pick tea.

DEVELOPING NATIONS In particular, Lewis challenged the prevailing view that the supply of labor in developing nations was upward sloping, so that an increase in the demand for labor resulted in an increase in wages.

Real wages, noted Lewis, tended to stay at low levels for many developing nations regardless of the increases in demand for labor. The only solution, he reasoned, was that the supply curve for labor had to be perfectly elastic— or horizontal rather than upward sloping—so that an increase in demand would leave wages unchanged. His theory explained why countries such as Sri Lanka are still underdeveloped, although they have been developing for nearly 100 years.

Lewis did not claim to have solved the problems of the developing countries. His contri-

butions, however, have made existing economic models and theory more applicable to realistic conditions.

TRANSITION Lewis explained how he felt about his illustrious career:

I had never meant to be an economist. . . . What was this economics? I had never heard of it before, and nobody in St. Lucia knew what it was. . . . Looking backward . . . I have lived through a period of transition. . . . I have been subject to all the usual disabilities—refusal of accommodations, denial of jobs for which I had been recommended, generalized discourtesy, and the rest of it. All the same, some doors that were supposed to be closed opened as I approached them. I have got used to being the first black to do this or that, which gets to be more difficult as the transition opens up new opportunities. Having to be a role model is a bit of a strain, but I try to remember that others are coming after me, and that whether the door will be shut in their faces as they approach will depend to some small extent on how I conduct myself.

—from *Lives of the Laureates*, by Spencer and Breit, 1990

Examining the Profile

1. **Demonstrating Reasoned Judgment** Why would an increase in demand for labor not increase the wage rate in developing countries?

2. **For Further Research** Find out more about the economy of Sri Lanka.

TEACHING
PROFILES

Background

Point out that the fullest discussion of Lewis's ideas on development may be found in his *The Theory of Economic Growth* (1955).

TEACH

Have students turn to Figure 17.6 on page 429. Imagine that AD and AS represent the demand and supply for labor in a developing country. If the demand for labor increases from AD_0 to Ad_1, there is very little increase in price. If the supply curve has a perfectly elastic (absolutely horizontal) range, as hypothesized by Lewis, there would be no increase in the equilibrium wage received by labor.

Answers to Examining the Profile

1. According to Lewis, the supply of labor is perfectly elastic—in graphic terms, a horizontal line. Therefore, wages would remain unchanged if demand changes.

2. Have students present their findings in an illustrated report.

SECTION 2
A Framework for Development

FOCUS

Section Objectives

1. Explain the stages of economic development.

2. Describe the steps industrialized countries need to take to help developing countries.

3. Describe the steps developing countries need to follow to help themselves.

Bellringer

Prior to taking roll at the beginning of the class period, display Focus Activity Transparency 93 on the overhead projector and assign the accompanying Student Activity 93.

Motivational Activity

Discuss students' responses to the activity sheet that accompanies Focus Activity Transparency 93.

Preteaching Vocabulary

Direct students to locate the key terms in the text. Then have them use each term in a sentence. **LEP**

Use the **Vocabulary PuzzleMaker** to create crossword and word search puzzles.

SECTION 2
A Framework for Development

Section Preview

Objectives

After studying this section, you will be able to:

1. **Explain** the stages of economic development.

2. **Describe** the steps industrialized countries need to take to help developing countries.

3. **Describe** the steps developing countries need to follow to help themselves.

Key Terms

primitive equilibrium, takeoff, World Bank

Applying Economic Concepts

Primitive Equilibrium *Primitive equilibrium* is the first stage on the road to a nation's economic development. It is called *primitive* because no formal economic organization exists. It is called *equilibrium* because nothing is changing.

Economic development is a formidable task. Many approaches have been suggested and implemented with various levels of success. The steps below outline how a country might develop from a primitive economy to an industrialized one.

Stages of Economic Development

Some economists have suggested that developing countries normally pass through several stages on their way to economic development. Others have argued that the process is not uniform for all countries. A country, for example, may not go from one stage to the next in a logical manner. It may skip one stage altogether, or it may be in more than one stage at the same time. It is helpful to think of economic development as occurring in stages, and the boundaries between these stages are not always clear-cut.

Primitive Equilibrium

The first stage toward economic development is **primitive equilibrium**. It is primitive in the sense that the society has no formal economic organization. An example might be the Inuit of the past century who shared the spoils of the hunt with other families in the village.

A people—or country—in primitive equilibrium often have no monetary system and may not be economically motivated. No real capital investment exists. The society is in equilibrium, in which nothing changes. Rules are handed down from one generation to the next, and culture and tradition direct economic decision making.

Breaking With Primitive Equilibrium

The second stage of economic development is one of transition. It consists of a break with primitive equilibrium and a move toward economic and cultural changes. The break may be brief and sudden, or it may take many years.

Generally, the break results from outside forces showing a different, more attractive way of life. Missionaries and tourists, as well as war, travel, and business ventures with other countries, reveal to the people different ways of living. **1**

A country does not grow economically in this transition stage, but old customs begin to crumble. People begin to question their traditions, and they observe new patterns of living. Social unrest often accompanies this stage.

Takeoff

The third stage of development—**takeoff**—is not reached until the barriers of primitive equilibrium are

---

overcome. A country in the takeoff stage begins to grow more rapidly than before. Still, that nation is far from reaching maturity or developing its greatest economic potential.

Several reasons explain the economic growth that occurs during this stage. One reason is that customs have been put aside, and people have begun to seek new and better ways of doing things. Another reason is that the people have begun to imitate the new or different techniques that outsiders have brought into the country. Still another reason is that outside help from an industrial nation may be providing financial, educational, or military aid.

During the takeoff stage, a country starts to save and invest more of its national income. New industries grow rapidly, and profits are reinvested in them. Industry uses new production techniques, and agricultural productivity greatly improves. Although the country still is not developed, it is moving away from economic stagnation.

Semidevelopment

The fourth stage is semidevelopment. In it, the makeup of the country's economy changes. National income grows faster than population, which leads to higher per capita income. At the same time, the core of the country's industry is built. The nation spends heavily on capital investment, and technological advances are made.

As industry grows, so does transportation, communications, medicine, law, and other services. The country begins to find its place in the international economy. It starts to make the goods it once bought from other countries. Before long, the semideveloped country starts to sell finished products to other nations.

High Development

The final stage of development is that of being highly developed. In this stage, efforts to obtain food, shelter, and clothing are more than successful. Most people have their basic needs and wants met. They turn their attention to services and such consumer goods as washing machines, refrigerators, and televisions.

The nation no longer emphasizes industrial production. Instead, it increases services and provides more public goods. Mature service and manufacturing sectors are signs of a highly developed economy.

Priorities for Industrialized Nations

The International Bank for Reconstruction and Development, also known as the **World Bank,** is an agency designed to channel funds from industrialized nations to developing ones. As a result of its considerable experience with developing nations, the World Bank has a list of recommendations for industrialized countries. 2

Reduce Trade Barriers

Trade barriers, especially nontariff barriers, need to be reduced or eliminated. In the United States, reducing barriers would result in such actions as importing more beef from Argentina. The World Bank has estimated that eliminating trade barriers would generate as much as $50 billion annually in export earnings for the developing countries.

Checking Understanding	Applying Economic Concepts
1. What generally causes the break with primitive equilibrium? 2. What is the function of the World Bank?	**World Bank** After World War II, with aid from the United States and the World Bank, Japan emerged as the dominant economy of Asia. From 1953 to 1966, Japan was an active borrower from the World Bank. By 1970 Japan had become a major lender.

Meeting Special Needs

Attention Deficiency   Inattention is sometimes caused by the difficulty of the material that confronts the students. It is, of course, easier for a student to pay attention if he or she is working at an appropriate instructional level (only 5 to 10 percent of the material is new). Have students preview Section 2 to assess components that might be difficult for them. Discuss with them what factors might affect maintaining attention.

TEACH

Guided Practice

L3   *Publicity Campaign* Call on students to identify the priorities for industrialized countries and for developing countries in promoting economic development. Note their responses on the chalkboard. Then have students work in small groups to develop a publicity campaign to inform industrialized and developing countries about the steps they should take to encourage development. Have groups present and explain their campaigns.

Economics in Action

Chapter 28
Disc 2, Side 2

Title: *Developing Countries*

Subject: Strengthening developing economies

Ask: How has the United States traditionally helped developing countries? *(with foreign aid— grants of money or low-interest loans)*

Also available in VHS.

Independent Practice

🗂 *Guided Reading* Assign Guided Reading Activity for Section 2. **LEP**

ANSWERS

1. outside forces showing a different, more attractive way of life
2. to channel funds from industrialized nations to developing nations

ASSESS

Check for Understanding

Assign Section 2 Review as homework or an in-class activity.

🖥 Use **Chapter Challenger Interactive Review Software** to review Section 2.

MEETING LESSON OBJECTIVES

Each objective below is tested by the questions that follow it in parentheses.

1. **Explain** the stages of economic development. **(1, 2, 5, 6)**

2. **Describe** the steps industrialized countries need to take to help developing countries. **(3, 5)**

3. **Describe** the steps developing countries need to follow to help themselves. **(4)**

Evaluate

📁 📁 🖥 Assign the Section 2 Quiz in the TCR or use the *Economics: Principles and Practices* Testmaker to create a customized quiz. Spanish Section Quizzes also are available in the Spanish Resources Binder.

506

Reform Macroeconomic Policy

Macroeconomic policies in the industrialized countries that reduce deficits, stabilize inflation, lower interest rates, and stabilize foreign currency fluctuations would greatly improve world economic development. If the industrialized economies grow, their increased international trade often includes and benefits the developing economies.

Increase Financial Support

The industrialized nations need to provide more external financing to the developing countries. This financing could be direct aid, or it could be indirect aid to international agencies such as the World Bank or the International Monetary Fund (IMF), which also works with developing nations.

Traditionally, the majority of United States foreign aid has been granted to achieve political aims. Between one-half and two-thirds of all United States foreign aid has been paid for military supplies and training, either directly or indirectly. More than 50 percent of all indirect military aid is paid to Israel and Egypt.

Support Policy Reform

The industrialized countries are encouraged to support the internal policy reforms of the developing countries, especially when the countries are trying to develop freer and more efficient market economies. Transactions on common economic grounds lead to a more favorable business climate between the industrialized and developing countries.

Priorities for the Developing Countries

The World Bank also has a list of recommendations for the developing countries. The developing countries face the responsibility for directing their own economic development and future.

HELP WANTED

Peace Corps Volunteer
▼

We offer minimal pay for hard work in unfamiliar surroundings. But if you are a dedicated individual who can work effectively with people, this will be the hardest job you'll ever love. The Peace Corps is seeking volunteers for 2-year assignments overseas. You will receive from 8 to 14 weeks of training in the history, culture, and language of the country in which you will serve. Your duties will include working with the people of your host country to improve food production, health care, and other basic needs. College training is not required, but assignments may be made on the basis of your experience or skills.
▼
Requirements: United States citizen, at least 18 years old
Salary: An allowance for living costs (housing, medical care, and transportation are provided)

Invest in People

Governments in developing countries need to invest more in education, family planning, nutrition, and basic health care. The wealth of any nation resides in the strength and vitality of its people.

Improve the Climate for Free Enterprise

Many of the price controls, subsidies, and other regulations that restrict the free development of markets should be removed. The World Bank suggests that competitive markets—not politicians—make the allocation decisions.

Open Economies to International Trade

Many developing economies have quotas, tariffs, and other barriers to trade. These barriers are used to

---

💲 Free Enterprise Activity 💲

Ask students to imagine they have been hired as economic consultants to a developing country that is in the takeoff stage of economic development. Have students use the World Bank recommendations as the basis for a plan that would encourage economic growth and the development of a free enterprise economy in the developing country. Call on students to share and explain their plans.

Investment in People *The World Bank encourages developing nations to invest in their people by providing basic health care.* **What is the reasoning for investing in people?**

protect domestic jobs and to protect infant industries. At the same time, however, the trade barriers protect inefficient industries and hold down a country's standard of living. Countries that open their markets to the world will benefit from comparative advantage and will ultimately develop competitive specialties of their own.

Revise Macroeconomic Policies

Developing countries, like the industrialized ones, need to follow policies curbing inflation, reducing borrowing, and decreasing deficits. Their policies also must allow market incentives such as profits, so that the economies can begin to sustain their own growth.

Ask students to draw an annotated flow chart showing the stages of economic development. Have students compare their charts.

Enrich

Have students write a book report on W.W. Rostow's *The Stages of Economic Growth* (Cambridge University Press, 1971). Suggest that they focus their report on a comparison between Rostow's stages and the stages described in this section.

CLOSE

Have students discuss the most important steps the U.S. can take to encourage economic growth in developing nations.

VISUAL INSTRUCTION

Point out that investment in people, also known as human capital investment, improves people's skills and health. As a result, productivity increases.

Answer to Caption:
The wealth of any nation resides in the strength and vitality of its people.

SECTION 2 REVIEW

Reviewing Terms and Facts

1. **Define** primitive equilibrium, takeoff, World Bank.
2. **List** the stages of economic development.
3. **Describe** four recommendations that the World Bank has for developed countries.
4. **Describe** four recommendations that the World Bank has for developing countries.

Critical Thinking

5. **Making Inferences** The International Bank for Reconstruction and Development was organized near the end of World War II. Why do you think it was originally founded?

Applying Economic Concepts

6. **Primitive Equilibrium** Imagine that a society is in primitive equilibrium—nothing is changing internally to begin economic development. Describe an event that could be a potential source of change.

CHAPTER 20: *Developing Countries* **507**

Answers to SECTION 2 REVIEW

1. All words are defined in the Glossary.

2. primitive equilibrium, breaking with primitive equilibrium, takeoff, semidevelopment, high development

3. reduce trade barriers, reform macroeconomic policy, increase financial support for developing nations, support market policy reform

4. Invest more in education, family planning, nutrition, and basic health care. Remove regulations that restrict the free development of markets. Open economies to international trade. Institute macroeconomic reforms, reduce borrowing, decrease deficits, and allow for market incentives.

5. to help countries recover from WWII

6. Answers may vary. Students may cite missionaries and tourists, war, travel, or business ventures with other countries.

Building a Database

Have you ever collected baseball cards or cataloged the CDs in your collection? Have you kept a list of the names and addresses of your friends? If you have, then you have created a database—an organized collection of information on a given subject or topic.

Ask students to list at least 10 ideas for a database. For each idea, they should suggest three or more fields to use in organizing the information. Then have them identify each field as a text, number, date, or time field.

Some examples include:
State—text field
When Admitted—date field
Capital—text field
State Bird—text field
State Motto—text field
State Flower—text field

Mountain—text field
Country—text field
Elevation—number field

Book Title—text field
Author—text field
Copyright—date field
Publisher—text field

Skills Practice For additional practice, have students complete Reinforcing Economic Skill 20.

Explanation

An electronic database is stored in files on the computer, which makes it easy to find, add, delete, and sort information. In a database, one category of information is called a *field.* A field is given a name that describes in a general way the main subject or idea of the category. If you were to convert the data in Figure 20.3 into a database, you would have three fields: *Donor Country, ODA as percentage of GNP, Total ODA.*

A *record* is a group of fields that are all related to the same topic or idea. For example, all the statistics referring specifically to France in Figure 20.3 make up one record. Together, all the records make up the database.

The first step in creating a database is to obtain a database management system (DBMS)—special software developed for record keeping. It provides instructions on how to define and name your fields according to the type of information they hold. A field that holds letters, for example, is a text field. A field that holds numbers is a number field. After entering the information, you give commands to the computer telling it what to do with the data, and it follows your commands.

Practice

Enter the statistics in Figure 20.3 into an electronic database, then answer the questions that follow.

1. If you sorted the data alphabetically, which record would appear first?
2. If you sorted your records according to total aid provided, which donor country would appear first? In what order would the United States appear?
3. If you sorted your records according to aid as a percentage of GNP, which donor country would appear first? In what place would the United States fall?

Figure 20.3
Net Official Development Assistance (ODA) from Major Sources

Donor Country	ODA as percentage of GNP 1996	Total ODA (billions of dollars) 1996	Donor Country	ODA as percentage of GNP 1996	Total ODA (billions of dollars) 1996
France	0.55	8.4	Australia	0.36	1.2
Germany	0.31	7.5	Austria	0.33	0.8
Italy	0.15	1.6	Canada	0.38	2.1
United Kingdom	0.28	3.2	Finland	0.32	0.4
Netherlands	0.81	3.2	Japan	0.28	14.5
Denmark	0.96	1.6	New Zealand	0.23	0.1
Spain	0.24	1.3	Norway	0.87	1.2
Belgium	0.38	1.0	Sweden	0.77	1.7
Portugal	0.27	0.3	Switzerland	0.34	1.1
Ireland	0.29	0.2	Greece	0.13	0.2
Luxembourg	0.36	0.1	United States	0.10	7.4

Source: OECD, *1996 Report*

Additional Practice

For further practice in building a database, complete the Reinforcing Skills exercise in the Chapter 20 Review on page 517.

Answers to SKILL

1. Australia
2. Japan; U.S. would appear fourth
3. Denmark; U.S. would appear in 22nd place

Financing Economic Development

Section Preview

Objectives

After studying this section, you will be able to:

1. **Describe** one internal and two external sources of funds for economic development.

2. **Explain** the role of international lending and developing agencies.

3. **Explain** how regional cooperation can assist economic growth.

Key Terms

expropriation, free-trade area, customs union, European Union, European Community, euro, ECU, cartel, population density

Applying Economic Concepts

Growth and Development Sound economic development depends on more than the infusion of large amounts of capital into developing countries. These nations must also address such issues as saving, investing, and providing incentives for their people.

For a developing country to foster industries in which it has a comparative advantage, it needs capital. Funds may be needed, for example, to provide irrigation for farms or heavy equipment for mining. Without capital, a developing country may not be able to build roads and highways needed for bringing products to ports for shipment to the rest of the world.

This financial capital generally can come from three different sources. It can be generated internally, lent or supplied by outside agencies, or obtained as a result of regional cooperation.

Development With Internal Funds

Internal funds are a source of capital. In many cases, they may be the only source of capital for a developing country. To generate these internal funds or savings, an economy must produce more than it consumes.

Savings in a Market Economy

If a developing country is modeled after a market economy, the incentive to save stems from the profit motive. Entrepreneurs are free to pursue the most profitable activities. Banks, for example, pay varying interest rates that are set by the forces of supply and demand. If the demand for money is high, the rate

Internal Funds *Generating internal funds has made Hong Kong an economic power.* **What must an economy do to generate internal funds?**

CHAPTER 20: *Developing Countries* **509**

Classroom Resources for SECTION 3

Reproducible Lesson Plan 20-3
Guided Reading Activity 20-3
Section Quiz 20-3
Spanish Section Quiz 20-3
Focus Activity Transparency 95
NBR's Economics in Action Video Program
Enrichment Activity 20
Reteaching Activity 20
Spanish Reteaching Activity 20

Economic Vocabulary Activity 20
Spanish Economic Vocabulary Activity 20
Chapter 20 Test, Form A and Form B
English and Spanish Audiocassettes
Testmaker
Vocabulary PuzzleMaker
Chapter Challenger Interactive Review Software
Mindjogger Videoquiz

TEACH

Guided Practice

L2 *Analyzing Ideas* On the chalkboard draw a table with *Internal Funds, External Funds,* and *Regional Cooperation* as vertical headings, and *Advantages* and *Disadvantages* as horizontal headings. Call on students to identify the advantages and disadvantages of the three sources of financial capital for development. Record their responses on the table. Then lead the class in a discussion of which methods of financing economic development are most efficient. **LEP**

GLENCOE
TECHNOLOGY

NIGHTLY BUSINESS REPORT

Economics in Action

Chapter 28
Disc 2, Side 2

Title: *Developing Countries*

Subject: Opportunities for developed countries

Ask: Why are manufacturers and investors from industrialized countries interested in developing nations? *(because as developing nations continue to develop, the citizens will consume more goods and spend more money on items produced at home and abroad; in addition, developing nations have lower labor costs)*

Also available in VHS.

will rise, and more saving will be encouraged. Saving, in turn, produces financial capital.

One economy that developed in this way was Hong Kong, one of the freest market economies in the world before the 1997 reunification with China. Before reunification, government interfered very little, and people were free to pursue almost any economic activity they desired. By 1997, Hong Kong's per capita GNP was about 85 percent of that of the United States, and more than 37 times greater than China's.

Many developing countries are so poor that there is barely enough production to fulfill basic consumption. It takes longer for savings to be obtained, but some countries have developed in this manner.

Savings in a Command Economy

Other developing countries, such as Cuba, the Dominican Republic, El Salvador, and Uganda, have had command economies at one time or another. In each case, a dictator tried to force saving on the economy. The governments of these countries argued that individual citizens were so poor that they did not have the incentive to save on their own. As a result, the governments felt they had to mobilize resources themselves.

Many people were forced to work on farms, roads, or other projects the government thought were needed

DID YOU KNOW?

▶ **Bikes Not Bombs** The Institute for Transportation and Development Policy (ITDP) promotes bicycle transportation in developing nations. ITDP points out that bicycles have the following advantages over automobiles: They cost much less, are easy to manufacture, use no fuels, and are friendly to the environment. They provide access to remote areas, and they are a source of jobs. The "Bikes Not Bombs" campaign provided thousands of used bicycles to health, education, and other civilian workers of Nicaragua.

for economic development. To boost agricultural output, China's government at one time forced people out of the cities and factories to work on farms.

History shows that although command economies can mobilize resources, they do not always use them to promote economic growth. Resources often are mobilized for political reasons. In addition, nearly all forced mobilizations fail to instill long-term incentives in the people. When resources are mobilized for the wrong reasons, the cost in personal, economic, and political freedoms is higher than most people want to pay. **1**

Development With External Funds

No matter what system of government a less developed country has, it is never easy for it to develop economically with internal funds. Therefore, some developing countries try to obtain external funds. There are three ways they can do this.

Attracting Private Investment

One way a country can obtain external funds is to attract private funds from foreign investors who might be interested in the country's natural resources. This happened in the Middle East with its abundance of oil, in Chile with its abundance of copper, and in Asia with its abundance of mahogany and teakwood.

A country rich in mineral resources might grant exclusive mining rights or favorable tax rates to foreign companies or investors willing to build factories on its soil. The country also might be able to provide low-cost labor, which would make investment even more attractive.

Foreign investments should be beneficial to both the investor and the host country. The developing country wants projects that will foster development, not exploit scarce resources. Investors want a reasonable return on their investment. Many corporations have not forgotten the billions of dollars lost during the takeover of American oil facilities in Iran, copper mines in Chile, and agricultural plantations in Cuba. Many investors no longer are willing to take major risks unless they are sure that the developing country is politically stable. ✓

Meeting Special Needs

Learning Disability Students with learning disabilities in reading or with other reading comprehension problems often do not practice or use good self-appraisal and self-management skills while they read. Encourage these skills by making students aware of the need for these unconscious activities. As students read Section 3, tell them to be aware of processes they use to help them understand the material. Have them note the number of times they reread phrases or sentences. Explain that rereading is important for understanding.

Developing countries that follow a policy of **expropriation**—the taking over of foreign property without some sort of payment in return—make it harder for all developing nations to attract foreign capital from industrialized countries.

Assistance From Industrialized Countries

Another way a country can obtain external funds is through grants or borrowing from foreign governments. The United States and other industrialized countries, including Canada and those in western Europe, grant aid to developing countries.

The former Soviet bloc also gave economic assistance to developing countries. More than 50 percent of its aid, however, went to Cuba, Ethiopia, Afghanistan, and Iraq. Like much of the foreign aid other nations grant, it was given mostly to promote political, rather than economic, ends.

Some economic aid also is provided by the OPEC nations—members of the Organization of Petroleum Exporting Countries. These nations generally limit aid to only a few countries and organizations. The OPEC nation of Saudi Arabia, for example, sends most of its foreign aid to Syria and the Palestine Liberation Organization.

Borrowing From International Agencies

A third way a country can get external financial assistance is by obtaining a loan from an international agency. Two such agencies are important to global economic development.

The International Bank for Reconstruction and Development—the World Bank—was mentioned earlier. The World Bank helps developing countries with loans and guarantees of loans from private sources. It is a corporation owned by the member nations of the International Monetary Fund, and it lends nearly $23 billion annually to developing countries. One of the owners is the United States, which contributes more than $1 billion annually.

In the past, many of the loans have been for projects such as dams, roads, and factories. More recently, loans have been made to developing nations in an effort to get them to change their economic policies. Rather than lend money for a particular project, the World Bank may grant a general loan that the borrowing country can use any number of ways. In return, the World Bank may ask the country to lower a tariff barrier, end a budget deficit, or reduce the level of inflation.

The World Bank has several affiliates. One is the International Finance Corporation (IFC)—an agency that invests in private businesses and other enterprises. The International Development Association (IDA) makes soft loans—loans that may never be paid back—to the neediest countries. The rates on IDA loans are interest-free and may be for periods of 35 or 40 years. The IDA is the lender of last resort for countries that cannot get external financing elsewhere.

The International Monetary Fund (IMF) was formed in 1944 by countries wanting to set up an international system of fixed exchange rates. Each country agreed to contribute a pool of currency and gold for use in fixing exchange rates at agreed-upon levels.

When the world went to a system of flexible rates in 1971, the IMF adjusted its role. Today it offers advice to all nations on monetary and fiscal policies. It also helps support the currency of some developing nations with loans so that the countries can compete in an open market. **2**

After the Berlin Wall came down and the Soviet Union collapsed, a number of former Soviet bloc countries wanted to trade their currencies on global exchanges. The IMF provided loans to help with the conversion. Today, the Hungarian *forint*, the Polish

Checking Understanding	Applying Economic Concepts
1. What may result if resources are mobilized for the wrong reasons? 2. What is the function of the IMF?	✓ **Foreign Investment** By the early 1950s, U.S. corporations virtually controlled Cuba. Nearly 90 percent of its mines, ranches, and oil; half of its sugar crop; and 3 million acres of its land belonged to Americans. At the same time, most Cubans suffered tremendous poverty.

CHAPTER 20: *Developing Countries* **511**

Independent Practice

📂 *Guided Reading* Assign Guided Reading Activity for Section 3. **LEP**

L2 *Time Line* Have students research economic development in South Korea. Direct students to use their findings to construct a time line showing South Korea's economic growth from the end of the Korean War to the present day. Have students compare their time lines. **LEP**

ANSWERS

1. The cost in personal, economic, and political freedoms is higher than most people want to pay.

2. It offers advice to all nations on fiscal and monetary policies. It also helps to support currencies of some developing nations.

? DID YOU KNOW

Insects and other pests are an enormous threat to economic development. Today more than 60 countries in Africa and the Middle East are threatened by locust plagues. In a single day, swarming locusts can travel up to 125 miles (200 km) and destroy crops that could have fed more than 100,000 people.

$ Free Enterprise Activity $

Have students write an essay comparing and contrasting the three sources of capital for developing countries with sources of capital for industrialized countries. Call on volunteers to read their essays to the class. Then have students discuss why it is easier for industrialized countries to raise financial capital for development.

ASSESS

Check for Understanding

Assign Section 3 Review as homework or an in-class activity.

 Use **Chapter Challenger Interactive Review Software** to review Section 3.

MEETING LESSON OBJECTIVES

Each objective below is tested by the questions that follow it in parentheses.

1. **Describe** one internal and two external sources of funds for economic development. **(1, 2, 5, 6)**

2. **Explain** the role of international lending and developing agencies. **(3)**

3. **Explain** how regional cooperation can assist economic growth. **(4)**

VISUAL INSTRUCTION

Point out to students that the founding members of what today is known as the European Union were Belgium, France, Germany, Italy, Luxembourg, and Netherlands.

Answer to Caption:

Citizens can hold common passports, can vote in European elections, and can travel anywhere in the EU to work, shop, save, and invest.

Figure 20.4
The European Union

The 16 members of the EU currently make up the largest single market in the world with more than 370 million people. A number of other nations have applied for membership, and even more from the former Soviet-bloc nations are eventually expected to join. **What are benefits of being a citizen in the EU?**

Source: European Commission, 1997.

Euro coin

16 Existing Members:
Austria 1995
Belgium 1952
Cyprus 1998
Denmark 1973
Finland 1995
France 1952
Germany 1952
Greece 1981
Ireland 1973
Italy 1952
Luxembourg 1952
Netherlands 1952
Portugal 1986
Spain 1986
Sweden 1995
United Kingdom 1973

To be considered for Membership, 2002-2006
Czech Republic
Estonia
Hungary
Poland
Slovenia

---

zloty, and the Czech Republic's *koruna* are all listed on world markets. This is important because investors must be able to purchase the currencies of these countries to conduct international trade with them.

Regional Cooperation

Some developing countries have joined together to form a **free-trade area**—an agreement in which two or more countries reduce trade barriers and tariffs among themselves. The free-trade area does not try to set uniform tariffs for nonmembers. Other countries have formed a **customs union**—an agreement in which two or more countries abolish tariffs and trade restrictions among themselves and adopt uniform tariffs for nonmember countries.

The European Union

One of the most successful examples of regional cooperation in the world today is the **European**

Union (EU). The EU, formerly known as the **European Community** (EC), consists of the 16 member nations shown in **Figure 20.4**.

In January 1993, the EC became the single largest unified market—in terms of population and GDP—in the world, even larger than the United States. It is a single market because no internal barriers regulate the flow of workers, financial capital, or goods and services. On November 1, 1993, as a result of the Maastricht Treaty, the EC became the European Union. Citizens of the EU hold common passports, can vote in European elections, and can travel anywhere in the EU to work, shop, save, and invest.

The EU collects revenues in the form of a VAT (Value Added Tax) and then distributes the funds to its members on the basis of need. Hundreds of billions of dollars have been redistributed in this manner and have been used to build highways, rail systems, and other public goods that will benefit the EU.

The final stage of European integration is scheduled for 2002 when the EU introduces a single cur-

---

Extending the Content

Cartels Cartels usually are successful when they sell a product that has an inelastic demand, such as oil. Conversely, they have been least successful with products that have an elastic demand. Even the most successful cartels have a limited life. One reason for this is that it is relatively easy for members to violate one or more of the selling conditions agreed to by the association. Indeed, OPEC has lost much of its power in recent years because a number of its members have regularly exceeded established output levels.

Figure 20.5
OPEC Members

The countries that belong to the Organization of Petroleum Exporting Countries (OPEC) represent a widely separated group of nations who have formed a cartel to keep the price of oil high. **What is a cartel?**

Evaluate

🗂 🗂 💻 Assign the Section 3 Quiz in the TCR or use the *Economics: Principles and Practices* Testmaker to create a customized quiz. Spanish Section Quizzes also are available in the Spanish Resources Binder.

◎ VISUAL INSTRUCTION

Have students identify the regions where most OPEC members are located. (*Africa, Middle East*)

Answer to Caption:

group of producers or sellers who agree to limit production or sale of product to control prices

rency—the **euro**—to replace the individual national currencies now issued by the member nations. The move to a common currency is one of the most difficult aspects of unification, and it has proceeded in stages.

The first stage was the creation of the **ECU**—European Currency Unit—a measure of value rather than a form of currency. During this stage, many EU countries priced products in terms of ECUs.

The second stage featured the creation of the European Monetary Union (EMU) in 1999. During this phase, all but four or five EU countries were to adopt a system of fixed exchange rates among themselves.

In 2002, the national currencies issued by EMU countries will be replaced by euro notes and euro coins. The remaining EU countries, such as the United Kingdom and Sweden, are expected to join the EMU eventually—and to give up their national currencies when they become members.

Finally, a European central bank will be created to manage the euro the same way that the Fed manages the dollar. Monetary policy will then be conducted from a single European point of view, rather than from many national points of view.

OPEC

A number of oil-producing nations have joined to form a **cartel**—a group of producers or sellers who agree to limit the production or sale of a product to control prices. Shown in Figure 20.5, OPEC's members were able to take advantage of a natural monopoly and push up world oil prices. Since it was organized in 1960, OPEC has successfully transferred trillions of dollars from the industrialized nations to the OPEC members as a result of higher prices paid for oil.

Even with all this financial capital, however, the growth rates of most OPEC nations were low by most standards. In Iran, revolution interrupted the development of the domestic economy. Kuwait was overrun by Iraq, and Iraq suffered huge losses during the Persian

CHAPTER 20: *Developing Countries* **513**

Cultural Diversity and Economics

European Union The EU has sought to develop a European identity among citizens of member nations through the use of the EU flag (a circle of 12 gold stars on a blue background), the EU anthem (the "Ode to Joy" from Beethoven's Ninth Symphony), and such documents as the European passport and driver's license. At the same time, however, the EU encourages national and regional cultural identities by using 9 official languages and by supporting the languages of ethnic minorities living in member nations.

Reteach

Have students write on index cards three questions about sources of funds for economic development. Collect and shuffle the cards and work through them, selecting students at random to answer the questions.

👉 👉 Have students complete Reteaching Activity 20. Spanish Reteaching Activities also are available in the Spanish Resources Binder.

Enrich

Ask students to write a research paper on the development of either the EU or OPEC.

👉 Have students complete Enrichment Activity 20.

CLOSE

Have students speculate on how NAFTA will assist economic development in the Western Hemisphere.

Gulf War. Overproduction by OPEC also pushed oil prices down. The World Bank estimated that from 1980 to 1991, the only OPEC member to have positive per capita GNP growth was Indonesia.

Most OPEC nations were not able to absorb their oil wealth in a balanced way. They bought many products for immediate consumption. Investment in other sectors of the economy was ignored, however.

The growth rates of OPEC for 1980 to 1997 show that huge amounts of capital alone do not solve the problems of developing countries. To have sound economic development, countries must also address such issues as saving, investment, and the incentives that cause people to work and improve their lives.

The South Korean Success Story

One of the most successful developing nations is the Republic of Korea, also known as South Korea. Despite its bleak prospects nearly 40 years ago, it overcame overwhelming odds to become the third-largest economic power in Asia and the nineteenth-largest economy in the world. From the late 1950s until the mid-1980s, South Korean exports grew at a rate of 25 percent per year. In addition, its real per capita GNP growth was in the 5 to 10 percent range.

In the early 1950s, South Korea was one of the poorest nations in Asia. It had the highest **population density**—number of people per square mile of land area—in the world. It also had a war-torn economy that had to be rebuilt.

After the Korean War, the United States sent foreign aid to South Korea for strategic and humanitarian reasons. Because the South Korean economy was ruined, however, even massive amounts of foreign aid would have done little more than maintain the country's low standard of living. For growth to take place, the South Koreans had to do more than rely on foreign aid.

The South Korean government decided to focus on labor-intensive industries and open its markets to free trade. It gave businesses incentives to follow this strategy. In addition, the government did not try to do everything at once. Instead, it focused on a few industries so that its people could gain experience producing and exporting for world markets.

Taking these steps, businesses in the South Korean economy first began to produce inexpensive toys and consumer goods for the world market. Next, they moved into textiles such as shirts, dresses, and sweaters. Then they invested in heavy industry, such as shipbuilding and steel manufacturing. Later, South Korea produced consumer and electronic goods such as radios, televisions, microwave ovens, and home computers. Most recently, the country has been making a strong bid as a leading producer of automobiles. The South Korean experience shows that a country can change a war-damaged economy to a well-developed, highly industrial one.

SECTION 3 REVIEW

Reviewing Terms and Facts

1. **Define** expropriation, free-trade area, customs union, European Union, European Community, euro, ECU, cartel, population density.
2. **Describe** two external sources of funds for economic development.
3. **List** two important international lending and development agencies.

4. **Identify** an example of regional cooperation for economic growth.

Critical Thinking

5. **Drawing Conclusions** Developing nations often need capital from foreign investors. What economic and political conditions serve to encourage this kind of investment?

Applying Economic Concepts

6. **Growth and Development** Provide an example to support the following statement: Economic growth in developing nations is often slowed by internal political problems and external political goals of industrialized nations.

Answers to SECTION 3 REVIEW

1. All vocabulary words are defined in the Glossary.
2. Students may choose two of the following: private funds from foreign investors, grants or borrowing from foreign governments of industrialized countries, borrowing from an international agency such as the World Bank.
3. World Bank and International Monetary Fund
4. European Union or OPEC

5. Strong economic development opportunities that address saving, investments, and worker incentives and a stable political climate encourage foreign investment.
6. Investors run the risk of losing their investment in developing nations with internal political problems. External political goals may be in conflict with the goals of the government or people of a developing nation.

ECONOMICS IN ACTION

Developing Countries

Setting Up the Video

With your classmates, view "Developing Countries" on the videodisc *Economics in Action.* The video focuses on the economic challenges of developing nations, which typically have agricultural-based economies and low GDPs. A news report on Chrysler's efforts to do business in China illustrates the problems that modern corporations face when setting up operations in developing countries.

Chapter 28
Disc 2, Side 2

Scan the bar code or enter the chapter number on your keypad and press Search. *(Also available in VHS format.)*

Hands-On Activity

Select a nation of the world that is currently classified as a developing nation. Use resources in the library or on the Internet to learn about the economic conditions in your chosen nation. You should list the nation's natural resources, then outline an economic plan that would create a healthy balance of trade with other nations. Prepare an oral presentation of your findings in which you answer the following questions: How would you market this nation's natural resources? How would you attract foreign businesses?

SURFING THE "NET"

Developing Countries

The World Bank recommends that industrialized nations help developing countries by reducing trade barriers, reforming macroeconomic policies, increasing financial support, and supporting their policy reforms. The World Bank also recommends that the developing nations help themselves by investing in their people, improving the climate for free enterprise, opening their economies through international trade, and revising their economic policies. Use the Internet to find out what successes specific countries have had in improving their developing economies.

Getting There

1. Use a search engine. Type in the words *developing countries* or *emerging economy.*

2. Next, enter words like the following to focus your search: *Third World, international trade, economic policies,* and *World Bank.*

3. The search engine will provide you with a number of links to follow. Links are "pointers" to different sites on the Internet and often appear as blue, underlined words.

What to Do When You Are There

Click on the links to navigate through the pages of information. Gather your findings. Use the findings to write several paragraphs describing how a specific country is improving its developing economy.

515

GLENCOE
TECHNOLOGY

Economics in Action

Chapter 28
Disc 2, Side 2

Title: *Developing Countries*

If you do not have access to a videodisc player, the **Economics in Action** programs are also available in VHS.

INTERNET SITES

The following are possible sites for completing the "Net" activities:

World Bank
http://www.worldbank.org/

The World Factbook Home Page
http://www.odci.gov/cia/publications/nsolo/wfb-all.htm

G7 Conference 1997
http://www.G7.com/

Not on the "Net"...

If students have limited or no access to the Internet, have them complete the activity "Developing Countries" by using *Readers' Guide to Periodical Literature* at the school or local library. Students should look for articles about developing nations or emerging economies. They should then find the articles and other resources they need to complete their research.

INTERNET ADDRESS BOOK

Internet addresses that you find useful can be noted in the space below for quick reference.

_____   _____
_____   _____
_____   _____
_____   _____
_____   _____
_____   _____

Answers

Reviewing Key Terms

1. h.
2. g.
3. b.
4. i.
5. d.
6. c.
7. j.
8. e.
9. f.
10. a.

Reviewing the Facts

1. moral responsibility to help those who have less; to ensure a stable supply of certain raw materials; to gain allies and attain greater political strength

2. A government that changes often or one in which officials are corrupt impedes planning, frightens investors, and slows economic development.

3. zero population growth

4. Corrupt officials smuggle money out of the country and deposit it abroad; people living in borrowing countries have no faith in their government or the future of the country's economy.

Reviewing Key Terms

Write the key term that best completes the following sentences.

a. population density   f. expropriation
b. customs union   g. free-trade area
c. primitive equilibrium   h. cartel
d. external debt   i. crude birthrate
e. capital flight   j. takeoff

1. A _____ is the formal arrangement to limit the production of a product.
2. A cooperative trade arrangement among nations that does not set uniform tariffs for nonmembers is called a _____.
3. A _____ is a cooperative trade arrangement among nations that sets uniform tariffs for nonmembers.
4. A developing country may have a very high _____ , contributing to rapid population growth.
5. When _____ becomes too large, countries have difficulty paying the interest.
6. The least developed stage in economic development is called _____.
7. The third stage of economic development is the _____.
8. The problem of _____ occurs when corrupt officials take money out of the country and deposit it abroad.
9. When _____ takes place, it is harder for developing nations to attract foreign capital from industrialized countries.
10. The number of people per square mile of land is a measure of _____.

Reviewing the Facts

SECTION 1 *(pages 498–502)*
1. **Identify** three reasons why industrialized countries are concerned about the problems of developing nations.
2. **Explain** why government can be an obstacle to economic development.

---

3. **Name** the condition in which the average number of births and deaths are approximately equal.
4. **Identify** two reasons for the occurrence of capital flight.

SECTION 2 *(pages 504–507)*
5. **Describe** what happens in a developing country in the stage of breaking with primitive equilibrium.
6. **Identify** four changes that take place in the take-off stage of economic development.
7. **List** the four World Bank recommendations for developing nations.

SECTION 3 *(pages 509–514)*
8. **Name** three sources of financial capital for development.
9. **Explain** how a developing country can attract foreign capital.
10. **List** three international agencies that provide funds for economic development.

Critical Thinking

1. **Predicting Consequences** What do you think would happen if industrialized nations and international agencies chose to withdraw support for developing nations?
2. **Demonstrating Reasoned Judgment** Would it be effective policy for the United States to increase financial aid to developing nations, regardless of their internal political conditions or economic policies? Explain the reasoning behind your answer.

Applying Economic Concepts

1. **Primitive Equilibrium** Why is it increasingly unlikely that countries in the world today may remain in the primitive equilibrium stage of economic development?
2. **Growth and Development** How will the economic growth and development of developing countries affect you in the future?

---

5. People become dissatisfied with the way things are, old customs begin to crumble, traditions are questioned, and new patterns of living are observed.

6. A country starts to save and invest more of its national income. New industries grow rapidly. Industry uses new production techniques. Agricultural productivity greatly improves.

7. Invest more in education, family planning, nutrition, and basic health care. Remove price controls, subsidies, and other regulations that restrict the free development of markets. Open economies to international trade in order to benefit from comparative advantage and to encourage the development of competitive specialties. Institute macroeconomic reforms that curb inflation, reduce borrowing, decrease deficits, and allow for market incentives.

8. internal funds, external funds, regional cooperation through free-trade areas or customs unions

Reinforcing Skills

BUILDING A DATABASE

Enter the statistics in **Figure 20.6** into an electronic database, then answer the questions that follow.

1. How many fields will you enter into your database?
2. How many records are given in the chart?
3. If you sorted the data alphabetically by language, which record would appear first?
4. If you sorted your records according to total number of speakers, which language would appear first?
5. Which state has the highest number of Portuguese speakers? Of Korean speakers?

Figure 20.6
Languages in the United States

Language	Number of Speakers	State with Highest %
1. Spanish	17,339,172	New Mexico
2. French	1,702,176	Maine
3. German	1,547,099	North Dakota
4. Italian	1,308,648	New York
5. Chinese	1,249,213	Hawaii
6. Tagalog	843,251	Hawaii
7. Polish	723,483	Illinois
8. Korean	626,478	Hawaii
9. Vietnamese	507,069	California
10. Portuguese	429,860	Rhode Island
11. Japanese	427,657	Hawaii
12. Greek	388,260	Massachusetts
13. Arabic	355,150	Michigan
14. Hindi	331,484	New Jersey
15. Russian	241,798	New York
16. Yiddish	213,064	New York
17. Thai/Lao	206,266	California
18. Persian	201,865	California
19. French Creole	187,658	Florida
20. Armenian	149,694	California

Source: Bureau of the Census, October 1997

Individual Activity

Economic growth is only one measure of progress. For you as an individual, growth and progress can be measured in terms of physical size and skills, mental achievement, economic gains, and social skills. Write a paragraph comparing your present self with yourself two years ago. What "stages" have you gone through to become the person you are? What are your future goals?

Cooperative Learning Activity

Organize into three groups, each choosing one of the following regions: Latin America, Africa, and Asia. Each student in the group should research a different nation in his or her region. Determine the relative progress of the country based on per capita GNP, life expectancy, literacy rate, and rate of economic growth. Compare your findings.

Technology Activity

Using E-Mail

In the **Journal Writing** activity on page 497, you tracked economic problems of foreign nations that you heard reported in the news. Using the information you collected, write a plan detailing how the United States could assist in alleviating some of the economic problems of a specific country. E-mail your plan to your local representative or legislator. Be sure to support your proposal or solution with statistics, facts, quotes, and historical events.

leadership could change frequently or a war could begin, and the developing nations would not benefit fully from the aid.

Applying Economic Concepts

1. Answers will vary. Students may argue that improvements in communication and travel, along with heightened social conscience, have enabled people and information to go into areas with primitive equilibrium and reveal different ways of living.
2. Answers will vary. Economic growth and development of developing countries should have a favorable impact because international trade will increase.

Reinforcing Skills

1. three fields: Language, Number of Speakers, State with Highest Percentage
2. twenty records
3. Arabic
4. Spanish
5. Rhode Island; Hawaii

? BONUS TEST QUESTION

Organize the items below in their correct order. Then explain the five stages in economic development.

1. Breaking with primitive equilibrium
2. High development
3. Primitive equilibrium
4. Semidevelopment
5. Takeoff

(3, 1, 5, 4, 2. Paragraphs will vary; see pages 504–505 for discussion of stages of economic development.)

9. Developing countries can attract private funds from foreign investors interested in the country's natural resources, secure grants or loans from industrialized nations that have political gains to make, or borrow from international agencies with a promise to change their economic policies.

10. Students may choose three of the following: World Bank, International Monetary Fund, International Finance Corporation, International Development Association.

Critical Thinking

1. Answers will vary. Developing countries would most likely be unable to change their economic situation because they would not have capital necessary to institute agricultural or industrial changes or even to build roads to get their products to the rest of the world.

2. No. If the United States increased financial aid to a country experiencing political turmoil, political

CHAPTER ORGANIZER

Daily Objectives	Reproducible Resources	Multimedia Resources
Section 1 **The Global Demand for Resources** 1. **Explain** Malthus's views on population growth. 2. **Explain** the importance of conserving nonrenewable resources. 3. **List** ways that people are using renewable energy resources to conserve scarce resources.	📁 Reproducible Lesson Plan 21-1 📁 Guided Reading Activity 21-1 📁 Cooperative Learning Activity 22 📁 Math Practice for Economics 28 📁 Primary and Secondary Source Reading 22 📁 Economic Simulation 6 📁 Economic Laboratory 6 📁 Performance Assessment Activity 21 📁 Section Quiz 21-1*	📽 Focus Activity Transparency 96 💾 Vocabulary PuzzleMaker 💾 Chapter Challenger Interactive Review Software 💾 Testmaker 💿 MindJogger Videoquiz 💿 NBR's Economics in Action Video Program
Section 2 **Economic Incentives and Resources** 1. **Explain** how the price system helps conserve water, natural gas, and oil. 2. **Describe** government efforts to limit pollution. 3. **State** the importance of using resources wisely.	📁 Reproducible Lesson Plan 21-2 📁 Guided Reading Activity 21-2 📁 Reinforcing Economic Skill 21 📁 Section Quiz 21-2*	📽 Focus Activity Transparency 97 💾 Vocabulary PuzzleMaker 💾 Chapter Challenger Interactive Review Software 💾 Testmaker 💿 NBR's Economics in Action Video Program
Section 3 **Applying the Economic Way of Thinking** 1. **Explain** why economics has become a generalized theory of choice. 2. **Understand** how our market economy will be able to cope with the future.	📁 Reproducible Lesson Plan 21-3 📁 Guided Reading Activity 21-3 📁 Section Quiz 21-3*	📽 Focus Activity Transparency 98 💾 Vocabulary PuzzleMaker 💾 Chapter Challenger Interactive Review Software 💾 Testmaker 💿 NBR's Economics in Action Video Program
Chapter Review and Evaluation	📁 Enrichment Activity 21 📁 Reteaching Activity 21* 📁 Economic Vocabulary Activity 21* 📁 Chapter 21 Test, Forms A and B	🎧 Chapter Digests Audiocassette Activities and Tests* 💾 Testmaker 💿 MindJogger Videoquiz

*Also available in Spanish

 Blackline Master   Transparency   CD-ROM   Software   Videodisc   Audiocassette

⏱ OUT OF TIME? Assign the Chapter 21 Digest Audiocassette and the corresponding Chapter Digest activities and tests.

National Council on Economic Education

VOLUNTARY NATIONAL CONTENT STANDARDS IN ECONOMICS
Emphasized in Chapter 21

Content Standard 1 *Students will understand that:*
Productive resources are limited. Therefore, people cannot have all the goods and services they want; as a result, they must choose some things and give up others.

Content Standard 4 *Students will understand that:*
People respond predictably to positive and negative incentives.

EconomicsAmerica *Resources Available From NCEE*

- *Capstone: The Nation's High School Economics Course*
- *Civics and Government: Focus on Economics*
- *Economics and the Environment*
- *Focus: High School Economics*
- *Geography: Focus on Economics*
- *Personal Decision Making: Focus on Economics*
- *United States History: Eyes on the Economy, Vol. II*

To order these materials, or to contact your state Council on Economic Education about workshops and programs, call 1-800-338-1192 or visit http://www.nationalcouncil.org.

PERFORMANCE ASSESSMENT

The following chapter projects may be assigned at the beginning of the chapter and used for performance assessment.

Multicultural Heritage Stress that conflict in one country can have an impact far beyond its borders. Ask students to identify current areas of conflict around the world. Have them investigate the number of people displaced by the conflict, the countries to which they are fleeing, and the social, political, and economic impact these refugees are having on their destination countries. Suggest that students present their findings in an illustrated report.

Cooperative Learning Organize students into five groups and assign one of the following topics to each group: Malthus's views on population growth, nonrenewable resources, renewable resources, the role of price in conserving resources, and the application of cost-benefit analysis. Have groups develop lesson plans for teaching their assigned topics to the rest of the class. Point out that in teaching the topics, groups must have students apply the information in some way. For example, with Malthus's views on population, students might compare geometric and arithmetic progression of numbers; or with nonrenewable and renewable resources, students might keep records of the ways in which these resources are used in the community. Have groups teach their topics to the rest of the class. Test students on these topics to evaluate groups' performance.

ADDITIONAL RESOURCES

Readings for the Student

Epping, Randy Charles. *A Beginner's Guide to the World Economy.* New York: Vintage Books, 1992. Provides answers to 71 questions about world economies.

Siebert, Horst. *Economics of the Environment: Theory and Policy.* New York: Springer-Verlag, 1992. Approaches the environment as a scarce resource; analyzes alternative policies for dealing with environmental problems.

Readings for the Teacher

Cairncross, Frances. *Costing the Earth: The Challenge for Governments, the Opportunities for Business.* Boston: Harvard Business School Press, 1991. Economic policies applied to environmental problems.

Smith, Denis, ed. *Business and the Environment: Implications of the New Environmentalism.* New York: St. Martin's Press, 1993. A series of essays analyzing the environmental movement from the perspective of economics, law, marketing, and risk assessment.

Multimedia

Decisions, Decisions: The Environment. Tom Snyder Productions, Inc., 80 Coolidge Hill Road, Watertown, MA 02172. Software in Apple, IBM, and Macintosh formats. Simulation, combining science and social studies, that requires students to address crucial environmental problems.

Earth: The Changing Environment. WETA/The World Bank, 1818 H Street NW, Washington, DC 20433. Color video, 28 mins. Argues for environmentally sound approaches to economic development in developing nations.

Chapter Overview

Chapter 21 discusses population and the application of economics to the problem of limited resources in a modified free market economy. **Section 1** explains Malthus's views on population and discusses nonrenewable and renewable energy resources. **Section 2** describes the roles of market prices in the conservation of resources and explains how economic incentives can reduce pollution. **Section 3** presents the five steps in the economic decision-making process.

GLENCOE
TECHNOLOGY

VIDEODISC
MindJogger Videoquiz

Use MindJogger to preview the Chapter 21 content.

Chapter 21
Disc 3, Side A

Also available in VHS.

interNET
CONNECTION

Resources for Chapter 21 on the World Wide Web*

National Council on Economic Education

http://www.nationalcouncil.org/

Sustainable Business Network

http://www.envirolink.org/pbn

Energy Information Administration

http://www.eia.doe.gov/

*Sites subject to change.

Power generated by windmills is considered an alternative energy source.

⊞ Extra Credit Project

Tell students to imagine they have been asked to design a time capsule to be opened in the year 2100. Have them select 10 items they would include in the time capsule that would show the global economic challenges we face today. Have them write an explanation of why they selected these items.

CHAPTER 21

Global Economic Challenges

SECTION 1
The Global Demand for Resources

SECTION 2
Economic Incentives and Resources

SECTION 3
Applying the Economic Way of Thinking

CHAPTER PREVIEW

People to Know

- Thomas Malthus
- Economic Geographer

Applying Economic Concepts to Your Life

Trade-Offs An empty lot is scheduled to be sold. The school board wants to buy the spot to build a new athletic facility. Local businesses want the land to add parking spaces for their customers. The city wants to build a park. Clearly, a limited resource—land— has more than one alternative use. *Trade-offs* are involved, and a choice has to be made. That's why we study economics—to become better decision makers.

Journal Writing

For one week, keep a journal of all the natural resources you use. Classify each as a renewable or nonrenewable resource.

CHAPTER 21: *Global Economic Challenges* **519**

Connecting to Past Learning

Chapter 21 reintroduces such basic economic concepts as scarcity and trade-offs. Call on students to briefly explain these two concepts. Then lead students in a discussion of how scarcity and trade-offs might be applied to such issues as energy resources and pollution.

Applying Economics

For a period of one day, have students record any examples of resource conservation— recycling aluminum cans or carpooling, for example—that they observe. In a class discussion, ask students to speculate how the actions they observed might have been motivated by economic reasons.

PERFORMANCE ASSESSMENT

Refer to page **518B** for a Performance Assessment activity for this chapter. Also see the **Performance Assessment Activities** booklet for additional suggestions.

VISUAL INSTRUCTION

Ask: Does the photograph illustrate a nonrenewable or renewable energy source? Why? *(renewable; because its supply is not depleted with use)*

Economic Portfolio

As students make their **Journal Writing** entries, have them consider how the resources they are using might be preserved and what actions they, personally, might take to aid this preservation.

Mention that this will help them complete the writing activity in the Chapter Review. Refer students to the **Technology Activity** in the Chapter 21 Review on page 537.

Key to Ability Levels — Teaching strategies have been coded for varying learning styles and abilities:
L1 - Basic (activities for all students)   **L2 - Average** (activities for average to above-average students)
L3 - Challenging (activities for above-average students)   **LEP - Limited English Proficiency**

FOCUS

Section Objectives

1. Explain Malthus's views on population growth.

2. Explain the importance of conserving nonrenewable resources.

3. List ways that people are using renewable energy resources to conserve scarce resources.

Bellringer

Prior to taking roll at the beginning of the class period, display Focus Activity Transparency 96 on the overhead projector and assign the accompanying Student Activity 96.

Motivational Activity

Discuss students' responses to the activity sheet that accompanies Focus Activity Transparency 96.

Preteaching Vocabulary

Call on volunteers to define the key terms in the Section Preview. Have other students check the accuracy of these definitions in the Glossary. **LEP**

Use the **Vocabulary PuzzleMaker** to create crossword and word search puzzles.

SECTION 1
The Global Demand for Resources

Section Preview

Objectives

After studying this section, you will be able to:

1. **Explain** Malthus's views on population growth.

2. **Explain** the importance of conserving nonrenewable resources.

3. **List** ways that people are using renewable energy resources to conserve scarce resources.

Key Terms

subsistence, embargo, gasohol, aquifer

Applying Economic Concepts

Scarcity Do you live in an area that has a water shortage? Has your local government ever passed temporary laws restricting lawn watering and washing cars? If so, you have experienced the economic principle of *scarcity* firsthand.

Scarcity has been defined as the fundamental economic problem. You experience scarcity at the personal level. Scarcity is also a problem at the national level, even for relatively prosperous nations such as the United States. At the global level, scarcity reveals itself through food and energy shortages, which are compounded as world population grows.

In many respects, the earth is a very small planet. A global perspective helps us to use our economic knowledge to make the world a better place in which to live.

The Population Issue

The issue of population growth has fascinated the world since Thomas Malthus published his *Essay on the Principles of Population* in 1798. His views, published nearly 200 years ago, are still relevant because of the earth's growing population and its demand for resources.

Malthus's Views on Population

Thomas Malthus argued that population would grow faster than its ability to feed itself. The problem, he stated, was that population tended to grow geometrically, or at a rapidly increasing rate, as in the numbers 1, 2, 4, 8, 16, 32, 64, and so on. The ability of the earth to feed people, however, would grow at a

slower constant rate, such as 1, 2, 3, 4, 5. . . . He feared that if population growth were not checked, the future would be bleak:

Famine seems to be the last, the most dreadful resource of nature. The power of population is so superior to the power of the earth to provide subsistence . . . that premature death must in some shape or other visit the human race. The vices of mankind are active and able ministers of depopulation. . . . But should they fail in this war of extermination, sickly seasons, epidemics, pestilence, and plague advance in terrific array and sweep off thousands and tens of thousands. Should success still be incomplete, gigantic inevitable famine stalks in the rear, and with one mighty blow, levels the population with the food of the world.

—Thomas Malthus, *Essay on Population*, 1798

Eventually, the masses of the world would be reduced to a condition of **subsistence**—the state in which a population produces barely enough to support itself.

In many countries—especially in the larger cities—poverty is widespread. The Indian city of Calcutta, for example, has about 12 million people, and its population is expected to reach 14 million by the year 2000. Calcutta is one of the most crowded and poorest cities in the world. Hundreds of thousands of street dwellers beg and search for food in the city dumps and refuse piles. At night they sleep in the streets. Similar conditions exist in other parts of the world. In these places, the Malthusian prediction of a subsistence standard of living is a cruel reality.

Classroom Resources for SECTION 1

- Reproducible Lesson Plan 21-1
- Guided Reading Activity 21-1
- Cooperative Learning Activity 22
- Math Practice for Economics 28
- Primary and Secondary Source Reading 22
- Economic Simulation 6
- Economic Laboratory 6
- Performance Assessment Activity 21
- Section Quiz 21-1
- Spanish Section Quiz 21-1

- Focus Activity Transparency 96
- NBR's Economics in Action Video Program
- Testmaker
- Vocabulary PuzzleMaker
- Chapter Challenger Interactive Review Software
- MindJogger Videoquiz

Was Malthus Wrong?

In many other parts of the world, conditions are much better. Malthus did not foresee the enormous advances in productivity, which have allowed an increasing standard of living to accompany a growing population. He also did not foresee that families might choose to have fewer children.

Malthus's predictions may not have been entirely accurate for the industrialized countries, but they still have long-run consequences for all nations. Today, for example, population pressures in other parts of the world are causing problems for many industrialized countries, including the United States, which is besieged by many illegal immigrants from China and Haiti. As a result, many experts argue that it is in everyone's interest to control global population growth.

World Population Trends

Figure 21.1 shows the rate of population growth for various nations during the 1990s. The world

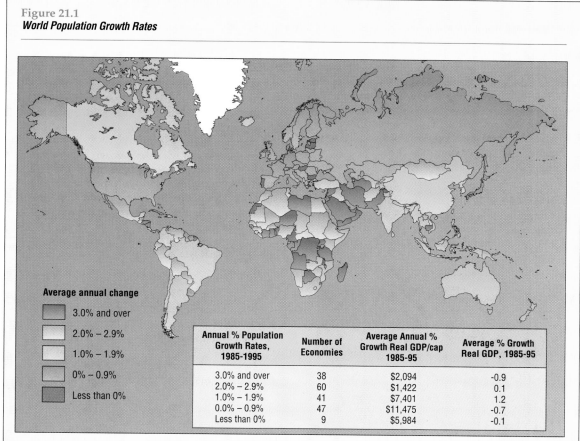

Figure 21.1
World Population Growth Rates

Average annual change
- 3.0% and over
- 2.0% – 2.9%
- 1.0% – 1.9%
- 0% – 0.9%
- Less than 0%

Annual % Population Growth Rates, 1985-1995	Number of Economies	Average Annual % Growth Real GDP/cap 1985-95	Average % Growth Real GDP, 1985-95
3.0% and over	38	$2,094	-0.9
2.0% – 2.9%	60	$1,422	0.1
1.0% – 1.9%	41	$7,401	1.2
0.0% – 0.9%	47	$11,475	-0.7
Less than 0%	9	$5,984	-0.1

Source: *The World Bank Atlas,* 1997

Population growth is highest in many of the countries that have the lowest standards of living. Conversely, population growth is lowest in countries with high standards of living. **What was Malthus's view on population?**

CHAPTER 21: *Global Economic Challenges* **521**

TEACH

Guided Practice

L2 *Analyzing Ideas* Have students review Thomas Malthus's views about population growth. Then write the following statement on the chalkboard: *Malthus was both right and wrong.* Ask students to discuss how this statement applies to Malthus's predictions about population and the supply of food. Provide guidance by asking students to consider the following questions: How do Malthus's views apply directly to poorer countries? How do these views apply directly to industrialized countries? Might rapid population growth have an indirect impact on the industrialized world? Suggest that students take notes during the discussion. Have them use these notes to write a brief essay titled "Thomas Malthus: Right and Wrong?"

Cooperative Learning
Assign Cooperative Learning Activity 22.

 VISUAL INSTRUCTION

Have students identify the areas where population growth is highest. (*Africa, Asia, Latin America*)

Answer to Caption:

that population would grow faster than its ability to feed itself

---

Meeting Special Needs

Learning Disability Students who have difficulty concentrating while they read will experience more frustration if they are asked to read *and* take notes. For them, it may be easier to finish reading and then review the text to take notes. Have these students read Section 1. As they read, have them use a signal—removable highlighting tape, for example—to mark important points. Then have them review the text to take notes.

GLENCOE TECHNOLOGY

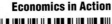

NIGHTLY BUSINESS REPORT

Economics in Action

Chapter 29

Disc 2, Side 2

Title: *Global Economic Challenges*

Subject: Opportunities of a global economy

Ask: What factors encourage American companies to establish business operations in foreign nations?
(Companies go where the costs of making their products will be low. They also go where their products will be in demand.)

Also available in VHS.

Independent Practice

📂 ***Guided Reading*** Assign Guided Reading Activity for Section 1. **LEP**

L3 ***Library Research*** Have students prepare an illustrated report on one of the following energy resources—oil, coal, natural gas, solar power, hydroelectric power, wind power, nuclear energy, or gasohol. Suggest that students focus their reports on such topics as history and development, reserves, and possible future use. Call on students to share their reports with the rest of the class.

---

population is growing at about 1.7 percent a year. Although this amount may not seem very large, the consequences can be enormous over time. Every year, the population increase is equivalent to adding another Mexico to the world. If the population keeps growing at this rate, it will be about 6.3 billion by the end of the century, more than 8 billion by 2020, and nearly 15 billion by 2050. At this rate, the population of the world will more than double from the time you graduate from high school until you retire at age 65. ☑

Nonrenewable Energy Sources

The depletion of many important resources compounds population pressures. Energy is one of these resources. As a factor of production, energy belongs to the category called *land* and is necessary for production to take place. Energy also makes life more comfortable. In the form of gasoline, it powers cars. In the form of electricity, it heats and cools homes. **1**

Nonrenewable resources occur in several forms—including oil, natural gas, and coal. Historically, low prices encouraged the consumption of each.

Oil

Between 1900 and 1970, energy consumption in the United States doubled almost every 14 years. Oil was refined into gasoline, and because prices were relatively low, automobiles were large, heavy, and got poor gas mileage.

> ### DID YOU KNOW?
>
> **Catch Those Rays!** The use of solar energy is growing rapidly in developing nations. Developing countries have been the biggest buyer of solar energy equipment sold by American companies. Solar stations supply power to homes and schools as well as to telecommunications systems, water pumping stations, and refrigerators for medical supplies. The governments of Guatemala, Panama, El Salvador, and Mexico are among those that recognize the advantages of solar power.

The low cost of oil even affected living habits. People tended to live some distance from where they worked, and many spent hours traveling to and from their jobs. Heating oil was inexpensive, so houses tended to be large, spacious, and poorly insulated.

In 1973, however, the oil-producing countries of the Middle East placed an **embargo**—a restriction on the export or import of a commodity in trade—on oil sales to the West. The embargo caused energy shortages in many parts of the world, which drove up prices. During the embargo, the price of oil went from less than $5 to more than $35 a barrel. Oil prices have decreased since then, but the oil that was consumed when prices were low will never be recovered.

Natural Gas

To protect consumers, the federal government followed a policy of controls that kept the price of natural gas low for many years. Policies were eventually changed in the late 1960s, but the artificially low prices had significant side effects.

When natural gas was inexpensive, people found many ways to use it. They heated their homes and swimming pools with it and built their factories and technology around it. Because natural gas was so inexpensive, it was even burned off at the wellhead to allow drillers to get to the more valuable oil. Over the years, trillions of cubic feet of natural gas were wasted because it was so inexpensive.

Coal

Another nonrenewable resource is coal. Today, nearly two-thirds of the world's known coal reserves are in the United States, Russia, and China. Although coal is plentiful, it too will eventually run out. Estimates based on the present rate of consumption indicate that the reserves will last about 200 years.

Renewable Energy Sources

Before 1973, little incentive to develop renewable energy sources such as solar, hydroelectric, or wind power existed. The oil embargo and soaring oil prices, however, provided this incentive. Americans became

---

$ *Free Enterprise Activity* $

Have students survey business owners and managers in the community to discover what measures they are taking to conserve resources. Suggest that students ask such questions as: What types of resources are you conserving? What conservation methods are you using? What methods might you adopt in the future? Why are you taking steps to conserve resources? Have students summarize their findings and present them to the class.

Natural Resources *The demand for scarce resources is one of the most pressing problems facing all nations. As cities expand in the United States, suburbs encroach upon farmland.* **What alternative energy sources are Americans considering?**

 VISUAL INSTRUCTION

Point out that in the 1950s, when the major exodus to the suburbs took place, close to 3,000 acres of forest and farmland were cleared each day for suburban developments.

Answer to Caption:

solar power, hydroelectric power, wind power, nuclear energy, and other fuels such as gasohol

---

concerned about the cost of energy and their dependence on foreign countries. As a result, they began to look for alternatives.

Solar Power

One alternative is solar power, which for many years interested mostly inventors and scientists. After the embargo, however, the federal government began issuing grants to researchers to find ways to reduce solar energy costs. Congress passed laws giving taxpayers credits for installing energy-saving devices in

their homes. This legislation encouraged many homeowners to insulate, install storm windows, and equip their homes with solar-powered water heaters. **2**

Hydroelectric Power

Another alternative is hydroelectric power, which historically had been used to power the mills and factories of the Northeast. The power was reliable, and its source—water—was free at the time. The drawback was that most dams were small and could not distribute power very efficiently to other locations.

 ANSWERS

1. land
2. It gave taxpayers credits for installing energy-saving devices in their homes.

 QUICK CHECK

Checking Understanding

1. Energy is considered part of which factor of production?
2. How did federal legislation encourage the development of solar power?

Applying Economic Concepts

✓ **Population Growth** You can use the "rule of 70" to find out how long it takes anything to double. Divide 70 by the rate of growth to find the number of years. For example, population would double in 70 ÷ 1.7, or 41.2 years.

CHAPTER 21: *Global Economic Challenges* **523**

Extending the Content

The U.S. Department of Energy The Department of Energy was created in 1977 mostly as a response to the 1973 embargo that forced up the price of oil. The purpose of the department is to

plan energy policy and research and develop new energy technology. The goal of the department is to reduce the country's vulnerability to future disruptions in oil markets.

ASSESS

Check for Understanding

Assign Section 1 Review as homework or an in-class activity.

○ Use **Chapter Challenger Interactive Review Software** to review Section 1.

MEETING LESSON OBJECTIVES

Each objective below is tested by the questions that follow it in parentheses.

1. **Explain** Malthus's views on population growth. **(2)**

2. **Explain** the importance of conserving nonrenewable resources. **(1, 3, 5, 6, 7)**

3. **List** ways that people are using renewable energy resources to conserve scarce resources. **(1, 4, 6)**

VISUAL INSTRUCTION

Point out that the nuclear clean-up is one of the major environmental challenges facing former communist countries.

Answer to Caption:

pros: provides about 10 percent of commercial electricity in the U.S.; cons: hazardous by-products, expensive to set up, may be dangerous to health and environment

---

Figure 21.2
The Most Dangerous Nuclear Reactors

Western governments have identified 9 nuclear power plants in the former Soviet Union and Eastern Europe, with a total of 24 reactors, that must be permanently closed. **What are the pros and cons of nuclear energy?**

Source: *Business Week*, June 8, 1993

When oil was obtained cheaply from the Middle East, waterpower became less important. By the late 1950s, most of the commercial power dams in the United States had been abandoned. When oil became more expensive, however, steps were taken to bring some of the dams back into use. Today, it is estimated that hydroelectric power could reduce imported oil usage by about 20 percent.

Wind Power

A third alternative is wind-generated electricity. In the early 1980s, sales of wind-driven equipment for generating electricity amounted to hundreds of millions of dollars. Many wind farms were built, producing enough electricity to power a medium-sized city.

Nuclear Energy

Interest also grew in nuclear energy, which generates about 10 percent of the commercial electricity used in the United States. The future of nuclear power, however, is uncertain for several reasons. Nuclear energy produces highly hazardous by-products, the safe disposal of which poses a major problem. In addition, construction costs of nuclear reactors are staggering. Lastly, many people are convinced that nuclear power presents a danger to health and the environment. The 1986 meltdown of the reactor in Chernobyl, Ukraine, reminded the world of the hazards of nuclear power.

Other Fuels

Other alternative energy sources include wood and **gasohol**—a fuel that is a mixture of 90 percent unleaded gasoline and 10 percent grain alcohol. Although gasohol has not been accepted as quickly as supporters first hoped, it still has a small share of the market in some areas. Wood stoves, in contrast, have grown rapidly in popularity, especially in high-cost energy areas such as the industrial Northeast.

Private industry has developed other lesser-known alternatives. Major food firms have made progress in converting chicken waste to fuel in the form of methane gas. This gas can then be recycled for industrial and commercial use.

Other Resources

Resources other than those used to generate energy also may be in danger. These include water and land.

Water

In the past, American concern with water focused mainly on the pollution of the country's waterways. Today, however, the focus is on the availability of water and the realization that water is in critical supply in many parts of the country.

More than 80 percent of the water consumed in the United States is used in agriculture. Most of this water is used in surface irrigation, which has a high evaporation rate. As a result, much water is lost into the atmosphere.

Cultural Diversity and Economics

Nuclear Costs Economic and human costs were completely ignored when the Soviet Union began its drive to develop nuclear energy in the years following World War II. Economic plans were adjusted to accommodate this new goal. Consumer goods, already relegated to a secondary status in the drive to industrialize, were further ignored. Test explosions were carried out near populated areas, and little care was taken in the disposal of nuclear waste. In the rush to get nuclear power plants into operation, little was done to establish safety standards. This approach, one Russian scientist noted, "was irresponsible and immoral." As a result, future generations will bear the cost—radioactive contamination is Russia's major environmental problem.

Farmers have been able to tap large sources of water from rivers, streams, ponds, and **aquifers**—underground water-bearing rock formations. Aquifers supply nearly 40 percent of the water that farmers use and are the source of fresh water for many communities.

One of the largest aquifers in the country is the Ogallala Aquifer, which supplies water to the High Plains states from Texas to Nebraska. So much water has been pumped out, however, that the aquifer's water table has been dropping about 3 feet a year. Some experts even predict that it will run out of water within the next 40 or 50 years.

The shortage of water is also a problem in Southern California. Over the years, some plans have been proposed and projects have been undertaken to bring in water from areas hundreds of miles away.

When water was plentiful at very low prices, farmers used a great deal of it in areas not otherwise suitable for farming. Consumers also used it freely. They watered their lawns, washed cars, used large-capacity washing machines, filled bathtubs, and ran showers for long periods of time. When water became scarce and its price went up, however, consumers began to conserve by washing their cars less often, installing water-saving devices in the bathroom, and reducing other usage of water around the home.

Land

Another valuable natural resource subject to the demands of a growing world population is land. Land, however, is different from other resources because there is a fixed supply of land that cannot be moved from one place to another.

A growing population often occupies the best farmland, which reduces the amount of land to be farmed. Many early settlers, for example, located in river valleys because the land was fertile and the rivers provided transportation. As the population grew, towns and cities replaced the early river settlements. As communities grew, factories, roads, and houses were built on the fertile land near the rivers. The development of this land forced the farmers to move to the outskirts.

This growth pattern repeated itself many times, and some of the finest farmland eventually ended up beneath expressways, shopping centers, and housing developments. Because many farmers willingly sold their land to industrial and housing interests, this trend would be nearly impossible to reverse today.

When the farmers sold their land, they often relocated to areas where the land was less fertile but also inexpensive. Since then, the development and availability of fertilizers, pesticides, herbicides, and other technological advances have kept the farmers' productivity very high.

CHAPTER 21
SECTION 1

Evaluate

Assign the Section 1 Quiz in the TCR or use the *Economics: Principles and Practices* Testmaker to create a customized quiz. Spanish Section Quizzes also are available in the Spanish Resources Binder.

Reteach

Have students write newspaper headlines that summarize the main points of the section. Call on volunteers to read and discuss their headlines.

Enrich

Direct students to research the locations of major reserves of nonrenewable energy sources. Have them record their findings on an outline map of the world. Remind students that their maps will need a title, labels, and a key. Call on volunteers to display their maps.

CLOSE

Have students discuss the problem of dwindling energy resources by considering these questions: What are we doing about this problem? What should we do about this problem?

SECTION 1 REVIEW

Reviewing Terms and Facts

1. **Define** subsistence, embargo, gasohol, aquifer.
2. **Describe** how Malthus believed population growth would affect the future of the planet.
3. **Explain** how the oil embargo affected gasoline consumption.
4. **List** the renewable sources of energy that are providing alternatives to nonrenewable resources.

5. **Describe** the effects that a growing population has on scarce resources such as aquifers.

Critical Thinking

6. **Making Comparisons** How do renewable resources differ from nonrenewable resources?

Applying Economic Concepts

7. **Scarcity** During the oil embargo, many people openly advocated nonprice gasoline rationing. Some favored allowing each automobile owner to use 10 gallons per week. What are the pros and cons of such a mandatory rationing program?

CHAPTER 21: *Global Economic Challenges* **525**

Answers to SECTION 1 REVIEW

1. All words are defined in the Glossary.

2. Malthus believed that population would grow geometrically but that the ability of the earth to feed people would grow at a slower constant rate, eventually leading to worldwide starvation.

3. It caused a shortage, which drove up gasoline prices and reduced consumption of gasoline.

4. solar power, hydroelectric power, wind power, nuclear energy, wood, methane gas

5. It quickly depletes scarce resources.

6. Nonrenewable resources will eventually run out, but renewable resources can be used, grown, replaced, or generated again.

7. Pros: forced conservation of a nonrenewable resource; decreased pollution. Cons: opens the door for black market trading of gasoline rations; government interference in people's right to choose; people whose career depends on travel would need special consideration or their earning potential would suffer.

Background

Malthus's treatise essentially argued that the perfectibility of society was impossible. Interestingly enough, the social utopians whose ideas he dismissed seized on his treatise as an argument for social reform. Progress toward utopia, they said, could be achieved through population control.

TEACH

Mention that one argument offered in opposition to Malthus's ideas was that every mouth that needed to be fed had a pair of hands that could be put to work. Have students discuss the validity of this argument.

? DID YOU KNOW

When Malthus's *Essay on the Principle of Population* was published, it did more than destroy the popular utopian vision of the period. Thomas Carlyle, a contemporary nineteenth-century essayist and historian, read the essay and promptly labeled economics "the dismal science," a title occasionally used even today.

PROFILES IN ECONOMICS

THOMAS MALTHUS
(1766–1834)

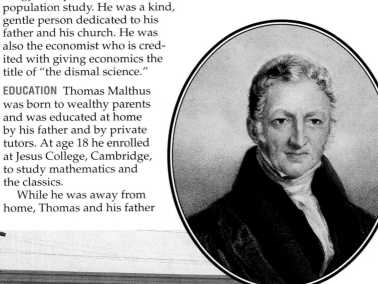

Thomas Malthus was an English economist, sociologist, and member of the clergy who pioneered modern population study. He was a kind, gentle person dedicated to his father and his church. He was also the economist who is credited with giving economics the title of "the dismal science."

EDUCATION Thomas Malthus was born to wealthy parents and was educated at home by his father and by private tutors. At age 18 he enrolled at Jesus College, Cambridge, to study mathematics and the classics.

While he was away from home, Thomas and his father

The government of China took strong steps to encourage smaller families.

became fascinated with a popular utopian vision that promised eventual peace, prosperity, and equality for all. Thomas attacked the argument in a 50,000-word letter to his father. The elder Malthus was so impressed that he encouraged Thomas to publish the treatise for others to read. The result was *An Essay on the Principle of Population as It Affects the Future Improvement of Society,* published in 1798.

POPULATION THEORY The book was an instant success that was to

often exchanged letters debating the popular issues of the day. At one point, the elder Malthus

forever change the way people viewed population. In it, Malthus argued that poverty and distress would be the eventual fate of people, not the popular utopian vision. He reasoned that population would increase at a geometric rate (1, 2, 4, 8, 16, . . .), while food supplies would increase at an arithmetic rate (1, 2, 3, 4, 5, . . .).

SUBSISTENCE STANDARD OF LIVING According to this progression, population growth would eventually outstrip the available food supply, resulting in famine, misery, and a subsistence standard of living for the masses.

At first, Malthus thought only three factors could check the growth of population: war, famine, and disease. Several years later, he added a fourth check: moral restraint. Separately or together, these factors could raise the death rate and/or lower the birthrate. In Malthus's view, however, these restraints on population growth would not be enough to prevent most of the world from forever remaining at the subsistence level. Despite his considerable accomplishments in other aspects of economics, Malthus is best remembered for his pessimistic views on population.

Examining the Profile

1. **Evaluating Information** Do you agree or disagree with Malthus's predictions about population? Why or why not?

2. **For Further Research** Find out what Malthus's other contributions to economics were.

Answers to Examining the Profile

1. Answers will vary. Some students might disagree, pointing out that birth control methods can effectively regulate population growth and new technology can improve food production. Others might agree, saying that in developing countries more and more children are needed to increase the food a family can produce.

2. Suggest that Robert L. Heilbroner's *The Worldly Philosophers* (Touchstone, 1986) is a useful source of such information.

Section Preview

Objectives

After studying this section, you will be able to:

1. **Explain** how the price system helps conserve water, natural gas, and oil.
2. **Describe** government efforts to limit pollution.
3. **State** the importance of using resources wisely.

Key Terms

deep gas, glut, pollution, acid rain, pollution permit

Applying Economic Concepts

Markets and Prices Have you ever planned a trip? Did you budget how much you would have to spend on gasoline? Did you pay attention to where you could get the cheapest price per gallon? Shopping for the best price is an example of how *markets and prices* operate in the free enterprise system.

Most economic systems require incentives to make them work smoothly. In a market economy, incentives such as the profit motive and prices can be used to preserve scarce resources.

The Price System

Before the oil embargo of the 1970s, energy prices were low, a situation that encouraged consumption. When prices jumped after the oil crisis, people became much more energy conscious. Cars became more fuel efficient, houses became more energy efficient, and entire industries began to think about ways to save energy. These actions helped prolong the existing supplies of nonrenewable resources and encouraged the development of new energy sources. The examples below show how the price system helps promote the conservation of scarce resources.

Irrigation

When farmers pump water out of the ground to water their crops, they use pumps driven by electricity or natural gas. When water tables fall because of pumping, it costs more to pump the water. As long as farmers continue to make a profit on their crops, they will pay the higher price for the water.

Initially, the higher cost of water will make everyone use it more efficiently, thus saving a scarce resource. In time, the falling water table will make some of the shallow wells useless. Deeper, more costly wells will be drilled instead. At this point, the price system will become relevant again. Deeper wells will be dug for profitable crops, while unprofitable crops will be abandoned.

Ultimately, the price system works to establish an equilibrium between the rising cost of recovering water and the depleted water tables. Although some crops and fields will be abandoned, they are likely to be the ones that were the least productive in the first place. As a result, the actual amount of agricultural output will not be much less than it is at present.

Deregulating Natural Gas

When the price of natural gas was low in the 1960s, the quantity demanded was high. Because government regulated the price, however, producers had little incentive to increase its production. Congress tried to stimulate gas discovery and production by lifting the price controls on **deep gas**—pockets of natural gas 15,000 feet or more below the earth's surface. This incentive increased its price to 3 or 4 times that of gas found above 15,000 feet. As a result, exploration for gas increased. Later, all gas price controls were removed, which encouraged even more production.

The lack of interest on the part of oil and gas producers in drilling for shallow gas was consistent with the law of supply, which maintains that the lower the price

CHAPTER 21: *Global Economic Challenges* **527**

the factory. Have students write a paragraph explaining how a person in their role might view the pollution tax. Have representatives of each role read their paragraphs to the class.

GLENCOE
TECHNOLOGY

NIGHTLY
BUSINESS
REPORT

Economics in Action

Chapter 29

Disc 2, Side 2

Title: *Global Economic Challenges*

Subject: Opportunities of a global economy

Ask: How can a global economy encourage companies to adopt sound environmental practices? *(Some consumers refuse to do business with firms that have poor environmental records, which encourages businesses to improve their records.)*

Also available in VHS.

VISUAL INSTRUCTION

Point out that in states where irrigation is used extensively—California, for example—water prices are a political as well as an economic issue.

Answer to Caption:

If people have to pay higher prices for water, they will use it more efficiently, thus conserving this scarce resource.

Irrigation *Surface irrigation systems are fairly common in the United States.* **How can the price system be used to preserve water?**

paid to producers, the less will be brought to market. Also consistent with the law of supply was the effort by producers to produce the deregulated deep gas.

Post-Embargo Oil Production

The higher price for oil after 1973 dramatically affected the production of oil. When oil was priced below $5 a barrel, few countries were willing to devote large resources to retrieve it. When the price increased to $35 and more, many countries increased their production almost overnight. **1**

By 1981, prices began to fall because of a worldwide **glut**—a substantial oversupply—of oil. A decline in demand caused by a recession contributed to the worldwide oversupply of oil. People had also learned to conserve energy, which further reduced the demand for oil. The collective impact of the increase in world supply and the decline in demand caused OPEC to lose some of its ability to control the supply of oil. This control slipped even further after the Persian Gulf War, when some OPEC members increased oil production to replenish their financial reserves depleted during the war.

Pollution and Economic Incentives

Pollution is the contamination of air, water, or soil by the discharge of poisonous or noxious substances.

Pollution is a problem that most countries today must face.

The Incentive to Pollute

For years, factories have located along the banks of rivers so they could dump their refuse into the moving waters. Some factories, which generated smoke and other air pollutants, located farther from the water, but their tall smokestacks still blew the pollutants long distances. Others tried to avoid the problem by digging refuse pits on their property and burying their toxic wastes.

In all three situations, factory owners were trying to lower production costs by using the environment as a giant waste-disposal system. From an economic point of view, the reasoning was sound. Firms get ahead when they lower production costs. Those who produce the most at the least cost make the most profits.

The costs of pollution to society as a whole, however, are huge. For example, **acid rain**—a mixture of water and sulfur dioxide that makes a mild form of sulfuric acid—falls over much of North America, damaging countless rivers and streams. Ecosystems in other areas may be poisoned by fertilizer buildup and raw sewage runoff.

The damage caused by pollution is extensive, but it can be controlled. One way to control pollution is through legislated standards. Another way is through economic incentives.

Meeting Special Needs

Writing Disability Many students with writing disabilities have difficulty organizing answers to questions that require written responses. Although they have usually studied "topic" or "lead" sentences, they often do not know how to form one independently. Read just the headings in this section aloud. As a group, have students write a topic sentence related to the role of economic incentives to reduce pollution.

Legislated Standards

Legislated standards include laws that specify the minimum standards of purity for air, water, and auto emissions. Congress, for example, has declared that all automobiles sold in the United States must meet certain pollution standards. If they do not meet the standards, the Environmental Protection Agency will not certify them, and they cannot be sold domestically.

Although affected industries have objected to them, some legislated standards have worked quite well. The auto industry complained loudly for years that it could not meet the tougher clean air standards. When pressed to do so, however, most auto manufacturers managed to meet them. Some other companies did not fare as well. They decided to close down rather than to spend the money needed to upgrade their aging capital stock.

A Pollution Tax

Besides legislation, another method of controlling pollution is to have companies pay taxes on the amount of pollutants they release. The size of the tax would depend on the severity of the pollution and the quantity of toxic substances being released. **2**

Suppose a community wants to reduce air pollution caused by 4 factories, each of which releases large quantities of coal dust. A tax of $50 for every ton of coal dust released into the air would be applied to each factory. The total tax paid over the course of the year depends on the number of tons discharged. Devices attached to the top of the factory's smokestacks would measure the amount during a one-week period. After the average rate of discharge is established, the factory would be billed accordingly.

Each company would have the choice of paying the tax or removing the pollutants themselves. Suppose

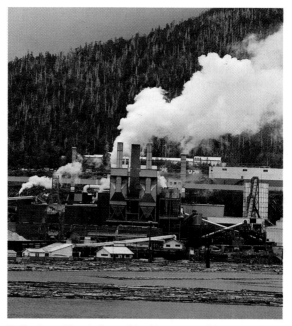

Pollution *Chemicals used in this paper mill have killed the surrounding forest as well as polluted the adjoining river.* **What is acid rain?**

two factories find that if they install scrubbers, they can remove the coal dust for $40 a ton—$10 a ton less than the tax would cost. More than likely, they would choose to install the scrubbers rather than pay the tax. The community would then be left with only two factories still polluting its air. If the quality of the air meets the standard, nothing further needs to be done.

If, however, air quality still is below the desired level, the tax can be raised to $60 or $70 a ton. Eventually, this tax hike might cause a third factory to install its own pollution equipment. If the air still is not clean

Checking Understanding	**Applying Economic Concepts**
1. How did the oil embargo affect the production of oil?	**Role of Government** The Environmental Protection Agency enforces the Clean Air Act, originally passed in 1963 and amended since then. The law sets standards for clean air and penalizes industries that pollute air and water.
2. What is a pollution tax?	

CHAPTER 21: *Global Economic Challenges* **529**

Select about 10 students and organize them into 2 teams. Have the teams take opposite sides and debate the following: Limits on pollution should be established by market forces, not by government legislation. Have students not directly involved in the debate act as judges and list the major arguments presented in the debate. At the conclusion of the debate, call on a number of judges to share their lists with the class. Then have students use this information to write a short paper supporting or opposing the proposal.

Independent Practice

 Guided Reading Assign Guided Reading Activity for Section 2. **LEP**

L2 *Applying Ideas* Have students research pollution problems in their community. Ask them to write a report on their findings noting the type of pollution, its causes, and possible remedies. Encourage students to share their reports with the rest of the class.

ASSESS

Check for Understanding

Assign Section 2 Review as homework or an in-class activity.

VISUAL INSTRUCTION

Point out that air pollution aggravates emphysema, pneumonia, and many other respiratory diseases.

Answer to Caption:

a mixture of water and sulfur dioxide that makes a mild form of sulfuric acid

ANSWERS

1. Many countries increased their oil production almost overnight.
2. a tax on the amount of pollutants a company releases

MEETING LESSON OBJECTIVES

Each objective below is tested by the questions that follow it in parentheses.

1. **Explain** how the price system helps conserve water, natural gas, and oil. **(2, 5)**

2. **Describe** government efforts to limit pollution. **(1, 3, 4)**

3. **State** the importance of using resources wisely. **(3)**

Evaluate

▱ ▱ ◉ Assign the Section 2 Quiz in the TCR or use the *Economics: Principles and Practices* Testmaker to create a customized quiz. Spanish Section Quizzes also are available in the Spanish Resources Binder.

Reteach

Have students use the key terms to write a paragraph that summarizes the section.

Enrich

Have students work individually or in small groups to create a four-page pictorial essay on the economic aspects of pollution. Encourage students or groups to display their essays on the bulletin board.

CLOSE

Have students discuss, from an economic perspective, the following statement made by Ralph Waldo Emerson: "We do not inherit the earth from our ancestors, we borrow it from our children."

---

enough, the community then could raise the tax again until the fourth factory decides to install scrubbers.

This tax approach, suggested by many economists, does not try to remove all pollution. It does, however, allow individual companies freedom of choice. It also provides flexibility that legislated standards lack and may prevent some plants from closing entirely.

Some firms would rather pay the tax than clean up their own pollution. These firms, however, help fund the pollution clean-up campaign. Consumers will not have to fund the effort out of their income, sales, or property taxes.

Pollution Permits

The Environmental Protection Agency (EPA) uses a similar system to reduce sulfur dioxide emissions, a key component of acid rain. The EPA's target is to ultimately reduce sulfur dioxide emissions to a level of 9 million tons per year.

The EPA started its program by issuing sulfur dioxide permits to utilities in 1993. The **pollution permits** allowed the utilities to release emissions into the air, and the utilities are not allowed to operate without the permits. If a utility has more permits than it needs, it can sell them in 1-ton increments. Thus, utilities that want to spend money on emissions cleanup could sell their permits, and use the cash to clean up their production. Those who prefer to purchase and use the permits are also allowed to do so.

The first set of pollution permits went on sale in March 1993 at the Chicago Board of Trade. The 1-ton permits brought prices ranging from $122 to $450

each. Several environmental groups also purchased the pollution permits. They planned to retire the permits to make them scarcer, and therefore more expensive, for the utilities.

The EPA will issue additional permits in successive years, but fewer permits will be issued as time goes on. Ultimately, the utilities will either have to pay very high prices for the permits, or they will have to buy antipollution devices.

Using Resources Wisely

The resource challenge is vital to the study of economics. Resources become scarce when the quantity demanded for them is greater than the quantity supplied. In a market economy, the price system plays a major role in the allocation of resources. It tells consumers when resources are scarce. It also helps decision makers allocate resources more wisely. For this reason, economists who believe in a market economy are optimistic about the future, especially if the price system is allowed to function and fulfill its role in the economy.

Even the amount of energy reserves is a function of price. Not long ago, it was thought that the United States natural gas reserves would last only another 30 years. That prediction, however, was made when the price of natural gas was low. When the price increased, less natural gas was bought, and the given reserves stretched further. At the same time, the higher price encouraged more exploration, and more reserves were found. As a result, supplies will last longer.

SECTION 2 REVIEW

Reviewing Terms and Facts

1. **Define** deep gas, glut, pollution, acid rain, pollution permit.
2. **Describe** how deregulation has affected the natural gas industry.
3. **Explain** how a pollution tax encourages industries to stop polluting.

Critical Thinking

4. **Making Comparisons** How do legislated standards and economic incentives differ in regard to pollution control?

Applying Economic Concepts

5. **Markets and Prices** Suppose that the demand for natural gas increases sharply because of a series of extremely harsh winters. How would a price increase affect gas usage as well as research efforts by natural gas companies?

Answers to SECTION 2 REVIEW

1. All words are defined in the Glossary.

2. The price of natural gas increased, thus encouraging production and reducing consumption.

3. Companies must pay taxes on the amount of pollutants they release. These companies can choose to pay the tax or take steps to remove the pollutants themselves. Either way, the companies must pay to clean up their pollution.

4. Legislated standards specify minimum standards of purity for air, water, and auto emissions and are inflexible. This may cause some companies to close if they cannot afford to comply. Economic incentives include pollution taxes and pollution permits. Incentives offer choices so companies can comply in the way that is best for them and still stay in business.

5. People would find ways to limit their use of natural gas, and natural gas companies would look for ways to increase production.

ECONOMIC SKILL

Analyzing Trends

The business section of a newspaper reports a trend toward lower interest rates. An automobile dealer advertises a trend in smaller cars. In some cases, a trend is a short-lived fad. In other cases, a trend is a general change in patterns that indicates long-term progress or decline.

Explanation

Trends can be determined by studying statistical information over a period of time. To analyze a trend, you should ask the following questions:
1. What definite patterns or directions can be seen on the graph?
2. Does the information extend over a significant period of time so that trends can be clearly determined?
3. What could be some underlying causes of the trends shown on the graph?
4. What additional information would make the graph more helpful in analyzing trends?

Practice

The bar graph that follows shows changes in "environmental" behavior for adults aged 18 years and older.

Study the trends indicated on the graph below, then answer the questions that follow.

1. What is the title of this graph?
2. What years are compared?
3. Describe the general trend in adults' environmental behaviors.
4. Which behavior had the greatest percentage change? By how much did the behavior change?
5. What could be some underlying causes of the trends shown on the graph?

TEACHING SKILLS

TEACH

Point out that economists often use trends to help them make generalizations about changes taking place at the moment. They also use trends as the basis for making predictions about the future. Ask students to review business periodicals and the business pages of newspapers to find examples of these two uses of trends.

📁 **Skills Practice** For additional practice, have students complete Reinforcing Economic Skill 21.

Figure 21.3

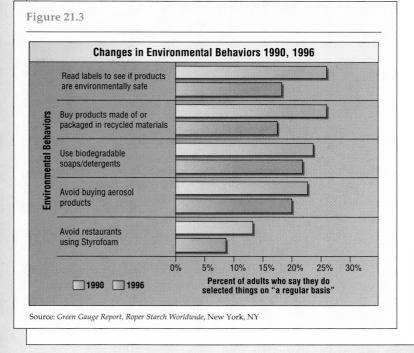

Changes in Environmental Behaviors 1990, 1996

Environmental Behaviors:
- Read labels to see if products are environmentally safe
- Buy products made of or packaged in recycled materials
- Use biodegradable soaps/detergents
- Avoid buying aerosol products
- Avoid restaurants using Styrofoam

Percent of adults who say they do selected things on "a regular basis"

☐ 1990   ☐ 1996

Source: *Green Gauge Report, Roper Starch Worldwide*, New York, NY

Additional Practice

For further practice in analyzing trends, complete the Reinforcing Skills exercise in the Chapter 21 Review on page 537.

Answers to SKILL

1. Changes in Environmental Behaviors
2. 1990, 1996
3. Adults are not as vigilant about environmentally-driven purchases as they used to be.
4. Buying products made of or packaged in recycled materials; reduced by about 10 percent from 1990 to 1996

5. Perhaps adults cared less about the environment in 1996 than they did in 1990. Perhaps they feel they can relax because they see companies making changes, such as fast-food restaurants switching to recycled packaging.

FOCUS

Section Objectives

1. Explain why economics has become a generalized theory of choice.
2. Understand how our market economy will be able to cope with the future.

Bellringer

Prior to taking roll at the beginning of the class period, display Focus Activity Transparency 98 on the overhead projector.

Motivational Activity

Discuss students' responses to the activity sheet that accompanies Focus Activity Transparency 98.

Preteaching Vocabulary

Ask students to explain, in their own words, the meaning of the key terms. **LEP**

Use the **Vocabulary PuzzleMaker** to create crossword and word search puzzles.

TEACH

Guided Practice

L2 *Applying Economics*
Have students identify an economic choice they made recently. Ask them to apply the five steps of economic decision making outlined on page 532 to their economic choice. Call on students to relate whether, after using the five-step approach, their choices have changed. **LEP**

532

Section Preview

Objectives	Key Terms	Applying Economic Concepts
After studying this section, you will be able to: 1. **Explain** why economics has become a generalized theory of choice. 2. **Understand** how our market economy will be able to cope with the future.	cost-benefit analysis, modified free enterprise economy	**Cost-Benefit Analysis** Have you ever decided not to do something because the cost of doing it was greater than the benefits that would be received? Economists call this *cost-benefit analysis*—and they use this analysis often. Perhaps you are starting to think like an economist.

As a science, economics is concerned with the way in which people cope with scarcity. Because scarcity is a universal problem, the study of economics is important to everyone.

A Framework for Decision Making

Through the study of economics, you learn that choices must be made. You begin to discover different ways to analyze a problem and that alternatives must be considered. The late economist Kenneth Boulding observed that economics has evolved to the point that it has now become a generalized theory of choice. Economics provides a framework for decision making and helps people to become better decision makers.

A Reasoned Approach

Economic decision making requires a careful, reasoned approach to problem solving. The National Council on Economic Education, an organization dedicated to the improvement of economic literacy in the United States, recommends five steps to economic decision making:

1. *State the problem or issue.*
2. *Determine the personal or broad social goals to be attained.*
3. *Consider the principal alternative means of achieving the goals.*

4. *Select the economic concepts needed to understand the problem and use them to appraise the merits of each alternative.*
5. *Decide which alternative best leads to the attainment of the most goals or the most important goals.*
   —*A Framework for Teaching the Basic Concepts*, 1996

These steps provide useful guidelines to decision making. Life is full of trade-offs, and you will be better equipped to deal with the future if you know how to analyze the problems you will encounter.

Decision Making at the Margin

Economists use a number of tools to help them make decisions. Some of these tools include production possibilities curves, supply and demand curves, production functions, and the National Income and Product Accounts.

One of the most important decision-making tools is the concept of marginal analysis. For example, when a firm makes a decision to produce additional output, it compares the extra cost of production with the extra benefits to be gained. If the benefits outweigh the costs, the firm decides to continue with the additional production. If the costs outweigh the benefits, the firm decides not to produce the additional output. 1

This process—**cost-benefit analysis**—involves comparing the costs of a course of action to its benefits. Firms use cost-benefit analysis when they make decisions to produce or purchase additional capital equipment. Many government agencies use it when they

---

Classroom Resources for SECTION 3

- Reproducible Lesson Plan 21-3
- Guided Reading Activity 21-3
- Section Quiz 21-3
- Spanish Section Quiz 21-3
- Focus Activity Transparency 98
- Enrichment Activity 21
- Reteaching Activity 21
- Spanish Reteaching Activity 21

- Economic Vocabulary Activity 21
- Spanish Economic Vocabulary Activity 21
- Chapter 21 Test, Form A and Form B
- Unit 5 Test
- English and Spanish Audiocassettes
- Testmaker
- Vocabulary PuzzleMaker
- Chapter Challenger Interactive Review Software
- MindJogger Videoquiz

evaluate programs. Individuals also use it when they make decisions. Cost-benefit analysis is even used to make choices among economic goals. Some choices will work against one goal while favoring another, but evaluating the costs and benefits of each choice helps in making decisions.

Coping With the Future

Everyone wants to know what will happen to the economy in the future. How will it adjust, and what course will it take in the future? Part of the answer can be found by examining the past.

The Triumph of Capitalism

During the 1930s, the forces of socialism and communism were sweeping the world, while capitalist countries were in economic depression. Communism in the Soviet Union had considerable impact upon the world, and socialist parties were on the rise in the European colonies in Africa.

Since then, communism in the former Soviet Union has collapsed under the weight of its own inefficiencies. Many socialist countries have embraced capitalism and the discipline of the market system. In addition, many developing countries have chosen capitalism as their economic system. Many emerging economic powers—including Hong Kong, Singapore, South Korea, and Taiwan—owe much of their remarkable growth to capitalism. ☑

Capitalism is now the dominant economic force in the world, but it is not the laissez-faire capitalism of the past. Capitalism has changed because people have addressed some of the weaknesses that Karl Marx and others discovered many years ago.

The capitalism of the 1930s was ruthlessly efficient in that it provided only for those who produced or

earned enough to buy the necessities of life. Early capitalism had little room for the elderly, the ill, or the incapacitated. Many economies today, including that of the United States, have a **modified free enterprise economy,** or modified private enterprise system. This is a free-market economy based on capitalism, yet modified by its people to satisfy the economic goals of freedom, efficiency, equity, security, full employment, price stability, and economic growth. 2

Markets and Prices

A modified free enterprise economy allows buyers and sellers to freely make the decisions that satisfy their wants and needs. The forces of supply and demand interact to establish prices in a market.

QUICK CHECK

Checking Understanding

1. What is marginal analysis?
2. How was American capitalism of the past different from American capitalism today?

Applying Economic Concepts

☑ **Comparative Systems** The intense rivalry between capitalism in the United States and communism in the former Soviet Union dominated global politics from 1945 to the early 1990s. Known as the cold war, the rivalry ended with the collapse of the Soviet Union.

CHAPTER 21: *Global Economic Challenges* **533**

Independent Practice

📂 **Guided Reading** Assign Guided Reading Activity for Section 3. **LEP**

L2 **Daily Life** Lead the class in a discussion of how a knowledge of economics will help them cope with everyday life in the future. Then have them write a brief essay explaining their views on this topic.

ASSESS

Check for Understanding

Assign Section 3 Review as homework or an in-class activity.

💿 Use **Chapter Challenger Interactive Review Software** to review Section 3.

MEETING LESSON OBJECTIVES

Each objective below is tested by the questions that follow it in parentheses.

1. **Explain** why economics has become a generalized theory of choice. **(1, 2, 5)**
2. **Understand** how our market economy will be able to cope with the future. **(3, 4)**

QUICK CHECK

ANSWERS

1. comparing extra benefits to extra costs of an action
2. Early capitalism had little room for the elderly, the ill, the incapacitated. Modern capitalism has modified to accommodate the seven economic goals.

Meeting Special Needs

Writing Disability Students with writing problems often copy answers directly from the book and have difficulty when they come to questions that require interpretation. Practice "reading between the lines" in the text, not only to have students make interpretations but also to have them learn to recognize bias.

Evaluate

 Assign the Section 3 Quiz in the TCR or use the *Economics: Principles and Practices* Testmaker.

Reteach

Have students write a paragraph explaining how to apply the economic way of thinking to problems.

Have students complete Reteaching Activity 21. Spanish Reteaching Activities also are available in the Spanish Resources Binder.

Enrich

Invite the manager of a local business to explain to the class how he or she uses cost-benefit analysis in his or her job.

Have students complete Enrichment Activity 21.

CLOSE

Have students develop a one-sentence description of economics. As an example, suggest: Economics is simply the study of choice. Have students compare their definitions.

VISUAL INSTRUCTION

Stress that the forces of supply and demand will determine this reallocation of resources.

Answer to Caption:

through the interaction of supply and demand and the signals sent by the price system

Alternatives *As the twenty-first century approaches, solar power will become a priority. As in the past, the capitalist system will allow producers and consumers to reallocate resources.* **How does change occur in a market economy?**

Prices, in turn, act as signals, causing producers and consumers to alter their spending decisions.

Prices also influence the allocation of resources across markets. The high price of oil in the 1970s made other energy sources competitive. In the 1980s, the high prices of personal computers attracted producers. Competition soon lowered prices and made the same computers affordable to mass markets.

A market economy has many advantages, including the ability to adjust to change gradually, without the need for government intervention. As long as the forces of supply and demand are allowed to function, they will send producers and consumers the signals needed to reallocate resources. Although no one knows what the future will bring, to date capitalism has demonstrated its ability to adapt.

SECTION 3 REVIEW

Reviewing Terms and Facts

1. **Define** cost-benefit analysis, modified free enterprise economy.
2. **Describe** the reasoned approach to decision making.
3. **Explain** how a market economy adapts to change.

Critical Thinking

4. **Synthesizing Information** Provide an example of how prices act as a signal to you as a buyer and/or seller.

Applying Economic Concepts

5. **Cost-Benefit Analysis** Think of a decision you must make in the next few days. How will you use your estimates of the costs and benefits to make your decision?

534 UNIT 5: *International and Global Economics*

Answers to SECTION 3 REVIEW

1. All vocabulary words are defined in the Glossary.

2. It involves the five steps put forth by the NCEE as guidelines to decision making.

3. In a market economy, supply and demand adjust to cause price changes, which act as signals to producers and consumers, causing them to reallocate resources.

4. Low prices encourage buyers to buy more. Higher prices encourage sellers to produce more.

5. Answers will vary. Students' answers should reflect an understanding of cost-benefit analysis and point out that they must weigh the cost of their decision against the benefits.

ECONOMICS IN ACTION

Global Economic Challenges

Setting Up the Video

With your classmates, view "Global Economic Challenges" on the videodisc *Economics in Action.* The video focuses on the challenges and opportunities of a global economy. Corporations set up plants where they can obtain the most efficient use of labor and capital resources and where their products will be in demand. A news report describes McDonald's expansion into 101 countries. The video also suggests

that a global economy can encourage companies to be socially responsible in response to boycotts.

Hands-On Activity

Clip two articles from a recent newspaper or magazine. One article should describe a foreign business that has established a company in the United States. The other should describe an American business that has established a company in a foreign country. Compare the two articles and prepare a brief oral report summarizing each article.

**Chapter 29
Disc 2, Side 2**

Scan the bar code or enter the chapter number on your keypad and press Search. *(Also available in VHS format.)*

SURFING THE "NET"

Global Demand for Resources

As the world population increases, people are becoming increasingly concerned about the rapid depletion of nonrenewable energy sources such as oil, natural gas, and coal. Many Americans became acutely aware of this depletion in the 1970s after the OPEC nations started an oil embargo. The embargo encouraged Americans to seek alternative energy sources. Use the Internet to find out the resources Americans are investigating as alternatives to nonrenewable resources.

Getting There

1. Use a search engine. Type in the words *alternative energy sources.*
2. Next, enter words like the following to focus your search: *solar power, wind power, nuclear energy,* and *hydroelectric power.*
3. The search engine will provide you with a number of links to follow. Links are "pointers" to different sites on the Internet and often appear as blue, underlined words.

What to Do When You Are There

Click on the links to navigate through the pages of information. Gather your findings. Use the findings to develop a brochure describing several of the alternatives to nonrenewable resources that are currently being investigated. Add clip art to your brochure and make extra copies to distribute in class.

535

NIGHTLY BUSINESS REPORT

Economics in Action

Chapter 29
Disc 2, Side 2
Title: *Global Economic Challenges*

If you do not have access to a videodisc player, the **Economics in Action** programs are also available in VHS.

INTERNET SITES

The following are possible sites for completing the "Net" activities:

Environmental Defense Fund
http://www.edf.org/

Solstice: Sustainable Energy and Development Online!
http://solstice.crest.org/

United Nations Environment Programme
http://www.unep.ch/

U.S. Environmental Protection Agency
http://www.epa.gov/

Not on the "Net"...

If students have limited or no access to the Internet, have them complete the activity "Global Demand for Resources" by using *Readers' Guide to Periodical Literature.* Students should look for articles about solar power, wind power, nuclear energy, and hydroelectric power. They should then find the articles they need to complete their research.

INTERNET ADDRESS BOOK

Internet addresses that you find useful can be noted in the space below for quick reference.

GLENCOE
TECHNOLOGY

VIDEODISC
MindJogger Videoquiz

Use MindJogger to review
the Chapter 21 content.

Chapter 21
Disc 3, Side A

Also available in VHS.

Answers

Reviewing Key Terms

1. j.
2. c.
3. h.
4. i.
5. g.
6. b.
7. d.
8. f.
9. e.

Reviewing the Facts

1. He did not foresee advances in productivity, which have allowed an increasing standard of living to accompany a growing population. He also did not foresee that some families would decide to have fewer children.

2. in many of the countries that have the lowest standards of living

3. oil, natural gas, coal

4. It produces highly hazardous by-products, which are difficult to dispose of safely.

5. Consumers consumed less, and the automobile industry started making smaller, more energy-efficient cars.

6. The law of supply maintains that the lower the price for a product, the less will be brought to market. Shallow gas was inexpensive, so producers had no

Reviewing Key Terms

Write the term that best completes the following sentences.

a. pollution permits
b. deep gas
c. modified free enterprise economy
d. glut
e. acid rain
f. pollution
g. aquifer
h. embargo
i. gasohol
j. subsistence

1. The state in which the population produces barely enough to support itself is _____ .
2. The United States has a _____, a system that has been altered by its people to satisfy economic goals.
3. A restriction on the export or import of a commodity in trade is a(n) _____.
4. _____ is a mixture of 90 percent unleaded gasoline and 10 percent grain alcohol.
5. An underground water-bearing rock formation is a(n) _____.
6. Natural gas found in pockets 15,000 feet or more beneath the earth's surface is _____.
7. By 1981, oil prices began to fall because of a worldwide _____ , or a substantial oversupply.
8. _____ is the contamination of air, water, or soil by the discharge of poisonous or noxious substances.
9. A mixture of water and sulfur dioxide that makes a form of sulfuric acid is _____ .

Reviewing the Facts

SECTION 1 *(pages 520–525)*
1. **Describe** why, despite Malthus's predictions, certain parts of the world have enjoyed steadily increasing standards of living.
2. **Explain** where the most rapid rates of population growth are found.
3. **List** the three major nonrenewable energy resources.
4. **Describe** the major drawback of nuclear energy.

SECTION 2 *(pages 527–530)*
5. **Explain** how American consumers and the automobile industry reacted to the oil price increases of the 1970s.
6. **Explain** how the reluctance of oil and gas producers to drill for shallow gas was consistent with the law of supply.
7. **Describe** what the Environmental Protection Agency hopes to accomplish by issuing pollution permits.
8. **State** how the price system in a market economy helps ensure that resources are used wisely.

SECTION 3 *(pages 532–534)*
9. **List** the steps involved in economic decision making.
10. **State** the importance of cost-benefit analysis.
11. **State** why adapting to change is important for an economic system.

Critical Thinking

1. **Making Predictions** In what ways can Americans ensure the wise use of resources? How might the world be different in 50 years if we do not use resources wisely today?
2. **Analyzing Information** How do the laws of supply and demand apply to the resource challenge?

Applying Economic Concepts

1. **Modified Free Enterprise Economy** The United States has a modified free enterprise economy in which the government regulates some industries. Do you think the government should play a smaller or larger role in regulating the American economy? Give reasons to support your answer.
2. **Scarcity** Scarce natural resources are a problem that concerns citizens throughout the world. What can you personally do to help conserve resources?

economic incentive to produce more.

7. They hope eventually to make the permits scarce enough to be cost-prohibitive, forcing industries to choose to clean up their own pollution.

8. The price system tells consumers when resources are scarce, and helps decision makers allocate resources more wisely.

9. 1. State the problem. 2. Determine the goals to be attained. 3. Consider principal alternative means of achieving the goals. 4. Select the economic con-

cepts needed to understand the problem and use them to appraise the alternatives. 5. Decide which alternative best leads to the attainment of the most goals or the most important goals.

10. Cost-benefit analysis is based on marginal analysis, a comprehensive approach that compares the extra cost of doing something with the extra benefits to be gained.

11. Adapting to change allows an economic system to survive in a changing world.

Figure 21.4
The Spread of Products Into American Households

[Graph showing Percent Ownership (y-axis, 0 to 100) versus Years Since Product Invented (x-axis, 5 to 120). Product curves labeled: Internet, Cell phone, PC, Microwave, VCR, Television, Radio, Electricity, Telephone, Automobile.]

Sources: Bureau of the Census, *The World Almanac,* Cellular Telecommunications Industry Assoc.

Reinforcing Skills
ANALYZING TRENDS

Analyze the graph above, then answer these questions.

1. What patterns can be seen on the graph?
2. About how long did it take 30 percent of American households to own an automobile? A television? A personal computer?
3. What could be some underlying causes of the trends shown on the graph?

Individual Activity

Research the process of using radiation for preserving and growing food. List the types of food products that are affected and the government agencies regulating the process. What are the benefits and possible side-effects of the radiation? Report your findings to the class.

Cooperative Learning Activity

Organize into two groups. One group opposes the extension of a plant that uses nuclear energy. It fears that an expanded facility will be unsafe. The other group states that the expansion will add 500 jobs to the local economy. Together, devise a plan that is safe, yet still helps the economy.

Technology Activity
Building a Database

Create a database on recycling centers in your community. Look in the telephone book to locate the nearest recycling centers. Find out the name, address, phone number, and operation hours of each service. Use this information to create a database, making separate fields for the materials, the locations, and the rebates paid for recycled items. Print and distribute your database to the rest of the class.

CHAPTER 21: *Global Economic Challenges* **537**

teeth, take short showers instead of baths, walk instead of drive, wear clothing until it is worn out, or recycle aluminum, newspaper, glass, and plastic.

Reinforcing Skills

1. As the economy evolves, it takes less and less time for new products to spread into the population.

2. 30 percent to own an automobile—about 65 years; 30 percent to own a television—about 25 years; 30 percent to own a PC—about 20 years

3. Answers will vary. Students may cite increased technology, economic factors, higher standard of living, greater population, and so on.

4. Answers will vary.

BONUS TEST QUESTION

Remind students that in Chapter 7, pollution was identified as an externality, or something that is not reflected in the price mechanism between buyers and sellers. Ask students how pollution taxes might internalize the cost of pollution. *(Taxes, or purchasing new, nonpolluting equipment to avoid taxes, are counted as costs by sellers and will be reflected in the prices buyers have to pay.)*

Critical Thinking

1. Answers will vary. Americans can conserve resources, lowering the demand and encouraging the wise use of resources. In 50 years, forced restrictions might be in place, some resources might be at dangerously low levels, or alternative energy sources might be very costly.

2. When the supply of a resource is plentiful, prices are low and people use the resource freely. As the resource becomes more scarce, the price goes up and the quantity demanded goes down, thus saving valuable resources and encouraging more exploration and production of or alternatives to nonrenewable resources.

Applying Economic Concepts

1. Answers will vary. Students should support their answers with examples and logical arguments.

2. Answers will vary. Students should cite specific examples such as turn off lights that are not being used, turn off the water while they brush their

Issues in Free Enterprise

PROTECTING DOMESTIC INDUSTRIES AGAINST FOREIGN COMPETITION

The winners in free trade are the consumers who get a wider variety of lower-priced goods from which to choose. The losers are the domestic industries that cannot produce as efficiently as the same industries in other nations. The recent economic success of Japan, which thrives on trade but goes to extreme measures to protect its domestic industries, has created the impression that protectionism can promote growth. As a result, the question arises: Should we protect our basic industries against foreign competition?

▲ *Caterpillar tractors are exported to Japan.*

Pro

The classical theory of free trade . . . doesn't deal with the fact that much "comparative advantage" today is created not by markets but by government action. If Boeing got a head start on the 707 from multibillion-dollar military contracts, is that a sin against free trade? Well, sort of. . . . If Japan uses public capital, research subsidies, and market-sharing cartels to launch a highly competitive semiconductor industry, is *that* protection? Maybe so, maybe not.

. . . [I]n a world where technology is highly mobile and interchangeable, there is a real risk that comparative advantage comes to be defined as whose work force will work for the lowest wage.

. . . Our competitors, increasingly, are not free marketeers in our own mold. It is absurd to let foreign mercantilist enterprise overrun U.S. industry in the name of free trade. . . .

[S]urely it is reasonable to fashion plans for [protecting] particular key sectors like steel, autos, machine tools, and semiconductors. The idea is not to close U.S. markets, but to limit the rate of import growth in key industries.

— FROM ROBERT KUTTNER'S "THE FREE TRADE FALLACY," *THE NEW REPUBLIC*

▼ *Protectionists believe that the United States should protect key industries such as steel.*

A customs official inspects Mexican-made Dodge trucks as they enter the United States.

Chiquita bananas are unloaded in Gulfport, Mississippi.

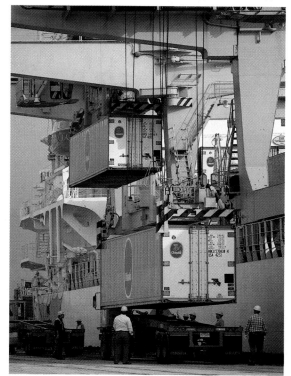

Con

Protectionism is, in effect, a "make work" jobs program—but a ridiculously expensive one, both directly and indirectly.

. . . [S]teelworkers (when they are working) make more than the median American income. Protectionism to preserve wage levels is just a redistribution of national wealth; it creates no new wealth. Nothing is wrong with redistribution, but . . . it's hard to see why the government should intervene to protect steelworker's wages at the expense of general national prosperity. This is especially true when millions are unemployed who would happily work for much less, and there is no jobs program for them.

. . . After you add the few hopeless loser industries where we must allegedly create barriers to save American wages, you've got the whole economy locked up, and whether this will actually encourage efficiency or the opposite is, at the very least, an open question. And if every major country protects every major industry, there will be no world market for any of them to conquer.

—FROM MICHAEL KINSLEY'S "KEEP FREE TRADE FREE," *THE NEW REPUBLIC*

Analyzing the Case Study

1. Who benefits most from international trade?
2. What evidence does Robert Kuttner cite to explain that protectionism is needed to protect basic industries from foreign competition?
3. What evidence does Michael Kinsley cite to explain that protectionism will negatively affect the United States economy?
4. With which opinion do you agree? Why?

CHAPTER 21: *Global Economic Challenges* **539**

Issues in Free Enterprise

L2 *Writing a Letter* Have students review Kuttner's and Kinsley's arguments. Then ask them to take a position on the issue and write a letter to the editor of their local newspaper that states and explains their position on protecting domestic industries against foreign competition. Call on students from both sides of the issue to read their letters to the class.

ASSESS

Have students answer the questions listed under "Analyzing the Case Study."

CLOSE

Refer students to the question they were asked to consider in the Focus activity. Ask them to consider the question once again. Conclude by asking students to discuss the following: If you believe the government does have a responsibility, what actions should it take to offer protection for domestic industries? If you believe the government has no responsibility, what actions can be taken to encourage domestic industries in areas that are dominated by foreign competition?

Answers to Analyzing the Case Study

1. consumers, who have a wider variety of lower-priced goods from which to choose
2. that a foreign company's advantage may have been created by government action rather than free operation of markets
3. Protectionism does little more than preserve the workers' wages. This constitutes a redistribution of the national wealth, not the creation of new wealth.

4. Answers will vary. Some may agree with Kuttner, pointing out that foreign competitors have an advantage in the market because of government support of some kind. Others may agree with Kinsley, arguing that protectionism simply prolongs the life of inefficient industries and adds nothing to the national wealth.

APPENDIX

Contents

PACK ICE

ICE CAP

TUNDRA

MOUNTAINS

EVERGREEN FOREST

Shallow water

3000 meters

5000 meters

ARID

MIXED FOREST

GRASSLAND

Inland water

Shallow water

3000 meters

5000 meters

ATLAS KEY

OCEANS AND SEAS

SYMBOL KEY

◉ National capital

★ State/province capital

● Major city

○ Other city

━━━ International boundary

----- Disputed boundary

.... Undefined boundary

──── State/province/republic boundary

☐ Non-subject

┼┼┼ Canal/waterway

Waterfall

▲ Peak

ATLAS

THE WORLD PHYSICAL/POLITICAL

- ● World's most populous cities
- —— International boundary
- ----- Disputed boundary
- ········· Undefined boundary

0   1000   2000 Miles

0   1000   2000 Kilometers

Projection: Robinson

ARCTIC OCEAN

Point Barrow

BEAUFORT SEA

BAFFIN BAY

Yukon R.
ALASKA (U.S.)
Mt. McKinley
20,320 ft.
(6,194 m.)
Bering Strait

Great Bear Lake
Great Slave Lake

HUDSON BAY

Davis Strait

Cape Farvel

NORTH AMERICA

CANADA

LABRADOR SEA

GULF OF ALASKA

ROCKY MOUNTAINS

Lake Winnipeg

Great Lakes

Cape Mendocino

GREAT PLAINS

Chicago ●

● New York

UNITED STATES

Missouri R.

Mississippi R.

APPALACHIAN MTS.

Cape Hatteras

ATLANTIC OCEAN

Los Angeles ●

BERMUDA (U.K.)

Tropic of Cancer

MEXICO

GULF OF MEXICO

See inset below

HAWAIIAN IS. (U.S.)

Mexico City ●

CARIBBEAN SEA

VENEZUELA

GUYANA
SURINAME
FRENCH GUIANA (FRANCE)

COLOMBIA

Cape São Roque

PACIFIC OCEAN

Equator

GALÁPAGOS IS. (ECUADOR)

ECUADOR

AMAZON BASIN

Amazon R.

SOUTH AMERICA

Pariñas Point

PERU

BRAZIL

MATO GROSSO PLATEAU

SAMOA

BOLIVIA

TONGA

Tropic of Capricorn

PARAGUAY
GRAN CHACO

Paraná R.

Rio de Janeiro ●

São Paulo ●

Mt. Aconcagua
22,834 ft.
(6,960 m.)

URUGUAY

● Buenos Aires

ANDES MOUNTAINS

CHILE **ARGENTINA**

West Longitude

FALKLAND IS. (U.K.)

Strait of Magellan

Cape Horn

SOUTH GEORGIA I. (U.K.)

Drake Passage

Antarctic Circle

International Date Line (Sunday)

CENTRAL AMERICA AND WEST INDIES

Projection: Bipolar Oblique Conic Conformal

THE BAHAMAS

Tropic of Cancer

GULF OF MEXICO

CUBA

TURKS AND CAICOS IS. (U.K.)

ATLANTIC OCEAN

VIRGIN ISLANDS (U.S. AND U.K.)

MEXICO

HAITI
DOMINICAN REPUBLIC

ANTIGUA AND BARBUDA

BELIZE

JAMAICA

PUERTO RICO (U.S.)

ST. KITTS AND NEVIS

GUADELOUPE (FRANCE)

DOMINICA

GUATEMALA

CARIBBEAN SEA

MARTINIQUE (FRANCE)

ST. LUCIA

HONDURAS

EL SALVADOR

ST. VINCENT AND THE GRENADINES

BARBADOS

NICARAGUA

ARUBA (NETHERLANDS)

NETHERLANDS ANTILLES (NETHERLANDS)

GRENADA

PACIFIC OCEAN

TRINIDAD AND TOBAGO

N

COSTA RICA

0   250   500 Miles

0   250   500 Kilometers

PANAMA

COLOMBIA

VENEZUELA

GUYANA

UNITED STATES MAP **545**

LIFE SKILL
Budgeting

To increase your wealth, financial planners recommend that you control your expenditures to live within your means. You can accomplish this by making a **budget**—a plan that matches expenditures with income. Budgeting can help you manage your money better and prevent you from buying goods and services you do not really need or cannot afford.

The first step in setting up a budget is to obtain a **spreadsheet**—a large sheet of paper with columns for weeks and months, and rows for different categories of expenditures. You can buy spreadsheets in an office supply store, make one of your own, or use a computer software program designed for this purpose.

Next, decide whether you want to set up your budget on a weekly, monthly, or yearly basis. If you get paid every two weeks, you might want to set up an annual budget with 26 biweekly columns. If you get paid monthly, you might prefer to set up an annual budget with 12 monthly columns, like the one illustrated below.

The first row of your budget should consist of the income you expect to have for each period. Be sure to record your **net income**—the income received after taxes have been taken out. The remainder of the rows should be used to list your expenditures.

List your monthly expenditures, such as rent and utility bills. Then list miscellaneous expenditures,

such as clothing or gifts. Because you do not know how many unexpected expenditures you will have, allow 5 to 10 percent of your net income for this category. Set up an additional category for repairs or maintenance of items you may own, such as a car. These items likely are too large to be included in the miscellaneous category.

Keep in mind that it is more efficient and sometimes easier to spread larger expenditures across time. Your car insurance, for example, may be due every six months. Rather than try to budget the entire payment in one or two periods, set aside enough money each period so that you have the entire amount on hand when the bill arrives.

Monitor your budget to make sure that the amounts you have allotted for each expenditure are reasonable. If you find that a category does not reflect your actual spending, adjust it. A benefit of a budget is that it can show you where you need to increase or decrease your spending.

Applying Life Skills

1. Why is making a budget important?

2. What are the steps involved in making a budget?

3. What does it mean to monitor a budget?

	Jan	Feb	March	April	May	June	July	Aug	Sep	Oct	Nov	Dec
Net Income												
Rent												
Auto												
Telephone												
Utilities												
Cable												
Food												
Clothing												
Entertainment												
Miscellaneous												

546 LIFE SKILL

Answers to SKILL

1. to increase your wealth, manage your money better, and prevent you from buying goods and services you do not really need or cannot afford

2. obtain a spreadsheet; organize your budget on a specific time basis, such as when you receive your

paycheck; list your net income and monthly expenditures; monitor your budget by category

3. analyzing and adjusting your spending to make sure your allotments for each expenditure are reasonable and obtainable

LIFE SKILL
Maintaining a Checking Account

Properly maintaining a checking account takes time and effort. Checking accounts generally are not free unless you are able to deposit—and not use—a minimum sum of money, which generally varies from $500 to $1,000. If you do not maintain the required minimum, you may pay a monthly fee.

Contact several banks to compare the terms of their checking accounts. Then order checks printed with your full name, current address, and telephone number. When you write checks, make all figures and amounts legible. Write the amount in the box on the extreme right and on the line on the left, using all the space available so that no one can change the amount. Be sure to date the checks correctly and sign them clearly and accurately. Immediately record in your checkbook the date the check was written, to whom it was written, and the amount for which it was written.

You should balance your checkbook every month after receiving a statement from the bank. The statement will tell you which checks the bank has received and which deposits it has recorded. It will also tell you what the balance of your account is at the time the statement was issued. It is your responsibility to **reconcile** your account—make sure your balance agrees with the bank's balance. To reconcile your account, follow these steps:

1. In your checkbook, mark each check entry listed on your bank statement with an *X* to show that the check has been processed. As you do this, make sure the amount of each check recorded in your checkbook matches the amount on the statement.
2. List the checks you wrote but that were not processed. Total the amounts of these checks, then add the total to the balance you have written in your checkbook.

3. Subtract any fees or charges indicated on the bank statement, such as a monthly service charge or a charge for new checks.
4. Subtract any cash withdrawals you made from automatic teller machines (ATMs).
5. Compare this balance with the balance on your bank statement. If no mistakes were made, your balance should match the bank's.

If the two balances do not match, look for mistakes. If you do not clear up the error immediately,

Tom Smith
1427 Blackwood Drive
Copper Canyon, TX 75067
(817) 555-1140

001

Feb. 2   19xx   1-32
                                      280

Pay to the
Order of: _____ Jack Jones _____ 54.00

Fifty-Four and ___No___ _____ Dollars
                    100s

FIRST STATE BANK
DALLAS, TEXAS

Tom Smith

⑈011000044⑈ 183506844 ⑈'

call the bank. The error may carry over to the next month and make balancing your checkbook even more difficult. If the balance gets too far out of line, a check may **bounce,** or be returned for insufficient funds, which will cost you a fee of $10 or $20. If a number of checks bounce, it could give you a bad credit rating.

Applying Life Skills

1. Why is having a checking account convenient for many consumers?
2. How do you balance a checkbook?
3. What does it mean when a check bounces?

LIFE SKILL **547**

Answers to SKILL

1. Answers will vary but may include the following: Most consumers do not feel comfortable carrying large amounts of cash. Most consumers pay their bills through the mail, and checks are much safer than cash to send in the mail.

2. Mark each entry you made against the bank's statement. Total the amount of checks you wrote but that were not processed. Subtract any fees, charges, or ATM withdrawals. Compare your balance with the bank's.

3. It is returned because the issuer did not have sufficient funds in his or her account.

Economics in Action

Chapter 13

Disc 1, Side 2

Title: *The American Tax System*

Subject: Compare a value added tax to a sales tax

Ask: What is the difference between sales tax and value added tax?
(Sales tax is a percentage of a product's price that is added when a consumer purchases a product. Value added tax is based on the difference between the product's selling price and the price of its various components.)

Also available in VHS.

LIFE SKILL
Filing an Income Tax Return

If you work, you probably have to file income tax forms with the federal government and, in some cases, with the state and/or city in which you live or work. The first step in filing income tax forms is to fill out a withholding statement with your employer. The federal withholding form, known as a W-4, asks for such information as your name and address, social security number, marital status, and any special allowances for disabilities or dependents. This form is shown below. The purpose of the W-4 is to help your employer determine how much money to withhold from each of your paychecks. If you do not complete the form properly, your employer may not withhold enough money, and you will have to pay additional taxes.

as union dues or uniforms, and uninsured losses from theft or natural disasters.

At the beginning of each year, the Internal Revenue Service sends out tax forms with detailed instructions on how to complete them. You can find the same forms at most post offices, public libraries, or banks. You may complete the forms yourself or have them completed by a professional tax preparer. The fee for

Form **W-4** Department of the Treasury Internal Revenue Service	**Employee's Withholding Allowance Certificate** ▶ For Privacy Act and Paperwork Reduction Act Notice, see reverse.		OMB No. 1545-0010 **1993**
1 Type or print your name and middle initial	Last name		2 Your social security number
Home address (number and street or rural route)		3 ☐ Single ☐ Married ☐ Married, but withhold at higher Single rate **Note:** *If married, but legally separated, or spouse is a nonresident alien, check the Single box.*	
City or town, state, and ZIP code		4 If your last name differs from that on your social security card, check here and call 1-800-772-1213 for more information . . . . ▶ ☐	

5 Total number of allowances you are claiming (from line G above or from the worksheets on page 2 if they apply) **5**
6 Additional amount, if any, you want withheld from each paycheck . . . . **6** $
7 I claim exemption from withholding for 1993 and I certify that I meet ALL of the following conditions for exemption:
   • Last year I had a right to a refund of **ALL** Federal income tax withheld because I had **NO** tax liability; **AND**
   • This year I expect a refund of **ALL** Federal income tax withheld because I expect to have **NO** tax liability; **AND**
   • This year if my income exceeds $600 and includes nonwage income, another person cannot claim me as a dependent.
   If you meet all of the above conditions, enter "EXEMPT" here . . . . ▶ **7**

Under penalties of perjury, I certify that I am entitled to the number of withholding allowances claimed on this certificate or entitled to claim exempt status.

Employee's signature ▶   Date ▶   , 19

8 Employer's name and address (Employer: Complete 8 and 10 only if sending to the IRS) | 9 Office code optional | 10 Employer identification number

Cat. No. 10220Q

Keep your pay stubs and the receipts for your expenditures together in a safe place. By law, every January your employer must provide you with a W-2 form, which summarizes your earnings for the year. You should check the information on your pay stubs against the information on the W-2. Some expenditures are tax deductible and will save you money by lowering your taxes. You must be able to prove, however, that you actually made the expenditures. Your proof is the receipts that you have saved.

Depending on the current tax laws, deductible expenses may include mortgage interest, medical bills and pharmaceutical expenses, child-care expenses, charitable contributions, such work-related expenses

this service varies according to the complexity of your tax return and the amount of time it takes to prepare it. You generally must file the completed forms by midnight, April 15.

Applying Life Skills

1. What is a W-4 form? What is its purpose?
2. In preparing to file an income tax form, why are receipts important?
3. What are some examples of tax deductible expenses?

Answers to SKILL

1. a federal tax withholding form that entitles your employer to withhold and send to the government a certain amount of taxes

2. They help prove that you made the expenditures you claim you did.

3. mortgage interest, medical bills and pharmaceutical expenses, child-care expenses, charitable contributions, some work-related expenses, uninsured losses from theft or natural disasters

LIFE SKILL

Renting an Apartment

If you decide to rent an apartment, take time to choose wisely. Determine the best location in terms of getting back and forth from work or school and convenience for shopping. Decide if you want a furnished or unfurnished apartment. Consider how much space you need to have adequate storage and be comfortable. Most importantly, determine how much rent you can afford to pay. Monthly rent plus related expenses should not be more than one week's take-home pay.

To find an apartment, consult the classified section of newspapers, ask friends for recommendations, or hire a rental agent. Never agree to rent an apartment until you have personally seen it. The best time to do this is during an evening or on a weekend, which will reveal the surrounding noise level and what the neighbors are like. If possible, talk to some of the people in the apartment complex to learn the advantages and disadvantages of moving into the area.

Inspect the apartment and the surrounding area carefully for the following:

1. Is the building well-built, well-maintained, and well-lit?
2. Is the apartment the right size? Does it have a convenient floor plan, enough wall space for your furniture, and adequate lighting and electrical outlets?
3. How many windows are there? Do they open and close easily? Are there screens and storm windows?
4. Is the apartment air-conditioned? Does it have its own heating and cooling controls?
5. Are major appliances, such as a stove and refrigerator, in good working condition?
6. Is the apartment carpeted? Are there drapes, blinds, or shades for the windows?
7. Does the building have fire walls? Smoke alarms?
8. Are laundry equipment and storage facilities available?
9. Is there trash collection or disposal? Where? How often? By whom? Who pays for it?
10. What kind of burglary protection is there?
11. What are the parking facilities?

After you have selected the apartment you want, you probably will have to sign a **lease,** a written agreement between you and the landlord that states the major terms of your occupancy. It generally includes a description of the rental property; the amount of rent to be paid and when it is due; how much deposit is required, what it covers, and under what conditions it may be forfeited; and how long the lease is in force and under what conditions it may be renewed. The lease also should include the terms for rent increases; who pays for specific utilities and repairs; what alterations you can make on the property; how much notice you must give before moving; whether you can rent the apartment to someone else; and whether children, pets, or roommates are allowed.

Before signing a lease, inspect the apartment with the landlord. Point out and write down all the damage to walls, floors, appliances, and fixtures. Attach a copy of this list to the lease so that you cannot be held responsible for damage done before you moved into the apartment. Check to see if a security deposit is required in addition to the rental deposit. If it is, determine the amount and under what conditions it will be returned. Insist that this information be included in the lease. Find out who pays for personal injury or loss of personal property due to the landlord's negligence. Make sure all the blanks in the lease are filled in or crossed out and all verbal contracts you made with the landlord are included.

Applying Life Skills

1. What are some things to consider if you decide to rent an apartment?
2. When is the best time to look for an apartment?
3. What is a lease? What does it include?

LIFE SKILL **549**

Answers to SKILL

1. location, furnished or unfurnished, space you need for storage and to be comfortable, how much rent you can afford to pay
2. during an evening or on a weekend
3. A lease is a written agreement between you and the landlord that states the major terms of your occupancy. It includes a description of the rental property; the amount of rent to be paid and when it is due; how much deposit is required, what it covers, and under what conditions it may be forfeited; how long the lease is in force; terms for rent increases; who pays for specific utilities and repairs; what alterations you may make on the property; how much notice you must give before moving; whether you can rent the apartment to someone else; and whether children, pets, or roommates are allowed.

GLENCOE
TECHNOLOGY

NIGHTLY BUSINESS REPORT

Economics in Action

Chapter 5

Disc 1, Side 1

Title: *Going Into Debt*

Subject: Different methods of using credit

Ask: What are the disadvantages of making purchases with credit cards?

(If you do not pay your credit card bill in full at the end of the month, you will pay interest on the unpaid portion of the bill. Interest rates for credit cards are usually higher than those for bank loans.)

 Also available in VHS.

LIFE SKILL
Borrowing Money

When borrowing money, you assume some risks. Being in debt is dangerous and can lead to personal bankruptcy. Before you decide to borrow money, keep the following factors in mind:

1. Do not borrow so much that if you become ill or lose your job, you no longer will be financially stable.
2. Stagger your debts. Spread out your payments so they are not all due at the same time.

If you have a legitimate need to borrow money, you might consider asking a family member or a friend for a loan. Life insurance companies, savings institutions, credit unions, commercial banks, retail organizations, and finance companies also lend money. The many types of loans that are available to consumers include the following:

- **Installment sales credit,** the most common type of loan available, is generally taken out to buy such merchandise as household furniture or appliances. The consumer makes an initial deposit on the goods and agrees to pay the balance, plus interest and service charges, in equal installments over a period of time.
- **Installment cash credit** is a direct cash loan often used for vacations, home improvements, or other personal expenses. No down payment is required, but the loan, plus interest and other charges, must be repaid in equal installments over a specified period of time.
- **Single lump sum credit** is a direct cash loan requiring that the amount borrowed plus interest be repaid on a specified day.
- **Open-ended or revolving credit** allows consumers to purchase goods and services from merchants on credit, often without a down payment. In some cases, the consumer may repay the entire balance within 30 days without any interest charges. Monthly payments are required thereafter, with interest being computed on the outstanding balance.
- **Credit card loans** are loans made through the use of a bank credit card. The payment plans for this type of loan vary widely. In some cases, the con-

sumer pays an annual fee for the use of the card. In other cases, the consumer may have to pay the balance in full at the end of the month, or make monthly installment payments.

Regardless of the type of loan you obtain, you are entitled by law to information about the cost of credit. First, you are entitled to know the **finance charge**—the total dollar amount the credit will cost, including interest charged plus any carrying or service charge. Second, you are entitled to know the **annual percentage rate (APR)**—the interest cost of the loan on a yearly basis. Because repayment schedules differ, the APR is your guide to the true cost of the loan.

To obtain a loan, you must be a good credit risk. The lender checks on your character, your ability to repay the loan, and your capital assets. To determine your creditability, lenders often check with a **credit bureau**—an agency that collects credit information on consumers. If your **credit rating**—a record of debt and payment history—is not good or is in doubt, you probably will be denied credit. Thus, to maintain a good credit rating, you should pay debts on time.

If your request for a loan is granted, you should check to make sure that the contract for the loan does not include any of the following:

1. An **add-on clause,** which allows the seller to keep title to an entire list of items until all payments on the loan have been completed.
2. A **balloon clause,** which makes the final payment larger than the other monthly payments.
3. An **acceleration clause**, which allows the lender to demand an immediate payment in full if one payment is not made.

Applying Life Skills

1. What are some wrong reasons for borrowing?
2. What kinds of loans are available for consumers?
3. What is a credit rating? Why is it important to maintain a good one?

Answers to SKILL

1. Answers will vary but may include to impress others with your purchases, to buy impulsively, or to pay off other debts.
2. installment sales credit, installment cash credit,

single lump sum credit, open-ended or revolving credit, credit card loans
3. a record of debt and payment history; if you don't, you may be denied credit

LIFE SKILL

Buying Insurance

Almost everyone needs some kind of insurance. Your parents, for example, may have several types of insurance—homeowners insurance in case of theft, fire, or natural disaster; automobile insurance in case of accident or disability; and health insurance to cover them if they are hospitalized or ill for a long time.

You need insurance to protect yourself. How much and what kind of insurance you need depends on your lifestyle, your job, your age, and many other factors. You need enough insurance to protect your belongings and potential income, but not so much that paying for it strains your budget.

There are six major types of insurance that you should consider:

- **Whole life insurance**, sometimes called ordinary life insurance, pays money to your survivors in the event of your death. It also carries a provision for savings against which you can borrow. You may collect the savings in one lump sum when you retire. Although this type of insurance can be expensive, it offers a combination of coverage to those who cannot buy individual coverage.

- **Term insurance** offers one type of coverage only—payment to your survivors in the event of your death.

- **Health insurance** covers medical and hospital bills if you become ill. Some health insurance policies also cover medication. A good policy covers approximately 80 percent of medical expenses.

- **Automobile insurance** can provide several different kinds of coverage: **Liability** coverage protects you from claims and lawsuits if you cause an accident. **Collision** covers damage to your automobile if another vehicle hits it.

- **Homeowners insurance** covers a homeowner when his or her home or property has been damaged. Mortgage lenders generally insist that a homeowner carry this type of insurance until his or her mortgage has been paid in full.

- **Property liability** protects renters and homeowners against claims of negligence filed by others when an accident occurs on the renter's or homeowner's property.

Deciding exactly what insurance to buy can be confusing. Different insurance companies often offer the same type of insurance under different names, which makes it difficult to know if separate insurance companies are talking about the same kind of policy. In addition, the product—coverage—is invisible. The consumer cannot tell how much the policy will pay until something happens for which he or she wants to collect payment.

When you are buying insurance, keep the following factors in mind:

1. Group policies—policies offered to a group of people, generally by an employer or organization—tend to be less expensive than individual policies purchased from an insurance agent.

2. Always consult more than one agent before buying a policy. Describe your needs carefully to each agent, and ask each to recommend a policy and provide a written list of benefits and estimates of costs. Inform each agent that you are consulting other agents and intend to compare costs and benefits before making any decision. Base your decision to buy a policy on the results of your comparison.

Applying Life Skills

1. Why do consumers need insurance?
2. What are six major types of insurance?
3. What factors should you consider when buying insurance?

LIFE SKILL **551**

Answers to SKILL

1. to protect themselves, their belongings, and potential income

2. whole life insurance, term insurance, health insurance, automobile insurance, homeowners insurance, property liability

3. group policies vs. individual policies; consult more than one agent before buying a policy; compare costs and benefits

LIFE SKILL
Paying for College

College costs have risen steadily in recent years. If you need financial aid, regardless of the reason, start researching for aid in your junior year or early in your senior year of high school. Check with your guidance counselor about federal aids and state, military, ethnic, and fraternal grants.

Generally, students from low-income families are eligible for some aid even if their grades are low. Students from middle-income families generally are eligible for less aid and then only if they have good grades. These students will have to rely more on subsidized student loans and special scholarships. Students from high-income families generally are not eligible for aid.

Financial aid comes in three basic forms—loans, which must be repaid; scholarships and grants, which need not be repaid; and jobs. Most financial-aid sponsors distribute their money through colleges. Therefore, contact the financial aid office of the college(s) of your choice. Because most colleges send out financial aid applications only upon request, you should obtain these forms early and then file them with your application for admission. Missing the appointed deadline will reduce your chances for aid.

LOANS There are four major types of student loans. The *National Direct Student Loan* is granted only to needy students. The funds come from the federal government, but individual colleges choose the students who receive them. The loan is interest-free while you are in school. After graduating, you have 10 years to

repay the loan at low interest. To apply for this type of loan, contact the financial aid office at the college(s) of your choice.

The *Government Guaranteed Student Loan* is made by financial institutions, which are guaranteed repayment by the federal government. While you are in school, the government pays the interest, which is generally 9 percent. After you graduate, you have 10 years to repay the loan. Like the National Direct

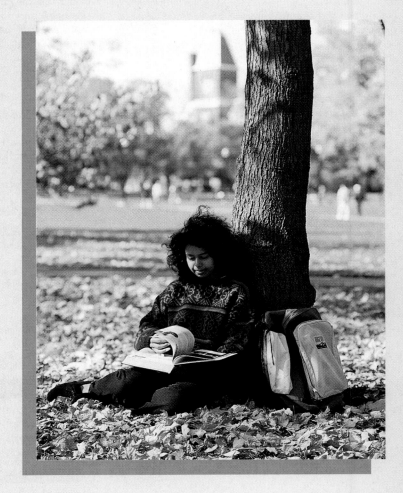

Answers to SKILL

1. in your junior year or early in your senior year
2. loans, scholarships and grants, and jobs
3. national, state, and college merit scholarships; athletic scholarships; talent scholarships; Reserve Officers' Training Corps scholarships

Student Loan, this loan is granted to you rather than to your parents. To apply, contact financial institutions.

A *bank loan* requires you or your parents to begin repayment while you are still in college. Although interest rates vary on this type of loan, they generally are higher than those on government loans.

A *special student loan* is one offered by colleges, civic and professional groups, and other organizations. The interest rates vary on these loans.

SCHOLARSHIPS AND GRANTS

Scholarships provide another source of financial aid. In most cases, income plays no part in eligibility. Some available scholarships include:

- *national, state, and college merit scholarships* awarded on the basis of academic excellence.
- *athletic scholarships* awarded to students who excel in a sport or sports.
- *talent scholarships* awarded to students gifted in the arts.
- *Reserve Officers' Training Corps scholarships* awarded to students willing to spend four years in the armed forces after graduation.

Grants also are available, but they generally are for the needy only. For those who qualify, *Pell Grants* can be used at any accredited college, vocational school, technical institute, nursing school, and the like. Grades play no role in eligibility.

WORK AND STUDY

The third basic kind of financial aid is in the form of a job. Several different programs fall into this category. One is the *College Work-Study Program* sponsored by the federal government. To be eligible, you must be a full-time student who would not be able to attend school without the job. Another program is *cooperative education*. Under this program, you work six months and go to school six months each year. What you earn on the job will pay your tuition.

If you are seeking financial aid for college, keep the following in mind:

- Start your investigation early.
- Apply for every scholarship or grant for which you may qualify.
- You can borrow from more than one program.

Applying Life Skills

1. If you need financial aid for college, when should you begin your search?

2. What are three forms of financial aid?

3. What kinds of scholarships are available?

LIFE SKILL
Preparing a Resume

One of the most critical parts of finding a job is preparing a resume. A good resume provides a brief history of your strengths, abilities, and accomplishments. A prospective employer's decision to interview you often depends on his or her reaction to your resume.

Before writing your resume, conduct an inventory of your strengths and weaknesses by asking yourself questions such as: What kinds of skills and talents do I have? What is my work history? How much formal education have I had? What were my grades and class standings? In what activities have I participated? What are my goals? What kind of work do I want? What salary would I be willing to accept?

When you have answered these questions, organize the entries on your resume. Begin with your name, address, and telephone number. Indicate the position or kind of position you are seeking. List all your relevant work experience, beginning with your most recent job. Include the dates of your employ-

ment, the names of the companies for which you worked, and the positions you held.

List the schools you have attended. Include any special honors or awards you have received and any activities in which you have been or are involved.

Provide at least three references, all of whom know you well enough to vouch for your abilities or strengths. Do not use relatives as references, and do not use more than two teachers. Keep in mind that you may adjust the format of your resume.

Applying Life Skills

1. Why is a resume an important step in finding a job?
2. What kinds of questions should you ask yourself when preparing a resume?
3. What kinds of items should you list on a resume?

Writing a Cover Letter

When you send a resume, it should be accompanied by a cover letter. A cover letter identifies and explains anything you are sending to someone. It may be as short as two sentences or as long as several paragraphs, commenting on the enclosed resume.

HOW TO SAY IT
- State briefly what is enclosed, but contain enough information to make the reader want to look at the attached resume.
- Mention why you are sending the resume—in response to an advertisement, because of a third person's suggestion, or to introduce yourself.
- Indicate any response you are expecting or any future action you will be taking.
- All cover letters should be typed on good quality paper.
- Address the person by name (instead of using "To Whom It May Concern").
- Sign each letter individually.

WHAT NOT TO SAY
Avoid duplicating the information listed on your resume. Summarizing a resume or mentioning the important points is helpful in orienting the reader, but repeating sentences may lead the reader to skip over those parts later while reading the resume.

Dear Ms. Jones,

I am responding to your advertisement in Sunday's paper for a computer programmer. As you will see from my attached resume, I have a great deal of experience in programming development. My work skills include an affinity for detail and previous experience in a programmer environment. Previous employers have found me responsible and innovative. I would appreciate the opportunity of discussing this position with you. May I call you next week to set up an interview for the computer programmer position?

Sincerely,
Bobby Little

—From Rosalie Maggio's *How to Say It: Choice Words, Phrases, Sentences & Paragraphs for Every Situation.* ©1990 by Prentice Hall, Englewood Cliffs, New Jersey

Answers to SKILL

1. A prospective employer's decision to interview you often depends on his or her reaction to your resume.

2. What kinds of skills and talents do I have? What is my work history? How much formal education have I had? What were my grades and class standings? In what activities have I participated? What are my goals? What kind of work do I want? What salary would I be willing to accept?

3. relevant work experience, schools you have attended, special awards or honors you have received, activities in which you are involved, references

Bobby Little
4144 Valley Court
Cranston, Illinois 60505
(708) 555-2242

Position Desired

Seeking part-time employment during the school year: Prefer to work one afternoon or evening per week plus one day of the weekend; willing to work full-time during the summer.

Work Experience

June 1992–Present: Part-time Cook, McDonald's, Inc., Cranston, Illinois

January 1992–May 1992: Part-time Stock Clerk, Brown's Hardware Store, Cranston, Illinois

Education

Senior at Scott High School, Class of 1994, currently an honors student

Honors and Awards

First Place medal (computer division), State of Illinois Science Fair, for project entitled "NYSE: The Stock Market Simulation," April 1994

Air Force Best Overall Project Award, State of Illinois Science Fair, April 1994

First Place, Computer Division, Blake County Science Fair, May 1994

Outstanding Physical Education/Health Student Award, Scott High School, Spring 1992

Special Interests

Computers, strategy games, playing the guitar

Member of Scott High School Chess Club (September 1992-May 1994)

Member of Scott High School Spanish Club (September 1991-May 1994)

References

Ms. Alice Williamson, Department of Science, Scott High School, Cranston, Illinois 60505 (708) 555-3414

Mr. John Brown, Owner, Brown's Hardware Store, Cranston, Illinois 60505 (708) 555-3633

Mr. Richard Adams, McDonald's, Inc., Cranston, Illinois 60505 (708) 555-8970

A

ability-to-pay principle of taxation belief that taxes should be paid according to level of income regardless of benefits received (p. 214)

absolute advantage country's ability to produce more of a given product than can another country (p. 450)

accelerated depreciation schedule that spreads depreciation over fewer years than normal to generate larger tax reductions (p. 231)

accelerator change in investment spending caused by a change in overall spending (p. 428)

acid rain pollution in form of rainwater mixed with sulfur dioxide, a mild form of sulfuric acid (p. 528)

agency shop arrangement under which non-union members must pay union dues (p. 190)

aggregate demand curve hypothetical curve showing different levels of real GDP that could be purchased at various price levels (p. 424)

aggregate supply curve hypothetical curve showing different levels of real GDP that could be produced at various price levels (p. 422)

agricultural bank commercial bank with more than 25 percent of its loans in agriculture (p. 313)

alternative minimum tax personal income tax rate that applies to cases where taxes would otherwise fall below a certain level (p. 231)

appropriations bill legislation earmarking funds for certain purposes (p. 243)

aquifer underground water-bearing rock formation (p. 525)

arbitration see **voluntary arbitration** and/or **compulsory arbitration** (p. 191)

articles of partnership formal legal papers specifying the arrangements between partners, including the way profits and losses are divided (p. 57)

assets properties, possessions and claims on others; usually listed as entries on a balance sheet (p. 302)

automatic stabilizer program that automatically provides benefits to offset a change in people's incomes; unemployment insurance, entitlement programs (p. 429)

automation production with mechanical or other processes that reduces the need for workers (p. 396)

average tax rate total taxes paid divided by the total taxable income (p. 215)

B

baby boom historically high birthrate years in the United States from 1946 to 1964 (p. 373)

balance of payments difference between money paid to, and received from, other nations in trade; *balance on current account* includes goods and services, *merchandise trade balance* counts only goods (p. 456)

balance sheet condensed statement showing assets, liabilities, and net worth of an economic unit (p. 302)

balanced budget annual budget in which expenditures equal revenues (p. 258)

balanced budget amendment constitutional amendment requiring government to spend no more than it collects in taxes and other revenues, excluding borrowing (p. 249)

bank holding company corporation that owns one or more banks (p. 296)

bank holiday brief period during which all banks or depository institutions are closed to prevent bank runs (p. 281)

bankruptcy court-granted permission to an individual or business to cease or delay payment on some or all debts for a limited amount of time (p. 61)

barter economy moneyless economy that relies on trade or barter (p. 266)

base year year serving as point of comparison for other years in a price index or other statistical measure (p. 204)

benefit principle of taxation belief that taxes should be paid according to benefits received regardless of income (p. 213)

Better Business Bureau business-sponsored nonprofit organization providing information on local companies to consumers (p. 71)

bill consolidation loan popular type of consumer loan used to pay off multiple existing loans (p. 322)

black market market in which economic products are sold illegally (p. 486)

blue-collar worker industrial or factory worker who receives a wage rather than a salary (p. 407)

board of directors representatives of common shareholders elected to set policies and goals, hire professional managers for a corporation (p. 60)

bond formal contract to repay borrowed money and interest on the borrowed money at regular future intervals (p. 61)

boycott protest in the form of a refusal to buy, including attempts to convince others to join (p. 184)

break-even point production needed if the firm is to recover its costs; production level where total cost equals total revenue (p. 122)

bullion ingots or bars of precious metals, usually gold or silver (p. 268)

business cycle systematic changes in real GDP marked by alternating periods of expansion and contraction (p. 383)

business fluctuation changes in real GDP marked by alternating periods of expansion and contraction that occur on a less than systematic basis (p. 383)

business organization profit-seeking enterprise that produces goods and/or services; includes sole proprietorships, partnerships, corporations (p. 54)

C

call option contract giving investors the option to buy commodities, equities, or financial assets at a specific future date using a price agreed upon today (p. 338)

capital tools, equipment, and factories used in the production of goods and services; one of four factors of production (p. 9)

capital consumption allowances wear and tear on capital equipment that is subtracted from GNP to get NNP (p. 355)

capital flight legal or illegal export of a nation's currency and foreign exchange (p. 500)

capital good tool, equipment, or other manufactured good used to produce other goods and services; a factor of production (p. 20)

capital-intensive production method requiring relatively large amounts of capital relative to labor (p. 488)

capital market market in which financial capital is loaned and/or borrowed for more than one year (p. 332)

capitalism market economy in which the factors of production are privately owned (p. 43)

capital-to-labor ratio measure obtained by dividing the total capital stock by the labor force (p. 379)

cartel group of sellers or producers acting together to raise prices by restricting availability of a product; OPEC (p. 513)

cease and desist order ruling requiring a company to stop an unfair business practice that reduces or limits competition (p. 169)

census complete count of population, including place of residence (p. 370)

center of population point where the country would balance if it were flat and everyone weighed the same (p. 372)

central bank bank that can lend to other banks in times of need, a "bankers' bank" (p. 280)

certificate of deposit receipt showing that an investor has made an interest-bearing loan to a financial institution (p. 304)

chamber of commerce nonprofit organization of local businesses whose purpose is to promote their interests (p. 71)

change in demand consumers demand different amounts at every price, causing the demand curve to shift to the left or the right (p. 88)

change in quantity demanded movement along the demand curve showing that a different quantity is purchased in response to a change in price (p. 86)

change in quantity supplied change in amount offered for sale in response to a price change; movement along the supply curve (p. 106)

change in supply different amounts offered for sale at each and every possible price in the market; shift of the supply curve (p. 106)

charter written government approval to establish a corporation; includes company name, address, purpose of business, number of shares of stock, and other features of the business (p. 59)

civilian labor force non-institutionalized part of the population, aged 16 and over, either working or looking for a job (p. 182)

closed shop illegal arrangement under which workers must join a union before they are hired (p. 190)

coins metallic forms of money such as pennies, nickels, dimes, and quarters (p. 300)

collateral property or other security used to guarantee repayment of a loan (p. 308)

collective bargaining process of negotiation between union and management representatives over pay, benefits, and job-related matters (p. 70)

collective farm small farms in the former Soviet Union owned by the state, but operated by families who shared in some of the profits (p. 479)

collectivization forced common ownership of factors of production; used in the former Soviet Union in agriculture and manufacturing under Stalin (p. 478)

collusion agreements, usually illegal, among producers to fix prices, limit output, or divide markets (p. 157)

command economy economic system characterized by a central authority that makes most of the major economic decisions (p. 33)

commercial bank depository institution that, until the mid-1970s, had the exclusive right to offer checking accounts (p. 281)

commodity money money that has an alternative use as a commodity; gunpowder, flour, corn (p. 267)

common stock certificate of ownership in a corporation entitling owner to vote for board of directors, but has last claim on dividends and assets (p. 60)

communism economic and political system in which factors of production are collectively owned and directed by the state; theoretically classless society in which everyone works for the common good (p. 474)

company union union organized, supported, and even financed by an employer (p. 184)

comparable worth doctrine stating that equal pay should be given for jobs of comparable difficulty (p. 200)

comparative advantage country's ability to produce a given product relatively more efficiently than another country; production at a lower opportunity cost (p. 451)

competition the struggle among sellers to attract consumers while lowering costs (p. 43)

complements products that increase the value of other products; products related in such a way that an increase in the price of one reduces the demand for both (p. 89)

compulsory arbitration situation forcing labor and management to use a mediator to reach a binding settlement (p. 191)

conglomerate firm with four or more businesses making unrelated products, with no single business responsible for a majority of its sales (p. 65)

conspicuous consumption use of an expensive good or service to impress others (p. 21)

constant dollars dollar amounts or prices that have been adjusted for inflation; same as real dollars (p. 204)

consumer person who uses goods and services to satisfy wants and needs (p. 21)

consumer cooperative nonprofit association that buys bulk amounts of consumer goods so that its members can purchase at prices below those charged by regular businesses;

same as co-op (p. 69)

consumer good good intended for final use by consumers rather than businesses (p. 20)

consumer price index index used to measure price changes for a market basket of frequently used consumer items (p. 362)

consumer sovereignty role of consumer as ruler of the market when determining the types of goods and services produced (p. 47)

consumption process of using up goods and services to satisfy wants and needs (p. 21)

consumption function schedule showing relatively constant and stable spending patterns by the consumer sector at different levels of income (p. 427)

co-op see **cooperative** (p. 69)

cooperative nonprofit association performing some kind of economic activity for the benefit of its members; includes consumer, service, and producer cooperatives (p. 69)

copyright exclusive right given to an author or artist to sell, publish, or reproduce his or her work for their lifetime plus 50 years (p. 160)

corporate income tax tax on corporate profits paid by corporations (p. 219)

corporation form of business organization recognized by law as a separate legal entity with all the rights and responsibilities of an individual, including the right to buy and sell property, enter into legal contracts, sue and be sued (p. 59)

cost-benefit analysis way of thinking that compares the cost of an action to its benefits (p. 532)

Council of Economic Advisers three-member group that devises strategies and advises the President of the United States on economic matters (p. 437)

coupon stated interest on a corporate, municipal or government bond (p. 326)

craft union labor union whose workers perform the same kind of work; same as trade union (p. 184)

credit union nonprofit service cooperative that accepts deposits, makes loans, and provides other financial services (p. 70)

creditor person or institution to whom money is owed (p. 312)

creeping inflation relatively low rate of inflation, usually 1 to 3 percent annually (p. 400)

crowding-out effect higher than normal interest rates and diminished access to financial capital faced by private investors when government increases its borrowing in financial markets (p. 258)

crude birthrate number of live births per 1,000 people (p. 499)

currency paper component of the money supply, today consisting of Federal Reserve notes (p. 300)

current dollars dollar amounts or prices that are not adjusted for inflation (p. 202)

current GDP Gross Domestic Product measured in current prices, unadjusted for inflation (p. 363)

current yield bond's annual coupon interest divided by purchase price; measure of a bond's return (p. 327)

customs duty tax on imported products (p. 220)

customs union group of countries that have agreed to reduce trade barriers among themselves and adopt uniform trade barriers for nonmembers (p. 512)

cyclical unemployment unemployment directly related to swings in the business cycle (p. 396)

D

deep gas natural gas located 15,000 feet or more below the earth's surface (p. 527)

deficiency payment cash payment making up the difference between the market price and the target price of an agricultural crop (p. 145)

deficit spending annual government spending in excess of taxes and other revenues (p. 253)

deflation decrease in the general level of prices (p. 399)

demand combination of desire, ability, and willingness to buy a product (p. 82)

demand curve graph showing the quantity demanded at each and every possible price that might prevail in the market at a given time (p. 84)

demand deposit account (DDA) account whose funds can be removed by writing a check and without having to gain prior approval from the depository institution (p. 281)

demand elasticity measure of responsiveness relating change in quantity demanded (dependent variable) to a change in price (independent variable) (p. 92)

demand schedule listing showing the quantity demanded at all possible prices that might prevail in the market at a given time (p. 84)

demographer person who studies growth, density, and other characteristics of the population (p. 372)

dependency ratio ratio of children and elderly per 100 persons in the 18-64 working age bracket (p. 374)

depreciation gradual wear on capital goods during production (p. 118)

depression state of the economy with large numbers of unemployed, declining real incomes, overcapacity in manufacturing plants, general economic hardship (p. 384)

depression scrip currency issued by towns, chambers of commerce, and other civic bodies during the Great Depression of the 1930s (p. 385)

deregulation relaxation or removal of government regulations on business activities (p. 284)

devaluation action taken by a country to make its currency worth less in terms of gold or another currency (p. 462)

developing country country whose average per capita income is only a fraction of that in more industrialized countries (p. 498)

diminishing marginal utility decreasing satisfaction or usefulness as additional units of a product are acquired (p. 90)

diminishing returns stage of production where output increases at a decreasing rate as more units of variable input are added (p. 115)

discomfort index unofficial statistic that is the sum of monthly inflation and the unemployment rate; same as **misery index** (p. 419)

discount rate interest rate the Federal Reserve System charges on loans to financial institutions (p. 307)

discount window physical location at the Federal Reserve System where loans are made to depository institutions (p. 308)

disposable personal income personal income less individual income taxes; total income available to the consumer sector after income taxes (p. 356)

distribution of income way in which the nation's income is divided among families, individuals, or other designated groups (p. 240)

dividend check paid to stockholders, usually quarterly, representing portion of corporate profits (p. 59)

division of labor division of work into a number of separate tasks to be performed by different workers; same as **specialization** (p. 23)

DJIA see **Dow-Jones Industrial Average** (p. 337)

Dow-Jones Industrial Average (DJIA) statistical series of 30 representative stocks used to monitor price changes on the New York Stock Exchange (p. 337)

dual banking system situation from 1863 to the present that allows banks to choose federal or state charters (p. 279)

durable good good that lasts more than three years when used regularly; can include a capital or a consumer good (p. 20)

E

easy money policy monetary policy resulting in lower interest rates and greater access to credit; associated with an expansion of the money supply (p. 306)

econometric model macroeconomic model using algebraic equations to describe how the economy behaves and is expected to perform in the future (p. 387)

economic institution organization or group that uses, and sometimes represents, the factors of production (p. 54)

economic interdependence economic activities in one part of the country or world affect what happens elsewhere (p. 23)

economic model set of assumptions in a table, graph, or equations used to describe or explain economic behavior (p. 134)

economic product good or service that is useful, relatively scarce, and transferable to others (p. 20)

economic system organized way a society provides for the wants and needs of its people (p. 32)

economics social science dealing with the study of how people satisfy seemingly unlimited and competing wants with the careful use of scarce resources (p. 11)

economies of scale increasingly efficient use of personnel, plant, and equipment as a firm becomes larger (p. 159)

economy see **economic system** (p. 32)

ECU European Currency Unit; monetary unit used by the European Union (p. 513)

Efficient Market Hypothesis (EMH) argument that stocks are always priced about right, and that bargains are hard to find because they are closely watched by so many investors (p. 334)

elastic type of elasticity where the percentage change in the independent variable (usually price) causes a more than proportionate change in the dependent variable (usually quantity demanded or supplied) (p. 92)

embargo prohibition on the export or import of a product (p. 522)

energy bank commercial bank with more than 25 percent of its loans in energy (p. 313)

enterprise zone economically depressed areas where government regulations have been suspended in an effort to attract business (p. 412)

entitlement program or benefit using established eligibility requirements to provide health, nutritional, or income supplements to individuals (p. 260)

entrepreneur risk-taking individual in search of profits; one of four factors of production (p. 10)

equilibrium price price where quantity supplied equals quantity demanded; price that clears the market (p. 138)

equilibrium wage rate wage rate leaving neither a surplus nor a shortage in the market (p. 195)

equities stocks that represent ownership shares in corporations (p. 334)

estate tax tax on the transfer of property when a person dies (p. 220)

euro single currency of European Union (p. 513)

European Community former customs union made up of 12 European nations; became the European Union in November of 1993 (p. 512)

European Union successor of the European Community established in 1993 by the Maastricht Treaty (p. 512)

excess reserves financial institution's cash, currency, and reserves not needed to back existing loans; potential source of new loans (p. 303)

excise tax general revenue tax levied on the manufacture or sale of selected items (p. 219)

expansion period of growth of real GDP; recovery from recession (p. 383)

expropriation government confiscation of private- or foreign-owned goods without compensation (p. 511)

external debt borrowed money that a country owes to foreign countries and banks (p. 500)

externality economic side effect that affects an uninvolved third party (p. 166)

F

fact-finding agreement between union and management to have a neutral third party collect facts about a dispute and present non-binding recommendations (p. 191)

factor market market where productive resources are bought and sold (p. 24)

factors of production productive resources that make up the four categories of land, capital, labor, and entrepreneurship (p. 9)

family two or more persons living together that are related by blood, marriage, or adoption (p. 357)

federal budget annual plan outlining proposed expenditures and anticipated revenues (p. 243)

federal budget deficit excess of federal expenditures over tax and revenue collections (p. 243)

federal debt total amount of money the federal government has borrowed from others (p. 254)

Federal Reserve note currency issued by the Fed that eventually replaced all other types of federal currency (p. 280)

Federal Reserve System privately owned, publicly controlled, central bank of the United States (p. 280)

fertility rate number of births that 1,000 women are expected to undergo in their lifetime (p. 372)

fiat money money by government decree; has no alternative value or use as a commodity (p. 267)

FICA Federal Insurance Contributions Act; tax levied on employers and employees to support Social Security and medicare (p. 218)

finance company firm that makes loans directly to consumers and specializes in buying installment contracts from merchants who sell on credit (p. 322)

financial asset document that represents a claim on the income and property of the borrower; CDs, bonds, Treasury bills, mortgages (p. 321)

financial capital money used to buy the tools and equipment used in production (p. 9)

financial intermediary institution that channels savings to investors; banks, insurance companies, savings and loan associations, credit unions (p. 321)

financial system network of savers, investors, and financial institutions that work together to transfer savings to investment uses (p. 320)

fiscal policy use of government spending and revenue collection measures to influence the economy (p. 427)

fiscal year 12-month financial planning period that may not coincide with the calendar year; October 1 to September 30 for the federal government (p. 243)

Five-Year Plan comprehensive centralized economic plan used by the Soviet Union and China to coordinate development of agriculture and industry (p. 478)

fixed cost cost of production that does not change when output changes (p. 118)

fixed exchange rate system under which the value of currencies were fixed in relation to one another; the exchange rate system in effect until 1971 (p. 461)

fixed income income that does not increase even though prices go up (p. 40)

flexible exchange rate system that relies on supply and demand to determine the value of one currency in terms of another; exchange rate system in effect since 1971, same as **floating exchange rate** (p. 463)

floating exchange rate see **flexible exchange rate** (p. 463)

floor price see **price floor** (p. 142)

food stamps government-issued coupons that can be exchanged for food (p. 411)

foreign exchange foreign currencies used by countries to conduct international trade (p. 461)

foreign exchange futures contracts allowing individuals to buy foreign currencies at some future date, at a price agreed upon today (p. 464)

foreign exchange market market where foreign currencies

used in trade are bought and sold (p. 461)

foreign exchange rate price of one country's currency in terms of another currency (p. 461)

fractional reserve system system requiring financial institutions to set aside a fraction of their deposits in the form of reserves (p. 302)

franchise exclusive right to produce or sell a certain product in an area or region (p. 159)

free enterprise economy market economy in which privately owned businesses have the freedom to operate for a profit with limited government intervention; same as **private enterprise economy** (p. 25)

free product relatively plentiful and abundant product not scarce enough to be a major concern in the study of economics; includes sunshine, rainfall (p. 20)

free-trade area group of countries that have agreed to reduce trade barriers among themselves, but lack a common tariff barrier for nonmembers (p. 512)

frictional unemployment unemployment caused by workers changing jobs or waiting to go to new ones (p. 395)

fringe benefit benefit received by employees in addition to wages and salaries; includes paid vacations, sick leave, retirement, insurance (p. 57)

full employment lowest sustainable unemployment rate thought possible in the economy (p. 397)

futures contracts to buy or sell commodities or financial assets at a specific future date, using a price agreed upon today (p. 338)

futures market market where futures contracts are bought and sold (p. 338)

G

galloping inflation relatively intense inflation, usually ranging from 100 to 300 percent annually (p. 400)

gasohol mixture of 90 percent unleaded gasoline and 10 percent grain alcohol (p. 524)

GATT see **General Agreement on Tariffs and Trade** (p. 458)

GDP gap difference between what the economy can and does produce; annual opportunity cost of unemployed resources (p. 419)

GDP in constant dollars Gross Domestic Product after adjustments for inflation; same as **real GDP** (p. 364)

General Agreement on Tariffs and Trade (GATT) agreement signed in 1947 between 23 countries that extended tariffs concessions and worked to do away with import quotas (p. 458)

general partnership see **partnership** (p. 57)

geographic monopoly market situation where a firm has a monopoly because of its location or the small size of the market (p. 159)

gift tax tax on donations of money or wealth that is paid by the donor (p. 220)

giveback wage, fringe benefit, or work rule given up when renegotiating a contract (p. 199)

glass ceiling seemingly invisible barrier hindering advancement of women and minorities in a male-dominated organization (p. 200)

glut substantial oversupply of a product (p. 528)

gold certificate paper currency backed by gold; issued in 1863 and popular until recalled in 1934 (p. 275)

gold standard monetary standard under which a country's currency is equivalent to, and can be exchanged for, a specified amount of gold (p. 275)

good tangible economic product that is useful, relatively scarce, transferable to others; used to satisfy wants and needs (p. 20)

Gosplan central planning authority in former Soviet Union that devised and directed Five-Year plans (p. 478)

government monopoly monopoly created and/or owned by the government (p. 160)

grant-in-aid transfer payment from one level of government to another not involving compensation (p. 240)

Great Depression greatest period of economic decline in United States history, lasting from approximately 1929 to 1939 (p. 185)

Great Leap Forward China's disastrous second five-year plan begun in 1958 that forced collectivization of agriculture and rapid industrialization (p. 487)

greenback paper currency not backed by gold that was printed by the United States government in 1861; notes were printed front and back in green ink (p. 274)

grievance procedure contractual provision outlining the way future disputes and grievance issues will be resolved (p. 191)

Gross Domestic Product (GDP) dollar value of all final goods, services, and structures produced within a country's national borders during a one-year period (p. 256)

Gross National Product (GNP) total dollar value of all final goods, services, and structures produced in one year with labor and property supplied by a country's residents, regardless of where the production takes place; largest measure of a nation's income (p. 354)

gross private domestic investment total expenditures by the investment sector in the output-expenditure model (p. 358)

growth triangle table showing the rates of growth of a statistical series between any two dates (p. 376)

H

horizontal merger combination of two or more firms producing the same kind of product (p. 65)

household basic unit of consumer sector consisting of all persons who occupy a house, apartment, or separate living quarters (p. 356)

human capital sum of peoples' skills, abilities, health, and motivation (p. 23)

hyperinflation abnormal inflation in excess of 500 percent per year; last stage of a monetary collapse (p. 400)

I

imperfect competition market structure where all conditions of pure competition are not met; monopolistic competition, oligopoly, and monopoly (p. 155)

implicit GDP price deflator index used to measure price changes in Gross Domestic Product (p. 363)

incidence of a tax final burden of a tax (p. 228)

income effect that portion of a change in quantity demanded caused by a change in a consumer's real income when the price of a product changes (p. 87)

income-to-poverty ratio ratio of family income divided by poverty level; measure used to compensate for differences in family sizes (p. 408)

inconvertible fiat money standard fiat money that cannot be exchanged for gold or silver; Federal Reserve notes today (p. 276)

incorporate process required to form a corporation, involves permission from federal government or state where the business will have its headquarters (p. 59)

independent pricing pricing policy by an imperfect competitor that ignores other producers and some market conditions (p. 157)

independent union labor union not affiliated with the AFL-CIO (p. 187)

index of leading indicators composite index of 11 economic series that move up and down in advance of changes in the overall economy; statistical series used to predict business cycle turning points (p. 388)

indexing adjustment of tax brackets to offset the effects of inflation (p. 217)

indirect business tax tax paid as a cost of doing business; license fees, property taxes, customs duties (p. 356)

individual income tax tax levied on the wages, salaries, and other income of individuals (p. 216)

Individual Retirement Account (IRA) retirement account in the form of a long-term time deposit, with annual contributions of up to $2,000 per year not taxed until withdrawn during retirement (p. 331)

industrial union labor union whose workers perform different kinds of work (p. 184)

industry collectively, all firms producing in a market; the supply side of the market (p. 152)

inelastic type of elasticity where the percentage change in the independent variable (usually price) causes a less than proportionate change in the dependent variable (usually quantity demanded or supplied) (p. 92)

infant industries argument argument that new and emerging industries should be protected from foreign competition until they are strong enough to compete (p. 455)

inflation rise in the general level of prices (p. 40)

injunction court order issued to prevent a company or union from taking action during a labor dispute (p. 192)

intangible personal property ownership rights to property as opposed to the property itself; includes stocks, bank accounts (p. 224)

interest payment made for the use of borrowed money; usually paid at periodic intervals for long-term bonds or loans (p. 61)

intergovernmental revenue funds one level of government receives from another level of government (p. 222)

intermediate products products directly excluded from GDP computations because they are components of other final products included in GDP; new tires and radios for use on new cars (p. 349)

Internal Revenue Service (IRS) branch of Treasury Department that collects taxes (p. 216)

International Bank for Reconstruction and Development see **World Bank** (p. 505)

inventory stock of goods held in reserve; includes finished goods waiting to be sold and raw materials to be used in production (p. 56)

investment tax credit tax credit given for purchase of equipment (p. 231)

J

jumbo CD certificate of deposit of $100,000 or more (p. 328)

junk bond corporate bond, generally rated as lower than medium or speculative grade, that pays high returns to compensate for the high risk of default (p. 328)

jurisdictional dispute disagreement, usually between unions, as to which has authority to perform certain kinds of work (p. 187)

K

keiretsu independently owned group of Japanese firms joined and governed by an external board of directors in order to regulate competition (p. 488)

Keynesian economics government spending and taxation policies suggested by John Maynard Keynes to stimulate the economy; synonymous with fiscal policies or demand-side economics (p. 427)

L

labor people with all their abilities and efforts; one of four factors of production, does not include the entrepreneur (p. 10)

labor mobility ability and willingness of labor to relocate, usually for higher wages (p. 196)

labor productivity growth rate of total output per unit of labor input; measure of productive efficiency (p. 380)

labor union organization that works for its members' interests concerning pay, working hours, health coverage, fringe benefits, other job related matters (p. 70)

Laffer curve graph showing that lower tax rates will supposedly stimulate higher tax revenues (p. 432)

laissez-faire philosophy that government should not interfere with business activity (p. 152)

land natural resources or "gifts of nature" not created by human effort; one of four factors of production (p. 9)

Law of Demand rule stating that more will be demanded at lower prices and less at higher prices; inverse relationship between price and quantity demanded (p. 86)

Law of Supply rule stating that more will be offered for sale at high prices than at lower prices (p. 106)

Law of Variable Proportions rule stating that short-run output will change as one input is varied while others are held constant (p. 111)

legal reserves currency and deposits used to meet the reserve requirement (p. 302)

legal tender fiat currency that must be accepted for payment by decree of government (p. 274)

liabilities debts and obligations owed to others; usually listed as entries on a balance sheet (p. 302)

life expectancy average remaining life span in years for persons who attain a given age (p. 372)

limited liability situation in which an owner's responsibility for a company's debts are limited to the size of the owner's investment in the firm; applies to common shareholders and limited partners in a limited partnership (p. 59)

limited life situation in which a firm legally ceases to exist when an owner dies, quits, or a new owner is added; applies to sole proprietorships and partnerships (p. 57)

limited partnership form of partnership where one or more partners are not active in the daily running of the business, and whose liability for the partnership's debt is restricted to the amount invested in the business (p. 57)

liquidity potential for being readily convertible into cash or other financial assets (p. 304)

lockout management refusal to let employees work until company demands are met (p. 184)

long run production period long enough to change amount of variable and fixed inputs used in production (p. 111)

Lorenz curve curve showing how much the actual distribution of income differs from an equal distribution (p. 405)

loss leader item intentionally sold below cost to attract customers (p. 138)

luxury good good for which demand increases faster than income when income rises (p. 220)

M

M1 money supply components conforming to money's role as medium of exchange; coins, currency, checks, other demand deposits, traveler's checks (p. 312)

M2 money supply components conforming to money's role as a store of value; M1, savings deposits, time deposits (p. 312)

macroeconomic equilibrium level of real GDP consistent with a given price level; intersection of aggregate supply and aggregate demand (p. 425)

macroeconomics that part of economic theory dealing with the economy as a whole and decision making by large units such as governments and unions (p. 182)

margin requirement minimum deposits left with a stockbroker to be used as partial payment on other securities (p. 300)

marginal analysis decision making that compares the extra cost of doing something to the extra benefits gained (p. 121)

marginal cost extra cost of producing one additional unit of production (p. 119)

marginal product extra output due to the addition of one more unit of input (p. 114)

marginal revenue extra revenue from the sale of one additional unit of output (p. 121)

marginal tax rate tax rate that applies to the next dollar of taxable income (p. 215)

marginal utility satisfaction or usefulness obtained from acquiring one more unit of a product (p. 89)

market meeting place or mechanism allowing buyers and sellers of an economic product to come together; may be local, regional, national, or global (p. 23)

market basket representative collection of goods and services used to compile a price index (p. 362)

market economy economic system in which supply, demand, and the price system help people make decisions and allocate resources; same as **free enterprise economy** (p. 34)

market equilibrium condition of price stability where the quantity demanded equals the quantity supplied (p. 134)

market failure market where any of the requirements for a competitive market—adequate competition, knowledge of prices and opportunities, mobility of resources, and competitive profits—are lacking (p. 163)

market structure market classification according to number and size of firms, type of product, and type of competition (p. 152)

maturity life of a bond or length of time funds are borrowed (p. 326)

measure of value one of the three functions of money that allows it to serve as a common denominator to measure value (p. 266)

mediation process of resolving a dispute by bringing in a neutral third party (p. 191)

medicaid joint federal-state medical insurance program for low-income people (p. 246)

medicare federal health-care program for senior citizens, regardless of income (p. 218)

medium of exchange money or other substance generally accepted in exchange; one of the three functions of money (p. 266)

member bank bank belonging to the Federal Reserve System (p. 294)

member bank reserves reserves kept by member banks at the Fed to satisfy reserve requirements (p. 302)

merger combination of two or more business enterprises to form a single firm (p. 64)

microeconomics branch of economic theory that deals with behavior and decision making by small units such as individuals and firms (p. 82)

minimum wage lowest legal wage that can be paid to most workers (p. 142)

misery index unofficial statistic that is the sum of monthly inflation and the unemployment rate; same as **discomfort index** (p. 419)

mixed economy see **modified private enterprise economy** (p. 48)

modified free enterprise economy free enterprise system with some government involvement; same as **modified private enterprise economy** (p. 533)

modified private enterprise economy free enterprise market economy where people carry on their economic affairs freely, but are subject to some government intervention and regulation (p. 48)

modified union shop arrangement under which workers have the option to join a union after being hired (p. 190)

monetarism school of thought stressing the importance of stable monetary growth to control inflation and stimulate long-term economic growth (p. 433)

monetary policy actions by the Federal Reserve System to expand or contract the money supply in order to affect the cost and availability of credit (p. 302)

monetary standard mechanism that keeps a money supply durable, portable, divisible, and stable in value; gold standard, silver standard, fiat money standard (p. 272)

monetary unit standard unit of currency in a country's money supply; American dollar, British pound (p. 269)

monetizing the debt process of creating enough additional money to offset federal borrowing so that interest rates remain unchanged (p. 310)

money anything that serves as a medium of exchange, a measure of value, and a store of value (p. 266)

money market market in which financial capital is loaned and/or borrowed for one year or less (p. 332)

money market mutual fund firm that pools funds collected from small savers to make larger loans to investors willing to pay high rates of return (p. 330)

monopolistic competition market structure having all conditions of pure competition except for identical products; form of imperfect competition (p. 155)

monopoly market structure characterized by a single producer; form of imperfect competition (p. 158)

moral suasion Federal Reserve System's use of persuasion to accomplish monetary policy; Congressional testimony, press releases (p. 308)

most favored nation clause trade law allowing a third country to enjoy the same tariff reductions the United States negotiates with another country (p. 458)

multinational corporation producing and selling without regard to national boundaries and whose business activities are located in several different countries (p. 66)

multiplier change in overall spending caused by a change in investment spending (p. 427)

municipal bond bond, often tax exempt, issued by state and local governments; known as *munis* (p. 329)

mutual fund company that sells stock in itself and uses the proceeds to buy stocks and bonds issued by other companies (p. 323)

mutual savings bank depositor-owned savings institution operated for the benefit of depositors (p. 281)

N

NAFTA see **North American Free Trade Agreement** (p. 459)

national bank commercial bank chartered by the National Banking System; member of the Fed (p. 274)

National Bank note currency backed by government bonds, issued by national banks starting in 1863 and generally disappearing from circulation in the 1930s (p. 274)

National Banking System system of federally chartered, inspected, and regulated banks established in 1863, now members of the Fed (p. 274)

national currency   see **National Bank note** (p. 274)

national income   net national product less indirect business taxes; measure of a nation's income (p. 356)

national income accounting   system of accounts used to track the nation's production, consumption, savings, and income statistics (p. 348)

natural monopoly   market where average costs are lowest when all output is produced by a single firm (p. 158)

need   basic requirement for survival; includes food, clothing, and/or shelter (p. 20)

negative externality   harmful side effect that affects an uninvolved third party; external cost (p. 166)

negative income tax   tax system that would make cash payments in the form of tax refunds to individuals when their income falls below certain levels (p. 411)

Negotiable Order of Withdrawal (NOW)   type of checking account that pays interest (p. 282)

net exports of goods and services   net expenditures by the output-expenditure model's foreign sector (p. 359)

net immigration   net population change after accounting for those who leave as well as enter a country (p. 372)

net national product (NNP)   Gross National Product minus depreciation charges for wear and tear on capital equipment; measure of net annual production generated with labor and property supplied by a country's citizens (p. 355)

net worth   excess of assets over liabilities, usually listed as a separate summary on a balance sheet; measure of the value of a business (p. 302)

nominal GDP   see **current GDP** (p. 363)

nonbank financial institution   nondepository institution that channels savings to investors; finance companies, insurance companies, pension funds (p. 322)

noncompeting labor grades   broad groups of unskilled, semi-skilled, skilled, and professional workers who do not compete with one another (p. 194)

nondurable good   item that lasts for less than three years when used regularly; can be a capital or a consumer good (p. 20)

nonmarket transaction   economic activity not taking place in the market and, therefore, not included in GDP; services of homemakers, work around the home (p. 351)

nonprice competition   competition involving the advertising of a product's appearance, quality, or design, rather than its price (p. 156)

nonprofit organization   economic institution that operates like a business but does not seek financial gain; schools, churches, community service organizations (p. 69)

non-recourse loan   agricultural loan that carries neither a penalty nor further obligation to repay if not paid back (p. 144)

North American Free Trade Agreement (NAFTA)   agreement signed in 1993 to reduce tariffs between the United States, Canada, and Mexico (p. 459)

NOW Account   see **Negotiable Order of Withdrawal** (p. 282)

O

oligopoly   market structure in which a few large sellers dominate and have the ability to affect prices in the industry; form of imperfect competition (p. 156)

open market operations   monetary policy in the form of bond sales or purchases in bond markets (p. 307)

opportunity cost   cost of the next best alternative use of money, time, or resources when one choice is made rather than another (p. 15)

options   contracts giving investors an option to buy or sell commodities, equities, or financial assets at a specific future date using a price agreed upon today (p. 338)

options markets   markets where options, including put options and call options, are traded (p. 338)

organizational chart   visual representation of a company's structure showing how different parts of the organization are related (p. 61)

output-expenditure model   macroeconomic model describing aggregate demand by the consumer, investment, government, and foreign sectors; GDP = C + I + G + F (p. 358)

overhead   broad category of fixed costs that includes interest, rent, taxes, and executive salaries (p. 118)

Over-The-Counter market (OTC)   electronic marketplace for securities not listed on organized exchanges such as the New York Stock Exchange (p. 336)

P

par value   principal of a bond or total amount borrowed (p. 326)

paradox of value   apparent contradiction between the high value of nonessentials and low value of essentials (p. 22)

partnership   unincorporated business owned and operated by two or more people who share the profits and have unlimited liability for the debts and obligations of the firm; same as **general partnership** (p. 57)

patent   exclusive government-granted right to sell or use any new art, machine, item of manufacture, or composition (p. 160)

payroll withholding statement   document attached to a paycheck summarizing pay and deductions (p. 225)

payroll withholding system   system that automatically deducts income taxes from paychecks on a regular basis (p. 216)

peak   point in time when real GDP stops expanding and begins to decline (p. 383)

pension   regular allowance for someone who has worked a certain number of years, reached a certain age, or who has suffered from an injury (p. 323)

pension fund   fund that collects and invests income until payments are made to eligible recipients (p. 323)

per capita   per person basis; total divided by population (p. 238)

perestroika   fundamental restructuring of the Soviet economy; policy introduced by Gorbachev (p. 480)

personal consumption expenditures   total consumer sector expenditures that consist of households and unrelated individuals (p. 358)

personal income total amount of income going to the consumer sector before individual income taxes are paid (p. 356)

picket demonstration before a place of business to protest a company's actions (p. 184)

piecework compensation system that pays workers for units produced, rather than hours worked (p. 480)

pollution contamination of air, water, or soil by the discharge of a poisonous or noxious substance (p. 528)

pollution permit federal permit allowing a public utility to release pollutants into the air; a form of pollution control (p. 530)

population density number of people per square mile of land area (p. 514)

population pyramid diagram showing the breakdown of population by age and sex (p. 373)

portfolio diversification strategy of holding several investments to protect against risk (p. 334)

positive externality beneficial side effect that affects an uninvolved third party (p. 167)

poverty threshold annual dollar benchmark used to evaluate the money income received by families and unrelated individuals (p. 407)

preferred stock nonvoting ownership stock whose claim on the income and assets of the corporation come ahead of the common shareholder (p. 60)

premium monthly, quarterly, semiannual, or annual price paid for an insurance policy (p. 323)

price ceiling maximum legal price that can be charged for a product (p. 141)

price discrimination illegal practice of charging customers different prices for the same product (p. 169)

price-fixing agreement, usually illegal, by firms to charge a uniform price for a product (p. 157)

price floor lowest legal price that can be charged for a product (p. 142)

price index statistical series used to measure changes in the price level over time (p. 361)

price leadership independent pricing decisions made by a dominate firm on a regular basis that results in generally uniform industry-wide prices (p. 157)

price level relative magnitude of prices at a given point in time as measured by a price index (p. 399)

price war fierce price competition between sellers, sometimes to the point where price is below the cost of the product (p. 157)

primary market market in which only the original issuer will repurchase a financial asset; government savings bonds, IRAs, small CDs (p. 332)

prime rate best or lowest interest rate commercial banks charge their customers (p. 309)

primitive equilibrium first stage of economic development during which the economy is static (p. 504)

principal amount borrowed when getting a loan or issuing a bond (p. 61)

private enterprise economy see **free enterprise economy** (p. 25)

private property concept giving people the right to control their possessions as they wish; characteristic of capitalism and free enterprise (p. 45)

private sector that part of the economy made up of private individuals and businesses (p. 239)

privatization conversion of state-owned factories and other property to private ownership (p. 483)

problem bank list banking regulator's confidential list of weak and potentially unsound banks (p. 312)

producer cooperative nonprofit association of producers helping members sell or market products; found mostly in agriculture (p. 70)

producer price index index used to measure prices received by domestic producers; formerly called the **wholesale price index** (p. 362)

product differentiation real or imagined differences between competing products in the same industry (p. 155)

product market market where goods and services are offered for sale (p. 24)

production process of creating goods and services with the combined use of land, capital, labor, and entrepreneurship (p. 22)

production function graphic portrayal showing how a change in the amount of a single variable input affects total output (p. 112)

production possibilities frontier diagram representing maximum combinations of goods and/or services an economy can produce when all productive resources are fully employed (p. 16)

productivity degree to which productive resources are used efficiently; normally refers to labor, but can apply to all factors of production (p. 22)

professional association nonprofit organization of professional or specialized workers seeking to improve working conditions, skill levels, and public perceptions of its profession (p. 71)

professional labor workers with a high level of professional and managerial skills (p. 194)

profit extent to which persons or organizations are better off at the end of a period than they were at the beginning; usually measured in dollars (p. 46)

profit-maximizing quantity of output level of production where marginal cost is equal to marginal revenue (p. 122)

profit motive driving force that encourages people and organizations to improve their material well-being; characteristic of capitalism and free enterprise (p. 46)

progressive tax tax where percentage of income paid in tax rises as level of income rises (p. 215)

property tax tax on tangible and intangible possessions such as real estate, buildings, furniture, stocks, bonds, and bank accounts (p. 224)

proportional tax tax in which percentage of income paid in tax is the same regardless of the level of income (p. 215)

proprietorship see **sole proprietorship** (p. 54)

protectionist person who would protect domestic producers with tariffs, quotas, and other trade barriers (p. 454)

protective tariff tax on an imported product designed to protect less efficient domestic producers (p. 453)

proxy ballot allowing a shareholder's representative to vote on corporate matters (p. 60)

public disclosure requirement forcing a business to reveal information about its products or its operations to the public (p. 170)

public good economic product that is consumed collectively; highways, national defense, police and fire protection (p. 167)

public sector that part of the economy made up of the local, state, and federal governments (p. 239)

public utility company providing essential services such as water and electricity to consumers, usually subject to some government regulations (p. 72)

pure competition market structure characterized by a large number of independent and well-informed buyers and sellers of an identical product—none of which are large enough to influence the price—along with relative ease of entry and exit in the industry (p. 152)

put option contract giving investors the option to sell commodities, equities, or financial assets at a specific future date using a price agreed upon today (p. 338)

Q

quantity supplied amount offered for sale at a given price; point on the supply curve (p. 106)

quantity theory of money hypothesis that the supply of money directly affects the price level over the long run (p. 309)

quota limit on the amount of a good that can be allowed into a country (p. 453)

R

ration coupon certificate allowing holder to receive a given amount of a rationed product (p. 131)

rationing system of allocating goods and services without prices (p. 131)

raw materials unprocessed natural resources used in production (p. 112)

real dollars see **constant dollars** (p. 204)

real estate investment trust (REIT) company organized to make loans to home builders (p. 323)

real GDP Gross Domestic Product after adjustments for inflation; same as **GDP in constant dollars** (p. 364)

real GDP per capita Gross Domestic Product adjusted for inflation and divided by the total population; total dollar amount of all final output produced for every person in the country after compensating for inflation (p. 376)

real property wealth in the form of real estate, buildings, and permanent attachments (p. 224)

rebate partial refund of the original price of a product (p. 140)

recession decline in real GDP lasting at least two quarters or more (p. 383)

regressive tax tax where percentage of income paid in tax goes down as income rises (p. 215)

Regulation Q federal regulation that once set maximum interest rates that could be paid on demand deposits (p. 285)

Regulation Z provision extending truth-in-lending disclosures to consumers (p. 299)

renewable resources natural resources that can be replenished for future use (p. 379)

reserve requirement formula used to compute the amount of a depository institution's required reserves (p. 302)

retained earnings corporate earnings kept by a corporation rather than being paid out to shareholders; same as **undistributed corporate profits** (p. 356)

revenue firm's receipts from the sale or rental of its product, also includes money from other sources such as dividends and interest (p. 62)

revenue tariff tax placed on imported goods to raise revenue (p. 453)

right-to-work law state law making it illegal to require a worker to join a union (p. 186)

risk situation in which the outcome is not certain, but the probabilities can be estimated (p. 325)

run on the bank sudden rush by depositors to withdraw all deposited funds, generally in anticipation of bank failure or closure (p. 281)

rural population those persons not living in urban areas (p. 370)

S

S&P 500 see **Standard & Poor's 500** (p. 337)

sales tax general state or city tax levied on a product at the time of sale (p. 222)

saving absence of spending that frees resources for use in other activities or investments (p. 320)

savings the dollars that become available for investors to use when others save (p. 320)

savings account interest-bearing deposit not requiring prior notice before making a withdrawal (p. 304)

savings and loan association (S&L) depository institution that historically invested the majority of its funds in home mortgages (p. 282)

savings bank savings institution owned by stockholders rather than by depositors (p. 282)

savings bond low-denomination, non-transferable bond issued by the federal government, usually through payroll-savings plans (p. 329)

scarcity fundamental economic problem facing all societies that results from a combination of scarce resources and people's virtually unlimited wants (p. 8)

seasonal unemployment unemployment caused by annual changes in the weather or other conditions that prevail at certain times of the year (p. 396)

seat membership in a stock exchange such as the New York Stock Exchange (p. 335)

secondary market market in which all financial assets can be sold to someone other than the original issuer; corporate bonds, government bonds (p. 332)

secondhand sales sales of used goods; category of activity not included in GDP computation (p. 349)

securities exchange physical place where buyers and sellers meet to exchange securities (p. 335)

seizure temporary government takeover of a company to keep it running during a labor-management dispute (p. 192)

selective credit controls rules pertaining to loans for specific commodities or purchases such as margin requirements for common stock (p. 308)

semiskilled labor workers who can operate machines requiring a minimum amount of training (p. 194)

seniority length of time a person has been on a job (p. 196)

service work or labor performed for someone; economic product that includes haircuts, home repairs, forms of entertainment (p. 20)

service cooperative nonprofit association of consumers dealing with services rather than goods; includes credit unions, some insurance and credit agencies (p. 70)

set-aside contract guaranteed contract or portion thereof reserved for a targeted, usually minority, group (p. 201)

share draft checking account offered by a credit union (p. 283)

shareholder see **stockholder** (p. 59)

short run production period so short that only variable inputs can be changed (p. 111)

shortage situation where quantity supplied is less than quantity demanded at a given price (p. 136)

silver certificate paper currency backed by, and redeemable for, silver from 1886 to 1968 (p. 275)

sin tax relatively high tax designed to raise revenue and discourage consumption of a socially undesirable product (p. 210)

skilled labor workers who can operate complex equipment and require little supervision (p. 194)

Social Security federal program of disability and retirement benefits that covers most working people (p. 40)

socialism economic system in which government owns some factors of production and has a role in determining what and how goods are produced (p. 473)

sole proprietorship unincorporated business owned and run by a single person who has rights to all profits and unlimited liability for all debts of the firm; most common form of business organization in the United States (p. 54)

Solidarity independent Polish labor union founded in 1980 by Lech Walesa (p. 485)

specialization assignment of tasks so that each worker performs fewer functions more frequently; same as division of labor (p. 22)

specie money in the form of gold or silver coins (p. 268)

spot market market in which a transaction is made immediately at the prevailing price (p. 338)

stages of production phases of production—increasing, decreasing, and negative returns (p. 114)

stagflation combination of stagnant economic growth and inflation (p. 419)

Standard & Poor's 500 (S&P 500) statistical series of 500 stocks used to monitor prices on the NYSE, American Stock Exchange, and OTC market (p. 337)

standard of living quality of life based on ownership of necessities and luxuries that make life easier (pp. 24, 377)

state bank bank that receives its charter from the state in which it operates (p. 272)

state farm large farms owned and operated by the state in the former Soviet Union (p. 479)

stock certificate of ownership in a corporation; common or preferred stock (p. 59)

stock certificate see **stock** (p. 59)

stockbroker person who buys or sells securities for investors (p. 335)

stockholder person who owns a share or shares of stock in a corporation; same as shareholders (p. 59)

store of value one of the three functions of money allowing people to preserve value for future use (p. 266)

storming Soviet practice of rushing production at month's end to fulfill quotas, often resulting in production of shoddy goods (p. 480)

strike union organized work stoppage designed to gain concessions from an employer (p. 184)

structural unemployment unemployment caused by a fundamental change in the economy that reduces the demand for some workers (p. 395)

structures category in the national income and product accounts that includes residential structures, apartments, and commercial buildings (p. 348)

subsidy government payment to encourage or protect a certain economic activity (p. 108)

subsistence state in which a society produces barely enough to support itself (p. 520)

substitutes competing products that can be used in place of one another; products related in such a way that an increase in the price of one increases the demand for the other (p. 88)

substitution effect that portion of a change in quantity demanded due to a change in the relative price of the product (p. 87)

supply schedule of quantities offered for sale at all possible prices in a market (p. 104)

supply curve graphical representation of the quantities produced at each and every possible price in the market (p. 105)

supply elasticity responsiveness of quantity supplied to a change in price (p. 109)

supply schedule tabular listing showing the quantities produced or offered for sale at each and every possible price in the market (p. 105)

supply-side economics economic policies designed to increase aggregate supply or shift the aggregate supply curve to the right (p. 431)

surcharge additional tax or charge added to other charges already in place (p. 231)

surplus situation where quantity supplied is greater than quantity demanded at a given price (p. 135)

T

takeoff third stage of economic development during which barriers of primitive equilibrium are overcome (p. 504)

tangible personal property all tangible items of wealth not permanently attached to land or buildings (p. 224)

target price agricultural floor price set by the government to stabilize farm incomes (p. 144)

tariff tax placed on an imported product (p. 453)

tax assessor person who examines and values property for tax purposes (p. 224)

tax base incomes and properties that are potentially subject to tax by local, state, or federal governments (p. 377)

tax-exempt income from a bond or other investment not subject to tax by federal or state governments (p. 329)

tax loophole exception or oversight in the tax law allowing taxpayer to avoid taxes (p. 212)

tax return annual report filed with local, state, or federal government detailing income earned and taxes owed (p. 216)

technological monopoly market situation where a firm has a monopoly because it owns or controls a manufacturing method, process, or other scientific advance (p. 159)

technological unemployment unemployment caused by technological developments or automation that make some worker's skills obsolete (p. 396)

theory of negotiated wages explanation of wage rates based on the bargaining strength of organized labor (p. 196)

theory of production theory dealing with the relationship between the factors of production and the output of goods and services (p. 111)

thrift institution savings & loan associations, mutual savings banks, and other depository institutions historically catering to savers (p. 281)

tight money policy monetary policy resulting in higher interest rates and restricted access to credit; associated with a contraction of the money supply (p. 306)

time deposit interest-bearing deposit requiring prior notice before a withdrawal can be made, even though the requirement may not always be enforced (p. 304)

total cost variable plus fixed cost; all costs associated with production (p. 119)

total product total output or production by a firm (p. 113)

total revenue total receipts; price of goods sold times quantity sold (p. 121)

trade deficit balance of payments outcome when spending on imports exceeds revenues received from exports (p. 456)

trade-offs alternatives that must be given up when one is chosen rather than another (p. 14)

trade union see **craft union** (p. 184)

trade-weighted value of the dollar index showing strength of the United States dollar against a market basket of other foreign currencies (p. 465)

trading desk physical location at the New York Federal Reserve district bank where the purchase and sale of government bonds is managed (p. 307)

traditional economy economic system in which the allocation of scarce resources and other economic activity is the result of ritual, habit, or custom (p. 32)

traditional theory of wage determination explanation of wage rates relying on theory of supply and demand (p. 195)

transfer payment payment for which the government receives neither goods nor services in return (p. 239)

Treasury bill short-term United States government obligation with a maturity of one year or under in denominations of $10,000 (p. 331)

Treasury bond United States government bond with maturity of 10 to 30 years (p. 330)

Treasury coin note paper currency printed from 1890 to 1893, redeemable in both gold and silver (p. 275)

Treasury note United States government obligation with a maturity of 2 to 10 years (p. 330)

trend line growth path the economy would follow if it were not interrupted by alternating periods of recession and recovery (p. 384)

trough point in time when real GDP stops declining and begins to expand (p. 383)

trust illegal combination of corporations or companies organized to hinder competition (p. 169)

trust fund special account used to hold revenues designated for a specific expenditure such as Social Security, medicare, or highways (p. 256)

truth-in-lending laws federal laws requiring that complete and accurate loan disclosures be made to consumers (p. 299)

two-tier wage system wage scale paying newer workers a lower wage than others already on the job (p. 199)

U

underground economy unreported legal and illegal activities that do not show up in GDP statistics (p. 351)

undistributed corporate profits see **retained earnings** (p. 356)

unemployed state of working for less than one hour per week for pay or profit in a non-family owned business, while being available and having made an effort to find a job during the past month (p. 394)

unemployment insurance government program providing payments to the unemployed; an automatic stabilizer (p. 429)

unemployment rate ratio of unemployed individuals divided by total number of persons in the civilian labor force, expressed as a percentage (p. 394)

union shop arrangement under which workers must join a union after being hired (p. 190)

unit elastic elasticity where a change in the independent variable (usually price) generates a proportional change of the dependent variable (quantity demanded or supplied) (p. 94)

United States note paper currency with no backing, first printed by the United States government in 1862 to finance the Civil War (p. 274)

unlimited liability requirement that an owner is personally and fully responsible for all losses and debts of a business; applies to proprietorships, general partnerships (p. 56)

unlimited life condition of continued legal existence of a corporation when an owner dies, sells, or transfers ownership (p. 62)

unrelated individual person living alone or with nonrelatives even though that person may have relatives living elsewhere (p. 357)

unskilled labor workers not trained to operate specialized machines and equipment (p. 194)

urban population those persons living in incorporated cities, towns, and villages with 2,500 or more inhabitants (p. 370)

user fee fee paid for the use of good or service; form of a benefit tax (p. 220)

utility ability or capacity of a good or service to be useful and give satisfaction to someone (p. 22)

V

value worth of a good or service as determined by the market (p. 21)

value added tax tax on the value added at every stage of the production process (p. 229)

variable cost production cost that varies as output changes; labor, energy, raw materials (p. 118)

vertical merger combination of firms involved in different steps of manufacturing or marketing (p. 65)

voluntary arbitration agreement by labor and management to place a dispute before a third party for a binding settlement (p. 191)

voluntary exchange act of buyers and sellers freely and willingly engaging in market transactions; characteristic of capitalism and free enterprise (p. 44)

W

wage-price controls policies and regulations making it illegal for firms to give raises or raise prices (p. 434)

wage rate prevailing pay scale for work performed in a given area or region (p. 195)

wampum form of money made from shells and devised by Native Americans, used widely in early colonial America (p. 267)

want way of expressing or communicating a need; a broader classification than needs (p. 20)

wealth sum of tangible economic goods that are scarce, useful, and transferable from one person to another; excludes services (p. 22)

welfare government or private agency programs that provide general economic and social assistance to needy individuals (p. 409)

white-collar worker clerical, business, or professional worker receiving a salary rather than a wage (p. 407)

wholesale price index see **producer price index** (p. 362)

wildcat bank generally fraudulent bank that operated in remote areas in the early 1800s (p. 273)

workfare program requiring welfare recipients to provide labor in exchange for benefits (p. 412)

World Bank international agency that makes loans to developing countries; formally the International Bank for Reconstruction and Development (p. 505)

Z

zero population growth condition in which the average number of births and deaths balance so that population size is unchanged (p. 499)

A

ability-to-pay principle of taxation/principio de tributación sobre la solvencia creencia que los impuestos se deben pagar de acuerdo al nivel de ingresos sin considerar los beneficios recibidos (p. 214)

absolute advantage/ventaja absoluta habilidad de un país para producir más de un producto en particular que los otros países (p. 450)

accelerated depreciation/depreciación acelerada programa que extiende la depreciación a lo largo de menos años de lo normal para generar mayores reducciones de impuestos (p. 231)

accelerator/acelerador cambio en el gasto causado por un cambio en el gasto global (p. 428)

acid rain/lluvia ácida contaminación en la forma de agualluvia mezclada con dióxido de sulfuro, forma leve de ácido sulfúrico (p. 528)

agency shop/taller gremial arreglo bajo el cual miembros que no son de la unión tienen que pagar cuotas de unión (p. 190)

aggregate demand curve/curva de demanda global curva hipotética que muestra distintos niveles del PIB real que se podrían producir a distintos niveles de precio (p. 422)

aggregate supply curve/curva de oferta global curva hipotética que muestra distintos niveles del PIB real que se podrían producir a distintos niveles de precio (p. 422)

agricultural bank/banco de crédito agrícola banco comercial con más de 25 por ciento de sus préstamos para la agricultura (p. 313)

alternative minimum tax/impuesto mínimo alternativo índice de impuesto sobre la renta que se aplica a casos en que los impuestos de otro modo caerían por debajo de cierto nivel (p. 231)

appropriations bill/proyecto de ley para asignación de fondos legislación para asignar fondos para ciertos propósitos (p. 243)

aquifer/acuífero formación subterránea rocosa que contiene agua (p. 525)

articles of partnership/contrato de asociación documento legal que especifica formalmente los acuerdos entre socios, incluyendo la forma en que se han de dividir las ganancias y las pérdidas (p. 57)

assets/haberes propiedades, posesiones y demandas a otras personas; generalmente, aparecen anotadas como asiento en el estado de cuentas (p. 302)

automatic stabilizer/estabilizador automático programa que automáticamente provee beneficios para compensar por un cambio en los ingresos de la gente; seguro de desempleo, programas de derecho a gratificación (p. 429)

automation/automatización producción, tanto mecánica como de otros procesos, que reduce la necesidad de trabajadores (p. 396)

average tax rate/tasa impositiva media total de impuestos pagados divididos por el total de renta imponible (p. 215)

B

baby boom/auge de bebés años en Estados Unidos, entre 1946 y 1964, en que hubo una alta tasa de natalidad (p. 373)

balance of payments/balanza de pagos diferencia entre dinero que se paga o que se recibe de otras naciones en actividad comercial; *balance de cuenta corriente* incluye bienes y servicios, *balanza comercial de mercancía* toma en cuenta sólo los bienes (p. 456)

balance sheet/estado de cuentas extracto de cuenta que muestra el activo y el pasivo y el valor neto de una unidad económica (p. 302)

balanced budget/presupuesto balanceado presupuesto anual en el que los gastos están a la par con los ingresos (p. 258)

balanced budget amendment/enmienda al presupuesto balanceado enmienda constitucional estatal o federal que requiere que el gobierno no gaste más de lo que recauda en impuestos y otros ingresos, a exclusión de préstamos (p. 249)

bank holding company/sociedad inversionista bancaria corporación que posee uno o más bancos (p. 296)

bank holiday/cierre bancario breve período durante el cual todos los bancos o instituciones de depósitos cierran para evitar los pánicos bancarios (p. 281)

bankruptcy/quiebra permiso que concede la corte a una persona o a un negocio para cesar o aplazar pago de algunas o todas las deudas durante un tiempo limitado (p. 61)

barter economy/economía de trueque economía sin dinero que depende del comercio o trueque (p. 266)

base year/año base año que sirve como punto de comparación para otros años en un índice de precios u otra estadística (p. 204)

benefit principle of taxation/principio de tributación acerca de beneficios creencia de que los impuestos se deben pagar de acuerdo con los beneficios que se reciban independiente del nivel de ingreso (p. 213)

Better Business Bureau organización sin fines de lucro patronizada por el comercio la cual provee al consumidor información acerca de las compañías locales (p. 71)

bill consolidation loan/préstamo para la consolidación de cuenta tipo popular de préstamo al consumidor que se usa para saldar múltiples préstamos en existencia (p. 322)

black market/mercado negro mercado en que se venden productos económicos ilegalmente (p. 486)

blue-collar worker/obrero trabajadores industriales o de factoria quienes reciben jornal en vez de salarios (p. 407)

board of directors/junta de directores representantes de accionistas ordinarios elegidos para instituir políticas y metas, alquilar gerentes profesionales para una corporación (p. 60)

bond/fianza contrato formal para devolver el dinero y los intereses sobre dinero prestado durante intervalos sistemáticos en el futuro (p. 61)

boycott/boicot protesta en la forma de rehusar a comprar, que incluye el esfuerzo para convencer a otras personas a tampoco comprar (p. 184)

break-even point/punto muerto producción necesaria si la firma ha de recuperar sus costos; nivel de producción en que el costo total equivale al ingreso total (p. 122)

bullion/lingote barras de metales nobles sin acuñar, por lo general oro o plata (p. 268)

business cycle/ciclo comercial cambios sistemáticos en el PIB real acentuados por periodos alternantes de expansión y contracción (p. 383)

business fluctuation/fluctuación comercial cambios en el PIB acentuados por períodos alternantes de expansión y contracción que ocurren en una base menos que sistemática (p. 383)

business organization/organización comercial empresa en pos de ganancias que produce bienes y/o servicios; incluye propietarios exclusivos, sociedades, corporaciones (p. 54)

C

call option/opción de compra contrato que da a los inversionistas la opción de comprar productos, acciones o bienes financieros en una fecha específica en el futuro y usando el precio que se acordó hoy (p. 338)

capital/capital implementos, equipo y fábricas que se usan en la producción de bienes y servicios; uno de cuatro factores de producción (p. 9)

capital consumption allowances/reservas para depreciación uso y desgaste de bienes de capital que se resta del PNB para obtener el PNN (p. 355)

capital flight/fuga de capitales exportación legal o ilegal de la moneda y las divisas de una nación (p. 500)

capital good/bienes de capital implemento, equipo u otros bienes fabricados que se emplean para producir otros bienes y servicios; un factor de producción (p. 20)

capital-intensive/con gran intensidad de capital método de producción que requiere relativamente grandes cantidades de capital con relación a la mano de obra (p. 488)

capital market/mercado de capital mercado en el que el capital financiero se presta por más de un año (p. 332)

capitalism/capitalismo economía mercantil en la cual los factores de producción son de propiedad privada (p. 43)

capital-to-labor ratio/relación capital-trabajo medida obtenida al dividir el total de las acciones de capital por la fuerza de trabajo (p. 379)

cartel/cartel grupo de vendedores o productores que obran conjuntamente para subir los precios al restringir la disponibilidad de un producto; OPEC (p. 513)

cease and desist order/orden de cesar y desistir fallo que ordena que una compañía pare una práctica comercial injusta que reduce o limita la competencia (p. 169)

census/censo cuenta completa de la población, incluyendo el lugar de residencia (p. 370)

center of population/centro de población punto donde el país se equilibraría si fuera plano y todo el mundo pesara lo mismo (p. 372)

central bank/banco central banco que le presta a otros bancos en momentos de necesidad, el "banco de los banqueros" (p. 280)

certificate of deposit/certificado de depósito recibo que indica que un inversionista ha hecho un préstamo con

intereses a una institución financiera (p. 304)

chamber of commerce/cámara de comercio organización sin fines de lucro cuyo propósito es promover los intereses comunes de los negocios locales (p. 71)

change in demand/cambio en demanda los consumidores demandan distintas cantidades en cada precio, haciendo que la curva de demanda cambie hacia la izquierda o la derecha (p. 88)

change in quantity demanded/cambio en cantidad demandada un movimiento en la curva de relación entre demanda y precio que demuestra que se está comprando una cantidad distinta debido a un cambio de precio (p. 86)

change in quantity supplied/cambio en la cantidad suplida cambio en la cantidad que se ofrece a la venta en respuesta a un cambio de precio; movimiento a lo largo de la curva de abastecimiento (p. 106)

change in supply/cambio en abastecimiento distintas cantidades ofrecidas a la venta a todos los precios posibles del mercado; cambio en la curva de abastecimiento (p. 106)

charter/carta constitucional aprobación escrita del gobierno para establecer una corporación; incluye el nombre de la compañía, la dirección, propósito del negocio, número de acciones y otros aspectos del negocio (p. 59)

civilian labor force/fuerza de trabajo civil parte de la población no institucionalizada, entre los 16 y 65 años, que está trabajando o buscando trabajo (p. 182)

closed shop/taller cerrado arreglo ilegal bajo el cual los trabajadores tienen que ser miembros de una unión antes de que los emplee (p. 190)

coins/monedas formas metálicas de dinero tal como el centavo, las monedas de cinco, diez y de 25 centavos (p. 300)

collateral/fianza propiedad u otra seguridad que se usa para garantizar el pago de un préstamo (p. 308)

collective bargaining/negociación colectiva proceso de negociación entre la unión y los representantes administrativos acerca de pago, beneficios y asuntos relacionados al trabajo (p. 70)

collective farm/granja colectiva en la antigua Unión Soviética, pequeñas granjas de propiedad del estado, pero operadas por familias que participaban en algunas de las ganancias (p. 479)

collectivization/colectivización propiedad común forzada de los factores de producción; se usó en la antigua Unión Soviética en la agricultura y en la industria manufacturera bajo Stalin (p. 478)

collusion/colusión acuerdos, por lo general ilegales, entre los productores para fijar los precios, limitar la producción o dividir los mercados (p. 157)

command economy/economía de mando sistema económico que se caracteriza por una autoridad central que hace la mayoría de las decisiones económicas (p. 33)

commercial bank/banco comercial institución depositoria que, hasta mediados de los años 70, tenía el derecho exclusivo de ofrecer cuentas de cheques (p. 281)

commodity money/dinero como producto dinero que tiene un uso alternativo como producto; pólvora, harina, maíz (p. 267)

common stock/acciones ordinarias certificado de propiedad en una corporación que autoriza al dueño a votar por la junta de directores, pero que tiene la última reclamación acerca de los dividendos y el capital (p. 60)

communism/comunismo sistema económico y político en el que los factores de producción son de propiedad colectiva y dirigidos por el estado; teoréticamente, una sociedad sin clases en que todos trabajan para el bien común (p. 474)

company union/sindicato de empresa unión organizada, sostenida y hasta financiada por el patrón (p. 184)

comparable worth/valor comparable doctrina que declara que se debe pagar lo mismo por trabajos de comparable dificultad (p. 200)

comparative advantage/ventaja comparativa habilidad del país de producir un cierto producto con relativamente más eficiencia que otro país; la oportunidad de producción al costo más bajo (p. 451)

complements/complementos productos que aumentan la utilidad o valor de otros productos; productos relacionados de tal modo que el aumento del precio de uno reduce la demanda de ambos (p. 89)

compulsory arbitration/arbitraje obligatorio situación que fuerza a los trabajadores y a la administración a usar un mediador para alcanzar un arreglo obligatorio (p. 191)

conglomerate/conglomerado de empresas firma con cuatro o más negocios que hacen productos no relacionados, sin ningún negocio en particular que sea responsable de la mayoría de sus ventas (p. 65)

conspicuous consumption/consumo suntuario uso de bienes y servicios caros para impresionar a las otras personas (p. 21)

constant dollars/dólares constantes las cantidades o precios al que se ajusta el dólar debido a la inflación; igual que **dólares reales** (p. 204)

consumer/consumidor persona que usa bienes y servicios para satisfacer sus necesidades y deseos (p. 21)

consumer cooperative/cooperativa de consumidor asociación sin fines de lucro que compra bienes de consumidor en grandes cantidades para que así sus miembros puedan comprar a precios por debajo de los que cobran los negocios regulares (p. 69)

consumer good/bienes del consumidor bienes cuyo fin está dirigido a los consumidores en vez del comercio (p. 20)

consumer price index/índice de precios de consumidor índice que se usa para medir los cambios de precio de la cesta de compra de los productos que el consumidor usa con más frecuencia (p. 362)

consumer sovereignty/soberanía del consumidor papel del consumidor como soverano del mercado a la hora de determinar los tipos de bienes y servicios que se producen (p. 47)

consumption/consumo proceso de consumir bienes y servicios para satisfacer las necesidades y deseos (p. 21)

consumption function/función del consumo gráfica que indica que para los distintos niveles económicos del sector del consumidor, los patrones de gasto son relativamente constantes y estables (p. 427)

co-op ver **cooperativa** (p. 69)

cooperative/cooperativa asociación sin fines de lucro que lleva a cabo algún tipo de actividad económica para el beneficio de sus miembros; incluye las cooperativas de consumidor, de servicios y de productores (p. 69)

copyright/derecho de autor derecho exclusivo que se concede a un autor o artista para vender, publicar o reproducir su trabajo durante su vida más 50 años (p. 160)

corporate income tax/impuesto sobre la renta de corporación impuesto que pagan las corporaciones sobre sus ganancias de corporación (p. 219)

corporation/corporación una forma de organización comercial reconocida por la ley como una entidad legal independiente con todos los derechos y responsabilidades de individuo, inclusive el derecho de comprar y vender propiedad, entrar en contratos legales, demandar y ser demandada (p. 59)

cost-benefit analysis/análisis de costo-ventajas forma de pensar que compara el costo de una acción con sus ventajas (p. 532)

Council of Economic Advisers/Consejo de Asesores Económicos grupo de tres miembros que idea estrategias y aconseja al Presidente de los Estados Unidos acerca de asuntos económicos (p. 437)

coupon/cupón interés declarado de un bono de una corporación, de un municipio o del gobierno (p. 326)

craft union/sindicato de artesanos gremio laboral cuyos trabajadores llevan a cabo el mismo tipo de trabajo; igual que un **sindicato gremial** (p. 184)

credit union/cooperativa de crédito cooperativa de servicios sin fines de lucro que acepta depósitos, hace préstamos y provee otros servicios financieros (p. 70)

creditor/acreedor persona o institución a quien se le debe dinero (p. 312)

creeping inflation/inflación reptante índice de inflación bajo, generalmente de 1 a 3 por ciento anualmente (p. 400)

crowding-out effect/efecto de exclusión tasas de interés más altas de lo normal y disminución del acceso al capital financiero a que se enfrentan los inversionistas privados cuando el gobierno aumenta sus préstamos en los mercados financieros (p. 258)

crude birth rate/tasa de natalidad bruta número de nacimientos por 1,000 personas (p. 499)

currency/efectivo componente de papel del abastecimiento de dinero, hoy consiste en billetes de la Reserva Federal (p. 300)

current dollars/dólares corrientes cantidades o precios del dólar que no han sido ajustados para reflejar la inflación (p. 202)

current GDP/PIB imperante Producto Interno Bruto que se mide por los precios imperantes, sin ajustarlos para reflejar la inflación (p. 363)

current yield/rendimiento imperante el interés anual del cupón de un bono dividido por el precio de compra; medida de las ganancias de un bono (p. 327)

customs duty/derechos aduaneros impuestos sobre productos importados (p. 220)

customs union/unión aduanera grupo de países que han acordado reducir las barreras de intercambio comercial entre sí y han adoptado barreras comerciales uniformes para los países que no son miembros (p. 512)

cyclical unemployment/desempleo cíclico desempleo directamente relacionado a oscilaciones en el ciclo económico (p. 396)

D

deep gas/gas profundo gas natural situado a 15,000 pies o más debajo de la superficie de la tierra (p. 527)

deficiency payment/aportación para enjugar un déficit aportación en efectivo para alcanzar la diferencia entre el precio del mercado y el precio indicativo de una cosecha agrícola (p. 145)

deficit spending/gastos deficitarios gastos anuales del gobierno en exceso de los impuestos y otros ingresos (p. 253)

deflation/deflación disminución en el nivel general de los precios (p. 399)

demand/demanda combinación de deseo, habilidad y voluntad de comprar un producto (p. 82)

demand curve/curva de demanda gráfica que ilustra la cantidad que se demanda a cada precio que puede prevalecer en el mercado en cualquier momento dado (p. 84)

demand deposit account/cuentas de depósito a la vista (CDV) cuentas cuyos fondos pueden retirarse al escribirse un cheque y sin la previa aprobación de la institución depositoria (p. 281)

demand elasticity/elasticidad de demanda medida de responsividad que relaciona el cambio en la cantidad demandada (variable dependiente) a un cambio en precio (variable independiente) (p. 92)

demand schedule/programa de demanda lista que indica la cantidad demandada a todos los precios posibles que pueden prevalecer en el mercado en cualquier momento dado (p. 84)

demographer/demógrafo persona que estudia el crecimiento, la densidad y otras características de la población (p. 372)

dependency ratio/relación de dependencia relación de niños a envejecientes por 100 personas dentro de la categoría de trabajo de las edades entre los 18-64 años (p. 374)

depreciation/depreciación desgaste gradual de los bienes de capital durante la producción (p. 118)

depression/depresión estado de la economía con grandes números de desempleados, disminución de ingresos reales, exceso de capacidad en las plantas manufactureras, dificultades económicas generales (p. 384)

depression scrip/vale de depresión moneda emitida por los pueblos, las cámaras de comercio y otras entidades cívicas durante la Gran Depresión de los años 30 (p. 385)

deregulation/eliminación de restricciones relajamiento o eliminación de los reglamentos del gobierno sobre las actividades comerciales (p. 284)

devaluation/devaluación acción que toma un país para que su moneda valga menos en relación al oro u otra moneda (p. 462)

developing country/país en desarrollo país cuyo promedio de ingresos per cápita es tan sólo una fracción del de los países más industrializados (p. 498)

diminishing marginal utility/utilidad marginal decreciente satisfacción o utilidad decreciente a medida que se van adquiriendo unidades adicionales de un producto (p. 90)

diminishing returns/rendimientos decrecientes etapa de producción en la que el rendimiento aumenta a un ritmo disminuyente a medida que se añaden más unidades de insumo variable (p. 115)

discomfort index/índice de incomodidad estadística no oficial de la suma de la inflación mensual y el índice de desempleo; igual al **índice de miseria** (p. 419)

discount rate/tasa de descuento tasa de interés que el Sistema de Reserva Federal cobra a las instituciones financieras por los préstamos (p. 307)

discount window/ventana de descuento local físico en el Sistema de Reserva Federal donde se hacen los préstamos a las instituciones depositorias (p. 308)

disposable personal income/ingreso personal disponible el ingreso personal menos los impuestos personales; todo el ingreso disponible al sector consumidor después de los impuestos (p. 356)

distribution of income/distribución de ingresos modo por el cual los ingresos de la nación se dividen entre familias, individuos u otros grupos designados (p. 240)

dividend/dividendo cheque que se paga a los accionistas, por lo general trimestralmente, representa una porción de las ganancias de la corporación (p. 59)

division of labor/división de trabajo división de trabajo en un número de tareas separadas para llevarse a cabo por distintos trabajadores; igual que **especialización** (p. 23)

DJIA ver **Dow-Jones Industrial Average** (p. 337)

Dow-Jones Industrial Average (DJIA) serie de estadísticas representativas de 30 acciones que se usan para seguir los cambios de precio en la New York Stock Exchange (p. 337)

dual banking system/sistema bancario doble situación desde 1863 hasta el presente que permite que los bancos elijan cartas constitucionales federales o del estado (p. 279)

durable goods/bienes durables bienes que duran más de tres años con uso regular; puede incluir capital o un objeto de consumidor (p. 20)

E

easy money policy/política de dinero abundante política monetaria que resulta en tasas de interés más bajas y mayor acceso a crédito; se asocia con la expansión del abastecimiento de dinero (p. 306)

econometric model/modelo econométrico modelo macroeconómico que usa ecuaciones algebraicas para describir cómo la economía se conduce y cómo se espera que se conduzca en el futuro (p. 387)

economic institution/institución económica organización o grupo de personas que usan y a veces representan los factores de producción (p. 54)

economic interdependence/interdependencia económica las actividades económicas en una parte del país o del mundo afectan lo que sucede en otro lugar (p. 23)

economic model/modelo económico conjunto de suposiciones en una tabla, gráfica o ecuaciones que se usan para describir o explicar la conducta económica (p. 134)

economic product/producto económico bienes o servicios útiles, relativamente escasos y transferibles a otras personas (p. 20)

economic system/sistema económico manera organizada de una sociedad proveer las necesidades de sus integrantes (p. 32)

economics/economía ciencia social que trata acerca del

estudio de cómo la gente satisface los aparentemente ilimitados y competitivos deseos mediante el uso cuidadoso de escasos recursos (p. 11)

economies of scale/economías de escala aumento de la eficacia del uso del personal, la planta y el equipo a medida que la empresa aumenta de tamaño (p. 159)

ECU Unidad monetaria europea; unidad monetaria que usa la Unión Europea (p. 513)

Efficient Market Hypothesis/Hipótesis de Mercado Eficiente (HME) argumento acerca de que las acciones siempre tienen el precio adecuado, y que las rebajas son difíciles de hallar porque muchísimos inversionistas siempre las están vigilando (p. 334)

elastic/elástico tipo de elasticidad en que el cambio de porcentaje en la variable independiente (generalmente el precio) causa un cambio más que proporcionado en la variable dependiente (generalmente la cantidad demandada u ofrecida) (p. 92)

embargo/embargo prohibición de la exportación o importación de un producto (p. 522)

energy bank/banco de energía banco comercial con más del 25 por ciento de sus préstamos en energía (p. 313)

enterprise zone/zona de iniciativa áreas económicamente deprimidas donde se han suspendido las reglamentaciones del gobierno para poder atraer el comercio (p. 412)

entitlement/titularidad programa o beneficio que usa los requerimientos de la eligibilidad establecida para proveer suplementos de salud, de alimentación o de ingresos a individuos (p. 260)

entrepreneur/empresario individuo arriesgado en busca de ganancias; uno de cuatro factores de producción (p. 10)

equilibrium price/precio de equilibrio precio en que la cantidad ofrecida equivale a la cantidad demandada; precio que aprueba el mercado (p. 138)

equilibrium wage rate/índice del equilibrio salarial índice salarial que no deja ni exceso ni escacez en el mercado (p. 195)

equities/capital accionario acciones que representan acciones de propiedad en las corporaciones (p. 334)

estate tax/impuesto sucesorio impuesto por el traspaso de propiedad cuando una persona muere (p. 220)

European Community/Comunidad Europea antigua unión aduanera compuesta de 12 naciones europeas; se convirtió en la Unión Europea en noviembre del 1993 (p. 512)

European Union/Unión Europea la sucesora de la Comunidad Europea que estableció el Tratado de Maastricht en noviembre del 1993 (p. 512)

excess reserves/reservas excesivas dinero efectivo, divisas y reservas de una institución financiera que no se necesitan para respaldar préstamos en existencia; fuente potencial de nuevos préstamos (p. 303)

excise tax/impuesto sobre el consumo impuesto sobre ingresos generales recaudado sobre la manufactura o venta de objetos selectos (p. 219)

expansion/expansión periodo de crecimiento del PIB real; recuperación de la recesión (p. 383)

expropriation/expropiación cuando el gobierno confisca bienes de propiedad privada o extranjera sin compensación (p. 511)

external debt/deuda externa dinero prestado que un país

debe a países y bancos extranjeros (p. 500)

externality/factores externos efecto secundario de la economía que afecta a un tercero que no está envuelto (p. 166)

F

fact-finding/indagación de los hechos acuerdo entre la unión y la empresa de pedirle a un tercero recoja los hechos acerca de una disputa y presente recomendaciones sin obligaciones (p. 191)

factor market/mercado de factor mercado en que se venden y se compran recursos productivos (p. 24)

factors of production/factores de producción recursos productivos que componen las cuatro categorías de tierra, capital, trabajo y espíritu empresarial (p. 9)

family/familia dos o más personas que viven juntas y que están vinculadas por sangre, matrimonio o adopción (p. 357)

federal budget/presupuesto federal plan anual que traza los gastos propuestos y las ganancias que se anticipan (p. 243)

federal budget deficit/déficit del presupuesto federal exceso de gastos federales sobre la recaudación de impuestos e ingresos (p. 243)

federal debt/deuda federal cantidad total de dinero que el gobierno federal ha pedido prestado de los demás (p. 254)

Federal Reserve Note/vale de la Reserva Federal moneda emitida por la Reserva Federal que con el tiempo sustituyó a todos los otros tipos de moneda federal (p. 280)

Federal Reserve System/Sistema de Reserva Federal banco central de los Estados Unidos, de propiedad privada y cuyo control es público (p. 280)

fertility rate/tasa de fecundidad número de alumbramientos que se espera que 1,000 mujeres experimenten en sus vidas (p. 372)

fiat money/moneda fiduciaria dinero por decreto del gobierno; no tiene valor alternativo ni uso como producto básico (p. 267)

FICA Acta de Contribuciones del Seguro Federal; gravamen impuesto sobre los patrones y empleados para sostener al Seguro Social y al Medicare (p. 218)

finance company/compañía financiera firma que hace préstamos directamente a los consumidores y que se especializa en la compra de contratos a plazos de los comerciantes que venden a crédito (p. 322)

financial asset/haber financiero documento que representa un derecho a los ingresos y la propiedad del prestatario; CDs, bonos, letras del Tesoro, hipotecas (p. 321)

financial capital/capital financiero dinero que se usa para comprar implementos y equipo que se usa en la producción (p. 9)

financial intermediary/intermediario financiero institución que canaliza los ahorros a los inversionistas; bancos, compañías de seguro, sociedades de ahorro y préstamo, cooperativas de crédito (p. 321)

financial system/sistema financiero red de personas que ahorran, inversionistas e instituciones financieras que colaboran para transferir los ahorros a usos de inversión (p. 320)

fiscal policy/política fiscal el uso de las medidas que usa el gobierno para gastos y recaudación de ingresos para influenciar la economía (p. 427)

fiscal year/año fiscal periodo de 12 meses para la planificación financiera que no necesariamente coincide con el año civil; del 1 de octubre al 30 de septiembre para el gobierno federal (p. 243)

Five-Year Plan/Plan de Cinco Años plan económico centralizado y abarcante que usó la Unión Soviética y la China para coordinar el desarrollo de la agricultura y la industria (p. 478)

fixed cost/costo fijo costo de producción que no cambia cuando cambia la producción (p. 118)

fixed exchange rate/cotización de divisa fija sistema bajo el cual el valor de una divisa se fijó en relación al de las otras; sistema de cotización que estuvo en efecto hasta el 1971 (p. 461)

fixed income/renta fija renta que no aumenta aunque los precios suban (p. 40)

flexible exchange rate/cotización de divisa flexible sistema que depende de oferta y demanda para determinar el valor de una moneda en términos de otra; sistema de cotización en efecto desde el 1971, igual a la **cotización flotante** (p. 463)

floating exchange rate/cotización flotante ver **cotización de divisa flexible** (p. 463)

floor price/precio mínimo precio legal más bajo que se puede cobrar por un producto (p. 142)

food stamps/sellos para la compra de alimentos cupones que emite el gobierno y que se canjean por alimentos (p. 411)

foreign exchange/divisas divisas que usan los países para conducir comercio internacional (p. 461)

foreign exchange futures/letras para entrega futura contratos que permiten que una persona compre divisas para una fecha futura, al precio que se fija hoy (p. 464)

foreign exchange market/mercado de divisas mercado en que se compran y venden las divisas que se usan para el intercambio comercial (p. 461)

foreign exchange rate/cotización de divisas precio de la moneda de un país en relación a la moneda de otro país (p. 461)

fractional reserve system/sistema de reserva fraccionada sistema que dicta que las instituciones financieras aparten una fracción de sus depósitos en la forma de reservas (p. 302)

franchise/franquicia derecho exclusivo para producir o vender cierto producto en un área o región (p. 159)

free enterprise economy/economía de libre empresa economía de mercado en la que los comercios privados tienen la libertad de operar para obtener ganancias con intervención limitada del gobierno; lo mismo que **economía de empresa privada** (p. 25)

free product/producto liberal producto relativamente abundante no lo suficientemente escaso para causar una gran preocupación en el estudio de economía; incluye el sol y la lluvia (p. 20)

free-trade area/zona de comercio libre grupo de países que han acordado reducir las barreras comerciales entre sí, pero que carecen de una barrera arancelaria para los países no miembros (p. 512)

frictional unemployment/desempleo friccional desempleo causado por trabajadores cuando cambian de trabajo o al

esperar ir a nuevos empleos (p. 395)

fringe benefit/beneficio complementario beneficio que recibe el empleado además de sueldos y salarios; incluye vacaciones pagas, licencia por enfermedad, retiro y seguro (p. 57)

full employment/empleo total la constante del índice de desempleo más bajo que se pueda pensar posible en la economía (p. 397)

futures/futuros contratos para comprar o vender mercancías o bienes financieros a una fecha específica en el futuro, usando un precio que se acordó hoy (p. 338)

futures market/mercado de futuros mercado donde se compran y se venden los contratos de futuros (p. 338)

G

galloping inflation/inflación galopante inflación relativamente intensa, generalmente alcanza desde 100 a 300 por ciento anualmente (p. 400)

gasohol mezcla de 90 por ciento gasolina sin plomo y 10 por ciento alcohol de grano (p. 524)

GATT/AGTC ver **Acuerdo General para Tarifas y Comercio** (p. 458)

GDP gap/laguna del PIB diferencia entre lo que la economía puede producir y lo que, de hecho, produce; costo de oportunidad anual de los recursos desempleados (p. 419)

GDP in constant dollars/PIB en dólares constantes el Producto Interno Bruto considerando la inflación; es igual al PIB (p. 364)

General Agreement on Tariffs and Trade/Acuerdo General para Tarifas y Comercio (AGTC) acuerdo firmado por 23 países en 1947 que extendía las conseciones de tarifas y que obró para eliminar las cuotas de.importación (p. 458)

general partnership/asociación general ver **asociación** (p. 57)

geographic monopoly/monopolio geográfico situación del mercado en la que una firma tiene un monopolio debido al sitio en que está situada o a la pequeñez del mercado (p. 159)

gift tax/impuesto sobre donaciones y legados impuesto sobre donaciones de dinero o riquezas que tiene que pagar el donante (p. 220)

giveback/devolución de beneficios en la renegociación de un contrato, sueldo, beneficio complementario o regla de trabajo que se pierde (p. 199)

glass ceiling/techo de cristal barrera aparentemente invisible que impide que las mujeres y las minorías avancen en una organización dominada por los hombres (p. 200)

glut/abarrotamiento superabundancia de un producto (p. 528)

gold certificate/certificado de oro billete de banco respaldado por oro; emitido en 1863 y popular hasta que fue retirado en 1934 (p. 275)

gold standard/patrón de oro patrón monetario bajo el cual la moneda de un país equivale a, y se puede cambiar por, una cantidad específica de oro (p. 275)

good/bien producto económico tangible y útil, relativamente escaso, transferible a otras personas; se usa para satisfacer necesidades y deseos (p. 20)

Gosplan autoridad central de planificación en la antigua Unión Soviética que ideó y dirigió los planes de Cinco Años (p. 478)

government monopoly/monopolio fiscal monopolio creado por/o de la propiedad del gobierno (p. 160)

grant-in-aid/donativo del gobierno transferencia de pago desde un nivel del gobierno a otro y que no incumbe compensación (p. 240)

Great Depression/Gran Depresión el periodo de mayor disminución económica en la historia de los Estados Unidos, duró aproximadamente desde 1929 hasta 1939 (p. 185)

Great Leap Forward/Gran Salto Adelante el segundo desastroso plan de cinco años de la China iniciado en 1958, forzó la colectivización de la agricultura y la rápida industrialización (p. 487)

greenback billete de banco no respaldado por oro que el gobierno de los Estados Unidos emitió en 1861; el frente y el dorso de los billetes estaban imprimidos con tinta verde (p. 274)

grievance procedure/procedimiento para la presentación de reclamaciones provisión contractual que delínea la forma en que se resolverán futuras disputas y asuntos de quejas (p. 191)

Gross Domestic Product/Producto Interno Bruto (PIB) valor en dólar de todos los productos, servicios y estructuras finales dentro de las fronteras nacionales de un país durante el periodo de un año (p. 256)

Gross National Product/Producto Nacional Bruto (PNB) valor total en dólar de todos los productos, estructuras y servicios finales producidos en un año con la mano de obra y la propiedad suplidas por los residentes de un país, sin importar donde toma lugar la producción; la mayor medida de los ingresos de una nación (p. 354)

gross private domestic investment/inversión interna privada bruta en el modelo producción-gastos, gasto total de parte del sector inversionista (p. 358)

growth triangle/triángulo de crecimiento tabla que muestra los índices de crecimiento de una serie estadística entre dos fechas cualquiera (p. 376)

H

horizontal merger/fusión horizontal combinación de dos o más empresas que producen el mismo producto (p. 65)

household/unidad familiar unidad básica del sector del consumidor que consiste de todas las personas que ocupan una casa, apartamento o vivienda separada (p. 356)

human capital/capital humano suma de las destrezas, habilidades, salud y motivación (p. 23)

hyperinflation/hiperinflación inflación anormal en exceso de 500 por ciento por año; última etapa de un colapso monetario (p. 400)

I

imperfect competition/competencia imperfecta estructura mercantil en la que no se satisfacen todas las condiciones de competencia pura; competencia monopolística, olipolio y monopolio (p. 155)

implicit GDP price deflator/deflactor implícito del precio PIB índice que se usa para medir los cambios de precio del Producto Interno Bruto (p. 363)

incidence of a tax/incidencia de un impuesto carga final de un impuesto (p. 228)

income effect/efecto de ingreso aquella porción de un cambio en cantidad demandada causada por un cambio en el ingreso real de un consumidor cuando el precio de un producto cambia (p. 87)

income-to-poverty ratio/relación ingreso-pobreza relación del ingreso familiar dividido por el nivel de pobreza; medida que se usa para compensar por las diferencias en los tamaños de familia (p. 408)

inconvertible fiat money standard/estándar inconvertible de la moneda fiduciaria moneda fiduciaria que no se puede cambiar por oro o plata; los vales de la Reserva Federal de hoy en día (p. 276)

incorporate/incorporar proceso requerido para formar una corporación, involucra permiso del gobierno federal o el estado donde el negocio tendrá su sede (p. 59)

independent pricing/fijación independiente de precios política de fijación de precios por parte de un competidor imperfecto que ignora a los otros productores y ciertas condiciones del mercado (p. 157)

independent union/unión independiente gremio no afiliado con la AFL-CIO (p. 187)

index of leading indicators/índice de indicadores anticipados índice compuesto de 11 series económicas que suben y bajan en anticipo a cambios en la economía global; series estadísticas que se usan para predecir los puntos críticos del ciclo comercial (p. 388)

indexing/indización ajuste de las escalas de impuestos para contrarrestar los efectos de la inflación (p. 217)

indirect business tax/impuesto comercial indirecto impuesto que se paga como un gasto por hacer negocios; gastos de licencia, impuestos de propiedad, derechos de aduana (p. 356)

individual income tax/impuesto sobre la renta personal impuesto sobre jornales, salarios y otros ingresos de las personas (p. 216)

Individual Retirement Account (IRA) cuenta de retiro personal, cuenta de retiro en la forma de depósito a largo plazo, con contribuciones anuales de hasta $2,000 exemptas de impuestos hasta que se saquen durante el retiro (p. 331)

industrial union/unión industrial gremio cuyos trabajadores llevan a cabo distintos tipos de trabajo (p. 184)

industry/industria colectivamente, todas las firmas que producen en un mercado; en el mercado, el lado que hace la oferta (p. 152)

inelastic/no elástica tipo de elasticidad en el cual el porcentaje de cambio en la variable independiente (usualmente el precio) causa un cambio menos que proporcionado en la variable dependiente (usualmente la cantidad demandada u ofrecida) (p. 92)

infant industries argument/argumento de las industrias nacientes argumento de que a las industrias nuevas que están surgiendo se las debe proteger de la competencia extranjera hasta que estén lo suficiente fuertes para competir (p. 455)

inflation/inflación aumento en el nivel general de los precios (p. 40)

injunction/mandato judicial orden de la corte dictada para evitar que una compañía o unión tome acción durante una disputa laboral (p. 192)

intangible personal property/propiedad personal intangible derechos de propiedad de bienes en contraste con la propiedad en sí; incluye acciones, cuentas bancarias (p. 224)

interest/interés pago que se hace por el uso de dinero prestado; usualmente se paga a intervalos periódicos para bonos o préstamos de largo plazo (p. 61)

intergovermental revenue/ingresos intergubernamentales fondos, que en el gobierno, se reciben de un nivel a otro (p. 222)

intermediate products/productos intermediarios productos directamente excluidos de las computaciones del PIB ya que son componentes de otros productos finales incluidos en el PIB; llantas y radios nuevos para usarse en autos nuevos (p. 349)

Internal Revenue Service (IRS)/Servicio de Rentas Internas rama del Departamento de Tesorería que recauda impuestos (p. 216)

International Bank for Reconstruction and Development/Banco Internacional para Reconstrucción y Desarrollo ver **World Bank** (p. 505)

inventory/inventario abastecimiento de bienes en reserva; incluye bienes terminados esperando venderse y materias primas que se usan en producción (p. 56)

investment tax credit/crédito impositivo de inversión crédito impositivo que se da para la compra de equipo (p. 231)

J

jumbo CD/CD jumbo certificado de depósito de $1,000,000 o más (p. 328)

junk bond/bono especulativo bono de corporación, generalmente considerado por debajo del grado mediano o especulativo, que paga grandes ganancias para compensar los grandes riesgos de incumplimiento (p. 328)

jurisdictional dispute/controversia sobre jurisdicción desacuerdo, por lo general entre uniones, en cuanto a quién tiene la autoridad para efectuar ciertos tipos de trabajo (p. 187)

K

keiretsu grupo de firmas japonesas de propiedad privada unidas y gobernadas por una junta directiva exterior para poder regular la competencia (p. 488)

Keynesian economics/economía keynesiana políticas del gobierno para gastos e impuestos sugeridas por John Maynard Keynes para estimular la economía; sinónimo de las políticas fiscales o de la economía del lado de la demanda (p. 427)

L

labor/trabajo la gente con todas sus habilidades y esfuerzos; uno de los cuatro factores de producción, no incluye al empresario (p. 10)

labor mobility/mobilidad laboral habilidad y voluntad laboral de reubicarse, por lo general por sueldos más altos (p. 196)

labor productivity/productividad laboral índice de crecimiento del rendimiento total por unidad de insumo; medida de la eficiencia de productividad (p. 380)

labor union/sindicato obrero organización que obra en beneficio de los intereses de sus miembros respecto a pago, horas de trabajo, seguro médico, beneficios complementarios y otros asuntos relacionados al trabajo (p. 70)

Laffer curve/curva Laffer gráfica que muestra que las tasas impositivas más bajas supuestamente estimulan mayores recaudaciones impositivas (p. 432)

laissez-faire/liberalismo filosofía de que el gobierno no debe interferir con las actividades comerciales (p. 152)

land/tierra recursos naturales o "dones de la naturaleza" no creados por el esfuerzo humano; uno de cuatro factores de producción (p. 9)

Law of Demand/Ley de Demanda regla que dicta que se demanda más a precios bajos y menos a precios altos; relación inversa entre precio y cantidad demandada (p. 86)

Law of Supply/Ley de Oferta regla que dicta que se ofrece más a la venta a precios altos que a precios bajos (p. 106)

Law of Variable Proportions/Ley de Proporciones Variables regla que dicta que la producción a corto plazo cambia a medida que un insumo es variado mientras otros se mantienen constante (p. 111)

legal reserves/reservas legales moneda y depósitos que se usan para cumplir con los requisitos de reserva (p. 302)

legal tender/moneda legal moneda fiduciaria que por decreto del gobierno hay que aceptar por pago (p. 274)

liabilities/compromisos deudas y obligaciones que se le deben a otras personas; usualmente anotadas como partidas en el estado de cuentas (p. 302)

life expectancy/expectativa de vida promedio de la duración de vida restante en años para personas que logran una cierta edad (p. 372)

limited liability/responsabilidad limitada situación en la cual la responsabilidad de un dueño por las deudas de una compañía están limitadas al tamaño de su inversión en la firma; se aplica a accionistas ordinarios y socios limitados en una sociedad en comandita simple (p. 59)

limited life/vida limitada situación en la cual una firma deja de existir legalmente al morir o renunciar un dueño o al agregarse uno nuevo; se aplica a propietarios únicos y a sociedades (p. 57)

limited partnership/sociedad limitada forma de sociedad en la que uno o más socios no participan activamente en el funcionamiento diario del negocio y cuyas responsabilidad por la deuda de la sociedad se limita a la cantidad invertida en el negocio (p. 57)

liquidity/liquidez potencial para conversión rápida a efectivo u otros bienes financieros (p. 304)

lockout/cierre patronal rehuso patronal de dejar que los empleados trabajen hasta que se cumplan las demandas de la compañía (p. 184)

long run/largo plazo periodo de producción lo bastante largo para cambiar la cantidad de insumos variables y fijos que se usan en la producción (p. 111)

Lorenz curve/curva de Lorenz curva que muestra cuánto la distribución en sí de los ingresos varía de una distribución igual (p. 405)

loss leader/artículo de promoción artículo que se vende intencionalmente por debajo de costo para atraer a los clientes (p. 138)

luxury good/bienes de lujo bienes cuya demanda aumenta mucho más rápido de lo que aumentan los ingresos (p. 220)

M

M1 componentes del abastecimiento de dinero que se conforman al papel del dinero como medio de intercambio; monedas, divisas, cheques, otros depósitos a la vista, cheques de viajeros (p. 312)

M2 componentes del abastecimiento de dinero que se conforman al papel del dinero como fuente de valor; M1, depósitos de ahorros, depósitos a plazo (p. 312)

macroeconomic equilibrium/equilibrio macroeconómico nivel de PIB consistente con un nivel de precio dado; intersección de oferta y demanda globales (p. 425)

macroeconomics/macroeconomía esa parte de la teoría económica que trata con la economía como un total y con la adopción de decisiones por grandes unidades como los gobiernos y las uniones (p. 182)

margin requirement/requerimiento marginal depósitos mínimos que se quedan con el corredor para usarlos como pago parcial de otros valores (p. 300)

marginal analysis/análisis marginal adopción de decisión que compara el costo extra de hacer algo con los beneficios extras que se obtienen (p. 121)

marginal cost/costo marginal costo extra de producir una unidad de producción adicional (p. 119)

marginal product/producto marginal producción extra debida a adición de una unidad más de insumo (p. 114)

marginal revenue/ingreso marginal ingreso extra de la venta de una unidad de producto adicional (p. 121)

marginal tax rate/tasa impositiva marginal tasa impositiva que se aplica al próximo dólar de ingreso sujeto a impuesto (p. 215)

marginal utility/utilidad marginal satisfacción o utilidad que se obtiene de adquirir una unidad más de un producto (p. 89)

market/mercado lugar de encuentro o mecanismo que permite que los compradores y vendedores de un producto económico se reunan; puede ser local, regional, nacional o global (p. 23)

market basket/cesta de mercado colección representativa de los bienes y servicios que se usan para compilar un índice de precios (p. 362)

market economy/economía de mercado sistema económico en el cual la oferta y la demanda y el sistema de precios ayudan a la gente a tomar decisiones y a asignar los recursos; lo mismo que **economía de libre comercio** (p. 34)

market equilibrium/equilibrio del mercado condición de la estabilidad del precio en que la cantidad demandada es igual a la cantidad ofrecida (p. 134)

market failure/fallo del mercado mercado que carece de cualquiera de los requisitos de un mercado competidor, como competencia adecuada, conocimiento de precios y oportunidades, mobilidad de recursos y ganancias competitivas (p. 163)

market structure/estructura del mercado clasificación del mercado de acuerdo al número y tamaño de las firmas, tipo de producto y tipo de competición (p. 152)

maturity/madurez vida de un bono o longitud del tiempo que los fondos están prestados (p. 326)

measure of value/medida de valor una de las tres funciones del dinero que le permite servir como denominador común para medir el valor (p. 266)

mediation/mediación proceso de resolver un conflicto al incluir a un tercero neutral (p. 191)

medicaid programa de seguro médico del gobierno federal y el estado para personas de ingresos bajos (p. 246)

medicare programa federal de cuidados de salud para envejecientes, que no toma en cuenta sus ingresos (p. 218)

medium of exchange/medio de cambio dinero u otra sustancia generalmente aceptada en intercambio; una de las tres funciones del dinero (p. 266)

member bank/banco miembro banco que pertenece al Sistema de Reserva Federal (p. 294)

member bank reserves/reservas de banco miembro reservas que mantienen los bancos miembros en la Reserva Federal para satisfacer los requisitos de reserva (p. 302)

merger/fusión combinación de dos o más empresas comerciales para formar una sóla firma (p. 64)

microeconomics/microeconomía rama de la teoría de la economía que trata con la conducta y las decisiones que adoptan las pequeñas unidades tales como los individuos y las firmas (p. 82)

minimum wage/sueldo mínimo sueldo legal más bajo que se le puede pagar a la mayoría de trabajadores (p. 142)

misery index/índice de miseria estadística no oficial que es la suma de la inflación mensual y la tasa de desempleo; igual al **índice de incomodidad** (p. 419)

mixed economy/economía mixta ver **economía de empresa privada modificada** (p. 48)

modified free enterprise economy/economía de libre empresa modificada sistema de libre empresa con un poco de participación del gobierno; igual que **economía de empresa privada modificada** (p. 533)

modified private enterprise economy/economía de empresa privada modificada economía de mercado de libre empresa donde la gente lleva a cabo sus asuntos económicos libremente, pero están sujetos a algunas intervenciones y regulaciones del gobierno (p. 48)

modified union shop/empresa de exclusividad gremial modificada arreglo bajo el cual los trabajadores tienen la opción de unirse a una unión luego de habérseles empleado (p. 190)

monetarism/monetarismo escuela de pensamiento que enfatiza la importancia del crecimiento monetario estable para controlar la inflación y estimular el crecimiento económico de largo plazo (p. 433)

monetary policy/política monetaria acciones que toma el Sistema de Reserva Federal para ampliar o reducir el abastecimiento de dinero para afectar el costo y disponibilidad de crédito (p. 302)

monetary standard/estándar monetario mecanismo que mantiene un abastecimiento de dinero, durable, portátil, divisible y estable en valor; el estándar del oro, el estándar de la plata, el estándar de la moneda fiduciaria (p. 272)

monetary unit/unidad monetaria unidad monetaria estándar del abastecimiento monetario de un país; el dólar americano, la libra británica (p. 269)

monetizing the debt/monetización de la deuda proceso de crear suficiente dinero adicional para contrarrestar los préstamos del gobierno de modo que las tasas de interés permanezcan sin cambiar (p. 310)

money/dinero cualquier cosa que sirva como medio de intercambio, una medida de valor y un abastecimiento de valor (p. 266)

money market/mercado monetario mercado en el cual el capital financiero se ha prestado por un año o menos (p. 332)

money market mutual fund/fondo común de inversiones firma que une los fondos que recoge de los pequeños ahorradores para hacerle préstamos grandes a inversionistas dispuestos a pagar altas tasas de rendimiento (p. 330)

monopolistic competition/competición monopolística estructura mercantil que posee todas las condiciones de competición pura a excepción de tener productos idénticos; una forma de competición imperfecta (p. 155)

monopoly/monopolio estructura mercantil caracterizada por un solo productor; una forma de competición imperfecta (p. 158)

moral suasion/persuasión moral el uso que el Sistema de Reserva Federal hace de la persuasión para lograr política monetaria; testimonio congresional, comunicados de prensa (p. 308)

most favored nation clause/cláusula de la nación más favorecida derecho mercantil que permite a un país tercero disfrutar las mismas rebajas de tarifas que los Estados Unidos negocia con otro país (p. 458)

multinational/multinacional corporación que produce y vende sin importarle las fronteras nacionales y cuyas actividades comerciales están situadas en varios países diferentes (p. 66)

multiplier/multiplicador cambio en el gasto global causado por un cambio en el gasto de inversión (p. 427)

municipal bond/bono municipal bono, a menudo exempto de impuestos, emitido por el gobierno estatal o local; conocido como *munis* (p. 329)

mutual fund/fondo mutuo compañía que vende acciones de sí misma y usa las ganancias para comprar acciones y bonos emitidos por otras compañías (p. 323)

mutual savings bank/banco mutualista de ahorro institución de ahorro de propiedad de los depositantes que opera para beneficio de ellos (p. 281)

N

NAFTA ver **Acuerdo Norteamericano de Comercio Libre** (p. 459)

national bank/banco nacional un banco comercial establecido por el Sistema Bancario Nacional; miembro del Fed (p. 274)

National Bank Note/billete del Banco Nacional moneda respaldada por bonos del gobierno, emitida por bancos nacionales comenzando en 1863 y que por lo general desapareció de circulación alrededor de los años 30 (p. 274)

National Banking System/Sistema Bancario Nacional sistema de bancos constituidos, inspeccionados y regulados federalmente que se estableció en 1863, ahora son miembros del Sistema Federal (p. 274)

national currency/moneda nacional ver **billete del Banco Nacional** (p. 274)

national income/ingresos nacionales producto nacional neto menos los impuestos comerciales indirectos; medida de los ingresos de una nación (p. 356)

national income accounting/contabilidad de los ingresos nacionales sistema de cuentas que se usa para seguir la producción, el consumo, los ahorros, las estadísticas de los ingresos de la nación (p. 348)

natural monopoly/monopolio natural mercado en que los costos promedios son más bajos cuando toda la producción la produce una sola firma (p. 158)

need/necesidad requisito básico para supervivencia; incluye comida, ropa y/o albergue (p. 20)

negative externality/factores externos negativos efectos secundarios negativos que afectan a un tercero no partícipe; costo externo (p. 166)

negative income tax/impuesto negativo sobre la renta sistema de impuestos que hace pagos efectivos en la forma de reembolsos de impuestos cuando los ingresos de las personas caen por debajo de ciertos niveles (p. 411)

Negotiable Order of Withdrawal (NOW) orden negativa de retiro, tipo de cuenta de cheques que paga intereses (p. 282)

net exports of goods and services/exportaciones netas de bienes y servicios gastos netos según el modelo de producción-gastos del sector extranjero (p. 359)

net immigration/inmigración neta carga de población neta después de tomar en cuenta las personas que salen o entran del país (p. 372)

net national product/producto interno neto (PIN) Producto Interno Bruto menos los cargos de depreciación por uso y desgaste del equipo capital; medida de la producción anual neta generada con la mano de obra y la propiedad suplida por los ciudadanos de un país (p. 355)

net worth/valor neto exceso de bienes por encima de las responsabilidades, usualmente anotados como un resumen separado en el estado de cuentas; medida del valor de un negocio (p. 302)

nominal GDP ver **PIB imperante** (p. 363)

nonbank financial institution/institución financiera no bancaria institución no depositoria que canaliza los ahorros a los inversionistas; compañías financieras, compañías de seguro, fondos de pensiones (p. 322)

noncompeting labor grades/grados de mano de obra no competitivos amplios grupos de trabajadores no calificados, semicalificados, calificados y profesionales que no compiten entre sí (p. 194)

nondurable good/bienes perecederos objetos que duran menos de tres años con uso regular; pueden ser bienes capitales o del consumidor (p. 20)

nonmarket transaction/transacción fuera del mercado actividad económica que no toma lugar en el mercado y, por lo tanto, no está incluída en el PIB; los servicios de las amas de casa, trabajo del hogar (p. 351)

nonprice competition/competición sin precio competición que implica la publicidad de la apariencia de un producto, su calidad o diseño en vez de su precio (p. 156)

nonprofit organization/organización sin fines de lucro institución económica que opera como un negocio pero que no busca ganancias; escuelas, iglesias, organizaciones de servicios para la comunidad (p. 69)

non-recourse loan/préstamo sin recurso préstamo de agricultura que no lleva ni penalidad ni demás obligaciones de pago (p. 144)

North American Free Trade Agreement/Tratado Norteamericano de Libre Comercio (NAFTA) tratado firmado en 1993 para reducir las tarifas entre los Estados Unidos, Canadá y México (p. 459)

NOW ACCOUNT ver **Negotiable Order of Withdrawal** (p. 282)

O

oligopoly/oligarquía estructura mercantil en la que unos cuantos vendedores grandes dominan la industria y tienen la habilidad de afectar los precios; forma de competición imperfecta (p. 156)

open market operations/operaciones de mercado abierto política monetaria en la forma de compra y venta de bonos en el mercado de bonos (p. 307)

opportunity cost/costo de oportunidad cuando se hace una elección en lugar de otra, el costo de la mejor alternativa que sigue para el uso del dinero, tiempo o recursos (p. 15)

options/opciones contratos que dan al inversionista una opción de comprar o vender bienes, capitales o bienes financieros a una fecha específica en el futuro usando el precio acordado hoy (p. 338)

options market/mercado de opciones mercados donde las opciones, incluso las opciones de venta y de compra, se intercambian (p. 338)

organizational chart/gráfica organizacional representación visual de la estructura de una compañía que muestra cómo las distintas partes de la organización se relacionan (p. 61)

output-expenditure model/modelo de producción-gastos modelo macroeconómico que describe la demanda total del consumidor, la inversión, gobierno y los sectores extranjeros; PIB = C + I + G + SE (p. 358)

overhead/gastos generales categoría amplia de gastos fijos que incluyen intereses, alquiler, impuestos y salarios de ejecutivos (p. 118)

Over-The-Counter market (OTC) mercado electrónico extrabursátil para valores no anotados en casas de cambio organizadas como la New York Stock Exchange (p. 336)

P

par value/valor a la par capital de un bono o la cantidad total pedida en préstamo (p. 326)

paradox of value/paradoja de valores contradicción aparente entre el alto valor de objetos no esenciales y el bajo valor de los esenciales (p. 22)

partnership/sociedad negocio no incorporado operado por dos o más dueños quienes comparten las ganancias y que tienen responsabilidad ilimitada por las deudas y obligaciones de la firma; igual que **sociedad colectiva** (p. 57)

patent/patente derecho exclusivo concedido por el gobierno para vender o usar cualquier arte nuevo, máquina, objeto de manufactura o composición (p. 160)

payroll withholding statement/estado de cuenta de retención de nómina documento adherido al cheque de pago que resume el pago y las deducciones (p. 225)

payroll withholding system/sistema de retención de

nómina sistema periódico que automáticamente deduce del cheque de pago los impuestos sobre la renta (p. 216)

peak/apogeo punto en el tiempo cuando el PIB cesa de aumentar y comienza a declinar (p. 383)

pension/pensión pago regular para alguien que ha trabajado cierto número de años, ha alcanzado cierta edad o ha sufrido algún daño (p. 323)

pension fund/fondo de pensiones fondo que recauda e invierte ingresos hasta que se hacen pagos a los titulares que tienen derecho (p. 323)

per capita/per cápita en base a persona; el total dividido por la población (p. 238)

perestroika reestructuramiento fundamental de la economía soviética; política introducida por Gorbachev (p. 480)

personal consumption expenditures/gastos de consumo personal gastos globales del sector del consumidor que consisten de las unidades familiares y personas no relacionadas (p. 358)

personal income/ingresos personales cantidad total de ingresos que van al sector del consumidor antes de que se paguen los impuestos sobre la renta (p. 356)

picket/piqueteo demostración ante un establecimiento comercial para protestar las acciones de una compañía (p. 184)

piecework/trabajo por pieza sistema de compensación que paga a los trabajadores por las unidades producidas, en vez de las horas trabajadas (p. 480)

pollution/polución contaminación del aire, agua o tierra por la descarga de una sustancia venenosa o nociva (p. 528)

pollution permit/permiso de polución permiso federal que permite que las empresas de servicios públicos liberen polutantes en el aire; una forma de controlar la contaminación (p. 530)

population density/densidad demográfica número de personas por milla cuadrada de área de terreno (p. 514)

population pyramid/pirámide demográfica diagrama que muestra la distribución de la población por edad y sexo (p. 373)

portfolio diversification/diversificación de cartera estrategia de retener varias inversiones para protección contra riesgos (p. 334)

positive externality/factores externos positivos efectos secundarios beneficiosos que afectan a un tercero no involucrado (p. 167)

poverty threshold/umbral de pobreza cota de referencia anual del dólar usada para evaluar el ingreso monetario recibido por familias e individuos no relacionados (p. 407)

preferred stock/acciones preferidas acciones de dueños que no votan y cuyo reclamo a los ingresos y a los bienes de la corporación viene por encima de los accionistas ordinarios (p. 60)

premium/prima precio que se paga mensualmente, trimestralmente, semianual o anual por una póliza de seguro (p. 323)

price ceiling/precio máximo máximo precio legal que se puede cobrar por un producto (p. 141)

price discrimination/descriminación de precio práctica ilegal de cobrarle a los clientes distintos precios por el mismo producto (p. 169)

price-fixing/fijación de precios acuerdo, usualmente ilegal, que hacen las compañías para cobrar un precio uniforme por un producto (p. 157)

price floor/precio mínimo precio legal más bajo que se puede cobrar por un producto (p. 142)

price index/índice de precios serie estadística que se usa para medir cambios en el nivel de los precios a lo largo del tiempo (p. 361)

price leadership/liderazgo de precios decisiones que una firma dominante toma periódicamente sobre la fijación de precios y que resulta en precios que por lo general son uniformes por toda la industria (p. 157)

price level/nivel de precios magnitud relativa de los precios en un momento determinado según los mide un índice de precios (p. 399)

price war/guerra de precio competencia de precio encarnizada entre vendedores, hasta el punto que el precio baja por debajo del costo del producto (p. 157)

primary market/mercado primario mercado en que sólo el emisor original volverá a comprar un haber financiero; bonos de ahorros del gobierno, los IRA, pequeños CD (p. 332)

prime rate/tasa preferencial tasa de interés mejor o más baja que los bancos comerciales cobran a sus clientes (p. 309)

primitive equilibrium/equilibrio primitivo primera etapa del desarrollo económico durante la cual la economía está estática (p. 504)

principal/capital cantidad que se pide prestada cuando se obtiene un préstamo o se emite un bono (p. 61)

private enterprise economy/economía de empresa privada ver **economía de empresa libre** (p. 25)

private property/propiedad privada concepto que les da a las personas el derecho de controlar sus posesiones como deseen; característica del capitalismo y el libre comercio (p. 45)

private sector/sector privado aquella parte de la economía compuesta por personas privadas y negocios (p. 239)

privatization/privatización conversión de factorías y otras propiedades del gobierno a propiedad privada (p. 483)

problem bank list/lista de bancos problemas de los reguladores bancarios, lista confidencial de bancos débiles y posiblemente poco firmes (p. 312)

producer cooperative/cooperativa de productores asociación sin fines de lucro de productores que ayuda a sus miembros a vender o mercadear sus productos; mayormente se halla en la agricultura (p. 70)

producer price index/índice de precios de productor índice que se usa para medir los precios recibidos de los productores domésticos; anteriormente denominado **índice de precios al por mayor** (p. 362)

product differentiation/diferenciación de precios diferencias reales o imaginadas entre productos que compiten en la misma industria (p. 155)

product market/mercado de productos mercado donde se ponen a la venta los bienes y servicios (p. 24)

production/producción proceso de crear bienes y servicios con el uso combinado de tierra, capital, mano de obra y espíritu empresarial (p. 22)

production function/función de producción rendimiento gráfico que muestra cómo un cambio en la cantidad de una sola variable de insumo afecta la producción total (p. 112)

production possibilities frontier/frontera de posibilidades de producción diagrama que representa el máximo de combinaciones de bienes y/o servicios que una economía puede producir cuando se emplean a plenitud todos los recursos (p. 16)

productivity/productividad grado hasta cual los recursos productivos se usan eficientemente; normalmente se refiere a mano de obra, pero puede aplicarse a todos los factores de producción (p. 22)

professional association/asociación profesional organización sin fines de lucro de trabajadores profesionales o especializados que buscan mejorar las condiciones de trabajo, los niveles de habilidades y la percepción pública de su profesión (p. 71)

professional labor/trabajo profesional trabajadores con un alto nivel de habilidades profesionales y gerenciales (p. 194)

profit/ganancias nivel al que personas y organizaciones mejoran al cabo de un periodo de lo que estaban al principio; usualmente se mide en dólares (p. 46)

profit-maximizing quantity of output/cantidad de producto para el máximo de ganancias nivel de producción en que el costo marginal equivale al ingreso marginal (p. 122)

profit motive/motivo de ganancia fuerza motriz que anima a la gente y organizaciones a mejorar su bienestar material; característica del capitalismo y el libre comercio (p. 46)

progressive tax/tributación progresiva tributación en que un porcentaje del ingreso que se paga en impuestos sube al subir el nivel de ingreso (p. 215)

property tax/impuesto sobre los bienes impuesto sobre posesiones tangibles e intangibles como bienes raíces, edificios, muebles, acciones, bonos y cuentas bancarias (p. 224)

proportional tax/impuesto proporcional tributación en que un porcentaje de los ingresos que se paga en impuestos es igual sin importar el nivel de ingreso (p. 215)

proprietorship/patrimonio ver **patrimonio personal** (p. 54)

protectionist/proteccionista persona que proteje a los productores domésticos con tarifas, cuotas y otras barreras comerciales (p. 454) ·

protective tariff/arancel proteccionista impuesto sobre un producto importado diseñado para proteger a los productores domésticos menos eficientes (p. 453)

proxy/poderes papeleta de poder que permite que el representante de un accionista vote en asuntos de empresas (p. 60)

public disclosure/revelación pública requisito que fuerza a un negocio a que revele al público información acerca de sus productos u operaciones (p. 170)

public good/bien público producto económico que se consume colectivamente; autopistas, defensa nacional, protección de la policía y de los bomberos (p. 167)

public sector/sector público esa parte de la economía compuesta de los gobiernos locales, estatales y federales (p. 239)

public utility/empresa de servicios públicos compañía que provee servicios esenciales como el agua y la electricidad a los consumidores, usualmente sujeta a algunas regulaciones del gobierno (p. 72)

pure competition/competencia pura estructura mercantil caracterizada por un gran número de independientes y bien informados compradores y vendedores de un producto idéntico—ninguno de los cuales es lo suficientemente grande para influenciar el precio—asímismo con relativa facilidad de entrada y salida de la industria (p. 152)

put option/opción de venta contrato que da a los inversionistas la opción de vender productos, valores o bienes finacieros a una fecha específica en el futuro usando el precio que se acordó hoy (p. 338)

Q

quantity supplied/cantidad ofrecida cantidad ofrecida en venta a un precio dado; punto en la curva de oferta (p. 106)

quantity theory of money/teoría de la cantidad del dinero hipótesis de que a largo plazo el abastecimiento de dinero afecta directamente el nivel del precio (p. 309)

quota/cuota límite de cantidad de bienes que se pueden permitir en un país (p. 453)

R

ration coupon/cupón de raciones certificado que permite al portador recibir una cantidad específica de un producto racionado (p. 131)

rationing/racionamiento sistema de distribución de bienes y servicios sin precios (p. 131)

raw materials/materias brutas recursos naturales sin procesar que se usan en la producción (p. 112)

real dollars/dólares reales ver **dólares constantes** (p. 204)

real estate investment trust/compañía fiduciaria de inversiones en bienes raíces compañía organizada para hacer préstamos a los constructores de casas (p. 323)

real GDP/PIB real Producto Interior Bruto después de ajustes para la inflación; igual que **PIB en dólares constantes** (p. 364)

real GDP per capita/PIB real per cápita Producto Interior Bruto ajustado para la inflación y dividido por la población total; cantidad total de dólar de todo producto final producido para cada persona en el país después de compensar por la inflación (p. 376)

real property/propiedad real riquezas en la forma de bienes raíces, edificios y accesorios permanentes (p. 224)

rebate/descuento devolución parcial del precio original de un producto (p. 140)

recession/recesión reducción en el PIB real que dura al menos dos trimestres o más (p. 383)

regressive tax/impuesto regresivo impuesto en que un porcentaje del ingreso que se paga en imposiciones baja cuando los ingresos suben (p. 215)

Regulation Q/Regulación Q regulación federal que una vez fijó tasas de interés máximo que se podían pagar sobre depósitos a la vista (p. 285)

Regulation Z/Regulación Z provisión que extiende a los consumidores revelaciones de veracidad de préstamos (p. 299)

renewable resources/recursos renovables recursos naturales que se pueden reabastecer para uso futuro (p. 379)

reserve requirement/requisito de reserva fórmula que se usa para calcular la cantidad de reservas que requiere una institución depositoria (p. 302)

retained earnings/utilidades no distribuidas ganancias de sociedad que una corporación retiene en vez de pagárselas a los accionistas; igual que **ganancias de corporación no**

distribuidas (p. 356)

revenue/ingresos los recibos de venta o alquiler de los productos de una compañía, también incluye dinero de otras fuentes como dividendos e intereses (p. 62)

revenue tariff/tarifa de ingresos impuesto sobre bienes importados para recaudar fondos (p. 453)

right-to-work law/ley de derecho al trabajo ley estatal que hace ilegal el requerir que un trabajador sea miembro de una unión (p. 186)

risk/riesgo situación en la cual el resultado no es cierto, pero las probabilidades se pueden estimar (p. 325)

run on the bank/pánico bancario prisa repentina de los depositantes por sacar todos sus fondos, generalmente en anticipación al fallo o cierre del banco (p. 281)

rural population/población rural aquellas personas que no viven en áreas urbanas (p. 370)

S

S&P 500 ver **Standard & Poor 500** (p. 337)

saving/ahorrar ausencia de gastos que libera los recursos para usarlos en otras actividades o inversiones (p. 320)

savings/ahorros los dólares que se hacen disponibles para que los inversionistas los usen cuando otras personas ahorran (p. 320)

savings account/cuenta de ahorros depósito que paga interés y que no requiere aviso previo antes de retirarse (p. 304)

savings and loan association/sociedad de ahorro y préstamo institución depositoria que históricamente invierte la mayoría de sus fondos en hipotecas de casas (p. 282)

savings bank/banco de ahorros institución de ahorros propiedad de los accionistas en vez de los depositantes (p. 282)

savings bond/bono de ahorros bono, no transferible, de baja denominación emitido por el gobierno federal, usualmente a través de planes de ahorros de nómina (p. 329)

scarcity/escasez problema económico fundamental que enfrentan todas las sociedades como resultado de una combinación de escasos recursos y las necesidades ilimitadas de la gente (p. 8)

seasonal unemployment/desempleo estacional desempleo causado por cambios anuales en el clima y otras condiciones que prevalecen durante ciertas épocas del año (p. 396)

seat/asiento afiliación en una bolsa de valores como la New York Stock Exchange (p. 335)

secondary market/mercado secundario mercado en el que todos los bienes finacieros se pueden vender a alguien excepto al emisor original; bonos de empresa privada, bonos del gobierno (p. 332)

secondhand sales/ventas de segunda mano venta de bienes usados; categoría de actividad no incluida en la computación del PIB (p. 349)

securities exchange/bolsa de valores lugar físico donde los compradores y los vendedores se reunen para intercambiar valores (p. 335)

seizure/incautación cuando el gobierno toma temporáneamente una compañía para mantenerla operando durante un conflicto obrero-patronal (p. 192)

selective credit controls/controles de crédito selectivo reglas que atañen a préstamos para productos específicos o compras como requisitos marginales para acciones ordinarias (p. 308)

semiskilled labor/mano de obra semientrenada trabajadores que pueden operar máquinas que requieren la mínima cantidad de entrenamiento (p. 194)

seniority/antigüedad cantidad de tiempo que una persona ha estado en un puesto de trabajo (p. 196)

service/servicio obra o trabajo efectuado por alguien; producto económico que incluye cortes de pelo, reparaciones del hogar, formas de entretenimiento (p. 20)

service cooperative/cooperativa de servicio sociedad de consumidores sin fines de lucro que trata con servicios en vez de con bienes; incluye las cooperativas de crédito y algunas agencias de seguro y de crédito (p. 70)

set-aside contract/contrato de destinación especial contrato o parte de un contrato garantizado reservado para un grupo señalado, usualmente un grupo minoritario (p. 201)

share draft/giro de acción cuenta de cheques ofrecida por una cooperativa de crédito (p. 283)

shareholder/accionista persona que es dueña de acciones en una corporación (p. 59)

short run/corto plazo periodo de producción tan corto que sólo se pueden cambiar los insumos variables (p. 111)

shortage/escasez situación donde la cantidad ofrecida es menor que la cantidad demandada a un precio dado (p. 136)

silver certificate/certificado de plata papel moneda respaldado y redimible con plata desde 1886 hasta 1968 (p. 275)

sin tax/impuesto de pecado impuesto relativamente alto diseñado para recaudar ingresos y desanimar el consumo de productos socialmente indeseables (p. 210)

skilled labor/mano de obra adiestrada trabajadores que pueden operar equipo complejo y que requieren poca supervisión (p. 194)

Social Security/Seguro Social programa federal de beneficios de invalidez y retiro que cubre a la mayoría de las personas que trabajan (p. 40)

socialism/socialismo sistema económico en el cual el gobierno es dueño de algunos factores de producción y tiene un papel en la determinación de qué bienes se producirán y cómo (p. 473)

sole proprietorship/propietario contable único de empresa negocio no incorporado de la propiedad y operación de una sóla persona quien tiene el derecho a todas las ganancias y responsabilidades sin límite por todas las deudas de la firma; la forma más común de organización comercial en los Estados Unidos (p. 54)

Solidarity/Solidaridad gremio obrero independiente de Polonia fundado en 1980 por Lech Walesa (p. 485)

specialization/especialización asignación de tareas para que cada trabajador haga menos funciones más frecuentemente; igual que **división de trabajo** (p. 22)

specie/especie dinero en la forma de monedas de oro o plata (p. 268)

spot market/mercado de entrega immediata mercado en el cual se hace una operación inmediatamente al precio imperante (p. 338)

stages of production/etapas de producción fases de producción—aumento, disminución y rendimiento negativo (p. 114)

stagflation combinación de estancamiento del crecimiento económico y la inflación (p. 419)

Standard & Poor's 500/Las 500 de Standard & Poor (S&L 500) serie estadística de las 500 acciones que se usan para observar los precios en la bolsa de valores de la NYSE, American Stock Exchange y el mercado extrabursátil (p. 337)

standard of living/estándar de vida calidad de vida basada en la propiedad de necesidades y lujos que hacen la vida más fácil (pp. 24, 377)

state bank/banco del estado banco que recibe su escritura de constitución del estado en que opera (p. 272)

state farm/granja del estado granjas enormes de la propiedad y operación del estado en la antigua Unión Soviética (p. 479)

stock/acción certificado de propiedad en una corporación; acciones preferidas y ordinarias (p. 59)

stockbroker/agente de bolsa persona que compra y vende valores para los inversionistas (p. 335)

stockholder/accionista La persona dueña de acciones de una corporación (p. 59)

store of value/fuente de valor una de las tres funciones del dinero que permite a las personas que preserven el valor para uso futuro (p. 266)

storming/tempestear práctica soviética de apresurar la producción al final del mes para cumplir las cuotas, con frecuencia resultando en la producción de chapucería (p. 480)

strike/huelga paro del trabajo organizado por la unión diseñado para obtener concesiones del patrón (p. 184)

structural unemployment/desempleo estructural desempleo causado por un cambio fundamental en la economía que reduce la demanda de algunos trabajadores (p. 395)

structures/estructuras categoría en los ingresos y cuentas de productos de la nación que incluye las estructuras residenciales, apartamentos y edificios comerciales (p. 348)

subsidy/subsidio pago del gobierno para animar o proteger cierta actividad económica (p. 108)

subsistence/subsistencia estado en que una sociedad escasamente produce lo suficiente para sostenerse (p. 520)

substitutes/sustitutos productos de competición que se pueden intercambiar; productos relacionados de tal forma que un aumento en el precio de uno aumenta la demanda por los otros (p. 88)

substitution effect/efecto de sustitución esa porción de un cambio en la cantidad de la demanda debido a un cambio en el precio relativo del producto (p. 87)

supply/oferta curva de cantidades que se ofrecen a la venta a todos los precios posibles del mercado (p. 104)

supply curve/curva de oferta gráfica de las cantidades producidas en cada uno de los precios del mercado (p. 105)

supply elasticity/elasticidad de oferta sensibilidad de la cantidad ofrecida al cambio de precio (p. 109)

supply schedule/tabla de oferta tabla que muestra las cantidades producidas u ofrecidas a la venta a cada precio del mercado (p. 105)

supply-side economics/economía de oferta política económica diseñada para aumentar la oferta global o para desplazar la curva de oferta global hacia la derecha (p. 431)

surcharge/sobretasa impuesto adicional o carga que se añade a otros cargos ya establecidos (p. 231)

surplus/superávit situación en que la cantidad ofrecida es mayor que la cantidad demandada a un precio dado (p. 135)

T

takeoff/despegue tercer etapa de desarrollo económico durante el cual las barreras de equilibrio primitivo se han vencido (p. 504)

tangible personal property/bienes personales tangibles todos los objetos tangibles de riquezas no empotradas en la tierra o los edificios (p. 224)

target price/precio indicativo precio más bajo de agricultura fijado por el gobierno para estabilizar los ingresos agrarios (p. 144)

tariff/tarifa impuesto sobre productos importados (p. 453)

tax assessor/tasador de impuestos persona que examina y evalúa propiedades para propósitos de impuestos (p. 224)

tax base/base impositiva ingresos y propiedades que están potencialmente sujetas a impuestos locales, estatales y del gobierno federal (p. 377)

tax-exempt/exento de impuestos ingresos de bonos u otras inversiones no sujetas a impuestos por el gobierno del estado y el federal (p. 329)

tax loophole/laguna tributaria excepción o descuido en la ley de impuestos que permite que los contribuyentes eviten impuestos (p. 212)

tax return/declaración de impuestos reporte anual que se registra con el gobierno local, el estatal o el federal y que detalla los ingresos que se ganaron y los impuestos que se deben (p. 216)

technological monopoly/monopolio tecnológico situación mercantil en que una firma tiene el monopolio porque es propietaria de/o controla un método o un proceso de manufactura u otro adelanto científico (p. 159)

technological unemployment/desempleo tecnológico desempleo causado por desarrollos tecnológicos o automatización que hace que las destrezas de algunos trabajadores sean obsoletas (p. 396)

theory of negotiated wages/teoría de salarios negociados explicación de las escalas de salarios basada en la fuerza de negociación del movimiento sindical (p. 196)

theory of production/teoría de producción teoría que trata con la relación entre los factores de producción y la producción de bienes y servicios (p. 111)

thrift institution/institución de pequeños ahorros sociedades de ahorros y préstamo, bancos mutualista de ahorro y otras instituciones depositorias que históricamente han provisto a los ahorradores (p. 281)

tight money policy/política de dinero escaso política monetaria que resulta en tasas de interés más altas y acceso restringido al crédito; se asocia con la contracción del abastecimiento de dinero (p. 306)

time deposit/depósito a plazo depósito que paga intereses y que requiere previo aviso antes de poder sustraerlo, aunque no siempre se cumple el requisito (p. 304)

total cost/costo total costo variable y costo fijo; todos los gastos asociados a la producción (p. 119)

total product/producto total rendimiento o producción total de una firma (p. 113)

total revenue/ingreso total total de recibos; precio de los bienes vendidos por la cantidad vendida (p. 121)

trade deficit/déficit comercial resultados de la balanza de pagos cuando los gastos de las importaciones exceden los ingresos recibidos de las exportaciones (p. 456)

trade-offs/compensación alternativas a las que hay que renunciar cuando se escoge una en lugar de otra (p. 14)

trade union/sindicato gremial ver **sindicato de artesanos** (p. 184)

trade-weighted value of the dollar/valor del dólar ponderado según el comercio exterior índice que indica la fuerza del dólar americano contra la cesta de mercado de otras divisas (p. 465)

trading desk/oficina de cambio sitio actual en el banco del distrito de la Reserva Federal de Nueva York donde se efectúa la compra y venta de bonos del gobierno (p. 307)

traditional economy/economía tradicional sistema económico en el que la distribución de escasos recursos y otra actividad económica es el resultado de rito, hábito o costumbre (p. 32)

traditional theory of wage determination/teoría tradicional de determinación de salario explicación del índice salarial basado en la teoría de oferta y demanda (p. 195)

transfer payment/transferencia de pago pago por el cual el gobierno no recibe ni bienes ni servicios de vuelta (p. 239)

Treasury bill/letra del Tesoro bono de corto plazo del gobierno de los Estados Unidos que madura al año o menos, en denominaciones de $10,000 (p. 331)

Treasury bond/bono del Tesoro bono del gobierno de los Estados Unidos que madura entre 10 y 30 años (p. 330)

Treasury coin note/pagaré del Tesoro en moneda papel moneda emitido desde 1890 hasta 1893, redimible tanto en oro o plata (p. 275)

Treasury note/pagaré del Tesoro obligación del gobierno de los Estados Unidos que madura entre 2 a 10 años (p. 330)

trend line/tendencia rumbo de crecimiento que seguiría la economía si no se interrumpiera por periodos alternantes de recesión y recuperación (p. 384)

trough/sima punto en el tiempo cuando el PIB real deja de declinar y comienza a ensanchar (p. 383)

trust/sociedad fiduciaria combinación ilegal de corporaciones o compañías que se organizan para impedir la competición (p. 169)

trust fund/fondo fiduciario cuenta especial que se usa para retener ingresos designados para un gasto específico como el Seguro Social, medicare o las autopistas (p. 256)

truth-in-lending laws/leyes de veracidad para préstamos leyes federales que requieren que a los consumidores se les haga una divulgación completa y precisa de la información acerca de los préstamos (p. 299)

two-tier wage system/sistema de salario de dos niveles escala de salario que paga a los nuevos trabajadores un sueldo más bajo que a los que ya estaban trabajando (p. 199)

U

underground economy/economía subterránea actividades ilegales sin reportar que no aparecen en las estadísticas del PIB (p. 351)

undistributed corporate profits/ganancias de corporación no distribuidas ver **utilidades no distribuidas** (p. 356)

unemployed/desempleado condición de trabajar por menos de una hora por semana por paga o provecho en un negocio que no es de la familia, en tanto que se está disponible y se ha hecho el esfuerzo de hallar trabajo durante el mes pasado (p. 394)

unemployment insurance/seguro de desempleo programa de gobierno que provee pagos a los desempleados; un estabilizador automático (p. 429)

unemployment rate/índice de desempleo relación de personas desempleadas dividida por el número total de personas en la fuerza de trabajo civil, expresado como un porcentaje (p. 394)

union shop/empresa de exclusividad gremial arreglo bajo el cual los trabajadores tienen que unirse a una unión tras ser empleados (p. 190)

unit elastic/elasticidad de la unidad elasticidad en que un cambio en la variable independiente (usualmente el precio) genera un cambio proporcional de la variable dependiente (cantidad demandada u ofrecida) (p. 94)

United States note/pagaré de los Estados Unidos papel moneda sin respaldo, emitida por el gobierno de los Estados Unidos inicialmente en 1862 para financiar la Guerra Civil (p. 274)

unlimited liability/responsabilidad sin límite requisito de que un propietario es personal y plenamente responsable por todas las pérdidas y deudas de un negocio; se aplica a propietarios, sociedades generales (p. 56)

unlimited life/vida sin límite condición de la existencia legal continuada de una corporación cuando el dueño muere, vende o transfiere la propiedad (p. 62)

unrelated individual/individuo no relacionado persona que vive sola o con personas que no son sus parientes aunque esa persona tenga parientes que vivan en otro lugar (p. 357)

unskilled labor/mano de obra no adiestrada trabajadores no entrenados para operar máquinas y equipo especializados (p. 194)

urban population/población urbana aquellas personas que viven en ciudades incorporadas, pueblos y aldeas con 2,500 ó más habitantes (p. 370)

user fee/tarifas para el usuario tarifa que se paga por usar unos bienes o servicios; forma de un impuesto de beneficio (p. 220)

utility/utilidad habilidad o capacidad de un bien o de un servicio para ser útil y darle satisfacción a alguien (p. 22)

V

value/valor valor de un bien o servicio según lo determina el mercado (p. 21)

value added tax/impuesto de valor agregado impuesto sobre el valor agregado a cada etapa del proceso de producción (p. 229)

variable cost/costo variable costo de producción que varía según cambia la producción; la mano de obra, la energía, la materia prima (p. 118)

vertical merger/fusión vertical combinación de firmas envueltas en distintos pasos de la manufactura o el mercadeo (p. 65)

voluntary arbitration/arbitraje voluntario acuerdo por parte de los sindicatos laborales y la administración de colocar una disputa delante de un tercero para llegar a un arreglo en firme (p. 191)

voluntary exchange/intercambio voluntario hecho en el cual los compradores y los vendedores participan libre y voluntariamente en operaciones mercantiles; característica del capitalismo y el libre comercio (p. 44)

W

wage-price controls/controles de salario-precio políticas y regulaciones que hacen ilegal el que las firmas den aumento o suban los precios (p. 434)

wage rate/escala de salarios escala de pago prevalente para trabajo efectuado en una cierta área o región (p. 195)

wampum forma de dinero hecho de conchas e ideado por los indios americanos, se usó ampliamente en los tiempos coloniales en los Estados Unidos (p. 267)

want/carencia modo de expresar o comunicar una necesidad; una clasificación más amplia que necesidades (p. 20)

wealth/riquezas suma de los bienes económicos tangibles que son escasos, útiles y transferibles de una persona a otra; excluye servicios (p. 22)

welfare/asistencia social programas del gobierno o de las agencias privadas que proveen asistencia económica y social a personas necesitadas (p. 409)

white-collar worker/empleado de corbata trabajador de oficina, comercial o profesional que percibe un salario y no un jornal (p. 407)

wholesale price index/índice de precios al por mayor ver **índice de precio de productor** (p. 362)

wildcat bank/banco especulador generalmente, banco fraudulento que operaba en áreas remotas a principios de los 1800 (p. 273)

workfare programa que requiere que los beneficiarios de asistencia social provean trabajo en cambio por los beneficios (p. 412)

World Bank/Banco Mundial agencia internacional que hace préstamos a países en vías de desarrollo; antiguamente el Banco Internacional para Reconstrucción y Desarrollo (p. 505)

Z

zero population growth/crecimiento demográfico nulo condición en la que el número promedio de nacimientos y muertes se equilibran de modo que el tamaño de la población no cambia (p. 499)

Vocabulario

Los siguientes términos se definen en el Capítulo 1:

SECCIÓN UNO
- escasez *(p. 8)*
- factores de producción *(p. 9)*
- tierra *(p. 9)*
- capital *(p. 9)*
- capital financiero *(p. 9)*
- trabajo *(p. 10)*
- empresario *(p. 10)*
- economía *(p. 11)*

SECCIÓN DOS
- compensaciones *(p. 14)*
- costo de oportunidad *(p. 15)*
- límites de posibilidades de producción *(p. 16)*

SECCIÓN TRES
- necesidad *(p. 20)*
- deseo *(p. 20)*
- producto gratis *(p. 20)*
- producto económico *(p. 20)*
- bienes *(p. 20)*
- bienes de consumidor *(p. 20)*
- bienes capital *(p. 20)*
- bienes durables *(p. 20)*
- bienes no durables *(p. 20)*
- servicio *(p. 20)*
- consumidor *(p. 21)*
- consumo *(p. 21)*
- consumo suntuario *(p. 21)*
- valor *(p. 21)*
- paradoja de valores *(p. 22)*
- utilidad *(p. 22)*
- riqueza *(p. 22)*
- producción *(p. 22)*
- productividad *(p. 22)*
- especialización *(p. 22)*
- división del trabajo *(p. 23)*
- capital humano *(p. 23)*
- interdependencia económica *(p. 23)*
- mercado *(p. 23)*
- mercado de factor *(p. 24)*
- mercado de producto *(p. 24)*
- economía de libre empresa *(p. 24)*

Sección uno

La escasez y la ciencia de la economía (páginas 8-12)

La mayoría de las cosas en la vida no son gratis. Los maestros de economía usan el término "no hay nada gratis" *(TINSTAAFL—There is No Such Thing As A Free Lunch)*— para describir este concepto.

El problema económico fundamental es la **escasez,** el resultado de recursos limitados en un mundo de deseos sin límite. Estos recursos o **factores de producción** son **la tierra, el capital, el trabajo** y **la empresaría.** Estos proveen los medios con los que una sociedad puede producir y distribuir sus bienes y servicios. Es debido a la escasez que todas las sociedades deben enfrentar las tres preguntas básicas de QUÉ, CÓMO y PARA QUIÉN producir.

Repasar la idea principal

¿Cómo se relaciona el término "no hay nada gratis" *(TINSTAAFL)* a la escasez?

Sección dos

Compensaciones y costo de oportunidad (páginas 14-17)

Las personas hallan **compensaciones** entre las alternativas. El **costo de oportunidad** de una decisión económica es la alternativa que se pierde cuando se escoge una acción sobre otra. Los países tienen que aceptar compensaciones al decidir producir ciertos bienes en vez de otros. Los economistas usan los **límites de posibilidades de producción** para ilustrar el concepto del costo de oportunidad.

Repasar la idea principal

¿Cómo se mide el costo? ¿Cómo puede ser ilustrado?

Sección tres

Conceptos económicos básicos (páginas 19-26)

Todas las personas tienen **necesidades** básicas, tales como el deseo de sobrevivir y necesidades de un nivel más alto, tales como el éxito y el amor. El **deseo** es una forma de expresar una necesidad, pero su concepto abarca mucho más que una necesidad.

El estudio de la economía trata acerca de aquellos **bienes** y **servicios** que son útiles, relativamente escasos y transferibles a otros. La **riqueza** tiene valor monetario e incluye recursos naturales, **bienes del consumidor** y **bienes de capital.**

Los **consumidores** ayudan a determinar cuales bienes y servicios serán producidos. Los factores de producción deben ser usados para que la **producción** pueda ocurrir. La **productividad** trata del uso eficiente de los recursos. La productividad tiende a aumentar cuando los trabajadores se especializan en lo que pueden hacer mejor y cuando se hacen inversiones en el **capital humano.**

El estudio de la economía ayuda a las personas a hacer decisiones de consumidor y de negocios con más conocimiento. También los ayuda a comprender cómo una **economía de libre empresa**—en la cual los consumidores y los negocios privados, no el gobierno—juntos hacen las decisiones del QUÉ, CÓMO y PARA QUIÉN.

Repasar la idea principal

¿Cuáles son los cinco conceptos económicos clave?

Sistemas económicos y adopción de decisiones

Vocabulario

Los siguientes términos se definen en el Capítulo 2:

SECCIÓN UNO
- sistema económico (*p. 32*)
- economía tradicional (*p. 32*)

- economía autoritaria (*p. 33*)
- economía de mercado (*p. 34*)

SECCIÓN DOS
- Seguro Social (*p. 40*)
- inflación (*p. 40*)
- renta fija (*p. 40*)

SECCIÓN TRES
- capitalismo (*p. 43*)
- intercambio voluntario (*p. 44*)
- propiedad privada (*p. 45*)
- provecho (*p. 46*)
- afán de lucro (*p. 46*)
- soveranía del consumidor (*p. 47*)
- economía mixta (*p. 48*)

- economía de empresa privada modificada (*p. 48*)

Sección uno

Sistemas económicos (páginas 32-36)

Los **sistemas económicos** ayudan a las sociedades a realizar sus deseos y a satisfacer las necesidades de su población. Los tres sistemas de economía que han evolucionado con el tiempo son la tradicional, la autoritaria y la de mercado.

En una **economía tradicional,** las preguntas de QUÉ, CÓMO y PARA QUIÉN se contestan por medio de las tradiciones y costumbres pasadas de generación a generación. Todos tienen un papel específico, pero esto puede resultar en una economía que permanece estancada.

En una **economía autoritaria,** una autoridad central decide las tres preguntas básicas. El individuo tiene un papel mínimo, o ninguno, en el planeamiento económico. Sin embargo, las economías autoritarias tienen una ventaja grande—la habilidad de cambiar los planes de producción rápidamente.

La **economía de mercado** se caracteriza por la libertad y la descentralización en hacer decisiones. Las economías de mercado tienen varias ventajas. Entre éstas se encuentra la habilidad de ajustarse a los cambios gradualmente, la libertad personal, una gran falta de intervención del gobierno y una gran variedad de bienes y servicios disponibles al consumidor.

Repasar la idea principal
¿Por qué es necesaria la decisión económica?

Sección dos

Evaluar el rendimiento económico (páginas 38-41)

Una sociedad puede usar sus metas para evaluar su sistema económico. En Estados Unidos, estas metas incluyen la libertad económica, la eficiencia económica, la igualdad económica, la seguridad económica, el empleo para todos, la estabilidad de precios y el crecimiento económico.

Aunque casi todos los americanos están de acuerdo con estas metas, no es siempre posible satisfacer a todos al mismo tiempo. Las metas de las personas también van a cambiar en el futuro mientras nuestra economía evoluciona.

Repasar la idea principal
¿Qué diferencias hay entre las decisiones económicas hechas en las economías tradicionales, autoritarias y de mercado?

Sección tres

El capitalismo y la libre empresa (páginas 43-48)

El sistema económico de Estados Unidos se basa en **el capitalismo** y la libre empresa. Las características del capitalismo incluyen cuatro partes principales: libertad económica, el **intercambio voluntario,** la **propiedad privada** y el **afán de lucro.**

La fuerza movilizadora de la economía es el empresario en busca de provecho propio. Los consumidores también desempeñan un papel primordial en ayudar a determinar QUÉ producir. El gobierno desempeña el papel de protector, proveedor y consumidor de bienes y servicios, regulador y promovedor de metas. La economía de los Estados Unidos hoy en día es una **economía mixta** o **economía de empresa privada modificada,** en la cual las personas proceden con sus asuntos económicos libremente pero con ciertas regulaciones gubernamentales.

Repasar la idea principal
¿Qué papel desempeña el empresario en la economía de Estados Unidos? ¿El papel del consumidor? ¿El papel del gobierno?

Vocabulario

Los siguientes términos se definen en el Capítulo 3:

SECCIÓN UNO
- institución económica (p. 54)
- organización comercial (p. 54)
- propiedad exclusiva (p. 54)
- responsabilidad general (p. 56)
- inventario (p. 56)
- beneficios complementarios (p. 57)
- vida limitada (p. 57)
- sociedad (p. 57)
- sociedad general (p. 57)
- sociedad en comandita simple (p. 57)
- contrato de asociación (p. 57)
- responsabilidad limitada (p. 59)
- corporación (p. 59)
- incorporar (p. 59)
- carta constitucional (p. 59)
- acciones (p. 59)
- accionista (p. 59)
- dividendo (p. 59)
- acciones ordinarias (p. 60)
- junta directiva (p. 60)
- acciones preferidas (p. 60)
- sustituto (p. 60)
- bono (p. 61)
- capital (p. 61)
- interés (p. 61)
- gráfica institucional (p. 61)
- quiebra (p. 61)
- vida sin límite (p. 62)
- ingreso (p. 62)

SECCIÓN DOS
- fusión (p. 64)
- fusión horizontal (p. 64)
- fusión vertical (p. 64)
- conglomerado (p. 65)
- multinacional (p. 66)

SECCIÓN TRES
- organización sin fines de lucro (p. 69)
- cooperativa (p. 69)
- cooperativa de consumidores (p. 69)
- cooperativa de servicios (p. 70)
- cooperativa de crédito (p. 70)
- cooperativa de productores (p. 70)
- gremio (p. 70)
- negociación colectiva (p. 70)
- asociación profesional (p. 71)
- cámara de comercio (p. 71)
- Better Business Bureau (p. 71)
- servicios públicos (p. 72)

Sección uno

Organizaciones comerciales (páginas 54-62)

Una **organización comercial** se puede establecer como una **propiedad exclusiva**, una **sociedad** o una **corporación.** Las propiedades exclusivas son empresas pequeñas y fáciles de administrar, donde sólo una persona es el dueño. Las sociedades tienen dos o más dueños y son, en su mayoría, un poco más grandes en tamaño que las propiedades exclusivas. Los inversionistas individuales, llamados **accionistas,** son los dueños de las corporaciones. Los dueños de **acciones ordinarias** votan para elegir a la **junta directiva,** quien, a su vez, selecciona a un equipo profesional de administración para efectuar las normas de la corporación.

Repasar la idea principal

¿Cuáles son las tres formas de organización comercial?

Sección dos

Crecimiento y expansión comercial (páginas 64-67)

Los comercios pueden expandirse a través de uniones llamadas **fusiones.** Las fusiones se llevan a cabo debido a que las compañías desean ser más grandes y eficientes. Una **fusión horizontal** ocurre cuando dos compañías similares se unen. Una **fusión vertical** es la que envuelve a dos o más compañías que están en diferentes etapas de la fabricación del producto.

Varias fusiones a veces pueden resultar en un **conglomerado,** una compañía muy grande que contiene por lo menos cuatro negocios diferentes, ninguno de los cuales es responsable por la mayoría de las ventas. Una **multinacional** puede ser una corporación corriente o un conglomerado, pero debe tener operaciones de manufactura o de servicio en un número de países diferentes.

Repasar la idea principal

¿Por qué y cómo puede expandir un comercio sus operaciones?

Sección tres

Otras organizaciones e instituciones (páginas 69-72)

Las **organizaciones sin fines de lucro** operan como un comercio, pero sin fines lucrativos. Más bien, su propósito es el contribuir al beneficio de una buena causa o el beneficiar a sus miembros. Las organizaciones sin fines de lucro incluyen a iglesias, hospitales, escuelas y **cooperativas.** También incluyen a las **negociaciones colectivas, asociaciones profesionales,** asociaciones comerciales y el gobierno.

Repasar la idea principal

¿Cuáles son las características de las organizaciones sin fines de lucro?

La demanda

Vocabulario

Los siguientes términos se definen en el Capítulo 4:

SECCIÓN UNO
- demanda (p. 82)
- microeconomía (p. 82)

- lista de demanda (p. 84)
- curva de relación entre demanda y precio (p. 84)

SECCIÓN DOS
- Ley de demanda (p. 86)
- cambio en cantidad demandada (p. 86)
- efecto de ingreso (p. 87)

- efecto de sustitución (p. 87)
- cambio de demanda (p. 88)
- sustitutos (p. 88)
- complementos (p. 89)
- utilidad marginal (p. 89)
- disminución de la utilidad marginal (p. 90)

SECCIÓN TRES
- elasticidad de demanda (p. 92)
- elástica (p. 92)
- inelástica (p. 92)
- elástica por unidad (p. 94)

Sección uno

¿Qué es la demanda? (páginas 82-84)

La **demanda** se mide en el mercado cuando el deseo por un producto se une a la habilidad y la intención de pagar por él. Esta doctrina económica puede ser ilustrada con una **lista de demanda** que muestra la cantidad de un producto que las personas desean comprar a diferentes precios, y con una **curva de relación entre demanda y precio,** la cual ilustra gráficamente la misma relación.

Repasar la idea principal

Represente el concepto de la demanda usando una lista y una ilustración.

Sección dos

La Ley de Demanda (páginas 86-90)

La **ley de demanda** afirma que las personas comprarán más de un producto a un precio bajo que a un precio más alto. El **cambio en cantidad demandada** significa que las personas compran diferentes cantidades de un producto si su precio cambia. Esta norma se demuestra en la ilustración con un movimiento en la curva de relación entre demanda y precio.

Cada vez que el precio de un producto cambia, ocasiona tanto un **efecto de ingreso** como un **efecto de sustitución.** Ambos ayudan a explicar por qué la curva de relación entre demanda y precio se mueve hacia abajo.

Un **cambio de demanda** significa que las personas han cambiado su decisión sobre la cantidad del producto que comprarán a cada precio diferente. Un aumento en la demanda es ilustrado con el movimiento de toda la curva hacia la derecha, una disminución se muestra con un movimiento hacia la izquierda. Los cambios de demanda ocurren debido a cambios en los ingresos de los consumidores, los gustos o los precios de bienes similares, tales como los **sustitutos** y los **complementos.**

La **utilidad marginal** tiende a disminuir con cada compra consecutiva. La norma de **disminución de la utilidad marginal** ayuda a explicar por qué la curva de relación entre demanda y precio tiene un movimiento hacia abajo. Esta afirma que los consumidores normalmente siguen comprando un producto hasta llegar a un punto en el cual el último producto comprado les da suficiente satisfacción como para justificar el precio.

Repasar la idea principal

¿Cuál es la diferencia entre un cambio de demanda y un cambio en la cantidad demandada?

Sección tres

La elasticidad de demanda (páginas 92-98)

La **elasticidad de demanda** es un concepto que relaciona los cambios en la cantidad demandada a los cambios en el precio de un producto. Si el cambio en precio produce un cambio relativamente mayor en la cantidad demandada, la demanda es **elástica.** Si el cambio en precio produce un cambio relativamente menor en la cantidad demandada, la demanda es **inelástica.** La demanda es **elástica por unidad** si un cambio en el precio no afecta los ingresos de la venta de un producto.

Es importante saber acerca de la elasticidad de demanda porque ésta les dice a los comercios cómo un cambio de precio afectará sus ingresos finales. También ayuda a predecir los cambios futuros de precio. La elasticidad de demanda es influenciada por la habilidad de posponer una compra, los productos sustitutos disponibles y el porcentaje de ingreso que la compra requiere.

Repasar la idea principal

¿Cómo los tres determinantes de la elasticidad de demanda ayudan a clasificar la naturaleza elástica o inelástica de la demanda por un producto?

Vocabulario

Los siguientes términos se definen en el Capítulo 5:

SECCIÓN UNO
- oferta (p. 104)
- lista de oferta (p. 105)
- curva de oferta (p. 105)
- Ley de oferta (p. 106)
- cantidad suplida (p. 106)
- cambio de cantidad suplida (p. 106)
- cambio de oferta (p. 106)

- subsidio (p. 108)
- elasticidad de oferta (p. 109)

SECCIÓN DOS
- teoría de producción (p. 111)
- a corto plazo (p. 111)
- a largo plazo (p. 111)
- Ley de proporciones variables (p. 111)
- función de producción (p. 112)
- materias primas (p. 112)

- producto total (p. 113)
- producto marginal (p. 114)
- etapas de producción (p. 114)
- rendimientos decrecientes (p. 115)

SECCIÓN TRES
- costo fijo (p. 118)
- gastos generales (p. 118)
- depreciación (p. 118)
- costo variable (p. 118)
- costo total (p. 119)

- costo marginal (p. 119)
- ingreso total (p. 121)
- ingreso marginal (p. 121)
- análisis marginal (p. 121)
- punto de equilibrio (p. 122)
- cantidad de producción para ganancia máxima (p. 122)

Sección uno

¿Qué es la oferta? (páginas 104-109)

La **oferta** es la cantidad de productos que los fabricantes llevarán al mercado a cada precio sin excepción. La oferta puede ser representada por una **lista de oferta** o una **curva de oferta.** La **ley de oferta** afirma que la cantidad de un producto económico ofrecido a la venta varía directamente con su precio. Si los precios están altos, los suplidores ofrecerán mayores cantidades a la venta. Si los precios están bajos, ellos ofrecerán menores cantidades a la venta.

Un **cambio de la cantidad suplida** es representado por un movimiento en la curva de oferta. Un **cambio de oferta** es un cambio en la cantidad que será ofrecida a cada precio sin excepción.

Un aumento en la oferta es ilustrado con el movimiento de la curva de oferta hacia la derecha. Una disminución en la oferta aparece como un movimiento de la curva hacia la izquierda.

Repasar la idea principal
¿Qué se entiende por oferta?

Sección dos

La teoría de producción (páginas 111-115)

La **ley de proporciones variables** afirma que la cantidad del producto final varía a la vez que se añaden más unidades provenientes de una sola fuente. Esta ley se encuentra ilustrada en la **función de producción.**

Las dos medidas más importantes del producto final son el **producto total** y el **producto marginal.** Las tres etapas de producción—rendimientos crecientes, **rendimientos decrecientes** y rendimientos negativos—muestran la manera en que el producto marginal cambia a la vez que se le añaden los ingredientes variables. La gran parte de la producción se lleva a cabo en la Etapa II bajo las condiciones de rendimientos decrecientes.

Repasar la idea principal
¿Cuáles son las tres etapas de producción?

Sección tres

La oferta y el papel que desempeña el costo (páginas 117-122)

Existen varias formas importantes de medir el costo. La primera es el **costo total,** la cual consiste del **costo fijo** y el **costo variable.** El **costo marginal** es el aumento en costos variables que proceden del producir una unidad adicional de producto final.

La combinación de costos variables y fijos a la que un comercio se enfrenta afecta la manera en la que éste opera. Cuando los costos marginales son bajos, los comercios tienden a permanecer abiertos por más tiempo. Lo opuesto tiende a pasar cuando los costos marginales son altos.

Los comercios usan dos formas de medir los ingresos para decidir qué cantidad de producto final les traerá las mayores ganancias. Estas dos medidas son el **ingreso total** y el **ingreso marginal,** el cual es el cambio en el ingreso total cuando se vende una unidad más de producto final. Un comercio aumenta al máximo sus ganancias cuando el costo marginal es exactamente igual al ingreso marginal. Puede que otras cantidades del producto final produzcan la misma ganancia, pero ningunas darán más.

Repasar la idea principal
¿Cuáles son las cuatro medidas principales del costo?

Vocabulario

Los siguientes términos se definen en el Capítulo 6:

SECCIÓN UNO
- racionamiento *(p. 131)*
- cupón de racionamiento *(p. 131)*

SECCIÓN DOS
- modelo económico *(p. 134)*
- equilibrio del mercado *(p. 134)*

- superávit *(p. 135)*
- escasez *(p. 136)*
- precio equilibrado *(p. 138)*
- artículos de promoción *(p. 138)*

SECCIÓN TRES
- descuento *(p. 140)*
- precio tope *(p. 141)*
- salario mínimo *(p. 142)*

- precio mínimo *(p. 142)*
- precio meta *(p. 144)*
- préstamo sin recursos *(p. 144)*
- aportación para déficit *(p. 146)*

Sección uno

Los precios como señales (páginas 128-132)

Los precios sirven como señales tanto para los productores como para los consumidores. Los precios altos son una señal para que se produzca más y se compre menos. Los precios bajos son una señal para que se produzca menos y se compre más.

Los precios tienen varias ventajas, incluyendo la neutralidad, la flexibilidad, la libertad de selección, la ausencia de gastos administrativos y la eficiencia. Los precios también tienen la ventaja de que todos los comprenden fácilmente.

Se pueden usar otros métodos de repartición que no están relacionados con los precios, incluyendo el **racionamiento.** Estas reparticiones que no están relacionadas con precios, sin embargo, causan problemas con respecto al ser justas, a los costos altos de administración y a los incentivos aminorados para trabajar y producir.

Repasar la idea principal

¿Cómo sirven los precios de señales tanto para los consumidores como para los productores?

Sección dos

Cómo se determinan los precios (páginas 134-138)

En un mercado competitivo, las fuerzas de la oferta y la demanda establecen los precios. Si el precio es demasiado alto, un **superávit** temporal aparece hasta que el precio baje. Si el precio es demasiado bajo, una **escasez** temporal aparece hasta que el precio suba. Eventualmente, el mercado alcanza un **precio equilibrado,** el cual no causa ni escasez ni superávit.

La teoría de poner precios competitivos representa en teoría un ideal que casi nunca se puede alcanzar. Aún así, una competencia absolutamente pura no es necesaria para que la teoría sea práctica.

Repasar la idea principal

¿Cómo funciona el proceso de ajuste en un mercado cuando se está determinando un precio equilibrado?

Sección tres

El sistema de precios en acción (páginas 140-146)

Una economía de mercado está compuesta de muchos mercados diferentes y hay diferentes precios que prevalecen en cada uno. El cambio en un precio afecta a más de la repartición de recursos en ese mercado. Un cambio de precio afecta la repartición de recursos entre los mercados.

Los gobiernos a veces fijan los precios a niveles sobre o bajo el precio equilibrado. Si un precio fijo es un **precio tope,** así como con los controles de rentas, la escasez normalmente aparecerá mientras que el precio permanezca fijo. Si el precio legal es un **precio mínimo,** como en el caso del **salario mínimo,** el resultado es normalmente un superávit.

Un cambio en la oferta o la demanda puede cambiar los precios. La elasticidad de la curva de relación entre demanda y precio afecta cuán grande será el cambio de precio. Mientras más elástica sea la curva, más pequeño el cambio de precio. Mientras menos elástica sea la curva, más grande el cambio de precio.

Los respaldos de precios agriculturales crecieron dramáticamente durante los años 1930 para contribuir a los ingresos agrícolas. Los programas de apoyo de la CCC permitieron que los agricultores pidieran préstamos repaldados por sus cosechas, retuvieran el préstamo y perdieran la cosecha si los precios del mercado estaban bajos. La **aportación para déficit** se usa con más frecuencia, proveyendo al granjero con un cheque que proporciona la diferencia entre el **precio meta** y el precio actual recibido por el producto.

Repasar la idea principal

¿Cómo funcionan los precios en forma colectiva para repartir los recursos entre los mercados?

Vocabulario

Los siguientes términos se definen en el Capítulo 7:

SECCIÓN UNO
- liberalismo *(p. 152)*
- industria *(p. 152)*
- estructura del mercado *(p. 152)*
- competencia pura *(p. 152)*
- competencia imperfecta *(p. 155)*
- competencia monopolista *(p. 155)*
- diferenciación del producto *(p. 155)*
- competencia sin precio *(p. 156)*
- oligopolio *(p. 156)*
- colusión *(p. 157)*
- fijación de precios *(p. 157)*
- guerra de precios *(p. 157)*
- fijación de precios independiente *(p. 157)*
- liderazgo de precio *(p. 157)*
- monopolio *(p. 158)*
- monopolio natural *(p. 158)*
- franquicia *(p. 159)*
- economías de escala *(p. 159)*
- monopolio geográfico *(p. 159)*
- monopolio tecnológico *(p. 159)*
- patente *(p. 160)*
- derecho de autor *(p. 160)*
- monopolio fiscal *(p. 160)*

SECCIÓN DOS
- fallo del mercado *(p. 163)*
- factor externo *(p. 166)*
- factor externo negativo *(p. 166)*
- factor externo positivo *(p. 167)*
- bienes públicos *(p. 167)*

SECCIÓN TRES
- fideicomiso *(p. 169)*
- descriminación de precio *(p. 169)*
- orden de cesar y desistir *(p. 169)*
- divulgación pública *(p. 170)*

Sección uno

Competencia y estructuras del mercado
(páginas 152-161)

La **competencia pura** es una **estructura del mercado** con muchos compradores y vendedores, productos económicos idénticos, acción independiente por los compradores y vendedores, participantes que están bien informados y libertad para que las compañías entren o dejen el mercado. La **competencia monopolista** tiene todas las características de la competencia pura menos la **diferenciación del producto.** El **oligopolio** es una estructura de mercado dominada por unas cuantas compañías muy grandes. El **monopolista** es un solo productor que posee el mayor control sobre la oferta y el precio. Todas las compañías, sin tener en cuenta la estructura del mercado, aumentan al máximo sus ganancias produciendo la cantidad de producto final donde el costo marginal sea igual al ingreso marginal.

Repasar la idea principal
¿Cuáles son los cuatro tipos de estructuras de mercado?

Sección dos

Fallos del mercado (páginas 163-167)

Los **fallos del mercado** ocurren cuando hay grandes desviaciones de una o más de las condiciones requeridas para la competencia pura. La competencia inadecuada es una de las características de los fallos del mercado y puede llevar al oligopolio o a los monopolios. La existencia de información inadecuada representa otro fallo del mercado. La inmovilidad de los recursos, representada por factores de producción que no pueden o quieren ser movidos a otros mercados, también presenta un obstáculo a la distribución eficiente de los recursos.

Algunas de las actividades ocasionan factores externos, o efectos económicos secundarios a terceros partidos. Los factores externos no están reflejados en los precios de las actividades que causaron los efectos secundarios en primer lugar, y por lo tanto representan una característica del fallo del mercado. Los **bienes públicos,** otro tipo de fallo del mercado, son suplidos por el gobierno porque el mercado no puede reusarle provisiones a aquellos que se niegan a pagar.

Repasar la idea principal
¿Cuáles son los cinco tipos principales de fallos del mercado?

Sección tres

El papel del gobierno (páginas 169-172)

El gobierno toma parte en los asuntos económicos que promueven y estimulan la competencia. Su actividad por medio de legislatura antimonopolista, otras clases de regulaciones y **divulgación pública** ha modificado la economía de libre empresa. Como resultado, la economía moderna es una combinación de diferentes estructuras de mercado, diferentes tipos de organizaciones comerciales y cierto grado de regulación gubernamental.

Repasar la idea principal
¿Cómo promueve el gobierno la competencia?

Vocabulario

Los siguientes términos se definen en el Capítulo 8:

SECCIÓN UNO
- macroeconomía *(p. 182)*
- fuerza de trabajo civil *(p. 182)*
- sindicato de artesanos o gremial *(p. 184)*
- sindicato industrial *(p. 184)*
- huelga *(p. 184)*
- piqueteo *(p. 184)*
- boicot *(p. 184)*
- cierre patronal *(p. 184)*
- sindicato de empresa *(p. 184)*
- la Gran Depresión *(p. 185)*
- ley de derecho de trabajo *(p. 186)*

- controversia sobre jurisdicción *(p. 187)*
- sindicato independiente *(p. 187)*

SECCIÓN DOS
- empresa de exclusividad gremial *(p. 190)*
- empresa sin exclusividad gremial inicial *(p. 190)*
- empresa gremial modificada *(p. 190)*
- empresa de agencia *(p. 190)*
- procedimiento de reclamación *(p. 191)*
- mediación *(p. 191)*
- arbitraje voluntario *(p. 191)*
- arbitraje obligatorio *(p. 191)*
- investigación *(p. 191)*

- mandato *(p. 192)*
- incautación *(p. 192)*

SECCIÓN TRES
- mano de obra no calificada *(p. 194)*
- mano de obra semicalificada *(p. 194)*
- mano de obra calificada *(p. 194)*
- mano de obra profesional *(p. 194)*
- grados de mano de obra no competitiva *(p. 194)*
- escala de salarios *(p. 195)*
- teoría tradicional de determinación de salarios *(p. 195)*
- escala de salarios equilibrada *(p. 195)*

- teoría de salarios negociados *(p. 196)*
- antigüedad *(p. 196)*
- movilidad de la mano de obra *(p. 196)*

SECCIÓN CUATRO
- devolución de beneficios gremiales *(p. 199)*
- sistema salarial de dos niveles *(p. 199)*
- barrera de vidrio *(p. 200)*
- valor comparable *(p. 200)*
- contrato de destinación especial *(p. 201)*
- dólares de valor corriente *(p. 202)*
- dólares de valor real o constante *(p. 204)*
- año base *(p. 204)*

Sección uno El Movimiento Laboral (páginas 182-187)

El crecimiento de los sindicatos fue lento en un principio porque la nación estaba compuesta en su mayoría de granjeros y dueños de negocios pequeños. El **sindicato de artesanos o gremial** fue el primero en surgir, seguido por los **sindicatos industriales.**

Las actitudes del público hacia los obreros cambiaron mucho después de **la Gran Depresión.** Durante los años 1930, el Acta Norris-LaGuardia, el Acta Wagner y el Acta de Estándares Justos de Trabajo cambieron la opiñion pública a favor de los obreros. El pasaje del Acta Taft-Hartley después de la Segunda Guerra Mundial limitó las actividades de los sindicatos.

Repasar la idea principal ¿Cuáles actas afectaron a los obreros después de la Depresión?

Sección dos Cómo resolver las diferencias entre los sindicatos y la administración (páginas 189-192)

Hay cuatro tipos de sindicatos: la **empresa de exclusividad gremial**, la **empresa sin exclusividad gremial inicial**, la **empresa gremial modificada** y la **empresa de agencia.** Hay varios métodos disponibles para resolver las polémicas entre los obreros y la administración si la negociación colectiva fracasa: la **mediación**, el **arbitraje,** la **investigación,** el **mandato** y la **incautación**.

Repasar la idea principal ¿Cómo pueden ser resueltas las polémicas entre los obreros y la administración?

Sección tres Trabajo y sueldo (páginas 194-197)

Los economistas dividen el trabajo entre cuatro **grados de mano de obra no competitiva—mano de obra no calificada, mano de obra semicalificada, mano de obra calificada** y **mano de obra profesional.** La **teoría tradicional de determinación de salarios** usa la influencia de la oferta y la demanda en el mercado para explicar la tasa de salarios. La **teoría de salarios negociados** asegura que la fortaleza de los sindicatos sea también un factor en la determinación de los salarios.

Repasar la idea principal ¿Cómo se diferencian las teorías de determinación de salarios?

Sección cuatro Tendencias y tópicos sobre el empleo (páginas 198-204)

Los sindicatos han decaído por tres razones: los dueños de empresas han tomado pasos muy agresivos para evitar los sindicatos, los que han entrado recientemente a la fuerza laboral tienen poca lealtad a los sindicatos de obreros y los sindicatos han cobrado demasiado en algunas industrias.

La mujer encuentra que hay una gran diferencia entre el salario que ella recibe y el que recibe el hombre. El **valor comparable** y los **contratos de destinación especial** son medidas para corregir esta diferencia.

Repasar la idea principal ¿Cuáles son los dos tópicos de empleo?

Vocabulario

Los siguientes términos se definen en el Capítulo 9:

SECCIÓN UNO
- impuesto de pecado (p. 210)
- laguna tributaria (p. 212)
- principio del beneficio de tributación (p. 213)
- principio de tributación y solvencia (p. 214)
- tributación proporcional (p. 215)
- tasa impositiva media (p. 215)
- tributación progresiva (p. 215)
- tasa impositiva marginal (p. 215)
- tributación regresiva (p. 215)

SECCIÓN DOS
- impuestos sobre la renta (p. 216)
- sistema de retención sobre nóminas (p. 216)
- Servicio de Rentas Internas (SRI) (p. 216)
- declaración de renta (p. 216)
- indización (p. 217)
- FICA (p. 218)
- medicare (p. 218)
- impuestos sobre las utilidades (p. 219)
- impuestos sobre el consumo (p. 219)
- artículo de lujo (p. 220)
- impuesto sucesorio (p. 220)
- impuestos sobre donaciones y legados (p. 220)
- derechos aduaneros (p. 220)
- tarifas a los usuarios (p. 220)

SECCIÓN TRES
- rentas intergubernamentales (p. 222)
- impuesto sobre las ventas (p. 222)
- impuesto sobre los bienes (p. 224)
- bienes inmuebles (p. 224)
- bienes personales tangibles (p. 224)
- bienes personales intangibles (p. 224)
- tasador de impuestos (p. 224)
- declaración de retención sobre nómina (p. 225)

SECCIÓN CUATRO
- frecuencia de un impuesto (p. 228)
- impuesto al valor agregado (p. 229)
- depreciación acelerada (p. 231)
- crédito tributario para inversión (p. 231)
- sobrecargo (p. 231)
- impuesto mínimo alternativo (p. 231)

Sección uno La economía de tributación (páginas 210-215)

El gobierno recauda miles de millones de dólares a través de tributaciones, cuotas por licencias, cuotas por la instrucción y derechos aduaneros. Los economistas usan tres criterios — la imparcialidad, la simplicidad y la eficiencia—para juzgar la efectividad de una tributación. **El principio del beneficio de tributación** y el **principio de tributación y** la **solvencia** ayudan a decidir el grupo o grupos que deberán recibir la tributación. Las tasas pueden ser divididas en tres grupos—**proporcional, progresiva** y **regresiva.**

Repasar la idea principal
¿Cuáles son los tres criterios de las tributaciones y los dos principios de tasación?

Sección dos El sistema federal de tributación (páginas 216-220)

La fuente principal de ingresos para el gobierno federal es el **impuesto sobre la renta,** una tributación progresiva la cual es administrada a través del **sistema de retención sobre nóminas.** El segundo componente más grande de los ingresos federales es el FICA, el cual se recauda para cubrir el seguro social y el **medicare.** El **impuesto sobre las utilidades** es la tercera fuente principal de ingreso federal.

Repasar la idea principal
¿Cuáles son las fuentes principales de ingreso del gobierno federal?

Sección tres Sistemas de tributación a nivel del estado y local (páginas 222-226)

Los gobiernos estatales reciben la mayoría de sus ingresos en forma de **impuestos sobre las ventas, rentas intergubernamentales,** impuestos sobre las rentas y contribuciones al retiro de sus empleados. Los gobiernos locales reciben ingresos de los **impuestos sobre los bienes,** los servicios públicos, tiendas de licores, impuestos sobre las ventas y de los gobiernos estatales y federales.

Repasar la idea principal
¿Cuáles son las fuentes principales de ingreso de los gobiernos estatales y locales?

Sección cuatro Tópicos de impuestos de actualidad (páginas 228-232)

Ha habido tres grandes modificaciones a las leyes de impuestos, las cuales han estado vigentes desde el año 1980. El Acta de Impuestos para la Recuperación Económica de 1981 ocasionó una gran reducción en la tasa de tributaciones del individuo y de corporaciones. La ley de reforma de impuestos del 1986 cerró unos escapes a la ley que habían sido abiertos en el 1981 e hizo el código de impuesto individual más proporcional. El Acta de Reconciliación de Presupuesto Omnibus del 1993 añadió varias categorías de impuestos marginales al código de impuestos del individuo.

Repasar la idea principal
¿Cómo ha sido cambiada la reforma de impuestos desde el año 1980?

Gastos del gobierno

Vocabulario

Los siguientes términos se definen en el Capítulo 10:

SECCIÓN UNO
- per cápita *(p. 238)*
- sector público *(p. 239)*
- sector privado *(p. 239)*
- pago de traslado *(p. 239)*
- donativo del gobierno *(p. 240)*
- distribución de ingresos *(p. 240)*

SECCIÓN DOS
- presupuesto federal *(p. 243)*
- año fiscal *(p. 243)*
- déficit presupuestario federal *(p. 243)*
- proyecto de ley para asignación de fondos *(p. 243)*
- medicaid *(p. 246)*

SECCIÓN TRES
- enmienda para equilibrar el presupuesto *(p. 249)*

SECCIÓN CUATRO
- gastos deficitarios *(p. 253)*
- deuda federal *(p. 254)*
- fondo fiduciario *(p. 256)*
- Producto Interno Bruto *(p. 256)*
- efecto de exclusión *(p. 258)*
- presupuesto equilibrado *(p. 258)*
- derecho de titularidad *(p. 260)*

Sección uno

La economía de gastos del gobierno (páginas 238-241)

Los gastos en todos los niveles del gobierno a mediados del año 1997 excedían $2.6 billones, o $9,610 per cápita. La gran mayoría del aumento tuvo lugar después de los años 1930, pero hoy en día muchas personas creen que los gastos del gobierno han crecido demasiado. El gobierno paga por los bienes y servicios, algunos de los cuales pertenecen al **sector público** y por los **pagos de traslado,** tales como los **donativos del gobierno,** por los cuales el gobierno no recibe nada en cambio.

Repasar la idea principal

¿Cómo ha afectado el aumento de los gastos del gobierno a la economía en general?

Sección dos

Los gastos del gobierno federal (páginas 243-247)

El Presidente es el responsable de desarrollar el **presupuesto federal** para el **año fiscal,** el cual comienza cada 1° de octubre. Los tres componentes más grandes del presupuesto federal, que representa a más de la mitad de todos los gastos federales, son la defensa nacional, el Seguro Social y el interés de la **deuda federal.** La seguridad de ingresos, medicare y la salud son las categorías que le siguen.

Repasar la idea principal

¿Cuáles son las principales categorías de gastos del gobierno federal, desde las más importantes hasta las menos importantes?

Sección tres

Los gastos del gobierno a nivel estatal y local (páginas 249-252)

Los presupuestos estatales pasan por un proceso de aceptación el cual varía de estado a estado. Los gastos estatales más grandes incluyen el bienestar público, los estudios universitarios y las contribuciones de seguros. Otros programas incluyen las carreteras, los hospitales y el interés de la deuda estatal.

La categoría principal de gastos para los gobiernos locales es la educación elemental y secundaria. Los servicios públicos, los hospitales, el interés de la deuda estatal, el departamento de la policía, el bienestar público y otros gastos siguen a la educación.

Repasar la idea principal

¿Cuáles son las principales categorías de gastos estatales, desde las más importantes hasta las menos importantes?

Sección cuatro

Déficit federales y la deuda nacional (páginas 253-260)

La deuda federal afecta la economía de varias maneras. Los impuestos que se necesitan para pagar el interés de la deuda afecta la distribución de ingresos y también transfieren el poder de adquisición del sector privado al sector gubernamental. Los incentivos del individuo para trabajar, ahorrar e invertir también pueden afectarse. Finalmente, cuando el gobierno compite con el sector privado por fondos, es posible que la tasa de interés suba.

Repasar la idea principal

¿Cómo afectan los impuestos a la distribución de recursos?

Vocabulario

Los siguientes términos se definen en el Capítulo 11:

SECCIÓN UNO
- economía de trueque (p. 266)
- dinero (p. 266)
- medio de cambio (p. 266)
- medida de valor (p. 266)
- almacenaje de valor (p. 266)
- moneda como producto básico (p. 267)
- moneda fiduciaria (p. 267)
- wampum (p. 267)
- efectivo (p. 268)
- lingotes (p. 268)

- unidad monetaria (p. 269)

SECCIÓN DOS
- estándar monetario (p. 272)
- banco estatal (p. 272)
- banca arriesgada (p. 273)
- moneda legal (p. 274)
- greenbacks (p. 274)
- billete de los EE.UU. (p. 274)
- Sistema Bancario Nacional (p. 274)
- banco nacional (p. 274)
- billete del Banco Nacional (p. 274)
- moneda nacional (p. 274)
- certificado de oro (p. 275)
- certificado de plata (p. 275)
- billetes de la divisa de tesorería (p. 275)
- estándar de oro (p. 275)
- estándar inconvertible de la moneda fiduciaria (p. 276)

SECCIÓN TRES
- sistema bancario dual (p. 279)
- Sistema de Reserva Federal (p. 280)
- banco central (p. 280)
- billete de la Reserva Federal (p. 280)
- pánico bancario (p. 281)
- cierre bancario (p. 281)
- banco comercial (p. 281)
- cuenta de depósito a la vista (p. 281)
- institución de pequeño ahorro (p. 281)
- banco mutualista de ahorro (p. 281)
- banco de ahorro (p. 282)
- Orden Negociable de Retiro (p. 282)
- sociedad de ahorro y préstamo (p. 282)
- giro de acción (p. 283)

SECCIÓN CUATRO
- eliminación de restricciones (p. 284)
- Regulación Q (p. 285)

Sección uno

La evolución del dinero (páginas 266-270)

El **dinero** es cualquier materia que sirva como medio de trueque, una medida de valor y un almacén de valor. Todos los dineros útiles tienen 4 características: portabilidad, durabilidad, divisibilidad y estabilidad de valor.

Repasar la idea principal
¿Cuáles son las características y funciones del dinero?

Sección dos

La banca de ayer y los estándares monetarios (páginas 272-277)

Los países usan un **estándar monetario** para mantener el valor de su moneda. Desde la Revolución hasta la Guerra Civil, los bancos fundados por el estado con dueños privados, emitían papel monetario. En el año 1861 el gobierno nacional vendió bonos e imprimió **greenbacks** para financiar la Guerra Civil. Más tarde, otras monedas federales fueron populares, incluyendo los **certificados de oro, certificados de plata, billetes de la divisa de tesorería** y la **moneda nacional.**

El **estándar de oro** se adoptó en el año 1900. En 1934, sin embargo, la nación adoptó un **estándar inconvertible de la moneda fiduciaria,** lo que significaba que los **billetes de la Reserva Federal** y los *greenbacks* no se podrían convertir en oro.

Repasar la idea principal
¿Por qué usa un país un estándar monetario?

Sección tres

El desarrollo de la banca moderna (páginas 279-283)

El establecimiento del Sistema Nacional de la Banca (National Banking System) en 1863 trajo uniformidad al sistema bancario. El jefe de contaduría monetaria inspeccionó a los bancos miembros. La nación también tenía un **sistema bancario dual** porque muchos de los bancos fundados por los estados no se unieron al NBS. Además de los **bancos comerciales,** otras instituciones de depósito incluyeron a los **bancos mutualistas de ahorro, sindicatos de crédito** y **sociedades de ahorro y préstamo.**

Repasar la idea principal
¿Dónde se podía depositar dinero después del año 1863?

Sección cuatro

Crisis, reforma y evolución en los años 1980s (páginas 284-288)

La **eliminación de restricciones,** la tasa de intereses altos, reservas financieras inadecuadas y el fraude en los 1980 afectaron a las sociedades de ahorro y préstamo. El Congreso eliminó el estado independiente de la industria en 1989. La autoridad supervisora fue transferida a la Oficina de Supervisión de Economía.

Repasar la idea principal
¿Cómo afectó la eliminación de restricciones a las instituciones financieras?

El Sistema de la Reserva Federal y la política monetaria

Vocabulario

Los siguientes términos se definen en el Capítulo 12:

SECCIÓN UNO
- banco afiliado *(p. 294)*
- sociedad inversionista bancaria *(p. 296)*
- ley de veracidad sobre préstamo *(p. 299)*
- Regulación Z *(p. 299)*
- dinero *(p. 300)*
- monedas *(p. 300)*
- requisito marginal *(p. 300)*

SECCIÓN DOS
- política monetaria *(p. 302)*
- sistema de reserva fraccional *(p. 302)*
- reserva obligatoria *(p. 302)*
- reservas legales *(p. 302)*
- reservas de banco afiliado *(p. 302)*
- responsabilidades *(p. 302)*
- haberes *(p. 302)*
- estado de cuentas *(p. 302)*
- capital líquido *(p. 302)*
- reservas excesivas *(p. 303)*
- liquidez *(p. 304)*
- certificado de depósito *(p. 304)*
- cuenta de ahorros *(p. 304)*
- depósito a plazo *(p. 304)*
- política de dinero abundante *(p. 306)*
- política de dinero caro *(p. 306)*
- operaciones de mercado abierto *(p. 307)*
- despacho mercantil *(p. 307)*
- tasa de descuento *(p. 307)*
- ventanilla de descuento *(p. 308)*
- garantía *(p. 308)*
- persuasión moral *(p. 308)*
- controles selectivos de crédito *(p. 308)*

SECCIÓN TRES
- tasa preferencial *(p. 309)*
- teoría sobre la cantidad de dinero *(p. 309)*
- monetización de la deuda *(p. 310)*
- M1 *(p. 312)*
- M2 *(p. 312)*
- lista de banco problemático *(p. 312)*
- acreedor *(p. 312)*
- banco de crédito agrícola *(p. 313)*
- banco de energía *(p. 313)*

Sección uno

El Sistema de la Reserva Federal (páginas 294-300)

El Sistema de la Reserva Federal *(Fed)* es el banco central de la nación, cuyas acciones son propiedad de sus bancos miembros. Su estructura consiste de una **Junta de Directores;** un **Comité Federal de mercado abierto** que consiste de 7 miembros de la Junta y 5 presidentes de distrito; y la **Consultoría Federal** con 12 miembros.

Además de supervisar a los bancos miembros de cada estado, el *Fed* tiene gran autoridad sobre las **sociedades inversionistas bancarias,** las operaciones internacionales de todos los bancos comerciales, algunas fusiones, la autorización de cheques, la legislación del consumidor concerniente a las **leyes de veracidad sobre préstamo,** el mantenimiento de la moneda nacional y los **requisitos marginales.**

Repasar la idea principal
¿Cómo está organizado el *Fed*?

Sección dos

La política monetaria (páginas 302-308)

La **política monetaria** y la banca comercial moderna operan con un **sistema de reserva fraccional.** Las **reservas legales** que un banco mantiene determina la cantidad de préstamos que éste puede hacer. El **capital líquido** de un banco es igual a la diferencia entre su **haberes** y sus **responsabilidades.** Cuando un banco recibe un depósito, se separa cierta cantidad del depósito a un lado como una reserva contra el depósito. Si existen algunas **reservas excesivas,** el banco puede hacer préstamos nuevos.

La política monetaria afecta el tamaño de la oferta monetaria y así el nivel de la tasa de intereses, usando el sistema de reserva fraccional. El primer recurso de la política monetaria es el cambio en la **reserva obligatoria,** el cual casi nunca se usa. El segundo recurso y el más popular es las **operaciones de mercado abierto.** Un cambio en la **tasa de descuento** es el tercer recurso importante. Dos de los recursos menos usados incluyen la **persuasión moral** y los **controles selectivos de crédito** tales como los **requisitos marginales.**

Repasar la idea principal
¿Cómo le permite el sistema de reserva fraccional al *Fed* manejar la política monetaria?

Sección tres

La política monetaria, la banca y la economía (páginas 309-313)

A corto plazo, los cambios en la oferta monetaria trabajan en combinación con la demanda de dinero para impactar la tasa de intereses. A largo plazo, el impacto de la política monetaria es en la inflación.

Debido a que las personas guardan su dinero en tantas formas diferentes y en tantos tipos distintos de cuentas, el Fed ha instituido dos definiciones adicionales para el dinero. La primera es el **M1,** el cual representa el componente de transacciones monetarias. El segundo es el **M2,** el cual representa el papel que desempeña el dinero como reserva de valor.

Repasar la idea principal
¿Cuáles son los efectos a corto y largo plazo de los cambios en la oferta monetaria?

Vocabulario

Los siguientes términos se definen en el Capítulo 13:

SECCIÓN UNO
- ahorrar *(p. 320)*
- ahorros *(p. 320)*
- sistema financiero *(p. 320)*
- activo financiero *(p. 321)*
- intermediario financiero *(p. 321)*
- institución financiera no bancaria *(p. 322)*
- compañía financiera *(p. 322)*
- préstamo de consolidación de cuenta *(p. 322)*
- prima *(p. 323)*

- fondo mutuo *(p. 323)*
- pensión *(p. 323)*
- fondo de pensiones *(p. 323)*
- fondo de inversión de bienes raíces *(p. 323)*

SECCIÓN DOS
- riesgo *(p. 325)*
- cupón *(p. 326)*
- vencimiento *(p. 326)*
- paridad *(p. 326)*
- rendimiento vigente *(p. 327)*
- CD gigante *(p. 328)*
- bono arriesgado *(p. 328)*
- bono municipal *(p. 329)*
- exento de impuestos *(p. 329)*
- bono de ahorros *(p. 329)*

- fondo común de inversiones *(p. 330)*
- pagaré del Tesoro *(p. 330)*
- bono del Tesoro a largo plazo *(p. 330)*
- bono del Tesoro a corto plazo *(p. 331)*
- Cuenta de retiro individual *(p. 331)*
- mercado de capital *(p. 332)*
- mercado monetario *(p. 332)*
- mercado primario *(p. 332)*
- mercado secundario *(p. 332)*

SECCIÓN TRES
- capitales *(p. 334)*
- Hipótesis de Mercado Eficiente *(p. 334)*
- diversificación de cartera *(p. 334)*
- agente de bolsa *(p. 335)*
- bolsa de valores *(p. 335)*
- asiento *(p. 335)*
- mercado extrabursátil *(p. 336)*
- DJIA *(p. 337)*
- 500 de S&P *(p. 337)*
- mercado al contado *(p. 338)*
- futuros *(p. 338)*
- mercado de futuros *(p. 338)*
- opciones *(p. 338)*
- opción de compra *(p. 338)*
- optición de venta *(p. 338)*
- mercados de opciones *(p. 338)*

Sección uno

Los ahorros y el sistema financiero (páginas 320-323)

El **ahorrar** es un proceso que hace posible el que haya ahorros disponibles para otros que quieran invertir. La economía tiene un **sistema financiero** que transfiere los ahorros a los inversionistas. Los **activos financieros** que se generan en el proceso son instituidos por comercios, gobiernos e **intermediarios financieros** para facilitar la transferencia de fondos de los que ahorran a los que invierten. Los intermediarios financieros incluyen **compañías financieras,** compañías de seguro de vida, **fondos mutuos, fondos de pensiones** y **fondos de inversión de bienes raíces.**

Repasar la idea principal

¿Qué intermediarios financieros existen para transferir fondos de los que ahorran a los que invierten?

Sección dos

Invertir en los activos financieros (páginas 325-332)

Hay un gran número de activos financieros disponible a los inversionistas. Los bonos instituidos por corporaciones, gobiernos estatales y locales, el gobierno de Estados Unidos y otros gobiernos forman una gran parte de los activos financieros. Los certificados de depósitos, el **mercado monetario de fondos mutuos,** y las **cuentas de retiro individual** son otros activos financieros instituidos por varias agencias privadas.

Repasar la idea principal

¿Qué activos financieros hay disponibles para los inversionistas?

Sección tres

Invertir en capitales, futuros y opciones (páginas 334-338)

Los **capitales,** o acciones, difieren de los activos financieros en que los capitales representan posesión de una corporación en vez de un préstamo. Muchos valores se intercambian en **bolsas de valores** organizadas, donde los miembros se reúnen para comprar y vender acciones.

Los inversionistas leen el **DJIA** para seguir el rendimiento de las acciones en el NYSE. El índice de **500 de Standard & Poor** muestra un grupo de 500 acciones ejemplares, las cuales están alistadas en varias bolsas de valores y también incluyen al **mercado al contado.**

Históricamente, los granjeros y compradores de productos agrícolas ingeniaron la manera de extender los contratos por más tiempo. Hoy en día, los contratos **futuros** se usan mucho. Si un inversionista desea tener la opción de salirse de la obligación de una entrega futura especificada en un contrato escrito hoy, puede que él o ella esté más interesado en un contrato de **opción.**

Repasar la idea principal

¿En qué se diferencian los capitales de los activos financieros y dónde se intercambian los capitales?

Vocabulario

Los siguientes términos se definen en el Capítulo 14:

SECCIÓN UNO

- contabilidad del ingreso nacional *(p. 348)*
- estructuras *(p. 348)*
- productos intermediarios *(p. 349)*
- ventas de segunda mano *(p. 349)*
- transacción fuera del mercado *(p. 351)*
- economía oculta *(p. 351)*

SECCIÓN DOS

- Producto Nacional Bruto *(p. 354)*
- producto nacional neto *(p. 355)*
- descuento del consumo de capital *(p. 355)*
- ingreso nacional *(p. 356)*
- impuesto comercial indirecto *(p. 356)*
- ingreso personal *(p. 356)*
- utilidades incorporadas *(p. 356)*
- ganancias empresariales no distribuidas *(p. 356)*
- ingreso personal disponible *(p. 356)*
- casa *(p. 356)*
- individuo no relacionado *(p. 357)*
- familia *(p. 357)*
- modelo de producción-gastos *(p. 358)*
- gastos de consumo personal *(p. 358)*
- inversión interna bruta del sector privado *(p. 358)*
- exportación neta de bienes y servicios *(p. 359)*

SECCIÓN TRES

- índice de precios *(p. 361)*
- cesta de mercado *(p. 362)*
- índice de precios del consumidor *(p. 362)*
- índice de precios del productor *(p. 362)*
- índice de precios al por mayor *(p. 362)*
- deflactor implícito de precios del PIB *(p. 363)*
- PIB vigente *(p. 363)*
- PIB nominal *(p. 363)*
- PIB real *(p. 364)*
- PIB en dólares constantes *(p. 364)*

Sección uno

La medida de la producción nacional (página 348-352)

El **PIB** es la medida más abarcadora de la producción total de la nación. Esta sólo cuenta los productos finales, servicios y las estructuras que son producidas en Estados Unidos, sin importar quién es el dueño de los recursos. Como ésta cuenta sólo los productos finales, los **productos intermediarios** y las **ventas de segunda mano** están excluidas.

El **PIB** no nos deja saber nada respecto a la composición de la producción o el estándar de vida. Algunas actividades no relacionadas con el mercado, tales como los servicios que ejecutan las amas de casa, se excluyen de la cantidad. Otras actividades son ilegales o no son declaradas, y por lo tanto, pertenecen a la **economía oculta.**

Repasar la idea principal

¿Cómo mide el PIB la producción total de la economía?

Sección dos

La medida del ingreso nacional (páginas 354-359)

La diferencia entre el PIB y el PNB es que el PIB cuenta sólo la producción en Estados Unidos, sin importar quién posee los recursos. Por contraste, el PNB es la medida del ingreso que reciben los ciudadanos americanos, sin importar dónde están localizados sus recursos.

Hay cinco formas de medir el ingreso, incluyendo el PIB. Éstas incluyen el **producto nacional neto,** el **ingreso nacional,** el **ingreso personal** y el **ingreso personal disponible.**

La economía también se puede organizar como el **sector casero** o del consumidor, el sector comercial o de inversionistas, el sector gubernamental y el sector extranjero. El **modelo de producción-gastos,** que se expresa como PIB = C + I + G + E, demuestra como el PIB es consumido por los cuatro segmentos de la economía.

Repasar la idea principal

¿Cuál es la diferencia entre el PIB y el PNB?

Sección tres

El PIB y los cambios en el nivel del precio (páginas 361-364)

Los economistas usan un **índice de precios** para seguir el movimiento de los precios al pasar del tiempo. Los índices de precios están basados en una **cesta de mercado** con productos representantes que se seleccionan en cierto año usado como base.

Los índices de precios pueden ser preparados para cualquier producto, grupo de productos o grupos de consumidores. Tres de los más populares incluyen el **índice de precios del consumidor,** el **índice de precios del productor** y el **deflactor implícito de precios del PIB.**

Repasar la idea principal

¿Cuál es el propósito del índice de precios?

Población, crecimiento económico y ciclos económicos

Vocabulario

Los siguientes términos se definen en el Capítulo 15:

SECCIÓN UNO
- censo *(p. 370)*
- población urbana *(p. 370)*
- población rural *(p. 370)*
- centro de población *(p. 372)*
- demógrafo *(p. 372)*
- índice de fertilidad *(p. 372)*

- expectativa de vida *(p. 372)*
- inmigración neta *(p. 372)*
- *baby boom (p. 373)*
- pirámide demográfica *(p. 373)*
- relación de dependencia *(p. 374)*

SECCIÓN DOS
- PIB real per cápita *(p. 376)*
- triángulo de crecimiento *(p. 376)*

- estándar de vida *(p. 377)*
- base impositiva *(p. 377)*
- recursos renovables *(p. 379)*
- relación capital-trabajo *(p. 379)*
- productividad de la mano de obra *(p. 380)*

SECCIÓN TRES
- ciclo económico *(p. 383)*
- fluctuación económica *(p. 383)*

- recesión *(p. 383)*
- máximo *(p. 383)*
- sima *(p. 383)*
- expansión *(p. 383)*
- tendencia *(p. 384)*
- depresión *(p. 384)*
- vale de depresión *(p. 385)*
- modelo econométrico *(p. 387)*
- índice de indicadores anticipados *(p. 388)*

Sección uno

Población (páginas 370-374)

La constitución de Estados Unidos requiere un **censo** de la población cada 10 años. El Departamento del Censo hace la cuenta. Éste clasifica la población de diferentes maneras; incluyendo la división en **poblaciones urbanas** y **rurales.** El porcentaje anual de crecimiento de la población era más de 3 por ciento hasta la Guerra Civil, pero ha bajado constantemente desde entonces.

El Departamento del Censo ha proyectado la continuación de la bajada en el porcentaje de crecimiento de la población hasta el año 2050. Los factores que contribuyen a esta tendencia son un **índice de fertilidad** con nivel de reemplazo, una **expectativa de vida** un poco más larga y una **inmigración neta.** Las proyecciones de edad y sexo demuestran la continua influencia del *baby boom,* una generación muy abundante que al final aumentará la **relación de dependencia.** La mezcla racial y étnica también cambiará.

Repasar la idea principal

¿Por qué son los cambios en la población importantes para cualquier país?

Sección dos

Desarrollo económico (páginas 376-381)

Debido a los cambios en la población, el desarrollo económico a largo plazo es normalmente medido en términos del **PIB real per cápita.** Para períodos más cortos, de año a año, se usa el PIB real no-ajustado para tomar en cuenta la población. El desarrollo económico es importante por cinco razones. Primero, aumenta el **estándar de vida** de todos. Segundo, aumenta la **base impositiva** y le facilita al gobierno a desarrollar varios programas. Tercero, ayuda a aliviar algunos problemas domésticos que son causados por la falta de trabajos. Cuarto, ayuda a las economías de otras naciones. Finalmente, el desarrollo económico en casa hace del sistema económico y político de Estados Unidos un modelo para los países en desarrollo del mundo.

Repasar la idea principal

¿Por qué es el desarrollo económico una de las siete mayores metas de la economía de Estados Unidos?

Sección tres

Ciclos económicos y Fluctuaciones (páginas 383-388)

El rendimiento económico en términos del PIB real varía al pasar del tiempo en un patrón llamado **ciclo económico.** Las dos fases del ciclo son la **recesión** y la **expansión.** La economía alcanza lo **máximo** cuando una expansión termina y una **sima** cuando una recesión termina.

Los ciclos económicos son resultado de un número de factores—incluyendo los cambios en el capital y los gastos de inventario por comercios, el estímulo suplido por las innovaciones e imitaciones, factores monetarios y acontecimientos externos inesperados.

Los economistas usan **modelos econométricos** para predecir la actividad económica futura. Los modelos simulan la actividad económica y proveen predicciones a corto plazo bastante precisas.

Repasar la idea principal

¿Qué son los ciclos económicos?

Vocabulario

Los siguientes términos se definen en el Capítulo 16:

SECCIÓN UNO
- desempleo (p. 394)
- índice de desempleo (p. 394)
- desempleo friccional (p. 395)
- desempleo estructural (p. 395)
- desempleo cíclico (p. 396)
- desempleo estacional (p. 396)
- desempleo tecnológico (p. 396)
- automatización (p. 396)
- empleo total (p. 397)

SECCIÓN DOS
- nivel de precios (p. 399)
- deflación (p. 399)
- inflación reptante (p. 400)
- inflación galopante (p. 400)
- hiperinflación (p. 400)

SECCIÓN TRES
- Curva de Lorenz (p. 405)
- obrero (p. 407)
- oficinista (p. 407)

- umbral de pobreza (p. 407)
- relación ingresos-pobreza (p. 408)
- asistencia social (p. 409)
- sellos para la compra de alimentos (p. 411)
- impuesto sobre la renta negativo (p. 411)
- zona de iniciativa (p. 412)
- *workfare* (p. 412)

Sección uno

El desempleo (páginas 394-397)

El Departamento del Censo identifica a las personas desempleadas en muestras mensuales que toman de aproximadamente 55,800 hogares en toda la nación. El número de desempleados es dividido entre la fuerza trabajadora civil para expresar el desempleo por medio de un porcentaje. El **índice de desempleo** es abarcador, pero no cuenta a los que desisten en buscar empleo ni distingue entre el empleo de tiempo completo y el empleo por horas.

Los tipos de desempleo incluyen el **desempleo friccional, desempleo estructural, desempleo cíclico, desempleo estacional** y el **desempleo tecnológico.**

Repasar la idea principal
¿Qué es el desempleo y cómo es tabulado?

Sección dos

La inflación (páginas 399-403)

Los economistas miden el **nivel de precios** con el CPI, el deflactor implícito de precios del PIB y el índice de precios del productor. El cambio en el nivel de precios es la tasa de inflación, la cual se expresa normalmente en términos de porcentajes de cambio. La **inflación reptante, inflación galopante** e **hiperinflación** son términos usados para describir el grado de severidad de la inflación.

Condiciones de crédito muy favorables y el aumento excesivo de la oferta monetaria son las causas bajo la inflación. Cuando estas condiciones están presentes, varios tipos de inflación—incluyendo la demanda-tirante, gastos del déficit, costo-empuje y el espiral de salario y precio—pueden ocurrir. La inflación errode el valor del dinero y obliga a los consumidores y comercios a cambiar sus hábitos de compras.

Repasar la idea principal
¿Qué causa la inflación y cómo desestabiliza a la economía?

Sección tres

La pobreza y la distribución de ingresos (páginas 405-412)

Una serie de factores causan la desigualdad en la distribución de ingresos, estos incluyen los niveles educacionales, la riqueza, la discriminación, la habilidad y el poder del monopolio. La pobreza es una medida relativa la cual se determina comparando la cantidad de dinero por ingresos que ganan las familias con el **umbral de pobreza.** La **relación ingresos-pobreza** también se usa para compensar por las diferencias en el tamaño de las familias y todas las medidas muestran una diferencia creciente entre los ingresos.

Varios programas para combatir la pobreza han sido introducidos para ayudar a los necesitados. Los programas de ayuda del gobierno incluyen la Ayuda a Familias con Niños Pequeños, Ingreso de Seguridad Suplemental, los **sellos para la compra de alimentos** y otros programas. Los economistas han propuesto un **impuesto negativo sobre la renta,** mientras que otros han propuesto **zonas de iniciativa** y *workfare.*

Repasar la idea principal
¿Qué es la pobreza y qué programas pueden usarse para aliviarla?

Vocabulario

Los siguientes términos se definen en el Capítulo 17:

SECCIÓN UNO
- estancamiento e inflación *(p. 419)*
- laguna del PIB *(p. 419)*
- índice de miseria *(p. 419)*
- índice de incomodidad *(p. 419)*

SECCIÓN DOS
- curva de abastecimiento global *(p. 422)*
- curva de demanda global *(p. 424)*
- equilibrio de macroeconomía *(p. 425)*

SECCIÓN TRES
- política fiscal *(p. 427)*
- economía keynesiana *(p. 427)*

- función del consumo *(p. 427)*
- multiplicador *(p. 427)*
- acelerador *(p. 428)*
- estabilizador automático *(p. 429)*
- seguro de desempleo *(p. 429)*
- economía de oferta *(p. 431)*
- curva de Laffer *(p. 432)*
- monetarismo *(p. 433)*

- controles de los salarios con los precios *(p. 434)*

SECCIÓN CUATRO
- Consejo de Asesores Económicos *(p. 437)*

Sección uno

El costo de la inestabilidad económica (páginas 418-421)

La falta de desarrollo e instabilidad económica tiene costos tanto económicos como sociales. Los costos económicos pueden ser medidos como **estancamiento e inflación** o **laguna del PIB.** Los costos sociales incluyen la frustración por estar desempleados, la posible instabilidad política, el aumento en el crimen y el daño a los valores familiares. Un gran desarrollo económico es más que un ideal económico. Es uno de los pilares fundadores de una sociedad vibrante.

Repasar la idea principal
¿Cuáles son los costos económicos y sociales de la instabilidad económica?

Sección dos

Equilibrio de macroeconomía (páginas 422-425)

El equilibrio de macroeconomía puede ser analizado con la ayuda de la **curva de abastecimiento global** y la **curva de demanda global.** La curva de abastecimiento global representa la suma de toda la producción que podría llevarse a cabo a cada nivel de precio. La demanda global representa la demanda total de todos los sectores de la economía a todos los niveles de precio posibles. Cuando la oferta y la demanda global son combinadas, su intersección se define como el **equilibrio de macro-economía.**

Repasar la idea principal
¿Cómo se parece el equilibrio de macroeconomía al equilibrio en los mercados individuales?

Sección tres

Políticas de estabilización (páginas 427-434)

Las políticas de la demanda, también conocidas como **políticas fiscales,** están diseñadas para que afecten la curva de demanda global a través del gasto federal y los impuestos. Las políticas de la oferta afectan la curva de abastecimiento global. Éstas incluyen un papel menos importante para el gobierno, una estructura de impuestos federales más baja y otras medidas para reducir el papeleo y la regulación en el sector comercial. Las políticas monetarias incluyen operaciones en el mercado abierto, cambios en la tasa de descuentos y en circunstancias extremas, cambios en la reserva obligatoria.

Repasar la idea principal
¿Cuáles son los tres procedimientos principales para la estabilización y el desarrollo?

Sección cuatro

La economía y la política (páginas 436-438)

Los Estados Unidos tienen una autoridad monetaria independiente—el Sistema de Reserva Federal. Mientras el *Fed* tenga la responsabilidad de establecer la política monetaria y los funcionarios tengan la responsabilidad de la política fiscal, puede que los dos no estén de acuerdo. Aunque la economía por sí misma es una ciencia social, los campos de la economía y política están muy relacionados. El Presidente tiene un **Consejo de Asesores Económicos,** pero en ocasiones él no puede seguir sus consejos por razones políticas.

Repasar la idea principal
¿Qué revela el registro histórico acerca de la conducta de la política económica?

Vocabulario

Los siguientes términos se definen en el Capítulo 18:

SECCIÓN UNO
- ventaja absoluta *(p. 450)*
- ventaja comparativa *(p. 451)*

SECCIÓN DOS
- tarifa *(p. 453)*
- cuota *(p. 453)*
- arancel proteccionista *(p. 453)*
- tarifa de ingreso *(p. 453)*
- proteccionista *(p. 454)*
- argumento de las industrias nacientes *(p. 455)*
- balanza de pagos *(p. 456)*
- déficit comercial *(p. 456)*
- cláusula de la nación más favorecida *(p. 458)*
- GATT *(p. 458)*
- TLC *(p. 459)*

SECCIÓN TRES
- divisas *(p. 461)*
- mercado de divisas *(p. 461)*
- cotización de la divisa *(p. 461)*
- cotización de la divisa fija *(p. 461)*
- devaluación *(p. 462)*
- cotización de la divisa flotante *(p. 463)*
- cotización de la divisa flexible *(p. 463)*
- letras para entrega futura *(p. 464)*
- valor ponderado del dólar según el comercio exterior *(p. 465)*

Sección uno

Ventaja absoluta y comparativa (páginas 448-451)

Los Estados Unidos están muy envueltos en el mercado internacional. En 1993 el americano promedio gastó más de $2,300 en bienes y servicios importados. **Ventaja absoluta** significa que un país puede producir más cantidad de un producto que otro país. La base para el mercado de hoy es la **ventaja comparativa.** Si las personas y los países se especializan en las cosas que ellos saben hacer con más eficiencia y usan el trueque para conseguir aquellas cosas que no pueden producir, entonces la producción global aumentará.

Repasar la idea principal

¿Qué concepto económico explica las ganancias mutuas del comercio?

Sección dos

Barreras del comercio internacional (páginas 453-459)

En el pasado, las barreras del comercio incluían las **tarifas** y las **cuotas.** En años recientes, otras barreras sin tarifas—que incluyen las licencias, certificaciones de salud y cuotas voluntarias—se han usado para restringir el paso libre de los productos.

Los que están de acuerdo con las barreras de comercio lo hacen a menudo pensando en la defensa nacional, el argumento de las industrias nacientes, la protección de trabajos domésticos, el mantener la moneda localmente y el ayudar a la **balanza de pagos.** Las personas a favor del mercado libre creen que todos estos argumentos son erróneos, con la excepción del argumento de las industrias nacientes. Para que el argumento de las industrias nacientes sea válido, la protección debe ser eliminada eventualmente para que la industria pueda competir por sí misma.

Las barreras de comercio contribuyeron a que las condiciones durante la Gran Depresión fueran aún peor. Desde 1934 el mundo se ha acercado más al comercio libre. El **GATT** contribuyó mucho al progreso mundial, y los que proponen el **TLC** desearían eliminar todas las barreras de comercio en Norteamérica.

Repasar la idea principal

¿Cómo han sido eliminadas las barreras de comercio a través de los años?

Sección tres

El financiamiento y el déficit comercial (páginas 461-466)

Las **divisas** son la base de las transacciones internacionales. El valor de las divisas se determina en los mercados donde las monedas extranjeras se compran y se venden. El sistema actual de **cotización de la divisa flexible** significa que el valor de las monedas extranjeras fluctúa con su oferta y demanda.

Los **déficits comerciales** a mediados de los años 1980 resultó en parte por un dólar poderoso. Cuando el **valor ponderado del dólar según el comercio exterior** disminuyó, el déficit comercial mejoró. Debido a que los déficits tienden a corregirse por sí mismos, la mayoría de las naciones ya no diseñan políticas económicas sólo para mejorar la balanza de pagos.

Repasar la idea principal

En un mundo de cotizaciones de la divisa flexible, ¿cómo reaccionan las naciones a la falta de equilibrio comercial?

Vocabulario

Los siguientes términos se definen en el Capítulo 19:

SECCIÓN UNO
- socialismo *(p. 473)*
- comunismo *(p. 474)*

SECCIÓN DOS
- Plan de Cinco Años *(p. 478)*
- colectivización *(p. 478)*
- Gosplan *(p. 478)*
- granja estatal *(p. 479)*
- granja colectiva *(p. 479)*
- trabajo por pieza *(p. 480)*
- tempestear *(p. 480)*

- *perestroika (p. 480)*

SECCIÓN TRES
- privatización *(p. 483)*
- Solidaridad *(p. 485)*
- mercado negro *(p. 486)*
- Gran Salto Adelante *(p. 487)*

SECCIÓN CUATRO
- con uso intensivo de capital *(p. 488)*
- *keiretsu (p. 488)*

Sección uno

El espectro de sistemas económicos (páginas 472-475)

El sistema económico global puede mostrarse en un espectro que se extiende desde los sistemas con un control gubernamental casi total, a aquellos que incluyen muy poca regulación de gobierno. Bajo el capitalismo, los individuos poseen los medios de producción, y la interacción de la oferta y la demanda determina los precios. Bajo el **socialismo,** el gobierno posee muchos de los medios de producción y los funcionarios públicos reparten y administran estos recursos. Por otra parte, el gobierno posee todos los medios de producción bajo el **comunismo** puro.

Repasar la idea principal

¿Cómo se diferencia la posesión de recursos bajo el capitalismo, el socialismo y el comunismo?

Sección dos

El ascenso y la caída del comunismo (páginas 477-481)

En 1917 una revolución derrocó al gobierno de Rusia e instituyó un sistema comunista. Ya para 1927, el país estaba bajo el control del partido comunista y había cambiado su nombre al de la Unión Soviética. En una serie de **Planes de Cinco Años,** los líderes comunistas trataron de alcanzar rápidamente la industrialización. Los planes incluían la **colectivización** de la agricultura y la trasformación de la industria—las cuales estaban bajo el control total del gobierno. **Gosplan,** la autoridad planificadora central, determinaba todos los aspectos de la producción industrial y agrícola. A pesar de los esfuerzos para incrementar la producción, que incluían el **trabajo por pieza** y las cuotas, la economía autoritaria resultó ser un fracaso miserable. Al principio de los 1990, el sistema económico Soviético se había ya desplomado.

Repasar la idea principal

¿Cómo trataron los comunistas de incrementar el desarrollo agrícola e industrial?

Sección tres

La transición hacia el capitalismo (páginas 483-487)

Los sistemas que eran comunistas se deberán enfrentar a varios retos a la vez que tratan de mobilizarse hacia el capitalismo. Estos retos incluyen la **privatización** de los recursos de capitales, el cambio en el poder político de los comunistas al de funcionarios elegidos por voto y a los nuevos incentivos de una economía capitalista. Rusia y Europa del este han tenido cierta cantidad de éxito en este cambio hacia el capitalismo. Al mismo tiempo, otros sistemas económicos a través del mundo han estado experimentando con la movida hacia la economía capitalista.

Repasar la idea principal

¿A qué retos se enfrentan las naciones a la vez que tratan de instituir el sistema capitalista?

Sección cuatro

Las diferentes caras del capitalismo (páginas 488-492)

Desde la Segunda Guerra Mundial, muchas naciones se han movido hacia el capitalismo, aunque su forma exacta varíe de país en país. Japón, que ha sido un sistema capitalista por largo tiempo, alcanzó un desarrollo económico fenomenal con la combinación de lealtad a las corporaciones, tecnología nueva e impuestos bajos. Las economías de los "tigres asiáticos"—Singapur, Taiwan, Hong Kong y Corea del Sur—también crecieron. Al mismo tiempo, Suecia se alejó del socialismo.

Repasar la idea principal

¿Qué factores ayudaron a que la economía del Japón creciera?

Vocabulario

Los siguientes términos se definen en el Capítulo 20:

SECCIÓN UNO
- países en desarrollo *(p. 498)*
- tasa bruta de natalidad *(p. 499)*

- crecimiento demográfico nulo *(p. 499)*
- deuda externa *(p. 500)*
- fuga de capitales *(p. 500)*

SECCIÓN DOS
- equilibrio primitivo *(p. 504)*
- despegue *(p. 504)*
- Banco Mundial *(p. 505)*

SECCIÓN TRES
- expropiación *(p. 511)*
- zona de comercio libre *(p. 512)*
- unión aduanera *(p. 512)*
- Unión Europea *(p. 512)*
- Comunidad Europea *(p. 512)*
- ECU *(p. 512)*
- cartel *(p. 513)*

- densidad demográfica *(p. 514)*

Sección uno

El desarrollo económico (páginas 498-502)

Los **países en desarrollo** tienen los mismos problemas que tienen los países industrializados—la mayor diferencia está en que sus problemas son mucho peor. La preocupación sobre el bienestar de los países en desarrollo es humanitario tanto como político. En 1991, eran 43 países representando a más de la mitad de la población mundial, cada uno con un PIB per cápita de menos de $500.

Los países en desarrollo se enfrentan a varios retos, que incluyen las **tasas brutas de natalidad** y el aumento en la expectativa de vida. La escasez de recursos naturales, la educación y la tecnología limitada, la carga enorme de la **deuda externa**, la **fuga de capitales** y los gobiernos corruptos y poco eficientes aumentan sus problemas.

Repasar la idea principal

¿En qué se diferencian los problemas de los países en desarrollo a los problemas de los países más industrializados?

Sección dos

Estructura para el desarrollo (páginas 504-507)

Ayuda el pensar que el desarrollo económico ocurre en etapas, aunque cada nación no sigue las mismas etapas. Las etapas incluyen el **equilibrio primitivo,** apartándose del equilibrio primitivo, **despegue,** desarrollo medio y desarrollo alto.

El Banco Mundial recomienda que las naciones industrializadas reduzcan sus barreras de comercio, reformen sus políticas macroeconómicas, aumenten su ayuda financiera y apoyen las políticas de reforma de los países en desarrollo.

El Banco Mundial también recomienda que los países en desarrollo inviertan sus propios recursos en educar a su gente, mejoren el clima para la empresa, abran sus economías al comercio internacional y cambien sus políticas económicas.

Repasar la idea principal

¿Qué pueden hacer las naciones industrializadas para ayudar a los países en desarrollo y qué pueden hacer los países en desarrollo para ayudarse a sí mismos?

Sección tres

El financiamiento del desarrollo económico (páginas 509-514)

Los países en desarrollo necesitan estimular el ahorro para poder proveer su propia fuente de fondos para inversiones. Las economías autoritarias tratan a menudo de forzar el ahorro mobilizando los recursos de una manera que ignora las libertades del individuo. Los intentos por asegurar el capital a través de la **expropiación** a menudo resultan mal, porque los inversionistas extranjeros comienzan a tenerle miedo a la inversión.

Los gobiernos y bancos extranjeros a veces proveen fondos externos de dinero. Otras instituciones, como el Banco Mundial y el Fondo de Moneda Internacional, también ofrecen ayuda.

Algunos países han podido ayudarse entre sí a través de la cooperación a nivel regional. Esta ayuda a veces toma la forma de unas **zonas de comercio libre** o una **unión aduanera,** tal como la de la **Comunidad Europea,** ahora llamada la **Unión Europea.** Las naciones productoras de petróleo organizaron el **cartel** de la OPEC para aumentar el precio del petróleo.

Repasar la idea principal

¿Cómo puede un país en desarrollo asegurar los fondos necesarios para alcanzar prosperidad económica?

Vocabulario

Los siguientes términos se definen en el Capítulo 21:

SECCIÓN UNO
- subsistencia *(p. 520)*
- embargo *(p. 522)*

SECCIÓN DOS
- gas profundo *(p. 527)*
- saturación *(p. 528)*
- contaminación *(p. 528)*

- gasohol *(p. 524)*
- acuífero *(p. 525)*

- lluvia ácida *(p. 528)*
- permiso de contami- nación *(p. 530)*

SECCIÓN TRES
- análisis costo-beneficio *(p. 532)*

- economía de libre empresa modificada *(p. 533)*

Sección uno

La demanda global de recursos (páginas 520-525)

A pesar de las predicciones de Thomas Malthus hace casi 200 años, muchas regiones han logrado que su están- dar de vida haya crecido constantemente, principalmente debido a la tecnología. Las naciones en desarrollo, con sus altos por cientos de nacimientos, sin embargo, se enfrentan a la amenaza de un estándar de vida inferior.

A la vez que la población mundial ha aumentado a través de los años, las personas se han preocupado cada vez más acerca de la reducción de las fuentes no reno- vables de energía como el petróleo, el gas natural y el car- bón. Muchos americanos se percataron agudamente de esta reducción en los años 1970 después que los países del Medio Oriente comenzaron el **embargo** de petróleo. El embargo motivó a los americanos a buscar otras fuentes de energía. Estas fuentes renovables incluyen la energía solar, energía hidroeléctrica, energía de viento, energía nuclear y **gasohol**—una combinación de gasolina sin plomo y alcohol de grano. Los americanos también están buscando diferentes formas de conservar agua y asegurar el uso prudente de las riquezas de la tierra.

Repasar la idea principal

¿Qué fuentes de energía renovables están investi- gando los americanos como alternativas a las fuentes no renovables?

Sección dos

Incentivos y recursos económicos (páginas 527-530)

Desde el embargo de petróleo de los 1970, los precios crecientes de gasolina han servido de gran motivación para preservar los recursos naturales. El sistema de pre- cios de nuestra economía de mercado también es un incentivo para conservar otros recursos. La eliminación de restricciones del gas natural, por ejemplo, ha motivado a los productores a buscar **gas profundo.** A la vez que la población americana ha crecido y usado más formas de energía, las personas se han empezado a preocupar acerca de la **contaminación,** ya sea del aire, agua o de la tierra por el derrame de substancias tóxicas o nocivas. Como respuesta a esta preocupación, el gobierno ha pasado legis- lación e incentivos económicos—que incluyen los **per- misos de contaminación**—para limpiar el ambiente. Toda esta legislación fue hecha con el propósito de motivar a las personas a usar los recursos naturales con prudencia.

Repasar la idea principal

¿Cómo motiva el sistema de precios a la preservación de recursos naturales en una economía de mercado?

Sección tres

La aplicación de la forma económica de pensar (páginas 532-534)

La economía se ha convertido en una teoría general- izada predilecta y en una estructura para tomar deci- siones. El Consejo Nacional de Educación Económica ha recomendado un sistema de cinco puntos para tomar deci- siones. La decisión final está relacionada con el **análisis costo-beneficio,** el cual compara el costo de una decisión a los beneficios ganados.

El capitalismo es el tipo de organización económica dominante en el mundo de hoy. La oferta y la demanda establecen los precios y los precios sirven de señal a los productores y a los consumidores. Los mercados son flexi- bles porque los cambios futuros afectan los precios y, así, la distribución de recursos. Esta flexibilidad hace posible que nuestra **economía de libre empresa modificada** se ajuste a los eventos en el futuro.

Repasar la idea principal

¿Cómo ayuda la forma económica de pensar a que las personas tomen mejores decisiones?

INDEX

The following abbreviations are used in the index: *crt* = cartoon; *fig* = figure, chart, graph; *m* = map; *p* = photograph; *q* = quote.

prices; absorbing unexpected shocks, 128; adjustment of, *fig137*; advantages of, 128-130; artificially low in command economies, 129; as a system, 140-41; *crt130*; as signals, 534; flexibility of, 128; neutrality of, 128; used to control traffic, 130

primary market; compared to other markets, *fig331*; defined, 332

primary regulators; and the Fed as, 294; of depository institutions, 294

prime rate; defined, 309

primitive equilibrium; and Inuit, 504; as stage of economic development, 504; defined, 504

principal; defined, 61

principles of taxation, see benefit principle of taxation and ability-to-pay principle

private bank notes; and the Constitution of the United States, 272; during the Revolutionary War, 272

private enterprise economy, 25; also see free enterprise economy

private property; 14th Amendment and, 44; 5th Amendment and, 44; and incentive to work, save and invest, 45; as characteristic of capitalism, *fig44*, 49; defined, 45

private sector; defined, 239

privatization; as problem during communist transition to capitalism, 483; defined, 483; example of, 483; vouchers used during, 483-84, 485

problem bank list; defined, 312; and FDIC, 312

produce; questions concerning WHAT, HOW and FOR WHOM, 10-11

producer cooperative; defined, 70

producer price index; and wholesale price index, 362; base year for, 363; defined, 362; number of commodities in, 363

product differentiation, 152; and monopolistic competition, 155-56; as condition of market structure, *fig159*; defined, 155

product market; defined, 24; *fig25*

production; Adam Smith and, 18; defined, 22

production function, 112-15; and marginal product, 114; and total product, 113; defined, 112; illustrated, *fig112*; *p113*; stages of, 114-115

production possibilities frontier,

16-17; and the GDP gap, *fig418*; defined, 16; *fig16*

production quotas; former U.S.S.R., 34

productivity, 22-23; Adam Smith's views on, 18; and a change in supply, 106; and communism, 475; and cost of inputs, 117; and division of labor, 113; and economic growth, 380-81; and Henry Ford, 113; *crt111*; as issue in free enterprise economy, 442-43; defined, 22; effects of productivity, 380; historical record, 380; not foreseen by Malthus, 521

productivity and growth; and economic impact of taxes, 212

products; economic products, 20; free products, 20; illustrated, *fig20*; shoddy under communism, 475

professional association; defined, 71

professional business association, see business association

professional labor; defined, 194

profit; defined, 46

profit maximization; discussed, 122; for monopolistic competition, 156; for monopoly, 161, *fig160*; for oligopoly, 157-58; for perfectly competitive firm, *fig154*; illustrated, *fig119*; quantity of output that maximizes, 122

profit maximizing quantity of output; defined, 122; for monopolists, *fig160*; illustrated, *fig119*

profit motive; as characteristic of free enterprise and capitalism, *fig44*, 45-46; defined, 46

progressive tax; and marginal tax rates, 215; defined, 215; examples of, 215, 216-217; illustrated, *fig214*; marginal brackets for, *fig218*

proletariat; and Karl Marx on, 476; defined, 476

property taxes; and Boston, *p226*; as indirect business tax, 356; as percent of state and local government revenues, *fig223*; defined, 224; in California, 225; in Massachusetts, 225

proportional tax; and average tax rates, 215; defined, 215; examples of, 215, *fig214*

proprietorship, see sole proprietorship

protecting industry against foreign competition; as issue in free enterprise, 538-39; con, *q539*; pro, *q538*

protectionism; and American jobs, *p454*; *crt455*; Michael Kinsley on, *q539*

protectionism, arguments for, 454-57; national defense, 454; infant industries, 455; protecting domestic jobs, 455-56; keeping the money home, 456; helping the balance of payments, 456-57

protectionism in Japan; and cost of rice and consumer goods, 489; and high cost of living, 489-90

protectionist; defined, 454

protective tariff; defined, 453

prounion legislation; examples of, 186

proxy; defined, 60

public debt; foreign ownership of, 257; also see federal debt

public disclosure; and banks, 170; and Food and Drug Administration, 170; and the Securities Exchange Commission, 170; defined, 170; for credit cards and loan terms, 169

public goods, 173; and market failures, 167; defined, 167; described, 239; neglect of as disadvantage of capitalism, 473

public opinion; and fact-finding, 191

public sector; defined, 239

public utilities; as local government expenditure, 251

public utility; defined, 72

public welfare; as local government expenditure category, 252; as percent of direct state and local expenditures, *fig250*; as state expenditure category, 249

Pueblo; Native American artist, *p33*

Puerto Rico; as served by the Fed, *m295*

pure competition, 152-55; and profit maximization, 153-54, *fig154*; characteristics of, *fig159*; defined, 152; conditions for, 152-53; farm market as example of, *p153*

pure monopoly, characteristics of, *fig159*; also see monopoly

purely competitive firm; and profit maximization, *fig154*

put option; defined, 338

──────── Q ────────

quality of life; and Gross Domestic Product, 350-51

quantity of money theory; and historical precedents, 309-10; and the long-run, 309-10; defined, 309

quantity supplied; defined, 106; illustrated, *fig105*

quintiles; and average income-

to-poverty ratios, *fig408*; and distribution of family incomes, *fig406*

quotas; and perestroika, 480-81; as barriers to international trade, 453-54; compared to tariffs, 453-54; defined, 453; in the Soviet economy, 480

──────── R ────────

rain forests; support for, 42

rate of inflation; during the business cycle, *fig401*

ration coupon; defined, 131

rationing; and diminished incentives, 132; and administrative cost of, 132; and ration coupons, 131; defined, 131; during World War II, 131; of gasoline, 131; *p132*; problem of fairness, 131

raw materials; defined, 112

Reagan administration; and deregulation, 284, 285, 431; and federal deficits, 254

Reagan presidency; weakened automatic stabilizers during, 433

Reagan, President; and 1981 air traffic controllers strike, 192; and deregulation of financial institutions, 284, 285-86; and user fees, 220; voluntary auto imports, 454

real dollars, see constant dollars

real estate agent; help wanted ad for, *fig45*

real estate investment trust (REIT), 339; and home construction, 323; as nonbank financial intermediary, 323; as part of the financial system, *fig321*; defined, 323

real GDP; compared to real GDP per capita, *fig377*; comparing GDP in different years, 364; converting to real GDP, 364; defined, 364; versus current GDP, *fig363*

real GDP per capita; compared to real GDP, *fig377*; defined, 376; growth triangle for, *fig378*

real property; defined, 224

rebate; defined, 140; legality under Robinson Patman Act, *fig170*

recession; average length of, 386; defined, 383; illustrated, *fig383*

Reciprocal Trade Agreements Act; described, 458; and most-favored nation clause, 458

regional stock exchanges; and needs of smaller corporations, 336; examples of 335-36, *fig335*

regressive tax; defined, 215;

ACKNOWLEDGMENTS

Cover, KS Studios; iv, Ed Bock/The Stock Market; vi, (top, l to r) The Granger Collection New York, David Levenson/Black Star, (center, l to r) courtesy American Express, Houston Chronicle, courtesy Wendy's International, courtesy The University of Chicago, (bottom, l to r) George Lange/Onyx, UPI/Bettmann, AP/Wide World Photos; vii, (top, l to r) Cynthia Johnson/Gamma-Liaison, Kevin Horan/Picture Group, Brad Markel/Gamma-Liaison, Robert Milazzo, (center, l to r) UPI/Bettmann, courtesy George Mason University, Steve Jennings/Picture Group, Bill Nation/Sygma, (bottom, l to r) Peter Sibbald/Sygma, The Granger Collection New York, courtesy Princeton University, The Granger Collection New York; ix, (r) Lester Lefkowitz/Tony Stone Images, (l) David R. Frazier/Photo Researchers; xi, (l) Greg Stott/Masterfile, (r) Thomas Braise/The Stock Market; 4-5, Uniphoto/Pictor; 6-7, Henry Horenstein/Stock Boston; 10, (l) Tom McHugh/Photo Researchers, (lc) Wolfgang Volz/Bilderberg/The Stock Market, (rc) Doug Martin, (r) Matt Meadows; 14, Bob Daemmrich/Tony Stone Images; 17, by permission of Johnny Hart and Creators Syndicate, Inc.; 18, (t) The Granger Collection New York, (b) The Bettmann Archive; 19, Doug Martin; 21, David R. Frazier; 24, (l) Erik Svenson/Tony Stone Images, (r) Jeff Bates; 26, Wally McNammee/Sygma; 27, (t)(b) Mark Burnett; 30-31, J. Messerschmidt/FPG International; 33, Renee Lynn/Photo Researchers; 37, Clark James Mishler/Alaska Stock Images; 38, Gabe Palmer/The Stock Market; 39, Mark Lyons/Lyons Photography; 40, King Features Syndicate; 41, George Herben/Alaska Stock Images; 42, (t) David Levenson/Black Star, (b) courtesy The Body Shop; 43, Doug Martin; 46, courtesy Johnson Publishing Company, Inc.; 47, Tim Courlas; 52-53, Matt Meadows; 54, Randy Schieber; 55, Robert Mullenix; 56, Doug Martin; 57, Matt Meadows; 58, file photo; 61, Bruce Ayres/Tony Stone Images; 68, (t) courtesy American Express, (b) Mark Burnett; 72, Michael Howell/Profiles West; 76, (t) Mark Burnett, (b) Garfield MR/The Stock Market; 77, (l) Kevin Horan/Zuma, (r) Marie Dorigny/SABA; 78-79, Jose L. Pelaez/The Stock Market; 80-81, Yvonne Hemsey/Gamma-Liaison Network; 82, Matt Meadows; 85, Robin Smith/Tony Stone Images; 86, Doug Martin; 88, courtesy Pepsi-Cola Co.; 90, Doug Martin; 91, (t) Houston Chronicle, (b) Dan Ford Connolly; 96, Dean Abramson/Stock Boston; 98, Hodgins in New York Daily News; 102-103, Lester Lefkowitz/Tony Stone Images; 104, Jeff Spielman/The Image Bank; 111, Robert Weber; 113, Matt Meadows; 114, Tom Tracy/FPG International; 116, (t)(b) courtesy Wendy's International; 118, Doug Martin; 126-127, Matthew McVay/Stock Boston; 129, (l) courtesy Apple Computer, Inc., (r) John Greenleigh/courtesy Apple Computer, Inc.; 130, (t) From The Wall Street Journal/Permission by Cartoon Feature Syndicate, (b) Reuters/Bettmann; 132, AP/World Wide Photos; 133, Danziger in The Christian Science Monitor ©1992 TCSPS; 136, Matt Meadows; 139, (t) courtesy The University of Chicago, (b) Jon Feingersh/The Stock Market; 140, Alvis Upitis/The Image Bank; 149, Reprinted by permission of Gill Fox/Connecticut Post; 150-151, Brent Turner/BLT Productions; 153, Julie Houck/Stock Boston; 155, Aaron Haupt Photography; 156, Reprinted with permission of NIKE, Inc. (Photo by Walter Iooss); 158, Chris Arend/Alaska Stock Images; 162, (t) George Lange/Onyx, (b) Courtesy Computer Associates; 164, courtesy Lockheed Corp.; 165, David Butow/Black Star; 166, John Coletti/Stock Boston; 176, (t) Mark Wilson/Archive Photos, (b) David R. Frazier/Photo Researchers; 177, (l) Brian K. Diggs/AP/Wide World Photos, (r) Joseph Nettis/Photo Researchers; 178-179, Frank Saragnese/FPG International; 180-181, Mark Reinstein/Gamma-Liaison Network; 186, Keystone/FPG International; 188, UPI/Bettmann; 189, Archives of Labor and Urban Affairs, Wayne State University; 195, Jeff Bates; 202, (l) Wynn Miller/Tony Stone Images, (r) Billy E. Barnes/Stock Boston; 208-209, Bob Daemmrich/Stock Boston; 213, (l) George Anderson, (r) Doug Martin; 220, Greg Smith/Gamma-Liaison Network; 221, (t) AP/Wide World Photos, (b) Walter Hodges/Westlight; 226, Jeff Greenberg/Photo Researchers; 232, BORN LOSER reprinted by permission of NEA, Inc.; 236-237, J. Richardson/Westlight; 240, FRANK & ERNEST reprinted by permission of NEA, Inc.; 241, Jeff Bates; 242, (t) Cynthia Johnson/Gamma-Liaison, (b) Ruth Frenson/AP/Wide World Photos; 247, Frank Rossotto/The Stock Market; 252, file photo; 253, Reprinted by permission Tribune Media Services; 259, The Boston Globe, © Jerry Holbert; 264-265, Ed Bock/The Stock Market; 267, Reprinted by permission News America Syndicate; 268, Wolfgang Kaehler; 271, Aaron Haupt; 273, 274, file photo; 276, Mark Burnett; 278, (t) Kevin Horan/Picture Group, (b) Scott McKiernan/Gamma-Liaison Network; 284, Matt Meadows; 285, Ed Zirkle; 286, The Wall Street Journal, Cartoon Features Syndicate; 287, Bob Daemmrich/Uniphoto; 292-293, Mike Mazzaschi/Stock Boston; 296, G. Parker; 301, (t) Brad Markel/Gamma-Liaison, (b) Jose L. Pelaez/The Stock Market; 318-319, Greg Stott/Masterfile; 324, (t) Robert Milazzo, (b) file photo; 342, (t) UPI/Bettmann, (b) Ed Lallo/Gamma-Liaison Network; 343, (l) Kurgan-Lisnet/Gamma-Liaison Network, (r) Aaron Haupt Photography; 344-345, Jean Miele/The Stock Market; 346-347, Gabe Palmer/The Stock Market; 350, Mark Burnett/Stock Boston; 352, Reprinted by permission Tribune Media Services; 353, (t) UPI/Bettmann, (b) Mural by Maxwell B. Starr, courtesy Rockdale Post Office, photo by Bob Daemmrich; 359, Dave Davidson/The Stock Market; 360, John Henley/The Stock Market; 364, From The Wall Street Journal-permission, Cartoon Features Syndicate; 368-369, Jordan Coonrad/Airborne; 373, Doug Martin; 382, (t) courtesy George Mason University, (b) Robin Moyer/Gamma-Liaison Network; 392-393, Eugene Richards/Magnum Photos; 397, From The Wall Street Journal/Permission by Cartoon Features Syndicate; 398, (t) Steve Jennings/Picture Group, (b) James Schnepf/Gamma-Liaison Network; 402, Jon Levy/Gamma-Liaison Network; 409, Richard Hutchings/Photo Researchers; 412, Greig Cranna/Stock Boston; 416-417, Armen Kachaturian/Gamma-Liaison Network; 420, Doug Martin; 426, Mark Burnett; 428, Bob Daemmrich/Uniphoto; 435, (t) Bill Nation/Sygma, (b) Don Smetzer/Tony Stone Images; 437, Doug Martin; 442, (t) Mak-1, (b) Gabe Palmer/The Stock Market; 443, (l) Howard Grey/Tony Stone Images, (r) Stephen Marks/The Image Bank; 444-445, Ron McMillan/Gamma-Liaison Network; 446-447, Cathlyn Melloan/Tony Stone Images; 448, Fred Ward/Black Star; 452, (t) Peter Sibbald/Sygma, (b) file photo; 454, Cynthia Johnson/Gamma-Liaison Network; 455, BERRY'S WORLD reprinted by permission of NEA, Inc.; 456, Greg Davis/The Stock Market; 457, Joseph Nettis/Photo Researchers; 464, Fisher, ©1992/The New Yorker Magazine; 465, Bob Daemmrich/Uniphoto; 470-471, Dallas & John Heaton/Uniphoto; 475, Sovfoto; 476, (t) The Granger Collection New York, (b) Pablo Ibarra/Gamma-Liaison Network; 478, Sovfoto; 481, Lisa Quinones/Black Star; 484, Eric Bouvet/Gamma-Liaison Network; 486, Dilip Menta/The Stock Market; 489, Martin Rogers/Uniphoto; 496-497, David Ball/The Stock Market; 503, (t) courtesy Princeton University, (b) Travelpix/FPG International; 507, Martin Rogers/Uniphoto; 509, Adina Tovy/Robert Harding Picture Library; 512, AP/Wide World Photos; 518-519, Thomas Braise/The Stock Market; 523, Henley & Savage/Uniphoto; 526, (t) The Granger Collection New York, (b) M.E. Warren/Uniphoto; 528, Jeff Lepore/Photo Researchers; 529, Harry M. Walker/Alaska Stock; 534, Thomas Braise/The Stock Market; 538, (t) Robert Harding Picture Library, (b) Jim Pickerell/Gamma-Liaison Network; 539, (l) Zigy Kaluzny, (r) Chris Jones/The Stock Market; 540, Ed Honowitz/Tony Stone Images; 552, Doug Martin.